Contents at a Glance

Contents

▓CHAPTER 8 Scope and Visibility 243

▓CHAPTER 9 Using Modules 261

■CHAPTER 13   Files and Directories 447

■CHAPTER 14   Command Line and Shell Interaction 501

About the Author

PETER WAINWRIGHT is a developer and software engineer who has worked extensively with Perl, Apache, and other open-source projects over a career spanning fifteen-plus years. He currently manages a Perl development team for Bloomberg LP, a financial services corporation.

When he is not engaged in either development or writing books, he maintains the Space Future Web site at http://www.spacefuture.com. He is an active proponent of commercial passenger space travel as well as a co-founder of Space Future Consulting, an international space tourism consultancy firm with representatives in the United States, Europe, and Asia.

In addition to *Pro Perl*, he is also the author of *Pro Apache* (Apress, 2004), now in its third edition, as well as a contributing author to *Beginning Perl* (Wrox Press, 2000) and *Professional Perl Development* (Wrox, 2001).

A former resident of both London and Zürich, he now lives and works in New York City with his wife, a writer and editor. He can be contacted through his Web site at http://www.cybrid.net or e-mailed at Peter.Wainwright@cybrid.net.

About the Technical Reviewer

ANDY LESTER is a programmer, manager, writer, speaker, and Perl evangelist. Almost 20 years of working on web applications has turned him into a fan of automated testing, which he talks about at conferences and user group meetings around the US. He's also the leader of the Chicago Perl Mongers.

Andy maintains over 20 modules on CPAN related to software development, testing, web applications, or a little of each. He also writes for *The Perl Journal* and *The Perl Review*, and has edited or contributed to many books.

Andy lives in McHenry, IL, with his wife, Amy, his daughter, Quinn, and Baxter, the world's neediest dog. His web site is at `http://petdance.com/`.

Introduction

Perl is an enduringly popular language, but one whose capabilities are often underestimated: while many programmers gain enough experience to write quick Perl scripts to solve problems, some never develop their understanding of the language to the point where writing modules or object orientation becomes second nature. *Pro Perl* demonstrates that Perl is not only a powerful tool for solving problems at the scripting level, but also a full-featured language for application development.

Pro Perl is aimed at intermediate-to-experienced programmers who have a good, basic understanding of programming concepts but may have little or no previous knowledge of Perl itself. The primary focus of the book is Perl 5.8, the current production release of the language. When an aspect of the language is expected to evolve in Perl 5.10, and especially in Perl 6, enhancements and possible changes in behavior are noted so that future-cognizant programmers can plan ahead. Conversely, there are still many cases, especially in business, where older versions of Perl—both 5.6 and even 5.005—are still thriving, with no need or expectation of upgrading. Therefore, *Pro Perl* does not assume that the latest cutting-edge features of Perl are always going to be available, and it takes time to note backward-compatibility issues, as well as point out ways to enable newer techniques to work even on earlier versions of Perl.

Pro Perl follows a depth-first approach; wherever possible, topics are explored completely in one place, rather than splitting "basic" and "advanced" concepts into different chapters. This allows the reader to easily discover and absorb more advanced aspects of a subject alongside the basics. *Pro Perl* is designed as a reference/tutorial that readers can access for information at any point, and then read on to discover more advanced information or branch out to related areas.

Chapter 1 provides an introduction to Perl and covers how to get and install a new Perl distribution. Much of this chapter is aimed at those interested in installing Perl themselves, and it covers basic and advanced techniques for customizing Perl, including building Perl from source and adjusting the build configuration features like threads and 64-bit integers (even on a 32-bit platform).

Chapters 2 to 11 cover the fundamentals of Perl. Chapter 2 serves as a primer for newcomers to Perl, providing an introduction to the fundamentals of the language, which are covered in depth in Chapters 3 to 11. This section includes material on Perl's data types and variables; the structure of Perl programs, including blocks, loops, conditions, and subroutines; using and writing modules and packages; and Perl's possibly most well-known features, interpolation and regular expressions.

Chapters 12 to 19 build on the knowledge gained in the first half of the book to examine intermediate-level subjects like files and filehandles, debugging Perl, generating and managing warnings and errors, and object-oriented programming with Perl.

Chapters 20 to 23 cover more advanced topics, including processes and threads, integrating Perl with other programming languages, network programming, and making use of Perl's support for Unicode, locale, and internationalization.

This is the second edition of *Pro Perl*; the first edition was published as *Professional Perl Programming* (Wrox Press, 2001). Since the first edition, every chapter has been updated with material to cover the latest features of Perl 5.8, with new content and examples throughout. Some material has been redistributed and reorganized, resulting in an expanded manuscript of 23 chapters in place of the original 26. New content has been written to cover embedded Perl programming and XSUBs (in Chapter 20) and working with Unicode, locale, and internationalization (in Chapter 23).

CHAPTER 1

███

Introducing Perl

In this introductory chapter, we cover the background of Perl and what makes it a popular programming language. We also look at installing a standard Perl distribution, as well as building it from source. For those who already have Perl installed, these sections can be skipped, though if we want to use optional features like *threading*, it may still be advantageous to build Perl from a source distribution, a process which is less daunting than it might at first seem.

Once Perl is installed, we look at how to run Perl scripts, and what needs to be done to get the operating system to recognize Perl scripts. We spend some time with the Perl command line and special environment variables, and see how Perl can be used as a versatile command-line tool to execute snippets of Perl without the involvement of any scripts. Even though Perl is ubiquitous, we also take a look at one way to create stand-alone Perl applications that can run without the benefit of a Perl installation.

There is far more to Perl than the standard distribution. In the last part of the chapter, we cover downloading installing new Perl modules from the *Comprehensive Perl Archive Network* (CPAN), the first—and frequently only—port of call for all Perl extensions and add-ons. As many Perl modules are a mixture of Perl plus C, we also cover some of the options for installing packages containing C, including ActivePerl's PPM package tool for Windows.

Introduction

Perl, the Practical Extraction and Reporting Language, is a tremendously versatile language that combines an extremely versatile syntax with a powerful range of features. Inspired by Unix text-processing tools like sed and awk, and shell scripting languages, Perl combines their power with a C-like syntax and the flexibility of Lisp to provide a development environment that is vastly more powerful, while also being easier to learn and faster to develop in.

Perl's versatility is one of its greatest strengths, but it can also be a liability if used unwisely. Unlike languages that have a strong opinion on what is the right way or the wrong way to do things, Perl is adaptable enough to adopt almost any approach—"There's More Than One Way to Do It," as the Perl motto goes. This lets Perl adapt to the programming style of the programmer, and not the other way around. In the eyes of Perl programmers, this is a good thing; in the eyes of advocates of some other languages, it isn't. Perl's anti-motto really ought to be "Just Because You Can Do It, Doesn't Mean You Should"; Perl does not impose good programming practices, so it is also easy to write badly constructed and hard-to-read code through sloppy programming.

Perl is a practically minded language, and takes a no-frills approach to almost everything, including features like object-oriented programming, which is pivotal to the entire ethos of other programming languages. Again, this is both a boon and a potential pitfall for the unwary. Perl is also the language of a thousand handy shortcuts, many of which are intuitive, and others of which are indispensable once they are known. We have tried to cover as many as we can during the course of this book.

Key Features

Perl has many features that contribute to its popularity. Some of them are obvious to anyone with familiarity with Perl—an easy learning curve, powerful text manipulation features, and cross-platform availability.

Ironically, experienced programmers sometimes have a harder time than newcomers; Perl makes some things so easy it is necessary to do a double-take and start from scratch rather than attempting to use familiar coding styles from other languages. This is especially true of the regular expression engine.

Others are hidden strengths—its open source credentials and licensing, independence from commercial interferences, and active online communities. Here are a few items for those who are less familiar with Perl to ponder:

- Perl has a relatively simple and intuitive syntax that makes it extremely quick to learn and lends itself to very rapid prototyping, especially compared to languages that involve an explicit compilation step. This is one reason it is popular as a scripting language—it can be faster to code a Perl tool than find and learn how to use an existing one.

- Perl is a cross-platform language, supported on almost any operating system of sufficient complexity. This means that, with a few caveats, a Perl program written on one platform will usually run on another with little or no modification. Perl's standard library contains considerable support for handling different platforms in such a way that Perl applications frequently need little or no additional effort to handle multiple platforms.

- Perl's versatility allows programmers to learn the language and adapt it to their own particular styles. Conversely, of course, Perl won't magically straighten out poor style.

- Perl contains a powerful suite of features to manipulate text. The regular expression engine, when properly used, is capable of almost any kind of textual transformation conceivable, and text manipulation is one reason for Perl's popularity both as a command-line tool and a web programming language.

- Perl's standard library comes with comprehensive support for many common programming problems. In addition, CPAN and ActiveState distribute modules for Linux and Windows respectively, which provide many powerful extensions to the standard library including very comprehensive XML support, graphical user interfaces, and several flavors of embedded Perl scripting. Perl can also be integrated into several different web servers.

- Perl supports references but doesn't support directly addressable pointers, one of the biggest sources of pain in C programming. References allow the easy construction of complex data structures, but without the dangers inherent in pointer arithmetic. As an adjunct to this, like most reference-based languages (Java is another), Perl has a garbage collector that counts references and removes data when it is no longer required.

- Perl has a flexible object-oriented programming syntax, which is both powerful and at the same time extremely simple. Its simplicity comes at the price of not implementing some of the more advanced object-oriented concepts available in other languages, but it is capable of a lot more than it is often given credit for.

- Perl is not commercially oriented. This is an important point and should not be overlooked. Perl has no commercial agenda, and does not have features added to boost anyone's market position at the expense of the language itself. This gives it a major advantage over commercial scripting languages (certain examples may spring to mind) that are not developed by the communities that use it.

- Perl is an open source project, developed by the community of programmers who use it. Its license allows it to be used and copied freely, under the terms of either the Artistic or GNU Public Licenses, whichever suits better. This means that it cannot be commercially coerced, and it also allows it to benefit from the input of thousands of programmers around the world. Even so, commercial support is available from several companies both on Unix and Windows for those that require it.

- Finally, Perl is not just a programming language but also a thriving online community. One of the most obvious faces of the community is CPAN (headquartered at http://cpan.org, but mirrored around the world) and its comprehensive repository of Perl programming libraries and modules. Others worthy of mention include the Perl Mongers, http://www.pm.org, a network of regional Perl clubs and societies; and the Perl Foundation, http://www.perlfoundation.org, which helps to coordinate YAPC (Yet Another Perl Conference) gatherings around the world.

Supported Platforms

Perl is supported on many platforms, and ports exist to more or less every operating system that still has life in it (and a few that don't). The most commonly used of these are:

- *Unix*: More or less every Unix or Unix-like operating system ever created, notably AIX, IRIX, HP/UX, BSD, Linux, Solaris, and Tru64
- *MS Windows*: DOS, Windows 3.1, 95, 98, NT, and 2000, and the Cygwin and MinGW Unix-on-Windows compatibility environments
- *Other desktop OSs*: Apple Macintosh (68k and PPC, both pre– and post–MacOS X), Acorn Risc OS, Amiga, BeOS, OS/2, and many others
- *Mainframes*: AS/400, OS390, VMS and OpenVMS, Stratus (VOS), and Tandem
- *PDAs*: EPOC (Psion/Symbian), Windows CE and PocketPC, but not PalmOS at time of writing

Binary versions of Perl for all of these operating systems and many others are available from the Ports page on CPAN at http://cpan.org/ports/index.html. Where possible, however, building from source is preferred and recommended.

Perl also builds from source on many of these platforms. This is generally preferable because binary distributions tend to lag behind the source code in version number (the delay depends a lot on the platform—Unix is near instantaneous). For Unix-like platforms, building from source should not be a problem, and may even be educational. Other platforms that should be able to compile Perl directly from source include DOS, OS/2, BeOS, EPOC, VMS, and Windows; see later in the chapter for details.

When built from source, Perl is often able to take advantage of additional facilities on the platform, like 64-bit integers (even on 32-bit architectures). It also allows the possibility of including support for threads and other features that are often not enabled by default in binary distributions.

Perl History and Versions

Perl is an evolving language, continuously updated with support for new features. Despite this, it is still an easy language to learn and has not lost its basic simplicity, despite evolving from a simple scripting tool into a full-fledged object-oriented application development language.

Perl evolved hand-and-glove with the Internet, and gained rapid popularity in its early days as a language for writing quick utility scripts. This was thanks in part to its powerful text handling features and familiarity to programmers used to the sed and awk tools by which it was partly inspired. Perl has an obvious relationship to C, but it also has characteristics derived from Lisp. It gained popularity as a language for writing server-side CGI scripts for web servers, again because of its text handling abilities and also because of its rapid prototyping. This culminated in version 4 of Perl.

Release 5 of Perl took Perl to a new level by introducing object-oriented programming features. Like the language itself, Perl's support for objects applies itself to getting the job done rather than worrying overly about ideology, but nonetheless turns out to be very capable. The ability to support objects derived principally from the introduction of hard references to the language. Up until this point, Perl only had symbolic references, which are now deprecated (and indeed disallowed with the strict module). It was in version 5 that Perl became more than just a language for writing short utility scripts and became a language in which serious applications could be developed.

Version 5.005 introduced initial support for threaded programming, albeit only inside the interpreter itself. This gave Windows, and other platforms that did not support child processes, an emulation of the Unix fork system call, thus greatly improving Perl's support on those platforms.

In version 5.6, Perl revised its version numbering system to be more in line with version numbers elsewhere. In particular, it adopted the Linux system of numbering stable and development releases with even and odd release numbers—in this scheme the previous stable release is now retrospectively known as Perl 5.5, the odd number notwithstanding. Version 5.6 introduced a number of important improvements, the main ones being much better support of Unix idioms under Windows and initial support for Unicode character sets. From version 5.6, experimental support for threads in user-level programming was first introduced, but only if built from source and requested at that time.

Perl 5.8 brings an improved implementation of threads known as *interpreter threads*. It also brings full support for Unicode, support for PerlIO and filehandle layers, restricted hashes as a replacement for pseudohashes, improved signal handling, further improved support for Windows, and a much more extensive regression test suite. The development version is Perl 5.9, and the next stable release will be (or may now be) Perl 5.10.

In the future is Perl 6, a complete and fully object-oriented reimplementation and expansion of Perl from the ground up, and the Parrot virtual machine on which it will run. While radically different under the hood, Perl 6 will be sufficiently like Perl 5 that it will be possible to run most if not all Perl 5 programs under it. A port of Perl 5 to the Parrot virtual machine called Ponie, which will be identically compatible with Perl 5.10, is also in the works—see http://www.poniecode.org for information. For more information on Parrot, see http://www.parrotcode.org. For Perl 6, see http://dev.perl.org/Perl6.

Finding Help

Perl comes with a lot of documentation as standard, including a complete set of manual pages that can be accessed with the perldoc utility. For an index of all available pages, use the command line

```
> perldoc perl
```

This should return a list of the many standard Perl manual pages available as part of every Perl installation. Where documentation refers to a Perl manual page, we can use perldoc to read it. For example, to read about Perl's command-line options or its C-based interfaces:

```
> perldoc perlrun
> perldoc perlapi
```

The perldoc script is quite versatile and is used for accessing all kinds of Perl documentation from a variety of sources, through various command-line options. Using perldoc -h will generate a brief summary of all these options, but as perldoc is a valuable tool to know how to use, we will cover a few of the ways it can be used here.

The most immediately useful variants of the perldoc command worth knowing are those that enable search and query modes.

```
> perldoc -f funcname    # look up a Perl function
> perldoc -q pattern     # search the questions in the Perl FAQ
> perldoc -r pattern     # search documentation recursively
```

The -f and -q options provide focused access to the perlfunc and perlfaq manual pages. The options let us extract only the text for a specific query, avoiding the need to search through the entire rather long document. For example:

```
> perldoc -f split
> perldoc -q '(mail|address)'
> perldoc -q -r '(un)pack'
```

This last command searches both the questions and the answers of the Perl FAQ (of which there are several numbered sections). Without the -r, it searches only the questions.

The other major use of perldoc is to display the documentation for modules, Perl's reusable libraries. For example:

```
> perldoc IO::File
```

Commands and scripts can also have documentation extracted from them, assuming they are written in Perl, of course. If the command is on the search path of the shell, we do not even need to tell perldoc where it is. As a self-referential example, we can read up on perldoc itself with

```
> perldoc perldoc
```

All of these commands will extract and display any embedded Perl documentation (technically, Plain Old Documentation or POD) present in the module or script. Even Perl's manual pages are written in this embedded documentation syntax. Just occasionally, we want to look at the actual source code of a Perl library though, which we can do with the -m option. This will give us the actual file contents, including POD documentation and Perl code.

```
> perldoc -m IO::File
```

If we just want to know where the file is, rather than display it, we can use -l instead of -m.

```
> perldoc -l IO::File
```

Finally, if we are not sure of the exact mixture of cases in the name of the module or script we are looking for, we can use the -i option to make a case-insensitive query. The -i option will also work with -q or -r to perform case-insensitive searches.

```
> perldoc -i exutils::makemaker
> perldoc -i -q CGI
```

A complete set of manual pages for Perl in HTML, PDF, PostScript, and plain text formats is available from CPAN's documentation page at: http://cpan.org/doc/index.html, or from http://www.perldoc.com. Users of ActivePerl can also use ActivePerl ➤ Online Documentation accessed through the Windows Start menu.

Talking of HTML, also available from http://cpan.org/doc/index.html is the current version of the Perl FAQ, along with many other useful essays that go beyond the basic Perl documentation.

Building and Installing Perl

Perl is released in two different versions, the stable version, also known as the maintenance version, and a development version. Both versions update in small ways from time to time, and occasionally take a big leap. The last such big leap was from Perl version 5.6.1 to Perl 5.8.0; the new development release, as mentioned earlier, became Perl 5.9.0. This does not mean Perl 5.9 is better than Perl 5.8, it just means it is more experimental. Ultimately it will become Perl 5.10, the next stable release.

Some development releases are more stable than others, but only officially stable releases are recommended for production environments. The new numbering scheme means that the latest stable version will always have an even second digit—incremental updates for Perl 5.8 are in the 5.8.X series, while the next major release will be 5.10. While we usually want to stick to the current stable release, looking at the perldelta document for the current development release (available on CPAN) can be useful to find out what the next stable release is likely to contain.

Getting the most current maintenance release is almost always a good idea. New maintenance versions of both stable and development releases increment the last digit; depending on what is in them we may or may not need to care about upgrading Perl immediately.

Before fetching and installing a Perl distribution, it is worth taking time to consider whether a binary distribution is suitable or whether it would be worth building from source. Source distributions include the following advantages:

- They can be built to take advantage of the underlying hardware; for example, Pentium+ class processor instructions. Binary distributions are frequently "dumbed down" in terms of processor capabilities in order to be more widely installable.

- Enhanced and experimental features such as extended precision integers and floating point numbers, and user-level threads can be included in the Perl interpreter on Unix platforms (Perl on Windows is always threaded).

- Support for additional packages like the GNU DBM (GDBM) and Berkley DB (DB) libraries can be built as part of the installation process if they are present on the system at the time Perl's build is configured.

Disadvantages of source distributions are that they take longer to carry out and require a compiler and supporting tools for the build process. They are also not always immediately portable to all the platforms on which Perl can run, while binary distributions have already solved the installation issues for their target platform. Having said this, the source is quite capable of being built on the bulk of platforms that we are likely to be using.

Installing Prebuilt Perl Distributions

Perl is available from many websites and FTP servers. Two places to look for it are http://www.perl.org and http://cpan.org, both of which carry the latest releases and links to all distributions, free and commercial, for all platforms on which Perl is known to work. Note that it is generally a good idea to pick a local mirror before downloading, for reasons of both speed and good neighborliness. The main CPAN site automatically tries to redirect browsers to a local site.

Binary distributions are available from a number of places, most notably CPAN's binary ports page at http://cpan.org/ports/index.html, which contains links to a large number of binary ports and incidental notes on availability. Some platforms lag behind the current source code release by a few version points—if this is important, consider building from source instead.

Many platforms can take advantage of prebuilt packages that will install onto a system using standard installation tools. Linux, for example, has both .deb and RPM packages, both of which are commonly available from the websites of the respective distributions (Debian and distributions based on it use .deb packages, while Red Hat and SuSE use RPM). Additionally, RPMs can be found at ftp.rpmfind.net and can be searched for with the rpmfind utility. Solaris packages can be installed with the pkgadd facility, and so on.

In general, packages keep up to date with the current Perl release, but check first and make a note of any changes that may mean getting a more up-to-date release.

Installing Perl on Unix

Installing a binary distribution of Perl is trivial—we just need to unpack it into the place we want it to live; to install it into a system-wide place like /usr/local or /usr/lib we will need root privileges, of course, which is usually denoted by the prompt # on the command line.

Most Unix vendors supply a binary Perl package for their particular platform, and many of them have Perl installed by default. If Perl is not already installed, it makes most sense to pick up the appropriate package from the vendor's web or FTP site.

Additionally, the latest versions of the standard package in both RPM and Debian formats can be tracked down at http://www.activestate.com. After retrieving the correct package, the following command lines for .rpm and .deb files will place them in the relevant location and, therefore, install Perl for us:

```
# rpm -i ActivePerl-5.8.4.810-i686-linux-thread-multi.rpm
# dpkg -i ActivePerl-5.8.5.810-i686-linux-thread-multi.deb
```

A .tar.gz archive is also available, if neither of these formats suits our needs.

If we want to run Perl (and attendant scripts like perldoc) from the command line, we need to either place the executables into a directory that is on the system path or adjust our own path so that we can run Perl from an installation directory of our own choosing. This latter approach is sometimes appropriate even if we could install to a system location, in order to have a second Perl installation independent of a preexisting vendor-supplied Perl. We can use the new copy for development without the risk of upsetting any operating system scripts that might rely on the Perl environment set up by the vendor.

Installing Perl on Windows

There are three main ports of Perl to Windows: the native port, the ActiveState port, and the Cygwin port. The native port can be built straight from the source, which is the preferred alternative; a straight binary port is available from the ports page for those who really can't build from source and can't (or won't) use one of the available alternative binary ports.

The ActiveState port, ActivePerl, is very popular and is freely available from http://www.activestate.com. If we are using Windows 9x, we will need the Microsoft Windows Installer (Windows 2000/XP and ME onwards have this as standard). It is available from the Windows Download page at ActiveState's website: http://www.activestate.com/Products/ActivePerl/Download.html. Select the appropriate Installer and install it first if necessary. We can then download the binary distribution from the Windows Download page or retrieve by FTP from ftp://ftp.activestate.com/ActivePerl/Windows/5.8.

The Cygwin port for the Cygwin Unix compatibility environment is available from http://sourceware.cygnus.com/cygwin. The Cygwin Port has the advantage of supporting (and indeed coming supplied with) many of the GNU utilities, including gcc, gzip, make, and tar, which the CPAN module CPAN.pm prefers to use.

Installing Perl on Macintosh

MacOS X is well provided for in terms of Perl as it is a Unix-based platform. Indeed, Perl comes preinstalled, and we do not need to do anything more to make use of it. In addition, since MacOS X is Unix-based underneath, most of the details for managing Unix installations apply to it also, including *shebang* lines for script identification (#!/usr/local/bin/perl -Tw). However, since Perl is used by some standard system utilities, it can sometimes be advantageous to install a second copy of Perl for development use so as not to accidentally disturb the vendor-supplied version.

The OS 9 port of Perl, also known as *MacPerl*, comes in several different forms, divided into two stand-alone versions and either a binary or source distribution based around the Macintosh Programmer's Workbench (MPW). Either version works on any version of MacOS from 7 through 9. All of the files needed can be found at a mirror of http://cpan.org/ports/mac. Additional information is available at the MacPerl homepage at http://www.macperl.org/.

Building Perl from Source

Building Perl from source is not required for most platforms, so this section can be skipped by those who would prefer not to experiment with compilers or are simply impatient to get on to actually writing Perl code. This section is therefore an introduction to building Perl for those who are curious about building Perl from source, or want to do more than the standard binary installations allow, such as enabling support for threads under Unix.

Source distributions are available from many places, most notably CPAN's Perl source code page at `http://cpan.org/src/index.html`. The current production release is always available as `stable.tar.gz` and `stable.zip`. Development releases are available as `devel.tar.gz` and `devel.zip`. In both cases, the actual version number is not reflected in the filename but is in the name of the directory archived inside, which unpacks as `perl-<version>` (for example, perl-5.8.5).

System administrators who are concerned with the accounting of the files they install can use a source package installation. These provide the advantage of having Perl installed as an accountable package, while at the same time taking advantage of the benefits of compiling it from source. Rather than install a binary RPM, for example, we can acquire the source RPM or SRPM (use `--sources` as an argument to `rpmfind` to locate one) and use `rpm --rebuild perl.srpm` to build a new binary package we can then install.

Building Perl is mostly just a matter of unpacking the source archive (stable or development version) and choosing how to configure the build process. Before moving on to configure the installation, we need to extract the archive. For example, assuming we have the `gzip` source archive on a Unix system, we use the following command lines:

```
> gunzip -c stable.tar.gz | tar -xvf -
> cd perl-5.6.0
```

If we have the GNU version of `tar`, we can also do the unpacking in one step with

```
> tar -xzvf stable.tar.gz
```

Perl builds easily on most Unix platforms; the majority of these can use the supplied `Configure` script to set up and compile Perl with the features and installation locations they want. Other platforms supported by the source bundle are documented in one of the `README` files available in the top-level directory of the source tree. For instance, instructions and additional details for building Perl on Windows are contained in the `README.win32` document. If the platform we want to build on has an associated `README` file, we can build and install Perl on it, but there may be more involved than simply running `Configure`.

Configuring the Source

The `Configure` script sets up the source distribution for compilation on the target platform. It has two modes of operation. The first is an interactive step-by-step question-and-answer session that asks us how we want to build the interpreter, where we want to install it, and the libraries that come with it. At any stage, where a reasonable default can be assumed, the script does so. We usually change just the options we care about and accept the defaults for the rest. At its simplest we can use `Configure` this way by entering

```
> ./Configure
```

The second mode of operation skips the question-and-answer session and assumes the defaults for all questions. Without qualification this will build a standard Perl that installs into the default place (`/usr/lib/perl5` on most systems) when we subsequently carry out the installation. To run `Configure` in this way, we use the `-d` option, for "default."

```
> ./Configure -d
```

In either mode, if we want to have `Configure` automatically start the compilation process after finishing the initial setup, we can specify the `-e` option. To stop `Configure` being concerned about the less important issues regarding how and why it is making its decisions, we can also specify `-s`, for "silent." These are both good options to specify with `-d` to configure and build Perl with minimal fuss.

```
> ./Configure -des
```

Both modes also allow us to specify configuration options on the command line. In the interactive mode, this changes the default option presented to us when Configure asks us the appropriate question; we can change our minds again then if we want to. In the noninteractive mode this is the only chance we get to determine how the resulting Perl is built.

There are many options that can be specified; the question-and-answer session displays most of the ones that it sets, so it is worth running through an interactive configuration once just to see what options a question sets. The most common option to specify is the prefix option, which determines where Perl is installed after it is built and presets the values of many other options. Configuration options are set with the -D flag, so to tell Perl to install itself in /usr/local/perl58 rather than the default location we would use

> ./Configure -des -Dprefix=/usr/local/perl58

This example uses the noninteractive mode of Configure to install Perl under the /usr/local directory. We might do this, for example, if we already have a Perl installation and we do not want to disturb it. Similarly, we can use -DDEBUGGING to enable a debug version of Perl and enable the -D option.

> ./Configure -des -Dprefix=/usr/local/perl58dbg -DDEBUGGING

Another option to combine with prefix that ensures we don't upset an existing installation is the installusrbinperl option. By default this is now disabled, although prior to Perl 5.8 it was enabled. It causes the installation stage to copy Perl and a few supporting scripts into the default place for system executables. Unless we change it, this default is /usr/bin. To disable an option we use -U, so to set up Perl 5.6 or earlier to install elsewhere and leave the existing installation untouched, we would use

> ./Configure -des -Dprefix=/usr/local/perl56 -Uinstallusrbinperl

Or to have Perl 5.8 do the extra installation work:

> ./Configure -des -Dprefix=/usr/local/perl58 -Dinstallusrbinperl

The PerlIO support in Perl 5.8 and later can similarly be disabled (if we have good reason to believe that the native support is better) with -Uuseperlio.

A complete list of Configure's options can be viewed by using the -h or --help option on the command line.

> ./Configure --help

If we have been through the configuration process at least once before, there will be a config.sh file present. In the interactive mode, Configure will ask if we want to use it, and then preset itself with defaults from the previous run. This file contains all the names of the options that we can supply on the command line too, so it can be handy for finding out how to set options. Note that if we are rebuilding Perl with different options, we should additionally execute a make distclean before we configure and build Perl a second time.

> make distclean
> ./Configure

Building the Source

Once configuration is complete, we actually build and install Perl by typing

> make

Perl builds itself in several steps. The first step is a stripped-down version of Perl called miniperl. This is a feature-complete version of the interpreter, but at this point none of the extension modules involving C code (for example, Socket) have been built yet.

The miniperl interpreter generates the Config module, which provides the information needed to build the extensions. The one critical extension that is built is DynaLoader, which provides support for dynamically loading extensions. We can configure which extensions are built, and whether they are built dynamically or statically, by configuring the build appropriately with options like -Dnoextensions=DB_file or -Donlyextensions=Dynaloader,Socket or answering the interactive questions appropriately.

The penultimate build step is to generate the scripts that come with Perl such as cpan, perldoc, and perlcc. Finally, the manual pages are generated and Perl is ready to be installed. To install to a privileged location, we will usually need root or administrator privileges. Assuming we do, we can just enter

```
# make install
```

This will build and install Perl according to the choices we made at the configuration stage. If we are overwriting an existing installation and prudently want to test the new build before we wreck anything, we can build Perl without installing it, test it, and then install it only if we are happy.

```
> make
> make test
> su
```

```
Password:
```

```
# make install
```

To verify that the installation is complete (and to reverify it later, if need be), use the perlivp "installation verification procedure" tool.

```
> perlivp -p
```

This will print out a series of "OK" messages if all is well, or generate appropriate messages if any problems are found. The -p is optional; it prints out the meaning of each test before it is run. We can also use -v to generate verbose output of what is being checked, if necessary.

Building a Binary Distribution

If we want to create a built Perl distribution for installation elsewhere, we can use the DESTDIR makefile macro to send the installed files to a different directory than the default.

```
> make install DESTDIR=/tmp/perl58dist
> cd /tmp/perl58dist
> tar cvf perl58dist.tar *
```

At the end of the build process a shell script called myconfig is generated with complete details of the configuration used to build Perl. This is handy for checking what actually was used to build Perl; a similar output can be generated from Perl itself with the -V option.

```
> perl -V
```

Individual options can be checked by qualifying the option. For example:

```
> perl -V:usethreads
```

The usethreads value is a Boolean one, so this command will come back with a line containing the word define if the option was set, or undef if it was not. Other options like cc or osname return string values.

The information provided by the -V option can also be accessed from the Config.pm module, which is generated from the contents of config.sh when Perl was built. Supporting scripts like h2xs and xsubpp use it to configure the build environment for building extension modules.

Building a Threaded Perl Interpreter

One specific reason for building Perl from the source distribution rather than installing a precompiled binary is to enable support for threads. Threads are a powerful way to write multitasking applications without the overheads of multiple processes, and are fundamental to languages such as Java. In Perl, threads are technically still considered experimental (although from Perl 5.8 they are in fact fully mature), so they are not built by default.

The Configure script poses two questions about threads: firstly, Build a threading Perl?, and secondly, Use interpreter-based threads? You'll almost certainly want to answer y and y respectively. (For Perl 5.6 and before, the answer to the second question should be n to use 5.005 threads, but unless legacy code needs it, this older thread implementation is deprecated and should be avoided if at all possible.)

Unfortunately, this will not on its own result in a working threaded Perl interpreter due to technical issues surrounding the configuration process. We must also select thread support on the command line with the usethreads option. Here is how we would do that before entering an interactive question and answer session:

> **./Configure -des -Dusethreads**

(If 5.005 threads are really necessary, also add -Duse5005threads to the end of this command.)

To build a threaded version of Perl noninteractively and in a different location as described earlier:

> **./Configure -des -Dusethreads -Dprefix=/usr/local/perl58thr**

Either way, we should eventually create a threaded Perl interpreter. If all has gone well, we should have a threads module in the standard library (for 5.005 threads, the module is instead called Thread—it should not be possible to have both modules installed simultaneously). We can check that it is present by executing

> **/usr/local/perl58/bin/perldoc threads**

See the latter part of Chapter 21 for a description of threads and why we might want to use them, and also the threaded network server example in Chapter 22.

Supporting 64-Bit Integers and Long Doubles

If Perl's build configuration script finds itself running on a natively 64-bit platform, Perl's own integers will automatically be 64 bit too. Otherwise, 32-bit integers are assumed.

Some 32-bit platforms can provide simulated 64-bit integers, for example, if the underlying C compiler (with which Perl is built) understands the long long type. To enable basic but minimal support for 64-bit integers, enable the use64bitint option.

> **./Configure -des -Duse64bitint ...**

This will give Perl 64-bit-wide scalar integers, although the underlying support for them may not be all that efficient. To get fully 64-bit integer support, use use64bitmax instead.

> **./Configure -des -Duse64bitint ...**

This hopefully will result in true 64-bit support not just for integers, but for internal pointers too, but depending on the actual support provided by the operating system we may find that every dependant library also needs to be rebuilt to support 64-bit integers, or that the resulting Perl executable does not work at all—*caveat machinator*.

Long doubles may be similarly enabled, even if the platform does not appear to natively handle them, with the uselongdouble option.

```
> ./Configure -des -Duselongdouble ...
```

Finally, to enable both long doubles and minimal 64-bit integer support we can also say

```
> ./Configure -des -Dusemorebits ...
```

Specifying Extra Compiler and Linker Flags

For the most part there will be few reasons why we might want to change the flags that the configuration script calculates for compiling and linking Perl. However, should the need arise, we can add our own flags with the -A option. While -D defines an option and -U undefines it, -A allows us to change it in almost any way we like. While it can change any configuration option, it is usually used to manipulate the compiler and linker flags that Configure does not give us direct control over. For example:

```
> ./Configure -Accflags=-DPERL_DEBUGGING_MSTATS -Dusemymalloc=y
```

This enables an additional symbol during compilation that enables support for the mstat function in the Devel::Peek module, which in turn allows us to study Perl's use of memory. It only works with Perl's internal memory allocator so we tell Configure to turn it on too. (Normally Configure will choose which malloc to use based on what it thinks of the platform's native implementation.)

We can override many low-level options this way, including ldflags, libs, and so on. In normal use -A appends a value to the existing definition separated by a space, since this is normally what we need (-D and -U are more convenient if we just want to override a value). However, we can qualify the value with append: or prepend: to directly attach the new text to the end or start of the existing value too, if need be. For information on these and other usage modes, see Configure -h.

One specialized option that affects the compiler flags is optimize. We can use it to control the optimization level the compiler applies to Perl. To build Perl with debugging information (which also switches on the DEBUGGING option as a side effect), we can say

```
> ./Configure -Doptimize='-g'
```

If we happen to know of additional optimization options beyond that which the configuration script knows about, we can try them here too.

Installing Extra Modules

If we specify the extras option (or answer y to the question in an interactive session), we can have Configure automatically download and install additional modules, typically extensions with a C-based component, into the standard Perl library. For example:

```
> ./Configure -des -Dextras="DBI Bundle::DBD::mysql" ...
```

The extras option uses the CPAN module (covered in more detail later in the chapter) to find the requested modules and so will only work if we have access to CPAN via the Internet, or a local module repository.

Extending the Default Library Search Path

Perl by default searches a standard list of directories whenever we ask it to load in a module. This list is held in the special variable @INC and can be seen by running perl -V. While there are many ways to augment @INC from the command line, environment, or within Perl code, it is sometimes handy to be able to add additional locations to the default list. We might want to do this, for example, if we have a standard location for specific shared Perl modules that are maintained outside the standard installation locations.

To add additional paths, we need to tell `Configure` about them. Probably the easiest way is the `otherlibdirs` option. For instance:

```
> ./Configure -des -Dotherlibdirs=/home/share/lib/perl:/home/share/lib/site-perl
```

These directories are added to the end of the list, so they provide additional search locations but will not override a system-installed library (since the system locations are searched first). To put additional locations at the front of the list, we need to append to the `CCFLAGS` makefile macro, which we can do like this (both lines that follow should be typed as a single command):

```
> ./Configure -des -Accflags=
```

```
'-DAPPLLIB_EXP=\"/home/share/lib/perl:/home/share/lib/site-perl\"'
```

We do not need to worry about specifying architecture-specific subdirectories with either option; they will automatically be extrapolated from the base paths we provide.

Reusing and Overriding a Previous Configuration

The final result of running `Configure` is, among other files, a script named `config.sh`. This contains all the answers to the questions we answered in interactive mode, or specified or left as the default on the command line. If we run `Configure` a second time, it will see this file and automatically make use of it.

If we have specific requirements that are difficult to manage as command-line options to the configuration script, we can instead create a second script in the manner of `config.sh` called `config.over`. This script, if present, is run at the end of the configuration phase (whether we chose to answer questions interactively or not) and just before the `config.sh` file is written. We can therefore use it to automatically override any number of configuration options. For example, to force support for 64-bit integers:

```
use64bitint='define';
```

Alternatively, we can use the -O option to override `config.sh` for a specified option. With this in place, we can use -U and -D to specify new values for options and override the previously saved answers recorded in `config.sh`. Without it, `config.sh` will override the command-line options unless we tell `Configure` to disregard it.

To use an alternate configuration file, for example, a `config.sh` copied to a backup name for later reuse, use the -f option.

```
> ./Configure -des -f perl58thr64.sh
```

Note that `config.over` cannot be called another name, however.

Differences for Windows and Macintosh

Building Perl from source on Windows is broadly similar to building it on Unix with the primary difference being the choice of compiler and make utility used. Running `perldoc perlwin32` provides some reasonably detailed information on the options available. For those without a Perl to use to run `perldoc`, the pages can be found in the unpacked distribution and read as unprocessed `.pod` files (which are reasonably legible even so) and are also available in HTML at `http://cpan.org`.

To build Perl for MacOS X is the same process as for Unix. For OS 7 to 9, it first requires installing the base packages and then compiling the source code with the MPW. Refer to the earlier section titled "Installing Perl on Macintosh" for details on which files to get and install.

Other Platforms

Other than generic Unix support and Windows, several other platforms are supported by the source distribution. Each of these has a `README` file located in the top of the tree that provides information to get Perl built and installed on that platform. For example, `README.cygwin` provides notes on building Perl for the Cygwin Unix compatibility environment on Windows.

Windows has more than one option, depending on whether we want to use the native Win32 port, the Cygwin support libraries, MinGW, or the DOS version (which requires the `djgpp` compiler available from `http://www.midpec.com/djgpp/`). Less common platforms are more or less functional but don't necessarily expect them to work completely, especially very old, very new, or very obscure platforms.

Running Perl

Having installed Perl, it is time to run some programs. The core of Perl is the Perl interpreter, the engine that actually interprets, compiles, and runs Perl scripts. Perl is not a traditional interpreted language like shell scripts; instead the interpreter compiles it from the original human-readable version into a condensed internal format generically known as *bytecode*. This bytecode is then executed by the interpreter. All Perl programs therefore go through two phases: a compile phase where the syntax is checked and the source code—including any modules used—is converted into bytecode; and a runtime phase, where the bytecode is executed.

Perl tries hard to be platform independent, but every platform has its own way of doing things, including its own way of running Perl. The first item on the agenda is usually to teach the operating system how to recognize a Perl script as a Perl script. Unix-like platforms have it easiest since Perl grew up there. Windows, Macintosh, and other platforms can be set up to handle Perl too, in their own particular ways.

The Perl interpreter supports several command-line options that affect its behavior in both the compile and runtime phases. These include essential features like enabling warnings or extracting configuration information, and less obvious but still useful features like implicit loops and automated input parsing that allow us to use Perl as a generic command-line tool. Since we do not always want to specify command-line options directly, Perl allows us to set them, as well as some of Perl's other default values, through environment variables. On Windows, we can set some values via the registry too.

Starting Perl Applications

In order for a Perl script to run, it must be given to the Perl interpreter to execute. Depending on the platform, there are various different ways this can happen. The simplest way, which works on all platforms that have a shell or equivalent command-line mechanism, is to run Perl directly, and supply the script name as an argument.

```
> perl myscript.pl
```

This presumes, of course, that the Perl interpreter `perl`, `perl.exe`, etc., is somewhere on the path defined for the shell. We can also supply command-line switches to Perl when we run it directly. For example, to enable warnings:

```
> perl -w myscript.pl
```

However, we usually want to run a Perl application directly, that is, to type

```
> myscript.pl
```

For this to work, the shell has to know that `myscript.pl` is a Perl script, find and execute the Perl interpreter, and feed the program to it. Because Perl tries to be helpful, it will actually tell us the best way to start up an application this way if we ask it using the -V option.

```
> perl -V:startperl
```

If the platform supports a form of implicit indication that allows a script to indicate that it is a Perl script and not some other form of executable, this will produce the information required, adjusted for the location that Perl is installed in. For example, on a Unix system we get something like

```
> startperl='#!/usr/bin/perl';
```

This indicates that #!/usr/bin/perl can be added to the start of any script to enable it to start up using Perl automatically.

Perl on Unix

Unix systems have it easiest when it comes to setting up scripts to run with Perl automatically, largely in part due to its close and long-term relationship with shells.

When the operating system comes to execute a Perl script, it doesn't know it is a Perl script, just a text file. However, when it sees that the first line starts with #!, it executes the remainder of the line and passes the name of the script to it as an argument, for example:

```
#!/usr/bin/perl -w
... rest of script ...
```

In this case the command happens to run the Perl interpreter. So, to start a script up directly on Unix systems we need to add this line, (possibly embellished with additional command-line options) to the start of a Perl script and make the script file executable.

This technique is standard on Unix platforms. Shells on other platforms don't understand the significance of a first line beginning #! and so we have to adopt other approaches.

Perl on Windows

MS Windows 9x/ME and Windows NT/2000/XP can make use of file extension associations stored in the registry to associate the .pl extension with the Perl interpreter. Handily, the ActiveState distribution offers to do this automatically at installation, and also makes sure that command-line arguments are passed correctly. While the shebang line is not used to locate the interpreter, trailing options are detected and used.

Otherwise, we need to follow the following instructions: select Settings ➤ Folder Options from the Start menu and click the File Types tab. From here click the New Type button and a new dialog box will appear. Click the New Icon button and type in the location. Now fill in the relevant boxes appropriately, using the .pl extension. When we click the New button to create a new action, we have the option to give the action a name and specify the path of the Perl interpreter, in this case.

Alternatively, we can simply convert a Perl script into a batch file. We can do this by using the supplied executable pl2bat. This makes the script stand-alone, but leaves the original file untouched also. It also changes the script name, so $0 (the batch file variable which refers to the name of itself) will be different inside scripts. Alternatively, if the script has no extension, we can copy the supplied batch file, runperl.bat, to another batch file with the same name as the Perl script. This achieves exactly the same result as it uses the $0 variable to call the Perl script via the Perl interpreter.

One problem with most Windows shells is that they do not do command-line expansion of wildcards like Unix shells do, instead opting to leave this task to the application. We do not have to put up with this, though. To fix the problem we can make use of the File::DosGlob module in a small utility module that we can preload by setting the variable PERL5OPT in the system's default environment. See perldoc perlwin32 for details of how to do this.

There is also a commercial package called perl2exe, which will convert the Perl script into a stand-alone executable, which may be appropriate for some needs.

Perl on Macintosh

MacOS X is based on Unix, so we can run any Perl script using Unix conventions like shebang lines.

Running Perl programs on Macintoshes with MacOS versions 7 to 9 is simple—each script just needs to have the appropriate creator and type attributes set and the operating system will automatically recognize it for a Perl script and invoke the interpreter. Running Perl from the command line is also simple, or rather, impossible since there is no command line. However, MacPerl provides the ability to save scripts as "applets," which can be executed by the usual double click or even just packaged up into a fully self-contained executable file. For more information on all issues concerning MacPerl, consult the website http://www.macperl.com.

The Command Line

Whether or not we invoke Perl directly or implicitly, we can supply it with a number of command-line options. We do not always have to supply command-line options explicitly. For systems that support shebang lines, we can add them to the end of the command contained in the first line.

```
#!/usr/bin/perl -Tw
...
```

Alternatively, and on systems that don't support shebang lines, we can set an environment variable. Perl examines several of these when it starts up and configures itself according to their contents. For command-line options, the special environment variable is PERL5OPT, which may contain command-line options, exactly as if they were appearing on a real command line. Here is how we can use it to cause Perl to enable warnings (-w) and taint mode (-T), and load the strict module for strict syntax checks:

```
rem Windows
set PERL5OPT = wMstrict

# Unix - csh-like
setenv PERL5OPT "-Mstrict -wT"

# Unix - Bourne shell-like
export PERL5OPT="-Mstrict -wT"
```

We can set PERL5OPT in a shell startup script or batch file (.profile or similar for Unix shells, AUTOEXEC.BAT for Windows 9x, or alternatively the registry for Windows in general).

Command-Line Options

Perl's command-line options are detailed on the perlrun manual page, which we can read with perldoc perlrun. We can also obtain a short list of options with

```
> perl -h
```

For completeness, here is the output of running this command:

```
-0[octal]        specify record separator (\0, if no argument)
-a               autosplit mode with -n or -p (splits $_ into @F)
-C[number/list]  enables the listed Unicode features
-c               check syntax only (runs BEGIN and CHECK blocks)
-d[:debugger]    run program under debugger
-e program       one line of program (several -e's allowed, omit programfile)
-F/pattern/      split() pattern for -a switch (//'s are optional)
-i[extension]    edit <> files in place (makes backup if extension supplied)
-Idirectory      specify @INC/#include directory (several -I's allowed)
```

```
-l[octal]       enable line ending processing, specifies line terminator
-[mM][-]module  execute 'use/no module...' before executing program
-n              assume 'while (<>) { ... }' loop around program
-p              assume loop like -n but print line also, like sed
-P              run program through C preprocessor before compilation
-s              enable rudimentary parsing for switches after programfile
-S              look for programfile using PATH environment variable
-t              enable tainting warnings
-T              enable tainting checks
-u              dump core after parsing program
-U              allow unsafe operations
-v              print version, subversion (includes VERY IMPORTANT perl info)
-V[:variable]   print configuration summary (or a single Config.pm variable)
-w              enable many useful warnings (RECOMMENDED)
-W              enable all warnings
-x[directory]   strip off text before #!perl line and perhaps cd to directory
-X              disable all warnings
```

If we build a debugging Perl, the -D option will also be available, as mentioned earlier. This is generally of interest only to programmers who are interested in working on Perl itself, or writing C-based extensions. The -C option is new to Perl 5.8. We won't cover every option here (they are all covered somewhere in the book, however), though we look at several in the following text. Detailed information on each option is available from the perlrun manual page that comes with Perl.

Command-Line Syntax

The simplest use of Perl is to run a script with no arguments, like this:

> `perl myscript.pl`

Assuming myscript.pl is the following simple example:

```
#!/usr/bin/perl
print "Hello Perl World!\n";
```

This will produce the traditional greeting

```
Hello Perl World!
```

Perl expects to see a script name at some point on the command line, otherwise it executes whatever input it receives. We can also therefore say

> `perl < myscript.pl`

Command-line options, if we choose to specify them, go before the script. This command enables warnings, taint mode, and includes the strict module:

> `perl -w -T -Mstrict myscript.pl`

The non-fatal version of taint mode, available from Perl 5.8 onwards, is enabled instead with a lowercase -t.

> `perl -w -t -Mstrict myscript.pl`

Some command-line options take an argument. For example, -e takes a string of code to evaluate, enclosed in quotes. Some options (-e included) allow a space after them. Others, like -m and -M do not—if we try to do so Perl will return an error.

```
No space is allowed after -M
```

Command-line options that take no argument may be grouped together, so `-w` and `-T` can be grouped into either `-wT` or `-Tw`. We can also add one command with an argument, such as `-M`, if it is the last in the group. For example:

```
> perl -TwMstrict myscript.pl
```

Supplying Arguments to Scripts

If we run a script directly, we can pass arguments to it that can be read inside the program (by examining the special array variable @ARGV).

```
> myscript.pl -testing -1 -2 -3
```

If we run a script via the Perl interpreter explicitly, we cannot just add options to the end of the command line, because Perl will absorb them into its own command line. However, if we add the special sequence `--` Perl will stop processing at that point and any further arguments will be passed to the script instead.

```
> perl -TwMstrict myscript.pl -- -testing -1 -2 -3
```

If the script's arguments do not look like options (that is, are not prefixed with a minus), there is no problem and we can say

```
> perl -TwMstrict myscript.pl testing 1 2 3
```

Even though this works, it is often a good idea to include the `--` sequence anyway, just in case we come back to edit the command and add minus-prefixed arguments later on. We will discuss and expand on the special variable @ARGV and sequence `--` later on in Chapter 6.

Using Perl As a Generic Command-Line Utility

With a little imagination, we can make Perl do a lot with just a few of its command-line options.

In particular, the `-e`, `-n`, `-p`, and `-l` options allow us to perform fairly powerful functions with a single command. The `-e` option allows us to execute code directly, rather than specifying a program file, so we don't need to actually write a program, save it to a file, and then execute it. The `-n` and `-p` options place an implicit `while` loop around the code we specify that reads from standard input, turning it into the body of the loop. The `-l` option strips off the terminator from each line read, then configures `print` to put it back afterwards.

By combining these options creatively, we can produce any manner of quick one-line text processing commands using Perl. Say we wanted to add line numbers to the start of every line of a program. We could write a program to do that, but we could also just type

```
> perl -ne 'print "$.: $_"' < in.pl > out.txt
```

The same command in MS Windows would be

```
> perl -ne "print ""$.: $_ """ <in.pl >out.txt
```

The special variable $. holds the line number, and $_ the contents of the line just read from the input. The option `-n` puts the whole thing in a loop, and the rest is redirection. If for some reason we wanted the line numbers on the end, we enter this command for the Bourne shell in Unix:

```
> perl -nle 'print "$_ [$.]"' < in.pl > out.txt
```

Here `-l` strips the original line ending, but redefines Perl's output formatting so that the `print` puts it back. Of course, these are just simple examples, but throw in a regular expression or a module loaded by the `-m` or `-M` flag and we can do some surprising things. For example, this command pulls a web page from a remote server and prints it out using the `LWP::Simple` module (available from CPAN):

```
> perl -MLWP::Simple -e 'getprint "http://www.myserver.com/img.gif"'
```

Other options we can use in these kinds of super-simple scripts are -a and -F, which enable and configure autosplit mode. This, among other things, allows us to tell Perl to automatically break down lines into individual words. Another useful option is -i, which edits a file in-place, so that transformations we perform on what we read from it are actually enacted on the file itself.

Finally, we can use the Perl debugger as a generic Perl shell by passing -d and -e with a trivial but valid piece of Perl code such as 1, and possibly -w to enable warnings.

```
> perl -dwe1
```

See Chapter 17 for more on the debugger and the features available from this "shell."

The Perl Environment

All environment variables present in the shell that executes Perl are made available inside Perl scripts in the special hash variable %ENV. In addition, Perl pays special attention to several environment variables and adjusts its configuration according to their contents.

Windows machines may (but are not required to) specify environment information in the registry, under either

HKEY_CURRENT_USER\Software\Perl

or

HKEY_LOCAL_MACHINE\Software\Perl

In the case of duplicate entries, the local machine settings are overridden by the current user settings. Entries are of type REG_SZ or REG_EXPAND_SZ and may include any of the standard Perl environment variables (that is, any variable starting with PERL) as described in Table 1-1. We can also specify additional path information to the library include path @INC, in both generic and version specific forms (we use version 5.8.5 here for example purposes) by setting some or all of the entries in Table 1-1.

Table 1-1. *Windows Registry Entries for Extending @INC*

Entry	Description
lib	Standard library path extension
sitelib	Site library path extension
vendorlib	Vendor library path extension
lib-5.8.5	Version-specific standard library path extension
sitelib-5.8.5	Version-specific site library path extension
vendorlib-5.8.5	Version-specific vendor library path extension

General Environment Variables Used by Perl

There are three general environment variables that are used by Perl, which we should consider here. The first of these is PATH. This is actually the standard shell search path that Perl uses to locate external commands when executed from Perl scripts. Sensible programs often set this variable internally and do not rely on the supplied value. It is also used by the -S command-line option that causes Perl to search for the specified script using the path.

The other two variables are HOME and LOGDIR. If the chdir function is used in Perl without an argument, then Perl checks the value of HOME and changes to that directory if set. If HOME is not set, Perl checks LOGDIR as a last resort. If neither is set, chdir does nothing.

Perl-Specific Environment Variables

Perl looks for and reads the values of several environment variables that, if present, we can use to control the behavior of the interpreter when it starts up. Almost all of these start with PERL5 and the most commonly used of them are PERL5LIB and PERL5OPT.

The variable PERL5LIB defines the library search path, a list of directories that Perl searches when the do, require, or use statement is used. The value of this variable becomes @INC inside the program. (The old name for this variable, PERLLIB, is only used if it is set and PERL5LIB is not.) We can also modify the default value of @INC, defined when Perl was built, using the -I flag.

The environment variable PERL5OPT, as its name may suggest, may contain a list of the command-line options, in the same format as they would be if supplied directly.

The variable PERL5DB specifies the command used to load the debugger when the -d option is used. By default this is set to

```
BEGIN { require 'perl5db.pl' }
```

If we have created our own modified debugger, we can set this variable to have Perl use it by default. Setting it to nothing effectively disables the -d option altogether.

The last of the most commonly used Perl environment variables, PERL5SHELL, is a Windows-specific variable that allows us to override the default shell used to execute external commands when executing external commands with backticks or the qx operator. Perl uses its own variable rather than relying on the value of COMSPEC as the latter is not always set to a desirable value for a Perl-created subshell process. The default is

command.com /c	Windows 9x/ME
cmd.exe /x/d/c	Windows NT/2000/XP

(In general it is desirable to avoid starting an external shell at all, and we devote some time in Chapter 14 to the why and how of avoiding shells.)

Less commonly used, and generally only of interest to those involved in developing or debugging Perl itself, are the PERL_DESTRUCT_LEVEL and PERL_DEBUG_MSTATS variables, both of which are advanced options. If the Perl interpreter supports the -D flag, PERL_DESTRUCT_LEVEL controls the behavior of Perl's garbage collector for the destruction of references. If Perl was built to use the malloc library that comes supplied with it (perl -V:d_malloc), PERL_DEBUG_MSTATS enables an additional memory statistics debugging mode for the -D flag (which must also be available). If set to a false value, statistics are dumped after the program completes. If set to a true value, statistics are also dumped after the compilation stage and before the execution stage.

If PerlIO is supported by the interpreter (the default from Perl 5.8), then the environment variable PERLIO can be used to control the default layers set on filehandles. See Chapter 12 for more information.

Plenty of Perl modules respond to their own special environment variables. For example, to pick a module that is close to the core of Perl, the Perl debugger examines the PERL5DB_OPTS environment variable for configuration information. See perldoc perlrun for a full and exhaustive list of standard variables.

Certain Perl features are also sensitive to certain locale environment variables if the use locale directive is specified. We cover locale and internationalization at the end of the book.

Installing Modules

Once we have a working Perl installation, we can install additional Perl modules to expand upon the features provided by the standard library that comes with the interpreter. The majority of Perl modules are available from CPAN, which has mirrors worldwide, and take the form of prepackaged archives containing the module code itself, supporting scripts or data files (if any), and an installation script called Makefile.PL that is used to generate a makefile to actually carry out the installation.

It is relatively easy to download a Perl module distribution and then install it by hand, either directly into the standard library, or into a local or site installation directory. However, Perl provides the cpan tool to automate the process of finding, downloading, building, installing, and testing a new module distribution.

Perl module distributions come in two distinct forms—those that bind to C (or C++) and require a C compiler to install, commonly called *extensions*, and pure-Perl modules that don't. While the latter can be installed almost anywhere, extensions obviously need a functional compiler available. For most Unix-like platforms, this is rarely an issue, but for Windows it is easier to use the PPM tool, which is essentially "CPAN for Windows" and which retrieves precompiled CPAN modules from the ActiveState PPM repository, eliminating the need for a compiler or other build tools.

In this section, we will first look at installing modules by hand, before moving on to see how the cpan and PPM tools can automate much of the manual labor for us.

Installing Modules by Hand

The process of installing modules is essentially the same for every platform; the most significant difference between different platforms is the tools required to perform each step of unpacking, building, and installing a module.

Installing Modules on Unix

Unix systems can install module packages downloaded directly from a CPAN mirror (see http://cpan.org). The package filename usually takes the form Some-Module-1.23.tar.gz, that is, a *gzipped tarball*. To install it, we first unpack it.

```
> gunzip -c (or gzip -dc ) Some-Module-1.23.tar.gz | tar xvf -
```

If we have the GNU version of tar (any Linux- or BSD-based system should have this), we can perform both steps in one go with

```
> tar -zxvf Some-Module-1.23.tar.gz
```

Either approach extracts the files from the archive without decompressing the archive file itself.

Having unpacked the module, we go into the source directory (which should have the same name, minus the tar.gz suffix) and generate Makefile from the supplied Makefile.PL file.

```
> cd Some-Module-1.23
> perl Makefile.PL
```

Next, we install and test the module using make.

```
> make
> make test
> su
```

```
Password:
```

```
# make install
```

Finally, if we want to keep the original source directory but clean out all the additional files created by the building and installation process, we can use the standard

```
> make clean
```

If we change our minds and still have the source at hand, we can also uninstall the package again.

```
# make uninstall
```

Installing Modules on Windows

To install CPAN modules by hand on Windows, we use the same general technique as with Unix, only with different decompression software. The .zip package files can be decompressed using the popular WinZip, infozip, or any other ZIP-compatible decompression tool. Most of these tools can also handle Unix-style .tar.gz files of the kind supplied by CPAN.

We can install the unpacked distribution with a make tool (such as nmake) in the usual way. For example, assuming dmake:

```
> nmake
> nmake test
> nmake install
> nmake clean
```

This of course relies on a functional C compiler being available if the module happens to contain C code. For pure Perl modules, this isn't a problem.

If we don't have a make equivalent, and we don't have any C code to deal with, we can sometimes get away with simply copying the files that were unpacked into an appropriate part of the standard library tree, for instance the \site\lib branch. However, some modules use a module called AutoSplit on installation to carve up the module source. (Another module, AutoLoad, then loads and compiles pieces of the module on demand.) Since we are unable to make use of the standard installation process, we need to perform a split ourselves to completely install the module. If a module file uses the AutoLoad module, we will need to run the following from the top of Perl's installation to finish the installation:

```
> perl -MAutoSplit -e "autosplit site\lib\ to \module.pm site\lib\auto"
```

(The AutoLoad and AutoSplit modules are covered in more detail in Chapter 10.)

Installing Modules on Macintosh

Again, MacOS X is just a particular case of the more general Unix case. Only the default install locations differ as the layout is a little different from most other Unix platforms.

Precompiled binary versions of some packages for OS 9 and earlier created by Chris Nandor are also available from http://cpan.org/authors/id/CNANDOR/. As usual, use a mirror of http://cpan.org if possible. Also available from this page is cpan-mac, a package of utilities that makes it possible to use the CPAN module with MacPerl. (The very latest versions of MacPerl include this functionality into the distribution.) However, it will not build modules that contain C code.

OS 9 systems can unpack source package files with Stuffit or one of its many cousins to get the unpacked source. If the package requires building C source, then things get tricky—a copy of the MPW is required, plus a certain amount of dexterity. The MacPerl homepage, http://www.macperl.com/, offers some advice and links that may help with this, as well as installing MacPerl itself.

If the package does not contain C code, then we can install it by manually moving the package files to the Perl library, generally under the site_perl folder, replicating the directory structure of the package as we go. Note that the line endings of the source files need to be Apple format—LF/CR, rather than CR/LF or just LF. The decompression should handle this automatically.

As with Windows, we may also need to manually split the module to complete its installation. This will be the case if the module file uses the AutoLoad module. Since there is no command line on a Macintosh, we will need to create and run the following to finish the installation:

```
#!perl -w
use AutoSplit;
autosplit "${MACPERL}site_perl:Path:To:Module.pm",
   "${MACPERL}site_perl:auto";
```

Installing Modules on Other Platforms

The CPAN website contains some instructions for installing modules on several platforms on the Installing CPAN Modules page at http://cpan.org/modules/INSTALL.html. Some of this information is also available from perldoc perlmodinstall, both sources with varying degrees of concurrency.

Installing Modules from CPAN

The CPAN module and cpan command provide a Perl-based interface to the CPAN archive for Unix-like platforms. We can use either the module or the tool to scan CPAN for new packages, check for updates on existing packages, and install new ones, including dependent modules and module bundles.

For Windows, ActivePerl provides the PPM tool, which provides a repository of many Perl modules from CPAN, preconfigured and built for several different Windows platforms. PPM is covered near the end of the chapter.

A new alternative interface to the CPAN repository is the *CPAN++*, a.k.a. *CPANPLUS* project. While this is currently still in development, it can be downloaded from CPAN and installed like any other module. It provides a cpanp tool in place of cpan, and will become the replacement for the CPAN module from Perl 5.10 onwards. While not yet ready for general release, CPANPLUS is well worth a look for those already familiar with the CPAN module or in search of a better tool for the job. For more information, see http://cpanplus.sourceforge.net/.

Starting and Configuring CPAN

To start the CPAN module from the command line, we can invoke the shell mode with

```
# perl -MCPAN -e shell
```

This command runs Perl, loading the CPAN module into memory and running the shell subroutine, which provides an interactive interface. If we don't want to use the shell, we can also use the cpan utility to run one command at a time. While its usage is very slightly different, the utility provides access to all the same underlying features as the module.

If we have Perl installed in a privileged place, we will need to be superuser to actually install a module (though we can still perform queries). If CPAN has never been configured, it will run through a set of questions to set itself up. Like Perl's build configuration, most of these are self-evident, and others are computed by default. However, the module needs to fetch several resources, including a current list of CPAN mirrors during the installation process, so it is very helpful (though not absolutely necessary) to have an active Internet connection during the configuration process.

Unix systems will generally have no trouble, but non-Unix systems will need to make sure that they have acceptable versions of at least some of the following command-line utilities:

- A copy of gzip.
- A tar program.
- A zip/unzip program like WinZip or infozip.
- A make program, e.g., dmake or nmake for Windows. nmake can be downloaded from http://www.microsoft.com and comes as standard with many Visual Studio products and the freely downloadable Microsoft Visual C++ Toolkit 2003 available at http://msdn.microsoft.com/visualc/vctoolkit2003/.

- A copy of the open source *lynx* browser (this is only necessary if Net::FTP is not installed yet).
- An noninteractive FTP command-line client (e.g., ncftpget, freely available and installed on many Linux and other Unix-like platforms).

The configuration process will also ask about FTP and HTTP proxies, and then fetch a list of mirrors from which we should pick two or three in the local area. This is the only part of the configuration process that requires us to make some considered choices, rather than entering return to accept the default. Select the appropriate region and country, then enter three or more numbers for the servers that will be used to download modules.

Note that any of these options can be changed later with the o command in shell mode.

The CPAN module supports command-line editing and history, if supplied by the Term::ReadLine module. This, and the Term::ReadKey module, can of course be installed with the CPAN module.

Once we have the CPAN module configured, we should have a cpan> prompt at which we can enter a variety of commands. Typing h or ? will generate a helpful list of available commands. If we have Term::ReadLine and Term::ReadKey installed and the GNU readline library available (see Chapter 15 for more on all of these), the prompt should be highlighted and underlined, otherwise we can install them.

```
cpan> install Term::ReadKey
...

cpan> install Term::ReadLine
...
```

We can also install modules directly from the command line using the cpan utility.

```
> cpan Term::ReadKey Term::ReadLine
```

Installing these modules significantly improves the CPAN shell by adding better interaction and a command-line history. Alternatively, we can install the CPAN bundle, which contains all the modules that CPAN can use, using the following command:

```
cpan> install Bundle::CPAN
...
```

Either way, the CPAN module will try to fetch the module or modules we requested. If we do not have an up-to-date copy of the Net::FTP or LWP module (for FTP or HTTP transfers, respectively) installed, then it will try to use the lynx browser to fetch it. If we don't have any of these installed, we will have to use an FTP client to fetch and install at least one of them manually. We should use reload cpan after executing any of the preceding commands to update the running CPAN shell.

Installing Modules

The CPAN module provides four commands related to installation. The main one, and in practice the one we tend to use the most often, is install. This takes a bundle, distribution, or module name (it is not practical to install an author, although it would be an intriguing concept) and determines the appropriate distribution file or files to fetch, build, and install. This means we can install modules without needing to worry about which actual distribution file they belong in. For example, we can say

```
cpan> install Apache::Registry
```

Installation is a multistep process:

1. The currently installed version (if any) is compared with that available from CPAN. If the installation is up-to-date and we are not doing a force (see "Installing Modules in Stages" later in this chapter), then the installation terminates.

2. The distribution file (named explicitly, by bundle, or inferred from the module requested) is fetched from the first configured CPAN mirror and unpacked.

3. Next, the module is built using perl Makefile.PL followed by make.

4. Next, the module is tested using make test. For most distributions, this executes a test suite implemented using the Test and Test::Harness modules. If this stage fails, the module installation aborts with an error, unless we used the force modifier, which is explained shortly.

5. Finally, if the distribution passed the test stage, it is installed in Perl's library.

We can, if we choose, also carry out these stages individually, but this is usually only done if there is a problem with the automatic installation.

Module Prerequisites

Many modules have prerequisites, other modules that must be installed first. If we try to install a module with missing prerequisites, the CPAN module can install them for us, either prompting us (in ask mode), downloading and installing them automatically (in follow mode), or ignoring them (in ignore mode, though it is unlikely a module will install if any of its prerequisites are missing). The default behavior is set when we first configure the module, and can be changed later with, for example:

```
cpan> o conf prerequisites_policy follow
```

Installing Modules in Stages

Instead of using the install command to fetch, build, test, and install a module in one go, we can use the get, make, and test commands to perform individual steps, and then finish with install. This can be occasionally useful for examining the outcome of each stage before proceeding to the next; generally useful if the automated install process fails for some reason.

If an installation fails in the test phase, or CPAN thinks that a module or distribution is already installed and up to date, it will decline to do so a second time. We can override this with force, for example:

```
cpan> force install Term::ReadLine
```

It is perfectly fine to do this, but please be aware that the distribution might not function entirely correctly (or in extreme cases, at all). Some test failures may involve features that are not applicable to a particular site or operating system. Read the output of the test phase carefully before deciding whether to use force.

Examining the Contents of a Distribution

It is rare that we would actually want to examine the contents of an unpacked distribution directly, but if we want to it's possible using the look command. This opens a system shell in the root directory of the unpacked distribution where the files can be listed:

```
cpan> get CGI
...

cpan> look CGI
> ls
...
```

We can also execute make commands from here directly, if necessary (for example, make install UNINST=1 to install a new module removing any older installed versions at the same time). However, look does not perform any kind of remote access; if we try to look for something that we don't have installed, then it must be fetched and downloaded first.

Cleaning Up

Once a package has been installed, we can clean up the files generated during the build process with `clean`. This accepts a bundle, module, or distribution as an argument and issues a `make clean` on the unpacked sources cached by the `CPAN` module. Clearly this makes sense only if the package has actually been installed recently. For example:

```
cpan> clean Net::FTP
```

Cleaning up is useful if we are very short of disk space, otherwise this step can usually be skipped as the `CPAN` module automatically clears out the oldest build sources. This occurs whenever the total exceeds the cache size specified when we configured it at the module startup.

Scanning and Searching CPAN

CPAN categorizes its archive in four different ways: by author, by bundle, by distribution, and by module.

- *Author*: These are the authors of the distributions available on CPAN, listed by code and full name.

- *Bundle*: Groups of module distributions that are commonly installed together are collected into special distributions called bundles, which simply list a set of related distributions. Installing a bundle saves time and effort by avoiding the need to install a collection of modules one by one. Note that bundles do not contain any source code themselves; they are just a list of other distributions to install. All bundles are given names starting "Bundle::" to distinguish them from "real" packages.

- *Distribution*: The actual distribution files for Perl packages, including the directory prefixes for the author whose distribution it is.

- *Module*: As well as a list of distributions, CPAN keeps track of all the modules provided by those distributions. Since we can install distributions by naming a module inside them, we rarely need to actually type in a distribution name.

To search CPAN and list records, the `CPAN` module provides the a, b, d, and m commands for specific categories, or the i command, which returns information on all of these categories. On its own, the i command will return a complete list of every record on CPAN.

```
cpan> i
```

This of course takes time and produces a very long and unwieldy list, even though the information is fetched from the mirror and stored locally. More usefully, we can narrow down the result by supplying a literal string or a regular expression. The literal string must match exactly.

```
cpan> i CGI
```

A regular expression (covered in Chapter 11) can be more specific as well as more flexible. To search for anything with "CGI" in it (case insensitively, incidentally):

```
cpan> i /CGI/
```

To search for anything that begins with "CGI", "cgi", "Cgi", and so on, use

```
cpan> i /^CGI/
```

To search for anything in the CGI module hierarchy:

```
cpan> i /^CGI::/
```

Alternatively, we can use the a, b, d, or m command to search for specific authors, bundles, distributions, or modules. These work identically to the i command but only return information for the specified category. For example, to list all modules containing XML but not distributions:

```
cpan> m /XML/
```

To find information for a particular author:

```
cpan> a DOUGM
```

To find all authors called Bob:

```
cpan> a /^Bob/
```

To find distributions with a version number of 1.x:

```
cpan> d /-1.\d/
```

Finally, to list all available bundles:

```
cpan> b
```

Listing Out-of-Date Modules

We can find out which modules and distributions have been updated on CPAN compared to our locally installed copies with the r command.

```
cpan> r
```

Package namespace	installed	latest	in CPAN file
CGI	3.00	3.05	L/LD/LDS/CGI.pm-3.05.tar.gz
DBI	1.41	1.45	T/TI/TIMB/DBI-1.45.tar.gz
Devel::Cover	0.47	0.50	P/PJ/PJCJ/Devel-Cover-0.50.tar.gz
Storable	2.08	2.13	A/AM/AMS/Storable-2.13.tar.gz
URI	1.23	1.34	G/GA/GAAS/URI-1.34.tar.gz

Since this command requires that the entire contents of the locally installed Perl library are examined for version numbers and compared to the current versions available at CPAN, it takes a short while to execute. We can narrow down the list we want to check for by supplying a string or regular expression. For example, to check for all out-of-date XML modules, the following works:

```
cpan> r /XML/
```

This regular expression simply matches any module with "XML" in the title. If we only want to know about XML modules in the XML hierarchy, we can specify a more explicit expression by anchoring it at the front.

```
cpan> r /^XML::/
```

Listing Available Modules

In a similar manner to the r command, we can also list all available but not yet installed modules with u. Not surprisingly, this generates a rather large list of modules, so it is more useful with a regular expression. For example, to find all uninstalled modules in the "XML" family:

```
cpan> u /^XML::/
```

Reading Documentation Without Installing

If we want to find out more about a module before installing it, since there are often multiple modules available for some tasks, we can use the readme command. This will look for the readme file within the distribution and, if present, fetch and display it to us without installing the module.

```
cpan> readme Apache::Session
```

Reloading CPAN

We can reload both the index information and the CPAN module itself with the reload command, should either be out of date (it is possible, though perhaps not likely, to have a permanent CPAN shell active on a server; updating the index from time to time would then be useful). To reload the index, use

```
cpan> reload index
```

To reload the CPAN and associated modules, use reload cpan. For example, to upgrade CPAN itself we can use

```
cpan> install Bundle::CPAN
cpan> reload cpan
```

The module will even prompt us to do this if our version of the CPAN module has been superseded.

Configuring CPAN Options

The o command configures CPAN options, and allows us to change any choice that we made during the original setup. To list all current configurations, use

```
cpan> o conf
```

To view a specific option, name the option. For example, to find the size of the build cache (where unpacked distribution sources are kept):

```
cpan> o conf build_cache
```

```
build_cache    10
```

To set an option, name the option and the new value. For example, to increase the build cache to 20 megabytes:

```
cpan> o conf build_cache 20
```

We can also set debugging options for various parts of the CPAN module. For general usage we would not normally want to do this, but a list of debugging options can be generated with

```
cpan> o debug
```

The cpan utility is convenient for Windows too, if we are using an environment like Cygwin. But for more traditional Windows setups, the ppm tool is an easier option.

Installing Modules on Windows with PPM

As mentioned earlier, the ActiveState port of Perl, ActivePerl, comes with the PPM package tool. The primary interface is the ppm command-line utility, which installs PPM modules, which are CPAN modules prebuilt and repackaged, ready for installation on Windows platforms. The distinction between a PPM module and a CPAN module is moot in the case of pure-Perl modules, but for modules that contain C or C++ code, PPM avoids the need to have a compiler available. The ppm tool works in a very similar way to the CPAN module and cpan command that inspired it, but rather than talking to a CPAN mirror, it by default connects to the PPM archive at http://www.activestate.com/PPMPackages/5.8/.

An example of its simplicity of use is as follows. Say we wish to install a package named Math::Matrix, which is not installed by default. Then we simply have to issue the command line at the prompt.

```
> ppm install Math::Matrix
```

As if by magic, and in a similar fashion to the CPAN module for Unix, the package is retrieved and installed automatically ready for our use and abuse.

The ppm tool is one of the most attractive reasons to use ActivePerl to run Perl applications on Windows. More information and a list of alternative mirrors is available in the PPM FAQ document at http://ASPN.ActiveState.com/ASPN/docs/ActivePerl/faq/ActivePerl-faq2.html. An excellent resource for an up-to-date list of modules available for use with PPM is http://www.activestate.com/ppmpackages/5.8/.

Summary

In this chapter, we looked at the key features and history of Perl, and saw how to download and install Perl binary distributions. We also examined some of the reasons why we might want to build Perl from source, and the various ways that we can control the features of the resulting Perl interpreter. One significant reason to build Perl from source on Unix systems is to enable support for threads, but there are others too, including 64-bit integer support (even on 32-bit platforms) or customizing the default library search path.

Once Perl is installed, we are ready to run Perl applications and scripts. We looked at starting applications on Unix, Windows, and Macintosh platforms, and covered Perl's many command-line options. Perl is surprisingly versatile run directly from the command line, and we also spent some time looking at Perl's role as a generic command-line utility.

There is more to Perl than the standard Perl distribution, and in the final part of the chapter we looked at CPAN, the Comprehensive Perl Archive Network, and saw how to download and install new modules, either by hand, or using the CPAN module and cpan utility under Unix, or the ppm utility on Windows platforms.

CHAPTER 2

■ ■ ■

Basic Concepts

In the next few chapters, Chapters 3 to 11, we cover the fundamentals of the Perl programming language in depth. This chapter is an introduction to the basics of Perl that newcomers to the language can use to familiarize themselves before we get into the details.

All the subjects covered here are examined in detail in later chapters, so this chapter is only really required reading for those totally new to Perl, or who need a quick refresher without getting bogged down in too much detail early on.

The topics covered here are as follows:

- Variables and Values
- Comments and Whitespace
- Operators and Built-In Functions
- Expressions and Statements
- Perl's Data Types
- Evaluation Context
- Perl's Special Variables
- String Interpolation
- Matching, Substitution, and Transliteration
- Blocks, Loops, and Conditions
- Subroutines
- Modules and Packages
- Enabling Warnings and Strictness
- Variable Declarations, Scope, and Visibility

The following is a short example Perl program that, once we have mastered the basics covered in this chapter, we will be fully able to understand:

```
#!/usr/bin/perl
# helloperl.pl
use strict;
use warnings;

sub hello {
    my ($argument)=@_;
    # the traditional salutation
    print "Hello $argument World!\n";
}
```

```
$ARGV[0] = "Brave New" unless scalar(@ARGV)>0;
```

```
hello($ARGV[0]);
```

If we save this program as hello.pl, we should be able to run it like this:

```
> hello.pl Perl
Hello Perl World!
```

Programmers who already have some experience in Perl will discover things they didn't know in the chapters that follow, but can nonetheless safely skip this introduction.

Values and Variables

Values are simply any single item of data that can be used in an expression to produce a new value or generate some kind of result. The following are all values:

```
1066
3.1415926
"Hello World"
```

These are literal or anonymous values, which means they are written directly into the source code. They are not associated with any label or identifier—they just are. As such, they are constants that we cannot manipulate. In order to do that, we need variables.

Variables are named identifiers that store a value. The value of a variable can be read or changed through the variable's name. In Perl, the data type of the variable is indicated by prefixing the name with a punctuation symbol. This is different from languages like C, which rely on a type specification in the declaration of a variable. However, Perl is not concerned with the precise type of a variable, whether it is an integer or a string or a reference and so on, but only its storage type: scalar, array, or hash.

Scalar variables store a single value, such as the preceding ones, and are prefixed with a $. Consider this example:

```
$counter
```

Array and hash variables look similar, but can store multiple values. We'll return to Perl's other data types shortly, so here are some examples in the meantime:

```
@array
%hash
```

A variable name can consist of any mixture of alphanumeric characters, including the under-score character, up to a total of 251 characters. From Perl 5.8 onward variables may even have accented and Unicode characters in their names. However, there are some limitations, notably that a variable name cannot start with a number. Here are some valid scalar variable names:

```
$A_Scalar_Variable
$scalarNo8
$_private_scalar
```

These, on the other hand, will cause Perl to complain:

```
$64bitint          (leading numbers not legal)
$file-handle       (minus sign not legal)
$excangeratetof    (pound symbol not legal)
```

Assigning values to variables is done with the assignment operator (i.e., an equals sign).

```
$variable = 42; # a Perl statement
```

This is a Perl statement, consisting of a variable, a value, an operator, and terminated by a semicolon to mark the end of the statement. It uses whitespace to improve the legibility of the statement, and is followed by a descriptive comment. Let's look at each of these concepts next, starting with comments and whitespace.

Comments and Whitespace

In the preceding examples, we surrounded the assignment with space characters. While not a requirement, it does improve readability. *Whitespace* is so called because it refers to anything that is just filler—literally, the white parts of a printed page. Perl is very forgiving when it comes to the use of whitespace (tabs, spaces, and newlines), so use it wherever it improves legibility.

Comments, indicated with a #, are segments of text that have no effect on the program at either compile or run time. They are provided to—hopefully—describe what the program is doing at that point. They are discarded by Perl during the compilation of the code and do not affect program execution in any way.

We can use whitespace and comments to improve the legibility of our code. As these two equivalent statements illustrate, whitespace can be used to help visually separate out matching parentheses in a complex expression. A comment allows us to document what the code actually does.

```
print 1+2*(3*(rand(4)-5))+6;
print 1 + 2 * ( 3*(rand(4)-5) ) + 6; # print expression
```

Perl's tendency to use punctuation for almost everything can result in often illegible code—see the section "Special Variables" later in this chapter. Judicious use of whitespace can make the difference between maintainable code and an illegible mess.

However, use of whitespace is not without restrictions. Specifically, whitespace cannot be used in places where it can confuse the interpreter. For instance, we cannot use whitespace in file names, so the following file name is not legal:

```
$sca lar;      # ERROR: we may use $scalar or $sca_lar instead.
```

In Perl, comments are also considered whitespace from the perspective of parsing source code. That means that whenever we can split a statement across multiple lines we can place a comment at the end of any line.

```
$string="one".  # first part
       "two".   # second part
       "three"; # after the statement
```

Variables and values are not very useful unless we have a means to manipulate them, such as the print function and arithmetic operators we used earlier. We will take a look at operators and functions next.

Operators and Functions

Operators are the fundamental tools with which we can process values and variables to produce new values. Numerical operators include addition, subtraction, multiplication, division, modulus, and raising powers (exponentiation) as shown in the following examples:

```
$number = 4 + 5;     # 4 plus 5 is 9
$number = 4 / 5;     # 4 divided by 5 0.8
$number = 4 % 5;     # 4 modulus 5 is 0
$number = 4 ** 0.5;  # 4 to the power of 0.5 is 2
$number = -4;        # negative 4 is -4
```

String operators include the concatenation operator:

```
$string = "P" . "e" . "r" . "l";
```

We should also not forget the comparison operators like <, >=, and == for numbers (and their equivalents lt, ge, and eq for strings).

```
$under_a_hundred = $number < 100;
$middle_or_higher = $string ge "middle"
```

The values that operators manipulate are called *operands*. Binary operators like addition have a left operand and a right operand. Unary operators like the unary minus earlier have a single right operand.

Perl has many built-in *functions* that can be used like operators. Some functions are *unary operators*, also called scalar operators, because they take a single value to process. Others are *list operators* that take either a fixed or arbitrary number of values. Either way, these values are always on the right-hand side. The print function is a good example of an arbitrary list operator, since it will print any quantity of values given to it:

```
print "A","list","of",5,"values","\n";
```

Perl has many built-in functions, all of which are either list operators or scalar operators, the latter taking only one value to process. A scalar operator is therefore just another term for a unary operator.

Operators have precedence and associativity, which control the order in which Perl will process them and whether the left- or right-hand side of a binary operator will be evaluated first. Multiplication has a higher precedence than addition, while both addition and subtraction have left associativity (meaning that the evaluation of the left operand is looked at first by Perl). For example, in this calculation the multiplication happens first, then the subtraction and addition, in that order:

```
$result = 1 - 2 + 3 * 4;     # 3*4 gives 12, 1-2 gives -1, -1+12 gives -11
```

Parentheses can be used to force a precedence other than the default.

```
$result = (1 - (2 + 3)) * 4;  # 2+3 gives 5, 1-5 gives -4, -4*4 gives -16
```

The assignment operator = also returns a result, in this case the value assigned to the left-hand side. It is perfectly normal to ignore this result because it is generally a side effect of the assignment. Even print returns a result to indicate whether or not it printed successfully, so it too qualifies as an operator.

We will read more on operators in Chapter 4. For now, we can take our knowledge of values, variables, and operators, and use it to start creating expressions and statements.

Expressions and Statements

An *expression* is any language construct that returns a value. Every example involving an operator in the previous section is an expression. A *statement* is just an expression whose return value is not used. Instead, it produces some other effect.

Values and variables are the simplest form of expression, but any combination of values, variables, and operators is also an expression. Since expressions return values, they can be combined into even larger expressions. For instance, this code is made up of several expressions:

```
print 1 + 2 / ( 3*(rand(4)-5) ) + 6; # combine values to make expressions
```

This example demonstrates the use of parentheses to explicitly control how a compound expression is evaluated. Working outwards, 4 is an expression, rand(4) is also an expression, as is rand(4)-5. The parentheses group the operator - and its operands, making them an expression that excludes the 3. The outer set of parentheses then groups the multiplication by 3, and returns its own value, which is divided into 2. The outermost expression consists of 1 plus the value of this expression, plus 6. Well, not quite the outermost. That's technically the print function, but its return value is ignored.

A statement produces an effect other than returning the result of a calculation. The preceding code has an effect: it prints out the result of its calculation to standard output. Statements are separated from each other by semicolons, which tell Perl where one statement ends and the next begins. Here is the same code again, this time rewritten in multiple statements:

```
$number = rand(4)-5;
$number = 3 * $number;
$number = 1+ $number + 6;
print $number;
```

As Perl does not care what kind of whitespace is used to separate expressions, or even if any is used, the preceding could be put all on one line instead:

```
$number = rand(4)-5; $number=3*$number; $number=1+$number+6; print $number
```

The very last statement of all does not need a semicolon because nothing comes after it. However, including the semicolon after each statement is good practice, just in case we add more code afterward. Combining statements into one line like this is valid Perl but not as legible as putting them on separate lines. In general, only consider it for very short statements where the meaning is clear.

A statement is an expression whose value is ignored. We call this evaluating the expression in a void context. We'll discuss context in a moment, after we consider the different ways Perl allows us to store data through its built-in data types.

Data Types

Perl is commonly described as defining three basic data types: *scalars*, *arrays*, and *hashes* (also known as *associative arrays* in other languages). These three data types cover most of the kinds of data that a Perl program will manipulate. However, this is not the whole story. Perl also understands the concept of *filehandles*, *typeglobs* (an amalgam of all the other types), and the *undefined value*, all of which are fundamental to the language. Scalars are categorized by the kind of value they store—integer, floating point number, text string, or reference (which also includes objects). While *references* and *objects* are both technically types of scalar value, the manner in which Perl treats them means that they should be considered separately.

Scalars

Scalars are solitary values, such as a number, or a string of text. Unlike more strongly typed languages like C, Perl makes no distinction between numbers and strings and provides no mechanism to define the "type" of a scalar. Instead Perl freely and automatically converts between different scalar types when they are used, caching the conversion for later reuse. The following are legal assignments of simple values to scalar variables:

```
$scalarint = 42;
$scalarfp  = 1.01;
$scalarstr = "A string is a scalar";
```

Although we will read more about numeric and string scalars in Chapter 3, we will cover references later in this chapter.

Arrays

The second data type is the *array*. An array is an indexed list of values with a consistent order. Names of arrays are prefixed with @. These are examples of arrays:

```
@first_array = (1, 2, 3, 4);
@second_array = ('one', '2', 'three', '4', '5');
```

To access an element of an array, we use square brackets around the index of the element we want, counting from zero. Notice that the data type of the element is scalar, even though it is in an array, so the correct prefix for the array element access is a dollar sign, not an at-sign:

```
$fifth_element = $array[4];
```

Being *ordered* lists of values, the following arrays are not the same:

```
@array1 = (1, 2, 3, 4);
@array2 = (1, 2, 4, 3);
```

Perl provides many functions for manipulating arrays, including pop, push, shift, unshift, splice, and reverse. All these and more are covered in Chapter 5.

Hashes

Hashes, also called *associative arrays*, are tables of key-value pairs. Names of hashes are prefixed with %. For example:

```
%hash = ('Mouse', 'Jerry', 'Cat', 'Tom', 'Dog', 'Spike');
```

Here Mouse is a key whose value is Jerry, Tom is the value for the key Cat, and Dog is the key of the value Spike. Since hash keys can only be strings, we can omit the quotes around them because Perl will treat them as constant strings. This fact allows us to use the => operator as an alternative to the comma that separates a key from its value, which lets us omit the quotes from the key.

```
%hash = (Mouse => 'Jerry', Cat => 'Tom', Dog => 'Spike');
```

To access a value in a hash we must provide its key. Just as with arrays, the value is scalar (even if it is a reference to an array or hash) so we prefix the accessed element with a dollar sign.

```
$canine = $hash{Dog};
```

As hash keys are always strings, we can omit the quotes here too. If we use a variable or expression as the key, Perl will evaluate it as a string and use that as the key.

Unlike elements in arrays, the key-value pairs in a hash are not ordered. So, while we can say that the "first" element in @array1 has the index 0 and the value 1, we cannot talk about the "first" key-value pair. We can access a list of the keys in a hash with the keys function, and a list of the values with values, but the order in which we receive them is not defined.

References

References are not strictly a separate data type, merely a kind of scalar value. A reference is an immutable pointer to a value in memory, which may be any data type: scalar, array, hash, and so on. Perl references are not so different from references in other languages like C++ or Java, and differ from C-style pointers in that we cannot perform arithmetic on them to change where they point.

We create a reference to an existing variable or value by putting a backslash in front of it, as in the following examples:

```
$scalarref = \$scalar;
$arrayref = \@array;
$hashref = \%hash;
$reftostring = \"The referee";
```

To get to the original value, we *dereference* the reference by prefixing it with the symbol of the underlying data type.

```
print $$reftostring;
@new_array = @$arrayref;
```

We can use braces to indicate exactly what we are dereferencing, or simply to make the code clearer. In this example, we use braces to indicate that we want to dereference an array reference, and then extract the element at index 4:

```
$fifth_element = @{$array}[4];
```

Without the braces, this statement would attempt to access the element at index 4 of an array called @array, then dereference the element value, quite a different meaning. A better way to keep this clear is to use the -> dereference operator.

```
$fifth_element = $array->[4];
$value = $hashref->{key};
```

References give us the ability to create hashes of hashes and arrays of arrays, and other more complex data structures. Arrays, hashes, and references are investigated in detail in Chapter 5.

Another very important property of references is that they are the basis of objects in Perl, through the bless keyword. An *object* in Perl is a reference that has been marked to be in a particular Perl package. So, it is a specialized type of reference, which is in turn a specialized form of scalar. Objects, therefore, are really scalars. Perl also enables objects to be treated as scalars for the purposes of operations like addition and concatenation. There are two mechanisms for doing this: using Perl's tie function to conceal the object behind a normal-seeming scalar variable, and overloading Perl's operators so the object can be treated like a scalar in some contexts. Objects are covered in Chapter 19.

The Undefined Value

The *undefined value*, which is also not strictly a data type, represents a lack of value or data type. It is neither a scalar, list, hash, nor any other data type, though if it had to be categorized it would be a scalar since it is by nature the simplest possible value—it certainly doesn't have elements. We can assign the undefined value to a variable explicitly using the undef function, or implicitly by simply declaring it but not initializing.

```
$a = undef;
$a;
```

The undef keyword is also a function, or to be more accurate, it is always a function and we sometimes just use its return value, which is undefined, which seems only appropriate. Another equivalent way to write the preceding statements is

```
undef $a;
```

Be wary of trying to empty an array by setting it to undef—it won't empty the array. Instead, we get an array with a single undefined element, which is a different thing entirely.

Typeglobs

The *typeglob* is a strange beast unique to Perl. It is a kind of super-value, an amalgam of exactly one of each of the other primary data types: scalar, array, hash, filehandle. In addition a typeglob can hold a code reference that is a pointer to a piece of Perl code, for example, a subroutine. It can also hold a format, which is a template that can be used with the write function to generate formatted and paginated output. The typeglob is not a single reference to something, rather it has six slots that can contain six different references all at once. It is prefixed with a *, so the typeglob *name contains the values of $name, @name, and %name, and other values as well.

Typeglobs are most often used for their ability to hold file and directory handles, since these are sometimes difficult to manipulate otherwise.

The other Perl data type is *filehandles*. A filehandle represents a channel for input and/or output within a Perl program, for instance, an open file or a network connection. Unlike the previous data types, filehandles are not prefixed with a special character. One way to create a filehandle is to use the open function:

```
open FILEHANDLE, $filename;
```

This example opens a filehandle called FILEHANDLE to the file called filename, so we can now manipulate this file using its handle.

We will read more about the undefined value, typeglobs, and filehandles in Chapter 5.

Context

An important concept in Perl is the idea of evaluation *context*. This is the context in which a Perl variable or section of Perl code is evaluated, and indicates the type of value that is wanted in a given situation.

Perl has three different contexts: scalar, list, and void. Which one applies depends on the way in which the value is being used (as opposed to what it actually is). In *scalar context*, a single scalar value is required. In *list context*, a list of values (zero or more) is required. Finally, when no value of any kind is required, we call this *void context*.

To illustrate the difference, here is an example of a list of three values being used in an assignment:

```
$count = (1,2,3);  # scalar context - counts the elements
@array = (1,2,3);  # list context - assigns @INC to another array
```

The list of three values is evaluated in scalar context in the first assignment and list context in the second. In both cases, the results of the assignments themselves are in void context. To make this clearer, in the next example, the leftmost assignment is in a void context but the rightmost is in list context (it is evaluated first and its result used by the leftmost assignment):

```
@array2 = @array1 = (1,2,3)
```

Several of Perl's built-in functions react differently when called in different contexts. For example, localtime returns a preformatted string containing the current time and date when used in scalar context, but a list of values (seconds, minutes, hours, and so on) when used in list context.

To force scalar context, we can use the scalar function, which is handy for things like printing out the time from localtime where the context from print would otherwise be list context:

```
print "The time is ",localtime,"\n";
```

Subroutines also have a context in which they are called, which they can detect with the built-in Perl function wantarray. We discuss that in Chapter 7.

Special Variables

Perl provides a number of *special variables* that are always available to any Perl script without declaration or qualification.

Some are set by context during program execution: $_ is used as the default loop control variable set by foreach, map, and grep loops, $. holds the current line number for the most recently read file, and @_ is defined to be the list of passed parameters on entry to subroutines. $! contains the most recent system error (if any). Others relate to Perl's environment: %ENV is a hash variable that contains environment variables in key-value pairs. We can both read it to find out how Perl was started, and alter it to control the environment of processes executed by Perl. @INC controls where Perl searches for reusable modules, and %INC stores the details of modules that were found and loaded. $0 contains the program name, while $$ contains the process ID.

Finally, several variables control how the interpreter works or manipulate aspects of the run-time environment: $| controls the buffering behavior of the current output filehandle, and $/ controls the input line terminator.

To see a special variable in action, issue the following command, which prints the default set of paths that Perl will search for libraries (Windows users need to replace the single quotes with double quotes, and replace "\n" with \"\n\"):

```
> perl -e 'foreach (@INC){print $_, "\n"}'
```

```
/usr/local/lib/perl5/5.8.5/i686-linux-thread-multi
/usr/local/lib/perl5/5.8.5
/usr/local/lib/perl5/site_perl/5.8.5/i686-linux-thread-multi
/usr/local/lib/perl5/site_perl/5.8.5
/usr/local/lib/perl5/site_perl
.
>
```

Likewise, the following example prints the value of the environment variable PATH. While the variable is a hash, the values in the hash are scalars, so the correct prefix to retrieve it is $:

```
> perl -e 'print $ENV{PATH}'
```

```
/usr/local/bin:/bin:/usr/bin:/usr/X11R6/bin>
```

Variables like %ENV and @ARGV, which hold the command-line arguments with which a program was executed, are reasonably self-explanatory. However, the majority of Perl's special variable names are comprised of punctuation marks, like $/. In theory, most of these are based on mnemonics, but since there are over 50 of them and only so much punctuation to go around, the intuitiveness of the mnemonic hints for some variables is a little stretched.

However, there is the English module, which provides a longer, descriptive name for each special variable. While we are not covering modules yet, this one is useful enough for newcomers to learn about now. After the English module is loaded with 'use English', $_ is given the alias $ARG, $. becomes $INPUT_LINE_NUMBER, and so on for every special variable Perl provides. Here is an example of how we can use it:

```
#!/usr/bin/perl -w
# whoami.pl

use English '-no-match-vars';

print 'I am', $PROGRAM_NAME, ' (', $PROCESS_ID, ')';
```

which is a lot more understandable than

```
print 'I am', $0, ' (', $$, ')';
```

■**Note** The `-no-match-vars` argument tells Perl not to provide aliases for special variables involved in regular expression matching. It is time consuming for Perl to manage these variables, so by not giving them English names we avoid making Perl do extra work. It is almost always a good idea to include `-no-match-vars`.

For a list of all of Perl's special variables and their English names, see Appendix B.

String Interpolation

Interpolation is a very useful property of strings in Perl. When a variable name is seen in a double-quoted string, Perl replaces that variable with its value. For instance, the `print` statement in the following example prints the value of the variable $today, which is sunny, rather than the word character that constitutes the variable name, which is Friday:

```
#!/usr/bin/perl
# interpolate.pl

$today = "Friday";
print "It is $today \n";
```

Next we'll execute the code, which in turn generates one line of output.

> **perl interpolate1.pl**

It is Friday

However, if we wanted to see the actual characters $today, we can prevent interpolation by escaping the variable name with a backslash:

```
print "It is \$today\n";
```

Now if we run this, we get It is \$today. Alternatively, we could use noninterpolating single quotes to prevent the variable from being interpolated. In that case, our `print` statement would look like this:

```
print 'It is $today \n';
```

The output we get from this is slightly different.

It is $today \n

Notice that Perl printed out the \n literally and that there is no linefeed, causing the command prompt (we assume > here) to appear on the end of the text. That is because it represents an end-of-line sequence only when interpolated. Perl has a number of special character combinations that are interpolated to their meanings when placed inside double quotes (or the equivalent qq operator). Perl supports the standard conventions for special characters like tabs and newlines first established by C. All of these are converted into the appropriate characters when they are seen by Perl in a double-quoted string. For example, for tabs and returns we use \t and \r.

Interestingly, interpolating a string containing the name of an array variable will cause each element of the array to be converted into text and placed into the resulting string, separated by spaces.

```
my @count=reverse (1..9);
print "Counting: @count ...";
# produces 'Counting: 9 8 7 6 7 4 3 2 1 ...'
```

This does not work for hash variables, though. Only scalar and array variables can be interpolated.

There is a lot more to interpolation than this, however, and it is in fact a more complex and versatile part of Perl than many people realize. Accordingly, we devote a good chunk of Chapter 11 to covering the subject of interpolation in depth, including inserting character codes, interpolating source code, and interpolating text more than once. Meanwhile, now that we have simple statements under control, it is time to introduce some structure to them.

Matching, Substitution, and Transliteration

One of Perl's best known features is its regular expression engine, which provides us with the ability to match input text against complex criteria, defined as regular expression strings, also called *patterns*. We can match text to see whether or not a given sequence of characters is present using the match operator m//, or just //.

```
my $input_text = "two pints of milk and a pot of yoghurt";
if ($input_text =~/milk/) {
    # got milk...
}
```

We can also substitute one string for another.

```
$input_text =~ /yoghurt/cream/;
```

Both matching and substitution can use a wide range of match criteria to search for arbitrarily complex sequences, return parts of the matched text, and match multiple times. As a taste of what is possible, this extracts all two- and three-letter words:

```
@words = $input_text =~ /\b(\w{2,3})\b/g;
```

Here \b means "match on a word boundary," and the parentheses cause the text that matches their contents to be returned. \w means a word character, any alphanumeric character plus underscores. It is qualified as \w{2,3}, which means match at least two but no more than three times.

Regular expressions are related to interpolation in two ways. Firstly, Perl interpolates regular expression patterns before it applies them, so we can use variables and special characters in patterns just like double-quoted strings. Secondly, regular expressions add their own special characters that look like interpolation special characters—\b, shown earlier, is an example. Regular expressions are a large subject, and we cover them in detail along with interpolation in Chapter 11.

Transliteration looks a lot like substitution. It allows us to exchange individual characters. For example, to capitalize all lowercase a, b, or c characters:

```
$input_text =~ /abc/ABC/;
```

or remove the t in Boston:

```
$input_text = "Boston";
$input_text =~/t//;
```

Transliteration really has nothing to do with regular expressions, but since the syntax is similar, we also cover it at the end of Chapter 11.

Blocks, Conditions, and Loops

A *block* in Perl is a unit that consists of several statements and/or smaller blocks. Blocks can exist either on their own, where they are known as *bare blocks*, or form the body of a control statement such as an if condition or a foreach loop.

Blocks are defined by enclosing their contents in curly braces, as in the following example:

```
#!/usr/bin/perl
# block.pl
use warnings;

{
    print "This is a first level block. \n";
    {
        print "   This is a second level block. \n";
    }
}
```

We do not need to end the block with a semicolon; it isn't a statement, but a way to group them. Blocks feature heavily in Perl programming: files are implicit blocks, and several of Perl's built-in functions can take blocks as arguments—map, grep, and sort being the most obvious examples.

```
@capitalised = map { ucfirst lc } ("some","MIXED","Case","sTrInGs");
```

Perl provides us with a number of constructs, which we can use to control how our program behaves under a given condition. These control constructs make use of the concept of blocks.

Conditional Blocks: if, else, and unless

The if statement allows us to execute the statements inside a block *if* a particular condition is met, as demonstrated in this example:

```
#!/usr/bin/perl
# if1.pl

$input=<>;
if ($input >= 5 ) {
    print "The input number is equal to or greater than 5 \n";
}
```

We use the operator >= to test whether our input was 5 or greater. If so, the block containing the print statement is executed. Otherwise, the program doesn't execute the block.

Note that we have used what is known as the readline operator, also called the diamond operator (<>), in the preceding example. This operator allows us to read a line at a time from a given filehandle. Normally a filehandle resides between the angle brackets, but if we are reading from standard input, we can omit it, leading to the diamond appearance.

We can create a more flexible version of if by combining it with else, as shown in the new version of our previous example.

```
#!/usr/bin/perl
# ifelse.pl

$input=<>;
if ($input >= 5 ) {
    print "The input number is equal to or greater than 5 \n";
} else {
    print "The input number is less than  5 \n";
}
```

The opposite of if is unless, which just inverts the sense of the condition, and is a linguistic aid to clarity when the body of the statement should be executed when the condition is false rather than true.

```
unless ($input >=5) {

}
```

Looping Blocks: foreach and while

The foreach statement loops through a list, executing a block for each value in that list.

```
#!/usr/bin/perl
# foreach1.pl
use warnings;

@array = ("one", "two", "three");
foreach $iterator (@array) {
    print "The value of the iterator is now $iterator \n";
}
```

When we run this, program we get

> **perl foreach.pl**

```
The value of the iterator is now one
The value of the iterator is now two
The value of the iterator is now three
```

Earlier we mentioned the special variable $_ and noted that that many functions read from this variable and write to it in the absence of any other variable. So, let's see how we can modify our previous example to use $_:

```
#!/usr/bin/perl
# foreach2.pl

@array = ("one", "two", "three", "four");
foreach (@array) {
    print "The value of the iterator is now $_ \n";
}
```

Having not stated explicitly our iterator, Perl has used $_ as the iterator, something that we can test by printing $_.

Perl's other main loop statement is while, which repeatedly executes a block until its control expression becomes false. For example, this short program counts from 10 down to 1. The loop exits when the counter variable reaches zero.

```
#!/usr/bin/perl
# while.pl
$count=10;
while ($count > 0) {
    print "$count...\n";
    $count = $count -1;
}
```

Like if, while has a counterpart, until, which simply inverts the sense of the condition. It loops while the condition is false and ends when it becomes true.

All the blocks described so far are executed as soon as Perl sees them. One important class of block that we have not yet covered is the subroutine, a block that is not executed on sight but which instead allows us to label the code inside for future reuse. We consider subroutines next; blocks, loops, and conditions are explored in depth in Chapter 6.

Subroutines

A *subroutine* is a block that is declared for reuse with the sub keyword. Unlike a regular bare block, which is executed as soon as Perl encounters it, a subroutine block is stored away for future use under the name used to declare it. This provides the ability to reuse the same code many times, a core value of good program design. Code can now call the subroutine by its name.

```
sub red_october {
    print "A simple sub\n";
}
```

To call this subroutine, we can now just write any of the following:

```
red_october;
&red_october;
red_october();
```

The first and third examples here are equivalent, but as we will see at the end of the chapter, the first will be disallowed if we enable "strict" subroutines. The second example shows an older way to call subroutines that is rarely seen in modern Perl but occasionally crops up in older code. (It also has a special property of passing the subroutine parameters given to the subroutine in which it is contained, but that is a detail we will come back to in Chapter 6.)

This simple example neither accepts parameters nor returns a value. More commonly subroutines are passed values and variables in order to perform a task and then return another value reflecting the result. For example, this subroutine calculates the factorial of the number passed to it and then returns the answer. Notice that there is no need to define the subroutine before we call it—Perl will figure it out for us.

```
#!/usr/bin/perl
# factorial.pl

$number=<>;      # read a number from the keyboard
chomp $number; # remove linefeed

# Call the subroutine with $number
$factorial=factorial($number);

# The subroutine
sub factorial {
    $input = shift; # read passed argument
    # return zero immediately if given 0 as input
    return 0 if $input==0;
    # otherwise do the calculation
    $result=1;
    foreach (1 .. $input) { # '..' generates a range
        $result *= $_;
    }
    return $result;
}

print "$number factorial is $factorial\n";
```

Subroutines can also be given prototypes, to control the type and number of parameters passed to them, and attributes, metadata that influences how the subroutine behaves. These and other details of subroutines can be found in Chapter 7.

All the variables in the preceding program are global package variables, because we did not declare any of them before using them. As a result, this program is vulnerable to both misspelling of variable names and the use of variables outside their intended context. In order to protect ourselves from potential problems like these, we should apply some warnings and strictness.

Modules and Packages

A *module* is a Perl library, a reusable collection of subroutines and variables. We can load a module into our program with `use`, which searches for a requested module in the paths present in the special variable `@INC`. For example, to load the `English` module, which provides English aliases for Perl's special variables, we write

```
use English;
```

A *package* is a Perl namespace, a logical subdivision of compiled code in which variables and subroutines can reside. Two variables, or subroutines, can exist with the same name at the same time, so long as they are in different packages. Even a simple Perl script has a namespace, the default package `main`.

Usually, a module creates a package with the same name as the module, with nested namespaces separated by semicolons. For the purposes of using the module, therefore, we can often treat the terms "module" and "package" as synonymous, or at least connected. For example:

```
use Scalar::Util;
```

The actual module file is `Scalar/Util.pm`, or `Scalar\Util.pm` on Windows, and is located in Perl's standard library. (We can find out exactly where with `perldoc -l Scalar::Util`.)

The `require` keyword also loads modules, but it simply loads code at run-time. The `use` keyword by contrast loads a module at compile time, before other code is compiled, and calls an import routine in the just-loaded module to import variables and subroutines into the package of the caller. While `require` does have uses, we generally want `use`. Take this example `use` statement:

```
use File::Basename 'basename','dirname';
```

After this statement we can use the subroutines `basename()` and `dirname()` in our program, because they have been imported from the `File::Basename` package, which is defined in the `File::Basename` module. We can also call a subroutine or refer to a variable directly in its original package.

```
$scriptdir=File::Basename::dirname($0); #find directory of script
```

There is a lot more to `use` than this of course, and we cover the subject of using modules in detail in Chapter 9. We can create our own modules too, which is the subject of Chapter 10.

Perl notionally divides modules into two kinds, which can be differentiated by their case. Functional modules start with an uppercase letter, and simply provide subroutines or define object classes. The `IO::File` and `CGI` modules are both examples of functional modules, as are `Scalar::Util`, `File::Basename`, `Math::Trig`, and so on. By contrast, pragmatic modules are all lowercase, and modify the behavior of Perl itself in some way. The `warnings` and `strict` modules are the most important of these, and we take a look at them next.

Warnings and Strictness

So far we have not enabled either warnings or strict compile checks in our code. For short demonstrations this might be OK, but in general it is highly recommended to enable both in order to maintain code quality and catch programming errors.

Warnings can be enabled in three ways: through the -w option, the special variable $^W, or the use warnings pragma. The first two control the same global setting that enables or disables all warnings in all code within the application, be it in the main script or loaded modules. The pragma allows finer grained control and only affects the file or block it is placed in.

Here's how you can specify the -w option on the command line:

```
> perl -w myscript.pl
```

This has the same effect as writing the following at the top of myscript.pl:

```
#!/usr/bin/perl
$^W=1;
```

It is standard on Unix systems to specify the name of the interpreter to use as the first line of the file—the so-called *hash-bang* line (because it starts with #!).

A common sight in many Perl scripts is the following, which enables warnings automatically:

```
#!/usr/bin/perl -w
```

Windows platforms will generally understand this convention too. If the file has a recognized file extension (such as .pl) and is passed to Perl to execute, the options specified on the end of the line are extracted and applied even though the path itself is not applicable.

We don't always want or need to enable warnings everywhere, though. The use warnings pragma is lexically scoped, so it only affects the file (or block) in which it appears.

```
#!/usr/bin/perl
use warnings;
use A::Module; #warnings not enabled inside loaded module
```

This is handy when we are trying to diagnose problems in our own code and want to ignore warnings being generated by modules we are just using. That doesn't mean the warnings aren't important, but it allows us to be selective. We can be more selective by switching on or off different categories of warnings, which we will discover how to do in Chapter 16.

Perl also provides the strict pragma. This enables additional checks that our code must pass at compile time before the interpreter will execute it. This is almost always a good thing to do and there are few reasons not to, except in very small scripts and one-liners. In fact there are three separate strict modes: vars, refs, and subs. A use strict without arguments gives us all three, but we can enable or disable each mode separately if we wish.

```
use strict;                 #enable all strict checks
use strict qw(vars refs subs); #same thing, explictly

no strict qw(refs);         #allow symbolic references
```

The vars mode enforces the declaration of variables before or at their first use; we touch on it some more in just a moment. The refs mode disables symbolic references, while the subs mode prevents us from using subroutines without parentheses or a & prefix, where their meaning and context can be ambiguous. We tackle these two subjects in Chapters 5 and 7, respectively.

Variable Declarations

One of the effects of use strict is to enforce variable *declarations*. Perl has two different kinds of variable, package and lexical, and several different ways to declare them. Although Perl has a keyword called local, it doesn't actually declare a local variable in the normally accepted sense of the term. In most cases, we want to use my:

```
use strict 'vars';
my $variable = "value";
```

With strict variables in effect, leaving off the my will cause a syntax error. The my tells Perl that this is a lexical variable, which only exists within the file or block in which it is declared. Declared at the top of a file, this means that it can be used from anywhere inside the file, including from within subroutines, but can't be accessed from code outside it, not even if that code was called from the place where it was declared. As this example shows, we can make an assignment to the variable at the same time we declare it.

The other kind of variable is a package variable, which is visible from anywhere as soon as it is given a value. If we do not enable strict variables and simply use a variable without declaring it, a package variable is the result. If we are not using packages, then the variable is in the default main package and is what we would normally think of as a global variable.

With strictness enabled, we can no longer create package variables just by using them. We must declare them with the older vars pragma or the more modern our keyword introduced in Perl 5.6.

The vars pragma merely tells Perl that we are going to be making use of the named package variable; it has no useful effect if strict variables are not enabled. Unfortunately, it does not allow us to declare and assign to the variable at the same time.

```
use vars '$variable';
$variable = "value";
```

The our keyword does, however. It declares a package variable, but only makes it visible lexically, just like my.

```
our $variable = "value";
```

The our keyword is intended as an improved, more intuitive replacement for use vars, but we often see the latter in older Perl code and code designed to run on a wide range of Perl versions.

So what about local? It provides the ability to temporarily hide a package variable with another variable of the same name, but holding a different value. Somewhat counterintuitively, the scope of the variable is lexical, so it persists only while the interpreter is executing code within the file or block in which it is declared. However, it is visible from anywhere so long as this remains true, notably within called subroutines. This isn't what most people are expecting, and is why my is usually what we want to use. In fact, local is most useful for temporarily overriding Perl's built-in variables, which are really special cases of package variables.

Scope and visibility are important concepts, so it is worth taking a moment to look at them a little more closely before the end of the chapter.

Scope and Visibility

The *scope* and *visibility* of a variable is determined by its nature, package or lexical, and where in a piece of code it resides. As we mentioned, Perl has two distinct types of variable in terms of scope: package variables, which are visible from anywhere in a program, and lexical variables, whose scope and visibility is constrained to the file or block in which they are first declared.

In the following example, the first mention of $scalar is a package variable. Because it exists at the top of the program and is not in a declared package, it is also what we traditionally think of as a global variable. Inside the block, we have a second $scalar. This one is declared to be a lexical variable through the use of the my keyword. The lexical variable obscures the package global within the block, but as soon as the block finishes, the original package variable reappears.

```
#!/usr/bin/perl
# scope.pl

our $scalar = "global";
print "\$scalar is a $scalar variable\n";
{
      my $scalar = "lexical";
      print "\$scalar is now a $scalar variable\n";
}
print "\$scalar is a $scalar variable again\n";
```

When we run this program, we get the following output:

> **perl scope.pl**

```
$scalar is a global variable
$scalar is now a lexical variable
$scalar is a global variable again
```

The subject of package and lexical variables is simple at first glance, rather more complex on closer examination. We can declare package variables lexically with our or hide one package variable with another using local, which differs from the my example earlier because its visibility would persist until execution leaves the block. We tackle all this in more detail in Chapter 8.

Summary

In this chapter, we introduced Perl's basic concepts. In the following chapters, 3 to 11, we will expand on all of these subjects in detail. The purpose of this chapter is to provide just enough information on each area that any of these chapters can be dipped into without recourse to the others. We started with the fundamentals of the language, values and variables, and passing through whitespace and comments, operators and functions, and expressions and statements. We then looked at Perl's data types—scalars, arrays, hashes, filehandles, and the special undefined value, with a quick glance at references and typeglobs, and also considered the context in which Perl evaluates expressions. We examined some of the many special variables Perl provides and saw how Perl can expand variables into strings using variable interpolation. We then took a brief look at the very large subject of regular expressions, and saw the match, substitution, and transliteration operations in action.

After a look at Perl's block constructs, including loops and conditional statements and expressions, we saw how to declare and use subroutines in Perl, then use modules, Perl's implementation of libraries, to make use of subroutines and variables defined externally to our program script.

All well-written Perl programs make use of warnings and strict checking, both of which were briefly covered. Finally, armed with this information, we saw how to properly declare the variables that up until now we had simply used by writing them down.

CHAPTER 3

■■■

Scalars: Integers, Floating-Point Numbers, and Strings

A scalar is a single atomic value, and the most basic of Perl's data types. Scalars in turn are divided into four distinct kinds: *integers, floating-point numbers, strings,* and *references*, which are pointers to values stored elsewhere. Of these, the first three are what we might call "normal" scalar values.

In Chapter 2, we introduced integers, floating-point numbers, and strings. In this chapter, we will focus on a detailed look at how Perl handles scalar numbers and strings, and the most important of the built-in operators and functions that Perl provides to manipulate them. If Perl has a specialty, it is probably string manipulation, and accordingly the end of the chapter is dedicated to a roundup of string functions, including `split`, `substr`, `printf`, `sprintf`, `pack`, and `unpack`.

There are many different ways to convert numbers to strings, and strings to numbers, and in this chapter we cover many of them. But although integers, floating-point numbers, and strings are fundamentally different kinds of values, Perl does not require the programmer to make a strong distinction between them. Instead, whenever a value is used in a context that requires a different kind of value—for example, attempting to add a string to a number, or taking the square root of an integer—Perl carries out an automatic conversion for us. Before we examine each of these types of scalar value individually, it is worth looking at how Perl manages them and handles this internal conversion.

Automatic Conversion: One Scalar Fits All

When a scalar is first created, an integer for example, only that representation is stored. When the scalar is used with an operator that expects a different representation, say a string, Perl automatically performs the conversion behind the scenes, and then caches the result. The original value is not altered, so the scalar now holds two representations. If the same conversion is needed again, Perl can retrieve the previously cached conversion instead of doing it all over again.

Both scalar variables and literal values have this ability; a variable merely allows its value to be changed. To illustrate how Perl handles conversions, consider the assignment of a literal integer value to a scalar variable:

```
$number = 3141;
```

This assigns an integer value to the scalar stored by the variable. The scalar is now combined into a string by concatenating it, using the dot operator, with another string.

```
$text = $number.' is a thousand PIs';
```

This statement causes Perl to convert the scalar into a string, since it currently only knows the integer value and concatenation only works between strings, not numbers. The converted string representation is now cached inside the scalar alongside the original integer. So, if the scalar is requested as a string a second time, Perl does not need to redo the conversion, it just retrieves the string representation.

The same principle works for floating-point numbers too. Here we divide the same scalar by 1.414, which requires that it be converted to a floating-point number:

```
$new_number = $number/1.414;
```

Our scalar variable now has three different representations of its value stored internally. It will continue to supply one of the three in any expression in which it is used, until it is assigned a new value. At this point, one of the representations is updated and the other two are marked as invalid.

```
$number = "Number Six";
```

In this case, the previous integer and floating-point number values of $number are now invalid; if we ask for the integer value of this variable now, Perl will recalculate it from the string value (getting a default result of zero since this string starts with a letter and not a digit).

All this behind-the-scenes shuffling may seem convoluted, but it allows Perl to optimize the retrieval and processing of scalar values in our programs. One benefit of this is that evaluation of scalars happens faster after the first time. However, the real point is that it allows us to write simpler and more legible programs, because we do not have to worry about converting the type of a scalar in order to meet the expectations of the language. This does not come without risk as Perl will happily let us use a string variable in a numeric context even if we had not intended it, but the advantage of transparent conversion within the scalar variable is that it allows us to avoid creating additional variables simply to store alternate representations and, in general, simplifies our code.

Numbers

As we stated earlier, numbers fall into one of two categories, integer or floating point. In addition, both types of number can be represented as a numerical string, which is converted to the appropriate format when used.

As well as handling integers in base 10 (decimal), numbers may be expressed and displayed in base 2 (binary), base 8 (octal), and base 16 (hexadecimal) formats, all of which Perl handles transparently. Conversely, displaying numbers in a different base requires converting them into a string with the correct representation, so this is actually a special case of integer-to-string conversion. Internally, integers are stored as 32-bit binary values (unless Perl had been built with native 64-bit integer support), so number bases are only relevant for input or output.

In many cases, calculations will produce floating-point results, even if the numbers are integers: for example, division by another integer that does not divide evenly. Additionally, the range of floating-point numbers exceeds that of integers, so Perl sometimes returns a floating-point number if the result of a calculation exceeds the range in which Perl can store integers internally, as determined by the underlying platform.

Integers

Integers are one of the two types of numerical value that Perl supports. In Perl code, integers are usually written in decimal (base 10), but other number bases and formats are also possible, as shown in Table 3-1.

Table 3-1. *Written Integer Formats*

Number	Format
123	Regular decimal integer
0b1101	Binary integer

Number	Format
0127	Octal integer
0xabcd	Hexadecimal integer
12_345	Underscore annotated integer
0xca_fe_ba_be	Underscore annotated hexadecimal integer

It is also possible to specify an integer value as a string. When used in an integer context, the string value is translated into an integer before it is used.

```
"123"   # regular decimal integer expressed as a string
```

The underscore notation is permitted in integers in order to allow them to be written more legibly. Ordinarily we would use commas for this.

```
10,023
```

However, in Perl, the comma is used as a list separator, so this would represent the value 10 followed by the value 23. In order to make up for this, Perl allows underscores to be used instead.

```
10_023
```

Underscores are not required to occur at regular intervals, nor are they restricted to decimal numbers. As the preceding hexadecimal example illustrates, they can also be used to separate out the individual bytes in a 32-bit hexadecimal integer. It is legal to put an underscore anywhere in an integer except at the start or, since Perl 5.8, the end. (It was found that the trailing underscore made the parser's job harder and was not actually very useful, so it was dropped.)

```
1_2_3  # ok
_123   # leading underscore makes '_123' an identifier - not a number!
123_   # trailing underscore ok prior to Perl 5.8, illegal from Perl 5.8 onwards
```

Integer Range and Big Integers

When Perl stores an integer value as an integer (as opposed to a numerical string), the maximum size of the integer value is limited by the maximum size of integers supported by the Perl interpreter, which in turn depends on the underlying platform. Prior to Perl 5.8, on a 32-bit architecture this means integers can range from

0 to 4294967295 (unsigned)

–2147483648 to 2147483647 (signed)

Perl can take advantage of 64-bit integers on platforms that support them—and from Perl 5.8 on 32-bit platforms too—but in either case only if the interpreter has been built with support for them.

If an integer calculation falls outside the range that integers can support, then Perl automatically converts the result into a floating-point value. An example of such a calculation is

```
print "2 to the power of 100:1 against and falling: ", 2**100;
```

This results in a number larger than integers can handle, so Perl produces a floating-point result and prints this message:

```
2 to the power of 100:1 against and falling: 1.26765060022823e+30
```

Because the accuracy of the floating-point number is limited by the number of significant digits it can hold, this result is actually only an approximation of the value 2**100. While it is perfectly possible to *store* a large integer in a floating-point number or a string (which has no limitations on the number of digits and so can store an integer of any length accurately), we cannot necessarily *use* that number in a numerical calculation without losing some of the precision. Perl must convert the string into an integer or, if that is not possible due to range limitations, a floating-point number in order to perform the calculation. Because floating-point numbers cannot always represent integers perfectly, this results in calculations that can be imprecise.

For applications in which handling extremely large integers is essential and the built-in integer support is not adequate, the `Math::BigInt` package is provided as part of the standard Perl library. This can be used explicitly, or via the `use bigint` or `use bignum` pragmas (the latter of which also pulls in `Math::BigFloat`) invoked automatically for any integer calculations.

```
use bignum; # or use bigint
print "2 to the power of 100:1 against and falling: ", 2**100;
```

This will print out the correct integer result of 1267650600228229401496703205376. However, unless the underlying platform actually allows native integer calculations on numbers of these sizes without a helping hand, it is also much slower.

Converting Integers into Floating-Point Numbers

In general we almost never need to explicitly convert integers to floating-point representations, since the conversion will be done for us automatically when needed. However, should you need to do so, the process is straightforward. No special function or operation is required; we can just multiply (or divide) it by 1.0.

```
$float = 1.0 * $integer;
```

This will store a floating-point value into `$float`, although if we print out we will still see an apparent integer value. This is because an integer is the most efficient way to display the result even if it is a floating-point value.

Converting Integers into Strings

Just as with floating-point numbers, we do not usually have to convert integers into strings since Perl will do it for us when the situation calls for it. However, at times you may genuinely want to impose a manual conversion. In this section, I'll discuss various issues surrounding this process.

For instance, one reason for manually converting a number into a string is to pad it with leading spaces or zeros (to align columns in a table, or print out a uniform date format). This is a task for `printf` and `sprintf`, generic string formatters inspired by and broadly compatible with (though not actually based on) the C function of the same names. They work using special tokens or "placeholders" to describe how various values, including numbers, should be rendered in character.

Formatting of integer values is carried out by the `%..d` and `%0..d` placeholders. For example, consider a numeric value that describes the desired width of the resulting text, i.e., `%4d` for a width of 4 characters. The 0, if present, tells `printf` to pad the number with leading zeros rather than spaces. Let's consider a few examples:

```
printf '%d/%d/%d', 2000, 7, 4;       # displays "2000/7/4"
printf '%d/%2d/%2d', 2000, 7, 4;     # displays "2000/ 7/ 4"
printf '%d/%02d/%02d', 2000, 7, 4;   # displays "2000/07/04"
```

Other characters can be added to the placeholder to handle other cases. For instance, if the number is negative, a minus sign is automatically prefixed, which will cause a column of mixed signs to be misaligned. However, if a space or + is added to the start of the placeholder definition, positive numbers will be padded, with a space or + respectively:

```
printf '% 2d', $number;   # pad with leading space if positive
printf '%+2d', $number;   # prefix a '+' sign if positive
```

The functions `printf` and `sprintf` are introduced in detail in the section "String Formatting with printf and sprintf" later in the chapter.

Converting Between Number Bases

As we briefly saw at the beginning of the chapter, Perl allows numbers to be expressed in octal, hexadecimal, binary, and decimal formats. To express a number in octal, prefix it with a leading zero. For example:

```
0123    # 123 octal (83 decimal)
```

Similarly, we can express numbers in hexadecimal using a prefix of `0x`.

```
0x123   # 123 hexadecimal (291 decimal)
```

Finally, from Perl 5.6 onwards, we can express numbers in binary with a prefix of `0b`.

```
0b1010011   # 1010011 binary (83 decimal)
```

Converting a number into a string that contains the binary, octal, or hexadecimal representation of that number can be achieved with Perl's `sprintf` function. As mentioned earlier, `sprintf` takes a format string containing a list of one or more placeholders, and a list of scalars to fill those placeholders. The type of placeholder defines the conversion that each scalar must undergo to be converted into a string. To convert into a different base, we just use an appropriate placeholder, %b, %o, %x, or %X.

```
$bintext = sprintf '%b', $number;   # convert to binary string (5.6.0+ only)
$octtext = sprintf '%o', $number;   # convert into octal string
$hextext = sprintf '%x', $number;   # convert into lowercase hexadecimal
$hextext = sprintf '%X', $number;   # convert into uppercase hexadecimal
```

The textual conversions are not created with the appropriate number base prefix (0, 0x, or 0b) in place, and so do not produce strings that convert back using the same base as they were created with. In order to fix this problem, we have to add the base prefix ourselves.

```
$bintext = sprintf '0b%b', 83;    # produces '0b1010011'
$octtext = sprintf '0%o', 83;     # produces '0123'
$hextext = sprintf '0x%bx', 83;   # produces '0x5'
```

The %b placeholder is only available from Perl version 5.6.0 onwards. Versions of Perl prior to this do not have a simple way to generate binary numbers and have to resort to somewhat unwieldy expressions using the `pack` and `unpack` functions. This is covered in more detail in the "Pack and Unpack" section later.

```
$bintext = unpack("B32", pack("N", $number));
```

This handles 32-bit values. If we know that the number is small enough to fit into a `short` (i.e., 16-bit) integer, we can get away with fewer bits.

```
$smallbintext = unpack("B16", pack("n", $number));
```

Unfortunately for small values, this is still likely to leave a lot of leading zeros, since `unpack` has no idea what the most significant bit actually is, and so it just ploughs through all 16 or 32 bits regardless. The number 3 would be converted into

```
'0000000000000011'   # '3' as a 16-bit binary string
```

We can remove those leading zeros using the string functions `substring` and `index`.

```
#hunt for and return string from the first '1' onwards
$smallbintext = substring($smallbintext, index($smallbintext, '1'));
```

A substitution works too.

```
$smallbintext =~ s/^0+//;
```

Though this works, it is certainly neither as elegant (nor as fast) as using `sprintf`; upgrading an older Perl may be a better idea than using this work-around.

Floating-Point Numbers

Perl allows real numbers to be written in one of two forms, fixed point and scientific. In the fixed-point representation, the decimal point is fixed in place, with a constant and unchanging number of available fractional digits. Prices are a common example of real-life fixed-point numbers. In the scientific representation, the number value is called the *mantissa*, and it is combined with an *exponent* representing a power of 10 that the mantissa is multiplied by. The exponent allows the decimal point to be shifted, and gives the scientific representation the ability to express both very small and very large numbers.

Either representation can be used to express a floating-point value within Perl, but depending on the application it is usually more convenient to use one over the other. Consider these examples:

```
123.45       # fixed point
-1.2345e2    # scientific, lowercase, negative
+1.2345E2    # scientific, uppercase, explicitly positive
```

Likewise, fractions can be expressed either in fixed-point notation or as a negative exponent.

```
0.000034     # fixed point
-3.4e-4      # scientific, lowercase, negative
+3.4E-4      # scientific, uppercase, explicitly positive
```

Floating-point numbers can be expressed over a very large range.

```
1e100        # a 'googol' or 1 x 10(100)
3.141        # 3.141 x 10(0)
1.6e-22      # 0.00000000000000000000016
```

■**Tip** A *googol* is actually the correct mathematical term for this number (1e100), believe it or not. Likewise, a *googolplex* is 10 to the power of a googol, or 10(10)(100), which is hard for both humans and programming languages to handle.

The distinction between "floating-point numbers" and "scientific representation" is these days one of implementation versus expression. On older hardware there was a speed advantage to using fixed-point numbers—indeed, integers could be pressed into duty as fixed-point reals when floating-point support was not available. So it made a difference whether or not a number was expressed in fixed-point or scientific form.

These days floating-point calculations are intrinsic to the CPU and there is no significant speed advantage to making fixed-point calculations with integers. As a result, even fixed-point numbers are now internally stored as (binary) floating-point values. There is still an advantage to writing in fixed-point notation for human consumption. We would rarely choose to write 15,000 as `1.5e4` or `15e3`, even if they are more natural floating-point representations.

Floating-point numbers are used to store what in mathematical terms are called real numbers, the set of all possible values. The accuracy of floating-point numbers is limited, so they cannot represent all real numbers. However, they are capable of a wider range of values than integers, both in terms of accuracy and in terms of scale. The preceding example of 1e100 is mathematically an integer, but it is one that Perl's internal integer representation is unable to handle, since one hundred consecutive zeros is considerably beyond the maximum value of 4,294,967,295 that integers can manage on most platforms. For a floating-point number however it is trivial, since an exponent of 100 coupled to a mantissa of 1 represents the value perfectly.

The standard C library of the underlying platform on which Perl is running determines the range of floating-point numbers. On most platforms floating-point numbers are handled and stored as *doubles*, double accuracy 8-byte (64-bit) values, though the actual calculations performed by the hardware may use more bits. Of these 64 bits, 11 are reserved for the exponent, which can range from 2 to the power of –1024 to +1024, which equates to a range of around 10 to the power of –308 to +308. The remaining 53 are assigned to the mantissa, so floating-point numbers can represent values up to 53 binary places long. That equates to 15 or 16 decimal places, depending on the exact value.

However, just because a value is within the range of floating numbers does not mean that it can represent them accurately. Unforeseen complications can arise when using floating-point numbers to perform calculations. While Perl understands and displays floating-point numbers in *decimal* format, it stores them internally in *binary* format. Fractional numbers expressed in one base cannot always be accurately expressed in another, even if their representation seems very simple. This can lead to slight differences between the answer that Perl calculates and the one we might expect.

To give an example, consider the floating-point number 0.9. This is easy to express in decimal, but in binary this works out to

0.111001101101101101101101101101101101101110 . . .

that is, a recurring number. But floating-point numbers may only hold a finite number of binary digits; we cannot accurately represent this number in the mantissa alone. As it happens, 0.9 *can* be accurately represented as 9e-1: a mantissa of 9 with an exponent of -1, but this is not true for every floating-point number. Consequently, calculations involving floating-point values, and especially comparisons to integers and other floating-point numbers, do not always behave as we expect.

Converting Floating Points into Integers

The quickest and simplest way to convert floating-point numbers into integers is to use the int function. This strips off the fractional part of the floating-point number and returns the integer part.

```
$int = int($float);
```

However, int is not very intelligent about how it calculates the integer part. First, it truncates the fractional part of a floating-point number and so only rounds down, which may not be what we want. Second, it does not take into account the problems of precision, which can affect the result of floating-point calculations. For example, the following calculation produces different results if the answer is returned as an integer, even though the resulting calculation ought to result in a round number:

```
$number = 4.05/0.05;
print "$number \n";    # returns 81, correct
print int($number);    # returns 80, incorrect!
```

Similarly, a comparison will tell us that $number is not really equal to 81.

```
$number = 4.15/0.05;
# if $number is not equal to 81 then execute the print statement
# in the block
if ($number != 81) {
   print "\$number is not equal to 81 \n";
}
```

The reason for this is that $number does not actually have the value 81 but a floating-point value that is very slightly less than 81, due to fact that the calculation is performed with binary floating-point numbers. When we display it, the conversion to string format handles the slight discrepancy for us and we see the result we expect.

To round the preceding to the nearest integer rather than the next highest or next lowest, we can add 0.5 to our value and then round it down.

```
print int($number+0.5);   # returns 81, correct
```

C programmers may be familiar with the floor and ceil functions of the standard C library that have a similar purpose (and the same rounding problems). In fact, using the POSIX module, we can gain direct access to these and C library functions defined by IEEE 1003.1, if we like. The difference is that the values returned from these functions are floating-point values, not integers. That is, though they appear the same to us, the internal representation is different.

Converting Floating Points into Strings

Perl automatically converts floating-point numbers into strings when they are used in a string context, for example:

```
print "The answer is $floatnum";
```

If the number can be represented as an integer, Perl converts it before printing.

```
$floatnum = 4.3e12;    # The answer is 4300000000000
```

Alternatively, if the number is a fraction that can be expressed as a fixed decimal (that is, purely in terms of a mantissa without an exponent), Perl converts it into that format.

```
$floatnum = 4.3e-3;    # The answer is 0.0043
```

Otherwise it is converted into the standard mantissa+exponent form.

```
$floatnum = 4.3e99;    # The answer is 4.3e99
```

Sometimes we might want to alter the format of the generated text, to force consistency across a range of values or to present a floating-point value in a different format. The sprintf and printf functions can do this for us, and provide several placeholder formats designed for floating-point output.

```
printf '%e', $floatnum;    #force conversion to fixed decimal format
printf '%f', $floatnum;    #force conversion to mantissa/exponent format
printf '%g', $floatnum;    #use fixed (as %e), if accurately possible, otherwise as %f
```

Perl's default conversion of floating-point numbers is therefore equivalent to

```
$floatstr = sprintf '%g', $floatnum;
```

■**Note** To be strictly accurate, the default conversion is %.ng, where n is computed at the time Perl is built to be the highest accurate precision available. In most cases this will be the same as %g. See also the discussion of $# at the end of this section.

A field width can be inserted into the format string to indicate the desired width of the resulting number text. Additionally, a decimal point and second number can be used to indicate the width of the fractional part. We can use this to force a consistent display of all our numbers.

```
printf '%6.3f', 3.14159;    # display a minimum width of 6 with 3
                            # decimal places; produces ' 3.142'
```

The width, 6, in the preceding example, includes the decimal point and the leading minus sign if the number happens to be negative. This is fine if we only expect our numbers to range from 99.999 to –9.999, but printf will exceed this width if the whole part of the number exceeds the width remaining (two characters) after the decimal point and three fractional digits have taken their share. Allowing a sufficient width for all possible values is therefore important if sprintf and printf are to work as we want them to.

Just as with integers, we can prefix the format with a space or + to have positive numbers format to the same width as negative ones.

```
printf '% 7.3f', 3,14159;      # pad with leading space if positive,
                               # produces '  3.142'
printf '%+7.3f', 3.14159;      # prefix a '+' sign if positive,
                               # produces ' +3.142'
printf '%07.3f', 3.14159;      # prefix with leading zeros,
                               # produces '003.142'
printf '% 07.3f', 3.14159;     # pad with a leading space, then leading zeros,
                               # produces ' 03.142'
printf '%+07.3f', 3.14159;     # pad with a leading +, then leading zeros,
                               # produces '+03.142'
printf '%.3f', 3.14159;        # leading digits with no padding,
                               # produces '3.142'
```

Interestingly, Perl's default conversion of floating-point numbers into strings can be overridden in a couple of ways. First, the special variable $# can be used to set the internal format for conversion (but note that use of $# has always been technically deprecated).

```
$#="%.3f"
print "1.6666666" # produces "1.667"
```

Second, for those who require exact and precise control over the conversion process, Perl can be built to use a different conversion function by overriding the d_Gconvert configuration option. See Chapter 1 and perldoc Configure for more information.

The use integer Pragma

We discussed earlier how Perl automatically converts between integers, strings, and floating-point numbers when required. However, we might specifically want an integer, either because we want a result in round numbers or simply for speed. One way to restrict the result of a calculation to integers is to use the int function, as shown in the earlier section, "Converting Floating Points into Integers."

This still causes Perl to do some calculations with floating-point numbers, since it does not always know to do different. If the underlying hardware does not support floating-point operations (rare, but still possible in embedded systems), this can result in unnecessarily slow calculations when much faster integer calculations could be used. To remedy this situation and allow Perl to intelligently use integers where possible, we can encourage integer calculations with the use integer pragma.

```
use integer;
$integer_result = $nominator / $divisor;
```

While use integer is in effect, calculations that would normally produce floating-point results but are capable of working with integers will operate interpreting their operands as integers.

```
use integer;
$PI = 3.1415926;
print $PI;          # prints '3.1415926'
print $PI + 5;      # prints '8'
```

We can disable integer-only arithmetic by stating no integer, which cancels out the effect of a previous use integer. This allows us to write sections (or blocks) of code that are integer only, but leave the rest of the program using floating-point numbers as usual, or vice versa. For example:

```
sub integersub {
  use integer;
  #integer-only code...
  {
      no integer;
      #floating point allowed in this block
  }
  #more integer-only code...
}
```

Using use integer can have some unexpected side effects. While enabled, Perl passes integer calculations to the underlying system (which means the standard C library for the platform on which Perl was built) rather than doing them itself. That might not always produce exactly the same result as Perl would, for example:

```
print -13 % 7;   # produces '1'

use integer;
print -13 % 7;   # produces '-6'
```

The reason for this behavior is that Perl and the standard C library have slightly different perspectives on how the modulus of a negative number is calculated. The fact that, by its nature, a modulus calculation cannot produce a floating-point result does not alter the fact that use integer affects its operation.

Even with use integer enabled, Perl will still produce a floating-point number if an integer result makes no sense or if the result would otherwise be out of range. For example:

```
use integer;
print sqrt(2);   # produces 1.4142135623731
print 2 ** 100;   # produces 1.26765060022823e+030
```

use integer has one final effect that is not immediately obvious: it disables Perl's automatic interpretation of bitwise operations as unsigned, so results that set the highest bit (that is, the 32nd bit in a 32-bit architecture) will be interpreted by Perl as signed rather than unsigned values.

```
print ~0, ' ',-1 << 0;   # produces '4294967295 4294967295'

use integer;
print ~0, ' ',-1 << 0;   # produces '-1 -1'
```

This can be useful behavior if we want it, but it is a potential trap for the unwary.

Mathematical Functions

Perl provides a number of built-in mathematical functions for managing numbers. Here is a quick summary of some of the more commonly encountered.

The abs function returns the absolute (unsigned) value of a number.

```
print abs(-6.3);   # absolute value, produces 6.3
```

Perl provides three functions for computing powers and logarithms, in addition to the ** exponentiation operator. These functions include sqrt, exp, and log.

```
print sqrt(6.3);   # square root of 6.3, produces 2.50998007960223
print exp(6.3);   # raise 'e' to the power of 6.3, produces 544.571910125929
print log(6.3);   # natural (base 'e') logarithm, produces 1.84054963339749
```

Perl's support for logarithms only extends to base(e), also called *natural*, logarithms. This is not a problem, though, since to work in other bases we just divide the natural log of the number by the natural log of the base, that is

```
$n=2;
print log($n) / log(10);   # calculate and print log(10)2
```

For the specific case of base 10 logarithms, the standard C library defines a base 10 logarithm function that we can use via the POSIX module as log10.

```
use POSIX qw(log10);
print log10($n);   # calculate and print log(10)2
```

Perl provides three built-in trigonometric functions, sin, cos, and atan2, for the sine, cosine, and arctangent of an angle, respectively. Perl does not provide built-in inverse functions for these three, nor does it provide the standard tan function, because these can all be worked out easily (ignoring issues of ranges, domains, and result quadrants).

```
atan2($n, sqrt(1 - $n ** 2))   # asin (inverse sine)
atan2(sqrt(1 - $n ** 2), $n)   # acos (inverse cosine)
sin($n) / cos($n)              # tan
```

We can easily define subroutines to provide these calculations, but to save us the trouble of writing our own trigonometric functions Perl provides a full set of basic trigonometric functions in the Math::Trig module, as well as utility subroutines for converting between degrees and radians and between radial and Cartesian coordinates. See the Math::Trig manual page for more information.

Strings

Perl provides comprehensive support for strings, including interpolation, regular expression processing, and even a selection of ways to specify them. Arguably, string processing is Perl's single biggest strength, and accordingly much of this book is concerned with it in one way or another. In this section, we will look at the basic features of strings and built-in functions Perl provides to handle them.

Quotes and Quoting

Literal strings—that is, strings typed explicitly into source code—can be written in a variety of different quoting styles, each of which treats the text of the string in a different way. These styles are listed in Table 3-2.

Table 3-2. *Quote Types and Operators*

Quote Type	Operator	Result
Single quotes	q	Literal string
Double quotes	qq	Interpolated string
N/A	qr	Regular expressions string
Backticks (``)	qx	Executes external program
N/A	qw	List of words

As the table shows, Perl provides two syntaxes for most kinds of strings. The ordinary punctuated kind uses quotes, but we can also use a quoting operator to perform the same function.

```
'Literal Text'          # is equivalent to q(Literal Text)
"$interpolated @text"   # is equivalent to qq($interpolated @text)
`./external -command`   # is equivalent to qx(./external -command)
```

One of the advantages of the quoting operators is that they allow us to place quote marks inside a string that would otherwise cause syntax difficulties. Accordingly, the delimiters of the quoting operators can be almost anything, so we have the greatest chance of being able to pick a pair of characters that do not occur in the string.

```
$text = q/a string with 'quotes' is 'ok' inside q/;
```

Perl accepts both paired and single delimiters. If a delimiter has a logical opposite, such as (and), < and >, [and], or { and }, the opposing delimiter is used for the other end; otherwise the same delimiter is expected again.

```
$text = qq{ "$interpolated" ($text) 'and quotes too' };
```

Other than their more flexible syntax, the quoting operators have the same results as their quote counterparts. Two quote operators, qw and qr, do not have quote equivalents, but these have more specialized purposes. More to the point, they do not produce strings as their output.

The *single quoted* string treats all of its text as literal characters; no processing, interpolation, or escaping is performed. The quoting operator for literal text is q, so the following are equivalent:

```
'This is literal text'
```

```
q/This is literal text/
```

Or with any other delimiter we choose, as noted previously.

The *double quoted* string interpolates its text, expanding scalar and array variables, and backslash-prefixed special characters like \n. The quoting operator for interpolated text is qq, so the following are equivalent:

```
"There are $count matches in a $thing.\n";
qq/There are $count matches in a $thing.\n/
```

Interpolation is a more advanced subject than it at first appears, and the first part of Chapter 11 is dedicated to exploring it in detail. Fortunately, if we do not have any variables in a double-quoted string, Perl will realize this at compile time and compile the string as a constant (as if it had been single quoted), so there is no substantive performance cost to using double quotes even for strings that do not need to be interpolated.

The qr operator, introduced in Perl 5.005, prepares regular expressions for use ahead of time. It accepts a regular expression pattern, and produces a ready-to-go regular expression that can be used anywhere a regular expression operator can.

```
# directly
$text =~ /pattern/;

# via 'qr':
$re = qr/pattern/;
$text =~ $re;
```

The qr operator also interpolates its argument in exactly the same way that double quoted strings and the qq operator do. Do not despair if this seems rather abstract at the moment; we will learn more about this in Chapter 11, where qr is covered in more detail.

Quoting a string with backticks, `, causes Perl to treat the enclosed text as a command to be run externally. The output of the command (if any) is captured by Perl and returned to us. For example:

```
#!/usr/bin/perl
# external.pl
use strict;
use warnings;
```

```
my $dir = "/home";
my $files = `ls -1 $dir`;    # or something like `dir c:` for DOS/Windows
print $files;
```

When run, this program produces the following output:

```
> perl external.pl
```

```
beeblebz
denta
prefectf
marvin
```

Interpolation is carried out on the string before it is executed, and then passed to a temporary shell if any shell-significant characters like spaces or quotes are present in the resulting string. The equivalent quoting operator for backticks is qx.

```
my $files = qx(ls -1 $dir);
```

There are serious security issues regarding the use of backticks, however. This is partly because they rely on environment variables like $PATH, which is represented in Perl as $ENV{PATH}, that we may not be able to trust. Additionally, the temporary shell can interpret characters in a potentially damaging way. For this reason, backticks and the qx operator are often considered deprecated in anything more complex than simple private-use scripts. See Chapter 21 for more on the issues as well as ways to avoid them.

The qw operator takes a whitespace-separated string and turns it into a list of values. In this respect it is unlike the other quoting operators, all of which return string values. Its purpose is to allow us to specify long lists of words without the need for multiple quotes and commas that defining a list of strings normally requires.

```
# Using standard single quotes
@array = ('a', 'lot', 'of', 'quotes', 'is', 'not', 'very', 'legible');

# much more legible using 'qw'
@array = qw(a lot of quotes is not very legible);
```

Both these statements produce the same list of single-word string values as their result, but the second is by far the more legible. The drawback to qw is that it will not interpolate variables or handle quotes, so we cannot include spaces within words. In its favor, though, qw also accepts tabs and newlines, so we can also say

```
@array = qw(
a lot
of quotes
is not
very legible
);
```

Note that with qw we need to avoid commas, which can be a hard habit to break. If we accidentally use commas, Perl will warn against it, since commas are just another character to qw and so comma-separated words would result in a single string, words, commas, and all.

```
@oops = qw(a, comma, separated, list, of, words);
```

If we try to do this, Perl will warn us (assuming we have warnings enabled) with

```
Possible attempt to separate words with commas at ...
```

If we actually want to use commas, we can, but in order to silence Perl, we will need to turn off warnings temporarily with no warnings and turn them back on again afterward (from Perl 5.6 onwards we can also turn off specific warnings, so we could do that too).

"Here" Documents

As we have just learned, the usual way to define literal text in source code is with quotes, or the equivalent quoting operators q and qq. Here documents are an additional and alternative way that is particularly well suited to multiple line blocks of text like document templates. Here documents are interpolated, and so make a convenient alternative to both concatenating multiple lines together and Perl formats, which also provide a document template processing feature, but in an entirely different way.

To create a here document, we use a << followed immediately by an end token, a bareword, or quoted string that is used to mark the end of the block. The block itself starts from the next line and absorbs all text, including the newlines, until Perl sees the end token, which *must* appear alone at the start of a new line. Normal Perl syntax parsing is disabled while the document is defined— although interpolation of variables still takes place—and parsing only continues after the end token is located.

```
$string = <<_END_OF_TEXT_;
Some text
Split onto multiple lines
Is clearly defined
_END_OF_TEXT_
```

This is equivalent to, but easier on the eye than

```
$string = "Some text \n".
"Split onto multiple lines \n".
"Is clearly defined \n";
```

The << and token define where the document is used, and tell Perl that it is about to start on the next line. There must be no space between the << and the token, otherwise Perl will complain. The token may be an unquoted bareword, like the preceding example, or a quoted string, in which case it can contain spaces, as in the following example:

```
# the end token may contain spaces if it is quoted
print <<"print to here";
This is
some text
print to here
```

If used, the type of quote also determines whether or not the body of the document is interpolated or not. Double quotes or no quotes causes interpolation. If single quotes are used, no interpolation takes place.

```
# this does not interpolate
print <<'_END_OF_TEXT_'
This %is @not %interpolated
_END_OF_TEXT_
```

Note that in all examples the here document is used within a statement, which is terminated by a semicolon, as normal. It is not true to say that the <<TOKEN absorbs all text following it; it is a perfectly ordinary string value from the point of view of the statement it appears in. Only from the next line does Perl start to absorb text into the document.

```
# a foreach loop on one line
foreach (split "\n", <<LINES) { print "Got $_ \n"; }
Line 1
```

```
Line 2
Line 3
LINES
```

Alternatively, we can define a here document within a statement if the statement spans more than one line; the rest of the lines fall after the end token:

```
#!/usr/bin/perl
# heredoc.pl
use warnings;
use strict;

# a foreach loop split across the 'here' document
foreach (split "\n", <<LINES) {
Line 1
Line 2
Line 3
LINES
    print "Got: $_ \n";
}
```

Since here documents are interpolated (unless we use single quotes to define the end token at the top, as noted earlier) they make a very convenient way to create templates for documents. Here is an example being used to generate an e-mail message with a standard set of headers:

```
#!/usr/bin/perl
# formate.pl
use warnings;
use strict;

print format_email('me@myself.net', 'you@yourself.org', "Wishing you were here",
                   "...instead of me!", "Regards, Me");

# subroutines will be explained fully in Chapter 7
sub format_email {
    my ($me, $to_addr, $subject, $body_of_message, $signature) = @_;

    return <<_EMAIL_;
To: $to_addr
From: $me;
Subject: $subject

$body_of_message
--
$signature
_EMAIL_
}
```

The choice of end token is arbitrary; it can be anything, including a Perl keyword. For clarity's sake, however, use an appropriately named token, preferably in capitals and possibly with surrounding underscores. The end token must also appear at the start of the line—if it is indented, Perl will not recognize it. Likewise, any indentation within the here document will remain in the document. This can present a stylistic problem since it breaks with the indentation of code in things like subroutines. For instance:

```
sub return_a_here_document {
    return <<DOCUMENT;
This document definition cannot be indented
if we want to avoid indenting
```

```
the resulting document too
DOCUMENT
}
```

If we do not mind indenting the document, then we can indent the end token by defining it with the indent to start with.

```
sub return_a_here_document {
    return <<'   DOCUMENT';
    This document is indented, but the
    end token is also indented, so it parses OK
    DOCUMENT
}
```

Although it uses the same symbol, the here document << has nothing whatsoever to do with the shift right operator. Rather, it is a unary operator with an unusual operand.

For large blocks of text, it is also worth considering the DATA filehandle, which reads data placed after the __END__ or __DATA__ tokens in source files, discussed in Chapter 12. This approach is less convenient in that it is used in place like a here document, but it does avoid the indentation problem mentioned previously and can often improve legibility.

Bareword Strings and Version Number Strings

The use strict pragma provides us with three separate additional checks on our Perl code. Two of them, to declare variables properly and forbid symbolic references, we already mentioned in Chapter 2, and will cover in detail in Chapter 8. The third restriction, strict subs, does not allow us to write a string without quotes, known as a *bareword* string, because of the potential for confusion with subroutines. Without strict subs we can in fact quite legally say

```
# 'use strict subs' won't allow us to do this
$word = unquoted;
```

instead of the more correct

```
$word = "unquoted";
```

The problem with the first example, apart from the fact we cannot include spaces in a bareword string, is that if at a future point we write a subroutine called unquoted, then our string assignment suddenly becomes a subroutine call. This is a fairly obvious example where we really ought to be using quotes, but it is easy (and perfectly legal) to use bareword strings in things like hash keys, because in these cases a string is required and expected.

```
$value = $hash{animal}{small}{furry}{cat};
```

The bareword is allowed because it is the most common case. What if we actually do want to call a subroutine called animal, however? We need to tell Perl by adding some parentheses, turning the bareword into an explicit subroutine call. For example:

```
$value = $hash{animal()}{small()}{furry()}{cat()};
```

There are a few other places where bareword strings are allowed. One is the qw operator, which we covered earlier.

```
qw(startword bareword anotherbareword endword);
```

A second place where barewords are allowed is on the left-hand side of the relationship (or digraph) operator. This is just a clever form of comma that knows it is being used to define paired keys and values, typically hashes. Since a hash key can only be a string, the left-hand side of a => is assumed to be a string if written as a bareword.

```
%hash = ( key => "value still needs quotes" );
```

(We can force a subroutine call instead by adding parentheses to key as before.)

Finally, Perl supports a very special kind of string called a version string, which in fact must be unquoted to be treated as such. The format of a version string must resemble a version number, and can only be made of digits and points.

```
$VERSION = 1.2.34;
```

Perl will see this as a version number, because it contains more than one decimal point and has no quotes. If the version number has no or only one decimal point, then we can currently use a v prefix to ensure that Perl does not interpret it as a regular integer or floating-point number.

```
$float   = 5.6;    # oops, that is a floating-point number
$VERSION = v5.6;   # force a version string (but see later)
```

Places where a version number is expected, such as the require and use keywords, do not need the prefix. Take the following line that states that Perl must be at least version 5.6 for the program to run:

```
require 5.6;       # always a version string
```

Version strings are likely to be replaced with version objects in Perl 5.10. While these will be semantically similar, the v prefix syntax will be retired and there may no longer be a direct equivalence between a version object and the string representation described previously. Instead, version objects will be created when the syntax expects one.

The special variable $^V ($PERL_VERSION) returns a version string. It contrasts with the older $], which returns a floating-point number for compatibility with older Perl versions (e.g., 5.003). It will return a version object in the future, though the usage will be the same.

The purpose of $^V is to allow version numbers to be easily compared without straying into the dangerous world of floating-point comparisons. Take this example that tests the version of Perl itself, and aborts with an error message if it is too old:

```
# 'require 5.6.0' is another way to do this:
die "Your Perl is too old! Get a new one! \n" if $^V lt 5.6.0;
```

The characters in a version string are constructed from the digits, so a 1 becomes the character Control-A, or ASCII 1. 5.6.0 is therefore equivalent to the interpolated string "\05\06\00" or the expression chr(5).chr(6).chr(0). This is not a printable string, but it is still a string, so we must be sure to use the string comparison operators like lt (less than) and ge (greater or equal to) rather than their numeric equivalents < and >=.

If we use a version string as the leading argument to the => operator, it is evaluated as a regular string and not a version number string, at least from Perl 5.8 onwards (prior to this it would be evaluated as a version number string). So this expression produces a hash with a key of U for Perl 5.8 and chr(64) for Perl 5.6:

```
my %hash=( v64 => "version 64");
```

Sometimes it is handy to know whether or not a scalar value conforms to a version number string. To find out, we can make use of the isvnumber routine from the Scalar::Util module.

```
use Scalar::Util qw(isvnumber);
...
print "Is a version number" if isvnumber($value);
```

As version strings will ultimately be replaced with version objects, code that relies on the string representation is risky and likely to break in future versions of Perl. Comparisons and isvumber will continue to work as they do now, but with the additional and more intuitive ability to make numeric rather than string comparisons.

Converting Strings into Numbers

As we have seen, Perl automatically converts strings into an integer or floating-point form when we perform a numeric operation on a string value. This provides us with a simple way to convert a string into a number when we actually want a number, for example, in a print statement, which is happy with any kind of scalar. All we have to do is perform a numeric operation on the string that doesn't change its value, multiplying or dividing by 1 for example. Adding zero is probably the simplest (and in fact is the traditional idiom in Perl).

```
# define a numeric string
$scalar = '123.4e5';

# evaluate it in original string context
print $scalar;   # produces '123.4e5'

# evaluate it in numeric context
print 0 + $scalar;   # produces '12340000'
```

If the string does not look like a number, then Perl will do the best job it can, while warning us that the string is not completely convertible and that some information is being lost with an "Argument isn't numeric at" message.

```
print "123.4e5abc" + 0   #   produces '12340000' and a warning
```

If we actually want to know in advance whether or not a string can be converted into some kind of numeric value, then there are a couple of ways we can do it. If we only need to know whether the string starts numerically, we could extract the numeric part with a regular expression—what pattern we use depends on what kind of numbers we are expecting to parse. For example, this checks for a string starting with an optional sign followed by at least one digit, and extracts it if present:

```
my $number = $string =~ /^([+-]?\d+)/;
```

This only handles integers, of course. The more diverse the range of number representations we want to match, the more complicated this becomes. If we want to determine whether the string is fully convertible (in the sense that no information is lost and no warning would be generated if we tried), then we can instead use the looks_like_number routine provided by Perl in the Scalar::Util module:

```
#!/usr/bin/perl
# lookslikenumber.pl
use Scalar::Util 'looks_like_number';

foreach (@ARGV) {
    print "$ARGV[0] ";
    print looks_like_number($ARGV[0])
        ? "looks" : "does not look";
    print " like a number\n";
}
```

looks_like_number will return 1 if the string can be completely converted to a numeric value, and 0 otherwise. It works by asking Perl's underlying conversion functionality what it thinks of the string, which is much simpler (and to the point) than constructing a regular expression to attempt to match all possible valid numeric strings.

Converting Strings into Lists and Hashes

Transforming a string into a list requires dividing it up into pieces. For this purpose, Perl provides the split function, which takes up to three arguments, a pattern to match on, the string that is to be carved up, and the maximum number of splits to perform. With only two arguments, the string is split as many times as the pattern matches. For example, this splits a comma-separated sequence of values into a list of those values:

```
#!/usr/bin/perl
# splitup.pl
use strict;
use warnings;

my $csv = "one, two, three, four, five, six";
my @list = split ', ' , $csv;
print "@list";
```

Although it is commonly used to split up strings by simple delimiters like commas, the first argument to split is in fact a regular expression, and is able to use the regular expression syntax of arbitrary delimiters.

```
@list = split /, /, $csv;
```

This also means that we can be more creative about how we define the delimiter. Without delving too deeply into regular expression syntax, to divide up a string with commas and arbitrary quantities of whitespace we can replace the comma with a pattern that absorbs whitespace—spaces, tabs, or newlines—on either side.

```
@list = split /\s*,\s*/, $csv;
```

This does not deal with any leading or trailing whitespace on the first and last items (and in particular any trailing newline), but it is effective nonetheless. However, if we want to split on a character that is significant in regular expressions, we have to escape it. The // style syntax helps remind us of this, but it is easy to forget that a pipe symbol, (|), will not split up a pipe-separated string.

```
$pipesv = "one | two | three | four | five | six";
print split('|', $pipesv);   # prints one | two | three | four | five | six
```

This will actually return the string as a list of single characters, including the pipes, because | defines alternatives in regular expressions. There is nothing on either side of the pipe, so we are actually asking to match on nothing or nothing, both of which are zero-width patterns (they successfully match no characters). split treats zero-width matches (a pattern that can legally match nothing at all) as a special case, splitting out a single character and moving on each time it occurs. As a result, we get a stream of single characters. This is better than an infinite loop, which is what would occur if Perl didn't treat zero-width matches specially, but it's not what we intended either. Here is how we should have done it:

```
print split('\|', $pipesv);   # prints one two three four five six
```

Having warned of the dangers, there are good uses for alternation too. Consider this split statement, which parses hash definitions in a string into a real hash:

```
$hashdef = "Mouse=>Jerry, Cat=>Tom, Dog=>Spike";
%hash = split /, |=>/, $hashdef;
```

Because it uses a regular expression, split is capable of lots of other interesting tricks, including returning the delimiter if we use parentheses. If we do not actually want to include the delimiters in the returned list, we need to suppress it with the extended (?:...) pattern.

```
# return (part of) delimiters
@list = split /\s*(, |=>)\s*/, $hashdef;
# @list contains 'Mouse', '=>', 'Jerry', ',' , 'Cat', ...
```

```
# suppress return of delimiters, handle whitespace, assign resulting
# list to hash
%hash = split /\s*(?:, |=>)\s*/, $hashdef;
```

Tip Both examples use more complex forms of regular expression such as \s to match whitespace, which we have not fully covered yet; see Chapter 11 for more details on how they work. The last example also illustrates how to define the contents of a hash variable from a list of values, which we will cover in detail when we come to hashes later.

If split is passed a third numeric parameter, then it only splits that number of times, preserving any remaining text as the last returned value.

```
my $configline = "equation=y = x ** 2 + c";
# split on first = only
my ($key, $value) = split (/=/, $configline, 2);
print "$key is '$value'";   # produces "equation is 'y = x ** 2 + c'"
```

split also has a special one and no-argument mode. With only one argument, it splits the default argument $_, which makes it useful in loops like the while loop that read lines from standard input (or files supplied on the command line), like the short program that follows:

```
#!/usr/bin/perl
# readconfig.pl
use warnings;
use strict;

my %config;

# read lines from files specified on command line or (if none)
# standard input
while (<>) {
    my ($key, $value) = split /=/;   # split on $_
    $config{$key} = $value if $key and $value;
}

print "Configured: ", join(', ', keys %config), "\n";
```

We can invoke this program with the following command:

> readconfig.pl configfile

Let's consider the following configfile:

```
first = one
second = two
```

Executing readconfig.pl using the supplied configfile, the following output is returned:

```
Configured: first, second
```

If no arguments are supplied at all, split splits the default argument on whitespace characters, after skipping any leading whitespace. The following short program counts words in the specified files or what is passed on standard input using the <> readline operator covered in Chapter 12:

```
#!/usr/bin/perl
# split.pl
```

```
use warnings;
use strict;

my @words;

# read lines from supplied filenames or (if none)
# standard input
while (<>) {
    # read each line into $_ in turn
    push @words, split; # split $_ into words and store them
}

print "Found ", scalar(@words), " words in input \n";
```

Functions for Manipulating Strings

Perl provides many built-in functions for manipulating strings, including split, which we discussed previously. Here is a short list and description of some of the most important of them:

Printing: print

Although perhaps the most obvious entry in the list, the ubiquitous print statement is not technically a string function, since it takes a list of arbitrary scalar values and sends them to a specified filehandle or otherwise standard output (technically, the currently selected filehandle). The general form is one of the following:

```
print @list;        # print to standard output
print TOFILE @list; # print to filehandle TOFILE
```

The details of using filehandles with print are covered in Chapter 12, but fortunately we can print to standard output without needing to know anything about them. Indeed, we have already seen print in many of the examples so far.

The output of print is affected by several of Perl's special variables, listed in Table 3-3.

Table 3-3. *Special Variables That Control Output*

Variable	Action
$,	The output field separator determines what print places between values, by default '' (nothing). Set to ',' to print comma-separated values.
$\	The output record separator determines what print places at the end of its output after the last value, by default '' (nothing). Set to '\n' to print out automatic linefeeds.
$#	The output format for all printed numbers (integer and floating point), in terms of a sprintf style placeholder. The default value is something similar to %.6g. To print everything to two fixed decimal places (handy for currency, for example) change to %.2f, but note that use of $# is now deprecated in Perl.
$|	The autoflush flag determines if line or block buffering should be used. If 0, it is block, if 1, it is line.

Although not directly related to print, it is worth noting that interpolated arrays and hashes use the special variable $" as a separator, rather than $, (a space by default).

Beware of leaving off the parentheses of print if the first argument (after the filehandle, if present) is enclosed in parentheses, since this will cause print to use the first argument as an argument list, ignoring the rest of the statement.

Line Terminator Removal: chop and chomp

The chop and chomp functions both remove the last character from a string. This apparently esoteric feature is actually very handy for removing line terminators. chop is not selective; it will chop off the last character irrespective of what it is or whether it looks like a line terminator or not, returning it to us in case we want to use it for something:

```
chop $input_string;
```

The string passed to chop must be an assignable one, such as a scalar variable (or more bizarrely, the return value of substr, shown in a bit, used on a scalar variable), since chop does not return the truncated string but the character that was removed. If no string is supplied, chop uses the default argument $_.

```
while (<>) {
   chop;
   print "$_ \n";
}
```

Note that if we want to get the string without the terminator but also leave it intact, we can use substr instead of chop. This is less efficient because it makes a copy of the line, but it preserves the original.

```
while (<>) {
   my $string = substr $_, 0, -1;
   print $string;
}
```

chomp is the user-friendly version of chop; it only removes the last character if it is the line terminator, as defined by the input record separator special variable $/, which defaults to \n.

```
chomp $might_end_in_a_linefeed_but_might_not;
```

Both chop and chomp will work on lists of strings as well as single ones.

```
# remove all trailing newlines from input, if present
@lines = <>;
chomp(@lines);
```

Giving either chop or chomp, a nonstring variable will convert it into a string. In the case of chomp, this will do nothing else; chop will return the last digit of a number and turn it into a string missing the last digit.

Although the line terminator can be more than one character wide, such as on Windows, chomp will still remove the line feed "character" correctly. However, if we happen to be reading text that was generated on a platform with a different concept of line ending, then we may need to alter Perl's idea of what a line terminator is.

```
@lines = <>;
{
    local $/ = "\015\012";
    chomp @lines;
}
```

Here we temporarily give $/ a different value, which expires at the end of the block in which it is placed. This code will strip DOS or Windows linefeeds from a file on a Unix platform within the block, but conversely it will not strip Unix linefeeds, since $/ does not match them within the block. A second chomp after the end of the block will deal with that.

Characters and Character Codes: ord and chr

The ord function produces the integer character code for the specified letter. If passed a string of more than one character, it will return the code for the first one. ord will also handle multibyte characters and return a Unicode character code.

```
print ord('A');   # returns 65
```

The inverse of ord is chr, which converts a character code into a character.

```
print chr(65);   # returns 'A'
```

■**Tip** Note that these examples will only produce this output if ASCII is the default character set. In Japan, for example, the output would be different.

The chr and ord functions will happily handle multibyte Unicode character codes as well as single-byte codes. For example:

```
my $capital_cyrillic_psi=chr(0x471);
```

See Chapter 23 for more information on Unicode.

Length and Position: length, index, and rindex

The length function simply returns the length of the supplied string.

```
$length = length($string);
```

If the argument to length is not a string, it is converted into one, so we can find out how wide a number will be if printed before actually doing so.

```
$pi = atan2(1, 0) * 2;   # a numeric value
$length_as_string = length($pi);   # length as string
```

The index and rindex functions look for a specified substring within the body of a string. They do not have any of the power of flexibility of a regular expression, but by the same token, they are considerably quicker. They return the position of the first character of the matched substring if found, or -1 otherwise (adjusted by the index start number $[, if it was changed from its default value 0).

```
$string = "This is a string in which looked for text may be found";
print index $string, "looked for";   # produces '26'
```

We may also supply an additional position, in which case index and rindex will start from that position.

```
print index $string, "look for", 30;   # not found, produces -1
```

index looks forward and rindex looks backward, but otherwise they are identical. Note that unlike arrays, we cannot specify a negative number to specify a starting point relative to the end of the string, nice though that would be.

Substrings: substr

The versatile substr extracts a substring from a supplied string in very much the same way that splice (covered in Chapter 5) returns parts of arrays, and indeed the two functions are modeled to resemble each other. substr takes between two and four arguments—a string to work on, an offset to start from, a length, and an optional replacement.

```
# return characters from position 3 to 7 from $string
print substr "1234567890", 3, 4;   # produces 4567
```

String positions start from 0, like arrays (unless we change the start position number by assigning a new value to the special variable $[). If the length is omitted, substr returns characters up to the end of the string.

```
print substr "1234567890", 3;    # produces 4567890
```

Both the offset and the length can be negative, in which case they are both taken relative to the end of the string.

```
print substr "1234567890", -7, 2;   # produces 45
print substr "1234567890", -7;      # produces 4567890
print substr "1234567890", -7, -2;  # produces 45678
```

We can also supply a replacement string, either by specifying the new string as the fourth argument, or more interestingly assigning to the substr. In both cases, the new string may be longer or shorter (including empty, if we just want to remove text), and the string will adjust to fit. However, for either to work we must supply an assignable value like a variable or a subroutine or function that returns an assignable value (like substr itself, in fact). Consider the following two examples:

```
$string = "1234567890";
print substr($string, 3, 4, "abc");
# produces '4567'
# $string becomes '123abc890'

$string = "1234567890";
print substr($string, 3, 4) = "abc";
# produces 'abc8'
# $string becomes '123abc890'
```

The difference between the two variants is in the value they return. The replacement string version causes substr to return the original substring before it was modified. The assignment on the other hand returns the substring after the substitution has taken place. This will only be the same as the replacement text if it is the same length as the text it is replacing; in the preceding example the replacement text is one character shorter, so the return value includes the next unreplaced character in the string, which happens to be 8.

Attempting to return a substring that extends past the end of the string will result in substr returning as many characters as it can. If the start is past the end of the string, then substr returns an empty string. Note also that we cannot extend a string by assigning to a substr beyond the string end (this might be expected since we can do something similar to arrays, but it is not the case).

Upper- and Lowercase: uc, lc, ucfirst, and lcfirst

Perl provides no less than four different functions just for manipulating the case of strings. uc and lc convert all character in a string into upper- and lowercase (all characters that have a case, that is) and return the result.

```
print uc('upper');   # produces 'UPPER'
print lc('LOWER');   # produces 'lower'
```

ucfirst and lcfirst are the limited edition equivalents; they only operate on the first letter.

```
print ucfirst('daniel');   # produces 'Daniel';
print lcfirst('Polish');   # produces 'polish';
```

If we are interpolating a string, we can also use the special sequences \U...\E and \L...\E within the string to produce the same effect as uc and lc for the characters placed between them. See the section "Interpolation" in Chapter 11 for more details. And speaking of interpolation . . .

Interpolation: quotemeta

The quotemeta function processes a string to make it safe in interpolative contexts. That is, it inserts backslash characters before any nonalphanumeric characters, including $, @, %, existing backslashes, commas, spaces, and all punctuation except the underscore (which is considered an honorary numeric because it can be used as a separator in numbers).

Pattern Matching, Substitution, and Transliteration: m//, s//, and tr//

Perl's regular expression engine is one of its most powerful features, allowing almost any kind of text matching and substitution on strings of any size. It supplies two main functions, the m// match and s/// substitution functions, plus the pos function and a large handful of special variables. For example, to determine if one string appears inside another ignoring case:

```
$matched = $matchtext =~ /some text/i;
```

Alternatively, to replace all instances of the word green with yellow:

```
$text = "red green blue";
$text =~ s/\bgreen\b/yellow/g;
print $text;    # produces 'red yellow blue'
```

Closely associated but not actually related to the match and substitution functions is the transliteration operator tr///, also known as y///. It transforms strings by replacing characters from a search list with the characters in the corresponding position in the replacement list. For example, to uppercase the letters a to f (perhaps for hexadecimal strings) we could write

```
$hexstring =~ tr/a-f/A-F/;
```

Entire books have been written on pattern matching and regular expressions, and accordingly we devote a large part of Chapter 11 to it.

Password Encryption: crypt

The crypt function performs a one-way transform of the string passed; it is identical to (and implemented using) the C library crypt on Unix systems, which implements a variation of the Data Encryption Standard (DES) algorithm. crypt is not always available, in which case attempting to use it will provoke a fatal error from Perl. Otherwise, it takes two arguments: the text to be encrypted and a *salt*, which is a two-character string made of random characters in the range 0..9, a..z, A..Z, /, or .. Here is how we can generate a suitable encrypted password in Perl:

```
@characters = (0..9, 'a'..'z' ,'A'..'Z', '.', '/');
$encrypted = crypt($password, @characters[rand 64, rand 64]);
```

Since we do not generally want to use the salt for anything other than creating the password, we instead supply the encrypted text itself as the salt for testing an entered password (which works because the first two characters are in fact the salt).

```
# check password
die "Wrong!" unless crypt($entered, $encrypted) eq $encrypted;
```

Note that for actually entering passwords it is generally a nice idea not to echo to the screen. See Chapter 15 for some ways to achieve this.

crypt is not suitable for encrypting large blocks of text; it is a one-way function that cannot be reversed, and so is strictly useful for generating passwords. Use one of the cryptography modules from CPAN like Crypt::TripleDES or Crypt::IDEA for more heavyweight and reversible cryptography.

Low-Level String Conversions: pack, unpack, and vec

Perl provides three functions that perform string conversions at a low level. The pack and unpack functions convert between strings and arbitrary machine-level values, like a low-level version of sprintf. The vec function allows us to treat strings as if they were long binary values, obviating the need to convert to or from actual integer values.

Pack and Unpack

The pack and unpack functions convert between strings and lists of values: the pack function takes a format or template string and a list of values, returning a string that contains a compact form of those values. unpack takes the same format string and undoes the pack, extracting the original values.

pack is reminiscent of sprintf. They both take a format string and a list of values, generating an output string as a result. The difference is that sprintf is concerned with converting values into legible strings, whereas pack is concerned with producing a byte-by-byte string representation of its input values. Whereas sprintf would turn an integer into a textual version of that same integer, for example, pack will turn it into a series of characters whose binary values in combination make up the integer.

```
$string = pack 'i', $integer;
```

The format string looks very different from the one used by sprintf. Here, i is just one of several template characters that handle integer values—we will cover the whole list of template characters in a moment. Combining several of these characters together into a format string allows us to convert multiple values and lists of mixed data types into one packed string. Using the same format we can later unpack the string to retrieve the original values.

Because pack and unpack work, but what order the bytes come out in depends on the processor architecture. V is a template like i, but which always packs integers "little-endian" irrespective of the underlying platform's native order. Here we use V and an explicit integer whose value we want to make sure comes out with the least significant byte first:

```
print pack 'V', 1819436368;    # produces the string 'Perl' (not 'lerP')
```

Why does this work? Well, the decimal number is really just an obscure way to represent a 32-bit value that is really 4 bytes, each representing a character code. Here is the same number in hexadecimal, where 60, the last byte, is the ASCII code for P:

```
print pack 'V', 0x6c726560;
```

To pack multiple integers we can put more is, or use a repeat count.

```
$string = pack 'i4', @integers[0..3];
```

If we supply too many items, the excess values are ignored. If we supply too few, Perl will invent additional zero or empty string values to complete the packing operation.

To pack as many items as the list can supply, we use a repeat count of *.

```
$string = pack 'i*', @integers;
```

We can combine multiple template characters into one template. The following packs four integers, a null character (given by x), and a string truncated to 10 bytes with a null character as a terminator (given by Z):

```
$string = pack 'i4xZ10', @integers[0..3], "abcdefghijklmnop";
```

We can also add spaces for clarity.

```
$string = pack 'i4 x Z10', @integers[0..3], "abcdefghijklmnop";
```

To unpack this list again, we would use something like the following:

```
($int1, $int2, $int3, $int4, $str) = unpack 'i4xZ10', $string;
```

Repeat counts can optionally be put in square brackets. Using square brackets also allows a repeat count to be expressed in terms of the size of another template character:

```
$intstring = pack 'i[4]', @integers; # same as before
$nullstring = pack 'x[d]'; # pack a double's-worth of null bytes
```

Note that there is a subtle difference between a repeated template character and a repetition count when the character encodes string data. This applies to the a/A and Z template characters. Each of these will absorb as many characters as the repeat count specifies from each input value. So 'a4' will get four characters from the first string value, whereas 'aaaa' will get one each from the first, second, third, and fourth.

```
print pack 'aaaa', 'First','Second','Third','Fourth'; # produces    'FSTF'
print pack 'a4', 'First','Second','Third','Fourth';   # produces    'Firs'
print pack 'a4a4a4a4', 'First','Second','Third','Fourth';
    # produces 'FirsSecoThirFour'
```

From Perl 5.8 pack and unpack can also use parentheses to group repeating sequences of template characters. To represent four integers, each prefixed by a single character, we could therefore use '(ci)4' with the equivalent meaning to 'cicicici'.

We can also encode and decode a repeat count from the format string itself, using the format count/sequence. Usually the count will be an integer and packed with n or N, while the sequence will be a string packed with a/A or passed with nulls using x. The following pair of statements will encode a sequence of strings provided by @inputstrings and then decode the resultant stream of data back into the original strings again in @outputstrings:

```
$stream = pack '(n/a*)*', @inputstrings;
@outputstrings = unpack '(n/a*)*', $stream;
```

■**Note** Technically the first * after the a is redundant for unpack, but harmless. Retaining it allows the same format string to be used for both packing and unpacking.

To encode the count value in readable digit characters instead of integers, simply pack the count using a string template instead.

```
$stream = pack '(a*/a*)*', 'one','two','three'; #creates '3one3two5three'
```

Unfortunately, pack is not smart enough to pad the numeric value, so '(a3/a*)*' will not produce '003one003two005three' as we would like and unpack isn't smart enough to decode a variable-length number prefix. So we would have to write a smarter decoder to handle the strings packed by the preceding example (and in addition no string can start with a digit or the decoder will not be able to tell where the count ends and the data begins).

pack and unpack can simulate several of Perl's other functions. For example, the c template character packs and unpacks a single character to and from a character code, in exactly the same way that ord and chr do.

```
$chr = pack 'c', $ord;
$ord = unpack 'c', $chr;
```

Just as with ord and chr, the c and C template characters will complain if given a value that is out of range. In the case of c, the range is –128 to 127. For C the range is 0 to 255. The advantage is, of course, that with pack and unpack we can process a whole string at once.

```
@ords = unpack 'c*', $string;
```

Similarly, here is how we can use x (which skips over or ignores, for unpack) and a (read as-is) to extract a substring somewhat in the manner of substr:

```
$substr = unpack "x$position a$length", $string;
```

pack and unpack support a bewildering number of template characters, each with its own properties, and a number of modifiers that alter the size or order in which they work. Table 3-4 provides a brief list; note that several only make sense with an additional count supplied along with the template character.

Table 3-4. *pack and unpack Template Characters*

Character	Properties
a	Arbitrary (presumed string) data, null padded if too short
A	Arbitrary (presumed string) data, space padded if too short
b	Bit string, ascending order (as used by vec)
B	Bit string, descending order
c	Signed character (8-bit) value
C	Unsigned character (8-bit) value
d	Double precision (64-bit) floating-point number
D	Long double precision (96-bit) floating-point number (Perl 5.8 onwards)
f	Single precision floating-point number
F	Perl internal floating-point number type, NV (Perl 5.8 onwards)
h	Hex string, byte order low-high
H	Hex string, byte order high-low
i	Signed integer value (length dependent on C)
I	Unsigned integer value (length dependent on C)
j	Perl internal integer number type, IV (Perl 5.8 onwards)
J	Perl internal unsigned number type, UV (Perl 5.8 onwards)
l	Signed long (32-bit) value
L	Unsigned long (32-bit) value
n	Unsigned short, big-endian (network) order
N	Unsigned long, big-endian (network) order
p	Pointer to null terminated string
P	Pointer to fixed-length string
q	Signed quad/long long (64-bit) value
Q	Unsigned quad/long long (64-bit) value
s	Signed short (16-bit) value
S	Unsigned short (16-bit) value
u	Unencoded string
U	Unicode character
v	Unsigned short, little-endian (VAX) order
V	Unsigned long, little-endian (VAX) order
w	BER (base 128) compressed integer
x	Null/ignore byte
X	Backup a byte

Character	Properties
Z	Null terminated string
@	Fill with nulls to absolute position (must be followed by a number)

If the format starts with `'U'`, then the input will be packed or unpacked in Unicode. This is true even if the repeat count is zero (so that the first item need not be a Unicode character). Similarly, if the first template character is `'c'` or `'C'`, Unicode does not become the default.

```
pack 'U8 N C20', $str1, $int, $str2;    # packs both strings as Unicode
pack 'U0 N C20', $int, $str;            # switches on Unicode, no initial string
pack 'C0 U8 N C20', $str1, $int, $str2; # packs first string as Unicode, not second
```

Neither pack or unpack have strong opinions about the size, alignment, or endianness of the values that they work with. If it is important to ensure that a string packed on one machine can be interpreted correctly on another, some steps to ensure portability are required.

First, Perl's idea of what size quantities like short integers are can be different from that of the underlying platform itself. This affects the s/S and l/L templates. To force Perl to use the native size rather than its own, suffix the template with an exclamation mark.

s	Signed short, Perl format
s!	Signed short, native format

To test whether or not Perl and the platform agree on sizes, compare the length of the strings produced by each of the preceding formats. If they are the same, there is agreement.

Second, as pack and unpack deal with strings, they obviously do not know or care about alignment of values. We usually care about this when the intent is to process argument lists and structures for C library routines, which Chapter 20 discusses. Adding an exclamation mark to x or X allows a format string to align forward or backward by the specified size (and therefore only makes sense with a repeat count). Typically, we would use a template character as the repeat count to indicate alignment according to the size of that value. To pack a character and a long in native format, we might use

```
$struct = pack 'c x![l!] l!', $char, $int;
```

This pads out the initial character to align to the boundary determined by the size of a long integer in the native format. Different platforms have different requirements for alignment, sometimes depending on what is being aligned, so it is important to remember that the preceding is stating an assumption that long integers align on boundaries that derived from the size of a long integer, which is not necessarily so.

Finally, pack and unpack will produce different results as a result of the endianness of the platform when asked to pack integers with s/S, i/I, or l/L. This is because the order of bytes can be different between processors, as we noted at the start when we used V in an example to print "Perl". The v/V (VAX) and n/N (network) template characters always pack short and long integers in the same order, irrespective of the processor architecture.

```
print pack 'V', 1819436368;    # produces the string 'Perl'
print pack 'N', 1819436368;    # produces the string 'lerP'
print pack 'i', 1819436368;    # warning! platform dependent!
```

If we want to pack structures for use with communication with C subroutines, we need to use the native formats i or I. If we want to be portable across machines and networks, we need to use a portable template character. As its name implies, the network-order n/N template character is the more logical choice. Unfortunately, floating-point numbers are notoriously difficult to pass between different platforms, and if we need to do this we may be better off serializing the data in some other way (for example, with Data::Dumper, though more efficient modules also exist).

Vector Strings

Perl also provides the vec function, which allows us to treat a string as if it were a long binary value rather than a sequence of characters. vec treats the whole string as a sequence of bits, with each character holding eight each. It therefore allows us to handle arbitrarily long bit masks and binary values without the constraints of integer size or assumption of byte order.

In operation, vec is somewhat like the substr function, only at the bit level. substr addresses a string by character position and length and returns substrings, optionally allowing us to replace the substring through assignment to a string. vec addresses a string by element position and length and returns bits as an integer, optionally allowing us to replace the bits through assignment to an integer. It takes three arguments: a string to work with, an offset, and a length, exactly as with substr, only now the length is in terms of bits and the offset is in multiples of the length. For example, to extract the tenth to twelfth bits of a bitstring with vec, we would write

```
$twobitflag = vec($bitstr, 5, 2);   # 5th 2-bit element is bits 10 to 12
```

The use of the word string with vec is a little stretched; in reality we are working with a stream of bytes in a consistent and platform-independent order (unlike an integer whose bytes may vary in order according to the processor architecture). Each byte contains 8 bits, with the first character being bits 0 to 7, the second being 8 to 15, and so on, so this extracts the second to fourth bits of the second byte in the string. Of course, the point of vec is that we do not care about the characters, only the bits inside them.

vec provides a very efficient way to store values with constrained limits. For example, to store one thousand values that may range between 0 and 9 using a conventional array of integers would take up 4 × 1000 bytes (assuming a 4-byte integer), and 1000 characters if printed out to a string for storage. With vec we can fit the values 0 to 9 into 4 bits, fitting 2 to a character and taking up 500 bytes in memory, and saved as a string. Unfortunately, the length must be a power of 2, so we cannot pack values into 3 bits if we only had to store values from 0 to 7.

```
# a function to extract 4-bit values from a 'vec' string
sub get_value {
    # return flag at offset, 4 bits
    return vec $_[0], $_[1], 4;
}

# get flag 20 from the bitstring
$value = get_value ($bitstr, 20);
```

It does not matter if we access an undefined part of the string, vec will simply return 0, so we need not worry if we access a value that the string does not extend to. Indeed, we can start with a completely empty string and fill it up using vec. Perl will automatically extend the string as and when we need it.

Assigning to a vec sets the bits from the integer value, rather like a supercharged version of chr. For example, here is how we can define the string Perl from a 32-bit integer value:

```
# assign a string by character code
$str = chr(0x50). chr(0x65). chr(0x72). chr(0x6c);   # $str = "Perl";

# the same thing more efficiently with a 32-bit value and 'vec'
vec ($str, 0, 32) = 0x50_65_72_6c;

# extract a character as 8 bits:
print vec ($str, 2, 8);  # produces 114 which is the ASCII value of 'r'.
```

Using this, here is the counterpart to the get_value subroutine for setting flags:

```
# a function to set 4-bit values into a 'vec' string
sub set_value {
   # set flag at offset, 4 bits
   vec $_[0], $_[1], 4;
}

# set flag 43 in the bitstring
$value = set_value ($bitstr, 43, $value);
```

String Formatting with printf and sprintf

We have already seen some examples of the printf and sprintf functions when we discussed converting numbers into different string representations. However, these functions are far more versatile than this, so here we will run through all the possibilities that these two functions afford us.

The two functions are identical except that sprintf returns a string while printf combines sprintf with print and takes an optional first argument of a filehandle. It returns the result of the print, so for generating strings we want sprintf.

sprintf takes a format string, which can contain any mixture of value placeholders and literal text. Technically this means that they are not string functions per se, since they operate on lists. We cover them here because their job is fundamentally one of string generation and manipulation rather than list processing.

For each placeholder of the form %... in the format, one value is taken from the following list and converted to conform to the textual requirement defined by the placeholder. For example:

```
# use the 'localtime' function to read the year, month and day
($year, $month, $day) = (localtime)[5, 4, 3];
$year += 1900;
$date = sprintf '%4u/%02u/%02u',  $year, $month, $day;
```

This defines a format string with three unsigned decimal integers (specified by the %u placeholder). All other characters are literal characters, and may also be interpolated if the string is double quoted. The first is a minimum of four characters wide, padded with spaces. The other two have a minimum width of two characters, padded with leading zeros.

printf and sprintf Placeholders

The printf and sprintf functions understand many placeholders for different types of value. Here they are loosely categorized and explained in Tables 3-5 to 3-11. To start with, Table 3-5 shows the placeholders for handling character and string values.

Table 3-5. *Character and String Placeholders*

Placeholder	Description
%c	A character (from an integer character code value)
%s	A string
%%	A percent sign

The placeholders for integer values, shown in Table 3-6, allow us to render numbers signed or unsigned, and in decimal, octal, or hexadecimal.

Table 3-6. *Integer and Number Base Placeholders*

Placeholder	Description
%d	Signed decimal integer
%I	(Archaic) alias for %d
%u	Unsigned decimal integer
%o	Unsigned octal integer
%x	Unsigned hexadecimal integer, lowercase a..f
%X	Unsigned hexadecimal integer, uppercase A..F
%b	Unsigned binary integer

In addition, all these characters can be prefixed with l to denote a long (32-bit) value, or h to denote a short (16-bit) value, for example:

%ld	Long signed decimal
%hb	Short binary

If neither is specified, Perl defaults to whatever size it was built to use (so if 64-bit integers are supported, %d will denote 64-bit integers, for example). The %D, %U, and %O are archaic aliases for %ld, %lu, and %lo. sprintf supports them, but their use is not encouraged.

Extra long (64-bit) integers may be handled by prefixing the placeholder letter with either ll (long long), L (big long), or q (quad).

%lld	64-bit signed integer
%qo	64-bit octal number

This is dependent on Perl supporting 64-bit integers, as we covered in Chapter 1.

Floating-point numbers can be represented as either scientific (fixed-point) values or floating-point values. We can either force one or the other representation, or request the best choice for the value being rendered, as shown in Table 3-7.

Table 3-7. *Floating-Point Placeholders*

Placeholder	Description
%e	Scientific notation floating-point number, lowercase e
%E	Scientific notation floating-point number, uppercase E
%f	Fixed decimal floating-point number
%F	(Archaic) alias for %f
%g	"Best" choice between %e and %f
%G	"Best" choice between %E and %f

By their nature, floating-point values are always double precision in Perl, so there is no l prefix. However, quadruple to store precision (long double) floating-point values can be handled with the ll or L prefixes.

| %llE | Long double scientific notation, uppercase E |
| %Lf | Long double fixed decimal |

As with 64-bit integers, this is dependent on Perl actually supporting long double values.

As the preceding tables show, much of the functionality of sprintf is related to expressing integers and floating-point numbers in string format. We covered many of its uses in this respect earlier in the chapter. In brief, however, placeholders may have additional constraints to determine the representation of a number or string placed by adding modifiers between the % and the type character, as shown in Table 3-8.

Table 3-8. *Width and Precision*

Modifier	Action
n	A number, the minimum field width.
*	Take the width for this placeholder from the next value in the list.
.m	Precision. This has a different meaning depending on whether the value is string, integer or floating point: String—The maximum width Integer—The minimum width Floating point—Digits after the decimal place
.*	Take the precision for this placeholder from the next value in the list.
n.m	Combined width and precision.
.	Take the width and precision for this placeholder from the next two values in the list.

If a string or character placeholder has a width, then strings shorter than the width are padded to the left with spaces (zeroes if 0 is used). Conversely, if a precision is specified and the string is longer, then it is truncated on the right. Specifying both as the same number gives a string of a guaranteed width irrespective of the value, for example, %8.8s.

A floating-point number uses the width and precision in the normal numerical sense. The width defines the width of the field as a whole, and the precision defines how much of it is used for decimal places. Note that the width includes the decimal point, the exponent, and the e or E—for example, %+13.3e.

The precision and width are the same for integers except that a leading . will pad the number with leading zeros in the same way in which 0 (shown later) does. If the integer is wider than the placeholder, then it is not truncated—for example, %.4d.

If asterisks are used either for width or precision, then the next value in the list is used to define it, removing it from the list for consideration as a placeholder value.

```
$a = sprintf "%*.*f", $float, $width, $precision;
```

Note that negative numbers for either will cause an additional implicit - (see Table 3-9).

Table 3-9. *Justification*

Character	Action
Space	Pad values to the left with spaces (right-justify)
0	Pad values to the left with zeros
-	Pad values to the right with spaces (left-justify)

Justification is used with a placeholder width to determine how unfilled places are handled when the value is too short. A space, which is the default, pads to the left with spaces, while 0 pads to the left with zeroes, shifting sign or base prefixes to the extreme left if specified. - pads with spaces to the right (even if 0 is also specified). For example:

%04d	Pad to four digits with 0
% 8s	Pad to eight characters with spaces
%8s	The same
%-8s	Pad to the right to eight characters with spaces

Number prefixes can be added to numbers to qualify positive numbers with a plus sign, and to indicate the base of nondecimal values, as shown in Table 3-10.

Table 3-10. *Number Prefixes*

Prefix	Action
+	Represent positive numbers with a leading +
#	Prefix nondecimal-based integers with 0, 0x, or 0b if they have a nonzero value

Either of these prefixes can be enabled (even on strings, though there is not much point in doing that) by placing them after the % and before anything else. Note that + is for signed integers and that # is for other number bases, all of which treat signed numbers as if they were very large unsigned values with their top bit set. This means that they are exclusive to each other, in theory at least. Both of them are counted in the width of the field, so for a 16-bit binary number plus prefix, allow for 18 characters. For example:

%+4d	Give number a sign even if positive
%+04d	Signed and padded with zeros
%#018hb	16-bit padded and prefixed short binary integer

Three placeholders do not easily fit into any of the categories so far. Table 3-11 lists them.

Table 3-11. *String Length, Pointers, and Version Numbers*

Placeholder	Description
%n	Write length of current output string into next variable
%p	Pointer value (memory address of value)
%v	Version number string

The %n placeholder is unique among all the placeholders in that it does not write a value into the string. Instead, it works in the opposite direction, and assigns the length of the string generated so far to the next item in the list (which must therefore be a variable).

The %p placeholder is not often used in Perl, since looking at memory addresses is not something Perl encourages, though it can occasionally be useful for debugging references.

Finally, the %v placeholder specifies that the supplied value is converted into a version number string of character codes separated by points, in the format defined by the placeholder (d for decimal, b for binary, and so on). A different separator may be used if a * is used before the v to import it.

Note that specifying the separator directly will not work, as v does not conform to the usual rules for placeholders. For example:

```
printf "v%vd", $^V;          # print Perl's version

printf "%v08b", 'aeiou';     # print letters as 8-bit binary digits
                             # separated by points

printf "%*v8o", '-', 'aeiou'; # print letters as octal numbers
                             # separated by minus signs
```

The version string placeholder is currently required to print a version string in a recognizable form, but Perl 5.10 is expected to provide a more convenient way with the introduction of version objects. See "Bareword Strings and Version Number Strings," earlier in this chapter, for more details.

Reordering the Input Parameters

From Perl 5.8 onwards, it is possible to reorder the input values so that they appear in the output string in a different order than they were supplied. To specify a particular input value, an order number is inserted in front of the width and separated from it by a dollar sign. Unordered placeholders are evaluated as normal, starting from the front of the list, so the third %s in this example produces 'one', not 'three':

```
printf '%2$5s,%1$5s,%s','one','two','three'; # produces 'two  ,one  ,one'
```

Be careful with the dollar signs; in a double-quoted string Perl will try to interpolate them, which is unlikely to produce the intended result. Remember to escape them with backslashes inside double quotes, or stick to single quotes to avoid accidents.

Schizophrenic Scalars

As we mentioned briefly in the introduction, it is possible to have a scalar variable with numeric and string values that are not direct conversions of each other. One of the more famous examples of this is the system error number or *Errno* variable $!, which Perl uses to store the result of built-in functions that call into the operating system—open and close are perhaps the most frequently seen cases. In numeric context, $! evaluates to the system error number itself. In string context, $! evaluates to a string describing the error number. This is an appropriate and useful alternate form for the error value to take, but not at all a direct conversion of any kind. The following example shows $! being used in both string and numeric contexts:

```
$opened_ok=open FILE,"doesnotexist.txt";
unless ($opened_ok) {
    print "Failed to open: $!\n"; #use of $! in string context
    exit $!; #use of $! in numeric context
}
```

We can create our own scalars with different alternate forms using the dualvar subroutine from the Scalar::Util package. It takes two arguments, the first of which is a number (either integer or floating point) and the second of which is a string. It returns a scalar with both values preset.

```
$PI=dualvar(3.1415926,"PI");
print "The value of $PI is", $PI+0; #produces "The value of PI is 3.1415926"
```

The string and numeric values will be used in their respective contexts with neither triggering a new conversion of the other. Perl will still convert the integer or floating-point number (whichever we set initially) to the other numeric type as required. It is important to realize that the dual-valued nature of such a variable is easily destroyed, however. If we assign a new integer value, for example, this will invalidate the string and force a conversion the next time the variable is used in string context. The advantage of dualvar is that it is just an interface to Perl's internal value-handling mechanism, and as such is just as fast as any normal scalar.

For more advanced forms of "clever" scalars we can resort to tie or the overload module, both of which allow us to create an object-oriented class that looks like a scalar but abstracts more complex behavior beneath the surface. We cover both subjects in Chapter 19. Be aware, however, that both of these solutions are intrinsically more heavyweight and much slower than a dual-valued variable.

Summary

In this chapter, we have talked about scalar numbers and strings, and their relationships to functions and modifiers. We were introduced to integers and floating-point numbers, and took a brief look at the use integer pragma. The different types of quotes and quoting operators were discussed, and we learned how to use a here document. We also saw what mathematical functions Perl provides. After seeing how to manipulate strings, we went on to look at low-level string conversions like pack and unpack, all of which has given us the foundation, for number and string manipulation, which we will need throughout the rest of the book.

In this chapter, we have looked at scalar numbers and strings, how Perl handles them internally, and how they are automatically converted into different forms on demand. We also looked at how to convert scalar values into different forms and the various built-in functions that Perl provides to help us. For integers, we additionally looked at number bases, the use integer pragma, and handling big integers. For floating-point numbers we also examined rounding issues and controlling the format of printed floating-point numbers. For strings, we covered quoting, here documents, bareword strings, version number strings, and the range of built-in functions that Perl provides for string manipulation, ranging from print and printf through to pack and unpack. Finally, we looked at a way to create scalars that carry different numeric and string values simultaneously using the dualvar subroutine.

CHAPTER 4

■■■

Operators

Operators allow us to both compute and compare values. Arithmetic operators like plus and minus, which indicate addition and subtraction, are typical computational operators, whereas "equal to" and "greater than" are typical comparative operators. Operators combine with values to make expressions, each of which has a value that is the result of its computation. These in turn may be combined into larger expressions (also called *compound expressions*) using additional operators. Values may be literal, held in variables, or returned as the result of subroutine calls or other expressions.

Operators require one or two (and in one case, three) input values to work on, producing a single output value as their result. With the exception of the eponymous ternary operator, operators are either unary, taking a single value and producing a new value from it, or binary, combining two expressions to produce a new value. An example of an unary operator is the logical not operator, !, which logically inverts the value supplied to it; an example of a binary operator is +, which adds its two values together to produce a value that is the sum. +, along with -, can also be unary, and indicate a positive or negative sign, so it is also an example of an operator with more than one mode of use.

The input values that operators work on are also known as *operands*. The value on the left of a binary operator is therefore the left operand and the value on the right is the right operand. These values may, in turn, be simple scalar or list values or expressions involving further operations. The order in which operators in the same expression are evaluated is determined by the rules of precedence, which are built into Perl.

In Perl, the distinction between operators and functions is not as clear-cut as it is in languages like C, C++, or Java. This is because it is perfectly valid to consider functions to be just another kind of operator, with the distinction that functions only take operands on their right side (but can often take multiple operands; such functions are also called *list operators*). Only a true binary operator can bind to operands on both its left and right, however. In this chapter, we are only going to talk about operators in the conventional sense of the term—basic operations that form the core essential abilities of the Perl language. + is essential, the readline operator <> is merely very useful.

Operator Types and Categories

Perl supplies around 70 operators in total, ranging from basic arithmetic operators, to operators for reference creation and file testing. In this section, we introduce these operators, dividing them into 14 convenient categories. Some are expansive—for instance, there are 15 different assignment operators—while others contain a single unique operator. For convenience, the categories are summarized here:

Assignment operator	=
Arithmetic operators	+ - * / % **
Shift operators	>> <<
String and list operators	. x
Logical operators	&& || ! and or xor not
Bitwise operators	& | ^ ~
Increment and decrement operators	++ --
Combination assignment operators	+= -= *= /= **= %= .= >>= &&= &= ^= x= <<= ||= |=
Comparison operators	== != < <= > >= <=> eq ne lt le gt ge cmp
Regular expression binding operators	=~ !~
Comma and relationship operators	=> ,
Reference and dereference operators	\ ->
Range operators	.. ...
Ternary operator	?

Assignment Operator

The assignment operator simply assigns the value of the expression on its right side to the variable (or more generally, lvalue) on its left.

```
$variable = "value";
```

The value returned from this operation is the value of the right-hand side. As a result it can be used in other expressions, as in

```
$c = $b = $a = 'This is the value of a, b and c';
```

The left-hand side of an assignment must be an lvalue, an entity that may be assigned to (the term literally means *left-hand-side value*, i.e., a value on the left of an assignment). Though usually a scalar variable, any lvalue is acceptable. Two obvious examples are assigning to an array element or a hash key.

```
@array[$index] = 42;
$hash{'key'} = "value";
```

A less obvious example of an lvalue is an array slice, to which we can assign a list (more on arrays in Chapter 5).

```
@array = (1, 2, 3, 4, 5);
@array[1..3] = (7, 8, 9);
print "@array";   # produces 1 7 8 9 5
```

A few built-in Perl functions also return lvalues, the most common of which is substr, which was introduced in Chapter 3. Perl 5.6 onwards also supports the lvalue attribute, a feature that allows us to define our own subroutines that return assignable values, just like substr. The lvalue attribute is covered in Chapter 7.

The precedence of the assignment operator is very low, so that all the expressions on its right will be evaluated first and the assignment will use the resulting value. There are some noteworthy exceptions, though. The comma and relationship operators, as well as the not, and, or, and xor operators, have lower precedence, so that statements like the following do what they appear to do:

```
@array = ($a = 1, $b = 2, $c = 3);   # assigns (1, 2, 3) to @array
```

Here $a is assigned the value 1, not the expression 1, $b.

The assignment operator is also the head of the family of combination assignment operators such as += and -=, which are coming up shortly.

Arithmetic Operators

Perl provides the standard set of mathematics operators for manipulating integers and floating-point numbers.

```
6 + 2       # addition, produces 8
6.3 - 2.8   # subtraction, produces 3.5
6*2         # multiplication, produces 12
6.3 * 2.8   # multiplication, produces 17.64
6 % 2       # modulus, produces 0
6.3 ** 2.8  # exponentiation, produces 173.04280186355
```

Multiplication and division tasks have a higher precedence than addition and subtraction, so the following produces 13, the sum of 4 and 9, rather than 21:

```
$result = 2*2 + 3*3;        # produces 2*2 plus 3*3 = 4 + 9 = 13
$result = (2*2) + (3*3);    # the same computation, explicitly
```

To force the precedence of the addition higher, we need to use parentheses.

```
$result = 2 * (2 + 3) * 3;   # produces 2 * 5 * 3 = 30
```

Other than this, all arithmetic operators have left associativity, which means they evaluate their left-hand side before their right. Multiplication and division have the same precedence, so associativity is used to determine which order to evaluate them in, from left to right. Therefore the following produces 7.5, not 0.3:

```
$result = 2 * 3 / 4 * 5;     # produces 2 * 3, /4, *5 = 7.5
$result = ((2 * 3) / 4) * 5; # the same thing, explicitly
```

To force the precedence of the second multiplication so 4 * 5 is evaluated first and then divided into 2 * 3, we again need to use parentheses.

```
$result = (2 * 3) / (4 * 5);  # produces 6 / 20 = 0.3
```

The modulus operator is a complement to the division operator; it divides the left operand by the right, but returns only the remainder.

```
print 4 % 2;   # produces 0, 2 divides evenly into 4
print 5 % 2;   # produces 1, 5 divided by 2 leaves a remainder of 1
```

% also works on negative numbers, but varies slightly depending on whether the use integer pragma is in effect or not. With it, modulus produces the same result that positive numbers would have. For example, take this statement:

```
print -13 % 7;   # produces 1
```

With the pragma in place, the result changes.

```
use integer;
print -13 % 7;   # produces -6, same as -(13 % 7)
```

Both results are correct, but from different perspectives, -13 divides by 7 with a remainder of 1 (it is short of -14 by -1), or a remainder of -6 (it is -6 more than -7). See the section entitled "The use integer Pragma" in Chapter 3 for more information on how it affects arithmetic and other operators.

The exponentiation operator, **, is also binary, with a higher precedence than all the other arithmetic operators. It raises the numeric value given as its left operand by the power of the right.

Both left and right operands can be floating point, in which case the result is also floating point (possibly converted to an integer for display purposes).

```
print 4 ** 0.5;    # produces 2
```

Both the + and - operators have a unary form, where they have no left-hand side. Typically these appear in assignments.

```
$negative = -3;
```

The unary minus has plenty of uses in this context. The unary plus, on the other hand, has no relevance at all except to stop parentheses being interpreted as part of a function.

```
print ("Hello"), " World";    # prints "Hello", returns " World"
print +("Hello"), " World";   # prints "Hello World"
```

This particular example is rather obvious, but in cases where parentheses are actually necessary for the first expression in a print statement this can be a useful trick, and it is an alternative to enclosing the whole argument list in parentheses.

Shift Operators

The >> and << shift operators manipulate integer values as binary numbers (floating-point values are processed into integer forms prior to evaluation), shifting their bits one to the left or one to the right, respectively. In integer terms this multiplies or divides the value by 2, omitting the remainder.

```
print 2 << 1;     # produces 4
print 2 << 3;     # produces 16
print 42 >> 2;    # produces 10 (40 >> 2)
```

The result of >> and << is treated as an unsigned integer, even if the topmost bit of the resulting value is set, so the following produce large positive values:

```
print -1 >> 1;    # produces 2147483647 (with 32 bit integers)
print -1 << 0;    # produces 4294967295 (with 32 bit integers)
```

If the use integer pragma has been used, then Perl uses signed integer arithmetic, and negative values behave more reasonably, rather than being treated as bit patterns.

```
use integer;
print -1 << 1;    # produces -2
print -1 >> 1;    # produces -1
```

The reason for the slightly odd-looking second result is that -1 is actually all ones in binary, so shifting it right 1 bit makes all bits except the topmost bit 1, and then the effect of use integer resets the top bit to 1 again.

Note that the shift operators have nothing to do with HERE documents, which were covered in the last chapter. These use << to assign all the text up to a specified token to the given string variable or operation, but this syntax is unrelated to the left shift operator.

String and List Operators

Perl provides the concatenation operator, ., and the repetition operator, x, for string variables. x is usually used for strings, but can also replicate lists.

The concatenation operator joins two strings together, returning the result.

```
$good_egg = "Humpty" . "Dumpty";    # produces "HumptyDumpty"
```

This is how Perl performs string addition. Adding strings with + actually converts both operands to integers (which in the preceding case would be 0 and 0) and then adds them, returning an integer result. If the strings happen to contain numeric values, then this may be what we want, otherwise we probably meant to use the concatenation operator.

The repetition operator, x, works on both strings and lists. If the left operand is a string, it is multiplied by the number given by the right operand.

```
print "abc" x 3;    # produces 'abcabcabc'
```

A common application of x is for generating padding for formatted text, like this example, which calculates padding in terms of tabs (presumed 8 characters wide) and spaces:

```
$width = 43;    # the padding width in characters
$padding = "\t" x ($width/8) . " " x ($width%8);
print $padding;
```

If the left operand is a list (enclosed in parentheses), then the values are replicated.

```
@array = (1, 2, 3) x 3;    # @array contains (1, 2, 3, 1, 2, 3, 1, 2, 3)
```

This is also a good way to produce a large list of identical values.

```
@columns = (1) x 80;    # produce an 80 element array of 1's
```

Note that if the left operand is an array, then it is taken in scalar context and the number of elements is repeated.

```
@array1 = (1, 2, 3);
@array2 = @array1 x 3;    # @array2 contains (3, 3, 3)
```

However, if the array is enclosed in parentheses, we get the desired result.

```
@array2 = (@array1) x 3;    # @array2 contains (1, 2, 3, 1, 2, 3, 1, 2, 3)
```

Correspondingly, if the right-hand side is a list or array, then it multiplies the left operand by the number of elements it contains.

```
print "string" x (1, 2, 3);    # produces "stringstringstring"
```

Finally, giving x a numeric value as its left operand causes it to be converted into a string for the replication.

```
print 3 x 3;    # produces 333
```

In addition to the concatenation and repetition operators, most other operators will work on strings, though many will convert them into integer or floating-point values before operating on them.

Logical Operators

The logical operators perform Boolean operations, returning 1 on success and 0 on failure. For instance, the following example demonstrates a Boolean AND operation:

```
$true = $a && $b;
```

This returns 1 (true) if both $a and $b are true. The meaning of *true* and *false* in this context is quite flexible, and we discuss it in more detail in the next chapter. For now though, it is enough to say that Perl generally does the "right thing" with its operands, so values like 0 and " " are false and others are true, while arrays and hashes are true if they have one or more elements and false if they have none. Numeric values are true if they have a value, positive or negative, and false if they are zero.

Perl supports two sets of logical operators, one appearing as conventional logic symbols and the other appearing as named operations. These two sets are identical in operation, but have dramatically different precedence:

&&	and	Return true if operands are both true.
||	or	Return true if either operand is true.
	xor	Return true if only one operand is true.
!	not	(Unary) Return true of operand is false.

Of the symbolic operators, the ! operator has a much higher precedence than even && and ||, and so expressions on the right of a ! almost always mean what they say.

```
!$value1 + !$value2;     # adds result of !$value1 to !$value2
!($value1 + !$value2);   # negates result of $value1 + !$value2
```

Conversely, the named operators not, and, or, and xor have the lowest precedence of all Perl's operators, with not having the highest precedence of the four. This allows us to use them in expressions without adding extra parentheses.

```
# ERROR: evaluates expression '"Done" && exit', which exits before the 'print'
print "Done" && exit;
# correct - prints "Done", then exits
print "Done" and exit;
```

All of the logical operators (excepting the unary not and !) are lazy in that they always evaluate the left-hand operand first. If they can determine their final result purely from the left operand, then the right is not evaluated *at all*. For instance, if the left operand of an or is true, then the result must be true. Similarly, if the left operand of an and is false, then the result must be false.

The efficiency of a Boolean expression can be dramatically different depending on how we express it.

```
# the subroutine is always called
expensive_subroutine_call(@args) || $variable;

# the subroutine is called only if '$variable' is false
$variable || expensive_function_call(@args);
```

The practical upshot of this is that it pays to write logic so that quickly evaluating expressions are on the left, and slower ones on the right. The countering problem is that sometimes we really do want the right side to be evaluated. For example, the following two statements operate quite differently:

```
# $tests will only be decremented if '$variable' is false.
do_test() if $variable || $tests--;
# $tests will always be (post-)decremented
do_test() if $tests-- || $variable;
```

Bitwise Operators

The bitwise operators, or bitwise logical operators, bear a strong resemblance to their Boolean counterparts, even appearing syntactically similar:

&	Bitwise AND
|	Bitwise OR
^	Bitwise exclusive OR (XOR)
~	Bitwise NOT

Unlike Boolean logic operators, bitwise operators treat their operands as binary values like the shift operators, and perform a logical comparison between the corresponding bits of each value. The result of the operation is a new value comprised of all the individual bit comparisons, hence the term *bitwise*. To demonstrate this, we can run the following short program:

```perl
#!/usr/bin/perl
# bitwise.pl
use warnings;
use strict;

my $a = 3;
my $b = 6;
my $r;

printf "$a = %03b \n", $a;
printf "$b = %03b \n", $b;

$r = $a & $b;    printf "$a & $b = %03b = %d\n", $r, $r;
$r = $a | $b;    printf "$a | $b = %03b = %d\n", $r, $r;
$r = $a ^ $b;    printf "$a ^ $b = %03b = %d\n", $r, $r;
$r = ~$a;        printf "~$a     = %03b = %d\n", $r, $r;
```

Executing this program displays the following output:

```
> perl bitwise.pl
```

```
3 =     011
6 =     110
3 & 6 = 010 = 2
3 | 6 = 111 = 7
3 ^ 6 = 101 = 5
~3    = 1111111111111111111111111111100 = -4
```

Bitwise operators can be used on any numeric value (floating-point values are processed into integers prior to the operation, as usual), but they are most often used for bitmasks and other values where the individual bits have specific meanings. For instance, the mode flag of the sysopen function is comprised of a series of flags, each of which sets a different bit. The fcntl and POSIX modules give us symbolic names for these values so we can write statements like

```perl
$mode = O_RDWR | O_CREAT | O_TRUNC;
```

What this actually does is combine three different values using a bitwise OR to create a mode value of the three bits. The symbols allow the statement to have an easily understandable meaning. Perl will spot that the symbols are constants and evaluate the whole expression at compile time, so this isn't any less efficient than specifying the numeric result directly. We can also apply bitwise logic to permissions masks like that used by sysopen, chmod, and umask.

```perl
# set owner-write in umask
umask (umask | 002);
```

This statement retrieves the current value of umask, bitwise ORs it with 2 (we could have just said 2 but permissions are traditionally octal, and 002 emphasizes that) and then sets it back again—in this case the intent is to ensure that files are created without other-write (that is, world-write) permissions.

The Bitwise Not Operator, ~

The bitwise not operator, ~, deserves a special mention. It returns a value with all the bits of the expression supplied inverted (up to the word size of the underlying platform). That means that on a 32-bit system, ~0 produces a value with 32 set bits. On a 64-bit system (or a 32-bit system where Perl has been specially built to use 64-bit integers), ~0 produces a value with 64 set bits. This can cause problems if we are manipulating bitmasks, since a 32-bit mask can suddenly grow to 64 bits if we invert it. For that reason, masking off any possible higher bits with & is a good idea.

```
# constrain an inverted bitmask to 16 bits
$inverted = ~$mask & (2 ** 16 - 1);
```

Note that space before the ~. This prevents =~ from being seen by Perl as the regular expression binding operator.

The result of all bitwise operations, including the unary bitwise not, is treated as unsigned by Perl, so printing ~0 will typically produce a large positive integer.

```
print ~ 0;    # produces 4294967295 (or 2 ** 32 - 1) with 32-bit integers.
```

This is usually an academic point since we are generally working with bitmasks and not actual integer values when we use bitwise operators. However, if the use integer pragma is in effect, results are treated as signed, which means that if the uppermost bit is set, then numbers will come out as negative two's-complement values.

```
use integer;
print ~3;    # produces -4
```

See Chapter 3 for more on the use integer pragma.

Bitwise String Operators

A feature of the bitwise operators that is generally overlooked is the fact that they can also work on strings. In this context they are known as *bitwise string operators*. In this mode they perform a character-by-character comparison, generating a new string as their output. Each character comparison takes the numeric ASCII value for the character and performs an ordinary bitwise operation on it, returning a new character as the result.

This has some interesting applications. For example, to turn an uppercase letter into a lowercase letter, we can bitwise OR it with a space, because the ASCII value for a space happens to be the difference in the ASCII value between upper- and lowercase letters.

```
print 'A' | ' ';    # produces 'a'
```

Examining this in terms of binary numbers shows why and how this works.

```
'A' = 10000001
' ' = 01000000
'a' = 11000001
```

The inverse of ' ', bitwise, is an underscore, which has the Boolean value 10111111, so ANDing characters with underscores will uppercase them.

```
print 'upper' & '_____';    # produces 'UPPER'
```

Similarly, bitwise ORing number strings produces a completely different result from bitwise ORing them as numbers.

```
print 123 | 456;    # produces '507'
print '123' | '456';    # produces '577'
```

The digit 0 happens to have none of the bits that the other numbers use set, so ORing any digit with 0 produces that digit.

```
print '2000' | '0030';   # produces '2030'
```

Note that padding is important here.

```
print '2000' | '30';   # produces '3000'
```

If one string is shorter than the others, then implicit zero bytes (or NULL characters, depending on our point of view) are added to make the string equal length, unless the operation is &, in which case the longer string is truncated to the shorter to avoid extra NULL characters appearing at the end of the resulting string.

Of course, in a lot of cases it is simpler and safer to use uc, lc, or simply add the values numerically, particularly if we cannot assume Latin-1 as the local character encoding (see Chapter 23). However, as an example that is hard to achieve quickly any other way, here is a neat trick for turning any text into alternating upper- and lowercase characters:

```
# translate every odd character to lowercase
$text |= " \0" x (length ($text) / 2 + 1);

# translate every even character to uppercase
$text &= "\377_" x (length($text / 2 + 1);
```

And here's a way to invert the case of all cased characters:

```
$text ^= ' ' x length $text;
```

Of course, both these examples presume normal alphanumeric characters and punctuation and a standard Latin-1 character set, so this kind of behavior is highly inadvisable when dealing with other character sets and Unicode. Even with Latin-1, control characters will get turned into something completely different, such as \n, which becomes an asterisk.

Primarily, the bitwise string operators are designed to work on vec format strings (as manipulated by the vec function), where the actual characters in the string are not important, only the bits that make them up. See the "Vector Strings" section in Chapter 3 for more on the vec function.

Increment and Decrement Operators

The ++ and -- operators are unary operators, and increment and decrement their operands (which must therefore be assignable lvalues), respectively. For instance, to increment the variable $number by one, we can write

```
$number ++;
```

The unary operators can be placed on either the left or right side of their operand, with subtly differing results. The effect on the variable is the same, but the value of the expression is different depending on whether the variable is modified before it is used, or used before it is modified. To illustrate, consider these examples in which we assume that $number starts with the value 6 each time we execute a new line of code:

```
print ++$number;   # preincrement variable, $number becomes 7, outputs 7
print $number++;   # postincrement variable, $number becomes 7, outputs 6
print --$number;   # predecrement variable, $number becomes 5, outputs 5
print $number--;   # postdecrement variable, $number becomes 5, outputs 6
```

Because of these alternate behaviors, ++ and -- are called *preincrement* and *predecrement operators* when placed before the operand, respectively. They are called *postincrement* and *postdecrement operators* when placed after them.

Somewhat surprisingly, Perl also allows the increment and decrement operators for floating-point variables, incrementing or decrementing the variable by 1 as appropriate. Whether or not the operation has any effect depends on whether the number's exponent allows its significant digits to resolve a difference of 1. Adding or subtracting 1 from a value like 2.8e33 will have no effect.

```
$number = 6.3;
print ++$number; # preincrement variable, $number becomes 7.3, outputs 7.3
print $number++; # postincrement variable, $number becomes 8.3, outputs 7.3
$number = 2.8e33;
print ++$number;    # no effect, $number remains 2.8e33
```

Interestingly, Perl will also allow us to increment (but not decrement) strings too, by increasing the string to the next "logical" value. For example:

```
$antenna_unit = "AE35";
print ++ $antenna_unit;  # outputs 'AE36'

# turn a benefit into a language into a haircut
$language = "Perk";
print ++ $language;       # outputs 'Perl'
print ++ $language;       # produces 'Perm'

# make a dated TV series (a bit) more current
$serial = "Space1999";
print ++ $serial;         # produce 'Space2000''
```

Only strings that are exclusively made up of alphanumeric characters (a–z, A–Z, and 0–9) can be incremented.

Combination Assignment Operators

Perl also supports C-style combination assignment operators, where the variable on the right of the assignment is also treated as the value on the right-hand side of the attached operator. The general syntax for such operators is this:

```
$variable <operator>= $value;
```

For example:

```
$variable += 2;
```

is a quicker way to write

```
$variable = $variable + 2;
```

There are 15 combination assignment operators in all, each of which is an assignment combined with the relevant binary operation as you can see in Table 4-1.

Table 4-1. *Combination Assignment Operators*

Arithmetic	String	Shift	Logical	Bitwise
+=	X=	<<=	||=	|=
-=	.=	>>=	&&=	&=
*=				^=
/=				
**=				
%=				

For illustration, this is how each of the arithmetic combination assignment operators changes the value of $variable from 10:

```
print $variable += 2;    # prints '12'
print $variable -= 2;    # prints '8'
print $variable *= 2;    # prints '20'
print $variable /= 2;    # prints '5'
print $variable **= 2;   # prints '100'
print $variable %= 2;    # prints '0'
```

This is also an example on concatenating one string onto another using the .= operator:

```
#!/usr/bin/perl
# concat.pl
use warnings;
use strict;

my $First = "One ";
my $First_Addition = "Two ";
my $Second_Addition = "Three";
my $string = $First;
print "The string is now: $string \n";
$string.= $First_Addition;
print "The string is now: $string \n";
$string.= $Second_Addition;
print "The string is now: $string \n";
```

Running this program displays the following output:

> **perl concat.pl**

```
The string is now: One
The string is now: One Two
The string is now: One Two Three
```

Beware of using combination assignments in other expressions. Without parentheses, they have lower precedence than the expression around them, causing unintended results.

```
$a = $b + $c += 2;       # syntax error, cannot assign to '$b + $c'
```

Because + has higher precedence than +=, this is equivalent to

```
$a = ($b + $c) += 2;    # the reason for the error becomes clear
```

What we really meant to say was this:

```
$a = $b + ($c += 2);    # correct, increments $c then adds it to $b
```

The regular expression binding operator looks a little like an assignment operator, it isn't. =~ is a binding operator, and ~= is a bitwise not assignment.

Comparison Operators

The comparison operators are binary, returning a value based on a comparison of the expression on their left and the expression on their right. For example, the equality operator, ==, returns true (1) if its operands are numerically equal, and false (") otherwise.

```
$a == $b;
```

There are two complimentary sets of these operators. The numeric comparison operators appear in conventional algebraic format and treat both operands as numeric, forcing them into numeric values if necessary.

```
print 1 < 2;        # produces 1
print "a" < "b";    # produces 0, since "a" and "b" both evaluate
                    # as 0 numerically, and 0 is not less than 0.
```

Note that if we have warnings enabled, attempting to compare strings with a numeric comparison operator will cause Perl to emit a warning.

```
Argument "a" isn't numeric in numeric lt (<) at ...
Argument "b" isn't numeric in numeric lt (<) at ...
```

The string comparison operators appear as simple mnemonic names, and are distinct from the numerical comparison operators in that they perform alphanumerical comparisons on a character-by-character basis. So, 2 is less than 12 numerically, but it is greater in a string comparison because the character 2 (as opposed to the number) is greater than the character 1. They are also dependent on locale (see Chapter 23), so the meaning of "greater than" and "less than" is defined by the character set in use.

```
print 2 > 12;   # numeric, produces 0
print 2 gt 12;  # string, produces 1 because the string "2" is
                # greater than "12"
```

Unlike the preceding counter example, comparing numbers with a string comparison operator does not produce an error.

There are seven comparison operations in all, each with a numeric and string version. Of these, the first six are standard Boolean tests that return true if the comparison succeeds and an empty value (" in string context, 0 numerically) otherwise. The seventh is the comparison operator, which is slightly different, as shown in Table 4-2.

Table 4-2. *Comparison Operators*

Numeric	String	Operation
!=	ne	Return true if operands are not equal.
>	gt	Return true if left operand is greater than right.
==	eq	Return true if operands are equal.
>=	ge	Return true if left operand is greater or equal to right.
<	le	Return true if left operand is less than right.
<=	lt	Return true if left operand is less than or equal to right.
<=>	cmp	Return -1 if left operand is less than right, 0 if they are equal, and +1 if left operand is greater than right.

The cmp and <=> operators are different from the other comparison operators because they do not return a Boolean result. Rather, they return one of three results depending on whether the left operand is less than, equal to, or greater than the right. Using this operator, we can write efficient code like

```
SWITCH: foreach ($a <=> $b) {
$_ == -1 and do {print "Less"; last;};
$_ == +1 and do {print "More"; last;};
print "Equal";
}
```

To do the same thing with ordinary if . . . else statements would take at least two statements. The <=> and cmp operators are frequently used in sort subroutines, and indeed the default sort operation uses cmp internally.

▌**Tip** The string comparison functions actually compare strings according to the value of the localization variable LC_COLLATE, including the implicit cmp of the sort function—see Chapter 23 for more details.

None of the comparison operators work in a list context, so attempting to do a comparison like @a1 == @a2 will compare the two arrays in scalar context; that is, the number of elements in @a1 will be compared to the number of elements in @a2. This might actually be what we intend, but it looks confusing. Writing $#a1 == $#a2 or using the scalar function would probably be a better way to go in this case.

Regular Expression Binding Operators

The regular expression binding operators =~ and !~ apply the regular expression function on their right to the scalar value on their left.

```
# look for 'pattern' in $match text
print "Found" if $match_text =~ /pattern/;
```

```
# perform substitution
print "Found and Replaced" if $match_text =~ s/pattern/logrus/;
```

The value returned from =~ is the return value of the regular expression function (1 if the match succeeded but no parentheses are present inside the expression), and a list of the match subpatterns (i.e., the values of $1, $2 . . . ; see "Regular Expressions" in Chapter 11) if any parentheses were used; it returns undef if the match failed. In scalar context, this is converted to a count of the parentheses, which is a true value for the purposes of conditional expressions.

The !~ operator performs a logical negation of the returned value for conditional expressions, that is, 1 for failure and " for success in both scalar and list contexts.

```
# look for 'pattern' in $match text, print message if absent
print "Not found" if $match_text !~ /pattern/;
```

Comma and Relationship Operators

We use the comma operator all the time, usually without noticing it. In a list context it simply returns its left- and right-hand side as parts of the list.

```
@array = (1, 2, 3, 4);        # construct a list with commas
mysubroutine(1, 2, 3, 4);     # send a list of values to 'mysubroutine'.
```

In a scalar context, the list operator returns the value of the right-hand side, ignoring whatever result is returned by the left:

```
return 1, 2, 3, 4;   # returns the value '4';
```

The relationship or *digraph* operator can be thought of as an intelligent comma. It has the same meaning as the comma operator but is intended for use in defining key-value pairs for hash variables. It also allows barewords for the keys.

```
# define a hash from a list, but more legibly
%hash = ('Tom'=>'Cat', 'Jerry'=>'Mouse', 'Spike'=>'Dog');
# define a hash from a list with barewords
%hash = (Tom=>'Cat', Jerry=>'Mouse', Spike=>'Dog');
```

Both operators bind less strongly than an assignment. In the following expression, $a is assigned the value 1, and $b is assigned the value 2:

```
$b=($a=1,2)
```

We'll return to both these operators when we come to lists, arrays, and hashes in Chapter 5.

Reference and Dereference Operators

The reference constructor \ is a unary operator that creates and returns a reference for the variable, value, or subroutine that follows it. Alterations to the value pointed to by the reference change the original value.

```
$number     = 42;
$numberref  = \$number;
$$numberref = 6;
print $number;   # displays '6'
```

To dereference a reference (that is, access the underlying value), we can prefix the reference, a scalar, by the variable type of whatever the reference points to; in the preceding example we have a reference to a scalar, so we use $$ to access the underlying scalar. To dereference a list, we would use @$, and to dereference a hash, %$. Since this sometimes causes precedence problems when used in conjunction with indices or hash keys, we can also explicitly dereference with curly braces.

```
$number = $$numberref;
$number = ${$numberref};
```

Alternatively, and often more legibly, we can use the *dereference*, or *arrow* operator.

The arrow operator, ->, has two meanings, depending on the nature of its left-hand side. The first occurs when the left-hand side is an array or hash reference, or something that returns one, such as a subroutine.

```
# look up a hash key
$value = $hashref -> {$key};

# take a slice of an array
@slice = $arrayref -> [7..11];

# get first element of subroutine returning array reference:
$result = sub_that_returns_an_arrayref() -> [0];
```

The arrow operator is also implicitly used whenever we stack indices or hash keys together. This lets us use multidimensional arrays (arrays of arrays) and hashes of hashes without excessive punctuation.

```
$element = $pixel3d[$x][$y][$z];
```

This is shorthand for

```
$element = $pixel3d[$x]->[$y]->[$z];
```

Interestingly, this is actually shorthand for the following, but without the need to create any intermediate variables:

```
my $yz_array = $pixel3d[$x];
my $z_array = $yz_array->[$y];
$element = $z_array->[$z];
```

This is because an array or hash can only contain scalars, so an array of arrays is really an array of array references. Perl is smart enough to know what we mean when we access a variable with stacked indices or hash keys though, so in this case we do not need the arrow operator. That said, it is still legal to put arrows in if we really want to.

The other application of the arrow operator is in object-oriented programming. It occurs when the left-hand side is either a Perl object or a package name and the right-hand side is a method (that is, a subroutine in the package). Chapter 19 covers this in detail, so for now we will just show two typical examples of the arrow operator in this mode:

```
My::Package::Name -> class_method(@args); # class method
$my_object -> method(@args); #object method
```

The arrow operator, ->, has nothing to do with the relationship (a.k.a. digraph) operator, =>, which is just a slightly smarter comma for use in defining key-value pairs. Confusing these two can be a plentiful source of syntax errors, so be sure to use the right one in the right place.

Range Operators

The range operator is one of the most poorly understood of Perl's operators. It has two modes of operation, depending on whether it is used in a scalar or list context. The list context is the most well known and is often used to generate sequences of numbers, as in

```
foreach (1..10) {
print "$_\n";    # print 1 to 10
}
```

In a list context, the range operator returns a list, starting with its left operand and incrementing it until it reaches the value on the right. So 1..10 returns the list (1, 2, 3, 4, 5, 6, 7, 8, 9, 10). The increment is done in the same manner as the increment operator, ++, so strings can also be incremented.

```
print "A".."E"    # returns ABCDE
```

If the left-hand side is equal to the right, then a single element list containing that value is returned. If it is greater, however, an empty list is returned, not a list in reverse. To generate a reverse list, we instead use the reverse function.

```
print reverse "A".."E"    # returns EDCBA
```

The use of the range operator in scalar context is less well understood, and consequently rarely used. It functions like a bistable flip-flop, and takes two Boolean expressions as operands—which is to say, the operator has a memory and remembers how it has been used previously. It initially returns 0 until its left-hand operand becomes true. Once this happens, it returns 1 unless and until the right-hand operand becomes true, after which it starts returning 0 again until the left-hand side becomes true, and so on ad infinitum.

The range operator's most common use is in conjunction with numeric operands, which as a convenience, Perl compares to the input line number (or *sequence number*) special variable $. For example, this loop prints out the first ten lines of input:

```
while (<>) {
1..10 and print;
}
```

In this example, the left side of the range operator becomes true on the first line of input, when the value of $. is 1. The right-hand side becomes true on the tenth line ($.==10), hence the result we expect. If the left- or right-hand operands are not literal numerics, then they are simply used as Boolean tests, and their value is used to switch the range operator to the other state. Consequently using scalar variables or expressions will not work.

```
# ERROR: this does NOT work
$start = 1; $end = 10;
while (<>) {
$start .. $end and print;
}
```

What happens here is that both the left and right operands always return true, so the range operator returns true for every line, flip-flopping to false and back to true each time. So this is just a hard way to print every line of input. What will work (usefully) are tests that involve either the sequence number variable $. or the current line, contained in $_. To make the preceding example work, we have to involve $. explicitly, as in this repaired (and complete) example:

```perl
#!/usr/bin/perl
use warnings;
use strict;

my $start = 2;
my $end = 4;

while (<>) {
    ($. == $start)..($. == $end) and print "$.: $_";
}
```

It is always possible to use the range operator with an explicit Boolean test like this; the previous example is simply shorthand that comes in useful for a particular class of solutions involving the reading of input lines. Another class of solutions with a shorthand version involves regular expressions, which return true if the associated string matches. Without an explicitly bound string (using =~ or !~), the default argument $_ is used, so we can create very effective and impressively terse code like the next example. This collects the header and body of an email message or an HTTP response—both of which separate the header and body with a blank line—into different variables.

```perl
$header = "";
$body = "";
while (<>) {
    1 .. /^$/ and $header. = $_;
    /^$/ .. eof() and $body. = $_;
    exit if eof;    # ensure we only pass through one file
}
```

When used with expressions that test $_, we can also make use of a variant of the range operator expressed as three dots rather than two.

```perl
(/^BEGIN/) ... (/END$/)
```

The three-dot form of the range operator is identical in all respects except that it will not flip state twice on the same line. Therefore, the second operand is not evaluated for truth on the same line that the first one transitions from false to true, and similarly the first operand is not reevaluated on the same line that the second operand evaluates to true. In the preceding example, the range operator will flip from false to true whenever BEGIN starts a line, and from true to false whenever END finishes a line; but if a line both starts with BEGIN and finishes with END, then only one of the two transitions will occur (whichever is waiting to flip next). For a more advanced example of how the range operator can be used with regular expressions, see "Extracting Lines with the Range Operator" in the discussion on regular expressions in Chapter 11.

Ternary Operators

The ternary ?: operator is an if statement that returns a value. It takes three expressions, and returns the second or third as its result, depending on whether the first is true or false respectively; the logic is essentially

```perl
if <expr1> then return <expr2> else return <expr3>:
```

Consider the following example:

```
$answer = $a ? $b : $c;    # assign $b if $a is true, otherwise assign $c
```

Here is another example that conditionally pluralizes "word" within a print statement:

```
# print 'word' or 'words'. '$#words' is 0 if @words has one element
print scalar(@words), " word", ($#words?'s':"), "\n";
```

The precedence of the ternary operator is low, just above that of assignment operators and the comma, so in general, operands that are expressions do not need parentheses. Conversely, however, the whole operator often does need to be parenthesized for the same reason. Otherwise, the rules of precedence can cause terms to the right to be swallowed up if they are higher precedence.

```
# result is $c + $d if $a is false
$result = $a ? $b : $c + $d;
```

```
# result is $b + $d or $c + $d
$result = ($a ? $b : $c) + $d;
```

Precedence and Associativity

We briefly discussed precedence and associativity earlier in the chapter, but we will discuss them in more detail here. For those just looking for a summary, there is also a table with all the operators and their precedence at the end of the section.

Precedence determines which operators evaluate their operands first. Arithmetic operators have a relatively high precedence, with multiplication having higher precedence than addition. The assignment operators like = have a very low precedence, so that they are only evaluated when the value of both their operands a result.

Associativity comes in to play when operators have the same precedence, as + and - do. It determines which operand—left or right—is evaluated first. All the arithmetic operators have left associativity, so they will always evaluate their left side before they evaluate their right. For example, multiplication, *, and division, /, have the same precedence, so they are evaluated left to right when found together.

```
1 / 2 * 3  =>  (1 / 2)*3  =>  1.5
```

If the association was to the right, the result would be

```
1/(2 * 3)  =>  1/6   =>  0.1666...
```

When Perl sees a statement, it works through all the operators contained within, working out their order of evaluation based on their precedence and associativity. As a more complete example, here is a sample of the kind of logic that Perl uses to determine how to process it. The parentheses are not actually added to the statement, but they show how Perl treats the statement internally. First, the actual statement as written:

```
$result = 3 + $var * mysub(@args);
```

The = operator has the lowest precedence, since the expressions on either side must obviously be evaluated before the = can be processed. In the compilation phase, Perl parses the expression starting from the lowest precedence operator, =, with the largest expressions and divides the surrounding expressions into smaller, higher precedence expressions until all that is left is terms, which can be evaluated directly.

```
($result) = ((3) + (($var) * (mysub(@args)) );
```

In the run-time phase, Perl evaluates expressions in order of highest precedence, starting from the terms and evaluating the result of each operation once the results of the higher precedence operations are known. A *term* is simply any indivisible quantity, like a variable name, literal value, or a subroutine call with its arguments in parentheses. These have the highest precedence of all, since their evaluation is unambiguous, indivisible, and independent of the rest of the expression. We don't often think of = as being an operator, but it returns a value, just like any other operator. In the case of =, the return value is the value of the assignment. Also like other binary operators, both sides must be evaluated first. The left-hand side must be assignable, but need not be a variable— functions like substr can also appear on the left of =, and need to be evaluated before = can assign to them (in the case of substr, the substring that it returns). Having established the concepts of precedence and associativity, we present Table 4-3, a complete list of all of Perl's basic operators in order of precedence (highest to lowest) and their associativity.

Table 4-3. *Precedence and Associativity of Perl Operators*

Associativity	Operators
Left	Terms, list operators
Left	->
None	++ --
Right	**
Right	! ~ \, + (unary) - (unary)
Left	=~ !~
Left	* / % x
Left	+ - .
Left	<< >>
None	Named unary operators (e.g., -X)
None	< > <= >= lt gt le ge
None	== != <=> eq ne cmp
Left	&
Left	| ^
Left	&&
Left	||
None	.. ...
Right	?:
Right	= += -= *= /= %= .= etc.
Left	, =>
None	List operators (to the right)
Right	not
Left	and
Left	or xor

Precedence and Parentheses

Parentheses alter the order of evaluation in an expression, overriding the order of precedence that would ordinarily control which operation gets evaluated first, so in the following expression the + is evaluated before the *:

4 * (9 + 16)

It is sometimes helpful to think of parentheses as a *precedence operator*, as they automatically push their contents to the top of the precedence rankings by making their contents appear as a term to the surrounding expression. Within the parentheses, operators continue to have the same precedence as usual, so the 9 and 16 have higher precedence than the + because they are terms.

We can nest parentheses to any depth we like, entirely overriding the rules of precedence and associativity if we wish.

```
(3 - ((4 + 5)*6))
```

Parentheses are multipurpose in Perl. They are also used to construct lists of values and delimit the arguments to subroutines and built-in functions. Whether as part of a subroutine or function argument list or as a simple list value, they still have the same effect of overriding precedence.

Functions and subroutines may be used with or without parentheses. With parentheses they are simply terms—atoms of evaluation—from the point of view of the rest of the statement, since the parentheses make the arguments indivisible from the function or subroutine call they belong to. Without parentheses, the behavior of functions and subroutines changes—they become in effect operators. Some functions take fixed numbers of arguments; if the number is one, they are called unary operators. Others, like push, and all subroutines that are declared without prototypes, are called *list operators*.

List operators are interesting in that they have high precedence to their left but low precedence to their right. The upshot of this is that anything to the right of a list operator is evaluated before the list operator is, and the list operator itself is then evaluated before anything to the left. Put another way, list operators tend to group as much as possible to their right, and appear as terms to their left. In other words

```
$result = $value + listop $value + $value, $value;
```

is always evaluated as if it were

```
$result = $value + (listop ($value + $value, $value));
```

This behavior makes sense when we recall that functions and subroutines can only ever process arguments to their right; they cannot have a left operand. As a result, and in particular, the comma operator has a higher precedence than list operators. Note, however, that even on their right side, list operators have a higher precedence than the named logical operators not, and, or, and xor, so we can say things like the following without requiring parentheses:

```
open FILEHANDLE, $filename or die "Failed to open $filename: $!";
```

Take care when using the algebraic form of logical operators with list operators, however. In the preceding example, replacing or with || would cause the open to attempt to open the result of $filename || die..., which would return the value of $filename in accordance with the shortcut rules of the logical operators, but which would swallow the die so that it was never called. This is a common mistake, and all the more so because it is hard to spot—the code may appear to be working correctly, the effects of the failed call to open manifesting in unpredictable ways later on.

Single-argument subroutines and functions also change their behavior with regard to precedence when used as operators. With parentheses, they are functions and therefore have term precedence. As operators, they have a lower precedence than the arithmetic operators but higher than most others, so that the following does what it looks like it does:

```
$name1 = "myfile"; $name2 = ".txt";
if (-f $name1.$name2) {
    print "A test for $name1$name2: The concatenation occurred first";
}
```

Assuming we have a file in our directory called myfile.txt, then the concatenated variables make up the filename, which -f then acts on and returns 1 because our file is present.

Using functions and subroutines without parentheses can sometimes make them more legible (and sometimes not). However, we can get into trouble if they swallow more expression into their argument list than we actually intended. The print function is one of the more common cases of inadvertently expansive expressions.

```
print "Bye! \n", exit if $quitting;
```

The problem with this statement is that exit has higher precedence than print, because print as a list operator gives higher precedence to everything on its right-hand side. So the exit is evaluated before print is called and the Bye! is never seen. We can fix this in two different ways, both using parentheses.

```
# turn 'print' into a function, making the arguments explicit
print("Bye! \n"), exit if $quitting;
# make the 'print' statement a term in its own right
(print "Bye! \n"), exit if $quitting;
```

As we noted earlier, if the next thing after a function or subroutine name is an open parenthesis, then the contents of the parentheses are used as the arguments and nothing more is absorbed into the argument list. This is the functional mode of operation, as opposed to the list-operator mode with no parentheses, and it is why the first example shown earlier produces the result we want. However, it can also trip us up. Consider the following seemingly equivalent statements:

```
# displays "<sum> is the sum of <value1> and <value2>"
print $value1 + $value2, "is the sum of $value1 and $value2 \n";
# ERROR: displays sum only, RETURNS string " is the sum of <value1> and <value2>"
print ($value1 + $value2), " is the sum of $value1 and $value2 \n";
```

The second statement tries to group the addition within parentheses to make it stand out from the rest of the statement. However, the laws of parentheses dictate that this means the contents are the specific arguments to print. Perl evaluates the comma operator first and we get the sum printed out (but not the rest of the line) as the call to print is its left operand. The comma operator then discards the result of the print call and returns the string "is the sum of . . ." as its value to the surrounding program, which ignores it.

To have this statement work as intended, we need to disambiguate the parentheses so that they are used to group only, rather than define an argument list. There are two ways to do this; either use more parentheses around the whole argument list or use operators.

```
# add parentheses
print (($value1 + $value2), "is the sum of $value1 and $value2 \n");
# disambiguate by adding zero
print 0 + ($value1 + $value2), "is the sum of $value1 and $value2\n";
# disambiguate with unary plus
print + ($value1 + $value2), "is the sum of $value1 and $value2 \n";
```

The last two examples work by simply preventing a parenthesis from being the first thing Perl sees after the print. The unary plus is a little friendlier to the eye (and this is in fact the only useful use of a unary plus). However, the more usual solution is the pragmatic one: we can just rewrite the print statement into an equivalent but less problematic form.

```
print "The sum of $value1 and $value 2 is ",($value1 + $value2);
```

Disabling Functions and Operators

Occasionally we might want to prevent certain operators or functions from being used. One possible reason for doing this is for scripts run by untrusted users such as CGI scripts on a web server.

Intriguingly, Perl makes this possible through the use ops and no ops pragmas, special modules that control the operation of the interpreter itself. These allow us to selectively enable or disable any of Perl's operators or functions. The typical use of the ops pragma is from the command line. For example, to disable the system function we can use

```
> perl -M-ops=system myprogram.pl
```

Notice the minus sign before ops, indicating that all operators should be enabled except those specified as the arguments, in this case just system.

The ops pragma controls how Perl compiles code, so it is not useful in code unless it is contained within a BEGIN block.

```
BEGIN {
    no ops qw(system);
}
```

An opcode is not the same thing as an operator, though there is a strong correlation. In this example, system, exec, and fork are directly comparable, but the backtick opcode relates to backticks (and the equivalent qx quoting operator). Opcodes are what Perl actually uses to perform operations, and all the operators and functions we use are mapped onto internal opcodes—sometimes directly and sometimes conditionally, depending on how the operator or function is used.

The ops pragma is an interface to the Opcode module, which provides a direct interface to Perl's opcodes, and thereby to its operators and functions. It defines several functions for manipulating sets of opcodes, which the ops pragma uses to enable and disable opcodes. It also defines a number of import tags that collect opcodes into categories that can be used to switch collections of opcodes on or off. For example, to restrict Perl to a default set of safe opcodes, we can use the :default tag.

```
> perl -Mops=:default myprogram.pl
```

If myprogram.pl contains any operators with opcodes outside this set, it will not compile under this command. Similarly, to disable the open, sysopen, and close functions, as well as binmode and umask, we can switch them off with the :filesys_open tag.

```
> perl -M-ops=:filesys_open myprogram.pl
```

We can also disable the system, backtick, exec, and fork keywords with the :subprocess tag.

```
> perl -M-ops=:subprocess myprogram.pl
```

Or, programmatically:

```
BEGIN { no ops qw(:subprocess); }
```

A reasonably complete list of tags defined by Opcode appears in Table 4-4.

Table 4-4. *Opcode Tags and Categories*

Tag	Category
:base_core	Core Perl operators and functions, including arithmetic and comparison operators, increment and decrement, and basic string and array manipulation.
:base_mem	Core Perl operators and functions that allocate memory, including the anonymous array and hash constructors, the range operator, and the concatenation operator. In theory, disabling these can prevent memory allocation problems like memory leaks or malicious attempts to cause programs to allocate excessive amounts of memory.

Continued

Table 4-4. *Continued*

Tag	Category
:base_loop	Looping functions such as while and for, grep and map, and the loop control statements next, last, redo, and continue. In theory, disabling these can prevents many kinds of CPU usage problems.
:base_io	Filehandle functions such as readline, getc, eof, seek, print, and readdir. Disabling these functions is probably not a useful thing to do. Disabling open and sysopen is a different matter, but they are not in this category.
:base_orig	Miscellaneous functions, including tie and untie, bless, the archaic dbmopen and dbmclose, localtime and gmtime, and various socket and network-related functions.
:base_math	The floating-point mathematical functions sin, cos, atan2, exp, log, and sqrt, plus the random functions rand and srand.
:base_thread	The threaded programming functions lock and threadsv.
:default	All of the preceding :base_ tags; a reasonably default set of Perl operators.
:filesys_read	Low-level file functions such as stat, lstat, and fileno.
:sys_db	Perl's functions for interrogating hosts, networks, protocols, services, users, and groups, such as getpwent. Note that the actual names of the opcodes differ from the functions that map to them.
:browse	All of the preceding tags, a slightly extended version of :default that also includes :filesys_read and :sys_db.
:filesys_open	open, sysopen, close, binmode, and umask.
:filesys_write	File modification functions like link and unlike, rename, mkdir and rmdir, chmod, chown, and fcntl.
:subprocess	Functions that start subprocesses like fork, system, the backtick operator (opcode backtick), and the glob operator. This is the set of opcodes that trigger errors in "taint" mode, and a particularly useful set of opcodes to disable in security-conscious situations like CGI scripts.
:ownprocess	Functions that control the current process, such as exec, exit, and kill.
:others	Miscellaneous opcodes, mostly to do with IPC, such as msgctl and shmget.
:dangerous	Also miscellaneous, but more dangerous, opcodes. Currently this contains syscall, dump, and chroot.

Many operators map to more than one opcode, depending on the types of value that they are asked to operate on. The addition operator, +, maps to the add and I_add opcodes, which do floating point and integer addition respectively. We can use the *opdump* function to generate a table of opcodes and descriptions. For example, to generate a complete (and very long) list of all opcodes and descriptions:

> **perl -MOpcode -e 'Opcode::opdump'**

This generates a table starting with

```
null   null operation
stub   stub
scalar scalar
pushmark pushmark
wantarray wantarray
const  constant item
gvsv   scalar variable
```

```
gv  glob value

    ....
```

Alternatively, to search for opcodes by description, we can pass in a string (actually, a regular expression). Any opcode whose description contains that string will be output. For example, to find the opcodes for all the logical operators:

> `perl -MOpcode=opdump -e 'opdump("logical")'`

This produces

```
and  logical and (&&)
or  logical or (||)
xor  logical xor
andassign  logical and assignment (&&=)
orassign  logical or assignment (||=)
```

Since the argument to opdump is a regular expression, we can also get a list of all logical operators, bitwise, and Boolean, with

> `perl -MOpcode=opdump -e 'opdump("bit|logic")'`

So, if we wanted to disable logical assignments, we now know that the andassign and orassign opcodes are the ones we need to switch off. Note that the description always contains the operator, or function names, for those opcodes that map directly to operators and functions. The Opcode module also contains a number of other functions for manipulating opcode sets and masks. Since these are unlikely to be of interest except to programmers working directly with the opcode tables, we will ignore them here. For more information, see perldoc Opcode and the related Safe module, covered in Chapter 17.

Overloading Operators

As well as disabling operators, we can override them with the overload pragmatic module. This implements an object-oriented technique called *overloading*, where additional meanings are layered over an operator. The overloaded meanings come into effect whenever an object that defines an overloaded operator is used as an operand of that operator. For example, consider a module that implements an object class called MyObject that starts with the following lines:

```
package MyObject;
use overload '+' => &myadd, '-' => &mysub;
...
```

Normally we cannot add or subtract objects because they are just references, and Perl does not allow us to perform arithmetic on references. However, if we try to perform an addition or subtraction involving objects of type MyObject, then the myadd and mysub methods in the MyObject package are called instead of Perl simply returning an error. This forms the basis of operator overloading for objects. Since overloading is fundamentally tied to object-oriented programming, we will not cover it further here. Overloading and the overload module are both covered in detail in Chapter 19.

Operators vs. Functions

Perl provides operators, like +, and it also has built-in functions, like abs. The distinction is apparently simple. Operators have an algebraic look and operate on operands. Functions take arguments, are referenced by name rather than a symbol, and use parentheses to group arguments together. Furthermore, operators are documented in the `perlop` manual page, and functions are in the `perlfunc` manual page. Simple.

However, it is actually not that simple. A character like + is clearly an operator because it is the universal symbol for addition, and addition is a mathematical operation. Additionally, in its binary form, + takes an operand on each side, something a function never does. So these cases are unambiguous. Conversely, `abs` is clearly a function because it has a name rather than being a piece of punctuation. But there are plenty of less obvious cases.

Many functions are called operators simply because they resemble operators. The file test functions `-f`, `-d`, `-l` and so on, also known as the `-X` operators, are one example. The readline operator, `<>`, is another. The `-X` operators are an example of a "named unary operator," an operator that has a name rather than a symbol and takes a single operand on its right. They resemble unary operators like `not`, which also has a name and takes a single operand on its right. So, the distinction between operators and functions is more vague than we might at first think. They also appear in *both* the `perlop` and `perlfunc` manual pages, just to keep things nicely ambiguous.

An alternative way to look at functions is to say that they are all either named unary operators (accepting a single argument) or named list operators (accepting a list of arguments), in either case on the right. This might seem arcane from a C programmer's perspective, but is quite familiar to anyone with experience with Lisp or any of its descendants, Perl included. How we talk about them then becomes a matter of how we use them: if we use parentheses, they are functions, and if we do not, they are (or at least, resemble) operators.

```
print -e($filename);   # file test '-e', functional style
print -e $filename;    # file test '-e', operator style
```

This is a useful idea because we can declare subroutines so that they also do not need parentheses, so they can be used as named list operators. With prototypes we can even implement subroutines that resemble named unary operators.

Summary

In this chapter, we looked at Perl's operators. First we examined the difference between an operator and a built-in function, and found that functions are really just a special class of list operators. We then took an in-depth look into the different types of operators, categorized into numerous loosely associated classes. We then covered precedence and associativity, and looked at the effect of parentheses on precedence. We then took a brief look at controlling the availability of operators and function with the `Opcode` module, and defining new operators behaviors using objects with the `overload` module. Finally, we considered the distinction between operators and functions in Perl, finding that in many cases the difference is only one of our perspective.

CHAPTER 5

■ ■ ■

Arrays, Hashes, References, and Typeglobs

Having introduced scalars in Chapter 3, we now consider in this chapter the remaining data types. Specifically, this chapter introduces arrays, hashes, references, and typeglobs. We will also examine the more complex data that can be created by mixing data types. Later in the chapter, we will also see how to define scalar, list, and hash constants, as well as check for their existence. Finally, we discuss one other special value, the undefined value.

Lists and Arrays

A *list* is a compound value that may hold any number of scalar values (including none at all). Each value, or element, in the list is ordered and indexed, it is always in the same place, and we can refer to it by its position in the list. An *array* provides dynamic storage for a list, and so can be grown, shrunk, and manipulated by altering its values. In Perl, we often use the terms "array" and "list" interchangeably, but the difference can be important.

Creating Lists and Arrays

In Perl, lists are written out using parentheses and the comma operator. For example:

```
(1, 2, 3, 4, 5, 6)
```

A list is simply a sequence of scalar values; we can copy it about, store it in arrays, and index it, but we can't alter its contents because it is not stored anywhere—the preceding list is just an expression in Perl code. To manipulate a list of values, we need to store the list in an array.

An array variable is prefixed with an at-sign, @, in the same way that scalar variables are prefixed with a dollar sign.

```
# define a six-element array from a six-element list
my @array = (1, 2, 3, 4, 5, 6);
```

The usual way of defining lists is with the comma operator, which concatenates scalars together to produce list values. We tend to take the comma for granted because it is so obvious, but it is in fact an operator performing an important function. However, defining arrays of strings can get a little awkward.

```
my @strings = ('one', 'two', 'three', 'four', 'five');
```

That's a lot of quotes and commas, an open invitation for typographic errors. A better way to define a list like this is with the list quoting operator, qw, which we briefly mentioned in Chapter 3. Here's the same list defined more legibly with qw:

```
my @strings = qw(one two three four five);
```

Or, defined with tabs and newlines:

```
my @strings = qw(
  one two
  three four
  five
);
```

As well as assigning lists to array variables, we can also assign them to a list of scalars variables.

```
my ($one, $two, $three) = (1, 2, 3);    # $one is now 1, $two 2 and $three 3
```

If there are too few variables to assign all the values, any remaining values will be discarded. This is a very common sight inside subroutines, where we will often encounter a first line like

```
my ($arg1, $arg2, @listarg) = @_;
```

When we declare an array with my or our, Perl will automatically create the array with zero elements unless we assign some at the time of declaration. An initial value of ( ) explicitly gives the new array zero elements (and in Perl 5.8 such an assignment is silently optimized away), so the following are equivalent declarations:

```
my @array=(); #explicit empty list
my @array; #implicit empty list
```

However, the following creates an array with a single undefined value, which may not be what we intended:

```
my @array=undef; # same as 'my @array=(undef)'
```

A mistake like this is relatively obvious written like this, but we can easily get tripped up if, for example, an array is assigned the return value of a subroutine that returns a list of zero or more values on success, but undef to indicate failure.

```
@array=a_subroutine_that_might_return_undef(); # beware!
die "failed!" if scalar(@array)==1
    and not defined $array[0]; # must check for undefined return value
```

Accessing Lists and Arrays

The array variable is a handle that we can use to access the values inside it, also known as array elements. Each element has an index number that corresponds to its position in the list. The index starts at zero, so the index number of an element is always one less than its place in the list. To access it, we supply the index number after the array in square brackets.

```
my @array = (1, 2, 3, 4, 5, 6);
# print the value of the fifth element (index 4, counting from 0)
print "The fifth element is $array[4] \n";
```

We can also place an index on the end of a list, for example:

```
print "The fifth element is ", (1, 2, 3, 4, 5, 6)[4];    # outputs 5
```

Of course, there isn't much point in writing down a list and then only using one value from it, but we can use the same approach with lists returned by functions like localtime, where we only want some of the values that the list contains.

```
$year = (localtime)[5] + 1900;
```

For the curious, the parentheses around localtime prevent the [5] from being interpreted as an anonymous array and passed to localtime as an argument. A drawback of Perl's flexible syntax rules is that sometimes precedence and associativity can bite in unexpected ways. Because the year value is given in years since 1900, we add 1900 to get the actual year.

The values of an array are scalars (though these may include references), so the correct way to refer to an element is with a dollar prefix, not an @ sign. It is the type of the returned value that is important to Perl, not where it was found.

```
print "The first element is $array[0] \n";
```

Given the @array earlier, this will reveal 1 to be the value of the first element.

If we specify a negative index, Perl rather smartly counts from the end of the array.

```
print "The last element is $array[-1] \n";
```

This accesses the last element of @array, earlier, which has a positive index of 5 and a value of 6.

We can also extract a list from an array by specifying a range of indices or a list of index numbers, also known as a *slice*.

```
print "The third to fifth elements: @array[2..4] \n";
```

This prints out the elements at indices 2, 3, and 4 with values 3, 4, and 5.

There is no need for a slice to be contiguous or defined as a range, and we can freely mix positive and negative indices.

```
print "The first two and last two elements: @array[0, 1, -2, -1] \n";
```

In our example six-element array, this prints out the values 1, 2, 5, and 6. Note that if we only had an array of three values, indices 1 and -2 would refer to the same element and we would see its value printed twice.

We can also retrieve the same index multiple times.

```
# replace array with first three elements, in triplicate
my @array = @array[0..2, 0..2, 0..2];
```

Arrays can only contain scalars, but scalars can be numbers, strings, or references to other values like more arrays, which is exactly how Perl implements multidimensional arrays. They can also contain the undefined value, which is and isn't a scalar, depending on how we look at it.

Manipulating Arrays

Arrays are flexible creatures. We can modify them, extend them, truncate them, and extract elements from them in many different ways. We can add or remove elements from an array at both ends, and even in the middle.

Modifying the Contents of an Array

Changing the value of an element is simple; just assign a new value to the appropriate index of the array.

```
$array[4] = "The Fifth Element";
```

We are not limited to changing a single element at a time, however. We can assign to more than one element at once using a list or range in just the same way that we can read multiple elements. Because this is a selection of several elements, we use the @ prefix, since we are manipulating an array value:

```
@array[3..5, 7, -1] = ("4th", "5th", "6th", "8th", "Last");
```

We can even copy parts of an array to itself, including overlapping slices.

```
@array = (1, 2, 3, 4, 5, 6);
@array[2..4] = @array[0..2];
print "@array \n"; # @array is now (1, 2, 1, 2, 3, 6);
```

We might expect that if we supply a different number of elements to the number we are replacing, then we could change the number of elements in the array, replacing one element with three, for example. However, this is not the case. If we supply too many elements, then the later ones are simply ignored. If we supply too few, then the elements left without values are filled with the undefined value. There is a logic to this, however, as the following example shows:

```perl
# assign first three elements to @array_a, and the rest to @array_b
@array_a[0..2], @array_b = @array;
```

Sometimes we do want to change the number of elements being replaced. Luckily, there is a function that does replace parts of arrays with variable-length lists. Appropriately enough it is called splice, and takes an array, a starting index, a number of elements, and a replacement list as its arguments.

```perl
splice @array, $from, $quantity, @replacement;
```

As a practical example, to replace element three of a six-element list with three new elements (creating an eight-element list), we would write something like

```perl
#!/usr/bin/perl
# splice1.pl
use strict;
use warnings;

my @array = ('a', 'b', 'c', ''d', 'e', 'f');
# replace third element with three new elements
my $removed = splice @array, 2, 1, (1, 2, 3);
print "@array \n";    # produces 'a b 1 2 3 d e f'
print "$removed \n";  # produces 'c'
```

This starts splicing from element 3 (index 2), removes one element, and replaces it with the list of three elements. The removed value is returned from splice and stored in $removed. If we were removing more than one element, we would supply a list instead.

```perl
#!/usr/bin/perl
# splice2.pl
use strict;
use warnings;

my @array = ('a', 'b', 'c', 'd', 'e', 'f');
# replace three elements 2, 3, and 4 with a different three
my @removed = splice @array, 2, 3, (1, 2, 3);
print "@array\n";    # produces 'a b 1 2 3 f'
print "@removed\n";  # produces 'c d e'
```

If we only want to remove elements without adding new ones, we just leave out the replacement list, shrinking the array.

```perl
#!/usr/bin/perl
# splice3.pl
use strict;
use warnings;

my @array = ('a', 'b', 'c', 'd', 'e', 'f');
# remove elements 2, 3 and 4
my @removed = splice @array, 2, 3;
print "@array\n";    # produces 'a b f'
print "@removed\n";  # produces 'c d e'
```

Leaving out the length as well removes everything from the specified index to the end of the list. We can also specify a negative number as an index, just as we can for accessing arrays, so combining these two facts we can do operations like this:

```perl
#!/usr/bin/perl
# splice4.pl
use strict;
use warnings;

my @array = ('a', 'b', 'c', 'd', 'e', 'f');
# remove last three elements
my @last_3_elements = splice @array, -3;
print "@array\n";    # produces 'a b c'
print "@last_3_elements\n";    # produces 'd e f'
```

splice is a very versatile function and forms the basis for several other, simpler array functions like pop and push. We'll be seeing it a few more times before we are done with arrays.

Counting an Array

If we take an array or list and use it in a scalar context, Perl will return the number of elements (including undefined ones, if any) in the array. This gives us a simple way to count array elements.

```perl
$count = @array;
```

It also lets us write conditions for testing whether or not an array has any values like this:

```perl
die "Usage: $0 <arg1> <arg2>\n" unless @ARGV == 2;
```

This said, accidentally using an array in scalar context is a common cause of errors in Perl. If we really mean to count an array, we are often better off using the scalar function, even though it is redundant in scalar context, just to make it clear that we are doing what we intended to do.

```perl
$count = scalar(@array);
```

We can find the index of the last element of the array using the special prefix $#. As indices start at zero, the highest index is one less than the number of elements in the list.

```perl
$highest = $#array; # $highest = scalar(@array)-1
```

This is useful for looping over ranges and iterating over arrays by index rather than by element when the position of an element is also important.

```perl
#!/usr/bin/perl
# byindex.pl
use strict;
use warnings;

my @array = ("First", "Second");
foreach (0..$#array) {
    print "Element number $_ contains $array[$_] \n";
}
```

Executing the code produces the following output:

```
Element number 0 contains First
Element number 1 contains Second
```

Adding Elements to an Array

Extending an array is also simple—we just assign to an element that doesn't exist yet.

```perl
#!/usr/bin/perl
# add1.pl
use strict;
use warnings;

my @array = ('a', 'b', 'c', 'd', 'e', 'f');
print "@array \n";    # produces 'a b 1 2 3 d e f'
$array[6] = "g";
print "@array \n";    # produces 'a b 1 2 3 d e f g'
```

We aren't limited to just adding directly to the end of the array; any missing elements in the array between the current highest index and the new value are automatically added and assigned undefined values. For instance, adding $array[10] = "k"; to the end of the preceding example would cause Perl to create all of the elements with indices 7 to 9 (although only notionally—no actual memory is allocated to hold the elements) as well as assign the value k to the element with index 10.

To assign to the next element, we could find the number of elements and then assign to the array using that number as the array index. We find the number of elements by finding the scalar value of the array.

```perl
$array[scalar(@array)] = "This extends the array by one element";
```

However, it is much simpler to use the push function, which does the same thing without the arithmetic.

```perl
push @array, "This also extends the array by one element";
```

We can feed as many values as we like to push, including more scalars, arrays, lists, and hashes. All of them will be added in turn to the end of the array passed as the first argument. Alternatively we can add elements to the start of the array using unshift.

```perl
unshift @array, "This becomes the zeroth element";
```

With unshift the original indices of the existing elements are increased by the number of new elements added, so the element at index five moves to index six, and so on.

push and unshift are actually just special cases of the splice function. Here are their equivalents using splice:

```perl
# These are equivalent
push @array, @more;
splice @array, @array,0,@more;

# These are equivalent
unshift @array, @more;
splice @array, 0, 0, @more;
```

Passing @array to splice twice might seem a bizarre way to push values onto the end, but the second argument is evaluated as a scalar by splice, so this is actually equivalent to writing scalar(@array). As we saw earlier, this is the number of elements in the array and one more than the current highest index. Even though we do not need it, using scalar explicitly may be a good idea anyway for reasons of legibility.

Resizing and Truncating an Array

Interestingly, assigning to $#array actually changes the size of the array in memory. This allows us to both extend an array without assigning to a higher element and also to truncate an array that is larger than it needs to be, allowing Perl to return memory to the operating system.

```
$#array = 999;  # extend @array to 1000 elements
$#array = 3;    # remove @elements 4+ from array
```

Truncating an array destroys all elements above the new index, so the last example is a more efficient way to do the following:

```
@array = @array[0..3];
```

This assignment also truncates the array, but by reading out values and then reassigning them. Altering the value of $#array avoids the copy.

Removing Elements from an Array

The counterparts of push and unshift are pop and shift, which remove elements from the array at the end and beginning, respectively.

```perl
#!/usr/bin/perl
# remove1.pl
use strict;
use warnings;
my @array = (1, 2, 3, 4, 5, 6);
push @array, '7';   # add '7' to the end
print "@array\n";   # array is now (1, 2, 3, 4, 5, 6, 7)
my $last = pop @array;   # retrieve '7' and return array to six elements
print "$last\n";   # print 7
unshift @array, -1, 0;
print "@array\n";   #  array is now (-1, 0, 1, 2, 3, 4, 5, 6)
shift @array;  # remove the first element of the array
shift @array;  # remove the first element of the array
print "@array\n";   #  array is now again (1, 2, 3, 4, 5, 6)
```

While the push and unshift functions will add any number of new elements to the array, their counterparts are strictly scalar in operation, they only remove one element at a time. If we want to remove several at once, we can use the splice function. In fact, pop and shift are directly equivalent to specific cases of splice.

```
splice(@array, -1);   # equivalent to 'pop @array'

splice(@array, 0, 1); # equivalent to 'shift @array'
```

From this we can deduce that the pop function actually performs an operation very similar to the following example:

```
# read last element and then truncate array by one - that's a 'pop'
$last_element = $array[$#array--];
```

Extending this principle, here is how we can do a multiple pop operation without pop or splice.

```
@last_20_elements = $array[-20..-1];
$#array-=20;
```

The simpler way of writing this is just

```
@last_20_elements = splice(@array, -20);
```

Both undef and delete will remove the value from an array element, replacing it with the undefined value, but neither will actually remove the element itself, and higher elements will not slide down one place. This would seem to be a shame, since delete removes a hash key just fine. Hashes, however, are not ordered and indexed like arrays.

To remove elements from the middle of an array, we also use the splice function, omitting a replacement list.

```
@removed = splice(@array, $start, $quantity);
```

For example, to remove elements 2 to 5 (four elements in total) from an array, we would use

```
@removed = splice(@array, 2, 4);
```

Of course, if we don't want to keep the removed elements, we don't have to assign them to anything.

As a slightly more creative example, here is how we can move elements from the end of the list to the beginning, using a splice and an unshift:

```
unshift @array, splice(@array, -3, 3);
```

Or, in the reverse direction:

```
push @array, splice(@array, 0, 3);
```

Removing All or Many Elements from an Array

To destroy an array completely, we can undefine it using the undef function. This is a different operation to undefining just part of an array as we saw previously.

```
undef @array;    # destroy @array
```

This is equivalent to assigning an empty list to the array:

```
@array = ();
```

It follows that assigning a new list to the array also destroys the existing contents. We can use that to our advantage if we want to remove lines from the start of an array without removing all of them.

```
@array = @array[-100..-1];    # truncate @array to its last one hundred lines
```

This is simply another way of saying

```
splice(@array, 0, $#array-100);
```

Reversing and Sorting Lists and Arrays

Perl supplies two additional functions for generating differently ordered sequences of elements from an array or list. The reverse function simply returns a list in reverse order.

```
# reverse the elements of an array
@array = reverse @array;

# reverse elements of a list
@ymd = reverse((localtime)[3..5]);    # return in year/month/day order
```

This is handy for all kinds of things, especially for reversing the result of an array slice made using a range. reverse allows us to make up for the fact that ranges can only be given in ascending order.

The sort function allows us to perform arbitrary sorts on a list of values. With only a list as its argument, it performs a standard alphabetical sort.

```
@words = ('here', 'are', 'some', 'words');
@alphabetical = sort @words;
print "@words";   # produces 'are here some words'
```

sort is much more versatile than this, however. By supplying a code or subroutine reference, we can sort the list in any way we like. sort automatically defines two special variables, $a and $b, that represent the values being sorted in custom sorting algorithms, so we can specify our own sort like this:

```
@alphabetical = sort {$a cmp $b} @words;
```

The $a and $b notation are unique to sort and originate in early versions of Perl, which is the reason for their slightly incongruous use here. The subroutine itself is defined by the opening and closing curly braces, and its return value is the result of the cmp operation.

The preceding sort subroutine using cmp is actually the behavior of the default sort algorithm that Perl uses when we specify no explicit algorithm of our own. In Perl 5.8, there are actually two underlying implementations, the older quicksort algorithm that was present in all Perl versions up to version 5.8, and the new default mergesort, which is more efficient, on average, for a larger range of cases. In some very special cases—typically where the same values appear many times in the list to be sorted—it might be more efficient to switch to the older algorithm. To do this, use

```
use sort _quicksort;
```

To reinstate the newer mergesort:

```
use sort _mergesort;
```

In the vast majority of cases, the distinction between these two algorithms is close to undetectable and will only be of interest to programmers who are critically concerned with performance and have datasets with many repeated values in them. Note also that this notation is likely to be transient while a better means of selecting the correct implementation is implemented, at which point the use sort pragma may go away again.

In order to be a correct and proper algorithm, the code must return -1 if $a is less than $b (however we define that), 0 if they are equal, and 1 if $a is greater than $b. This is exactly what cmp does for strings, and the numerical comparison operator <=> does for numbers.

We should take care to never alter $a or $b either, since they are aliases for the real values being sorted. At best this can produce an inconsistent result, at worst it may cause the sort to lose values or fail to return a result. The best sorts are the simple ones, such as

```
@ignoring_case = sort {lc($a) cmp lc($b)} @words;
@reversed = sort {$b cmp $a} @words;
@numerically = sort {$a <=> $b} @numbers;
@alphanumeric = sort {int($a) <=> int($b) or $a cmp $b} @mixed;
```

The last example is worth explaining. It first compares $a and $b as integers, forcing them into numeric values with int. If the result of that comparison is nonzero, then at least one of the values has a numeric value. If however the result is zero, which will be the case if $a and $b are both non-numeric strings, the second comparison is used to compare the values as strings. We can chain any number of criteria together like this. Parentheses are not required because or has a very low precedence, lower than any of the comparison operators.

Note that it is possible (though not necessarily sensible) to use a sort inside the comparison function of another sort. This will only work for Perl version 5.6.1 onwards, however. In earlier versions, the inner sort will interfere with the outer ones.

We can also use a named subroutine to sort with. For example, we can create a subroutine named reversed that allows us to invent a sort reversed syntax.

```
sub reversed {$b cmp $a};
@reversed = sort reversed @words;
```

Similarly, here is a subroutine called `numerically` that also handles floating point numbers, presented as a complete example:

```
#!/usr/bin/perl
# numericsort.pl
use strict;
use warnings;

# force interpretation of $a and $b as floating point numbers
sub numerically {$a*1.0 <=> $b*1.0 or $a cmp $b};

my @words = qw(1e2 2e1 3);
print 'Normal  sort:', join ', ', sort @words;
print 'Numeric sort:', join ', ', sort numerically @words;
```

Running this program results in the output

```
3, 2e1, 1e2
1e2, 2e1, 3
```

Note, however, that all these `sort` routines must be defined in the same package as they are used in order to work, since the variables $a and $b are actually package variables automatically defined by the `sort` function. Similarly, we should never declare $a and $b with `my` since these will hide the global variables. Alternatively, we can define a prototype, which provokes `sort` into behaving differently.

```
sub backwards ($$) {$_[0] cmp $_[1]};
```

The prototype requires that two scalars be passed to the `sort` routine. Perl sees this and passes the values to be compared through the special variable @_ instead of via $a and $b. This will allow the `sort` subroutine to live in any package, for example, a fictional `Order` package containing a selection of sort algorithms.

```
use Order;
@reversed = sort Order::reversed @words;
```

We'll see how to create package like this in Chapter 9.

First, Max, Min, Sum, Shuffle, and Reduce

Perl provides several list manipulation routines as part of the `List::Util` package. These perform common functions that are useful but not fundamental enough to be eligible for native support within the Perl interpreter itself.

- `first`: Return the first element of the list for which a condition is true.
- `max`, `min`: Return the highest and lowest numerical value, respectively.
- `maxstr`, `minstr`: Return the highest and lowest alphabetical value, respectively.
- `sum`: Return the sum of the list evaluated numerically.
- `shuffle`: Return the list in a random order.
- `reduce`: Reduce a list to a single value by arbitrary criteria.

The `first` function looks like grep, but instead returns only the first value in the list for which the condition is true.

```
print first { $_ > 10 } (5,15,11,21);    # produces '15'.
```

The max, min, maxstr, min, minstr, and sum functions all return a single value according to their purpose. For the preceding example list, replacing first with min would return 1, while minstr would return 11 (since 11 is alphabetically before 5), max and maxstr both 21, and sum 52.

The reduce function resembles sort, complete with a code block containing the implicit variables $a and $b. Here, however, $a represents the result so far, while $b represents each value of the list in turn. Each time the block is executed, the result is assigned to $a ready for the next iteration, until the list is processed. For example, the following reduce subroutine behaves like sum:

```
print reduce { $a + $b } (5,15,11,21);
```

This is just a convenient Perl-like way to express in a short statement what would otherwise take a loop. The preceding statement has the same effect as the short code snipped that follows using foreach. This example is slightly expanded to use a transient $a and $b in the same manner as the reduce statement:

```
print do {
    my $a=0;
    foreach my $b (5,15,11,21) { $a = $a + $b }
    $a; #value returned to print
}
```

Changing the Starting Index Value

Perl allows us to change the starting index value from 0 to something else by assigning to the special variable $[. This is not a recommended practice, however, not least because the change affects all array accesses, not just the arrays we want to modify. For example, to have our lists and arrays start at index 1 (as Pascal would) instead of 0, we would write

```
$[=1;
@array = (11, 12, 13, 14, 15, 16);
print $array[3];   # produces 13 (not 14)
```

The scope of $[is limited to the file that it is specified in, so subroutines and object methods called in other files will not be affected by the altered value of $[. Even so, messing with this special variable is dangerous and discouraged.

Converting Lists and Arrays into Scalars

Since lists and arrays contain compound values, they have no direct scalar representation—that's the point of a compound value. Other than counting an array by assigning it in scalar context, there are two ways that we can get a scalar representation of a list or array. First, we can create a reference to the values in the list or, in the case of an array, generate a direct reference. Second, we can convert the values into a string format. Depending on our requirements, this string may or may not be capable of being transformed back into the original values again.

Taking References

An array is a defined area of storage for list values, so we can generate or "take" a reference to it with the backslash operator.

```
$arrayref = \@array;
```

This produces a reference through which the original array can be accessed and manipulated. Alternatively, we can make a copy of an array and assign that to a reference by using the array reference constructor (also known as the anonymous array constructor), [. . .].

```
$copyofarray = [@array];
```

Both methods give us a reference to an anonymous array that we can assign to, delete from, and modify. The distinction between the two is important, because one will produce a reference that points to the original array, and so can be used to pass it to subroutines for manipulations on the original data, whereas the other will create a copy that can be modified separately.

Converting Lists into Formatted Strings

The other way to turn an array into a scalar is via the join, sprintf, or pack function.

join is the counterpart to split, which we covered under strings in Chapter 3. It takes a simple string as its separator argument, not a regular expression like split. It creates a string from the contents of the array, optionally separated by the separator string.

```
# join values into comma-separated-value string
$string = join ',', @array;

# concatenate values together
$string = join '', @array;
```

join is not a complicated function, but if we want to join the values in an array together with a space, we can instead use interpolation to equal effect.

```
# equivalent join and interpolating string
$string = join ' ', @array;
$string = "@array";
```

The sprintf and pack functions both take a format string and a list of values, and returns a string created from the values in the list rendered according to the specified format. Both functions are covered in detail in Chapter 3, so here we will just briefly recap. Here's an example of sprintf being used to generate a custom date string from localtime, which returns a list of values:

```
# get current date and time into array
@date = (localtime)[5, 4, 3, 2, 1, 0]; # Y, M, D, h, m, s
$date[0]+=1900; $date[1]++;           # fix year and month

# generate time string using sprintf
$date = sprintf "%4d/%02d/%02d %2d:%02d:%02d", @date;
```

The following example uses pack to construct the string "Perl" from the ordinal value of the characters expressed as numbers:

```
@codes = (80, 101, 114, 108);
$word = pack 'C*', @codes;
print $word;   # produces 'Perl'
```

Of course, there are many more applications of pack and sprintf than this, depending on what we have in mind. Refer to Chapter 3 for more details and examples.

Converting Lists and Arrays into Hashes

By contrast with scalars, converting a list or array into a hash of key-value pairs is extremely simple; just assign the array to the hash.

```
%hash = @array;
```

The values extracted from the array are assigned to the hash in pairs, with even elements (starting at index 0) as the keys and odd elements (starting at index 1) as their values. If the array contains an odd number of elements, then the last key to be assigned to the hash will end up with an undefined value as its value; if we have warnings enabled (as we should), Perl warns against this with

```
Odd number of elements in hash assignment ...
```

To understand what a hash is and why this warning occurs, we need to look at hashes in more detail.

Hashes

Hashes, also known as associative arrays, are Perl's other compound data type. While lists and arrays are ordered and accessed by index, hashes are ordered and indexed by a descriptive key. There is no first or last element in a hash like there is in an array (the hash does have an internal order, but it reflects how Perl stores the contents of the hash for efficient access, and cannot be controlled by the programmer).

Creating Hashes

Hashes are defined in terms of keys and values, or key-value pairs to use an alternative expression. They are stored differently from arrays internally, in order to allow for more rapid lookups by name, so there is no "value" version of a hash in the same way that a list is a "value" version of an array. Instead, lists can be used to define either arrays or hashes, depending on how we use them.

The following list of key-value pairs illustrates the contents of a potential hash, but at this point it is still just a list:

```
('Mouse', 'Jerry', 'Cat', 'Tom', 'Dog', 'Spike')
```

Because hashes always consist of paired values, Perl provides the => operator as an alternative to the comma. This helps differentiate the keys and values and makes it clear to anyone reading our source code that we are actually talking about hash data and not just a list. Hash values can be any scalar, just like array elements, but hash keys can only be strings, so the => operator also allows us to omit the quotes by treating its left-hand side as a constant string. The preceding list would thus be better written as

```
(Mouse => 'Jerry', Cat => 'Tom', Dog => 'Spike')
```

To turn this into a hash, we need to assign it to a hash variable. Hashes, like arrays and scalars, have their own special prefix, in this case the % symbol. So, to create and populate a hash with the preceding list we would write

```
my %hash = (Mouse => 'Jerry', Cat => 'Tom', Dog => 'Spike');
```

When this assignment is made, Perl accepts the keys and values supplied in the list and stores them in an internal format that is optimized for retrieving the values by key. To achieve this, Perl requires that the keys of a hash be string values, which is why when we use => we can omit quotes, even with strict vars in operation. This doesn't stop us from using a variable to store the key name, as Perl will evaluate it in string context, or a subroutine, if we use parentheses. However, it does mean that we must use quotes if we want to use a literal string containing spaces or other characters meaningful to Perl such as literal $, @, or % characters.

```
# using variables to supply hash keys
($mouse, $cat, $dog)=>('Souris', 'Chat', 'Chien');
my %hash = ($mouse => 'Jerry', $cat => 'Tom', $dog => 'Spike');

# using quotes to use nontrivial strings as keys (with and without interpolation)
%hash =('Exg Rate' => 1.656, '%age commission' => 2, "The $mouse" => 'Jerry');
```

■Tip This restriction on keys also means that if we try to use a nonstring value as a key, we will get unexpected results; in particular, if we try to use a reference as a key, it will be converted into a string, which cannot be converted back into the original reference. Therefore, we cannot store pairs of references as keys and values unless we use a symbolic reference as the key (see "References" later in the chapter for more on this subject).

Alternatively, we can use the `qw` operator and separate the keys and values with whitespace. A sensible layout for a hash might be

```
%hash = qw(
  Mouse   Jerry
  Cat     Tom
  Dog     Spike
);
```

Accessing Hashes

Note how this is very similar to creating an array. In fact, the assignment is identical, but the type of the variable means that Perl organizes the data differently in memory. We can now access elements of the hash, which we do by providing a key after the hash in curly brackets. Since the key must be a string, we can again omit the quotes even if use strict is in effect.

```
print "The mouse is ", $hash{Mouse};
```

This is similar in concept to how we index an array, but note that if we are using strict variables (courtesy of use strict), we ought to use quotes now; it is only the => operator that lets us get away with omitting the quotes when strict vars are in effect. Note that just like an array, a hash only stores scalars values. Consequently, the prefix for a hash key access is $, not %, just as it is for array elements.

We can also specify multiple keys to extract multiple values.

```
@catandmouse = @hash{'Cat', 'Mouse'};
```

This will return the list ('Tom', 'Jerry') into the array @catandmouse. Once again, note that the returned value is a list so we use the @ prefix.

We can even specify a range, but this is only useful if the keys are incremental strings, which typically does not happen too often; we would probably be better off using a list if our keys are that predictable. For example, if we had keys with names AA, AB . . . BY, BZ inclusive (and possibly others), then we could use

```
@aabz_values = @hash{'AA'..'BZ'};
```

We cannot access the first or last elements of a hash, since hashes have no concept of first or last. We can, however, return a list of keys with the keys function, which returns a list of the keys in the hash.

```
@keys = keys %hash;
```

The order of the keys returned is random (or rather, it is determined by how Perl chooses to store the hash internally), so we would normally sort the keys into a more helpful order if we wanted to display them. To sort lexically, we can just use sort keys %hash like this:

```
print "The keys are:";
print join(",", sort keys %hash);
```

We can also treat the keys as a list and feed it to a foreach loop.

```
# dump out contents of a hash
print "$_ => $hash{$_} \n" foreach sort keys %hash;
```

Hash Key Order

The order in which hash keys are stored and returned by keys and each is officially random, and should not be relied on to return keys in any expected fashion. Prior to Perl 5.8, however, it was true that repeatedly running a program that created a hash with the same keys would always return the keys in the same order. The order was highly dependent on the platform and build of Perl, so different Perl interpreters might give different results, but the same Perl executable would always create a hash the same way each time. The problem with this was that it opened up Perl applications to potential security issues due to the predictability of the key order. From Perl 5.8 onwards this is no longer true, and hash keys are always returned in a random order.

While this is not usually a problem, it is worth noting that for applications where we just want to know what order we added the keys in, we can make use of the Tie::IxHash module (Ix is short for *IndexedHash*). This module allows us to create hashes that internally record the order of hash keys so that we can retrieve it later. It is slower than a native hash since it is really a tied object pretending to be a hash (see Chapter 19), but other than the key order, it behaves just like a normal hash.

```perl
#!/usr/bin/perl
# orderedhash.pl
use strict;
use warnings;
use Tie::IxHash;

my %hash;
tie %hash, Tie::IxHash;
%hash = (one => 1, two => 2, three => 3);
print join(",",keys(%hash)),"\n"; # *always* produces 'one,two,three'
```

The semantics of this hash is identical to a normal hash, the only difference being that the return value of keys and each is now known and reproducible. The Tie::IxHash module also provides an object-oriented interface that, amongst other things, allows hash key-value pairs to be pushed, popped, shifted, and unshifted like an array, and also if necessary set to an entirely new order.

```perl
my $hashobj=tie %hash, Tie::IxHash;
...
$hashobj->Push(four => 4);
print join("=>",$hashobj->Shift()),"\n"; # produces 'one=>1'
$hashobj->Reorder('four','one','two');
print join(",",keys(%hash)),"\n"; # produces 'four,three,two'
```

Legacy Perl code may happen to depend on the order of keys in a hash—older versions of the Data::Dumper module have this problem, for example. For these cases, we can control the ordering of keys explicitly, so long as we appreciate that this may make a program vulnerable to hostile intents. First, we can set the environment variable PERL_HASH_SEED, which sets the initial seed of the pseudo-random number generator, to a constant value such as zero.

```
PERL_HASH_SEED=0 hashseed.pl
```

To find the seed with which Perl was initialized, use the hash_seed function from the Hash::Util module.

```perl
#!/usr/bin/perl -w
# hashseed.pl
use Hash::Util qw(hash_seed);
print hash_seed();
```

Setting PERL_HASH_SEED to this value will cause any subsequent invocation of Perl to create hashes in a reproducible way. Alternatively, we can build a Perl interpreter from source, specifying -DNO_HASH_SEED during the configuration step. This will permanently disable the random initial seed.

Before overriding the seed, bear in mind that overriding, storing, or passing the seed value elsewhere sidesteps the security purpose of randomizing the hash in the first place. This feature is only provided to for the sake of older Perl applications that require a predictable ordering to hash keys. Perl has always officially had random key orders, so such applications should ultimately be rewritten to remove their dependency on a predictable order.

Manipulating Hashes

We can manipulate hashes in all the same ways that we can manipulate arrays, with the odd twist due to their associative nature. Accessing hashes is a little more interesting than accessing arrays, however. Depending on what we want to do with them, we can use the keys and values functions, sort them in various different ways, or use the each iterator if we want to loop over them.

Adding and Modifying Hash Values

We can manipulate the values in a hash through their keys. For example, to change the value of the key Cat, we could use

```
$hash{'Cat'} = 'Sylvester';
```

If the key already exists in the hash, then its value is overwritten. Otherwise, it is added as a new key.

```
$hash{'Bird'} = 'Tweety';
```

Assigning an array (or another hash) produces a count of the elements, as we have seen in the past, but we can assign multiple keys and values at once by specifying multiple keys and assigning a list, much in the same way that we can extract a list from a hash.

```
@hash{'Cat', 'Mouse'} = ('Sylvester', 'Speedy Gonzales');
```

You can also use arrays to create and expand hashes.

```
@hash{@keys} = @values;
```

We can even use ranges to generate multiple keys at once; for example, the following assignment creates key-value pairs ranging from A=>1 to Z=>26:

```
@lettercodes{'A'..'Z'} = 1..26;
```

Keys and values are added to the hash one by one, in the order that they are supplied, so our previous example of

```
@hash{'Cat', 'Mouse'} = ('Sylvester', 'Speedy Gonzales');
```

is equivalent to

```
$hash{'Cat'} = 'Sylvester';
$hash{'Mouse'} = 'Speedy Gonzales';
```

This can be an important point to keep in mind, since it allows us to overwrite the values associated with hash keys, both deliberately and accidentally. For example, this code snippet defines a default set of keys and values and then selectively overrides them with a second set of keys and values, held in a second input hash. Any key in the second hash with the same name as one in the first overwrites the key in the resulting hash. Any keys not defined in the second hash keep their default values.

```perl
#!/usr/bin/perl
# hash1.pl
use strict;
use warnings;

# define a default set of hash keys and values
my %default_animals = (Cat => 'Tom', Mouse => 'Jerry');

# get another set of keys and values
my %input_animals = (Cat => 'Ginger', Mouse => 'Jerry');

# providing keys and values from second hash after those
# in default hash overwrites them in the result
my %animals = (%default_animals, %input_animals);
print "$animals{Cat}\n"; # prints 'Ginger'
```

Removing Hash Keys and Values

Removing elements from a hash is easier, but less flexible, than removing them from a list. Lists are ordered, so we can play a lot of games with them using the splice function amongst other things. Hashes do not have an order (or at least, not one that is meaningful to us), so we are limited to using undef and delete to remove individual elements.

The undef function removes the value of a hash key, but leaves the key intact in the hash.

```perl
undef $hash{'Bird'};   # 'Bird' still exists as a key
```

The delete function removes the key and value entirely from the hash.

```perl
delete $hash{'Bird'};   # 'Bird' removed
```

This distinction can be important, particularly because there is no way to tell the difference between a hash key that doesn't exist and a hash key that happens to have an undefined value as its value simply by looking at the result of accessing it.

```perl
print $hash{'Bird'};   # produces 'Use of uninitialized value in print ...'
```

It is for this reason that Perl provides two functions for testing hash keys, defined and exists.

Reversing Hashes

One special trick that is worth mentioning while we are on the subject of hashes is how to reverse the keys and values, so that the values become the keys and vice versa. This at first might seem to be a difficult, or at least a nontrivial task involving code similar to the following:

```perl
#!/usr/bin/perl
# reverse.pl
use strict;
use warnings;

my %hash = ('Key1' => 'Value1', 'Key2' => 'Value2');
print "$hash{Key1}\n";    # print 'Value1'
foreach (keys %hash) {
    # invert key-value pair
    $hash{$hash{$_}} = $_;

    # remove original key
    delete $hash{$_};
}
print "$hash{Value1}\n";    # print 'Key1'
```

Reversing, or *transposing*, a hash offers plenty of problems. If the values are references, turning them into keys will convert them into strings, which cannot be converted back into references. Also, if two keys have the same value, we end up with only one of them making it into the reversed hash, since we cannot have two identical keys.

We can't fix the problem with duplicate keys, since hashes do not allow them, but we can reverse the keys and values much more simply than the preceding code, and without endangering identical key-value pairs, by converting the hash into a list, reversing the list, and then assigning it back to the hash again.

```
# this does the same as the previous example!
%hash = reverse %hash;
```

We have to look closely to see the list in this example; it is returned by the %hash because reverse is a function that gives its argument(s) a list context. There is no such thing as hash context in Perl, for the same reason that there is no such thing as a hash value, as we noted at the start of this discussion. The reverse then reverses the list, which also happens to reverse the orientation of the keys and values, and then the reversed list is assigned back to the hash.

If more than one key has the same value, then this trick will preserve the first one to be found. Since that's entirely random (because we cannot sort the list), we cannot determine which key will be preserved as a value in the new hash. If we want to handle that, we will have to either process the hash the slow way, find a way to eliminate duplicates first, or use a different storage strategy. For simple hashes without duplicates, though, this is a very simple way to achieve the desired end.

Accessing and Iterating over Hashes

The simplest, or at least the most common, way of iterating across a hash is to use the keys function to return a list of the keys. This list is actually a copy of the hash keys, so we cannot alter the key names through this list. However, it provides a very simple way to iterate across a hash.

```
#!/usr/bin/perl
# iterate.pl
use strict;
use warnings;

my %hash = ('Key1' => 'Value1', 'Key2' => 'Value2');
# dump of hash
print "$_ => $hash{$_} \n" foreach keys %hash;
```

If we want a list for output, we probably want to sort it too.

```
# sorted dump of hash
print "$_ => $hash{$_} \n" foreach sort keys %hash;
```

We can also access the values directly through the value function.

```
@values = values %hash;
```

This provides a convenient way to process a hash when we do not care about the keys, with the caveat that we cannot easily find the keys if we need them, since hashes are one way, there is no "look up key by value" syntax.

```
# print list of sorted values
foreach (sort values %hash) {
    print "Value: $_ \n";
}
```

This returns a copy of the values in the hash, so we cannot alter the original values this way. If we want to derive a list of values that we can alter to affect the original hash, we can do so with a loop like this:

```
# increment all hash values by one
foreach (@hash{keys %hash}) {
    $_++;
}
```

This example makes use of *aliasing*, where the default argument variable $_ becomes a direct alias for, rather than a copy of, the value that it refers to.

The catch with foreach is that it pulls all of the keys (or values) out of the hash at one time, and then works through them. This is inefficient in terms of memory usage, especially if the hash is large. An alternative approach is offered by the each function, which returns the next key-value pair each time it is used. It is ideal for use in while loops.

```
while (($key, $value) = each %hash) {
print "$key => $value \n";
    $hash{$key}++;
}
```

The order of the key-value pairs produced by each is the same as that produced by keys and values. It works by moving an internal iterator through the hash, so that each subsequent call to each returns the next key-value pair. We cannot access the iterator directly, however. The index is reset after we reach the last key, or if we use keys to return the whole list.

Sorting and Indexing

If we want to generate an ordered list of hash keys and values, we can do so with the sort function. A simple alphabetical list of keys can be produced with sort keys %hash as we saw earlier. However, sort is a versatile function and we can play all sorts of tricks with it. One not so clever trick is simply to sort the values directly, as we saw earlier.

```
# print list of sorted values
foreach (sort values %hash) {
    print "Got $_ \n";
}
```

The catch with this is that we can't easily get back to the keys if we want to. The solution to this problem is to give sort a subroutine that accesses the values via the keys.

```
# sort a hash by values
foreach (sort { $hash{$a} cmp $hash{$b} } keys %hash) {
    print "$hash{$_} <= $_ \n";
}
```

This is important if we want to change the values in the hash, since values just returns a copy of the hash values, which we cannot assign to.

Creative uses of sort give us other possibilities too. For instance, we can create a hash with an index by replacing the values with references to two-element arrays or hashes containing an index value and the original value. This is an example of a complex data structure, which we cover later, so we'll just give a simple example of defining and then sorting such a hash.

```
#!/usr/bin/perl
# indexhash.pl
use warnings;
use strict;
# create a hash with integrated index
my %hash = (
    Mouse => { Index => 0, Value => 'Jerry'},
    Cat   => { Index => 1, Value => 'Tom'},
    Dog   => { Index => 2, Value => 'Spike'}
);
```

```
# sort a hash by integrated index
foreach (sort { $hash{$a} {'Index'} cmp $hash{$b}{'Index'} } keys %hash) {
    print "$hash{$_} {'Value'} <= $_ \n";
}
```

The only catch with this is that we will need to keep track of the index numbers ourselves, since unlike an array we don't get it done for us automatically. However, see tie and the Tie::Hash module in Chapter 19 for another way to create an indexed hash that solves some of these problems.

Named Arguments

Perl does not offer an official mechanism for passing named arguments to subroutines, but hashes allow us to do exactly this if we write our subroutines to use them.

```
sub animate {
    my %animals = @_;
    # rest of subroutine...
}

animate(Cat => 'Tom', Mouse => 'Jerry');
```

Some existing modules in the Perl library allow this and also adapt between ordinary or named arguments by prefixing the key names with a minus sign. Here is a quick example of how we can do it ourselves:

```
#!/usr/bin/perl
# arguments.pl
use warnings;
use strict;

# list form takes mouse, cat, dog as arguments, fixed order.
animate('Jerry', 'Tom', 'Spike');

# hash form takes animals in any order using '-' prefix to identify type,
# also allows other animal types
animate(-Cat => 'Sylvester', -Bird => 'Tweety', -Mouse => 'Speedy Gonzales');

# and the subroutine...
sub animate {
    my %animals;

    # check first element of @_ for leading minus...
    if ($_[0]!~/^-/) {
        # it's a regular argument list, use fixed order
        @animals{'-Mouse', '-Cat', '-Dog'} = @_;
    } else {
        # it's named argument list, just assign it.
        %animals = @_;
    }
    # rest of subroutine...
    foreach (keys %animals) {
        print "$_ => $animals{$_} \n";
    }
}
```

See Chapter 7 for more on this theme, as well as some improved examples that check arguments more closely.

Converting Hashes into Scalars

Evaluating a hash in scalar context returns 0 (false) if the hash is empty. If it contains data, we get a string containing a numeric ratio of the form N/M that describes in approximate terms how efficiently Perl has been able to store the keys and values in the hash. Loosely speaking, the numbers are a ratio and can be read as a fraction, the higher the first relative to the second, the more efficient the storage of the hash.

```perl
#!/usr/bin/perl
# convert1.pl
use warnings;
use strict;

my %hash = (one => 1, two => 2, three => 3, four => 4, five => 5);

# check the hash has data
if (%hash) {
    # find out how well the hash is being stored
    print scalar(%hash);   # produces '4/8'
}
```

Counting Hashes

While this is interesting if we are concerned with how well Perl is storing our hash data, it is unlikely to be of much use otherwise. We might have expected to get a count of the elements in the hash, or possibly the keys, but we can't count a hash in the same way that we can an array, simply by referring to it in scalar context. To count a hash we can use either keys or values and evaluate the result in scalar context. For example:

```perl
# count the keys of a hash
$elements = scalar(keys %hash);
```

If we really wanted to know the number of elements we would only need to multiply this result by 2.

Taking References

For a more useful scalar conversion, we can create a reference (also called taking a reference) to the hash with the backslash operator.

```perl
$hashref = \%hash;
```

Dereferencing a hash reference is very much like dereferencing an array reference, only with a key instead of an index.

```perl
$dog = $hash -> {'Dog'};
```

Alternatively, we can dereference the entire hash with a % prefix.

```perl
%hash == %$hashreference;
```

We can also create a hash reference with the {...} constructor, which creates a brand new anonymous hash with the same contents as the old one. This is different from, and produces a different result to, the array reference constructor, [...], because the reference points to an anonymous hash that is therefore organized and stored like one.

```perl
$hashref = {Mouse => 'Jerry', Cat => 'Tom', Dog => 'Spike'};
```

Since the contents of the constructor are just a list, we can also create a hash reference to an anonymous hash with the contents of an array, and vice versa.

```
$hashref = {@array};
$arrayref = [%hash];
```

Both constructors take lists as their arguments, but organize them into different kinds of anonymous compound value.

Converting Hashes into Arrays

Converting a hash into a list or array is very simple; we just assign it.

```
@array = %hash;
```

This retrieves all the keys and values from the hash in pairs, the order of which is determined by the internal structure of the hash. Alternatively, we can extract the hash as two lists, one of keys, and one of values.

```
@keys = keys %hash;
@values = values %hash;
```

This gives us two arrays with corresponding indices, so we can look up the value by the index of the key (and vice versa, something we cannot do with a hash).

A final option that is sometimes worth considering is turning the hash into an array of arrays or array of hashes, in order to create an index but preserve the key-value pairs in a single variable. Here is one way to do that:

```
my @array;
foreach (keys %hash) {
    push @array, { $_ => $hash{$_} };
}
```

This creates an array of hashes, each hash with precisely one key-value pair in it. Of course there are other, and arguably better, ways to create indexed hashes, one of which we covered earlier in this section. Again, it's a matter of preference, depending on whether we want to be able to look up the index and value by key, or the key and value by index.

Pseudohashes

A pseudohash is, essentially, an array that is pretending to be a hash. The object of the exercise is to have the flexibility of key-based access with the speed of an indexed array, while at the same time restricting the hash to only a specified set of keys. Deprecated in Perl 5.8, and scheduled to be removed entirely in Perl 5.10, pseudohashes have now been replaced by restricted hashes. However, old code may still be using pseudohashes, and so it is worth taking a quick look at what they are and how they work.

Properly speaking, pseudohashes should be called pseudohash *references*, since the feature only works through a reference. To create a pseudohash, we create a reference to an array whose first element is a hash describing the mapping of keys to array indices. Since the first element is taken up by the hash, the actual values start at index one. Here is a simple example:

```
my $pseudo=[{ one => 1, two => 2, three => 3}, 'first','second','third'];
```

The value 'first' can now be accessed by index or by key.

```
print $pseudo->{one}    # produces 'first'
print $pseudo->[1];     # also produces 'first'
```

Attempting to access or set a value in the hash with a key that is not in the index hash will cause an error, No such pseudo-hash field "key" at ....

It can be irritating and error-prone to get the right values associated with the right keys, so instead we can use the fields pragmatic module, which gives us more options in how we set up the pseudohash. It has two main routines: phash and new. Note that in Perl 5.10 onwards only new will be supported.

For example, to set up the same pseudohash as earlier, we can instead write

```
use fields;
my $pseudo_from_list=fields::phash(one=>'first',
                              two=>'second', three=>'third');
my $pseudo_from_2arefs=fields::phash([qw(one two three)],[qw(first second third)]);
my $no_values_pseudo=fields::phash(qw[one two thee]);
```

The semantics of pseudohashes are almost identical to ordinary hashes; we can use keys, values, each, and delete in the same way as usual.

```
my @keys=keys %$pseudo;
my @values=values %$pseudo;
while (my ($key,$value)=each %$pseudo) {
    print "$key => '$value'\n";
}
```

Deleting a pseudohash key is slightly more complex. Deleting the key directly only frees up the value; we have to delete the key in the embedded hash as well to remove it from the hash.

```
delete $pseudo->{three}; # free value
delete $pseudo->[0]{three}; # remove key
```

If we have code that makes extensive use of pseudohashes and we want to be able to continue to use it without a rewrite after pseudohashes are removed from the language, there is another option. The Class::PseudoHash module from CPAN reimplements the semantics of pseudohashes so that code that needs them will continue to run (albeit not as fast, since the native support has been removed).

```
# for Perl 5.10 +
use fields;
use Class::PseudoHash;

my $pseudo=fields::phash(key => 'value'); # still works
```

We can also create a pseudohash with new. This will create a new pseudohash (or from Perl 5.10 onwards, a restricted hash, described in the next section) with the fields specified to the fields pragma in the specified package.

```
{
    package My::Package;
    use fields qw(one two three _secret_four);
}

my $pseudo=fields::new(My::Package);
$pseudo={one => 'first', two => 'second', three => 'third'};
```

This creates a regular pseudohash, as described previously, but blessed into the My::Package class. However, a more natural way to access this feature is via a typed scalar, which we will touch on in a moment as it works just as well with restricted hashes.

Restricted Hashes

Restricted hashes are the replacement for pseudohashes, and the tools to manipulate them are provided by the Hash::Util module. From Perl 5.10 onwards, the fields pragma will also create restricted hashes rather than pseudohashes, but with the same usage semantics (apart from delete, which will now work as usual). The feature exists in Perl 5.8 and up, and the equivalent of a pseudo-hash can be created as a restricted hash using Hash::Util with the lock_keys function.

```perl
#!/usr/bin/perl
# restrictedhash.pl
use strict;
use warnings;
use Hash::Util qw(lock_keys);

%hash1=(one =>'first', two=>'second', three=>'third');
lock_keys(%hash1);              # lock hash to pre-existing keys
```

Whereas a pseudohash provided us with a hash with fixed keys and changeable values, restricted hashes also let us lock values, making them read-only, and we can choose to lock and unlock individual values or the whole hash at will. The functions to do this are unlock_keys, lock_value, and unlock_value. Adding these to the use statement and continuing the preceding example, we can lock and unlock individual keys and values with

```perl
unlock_keys(%hash1);           # unlock all keys

my %hash2;
lock_keys(%hash2,'one',two','six'); # lock empty hash with the specified keys

lock_value(%hash2,'one','two');   # lock the values of keys 'one' and 'two'
unlock_value(%hash2,'two');       # unlock the value of key 'two'
```

Notice that we can lock keys and values that do not yet exist. Here, locking the keys of an empty hash (%hash2 in this example) to a list supplied to lock_keys means that only those keys can subsequently be created, but as yet, they do not exist in the hash. Locking the value of a nonexistent key causes the key to be created and given a value of undef.

Attempting to delete a key from a locked hash will fail to change the hash, but will not generate an error and will return the value (assuming the key is present) as usual. Attempting to add a new key or change a locked value will provoke an error, of course. Attempting to lock a nonempty hash with a list of keys that does not include all the keys currently in the hash will also cause an error, but if we want to lock the hash with additional keys, we can just add them to the list at the time the hash is locked.

```perl
my %hash3=(oldkey1=>1, oldkey2=>2);
lock_keys(%hash,keys(%hash3),'newkey1','newkey2');
```

There is currently no function to lock more than one value at a time, but if we just want to lock the entire hash, we can use the lock_hash function. Similarly, to unlock all values and keys, we can use unlock_hash.

```perl
lock_hash(%hash3);             # lock hash keys and make all values read-only
unlock_hash(%hash3);           # turn back into a regular unrestricted hash
```

Note that it is not currently possible to lock values in a hash whose keys are not locked; Hash::Util deems this to be of little point. Interestingly, using lock_hash followed by unlock_keys leaves the hash mutable but all its values read-only, proving that it is indeed possible.

To do the same thing directly in Perl 5.8 onwards we could use Internals::SvREADONLY, which does all the hard lifting for Hash::Util.

```perl
Internals::SvReadOnly($hash3->{oldkey1} => 1); # read-only value
Internals::SvReadOnly($hash3->{oldkey1} => 0); # writable again
```

Intriguing though this is, it is also a little arcane. Another way to create an immutable scalar in any version of Perl is with tie, as we will see in Chapter 19.

Compile-Time Checking of Restricted Hashes

Perl has a special syntax for lexically declared scalar variables (that is, scalars declared with my or our) that allows them to be associated with a specific package. Perl does not have a strong sense of type on the basis that it is largely redundant, so giving a type to a lexical scalar merely acts to coax some extra features out of the Perl interpreter. Compile-time checking of restricted hashes and pseudohashes is one of those features (the other is package attributes, covered in Chapter 10).

Giving a type to a lexical scalar associated with a pseudohash or restricted hash allows the interpreter to check the validity of accesses to the hash with literal keys at compile time. In the case of a pseudohash, any hash-like access of the variable can then be silently converted into simple array accesses of the underlying array on which the pseudohash is based, with a corresponding improvement in run-time performance.

For this to work, we must make use of the package-based pseudohash via the fields::new function, since typing is a package-based syntax. Here is a simple one-line example:

```
# declare a typed scalar to cause compile-time optimization
my My::Package $pseudo_converts_to_array=fields::new(My::Package);
```

This idiom is not usually seen in application-level code, but it is quite common in object classes, including several provided by the standard Perl library. Since we won't cover objects in detail for a while, we will restrict ourselves to a simple example to illustrate the general point:

```
#!/usr/bin/perl
# typedscalar.pl
use strict;
use warnings;

{
    package My::Package;

    use fields qw(one two three);

    sub new {
        return fields::new({
            one => 1, two =>2, three => 3
        });
    }
}

print "This happens first?\n";
my My::Package $obj=new My::Package;
#my $obj=new My::Package;

$obj->{one}=5;  # Ok, exists
$obj->{four}=4; # Bad key
```

The creation of a new object happens in the call to new My::Package. When this is assigned to a typed scalar, we get a syntax error at the last line of the file during compilation. If we comment out this line and enable the untyped scalar assignment below it, the error is only detected at run time; we see "This happens first?" appear, and only then does Perl tell us we've tried to use an invalid key.

The only thing this particular object class does is generate restricted hashes with the keys one, two, and three, so if we need to create many restricted hashes with the same keys, this can be a good way to implement that hash. Unfortunately, typing in Perl really is no more than an invitation to the interpreter to do some optimization if possible. It won't cause Perl to complain if we assign something different to the scalar, even objects of a different class, but it will catch attempts to use literal invalid keys at compile time.

Typed scalars and restricted hashes are also used under the covers to implement other parts of Perl's syntax. A good example is the implementation of package-based attributes, in collusion with the attributes and Attribute::Handlers modules. We will take a look at implementing attributes in Chapter 10.

References

Rather than referring to a variable directly, Perl lets us refer to it by a reference—a pointer to the real value stored somewhere else. There are two kinds of references in Perl: hard references, which are immutable values in the style of C++ references, and symbolic references, which are simply strings containing the name of a variable or subroutine, minus the leading punctuation.

Of the two, hard references are by far the most common, and are the basis for complex data structures like arrays of arrays. Internally they are memory pointers, and we can access the value that they point to by following or *dereferencing* the reference. Perl provides a flexible syntax for doing this, involving the backslash and arrow operators.

Conversely, symbolic references are actually banned by use strict (more accurately, use strict refs) because they are a common source of bugs due to their malleable nature and resistance to compile-time error checking—by changing the contents of the string we change the thing that it points to. It is also possible to accidentally create a symbolic reference when we didn't mean to, especially if we fail to turn on warnings as well. Having made these points, symbolic references can be useful in the right places, so long as we are careful.

Hard References

Hard references, usually just called references, are not really a data type but just a kind of scalar value. They differ from integer, floating-point, or string values because they are pointers to other values, and are not malleable—unlike C, we cannot perform operations to change the value of a reference to make it point to something else. We can assign a new reference to a scalar variable, but that is all. Worldly programmers generally consider this a good thing.

Creating References

To create a reference for an existing value or variable, we use the backslash operator. This will convert any value or data type, be it scalar, array, hash, subroutine, and so forth, and create a scalar reference that points to it.

```
# references to values
$numberref = \42;
$messageref = \"Don't Drink The Wine!";
@listofrefs = \(1, 4, 9, 16, 25);

# references to variables
$scalarref = \$number;
$arrayref = \@array;
$hashref = \%hash;
$globref = \*typeglob;    # typeglobs are introduced later in the chapter

# reference to anonymous subroutine
$subref = \sub { return "This is an anonymous subroutine" };

# reference to named subroutine
$namedsubref = \&mysubroutine;
```

If we pass a list to the backslash operator, it returns a second list of references, each one pointing to an element of the original list.

```
@reflist = \(1, 2, 3);
```

This is identical to, but shorter than

```
@reflist = (\1, \2, \3);
```

We can declare a reference and initialize it to point to an empty list or hash with [ ] and { }.

```
my $arrayref=[]; # reference to empty array
my $hashref={};  # reference to empty hash
```

Note that both references are "true" because they point to something real, albeit empty.

References have implicit knowledge of the type of thing that they are pointing to, so an array reference is always an array reference, and we can demonstrate this by attempting to print a reference. For example, this is what we might get if we attempted to print $scalarref:

```
SCALAR(0x8141f78)
```

A common mistake in Perl is to try to use the backslash operator to create a reference to an existing list, but as we showed previously, this is not what backslash does. In order to create an array reference from a list, we must first place the list into an array. This causes Perl to allocate an array structure for the values, which we can then create a reference for—the original list is not stored as an array, so it cannot be referenced. This is essentially what the [. . .] construct does.

The [. . .] and { . . . } constructors also create a reference to an array or hash. These differ from the backslash operator in that they create a copy of their contents and return a reference to it, not a reference to the original.

```
$samearrayref = \@array;
$copyarrayref = [@array];
$samehashref = \%hash;
$copyhashref = {%hash};
```

The [. .] and { . . } constructors are not strictly operators and have the precedence of terms (like variable names, subroutines, and so on) which is the highest precedence of all. The contents of the constructors are always evaluated before they are used in other expressions.

The hash reference constructor constructs a hash, which requires key-value pairs, and so spots things like odd numbers of elements. We can't create hash references with the backslash operator either—we have to pass it a hash variable. But that's why we have the { . . . } constructor.

Confusing constructors with lists is a very common Perl error, especially as Perl is quite happy for us to do the following:

```
# this does not do what it might appear to
@array = [1, 2, 3, 4];
```

What this probably meant to do was assign @array a list of four elements. What it actually does is assign @array one element containing a reference to an anonymous array of four elements, i.e., it is actually the same as

```
@inner_array = (1, 2, 3, 4);
@array = \@inner_array;
```

When arrays and hashes do not appear to contain the values that they should, this is one of the first things to check. The error Reference found where even-sized list expected . . . is a clue that this may be happening during a hash definition, but for arrays we are on our own.

Perl sometimes creates references automatically, in order to satisfy assignments to complex data structures. This saves what would otherwise be a lot of monotonous construction work on our part. For instance, the following statements create several hash references and automatically chain them together to form a composite structure, a process known immemorially as *autovivification*:

```perl
my %hash;
$hash{'name'}{'address'}{'street'}{'number'} = 88;
```

Comparing References

References to the same underlying value are equal, but only if they point to the same actual value (literally, the same location in memory):

```perl
#!/usr/bin/perl
# ref1.pl
use warnings;
use strict;

my $text = "This is a value";

my $ref1 = \$text;
my $ref2 = \$text;

print $ref1 == $ref2    # produces '1'

$$ref1 = 'New value';
print $$ref2;    # produces 'New value'
```

Pointing to two values that happen to be equal will not result in equal references:

```perl
#!/usr/bin/perl
# ref2.pl
use warnings;
use strict;

my $text1 = "This is a value";
my $text2 = "This is a value";

my $ref1 = \$text1;
my $ref2 = \$text2;

print $ref1 == $ref2;    # produces ''

$$ref1 = 'New value';
print $$ref2;    # produces 'New value'
```

Dereferencing

A reference is only useful if we can access the underlying value, a process called dereferencing. We can extract the value and assign it to a variable, or we can simply work through the reference, a little like keyhole surgery.

Dereferencing is dependent on the type of the reference; we can only get a scalar from a scalar reference, and we can only get an array from an array reference. However, since all references, regardless of type, are scalars, Perl cannot perform compile-time syntax checks to ascertain whether a reference is being dereferenced with the correct type. This compels us to take a little care when using references, since incorrectly using a reference may only show up as a run-time error.

Dereferencing any reference can be done by prefixing the reference with the symbol appropriate for the underlying data type; the previous comparison example includes four scalar dereferences using $$. As a more complete example, here is how we can copy out the value pointed to by a scalar, array, hash, and typeglob reference into a new variable:

```
$value = $$ref;
@array = @$arrayref;
%hash = %$hashref;
*glob = *$globref;
```

Similarly, we can call a subroutine through a code reference like this (we will come back to code references in Chapter 7):

```
&$coderef(@args);
```

We cannot dereference with impunity—attempting to access an array or hash reference as a scalar produces a syntax error.

```
Not a SCALAR reference ...
```

Similarly, while a statement like @a=21 will create an array with one element (with the value 21), and might conceivably be what we intended, Perl is skeptical that we would ever want to create such an array by dereferencing, and so produces a run-time error if we say

```
@a = @$scalarref;
```

If we want to use the values held by a hash reference in the manner of an array, we have to re-create the reference (or generate a new one), because hashes are not organized in the same way as arrays. So the values must be extracted and stored in the other format.

```
$ref = {a=>1, b=>2, c=>3};
print %$ref;   # produces a1b2c3 (dependent on internal ordering of hash)
print @$ref;   # run-time error 'Not an ARRAY reference ...'

$ref = [ %$ref ];   # convert '$ref' from hash to array reference

print %$ref;   # run-time error 'Can't coerce array into hash ...'
print @$ref;   # produces a1b2c3 (dependent on order of hash)
```

Working with References

Instead of just pulling out the value from a reference and assigning it to something else, we can work directly through the reference. For example, to access a scalar value in an array or hash value, we would use

```
$element_2 = $$arrayref[1];
$hashvalue = $$hashref{'key_name'};
```

If we mentally replace the $arrayref and $hashref with array and hash, we can see that these are really just conventional array and hash accesses, just being done through a reference (the key-hole). Similarly, we can get an array slice via a reference.

```
@slice = @$arrayref[6..9];
```

This works well when we are accessing a scalar containing an array reference, but it can cause problems if we try to access an array containing array references. For example, consider the following nested array:

```
@array = (1, [2, 3, 4], 5);
```

This array contains an array reference as its second element (note that if we had not used an array reference constructor and just used parentheses, we would have ended up with a plain old five-element array). We might try to access that array with

```
@subarray = @$array[1];
```

Unfortunately this gives us an array with an array reference as its only element, not the three elements 2, 3, 4. This is because prefixes bind more closely than indices, and so the @ is applied before the [1]. The preceding is therefore actually equivalent to

```
@subarray = ($$array[1]);
```

This explains why we get a single array reference as the only element of @subarray. In order to get the index to happen first, we need to use curly braces to apply the dereferencing operation to the array element instead of to the array.

```
@subarray = @{$array[1]};
```

This more explicit dereferencing syntax also has its scalar, hash, code, and typeglob counterparts, for example:

```
%subhash = %{$hashofhashes{$hashkey}};
```

An alternative technique for dereferencing is the arrow or dereference operator. This is often more legible than the double prefix syntax.

```
$element_2 = $arrayref->[1];
$hashvalue = $hashref -> {'key_name'};
```

Multidimensional arrays and hashes can omit the arrow, since Perl is smart enough to translate adjacent indices or hash keys into an implicit dereference. The following are therefore equivalent, but the first is easier to read:

```
$value = $threedeepreference[9]{'four'}[1];
$value = $threedeepreference[9] -> {'four'} -> [1];
```

This only applies to the second and subsequent indices or hash keys, however. If we are accessing a reference, we still need to use the first arrow so Perl knows that we are going via a reference and not accessing an element or hash value directly.

Passing References to Subroutines

One of the major advantages of hard references is that they allow us to package up a compound value like an array or hash into a scalar. This allows us to create complex data structures, and it also allows us to pass arrays and hashes into subroutines, keeping them intact.

As we observed earlier, if we combine lists directly, then they merge together. This is handy if we want to create a combined list, but problematic if we want to pass, say, a couple of arrays to a subroutine, since inside the subroutine we will be unable to tell one from the other.

```
mysub (@array1, @array2);

sub mysub {
    my @combinedarray = @_;

    foreach (@combinedarray) {
        ...
    }
}
```

References solve this problem by replacing the arrays with array references.

```
mysub (\@array1, \@array2);

sub mysub {
    my ($arrayref1, $arrayref2) = @_;
```

```
foreach (@$arrayref1) {
    ...
}
foreach (@$arrayref2) {
    ...
}
}
```

Not only does this solve the problem, but it is also more efficient if the arrays happen to be large ones, because we pass two scalars, and not an indefinite number of values.

However, see the section "Typeglobs" later in this chapter for an alternative, and also subroutine prototypes in Chapter 7 for two alternative approaches to passing arrays and hashes without using references. Each has its merits and drawbacks.

Finding the Type of a Reference

Perl cannot perform syntax checks to ensure that references are being dereferenced with the correct prefix because the content of a scalar variable is defined at run time, and can change during the lifetime of a program. Consequently, it is occasionally useful to be able to check the type of a reference before we access it. Fortunately, we can find out the type of a reference with the ref function. This is analogous to a "type of" function, but only for references. Since nonreferences are implicitly typed by their prefix, this is all we need.

ref takes a single reference as an argument, or uses $_ if no argument is supplied. It returns a string containing the reference type, or undef if the argument is not a reference.

```
$ref = \[1, 2, 3];
print "The reference type of $ref is '", ref($ref),"' \n";
```

When executed, these lines produce a message of the form

```
The reference type of ARRAY(0x8250290) is 'ARRAY'
```

The string representation of a reference is the reference type followed by the memory address it points to. While useful for debugging, we cannot convert this back into a reference again, so it is rarely useful otherwise. Conversely, ref returns a string description of the reference type, which is more useful as well as being easier to use.

The values returned for references are strings containing the name of the reference. These are the same names produced when we print a reference, for example, SCALAR, and include those listed in Table 5-1.

Table 5-1. *Return Values of ref*

Value	Meaning
SCALAR	A scalar reference
ARRAY	An array reference
HASH	A hash reference
CODE	A reference to an anonymous subroutine
GLOB	A reference to a typeglob
IO (or IO::Handle)	A filehandle reference
REF	A reference to another reference
LVALUE	A reference to an assignable value that isn't a SCALAR, ARRAY, or HASH (e.g., the return value from substr)

In general, the first three reference types on this list are by far the most commonly encountered; see "Complex Data Structures" later in the chapter for an example that uses ref to recursively explore an arbitrarily complex structure of scalars, arrays, and hashes.

Finding the Type of a Blessed Reference

Blessed references are a very specific and important subclass of hard references, being the primary mechanism by which Perl implements objects and object-oriented programming. They are created by using the bless function on a hard reference to assign a package name to it, converting it from an ordinary reference into an object of the class defined by the package.

The ref function will return the name of the blessed class when called on an object, rather than the type of the underlying reference. In general, this is what we want, because the point of objects is that we treat them as opaque values that hide the details of their implementation from us. In the rare cases that we do want to know the underlying reference type (perhaps because we want to dump out the object's state or save it to a file on disk), we can use the reftype function, which can be found in both the Scalar::Util and attributes modules (attributes is automatically included if we use an attribute, Scalar::Util is the more natural choice if we aren't using attributes—see Chapters 7 and 10 for information on what they do).

```perl
#!/usr/bin/perl
# reftype.pl
use warnings;
use strict;

use Scalar::Util qw(reftype);

die "Usage: $0 <object module> ...\n" unless @ARGV;

foreach (@ARGV) {
    my $filename = $_;
    $filename =~ s|::|/|g;
    require "$filename.pm";
    my $obj = new $_;

    print "Object class ", ref($obj), " uses underlying data type ", reftype($obj),
    "\n";
}
```

We can use this script like this:

```
> perl reftype.pl CGI
```

```
Object class CGI uses underlying data type HASH
```

Reference Counting, Garbage Collection, and Weak References

Perl keeps a count of how many places a reference is stored, and will delete the item being referenced only when no more references to that item exist. This process is called *garbage collection*, and it is fundamental to Perl's memory management. Unfortunately, if two data structures contain references to each other, then neither of the references will ever reach a count of zero and the data structures will become immortal, at least until the program terminates.

```perl
my $node1={next => undef, last => undef, value => "First item" };
my $node2={next => undef, last => $node1, value => "Next Item"});
$node1{next}=$node2; # create a reference loop
$node1=undef; $node2=undef; # memory leak!
```

Here $node1 references a hash that at the end of this code contains a reference to the hash pointed to by $node2. At the same time, $node2 contains a reference to the hash pointed to by $node1. The result is that even if we undefine both variables, the hashes will continue to exist in memory. Since we can no longer access them, the memory they are using cannot be reclaimed—a memory leak.

In general, the solution to this problem is to avoid creating loops between referenced data structures, but this is not always a practical solution. In the case of structures like doubly-linked lists (of which the preceding code is a very compressed example), a loop might even be unavoidable. We could use a symbolic reference in place of the hard reference in one or both directions, since symbolic references aren't included in the reference count, but symbolic references are much slower and require that we turn off strict references.

Fortunately, there is a better solution. To help prevent memory leaks in cases like this, we can weaken a hard reference using the weaken routine provided by the Scalar::Util package. Similarly, we can test a reference to see whether it is weak or not with the isweak routine.

```perl
#!/usr/bin/perl -w
# weakreference.pl
use Scalar::Util qw(weaken isweak);

my $node1={next => undef, last => undef, value => "First item"};
my $node2={next => undef, last => $node1, value => "Next Item"};
$node1->{next}=$node2; # create a reference loop

weaken $node1->{next};
print "node1->next is ",
    (isweak($node1->{next})?"weak":"hard"),"\n"; # produces 'node1->next is weak'
print "node2 is ",(isweak($node2)?"weak":"hard"),"\n"; # produces 'node2 is hard'
$node1=undef; $node2=undef; # no more memory leak
```

Now when the variables $node1 and $node2 are changed to undef so that neither of the hashes they point to have any external references, the hash that $node2 originally pointed to has no more strong references to it, so Perl can garbage-collect it. This destroys the one remaining reference to the hash originally pointed to by $node1, so it is now also garbage-collected. Note that we need to weaken the copy of the reference stored in the hash, not the scalar variable $node2, for this to work. It is the reference, not the thing the reference points to, that is made weak. As a side note, we could make the preceding more efficient by weakening the reference at the moment we copy it.

```perl
weaken($node1->{next}=$node);
```

For more on garbage collection, see Chapter 19 and the special method DESTROY provided by Perl for object instances.

Symbolic References

Symbolic references, as opposed to hard references, are simply descriptions of variables represented as text. More accurately, they contain a label that holds the name of a typeglob, which in turn provides access to the scalar, array, hash, filehandle, or subroutine with that name.

For instance, the symbolic reference for the variable @array is the string "array". Here is an example of a symbolic reference in action:

```perl
#!/usr/bin/perl
# symbolic_ref.pl
use warnings;
use strict;
no strict 'refs';
our @array = (1, 2, 3);   # only package variables allowed
```

```
my $symref = 'array';
my $total = $#$symref;
$total++;
print "$symref has $total elements \n";
foreach (@$symref) {
    print "Got: $_ \n";
}
```

The notation for symbolic references is exactly the same as it is for hard references—in both cases we say things like @$arrayref to dereference the reference. The distinction is that in the case of a hard reference, the scalar variable contains an immutable pointer, whereas in the case of a symbolic reference, it contains an all-too-mutable string. We can even construct the reference name from pieces and evaluate the result, using braces to disambiguate the assembled reference from the surrounding code.

```
my %hash = ( "key" => "value" );
my $value=${"ha".lc('S').(++'g')}{key}; #assigns 'value';
```

A symbolic reference can only refer to a global variable, or to be more technical, a variable that exists in the symbol table, though the reference itself can be lexical. We cannot therefore refer to variables that have been declared with my. This is a significant caveat. If the symbolic reference is unqualified, it is presumed to be a reference to a variable in the current package; otherwise it refers to the variable in the named package.

```
my $symbolrefinotherpackage = 'My::Other::Package::variable';
```

Be careful if assembling a symbolic reference that contains double colons, though, especially if interpolating variables into a string—Perl will parse a double-colon the moment it sees it and will dereference a name within the string if it looks valid. Use backslashes to escape the colons to prevent this from happening, or construct the string in another way. Consider this faulty attempt to access a variable %hash in a package provided via a string variable, and the three different valid ways that follow it:

```
my $class="main";
my $value=${"$class::hash"}{value};    # ERROR - will dereference '$class::hash'
                                       # within the string

my $value=${"$class\:\:hash"}{value};  # no longer looks like symbolic ref, OK
my $value=${$class."::hash"}{value};   # concatenate strings, also OK
my $value=${${class}::hash"}{value};   # disambiguate with braces
                                       # also OK but hard to read
```

Since symbolic references do not have a type, we can dereference any variable whose name matches the reference by prefixing it with the appropriate symbol.

```
my $symref = "Package::variable";

my $scalar = $$symref;
my @array  = @$symref;
my %hash    = %$symref;
my $code    = &$symref;
my *glob    = *$symref;
```

Because symbolic references are mutable, they are not counted as references for the purpose of garbage collection (see the discussion of weak references earlier) and are banned by the strict module by default.

```
use strict;   # strict 'vars', 'subs' and 'refs'
```

To enable symbolic references, we therefore have to make special dispensation.

```
no strict 'refs';
```

Since this is not in general an advisable idea (we should generally use the strict pragma unless we are writing "throwaway" code), it is best to do this inside a subroutine or other lexically limited scope, where the range of permissibility of symbolic references is clearly defined.

The reason for restricting the use of symbolic references is that it is very easy to accidentally create a symbolic reference where we did not mean to, especially if we don't have warnings enabled (which we should never do globally anyway, but might do temporarily inside a subroutine). However, a few places do allow symbolic references as special cases, i.e., functions that take filehandles as arguments (like print).

Complex Data Structures

Combining lists and hashes with references allows us to create arbitrarily complex data structures such as lists of lists, hashes of hashes, and lists of hashes of lists of lists, and so on. However, Perl lacks the ability to explicitly declare things like multidimensional arrays, because lists and hashes can only contain scalar values.

The Problem with Nesting—My Lists Went Flat!

One consequence of not being able to declare multidimensional arrays explicitly is that nesting lists does not work the way we might expect it to. A seemingly obvious way to store one list in another would be to write

```
@inner = (3, 4);
@outer = (1, 2, @inner, 5, 6);
```

We would then like to be able to access the inner list by writing $outer[2] and then access its elements with something like $outer[2][1]. Unfortunately, this does not work because the preceding example does not produce a list containing another list. Instead the lists are "flattened," the inner list being converted into its elements and integrated into the outer list. The preceding example actually results in this:

```
@outer = (1, 2, 3, 4, 5, 6);
```

While this is a perfectly acceptable way to merge lists together, it does not produce the nested data structure that we actually intended. The heart of the problem is that Perl does not allow lists and hashes to store other lists or hashes as values directly. Instead we must store a reference (which is a scalar value) to the hash or list we want to nest.

We can fix the flattening problem using either of the modified examples that follow, the first using square brackets to construct a reference and the second using a backslash to get the reference to the original array.

```
@outer = (1, 2, [@inner], 5, 6);   # using square brackets
@outer = (1, 2, \@inner, 5, 6);    # using a backslash
```

Note that the second example avoids duplicating the inner array by taking a direct reference but assumes we only do this once. In a loop this would cause duplicated references, which we probably did not intend. For more on this issue, see "Creating Complex Data Structures Programmatically" later in this chapter.

Now we know how to construct complex data structures, we can go on to create more complex animals like lists of lists and hashes of hashes.

Lists of Lists and Multidimensional Arrays

The way to create a list of lists is to create a list of list *references*, either with the square bracket notation, [. . .], or using the backslash operator. Defining a list of lists is actually quite simple. The following example shows a list of lists defined using square brackets:

```
@array = (
   ["One", "Two", "Three"],
   ["Red", "Yellow", "Blue"],
   ["Left", "Middle", "Right"],
```

The important point to note about this is that the outer array contains a list of references—one for each inner list. The result is, in effect, a two-dimensional array that we can access using two sets of indices.

```
print $array[0][2];    #displays third element of first row - 'Three'
print $array[2][1];    #displays second element of third row - 'Middle'
```

This is actually a piece of Perl shorthand, in deference to languages like C where real multidimensional arrays can be laid out in memory as a contiguous block and accessed using multiple indices (which translate into pointer arithmetic). In Perl an index is just a count into an array, so the value of $array[0] is in fact a reference, which we should not be able to tack a [2] onto. In other words, we would expect to have to write

```
print $array[0] -> [2];
```

This does indeed work, because this is exactly what happens internally. Perl is clever enough to automatically spot multiple indices and do the additional dereferencing without having to be told explicitly.

We can retrieve an individual array row by using one index, which will give us a scalar array reference, as we just observed.

```
$second_row = $array[1];
```

We can dereference this reference to get an array.

```
@second_row = @{$array[1]};
```

There is an important difference between using $second_row and @second_row, however. $second_row is a reference to the second row of the original multidimensional array, so if we modify the array that $second_row points to, we are actually affecting the original array.

```
print $array[1][1];    #prints 'Yellow'
$second_row [1] = "Green";
print $array[1][1];    #prints 'Green'
```

By contrast, @second_row contains a copy of the second row (because the assignment is actually a straight array copy), so modifying it does not affect @array. This distinction can be very important when working with complex data structures since we can affect values we did not mean to, or conversely, not modify the contents of arrays that we meant to.

Instead of defining a straight list of lists, we can also define a reference to a list of lists, in which case we just have to modify the outer array definition by replacing the parentheses with square brackets and changing the variable type to a scalar, like so:

```
$arrayref = [
   ["One", "Two", "Three"],
   ["Red", "Yellow", "Blue"],
   ["Left", "Middle", "Right"],
];
```

Accessing the elements of this array can be done either by dereferencing the outer array reference $arrayref, or by using the dereferencing operator, ->, to access the underlying array, which is somewhat clearer to read.

```
print $$arrayref[0][2];
print $arrayref -> [0][2];   #using '->' is clearer
```

Accessing a row is similar to before, but with an extra layer of dereferencing. Either of the following will do the trick, though again the second is clearer:

```
$second_row = $$array[1];
$second_row = $array->[1];
```

Hashes of Hashes and Other Variations

Creating a hash of hashes is similar to creating a list of lists, differing only in our use of syntax. Here is an example of a three-deep nested hash of hashes:

```
%identities = (
   JohnSmith => {
      Name => { First=>"John", Last=>"Smith" },
      Phone => { Home=>"123 4567890", Work=>undef },
      Address => { Street => "13 Acacia Avenue",
      City => "Arcadia City",
      Country => "El Dorado",
      }
},
   AlanSmithee => {
      Name => { First=>"Alan", Last=>"Smithee" },
      Phone => { Work=>"not applicable" },
   }
);
```

Accessing this structure is similar too, and again Perl allows us to omit the dereferencing operator for consecutive hash keys.

```
$alans_first_name = $identities{'AlanSmithee'}{'Name'}{'First'};
```

Since nesting data structures is just a case of storing references, we can also create lists of hashes, hashes of lists, and anything in between.

```
#!/usr/bin/perl
# lists.pl
use warnings;
use strict;

my (@list_of_hashes, %hash_of_lists, %mixed_bag, $my_object);
my @my_list = (1,2,3,4,5);

@list_of_hashes = (
   { Monday=>1, Tuesday=>2, Wednesday=>3, Thursday=>4, Friday=>5 },
   { Red=>0xff0000, Green=>0x00ff00, Blue=>0x0000ff },
);
print "Tuesday is the $list_of_hashes[0]{Tuesday}nd day of the week.", "\n";

%hash_of_lists = (
   List_1 => [1, 2, 3],
   List_2 => ["Red", "Yellow", "Blue"],
);
```

```perl
print "The second element of List_1 is: $hash_of_lists{List_1}[1]", "\n";

%mixed_bag = (
    Scalar1 => 3,
    Scalar2 => "Hello World",
    List1 => [1, 2, 3],
    Hash1 => { A => 'Horses', C => 'Miles' },
    List2 => ['Hugh','Pugh',
    ['Barley-McGrew','Cuthbert'],
     'Dibble', 'Grubb'],
    Scalar3 => $my_object,
    Hash2 => { Time => [ gmtime ],
    Date => scalar(gmtime),
    },
List3 => @my_list[0..2],
);

print $mixed_bag{List2}[2][1]; # produces 'Cuthbert'
```

Adding to and Modifying Complex Data Structures

Manipulating nested data structures is essentially no different to manipulating simple ones; we just have to be sure to modify the correct thing in the right way. For example, to add a new row to our two-dimensional array, we can either define the row explicitly, or use the push function to add it. In either case we have to be sure to add a reference, not the list itself, or we will end up adding the list contents to the outer array instead.

```perl
# Right - adds a reference
$array[2] = \@third_row;    #backslash operator creates reference to array
push @array, ["Up", "Level", "Down"];    #explicit reference
push @array, \( "Large", "Medium", "Small" );    #backslashed reference

# ERROR: this is probably not what we want
$array[2] = (8, 9, 10);    # $array[2] becomes 10, the 8 and 9 are discarded
push @array, @third_row;    # contents of @third_row added to @array
```

In the first wrong example, we will get a warning from Perl about the useless use of a constant in void context. The second example, which is perfectly legal Perl, will not generate any warnings. This is consequently one of the commonest sources of bugs when manipulating complex data structures. The way to avoid it is to be extremely clear and consistent about the structure of the data, and to avoid complicated mixtures of scalars, lists, and hashes unless their use is transparent and obvious.

Modifying the contents of nested lists and hashes is likewise simple. We have already seen how to replace a row in a list of lists, but we can also replace individual elements and array slices.

```perl
# Right
$array[2][1] = 9;    #replace an individual element
$array[2][12] = 42;    #grow the list by adding an element

@{$array[2]} = (8, 9, 10);    #replace all the elements
@{$array[2]}[1..2] = (9, 10);    #replace elements 2 and 3, keeping 1

# ERROR: Wrong
$array[2][1..2] = (9, 10);    #cannot take a slice of a list reference
```

The essential point to remember is that this is no different from manipulating simple lists and hashes, so long as we remember that we are really working through references. Perl allows a shorthand for indices when accessing elements, but this doesn't extend to array slices or more complex manipulations, so we need to handle the reference ourselves in these cases.

Creating Complex Data Structures Programmatically

Explicitly writing the code to define a complex structure is one way to achieve our goal, but we might also want to generate things like lists of lists programmatically. This is actually straightforward, but a couple of nasty traps lurk for the unwary Perl programmer. Here is a loop that appears to create a list of lists, but actually constructs a list of integers:

```perl
#!/usr/bin/perl
# complex1.pl
use warnings;
use strict;

my (@outer, @inner);
foreach my $element (1..3) {
    @inner = ("one", "two");
    $outer[$element] = @inner;
}
print '@outer is ', "@outer \n";
```

Running this program produces the following output:

> **perl complex1.pl**

```
Use of uninitialized value in join at test.pl line 11.
@outer is  2 2 2
```

Although this might appear correct, we are in fact assigning a list in a scalar context. All that actually happens is that a count of the two elements in each of the three instances of the @inner array that the foreach loop reads is assigned to an element of the @outer array. This is why @outer consists of three twos rather than three @inner arrays, each of which has the two elements one and two.

The following variant is also defective—it suffers from list flattening, so the contents of all the inner arrays will be merged into the outer array:

```perl
#ERROR: list flattening
#!/usr/bin/perl
# complex2.pl
use warnings;
use strict;
my (@outer, @inner);
foreach my $element (1..3) {
    @inner = ("one", "two");
    push @outer, @inner;
}
print '@outer is ', "@outer \n";
```

If we run this program we see the following output:

> **perl complex2.pl**

```
@outer is one two one two one two
```

The correct thing to do is to assign references, not lists. The following loop does the task we actually wanted. Note the additional square brackets.

```perl
#!/usr/bin/perl
# complex3.pl
use warnings;
use strict;

my (@outer, @inner);
foreach my $element (1..3) {
    @inner = ("one", "two");
    push @outer, [@inner];   #push reference to copy of @inner
}
print '@outer is ', "@outer \n";
```

Running this program produces output like this:

> **perl complex3.pl**

@outer is ARRAY(0x176f0d0) ARRAY(0x176505c) ARRAY(0x17650bc)

Note that @outer consists of three *different* arrays despite the fact that @inner didn't change. The reason for this is that each of the three instances of @inner has a different address, which we used to create @outer.

We have already referred to the important distinction between creating a reference with square brackets and using the backslash operator to take a reference to the list. In the preceding code, the brackets make a copy of the contents of @inner and return a reference to the copy, which is pushed onto the end of @outer. By contrast, a backslash returns a reference to the original list, so the following apparently equivalent code would not work:

```perl
#!/usr/bin/perl
# complex4.pl
use warnings;
use strict;

my (@outer, @inner);
foreach my $element (1..3) {
    @inner = ("one", "two");
    push @outer, \@inner;   #push reference to @inner
}
print '@outer is ', "@outer \n";
```

When run, this program produces output like the following:

> **perl complex4.pl**

@outer is ARRAY(0x1765188) ARRAY(0x1765188) ARRAY(0x1765188)

What actually happens is that the @outer array is filled with the same reference to the @inner array three times. Each time the @inner array is filled with a new double of elements, but the elements of @outer all point to the same list, the current contents of @inner. At the end of the loop, all the elements of @outer are identical and only two different elements are actually stored in total.

Another way to approach this task, avoiding the pitfalls of accidentally creating duplicate references or counting lists we meant to assign as references, is to use references explicitly. This makes it much harder to make a mistake, and also saves a list copy.

```
#!/usr/bin/perl
# complex5.pl
use warnings;
use strict;

my (@outer, $inner_ref);
foreach my $element (1..3) {
    $inner_ref = ["one", "two"];
    push @outer, $inner_ref;   #push scalar reference
}
print '@outer is ', "@outer \n";
```

Running this program results in

> **perl complex5.pl**

@outer is ARRAY(0x176f0ac) ARRAY(0x1765044) ARRAY(0x17650a4)

Rather than redefining a list, this time we redefine a list reference, so we are guaranteed not to assign the same reference more than once. Finally, another way to ensure that we don't assign the same array is to create a new array each time by declaring @inner inside the loop.

```
#!/usr/bin/perl
# complex6.pl
use warnings;
use strict;

my @outer;
foreach my $element (1..3) {
    my @inner = ("one", "two");
    push @outer, \@inner;   #push reference to @inner
}
print '@outer is ', "@outer \n";
```

If we run this program, we see

> **perl complex6.pl**

@outer is ARRAY(0x17651b8) ARRAY(0x176f0d0) ARRAY(0x1765074)

Here @inner is declared each time around the loop, and remains in scope for that iteration only. At the start of each new iteration, the old definition of @inner is discarded and replaced by a new one (note that while the elements of @inner don't change, their addresses change). As with the explicit reference example, this is also more efficient than using square brackets since no additional array copy takes place; however, it is more prone to bugs if we omit warnings since there is nothing programmatically wrong with assigning the same reference multiple times, even if it wasn't what we actually intended.

Although we have only discussed lists of lists in this section, exactly the same principles also apply to any other kind of complex data structure such as hashes of hashes or hybrid structures; just substitute braces, {}, for square brackets and percent signs for @ signs where appropriate.

Traversing Complex Data Structures

Iterating over simple data structures is easy, as we saw when we covered arrays and hashes earlier. Traversing more complex structures is also simple if they are homogeneous (that is, each level of nesting contains the same type of reference and we don't have other data types like scalars or undefined values lurking). Here's a simple loop that iterates over a list of lists:

```perl
#!/usr/bin/perl
# simple1.pl
use warnings;
use strict;

my @outer = (['a1', 'a2', 'a3'], ['b1', 'b2', 'b3'], ['c1', 'c2', 'c3']);

foreach my $outer_el (@outer) {
   foreach (@{$outer_el}) {
      print "$_\n";
   }
   print "\n";
}
```

And here's one that iterates over a hash of hashes:

```perl
#!/usr/bin/perl
# simple2.pl
use warnings;
use strict;

my %outer = (A=> {a1=>1, a2=>2, a3=>3}, B=> {b1=>4, b2=>5, b3=>6},
             C=> {c1=>7,c2=>8, c3=>9});

foreach my $outer_key (keys %outer) {
   print "$outer_key => \n";
   foreach (keys %{$outer{$outer_key}} ) {
      print"\t$_ => $outer{$outer_key} {$_} \n";
   }
   print "\n";
}
```

Finally, here is another list-of-lists loop that also prints out the indices and catches undefined rows:

```perl
#!/usr/bin/perl
# simple3.pl
use warnings;
use strict;

my @outer;
@outer[1, 2, 5] = (['First', 'Row'], ['Second', 'Row'], ['Last', 'Row']);

for my $outer_elc (0..$#outer) {
   if ($outer [$outer_elc] ) {
      my $inner_elcs = $#{ $outer[$outer_elc] };
      print "$outer_elc : ", $inner_elcs+1," elements \n";
      for my $inner_elc (0..$inner_elcs) {
         print "\t$inner_elc : $outer[$outer_elc][$inner_elc] \n";
      }
   } else {
```

```perl
        print "Row $outer_elc undefined\n";
    }
}
```

Traversing other structures is just a matter of extending these examples in the relevant direction. Things become more complex, however, if our structures contain a mixture of different data types. In most cases when we have structures like this, it is because different parts of the structure have different purposes, and we would therefore not normally want to traverse the whole structure. But it can be useful for debugging purposes; so in order to handle structures that could contain any kind of data, we can resort to the ref function. The following recursive subroutine will print out nested scalars (which includes objects), lists, and hashes to any level of depth, using ref to determine what to do at each stage:

```perl
#!/usr/bin/perl
# print_struct.pl
use warnings;
use strict;

my $mixed = [
    'scalar', ['a', 'list', ['of', 'many'], 'values'],
    {And=>{'A Hash'=>'Of Hashes'}}, \'plus a scalar ref'
];

print_structure($mixed);

sub print_structure {
    my ($data, $depth) = @_;

    $depth=0 unless defined $depth; #for initial call

    foreach (ref $data) {
        /^$/ and print($data,"\n"), next;
        /^SCALAR/ and print('-> ', $$data, "\n"), next;
        /^HASH/ and do {
        print "\n";
        foreach my $key (keys %{$data}) {
            print "\t" x$depth, "$key => ";
            print_structure ($data->{$key}, $depth+1);
        }
        next;
    };

    /^ARRAY/ and do {
        print "\n";
        for my $elc (0..$#{$data}) {
            print "\t" x$depth, "[$elc] : ";
            print_structure ($data->[$elc], $depth+1);
        }
        next;
    };
    # it is something else - an object, filehandle or typeglob
    print "?$data?";
    }
}
```

If all we are interested in is debugging data structures, then we can have the Perl debugger do it for us, as this example demonstrates (there is much more on the Perl debugger in Chapter 17):

```
> perl -d -e 1;
```

```
Default die handler restored.

Loading DB routines from perl5db.pl version 1.07
Editor support available. Enter h or 'h h' for help, or 'man perldebug' for more
help.

main::(-e:1):    1
DB<1> $hashref={a=>1,b=>2,h=>{c=>3,d=>4},e=>[6,7,8]}

DB<2> x $hashref
0   HASH(0x82502dc)
   'a' => 1
   'b' => 2
   'e' => ARRAY(0x8250330)
      0  6
      1  7
      2  8
   'h' => HASH(0x80f6a1c)
      'c' => 3
      'd' => 4
DB<3>
```

Here we have just used the debugger as a kind of shell, created a hash containing an array and another hash, and used the x command of the Perl debugger to print it out in a nice legible way for us.

Several Perl modules perform similar functions. Notably, the Data::Dumper module generates a string containing a formatted Perl declaration that, when executed, constructs the passed data structure.

```
#!/usr/bin/perl
# datadumper.pl
use warnings;

use Data::Dumper;

my $hashref = {a=>1, b=>2, h=>{c=>3, d=>4}, e=>[6, 7, 8]};

print Dumper($hashref);
```

Running this program produces the output that follows:

```
> perl datadumper.pl
```

```
$VAR1 = {
   'e' => [
      6,
      7,
      8,
      ],
   'h' => {
      c' => 3,
      d' => 4
   },
```

```
  'a' => 1,
  'b' => 2
};
```

Note that the output of Data::Dumper is actually Perl code. We can also configure it in a variety of ways, most notably by setting the value of $Data::Dumper::Indent (which ranges from 0 to 4, each producing an increasing level of formatting, with 2 being the default) to control the style of output. Finally, if we want to store complex data structures in a file, then we will also want to look at modules like Data::Dumper, FreezeThaw and Storable, and possibly also the MLDBM module or DBM::Deep.

Typeglobs

The typeglob is a composite data type that contains one instance of each of the other data types; it is an amalgam (or in Perl-speak, glob) of all Perl's data types, from which it gets its name. It is a sort of super reference whose value is not a single reference to something but six slots that can contain six different references, all at once:

scalar	A reference to a scalar
array	A reference to an array
hash	A reference to a hash
code	A code reference to a subroutine
handle	A file or directory handle
format	A format definition

Typeglobs programming is a little obscure and rather lower level than many programmers are entirely happy with. It is actually quite possible (and even recommended) to avoid typeglobs in everyday Perl programming, and there are now few reasons to use typeglobs in Perl programs. In ancient days, before references were invented, typeglobs were the only way to pass arguments into subroutines by reference (so they could be assigned to) instead of by value.

The other common use of typeglobs was to pass filehandles around, since filehandles have no specific syntax of their own and so cannot be passed directly. The IO::Handle, IO::File, and IO::Dir modules have largely replaced typeglobs for dealing with filehandles, but since the IO:: family of modules is comparatively bulky to a fundamental built-in datatype, typeglobs are still a popular choice for dealing with filehandles and will often be seen in older Perl code.

Defining Typeglobs

Typeglobs are defined using an asterisk prefix, in exactly the same way as scalars are prefixed with a dollar sign, or arrays with an at-sign. To create a typeglob, we need only assign a value to it. The most obvious example is assigning a typeglob from another typeglob:

```
*glob = *anotherglob;
```

This copies all the six references (which need not all be defined) held in anotherglob to the typeglob glob. For example:

```
$message = "some text";
*missive = *message;
print $missive;    # produce "some text";
```

Alternatively, we can assign references individually.

```
*glob = \$scalar;
```

This creates a new typeglob containing a defined scalar reference, and an undefined value for the other five. We can access this new scalar value with

```
print $glob;   # access typeglob scalar reference
```

Assigning a scalar reference to a typeglob creates a new variable called $glob that contains the same value as the original scalar.

Interestingly, we can then fill other slots of the typeglob without affecting the ones currently defined (unless of course we overwrite one). Perl treats glob assignments intelligently, and only overwrites the part of the glob that corresponds to the reference being assigned to it, a property unique amongst Perl's data types. The following statement fills the array reference slot, but leaves the scalar reference slot alone:

```
*glob = \@array;
```

By filling in the array slot, we create a variable called @glob, which points to the same values as the original @array; changing either variable will cause the other to see the same changes. The same applies to our earlier $glob variable. Changing the value of $glob also changes the value of $scalar, and vice versa. This is called *variable aliasing*, and we can use it to great effect in several ways on variables, subroutines, and filehandles.

The upshot of this is that we rarely need to access a typeglob's slots directly, since we can simply access the relevant variable (the exception is, of course, filehandles, which do not have their own syntax for direct access), but we can play some interesting tricks by assigning to typeglobs.

Manipulating Typeglobs

We have already seen how we can create aliases for scalars and arrays (the same applies to hashes too, of course):

```
*glob = \$scalar;    # create $glob as alias for $scalar
*glob = \@array;     # create @glob as alias for @array
*glob = \%hash;      # create %glob as alias for %hash
```

If we assign the typeglob to a new name, we copy all three references. For example, the following statement invents the variables $glob2, @glob2, and %glob2, all of which point to the same underlying values as the originals:

```
*glob2 = *glob;
```

So far we have considered only the three standard variable types, but typeglobs also contain a code reference slot, which is how Perl defines subroutine names. A roundabout way to define a named subroutine is to assign a code reference to a typeglob.

```
*subglob = sub {return "An anonymous subroutine?"};
```

or

```
*subglob = \&mysubroutine;
```

Both of these assignments cause a subroutine called subglob to spring into existence. The first demonstrates that the only difference between a named and an anonymous subroutine (see Chapter 7 for more on subroutines) is a typeglob entry. The second creates an alias for the subroutine mysubroutine, so we can now call mysubroutine or subglob with equal effect.

```
# these two statements are identical
print mysubroutine(@args);
print subglob(@args);
```

Both typeglobs contain the same code reference, so the two names are simply two different ways to refer to the same thing.

Accessing Typeglobs

If we want to access the different parts of a typeglob, we can do so by casting it into the appropriate form. For example:

```
# assign a new KEY to %glob
${*glob}{$KEY} = $value;
```

The same approach works for ${*glob}, @{*glob}, and &{*glob}, which access the scalar, array, and subroutine parts of the typeglob, respectively. However, we cannot do the same for filehandles or report formats, since they do not have a prefix.

We can also access the different parts of a typeglob directly. This uses a notation similar to hashes, but with a typeglob rather than a scalar prefix. There are five slots in a typeglob that can be accessed (reports being the exception). Each has its own specific key that returns the appropriate reference, or undef if the slot is not defined.

```
$scalarref = *glob{SCALAR};
$arrayref = *glob{ARRAY};
$hashref = *glob{HASH};
$subref = *glob{CODE};
$fhref = *glob{IO};
```

We can also generate a reference to the typeglob itself with

```
$globref = *glob{GLOB};
```

The unqualified name of the typeglob, without any package prefix, is available via NAME.

```
$globname = *glob{NAME}; # returns the string 'glob'
```

Much of the time we do not need to access the contents of a typeglob this way. Scalar, array, hash, and code references are all more easily accessed directly. Perl's file handling functions are also smart, in that they can spot a typeglob and extract the filehandle from it automatically.

```
print STDOUT "This goes to standard output";

print *STDOUT "The same thing, only indirectly";
```

Assigning a typeglob to anything other than another typeglob causes it to be interpreted like a reference; that is, the name of the typeglob, complete with package specifier and asterisk prefix, is written into the scalar.

```
$globname = *glob;
print $globname;    # produces '*main::glob'
```

This is basically just a way to create a symbolic reference to a typeglob, which is getting dangerously abstract and obscure, and is exactly the sort of thing that use strict was implemented to prevent.

```
*$globname = *anotherglob;    # aliases '*anotherglob' to '*glob'
```

However, it does have one use, which comes about because we can refer to filehandles via their typeglobs, coupled with the fact that Perl's file handling functions accept the name of a filehandle (in a string) as a substitute for the filehandle itself.

We can take a reference to a typeglob in the usual manner, and then access it via the reference.

```
my $globref = \*glob;

$scalarref = $globref->{SCALAR};
```

Since a glob reference is very much like any other reference, a scalar, we can store it in an array element, a hash value, or even another glob.

```
*parentglob = $globref;
```

The Undefined Value

The undefined value is a curious entity, being neither a scalar, list, hash, nor any other data type. Although it isn't strictly speaking a datatype, it can be helpful to think of it as a special datatype with only one possible value. It isn't any of the other data types, and so cannot be confused for them. We can assign an undefined value to a scalar variable, or anywhere else a literal value may live, so the undefined value can also be considered a special case of a scalar value. Conveniently, it evaluates to an empty string (or zero, numerically), which is a false value, so we can ignore its special properties in Boolean tests if we wish, or check for it and handle it specially if we need to. This dual nature makes the undefined value particularly useful.

It is common to initialize a scalar variable with undef to indicate that it is not meant to have defined value initially. This is technically not necessary because when we declare a variable, Perl automatically initializes its value to undef unless we provide one (from Perl 5.8.4 onwards the assignment is even optimized away at compile time for efficiency). The following statements are therefore equivalent:

```
my $undefinedtostartwith=undef; # explicitly undefined
my $undefinedtostartwith;       # implicitly undefined
```

The concept of a value-that-is-not-a-value is common to many languages. In Perl, the undef function returns an undefined value, performing the same role as NULL does in C—it also undefines variable arguments passed to it, freeing the memory used to store their values. If we declare a variable without initializing it, it automatically takes on the undefined value too. Perl also provides the defined function that tests for the undefined value and allows us to distinguish it from an empty string or numeric zero.

```
$a = undef;          # assign undefined value to $a
$b;                  # assign undefined value to $b implicitly
$a = 1;              # define $a
print defined($a)    # produces '1'
undef $a             # undefine $a
print defined ($a)   # produces '0'
```

The undefined value is returned by many of Perl's built-in functions to indicate an error or an operation that did not complete. Since many operations cannot legally return any other value for failure, undef becomes a useful way to indicate failure because it is not a real value. We can distinguish between undef and zero with the defined function, as the following example demonstrates. The main code passes a filename to a subroutine called get_results and handles three different possible outcomes, one "success" and two different kinds of "failure."

```
#!/usr/bin/perl
# undef.pl
use warnings;
use strict;

# get a filename
my $file = $ARGV[0] or die "Usage $0 <result file> \n";

# process and return result
my $result = get_results($file);
```

```
# test result
if ($result) {
    print "Result of computation on '$file' is $result \n";
} elsif (defined $result) {
    print "No results found in file \n";
} else {
    print "Error - could not open file: $! \n";
}

# and the subroutine...
sub get_results {
    # return 'undef' to indicate error
    open RESULTS, $_[0] or return undef;

    # compute result (simple sum)
    my $file_result = 0;
    while (<RESULTS>) {
        $file_result += $_;
    }

    # return result, 0 if file empty
    return $file_result;
}
```

The get_results subroutine uses undef to distinguish between two different but equally possible kinds of nonresult. It is designed to read results from a file and performs a calculation on them (for simplicity, we've just used a simple sum), returning the result. It is possible that there are no results, so the calculation returns zero. This isn't actually an error, just a lack of result. If the results file is missing, however, that is an error. By passing back undef rather than zero for an error, we can distinguish between these two possible results of calling the subroutine and act accordingly. If we did not care about the reason for the nonresult, we could simplify our code to

```
if ($result) { # true
    print "Result of computation on '$file' is $result \n";
} else { # false or undef
    print "No results \n";
}
```

Without an argument to undefine, undef is very much like a value that happens to be undefined; we can treat it almost as a number with no value. However, it is always distinct from a scalar because it returns false when given to the defined function. Having said that, the undefined value does have some things in common with a scalar, it is a single value (in a manner of speaking) and we can even take a reference to it, just like a scalar or list.

```
my $undefref = \undef;
print defined($$undefref);    # produces '0'
```

Tests of Existence

The defined function tests a value to see if it is undefined, or has a real value. The number 0 and the empty string are both empty values, and test false in many conditions, but they are defined values unlike undef. The defined function allows us to tell the difference.

```
print "It is defined!" if defined $scalar;
```

defined comes up short when we use it on hashes, however, since it cannot tell the difference between a nonexistent key and a key with an undefined value, as noted previously. All it does is convert undef to an empty value (' ' or 0, depending on the context) and everything else to 1. In order to test for the existence of a hash key, we instead use the exists function.

```
my %hash = ('A Key' => 'A Value', 'Another Key' => 'Another Value');
print "It exists!" if exists $hash{'A Key'};
```

Or, in a fuller example that tests for definition as well:

```
#!/usr/bin/perl
# exists.pl
use strict;
use warnings;

my %hash = ('Key1' => 'Value1', 'Key2' => 'Value2');
my $key = 'Key1';

# the first if tests for the presence of the key 'Key1'
# the second if checks whether the key 'Key1' is defined
if (exists $hash{$key}) {
    if (defined $hash{$key}) {
        print "$key exists and is defined as $hash{$key} \n";
    } else {
        print "$key exists but is not defined \n";
    }
} else {
    print "$key does not exist\n";
}
```

In a sense, defined is the counterpart of undef and exists is the counterpart of delete (at least for hashes). For arrays, delete and undef are actually the same thing, and exists tests for array elements that have never been assigned to. exists is not applicable to scalar values; use defined for them.

Using the Undefined Value

If we do not define a variable before using it, Perl will emit a warning, if warnings are enabled.

```
my $a;
print "The value is $a \n";   # produces 'Use of uninitialized value ...'
```

If warnings are not enabled, undef simply evaluates to an empty string. A loop like the following will also work correctly, even if we do not predeclare the count variable beforehand, because on the first iteration the undefined variable will be evaluated as 0:

```
#!/usr/bin/perl
# no_warnings.pl;
# warnings not enabled...

while ($a<100) {
    print $a++, "\n";
}
```

Leaving warnings disabled globally is not good programming, but if we know what we are doing, we can disable them locally to avoid warnings when we know we may be using undefined values. In this case, we should really declare the loop variable, but for illustrative purposes we could use a warnings pragma, or a localized copy of $^W to disable warnings temporarily like this:

```
# warnings enabled here ...
{
    no warnings;   # use 'local $^W = 0' for Perl < 5.6
    while ($a < 100) {
```

```
        print $a++, "\n";
    }
}
# ... and here
```

Perl is smart enough to let some uses of the undefined value pass, if they seem to be sensible ones. For example, if we try to increment the value of an undefined key in a hash variable, Perl will automatically define the key and assign it a value without complaining about it. This allows us to write counting hashes that contain keys only for items that were actually found, as this letter counting program illustrates:

```
#!/usr/bin/perl
# frequency.pl
use warnings;
use strict;

sub frequency {
    my $text = join('', @_);
    my %letters;
    foreach (split //, $text) {
        $letters{$_}++;
    }
    return %letters;
}
my $text = "the quick brown fox jumps over the lazy dog";

my %count = frequency($text);

print "'$text' contains: \n";
foreach (sort keys %count) {
    print "\t", $count{$_}, " '$_", ($count{$_} == 1)? "'": "'s", "\n";
}
```

This will create a hash of letter keys with the frequency of each letter's occurrence as their values. Of note is the split statement, which uses an empty pattern //. This is a special case of split that returns characters one at a time by using a delimiter of nothing at all.

The trick to this program lies in the line $letters{$_}++. To start with, there are no keys in the hash, so the first occurrence of any letter causes a new key and value to be entered into the hash. Perl allows this, even though the increment implies an existing value. If a letter does not appear at all, there won't even be a key in the hash for it, eliminating redundant entries.

Using undef As a Function

Although we often use undef as if it were a value by assigning it or returning it from subroutines, it is in fact a function that returns the undefined value (for which there is no written equivalent). When used on variables, undef undefines them, destroying the value. The variable remains intact, but now returns undef when it is accessed. For example:

```
undef $scalar;
```

This is essentially the same as

```
$scalar = undef;
```

If the undef function is used on an array or a hash variable, it destroys the entire contents of the variable, turning it into an empty array or hash. The following two statements are therefore equivalent:

```
undef @array;
@array = ();
```

Undefining an array element, a slice of an array, or a hash key, undefines the value, but not the array element or hash key, which continues to exist.

```
undef $hash{'key'};    # undefine value of key 'key'
my $value = $hash{'key'};   # $value is now 'undef'
```

Similarly:

```
my @array = (1, 2, 3, 4, 5);   # define a five element array
@array[1..3] = undef;   # @array contains (1, undef, undef, undef, 5)
```

To actually remove the element or hash key, we use the delete function.

```
my @array = (1, 2, 3, 4, 5);   # define a five-element array
delete @array[1..3];   # no more second, third, and fourth elements
```

Constants

A constant is a value that remains unchanged throughout the lifetime of a program. By defining a named constant and then using it rather than the value, we can avoid retyping, and potentially mistyping, the value. In addition, it makes our code more legible. A good example of a constant is the value of pi, 3.14159265358979.... Clearly it would be preferable to just type PI in our programs than reel out a string of digits each time. A second reason for using a constant is that we can, if we wish, change it. By defining it in one place and then using the definition in every other place in our code, we can easily alter the value throughout the application from a single definition.

One simple but not very satisfactory way to define a constant is with a scalar variable. By convention, constants use fully capitalized names, for example:

```
# define constant '$PI'
$PI = 3.1415926;

# use it
$deg = 36;
print "$deg degrees is ", $PI*($deg/180), " radians";
```

However, this constant is constant in typography only. It's still a regular scalar variable and can be assigned a new value as normal. A more reliable way to define a scalar constant is by assigning a value, by reference, to a typeglob. Here is how we could define the constant $PI using this approach:

```
# define constant
*PI = \3.1415926;
```

This causes Perl to create the variable $PI, since the assigned reference is to a scalar. Because the reference is to a literal value rather than a variable, it cannot be redefined and so the scalar "variable" $PI is read-only, a true constant. Attempting to assign a new value to it will provoke an error from Perl.

```
# A more rational, if inaccurate, value of PI
$PI = 3;   # produces 'Modification of a read-only value attempted ...'
```

However, this still does not reinforce the fact that PI is supposed to be constant, because it looks like a regular scalar variable, even if we are prevented from altering it. What we would ideally like is constants that look constant, without any variable prefix character, which is what the constant pragma provides us with.

Declaring Scalar Constants with the constant Pragma

The constant pragmatic module allows us to define scalar constants that both look and behave like constants. Like any module, we use it through a use statement, providing the name and value of the constant we wish to define. To define a value for PI, we could write

```
use constant PI => 3.1415926;
```

This notation is an immediate improvement over using a scalar variable or a typeglob since it legibly declares to the reader, as well as to Perl, that we are defining a constant. The use of => is optional. We could equally have used a comma, but in this context => makes sense since we are defining an association. It also allows us to omit the quotes we would otherwise need if use strict is in effect, which is elegant since the result of this statement is to define a constant PI, which we can use like this:

```
print "$deg degrees is ", PI*($deg/180);
```

This is an immediate improvement over the first example, since PI is clearly a constant, not a variable like $PI. It also cannot be assigned to, since it is no longer a scalar variable. (For the curious, it is actually a subroutine, defined on-the-fly by the module that takes no arguments and returns the value we supplied. This makes a surprisingly effective constant even though it is not actually a built-in feature of the language.)

Constants are a good place to perform one-off calculations too. The definition of pi shown previously is adequate for most purposes, but it is not the best that we can do. We saw earlier that we can calculate pi easily using the expression 4*atan2(1, 1). We can use this expression to define our constant PI:

```
use constant PI => 4 * atan2(1, 1);
```

Although this is more work than just defining the value explicitly, Perl only evaluates it once, and we end up with the best possible value of pi that can be handled on any architecture that we run the program on without needing to rewrite the code.

Calculating constants is also useful for clarity and avoiding errors; it is easier to get the preceding expression right because it is shorter to type and errors are more obvious. Detecting one wrong digit in a 15-digit floating point number is not so simple. Similarly, computed values such as the number of seconds in a year look better like this:

```
use constant SECONDS_IN_YEAR => 60 * 60 * 24 * 365;
```

than this:

```
use constant SECONDS_IN_YEAR => 31536000;
```

Constants are conventionally defined in entirely uppercase, to enable them to be easily distinguished from functions that happen to take no arguments. This is not an enforced rule, but it is often a good idea to improve the legibility of our code.

Expressions used to define constants are evaluated in a list context. That means that if we want the scalar result of a calculation, we need to say so explicitly. For example, the gmtime function returns a list of date values in list context, but in a scalar context it instead returns a nicely formatted string containing the current date. To get the nicely formatted string, we need to use scalar to force gmtime into a scalar context.

```
use constant START_TIME => scalar(gmtime);
```

As a final note on scalar constants, we can also define a constant to be undefined.

```
use constant TERMINATION_DATE => undef;
use constant OVERRIDE_LIST => ();
```

Both of these statements create constants that evaluate to undef in a scalar context and () in a list context.

Declaring Constant Scalar Variables

It can sometimes be useful to create a variable that has a constant value. One particular use is in interpolation—we can embed the variable into a double-quoted string. We cannot do this with constants created by the constant pragma, and must resort to concatenation instead.

A constant scalar variable (which is admittedly twisting the term "variable") can be created in a number of ways. Perhaps the simplest is to assign a reference to a constant string to a typeglob.

```
#!/usr/bin/perl
use warnings;
use strict;

use vars qw($constantstring); # declare use of package scalar
*constantstring=\"immutable"; # assign constant string to scalar slot of glob
print $constantstring;        # produces 'immutable'
$constantstring='no!';        # Error
```

Alternatively, from Perl 5.8 we can use the built-in function Internals::SvREADONLY. As its name suggests, this function is somewhat secret and technically deemed to be unofficial. It is likely a friendlier and more official face will be put on it in the future since it is the underlying foundation of restricted hashes as provided by the Hash::Util module. For now:

```
my $constantstring='immutable';
Internals::SvREADONLY($constantstring => 1);
```

Finally, we can create a tied object class that overrides write operations, and we will see such a class in Chapter 21.

Declaring List and Hash Constants

Unlike the typeglob definition of constants, which only works for literal values and hence only defines scalar constants, the constant pragma also allows us to define constant arrays and constant hashes. Both of these work in essentially the same way as a scalar constant, with the values to be made constant passed to the module and a subroutine that is defined behind the scenes to implement the resulting constant. Here is how we can define a constant list of weekdays that we can use to retrieve the day names by index:

```
use constant WEEKDAYS=>('Monday', 'Tuesday', 'Wednesday', 'Thursday'', 'Friday');
```

Accessing the individual elements of a constant array can be tricky though, because the constant returns a list of values to us, not an array. Because of this, we cannot simply use an index to retrieve an element.

```
print "The third day is", WEEKDAYS[2]; #ERROR: syntax error
```

To solve this problem, we only need to add parentheses to make the returned list indexable.

```
print "The third day is", (WEEKDAYS)[2]; # works ok
```

A similar technique can be used to create hash constants, though the values are stored and returned as a list, so they cannot be accessed through a key without first being transferred into a real hash.

```
use constant WEEKABBR => (
    Monday=>'Mon', Tuesday=>'Tue', Wednesday=>'Wed',
    Thu=>'Thursday', Fri=>'Friday'
);
```

```
my %abbr = WEEKABBR;
my $day = 'Wednesday';
print "The abbreviation for $day is ", $abbr{$day};
```

Because of this limitation, constant hashes are better defined via a reference, which can hold a real hash as its value, rather than a simple list of keys and values that happen to resemble a hash. Given that, however, if we really want a reference to a constant hash, a pseudohash or restricted hash may be a better solution to the same problem.

Constant References

Since references are scalars, we can also define constant references. As a simple example, the preceding array could also have been declared as

```
use constant WEEKDAYS=>[ 'Monday', 'Tuesday', 'Wednesday', 'Thursday', 'Friday'];
```

Because the constant is a reference to an array, we must dereference it to access the elements, which is marginally more attractive (and certainly more legible) than adding parentheses.

```
print "The third day is ", WEEKDAYS->[2];
```

However, all that is being defined here is a constant reference. We cannot assign a new value to WEEKDAYS, but we can still alter the values in the array through the existing reference. The list is not truly constant, though it still looks like a constant.

```
WEEKDAYS->[0]='Lundi';   #this is perfectly legal
```

Depending on our programming goals, this might actually be a good thing, allowing us to secretly customize the value of a constant inside a package while presenting it as an unchanging and unmodifiable value to the outside world. However, this kind of behavior should be exercised with caution.

Listing and Checking for the Existence of Constants

To check for the existence of a constant, we can make use of the declared hash in the constant package to see if the constant exists or not.

```
unless (exists $constant::declared{'MY_CONSTANT'}) {
    use constant MY_CONSTANT => "My value";
}
```

We can also dump out a list of all the currently declared constants by iterating over the keys of the hash.

```
foreach (keys %constant::declared) {
    print "Constant $_ is defined as '$constant::declared{$_}'";
}
```

To detect a constant scalar such as a locked value in a restricted hash, we can use the readonly function from Scalar::Util.

```
#!/usr/bin/perl -w
# testforconstantscalar.pl
use Scalar::Util qw(readonly);
my $constant="immutable";
print "scalar is ",(readonly($constant)?"constant":"variable"),"\n";
Internals::SvREADONLY($constant => 1);
print "scalar is ",(readonly($constant)?"constant":"variable"),"\n";
```

Summary

We began this chapter by looking at lists and arrays. Specifically, we saw how to manipulate and modify them; count the number of elements; add, resize, and remove elements; and sort arrays. We also noted the essential difference between lists and arrays—lists are passed values, arrays are storage for lists.

We then took a similar look at hashes, and also saw how to convert them into scalars and arrays. We then covered two ways to create hashes with fixed and unchangeable keys: pseudohashes, now deprecated, and their replacement, restricted hashes. We also covered the `fields` pragma and the use of typed scalar variables to provide compile-time checks and optimization where pseudohashes or restricted hashes are in use.

From there we discussed references, both hard and symbolic, and learned how to create references and then dereference them. We also covered weak references and garbage collection, passing data to subroutines by reference, and finding the type of a reference.

Armed with this information, we dug into complex data structures, including problems inherent with nesting. We learned how to construct hashes of hashes, arrays of hashes, and more esoteric constructions. From there we learned how to create complex data structures programmatically and then navigate them. We also covered typeglobs and saw how to define and manipulate them. We looked at the undefined value, and, amongst other things, explored its use as a function.

Finally, we examined constants and put the `constant` pragma to use. We saw how to declare constant scalars, lists, hashes, and references, and how to detect constants in code.

■ ■ ■

## CHAPTER 6

Structure, Flow, and Control

In this chapter, we look at Perl's control structures, starting with the basic syntax of the language, expressions, and statements. We will then build these into more complex structures such as compound statements (also known as blocks) and conditional statements.

We will consider Perl's conditional statements, and then move on to read about loops in Perl. We will look at the various statements that we can use to create loops and how to use them in particular with lists, arrays, and hashes. We will also look into the modifiers provided by Perl to change the behavior of loops.

Declarations, Statements, Expressions, and Blocks

A Perl program consists of a mixture of statements, declarations, and comments. *Statements* are executed by the Perl interpreter at run time. *Declarations*, on the other hand, are directives that affect the way that the program is compiled. Therefore, a declaration's effect ends after compilation, whereas a statement will effect the program each time that section of code is run. The sub, my, and use keywords are the most obvious types of declarations.

Statements are made up of expressions, and can be combined together into a block or compound statement. An expression is any piece of Perl code that produces a value when it is evaluated; we saw plenty of these in the preceding chapters. For example, the number 3 is an expression because it produces 3 when evaluated. Operators combine expressions to form larger expressions. For example, 3+6 is an expression that produces the number 9. In Perl, however, the distinction between statements and expressions is rather arbitrary. Most statements are simply expressions whose return values are discarded rather than used. The distinction between statements and declarations is also somewhat arbitrary. Perl, like many other languages inspired by or derived from Lisp, allows code to be run during the compilation phase, prior to execution. This blurs the line between compilation and execution and between declarations and statements.

Blocks are just aggregations of statements, defined with the use of curly braces. A block defines its own scope, so variables declared inside a block only last so long as that block is being executed. More technically, blocks create a new stack frame, and variables allocated within it last only so long as that frame exists, unless a reference to them is retained by something outside the block. In that case, the variable persists (via the reference) so long as the reference does.

Declarations

Declarations take effect at compile time, rather than at run time. An important class of declaration is the inclusion of modules or source code with the use keyword. This includes both pragmatic modules like use integer and functional modules like use CGI. Another is declaring a subroutine ahead of its definition with sub. Other kinds of declaration include my and our statements and format definitions. The following are all examples of declarations:

```
sub mysubroutine ($);   # declare a subroutine with one scalar argument

my $scalar;   # declare a lexical variable (at compile-time)

# define a format for STDOUT
format =
@<<<< = @>>>>

$key, $value

use warnings;   # use pragmatic module

use strict;   # use pragmatic module

use CGI qw (:standard);   # use CGI module

BEGIN {
   print "This is a compile-time statement";
}
```

The BEGIN block is an interesting example, because it is the most obvious case of code being executed during the compilation rather than the execution of a program. The block behaves like a declaration, but the contents are statements. use also falls into this category; it is really a require statement and an import statement wrapped inside a BEGIN block that executes at compile time. So, arguably, use is not a declaration, but like BEGIN, a mechanism to execute code during the compile phase. Whether a BEGIN block is a declaration or not is a moot point, but it happens at the compile phase, so it is certainly not a regular block.

All of these examples demonstrate features of Perl covered later in the book, so for now we will just note their existence and move on. For the curious, subroutines are covered in Chapter 7; my and our in Chapter 8; use, require, and import in Chapter 9; and the BEGIN block (along with siblings END, CHECK, and INIT) is covered in more detail in Chapter 10. Formats can be found in Chapter 18.

Expressions and Simple Statements

An expression in Perl is any construct that returns a value (be it scalar, list, or even an undefined value). It can be anything from a literal number to a complex expression involving multiple operators, functions, and subroutine calls. That value can then be used in larger expressions or form part of a statement. Statements differ from expressions only in that they are separated from each other by semicolons. The chief distinction between a statement and an expression is that a statement does not return a value (for example, an if statement) or returns a value that is ignored (for example, a print statement).

This second kind of statement is really just an expression in disguise—Perl will detect that we don't use the return value and optimize the code accordingly, but we could still change our mind and use it if we choose to. In Perl terminology, these expressions are evaluated in *void context*. For example, the statement $b = $a is also an expression, which returns the value of the assignment ($a). We can see this in action by considering the following two statements:

```
$b = $a;       # $b = $a is a statement
$c = $b = $a;  # $b = $a is now an expression, and $a assigns to $c
```

Another way of looking at this is to say that a statement is an expression that is executed primarily because it performs a useful action rather than returns a result. A print statement is probably the most common example:

```
print "Hello World";
```

This is a statement by virtue of the fact that the return value from print is not used. Indeed, it is easy to forget that print does in fact return a value. In point of fact, print actually returns a true value if it succeeds and a false value if the filehandle to which it is printing is invalid. We rarely bother to check for this when printing to standard output, but if we wanted to, we could turn this statement into an expression by writing

```
$success = print "Hello World";
```

Now we have a print expression whose value is used in an assignment statement. For standard output this is usually not necessary, but if we were printing to a filehandle, and especially to one that could become invalid outside our control, like a network socket, this becomes more important.

Blocks and Compound Statements

The block is a Perl construct that allows several statements (which in turn may be simple statements or further blocks) to be logically grouped together into a compound statement and executed as a unit. Blocks are defined by enclosing the statements within curly braces with the final statement optionally terminated by a semicolon. The general form of a block is therefore

```
{ STATEMENT; STATEMENT; ... ; STATEMENT[;] }
```

This is the most obvious form of block. Less obvious is that a block is also created by the limits of a source file. A simple Perl script is a block that starts at the top of the file and ends at the bottom (or a __DATA__ or __END__ token, if one is present in the file; see Chapter 12 for more on these). Likewise, an included file that has been read in using require also defines a block corresponding to the included file.

The definition of a block is important because in addition to grouping statements together logically, a block also defines a new scope in which variables can be declared and used. Following are two short programs, one of which executes the other via require. Both files define their own scope, and in addition the explicit block in the second program child.pl defines a third. Here is the parent process:

```
#!/usr/bin/perl
# parent.pl
use warnings;
use strict;

my $text = "This is the parent";
require 'child.pl';
print "$text \n";    # produces "This is the parent"
```

and here is the child process:

```
#!/usr/bin/perl
# child.pl
use warnings;
use strict;

my $text = "This is the child";
{
    my $text = "This is block scoped";
    print "$text \n";    # produces "This is block scoped";
}
print "$text \n";    # produces "This is the child";
```

Variables that are defined within a particular scope only exist as long as that block is being executed and are not seen or usable by the wider scope outside the block. This has a lot of significant implications, as we will see.

Blocks in Perl Statements

Almost all of Perl's control structures (such as if statements, for and while loops, and subroutine declarations) can accept a block in their definitions, and many require it. For example, the if statement requires a block to encapsulate as the action that follows its condition; a simple statement will not do and will cause Perl to generate a syntax error.

```
if (EXPRESSION) { STATEMENT; STATEMENT; ... STATEMENT[;] }
```

Or, put more simply:

```
if (EXPRESSION) BLOCK
```

Note that a block is not the equivalent of a statement. As we just saw, blocks are accepted in places where simple statements are not. Also, blocks do not require a terminating semicolon after the closing brace, unlike the statements inside it. Significantly, in some contexts blocks can also return a value.

Naked Blocks

Although it is their most common application, blocks do not have to belong to a larger statement. They can exist entirely on their own, purely for the purposes of defining a scope. The following example shows a block in which several scalar variables are defined using my. The variables exist for the lifetime of the block's execution and then cease to exist.

```perl
#!/usr/bin/perl
# time.pl
use warnings;

# a bare block definition
{
    # define six scalars in new block scope:
    my ($sec, $min, $hour, $day, $month, $year) = localtime();
    # variables exist and can be used inside block
    print "The time is: $hour: $min. $sec \n";
    $month++;
    $year += 1900;
    print "The date is: $year/ $month/ $day \n";
    # end of block - variable definitions cease to exist
}

# produces 'uninitialized value' warning - $sec does not exist here
print "$sec seconds \n";
```

The output from this is

```
Name "main::sec" used only once: possible typo at d.pl line 18.
The time is: 2: 30. 5
The date is: 2000/ 12/ 15
Use of uninitialized value in concatenation (.) at d.pl line 18.
 seconds
```

Note that adding use strict would turn the preceding warning into a compile-time syntax error as strictness requires declaring all variables.

If we take a reference to a bare block, it can also be used to define an anonymous subroutine, a subject we will cover in Chapter 7.

Defining the Main Program As a Block

An interesting use of blocks is to put the main program code into a block within the source file. This helps to distinguish the actual program from any declarations or initialization code (in the shape of use statements and so forth) that may occur previously. It also allows us to restrict variables needed by the main program to the scope of the main program only, rather than turning them into global variables, which should be avoided. Consider the following simple but illustrative program:

```perl
#!/usr/bin/perl
# blockmain.pl

# Declarations First
use strict;
use warnings;

# Initialization code, global scope

my $global_variable = "All the World can see Me";
use constant MY_GLOBAL_CONSTANT => "Global Constant";

# Here is the main program code

MAIN: {
    # variable defined in the main program scope, but not global
    my $main_variable = "Not visible outside main block";
    print_variables ($main_variable);
}

# No one here but us subroutines...

sub print_variables {
    print $global_variable, "\n", MY_GLOBAL_CONSTANT, "\n";
    # print $main_variable, "\n";    #error!
    print $_[0], "\n";    # passed from main block, ok now
}
```

We have used a label MAIN: to prefix the start of the main program block to make it stand out. The use of the label MAIN: is entirely arbitrary—we could as easily have said MY_PROGRAM_STARTS_NOW:. However, MAIN: is friendlier to those coming from a C programming background where a main function is required. Of course, we could also create a real main subroutine, and we need to make sure that we call it.

The issue of scoping variables so they are invisible from subroutines is not a minor one. If we had failed to enable warnings and strict mode, and if we had uncommented the second line of print_variables, Perl would have happily accepted the undefined variable $main_variable and printed out a blank line. By placing otherwise global variables inside the scope of a main block, we prevent them from being accidentally referred to inside subroutines, which should not be able to see them.

Blocks As Loops

Bare blocks can sometimes be treated as loops, which are discussed in detail later in the chapter. A block that is not syntactically required (for example, by an if statement) or is part of a loop statement can be treated as a loop that executes only once and then exits. This means that loop control statements like next, last, and redo will work in a block. Because blocks are one-shot loops, next and last are effectively the same. However, redo will reexecute the block.

In short, these three loops all do the same thing, one with a while, one with a foreach, and one with a bare block and a redo:

```perl
#!/usr/bin/perl
# while.pl
use warnings;
use strict;

my $n = 0;

print "With a while loop:\n";
while (++$n < 4) {print "Hello $n \n";}

print "With a foreach loop:\n";
foreach my $n (1..3) { print "Hello $n \n"; }

print "With a bare block and redo: \n";
$n = 1; { print "Hello $n \n";
last if (++$n > 3); redo; }
```

The block of an if statement is required syntactically, and if is not a loop statement, so the redo statement here will not work:

```perl
#!/usr/bin/perl
# badblockloop.pl
use warnings;
use strict;

if (defined(my $line = <>)) {
    last if $line =~/quit/;
    print "You entered: $line";
    $line = <>;
    redo;
}
print "Bye! \n";
```

The fact that redo, next, and last do not work in if blocks is actually a blessing. Otherwise it would be hard, albeit not impossible, to break out of a loop conditionally. Instead we get a syntax error.

```
Can't "redo" outside a loop block at ./badblockloop.pl line 10, <> line 2.
```

However, we can nest blocks inside each other, so by adding an extra bare block we can fix the preceding program so that it will work.

```perl
#!/usr/bin/perl
# Blockloop.pl
use warnings;
use strict;

if (defined(my $line = <>)) { { # <- note the extra block
    last if $line =~/quit/;
    print "You entered: $line";
    $line = <>;
    redo;
} }
print "Bye! \n";
```

Using blocks as loops is an interesting approach to solving problems, but they are not always the simplest or easiest to understand. The preceding script could more easily be fixed simply by replacing the if with a while. This makes more sense and does not require an extra block because while is a looping statement:

```perl
#!/usr/bin/perl
# blockwhile.pl
use warnings;
use strict;

while (my $line = <>) {
    last if $line =~/quit/;
    print "You entered: $line";
}
print "Bye! \n";
```

We cover loops in more detail later in the chapter.

The do Block

Blocks do not normally return a value; they are compound statements, not expressions. They also provide a void context, which applies to the last statement in the block. This causes its value to be discarded, just as all the statements before it are. However, the do keyword allows blocks to return their values as if they were expressions, the value being derived from the last statement. Let's consider an example:

```perl
@words = do {
    @text = ("is", "he", "last");
    sort @text;
};
```

In this example, a list is generated and returned by the sort function. We could make this more explicit by adding a return beforehand as we do for subroutines, but it is not actually necessary. (return is not necessary in subroutines either, but it certainly adds clarity.)

Because prefixing do to a block turns it into an expression, it often needs to be followed by a semicolon when used as the final part of a statement. Omitting the final semicolon from statements like the preceding one is a common mistake, because in any other context a block does not require a following semicolon.

There is another, syntactic, reason for needing a do to return the value of a block. Without do Perl would have a hard time telling apart a bare block from a hash definition.

```perl
$c = do { $a = 3, $b = 6 };   # a block, $c = 6
{ $a = 3; $b = 6 }   # has a semicolon, therefore a block
# a hash definition, $c = {3 => 6}, test with 'print keys %{$c}'
$c = { $a = 3, $b = 6 };
```

Regarding the use of blocks as loops, do blocks are not considered loops by Perl, because the block is syntactically required by the do. Loop-control statements will therefore not work inside a do block. However, a do block can be suffixed with a loop condition such as while or until, in which case it is transformed into a loop.

```perl
do { chomp($line = <>); $input. = $line } until $line =~/^stop/;
```

The block is executed before the condition is tested, so in this example the word stop will be added to the end of $line before the loop terminates.

BEGIN and END Blocks

BEGIN and END blocks are special blocks that are executed outside the normal order of execution. We can use them in any application, though they are mostly used in modules, and accordingly we cover them in detail in Chapter 10. They are worth a brief examination here, because apart from the circumstances of their execution, they have a lot in common with regular bare blocks.

BEGIN blocks are executed during the compilation phase as they are encountered by the interpreter, so their contents are compiled and run before the rest of the source code is even compiled. We can define multiple BEGIN blocks, which are executed in the order the interpreter encounters them. This is especially relevant when we consider that the use statement uses an implicit BEGIN block to allow modules to export definitions before the main program code is compiled.

END blocks are the inverse of BEGIN blocks; they are executed by the interpreter after the application exits and before the exit of the interpreter itself. They are useful for "cleanup" duties such as closing database connections, resetting terminal properties, or deleting temporary files. We can also define multiple END blocks, in which case they are executed in reverse order of definition.

The following is a short script that shows both BEGIN and END blocks in action:

```perl
#!/usr/bin/perl
# begend.pl
use warnings;
use strict;

END {
    print "Exiting... \n";
}

print "Running! \n";

fun();

sub fun {
    print "Inside fun \n";
}

BEGIN {
    print "Compiling... \n";
    # can't call 'fun' - not compiled yet
    # fun();
}
```

When run, this program prints out the following:

> **perl begend.pl**

```
Compiling...
Running!
Inside fun
Exiting...
```

As the output shows, the BEGIN block was executed first. Since the fun subroutine had not yet been compiled when the BEGIN block gets executed, attempting to call fun from inside the BEGIN block would cause an error. On other hand, the END block, which defined first in the program, is executed last.

Perl actually defines five special block types, though only BEGIN and END are in widespread use. Two others are CHECK and INIT, which take place just after the compile phase and just before the run phase, respectively. Though these are rarely used in practice, we cover them in Chapter 10 also. The final special block is DESTROY, and it is used in object-oriented modules covered in Chapter 19.

Conditional Statements

Conditional statements execute the body of the statement (sometimes known as a *branch* or *branch of execution*) only if a given Boolean condition is met. The condition is an expression whose value is used to determine the course of execution. Perl's primary mechanism for conditional execution is the if statement and its related keywords, unless, else, and elsif. However, Perl being as flexible as it is, there are other ways we can write conditions too.

Multiple-branch conditions are implemented in other languages using special multiple-branch conditional statements like switch or case. Perl has no such equivalent, because it does not need one. As we will see, there are already plenty of ways to write a multiple-branch condition in Perl. However, for those who really must have a dedicated switch statement, Perl provides the Switch module.

Before embarking on a detailed look at these functions, it is worth taking a brief diversion to discuss the nature of truth in Perl.

What Is Truth?

Perl has a very broad-minded view of the meaning of true and false—in general, anything that has a "non-zero" value is true. Anything else is false. By "non-zero" we mean that the value is in some sense "set." Even 0 is information of a sort, especially compared to undef.

There are a few special cases. The string 0 is considered false even though it has a value, as a convenience to calculations that are performed in string context. The undefined value also evaluates to false for the purposes of conditions. However, a string of spaces is true, as is the string 00. The examples in Table 6-1 illustrate various forms of truth and falsehood.

Table 6-1. *True and False Values*

Value	True/ False
1	True
-1	True
"abc"	True
0	False
"0"	False
""	False
" "	True
"00"	True
"0E0"	True (this is returned by some Perl libraries)
"0 but true"	True (ditto)
()	False (empty list)
undef	False

To distinguish between the undefined value and other values that evaluate to false, we can use the defined function; for instance:

```
if (defined $var) {
    print "$var is defined";
}
```

The ability to handle undef as distinct from true and false is very useful. For example, it allows functions and subroutines that return a Boolean result to indicate an "error" by returning undef. If we want to handle the error, we can do so by checking for undef. If we do not care or need to know, we can just check for truth instead.

```
if (defined($var) && $var) {
    print "true \n";
}
```

if, else, and elsif

As we have already seen, basic conditions can be written using an if statement. The basic form of an if statement is as follows (note that a trailing semicolon is not required):

```
if (EXPRESSION) BLOCK
```

Here EXPRESSION is any Perl expression, and BLOCK is a compound statement—one or more Perl statements enclosed by curly braces. BLOCK is executed only if EXPRESSION is true. For instance, in the preceding example, the block that contains print "true \n" would be executed *only* if the expression (defined($var) && $var) evaluates to true, that is, only if $var is defined *and* true.

We can invert the syntax of an if statement and put the BLOCK first. In this case, we can omit both the parentheses of the condition and also replace the block with a bare statement or list of statements. The following forms of if statement are all legal in Perl:

```
BLOCK if EXPRESSION;
STATEMENT if EXPRESSION;
STATEMENT, STATEMENT, STATEMENT if EXPRESSION;
```

For example:

```
print "Equal" if $a eq $b;
```

```
print (STDERR "Illegal Value"), return "Error" if $not_valid;
```

```
close FILE, print ("Done"), exit if $no_more_lines;
```

```
return if $a ne $b;
```

The use of the comma operator here deserves a little attention. In a list context (that is, when placed between parentheses), the comma operator generates lists. However, that is not how it is being used here. In this context, it simply returns the right-hand side, discarding the left, so it becomes a handy way to combine several statements into one and relies on the fact that most statements are also expressions.

The inverted syntax is more suitable for some conditions than others. As Perl's motto has it, there is more than one way to do it (so long as the program remains legible). In the preceding examples, only the last return statement is really suited to this style; the others would probably be better off as normal if statements.

Beware declaring a variable in an inverted conditional statement, since the variable will only exist if the condition succeeds. This can lead to unexpected syntax errors if we have warnings enabled and unexpected bugs otherwise.

```
use warnings;
```

```
$arg = $ARGV[1] if $#ARGV;
if ($arg eq "help" ) {    #$arg may not be declared
    print "Usage: \n";
    ...
}
...
```

We would be unlikely to leave $arg undefined if we had written a conventional if statement because the declaration would be inside the block, making it obvious that the scope of the variable is limited. However, the inverted syntax can fool us into thinking that it is a declaration with wider scope.

If, then, and else conditions are implemented with the else keyword.

```
if (EXPRESSION) BLOCK else BLOCK
```

For example:

```
# First 'if else' tests whether $var is defined
if (defined $var) {
    # If $var is defined, the second 'if else' tests whether $var is true
    if ($var) {
        print "true \n";
    } else {
        print "false \n";
    }
} else {
    print "undefined \n";
}
```

However, it is not legal (and not elegant, even if it were) to invert an if statement and then add an else clause.

```
# ERROR!
return if $not_valid else { print "ok" };
```

If we have multiple mutually exclusive conditions, then we can chain them together using the elsif keyword, which may occur more than once and may or may not be followed by an else.

```
if (EXPRESSION) BLOCK elsif (EXPRESSION) BLOCK elsif...
if (EXPRESSION) BLOCK elsif (EXPRESSION) BLOCK else BLOCK
```

For example, to compare strings using just if and else we might write

```
if ($a eq $b) {
    print "Equal";
} else {
    if ($a gt $b) {
        print "Greater";
    } else {
        print "Less";
    }
}
```

The equivalent code written using elsif is simpler to understand, shorter, and avoids a second level of nesting:

```
if ($a eq $b) {
    print "Equal";
} elsif ($a gt $b) {
    print "Greater";
} else {
    print "Less";
}
```

Note that the else if construct, while legal in other languages such as C, is not legal in Perl and will cause a syntax error. In Perl, use elsif instead. Also note that if $a is less than $b most of the time, then we would be better off rewriting this statement to test $a lt $b first, then $a gt $b or

$a eq $b second. It pays to work out the most likely eventuality and then make that the fastest route through our code.

If the conditions are all testing the same expression with different values, then there are more efficient ways to do this. See "Switches and Multibranched Conditions" later in the chapter for some examples.

The if, unless, and elsif keywords all permit a variable to be declared in their conditions. For example:

```
if (my @lines = <HANDLE>) {   # test if there is a filehandle called HANDLE
    ...do something to file contents...
} else {
    "Nothing to process \n";
}
```

The scope of variables declared in this fashion is limited to that of the immediately following block, so here @lines can be used in the if clause but not the else clause or after the end of the statement.

unless

If we replace the if in an if statement with unless, the condition is inverted. This is handy for testing a condition that we want to act on if it evaluates to false, such as trapping error conditions.

```
# unless file filename is successfully opened then return a failure message
unless (open FILE, $filename) {
    return "Failed to open $filename: $!";
}
```

We can also invert the syntax of an unless statement, just as we can with if.

```
return "Failed to open $filename: $!" unless (open FILE, $filename);
```

This is exactly the same as inverting the condition inside the parentheses but reads a little better than using an if and not:

```
if (not open FILE, $filename) {
    return "Failed to open $filename: $!";
}
```

It is perfectly legal, though possibly a little confusing, to combine unless with an else or elsif as in the following:

```
unless (open FILE, $filename) {
    return "Failed to open $filename: $!";
} else {
    @lines = <FILE>;
    foreach (0..$#lines) {
        print "This is a line \n"
    }
    close FILE;
}
```

In this case, it is probably better to write an if-not expression or to invert the clauses, since unless-else is not a natural English construct.

Writing Conditions with Logical Operators

Perl's logical operators automatically execute a shortcut to avoid doing unnecessary work whenever possible, a feature Perl shares with most languages derived from or inspired by C (see Chapter 4). Take the following example:

```
$result = try_first() or try_second() or try_third ();
```

If try_first returns a true value, then clearly Perl has no need to even call the try_second or try_third functions, since their results will not be used; $result takes only one value, and that would be the value returned by try_first. So Perl takes a shortcut and does not call them at all.

We can use this feature to write conditional statements using logical operators instead of if and unless. For example, a very common construct to exit a program on a fatal error uses the die function that, upon failure, prints out an error message and finishes the program.

```
open (FILE, $filename) or die "Cannot open file: $!";
```

This is equivalent, but more direct, than the more conventional

```
unless (open FILE, $filename) {
   die "Cannot open file: $!";
}
```

We can also provide a list of statements (separated by commas) or a do block for the condition to execute on success. Here is an example that supplies a list:

```
open (FILE, $filename) or
    print (LOG "$filename failed: $!"), die "Cannot open file:$!";
```

Not every programmer likes using commas to separate statements, so we can instead use a do block. This also avoids the need to use parentheses to delineate the arguments to print.

```
open (FILE, $filename) or do {
   print LOG "$filename failed: $!";
   die "Cannot open file: $!";
};
```

When writing conditions with logical operators, it is good practice to use the low-precedence and, or, and not operators, instead of the higher priority &&, ||, and !. This prevents precedence from changing the meaning of our condition. If we were to change the previous example to

```
# ERROR! This statement ...
open (FILE, $filename)
    || print (LOG "$filename failed: $1"), die "Cannot open file:$!";
```

Perl's precedence rules would cause it to interpret this as a list containing a condition and a die statement.

```
# ERROR! ... actually means this
(open (FILE, $filename) || print (LOG "$filename failed: $1")),
    die "Cannot open file:$!";
```

As a result, this statement will always cause the program to die with a "Cannot open file" message, regardless of whether the open failed or succeeded.

Using a do block avoids all these problems and also makes the code easier to comprehend. Either a || or an or will work fine in this rewritten example:

```
open (FILE, $filename) || do {
   print LOG "$filename failed: $1";
   die "Cannot open file:$!";
};
```

Whether this is better than the original if form is questionable, but it does emphasize the condition in cases where the condition is actually the point of the exercise. In this case, the open is the most significant thing happening in this statement, so writing the condition in this way helps to emphasize and draw attention to it.

The drawback of these kinds of conditions is that they do not lend themselves easily to `else` type clauses. The following is legal, but tends toward illegibility:

```
open (FILE, $filename), $text = <FILE> or die "Cannot open file: $!";
```

It would also fail with a closed filehandle error if we used || instead of or; this has higher precedence than the comma and would test the result of `$text = <FILE>` and not the `open`.

The Ternary Operator

The ternary operator, `?:`, is a variant of the standard `if`-style conditional statement that works as an expression and returns a value that can be assigned or used in other expressions. It works identically to the ternary operator in C. The operator evaluates the first expression: if that expression is true, it returns the value of the second expression; and if the first expression was false, then the operator returns the value of the third expression. This is what it looks like:

```
result = expression1 ? expression2 : expression3
```

The ternary operator is very convenient when the purpose of a test is to return one of two values rather than follow one of two paths of execution. For example, the following code snippet adds a plural s conditionally, using a conventional `if-else` condition:

```perl
#!/usr/bin/perl
# plural_if.pl
use warnings;
use strict;

my @words = split ('\s+', <>);    #read some text and split on whitespace

my $count = scalar (@words);

print "There ";
if ($count == 1) {
    print "is";
} else {
    print "are";
}
print " $count word";

unless ($count == 1) {
    print "s";
}

print " in the text \n";
```

Running this program and entering some text produces messages like

```
There are 0 words in the text
There is 1 word in the text
There are 4 words in the text
```

The same code rewritten using the ternary operator is considerably simpler.

```perl
#!/usr/bin/perl
# plural_ternary.pl
use warnings;
use strict;
```

```
my @words = split ('\s+', <>);    #read some text and split on whitespace
my $words = scalar (@words);
```

print "There ", ($words == 1)?"is":"are"," $words word",
    ($words == 1)?"":"s","
in the text \n";

We can also nest ternary operators, though doing this more than once can produce code that is hard to read. The following example uses two ternary operators to compute a value based on a string comparison using cmp, which can return -1, 0, or 1:

```
#!/usr/bin/perl
# comparison.pl
use warnings;
use strict;

my @words = split ('\s+',<>);
die "Enter two words \n" unless scalar(@words) == 2;

my $result = $words[0] cmp $words[1];
print "The first word is ", $result ? $result>0 ? "greater than" :
    "less than" : "equal to "," the second \n";
```

This program checks that we have entered exactly two words, and if so it prints out one of the following three messages:

```
The first word is less than the second
The first word is greater than the second
The first word is equal to the second
```

The nested ternary operators know which ? and : belongs where, but it does not make for legible code. To improve upon this, the last line is probably better written with parentheses.

```
print "The first word is ", $result
    ? ($result > 0 ? "greater than" : "less than")
    : "equal to", " the second \n";
```

This makes it much simpler to see which expression belongs to which condition.

Be careful when combining the ternary operator into larger expressions. The precedence of operators can sometimes cause Perl to group the parts of an expression in ways we did not intend, as in the following example:

```
#!/usr/bin/perl
# plural_message.pl
use warnings;
use strict;

my @words = split ('\s+', <>);
my $words = scalar (@words);
#ERROR!
my $message = "There ". ($words==1) ? "is" :
  "are". " $words word".
    ($words == 1)?"" : "s". " in the text\n";

print $message;
```

This appears to do much the same as the previous example, except it stores the resulting message in an intermediate variable before printing it. But (unlike the comma operator) the precedence of the concatenation operator, ., is greater than that of the ternary ? or :, so the meaning of the statement is entirely changed. Using explicit parentheses, the first expression is equivalent to

```
"There ", (($words==1)? "is" : "are"), " $words word",
   (($words == 1)?"" : "s"), " in the text \n";
```

But with the concatenation operator, what we actually get is

```
("There ". ($words==1))? "is" : ("are". " $words word",
   ($words == 1)?"" : "s". " in the text \n");
```

The expression ("There ". ($words==1)) always evaluates to a true value, so the result of running this program will always be to print the word "is" regardless of the input we give it.

One final trick that we can perform with the ternary operator is to use it with expressions that return an lvalue (that is, an assignable value). An example of such an expression is the substr function.

```
#!/usr/bin/perl
# fix.pl
use warnings;
use strict;
my $word = "mit";
my $fix = "re";
my $before = int(<>);    #no warnings in case we enter no numeric text

($before ? substr($word, 0, 0): substr ($word, length($word), 0)) = $fix;
print $word, "\n";
```

In this program the contents of $fix are either prefixed or postfixed to the contents of the variable $word. The ternary operator evaluates to either the beginning or the end of the value in $word as returned from substr. This value is then assigned the value of $fix, modifying the contents of $word, which is then printed out.

The result of this program is either the word remit, if we enter any kind of true value (such as 1), or mitre, if we enter either nothing or a string that evaluates to false (such as "0", or a nonnumeric value).

Switches and Multibranched Conditions

A *switch* is a conditional statement that contains multiple branches of execution. It can be thought of as rotary switch with several different positions. A simple but crude way to implement a switch is with an if...elsif...else statement, as we have already seen.

```
if ($value == 1) {
    print "First Place";
} elsif ($value == 2) {
    print "Second Place";
} elsif ($value == 3) {
    print "Third Place";
} else {
    print "Try Again";
}
```

The problem with this kind of structure is that after a few conditions it becomes hard to understand. Perl does not have a built-in multiple-branch conditional statement like C or Java, but it does not really need one as there are many ways to achieve the same effect, including the Switch module for those who disagree. Here are two ways of writing the same set of conditions in a block:

```
SWITCH: {
    if ($value == 1) { print "First Place" };
    if ($value == 2) { print "Second Place" };
    if ($value == 3) { print "Third Place" };
    if ($value > 3)  { print "Try Again" };
```

```
}
SWITCH: {
    $value == 1 and print "First Place";
    $value == 2 and print "Second Place";
    $value == 3 and print "Third Place";
    $value > 3 and print "Try Again";
}
```

Here the block does not actually do anything useful except to allow us to group the conditions together for clarity. The SWITCH: label that prefixes the block likewise has no function except to indicate that the block contains a multiple-branch condition. Both of these examples are also less efficient than the original example because all conditions are tested, even if an earlier one matches. But as we saw earlier, bare blocks can be considered loops, so we can use the last loop control statements to break out of the block after the correct match.

```
SWITCH: {
    $value == 1 and print ("First Place"), last;
    $value == 2 and print ("Second Place"), last;
    $value == 3 and print ("Third Place"), last;
    print "Try Again";   # default case
}
```

As a bonus, the use of last, like break in C, guarantees that we cannot go on to match more than one condition, which in turn allows us to express later conditions a little more loosely, since they do not have to worry about avoiding matches against values now catered for by earlier cases.

We can also make use of the label to make our last statements more explicit.

```
SWITCH: {
    $value == 1 and print ("First Place"), last SWITCH;
    $value == 2 and print ("Second Place"), last SWITCH;
    $value == 3 and print ("Third Place"), last SWITCH;
    print "Try Again";   # default case
}
```

Here the meaning of last is clear enough, but the label can be very useful in longer clauses and particularly in multiple nested blocks and conditions.

If the cases we want to execute have only one or two statements and are similar, it is fine just to write them as a comma-separated list, as in this example. If the cases are more complex, however, this rapidly becomes illegible. A better solution in this case might be to use do blocks.

```
SWITCH: {
    $value == 1 and do {
        print "First Place";
        last;
    };

    $value == 2 and do {
        print "Second Place";
        last;
    };

    $value == 3 and do {
        print "Third Place";
        last;
    };

    print "Try Again";
}
```

Note that a do block does not count as a loop, so the `last` statements still apply to the switch block that encloses them. This is fortunate; otherwise we would have to say `last SWITCH` to ensure that right block is referred to. Of course, we can choose to use the label anyway for clarity if we choose, as noted previously.

If we are testing the value of a string rather than an integer, we can reproduce the preceding techniques but just replace the conditions with string equality tests.

```
SWITCH: {
    $value eq "1" and print ("First Place"), last;
    $value eq "2" and print ("Second Place"), last;
    $value eq "3" and print ("Third Place"), last;
    print "Try Again";
}
```

Having said this, if our strings are numeric, we can do a numeric comparison if need be. In this example, `$value eq "1"` and `$value == 1` have precisely the same result, thanks to Perl's automatic string number conversion. Of course, this only holds so long as we don't go past "9".

We can also use regular expression matching.

```
SWITCH: {
    $value =~/^1$/ and print("First Place"), last;
    $value =~/^2$/ and print("Second Place"), last;
    $value =~/^3$/ and print("Third Place"), last;
    print "Try Again";
}
```

This might not seem much of an improvement, but regular expressions have the useful feature that if they are not associated with a value, then they use the contents of the special variable $_ that Perl provides internally. As we mentioned earlier, it is the "default variable" that functions read or write from if no alternative variable is given. We will see in "Using foreach with Multibranched Conditions" how to use this with `foreach` to rewrite our switch.

The Switch Module

The `Switch` module gives Perl a bona fide `switch` and `case` statement, allowing us to write multi-branch conditions in a similar style to languages that provide them natively.

```
use Switch;

switch (10 * rand) {
    case 1 { print "First Place" }
    case 2 { print "Second Place" }
    case 3 { print "Third Place" }
    else   { print "...Also Ran" }
}
```

As this example illustrates, a default branch can also be created with `else`, which works just the same as it would in an `if...else` statement.

An advantage of this `switch` statement is that by default cases do not fall through, that is, once a given case matches the value, no further cases are considered. This differs from both C, where we must explicitly break out of the switch, and the examples earlier, where we had to use `last`. If we actually want to fall through to other cases, we can explicitly do so with `next`.

```
...
case 4 { print "Fourth Place"; next }
...
```

If the switch is given the value 4, it will now output `Fourth Place...Also Ran`.

Alternatively, to have all cases fall through by default(in the style of C) append 'fallthrough' to the use statement. To break out of the switch, we must now request it explicitly with last, as in the previous examples. The next example is equivalent to the previous one, with the additional case 4, but with fall through enabled as the default:

```
use Switch 'fallthrough';
```

```perl
switch (10 * rand) {
    case 1 { print "First Place", last }
    case 2 { print "Second Place", last }
    case 3 { print "Third Place", last }
    case 4 { print "Fourth Place" }
    else   { print "...Also Ran" }
}
```

The conditions can be almost anything and will be evaluated in the most appropriate way. We can use numbers, strings, and regular expressions. We can also use hashes and hash references (true if the value being tested exists as a key in the hash), array references (true if the value is in the array), code blocks, and subroutines. Here is an example that exercises most of the possibilities available:

```perl
#!/usr/bin/perl
# bigswitch.pl
use strict;
use warnings;
use Switch;

my $perl = "Perl";
my %hash = ( "pErl" => 2, "peRl" => 3 );
my $cref  = sub { $_[0] eq "pERl" };
sub testcase { $_[0] eq "peRL" };
my @array = (2..4);

my @values=qw[
    1 perl Perl 3 6 pErl PerL pERL pERl peRL PERL php
];

foreach my $input (@values) {
    switch ($input) {
        case 1                      { print "1 literal number" }
        case "perl"                 { print "2 literal string" }
        case ($perl)                { print "3 string variable" }
        case (\@array)              { print "4 array variable reference" }
        case [5..9]                 { print "5 literal array reference" }
        case (%hash)                { print "6 hash key" }
        case { "PerL" => "Value" }  { print "7 hash reference key" }
        case { $_[0] eq "pERL" }    { print "8 anonymous sub" }
        case ($cref)                { print "9 code reference (anonymous)" }
        case (\&testcase)           { print "A code reference (named)" }
        case /^perl/i               { print "B regular expression" }
        else                        { print "C not known at this address" }
    }
    print "\n";
}
```

The seventh and eighth cases in the previous example, hash reference and anonymous subroutine, bear a little closer examination. Both are delimited by curly braces, but the switch can tell them apart because of the operator in use (=> versus eq). This prescience is possible because the Switch module actually parses the source code just prior to execution and works out the most sensible thing to do based on what it sees.

The anonymous subroutine also bears examination because it refers to the variable $_[0], which is not otherwise defined in this program. What is actually going on here is hinted at by the fact that this case is called "anonymous subroutine." The block { $_[0] eq "pERL" } is actually a subroutine defined in place within the case statement, and $_[0] simply accesses the first argument passed to it, which is the value of $input. It is therefore exactly equivalent to the ninth and tenth "code reference" cases, just more concise.

Interestingly, the switch value can also be a code reference or subroutine, in which case the case tests are applied to it instead. There are limitations to this method, since there is no way to pass a conventional text value. Instead it must be written explicitly into the subroutine.

```perl
#!/usr/bin/perl -w
# switchonsub.pl
use strict;
use Switch;

my $input;

sub lessthan { $input < $_[0] };

$input=int(<>);
switch ( \&lessthan ) {
    case 10              { print "less than 10" }
    case (100-$input)    { print "less than 50" }
    case 100             { print "less than 100" }
}
```

There are friendlier ways to handle this kind of situation using a closure (see Chapter 7), and not every subroutine-based switch necessarily needs to reference a global variable the way this one does, but in a lot of cases there is likely to be a better way to express the problem, for instance with explicit case conditions like case { $_ < 10 }.

Perl 6 will provide a native multibranch statement, but using given and when in place of switch and case. The Switch module can be told to use Perl 6 terminology by appending 'Perl6' to the use statement.

```perl
use Switch 'Perl6';


given ($value) {
    when 1 { print "First Place" }
    when 2 { print "Second Place" }
    when 3 { print "Third Place" }
}
```

Returning Values from Multibranched Conditions

Simple if and unless statements do not return a value, but this is not a problem since we can write a conditional expression using the ternary operator. For multiple-branch conditions, we have to be more inventive, but again Perl provides several ways for us to achieve this goal. One way to go about it is with logical operators using a do block.

```
print do {
    $value == 1 && "First Place" ||
    $value == 2 && "Second Place" ||
    $value == 3 && "Third Place" ||
    "Try again"
}, "\n";
```

If this approach does not suit our purposes, we can always resort to a subroutine and use return to return the value to us.

```
sub placing {
    $_[0] == 1 and return "First Place";
    $_[0] == 2 and return "Second Place";
    $_[0] == 3 and return "Third Place";
    return "Try Again";
}
print placing ($value), "\n";
```

Or, using the ternary operator:

```
sub placing {
    return $_[0] == 1? "First place" :
           $_[0] == 2? "Second place" :
           $_[0] == 3? "Third place" :
            "Try Again";
}
```

While this works just fine, it does not scale indefinitely. For situations more complex than this, it can be easier to decant the conditions and return values into the keys and values of a hash, then test for the hash key. Finally, there is another solution involving using foreach, which we will also consider in "Using foreach with Multibranched Conditions."

Loops and Looping

A loop is a block of code that is executed repeatedly, according to the criteria of the loop's controlling conditions. Perl provides two kinds of loop:

- Iterating loops, provided by for and foreach
- Conditional loops, provided by while and until

The distinction between the two types is in the way the controlling conditions are defined.

The for and foreach loops iterate over a list of values given either explicitly or generated by a function or subroutine. The sense of the loop is "for each of these values, do something." Each value in turn is fed to the body of the loop for consideration. When the list of values runs out, the loop ends.

The while and until loops, on the other hand, test a condition each time around the loop. The sense of the loop is "while this condition is satisfied, keep doing something." If the condition succeeds, the loop body is executed once more. If it fails, the loop ends. There is no list of values and no new value for each iteration, unless it is generated in the loop body itself.

Both kinds of loop can be controlled using statements like next, last, and redo. These statements allow the normal flow of execution in the body of a loop to be restarted or terminated, which is why they are also known as loop modifiers. We have already talked about loop modifiers briefly in Chapter 2, but will learn more about them later in this chapter.

Because Perl is such a versatile language, there are also ways to create loop-like effects without actually writing a loop. Perl provides functions such as map and grep that can often be used to produce the same effect as a foreach or while loop—but more efficiently. In particular, if the object of a loop is to process a list of values and convert them into another list of values, map may be a more effective solution than an iterative foreach loop.

Writing C-Style Loops with for

The for and foreach keywords are actually synonyms, and typically differ only in how they get used. for is used, by convention, for loops that imitate the structure of the for loop in C. Here's how a for loop can be used to count from nine to zero:

```
for ($n = 9; $n >= 0; $n-) {
    print $n;
}
```

Any C programmer will recognize this syntax as being identical to C, with the minor exception of the dollar sign of Perl's scalar data type syntax. Similarly, to count from zero to nine we could write

```
for ($n = 0; $n < 10; $n++) {
    print $n, "\n";
    sleep 1;
}
print "Liftoff! \n";
```

The parenthesized part of the for loop contains three statements: an initialization statement, a condition, and a continuation statement. These are usually (but not always) used to set up and check a loop variable, $n in the first example. The initialization statement (here $n=0) is executed before the loop starts. Just before each iteration of the loop the condition $n<10 is tested. If true the loop is executed; if false the loop finishes. After each completion of the loop body, the continuation statement $n++ is executed. When $n reaches 10, the condition fails and the loop exits without executing the loop body, making 9 the last value of $n to be printed and giving $n the value 10 after the loop has finished.

In the preceding example, we end up with the scalar variable $n still available, even though it is only used inside the loop. It would be better to declare the variable so that it only exists where it is needed. Perl allows the programmer to declare the loop variable inside the for statement. A variable declared this way has its scope limited to the body of the for loop, so it exists only within the loop statement:

```
for (my $n = 0; $n < 10; $n ++) {
    print $n,' is ', ($n % 2)? 'odd' : 'even';
}
```

In this example, we declare $n lexically with my, so it exists only within the for statement itself. (For why this is a good idea and other scoping issues, see Chapter 8.)

As an aside, the for loop can happily exist with nothing supplied for the first or last statement in the parentheses. Remember, however, that the semicolons are still required to get C-style semantics since for and foreach are synonyms. The following is thus a funny looping while loop:

```
for (; eof (FILE) ;) {
    print <FILE>;
}
```

While we are on the subject and jumping ahead for a moment, the optional continue block is really the same construct as the last statement of a C-style for loop, just with a different syntax. Here is the equivalent of the earlier for loop written using while:

```
$n = 0;
while ($n < 10) {
    print $n, ' is ', ($n % 2)? 'odd': 'even';
```

```
} continue {
    $n ++;
}
```

Writing Better Loops with foreach

The C-style for loop is familiar to C programmers, but it is often unnecessarily complicated. For instance, one of the most common uses of a for loop in C is to iterate over the contents of an array using a loop variable to index the array. In the following example, the loop variable is $n, and it is used to index the elements of an array (presumed to already exist) called @array. The first element is at index 0, and the highest is given by $#array.

```
for (my $n = 0; $n < $#array; $n++) {
    print $array [$n], "\n";
}
```

However, we do not need to use an index variable. We can just iterate directly over the contents of the array instead. Although in practice for is usually used for the C style and foreach for the Perl style, the two keywords are actually synonyms, and both may be used in either the C and Perl syntaxes. The convention of using each in its allotted place is not enforced by Perl but is generally considered good practice anyway. Here is the foreach (i.e., Perl-style) version of the preceding loop:

```
my $element;
foreach $element (@array) {
    print $element, "\n";
}
```

Even better, foreach allows us to declare the loop variable in the loop. This saves a line because no separate declaration is needed. More importantly, it restricts the scope of the variable to the loop, just as with the for loop earlier. This means that if the variable did not exist beforehand, neither will it after.

```
foreach my $element (@array) {
    print $element,"\n";
}
# $element does not exist here
```

If the loop variable already happens to exist and we don't use my, Perl localizes the variable when it is used as a loop variable, equivalent to using the local keyword. When the loop finishes, the old value of the variable is reestablished.

```
#!/usr/bin/perl
# befaft.pl
use warnings;

$var = 42;
print "Before: $var \n";
foreach $var (1..5) {
    print "Inside: $var \n";
}
print "After: $var \n";    # prints '42', not '5'
```

This localization means that we cannot accidentally overwrite an existing variable, but it also means we cannot return the last value used in a foreach loop as we would be able to in C. If we need to do so this, we may be better off using a while loop or a map. Of course, giving a loop variable the same name as a variable that already exists is confusing, prone to error, and generally a bad idea anyway.

If we really want to index an array by element number, we can still do that with foreach. A foreach loop needs a list of values, and we want to iterate from zero to the highest element in the array. So we need to generate a list from zero to the highest element index and supply that to the foreach loop. We can achieve that easily using the range operator and the $#array notation to retrieve the highest index:

```
foreach my $element (0..$#array) {
    print "Element $element is $array[$element] \n";
}
```

Using a range is easier to read, but in versions of Perl prior to 5.005 it is less efficient than using a loop variable in a for (or while) loop, for the simple reason that the range operator creates a list of all the values between the two ranges. For a range of zero to one hundred million, this involves the creation of a list containing one-hundred-million integers, which requires at least four-hundred-million bytes of storage. Of course, it is unlikely that we are handling an array with one-hundred-million values in the first place. However, the principle holds true, so be wary of creating large temporary arrays when you can avoid them. From Perl 5.005 onwards the range operator has been optimized to return values iteratively (rather like each) in foreach loops, so it is now much faster than a loop variable. This can be considered a reason to upgrade as much as a programming point, of course.

If no loop variable is supplied, Perl uses the "default" variable $_ to hold the current loop value.

```
foreach (@array) {
    print "$_ \n";
}
```

This is very convenient, especially with functions that default to using $_ if no argument is supplied, like the regular expression operators.

```
foreach (@array) {
    /match_text/ and print "$_ contains a match! \n";
}
```

A final, somewhat unusual, form of the for/foreach loop inverts the loop to place the body before the for. This is the same syntax as the inverted if, but applied to a loop instead. For example:

```
/match_text/ and print ("$_ contains a match! \n") foreach @array;
```

This syntax can be convenient for very short loop bodies, but it is not really suitable if the foreach becomes obscured. The preceding example is borderline legible, for example, and a map or the former version would probably be better.

Using foreach with Multibranched Conditions

We have already mentioned that, when used with switches and multibranched conditions, regular expressions have the particularly useful feature of using $_ when they are not associated with a value. By combining this with a foreach loop, we can remove the test variable altogether. Without a defined loop variable, foreach assigns each value that it is given in turn to $_ inside the block that follows it. This means we can rewrite this statement:

```
SWITCH: {
    $value =~/^1$/ and print("First Place"), last;
    $value =~/^2$/ and print("Second Place"), last;
    $value =~/^3$/ and print("Third Place"), last;
    print "Try Again";
}
```

like this:

```
SWITCH: foreach ($value) {
    /^1$/ and print ("First Place"), last;
    /^2$/ and print ("Second Place"), last;
    /^3$/ and print ("Third Place"), last;
    print "Try Again";
}
```

Note that the SWITCH label helps to remind us that this isn't a foreach loop in the usual sense, but it is not actually necessary.

We have also seen how to return a value from multibranched conditions using a do block, subroutine, or the ternary operator. However, foreach also comes in very handy here when used with logical operators:

```
foreach ($value) {
    $message = /^1$/ && "First Place" ||
               /^2$/ && "Second Place" ||
               /^3$/ && "Third Place" ||
               "Try Again";
    print "$message \n";
}
```

Here we use a foreach to alias $value to $_, then test with regular expressions. Because $value is a scalar, not a list, the loop only executes once, but the aliasing still takes place. The shortcut behavior of logical operators will ensure that the first matching expression will return the string attached to the && operator. Note that if we were writing more complex cases, parentheses would be in order; for this simple example we don't need them.

This approach works only so long as the resulting values are all true. In this case we are returning one of the strings First Place...Try Again, so there is no problem. For situations involving zero, an undefined value, or an empty string (all of which evaluate to false), we can make use of the ternary operator to produce a similar effect.

```
foreach ($value) {
    $message = /^1$/? "First Place":
               /^2$/? "Second Place":
               /^3$/? "Third Place":
                   "Try Again";
    print "$message \n";
}
```

The regular expressions in this example are testing against $_, which is aliased from $value by the foreach.

Variable Aliasing in foreach Loops

If we are iterating over a real array (as opposed to a list of values), then the loop variable is not a copy but a direct alias for the corresponding array element. If we change the value of the loop variable, then we also change the corresponding array element. This can be a source of problems in Perl programs if we don't take this into account, but it can also be very useful. This example uses aliasing to convert a list of strings into a consistent capitalized form.

```
#!/usr/bin/perl
# capitalize.pl
use warnings;
use strict;

my @array = ("onE", "two", "THREE", "fOUR", "FiVe");
foreach (@array) {
    # lc turns the word into lowercase, ucfirst then capitalizes the first letter
```

```perl
    $_ = ucfirst lc;   # lc uses $_ by default with no argument
}
print join(',', @array);
```

Sometimes we might want to avoid the aliasing feature and instead modify a copy of the original array. The simplest way to do that is to copy the original array before we start.

```perl
foreach (@tmparray = @array) {
    $_ =~tr/a-z/A-Z/;
    print;
}
```

The assignment to a local lexically scoped variable creates a temporary array, which can be modified without affecting the original array. It is also disposed of at the end of the loop.

Conditional Loops—while, until, and do

The while and until loops test a condition and continue to execute the loop for as long as that condition holds. The only difference is that for while the condition holds while it is true, and for until it holds until it is false (i.e., until it is true). Here is an example of counting from 1 to 10 using a while loop rather than a for or foreach loop:

```perl
#!/usr/bin/perl
# count10.pl
use warnings;
use strict;

# count from 1 to 10 (note the post-increment in the condition)
my $n = 0;
while ($n++ < 10) {
    print $n, "\n";
}
```

The while and until loops are well suited to tasks where we want to repeat an action continuously until a condition that we can have no advance knowledge of occurs, such as reaching the end of a file. The following example shows a while loop being used to read the contents of a file line by line. When the end of the file is reached, the readline operator returns false and the loop terminates.

```perl
open FILE, "file.txt";
while ($line = <FILE>) {
    print $line;
}
close FILE;
```

If we replace while with until, the meaning of the condition is reversed, in the same way that unless reverses the condition of an if statement. This makes more sense when the nature of the question asked by the Boolean test implies that we are looking for a "no" answer. The eof function is a good example; it returns true when there is no more data.

```perl
open FILE, "file.txt";
until (eof(FILE)) {
    $line = <FILE>;
    print $line;
}
```

Variable Aliasing with while

while loops do not alias their conditions the way that a foreach loop does its controlling list, because there is no loop variable to alias with. However, a few Perl functions will alias their values to $_ if placed in the condition of a while loop. One of them is the readline operator. This means we can write a loop to read the lines of a file one by one without a loop variable.

```
open FILE, "file.txt";
while (<FILE>) {
    print "$.: $_";
}
```

Or, more tersely:

```
print "$.: $_" while <FILE>;
```

Looping Over Lists and Arrays with while

We can loop over the contents of an array with while if we don't mind destroying the array as we do it.

```
while ($element = shift @array) {
    print $element, "\n";
}
# @array is empty here
```

On the face of it, this construct does not appear to have any advantage over a more intuitive foreach loop. In addition, it destroys the array in the process of iterating through it, since the removed elements are discarded. However, it can have some advantages. One performance-related use is to discard large memory-consuming values (like image data) as soon as we have finished with them. This allows Perl to release memory that much faster.

There can also be computational advantages. Assume we have a list of unique strings and we want to discard every entry before a particular "start" entry. This is easy to achieve with a while loop because we discard each nonmatching string as we test it.

```
#!/usr/bin/perl
# startexp.pl
use warnings;
use strict;
# define a selection of strings one of which is "start"
my @lines = ("ignored", "data", "start", "the data", "we want");

# discard lines until we see the "start" marker
while (my $line = shift @lines) {
    last if $line eq 'start';
}

# print out the remaining elements using interpolation ($")
print "@lines";
```

Looping on Self-Modifying Arrays

We can use array functions like push, pop, shift, and unshift to modify the array even while we are processing it. This lets us create some interesting variations on a standard loop that are otherwise hard to achieve.

As an example, the following program oscillates indefinitely between two values. It works by shifting elements off an array one by one and adding them to the other end after subtracting each value from the highest value in the range, plus 1:

```
#!/usr/bin/perl
# oscillator.pl
use warnings;
use strict;
```

```perl
my $max = 20;
my @array = (1..$max-1);

while (my $element = shift @array) {
    push (@array, $max - $element);
    sleep 1;    # delay the print for one second to see the output
    print '*' x $element, "\n";   # multiply single '*' to get a bar of '*'s
}
```

A slight variation of this program produces a loop that counts from one to a maximum value, then back to one again, and terminates. The principal difference is that the array ranges from one to $max not one to $max-1:

```perl
#!/usr/bin/perl
# upanddown.pl
use warnings;
use strict;

my $max = 6;
my @array = (1..$max);

while (my $element = shift @array) {
    push (@array,$max - $element);
    print $element, " : ", join(",", @array), "\n";
}
```

Why should such a trivial difference cause the loop to terminate? This program produces the following output, which shows us why it terminates after passing through the array only twice:

```
1 : 2,3,4,5,6,5
2 : 3,4,5,6,5,4
3 : 4,5,6,5,4,3
4 : 5,6,5,4,3,2
5 : 6,5,4,3,2,1
6 : 5,4,3,2,1,0
5 : 4,3,2,1,0,1
4 : 3,2,1,0,1,2
3 : 2,1,0,1,2,3
2 : 1,0,1,2,3,4
1 : 0,1,2,3,4,5
```

We can see from this what is actually going on. The values of the array are each replaced with a value one lower. Since the first array element contained 1, this is reduced to 0. When it comes around for the second time, the result of the shift is a false value, because 0 is false. So the loop terminates.

These particular examples are chosen for simplicity and could also be implemented using simpler loops, for example, using an increment variable that oscillates between +1 and -1 at each end of the number range. While we have only used an ordered list for clarity, the oscillator will work even if the array does not contain ordered numbers.

Looping Over Hashes with while

We can iterate over a hash with while instead of foreach using the each function, which in a list context returns the next key-value pair in the hash, in the same order that keys and values return the keys and values, respectively. When there are no more key-value pairs, each returns undef, making it suitable for use in the condition of a while loop.

```
while (($key, $value) = each(%hash)) {
    print "$key => $value\n";
}
```

Using foreach and keys or while and each for this kind of task is mostly a matter of personal preference. However, foreach is generally more flexible as it allows sorting keys and aliasing with $_, neither of which are possible in a while/each loop. However, while avoids extracting the entire key list at the start of the loop and is preferable if we intend to quit the loop once a condition is met. This is particularly true if the hash happens to be tied to something that is resource-heavy (in comparison to an in-memory hash) like a DBM database.

Note that a foreach loop is a much safer option if we want to alter the contents of the array or hash we are iterating over. In particular, the internal iterator that each uses can get confused if the hash is modified during the course of the loop.

do . . . while and do . . . until

One problem with while and until loops is that they test the condition first and execute the loop body only if the test succeeds. This means that if the test fails on the first pass, the loop body is never executed. Sometimes, however, we want to ensure that the body is executed at least once. Fortunately, we can invert while and until loops by appending them to a do block to produce a do...while or do...until loop.

```
do {
    $input = <>; #read a line from standard input
    print "You typed: $input \n";
} while ($input !~ /^quit/);
```

The last line can be rewritten to use until to equal effect.

```
} until $input =~ /^quit/;
```

Note that parentheses around the condition are optional in an inverted while or until loop, just as they are in an inverted if.

Interestingly, this inverted loop structure applies to all the looping statements, even foreach:

```
# this works, but is confusing. Don't do it.
do {
    print;
} foreach (@array);
```

However, there is little point in doing this for foreach, first because it will not work except using $_, second because the loop body does not execute first as it needs the loop value to proceed, and third because it's just plain confusing. We mention it only because Perl allows it, and it is conceivably possible that we may encounter it in code.

Note that in the inverted form we cannot declare a variable in the conditional expression. We also cannot use loop control statements to control the loop's execution as these are not permitted in a do block—see "The Trouble with do" later in the chapter.

Controlling Loop Execution

Ordinarily a loop will execute according to its controlling criteria. Frequently, however, we want to alter the normal flow of execution from within the loop body itself, depending on conditions that arise as the loop body is executed. Perl provides three statements for this, collectively known as loop modifiers: next, which advances to the next iteration (retesting the loop condition); last, which immediately exits the loop; and redo, which restarts the current iteration (without retesting the loop condition).

The next statement forces the loop immediately onto the next iteration, skipping any remaining code in the loop body but executing the `continue` block if it is present. It is most often used when all the tasks necessary for a given iteration have been completed or the loop variable value for the current iteration is not applicable.

The following code snippet reads configuration parameters from the user, consisting of lines of `name = value` pairs. It uses `next` to skip past empty lines, comments (lines beginning with a #), and lines without an equals sign.

```perl
#!/usr/bin/perl
# config.pl
use warnings;
use strict;
my %config = ();
while (<>) {
    chomp;   #strip linefeed

    next if /^\s*$/;   #skip to the next iteration on empty lines
    next if /^\s*\#/;  #skip to the next iteration on comments
    my ($param, $value) = split("=", $_, 2);   #split on first '='
    unless ($value) {
        print ("No value for parameter '$_' \n");
        next;
    }

    $config{$param} = $value;
}

foreach (sort keys %config) {
    print "$_ => $config{$_} \n";
}
```

The `last` statement forces a loop to exit immediately, as if the loop had naturally reached its last iteration. A `last` is most often used when the task for which the loop was written has been completed, such as searching for a given value in an array—once found, no further processing is necessary. It can also be used in `foreach` loops pressed into service as multibranch conditions as we saw earlier. Here is a more conventional use of `last` that copies elements from one array to another until it hits an undefined element or reaches the end of the source array:

```perl
#!/usr/bin/perl
# last.pl
use warnings;

my @array = ("One", "Two", "Three", undef, "Five", "Six");

#copy array up to the first undefined element
my @newarray = ();
foreach my $element (@array) {
    last unless defined ($element);
    push @newarray, $element;
}

foreach (@newarray) {
    print $_." \n";   # prints One, Two, Three
}
```

The `redo` statement forces the loop to execute the current iteration over again. At first sight this appears similar to `next`. The distinction is that with `redo` the loop condition is not retested, and the continue block, if present, is not executed. In the case of a foreach loop, that means that the loop variable retains the value of the current loop rather than advances to the next. In the case of a while or until loop, the code in the conditional clause is not reexecuted, and any functions in it are not called. A redo is most often used when more than one iteration may be needed before the main body of a loop can be executed, for example, reading files with multiple-line statements.

```perl
#!/usr/bin/perl
# backslash.pl
use warnings;
use strict;
my @lines = ();
while (<>) {
    chomp;
    if (s/\\$//) {    #check for and remove a trailing backslash character
        my $line = <>;
        $_.= $line, redo;    # goes to the 'chomp' above
        }
        push @lines, $_;
    }

foreach (0..$#lines) {
    print "$_ : $lines[$_] \n";
}
```

In this example, the while statement reads a line of input with <> and aliases it to $_. The chomp removes the trailing newline, and the remainder of the line is checked for a trailing backslash. If one is found, another line is read and appended to $_.

Inside the if statement, the redo is called to pass execution back up to the chomp statement. Because redo does not reexecute the while statement, the value of $_ is not overridden, and the chomp is performed on the value of $_ that was assigned inside the if statement. This process continues so long as we continue to enter lines ending with a backslash.

All of the loop control statements next, last, and redo can be used in any kind of loop (for, foreach, while, until). One exception to this is the do...while and do...until loops. This is because loops built around do blocks do not behave quite the way we expect, as we will see shortly.

The continue Clause

All of Perl's loops can accept an additional continue clause. Code placed into the block of a continue clause is executed after the main body of the loop. Ordinarily this has no different effect from just adding the code to the end of the main loop, unless the loop body contains a next statement, in which case the continue block is executed before returning to the top of the loop. This makes a continue block a suitable place to increment a loop variable.

```perl
my $n = 0;

while ($n < 10) {
    next if ($n % 2);
    print $n, "\n";

} continue {
    # 'next' comes here
    $n++;
}

# 'last' comes here
```

Note, however, that a `last` statement will not execute the `continue` block before exiting the loop. Similarly, `redo` will not execute the `continue` block because it reexecutes the loop body on the same iteration, rather than continuing to the next.

There are actually few, if any, instances where a `continue` block is actually necessary, since most loops with a `continue` clause can be easily rewritten to avoid one. As we mentioned earlier, the `continue` clause is actually an explicit way to write the third part of a `for` loop, which deals with `next`, `last`, and `redo` in the same way as the `while...continue` loop earlier.

Controlling Nested Loops

So far we have just seen how to use loop control statements to affect the execution of the current loop. However, the `next`, `last`, and `redo` statements all accept an optional loop label as an argument. This allows us to jump to the start or end of an outer loop, so long as that loop has a name. To give a loop a name, we just prefix it with a label.

```
my @lines = ();
LINE: foreach (<>) {
    chomp;
    next LINE if /^$/;    #skip blank lines
    push @lines, $_;
}
```

Even in a simple loop this can enable us to write more legible code. Since the label indicates the purpose of the loop and of the control statements inside it, `next LINE` literally means "do the next line." However, if we have two nested loops, labeling the outer loop allows us to jump to the next iteration of the outer loop using `next`.

```
OUTER: foreach my $outer (@array) {
    INNER: foreach my $inner (@{$outer}) {
        next OUTER unless defined $inner;
    }
    # 'last' or 'last INNER' would come here
}
```

This is very similar to using a `last` statement, except that it will jump to the top of the outer loop rather than the end of the inner loop. If the outer loop contains more code after the inner loop, `next` will avoid it while `last` will execute it.

Similarly, we can use `last` to exit both loops simultaneously. This is a much more efficient way to exit nested loops than exiting each loop individually.

```
LINE: foreach my $line (<>) {
    chomp;
    ITEM: foreach (split /, /, $line) {
        last LINE if /^_END_/; #abort both loops on token
        next LINE if /^_NEXT_/; #skip remaining items on token
        next ITEM if /^\s*$/;   #skip empty columns
        #process item
        print "Got: $_ \n";
    }
}
```

Only the outer loop actually needs to be labeled, so loop control statements can apply themselves to the outer loop and not to the inner loop.

Perl allows labels to be defined multiple times. When a label is used, the label definition that is closest in scope is taken to be the target. For loop control statements, the first matching loop label in the stack of loops surrounding the statement is used. In general, we do not expect to be giving two loops the same name if one is inside the other, so it is always clear which label a loop control statement is referring to. Reusing labels is also handy for switch-style conditional statements and any other constructs where we want to make the purpose of the construct clear.

Strangely, we can jump to a loop label of an outer loop, even if there is a subroutine call in the way. This is really a very bad idea and is almost certainly not intended, so Perl will warn us if we do it inadvertently.

```
Exiting subroutine via next at ...
```

■Tip Although we would not expect to do this normally, it is possible to mistype the name of a label, especially if we copy and paste carelessly.

The Trouble with do

The fact that loop modifiers do not work in do...while, or do...until loops may seem strange. The reason for this is slightly obscure, but it comes about because unlike a normal while or until loop, the while and until conditions in a do...while or do...until loop are considered modifiers, which modify the behavior of the do block immediately before them. The do block is not considered to be a loop, so loop control statements do not work in them.

It is possible, though not terribly elegant, to get a next statement to work in a do...while loop through the addition of an extra bare block inside the do block, as in this example:

```perl
#!/usr/bin/perl
# even.pl
use warnings;
use strict;

# print out even numbers with a do...while loop
my $n = 0;
do { {
    next if ($n % 2);
    print $n, "\n";
} } while ($n++ < 10);
```

Unfortunately while this works for next, it does not work for last, because both next and last operate within the bounds of the inner block. All last does in this case is take us to the end of the inner block, where the while condition is still in effect. In addition, this is ugly and nonintuitive code. The better solution at this point is to find a way to rephrase this code as a normal while, until, or foreach loop and avoid the whole problem.

```perl
$n = 0;
while (++$n <= 10) {
    next if ($n % 2);
    print $n, "\n";
}
```

The goto Statement

The goto statement has two basic modes of operation. The simpler and more standard use allows execution to jump to an arbitrary labeled point in the code, just as in C and many other languages.

```perl
($lines, $empty, $comment, $code) = (0, 0, 0, 0);

while (<>) {
    /^$/ and $empty++, goto CONTINUE;
```

```
    /^#/ and $comment++, goto CONTINUE;
    $code++, goto CONTINUE;
CONTINUE:
    $lines++;
}
```

There are few, if any, reasons to use a goto with a label. In this case, we would be better off replacing goto with next statements and putting the continue code into a continue block.

```
while (<>) {
    /^$/ and $empty++, next;
    /^#/ and $comment++, next;
    $code++;
} continue {
    $lines++;
}
```

A goto statement can also take an expression as its argument. The result of the expression should be a label that execution can jump to. This gives us another, albeit rather ugly, way to write a compound switch statement.

```
$selection = int(3*rand);    # random integer between 0 and 2

@selections = ("ZERO", "ONE", "TWO");
goto $selections[$selection];

{ ZERO:
    print "None";
    next;
  ONE:
    print "One";
    next;
  TWO:
    print "Two";
    next;
}

print "...done \n";
```

Again, there are better ways to write compound statements. We covered these earlier, so we should not have to resort to goto here.

The second and more interesting use of goto is to call subroutines. When used in this context, the new subroutine entirely replaces the context of the calling one, so that on return from the second subroutine, execution is returned directly to the *caller* of the first subroutine. The primary use of this form is in autoloaded functions, which will be covered in Chapter 10.

It can also be used for so-called tau-recursion. This is where a subroutine can call itself recursively many times without causing Perl to create an ever-growing stack of subroutine calls. The final call returns directly to the original caller instead of returning a value through all of the intermediate subroutine calls. We will cover this in Chapter 7.

map and grep

The map and grep functions convert one list into another, applying a transform or condition to each element of the source list in turn. If the goal of a foreach or while loop is to generate a new list, we might be able to do the job better using map or grep. The syntax of map (and grep) takes one of two equivalent forms:

```
map EXPRESSION, LIST        grep EXPRESSION, LIST
map BLOCK LIST              grep BLOCK LIST
```

In each case the EXPRESSION or BLOCK is executed for each value of LIST, with the results returned as a new list.

The purpose of map is to convert the elements of a list one by one and to produce a new list as a result. The expression or block performs the conversion, so map is conceptually related to a foreach loop. Similarly, the purpose of grep is to return a list containing a subset of the original list. The expression or block is evaluated to a true or false value to see if the element is eligible for inclusion, so grep is conceptually related to a while loop. Both functions perform aliasing to $_ in the same way that foreach does.

map

To illustrate how map works, here is an example. Assume that we have a list of integers representing ASCII values, and we want to turn it into a list of character strings. We can do that with a foreach loop with a loop like this:

```
my @numbers = (80, 101, 114, 108);
my @characters;

foreach (@numbers) {
    push @characters, chr $_;
}

print @characters;
```

With map we can replace the loop with

```
my @characters = map (chr $_, @numbers);
```

Or, using the block syntax:

```
my @characters = map {chr $_} @numbers;
```

Even better, we can feed the list returned by the map into a join, then print the result in a single operation.

```
print join ('-', map {chr $_} @numbers);    # displays 'P-e-r-l'
```

Another common use for map is to construct a hash map of values to quickly determine if a given value exists or not. With an array we would have compare each element in turn.

```
#!/usr/bin/perl -w
# insequencemap.pl
use strict;

my @sequence=(1,1,2,3,5,8,13,21,34,55,89);
my %insequence=map { $_ => 1 } @sequence;
my $number=<>;
print "$number is ",($insequence{$number}?"":"NOT"),"in sequence\n";
```

Unlike foreach, map cannot choose to use an explicit loop variable and must use $_ within the block or expression. It also cannot make use of loop control variables, for the same reasons that a do block cannot, as we saw earlier.

In void context, the return value of map is discarded. Prior to Perl 5.8, this was perfectly functional code but not very efficient; the list of values to return would be constructed and then discarded again. From version 5.8.1 onwards Perl is smart enough to notice when it is asked to evaluate a map whose return value is not used and will optimize the map to avoid the redundant work. The following two statements are therefore equivalent and equally efficient.

```
ucfirst foreach @words; # foreach style self-modify list
map { ucfirst } @words; # map style self-modify list
```

From 5.8.4, assigning a map to a scalar value (which counts the number of values present) will also be optimized.

```
my $howmany = map { ucfirst } @words; # more efficient in Perl >= 5.8.4
```

Void context aside, map is usually used to convert one list into another of equal length, with one new value in the result for each value in the input. However, it is possible to persuade map not to return a new value by having it return ().

```
print map { ($_>110) ? () : chr($_) } @numbers; # displays 'Pel'
```

If the only object of the map is to selectively return values, however, we should really be using grep.

grep

The grep function gets its name from the Unix grep command, which scans text files and returns lines from them that match a given regular expression search pattern. The Perl grep function is similar in concept in that it returns a list containing a subset of the original list, though it does not directly have anything to do with regular expressions.

The syntax of grep is identical to map, but while the expression or block in a map statement is used to transform each value in a list, the corresponding expression or block in a grep statement is evaluated as a condition to determine if the value should be included in the returned list.

For example, the following while loop reads a list of lines from standard input and builds up a list of the lines that started with a digit:

```
my @numerics = ();
while (<>) {
    push @numerics, $_ if /^\d/;
}
print "@numerics\n";
```

We can simplify the preceding to just

```
@numerics = grep {/^\d/} <>;
```

Here we have used a regular expression as the condition, in keeping with the spirit of the Unix grep command, which works on a similar basis. However, since grep accepts any expression or block to test the condition, we can use any kind of condition we like.

Just because grep tests each value rather than manipulating it does not mean that it has to leave the value untouched. Just as map can be made to act like grep by returning (), grep can be made to act like map by assigning a new value to $_. However, doing this alters the original list. This is fine if we intend to discard the original list, but it can lead to problematic code if we forget. Here is an example where the source list is generated by reading from standard input. We can't subsequently access this list from anywhere else, so there is no risk of making a mistake.

```
@numerics = grep { s/^(\d+)/Line $1:/ } <>;
```

This example assigns the result of the substitution value to $_ for each matching line. The return value of the substitution is true if a match was made and false otherwise, so only the lines that were transformed are returned by the grep.

Just like map, grep can be used in a void context to change an original array without creating a new list of values. Also like map, from version 5.8.1 Perl will optimize such a grep so that no output values are generated to then get immediately discarded.

Chaining map and grep Functions Together

Both map and grep take lists as input and produce lists as output, so we can chain them together. The following example again reads a list of lines from standard input, and returns a list of all lines that were exactly five characters long (including the terminating linefeed), with each line lowercased and the first character capitalized (assuming it can be). Both ucfirst and lc will use $_ if given no explicit argument. We can write

```
@numerics = map { ucfirst } map { lc } grep { length($_)==5 } <>;
```

A chain like this can be a powerful way to quickly and concisely manipulate a list through several different stages, more so when the bodies are more complex (e.g., call subroutines) than the simplistic example given here. The drawback is that to make sense of the code we have to read it from back to front, which is a little counterintuitive.

This example also illustrates a typical situation where the block syntax of map and grep is much clearer than the expression syntax, which would require three sets of nested parentheses.

Summary

We started this chapter by exploring the basic structures of Perl. We covered statements, declarations, expressions, and blocks. We then looked in particular at the properties and facilities provided by blocks and the various ways in which they can be expressed and used. In particular, treating blocks as loops, defining do blocks, and working with BEGIN and END blocks are all discussed.

We covered Perl's conditional statements, if, else, elsif, and unless. After a short discussion on the nature of truth, we also looked in detail at how to create loops with for and foreach, while, until, do, do..while, and do...until and how to control loops with next, last, redo, and continue.

The chapter ended with a short discussion of the uses and disadvantages of goto, followed by a look at the map and grep functions, which turn a list of input values into a new list. We saw how to use both map and grep to implement code that both transforms and selectively removes values from the input list, plus how to chain multiple map and grep expressions together to achieve more complex kinds of list manipulation.

CHAPTER 7

■■■

Subroutines

Subroutines are autonomous blocks of code that function like miniature programs. They can be executed from anywhere within a program, and because they are autonomous, calling them more than once will also reuse them.

There are two types of subroutine, *named* and *anonymous*. Most subroutines are of the named persuasion, called by writing their names literally into the source code. Anonymous subroutines do not have a name by which they can be called but are stored and accessed through a code reference. Since a code reference is a scalar value, it can be passed as a parameter to other subroutines and built-in functions like sort.

The use of named subroutines is syntactically the same as the use of Perl's own built-in functions. We can use them in a traditional function-oriented syntax (with parentheses) or treat them as named list operators. Indeed, we can even override and replace most built-in functions with our own definitions provided as subroutines through the use of the use subs pragma.

Subroutines differ from ordinary bare blocks or do blocks in that they can be passed a list of parameters to process. This list appears inside subroutines as the special variable @_, from which the list of passed parameters (also known as *arguments*) can be extracted. Because the passed parameters take the form of a list, any subroutine can automatically read in an arbitrary number of values, but conversely the same flattening problem that affects lists that are placed inside other lists also affects the parameters fed to subroutines. The flexibility of the parameter-passing mechanism can cause problems if we want to actually define the type and quantity of parameters that a subroutine will accept. Perl allows us to define this with an optional prototype, which, if present, allows Perl to do compile-time syntax checking on how our subroutines are called.

Subroutines, like bare blocks, may return either a scalar or a list value to the calling context. This allows them to be used in expressions just as any other Perl value is. The way this value is used depends on the context in which the subroutine is called. The wantarray function allows a subroutine to detect this context and behave accordingly if required. Subroutines can also have attributes, which we consider at the end of the chapter.

Declaring and Calling Subroutines

Subroutines are declared with the sub keyword. When Perl encounters sub in a program, it stops executing statements directly, and instead it creates a subroutine definition that can then be used elsewhere. The simplest form of subroutine definition is the explicitly named subroutine:

```
sub mysubroutine {
    print "Hello subroutine! \n";
}
```

We can call this subroutine from Perl with the following:

```
# call a subroutine anywhere
mysubroutine();
```

In this case, we are calling the subroutine without passing any values to it, so the parentheses are empty. To pass in values we supply a list to the subroutine. Note how the subroutine parentheses resemble a list constructor:

```
# call a subroutine with parameters
mysubroutine("testing", 1, 2, 3);
```

Of course, just because we are passing values into the subroutine does not mean that the subroutine will use them. In this case, the subroutine entirely ignores anything we pass to it. We'll cover passing values in more detail shortly.

In Perl it does not matter if we define the subroutine before or after it is used. It is not necessary to predeclare subroutines (unless we are declaring a prototype, as we will see later). When Perl encounters a subroutine call it does not recognize, it searches all the source files that have been included in the program for a suitable definition, and then uses it. However, defining or predeclaring the subroutine first allows us to omit the parentheses and use the subroutine as if it were a list operator:

```
# call a previously defined subroutine without parentheses
mysubroutine;
mysubroutine "testing", 1, 2, 3;
```

Tip Note that calling subroutines without parentheses alters the precedence rules that control how their arguments are evaluated, which can cause problems, especially if we try to use a parenthesized expression as the first argument. See Chapter 4 for more information.

We can also use the archaic and now mostly deprecated & prefix to call a subroutine. In modern versions of Perl (that is, anything from Perl 5 onwards) this is strictly optional, but older Perl programs may contain statements like the following:

```
# call a Perl subroutine using the old syntax
&mysubroutine;
&mysubroutine();
```

The ampersand has the property of causing Perl to ignore any previous definitions or declarations for the purposes of syntax, so parentheses are mandatory if we wish to pass in parameters. It also has the effect of ignoring the prototype of a subroutine, if one has been defined. Without parentheses, the ampersand also has the unusual property of providing the subroutine with the same @_ array that the calling subroutine received, rather than creating a new localized one. In general, the ampersand is optional, and in these modern and enlightened times, it is usually omitted for simple subroutine calls.

Anonymous Subroutines and Subroutine References

Less common than named subroutines, but just as valid, are anonymous subroutines. As their name suggests, anonymous subroutines do not have a name. Instead they are used as expressions, which return a code reference to the subroutine definition. We can store the reference in a scalar variable (or as an element of a list or a hash value) and then refer to it through the scalar:

```
my $subref = sub { print "Hello anonymous subroutine"; };
```

In order to call this subroutine we use the ampersand prefix. This instructs Perl to call the subroutine whose reference this is and return the result of the call:

```
# call an anonymous subroutine
&$subref;
&$subref("a parameter");
```

This is one of the few places that an ampersand is still used. However, even here it is not required; we can also say the following:

```
$subref->();
$subref->("a parameter");
```

These two variants are nearly, but not quite, identical. First, &$subref passes the current @_ array (if any) directly into the called subroutine, as we mentioned earlier. Second, the ampersand disables any prototypes we might have defined for the subroutine. The second pair of calls retains the prototype in place so it is checked at compile time. (We cover both of these points later in the chapter.)

We can generate a subroutine reference from a named subroutine using the backslash operator:

```
my $subref = \&mysubroutine;
```

This is more useful than one might think, because we can pass a subroutine reference into another subroutine as a parameter. The following simple example demonstrates a subroutine taking a subroutine reference and a list of values, then returning a new list generated from calling the subroutine on each value of the passed list in turn:

```
#!/usr/bin/perl
# callsub.pl
use warnings;
use strict;

sub do_list {
    my ($subref, @in) = @_;

    return map { &$subref ($_) } @in;
}

sub add_one {
    return $_[0] + 1;
}

$, = ",";
print do_list (\&add_one, 1, 2, 3);   # prints 2, 3, 4
```

Some Perl functions (notably sort) also accept an anonymous subroutine reference as an argument. We do not supply an ampersand in this case because sort wants the code reference, not the result of calling it. Here is a sort program that demonstrates the different ways we can supply sort with a subroutine. The anonymous subroutine appearing last will not work with Perl 5.005:

```
#!/usr/bin/perl
# sortsub.pl
use warnings;
use strict;

# a list to sort
my @list = (3, 4, 2, 5, 6, 9, 1);

# directly with a block
print sort {$a cmp $b} @list;

# with a named subroutine
sub sortsub {
    return $a cmp $b;
}
```

```
print sort sortsub @list;

# with an anonymous subroutine
my $sortsubref = sub {return $a cmp $b;};
print sort $sortsubref @list;
```

Of course, since we can get a code reference for an existing subroutine, we could also have said

```
$sortsubref = \&sortsub;
```

The advantage of using the anonymous subroutine is that we can change the subroutine that sort uses elsewhere in the program, for example:

```
# define anonymous subroutines for different sort types:
$numericsort = sub {$a <=> $b};
$stringsort = sub {$a cmp $b };
$reversenumericsort = sub {$b <=> $a};

# now select a sort method
$sortsubref = $numericsort;
```

The disadvantage of this technique is that unless we take care to write and express our code clearly, it can be very confusing to work out what is going on, since without running the code it may not always be possible to tell which subroutine is being executed where. We can use print $subref to print out the address of the anonymous subroutine, but this is not nearly as nice to read as a sub-routine name, is not invariant between invocations, and tells us nothing about the subroutine.

It is also possible to turn an anonymous subroutine into a named one, by assigning it to a typeglob. This works by manipulating the symbol table to invent a named code reference that Perl thereafter sees as a subroutine definition. This creates a subroutine definition for namedsub using the code reference in $subref:

```
*namedsub = $subref;
```

This leads to the possibility of determining the actual code supported by a subroutine name at run time, which is handy for implementing things like state machines. This will be covered more fully in "Manipulating the Symbol Table" in Chapter 8. A generalized mechanism for dynamic sub-routine definition is also provided by the special AUTOLOAD subroutine introduced later in the chapter and developed in Chapter 10.

Strict Subroutines and the use strict subs Pragma

The strict pragma has three components, refs, vars, and subs, all of which are enabled with an unqualified use strict. The subs component affects how Perl interprets unqualified (that is, not quoted or otherwise identified by the syntax) words or "barewords" when it encounters them in the code.

Without strict subroutines in effect, Perl will allow a bareword and will interpret it as if it were in single quotes:

```
my $a = bareword;
print $a;    #prints "bareword";
```

The problem with this code is that we might later add a subroutine called bareword, at which point the preceding code suddenly turns into a function call. Indeed, if we have warnings enabled, we will get a warning to that effect:

```
Unquoted string "bareword" may clash with future reserved word at ...
```

Strict subroutines are intended to prevent us from using barewords in a context where they are ambiguous and could be confused with subroutines. To enable them, use one of the following:

```
use strict;      # enables strict refs, vars, and subs
use strict subs;  # enables strict subs only
```

Now any attempt to use a bareword will cause Perl to generate a fatal error:

```
Bareword "bareword" not allowed while "strict subs" in use at ...
```

Ironically, the second example contains the illegal bareword subs. It works because at the point Perl parses the pragma it is not yet in effect. Immediately afterwards, barewords are not permitted, so to switch off strict subs again we would have to use either quotes or a quoting operator like qw:

```
no strict 'subs';
no strict q(subs);
no strict qw(subs);
```

Predeclaring Subroutines

Perl allows subroutines to be called in two alternate syntaxes: functions with parentheses or list operators. This allows subroutines to be used as if they were one of Perl's built-in list operator functions such as print or read (neither of which require parentheses).

This syntax is only valid if Perl has already either seen the subroutine definition or a declaration of the subroutine. The following subroutine call is not legal, because the subroutine has not yet been defined:

```
debug "This is a debug message";    # ERROR: no parentheses
#...rest of program...
sub debug {
    print STDERR @_, "\n";
}
```

The intention here is to create a special debug statement, which works just like the print statement, but it prints to standard error rather than standard out, and ends with an automatic linefeed. Because we want it to work like print in all other respects, we would prefer to omit the brackets if we choose to, just as print does. To do this, we must predeclare the subroutine before we use it:

```
# predeclare subroutine 'debug'
sub debug;

debug "This is a debug message";    # no error
#...rest of program...

sub debug {
    print STDERR @_, "\n";
}
```

Subroutines are also predeclared if we import them from another package (see Chapter 10 for more on packages), as in

```
use mypackage qw(mysubroutine);
```

Overriding Built-In Functions

Another way to predeclare subroutines is with the use subs pragma. This not only predeclares the subroutine, but also it allows us to override Perl's existing built-in functions and replace them with our own. We can access the original built-in function with the CORE:: prefix. For example, the following is a replacement version of the srand function, which issues a warning if we use srand in a version of Perl of 5.004 or greater without arguments.

```perl
#!/usr/bin/perl
# srandcall.pl
use warnings;
use strict;
use subs qw(srand);

sub srand {
    if ($] >= 5.004 and not @_) {
        warn "Unqualified call to srand redundant in Perl $]";
    } else {
        # call the real srand via the CORE package
        CORE::srand @_;
    }
}
```

Now if we use srand without an argument and the version of Perl is 5.004 or greater, we get a warning. If we supply an argument, we are assumed to know what we are doing and are supplying a suitably random value.

Subroutines like this are generally useful in more than one program, so we might want to put this definition into a separate module and use it whenever we want to override the default srand:

```perl
#!/usr/bin/perl
# mysrand.pm

package mysrand;

use strict;

use vars qw(@ISA @EXPORT @EXPORT_OK);
use Exporter;

@ISA = qw(Exporter);
@EXPORT = qw(mysrand);
@EXPORT_OK = qw(srand);

sub mysrand {
    if ($] >= 5.004 and not @_) {
        warn "Unqualified call to srand redundant in Perl $]";

    } else {
        # call the real srand via the CORE package
        CORE::srand @_;
    }
}

use subs qw(srand);
sub srand {&mysrand;};    # pass @_ directly to mysrand
```

This module, which we would keep in a file called mysrand.pm to match the package name, exports the function mysrand automatically and the overriding srand function only if we ask for it.

```perl
use mysrand;    # import 'mysrand'
use mysrand qw(mysrand);    # import and predeclare mysrand
use mysrand qw(srand);    # override 'srand'
```

We'll talk about packages, modules, and exporting subroutines in Chapter 10.

The Subroutine Stack

Whenever Perl calls a subroutine, it pushes the details of the subroutine call onto an internal stack. This holds the context of each subroutine, including the parameters that were passed to it in the form of the @_ array, ready to be restored when the call to the next subroutine returns. The number of subroutine calls that the program is currently in is known as the "depth" of the stack. Calling subroutines are higher in the stack, and called subroutines are lower.

This might seem academic, and to a large extent it is, but Perl allows us to access the calling stack ourselves with the caller function. At any given point we are at the "bottom" of the stack, and we can look "up" to see the contexts stored on the stack by our caller, its caller, and so on, all the way back to the top of the program. This can be handy for all kinds of reasons, but most especially for debugging.

In a purely scalar context, caller returns the name of the package from which the subroutine was called, and undef if there was no caller. Note that this does not require that the call come from inside another subroutine—it could just as easily be from the main program. In a list context, caller returns the package name, the source file and the line number from which the subroutine was called. This allows us to write error traps in subroutines as follows:

```
sub mysub {
    my ($pkg, $file, $line) = caller;
    die "Called with no parameters at $file line $line" unless @_;
}
```

If we pass a numeric argument to caller, it looks back up the stack the requested number of levels and returns a longer list of information. This level can of course be "0", so to get everything that Perl knows about the circumstances surrounding the call to our subroutine we can write

```
@caller_info = caller 0;   # or caller(0), if we prefer
```

This returns a whole slew of items into the list, which may or may not be defined depending on the circumstances. They are, in order

- package: The package of the caller.

- filename: The source file of the caller.

- line: The line number in the source file.

- subroutine: The subroutine that was called (that is, us). If we execute code inside an eval statement, then this is set to eval.

- hasargs: This is true if parameters were passed (@_ was defined).

- wantarray: The value of wantarray inside the caller; see "Returning Values from Subroutines" later in the chapter.

- evaltext: The text inside the eval that caused the subroutine to be called, if the subroutine was called by eval.

- is_require: true if a require or use caused the eval.

- hints: Compilation details, internal use only.

- bitmask: Compilation details, internal use only.

In practice, only the first four items, package, file name, line, and subroutine, are of any use to us, which is why they are the only ones returned when we use caller with no arguments. Unfortunately we do not get the name of the calling subroutine this way, so we have to extract that from further up the stack:

```
# get the name of the calling subroutine, if there was one
$callingsub = (caller 1)[3];
```

Or, more legibly:

```
($pkg, $file, $line, $callingsub) = caller 1;
```

Armed with this information, we can create more informative error messages that report errors with respect to the caller. For example:

```
# die with a better error message

sub mysub {
    my ($pkg, $file, $line) = caller;
    die "Called from ", (caller(1)) [3],
        " with no parameters at $file line $line \n" unless @_;
    ...
}
```

If debugging is our primary interest, a better solution than all the preceding is to use the Carp module. The Carp module and other debugging aids are covered in Chapter 17.

One final point about the calling stack: if we try to access the stack above the immediate caller, we may not always get the right information back. This is because Perl can optimize the stack under some circumstances, removing intermediate levels. As we will see, the goto statement is often used to remove a level from the call stack. The result of this is that the output of caller is not always as consistent as we might expect, so a little caution should be applied to its use.

Recursion

Recursion happens when a subroutine calls itself, either directly or indirectly, via another subroutine (also known as *mutual recursion*). For example, consider this subroutine that calculates the Fibonacci sequence, where each number is equal to the sum of the previous two, up to a specified number of terms:

```
#!/usr/bin/perl
# fib1.pl
use warnings;
use strict;

sub fibonacci1 {
    my ($count, $aref) = @_;

    unless ($aref) {
        # first call - initialize
        $aref = [1,1];
        $count -= scalar(@{$aref});
    }

    if ($count-) {
        my $next = $aref->[-1] + $aref->[-2];
        push @{$aref}, $next;
        return fibonacci1($count, $aref);
    } else {
        return wantarray?@{$aref}: $aref->[-1];
    }
}

# calculate 10th element of standard Fibonacci sequence
print scalar(fibonacci1(10)), "\n";
```

```
# calculate 10th element beyond sequence starting 2, 4
print scalar(fibonacci1(10, [2, 4])), "\n";

# return first ten elements of standard Fibonacci sequence
my @sequence = fibonacci1(10);
print "Sequence: @sequence \n";
```

Each time the subroutine is entered, it calculates one term, decrements the counter by one, and calls itself to calculate the next term. The subroutine takes two arguments, the counter, and a reference to the list of terms being calculated. (As a convenience, if we don't pass in a reference, the subroutine initializes itself with the start of the standard Fibonacci sequence, 1, 1). We pass in a reference to avoid copying the list repeatedly, which is wasteful. When the counter reaches zero, the subroutine exits without calling itself again, and returns either the whole list or the last term, depending on how it was called.

This is an example of forward recursion, where we start at the beginning of the task and work our way towards the end. Elements are calculated one by one as we continue with our recursion. An alternative way of doing the same job is to use reverse recursion, which starts by trying to calculate the last term first:

```
#!/usr/bin/perl
# fib2.pl
use warnings;
use strict;

sub fibonacci2 {
    my ($count, $internal) = @_;

    if ($count <= 2) {
        # we know the answer already
        return $internal ? [1,1] : 1;
    } else {
        # call ourselves to determine previous two elements
        my $result = fibonacci2($count -1, 'internal');
        # now we can calculate our element
        my $next = $result->[-1] + $result->[-2];

        if ($internal) {
            push @{$result}, $next;
            return $result;
        } else {
            return $next;
        }
    }
}

foreach (1..20) {
    print "Element $_ is ", fibonacci2($_), "\n";
}
```

This time the subroutine starts by trying to work out the last term, starting at the end and reversing back towards the beginning, until we can determine the answer without a further call. If the requested term is the first or second, we just return the result, otherwise, it needs to work out the terms prior to the one we have been asked for, which it does by calling itself for the previous terms. In this model, we descend rapidly to the bottom of the recursion stack until we get the answer [1,1]. We then calculate each new term as we return back up.

Reverse recursion is not as obvious as forward recursion, but it can be a much more powerful tool, especially in algorithms where we do not know in advance exactly how the initial known results will be found. Problems like the Queen's Dilemma (placing eight queens on a chessboard such that no queen can take another) are more easily solved with reverse recursion, for example.

Both approaches suffer from the problem that Perl generates a potentially large call stack. If we try to calculate a sufficiently large sequence, then Perl will run out of room to store this stack and will fail with an error message:

```
Deep recursion on subroutine "main::fibonacci2" at ...
```

Some languages support "tail" recursion, an optimization of forward recursive subroutines where no code exists after the recursive subroutine call. Because there is no more work to do at the intermediate levels of the subroutine stack, they can be removed. This allows the final call to the recursed subroutine call to directly return to the original caller. Since no stack is maintained, no room is needed to store it.

Perl's interpreter is not yet smart enough to figure out this optimization automatically, but we can code it explicitly using a goto statement. The fibonnaci1 subroutine we showed first is a recursive subroutine that fits the criteria for tau-recursion, as it returns. Here is a modified version, fibonacci3, that uses goto to avoid creating a stack of recursed subroutine calls. Note that the goto statement and the line immediately before it are the only difference between this subroutine and fibonacci1:

```perl
#!/usr/bin/perl
# fib3.pl
use warnings;
use strict;

sub fibonacci3 {
    my ($count, $aref) = @_;

    unless ($aref) {
        # first call - initialize
        $aref = [1,1];
        $count -= scalar(@{$aref});
    }

    if ($count-) {
        my $next = $aref->[-1] + $aref->[-2];
        push @{$aref}, $next;
        @_ = ($count, $aref);
        goto &fibonacci3;
    } else {
        return wantarray?@{$aref}:$aref->[-1];
    }
}
# calculate 1000th element of standard Fibonacci sequence
print scalar(fibonacci3(1000)), "\n";
```

The goto statement jumps directly to another subroutine without actually calling it (which creates a new stack frame). The automatic creation of a localized @_ does not therefore happen. Instead, the context of the current subroutine call is used, including the current @_. In order to "pass" arguments, we therefore have to predefine @_ before we call goto. Examining the preceding code, we can see that although it would sacrifice legibility, we could also replace $count with $_[0] to set up @_ correctly without redefining it.

Recursion is a nice programming trick, but it is easy to get carried away with it. Any calculation that uses recursion can also be written using ordinary iteration too, so use recursion only when it presents the most elegant solution to a programming problem.

Checking for and Defining Subroutines On the Fly

We can check for the existence of a subroutine before we call it using Perl's defined function, or alternatively by examining the CODE slot of the corresponding typeglob. For example:

```
if (defined &capitalize) {
    capitalize(@countries);
}
```

Or equivalently:

```
capitalize(@countries) if *capitalize{CODE};
```

This is more useful than it might seem. For instance, when using a library that may or may not support a particular subroutine (depending on the installed version), we can safeguard against a possible exit from our program by checking that the library has the function before we try to call it. In combination with the use if pragma (covered in Chapter 9), we can first conditionally load a module, and then only use a subroutine from it if it was loaded.

If we are writing object-oriented Perl, we can use the special object method can, in order to do the same thing in a more object-oriented style:

```
$bean->jump('left') if $bean->can('jump');
```

We are not limited to just testing for the existence of subroutines. We can also substitute for them and even define them on-the-fly, by assigning an anonymous subroutine to a typeglob. This gives us the ability to define a subroutine in different ways depending on the circumstances. For instance, take this short program that defines a real debug routine or a stub that Perl can optimize away depending on whether an environment variable is set:

```
#!/usr/bin/perl
# conditionaldebug.pl
use strict;
use warnings;
use subs qw(debug);

unless (defined &debug) {
    if ($ENV{DEBUG_ENABLED}) {
        *debug = sub { print STDERR "@_\n" };
    } else {
        *debug = sub { };  #stub
    }
}

debug "In debug mode";
```

Since the debug subroutine is not defined at the time this program is first compiled, we predeclare the debug subroutine with a use subs statement to stop the last statement from generating a syntax error. An alternative approach would be to put the unless clause into a BEGIN block, to guarantee that the subroutine is defined before the last line is compiled. (If we placed the conditional code into a module and then loaded it with use, this would be taken care of for us.)

Alternatively, we can define an AUTOLOAD subroutine. If an AUTOLOAD subroutine exists in the same package as a nonexistent subroutine, Perl will call it, rather than exiting with an error. The name of the missing subroutine, complete with package name, is placed in the special package variable $AUTOLOAD, and the arguments passed to the subroutine are instead passed to AUTOLOAD.

As a trivial example, the following AUTOLOAD subroutine just returns the missing subroutine name as a string:

```
sub AUTOLOAD {
    our $AUTOLOAD;    # or 'use vars' for Perl < 5.6
    return $AUTOLOAD;
}
```

Because $AUTOLOAD is a package variable that we have not declared, we need to gain access to it with the our directive if use strict is in effect (Perl versions before 5.6 need to have use vars instead). The preceding example allows us to write strange looking statements like this:

```
$, = " ";
print "", Hello, Autoloading, World;
```

This is identical in effect to

```
print "main::Hello", "main::Autoloading", "main::World";
```

In other words, this AUTOLOAD subroutine interprets unqualified barewords as strings. A slightly more useful example of the same technique is shown by this HTML tag generator, which automatically creates matching start and end tags, with any supplied parameters sandwiched in between. Note the regular expression to strip off the package prefix:

```
sub AUTOLOAD {
    our ($AUTOLOAD);    # again, 'use vars' if Perl < 5.6
    $AUTOLOAD =~ s/^.*:://;    # strip the package name
    return "<$AUTOLOAD> \n". join("\n",@_). "</$AUTOLOAD> \n";
}
```

We can now write an HTML page programmatically using functions that we haven't actually defined, in a similar (and much shorter, albeit less sophisticated) way to the CGI module. Here is an example HTML document created using the preceding autoloader subroutine in a single line of code:

```
print html(head(title("Autoloaded HTML")), body(h1("Hi There")));
```

While functional, this example has a few deficiencies. For a start, we can invent any tag we like, including misspelled ones. Another problem is that it does not learn from the past; each time we call a nonexistent subroutine, Perl looks for it, fails to find it, then calls AUTOLOAD. It would be more elegant to define the subroutine so that next time it is called, Perl finds it. The chances are that if we use it once, we'll use it again. To do that, we just need to create a suitable anonymous subroutine and assign it to a typeglob with the same name as the missing function, which inserts the new subroutine into the symbol table for us. Here is a modified version that does this for us:

```
sub AUTOLOAD {
    our ($AUTOLOAD);
    no strict 'refs';
    my $tag = $AUTOLOAD;
    $tag =~s/.*:://;
    *$AUTOLOAD = sub {
        "<$tag> \n". join("\n", @_). "</$tag> \n";
    };

    &$AUTOLOAD;    # we can use a 'goto' here too – see below
}
```

Now, whenever a tag is asked for, a subroutine for that tag is defined. The next time the same tag is asked for, the newly defined subroutine catches the call and handles it.

Aside from the anonymous subroutine definition, the other interesting point about this autoloading subroutine is the call to the new subroutine at the end.

Since AUTOLOAD has to define the subroutine the first time it is called, it has to call it as well. We make use of the &subname; syntax to pass the contents of @_ directly to the new subroutine. However, $AUTOLOAD is a symbolic reference, so we use no strict refs at the top of the subroutine.

AUTOLOAD subroutines that define subroutines are one place where using goto does make sense. We can replace the last line of this subroutine with the following:

```
goto &$AUTOLOAD;
```

Why is this useful? Because it removes the AUTOLOAD subroutine itself from the calling stack, so caller will not see the AUTOLOAD subroutine, but rather the original caller. From the point of view of the rest of the program, it is as if AUTOLOAD were never involved. Consequently goto is a common sight in AUTOLOAD subroutines that define subroutines on-the-fly.

▨Tip Autoloading is quite handy in functional programming, but much more useful in modules and packages. Accordingly we cover it in more depth in Chapter 10.

Passing Parameters

Basic Perl subroutines do not have any formal way of defining their arguments. We say "basic" because we can optionally define a prototype that allows us to define the types of the arguments passed, if not their names inside the subroutine. However, ignoring prototypes for the moment, we may pass any number of parameters to a subroutine:

```
mysubroutine ("parameter1", "parameter2", 3, 4, @listparameter);
```

It is helpful to think of the parentheses as a conventional list definition being passed to mysubroutine as a single list parameter—remove mysubroutine from the preceding statement and what we are left with is a list. This is not far from the truth, if we recall that declaring a subroutine prior to using it allows us to use it as if it were a built-in list operator. Consequently, arrays and hashes passed as arguments to subroutines are flattened into one list internally, just as they are when combined into a larger list.

The parameters that are passed into a subroutine appear inside the subroutine as a list contained in the special variable @_. This variable is made local to each subroutine, just as $_ is inside nested foreach loops. The definition of @_ is thus unique to each subroutine, despite the fact that @_ is a package variable.

A simple and common way to extract the parameters passed to a subroutine is simply to assign @_ to a list of scalar variables, like so:

```
sub volume {
    my ($height, $width, $length) = @_;
    return $height * $width * $length;
}
```

This gives us three named scalar variables we can write code for more legibly, and also takes care of any aliasing problems that might otherwise occur (as we will see in a moment). Alternatively, we can use shift to pull values off the array one by one:

```
sub volume {
    my $height = shift;
    my $width = shift;
    my $length = shift;
    return $height * $width * $length;
}
```

This differs from the previous example in that it actually modifies @_, removing passed parameters from the front of the list. After all the shifts have been processed, @_ may be empty or it may contain further unhandled parameters. We can use that to our advantage to write subroutines that only use some parameters and pass the rest on. For example, here is a speculative object method that is a wrapper for the volume function:

```
sub volume {
    my $self = shift;              #remove object passed as first parameter
    return Functions::volume(@_);  #call sub with remaining parameters
}
```

If it is brevity we are after, we can avoid assigning the contents of @_ at all, and simply use its values. This version of volume is not as clear as the first, but makes up for it by being only one line long. As a result the workings of the subroutine are still fairly obvious:

```
sub volume { return $_[0] * $_[1] * $_[2]; } # HxWxD
```

The @_ array is a localized array defined when the subroutine is first entered. However, while the array itself is local, the *values* of @_ are aliases for the original parameters that were passed in to the subroutine. This is a moot distinction of a parameter was literal, but if the parameter was a variable modifying the value, @_ modifies the original variable, much as $_ will modify the values in an array looped over with foreach. If the purpose of a subroutine is to manipulate a list of values in a consistent and generic way, it can be surprisingly useful. Here is an example of such a subroutine that emulates the chomp function:

```
#strip the input line separator '$/' from the end of each passed string:
sub mychomp {
    s|$/$|| foreach @_;
}
```

This also happens to be a good demonstration of aliasing. The subroutine actually aliases twice over: once in the @_ array inside the subroutine, and again in the foreach loop that aliases the loop variable $_ to the values in the @_ array one by one.

We can call this subroutine in the same way as the real chomp:

```
mychomp $string;
mychomp @lines;
```

Modifying the passed arguments implies that they are modifiable in the first place. Passing a literal value rather than a variable will produce a syntax error. For example:

```
mychomp "you can't touch this \n";
```

This produces

```
Modification of a read-only value attempted at ...
```

When we come to discuss prototypes, we will see how we can define subroutines that can be checked for correct usage at compile time. This means we can create a subroutine like mychomp that will produce a syntax error if used on a literal variable at compile time, just like the real chomp.

Passing Lists and Hashes

We mentioned earlier, when we started on the subject of passed arguments, that passing lists and hashes directly into a subroutine causes list flattening to occur, just as it does with ordinary list definitions. Consequently, if we want to pass an array or hash to a subroutine, and keep it intact and separate from the other arguments, we need to take additional steps. Consider the following snippet of code:

```
my $message = "Testing";
my @count = (1, 2, 3);
testing ($message, @count);    # calls 'testing' - see below
```

The array @count is flattened with $message in the @_ array created as a result of this subroutine, so as far as the subroutine is concerned the following call is actually identical:

```
testing ("Testing", 1, 2, 3);
```

In many cases, this is exactly what we need. To read the subroutine parameters, we can just extract the first scalar variable as the message and put everything else into the count:

```
sub testing {
    my ($message, @count) = @_;
    ...
}
```

Or, using shift:

```
sub testing {
    my $message = shift;
    # now we can use @_ directly in place of @count
    ...
}
```

The same principle works for hashes, which as far as the subroutine is concerned is just more values. It is up to the subroutine to pick up the contents of @_ and convert them back into a hash:

```
sub testing {
    my ($message, %count) = @_;
    print "@_";
}
```

```
testing ("Magpies", 1 => "for sorrow", 2 => "for joy", 3 => "for health",
        4 => "for wealth", 5 => "for sickness", 6 => "for death");
```

However, this only works because the last parameter we extract inside the subroutine absorbs all the remaining passed parameters. If we were to write the subroutine to pass the list first and then the scalar afterwards, all the parameters are absorbed into the list and the scalar is left undefined:

```
sub testing {
    my (@count, $message) = @_;    # ERROR
    print "@_";
}
```

```
testing(1, 2, 3, "Testing");
# results in @count = (1, 2, 3, "Testing") and $message = undef
```

If we can define all our subroutines like this, we won't have anything to worry about, but if we want to pass more than one list, we still have a problem. If we attempt to pass both lists as-is, then extract them inside the subroutine, we end up with both lists into the first and the second left undefined:

```
sub testing {
    my (@messages, @count) = @_; # wrong!
    print "@_";
}
```

```
my @msgs = ("Testing", "Testing");
my @count = (1, 2, 3);
testing(@msgs, @count);
```

```
# results in @messages = ("Testing", "Testing", "Testing", 1, 2, 3)
# and @count = ();
```

The correct way to pass lists and hashes, and keep them intact and separate, is to pass references. Since a reference is a scalar, it is not flattened like the original value, and so our data remains intact in the form that we originally supplied it:

```
testing (["Testing", "Testing"], [1, 2, 3]);   # with two lists
testing (\@messages, \@count);   # with two array variables
testing ($aref1, $aref2);   # with two list references
```

Inside the subroutine we then extract the two list references into scalar variables and dereference them using either @{$aref} or $aref->[index] to access the list values:

```
sub testing {
    my ($messages, $count) = @_;

    # print the testing messages
    foreach (@ {$messages}) {
        print "$_ ... ";
    }
    print "\n";

    # print the count;
    foreach (@ {$count}) {
        print "$_!\n";
    }
}
```

Another benefit of this technique is efficiency; it is better to pass two scalar variables (the references) than it is to pass the original lists. The lists may contain values that are large both in size and number. Since Perl must store a local copy of the @_ array for every new subroutine call in the calling stack, passing references instead of large lists can save Perl a lot of time and memory.

Converting Scalar Subroutines into List Processors

Consider this subroutine, which capitalizes the first letter of the string that it is passed:

```
sub capitalize {
    $_[0] = ucfirst(lc $_[0]);
    print $_[0],"\n";
}

$country = "england";
capitalize($country);   # produces 'England'
```

Simple enough, but it only works on one string at a time. However, just because we wrote this subroutine to work as a scalar operator does not alter the fact that in reality it is working on a list. We have just limited it to handle the first value. With only a little extra effort, we can turn this subroutine into something that works on scalars and lists alike:

```
sub capitalize {
    foreach (@_) {
        $_=ucfirst lc;   # lc uses $_ if argument is omitted
        print $_,"\n";
    }
}
```

Or more efficiently, with map:

```
sub capitalize {
    map { print ucfirst lc; print "\n" } @_;
}
```

This version works identically for calls like the preceding that pass only one parameter, but happily it works on arrays too:

```
sub capitalize {
    map {$_ = ucfirst lc} @_;
    print "@_[0, 1, 2]";
}

@countries = ("england", "scotland", "wales");
capitalize (@countries);   # produces ("England", "Scotland", "Wales")
```

Passing @_ Directly into Subroutines

We said earlier that the @_ array is distinct to each subroutine and masks any previous definition. That is almost true—there is one exception provided, for reasons of efficiency, to the Perl programmers dedicated to optimizing their code. Normally @_ is defined locally, on entry to each subroutine. So, if we pass in no parameters at all, we get an empty array. However, if we call a subroutine using the & prefix and do not pass parameters or use braces, then the subroutine inherits the @_ array of the calling subroutine directly:

```
&mysubroutine;   # inherit @_ from parent
```

The problem with this technique is that it is rather arcane and not obvious to the reader of our code. Therefore, if we use it, a comment to the effect that this is what we are doing (such as the one earlier) is highly recommended.

As far as the subroutine is concerned, this is no different from passing the @_ array as a parameter:

```
mysubroutine(@_);
```

Although this may seem equivalent, in the second case the @_ array is copied each time the call is made. If @_ contains a large number of values, or many calls are made (for instance, in a recursive subroutine), then this is potentially expensive. The &mysubroutine; notation passes the @_ array directly without making a copy, and so it avoids the unnecessary work. However, if @_ only contains a few elements, it is probably better to live with the very minor inefficiency of copying the array and use the explicit version.

Note that the aliasing of the values in the @_ array to the original variables (if the parameter was a variable) happens in either case, so it is not necessary to resort to this practice if all we want to do is modify the variables that were passed to us.

Named Parameters

Unlike other languages such as C or Java, Perl does not have any way to define formal parameter names for subroutines. The closest it gets is prototypes combined with retrieving parameters as lexical variables, as in

```
sub surname {
    my ($scalar1, $scalar2, @listarg) = @_;
    ...
}
```

However, we can implement named parameters using a hash. This provides an elegant way to pass in parameters without having to define them formally. The trick is to assign the @_ array to a hash variable. This converts the passed list into key-value pairs:

```perl
sub volume {
    my %param = @_;
    return $param{height} * $param{width} * $param{length};
}
```

The disadvantage of this approach is that we have to name all the parameters that we pass. It is also slower, since hashes are inherently slower than arrays in use. The advantage is that we can add more parameters without forcing the caller to supply parameters that are not needed. Of course, it also falls upon us to actually check the arguments passed and complain if the caller sends us arguments that we do not use.

We can call this subroutine using the => operator to make it clear that we are passing named parameters:

```perl
volume (height => 1, width => 4, length => 9);
```

We can also write the subroutine so that it accepts both named parameters and a simple list. One common technique borrowed from Unix command line switches is to prefix named arguments with a minus, to distinguish them from unnamed arguments. To determine how the subroutine has been called, we just check the first character of the first parameter to see if it is a minus:

```perl
#!/usr/bin/perl
# namedorlistargs.pl
use strict;
use warnings;

sub volume {
    my %param;

    if ($_[0]=~/^-/) {
        # if the first argument starts '-', assume named arguments
        while (@_) {
            my ($key, $value)=(shift, shift);
            $key =~ s/^-//;    #remove leading minus
            $param{$key} = $value;
        }

    } else {
        # no '-' on first argument - assume list arguments
        $param{height} = shift;
        $param{width} = shift;
        $param{length} = shift;
    }

    # default any unspecified dimensions to 1
    foreach ('height', 'width', 'length') {
        unless (defined $param{$_}) {
            warn "Undefined $_, assuming 1";
            $param{$_} = 1;
        }
    }

    return abs($param{height} * $param{width} * $param{length});
}
```

```
print volume(2,5,10),"\n";
print volume(-height=>2,-width=>5,-length=>10),"\n";
```

In this version of the volume subroutine, we handle both simple and named parameters. For named parameters, we have also taken advantage of the fact that we know the names of the parameters to report a handy informative warning, if any of them are undefined.

Named parameters allow us to create a common set of parameters and then add or override parameters. This makes use of the fact that if we define a hash key twice, the second definition overrides the first:

```
# define some default parameters
%default = (-height => 1, -width => 4, -length => 9);

# use default
print volume(%default);

# override default
print volume(%default, -length => 16);
print volume(%default, -width => 6, -length => 10);

# specify additional parameters
print volume(%default, -color => "red", -density => "13.4");
```

Before leaving the subject of named parameters, it is worth briefly mentioning the Alias module, available from CPAN. Alias provides the subroutines alias and attr, which generates aliases from a list of key-value pairs. Both subroutines use typeglobs to do the job.

The alias subroutine takes a list of key-value pairs as its argument and is therefore suited to subroutines. The type of variable defined by the alias is determined by the type of value it is aliased to; a string creates a scalar, a list creates an array. Here is yet another volume subroutine that uses alias:

```
#!/usr/bin/perl
# volalias.pl
use warnings;
use strict;

no strict 'vars';
use Alias;

# subroutine using 'alias'
sub volume {
    alias @_;
    return $height * $width * $length;
}

# a call to the subroutine
print volume(height => 1, length => 9, color => 'red', width => 4);

# aliased variables visible here
print " = $height x $width x $length \n";
```

However, alias suffers from three serious deficiencies. The first is that it is not compatible with strict vars; if we want strict variables, we will have to declare all the aliased variables with use vars or (preferably) our. Another is that alias creates global aliases that persist outside the subroutine, which is not conducive to good programming. The third is that if we only use the variable once, we'll get a warning from Perl about it. The preceding script does not do that because of the last line. Comment out that line, and all three variables will generate used only once warnings.

attr takes a reference to a hash and creates aliases based on the keys and values in it. attr $hashref is similar to alias %{$hashref} but localizes the aliases that it creates. It is ideal to use with object methods for objects based around hashes, since each object attribute becomes a variable (hence the name):

```
#!/usr/bin/perl
# attr.pl
use warnings;
use strict;

{
    package Testing;
    use Alias;
    no strict 'vars';    # to avoid declaring vars

    sub new {
        return bless {
            count => [3, 2, 1],
            message => 'Liftoff!',
        }, shift;
    }

    sub change {
        # define @count and $message locally
        attr(shift);
        # this relies on 'shift' being a hash reference
        @count = (1, 2, 3);
        $message = 'Testing, Testing';
    }
}
my $object = new Testing;
print "Before: ", $object->{message}, "\n";
$object->change;
print "After : ", $object->{message}, "\n";
print $Testing::message, "\n";   # warning - 'attr' vars do not persist
close Testing::count;
```

We can also define "constants" with the const subroutine. This is actually just an alias for alias (it's even defined using alias inside the module, and must be imported explicitly):

```
# const.pl
use Alias qw(const);    # add 'alias' and/or 'attr' too, if needed

const MESSAGE => 'Testing';
print $MESSAGE, "\n";
```

Attempting to modify the value of a constant produces an error:

```
# ERROR: produce 'Modification of a read-only value attempted at ...'
$MESSAGE = 'Liftoff!';
```

■**Tip** The Alias module also provides several customization features, mainly for the attr subroutine, which allows us to control what gets aliased and how. Refer to perldoc Alias for a rundown and some more examples.

Prototypes

The subroutines we have considered so far exert no control over what arguments are passed to them; they simply try to make sense of what is passed inside the subroutine. For many subroutines this is fine, and in some cases it allows us to create subroutines that can be called in a variety of different ways. For example, we can test the first argument to see if it is a reference or not and alter our behavior accordingly. However, we are not enforcing a calling convention, so we will only discover our subroutines are being called incorrectly when we actually execute the call, and then only if we have written the subroutine to check its arguments thoroughly. Since some subroutine calls may not occur except under very specific circumstances, this makes testing and eliminating bugs very difficult.

Fortunately, there is a way to define compile-time restrictions on the use of subroutines through the use of prototype definitions. Although entirely optional, by specifying the types of the expected parameters, prototypes can eliminate a lot of the problems involved in ensuring that subroutines are called correctly. This allows us to specify what parameters a subroutine takes (scalars, lists/hashes, or code references), whether a parameter can be either a simple literal value, or whether it must be an actual variable. Good use of prototypes early in the development process can be invaluable.

A prototype definition is a parenthesized list of characters mirroring the Perl variable type syntax (that is, $, @, %, and so on). It is placed after the sub keyword and subroutine name but before anything else, be it a subroutine definition, declaration, or anonymous subroutine:

```
sub mysub (PROTOTYPE);         # subroutine declaration
sub mysub (PROTOTYPE) {...}    # subroutine definition
$subref = sub (PROTOTYPE) {...} # anonymous subroutine
```

Defining the Number of Parameters and Their Scope

Prototypes allow us to explicitly define how many arguments a subroutine expects to receive. This is something that for efficiency reasons we would clearly prefer to check at compile time. We do not have to wait until the subroutine call is used to find out that it is faulty, and passing the wrong number of parameters is an obvious candidate for a bug.

To illustrate, consider the volume subroutine that we defined in various different forms earlier. With the exception of the named argument example, the subroutine expects three scalar parameters. Using prototypes we can enforce this by adding ($$$), meaning three mandatory scalar arguments, to the subroutine definition:

```
sub volume ($$$) {
    # ... as before ...
}
```

With this prototype in place, volume can only be called with three scalar arguments. They can be literals or variables, but there must be three of them, and they must be scalar. Hence, this is legal:

```
print volume(1, 4, 9), "\n";   # displays 1 * 4 * 9 == 36
```

The following, however, is not. Even though it provides the right number of values, it doesn't supply them in a way that fits the prototype:

```
@size = (1, 4, 9);
print volume(@size), "\n";
```

Instead, we get this error:

```
Not enough arguments for main::volume at ... near @size
```

So far, so good. However, due to Perl's concept of context, prototypes do not enforce things quite as strictly as this might imply. The prototype does not actually enforce a data type—it *attempts* to force it. What the first $ in the prototype actually does is force @size to be interpreted in scalar context and not as a list; in other words, it is exactly as if we had written the following:

```
print volume(scalar @size), "\n";
```

Having turned the three element array into a scalar "3", the prototype goes on to interpret the second argument as a scalar also. It then finds there isn't one and produces an error. The fact that we passed an array is not relevant, since an array can be converted to a scalar. However, by passing just one array, we omitted two mandatory arguments, which is important. To illustrate this, the following actually works just fine, the array not withstanding:

```
print volume(@size, 4, 9);   # displays 3 * 4 * 9 == 108
```

We have not supplied three scalars, but we have supplied three values that can be interpreted as scalars, and that's what counts to Perl. We can also use @ and % in prototype definitions, and it is sometimes helpful to consider subroutines without prototypes as having a default prototype of (@); that is:

```
sub mysubroutine (@) {...}
```

Just like unprototyped subroutines, the single @ prototype will absorb all values, flattening any lists or hashes it finds. It follows from this that a prototype of (@,@) is just as invalid as it was before. However, if we want to enforce an array variable, as opposed to a mere list, that's a different story, as we will see shortly.

A @ or % prototype matches all parameters in the argument list from the point it is defined to the end of the list. Indeed, % and @ are actually identical in meaning to Perl, since passing a hash turns it into a list. Recall that there is no such thing as "hash context." It cannot check that passed parameters came from a hash due to flattening, nor that the remaining parameters divide evenly into pairs because that is a run-time issue. However, this does not mean they are of no use. It means that the only useful place for either prototype character is at the end of the prototype. As an example, here is a subroutine, which joins array elements incorporating a prefix and suffix. It takes a minimum of three parameters but has no maximum because of the @ prototype:

```
#!/usr/bin/perl
# join.pl
use warnings;

sub wrapjoin ($$$@) {
    my ($join, $left, $right, @strings) = @_;
    foreach (@strings) {
        $_ = $left. $_. $right;
    }
    return join $join, @strings;
}

print wrapjoin("\n", "[","]", "One", "Two", "Three");
```

Without the @ we could only pass three arguments. If we added more $ characters we could allow more, but then we would be forced to supply that many arguments. The @ allows an arbitrary number, so long as we also supply three scalars to satisfy the initial $$$.

Lists can validly be empty, so the prototype does not ensure that we actually get passed something to join. We could attempt to fix that by requiring a fourth scalar, like this:

```
sub wrapjoin ($$$$@) {
    my ($join, $left, $right, @strings) = @_;
    ...
}
```

However, a little thought reveals a flaw in this design. A literal list of strings works fine, but if the caller supplies an actual array variable for the fourth argument, it gets converted to a scalar. In effect, we have introduced a new bug by adding the prototype.

The moral here is that prototypes can be tricky and can even introduce bugs. They are not a universal band-aid for fixing subroutine calling problems. If we want to detect and flag an error for an empty list, prototypes cannot help us—we will have to write the subroutine to handle it explicitly at run time.

Prototyping Code References

Other than $ and @ (and the synonymous %), we can supply one other basic prototype character: &. This tells Perl that the parameter to be supplied is a code reference. This is not as far-fetched as it might seem; the sort function accepts such an argument, for example.

If the very first parameter is prototyped with &, then Perl allows it to be a bare block, rather than an anonymous subroutine. For the second and subsequent parameters, the code reference must actually be to a subroutine, anonymous or named. (If we actually want to disallow a code block, we can prototype with \& instead of &.)

Here is how we could prototype the do_list subroutine we introduced when we covered anonymous subroutines earlier:

```
sub do_list (&@) {
    my ($subref, @in) = @_;
    my @out;
    foreach (@in) {
        push @out, &$subref ($_);
    }
    return @out;
}
```

The prototype requires that the first argument be a code reference, since the subroutine cannot perform any useful function on its own. As it is the first parameter, either a subroutine reference or an explicit block will satisfy the prototype. For example:

```
@words = ("ehT", "terceS", "egasseM");
do_list { print reverse($_[0] =~/./g), "\n" } @words;
```

Note how this syntax is similar to the syntax of Perl's built-in sort, map, and grep functions.

Subroutines As Scalar Operators

We mentioned previously that subroutines can be thought of as user-defined list operators, used much in the same way as built-in list operator functions like print, chomp, and so on. However, not all of Perl's functions are list operators. Some, such as abs, only work on scalars and interpret their argument in a scalar context (or simply refuse to execute) if we try to supply a list.

Defining subroutines with a prototype of ($) effectively converts them from being list operators to scalar operators. Returning to our capitalize example, if we decided that, instead of allowing it to work on lists, we want to force it to only work on scalars, we would write it like this:

```
sub capitalize ($) {
    $_[0] = ucfirst (lc $_[0]);
}
```

Now, if the subroutine is passed more than one argument, Perl will generate a compile-time error. However, there is a sting in the tail. Before the prototype was added, this subroutine would accept a list and capitalize the string in the first element, coincidentally also returning it. Another programmer might be using it in the following way, without our knowledge.

```
capitalize(@list); # capitalizes the first element
```

While adding the prototype prevents multiple strings being passed in a list, an array variable still fits the prototype, as we saw earlier. It simply gets evaluated in a scalar context, which counts its elements. Suddenly, the previously functional `capitalize` turns the passed array into a scalar number:

```
@countries = ("england", "scotland", "wales");
capitalize (@countries);
```

The result of this is that the number "3" is passed into `capitalize`. Since this is not a variable, it causes a syntax error when we try to assign to `$_[0]`. If we chose to return a result rather than modifying the passed argument, then the code would be perfectly valid but badly bugged. However, a program that is used to print "England" might start printing "3" instead. This is more than a little confusing and not intuitively easy to track down.

The key problem here is not that we are passing an array instead of a scalar but that we are checking for a scalar value rather than a scalar variable, which is what we actually require. In the next section we will see how to do that.

Requiring Variables Rather Than Values

So far we have seen how to enforce a specific number of arguments and their scope, if not their data type. We can also use prototypes to require that an actual variable be passed. This is invaluable when we want to implement a subroutine that modifies its passed parameters, such as the `capitalize` example just shown.

To require a variable, we again use a $, @, and % character to specify the type, but now we prefix it with a backslash. This does not, as it might suggest, mean that the subroutine requires a reference to a scalar, array, or hash variable. Instead, it causes Perl to require a variable instead of merely a value. It also causes Perl to automatically pass the variable as a reference:

```
#!/usr/bin/perl
# varproto.pl
use warnings;
use strict;

sub capitalize (\$) {
    ${$_[0]} = ucfirst (lc ${$_[0]});
}

my $country = "england";
capitalize $country;
print $country, "\n";      # Ok, produces 'England'
# capitalize "scotland";  # ERROR: compile-time syntax error!
```

If we tried to call `capitalize` with a literal string value, we would get this error:

```
Type of arg 1 to main::capitalize must be scalar (not constant item) at ...,
  near ""england";"
```

The fact that Perl automatically passes variables as references is very important, because it provides a new way to avoid the problem of list flattening. In other words, prototypes allow us to pass arrays and hashes to a subroutine as-is, without resorting to references in the subroutine call.

The `push` function is an example of a built-in function that works by taking an array as its first argument. We do not need to treat that variable specially to avoid flattening, and we can replicate that syntax in our own code by defining a prototype of (\@@). The following subroutine uses the list-processing version of `capitalize` to produce a capitalizing `push` subroutine. First it removes the array variable using `shift`, then capitalizes the rest of the arguments and adds them to the variable with `push`. Perl, being versatile, lets us do the whole thing in one line:

```
sub pushcapitalize (\@@) {
    push @{shift}, capitalize(@_);
}
```

We can use this subroutine just like we use the push function:

```
pushcapitalize @countries, "england";
pushcapitalize @countries, "scotland", "wales";
pushcapitalize @countries, @places;    # no flattening here!
```

Note that we omitted the parentheses, which requires that the subroutine be either already defined or predeclared.

Hash variables are requested using \%, which unlike % does have a different meaning to its array counterpart \@. Here is an example that flips a hash variable around so that the keys become values and the values become keys. If two keys have the same value, one of them will be lost in the transition, but for the sake of simplicity we'll ignore that here:

```
sub flip (\%) {
    %{$_[0]} = reverse %{$_[0]};
}
```

This subroutine makes use of the fact that a hash is essentially just a list with an even number of values, and a little extra cleverness allows quick key access. So, to flip the hash, we turn it into a list and reverse it. This also reverses each key-value pair with respect to each other; we then turn it back into a hash again.

If we want to define a prototype that requires a variable arguments but that is flexible as to what kind—for example, a scalar, an array, or a hash variable—we can do so by grouping the prototype characters together with square braces. For example:

```
# requires a ref to scalar,array, or hash, plus scalar value
sub wantsascalararrayorhash (\[$@%]$);
```

Although Perl will automatically pass variables as references when a variable prototype is in effect, it will only allow an explicit reference if we dereference it first:

```
pushcapitalize @{$countries_ref}, "england";
flip %{$hash_ref};
```

We can avoid this slightly ugly syntax by calling the subroutine with an & prefix, since & disables prototypes. It is debatable whether this is an improvement, though, since disabling the prototype bypasses the protection it was intended to provide.

```
&flip $hashref; # OK - & disables prototype
```

Note that as we mentioned earlier, \& also has a meaning subtly different from &. It requires that the passed code reference be a reference to an actual subroutine, that is, a code reference defined using $coderef = sub {...} or $coderef = \&mysubroutine. A reference to an in-line bare block (such as in mysub {...} @list) will not be accepted.

Optional Parameters

A prototype such as ($$$@) allows us to define a subroutine with three required parameters and any number of optional ones, but it is something of an all-or-nothing solution. To define a variable number of parameters, say a subroutine that takes at least three but no more than four parameters, we use a semicolon to separate the mandatory parameters from the optional ones.

The following subroutine, which calculates mass, is a variation on the volume subroutine from earlier. It takes the same three dimensions and a fourth optional density parameter, which defaults to 1.

```
sub mass ($$$;$) {
    return volume($_[0],$_[1],$_[2]) * (defined($_[3])? $_[3]: 1);
}
```

Using a semicolon does not preclude the use of @ to gobble up any extra parameters. We can for instance define a prototype of ($$$;$@), which means three mandatory scalar parameters, followed by an optional scalar, followed by an optional list. That differs from ($$$;@) in that we don't have to pass a fourth argument, but if we do it must be scalar.

We can also define optional variables. A prototype of ($$$;\$) requires three mandatory scalar parameters and an optional fourth scalar variable. For instance, we can extend the volume subroutine to place the result in a variable passed as the fourth argument, if one is supplied:

```
sub volume ($$$;\$) {
    my $volume = $_[0] * $_[1] * $_[2];
    ${$_[3]} = $volume if defined $_[3];
}
```

And here is how we could call it:

```
volume(1, 4, 9, $result);   # $result ends up holding 36
```

From all this, we can deduce that the default prototype of an unprototyped subroutine is actually (;@).

Disabling Prototypes

All aspects of a subroutine's prototype are disabled if we call it using the old-style prefix &. Although this can occasionally be useful, it is also a potential minefield of confusion. To illustrate, assume that we had redefined our capitalize subroutine to only accept a single scalar variable:

```
sub capitalize (\$) {
    $_[0] = ucfirst (lc $_[0]);
}
```

Another programmer who had been calling the unprototyped version with a list to capitalize the first string now encounters a syntax error:

```
capitalize (@countries);      # ERROR: not a scalar variable
```

One way they could fix this is to just pass in the first element. However, they can also override the prototype and continue as before by prefixing their subroutine call with an ampersand:

```
capitalize ($countries[0]);   # pass only the first element
&capitalize @countries;       # disable the prototype
```

Naturally, this kind of behavior is somewhat dangerous, so it is not encouraged; that's the whole point of a prototype. However, the fact that an ampersand disregards a prototype means that we cannot generate a code reference for a subroutine and still enforce the prototype:

```
$subref = \&mysubroutine;    # prototype not active in $subref
```

This can be a real problem. For instance, the sort function behaves differently if it is given a prototyped sort function (with a prototype of ($$)), passing the values to be compared rather than setting the global variables $a and $b. However, defining a named subroutine with a prototype and then passing a reference to it to sort doesn't work. The only way to retain a prototype on a subroutine reference is to define it as an anonymous subroutine in the first place:

```
# capitalize as a anonymous subroutine
$capitalize_sub = sub (\$) {
    $_[0] = ucfirst (lc $_[0]);
};
```

And using reverse:

```
# an anonymous 'sort' subroutine - use as 'sort $in_reverse @list'
$in_reverse = sub ($$) {
    return $_[1] <=> $_[0];
}
```

Retrieving and Setting Prototypes Programmatically

We are not limited to giving our subroutines prototypes by typing them into the code explicitly. From Perl 5.8 we can both retrieve the prototype of a previously defined subroutine or built-in function, and set or change the prototype of a subroutine.

Retrieving Prototypes

To retrieve the prototype of a subroutine, we use the built-in prototype function. For example:

```
#!/usr/bin/perl
# getprototype.pl
use strict;
use warnings;

sub add_two ($$) {
    return $_[0]+$_[1];
}

print prototype(\&add_two),"\n"; # produces '$$'
print prototype('add_two'),"\n"; # likewise
```

If the subroutine does not yet have a prototype, an empty string is returned. If the subroutine does not exist, then undef is returned.

Similarly, to retrieve the prototype of a built-in function, we prefix the name of the function with CORE::, as in this example:

```
print prototype("CORE::substr"); # produces '$$;$$'
```

Not all built-in keywords resemble functions, and attempting to retrieve their prototypes will return undef—use is one such keyword. This generally also indicates that we cannot override the built-in function with a use subs pragma. Attempting to retrieve a prototype for a nonexistent built-in function will generate a "Can't find an opnumber for "foo"" error, however.

Setting Prototypes

There might seem little point in setting the prototype of a subroutine—after all, we could surely just have defined it with one in the first place. But there are occasions when we might create a subroutine on-the-fly and only know the correct prototype at that point. For instance, subroutines created by AUTOLOAD and called from an eval statement are a good candidate for this feature.

To set a prototype, we use the set_prototype function provided by the Scalar::Util module, which comes as standard with Perl 5.8 and above but is also available from CPAN for earlier versions. It takes two arguments, a code reference for the subroutine (named or anonymous) to be changed and a string containing the prototype specification, minus the parentheses. This short program shows it in action:

```
#!/usr/bin/perl
use strict;
use warnings;

use Scalar::Util qw(set_prototype);
```

```
sub add_list {
    @_ = @{$_[0]} if ref $_[0]; #accepts list or arrayref
    my $result=0;
    $result = $result + $_ foreach @_;
    return $result;
};

set_prototype \&add_list,'$$$';
print "add_list prototype is (",prototype("add_list"),")\n";
eval 'print "sum is ",add_list(1,2,3),"\n"'
    or die "eval failed: $@";

set_prototype \&add_list,'\@';
print "add_list prototype is (",prototype("add_list"),")\n";
my @list=(1,2,3,4,5);
eval 'print "sum is ",add_list(@list),"\n"'
    or die "eval failed: $@";

set_prototype \&add_list,'$$$$$';
print "add_list prototype is (",prototype("add_list"),")\n";
eval 'print "sum is ",add_list(1,2,3),"\n"'
    or die "eval failed: $@"; # error!
```

Because prototypes are only considered at compile time, it is pointless to set a prototype for a function after the code that uses it has already been compiled. Here we achieve this goal by making sure that the code that refers to our subroutine is only compiled at run time by placing it into a string and passing it to eval. This way, Perl only compiles the calls to add_list in each case after the prototype has been set. As a result, even though the subroutine is written to accept either a list of values or an array reference, the first call only accepts a list while the second only accepts a reference. The last of the three cases causes an error because the prototype at this point requires five scalars, and we only passed three. If we run this program, we get the following output:

> **setprototype.pl**

```
add_list prototype is ($$$)
sum is 6
add_list prototype is (\@)
sum is 15
add_list prototype is ($$$$$)
eval failed: Not enough arguments for main::add_list at (eval 5) line 1, near "3)"
```

Note that only the string form of eval works in this example, because only in the string form is the code first compiled at the time the eval is executed. If we use the block form, with curly braces instead of quotes, no error occurs because the block is compiled at the same time as the surrounding code.

Returning Values from Subroutines

Subroutines can return values in one of two ways: either implicitly, by reaching the end of their block, or explicitly, through the use of the return statement.

If no explicit return statement is given, then the return value of a subroutine is the value of the last statement executed (technically, the last expression evaluated), the same as for ordinary bare blocks. For example, the string "implicit return value" is returned by the following simple subroutine because it is the value of the last (and in this case, only) statement in the subroutine:

```perl
sub implicit_return {
    my $string = "implicit return value";
}
```

Or even just

```perl
sub implicit_return {
    "implicit return value";
}
```

To explicitly define the return value, we use the return statement; return takes an expression as its argument, and returns its value to the caller:

```perl
sub explicit_return {
    return "explicit return value";
}
```

It follows from this that it is never actually necessary to use return when passing back a value from the last statement in the subroutine. However, it is good practice to indicate that we know what we are doing and are aware of what the return value is. If a subroutine does not have an explicit return, the usual implication is that it does not return a value of use. An exception is very short subroutines such as sort subroutines, typically comprising of only one expression, whose return value is obvious from context.

There is nothing to stop us putting several return statements into the same subroutine. Whichever return statement is encountered first will cause the subroutine to exit with the value of the supplied expression, aborting the rest of the subroutine. The following simple subroutine illustrates this:

```perl
sub list_files {
    my $path = shift;
    return "" unless defined $path;       # return an empty string if no path
    return join(', ', glob "$path/ * ");  # return comma separated string
}
```

Here we have used two return statements. The first returns the undefined value if we fail to supply a pathname for the subroutine to look at. The second is only reached if a defined (but not necessarily valid or existent) path is supplied. We could call this subroutine with code that looks like this:

```perl
if (my $files = list_files ("/path/to/files")) {
    print "Found $files \n";
}
```

Multiple return statements are a convenient way to return values from a subroutine as soon as the correct value has been computed, but for large subroutines they should be used with caution. Many programming problems stem from overcomplex subroutines that have more than one return in them, causing a crucial piece of code to be skipped in some cases and not others. This is often a sign that the subroutine is too large to be easily maintained and should be split into smaller functional blocks. Otherwise, it is better to either funnel the execution of the subroutine to just one return statement at the end or else to make it very clear in the source where all the exits are.

The preceding list_files subroutine works, but it is a little clumsy. It does not allow us to distinguish between an undefined path and a path on which no files were found. It also returns the files found as a string rather than a list, which would have been more useful. The first of these we can fix by using the undefined value to indicate an error. The second we can fix by returning a list, or more cunningly, by detecting the calling context and returning a scalar or list value as appropriate. We will cover each of these in turn.

Returning the Undefined Value

Although it might seem a strange idea, it is quite common for subroutines and many of Perl's built-in functions to return the undefined value undef instead of a real (that is, defined) value.

The advantage of undef is that it evaluates to "false" in conditions, but is distinct from a simple zero because it returns false when given as an argument to defined. This makes it ideal for use in subroutines that want to distinguish a failed call from one that just happens to return no results. This modified version of list_files uses undef to flag the caller when no path is specified:

```perl
#!/usr/bin/perl
# findfiles.pl
use warnings;
use strict;
my $files = list_files ($ARGV[0]);

if (defined $files) {
    if ($files) {
        print "Found: $files \n";
    } else {
        print "No files found \n";
    }
} else {
    print "No path specified\n";
}

sub list_files {
    my $path = shift;

    return undef unless defined $path;  #return an empty list if no path
    return join(',', glob "$path/*");   #return comma separated string
}
```

If no path is supplied, the subroutine returns undef, which evaluates to false in the if statement. If the path was supplied but no files were found, the subroutine returns an empty string, which while false is still defined and so tests true in the if statement. We then test the value of $files with the ternary operator and print out an appropriate message if the string happens to be empty. Note that in this particular application checking @ARGV first would be the correct way to handle a lack of input, allowing us to simplify the subroutine by not requiring it to deal with an undefined path as a special case at all.

undef works well in a scalar context but is problematic in list context. While it is perfectly possible to assign undef to an array variable, it is confusing because what we end up with is an array of one value, which is undefined. These two statements are equivalent, and both of them result in an array of one element, not an empty array:

```perl
@list=undef;
@list=(undef);
```

If we naively try to convert our subroutine to return a list instead of a scalar string, we might write

```perl
sub list_files {
    my $path = shift;

    return undef unless defined $path;  #return undef if no path
    return glob "$path/*";              #return a list of files
}
```

Unfortunately, if we try to call this function in a list context and do not specify a defined path, we end up with anomalous behavior:

```
foreach (list_files $ARGV[0]) {   #if program executed with no argument...
    print "Found: $_\n";          #...called once with $_ == undef
}
```

If the path is undefined, this will execute the loop once, print "Found: ", and generate an uninitialized value warning. The reason for this is that undef is not a list value, so when evaluated in the list context of the foreach loop, it is converted into a list containing one value, which happens to be undefined. As a result, when the subroutine is called with an undefined path, the loop executes once, with the value of the loop variable $_ being undefined.

In order for the loop to behave the way we intended, and not execute even once when no results are found, we need to return an empty list. Here's another version of list_files that does this:

```
sub list_files {
    my $path = shift;
    return () unless defined $path;  #return empty list if no path
    return glob "$path/*";           #return list of files
}
```

This fixes the problem we had when returning undef, but at the cost of losing the ability to distinguish between an undefined path and a path that happens to contain no files. What we would really like to do is return either undef or the empty list depending on whether a scalar or list result is required. The wantarray function provides exactly this information, and we cover it next.

Responding to the Calling Context

Sometimes it is useful to know what the calling context is, so we can return different values based on the caller's requirements. The return statement already knows this implicitly, and makes use of the context to save time, returning a count of a returned list if the subroutine is called in a scalar context. This is more efficient than returning all the values in the list and then counting them—passing back one scalar is simpler when that is all the calling context actually requires.

Perl allows subroutines to directly access this information with the wantarray function. Using wantarray allows us to intelligently return different values based on what the caller wants. For example, we can return a list either as a reference or a list of values, depending on the way in which we were called:

```
return wantarray ? @files : \@files;
```

We can also use wantarray to return undef or an empty list depending on context, avoiding the problems of assigning undef to an array variable as we discussed earlier:

```
return wantarray ? () : undef;
```

As discussed in the previous section, the case of returning undef or an empty list according to context is important enough to warrant a special case use of the return function. If return is used without any argument at all, it automatically returns undef or an empty list if the calling context is scalar or list, respectively. If the calling context is void, then it does not bother to return a value at all. The preceding statement can therefore be rewritten to simply read

```
return;
```

This is very convenient, of course, but suffers from the problem that it is not easy to tell by reading the code whether or not we expect to return a value or not—we could just as easily be using return simply to exit the subroutine. As a result, some programmers prefer to use the wantarray expression shown earlier to make the intended behavior of the subroutine clearer.

Modifying our original subroutine to incorporate both these changes gives us the following improved version of list_files that handles both scalar and list context:

```
sub list_files {
    my $path = shift;

    return wantarray ? () : undef unless defined $path;
    # or simply: return unless defined $path;

    my @files = glob "$path/ *";
    return wantarray ? @files : \@files;
}
```

This is an example of Perl's reference counting mechanism in action; @files may go out of scope, but the reference returned in scalar context preserves the values it holds.

We can now call list_files with two different results. In list context we get either a list of files, an empty list if either no files were found or the path is undefined. This allows the return value to be used in a foreach loop. If we want to distinguish between a defined path with no files and an undefined path, we call list_files in scalar context. In return, we get a reference to a list of files, a reference to an empty list if no files were found, or the undefined value if the path was undefined. By additionally testing for the undefined value with defined, we can now distinguish all three cases:

```
# list context
@files = list_files ($ARGV[0]);
die "No path defined or no files found" unless @files;
print "Found: @files \n";
# scalar context
$files = list_files($ARGV[0]);
die "No path defined! \n" unless defined $files;
die "No files found! \n"" unless $files;
print "Found: @{$files} \n";
```

One final note about wantarray: If we want to find the number of files rather than retrieve a list, then we can no longer call the subroutine in scalar context to achieve it. Instead, we need to call the subroutine in list context and then convert it into a scalar explicitly:

```
$count = $#{list_files $ARGV[0]}+1;
```

This is much clearer, because it states that we really do mean to use the result in a scalar context. Why not use scalar, though? Because scalar forces its argument into a scalar context—that won't do what we want. By contrast, $# requires that its argument is a list and then counts it.

Handling Void Context

So far we have considered list and scalar contexts. If the subroutine is called in a void context, wantarray returns undef. We can use this fact to save time computing a return value or even to produce an error:

```
sub list_files {
    die "Function called in void context" unless defined wantarray;
    ...
}
```

This is particularly handy when writing subroutines that resemble map or grep; we can choose to modify the original values or generate new ones. But generating new values is expensive if the caller does not intend to use them, so we can save ourselves the trouble—and Perl a whole lot of pointless memory allocation and deallocation—by checking if wantarray is undefined.

A Context-Sensitive Example

Putting all the preceding together, here is a final version of list_files that handles both scalar, list, and void contexts, along with a sample program to test it out in each of the three contexts:

```perl
#!/usr/bin/perl
# listfile.pl
use warnings;
use strict;

sub list_files {
    die "Function called in void context" unless defined wantarray;
    my $path = shift;


    return unless defined $path;
    chomp $path;    #remove trailing linefeed, if present
    $path.='/*' unless $path =~/\*/;   #add wildcard if missing
    my @files = glob $path;
    return wantarray?@files:\@files;
}

print "Enter Path: ";
my $path = <>;

# call subroutine in list context
print "Get files as list:\n";
my @files = list_files($path);
foreach (sort @files) {
    print "\t$_\n";
}

# call subroutine in scalar context
print "Get files as scalar:\n";
my $files = list_files($path);
foreach (sort @{$files}) {
    print "\t$_ \n";
}

# to get a count we must now do so explicitly with $#...
# note that 'scalar would not work, it forces scalar context.
my $count = $#{list_files($path)}+1;
print "Count: $count files\n";

# call subroutine void context - generates an error
list_files($path);
```

■Tip The name wantarray is something of a misnomer, since there is actually no such thing as "array context," arrays being storage. A better name for it would have been wantlist.

Assigning Values to Subroutines

Some of Perl's built-in functions allow us to assign to them as well as use them in expressions. In programming parlance, the result of the function is an *lvalue*, or a value that can appear on the left-hand side of an assignment. The most common and obvious lvalues are variables, which we assign to all the time:

```
$scalar_value = "value";
```

Some Perl functions can also be assigned to in this way, for example, the substr function:

```
$mystring = "this is some text";
substr($mystring, 0, 7) = "Replaced";
print $mystring;   # produces "Replaced some text";
```

The substr function returns part of a string. If the string happens to be held in a variable, then this returned string segment is an lvalue, and can be assigned to. Perl does not even require that the new text be the same length, as the preceding example illustrates. It would be wonderful to be able to do this kind of thing in our own subroutines.

In fact, Perl does allow us to this, albeit only experimentally at the moment. Assignable subroutines make use of subroutine attributes, an experimental but currently stable feature of Perl from version 5.6 onwards. Since attributes are likely to evolve, this technique should be avoided for production code unless we are prepared for the possibility of having to do some code rework if we upgrade to a future Perl with different semantics for attributes. However, for the moment, to make a subroutine assignable, we can use the special attribute lvalue, as this simple assignable subroutine script demonstrates:

```
#!/usr/bin/perl
# assignable.pl
use warnings;
use strict;

my $scalar = "Original String";

sub assignablesub : lvalue {
    $scalar;
}

print $scalar, "\n";
assignablesub = "Replacement String";
print $scalar, "\n";
```

In order for an assignable subroutine to function correctly, it must return a variable. In addition, it must *not* use return, because with an assignable subroutine data can pass in as well as out. Currently (as of Perl 5.8) only scalar values may be used as assignable return values. This includes an array element or hash value, however.

Another potential problem with lvalue subroutines is that they cannot, by definition, control what happens to the value they return. The assignment occurs after the subroutine returns, so there is no way to control or check the assigned value. If we need to do this, then the returned value needs to be able to validate itself. We can possibly do that with a restricted hash or pseudohash, or otherwise with a tied object reference, but either solution adds complexity.

Attributes do not preclude prototypes. If we want to specify a prototype, we can do so after the subroutine, before any attributes. The following example shows a prototyped assignable subroutine that provides an example of assigning to an array via the returned lvalue:

```
my @array = (1, 2, 3);

sub set_element (\@$) : lvalue {
    @{$_[0]} [$_[1]];   # return element of passed array
    # @{$_[0]} is the array
```

```
    # [$_[1]] is the $_[1]th element of that array
}

set_element (@array, 2) = 5;
```

This is a simple and so not particularly useful example, of course, but it shows the way to more complex and powerful constructs.

Closures

Closures are subroutines that operate on variables created in the context in which they were defined, rather than passed in or created locally. This means that they manipulate variables outside their own definition, but within their scope. Here is a simple example of a closure at work:

```
my $count = 0;
sub count { return ++ $count; }
print count, count, count;   # produces '123'
```

Here the subroutine count uses the variable $count. But the variable is defined outside of the subroutine and so is defined for as long as the program runs. Nothing particularly remarkable so far, all we are doing is defining a lexical global variable. However, what makes closures useful is that they can be used to implement a form of memory in subroutines where the variable is global inside the subroutine but is invisible outside. Consider the following example:

```
{
    my $count = 0;
    sub count {return ++ $count;}
}
print count, count, count;   # still print 123
```

What makes this interesting is that the variable $count is no longer directly accessible by the time we get to the print statement. Ordinarily it would have ceased to exist at the end of the block in which it is defined because it is lexical and therefore bounded by the block's scope. However, it is referred to in the subroutine count, which is by nature a global definition. Consequently, Perl still has a reference to the variable, and so it persists. The only place the reference exists is in the subroutine count, so we have effectively created a persistent and private variable inside count.

A closure makes a handy way to store the result of an operation so that it does not have to be repeated—the previous result can simply be reused. While we can do the same with a global variable, the closure forces callers to go through the subroutine to get an answer. This short program caches the results of a random integer generated for each supplied range. Subsequent calls with the same range parameter will always return the same result. Callers of this routine cannot tell whether the value was just calculated or retrieved from the cache:

```
#!/usr/bin/perl -w
# constrandinrange.pl
use strict;

{
    my %cached;

    sub constrandinrange ($) {
        my $range=shift;
    unless ($cached{$range}) {
        $cached{$range}=int(rand $range+1);
    }
```

```perl
        return $cached{$range};
        }
}

print constrandinrange(10),"\n";
print constrandinrange(20),"\n";
print constrandinrange(10),"\n";
print constrandinrange(20),"\n";
```

Here is another example: a version of the factorial program we first gave back in Chapter 2. This time, the results of each factorial calculation are cached:

```perl
#!/usr/bin/perl
# factorial.pl
use warnings;
use strict;

# factorial closure
{
    my @cache=(0,1); # prep the cache

    # the subroutine
    sub factorial {
        my $input = shift; # read passed argument

        # get the number of the highest so far
        my $highest = $#cache;

        # do we already have the answer cached?
        if ($input > $highest) {
            # calculate remaining terms
            foreach ($highest+1 .. $input) {
                $cache[$_] = $cache[$_-1] * $_;
            }
        }

        # return answer
        return $cache[$input];
    }
}

my $number;
do {
    $number=<>;     # read a number from the keyboard
    chomp $number; # remove linefeed

    # call the subroutine with $number
    my $result=factorial($number);

    print "$number factorial is $result\n";
} while ($number > 0);
```

This application will loop, reading numbers from the keyboard and printing out their factorial until it gets zero or an input that does not have a numeric value. Since to calculate a given factorial we need to calculate all factorials of lower numbers, we only need to calculate from the point the highest previous calculation left off. If the requested number has already been calculated, we just return it.

Anonymous Closures

Closures get even more interesting when we create them in an anonymous subroutine. If we replace the block with a subroutine definition and count with an anonymous subroutine, we end up with this:

```
sub make_counter ($) {
    my $count = shift;
    return sub { return $count++; }
}
```

The outer subroutine make_counter accepts one scalar variable and uses it to initialize the counter variable. We then create an anonymous subroutine that refers to the variable (thus preserving it) and returns the code reference of the anonymous subroutine. We can now use make_counter to create and use any number of persistent counters, each using its own secret counter variable:

```
$tick1 = make_counter(0);    #counts from zero
$tick2 = make_counter(100);  #counts from 100

$, = ", ";
print &$tick1, &$tick2, &$tick1, &$tick2; # produces 0, 100, 1, 101
```

Just because the subroutine is anonymous does not mean that it cannot accept parameters—we just access the @_ array as normal. Here is a variation of make_counter that allows us to reset the counter variable by passing a number to the anonymous subroutine:

```
#!/usr/bin/perl
# closure.pl
use warnings;
use strict;

sub make_counter ($) {
    my $count = @_?shift:0;

    return sub {
        $count = $_[0] if @_;
        return $count++;
    }
}

my $counter = make_counter(0);
foreach (1..10) {
    print &$counter, "\n";
}
print "\n";   # displays 0, 1, 2, 3, 4, 5, 6, 7, 8, 9

$counter->(1000);   #reset the counter
foreach (1..3) {
    print &$counter, ""\n";
}
print "\n";   # displays 1000, 1001, 1002
```

Closures also provide a way to define objects so that their properties cannot be accessed from anywhere other than the object's own methods. The trick is to define the object's underlying data in terms of an anonymous subroutine that has access to an otherwise inaccessible hash, in the same way that the variable $count is hidden here. We will take a look at doing this in Chapter 19, along with tied objects, which would allow us to disguise a counter like the preceding one as a read-only scalar variable that increments each time we access it.

Attributes

Attributes are pieces of information associated with either variables or subroutines that can be set to modify their behavior in specific ways. Currently, Perl defines three built-in attributes for subroutines, lvalue, locked, and method, and one for our-declared variables, unique. We have already seen and discussed lvalue earlier in this chapter, and we cover locked and method in brief next.

Special Attributes

As of Perl 5.8, there are currently four attributes with special meanings:

lvalue

We discussed the lvalue attribute earlier in the chapter: it allows subroutines to return assignable values, rather like the substr function does when used on a variable.

locked

The locked attribute is deprecated in Perl version 5.8 onwards and is applicable only to threaded programming using the old thread model introduced in Perl 5.005. It allows simultaneous calls to the same subroutine to be serialized, so that only one thread can execute the body at a time:

```
# Perl 5.005 threads only
sub oneatatimeplease : locked {
    # Only one thread can execute this subroutine at a time.
}
```

From Perl 5.8 onwards, thread synchronization is handled instead by the lock function provided by the threads::shared module.

method

The method attribute prevents Perl from confusing it with a built-in function of the same name. We can therefore create a method called print and be sure that it will only be used when an object-oriented call to print is made. Only if the subroutine is called as an object method will Perl call it instead of the built-in function. In conjunction with locked (and therefore only with old-style threads), method is also used in object classes to indicate that a locked subroutine should lock on a per-object basis. It modifies the effect of the locked attribute to apply itself to the first argument of the subroutine, the blessed object reference:

```
sub objectmethodlock : locked : method {
    my $self = shift;
    # Perl 5.005 threads only
    # only one thread can execute this method on the same object
    # but different threads can execute it on different objects
}
```

We cover the method attribute in a little more detail when we discuss threaded programming in Perl in Chapter 21.

unique

The unique attribute is applied to package variables declared with our; it causes a variable to be shared between interpreters in situations where more than one may exist concurrently in the same application. We discuss it briefly in Chapter 8 and mention it here only for completeness.

Accessing Attributes

The mechanism for processing attributes is actually handled by the `attributes` module. Perl will automatically use `attributes` if we make use of an attribute in our code, so there is rarely any need to explicitly use the module unless we want to extract the list of defined attributes programmatically with the `get` function or find the underling type of a blessed reference with `reftype`:

```
use attributes qw(get reftype);    # import 'get' and 'reftype' subroutines
sub mylockedmethod : locked method {
    my $self=shift;
    my $class=ref($self);
    my $type=reftype($self);

    print "This is a locked method call for ",
        " object $self (class $class), true type $type\n";
}

my @attrlist = get \&mysubroutine;    # contains ('locked', 'method')
```

The `reftype` subroutine also takes a reference to a variable or subroutine. It returns the underlying reference type: `HASH` for a hash variable, `CODE` for a subroutine reference, and so on. Blessed references return the underlying data type, which makes `reftype` a potentially useful subroutine as a replacement for `ref` even if we are not using attributes, as we mentioned back in Chapter 4.

Package Attributes

We can create our own attributes for subroutines with the `Attribute::Handlers` module. Using this module we can also create handlers for lexically scoped variables, that is, variables declared with `my` or `our`. However, attributes for variables are a largely experimental feature and are thus not yet recommended for production use. Attributes created this way are package-based, the package providing the attribute handlers for declarations within that package (or in object-oriented cases, a subclass). This allows different modules to define attributes with the same name without conflicting. We cover them along with writing packages to create our own attributes for variables and subroutines in Chapter 10.

Summary

In this chapter we saw how to declare and call subroutines. Specifically, we looked at anonymous subroutines, subroutine references, and the `use strict subs` pragma. Next, we looked at predeclaring subroutines and learned how to override built-in functions. After this, we learned about the internal stack, which Perl uses to hold details of subroutines, and saw an example of a recursive subroutine.

We went on to examine how parameters are passed to subroutines, and in particular the passing of scalars, lists, and hashes, converting scalar subroutines into list processors, passing the special array @_ directly into subroutines and implementing named parameters. We also looked at Perl's support for subroutine prototypes, which provide compile-time checking of the number and type of parameters passed to a subroutine. We saw how to define the number of parameters, how to pass variables by reference instead of by value, making parameters optional, and when necessary, disabling prototypes in subroutines calls. Following this, we looked at how to return values from subroutines. We also saw how to return the undefined value and determine and respond to the calling context. Finally, we covered attribute lists and looked at defining attributes on subroutines, accessing attributes, special attributes, and package attributes.

CHAPTER 8

■■■

Scope and Visibility

We touched on the concept of scope briefly in Chapter 2 and mentioned it in following chapters from time to time without going into the full details. The scope of a variable is simply the range of places in code from which the variable can be accessed. However, there are two fundamentally different types of variable scope in Perl: *package scope* (also called *dynamic scope*) and *lexical scope*. Which one we use depends on how variables are declared. Named subroutines, on the other hand, always have package scope, as they are defined within a package. This is why we can call a subroutine in another package, and also why it makes no sense to define one subroutine inside another. Anonymous subroutine references are scalars, though, so they can be scoped like any other variable.

Package and lexical scope work in fundamentally different ways, and using both at the same time is frequently the source of much confusion. One useful rule-of-thumb for understanding the distinction is that package variables have a scope that is determined at run time from the current contents of the symbol table, which along with subroutine definitions represents the entirety of the Perl program in memory, whereas lexical variables have a scope that is determined at compile time based on the structure of the source code itself.

Package Variables

A package is defined as a namespace in which declarations of variables and subroutines are placed, confining their scope to that particular package. A great deal of the time we can avoid defining package variables at all by declaring all variables as lexical variables. This lets us define local variables in the way they are normally understood in other languages. However, we often use package variables without being aware of it, for example, the variables $_, @_, %ENV, and @ARGS are all package variables in the main package.

Defining Package Variables

Packages are defined by the package keyword. In and of itself, a package declaration does nothing, but it states that all further declarations of subroutines or package variables will be placed into the package designated by the declaration, until further notice. The notice in this case is either the end of the file, the end of the current block (if the package declaration was made inside one), or less commonly but perfectly legally, another package declaration. The package keyword takes one argument: a list of namespaces separated by double colons. For example:

```
package My::Package;
```

This declares that the variables and subroutines that follow will be in the Package namespace, inside the My namespace.

Package variables have the scope of the package in which they were declared. A package variable can be accessed from other packages by specifying the full package name, in the same way that we can refer to any file on a hard disk from the current directory by starting at the root directory and writing out the full path of the file. This code snippet creates and accesses package variables, both local to the current package and in other packages through their full name. It also defines two subroutines, one in the current package and one in a different package:

```
package My::Package;

$package_variable = "implicitly in 'My::Package'";
$My::Package::another_variable = "explicitly declared in 'My::Package'";
$Another::Package::variable = "explicitly declared in 'Another::Package'";

sub routine { print "subroutine in my package" }
sub Another::Package::routine { print "subroutine in another package" }

{
    package Yet::Another::Package;
    $yet_another_package_variable="blocks limit scope of package declaration";
}

$back_in_my_package = "back in 'My::Package' again";
```

The effect of a `package` declaration is to cause all unqualified package variables and (more significantly) subroutines that follow it to be located in the namespace that it defines. We don't have to use a `package` declaration though; we can define variables and subroutines with an explicit package name. As we showed in the preceding example, it just makes writing code a bit simpler if we do.

Package variables are defined simply by using them, as in the preceding example. No extra syntax or qualifier is needed. Unfortunately, this makes them very easy to define accidentally by misspelling the name of another variable. Perl prevents us from making this mistake with the `use strict 'vars'` pragma, introduced in Chapter 2 and covered in more detail later.

A package is not the same as a module, however, and certainly not the same as a file. In simple terms, a package defines a namespace in a data structure known as the *symbol table*. Whenever a new variable or subroutine is defined, a new entry is added to the table for the appropriate package (the current package if one is not explicitly prefixed to the variable or subroutine name). The same variable name in a different package is not confused with it because the namespaces of the two variables are different and they are defined in different parts of the symbol table.

Package scope is not the same as file scope. A package is most often defined in a single file (a module) to improve maintainability, but Perl does not enforce this and allows packages to be spread across many files. While uncommon, this is one approach we can take if we want to split up subroutines or methods in a package into separate functional files. We define one main module with the same name as the package, translated into a pathname, and `use` or `require` all the other supporting modules from it:

```
package My::Module;
require My::Module::Input;
require My::Module::Output;
require My::Module::Process;
```

The modules `Input.pm`, `Output.pm`, and `Process.pm` in this scheme would all contain a first line of `package My::Module;`, rather than a package that reflects the actual name of the file, such as `My::Module::Input` for `My/Module/Input.pm`. This allows them to add additional subroutine definitions to the `My::Module` namespace directly. Since there is no familial relationship between namespaces, adding definitions to `My::Module::Input` has no effect on the `My::Module` package, or vice versa. This is more efficient than the alternative, using the `Exporter` module to export all the names explicitly.

It follows from this that package variables must be global variables. In practice, what we usually think of as global variables are package variables that are accessed from within their own package, where the package prefix is not required. For instance, the variable $package_variable in the first example earlier is global within the package MyPackage. We can access it from anywhere in our code, so long as the contents of MyPackage have been compiled and executed by the interpreter. Within My::Module we can refer to it as $package_variable. From any other package, we merely have to fully qualify it as $My::Module::package_variable.

New package variables can be created by executing code, with existing variables given local temporary values. Both of these events modify the contents of the symbol table as the program executes. As a result, package scope is ultimately determined at run time and is dependent on the structure of the data in the symbol tables. This differs from lexical variables, whose scope is determined at compile time when the source code is parsed.

All subroutines and package variables must reside in a package, in the same way that all files in a filing system must have a directory, even if it is the root. In Perl, the "root" namespace is main, so any subroutine or package variable we define without an explicit package name or prior package declaration is part of the main package. In effect, the top of every source file is prefixed by an implicit

```
package main;
```

Perl's special variables, as well as the filehandles STDIN, STDOUT, and STDERR, are exempt from the normal rules of package scope visibility. All of these variables are automatically used in the main package, wherever they are used, irrespective of the package declaration that may be in effect. There is therefore only one @_ array, only one default argument $_, and only one %ARGV or @INC. However, these variables have a special status in Perl because they are provided directly by the language; for our own variable declarations and subroutines, the normal rules of packages and namespaces apply.

Using strict Variables

Since it is easy to accidentally define a new global variable without meaning to, Perl provides the strict module. With either of use strict or use strict 'vars', a compile-time syntax check is enabled that requires variables to either be declared lexically or be declared explicitly as package variables. This is generally a good idea, because without this check it is very easy to introduce hard-to-spot bugs, either by forgetting to define a variable before using it, creating a new variable instead of accessing an existing one, or by accessing a global variable when we actually meant to create and use a local copy.

With strict variables in effect, Perl will no longer allow us to define a variable simply by assigning to it. For instance:

```
#!/usr/bin/perl
# package.pl
use warnings;
use strict;

package MyPackage;

$package_variable = "This variable is in 'MyPackage'";   # ERROR
```

If we attempt to run this code fragment, Perl will complain with an error.

```
Global symbol "$package_variable" requires explicit package name at ...
```

Usually the simplest fix for this problem is to prefix the variable with my, turning the variable into a file-scoped lexical variable. However, if we actually want to define a global package variable, we now need to say so explicitly.

Declaring Global Package Variables

The traditional meaning of *global* variable is a variable that can be seen from anywhere—it has global visibility. In Perl, the distinction between package and lexical variables means that there are two different kinds of global variables, *package-global* and *file-global*.

A package variable is global within the package in which it is defined, as we have just seen. Any code in the same package can access the variable directly without qualifying it with a package prefix, except when the variable has been hidden by another variable with the same name (defined in a lower scope). By contrast, a lexical variable (declared with my) is a global variable if it is defined at the file level, outside a block, which makes it a global variable within the file. Only package variables are truly global, because they can always be accessed by referring to them via their full package-prefixed name in the symbol table.

The simplest way to define a package variable is to write it out in full, including the package name, for example:

```
$MyPackage::package_variable = "explicitly defined with package";
```

However, this can be inconvenient to type each time we want to define a new package variable and also causes a lot of editing if we happen to change the name of the package. We can avoid having to write the package name by using either use vars or our. These both define package variables in the current package, but work in slightly different ways.

Declaring Global Package Variables with use vars

To define a package variable with the vars pragma, we pass it a list containing the variables we want to declare. This is a common application of qw:

```
use vars ('$package_variable','$another_var','@package_array');
# using qw is often clearer
use vars qw($package_variable $another_var @package_array);
```

This defines the named variables in the symbol table for the current package. Therefore the variables are directly visible anywhere the package is defined, and they can be accessed from anywhere by specifying the full variable name including the package.

Because use takes effect at compile time, variables declared with use vars are added to the symbol table for the current package at compile time. Also, use pays no attention to enclosing declarations like subroutine definitions. As package variables know nothing about lexical scope, the following script defines the variable $package_variable at compile time and makes it immediately visible anywhere within the package, despite the fact the use is in a subroutine. The value is only assigned once the subroutine is executed, however:

```
#!/usr/bin/perl
# globpack.pl
use warnings;
use strict;

sub define_global {
    use vars qw($package_variable);
    $package_variable = "defined in subroutine";
}

print $package_variable;    # visible here but not yet defined
define_global;
print $package_variable;    # visible here and now defined
```

What we probably intended to do here was create a local package variable with our, which was introduced into Perl 5.6 for precisely this sort of occasion. Since understanding our requires an understanding of lexical scope, we'll leave discussing it until after we look at purely lexical my declarations.

Localizing Package Variables with local

Package variables can be temporarily localized inside subroutines and other blocks with the local keyword. This hides an existing package variable by masking it with a temporary value that exists for as long as the local statement remains in lexical scope. As a statement, local takes either a single variable name or a list enclosed in parentheses and optionally an assignment to one or more values:

```
local $hero;
local ($zip, @boing, %yatatata);
local @list = (1, 2, 3, 4);
local ($red, $blue, $green, $yellow) = ("red", "blue", "green");
```

The local keyword does not, as its name suggests, create a local variable; that is actually the job of my. The local keyword only operates on an existing variable, which can be either a global or a variable defined in the calling context. If no such variable exists, and we have use strict enabled, Perl will issue a compile-time error at us. Many programs simply avoided strict in order to use local, but now that our exists there is no longer a compelling reason to do this. In any event, most of the time when we want to create a local variable, we really should be using my instead.

Localized variables are visible inside subroutine calls, just as the variable they are masking would be if they had not been defined. They are global from the perspective of the subroutines in the call-chain below their scope, so they are not visible outside the subroutine call. This is because localization happens at run time and persists for the scope of the local statement. In this respect, they differ from lexical variables, which are also limited by the enclosing scope but which are not visible in called subroutines.

The following demonstration script illustrates how local works, as well as the differences and similarities between my, our, and use vars:

```perl
#!/usr/bin/perl
# scope-our.pl
use warnings;
use strict;

package MyPackage;

my  $my_var    = "my-var";       # file-global lexical variable
our $our_var   = "our-var";      # global to be localized with 'our'
our $local_var = "global-var";   # global to be localized with 'local'
use vars qw($use_var);           # define 'MyPackage::use_var' which exists
                                 # only in this package

$use_var = "use-var";

package AnotherPackage;

print "Outside, my_var is '$my_var' \n";        # display 'my-var'
print "Outside, our_var is '$our_var' \n";      # display 'our-var'
print "Outside, local_var is '$local_var' \n";  # display 'global-var'

#-----

sub sub1 {
    my $my_var       = "my_in_sub1";
    our $our_var      = "our_in_sub1";
    local $local_var = "local_in_sub1";

    print "In sub1, my_var is '$my_var'\n";        # display 'my_in_sub1'
    print "In sub1, our_var is '$our_var'\n";      # display 'our_in_sub1'
    print "In sub1, local_var is '$local_var'\n";  # display 'local_in_sub1'
```

```
        sub2();
    }

    sub sub2 {
        print "In sub2, my_var is '$my_var'\n";       # display 'my-var'
        print "In sub2, our_var is '$our_var'\n";      # display 'our-var'
        print "In sub2, local_var is '$local_var'\n"; # display 'local_in_sub1'
    }

    #-----

    sub1();

    print "Again outside, my_var is '$my_var' \n";       # display 'my-var'
    print "Again outside, our_var is '$our_var' \n";     # display 'our-var'
    print "Again outside, local_var is '$local_var' \n"; # display 'global-var'
```

Although it is often not the right tool for the job, there are a few instances when only local will do what we want. One is if we want to create a local version of one of Perl's built-in variables. For example, if we want to temporarily alter the output separator $ in a subroutine, we would do it with local like this:

```
#!/usr/bin/perl -w
# localbuiltinvar.pl
use strict;

sub printwith {
    my ($separator, @stuff)=@_;
    local $, = $separator;      # create temporary local $,
    print @stuff,"\n";
}

printwith("... ","one","two","three");
```

The output of this program is

```
one... two... three
```

This is also the correct approach for variables such as @ARGV and %ENV. The special variables defined automatically by Perl are all package variables, so creating a lexical version with my would certainly work from the point of view of our own code, but either this or the lexical version would be totally ignored by built-in functions like print. To get the desired effect, we need to use local to create a temporary version of the global variable that will be seen by the subroutines and built-in functions we call.

Another use for local is for creating local versions of filehandles. For example, this subroutine replaces STDOUT with a different filehandle, MY_HANDLE, presumed to have been opened previously. Because we have used local, both the print statement that follows and any print statements in called subroutine a_sub_that_calls_print() will go to MY_HANDLE. In case MY_HANDLE is not a legal filehandle, we check the result of print and die on a failure:

```
sub print_to_me {
    local *STDOUT = *MY_HANDLE;
    die unless print @_;
    a_sub_that_calls_print();
}
```

If we had used our, only the print statement in the same subroutine would use the new file-handle. At the end of the subroutine the local definition of STDOUT vanishes. Note that since STDOUT always exists, the use of local here is safe, and we do not need to worry about whether or not it exists prior to using local.

Curiously, we can localize not just whole variables, but in the case of arrays and hashes, elements of them as well. This allows us to temporarily mask over an array element with a new value, as in this example:

```
#!/usr/bin/perl
# localelement.pl
our @array=(1,2,3);
{
    local $array[1]=4;
    print @array,"\n"; # produces '143'
}
print @array,"\n",   # produces '123'
```

There might not immediately seem to be any useful applications for this, but as it turns out, there are plenty. For example, we can locally extend the value of @INC to search for modules within a subroutine, locally alter the value of an environment variable in %ENV before executing a subprogram, or install a temporary local signal handler into %SIG:

```
sub execute_specialpath_catchint ($cmd,@args) {
    local $ENV{PATH} = "/path/to/special/bin:".$ENV{PATH}
    local $SIG{INT}  = \&catch_sigint;
    system $cmd => @args;
}
```

A word of warning concerning localizing variables that have been tied to an object instance with tie. While it is possible and safe to localize a tied scalar, attempting to localize a tied array or hash is not currently possible and will generate an error (this limitation may be removed in future).

Automatic Localization in Perl

Perl automatically localizes variables for us in certain situations. The most obvious example is the @_ array in subroutines. Each time a subroutine is called, a fresh local copy of @_ is created, temporarily hiding the existing one until the end of the subroutine. When the subroutine call returns, the old @_ reappears. This allows chains of subroutines to call each other, each with its own local @_, without overwriting the @_ of the caller.

Other instances of automatically localized variables include loop variables, including $_ if we do not specify one explicitly. Although the loop variable might (and with strict variables in effect, must) exist, when it is used for a loop, the existing variable is localized and hidden for the duration of the loop:

```
#!/usr/bin/perl
# autolocal.pl
use warnings;
use strict;

my $var = 42;
my $last;
print "Before: $var \n";
foreach $var (1..5) {
    print "Inside: $var \n";   # print "Inside: 1", "Inside: 2" ...
    $last = $var;
}
```

```
print "After: $var \n";    # prints '42'
print $last;
```

It follows from this that we cannot find the last value of a foreach loop variable if we exit the loop on the last statement without first assigning it to something with a scope outside the loop, like we have done for $last in the preceding example.

Lexical Variables

Lexical variables have the scope of the file, block, or eval statement in which they were defined. Their scope is determined at compile time, determined by the structure of the source code, and their visibility is limited by the syntax that surrounds them. Unlike package variables, a lexical variable is not added to the symbol table and so cannot be accessed through it. It cannot be accessed from anywhere outside its lexical scope, even by subroutines that are called within the scope of the variable. When the end of the variable's scope is reached, it simply ceases to exist. (The value of the variable, on the other hand, might persist if a reference to it was created and stored elsewhere. If not, Perl reclaims the memory the value was using at the same time as it discards the variable.)

In this section, we are concerned with my. While the similar-sounding our also declares variables lexically, it declares package variables whose visibility is therefore greater than their lexical scope. We will come back to the our keyword once we have looked at my.

Declaring Lexical Variables

The following is a short summary of all the different ways in which we can declare lexical variables with my, most of which should already be familiar:

```
my $scalar;                          # simple lexical scalar
my $assignedscalar = "value";        # assigned scalar
my @list = (1, 2, 3, 4);             # assigned lexical array
my ($red, $blue, $green);            # list of scalars
my ($left, $right, $center) = (1, 2, 0); # assigned list of scalars
my ($param1, $param2) = @_;          # inside subroutines
```

All these statements create lexical variables that exist for the lifetime of their enclosing scope and are only visible inside it. If placed at the top of a file, the scope of the variable is the file. If defined inside an eval statement, the scope is that of the evaluated code. If placed in a block or subroutine (or indeed inside curly braces of any kind), the scope of the variable is from the opening brace to the closing one:

```
#!/usr/bin/perl
# scope-my.pl
use warnings;
use strict;

my $file_scope = "visible anywhere in the file";
print $file_scope, "\n";

sub topsub {
    my $top_scope = "visible in 'topsub'";
    if (rand > 0.5) {
        my $if_scope = "visible inside 'if'";
        # $file_scope, $top_scope, $if_scope ok here
        print "$file_scope, $top_scope, $if_scope \n";
    }
```

```
    bottomsub();
    # $file_scope, $top_scope ok here
    print "$file_scope, $top_scope\n";
}

sub bottomsub {
    my $bottom_scope = "visible in 'bottomsub'";
    # $file_scope, $bottom_scope ok here
    print "$file_scope, $bottom_scope \n";
}

topsub();

# only $file_scope ok here
print $file_scope, "\n";
```

In the preceding script, we define four lexical variables, each of which is visible only within the enclosing curly braces. Both subroutines can see $file_scope because it has the scope of the file in which the subroutines are defined. Likewise, the body of the if statement can see both $file_scope and $top_scope. However, $if_scope ceases to exist as soon as the if statement ends and so is not visible elsewhere in topsub. Similarly, $top_scope only exists for the duration of topsub, and $bottom_scope only exists for the duration of bottomsub. Once the subroutines exit, the variables and whatever content they contain cease to exist.

While it is generally true that the scope of a lexical variable is bounded by the block or file in which it is defined, there are some common and important exceptions. Specifically, lexical variables defined in the syntax of a loop or condition are visible in all the blocks that form part of the syntax:

```
#!/usr/bin/perl
# ifscope.pl
use strict;
use warnings;

if ( (my $toss=rand) > 0.5 ) {
    print "Heads ($toss)\n";
} else {
    print "Tails ($toss)\n";
}
```

In this if statement, the lexical variable $toss is visible in both the immediate block and the else block that follows. The same principle holds for elsif blocks, and in the case of while and foreach, the continue block.

Preserving Lexical Variables Outside Their Scope

Normally a lexically defined variable (either my or our) ceases to exist when its scope ends. However, this is not always the case. In the earlier example, it happens to be true because there are no references to the variables other than the one created by the scope itself. Once that ends, the variable is unreferenced and so is consumed by Perl's garbage collector. The variable $file_scope appears to be persistent only because it drops out of scope at the end of the script, where issues of scope and persistence become academic.

However, if we take a reference to a lexically scoped variable and pass that reference back to a higher scope, the reference keeps the variable alive for as long as the reference exists. In other words, so long as something, somewhere, is pointing to the variable (or to be more precise, the memory that holds the value of the variable), it will persist even if its scope ends. The following short script illustrates the point:

```
#!/usr/bin/perl
# persist.pl
use warnings;
use strict;

sub definelexical {
    my $lexvar = "the original value";
    return \$lexvar;    # return reference to variable
}

sub printlexicalref {
    my $lexvar = ${$_[0]};    # dereference the reference
    print "The variable still contains $lexvar \n";
}

my $ref = definelexical();
printlexicalref($ref);
```

In the subroutine definelexical, the scope of the variable $lexvar ends once the subroutine ends. Since we return a reference to the variable, and because that reference is assigned to the variable $ref, the variable remains in existence, even though it can no longer be accessed as $lexvar. We pass this reference to a second subroutine, printlexicalref, which defines a second, $lexvar, as the value to which the passed reference points. It is important to realize that the two $lexvar variables are entirely different, each existing only in its own scope but both pointing to the same underlying scalar. When executed, this script will print out

```
The variable still contains the original value.
```

Tip In this particular example, there is little point in returning a reference. Passing the string as a value is simpler and would work just as well. However, complex data structures can also be preserved by returning a reference to them, rather than making a copy as would happen if we returned them as a value.

The fact that a lexical variable exists so long as a reference to it exists can be extended to include "references to references" and "references to references to references." So long as the "top" reference is stored somewhere, the lexical variable can be hidden at the bottom of a long chain of references, each one being kept alive by the one above. This is in essence how lexical array of arrays and hashes of hashes work. The component arrays and hashes are kept alive by having their reference stored in the parent array or hash.

Lexically Declaring Global Package Variables with our

The our keyword is a partial replacement for use vars, with improved semantics but not quite the same meaning. It allows us to define package variables with a lexical scope in the same manner as my does. This can be a little tricky to understand, since traditionally lexical and package scope are usually entirely different concepts.

To explain, our works like use vars in that it adds a new entry to the symbol table for the current package. However, unlike use vars the variable can be accessed without a package prefix from any package so long as its lexical scope exists. This means that a package variable, declared with our at the top of the file, is accessible throughout the file using its unqualified name even if the package changes.

Another way to look at our is to think of it as causing Perl to rewrite accesses to the variable in other packages (in the same file) to include the package prefix before it compiles the code. For instance, we might create a Perl script containing the following four lines:

```
package MyPackage;
our $scalar = "value";    # defines $MyPackage::scalar

package AnotherPackage;
print $scalar;
```

When Perl parses this, it sees the lexically scoped variable $scalar and our invisibly rewrites all other references to it in the same file to point to the definition in MyPackage, that is, $MyPackage::scalar.

Using our also causes variables to disappear at the end of their lexical scope. Note that this does not mean it removes the package variable from the symbol table. It merely causes access through the unqualified name to disappear. Similarly, if the same variable is redeclared in a different package, the unqualified name is realigned to refer to the new definition. This example demonstrates both scope changes:

```
#!/usr/bin/perl -w
use strict;

package First;
our $scalar = "first";    # defines $First::scalar
print $scalar;            # prints $FirstPackage::scalar, produces 'first'

package Second;
print $scalar;            # prints $First::scalar, produces 'first'
our $scalar = "second";
print $scalar;            # prints $Second::scalar, produces 'second'

package Third;
{
    our $scalar = "inner"; # declaration contained in block
    print $scalar;        # prints $First::scalar, produces 'inner'
}
print $scalar;            # print $Second::scalar, produces 'second'
```

An our variable from another package may, but is not required to, exist, also unlike local, which under strict vars will only localize a variable that exists already. our differs from use vars in that a variable declared with use vars has package scope even when declared inside a subroutine; any value the subroutine gives it persists after the subroutine exits. With our, the variable is removed when the subroutine exits.

The our keyword behaves exactly like my in every respect except that it adds an entry to the symbol table and removes it afterwards (more correctly, it tells Perl to define the symbol in advance, since it happens at compile time). Like my, the added entry is not visible from subroutine calls, since it is lexically scoped. See the "Declaring Lexical Variables" section for more details on how my works.

The unique Attribute

The our pragma takes one special attribute that allows a variable to be shared between interpreters when more than one exists concurrently. Note that this is not the same as a threaded Perl application.

Multiple interpreters generally come about only when forking processes under threaded circumstances: Windows, which emulates fork, is the most common occurrence. Another is where a Perl interpreter is embedded into a multithreaded application. In both these cases, we can choose to have a package variable shared between interpreters, in the manner of threads, or kept separate within each interpreter, in the manner of forked processes:

```
# one value per interpeter
our $unshared_data = "every interpreter for itself";
# all interpreters see the same value;
our $shared_data : unique = "one for all and all for one";
```

Note that this mechanism doesn't allow us to communicate between interpreters. After the first fork, the shared value becomes strictly read-only. See Chapters 20 and 21 for more on embedding Perl and threaded programming, respectively.

The Symbol Table

We have seen that package variables are entered into the symbol table for the package in which they are defined, but they can be accessed from anywhere by their fully qualified name. This works because the symbol tables of packages are jointly held in a master symbol table, with the main:: package at the top and all other symbol tables arranged hierarchically below. Although for most practical purposes we can ignore the symbol table most of the time and simply let it do its job, a little understanding of its workings can be informative and even occasionally useful.

Perl implements its symbol table in a manner that we can easily comprehend with a basic knowledge of data types: it is really a hash of typeglobs. Each key is the name of the typeglob, and therefore the name of the scalar, array, hash, subroutine, filehandle, and report associated with that typeglob. The value is a typeglob containing the references or a hash reference to another symbol table, which is how Perl's hierarchical symbol table is implemented. In fact, the symbol table is the origin of typeglobs and the reason for their existence. This close relationship between typeglobs and the symbol table means that we can examine and manipulate the symbol table through the use of typeglobs.

Whenever we create a global (declared with our or use vars but not my) variable in Perl we cause a typeglob to be entered into the symbol table and a reference for the data type we just defined placed into the typeglob. Consider the following example:

```
our $variable = "This is a global variable";
```

What we are actually doing here is creating a typeglob called variable in the main package and filling its scalar reference slot with a reference to the string "This is a global variable". The name of the typeglob is stored as a key in the symbol table, which is essentially just a hash, with the typeglob itself as the value, and the scalar reference in the typeglob defines the existence and value of $variable. Whenever we refer to a global variable, Perl looks up the relevant typeglob in the symbol table and then looks for the appropriate reference, depending on what kind of variable we asked for.

The only thing other than a typeglob that can exist in a symbol table is another symbol table. This is the basis of Perl's package hierarchy, and the reason we can access a variable in one package from another. Regardless of which package our code is in, we can always access a package variable by traversing the symbol table tree from the top.

The main Package

The default package is main, the root of the symbol table hierarchy, so any package variable declared without an explicit package prefix or preceding package declaration automatically becomes part of the "main package":

```
our $scalar;    # defines $main::scalar
```

Since main is the root table for all other symbol tables, the following statements are all equivalent:

```
package MyPackage;
our $scalar;
```

```
package main::MyPackage;
our $scalar;

our $MyPackage::scalar;
our $main::MyPackage::scalar
```

Strangely, since every package must have main as its root, the main package is defined as an entry in its own symbol table. The following is also quite legal and equivalent to the preceding, if somewhat bizarre:

```
our $main::main::main::main::main::main::main::MyPackage::scalar;
```

This is more a point of detail than a useful fact, of course, but if we write a script to traverse the symbol table, then this is a special case we need to look out for.

In general, we do not need to use the main package unless we want to define a package variable explicitly without placing it into its own package. This is a rare thing to do, so most of the time we can ignore the main package. It does, however, allow us to make sense of error messages like

```
Name "main::a" used only once: possible typo at....
```

The Symbol Table Hierarchy

Whenever we define a new package variable in a new package, we cause Perl to create symbol tables to hold the variable. In Perl syntax, package names are separated by double colons, ::, in much the same way that directories are separated by / or \, and domain names by a dot. For the same reason, the colons define a location in a hierarchical naming system.

For example, if we declare a package with three package elements, we create three symbol tables, each containing an entry to the one below:

```
package World::Country::City;
our $variable = "value";
```

This creates a chain of symbol tables. The World symbol table created as an entry of main contains no actual variables. However, it does contain an entry for the Country symbol table, which therefore has the fully qualified name World::Country. In turn, Country contains an entry for a symbol table called City. City does not contain any symbol table entries, but it does contain an entry for a typeglob called *variable, which contains a scalar reference to the value value. When all put together as a whole, this gives us the package variable:

```
$main::World::Country::City::variable;
```

Since main is always the root of the symbol table tree, we never need to specify it explicitly. In fact, it usually only turns up as a result of creating a symbolic reference for a typeglob as we saw earlier. So we can also just say

```
$World::Country::City::variable;
```

This is the fully qualified name of the package variable. The fact that we can omit the package names when we are actually in the World::Country::City package is merely a convenience. There is no actual variable called $variable, unless we declare it lexically. Even if we were in the main package, the true name of the variable would be $main::variable.

Manipulating the Symbol Table

All global variables are really package variables in the main package, and they in turn occupy the relevant slot in the typeglob with that name in the symbol table. Similarly, subroutines are just code references stored in typeglobs. Without qualification or a package declaration, a typeglob is automatically in the main package, so the following two assignments are the same:

```
*subglob = \&mysubroutine;
*main::subglob = \&main::mysubroutine;
```

Either way we can now call mysubroutine with either name (with optional main:: prefixes if we really felt like it):

```
mysubroutine(); # original name
subglob();      # aliased name
```

We can, of course, alias to a different package too, to make a subroutine defined in one package visible in another. This is actually how Perl's import mechanism works underneath the surface when we say use module and get subroutines that we can call without qualification in our own programs:

```
# import 'subroutine' into our namespace
*main::subroutine = \&My::Module::subroutine;
```

Typeglob assignment works for any of the possible types that a typeglob can contain, including filehandles and code references. So we can create an alias to a filehandle this way:

```
*OUT = *STDOUT;
print OUT "this goes to standard output";
```

This lets us do things like choose from a selection of subroutines at runtime:

```
# choose a subroutine to call and alias it to a local name
our *aliassub = $debug? *mydebugsub: *mysubroutine;

# call the chosen subroutine via its alias
aliassub("Testing", 1, 2, 3);
```

All this works because package typeglobs are actually entries in the symbol table itself. Everything else is held in a typeglob of the same name. Once we know how it all works, it is relatively easy to see how Perl does the same thing itself. For example, when we define a named subroutine, we are really causing Perl to create a code reference, then assign it to a typeglob of that name in the symbol table. To prove it, here is a roundabout way to define a subroutine:

```
#!/usr/bin/perl
# anonsub.pl
use warnings;
use strict;

our $anonsub = sub {print "Hello World"};

*namedsub = \&{$anonsub};
namedsub();
```

Here we have done the same job as defining a named subroutine, but in explicit steps: first creating a code reference, then assigning that code reference to a typeglob. The subroutine is defined in code rather than as a declaration, but the net effect is the same.

We can create aliases to scalars, arrays, and hashes in a similar way. As this example shows, with an alias both variables point to exactly the same underlying storage:

```
#!/usr/bin/perl -w
# scalaralias.pl
use strict;

our $scalar1="one";
*scalar2=\$scalar1;
our $scalar2="two";
print $scalar1; # produces "two";
```

We use our to declare the variables here, in order to keep Perl happy under strict vars. As this is a manipulation of the symbol table, my won't do. Also note that the assignment to the typeglob does not require any declaration, and the declaration of $scalar2 actually comes after it. Typeglobs cannot be declared, and it would not make much sense to try, but if we want to access the scalar variable afterwards without qualifying it with main::, we need to ask permission to avoid running afoul of the strict pragma.

We can also create a constant scalar variable by taking a reference to a scalar (but see also "Constants" in Chapter 5 for more approaches):

```
*constantstring=\"I will not be moved";
our $constantstring="try to change";
# Error! 'Attempt to modify constant scalar...'
```

Be wary of assigning to a typeglob things other than references or other typeglobs. For example, assigning a string does have an interesting but not entirely expected effect. We might suppose the following statement creates a variable called $hello with the value world:

```
*hello = "world";
```

However, if we try to print $hello, we find that it does not exist. If we print out *hello, we find that it has become aliased instead:

```
print *hello;   # produce '*main::world'
```

In other words, the string has been taken as a symbolic reference to a typeglob name, and the statement is actually equivalent to

```
*hello = *world;
```

This can be very useful, especially since the string can be a scalar variable:

```
*hello = $name_to_alias_to;
```

However, it is also a potential source of confusion, especially as it is easily done by forgetting to include a backslash to create a reference. Assigning other things to typeglobs has less useful effects. An array or hash, for example, will be assigned in scalar context and alias the typeglob to a typeglob whose name is a number:

```
@array = (1, 2, 3);
*hello = @array;
print *hello;   # produces 'main::3' since @array has three elements
```

This is unlikely to be what we wanted, and we probably meant to say *hello = \@array in this case. Assigning a subroutine aliases the typeglob to the value returned by the subroutine. If that's a string, it's useful; otherwise it probably isn't:

```
*hello = subroutine_that_returns_name_to_alias_to(@args);
```

Examining the Symbol Table Directly

Interestingly, the symbol table itself can be accessed in Perl by referring to the name of the package with a trailing ::. Since symbol tables are hashes, and the hashes are stored in a typeglob with the same name, the hash that defines the main symbol table can be accessed with %{*main::}, or simply %{*::}, as this short script demonstrates:

```
#!/usr/bin/perl
# dumpmain.pl
use warnings;
use strict;
```

```perl
foreach my $name (sort keys %{*::}) {
    next if $name eq 'main';
    print "Symbol '$name' => \n";

    # extract the glob reference
    my $globref = ${*::} {$name};

    # define local package variables through alias
    local *entry = *{$globref};
    # make sure we can access them in 'strict' mode
    our ($entry, @entry, %entry);

    # extract scalar, array, and hash via alias
    print "\tScalar: $entry \n" if defined $entry;
    print "\tArray : [@entry] \n" if @entry;
    print "\tHash  : {", join(" ", {%entry}), "} \n" if %entry;

    # check for subroutine and handle via glob
    print "\tSub '$name' defined \n" if *entry{CODE};
    print "\tHandle '$name' (", fileno(*entry), ") defined \n"
    if *entry{IO};
}
```

The Dumpvalue module provides a more convenient interface to the symbol table and forms a core part of the Perl debugger. It does essentially the same thing as the preceding example, but more thoroughly and with a more elegant output. The following script builds a hierarchy of symbol tables and variables and then uses the Dumpvalue module to print them out:

```perl
#!/usr/bin/perl
# dumpval.pl
use warnings;
use strict;

use Dumpvalue;

# first define some variables
{
    # no warnings to suppress 'usage' messages
    no warnings;

    package World::Climate;
    our $weather = "Variable";

    package World::Country::Climate;
    our %weather = (
        England => 'Cloudy'
    );

    package World::Country::Currency;
    our %currency = (
        England => 'Sterling',
        France => 'Franc',
        Germany => 'Mark',
        USA => 'US Dollar',
    );
```

```perl
    package World::Country::City;
    our @cities = ('London', 'Paris', 'Bremen', 'Phoenix');

    package World::Country::City::Climate;
    our %cities = (
        London => 'Foggy and Cold',
        Paris => 'Warm and Breezy',
        Bremen => 'Intermittent Showers',
        Phoenix => 'Horrifyingly Sunny',
    );

    package World::Country::City::Sights;
    our %sights = (
        London => ('Tower of London','British Museum'),
        Paris => ('Eiffel Tower','The Louvre'),
        Bremen => ('Town Hall','Becks Brewery'),
        Phoenix => ('Arcosanti'),
    );
}

my $dumper = new Dumpvalue (globPrint => 1);
$dumper->dumpValue(\*World::);
```

While Dumpvalue can be pressed into service this way, it is worth considering the Symbol::Table module, available from CPAN, which provides a more focused interface.

Summary

Scope and visibility are important concepts in any programming language. Perl has two distinct kinds of scope, package scope and lexical scope, each of which has its own rules and reasons for being. A discussion of scope therefore becomes a discussion of package variables, and declarations, versus lexical variables.

We began with a discussion of package variables and their scoping rules, including defining them under strict, the distinction between package and global variables, declaring package variables lexically with our, overriding them temporarily with local, and why we probably meant to use my instead. We then talked about lexical variables, declaring them with my, and how they differ from package variables and variables declared with our.

We finished off with a look at the symbol table, which is the underlying structure in which not just package variables but subroutine declarations and file handles live. As it turns out, the symbol table is really just a big nested collection of typeglobs, so we also saw how to create new entries in the symbol table, how to create aliases for existing package variables and subroutines, and finally how to walk through the symbol table and examine its contents programmatically.

## CHAPTER 9

Using Modules

Modules are the basic unit of reusable code in Perl, the equivalent of libraries in other languages. Perl's standard library is almost entirely made up of modules. When we talk about Perl libraries, we usually mean modules that are included as part of the standard Perl library—the collection of Perl code that comes with the standard Perl distribution. Although the words "module" and "library" are frequently used interchangeably, they are actually not quite equivalent because not all libraries are implemented as modules. Modules are closely related to packages, which we have already been exposed to in previous chapters. In many cases a module is the physical container of a package— the file in which the package is defined. As a result, they are often named for the package they implement: the CGI.pm module implements the CGI package, for instance.

A library is simply a file supplied by either the standard Perl library or another package that contains routines that we can use in our own programs. Older Perl libraries were simple collections of routines collected together into a file, generally with a .pl extension. The do and require functions can be used to load this kind of library into our own programs, making the routines and variables they define available in our own code.

Modern Perl libraries are defined as modules and included into programs with the use directive, which requires that the module name ends in .pm. The use keyword provides additional complexity over do and require, the most notable difference being that the inclusion happens at compile time rather than run time.

Modules come in two distinct flavors, *functional* and *pragmatic*. Functional modules are generally just called modules or library modules. They provide functionality in the form of routines and variables that can be used from within our own code. They are what we usually think of as libraries. Conversely, pragmatic modules implement pragmas that modify the behavior of Perl at compile time, adding to or constraining Perl's syntax to permit additional constructs or limit existing ones. They can easily be told apart because pragmatic modules are always in lowercase and rarely more than one word long. Functional libraries use uppercase letters and often have more than one word in their name, separated by double semicolons. Since they are modules, they are also loaded using the use directive. The strict, vars, and warnings modules are all examples of pragmatic modules that we frequently use in Perl scripts. Some pragmatic modules also provide routines and variables that can be used at run time, but most do not.

In this chapter, we will examine the different ways of using modules in our scripts. In the next chapter, we will look inside modules, that is, examine them from the perspective of how they work as opposed to how to use them.

Loading Code Using do, require, and use

Perl provides three mechanisms for incorporating code (including modules) found in other files into our own programs. These are the do, require, and use statements, in increasing order of complexity and usefulness. Any code that is loaded by these statements is recorded in the special hash %INC (more about this later).

The simplest is do, which executes the contents of an external file by reading it and then evaling the contents. If that file happens to contain subroutine declarations, then those declarations are evaluated and become part of our program:

```
do '/home/perl/loadme.pl';
```

A more sophisticated version of do is the require statement. If the filename is defined within quotes, it is looked for as-is; otherwise it appends a .pm extension and translates any instance of :: into a directory separator:

```
# include the old-style (and obsolete) getopts library
require 'getopts.pl';
```

```
# include the newer Getopt::Std library
# (i.e. PATH/Getopt/Std.pm)
require Getopt::Std;
```

The first time require is asked to load a file, it checks that the file has not already been loaded by looking in the %INC hash. If it has not been loaded yet, it searches for the file in the paths contained in the special array @INC.

More sophisticated still is the use statement. This does exactly the same as require, but it evaluates the included file at compile time, rather than at run time as require does. This allows modules to perform any necessary initializations and to modify the symbol table with subroutine declarations before the main body of the code is compiled. This in turn allows syntax checks to recognize valid symbols defined by the module and flag errors on nonexistent ones. For example, this is how we include the Getopt::Std module at compile time:

```
# include Getopt::Std at compile time
use Getopt::Std;
```

Like require, use takes a bare unquoted module name as a parameter, appending a .pm to it and translating instances of :: or the archaic ` into directory separators. Unlike require, use does not permit any filename to be specified with quotes and will flag a syntax error if we attempt to do so. Only true library modules may be included via use.

The traditional way to cause code to be executed at compile time is with a BEGIN block, so this is (almost) equivalent to

```
BEGIN {
    require Getopt::Std;
}
```

However, use also attempts to call the import method (an object-oriented subroutine) in the module being included, if present. This provides the module with the opportunity to define symbols in our namespace, making it simpler to access its features without prefixing them with the module's package name. use Module is therefore actually equivalent to

```
BEGIN {
    require Module;
    Module->import;    # or 'import Module'
}
```

This one simple additional step is the foundation of Perl's entire import mechanism. There is no more additional complexity or built-in support for handling modules or importing variables and subroutine names. It is all based around a simple function call that happens at compile time. The curious thing about this is that there is no requirement to actually export anything from an import subroutine. Object-oriented modules rarely export symbols and so often commandeer the import mechanism to configure the class data of the module instead. A statement like use strict vars is a trivial but common example of this alternative use in action.

As the preceding expansion of use illustrates, the automatic calling of import presumes that the module actually creates a package of the same name. The import method is searched for in the package with the name of the module, irrespective of what loading the module actually causes to be defined.

Import Lists

As we just discussed, the major advantage that use has over require is the concept of importing. While it is true that we can import directly by simply calling import ourselves, it is simpler and more convenient with use.

If we execute a use statement with only a module name as an argument, we cause the import subroutine within the module to be called with no argument. This produces a default response from the module. This may be to do nothing at all, or it may cause the module to import a default set of symbols (subroutines, definitions, and variables) for our use. Object-oriented modules tend not to import anything, since they expect us to use them by calling methods. If a module does not provide an import method, nothing happens of course.

Function-oriented modules often import symbols by default and optionally may import further symbols if we request them in an import list. An import list is a list of items specified after the module name. It can be specified as a comma-separated list within parentheses or as a space-separated list within a qw operator. If we only need to supply one item, we can also supply it directly as a string. However, whatever the syntax, it is just a regular Perl list:

```
# importing a list of symbols with a comma-separated list:
use Module ('sub1', 'sub2', '$scalar', '@list', ':tagname');

# it is more legible to use 'qw':
use Module qw(sub1 sub2 $scalar @list :tagname);

# a single symbol can be specified as a simple string:
use Module 'sub1';

# if strict references are not enabled, a bareword can be used:
use strict refs;
```

The items in the list are interpreted entirely at the discretion of the module. For functional modules, however, they are usually symbols to be exported from the module into our own namespace. Being selective about what we import allows us to constrain imports to only those that we actually need. Symbols can either be subroutine names, variables, or sometimes tags, prefixed by a :, if the module in question supports them. These are a feature of the Exporter module, which is the source of many modules' import mechanisms. We discuss it from the module developer's point of view in Chapter 10.

We cannot import any symbol or tag into our code—the module must define it to be able to export it. A few modules like the CGI module have generic importing functions that handle anything we pass to them. However, most do not, and we will generate a syntax error if we attempt to export symbols from the module that it does not supply.

Suppressing Default Imports

Sometimes we want to be able to use a module without importing anything from it, even by default. To do that, we can specify an empty import list, which is subtly different from supplying no import list at all:

```
use Module;    # import default symbols
use Module();  # suppress all imports
```

When used in this second way, the import step is skipped entirely, which can be handy if we wish to make use of a module but not import anything from it, even by default (recall that we can always refer to a package's variables and subroutines by their fully qualified names). The second use statement is exactly equivalent to a require, except that it takes place at compilation time, that is

```
BEGIN { require Module; }
```

Note that we cannot suppress the default import list and then import a specific symbol—any import will trigger the default (unless of course the module in question has an import method that will allow this). Remember that the entire import mechanism revolves around a subroutine method called import in the module being loaded.

Disabling Features with no

no, which is the opposite of the use directive, attempts to unimport features imported by use. This concept is entirely module dependent. In reality, it is simply a call to the module's unimport subroutine. Different modules support this in different ways, including not supporting it at all. For modules that do support no, we can unimport a list of symbols with

```
no Module qw(symbol1 symbol2 :tagname);
```

This is equivalent to

```
BEGIN {
    require Module;
    unimport('symbol1', 'symbol2', ':tagname');
}
```

Unlike use, a no statement absolutely needs the subroutine unimport to exist—there would be no point without it. A fatal error is generated if this is not present.

Whether or not no actually removes the relevant symbols from our namespace or undoes whatever initialization was performed by use depends entirely on the module. It also depends on what its unimport subroutine actually does. Note that even though it supposedly turns off features, no still requires the module if it has not yet been loaded. In general, no happens after a module has been used, so the require has no effect as the module will already be present in %INC.

The if Pragma

An interesting variation on use is use if, which allows us to conditionally load a module based on arbitrary criteria. Since use happens at compile time, we must make sure to use constructs that are already defined at that time, such as special variables or environment variables. For example:

```
use if $ENV{WARNINGS_ON},"warnings";
```

This will enable warnings in our code if the environment variable WARNINGS_ON is defined. Functional modules can also be loaded the same way:

```
use if $ENV{USE_XML_PARSER},"XML::Parser";
use if !$ENV{USE_XML_PARSER},"XML::SAX";
```

The if pragma is, of course, implemented by the if.pm module and is a perfectly ordinary piece of Perl code. To do its magic, it defines an import that loads the specified module with require if the condition is met. From this we can deduce that it works with use, but not require, since that does not automatically invoke import.

If we need to specify an import list, we can just tack it on to the end of the statement as usual. The following statement loads and imports a debug subroutine from My::Module::Debug if the program name (stored in $0) has the word debug in its name. If not, an empty debug subroutine is defined, which Perl will then optimize out of the code wherever it is used.

```
use if $0=~/debug/ My::Module::Debug => qw(debug);
*debug = sub { } unless *debug{CODE};
```

An unimport method is also defined so we can also say no if:

```
use strict;
no if $ENV{NO_STRICT_REFS} => strict => 'refs';
```

This switches on all strict modes, but then it switches off strict references (both at compile time) if the environment variable NO_STRICT_REFS has a true value.

Testing for Module Versions and the Version of Perl

Quite separately from their usual usage, both the require and use directives support an alternative syntax, taking a numeric value as the first or only argument. When specified on its own, this value is compared to the version of Perl itself. It causes execution to halt if the comparison reveals that the version of Perl being used is less than that stated by the program. For instance, to require that only Perl version 5.6.0 or higher is used to run a script, we can write any of the following:

```
require 5.6.0;
use 5.6.0;
require v5.6.0;    # archaic as of Perl 5.8, see Chapter 3
```

Older versions of Perl used a version resembling a floating-point number. This format is also supported, for compatibility with older versions of Perl:

```
require 5.001;     # require Perl 5.001 or higher
require 5.005_03;  # require Perl 5.005 patch level 3 or higher
```

Note that for patch levels (the final part of the version number), the leading zero is important. The underscore is just a way of separating the main version from the patch number and is a standard way to write numbers in Perl, not a special syntax. 5.005_03 is the same as 5.00503, but more legible.

A version number may also be specified after a module name (and before the import list, if any is present), in which case it is compared to the version defined for the module. For example, to require CGI.pm version 2.36 or higher, we can write

```
use CGI 2.36 qw(:standard);
```

If the version of CGI.pm is less than 2.36, this will cause a compile-time error and abort the program. Note that there is no comma between the module name, the version, or the import list. As of Perl 5.8, a module that does not define a version at all will fail if a version number is requested. Prior to this, such modules would always load successfully.

It probably comes as no surprise that, like the import mechanism, this is not built-in functionality. Requesting a version simply calls a subroutine called VERSION() to extract a numeric value for comparison. Unless we override it with a local definition, this subroutine is supplied by the UNIVERSAL module, from which all packages inherit. In turn, UNIVERSAL::VERSION() returns the value of the variable $PackageName::VERSION. This is how most modules define their version number.

Pragmatic Modules

Pragmatic modules implement pragmas that alter the behavior of the Perl compiler to expand or constrict the syntax of the Perl language itself. One such pragma that should be familiar to us by now is the strict pragma. Others are vars, overload, attributes, and in fact any module with an all-lowercase name: it is conventional for pragmatic modules to be defined using all lowercase letters. Unlike functional modules, their effect tends to be felt at compile time, rather than run time. A few pragmatic modules also define functions that we can call later, but not very many.

It sometimes comes as a surprise to programmers new to Perl that all pragmas are defined in terms of ordinary modules, all of which can be found as files in the standard Perl library. The strict pragma is implemented by strict.pm, for example. Although it is not necessary to understand exactly how this comes about, a short diversion into the workings of pragmatic modules can be educational.

How Pragmatic Modules Work

Many of these modules work their magic by working closely with special variables such as $^H, which provides a bitmask of compiler "hints" to the Perl compiler, or $^W, which controls warnings. A quick examination of the strict module (the documentation for which is much longer than the actual code) illustrates how three different flags within $^H are tied to the use strict pragma:

```
package strict;
$strict::VERSION = "1.01";

my %bitmask = (
      refs => 0x00000002,
      subs => 0x00000200,
      vars => 0x00000400
);
sub bits {
    my $bits = 0;
    foreach my $s (@_){ $bits |= $bitmask{$s} || 0; };
    $bits;
}

sub import {
    shift;
    $^H |= bits(@_ ? @_ : qw(refs subs vars));
}

sub unimport {
    shift;
    $^H &=~ bits(@_ ? @_ : qw(refs subs vars));
}
1;
```

From this, we can see that all the strict module really does is toggle the value of three different bits in the $^H special variable. The use keyword sets them, and the no keyword clears them. The %bitmask hash variable provides the mapping from the names we are familiar with to the numeric bit values they control.

The strict module is particularly simple, which is why we have used it here. The entirety of the code in strict.pm is shown earlier. Chapter 10 delves into the details of import and unimport methods and should make all of the preceding code clear.

Scope of Pragmatic Modules

Most pragmatic modules have lexical scope, since they control the manner in which Perl compiles code—by nature a lexical process. For example, this short program illustrates how strict references can be disabled within a subroutine to allow symbolic references:

```
#!/usr/bin/perl
# pragmascope.pl
use warnings;
use strict;
```

```
# a subroutine to be called by name
sub my_sub {
    print @_;
}

# a subroutine to call other subroutines by name
sub call_a_sub {
    # allow symbolic references inside this subroutine only
    no strict 'refs';

    my $sub = shift;
    # call subroutine by name - a symbolic reference
    &$sub(@_);
}

# all strict rules in effect here
call_a_sub('my_sub', "Hello pragmatic world \n");
```

Running this program produces the following output:

> **perl pragmascope.pl**

```
Hello pragmatic world
```

The exceptions are those pragmas that predeclare symbols, variables, and subroutines in preparation for the run-time phase, or modify the values of special variables, which generally have a file-wide scope.

The Special Hash %INC

As mentioned earlier, any file or module that the do, require, and use statements load is recorded in the special hash %INC, which we can then examine to see what is loaded in memory. The keys of %INC are the names of the modules requested, converted to a pathname so that :: becomes something like / or \ instead. The values are the names of the actual files that were loaded as a result, including the path where they were found. Loading a new module updates the contents of this hash as shown in the following example:

```
#!/usr/bin/perl
# INC.pl
use strict;

print "\%INC contains: \n";
    foreach (keys %INC) {
    print "  $INC{$_}\n";
}

require File::Copy;
do '/home/perl/include.pl';

print "\n\%INC now contains: \n";
    foreach (keys %INC) {
    print "  $INC{$_}\n";
}
```

The program execution command and corresponding output follows:

```
> perl INC.pl
```

```
%INC contains:
 /usr/lib/perl5/5.8.5/strict.pm

%INC now contains:
 /usr/lib/perl5/5.8.5/strict.pm
 /usr/lib/perl5/5.8.5/vars.pm
 /usr/lib/perl5/5.8.5/File/Copy.pm
 /usr/lib/perl5/5.8.5/File/Spec/Unix.pm
 /usr/lib/perl5/5.8.5/warnings/register.pm
 /usr/lib/perl5/5.8.5/i586-linux-thread-multi/Config.pm
 /usr/lib/perl5/5.8.5/Exporter.pm
 /usr/lib/perl5/5.8.5/warnings.pm
 /usr/lib/perl5/5.8.5/File/Spec.pm
 /usr/lib/perl5/5.8.5/Carp.pm
```

Note that %INC contains Exporter.pm and Carp.pm, although we have not loaded them *explicitly* in our example. The reason for this is that the former is required and the latter is used by Copy.pm, also required in the example. For instance, the IO module is a convenience module that loads all the members of the IO:: family. Each of these loads further modules. The result is that no less than 29 modules loaded as a consequence of issuing the simple directive use IO.

It should also be noted that we did not specify in our example the full path to the modules. use and require, as well as modules like ExtUtils::Installed (more on this later in the chapter), look for their modules in the paths specified by the special array @INC.

The Special Array @INC

This built-in array is calculated when Perl is built and is provided automatically to all programs. To find the contents of @INC, we can run a one-line Perl script like the following for a Linux terminal:

```
> perl -e 'foreach (@INC) { print "$_\n"; }'
```

On a Linux Perl 5.6 installation, we get the following listing of the pathnames that are tried by default for locating modules:

```
/usr/local/lib/perl5/5.6.0/i686-linux-thread
/usr/local/lib/perl5/5.6.0
/usr/local/lib/perl5/site_perl/5.6.0/i686-linux-thread
/usr/local/lib/perl5/site_perl/5.6.0
/usr/local/lib/perl5/site_perl
```

Equivalently for Windows, the Perl script is

```
> perl -e "foreach (@INC) { print \"$_\n\";}"
```

```
C:/perl/ActivePerl/lib
C:/perl/ActivePerl/site/lib
.
```

When we issue a `require` or `use` to load a module, Perl searches this list of directories for a file with the corresponding name, translating any instances of `::` (or the archaic `` ` ``) into directory separators. The first file that matches is loaded, so the order of the directories in @INC is significant.

It is not uncommon to want to change the contents of @INC, to include additional directories into the search path or (less commonly) to remove existing directories. We have two basic approaches to doing this—we can either modify the value of @INC from outside the application or modify @INC (directly or with the `use lib` pragma) from within it.

Modifying @INC Externally

We can augment the default value of @INC with three external mechanisms: the `-I` command-line option and the `PERL5OPT` and `PERL5LIB` environment variables.

The `-I` option takes one or more comma-separated directories as an argument and adds them to the start of @INC:

```
> perl -I/home/httpd/perl/lib,/usr/local/extra/lib/modules perl -e 'print join
"\n",@INC'
```

```
/home/httpd/perl/lib
/usr/local/extra/lib/modules
/usr/local/lib/perl5/5.8.5/i686-linux-thread
/usr/local/lib/perl5/5.8.5
/usr/local/lib/perl5/site_perl/5.8.5/i686-linux-thread
/usr/local/lib/perl5/site_perl/5.8.5
/usr/local/lib/perl5/site_perl
```

We can define the same option to equivalent effect within `PERL5OPT`, along with any other options we want to pass:

```
> PERL5OPT="I/home/httpd/perl/lib,/usr/local/p5lib" perl -e 'print join "\n",@INC'
```

Note we do not include the leading minus in the environment variable; otherwise it is the same as specifying the option on the command line. However, if all we want to do is provide additional search locations, or we want to separate library paths from other options, we should use `PERL5LIB` instead. This takes a colon-separated list of paths in the same style as the `PATH` environment variable in Unix shells:

```
> PERL5LIB="/home/httpd/perl/lib:/usr/local/p5lib" perl -e 'print join "\n",@INC'
```

Modifying @INC Internally

Since @INC is an array, all of the standard array manipulation functions will work on it:

```
# add directory to end of @INC
push @INC, "/home/httpd/perl/lib";

# add current directory to start of @INC using the 'getcwd'
# function of the 'Cwd' module
use Cwd;
unshift @INC, getcwd();
```

However, since the `use` directive causes modules to be loaded at compile time rather than run time, modifying @INC this way will not work for used modules, only required ones. To modify @INC so that it takes effect at compile time, we must enclose it in a `BEGIN` block:

```
# add directory to start of @INC at compile-time
BEGIN {
    unshift @INC, '/home/httpd/perl/lib';
}

use MyModule;    # a module in 'home/httpd/perl/lib'...
...
```

The use lib Pragma

Since BEGIN blocks are a little clunky, we can instead use the lib pragma to add entries to @INC in a friendlier manner. As well as managing the contents of @INC more intelligently, this module provides both a more legible syntax and a degree of error checking over what we try to add. The use lib pragma takes one or more library paths and integrates them into @INC. This is how we could add the directory /home/httpd/perl/lib using the lib pragma:

```
use lib '/home/httpd/perl/lib';
```

This is almost but not quite the same as using an unshift statement inside a BEGIN block, as in the previous example. The difference is that if an architecture-dependent directory exists under the named path and it contains an auto directory, then this directory is assumed to contain architecture-specific modules and is also added, ahead of the path named in the pragma. In the case of the Linux system used as an example earlier, this would attempt to add the directories

```
/home/httpd/perl/lib/i386-linux/auto
/home/httpd/perl/lib
```

Note that the first directory is only added if it exists, but the actual path passed to lib is added regardless of whether it exists or not. If it does exist, however, it must be a directory; attempting to add a file to @INC will produce an error from the lib pragma.

We can also remove paths from @INC with the no directive:

```
no lib 'home/httpd/perl/lib';
```

This removes the named library path or paths, and it also removes any corresponding auto directories, if any exist.

The lib pragma has two other useful properties that make it a superior solution to a BEGIN block. First, if we attempt to add the same path twice, the second instance is removed. Since paths are added to the front of @INC, this effectively allows us to bump a path to the front:

```
# search for modules in site_perl directory first
use lib '/usr/lib/perl5/site_perl';
```

Second, we can restore the original value of @INC as built-in to Perl with the statement

```
@INC = @lib::ORIG_INC;
```

Note that the lib pragma only accepts Unix-style paths, irrespective of the platform—this affects Windows in particular.

Locating Libraries Relative to the Script

A common application of adding a library to @INC is to add a directory whose path is related to that of the script being run. For instance, the script might be in /home/httpd/perl/bin/myscript and the library modules that support it in /home/httpd/perl/lib. It is undesirable to have to hard-code this information into the script, however, since then we cannot relocate or install it in a different directory.

One way to solve this problem is to use the getcwd function from Cwd.pm to determine the current directory and calculate the location of the library directory from it. However, we do not need to, because Perl provides the FindBin module for exactly this purpose.

FindBin calculates paths based on the current working directory and generates six variables containing path information, any of which we can either import into our own code or access directly from the module. These variables are listed in Table 9-1.

Table 9-1. *FindBin Variables*

Variable	Path Information
$Bin	The path to the directory from which the script was run
$Dir	An alias for $Bin
$Script	The name of the script
$RealBin	The real path to the directory from which the script was run, with all symbolic links resolved
$RealDir	An alias for $RealBin
$RealScript	The real name of the script, with all symbolic links resolved

Using FindBin we can add a relative library directory by retrieving the $Bin/$Dir or $RealBin/$RealDir variables and feeding them, suitably modified, to a use lib pragma:

```
use FindBin qw($RealDir);   # or $Bin, $Dir, or $RealBin ...
use lib "$RealDir/../lib";
```

Using the FindBin module has significant advantages over trying to do the same thing ourselves with getcwd and its relatives. It handles various special cases for Windows and VMS systems, and it deals with the possibility that the script name was passed to Perl on the command line rather than triggering Perl via a #! header (and of course it's shorter too).

Variations on FindBin are available from CPAN. Two worth mentioning are FindBin::Real and FindBin::libs. FindBin::Real is a functional module with the same features as FindBin but with the variables replaced with subroutines. It handles cases where modules in different directories both attempt to determine the script path, and so is preferred for use in modules. (In typical use, only the script itself needs to find out where it came from.) FindBin::libs takes note of the fact that FindBin is mostly used to locate library directories and combines the two into a single module that first locates library directories relative to the script and then adds them to @INC.

Checking for the Availability of a Module

One way to check if a given module is available is to look in the %INC hash to see if the module is present. We can avoid fatal errors by checking for each module and using it only if already loaded. In the following example, if Module1 is loaded, then we use it, otherwise we look to see if Module2 is loaded:

```
if ($INC{'Module1'}) {
    # use some functions from Module1
} elsif ($INC{'Module2'}) {
    # use some functions from Module2
}
```

However, the simplest way would be to try to load it using require. Since this ordinarily produces a fatal error, we use an eval to protect the program from errors:

```
warn "GD module not available" unless eval {require GD; 1};
```

In the event that the GD module, which is a Perl interface to the libgd graphics library, is not available, eval returns undef, and the warning is emitted. If it does exist, the 1 at the end of the eval is returned, suppressing the warning. This gives us a way of optionally loading modules if they are present but continuing without them otherwise, so we can enable optional functionality if they are present. In this case, we can generate graphical output if GD is present or resort to text otherwise. The special variable $@ holds the syntax error message that is generated by the last eval function.

Note that a serious problem arises with the preceding approach if require is replaced with use. The reason is that eval is a run-time function, whereas use is executed at compile time. So, use GD would be executed before anything else, generating a fatal error if the GD module was not available. To solve this problem, simply enclose the whole thing in a BEGIN block, making sure that the whole block is executed at compile time:

```
BEGIN {
    foreach ('GD', 'CGI', 'Apache::Session') {
        warn "$_ not available" unless eval "use $_; 1";
    }
}
```

Finding Out What Modules Are Installed

We can find out which library module packages are installed and available for use with the ExtUtils::Installed module. This works not by scanning @INC for files ending in .pm, but by analyzing the .packlist files left by module distributions during the installation process. Not unsurprisingly, this may take the module a few moments to complete, especially on a large and heavily extended system, but it is a lot faster than searching the file system. Only additional modules are entered here, however—modules supplied as standard with Perl are not included.

Scanning .packlist files allows the ExtUtils::Installed module to produce more detailed information, for example, the list of files that should be present for a given module package. Conversely, this means that it does not deal with modules that are not installed but are simply pointed to by a modified @INC array. This is one good reason to create properly installable modules, which we discuss later in the chapter. The resulting list is of installed module packages, not modules, and the standard Perl library is collected under the name Perl, so on a standard Perl installation we may expect to see only Perl returned from this module.

To use the module, we first create an ExtUtils::Installed object with the new method:

```
use ExtUtils::Installed;
$inst = ExtUtils::Installed->new();
```

On a Unix-based system, this creates an installation object that contains the details of all the .packlist files on the system, as determined by the contents of @INC. If we have modules present in a directory outside the normal directories contained in @INC, then we can include the extra directory by modifying @INC before we create the installation object, as we saw at the start of the previous section.

Once the installation object is created, we can list all available modules in alphabetical order with the modules method. For example, this very short script simply lists all installed modules:

```
# list all installed modules;
print join "\n", $inst->modules();
```

On a standard Perl installation this will produce just the word "Perl", or possibly Perl plus one or two other modules in vendor-supplied installations, as standard library modules are not listed individually A more established Perl installation with additional packages installed might produce something like this:

```
Apache::DBI
Apache::Session
Archive::Tar
CGI
CPAN
CPAN::WAIT
Compress::Zlib
Curses
DBI::FAQ
Date::Manip
Devel::Leak
Devel::Symdump
Digest::MD5
...
```

The ExtUtils::Installed module does far more than simply list installed module packages, however. It provides the basics of library package management by providing us with the ability to list the files and directories that each module distribution created when it was installed, and to verify that list against what is currently present. In addition to new and modules we saw in action earlier, ExtUtils::Installed provides six other methods that are listed in Table 9-2.

Table 9-2. *ExtUtils::Installed Methods*

Method	Description

directories	Returns a list of installed directories for the module. For example:
	@dirs = $inst->directories($module);
	A second optional parameter of prog, doc, or all (the default) may be given to restrict the returned list to directories containing code, manual pages, or both:
	directories(module, 'prog'|'doc'|'all');
	Further parameters are taken to be a list of directories within which all returned directories must lie:
	directories(module, 'prog'|'doc'|'all', @dirs);
	For instance, this lists installed directories contained by @locations:
	@dirs = $inst->directories($module, 'prog', @locations);

directory_tree	Returns a list of installed directories for the module, in the same way as directories, but also including any intermediate directories between the actual installed directories and the directories given as the third and greater parameters: directory_tree(module, 'prog'|'doc'|'all', @dirs); For instance, the following example lists installed directories and parents under /usr: @dist = $inst->directories($module, 'all', '/usr');
files	Returns a list of installed files for the module, for example: @files = $inst->files($module); A second optional parameter of prog, doc, or all may be given to restrict the returned list to files containing code, documentation, or both: files (module, 'prog'|'doc'|'all') Further parameters are taken to be a list of directories within which all returned files must lie: files(module, 'prog'|'doc'|'all', @dirs) This is how we list the installed files contained by @dirs: @files = $inst->files($module, 'prog', @dirs);

Continued

Table 9-2. *Continued*

Method	Description
packlist	Returns an `ExtUtils::Packlist` object containing the raw details of the `.packlist` file for the given module: `packlist(module);` See the `ExtUtils::Packlist` documentation for more information.
validate	Checks the list of files and directories installed against those currently present, returning a list of all files and directories missing. If nothing is missing, an empty list is returned: `validate(module);` For instance: `$valid = $inst->validate($module)?0:1;`
version	Returns the version number of the module, or `undef` if the module does not supply one. The `CPAN` module uses this when the `r` command is used to determine which modules need updating, for example: `version(module);`

The ability to distinguish file types is a feature of the extended `.packlist` format in any recent version of Perl. Note that not every installed module yet provides a packing list that supplies this extra information, so many modules group all their installed files and directories under `prog` (the assumed default) and nothing under `doc`. To get a more accurate and reliable split between program and documentation files, we can use additional paths such as `/usr/lib/perl5/man` as the third and greater parameters.

As a more complete example of how we can use the features of `ExtUtils::Installed`, here is a short script to run on Unix that lists every installed module distribution, the files that it contains, and the version of the package, complete with a verification check:

```perl
#!/usr/bin/perl
# installedfiles.pl
use warnings;
use strict;

use ExtUtils::Installed;

my $inst = new ExtUtils::Installed;

foreach my $package ($inst->modules) {
    my $valid = $inst->validate($package)?"Failed":"OK";
    my $version = $inst->version($package);
    $version = 'UNDEFINED' unless defined $version;

    print "\n\n--- $package v$version [$valid] ---\n\n";
    if (my @source = $inst->files($package, 'prog')) {
        print "\t", join "\n\t", @source;
    }
    if (my @docs = $inst->files($package, 'doc')) {
        print "\n\n\t", join "\n\t", @docs;
    }
}
```

Postponing Module Loading Until Use with autouse

Modules can be very large, frequently because they themselves use other large modules. It can, therefore, be convenient to postpone loading them until they are actually needed. This allows a program to start faster, and it also allows us to avoid loading a module at all if none of its features are actually used.

We can achieve this objective with the autouse pragmatic module, which we can use in place of a conventional use statement to delay loading the module. To use it, we need to specify the name of the module, followed by a => (since that is more legible than a comma) and a list of functions:

```
use autouse 'Module' => qw(sub1 sub2 Module::sub3);
```

This will predeclare the named functions, in the current package if not qualified with a package name, and trigger the loading of the module when any of the named functions are called:

```
sub1("This causes the module to be loaded");
```

We can also supply a prototype for the subroutine declaration, as in

```
use autouse 'Module' => 'sub3($$@)';
```

However, there is no way for this prototype to be checked against the real subroutine since it has not been loaded, so if it is wrong we will not find out until we attempt to run the program.

There are two important caveats to bear in mind when using the autouse pragma. First, the module will only be loaded when one of the functions named on the autouse line is seen. Attempting to call another function in the module, even if it is explicitly called with a package name, will cause a run-time error unless the module has already been loaded. For instance, this does not delay loading the Getopt::Long module:

```
use autouse 'Getopt::Long';
# ERROR: ''Getopt::Long' is not loaded, so 'GetOptions' is unavailable
GetOptions(option =>\$verbose);
```

But this does:

```
use autouse 'Getopt::Long' => 'GetOptions';
# OK, 'GetOptions' triggers load of 'Getopt::Long'
GetOptions(option =>\$verbose);
```

Second, autouse only works for modules that use the default import method provided by the Exporter module (see Chapter 10). Modules that provide their own import method such as the CGI module cannot be used this way, unless they in turn inherit from Exporter. Any module that defines an export tag like :tagname falls into this category. Such modules frequently provide their own specialized loading techniques instead, CGI.pm being one good example.

A significant problem when using autouse is that initialization of modules that have been autoused does not occur until they are needed at run time. BEGIN blocks are not executed, nor are symbols imported. This can cause significant problems, as well as hiding syntax errors that would otherwise be found at compile time. For this reason, it is smart to include modules directly for development and testing purposes and to only use autouse in the production version (though we must still test that, we can at least eliminate autouse as a cause of problems in the debugging phase).

Alternatively, use a debug flag to switch between the two. Perl's -s option and the if pragma make a handy way to achieve this:

```
#!/usr/bin/perl -s -w
# debugorautouse.pl
use strict;
use vars '$debug';
```

```
use if  $debug,              'File::Basename' => 'basename';
use if !$debug, autouse => 'File::Basename' => 'basename';

print "Before: ",join(",",keys %INC),"\n";
my $prog=basename($0);
print "After : ",join(",",keys %INC),"\n";
```

If we execute this program with no arguments, we will see that File::Basename is not loaded before the call to basename but is loaded afterward. If on the other hand we run the program as

> **debugorautouse.pl -debug**

then the -s option that is specified on the first line causes the global variable $debug to be set. In turn this cases the module to be loaded immediately, so File::Basename appears in the list both before and after the call is made. If we want to actually process command-line arguments, the -s option is not so convenient, but we can as easily test for a suitable invented environment variable like $ENV{PLEASE_DEBUG_MY_PERL}.

If a module is already present when an autouse declaration is seen, it is translated directly into the equivalent use statement. For example:

```
use Module;
use autouse 'Module' => qw(sub1 sub2);
```

is the same as

```
use Module qw(sub1 sub2);
```

This means that it does no harm to attempt to autouse a module that is already loaded (something that might commonly happen inside a module, which has no idea what is already loaded), but conversely the autouse provides no benefit.

The autouse module is an attempt to provide load-on-demand based on the requirements of the user. The AUTOLOAD subroutine and the AutoLoader and Selfloader modules also provide us with the ability to load modules and parts of modules on demand, but as part of the module's design. See Chapter 10 for more details.

Summary

Over the course of this chapter, we examined what Perl modules are and how they related to files and packages. We started out with an examination of the do, require, and use statements and the differences between them. We then went on to look at the import mechanism provided by Perl and how it can be used to add definitions from modules that we use. We considered the difference between functional and pragmatic modules and found that pragmatic modules turn out to be very much like their functional brethren.

Perl searches for modules using the special array variable @INC and places the details of what was found where in the corresponding special hash variable %INC. We saw how to manipulate @INC in various ways, including directly, and the use lib pragma. We also found out how to ask Perl what modules have been added to the library that did not originally come with Perl.

Finally, we looked at delaying the loading of modules until they are needed with the autouse pragma. This has powerful possibilities for limiting the impact of a Perl application on memory, but not without drawbacks, notably that if a dependent module is not present we will not find out at compile time. Instead, we will only know the first time the application tries to use something from it, which could be a considerable time after it started.

CHAPTER 10

■■■

Inside Modules and Packages

We have already seen how modules work from the user's perspective through the do, require, and use statements. We have also seen the relationship between modules and packages. In this chapter, we examine the internals of implementing modules.

In order for modules to be easily reusable, they need to be well behaved. That means not defining variables and subroutines outside their own package unless explicitly asked to do so. It also means not allowing external definitions to be made unless the design of the module permits it. Exporting definitions from one package into another allows them to be used without prefixing the name of the original package, but it also runs the risk of a namespace collision, so both the module and the application need to be able to cooperate, to control what happens. They can do this through the import mechanism, which defines the interface between the module and the application that uses it.

At the application end, we specify our requirements with the use or require statements, with which we can pass a list of symbols (often, but not necessarily, subroutine names). Conversely, at the module end, we define an import subroutine to control how we respond to import (or, from our point of view, export) requests. The Exporter module provides one such import subroutine that handles most common cases for us. Either way, the interface defined through the import mechanism abstracts the actual module code, making it easier to reuse the module, and minimizing the chances of an application breaking if we made changes to the module.

Perl provides a number of special blocks that can be used in any Perl code but which are particularly useful for packages, and accordingly we spend some time discussing them in this chapter. The BEGIN, END, INIT, and CHECK blocks allow a module to define initialization and cleanup code to be automatically executed at key points during the lifetime of the module. The AUTOLOAD subroutine permits a package to react to unknown subroutine calls and stand in for them.

Modules and Packages

A package declaration is the naming of a new namespace in which further declarations of variables and subroutines are placed. A module is simply a library file that contains such a declaration and an associated collection of subroutines and variables. The link between package name and module file would therefore appear to be a strong one, but this is not necessarily true. As we saw in the last chapter, the module that is loaded corresponds to the named package, but this does not imply that the module actually defines anything in that package. As an example, many of Perl's pragmatic modules are purely concerned with compile-time semantics and do not contribute anything new to the symbol table.

In fact, a module doesn't have to include a package declaration at all. Any constructs it creates will simply be put into whatever package was in effect at the time it was loaded—main, if none has been declared yet. However, this is unusual. By including a package definition we are able to use many different modules without worrying about clashes between similarly named definitions. The notable exception are libraries that include several modules from one master module; the master defines the namespace and then loads all its children, none of which define a namespace and so place their definitions into the parent's namespace.

Similarly, the package declarations in a module don't have to correspond to the name of the module supplied to the use statement—they just usually do. In some cases, we might use a different package or define symbols in more than one package at the same time. Since a module file usually only contains declarations of subroutines and variables, rather than code that actually does something, executing it has no visible effect. However, subroutines and package variables are added to the symbol table, usually under the namespace defined by the package declaration.

Whatever else it does, in order for a module to be loaded successfully by either require or use, it must return a true value. Unless the module actually contains a return statement outside a subroutine definition, this must be the last statement in the file. Since a typical module contains mainly subroutine definitions (which don't return anything), we usually need to add an explicit return value to let Perl know that the module is happy. We can also add code for initialization that does do something actively and have that return a conditional value. This means we can, for example, programmatically have a module fail compilation if, say, an essential resource like a configuration file that it needs is missing.

Most modules do not have any initialization code to return a value, so in general we satisfy Perl by appending a 1—or in fact any true value—to the end of the module file. As the last statement in the file, this is returned to the use or require that triggered the loading of the module file, which tests the value for truth to determine whether or not the module loaded successfully. Taking all this together, the general form of a module file is simply

```
package My::Module;

... use other modules ...
... declare global variables ...
... define subroutines ...

1;
```

Note that here "global variables" can mean either lexically scoped file globals (which are global to the file but not accessible from outside it) or package variables that are in the namespace of the package but accessible from elsewhere by qualifying their name with a prefix of the package name.

Although Perl does not force the file name to follow the package name, this module would most likely be called Module.pm and placed in a directory called My, which in turn can be located anywhere that Perl is told to look for modules. This can be any of the paths in @INC, in our own personal location provided to Perl at run time through the use lib pragma, the -I option, or the PERL5LIB environment variable, or even added by other Perl modules.

Manipulating Packages

The package directive changes the default namespace for variables and subroutine declarations, but we are still free to define our own fully qualified definitions if we choose. For instance, rather than creating a module file containing

```
package My::Module;

sub mysub {
    return "Eep!\n";
}

1;
```

we could, with equal effect (but losing some maintainability), declare the subroutine to be in the package explicitly:

```
sub My::Module::mysub {
    return "Eep!\n";
}

1;
```

It isn't very likely that we would do this in reality—if the subroutine was copied to a different source file, it would need to be renamed. It has possibilities if we are generating subroutines on the fly, a subject we will cover in more detail when we discuss autoloading, but otherwise a package declaration is far more convenient. The same goes for our and use vars declarations, which are simply shorthand that use the package declaration to omit the full variable name.

Finding Package Names Programmatically

It can be occasionally useful for a subroutine to know the name of the package in which it is defined. Since this is a compile-time issue (package declarations are lexical, even though they affect run time scope), we could manually copy the package name from the top of the module or whichever internal package declaration the subroutine falls under.

However, this is prone to failure if the package name changes at any point. This is a more serious problem than it might at first appear because it will not necessarily lead to a syntax error.

To avoid this kind of problem, we should avoid ever naming the package explicitly except in the package declaration itself. Within the code, we can instead use the special bareword token __PACKAGE__ like so:

```
sub self_aware_sub {
    print "I am in the ",__PACKAGE__," package.\n";
}
```

As a more expressive but less functional example, the following series of package declarations shows how the value produced by __PACKAGE__ changes if more than one package is present in a given file:

```
package My::Module;
print __PACKAGE__,"\n";
package My::Module::Heavy;
print __PACKAGE__,"\n";
package My::Module::Light;
print __PACKAGE__,"\n";
package A::Completely::Different::Package;
print __PACKAGE__,"\n";
```

Each time the __PACKAGE__ token is printed out, Perl expands it into the current package name, producing My::Module, then My::Module::Heavy, and so on.

When Perl loads and compiles a file containing this token, the interpreter first scans and substitutes the real package name for any instances of __PACKAGE__ it finds before proceeding to the compilation stage. This avoids any potential breakages if the package name should change.

Manipulating Package Names Programmatically

The Symbol module provides subroutines for creating and manipulating variable names with respect to packages without dealing with the package name directly, notably the gensym and qualify subroutines.

The gensym subroutine generates and returns a reference to a fully anonymous typeglob—that is, a typeglob that does not have an entry anywhere in any symbol table. We can use the anonymous typeglob as we like, for example, as a filehandle (though IO::Handle does this better in these more enlightened days, and, as a point of fact, uses gensym underneath). It takes no arguments and just returns the reference:

```
use Symbol;

my $globref = gensym;
open ($globref, $filename);
...
```

More useful is the qualify subroutine, which provides a quick and convenient way to generate fully qualified names (and therefore symbolic references) for variables from unqualified ones. It operates on strings only, and with one argument it generates a name in the current package. For example:

```
#!/usr/bin/perl
# symbol1.pl
use warnings;

use Symbol;

my $fqname = qualify('scalar');
$$fqname = "Hello World\n";
print $scalar;   # produces 'Hello World'
```

Since this is a simple script without a package declaration, the variable created here is actually called $main::scalar. If we supply a package name as a second argument to qualify, it places the variable into that package instead.

```
#!/usr/bin/perl
# symbol2.pl
use warnings;

use Symbol;

my $fqname = qualify('scalar','My::Module');
$$fqname = "Hello World\n";
print $My::Module::scalar;
```

In both cases, qualify will only modify the name of the variable passed to it if it is not already qualified. It will correctly qualify special variables and the standard filehandles like STDIN into the main package, since these variables always exist in main, wherever they are used. This makes it a safer and simpler way than trying to make sure our symbolic references are correct and in order when we are assembling them from strings.

Unfortunately, qualify is not very useful if we have strict references enabled via use strict, since these are symbolic references. Instead, we can use qualify_to_ref, which takes a symbolic name and turns it into a reference for us, using the same rules as qualify to determine the package name:

```
#!/usr/bin/perl
# symbol3.pl
use warnings;
use strict;

use Symbol;

my $fqref = qualify_to_ref('scalar','My::Module');
$$fqref =\"Hello World\n";
print $My::Module::scalar;
```

All three of these examples work but produce a warning from Perl that the variable `main::scalar` (or `My::Module::scalar`) is only used once, which is true. Perl doesn't see that we defined the variable name through a reference, so it (correctly) points out that we appear to have used a variable we haven't defined. The correct thing to do would be to declare the variable so we can use it without complaint, as this modified example, complete with embedded package, illustrates:

```
#!/usr/bin/perl
# symbol4.pl
use warnings;
use strict;

use Symbol;

my $fqref = qualify_to_ref('scalar','My::Module');
$$fqref =\"Hello World\n";
print My::Module::get_scalar();

package My::Module;

our $scalar;    # provide access to scalar defined above

sub get_scalar {
    return $scalar;
}
```

Removing a Package

While it is rare that we would want to remove a package during the course of a program's execution, it can be done by removing all traces of the package's namespace from the symbol table hierarchy. One reason to do this might be to free up the memory used by the package variables and subroutines of a module no longer required by an application. For example, to delete the `My::Module` package, we could write

```
my $table = *{'My::Module::'}{'HASH'};
undef %$table;
my $parent = *{'My::'}{'HASH'};
my $success = delete $parent->{'Module::'};
```

This is more than a little hairy, but it basically boils down to deleting the entries of the symbol table for `My::Module` and removing the `Module` namespace entry from the `My` namespace. We delete the hash explicitly because we store the result of the `delete` in a variable, and thus the symbol table too. This is because Perl cannot reuse the memory allocated by it or the references contained in it, while something still holds a reference to it. Deleting the actual table means that `delete` returns an empty hash on success, which is still good for a Boolean test but avoids trailing a complete and unrecycled symbol table along with it.

Fortunately, the `Symbol` module provides a `delete_package` function that does much the same thing but hides the gory details. It also allows us more freedom as to how we specify the package name (we don't need the trailing semicolons, for instance, and it works on any package). To use it, we need to import it specifically, since it is not imported by default:

```
use Symbol qw(delete_package);

...

print "Deleted!\n" if delete_package('My::Module');
```

The return value from delete_package is undefined if the delete failed, or a reference is made to the (now empty) namespace.

If we wanted to create a package that we could remove programmatically, we could do so by combining delete_package with an unimport subroutine; see "Importing and Exporting" later in the chapter for an example.

BEGIN Blocks, END Blocks, and Other Animals

Perl defines four different kinds of special blocks that are executed at different points during the compile or run phases. The most useful of these is BEGIN, which allows us to compile and execute code placed in a file before the main compilation phase is entered. At the other end of the application's life, the END block is called just as the program exits. We can also define CHECK and INIT blocks, which are invoked at the end of the compilation phase and just prior to the execution phase respectively, though these are considerably rarer.

All four blocks look and behave like subroutines, only without the leading sub. Like signal handlers, they are never called directly by code but directly by the interpreter when it passes from one phase of existence to another. The distinction between the block types is simply that each is executed at a different phase transition. The precise order is

```
BEGIN
(compile phase)
CHECK
INIT
(run phase)
END
```

Before we examine each block type in more detail, here is a short program that demonstrates all four blocks in use and also shows how they relate to the main code and a __DIE__ signal handler:

```perl
#!/usr/bin/perl
# blocks.pl
use warnings;
use strict;

$SIG{__DIE__} = sub {
    print "Et tu Brute?\n";
};

print "It's alive!\n";
die "Sudden death!\n";

BEGIN {
    print "BEGIN\n";
}

END {
    print "END\n";
}

INIT {
    print "INIT\n"
}

CHECK {
    print "CHECK\n"
}
```

When run, this program prints out

```
BEGIN
CHECK
INIT
It's alive!
Et tu Brute?
Sudden death!
END
```

Note that in Perl versions before 5.6, CHECK blocks are ignored entirely, so we would not see the CHECK line. Apart from this, the program would run perfectly. Of course, if the CHECK block needs to perform vital functions, we may have a problem; therefore CHECK blocks are best used for checks that are better made after compilation but which can also be made, less efficiently perhaps, at run time too.

We can define multiple instances of each block; each one is executed in order, with BEGIN and INIT blocks executing in the order in which they are defined (top to bottom) and CHECK and END blocks executed in reverse order of definition (bottom to top). The logic for END and CHECK blocks executing in reverse is clearer once their purpose is understood. For example, BEGIN blocks allow modules to initialize themselves and may be potentially dependent upon the initialization of prior modules. Corresponding END blocks are executed in the reverse order to allow dependent modules to free their resources before earlier modules free the resources on which they rely—last in, first out.

As an example, consider a network connection to a remote application—we might open a connection in one BEGIN block and start a new session in another, possibly in a different module. When the application ends, we need to stop the session and then close the connection—the reverse order. The order in which the modules are loaded means the END blocks will execute in the correct order automatically. The new CHECK block has a similar symmetry with BEGIN, but around the compilation phase only, not the whole lifetime of the application. Likewise, INIT pairs with END across the run-time phase.

Additional blocks read in by do or require are simply added to the respective list at the time they are defined. Then, if we have a BEGIN and END block and we require a module that also has a BEGIN and END block, our BEGIN block is executed first, followed by the module's BEGIN block. At the end of the script, the module's END block is called first, then ours. However, if we include a module with use rather than require, the order of BEGIN blocks is determined by the order of the use relative to our BEGIN block and any other use statements. This is because use creates a BEGIN block of its own, as we have already seen.

Blocks nest too—a BEGIN inside a BEGIN will execute during the compilation phase of the outer block. A chain of use statements, one module including the next at compile time, does this implicitly, and similarly chains the END blocks (if any).

BEGIN Blocks

If we need to perform initialization within a module before it is used, we can place code inside the source file to perform whatever tasks we need to do, for example, loading a configuration file:

```
package My::Module;

return initialize();

sub initialize {
    ...
}

... other sub and var declarations ...
```

This module doesn't need a 1 at the end because its success or failure is returned explicitly. However, the initialization only takes place once the module starts to execute; we can't predefine anything before defining critical subroutines. A BEGIN block solves this problem. It forces execution of a module's initialization code before the rest of it compiles.

As an example, here is a module that computes a list of variables to export at compile time and exports them before the code that uses the module compiles. For simplicity, we have used a local hash to store the variable definitions and kept it to scalars, but it is easily extensible:

```
# My/SymbolExporter.pm

package My::SymbolExporter;

use strict;

BEGIN {
    use vars '@SYMBOLS';
    # temporary local configuration - we could read from a file too
    my %conf = (
        e => 'mc2',
        time => 'money',
        party => 'a good time',
    );

    sub initialize {
        no strict 'refs';
        foreach (keys %conf) {
            # define variable with typeglob
            *{__PACKAGE__.'::'.$_} = \$conf{$_};

            # add variable (with leading '$') to export list
            push @SYMBOLS, "\$$_";
        }
        return 1;
    }

    return undef unless initialize;
}

use Exporter;
our @ISA = qw(Exporter);
our @EXPORT = ('@SYMBOLS',@SYMBOLS);
```

Ordinarily, we'd use the Exporter module or an import method to deal with this sort of problem, but these are really just extensions to the basic BEGIN block. Just to prove it works, here is a script that uses this module and prints out the variables it defines:

```
#!/usr/bin/perl
# symbolexportertest.pl
use warnings;
use strict;

use My::SymbolExporter;

print "Defined: @SYMBOLS\n\n";

print "e = $e\n";
print "time = $time\n";
print "party = '$party'\n";
```

Another use of BEGIN blocks is to preconfigure a module before we use it. For example, the AnyDBM_File module allows us to reconfigure its @ISA array by writing something like the following:

```
BEGIN {
    @AnyDBM_File::ISA = qw(GDBM_File SDBM_File);
}

use AnyDBM_File;
```

Inside the module, the code simply checks to see if the variable is defined before supplying a default definition:

```
our @ISA = qw(NDBM_File DB_File GDBM_File SDBM_File ODBM_File) unless @ISA;
```

It is vital that we put our definition in a BEGIN block so that it is executed and takes effect before the use statement is processed. Without this, the implicit BEGIN block of the use statement would cause the module to be loaded before our definition is established despite the fact it appears first in the source.

END Blocks

The opposite of BEGIN blocks are END blocks. These are called just as Perl is about to exit (even after a __DIE__ handler) and allow a module to perform closing duties like cleaning up temporary files or shutting down network connections cleanly:

```
END {
    unlink $tempfile;
    shutdown $socket, 2;
}
```

The value that the program is going to exit with is already set in the special variable $? when the END blocks are processed, so we can modify $? to change it if we choose. However, END blocks are also not caught if we terminate on a signal and (obviously) not if we use exec to replace the application with a new one.

The CHECK and INIT Blocks

The CHECK and INIT blocks are considerably rarer than BEGIN and END, but they are still occasionally useful.

CHECK blocks execute in reverse order just after the compilation phase ends and correspond to the END blocks, which run at the end of the run phase. Their purpose is to perform any kind of checking that might be required of the compiled source before proceeding with the run phase. (However, they are not available in Perl prior to version 5.6.)

```
# Perl > = 5.6.0 for CHECK blocks
use 5.6.0;

# check that conditional compilation found at least one implementation
CHECK {
    die "No platform recognized" unless
    defined &Unixsub or
    defined &win32sub or
    defined &macsub or
    defined &os2sub;
}
```

This block will be called as soon as Perl has finished compiling all the main code (and after all BEGIN blocks have been executed), so it is the ideal point to check for the existence of required entities before progressing to the execution stage. By placing the code in a CHECK block rather than in the module's main source, we give it a chance to object before other modules—which may be used before it—get a chance to run.

The INIT blocks execute just before the run phase and just after the compile phase—CHECK blocks are also included if any are defined. They execute in order of definition and correspond to BEGIN blocks, which run just before the compile phase. Their purpose is to initialize variables and data structures before the main run phase starts:

```
# establish a package variable for all modules
INIT {
    $My::Module::start_time = time;
}
```

Both block types have little effect over simply placing code at the top of a file when only one of either type exists. However, if several modules define their own CHECK and INIT blocks, Perl will queue them up and run through them all before commencing execution of the main application code.

Autoloading

Normally when we try to call a nonexistent subroutine, Perl generates a syntax error, if possible at compile time. However, by defining a special subroutine called AUTOLOAD, we can intercept nonexistent calls and deal with them in our own way at run time.

Autoloading is a powerful aspect of Perl. When used wisely, it provides us with some very handy techniques, such as the ability to write one subroutine that handles many different cases and masquerade it as many subroutines each handling a single case. This is a great technique for allowing a module to be powerful and flexible without the expense of creating many possibly redundant routines with a corresponding cost in memory. We can also, with deft usage of the eval and sub keywords, generate new subroutines on demand.

The cost of autoloading is twofold, however: first, calling a subroutine not yet compiled will incur a speed penalty at that point, since Perl must call the AUTOLOAD subroutine to resolve the call. Second, it sidesteps the normal compile-time checks for subroutine existence, since there is no way for Perl to know if the subroutine name is valid or not until an attempt is made to call it during execution.

Several modules in the standard library take advantage of autoloading to delay the compilation of subroutines until the moment they are required. The autouse module introduced in the last chapter even provides a simple generic interface that delays loading an entire module until one of its subroutines is called. However, there is no granularity: when the module is loaded, it is all loaded at once. The AutoSplit and AutoLoader modules solve this problem. AutoSplit carves up a module file into separate subroutines, which the AutoLoader module can subsequently read and compile at the moment each routine is required. These modules are typically used during the distribution and installation of modules, since the extraction of subroutines from the original source by AutoSplit is a manual process. The SelfLoader module provides a simpler but easier solution. It allows us to store code as text inside the module file, compiling it at the time it is needed. While not as efficient as AutoLoader, which does not even load the subroutine code if it doesn't need it, it does not need any additional processing steps to work.

Autoloading Subroutines

Autoloading is automatically enabled in any package in which we define a subroutine called AUTOLOAD. This subroutine will automatically intercept all attempts to call nonexistent subroutines and will receive the arguments for each nonexistent subroutine. At the same time, the name of the missing subroutine is placed in the special package variable $AUTOLOAD. To illustrate, here is a short example that intercepts nonexistent subroutine calls and prints out the name and arguments passed:

```
#!/usr/bin/perl
# autoload.pl
use warnings;
use strict;

sub AUTOLOAD {
    our $AUTOLOAD;    # "use vars '$AUTOLOAD'" for Perl < 5.6
    $" = ',';
    print "You called '$AUTOLOAD(@_)'\n";
}

fee('fie','foe','fum');
testing(1,2,3);
```

When run, this script should produce

```
You called 'main::fee(fie,foe,fum)'
You called 'main::testing(1,2,3)'
```

We use our to declare interest in the package's $AUTOLOAD variable (Perl prior to version 5.6 needs to use use vars instead). Since only the AUTOLOAD subroutine needs to know the value of $AUTOLOAD, we place the our declaration inside the subroutine to define a temporary alias.

In general, creating an autoloader stymies compile-time checkers. But interestingly, defining a prototype for the autoloader is perfectly valid and can help eliminate subroutine calls that are simply a result of mistyping a call to a real subroutine. If all the subroutine calls we want to intercept have the same prototype, then calls whose parameters do not match the prototype will still fail at compile time, since Perl knows that the AUTOLOAD subroutine is not interested in handling them. In the preceding example, both example calls use three scalar arguments, so a prototype of ($$$) would be appropriate. Of course, a mistyped subroutine call can still match the prototype, so this does not completely save us from mistakes.

We can use AUTOLOAD subroutines in a variety of ways that break down into one of two general approaches: use the AUTOLOAD subroutine as a substitute for a collection of subroutines, or use the AUTOLOAD subroutine to define missing subroutines on the fly.

Using an AUTOLOAD Subroutine As a Substitute

The first and simplest use of the autoloader is simply to stand in for another subroutine or collection of similar subroutines. We can define the interface to a module in terms of these other calls but actually implement them in the AUTOLOAD subroutine. The disadvantage of this is that it takes Perl slightly longer to carry out the redirection to the autoloader subroutine (although conversely the compile time is faster). The advantage is that we can replace potentially hundreds of subroutine definitions with just one. This has benefits in maintainability as well as startup time.

Here is a simple example that illustrates the general technique with a few simple statistical calculations that sum, average, and find the biggest and smallest of a list of supplied numeric values:

```
#!/usr/bin/perl
# autostat.pl
use warnings;
use strict;

use Carp;

sub AUTOLOAD {
    our $AUTOLOAD;
```

```perl
    my $result;
    SWITCH: foreach ($AUTOLOAD) {
        /sum/ and do {
            $result = 0;
            map { $result+= $_ } @_;
            last;
        };
        /average/ and do {
            $result = 0;
            map { $result+= $_ } @_;
            $result/=scalar(@_);
            last;
        };
        /biggest/ and do {
            $result = shift;
            map { $result = ($_ > $result)?$_:$result } @_;
            last;
        };
        /smallest/ and do {
            $result = shift;
            map { $result = ($_ < $result)?$_:$result } @_;
            last;
        }
    }
    croak "Undefined subroutine $AUTOLOAD called" unless defined $result;
    return $result;
}

my @values = (1,4,9,16,25,36);

print "Sum: ",sum(@values),"\n";
print "Average: ",average(@values),"\n";
print "Biggest: ",biggest(@values),"\n";
print "Smallest: ",smallest(@values),"\n";
print "Oddest: ",oddest(@values),"\n";
```

This AUTOLOAD subroutine supports four different statistical operations and masquerades under four different names. If we call any of these names, then the autoloader performs the requested calculation and returns the result. If we call any other name, it croaks and exits. We use croak from the Carp module, because we want to return an error for the place from which the AUTOLOAD subroutine was called, as that is where the error really is.

This script also illustrates the problem with autoloading—errors in subroutine names are not caught until run time. With real subroutines, the call to oddest would be caught at compile time. With this script, it isn't caught until the autoloader is actually called and discovers that it isn't a name that it recognizes.

The preceding example demonstrates the general principle of substituting for a collection of other subroutines, but it doesn't really provide any benefit; it would be as easy to define the subroutines individually (or indeed just get them from List::Util, but that's beside the point), as the implementations are separate within the subroutine. However, we can be more creative with how we name subroutines. For example, we can use an autoloader to recognize and support the prefix print_ for each operation. Here is a modified version of the previous example that handles both the original four operations and four new variants that print out the result as well:

```perl
#!/usr/bin/perl
# printstat.pl
use warnings;
```

```perl
use strict;

use Carp;

sub AUTOLOAD {
    our $AUTOLOAD;

    my $subname; # get the subroutine name
    $AUTOLOAD =~/([^:]+)$/ and $subname = $1;

    my $print; # detect the 'print_' prefix
    $subname =~s/^print_// and $print = 1;

    my $result;
    SWITCH: foreach ($subname) {
        /^sum$/ and do {
            $result = 0;
            map { $result+= $_ } @_;
            last;
        };
        /^average$/ and do {
            $result = 0;
            map { $result+= $_ } @_;
            $result/= scalar(@_);
            last;
        };
        /^biggest$/ and do {
            $result = shift;
            map { $result = ($_>$result)?$_:$result } @_;
            last;
        };
        /^smallest$/ and do {
            $result = shift;
            map { $result = ($_<$result)?$_:$result } @_;
            last;
        };
    }
    croak "Undefined subroutine $subname called" unless defined $result;
    print ucfirst($subname),": $result\n" if $print;
    return $result;
}

my @values = (1,4,9,16,25,36);

print_sum(@values);
print_average(@values);
print_biggest(@values);
print_smallest(@values);
```

The subroutine name actually passed in the $AUTOLOAD variable contains the package prefix, main::, as well. In the previous example, we did not check from the start of the name, so this did not matter. Here we do care though, so we strip all possible package prefixes by extracting from the end of the name as much text as we can, not including a semicolon. This gives us the unqualified subroutine name.

Now we can detect and remove the print_ prefix. We take advantage of the fact that we are left with just the subroutine name to anchor the regular expressions at the start and end for a little extra efficiency—the first example worked only because we did not use anchors and none of our subroutine names contained another. If we wanted to be even more inventive, we could remove the trailing $ anchors and use a trailing suffix in the subroutine name to further adapt each function.

Defining Subroutines on the Fly

The run-time performance penalty of using the autoloader can be mitigated by having the autoloader define a new subroutine to perform the requested task, instead of handling the job itself. Any subsequent calls will now pass directly to the new subroutine and not the autoloader.

As an example, here is a simple autoloader that defines subroutines to return HTML syntax, much in the way that the CGI module can. It isn't nearly as feature-rich as that module, but it is a lot smaller too:

```perl
#!/usr/bin/perl
# autofly.pl
use warnings;
use strict;

sub AUTOLOAD {
    our $AUTOLOAD;

    my $tag;
    $AUTOLOAD =~ /([^:]+)$/ and $tag = $1;

    SWITCH: foreach ($tag) {
        /^start_(.*)/ and do {
            eval "sub $tag { return \"<$1>\@_\" }";
            last;
        };
        /^end_(.*)/ and do {
            eval "sub $tag { return \"</$1>\" }";
            last;
        };
        # note the escaping with \ of @_ below so it is not
        # expanded before the subroutine is defined
        eval "sub $tag { return \"<$tag>\@_</$tag>\" }";
    }
    no strict 'refs';
    &$tag; # pass @_ directly for efficiency
}

# generate a quick HTML document
print html(
    head(title('Autoloading Demo')),
    body(ul(
        start_li('First'),
        start_li('Second'),
        start_li('Third'),
    ))
);
```

This autoloader supports automatic tag completion, as well as generating the start and end of tags if start_ or end_ is prefixed to the subroutine name. It works by defining a subroutine to generate the new tag, then calling it. The first time start_li is called, the autoloader generates a new subroutine called start_li, then calls it. The second time start_li is called, the subroutine already exists, so Perl calls it directly, and the autoloader is not involved.

A little deftness with interpolation is required for the subroutines to be defined correctly. We want the tag name itself interpolated, both as the subroutine name and inside the returned string, but we want interpolation of the passed arguments delayed until the subroutine is actually called. To achieve that, we put double quotes around the returned string but escape both them and @_ so that they are not interpreted when the subroutine is defined—instead they only become active when it is actually called.

Self-Defining Instead of Autoloading Subroutines

A variation on the theme of delaying the definition of subroutines and methods when they are first called is to retrieve their definition from somewhere else and compile it when they are first called. For instance, we may have a large and complex module with many features, of which we may only actually use some. In order to avoid compiling all the subroutines redundantly, we can put aside compiling them until they are called. If they are never called, we need never define them.

The essence of this approach is to define a subroutine initially as a stub only, so that the subroutine is defined in the symbol table but does not as yet implement the feature it is intended to provide. The stub does not contain much code, so it is quick to compile and does not occupy much memory. When the stub is actually called, it compiles and replaces itself with the real subroutine. Here is a short program that shows one way to do this:

```perl
#!/usr/bin/perl
# autodefine.pl
use warnings;
use strict;

sub my_subroutine {
    print "Defining sub...\n";

    # uncomment next line and remove 'no warnings' for Perl < 5.6
    # local $^W = 0;
    eval 'no warnings; sub my_subroutine { print "Autodefined!\n"; }';

    &my_subroutine;
}

my_subroutine;  # calls autoloader
my_subroutine;  # calls defined subroutine
```

Running this program produces

```
Defining sub...
Autodefined!
Autodefined!
```

A variant of this approach would be to store all the subroutine definitions in a different file, or after a __DATA__ token, and read the subroutine code from there, which is the approach taken by SelfLoader. Alternatively, we can create a typeglob alias to an evaluated anonymous subroutine, with equal effect to the preceding example:

```perl
#!/usr/bin/perl
# globdefine.pl
use warnings;
use strict;
```

```
sub my_subroutine {
    print "Defining sub...\n";
    no warnings;
    # remove above and add the following for Perl < 5.6
    # local $^W = 0;

    *my_subroutine = eval {
        sub {
            print "Autodefined!\n";
        }
    };

    &my_subroutine;
}

my_subroutine;
my_subroutine;
```

In both cases we suppress the redefinition warning by switching off warnings locally with no warnings, or by locally clearing $^W. In this case, we know we want to redefine the subroutine, so we don't need Perl telling us about it.

The drawback of this approach compared to defining an AUTOLOAD subroutine is that we need to define a stub for each subroutine we want to delay compilation for. The advantage is that because a stub is present we don't lose the ability to syntax check subroutine names at compile time. This is particularly useful if we are also providing prototypes for our subroutines, since they clearly cannot be checked at compile time if they are only created at run time (unless they all have the same prototypes and we prototype the autoloader itself, as noted earlier). The contents of the subroutines are only checked at run time, however, an unavoidable compromise if we wish to avoid parsing them until they are used.

AutoLoader and SelfLoader

The Perl standard library provides three modules that implement the strategy of delayed loading of subroutines in two different ways. The autouse module we already looked at in the last chapter, as it is a mechanism for the calling rather than called module. Of the remaining two, the more complex is AutoLoader, which loads additional files containing subroutine definitions as required. For this to work, they must previously have been generated by the AutoSplit module using an AUTOLOAD subroutine. This implies that the module is split into separate pieces prior to being used, that is, an installation process is required.

The SelfLoader module operates along broadly similar lines, but it keeps all the subroutines to be loaded later inside the source file. The advantage is that we do not need to remember to use AutoSplit. Conversely, we must load all the source code into memory in an uncompiled form so that it can be compiled on demand.

Using the AutoLoader

In order to use the AutoLoader module, we need to adapt our modules to its requirements. The first and most important step is to place the subroutines we want to delay loading after an __END__ token. Anything before is compiled at compile time, anything after is compiled at run time on demand. This may require a little reorganization of the source, of course.

Once this is done, we add a use statement to include the AutoLoader module and import its AUTOLOAD subroutine, which does the work of retrieving the subroutines once they are split out. Note that importing the subroutine is important—the AutoLoader will not work without it:

```
use AutoLoader qw(AUTOLOAD);
```

(Why does AutoLoader not automatically export AUTOLOAD for us? Because we could implement our own AUTOLOAD routine to handle special cases and invoke AutoLoader's from it. This lets us control the autoloading process if we need to.)

The __END__ token causes the Perl interpreter to stop reading the file at this point, so it never sees the subroutines placed after it. To make them available again, we use the AutoSplit module to carve out the subroutines after the __END__ token into separate files placed in an auto directory relative to the module file. This often takes place in installation scripts and typically takes the form of a one-line Perl program. For example, to autosplit a module from the directory in which it is placed, use the following:

```
> perl -MAutoSplit -e 'autosplit qw(My/AutoModule.pm ./auto)'
```

This takes a module called My::AutoModule, contained in a file called AutoModule.pm, in a directory called My in the current directory, and splits it into parts inside an auto directory (which is created at the time if it doesn't already exist). Inside it we will now find the directories My/AutoModule. We in turn find within the directories an index file called autosplit.ix that describes the split-out subroutines. Along with it we find one file for each subroutine split out of the module, named for the subroutine with the suffix .al (for autoload).

Be aware that lexical my variables at file scope are not visible to autoloaded subroutines. This is obvious when we realize that the scope of the file has necessarily changed because we now have multiple files. On the other hand, variables declared with our (or use vars) will be fine, since they are package-scoped.

As an example of how AutoLoader is used, take this simple module file that implements a package called My::AutoModule:

```
# My/AutoModule.pm

package My::AutoModule;

use strict;
use Exporter;
use AutoLoader qw(AUTOLOAD);

our @ISA = qw(Exporter);
our @EXPORT = qw(one two three);

sub one {
    print "This is always compiled\n";
}

__END__

sub two {
    print "This is sub two\n";
}

sub three {
    print "This is sub three\n";
}

1;
```

The file, which in this case is named AutoModule.pm and is contained in a directory called My to match the package name, has three subroutines. The first, one, is a regular subroutine—it is always compiled. The others, two and three, are actually just text at the end of the file—the __END__ ensures that Perl never sees them and never even reads them in. Note that the only changes from a normal module are the use AutoLoader line and the __END__ token. The trailing 1; is not actually needed any longer, but we retain it in case we ever convert the module back into an unsplit one.

When we split the file, it creates three files, autosplit.ix, two.al, and three.al, all in the auto/My/AutoModule directory. Since we specified . as the installation directory, this new directory is immediately adjacent to the original AutoModule.pm file. If we had wanted to split a module that was installed into the Perl standard library tree, we would have used a different path here, according to the position of the file we want to split.

The autosplit.ix file contains the essential information about the subroutines that have been split out:

```
# Index created by AutoSplit for My/AutoModule.pm
#    (file acts as timestamp)
package My::AutoModule;
sub two;
sub three;
1;
```

Close inspection of this file reveals that it is in fact a snippet of Perl code that predeclares two subroutines, the two that were split out, in the package My::AutoModule. When the module is used in an application, the line use AutoLoader causes the AutoLoader module to be read in and initialized for that module. This has the effect of loading this index file, and thus declaring the subroutines.

The point of this may seem obscure, since the AUTOLOAD subroutine will seek the split-out files regardless, but it allows us to declare prototypes for subroutines and have them checked at compile time. It also allows us to call subroutines without parentheses, in the list operator style. Here is a short script that calls the subroutines defined by this module:

```
#!/usr/bin/perl
# automoduletest.pl
use warnings;
use strict;

use lib '.';
use My::AutoModule;

one;
two;
three;
```

The .al files contain the subroutines that were split out. Due to varying locations, slightly different scripts used, and so on, we may have small variations in the actual contents of the .al files obtained, but the following sample provides a rough idea of what can be expected:

```
# NOTE: Derived from My/AutoModule.pm.
# Changes made here will be lost when autosplit again.
# See AutoSplit.pm.
package My::AutoModule;

#line 18 "My/AutoModule.pm (autosplit into ./auto/My/AutoModule/two.al)"
sub two {
    print "This is sub two\n";
}

# end of My::AutoModule::two
1;
```

The AutoSplit module is smart enough to check that the AutoLoader module is actually used by a file before it attempts to split it. We can disable this check (if we insist), as well as determine whether old subroutine .al files are removed if they no longer exist, and check to see if the module has actually changed. To do this, we add one or more of three optional Boolean arguments to the autosplit subroutine:

```
> perl -MAutoSplit -e 'autosplit qw(My/AutoModule.pm ./auto), [keep], [check],
[changed]'
```

Substitute a 0 or 1 for the parameters to set or unset that argument. If any of these Boolean arguments are true, then the following actions occur:

- keep: Deletes any .al files for subroutines that no longer exist in the module (ones that do still exist are overwritten anyway). The default is 0, so .al files are automatically preserved.

- check: Causes the autosplit subroutine to verify that the file it is about to split actually contains a use AutoLoader directive before proceeding. The default is 1.

- changed: Suppresses the split if the timestamp of the original file is not newer than the timestamp of the autosplit.ix file in the directory into which the split files are going to be placed. The default is 1.

For example, the explicit version of the preceding two-argument call would be

```
> perl -MAutoSplit -e 'autosplit "My/AutoModule.pm","./auto", 0, 1, 1'
```

Again, the equivalent for Windows is

```
> perl -MAutoSplit -e "autosplit\"My/AutoModule.pm\",\"./auto\", 0, 1, 1"
```

We are not obliged to use the AutoLoader module's AUTOLOAD subroutine directly, but we need to use it if we want to load in split files. If we already have an AUTOLOAD subroutine and want to also use AutoLoader, we must not import the AUTOLOADER subroutine from AutoLoader but instead call it from our own AUTOLOAD subroutine:

```
use AutoLoader;

sub AUTOLOAD {
    ... handle our own special cases ...

    # pass up to AutoLoader
    $AutoLoader::AUTOLOAD = $AUTOLOAD;
    goto &AutoLoader::AUTOLOAD;
}
```

Note the goto—this is needed so that the call stack reflects the correct package names in the right place, or more specifically, doesn't include our own AUTOLOAD subroutine in the stack, which will otherwise confuse the AutoLoader module's AUTOLOAD subroutine. Of course, if we have our own AUTOLOAD subroutine, we might not need the module at all—multiple autoloading strategies in the same module or application is probably getting a little overcomplex.

Using the SelfLoader

The SelfLoader module is very similar in use to the AutoLoader module, but it avoids the need to split the module into files as a separate step. To use it, we use the SelfLoader module and place the subroutines we want to delay the loading of after a __DATA__ token. Here is a module called My::SelfModule that is modified from the My::AutoModule module given earlier to use SelfLoader instead:

```
# My/SelfModule.pm

package My::SelfModule;
```

```
use strict;
use Exporter;
use SelfLoader;

our @ISA = qw(Exporter);
our @EXPORT = qw(zero one two three);

sub one {
    print "This is always compiled\n";
}

__DATA__

sub two {
    print "This is sub two\n";
}
sub three {
    print "This is sub three\n";
}

1;
```

This module is identical to the AutoLoader version except for the two alterations. We replace use AutoLoader qw(AUTOLOAD) with use SelfLoader and __END__ with __DATA__. If we also want to place actual data in the module file, we can do so as long as it is read before loading the SelfLoader module, that is, in a BEGIN block prior to the use SelfStubber statement.

The SelfLoader module exports its AUTOLOAD subroutine by default, however, so if we want to define our own and call SelfLoader from it, we need to specify an explicit empty list:

```
use SelfLoader ();

sub AUTOLOAD {
    # ... handle cases to be processed here

    # pass up to SelfLoader
    $SelfLoader::AUTOLOAD = $AUTOLOAD;
    goto &SelfLoader::AUTOLOAD;
}
```

To test this module, we can use a script similar to the one used for My::AutoModule, except that My::SelfModule must be used instead. We also need to add parentheses to the subroutine calls because SelfLoader does not provide declarations (as we discover if we try to run it). To solve this problem, we can make use of the Devel::SelfStubber module to generate the declaration stubs we need to add:

```
> perl -MDevel::SelfStubber -e 'Devel::SelfStubber->stub("My::SelfModule",".")'
```

And for Windows:

```
> perl -MDevel::SelfStubber -e "Devel::SelfStubber->stub (\"My::SelfModule\",\".\")"
```

This generates the following declarations for our example module, which we can add to the module to solve the problem:

```
sub My::SelfModule::two ;
sub My::SelfModule::three ;
```

We can also regenerate the entire module, stubs included, if we first set the variable $Devel::SelfStubber::JUST_STUBS = 0. This gets a little unwieldy for a command line, but it is possible. Take as an example the following command (which should all be typed on one line):

```
> perl -MDevel::SelfStubber -e '$Devel::SelfStubber::JUST_STUBS
  = 0; Devel::SelfStubber->stub("My::SelfModule",".")' > My/SelfModule-stubbed.pm
```

For Windows, because of the different quoting conventions, this becomes

```
> perl -MDevel::SelfStubber -e "$Devel::SelfStubber::JUST_STUBS
  = 0; Devel::SelfStubber->stub(\"My::SelfModule\",\".\")" > My/SelfModule-stubbed.pm
```

This generates a new module, SelfModule-stubbed.pm, which we have named differently just for safety; it is still My::SelfModule inside. If all looks well, we can move or copy SelfModule-stubbed.pm over Selfmodule.pm. Note that running this command more than once can generate extra sets of stubs, which may cause problems or at least confusion, and we may even end up with an empty file if we forget to put the __DATA__ token in. For this reason, it is not advisable to attempt to replace a file with a stubbed version in one step.

Importing and Exporting

In the previous chapter, we looked at how to import symbols from one package into our own using the use and import statements. Now we will see the other side of the fence—the perspective of the module.

The term "importing" means taking symbols from another package and adding them to our own. From the perspective of the module being imported from, it is "exporting," of course. Either way, the process consists of taking a symbol visible in the namespace of one package and making it usable without qualifying it with a namespace prefix in another. For instance, even if we can see it, we would rather not refer to a variable called

```
$My::Package::With::A::Long::Name::scalar
```

It would be much better if we could refer to this variable simply as $scalar in our own code. From Chapter 5, we know that we can do this explicitly using typeglobs to create aliases:

```
my *scalar =\$My::Package::With::A::Long::Name::scalar;
```

Likewise, to create an alias for a subroutine:

```
my *localsub =\&My::Package::With::A::Long::Name::packagesub;
```

This is a simple case of symbol table manipulation, and it isn't all that tricky once we understand it; refer to Chapter 8 for more detail if necessary. However, this is clumsy code. We have to create an alias for every variable or subroutine we want to import. It is also prone to problems in later life, since we are defining the interface—the directly visible symbols—between this package and our own code, in our own code. This is very bad design because the package is not in control of how it is used. At best it is a maintenance nightmare; at worst, if the package is updated, there is a high chance our code will simply break.

Good programming practice dictates that packages should have a well-defined (and documented) interface and that all dependent code should use that interface to access it. The package, not the user of the package, should dictate what the interface is. Therefore, we need a way to ask the package to create appropriate aliases for us; this is the import mechanism that the use and no declarations invoke automatically. By passing responsibility for imports to the package, it gets to decide whether or not the request is valid, and reject it if not.

The import mechanism is not all that complex, and a basic understanding of it can help with implementing more complex modules with more involved export requirements. It is also applicable to simpler import mechanisms that, rather than actually exporting symbols, allow us to configure a package using the import list as initialization data. Object-oriented modules, which rarely export symbols, commonly use the import mechanism this way. However, if our requirements are simple, we can for the most part ignore the technicalities of the import mechanism and use the Exporter module to define our interface for us. For the majority of packages, the Exporter can handle all the necessary details. If we just want to export a few subroutines, skip part of the next section of this chapter and head straight to the section titled "The Exporter Module."

The Import Mechanism

Perl's mechanism for importing symbols is simple, elegant, and shockingly ad hoc, all at the same time. In a nutshell, we call a subroutine (actually an object method) called import in the package that we want to import symbols from. It decides what to do, then returns an appropriate value.

The import stage is a secondary stage beyond actually reading and compiling a module file, so it is not handled by the require directive; instead, it is a separate explicit step. Written out explicitly, we could do it like this:

```
require My::Module;    # load in the module
My::Module->import;    # call the 'import' subroutine
```

Since this is a call to an object method, Perl allows us to invert the package and subroutine names, so we can also say

```
import My::Module;
```

This doesn't mean we have to start programming everything as objects, however. It is just a convenient use of Perl's object-oriented syntax, just as the print statement is (to the surprise of many programmers). The syntax fools many programmers into thinking that import is actually a Perl keyword, since it looks exactly like require, but in fact it is only a subroutine. This typical import statement appears to be a core Perl feature for importing symbols, but in fact all it does is call the subroutine import in the package My::Module and pass the arguments subone, subtwo, and $scalar to it:

```
import My::Module qw(subone subtwo $scalar);
```

The import subroutine is rarely invoked directly because the use directive binds up a require and a call to import inside a BEGIN block. For example, use My::Module is therefore (almost) equivalent to

```
BEGIN {
    require My::Module;
    import My::Module;
}
```

Given that use does all the work for us, are there any reasons to need to know how to do the same job explicitly? Loading modules on demand during program execution can be easily achieved by using require and importing without the BEGIN block, as in the first example. This doesn't work with use because it happens at compile time due to the implicit BEGIN, and it disregards the surrounding run-time context.

Note that the preceding import has no parentheses; any arguments passed to use therefore get automatically passed directly to the import subroutine without being copied, as covered in Chapter 9. If there is no import subroutine defined, however, the preceding will complain, whereas use will not. A more correct import statement would be

```
import My::Module if My::Module->can('import');
# 'can' is a universal method (see Chapter 18)
```

Similarly, the no directive calls a function called unimport. The sense of no is to be the opposite of use, but this is a matter purely of convention and implementation, since the unimport subroutine is just another subroutine. In this case though, Perl will issue an error if there is no unimport method defined by the module. The no My::Module code is (roughly, with the same proviso as earlier) equivalent to

```
BEGIN {
    require My::Module;
    unimport My::Module;
}
```

It may seem strange that no incorporates a require within it, but there is no actual requirement that we use a module before we no parts of it. Having said that, the module may not work correctly if the import subroutine is not called initially. If use has already pulled in the module, the require inside no will see that the module is already in %INC, and so won't load it again. This means that in most cases no is just a way of calling unimport in the module package at compile time.

In the same way that aliasing can be done with typeglobs, removing aliases can be done by editing an entry out of the symbol table. Here is an example that does just that, using the delete_package subroutine of the Symbol module that we introduced previously:

```
# Uninstallable.pm
package Uninstallable;

use Symbol qw(delete_package);

our $message = "I'm here\n"; # package global

sub unimport {
    delete_package(__PACKAGE__);
}

1;
```

This module, which for the purposes of testing we shall call Uninstallable.pm (because we can uninstall it, not because we can't install it), defines one variable simply so we can tell whether or not it is present by testing for it. The next short script shows how. Note the BEGIN blocks to force the print statements to happen at the same time as use—otherwise the package would be uninstalled before the first print executes.

```
#!/usr/bin/perl
# uninstall.pl
use strict;

BEGIN { print "Now you see me: "; }
use Uninstallable;
BEGIN { print $Uninstallable::message; }

BEGIN { print "Now you don't!\n"; }
no Uninstallable;
BEGIN { print $Uninstallable::message; }
```

When run, presuming the module and script are both in the current directory:

> **perl -I. uninstall.pl**

you'll see the following output:

```
Now you see me: I'm here
Now you don't!
```

As interesting as this is, it is rare (though not impossible) that we would actually want to delete a package programmatically. Where they are implemented, most unimport subroutines simply clear flags that an import sets. Many of Perl's pragmatic modules like strict and warnings work this way, for example, and are actually very small modules in themselves.

Bypassing import

The use and no directives incorporate one extra trick: if we pass them an explicit empty parameter list, they don't call the import function at all. This means that we can suppress a module's default import if we only want to use some of its features. Take the CGI module as an example:

```
use CGI;                 # parse environment, set up variables
use CGI qw(:standard);   # import a specific set of features
use CGI ();              # just load CGI, don't parse anything
```

Suppressing the default import by passing an empty list is more useful than it might seem. The CGI module in the previous examples does rather a lot more than simply importing a few symbols by default; it examines the environment and generates a default CGI object for functional programming, as well as automatically generating a number of methods. If we just want to use the CGI module's HTML generation features, we don't need all that, so we can stop the module initializing itself by explicitly passing nothing to it.

Exporting

While most modules make use of the Exporter module covered later, they are not compelled to do so. Here is a simple exporting subroutine that illustrates how a module can implement a simple import subroutine:

```
# default import
sub import {
    my $caller = caller(1);                # get calling package
    *{"$caller\:\:mysub"} =\&mysub;        # export 'mysub'
    *{"$caller\:\:myscalar"} =\$myscalar;  # export '$myscalar'
    *{"$caller\:\:myhash"} =\%myhash;      # export '%myhash'
}
```

The principal technique is that we find the caller's package by inspecting the subroutine stack with caller. It so happens that when called in a scalar context, caller returns just the package name, so caller(1) returns the package of the caller—in other words, the place from which the use was issued. Once we know this, we simply use it to define typeglobs in the calling package filled with references to the variables we want to export.

This import subroutine doesn't pay any attention to the arguments passed to it (the first one of which is the package name). It just exports three symbols explicitly. This isn't very polite, as the calling package might not need all of them, and might even have its own versions of them. Here is a more polite and more versatile import subroutine that exports only the requested subroutines, if they exist:

```
# export if defined
sub import {
    my $caller = caller(1);    # get the name of the calling package
    my $package = shift;       # remove leading package argument from @_
    no strict refs;            # we need symbolic references to do this

    foreach (@_) {                              # for each request
        if (defined &{"$package\:\:$_"}) {      # if we have it...
            *{"$caller\:\:$_"} =\&{"$package\:\:$_"}   # ...make an alias
        } else {
```

```
            die "Unable to export $_ from $package\n"; # otherwise, abort
        }
    }
}
```

Usually, the package passed in is the package we are in anyway—we could as easily have said \&{$_} as \&{"$package\:\:$_"}. However, it is good practice to use the package name in case the import method is inherited by another package—by using the passed name, our import will also serve for any packages that inherit from it (via @ISA). This is exactly how the Exporter module works, in fact.

The preceding example only works for subroutines, so it only constructs subroutine references. A more versatile version would examine (and remove if appropriate) the first character of the symbol and construct a scalar, array, hash, code, or typeglob reference accordingly. Here is an example that does that, though for brevity, we have removed the check for whether the symbol actually exists:

```
# export arbitrary
sub import {
    my $caller = caller(1);   # get calling package
    my $package = shift;   # remove package from arguments
    no strict refs;   # we need symbolic references for this

    foreach (@_) {
        my $prefix;
        s/^([&%$@*])// and $prefix = $1;

        $prefix eq '$' and *{"$caller\:\:$_"} =\${"$package\:\:$_"}, last;
        $prefix eq '%' and *{"$caller\:\:$_"} =\%{"$package\:\:$_"}, last;
        $prefix eq '@' and *{"$caller\:\:$_"} =\@{"$package\:\:$_"}, last;
        $prefix eq '*' and *{"$caller\:\:$_"} =*{"$package\:\:$_"}, last;
        *{"$caller\:\:$_"} =\&{"$package\:\:$_"}, last;
    }
}
```

It is up to the import subroutine whether or not to carry out additional default imports when an explicit list is passed. In general, the answer is no, but it is usual to define a special symbol like :DEFAULT that imports all the default symbols explicitly. This allows the module user maximum flexibility in what to allow into their namespace:

```
sub import {
    my $package = shift;

    # if an empty import list, use defaults
    return _default_import() unless @_;

    foreach (@_) {
        /:DEFAULT/ and _default_import(), last;
        _export_if_present($package,$_);
    }
}

sub _default_import {
    # ... as above ...
}

sub _export_if_present {
    my ($package,$symbol) = @_;
    my $prefix;
```

```
        $symbol = s/^([&%$@*])// and $prefix = $1;

    if ($prefix and $prefix ne '&') {
        SWITCH: foreach ($prefix) {
            m'$' and do {
                if (defined ${"$package\:\:$_"}) {
                    *{"$caller\:\:$_"}=\${"$package\:\:$_"};
                    return;
                }
            };
            m'@' and do {
                # ... ditto for arrays ...
            };
            m'%' and do {
                # ... ditto for hashes ...
            };
            m'*' and do {
                # ... ditto for typeglobs ...
            };
        }
    } elsif (defined &{"$package\:\:$_"}) {
        *{"$caller\:\:$_"}=\&{"$package\:\:$_"}
    } else {
        die "Unable to export $_ from $package\n";
    }
}
```

The import method is not obliged to export symbols in response to being called. It can choose
to do anything it likes and treat the list of names passed to it in any way it sees fit. As an indication
of what else can be done with import lists, here is an import subroutine that invents generators for
HTML tags by defining a subroutine for any symbol passed to it that it doesn't recognize. (The CGI
module uses exactly this approach, though its HTML methods are a good deal more advanced. It is
also a much bigger module than these eight lines of code.)

```
sub import {
    my $package = shift;

    foreach (@_) {
        # for each passed symbol, generate a tag subroutine in the
        # caller's package.
        *{"$package\:\:$_"} = sub {
            "<$tag>\n".join("\n",@_)."</$tag>\n";
        };
    }
}
```

This is frequently a better way to handle automatic generation of subroutines than autoloading
is, since it is more controlled and precise. Also we have to declare the subroutines we want to use at
compile time (as use calls import then) where they can be subjected to syntax checking. Autoloading,
by contrast, actually disables compile-time checks, since it is perfectly valid for a subroutine not to
exist before it is called.

When to Export, When Not to Export

Having shown how to export symbols, it is worth taking a moment to consider whether we should.
The point of packages is to increase reusability by restraining the visibility of variables and subroutines. We can write application code in the main package free from worry about name clashes

because modules place their variables and subroutines into their own packages. Importing symbols goes against this strategy, and uncontrolled importing of lots of symbols pollutes code with unnecessary definitions that degrade maintainability and may cause unexpected bugs. In general we should take time to consider

- What should and should not be exported by default from a module (as little as possible)
- What should be allowed to be exported
- What should be denied export

These steps are an essential part of defining the interface to the package, and therefore a critical element of designing reusable code.

Object-oriented modules should usually not export anything at all; the entire point of object orientation is to work through the objects themselves, not to bypass them by importing parts of the module class into our own code. Additionally, exporting symbols directly bypasses the inheritance mechanism, which makes code that uses the exported symbols hard to reuse and likely to break. There are a few rare cases where modules provide both functional and object-oriented interfaces, but only in the simplest modules that are not intended to be inherited from is this a viable strategy.

In summary, the export list of a module is far more than just a list of symbols that will/may be imported into another package; it is the functional interface to the module's features, and as such should be designed, not gradually expanded. The Exporter module helps with this by allowing us to define lists of conditionally exported symbols.

The Exporter Module

The Exporter module provides a generic import subroutine that modules can configure to their own taste. It handles almost all possible issues that a traditional exporting module needs to consider, and for many modules it is all they need.

Using the Exporter

To use the Exporter, a module needs to do three things: use Exporter, inherit from it, and define the symbols eligible for export. Here is a very short module that demonstrates the basic technique, using fully qualified names for the package variables @ISA and @EXPORT:

```
# My/Module.pm
package My::Module;

use Exporter;

# inherit from it
@My::Module::ISA = qw(Exporter);

# define export symbols
@My::Module::EXPORT = qw(greet_planet);

sub greet_planet {
    return "Hello World\n";
}
```

Here we have an @ISA array that tells the interpreter that the module is a subclass of Exporter and to refer to it for any methods the module does not provide. Specifically that means import and unimport, of course. We don't need to worry too much about the object-oriented nature of inheriting from Exporter, unless we want to define our own import subroutine and still make use of the one provided by Exporter (we will get to that in a moment).

The @EXPORT array defines the actual symbols we want to export. When import is invoked for our module, the call is relayed up to the Exporter module, which provides the generic import method.

It in turn examines the definition of @EXPORT in our module, @My::Module::EXPORT and satisfies or denies the requested import list accordingly.

To illustrate, here's a short script that uses the preceding module, assuming it is in a file named Module.pm in a directory called My in the same directory as the script:

```
#!/usr/bin/perl
# import.pl
use warnings;
use strict;

use lib '.'; #look in current directory for My/Module.pm
use My::Module;

print greet_planet;
```

Importing from the Exporter

One advantage of the Exporter module is that the import method it provides is well developed and handles many different situations for us. Even if we decide to provide our own import subroutine, we may want to use Exporter too, just for the richness of the features it provides (and if we don't, we probably ought to document it). For example, it accepts regular expressions as well as literal symbol names, which means that we can define a collection of symbols with similar prefixes and then allow them to be imported together rather than individually. Here is how we can import a collection of symbols all starting with prefix_ from a module that uses the Exporter module:

```
use My::Module qw(/^prefix_/);
```

The Exporter also understands negations, so we can import all symbols that do not match a given name or regular expression:

```
# import everything except the subroutine 'greet_planet'
use My::Module qw(!greet_planet);

# import anything not beginning with 'prefix_'
use My::Module qw(!/^prefix_/);
```

We can also collect symbols together into groups and then import the groups by prefixing the group name with a colon. Again, this isn't a core Perl feature, it is just something that the Exporter module's import method does. For example:

```
use My::Module qw(:mygroup);
```

We'll see how to actually define a group in a moment.

Default and Conditional Exports

The @EXPORT variable defines a list of default exports that will be imported into our code if we use the module with no arguments, that is:

```
use My::Module;
```

But not either of these:

```
use My::Module ();
use My::Module qw(symbola symbolb symbolc);
```

If we give an explicit list of symbols to import, even if it is an empty list, Exporter will export only those symbols. Otherwise, we get the default, which is entirely up to the module (and hopefully documented).

Since exporting symbols automatically is not actually all that desirable (the application didn't ask for them, so we shouldn't spray it with symbols), Exporter also allows us to define conditional exports in the @EXPORT_OK array. Any symbol in this array may be exported if named explicitly, but it will not be exported by default.

In My::Module (Module.pm):

```
# change sub to be exported only on request
@EXPORT_OK = qw(greet_planet);
```

In application (import.pl):

```
# now we must import the sub explicitly
use My::Module qw(greet_planet);
```

The contents of the @EXPORT array are also checked when an explicit list is given, so any name or regular expression passed to import will be imported if it matches a name in either the @EXPORT or @EXPORT_OK list. However, any explicit list suppresses the exporting of the default list—which is the point, of course.

We can ask for the default symbols explicitly by using the special export tag :DEFAULT. The advantage is that we augment it with additional explicit requests. For example, this statement imports all the default symbols and additionally imports two more (presumably on the @EXPORT_OK list):

```
use My::Module qw(:DEFAULT symbola symbolb);
```

Alternatively, we can import the default list but skip over selected symbols:

```
use My::Module qw(:DEFAULT !symbola !symbolb);
```

Since this is a common case, we can also omit the :DEFAULT tag and simply put

```
use My::Module qw(!symbola !symbolb);
```

In fact, this is the same as the example of negation we gave earlier; in effect, an implicit :DEFAULT is placed at the front of the list if the first item in the list is negated.

As a working example of the different ways that import lists can be defined, here is a short demonstration module, called TestExport.pm, and a test script that we can use to import symbols from it in different ways. First the module, which exports two subroutines by default and two if asked:

```
# TestExport.pm

package TestExport;

use strict;
use Exporter;

our @ISA = qw(Exporter);
our @EXPORT = qw(sym1 sym2);
our @EXPORT_OK = qw(sym3 sym4);

sub sym1 {print "sym1\n";}
sub sym2 {print "sym2\n";}
sub sym3 {print "sym3\n";}
sub sym4 {print "sym4\n";}

1;
```

The following script contains a number of different use statements that import different symbols from the module, depending on their argument. To use it, uncomment one (and only one) use statement, and the script will print out the subroutines that were imported as a result. It also demonstrates a simple way of scanning the symbol table, as well as the use of %INC to check for a loaded module.

```perl
#!/usr/bin/perl
# testexport.pl
use warnings;
use strict;

# :DEFAULT import
#use TestExport;

# no imports
#use TestExport();

# just 'sym1'
#use TestExport qw(sym1);

# everything but 'sym1'
#use TestExport qw(!sym1);

# just 'sym3'
#use TestExport qw(sym3);

# everything but 'sym3'
#use TestExport qw(!sym3);

# implicit :DEFAULT
#use TestExport qw(!sym1 sym3);

# no implicit :DEFAULT
#use TestExport qw(sym3 !sym1);

unless (exists $INC{'TestExport.pm'}) {
    die "Uncomment a 'use' to see its effect\n";
}

foreach (keys %::) {
    print "Imported: $_\n" if /^sym/;
}
```

Note that in these examples we have concentrated on subroutines, since these are the symbols we most commonly export, though we are equally free to export variables too.

Export Lists

In addition to adding symbol names to @EXPORT and @EXPORT_OK, we can define collections of symbols as values in the hash variable %EXPORT_TAGS. The key is a tag name that refers to the collection. For example:

```perl
our (@EXPORT @EXPORT_OK %EXPORT_TAGS);

$EXPORT_TAGS{'subs'} = [qw(mysub myothersub subthree yellowsub)];
$EXPORT_TAGS{'vars'} = [qw($scalar @array %hash)];
```

Or, more succinctly:

```perl
our %EXPORT_TAGS = (
    subs => [qw(mysub myothersub subthree yellowsub)],
    vars => [qw($scalar @array %hash)],
);
```

Note that in accordance with the principles of nested data structures, we need to assign an array reference to each tag name key—otherwise we just count the list.

However, defining a list and assigning it to a tag does not automatically add the names in the list to either @EXPORT or @EXPORT_OK; in order for the tag to be imported successfully, the names have to be in one or other of the arrays too. Fortunately, Exporter makes this simple for us by providing a pair of subroutines to add the symbols associated with a tag to either list automatically. To add a tag to the default export list:

```
Exporter::export_tags('subs');
```

To add a tag to the conditional export list:

```
Exporter::export_ok_tags('vars');
```

We can now import various permutations of tags and symbol names:

```
# import two tags
use My::Module qw(:subs :vars);

# import the default list excepting the items in ':subs'
use My::Module qw(:DEFAULT !:subs);

# import ':subs' excepting the subroutine 'myothersub'
use My::Module qw(:subs !myothersub);
```

To show tags in action, here is a modified example of the TestExport module we gave earlier, rewritten to use tags instead. We define the default and on-request export lists using the export_tags and export_ok_tags subroutines:

```
# TestTagExport.pm

package TestTagExport;

use strict;
use Exporter;

our @ISA = qw(Exporter);
our %EXPORT_TAGS = (
    onetwo => ['sym1','sym2'],
    threefour => ['sym3','sym4'],
    onetwothree => [qw(sym1 sym2 sym3)],
    all => [qw(sym1 sym2 sym3 sym4)],
);

Exporter::export_tags('onetwo');
Exporter::export_ok_tags('threefour');

sub sym1 {print "sym1\n";}
sub sym2 {print "sym2\n";}
sub sym3 {print "sym3\n";}
sub sym4 {print "sym4\n";}

1;
```

Here is a script that tests out the export properties of the new module, concentrating on tags rather than symbols, though all the tests that applied to the first module will work with the same effect with this example:

```perl
#!/usr/bin/perl
# testtagexport.pl
use warnings;
use strict;

# import tag
#use TestTagExport;

# import symbol plus tag
#use TestTagExport qw(:threefour sym2);

# import tag minus symbol
#use TestTagExport qw(:onetwothree !sym2);

# import one tag minus another
#use TestTagExport qw(:onetwothree !:DEFAULT);

unless (exists $INC{'TestTagExport.pm'}) {
    die "Uncomment a 'use' to see its effect\n";
}

foreach (keys %::) {
    print "Imported: $_\n" if /^sym/;
}
```

Versions

The use and require directives support a version number syntax in addition to their regular use in module loading. The Exporter module also allows us to handle this usage by defining a require_version method that is passed the package name (because it is a method) and the version number requested:

```perl
our $VERSION = "1.23";

# this subroutine name has special meaning to Exporter
sub require_version {
    my ($pkg,$requested_version) = @_;
    return $requested_version ge $VERSION;
}
```

If we do not supply a require_version method, then a default definition provided by Exporter is used instead; this also tests the requested version against the value of $VERSION defined in the local package (if any is defined), but it uses a numeric comparison, which works well for comparing version number objects/strings (see Chapter 3).

Handling Failed Exports

The Exporter module automatically causes an application to die if it attempts to import a symbol that is not legal. However, by defining another array, @EXPORT_FAIL, we can define a list of symbols to handle specially in the event that Exporter does not recognize them. For example, to handle cross-platform special cases, we might define three different subroutines:

```perl
our (@EXPORT_FAIL);

@EXPORT_FAIL = qw(win32sub macsub Unixsub);
```

In order to handle symbols named in the failure list, we need to define a subroutine, or rather a method, called export_fail. The input to this method is a list of the symbols that the Exporter did not recognize, and the return value should be any symbols that the module was unable to process:

```
sub export_fail {
    my $pkg = shift;

    my @fails;
    foreach (@_) {
        # test each symbol to see if we want to define it
        push @fails,$_ if supported($_);
    }

    # return list of failed exports (none if success)
    return @fails;
}

sub supported {
    my $symbol = shift;
    ... test for special cases ...
    return $ok_on_this_platform;
}
```

If an export_fail method isn't defined, then Exporter supplies its own, which returns all the symbols, causing them all to fail as if the @EXPORT_FAIL array was not defined at all. Note that we cannot have Exporter call export_fail for any unrecognized symbol, only those listed in the @EXPORT_FAIL array. However, if we wanted to handle situations like this ourselves, we can always define our own import method, which we discuss next.

Using the Exporter with a Local import Method

If a module needs to do its own initialization in addition to using Exporter, we need to define our own import method. Since this will override the import method defined by Exporter, we will need to take steps to call it explicitly. Fortunately, the Exporter module has been written with this in mind.

Assuming we're familiar with object-oriented programming, we might guess that calling SUPER::import from our own import subroutine would do the trick, since SUPER:: is the named method in the parent package or packages. Unfortunately, although this works, it imports symbols to the wrong package, because Exporter's import method examines the package name of the caller to determine where to export symbols. Since that is the module, and not the user of the module, the export doesn't place anything in the package that issues the use statement. Instead, we use the export_to_level method, which traces back up the calling stack and supplies the correct package name to Exporter's import method. Here's how to use it:

```
our @ISA = qw(Exporter);
our @EXPORT_OK = qw(mysub myothersub subthree yellowsub);

sub import {
    my $package = $_[0];
    do_our_own_thing(@_);
    $package->export_to_level(1, @_);
}
```

The first argument to export_to_level is a call-stack index (identical to that passed to the caller function). This is used to determine the package to export symbols to, thereby allowing export_to_level to be completely package independent. Note that because the package information needs to be preserved intact, it is important that we do not remove the package name passed as the first argument, which is why we used $_[0] and not shift in the preceding example.

Debugging Exports

The Exporter module also has a special verbose mode we can use when we are debugging particularly complex import problems. To enable it, define the variable $Exporter::Verbose before using the module. Note that for this to be successful it needs to be in a BEGIN block:

```
BEGIN {
    $Exporter::Verbose = 1;
}
```

Note also that this will produce debug traces for all modules that use Exporter. Since a very large number of modules use Exporter, this may produce a lot of output. However, since BEGIN blocks (including the implicit ones in use statements) are executed in order, we can plant BEGIN blocks in between the use statements to restrain the reporting to just those modules we are interested in:

```
use Exporter;
use A::Module::Needed::First;

BEGIN { print "Loading...\n"; $Exporter::Verbose = 1;}
use My::Problematic::Exporting::Module;

BEGIN { print "...loaded ok\n"; $Exporter::Verbose = 0;}
use Another::Module;
```

Package Attributes

Package attributes are an extension to the predefined attribute mechanism provided by the attributes module and covered in Chapter 7. Perl only understands four native attributes by default (lvalue, locked, method, and unique, of which locked and method are now deprecated), but the idea of package attributes is that we can implement our own attributes that work on a package-wide basis. To implement them, we define specially named subroutines within the package. The easiest way to create these is with the Attribute::Handlers module, although the underlying mechanism is not (as is often the case in Perl) all that complex. The attribute mechanism is still somewhat experimental in Perl 5.8, so some of its more idiosyncratic properties are likely to be smoothed out over time.

Each data type may have a different set of attributes associated with it. For example, a scalar attribute is implemented by writing FETCH_SCALAR_ATTRIBUTES and MODIFY_SCALAR_ATTRIBUTES subroutines, and similarly for ARRAY, HASH, and CODE. The package may implement the details of storage and retrieval any way it likes based on the arguments passed.

FETCH_ subroutines are called by attributes::get whenever we use it on a reference of the correct type in the same package. They are passed a single argument, which is a reference to the entity being queried. They should return a list of the attributes defined for that entity.

MODIFY_ subroutines are called during the import stage of compilation. They take a package name and a reference as their first two arguments, followed by a list of the attributes to define. They return a list of unrecognized attributes, which should be empty if all the attributes could be handled.

Both FETCH_ and MODIFY_ subroutines may be accessed by corresponding routines in a package implementing a derived object class. The parent package is called with SUPER::FETCH_TYPE_ATTRIBUTES and SUPER::MODIFY_TYPE_ATTRIBUTES. The intent is that a subclass should first call its parent and then deal with any attributes returned. In the case of FETCH_, it should add its own attributes to the list provided by the parent and return it. In the case of MODIFY_, it should deal with the list of unrecognized attributes passed back from the parent. This is essentially the same mechanism that the Exporter module uses.

Attribute Handlers

With the `Attribute::Handlers` module, we can invent our own attributes and register handlers to be triggered when a variable or subroutine is declared with them, without any need to get involved in defining explicit `FETCH_` and `MODIFY_` subroutines. Here is a minimal example that shows an attribute handler in action:

```perl
#!/usr/bin/perl
use strict;
use warnings;
use Attribute::Handlers;

{

    package Time;

    sub Now : ATTR(SCALAR) {
        my ($pkg,$sym,$ref,$attr,$data,$when)=@_;
        $$ref=time;
    }
}

my Time $now : Now;
print $now; # produces the time in seconds since 1970/1/1
```

This creates a handler called `Now` in the `Time` package that can be applied to scalar attributes—attempting to declare this attribute on an array, hash, or subroutine will cause a syntax error. When a scalar variable is declared and typed to the `Time` package and then given `Now` as an attribute, the handler is called. Interesting though this syntax looks, Perl does not really support the typing of variables. Providing a scalar variable with a type is really just a suggestion to Perl to do something with the variable if the opportunity arises. Package attributes are one of the two features that provided a "something," the other being the compile-time checking of hash keys accesses in pseudohashes and restricted hashes. The effect of the type is only at compile time; it does not persist into the execution phase.

The handler is passed six values, of which the third, the reference, points to the scalar variable on which the attribute is being defined. The action of the handler is to assign the current time to the dereferenced variable. As a result, when we print the variable out, we find it already has a value of the current time (in seconds since January 1, 1970).

Observant readers will notice that the declaration of the handler subroutine is itself implemented using an attribute called ATTR. The data value associated with it is SCALAR, which tells the ATTR handler—defined in `Attribute::Handlers`—how to set up the `FETCH_` and `MODIFY_` subroutines to call the Now subroutine.

The other parameters are as follows:

- `$pkg`: The name of the package. In this case, it is `Time`, but it could also be the name of a package implementing a subclass.

- `$sym`: For package declarations, the symbolic name of the variable or subroutine being defined, qualified by its package. In the case of a lexical variable like the one shown previously, there is no symbol and so no name, so the string LEXICAL is passed.

- `$attr`: The name of the attribute, here Now.

- `$data`: The data passed with the attribute, if any. For ATTR it was SCALAR; for our Now attribute, we didn't pass any.

- `$when`: The phase of execution—BEGIN, INIT, CHECK, or END.

By default a handler is executed during the check phase transition of the interpreter, which is to say Perl compiles it as a CHECK block (see earlier in the chapter for more on what a CHECK block is). We can create handlers that execute at any of the four transition points BEGIN, CHECK, INIT, or END, all of them, or a selection. The following example defines a handler in the UNIVERSAL package that executes at BEGIN, INIT, and CHECK. It records the total startup time of all BEGIN blocks (including use statements) that are declared after it, everything that occurs in the CHECK phase transition, and any INIT handlers that were declared before it. For variety, it also defines an attribute for hash variables:

```perl
#!/usr/bin/perl
use strict;
use warnings;
use Attribute::Handlers;

{
    package UNIVERSAL;
    use Time::HiRes qw(gettimeofday);

    # calculate the startup time
    sub Startup : ATTR(HASH,BEGIN,INIT,CHECK) {
        my ($pkg,$sym,$ref,$attr,$data,$when)=@_;

        if ($when eq 'BEGIN') {
            # at begin, store current time
            my ($secs,$usecs)=gettimeofday();
            %$ref=( secs => $secs, usecs => $usecs );

            print "Startup BEGIN...\n";
        } elsif ($when eq 'INIT') {
            # at init, calculate time elapsed
            my ($secs,$usecs)=gettimeofday();
            $ref->{secs} = $secs - $ref->{secs};
            $ref->{usecs} = $usecs - $ref->{usecs};
            if ($ref->{usecs} < 0) {
                $ref->{usecs} += 1_000_000;
                $ref->{secs} -= 1;
            }

            print "Startup INIT...\n";
        } else {
            # we could do something time-consuming here
            print "Startup CHECK...\n";
        }
    }
}

our %time : Startup;

BEGIN { print "Beginning...\n";     sleep 1 }; #happens after Startup BEGIN
CHECK { print "Checking...\n";      sleep 1 }; #between Startup BEGIN and INIT
INIT  { print "Initialising...\n";  sleep 1 }; #happens after Startup INIT

print "BEGIN+CHECK took ",$time{secs}*1_000_000+$time{usecs},"uS\n";
```

Why is this handler declared in the UNIVERSAL package? In this case, mainly because typing a variable (by prefixing it with the name of a package) is an object-oriented mechanism that only works on scalar variables. It works fine for our first example because it is a SCALAR attribute, but this is a handler for hash variables.

Declaring a handler in UNIVERSAL has the useful property of making it available to any and all hashes, anywhere. However, it also allows for the possibility of collisions between different modules. Unfortunately, a colon is not a legal character in an attribute name, so we can't create a handler in the package Time and then declare constructs with it, unless we do so in a package that subclasses from the Time package via the @ISA array or use base pragma.

The preceding handler does not implement a clause for the END phase transition. This might seem like a useful thing to do—after all, we could time the running time of the program that way. But this won't work, because the hash is a lexically scoped variable. Even though it is declared with our and so exists as a package variable, the lexical scope ends before the END block is executed. Consequently, Attribute::Handlers cannot bind the attribute at this phase. As a consequence, we can only usefully define END handlers for subroutine declarations.

Attributes for different data classes can coexist peacefully, although we will need to say no warnings 'redefine' to stop Perl complaining that we have more than one subroutine with the same name. While this true, the Attribute::Handlers module resolves the problem because the attributes remap the subroutine calls into autogenerated FETCH_ and MODIFY_ subroutines. However, we cannot declare more than one attribute handler for the same type of data but at different phases:

```
use warnings;
no warnings 'redefine';
sub MyAttr : ATTR(SCALAR,BEGIN,INIT) {...} # first attribute handler is defined
sub MyAttr : ATTR(HASH,BEGIN,INIT {...}    # Redefine 'Now', different data type, OK
sub MyAttr : ATTR(HASH,CHECK) {...}        # ERROR: same data type again
```

Without qualification or with the special data type ANY, a handler will be called for all variables and code references. The ANY label allows the phase transitions to be specified, otherwise it is no different from the unqualified version. These handlers will execute for any variable or subroutine for which the attribute is declared:

```
sub MyAttr : ATTR {...}
sub MyAttr : ATTR(ANY)  {...}
sub MyAttr : ATTR(ANY,BEGIN,INIT) {...}
```

The data passed to a handler is natively presented as a string containing the whole text between the opening and closing parentheses; it is not treated as normal Perl syntax. However, Attributes::Handlers makes some attempt to parse the string if it looks like it might be defining something other than a string. A comma-separated list is not treated specially, but an opening square or curly brace is, if it is matched at the end. This example illustrates several valid ways to pass data arguments that will be parsed into corresponding data structures:

```
#!/usr/bin/perl
# attrhandler3.pl
use strict;
use warnings;
use Attribute::Handlers;

{
    package MyPackage;

    sub Set : ATTR(SCALAR) {
        my ($pkg,$sym,$ref,$attr,$data,$when)=@_;
        $$ref=$data;
    }
}
```

```perl
my MyPackage $list : Set(a,b,c);
print "@$list\n";    # prodices 'a b c'
my MyPackage $aref : Set([a,b,c]);
print "@$aref\n";    # produces 'ARRAY(0xNNNNNN)'
my MyPackage $string : Set('a,b,c');
print "$string\n";   # produces 'a,b,c'
my MyPackage $href : Set({a=>1,b=>2,c=>3});
print map {
    "$_ => $href->{$_}\n"
} keys %$href;        # produces 'a => 1' ...
my MyPackage $qwaref : Set(qw[a b c]);
print "@$qwaref\n";  # produces 'a b c'
```

Handlers also allow ways to make otherwise complex syntax simpler by encapsulating it, for example, the tie mechanism. The following example wraps an interface to tie an arbitrary DBM database with any of the standard DBM implementations inside an attribute handler that hides away the details and awkward syntax of the tie and replaces it with an intuitive attribute instead:

```perl
#!/usr/bin/perl
use strict;
use warnings;
use Attribute::Handlers;

{
    package UNIVERSAL;
    use Fcntl qw(O_RDWR O_CREAT);

    sub Database : ATTR(HASH) {
        my ($pkg,$sym,$ref,$attr,$data)=@_;

        my ($file,$type,$mode,$perm);
        if (my $reftype=ref $data) {
            die "Data reference not an ARRAY"
                unless $reftype eq 'ARRAY';
            $file = shift @$data;
            $type = shift(@$data) || 'SDBM_File';
            $mode = shift(@$data) || O_RDWR|O_CREAT;
            $perm = shift(@$data) || 0666;
        } else {
            $file = $data;
            ($type,$mode,$perm)=('SDBM_File',O_RDWR|O_CREAT,0666);
        }

        eval "require ${type}" or
            die "${type} not found";

        tie %$ref, $type, $file, $mode, $perm;
    }
}

my %sdbm : Database(mysdbmfile);
$sdbm{key} = 'value';

my %gdbm : Database('mygdbmfile.dbm',GDBM_File);
$gdbm{key} = 'value';
```

Since we can be passed either a single string (the database file name) or an array reference (file name plus mode plus permissions), the handler needs to check what data type the data parameter actually is. Either way, defaults are filled in if not specified. Other than this, there is not much in the way of real complexity here. Note the quotes on 'mygdbmfile.dbm', though—these are needed because without them the dot will be parsed as a string concatenation and silently disappear from the resulting file name.

If we just want to create a quick and dirty mapping to a tieable module, then we can create handlers automatically with the autotie and autotieref keywords, both of which allow us to construct one or more handlers by simply associating handler names with the module to be tied in a hash reference passed as an argument to the use statement of the Attribute::Handlers module:

```
#!/usr/bin/perl
# attrhandlerautotie.pl
use strict;
use warnings;
use Attribute::Handlers autotie => {Database => 'MLDBM'};
use Fcntl qw(O_RDWR O_CREAT);

my %dbm : Database(mydbmfile,O_RDWR|O_CREAT,0666);
$dbm{key} = 'value';
```

Here we use the MLDBM module to automatically use the most appropriate underlying DBM implementation (see perldoc MLDBM for how the selection is made). We lose the ability to supply helpful defaults, but we need to write no code at all to implement the handler.

The autotieref keyword works identically to autotie, but it passes the attribute's data arguments to the internally generate tie statement as an array reference rather than as a list of arguments. This is purely to satisfy those modules that actually require an array reference instead of a list; use whichever is appropriate to the circumstance.

Creating Installable Modules

An installable module is one that we can bundle up, take somewhere else, and then install by unpacking it and executing an installation script. If we want to make our scripts and modules easily portable between systems, it is far better to automate the process of installation than manually copy files into a library directory. In addition, if we want to distribute the module more widely or upload it to CPAN for the enjoyment of all, we need to make sure that the module is well behaved and has all the right pieces in all the right places. Fortunately, the h2xs utility supplied with Perl automates a great deal of this process for us, allowing us to concentrate on the actual code. (CPAN also has several modules that aim to expand on the features and ease-of-use of h2xs that may be worth investigating, for example, Module::Starter.)

The h2xs utility is technically designed for creating Perl interfaces to C or C++ libraries, but it is perfectly capable of setting up the basic infrastructure for a pure Perl module as well—we just don't avail ourselves of its more advanced features.

Note that an installable module doesn't have to just be one file. Typically a module distribution contains the main module plus a number of other supporting modules, which may or may not be directly usable themselves. The whole ensemble is "the module," whereas the one we actually load into our applications is the primary interface.

Well-Written Modules

When we are writing modules for our own personal use, we can be fairly lax about how they are structured; a package declaration at the top and a 1 at the bottom are all we really need. However, a well-written and well-behaved module for general consumption should have some essential attributes:

- *Its own unique package name*: In the case of modules designed for wider distribution, this should be not only chosen wisely but also checked against other modules already available from CPAN to see if it fits well with existing nomenclature. For modules destined for CPAN, consult the module distribution list at http://cpan.org/modules/01modules.index.html and the exhaustive list of uploaded modules in http://cpan.org/modules/03modlist.data.gz.

- *A version number*: The main module file should have a version number defined inside it, either in the package variable $VERSION or in a VERSION subroutine that returns a version number.

- *Strict mode*: No Perl code should really be without the strict pragma. It must be said that there are several examples of modules in the Perl standard library that do not adhere to these standards. Mostly these are tried and tested modules from early in the development of the standard library that are known to work. For new modules, strict mode is a good idea.

- *Documentation*: All subroutine calls, exported and exportable symbols, and configuration details should be written up and distributed along with the module, preferably in the form of Plain Old Documentation (POD) within the main module file (see Chapter 18 for more on POD documents). It is not necessary for every module to be documented if some modules only support modules and are not intended to be used directly, but all salient features should be there. To be properly structured, the POD document should contain at least the following sections:

  - NAME: The package name and brief description
  - SYNOPSIS: Code example of how the module is used
  - DESCRIPTION: A description of what the module does
  - EXPORT: What the module exports
  - SEE ALSO: Any related modules or Perl documentation
  - HISTORY: Optionally, a history of changes

Tools are written to look for these sections, such as the podselect utility and the translators that are based on it. These can use properly constructed documentation to extract information intelligently and selectively. Additional optional sections include BUGS, CHANGES, AUTHOR, COPYRIGHT, and SUPPORTED PLATFORMS.

Remembering to do all this can be irritating, which is why h2xs can create a skeleton module with all of the preceding already defined and in place for us. All we have to do is replace the content of each section with something more meaningful.

Creating a Working Directory

The first and main step to use h2xs to create an installable module is to create a working directory tree where the module source code will reside. This resembles a local library directory (and indeed we can use the module directly if we add it to @INC via Perl's -I option or the use lib pragma). In its most basic usage, h2xs creates a directory tree based on the package name we give it and creates an initial module file with all the basic attributes in place. We use -n to name both module and directory structure and -X to tell h2xs not to bother trying to wrap any C or C++ code. For example:

```
> h2xs -X -n Installable::Module
```

This creates a directory Installable-Module inside, which are the files and directories listed in Table 10-1.

Table 10-1. *Initial Contents of a Distributable Module Directory*

File	Description
lib/Installable/Module.pm	This is the Perl module itself.
Makefile.PL	This is a Perl script that generates a makefile script for the module. The makefile is generated by simply running Perl on this file, for example: > **perl Makefile.PL** In turn, the makefile defines various targets, notably dist, which creates a distribution file and install, which carries out the building, testing, and installation of the module.
t/Installable-Module.t	A test script to test the module's functionality, which is compatible with the Test::Harness module and which is executed (using Test::Harness) by the test makefile target. We can create our own tests using the Test or Test::Simple/Test::More modules and add them to this script.
Changes	A Changes file that documents the module's history. This file is suppressed by the -C option.
MANIFEST	A list of the files in the distribution. By adding files to this list, we can add them to the distribution that is created by the dist target.

The actual donkeywork of creating the makefile is done by a collection of modules in the ExtUtils family, the principal one being ExtUtils::MakeMaker. A single call to this module actually takes up the bulk of the Makefile.PL script:

```
use 5.008005;
use ExtUtils::MakeMaker;
# See lib/ExtUtils/MakeMaker.pm for details of how to influence
# the contents of the Makefile that is written.
WriteMakefile(
    NAME            => 'Installable::Module',
    VERSION_FROM    => 'lib/Installable/Module.pm', # finds $VERSION
    PREREQ_PM       => {}, # e.g., Module::Name => 1.1
    ($] >= 5.005 ?    ## Add these new keywords supported since 5.005
      (ABSTRACT_FROM => 'lib/Installable/Module.pm', # retrieve from module
       AUTHOR        => 'You <your@email>') : ()),
);
```

This is a newer Makefile.PL; older versions of h2xs create a slightly different directory structure and a Makefile.PL without the trailing definitions. However, the format and use is broadly similar.

Notice the use statement at the start of this file. It requires a Perl version of at least 5.8.5, but only because in this case it was the version of the interpreter that h2xs used. If we know our module doesn't need such a current version, we can override it with the -b option to h2xs. For example, for Perl version 5.005, or 5.5.0 in the new version numbering format, we would use

> **h2xs -X -n Installable::Module -b 5.5.0**

Sometimes we already have a module, and we just want to convert it into an installable one. The best option here is to create a new module source file and then copy the existing source code from the old module file into it. This way we get the extra files correctly generated by h2xs for us, each in its proper place, and each containing a valid structurally correct skeleton to aid in adapting the module to conform with the guidelines.

Either way, once we have the directory set up and the appropriate files created within it, we can create a functional and (preferably) fully documented module.

Building an Installable Package

To create an installable package file from our module source, we only need to create the makefile and then use make dist (or nmake or dmake on a Windows system) to create the distribution file:

```
> perl Makefile.PL
> make dist
```

If we have added other modules to our source code or additional files we want to include with the distribution, we add them to the MANIFEST file. At the start, this file contains just the files generated by h2xs, that is Changes, MANIFEST, Makefile.PL, Module.pm, and test.pl.

Assuming the make dist executes successfully, we should end up with an archived installation file comprising the package name (with colons replaced by hyphens) and the version number. On a Unix system, our example module gets turned into Installable-Module-0.01.tar.gz. To test it, we can invoke

```
> make disttest
```

We can now take this package to another system and install it with

```
> gunzip Installable-Module-0.01.tar.gz
> tar -xvf Installable-Module-0.01.tar
```

Once the source is unpacked, we create the makefile and run the install target from it.

```
> cd Installable-Module-0.01
> perl Makefile.PL
> make
> make test
> su
```

Password:

```
# make install
```

This will install files into the default installation location, which is usually the standard Perl library. We can instead opt to install the package into the site_perl directory under Perl's main installation tree with the install_site target:

```
> su
```

Password:

```
# make install_site
```

Alternatively, we can have install install the module into the site_perl directory automatically by adding a definition for INSTALLDIRS to the key-value pair of WriteMakefile:

```
use 5.005005;
use ExtUtils::MakeMaker;
# See lib/ExtUtils/MakeMaker.pm for details of how to influence
# the contents of the Makefile that is written.
WriteMakefile(
    'INSTALLDIRS' => 'site',
    ...as before...
);
```

The valid values for this parameter are perl, site, and vendor. Of the three, site is really the only good choice if we want to keep our own modules from entering the official Perl library. Note that we will need to have permission to actually install the file anywhere under the standard Perl library root. Once the installation is complete, we should be able to see details of it by running perldoc perllocal.

Alternatively, to install a module into our own separate location, we can supply the LIB or PREFIX parameters when we create the makefile. For example, to install modules into a master library directory lib/perl in our home directory on a Unix system, we could type

```
> cd Installable-Module-0.01
> perl Makefile.PL PREFIX=~/lib/perl
> su
```

Password:

```
# make install
```

The PREFIX parameter overrides the initial part of all installation paths, allowing installation into a different location. The various installation locations for modules, manual pages, and scripts are given sensible defaults derived from this initial path. Individual paths can then be overridden specifically if necessary with the following parameters:

- INST_ARCHLIB: Architecture-dependent files
- INST_LIB: Primary module source files
- INST_BIN: Binary executables
- INST_SCRIPT: Scripts
- INST_MAN1DIR: Section 1 manual pages
- INST_MAN3DIR: Section 3 manual pages

PREFIX is therefore ideal for installing a module into a private local directory for testing.

The LIB parameter allows the implementation files of a module to be installed in a nonstandard place, but with accompanying files such as scripts and manual pages sent to a default location or those derived from PREFIX. This makes the module findable by documentation queries (for example, the man command on Unix) while allowing it to reside elsewhere.

Adding a Test Script

The makefile generated by ExtUtils::MakeMaker contains an impressively larger number of different make targets. Amongst them is the test target, which executes the test script test.pl generated by h2xs. To add a test stage to our package, we only have to edit this file to add the tests we want to carry out.

Tests are carried out in the aegis of the Test::Harness module, which we will cover in Chapter 17, but which is particularly aimed at testing installable packages. The Test::Harness module expects a particular kind of output, which the pregenerated test.pl satisfies with a redundant automatically succeeding test. To create a useful test, we need to replace this pregenerated script with one that actually carries out tests and produces an output that complies with what the Test::Harness module expects to see.

Once we have a real test script that carries out genuine tests in place, we can use it by invoking the test target, as we saw in the installation examples earlier:

```
> make test
```

By default the `install` target does not include `test` as a dependent target, so we do need to run it separately if we want to be sure the module works. The CPAN module automatically carries out the test stage before the install stage, however, so when we install modules using it we don't have to remember the test stage.

Uploading Modules to CPAN

Once a module has been successfully turned into a package (and preferably reinstalled, tested, and generally proven), it is potentially a candidate for CPAN. Uploading a module to CPAN allows it to be shared among other Perl programmers, commented on, improved, and made part of the library of Perl modules available to all within the Perl community.

This is just the functional stage of creating a module for general distribution, however. Packages cannot be uploaded to CPAN arbitrarily. First we need to get registered so we have an upload directory to upload things into. It also helps to discuss modules with other programmers and see what else is already available that might do a similar job. It definitely helps to choose a good package name and to discuss the choice first. Remember that Perl is a community as well as a language; for contributions to be accepted (and indeed, noticed at all), it helps to talk about them.

Information on registration and other aspects of contribution to CPAN are detailed on the Perl Authors Upload Server (PAUSE) page at `http://cpan.org/modules/04pause.html` (or any mirror). The module distribution list is at `http://cpan.org/modules/01modules.index.html`, while details of all the modules currently held by CPAN and its many mirrors is in `http://cpan.org/modules/03modlist.data.gz`.

Summary

In this chapter, we explored the insides of modules and packages and how to write our own modules. We saw how packages affect the symbol table and looked at a few ways to take advantage of this knowledge to examine and even manipulate package contents programmatically.

We then looked at Perl's special phase transition blocks, `BEGIN`, `CHECK`, `INIT`, and `END`, and how we can use them to create modules that can initialize themselves and carry out various kinds of checks between phases of the interpreter's operation.

The next main topic discussed was the autoloading mechanism, which allows us to intercept calls to subroutines that do not exist and define them on the fly if we want to. From there we looked at importing and exporting, completing the discussion started in the previous chapter from the viewpoint of the module being imported from. We looked at the basics of the import mechanism, how we can use it to do other things than importing, and how to use the `Exporter` module to handle many common import and export requirements.

We also looked at package attributes and implementing our own attributes for subroutines and variables with the `Attribute::Handlers` module. Like the import/export mechanism, this completes the previous discussion started in Chapter 7, where we introduced using Perl's built-in attributes from the perspective of the implementing module.

Finally, we went through the process of creating an installable module, including the use of `h2xs` to create the initial working directory and files, bundling the completed module into a distributable archive, and then installing the archive on another platform.

■■■

## CHAPTER 11

Interpolation and Regular Expressions

Interpolation and regular expressions are two of Perl's most powerful features, providing us with the ability to match, substitute, and generally mangle and manipulate text in almost any way we can conceive. Interpolation is merely the process of evaluating variables within strings and substituting their names with the corresponding values. We can interpolate scalars directly, and handily we can also interpolate arrays to render all their elements into the string. We can also interpolate special characters such as linefeeds or instructions such as uppercasing all text that follows. More advanced use of interpolation allows us to interpolate code and subroutine calls too.

The regular expression engine in Perl provides the power behind the match and substitution operations, as well as other functions like split. Regular expressions define patterns describing sequences of characters in string data. By applying these patterns, we can detect and extract text that matches them or substitute new text in its place. The syntax of regular expressions is rich enough to allow the definition of very powerful patterns and to carry out complex analysis and manipulation of large quantities of text in very few lines of code.

A regular expression is itself a string of text, containing the pattern we wish to apply to the input text. We are not limited to supplying static strings as patterns, however, because Perl interpolates any pattern we use in a regular expression operation before supplying it to the regular expression engine. Before we tackle regular expressions, therefore, it makes sense to look at interpolation first.

String Interpolation

The literary definition of *interpolation* is the process of inserting additional words or characters into a block of text. In Perl, interpolation is just the process of substituting variables and special characters in strings. The concept was briefly introduced in Chapter 2, and we have seen several simple uses of interpolated strings since.

When Perl encounters a string that can be interpolated, it scans it for three significant characters: $, @, and \. If any of these are present and not escaped (prefixed with a backslash), they trigger interpolation of the text immediately following. What actually happens depends on the character, as described in Table 11-1.

Table 11-1. *Interpolation Metacharacters*

Character	Action
\	Interpolate a metacharacter or character code (compile time).
$	Interpolate a scalar variable or evaluate an expression in scalar context (run time).
@	Interpolate an array variable or evaluate an expression in list context (run time).

Perl will look to interpolate a string whenever it sees double quotes, the qq operator (which is equivalent to double quotes), backticks (which is equivalent to a [qx] operator), or a regular expression. If at compile time Perl notes that a string contains interpolatable content, it will expand any static content, such as special characters, and note the presence of any variables or other dynamic content that cannot be expanded until the code is executed. If the string contains no, or only static, interpolatable content, then the string is processed entirely at compile time. Perl will quickly figure out that a string does not need to be expanded at run time, so it costs us very little at compile time and nothing at run time to use double quotes around a string that does not interpolate.

Interpolating Metacharacters and Character Codes

The backslash character, \, allows us to insert characters into strings that would otherwise be problematic to type, not to mention display. The most common of these is \n, which we have used a great deal to produce a linefeed. Other common examples include \t for a tab character, \r for a return, and \e for escape. Table 11-2 provides a brief list of them.

Table 11-2. *Interpolation Metacharacters*

Character	Description
\000..\377	An ASCII code in octal.
\a	Alarm (ASCII 7).
\b	Backspace (ASCII 8).
\c<chr>	A control character (for example, \cg is ctrl-g, ASCII 7, same as \a).
\e	Escape character (ASCII 27).
\E	End effect of \L, \Q, or \U.
\f	Form feed (new page) character (ASCII 12).
\l	Lowercase next character.
\L	Lowercase all following characters to end of string or \E.
\n	Linefeed (newline) character (ASCII 10 on Unix, 10+13 on Windows, etc.).
\N{name}	A named character.
\Q	Escape (backslash) all nonalphanumeric characters to end of string or \E.
\r	Return character (usually ASCII 13).
\t	Tab character (ASCII 8).
\u	Uppercase next character.
\U	Uppercase all following characters to end of string or \E.
\x<code>	An ASCII code 00 to ff in hexadecimal.
\x{<code>}	A UTF8 Unicode character code in hexadecimal.
\\ \$ \@ \"	A literal backslash, dollar sign, at sign, or double quote. The backslash disables the usual metacharacter meaning. These are actually just the specific cases of general escapes that are most likely to cause trouble as unescaped characters.

Some metacharacters are specific and generate a simple and consistent character. Others, like \0..\7, \c, \x, and \N, take values that produce characters based on the immediately following text. The \l and \u metacharacters lower the case of, or capitalize, the immediately following character, respectively. Finally, the \L, \Q, and \U metacharacters affect all characters after them until the string ends or a \E is encountered.

The Magic Linefeed

The \n metacharacter is unusual in this list in that it does not evaluate to a single known character. Instead, it evaluates to whatever a linefeed is on the platform of execution. For Unix, it is the line-feed character, which is equivalent to ASCII code 10. On a Windows system, it is a return followed by a linefeed, equivalent to ASCII codes 12 + 10. On a Macintosh, it is the reverse. In practice, \n is defined by the underlying platform to do the right thing. For networking applications, however, we might be better off specifying newlines explicitly to get universally predictable results. Either octal codes or the \c metacharacter will do this for us. Note that the numbers are octal, not decimal, so 012 in the following example is really 10 in decimal, while 015 is 12 in decimal:

```
print "This is a new line in octal \012\015";
print "This is a new line in control characters \cM\cJ";
```

Special Effects: Uppercase, Lowercase, and Quotemeta

Perl provides five metacharacters, \l, \u, \L, \Q, and \U, that affect the text following them. The low-ercase characters affect the next character in the string, whereas the uppercase versions affect all characters until they are switched off again with \E or reach the end of the string.

The \l and \u characters modify the case of the immediately following character, if it has a case to change. Note that the definition of lower- and uppercase is locale dependent and varies between character sets. If placed at the beginning of a string, they are equivalent to the lcfirst and ucfirst functions:

```
print "\lPolish";    # produce 'polish'
print "\uperl";      # produce 'Perl'
```

The \L and \U characters by contrast affect all characters that follow and are equivalent to the lower and upper functions, stopping only if a \E, the opposing operation, or the end of the string is encountered:

```
print "This is \Uupper\E case\n";    # produces UPPER
print "This is \LLOWER\E case\n";    # produces lower
```

We can also combine both types of metacharacter. Putting \l or \u inside a \L...\E or \U...\E produces no useful effect, but we can immediately precede such a section to reverse the effect on the first character:

```
$surname = "rOBOTHAM";
print "\u\L$surname\E";    # produces 'Robotham'
```

This is equivalent to using print ucfirst(lower $surname) but avoids two function calls.

The \Q metacharacter is similar to \L and \U, and like them affects all following characters until stopped by \E or the end of the string. The \Q metacharacter escapes all nonalphanumeric characters in the string following it and is equivalent to the quotemeta function. We discuss it in more detail in the section "Protecting Strings Against Interpolation" later in this chapter. Note that there is no \q metacharacter, since a single backslash performs this function on nonalphanumeric characters, and alphanumeric characters do not need escaping.

Interpolating Variables

Other than embedding otherwise hard-to-type characters into strings, the most common use of interpolation is to insert the value of variables, and in particular, scalars. This is the familiar use of interpolation that we have seen so far:

```
$var = 'Hello World';
print "Greetings, $var \n";
```

There is no reason why we cannot chain several interpolated strings together, as in

```
$var = 'Hello';
$message = "$var World";
$full_message = "$message \n";
print "Greetings, $full_message";   # print 'Greetings, Hello World'
```

Conversely, there is no point to interpolating a string that contains just a scalar variable, like this:

```
open FILE, "$filename"; # pointless use of interpolation
```

While this statement works, the quotes perform no useful purpose and merely serve to obfuscate the code. The same is not true for arrays, however.

Arrays also interpolate, but not quite in the way that we might expect. One of Perl's many "smart" features is that it notices arrays and automatically separates their values with spaces when interpolating them into a string. This is more useful than directly concatenating the values, which we can in any case achieve by printing an array outside of interpolation where the values usually run together, as shown here:

```
@array = (1, 2, 3, 4);
$\ = "\n";

print @array;     # display '1234'
print "@array";   # display '1 2 3 4'
$, =', ';         # change the output field separator
print @array;     # display '1, 2, 3, 4'
print "@array";   # still display '1 2 3 4'
$"=':';           # change the interpolated list separator
print "@array";   # display '1:2:3:4'
```

Whereas printing an array explicitly uses the output field separator $,, just as an explicit list of scalars does, arrays and lists evaluated in an interpolative context use the interpolated list separator $", which is by default set to a space (hence the result of the first interpolation in the preceding example).

If we try to interpolate a variable name and immediately follow it with text, a problem arises. Perl will think that the text is part of the variable name because it has no reason to assume otherwise. It will end the variable name at the first character that is not legal in variable names. For instance, the following does not work (or at least, does not do what we expect):

```
$var = "Hello ";
print "Greetings, $varWorld \n";   # try to interpolate $varWorld
```

We can fix this by splitting the string into two after $var, but this rather defeats the point of interpolation. We can instead keep the string together by delimiting the variable name within curly braces:

```
print "Greetings, ${var}World \n";   # interpolate $var
```

Note that although this looks reminiscent of dereferencing a scalar reference, it actually has nothing to do with it. However, a related trick allows us to embed code into interpolated strings, as we will see in a moment.

Variable interpolation works on any valid variable name, including punctuation. This includes array indices, hash keys (but not hashes), and even the maximum-array-index notation $#:

```
@ary = (1, 2, 3, 4);
$aref = \@ary;
%hsh = @ary;        # 1=>2, 3=>4

print "$#ary";       # display 3 (number of elements)
print "$ary[2]";     # display 3 (the value of the third element)
```

```
print "$aref->[2]";    # same again, via a reference
print "@{$aref}[2]";   # same again, different syntax
print "$hsh{1}";       # displays key '1', value 2
```

Hashes are not interpolated by Perl. This is partly because there is no clear single representation of a hash in string form, partly because the keys of a hash are not extracted in a predictable order, and partly because to do so would require that a fourth character, %, would have to be given special meaning in interpolated strings.

Interpolating Code

We can interpolate code too. How we embed code depends on whether the result should be interpreted as a scalar or a list. This is not just a case of whether one value or several is expected. It's also a matter of the context, scalar or list, that the code runs in. To embed and evaluate code in a scalar context, we use the delimiters ${\ and }, which reads as a dereference of a scalar reference. The additional reference constructors (backslash and square brackets) are what distinguish embedded code from an explicitly defined variable name. For example:

```
# print out the data from first 10 characters of scalar 'gmtime'
print "Today is ${\ substr(scalar(gmtime), 0, 10) } \n";
```

To embed and evaluate in list context, we use @{[and]}, that is, a dereference of an anonymous array reference. For example:

```
# print out the keys of a hash
print "Keys: @{[keys %hash]}";
```

Here is a more complex example that calls gmtime and uses only the hours, minutes, and seconds out of the list of values it returns:

```
# print out the time, hms
print "The time is @{[reverse((gmtime)[0..2])]} exactly \n";
```

Note that the interpolated list separator $" applies to any list context, whether a literal interpolated array or the return values of code as just shown, so the hours, minutes, and seconds are separated by spaces in the output.

In order for code to embed properly, it must return a value. In other words, it must be an expression and not a statement. This means that we cannot use constructs like foreach loops to build lists or execute an if statement. However, it's possible to use alternate versions of these constructs that do return an expression. In the case of a condition, the ternary ?: operator will do just fine. In the case of a loop, the map or grep functions can do the same work as a foreach loop, but they return a value too. We are interpolating, after all, and to execute code with no effect on the string would be a strange thing to want to do. Here is an example of a map expression being interpolated:

```
# subtract each array element from its maximum index
print "Mapping \@ary:@{[map{$_ = $#ary-$_}@ary]}\n";
```

Rather than embedding expressions, we might consider calling out to subroutines to do most of the heavy lifting. The same rules apply as before; we need to define the context, scalar or list, that the subroutine is called with. For subroutines that return a scalar value, we use the scalar reference-dereference syntax, and for subroutines that return a list, we use the array reference-dereference syntax:

```
my $answer      = "The answer is ${\ get_answer($question) }.\n";
my $commandline = "You entered: @{[ get_options(@ARGV) ]}.\n";
```

Constants defined by the use constant pragma can also be conveniently expanded and interpolated, since they are subroutines:

```
use constant now => scalar localtime;
print "The time is ${\now()}\n";
```

Inside the subroutine we could react to the context with `wantarray` if we want to, and handle list context too, just as normal. However, if the subroutine actually returns a scalar or array reference, then we can use it without the reference creation part of the syntax, and just dereference it. Here is a trivial example of interpolating a subroutine that returns a reference to a string:

```
#!/usr/bin/perl
# interpscalarrefsub.pl
use warnings;
use strict;

sub now { return \scalar(localtime) };

print "The time is ${&now}\n";
```

Embedding code into strings is certainly possible, but before embarking on such a task, it is worth considering whether it is practical; for a start, it is not naturally inclined to legibility. It also bypasses Perl's compile-time syntax checking, since the code is not evaluated until Perl tries to interpolate the string at run time. In this sense it is (slightly) similar to an `eval`, except that it is evaluated in the current context rather than defining its own.

Where Interpolation Happens

Interpolation happens in a number of different places. The most obvious and common are double quotes and the double quote operator `qq`:

```
print "@ary";
print qq(@ary);
```

Backtick-quoted strings also interpolate their contents, as does the `qx` operator, which is their equivalent:

```
$files = `ls $directory`;    # Or 'dir' for a Windows system
$files = qx(ls $directory);
```

The `qx` operator can be prevented from interpolating if its delimiters are changed to a single quote. This is a mnemonic special case:

```
$ttytype = qx'echo $TERM';    # getting it from %ENV is simpler!
```

Note that `eval` statements will interpolate quotes inside the strings that they evaluate. This is not the same as simply giving `eval` a double-quoted string—that is just regular double-quoted interpolation, which is then passed to `eval`. What we mean is that double quotes inside string variables causes `eval` to interpolate the strings. We will see how useful that is in a moment.

While we are on the subject of quotes and quoting operators, the `qw` operator does not interpolate, and neither of course does `q`, which wouldn't be expected to, since it is the equivalent of a single quote as we noted back in Chapter 3.

Interpolation in Regular Expressions

The final place where interpolation occurs is in regular expressions, and these are the focusing points of this chapter. In the following example, `$pattern` is given a single-quoted value, yet it is interpolated when used as a regular expression:

```
$input = <>;
# match any pair of alphanumeric characters separated by space
$pattern = '\w\s\w';
```

```
# $pattern is interpolated when treated as a regular expression
print "Yes, got a match \n" if $input =~ /$pattern/;
```

Since the variable value may change, interpolation happens each time the regular expression is evaluated, unless we use the /o flag. This can be an important time saver, since interpolation can be an involved process, but it has its own caveats, as we shall see later in the chapter.

Interpolation does not just include regular expressions in match and substitution operations. It also includes functions like split, which (as many programmers forget and thereby end up being considerably confused) takes a regular expression as its first argument, and the qr operator.

Unfortunately, the syntax of regular expressions collides with ordinary variable names as seen in an interpolated string. In particular, an array index looks like a regular expression character class (which is denoted by a pair of square brackets):

```
$match = /$var[$index]/;
```

This could either mean the value of $var followed by one of the characters $, i, n, d, e, or x, or it could mean the $index element of the array variable @var. To resolve this, Perl tries to accommodate by looking for @var, and if it finds it, it will try to return an element if $index looks at all reasonable (the number 3 would be reasonable, a string value would not). If there is no @var, or $index does not look like an index value, then Perl will look for $var and treat the contents of the square brackets as a character class instead. Clearly this is prone to breakage as the program evolves, so we are better off rewriting the expression to avoid this guesswork if possible.

Substitutions also carry out interpolation in the replacement text, but only on a successful match, so embedded code in the replacement text will only be executed if a match is found.

```
$text =~ s/($this|$that|$other)/$spare/;
```

Interpolating Text Inside Variables

So far we have only looked at interpolation in literal strings. However, it is sometimes useful to cause Perl to interpolate over text in a string variable. Unfortunately, the trick to doing this is not immediately obvious—if we interpolate the variable name, we get the text that it contains as its value, but the text itself remains uninterpolated:

```
@array = (1, 2, 3, 4);
$text = '@array';   # note the single quotes!
print "$text";      # produce '@array'
```

In fact, the solution is simple once we see it—use eval and supply the variable to be interpolated directly to it:

```
print eval $text;   # produce 1234
```

This is not actually interpolation, but it points the way toward it. This particular example works because the content of $text is a valid Perl expression, that is, we could replace $text with its contents, sans quotes, and the resulting statement would still be legal. We can see that no quotes (and therefore no interpolation) are involved because the output is 1234, not 1 2 3 4, as it would be if $" had taken effect.

To produce interpolation inside string variables, we combine eval with double quotes inside the string, that is, around the string value:

```
$text = 'The array contains: @array';
print eval '"'.$text.'"'; # produce 'The array contains: 1 2 3 4'
print eval "\"$text\"";   # an alternative way to do the same thing
print eval qq("$text");   # and another
```

Adding literal double quotes to the string without causing a syntax error, disabling interpolation, or otherwise going wrong takes a little thought. Simply enclosing the whole string in single quotes stops the eval seeing double quotes as anything other than literal quote symbols. The correct way to interpolate is either to concatenate double quotes, as in the first example just shown, or use literal double quotes inside regular ones, as in the second and third.

Protecting Strings Against Interpolation

Sometimes we may want to protect part or all of a body of text against interpolation. The most obvious way to do that is to just use single quotes and combine variables into the string through concatenation:

```
$contents = '@array contains'. join(', ',@array). "\n";
```

It is easy to accidentally put characters that can be interpolated into a string. One common mistake is to forget the @ in e-mail addresses, as in the following example, which interpolates an array called @myself:

```
$email = "my@myself.com";
```

We can use a backslash to escape any dollar sign, at sign, or backslash that should be left alone:

```
print "\@array";   # produce '@array'
```

This is inconvenient, however, and prone to errors. It also does not take into account the fact that the text might have been generated dynamically. A better solution is to get Perl to do the job for us. One simple way of completely protecting a string is to pass it through a regular expression:

```
# escape all backlashes, at signs, and dollar characters
$text = 'A $scalar, an @array and a \backslash';
$text =~ s/([\$\@\\])/\\$1/mg;
print $text;   # produce 'A \$scalar, an \@array and a \\backslash'
```

Unfortunately, this regular expression requires many backslashes to make sure the literal characters remain literal, which makes it hard to read. Even in the character class we need extra backslashes because both $@ and @$ have meanings that can be interpolated. The \ in front of the @ symbol is the only one that is not actually required, but we have added it for consistency anyway. A better way to do the same thing is with Perl's built-in quotemeta function. This runs through a string using backslashes to escape all nonalphanumeric characters, so it also escapes quotes, punctuation, and spaces. While this might not be important for interpolation, it makes strings safe for passing to shells with reasonable quoting rules (which is to say most Unix shells, but not the various standard Windows shells). It also makes it safe to use user-inputted strings in a regular expression:

```
$text = '"$" denotes a scalar variable';
$text = quotemeta $text;
print $text;   # display '\"\$\"\ denotes\ a\ scalar\ variable'
print eval qq("$text");   # display '"$" denotes a scalar variable'
```

The quotemeta function uses $_ if no explicit variable is passed, making it possible to write loops like this:

```
foreach (@unescaped_lines) {
    print "Interpolating \"", quotemeta, "\" produces '$_' \n";
}
```

The quotemeta function can also be triggered in every part of a string by inserting the metacharacters \Q and \E around the text to be protected. This use of quotemeta is primarily intended for use in regular expressions. It allows us to protect sensitive characters in interpolated variables used in the search pattern from being interpreted as regexp syntax, as this example illustrates:

```
$text = "That's double+ good";
$pattern = "double+";
print "Matched" if $text =~ /\Q$pattern/; # return 'Matched'
$text = "That's double plus good";
print "Matched" if $text =~ /$pattern/;   # (incorrectly) return 'Matched'
print "Matched" if $text =~ /\Q$pattern/; # do not match, return nothing.
$pattern = quotemeta($pattern);
print "Matched" if $text =~ /$pattern/;   # now pattern doesn't match,
                                          # returns nothing.
```

Without the \Q, the pattern would match double (and doublee, and so on), which is not what we intended. As the last example shows, it is as easy to use quotemeta as it is to use \Q when we want to protect the entire string.

Although quotemeta also works on literal strings, the effects can be counterintuitive, since the special interpolation characters \, @, and $ will not be escaped—they are interpreted literally and the contents escaped instead:

```
$variable = "contains an @ character";
print "\QThis string $variable\E";
# produces 'This\ string\ contains\ an\ \@\ character'
```

Regular Expressions

The regular expression, also called *regex* or *regexp*, is a syntax for expressing search patterns for finding and extracting matches within text. Regexps have a long history, and Perl's implementation was inspired a great deal by the regexp engine of the Unix utility awk. A good understanding of Perl's regular expression engine is an invaluable skill for making the most of the language. Here is a simple example that uses . to match any character, just for illustration:

```
my $matchtext=<>;
print "Matched!" if $matchtext =~ /b.ll/;
# match 'ball', 'bell', 'bill', 'boll', 'bull', ...
```

The phrase "search pattern" seems simple enough—the preceding one means "find a 'b', then any character, then an 'l' followed by another 'l'"—but we can use them to state much more complex criteria. These can involve repetitions, alternative characters or words, character classes, look-ahead and look-behind conditions, and even rematching sequences of previously found text. Regular expression patterns may match more than once if we so choose, and we can write loops to handle each match or extract them all as strings into a list. We can control case sensitivity and the position from which subsequent match attempts start and find multiple matches allowing or disallowing overlapping. We also have the choice to use variables to define part or all of the pattern, because Perl interpolates the search pattern before using it. This interpolation can be an expensive process, so we also have means to optimize it.

A key to writing good regular expressions is to understand the guiding principles of how the engine seeks a match. Perl's regular expression engine works on three basic principles, in this order:

- *Eagerness*: It will try to match as soon as possible.

- *Greediness*: It will try to match as much as possible.

- *Relentlessness*: It will try every possible combination before giving up.

Programmers new to regexps are often surprised when their patterns do not produce the desired effects. Regexps are literal-minded—they will always match the first set of criteria that satisfies the pattern, irrespective of whether or not a "better" match might occur later. They will also find a match, even a wildly inappropriate one (from the point of view of the programmer), if we do not define our search pattern precisely enough. This is perfectly correct behavior, but to make use of regexps effectively, we need to think carefully about what we want to achieve.

During the course of this chapter, we will cover all the various aspects of regexps, from simple literal patterns to more complex ones. First we will take a brief look at how and where regexps are used.

Where Regular Expressions Occur

Regexps occur in a number of places within Perl. The most obvious are the match and substitution operators. However, a fact sometimes overlooked is that the split function also uses a regexp. We just don't notice if we don't split on a string that contains characters with meaning to Perl's regular expression engine.

We can also precompile regexps with the qr quoting operator. This operator does not actually trigger the regexp engine, but carries out the interpolation and compilation of a regexp so that it need not be repeated later. This allows us to prepare a potentially long and complex regexp ahead of time and then refer to it through a variable, which can provide an advantage in terms of both speed and legibility.

It is worth mentioning the transliteration operator tr (or equivalently, y) because it does not take a regular expression argument despite having a syntax that closely resembles the match and substitution operators. However, it does have some aspects in common, which are also covered here.

Matching and Substitution

The match operator, m//, and substitution operator, s///, are the main interfaces to Perl's regexp engine. Both operators attempt to match supplied text to a pattern and bind to the search text with the =~ or !~ operators. If the match succeeds, a substitution operation will then replace the text matched with the supplied substitution text.

As with the quoting operators, we can pick our own delimiters. For matching, but not substitution, we can drop the m if we stick to //. In the following case, we are looking for the text proton:

```
# true if $atom contains the text 'proton'
if ($atom =~ /proton/) {
    ...
}
```

A substitution uses the same regular expression pattern but also supplies the text for substitution:

```
# replace first occurrence of 'proton' with 'neutron'
$atom =~ s/proton/neutron/;
```

The result of the =~ operator is true if the regular expression matches, and false otherwise. In the first example, we use the result to control an if statement. In the substitution we don't bother to check the result, but we could if we choose to. The difference between =~ and !~ is only that the latter logically negates the result, so it returns true for a failed match. For example, to check that $atom does not in fact contain a proton, we could write

```
if ($atom !~ /proton/) {
    print "No protons here!";
}
```

The !~ operator is more useful than it might seem, since it turns out to be very hard to test for nonmatches within a regexp. This is due to the regexp engine's relentless checking of all possible matches before giving up. We will come back to this later.

It is important to realize that =~ is not a relative of the assignment operator =, even though it looks like one. Novice Perl programmers in particular sometimes write ~= by mistake, thinking that it follows the same pattern as combined operators, like +=. It is also important not to place a space between the = and ~. This would mean an assignment and a bitwise NOT, legal Perl but not what we intended.

If neither binding operator is used, both the match and substitution operators default to using $_ as their input. This allows us to write very concise Perl programs when used in combination with functions that set $_. For instance, this while loop uses a regexp to skip past lines that look like comments, that is, the first non-whitespace character is a #:

```
while (<>) {
    next if /^\s*#/;    # test $_ and reject comments
    print $_;
}
```

Similarly, this foreach loop applies the regular expressions to $_ in the absence of an explicit iterator:

```
foreach (@particles) {
    /proton/   and print("A positive match \n"), last;
    /electron/ and print("Negative influence \n"), last;
    /neutron/  and print("Ambivalent \n"), last;
}
```

The split Function

The split function also takes a search pattern as its first argument. Since Perl knows the first argument is a regular expression, we can use any valid quoting characters, including ordinary single or double quotes. Consequently, the regular expression nature of the first argument is not immediately obvious from many normal uses of split, as in

```
# split text into pieces around commas
@values = split (',',$text);
```

The search pattern here only matches a single comma, so we do not notice any special behavior. However, we can replace the comma with a regexp to remove whitespace from the returned items. This is done using the special whitespace metacharacter \s in combination with the * modifier, to match on zero or more occurrences. Consider the following example, written with single quotes and again with regexp-style forward slashes, just to underline the point that the first argument is a regular expression:

```
# split text into pieces around commas plus whitespace
@values = split('\s*,\s*',$text);

# the same statement written in a more regexp style
@values = split /\s*,\s*/,$text;
```

Note that this example does not handle leading whitespace at the start of the string or trailing whitespace at the end. We can fix that using a different regexp, which we will see in just a moment.

Just as with the matching and substitution functions, split binds to $_ if it is given no search text to work on. This lets us write split expressions with only one argument:

```
@csv = split /,/;    # split $_ on commas
```

▓**Tip** Before using this example to handle real comma-separated data, note this does not handle quoted commas. Use Text::CSV or Text::Balanced (covered in Chapter 18) instead.

If split is given no parameters at all, it splits $_ on whitespace. More accurately, it splits on the special pattern ' ' (which is special only to split). It is equivalent to \s+ except that it does not return an initial empty value if the match text starts with whitespace:

```
# split $_ on whitespace, explicitly (leading whitespace returns an empty
# value)
@words = split /\s+/,$_;

# split $_ on whitespace, implicitly (leading whitespace does not return an
# empty value)
@words = split;

# The same as 'split' on its own
@words = split ' ';
```

If we actually want to split on single spaces, we supply split with a literal regexp instead. This is the one time when it makes a difference what the delimiters are:

```
# split on individual spaces
@words = split / /;
```

The split function does not use =~ or !~, which is largely the point. Its functionality can be easily replicated using a match regexp, but split reads a lot better and pairs up with the join keyword that performs the opposite operation.

Precompiled Regular Expressions

The qr operator is a member of Perl's family of quoting operators. It takes a string and compiles it into a regexp, interpolating it as it goes unless a single quote is used as the delimiter. This is exactly the same way the match operator deals with it. For example, here is a particularly hairy piece of regexp (complete with some trailing modifiers, just for illustrative purposes):

```
# an arbitrary complex regexp, precompiled into $re
my $re = qr/^a.*?\b ([l|L]ong)\s+(and|&)\s+(?:$complex\spattern)/igsm;
```

Once compiled, we can use the regexp in our code without ever having to define it again:

```
# 'if' statement is much more legible...
if ($text =~ $re) { ... }
```

The qr operator has many more other advantages: it is more legible, and as it is not recompiled each time the regexp is used, it is faster. There are other things we can do with the qr operator in combination with other regexp features, as we will see.

Regular Expression Delimiters

All forms of regexp can use delimiters other than the forward slash, though the match operator must include them if any other delimiter is used:

```
$atom =~ /proton/;              # traditional match, no 'm'
$atom =~ m|proton|;             # match with pipes
$atom =~ m ?proton?;            # match with a space and question marks
$atom =~ s/proton/neutron/;     # traditional substitution
$atom =~ s|proton|neutron|;     # substitution with pipes
$atom =~ s'proton'neutron';     # substitution with single quotes
my @items = split m|\s+|,$text; # split using pipes
my @items = split(',',$text);   # traditional split using quotes
```

This last example explains why we can supply something like , to split and have it work. The single quotes are really regexp delimiters and not a single-quoted string. It just happens to look that way to the untutored eye. Single quotes also have an additional meaning, which we will come to in a moment.

Another reason for changing the delimiter is to avoid what is known as LTS or *Leaning Tooth-pick Syndrome*, where literal forward slashes must be escaped with backslashes to avoid them being misinterpreted as the end of the pattern:

```
# match expression with forward slashes
if ($path =~ /\/usr\/local\/lib\/perl5/) { ... }

# same expression using pipes
if ($path =~ m|/usr/local/lib/perl5/|) { ... }
```

We can even use a # as a delimiter, so long as a space is not inserted between the operator and the first delimiter:

```
$atom =~ s#proton#neutron#;     # substitution with '#' signs
$atom =~ s #proton#neutron#;    # ERROR: 's' followed by a comment
```

In fact, we can even use alphanumeric characters as a delimiter, but since regexps such as msg$mmsg are pathologically unfriendly, it is not encouraged. (That regular expression would be better written /sg$/msg, for those still trying to figure it out.)

The delimiters may also be paired characters like brackets and braces:

```
$atom =~ s{proton}{neutron};
```

All of the following character pairs can be used in this fashion:

```
()   []   {}   <>
```

Using a pair of characters provides another benefit when using the substitution operator; it allows the pattern and its replacement to be placed on separate lines:

```
$atom =~ s{proton}     # the pattern
          {neutron};    # the replacement
```

The only drawback to this style is that the braces might be mistaken for blocks of code, especially when the /e trailing modifier is involved. It is a good idea to make the delimiters stand out from the surrounding code as well; which one is the most suitable depends upon the circumstances.

It is not even necessary for the delimiters of the pattern to be the same as those of the replacement (though how comprehensible this might be is another matter):

```
$atom =~ s[proton]<neutron>;
```

If the delimiter is a single quote, then interpolation is not carried out on the pattern. This allows us to specify characters like dollar signs, at signs, and normal forward slashes and backslashes without using backslashes to escape them from special interpretation:

```
$atom =~ m/$proton/;   # match contents of $proton
$atom =~ m'$proton';   # match '$proton'
```

If the delimiter is a question mark, a special one-shot optimization takes place inside the regexp engine:

```
?proton?   # match proton once only
```

This pattern will never match again, even if we test it multiple times from inside a loop. The only way to reactivate it is with the no-argument form of reset, which resets all one-shot patterns in the same package scope:

```
reset;   # reset one-shot patterns in current package
```

This said, ?-delimited regexps are rare, and their benefits dubious. If the intent is to prevent a variable interpolation from occurring more than once, then similar (though not as thorough) effects can be obtained more traditionally with the /o pattern match modifier detailed later. It is even possible that this syntax may disappear completely one day.

Elements of Regular Expressions

Before getting into the details of regexp syntax, let's take a brief look at four of the most important elements of regexp syntax. We will cover each of these in much more detail shortly, so this is just a quick roundup to keep in mind as we progress. Once we have a preliminary idea of these four aspects of regexps, we will be able to use them in other examples before we get to the nitty-gritty of exactly what they are and what features they provide:

- Metacharacters
- Pattern match modifiers
- Anchors
- Extended patterns

The role of a regexp is to match within the text to which it is applied. The simplest regexps consist of nothing more than literal characters that must be present in the string for the match to succeed. Most of the regular expressions we have seen so far fall into this category. For example:

```
$match = $colors =~ /red/;   # literal pattern 'red'
```

Here the variable $match is set to 1 if the variable $colors contains the text red at any point and is undefined otherwise. Although this pattern is perfectly functional, it has some major limitations. It cannot discriminate between finding a word and part of another word, for instance, both shred and irredeemable are valid matches. One way to test for a specific word is to check for spaces around it. We could do that with an explicit space, or

```
$match = $colors =~ / red /;    # match ' red '
```

A better way of doing this is using metacharacters. Perl provides several metacharacters for regexps that handle common cases, including \s, which matches any whitespace character, including spaces, tabs, and newlines. These resemble interpolated metacharacters like \n, but they only have meaning within regular expressions. For instance, if we just want to pick out words, using \s is better than using a space, since it matches more cases.

```
$match = $colors =~ /\sred\s/;   # match ' red ', '<tab>red\n' ...
```

However, neither method is particularly effective, because they do not cater to cases such as the word occurring at the beginning or end of the text or even punctuation like quotes, colons, and full stops. A better solution is to use another metacharacter that matches the boundary between words and the surrounding text:

```
$match = $colors =~ /\bred\b/;
```

The boundary, defined by \b, is where a word character (defined as alphanumeric plus underscore) falls adjacent to a nonword character or at either end of the string. As a result, it catches many more cases than the previous examples. Interestingly, it does not match any actual text characters and is therefore what is called a *zero-width assertion*.

Finally, we might want to match the word red, regardless of its case. To do that, we can use a pattern match modifier (or trailing modifier) that is placed after the pattern of a regular expression. Other available modifiers include /g for multiple matches and /x to allow documentation within a search pattern (both of which are covered in detail shortly). In this case, we want the /i modifier to turn off case sensitivity:

```
$match = $colors =~ /\bred\b/i;   # match 'red', 'RED', 'rEd' ...
```

We can also anchor a regular expression so that it matches only at the beginning or the end of the match text. To anchor at the beginning, we prefix the pattern with a caret:

```
$match = $colors =~ /^red/;   # match 'red' at the start of the string
```

Likewise, to anchor at the end, we use a dollar sign:

```
$match = $colors =~ /red$/;   # match 'red' at the end of the string
```

We can even use both together, which on a simple pattern like this is equivalent to using the eq comparison operator:

```
$match = $colors =~ /^red$/;   # match whole line to 'red'
$match = ($colors eq 'red');   # the same thing, with 'eq'
```

Beyond the basic features of regular expressions, Perl also defines a whole range of so-called *extended patterns* that can be used to modify the nature of subpatterns (that is, parts of a pattern). Two that are particularly useful are the zero-width look-ahead assertion, which matches the text ahead without absorbing it, and the clustering modifier, which allows grouping without the other side effects of parentheses:

```
(?=zerowidth)              # match but do not move forward in text
(?:no|value|extracted|here)  # group terms but do not extract match
```

We will see more of all of those elements of regular expressions in the chapter.

More Advanced Patterns

Literal patterns are quite useful, but they are only the simplest form of regexps that Perl supports. In addition to matching literal characters, we have the ability to match any particular character, a range of characters, or those between alternative substrings. Additionally, we can define optional expressions that may or may not be present or expressions that can match multiple times. Most crucially, we can extract the matched text in special variables and refer to it elsewhere, even inside the regexp.

Matching Arbitrary Characters and Character Classes

Regexps may use the period, ., to match any single character. This immediately gives us more flexibility than a simple literal pattern. For example, the following regular expression (which we saw earlier in the chapter) will match several different words:

```
$matchtext =~ /b.ll/;   # match 'ball', 'bell', 'bill', 'boll', 'bull'...
```

Unfortunately, this is a little too flexible since it also matches bbll, and for that matter bsll bXll, b ll, and b?ll. What we really want to do is restrict the characters that will match to the lowercase vowels only, which we can do with a character class.

A *character class* is a sequence of characters, enclosed within square brackets, that matches precisely one character in the match text. For example, to improve the previous example to match on a lowercase vowel only, we could write

```
$matchtext =~ /b[aeiou]ll/;
# only match 'ball', 'bell', 'bill', 'boll', or 'bull'
```

Similarly, to match a decimal digit, we could write

```
$hasadigit =~ /[0123456789]/;   # match 0 to 9
```

Since matching a range of characters is a common requirement, we can specify the range with a hyphen (minus sign):

```
$hasdigit =~ /[0-9]/;   # also match 0 to 9 (as does the \d metacharacter)
```

Tip As a brief aside, ranges are sensitive to the character set that is in use, as determined by the `use locale` pragma, covered in Chapter 23. However, if we are using ASCII (or an ASCII-compatible character set like Latin-1), which is usually most of the time, this does not make too much difference.

If we want to match the minus sign itself we can, but only if we place it at the beginning or end of the character class. This example matches any math character and also illustrates that ranges can be combined with literal characters inside a character class:

```
$hasmath =~ /[0-9.+/*-]/;
```

Note that the `.` character loses its special meaning inside a character class, as does `*` (match zero or more times). Likewise, the `?`, `(`, `)`, `{`, and `}` characters all represent themselves inside a character class and have no special meanings. We can also replace the `0-9` range with the equivalent `\d` metacharacter within the set:

```
$hasmath =~ /[\d.+/*-]/;
```

Several ranges can be combined together. The following two regexps match any alphanumeric character (according to Perl's definition this includes underscores) and a hexadecimal digit, respectively:

```
$hasalphanum =~ /[a-zA-Z0-9_]/;
$hashexdigit =~ /[0-9a-fA-F]/;
```

Ranges are best used when they cover a simple and clearly obvious range of characters. Using unusual characters for the start or end of the range can lead to unexpected results, especially if we handle text that is expressed in a different character set.

Ranges like `a-z`, `A-Z`, and `0-9` are predictable because the range of characters they define is intuitively obvious. Ranges like `a-Z`, `?-!`, and `é-ü` are inadvisable, since it is not immediately obvious what characters are in the set, and it is entirely possible that a different locale setting can alter the meaning of the range. Even in the simpler case, `a-z` is only a very narrow definition of a lowercase letter. Consider using POSIX character classes like `[:alpha:]`, `[:alphanumeric:]`, or `[:upper:]` where cross-locale portability is important.

The sense of a character class can be inverted by prefixing it with a caret symbol, `^`. This regexp matches anything that is not a digit:

```
$hasnondigit =~ /[^0-9]/; # or equivalently [^\d]
```

Like the minus sign, if we actually want to match a caret, then we just need to place it anywhere but at the start of the class:

```
$hasdigitorcaret =~ /[0-9^]/;
```

If we want to match a closing bracket, we have to get a little more inventive. The backslash is allowed inside character classes and still escapes the character following it. To match a closing square bracket, we need to escape it with backslash, as this example shows:

```
$hasbrackets =~ /[[\]]/;
```

Interestingly, we do not need to escape an opening square bracket (though we can anyway, for clarity's sake) since Perl already knows we are in a character class, and character classes do not nest. Anywhere else in a regexp where we want a literal opening square bracket, we need to escape the special meaning to avoid starting a character class we don't want.

Characters that are meaningful for interpolation also need to be escaped if the search pattern is delimited with anything other than single quotes. This applies to any part of a regexp, not just within a character class. However, since characters like . and * lose their special meaning inside character classes, programmers often forget that $ and @ symbols do not:

```
$bad_regexp =~ /[@$]/;      # ERROR: try to use '$]'
$empty_regexp =~ /[$@]/;    # ERROR: use value of $@
```

We can match these characters by escaping them with a backslash, including the backslash itself:

```
$good_regexp =~ /[\$\@\\]/;  # matches $, @ or \
```

Strangely, the pattern [@] is actually valid, because Perl does not define @] as a variable and so correctly guesses that the closing bracket is actually the end of the character class. Relying on this kind of behavior, however, is dangerous, as we are bound to get tripped up by it sooner or later.

Table 11-3 presents a summary of the standard character class syntax and how different characters behave within it.

Table 11-3. *Character Class Syntax*

Syntax	Action
[	Begin a character class, unless escaped or a class has already been started.
n	Match character n.
n-m	Match characters from n to m.
-	At end of string, match -; otherwise, define a range.
. ? * ( ) { }	Match the literal characters ., ?, (,), { and }.
^	At beginning of string, negate sense of class.
$ @ \	Interpolate, unless escaped or pattern is single quoted.
]	End character class, unless escaped.

Some common classes have metacharacters like \w or \d as shortcuts. From Perl 5.6 onwards, regular expression patterns may also use POSIX and Unicode character class definitions, which understand international character sets and multibyte characters. See Chapter 23 for full details.

Repetition and Grouping

Literal characters and character classes permit us to be as strict or relaxed as we like about what we can match to them, but they still only match a single character. In order to allow repeating matches, we can use one of the three repetition modifiers listed in Table 11-4.

Table 11-4. *Repetition and Grouping Modifiers*

Character	Meaning
?	Match zero or one occurrences.
*	Match zero or more occurrences.
+	Match one or more occurrences

Each of these modifies the effect of the immediately preceding character or character class, in order to match a variable number of characters in the match text. For example, to match bell! or bells!, we could use

```
$ringing =~ /bells?!/;      # match 'bell!' or 'bells!
```

Alternatively, if we use the * modifier, we can match zero or more occurrences of a character:

```
$ringings =~ /bells*!/;    # match 'bell!', 'bells!', 'bellss!', etc.
```

Finally, if we use +, we require at least one match but will accept more:

```
$ringings =~ /bells+!/     # match 'bells!', 'bellss!', etc.
```

Repetition modifiers also work on character classes. For instance, here is one way to match a decimal number using a character class:

```
$hasnumber =~ /[0-9]+/     # match '1', '007, '1701', '2001', '90210', etc.
```

Grouping Optional or Repeated Sequences of Characters

We can use parentheses to define a string of characters, which allows us to match terms rather than just single characters. (Parentheses also extract the matched text, but we are not interested in that property here.) For example, we can match either of the strings such or nonesuch by defining none as an optional term:

```
$such =~ /(none)?such/;    # match either 'such' or 'nonesuch'
```

We can even nest parentheses to allow optional strings within optional strings. This regular expression matches such, nonesuch, and none-such:

```
$such =~ /(none(-)?)?such/  # match 'such', 'nonesuch' or 'none-such'
```

Note that in this case we could have omitted the nested parentheses since they are surrounding only one character. However, the parentheses help to emphasize this and improve the legibility of the pattern.

If we replace the question mark with an asterisk or plus sign, we can match on repeated sequences of characters:

```
$such =~ /(none(-)*)+such/  # match 'nonesuch', 'none-such', 'none--nonesuch',
                            # 'nonenonenone-none-none----none-such'
```

Grouping Alternatives

We can also use parentheses to group terms in a way that are analogous to character classes. The syntax is simple and intuitive; we simply specify the different terms within parentheses separated by a pipe symbol:

```
$such =~ /(none|all)such/;   # match 'nonesuch' or 'allsuch'
```

We can nest grouped terms to produce various interesting effects, for example:

```
$such =~ /(no(ne|t as )|a(ny|ll))such/; # match 'nonesuch', 'not as such',
                                        # 'anysuch', 'allsuch'
```

This regexp uses two inner groups nested inside the outer one. We could equally have used only one group and written

```
$such =~ /(none|not as |any|all)such/;
```

In theory, the first example is more efficient, since we have grouped similar terms by their common characters and only specified the differences. However, Perl's regexp engine is very good at optimizing things like this, and in reality both expressions will execute with more or less the same speed.

In fact, it is not always necessary to use parentheses around the alternatives. We needed it earlier to keep "such" outside the group, but the following is a perfectly legal way to match sharrow, miz, or dloan:

```
$who =~ /sharrow|miz|dloan/;
```

This works because there is no ambiguity about the start of the first term or the end of the last—they are determined by the ends of the pattern. Similarly, any regexp syntax like [ ], ( ), +, *, and so on will also end a set of alternatives:

```
$who =~ /^(.*)sharrow|miz|dloan/;
```

Even if parentheses are not required, many programmers include them anyway, to keep the meaning clear and protect against future extensions of the pattern, which would require the parentheses to be added anyway.

Specifying a Number of Repetitions

We can exercise a greater degree of control over the * and + modifiers by specifying a particular number or range of allowable repetitions. A single specified number of matches takes the form of a number in curly braces:

```
$sheep =~ /ba{2}!/;    # match 'baa!'
```

To define a range, we specify two numbers separated by a comma:

```
$sheep =~ /ba{2,4}!/    # match 'baa!', 'baaa!', or 'baaaa!'
```

We have included a trailing exclamation mark in this example, since without it anything can follow the search pattern, including more as, so the preceding two examples would have been equivalent in their ability to succeed. If we were extracting the matched text with parentheses, that would be another matter of course.

As a special case, if we use a comma to define a range of repetitions but omit the second value, the regexp engine interprets this as "no upper limit." We can match a sheep with unlimited lung volume with

```
$sheep =~ /ba{2,}!/;    # match 'baa!', 'baaaaaaaaaaaa!', etc...
```

From this, it follows that the standard repetition modifiers are just shorthand for the expanded versions shown in Table 11-5.

Table 11-5. *Repetition Modifiers, Expanded*

Character	Meaning
?	Equivalent to {0,1}
*	Equivalent to {0,}
+	Equivalent to {1,}

Note that using interpolation to specify a range with variables is perfectly acceptable, as it is anywhere else in a search pattern. For example, we can supply a variable range at the point of execution by writing something like the following:

```
($min, $max) = (2, 4);
$sheep= "baaa!";
if ($sheep =~ /ba{$min,$max}!/) {    # equivalent to '/ba{2,4}!/'
    print "match \n";
}
```

Number repetitions are useful when we want to find a specific occurrence within the match text. Here's an example that uses a repetition count to find the fourth (and only the fourth) word in a colon-separated list:

```
$text = "one:two:three:four:five";
# extract the 4th field of colon separated data
$text =~ /(([^:]*):?){4}/;
print "Got: $2\n"; # print 'Got: four'
```

What does this actually mean, though? This pattern looks for zero-or-more noncolon characters, followed (optionally) by a colon, and looks four times. The optional colon ensures that we will
match the last field on the line, while the greediness of the pattern ensures that if a colon is present,
everything up to it will be included by the match. Parentheses are used to group the noncolon characters and the colon into a single term for the repetition. They are also used to extract the part of
the text we are interested in (that is, not the colon).

The last line takes advantage of the fact that parentheses also extract the text they match and
make it available to us in a numbered variable. In the preceding example, the numbered variable
$1 represents the match of the *first* set of parentheses, that is, `(([^:]*):?)`. Printing $1, therefore,
would output four:. We are interested in the text matched by the *second* (inner) set of parentheses,
`[^:]*)`, so we print $2. We will be using numbered variable a few times in the next sections before
looking at them in detail in the section "Extracting Matched Text."

Eagerness, Greediness, and Relentlessness

As was mentioned earlier, Perl's regexp engine has three main characteristics that define its behavior. While these rules always hold, they become more important once we start adding repetitions
and groups to our regexps. Wherever a repetition or a group occurs in a search pattern, Perl will
always try to match as much as it can from the current position in the match text. It does this by
grabbing as much text as possible and then working backwards until it finds a successful match.

For instance, when given a regexp like baa+ and a match text of baaaaaaaa, Perl will always find
and return all the as in the match text, though depending on the circumstances, it might take the
engine more or less time to arrive at this final result. However, regexps also match as soon as possible. This means that the left-most match satisfying the search pattern will always be found first,
irrespective of the fact that a bigger match might occur later in the string:

```
$sheep = "baa baaaaa baaaaaaaaaa";
$sheep =~ /baa+/;   # match first 'baa'
```

This is rather like walking across stepping stones; the engine will try to take one really big
stride, and if it can't make it, it will try successively smaller ones until it finds a step it can take. But
that step will always be from wherever the engine is currently standing, which is the position in the
search text it has currently reached. In order to find the longest possible match, we will have to find
all possible matches with the /g pattern match modifier and then pick out the longest. The /g modifier causes the regular expression engine to remember where its position after the pattern has been
matched, then restart from that position the next time. By invoking the pattern repeatedly, such as
from within a loop condition, we extract each matching string in turn:

```
$sheep = "baa baaaaa baaaaaaaaaa";
while ($sheep =~ /(baa+)/g) {
    $match = $1 if length($1) > length($match);
}
# print 'The loudest sheep said 'baaaaaaaaaa''
print "The loudest sheep said '$match' \n";
```

Greediness can lead to counterintuitive results if we forget about it. For example, the following
regexp supposedly matches single-quoted text:

```
$text =~ /'.*'/;   # text contains a single quoted string
```

Unfortunately, although it does indeed do what it should, it does it rather too well. It takes
no account of the possibility that there might be more than one pair of quotes in the match text.

A quote can satisfy the . so the engine will take a big stride and work backwards until it finds the last quote. For example, assume we set $text to a value like

```
$text = "'So,' he said. 'What will you do?'";
```

The regexp /'.*'/ will match the first quote, grab as much as possible, match the last quote, and everything in between—the entire string in other words. One way to fix this is to use a nongreedy match, which we'll cover in a moment. Another is to be more precise about what we actually want. In this case, we don't want any intervening quotes, so our regexp would be better written as

```
$text =~ /'[^']*'/;   # a better match between quotes
```

This says "match a quote, zero or more characters that can be anything *but* a quote, and then another quote." When fed, the previous sample text it will match 'So,' as we intended. We are in trouble if we encounter any text with apostrophes in it, but that's another problem.

Writing regexps is full of traps like this. The regexp engine will always find a match any way it can, regardless of how apparently absurd that match might seem to us. In cases of disagreement, it is the engine that is right, and our search pattern that needs a rethink.

The zero-or-more quantifier, *, is especially good at providing unexpected results. Although it causes whatever it is quantifying to match as many times as possible, it is still controlled by the "as soon as possible" rule. It could also be expressed as "once we have matched as soon as possible, match as much as possible at that point." In the case of *, nothing at all may be the only match at the current position. To illustrate this, the following example attempts to replace spaces with dashes, again using the /g pattern match modifier to match all occurrences within the string:

```
$text =~ s/\s*/-/g;
```

If $text is given a value of something like "journey into space!", we might expect to get this result:

```
journey-into-space!
```

However, \s* matches zero or more spaces. That condition is satisfied not only between the words, but also between each letter (no spaces there) and even at the start and end of the string. So what we actually get is

```
-j-o-u-r-n-e-y-i-n-t-o-s-p-a-c-e-!-
```

This might have been what we wanted, but probably not. The solution in this case is simple, replace the * with a +. However, in larger patterns, problems like this are easier to introduce and harder to spot.

Lean (Nongreedy) Matches

Lean (or more conventionally, *nongreedy*) matches alter the configuration of the regexp engine to change one of the four fundamental rules. Instead of matching as much as possible, the engine will match as little as possible. To make any repetition nongreedy, we suffix it with a question mark. For example, the quantifiers in Table 11-6 are all nongreedy.

Table 11-6. *Nongreedy Patterns*

Pattern	Meaning
(word)??	Match zero or one occurrence.
(word)*?	Match zero or more occurrences.
(word)+?	Match one or more occurrence.
(word){1,3}?	Match one to three occurrences.
(word){0,}?	Match zero or more occurrences (same as *?).

These all have the same meaning as their greedy counterparts, but change the way the pattern tries to satisfy them. Following the rule of "as soon as possible," a regexp will normally grab as much text as possible and try to match "as much as possible." The first successful match is returned. With a nongreedy quantifier, the regexp engine grabs one character at a time and tries to match "as little as possible."

For example, another way we could have solved the single-quote finder we gave earlier would have been to make the "match any characters" pattern nongreedy:

```
$text =~ /'.*?'/    # nongreedy match between quotes
```

Lean matches are not a universal remedy to cure all ills, however, and they should not be used as a quick fix for a poorly designed pattern. For a start, they can be a lot slower than their greedy counterparts. If the preceding text happened to contain a very long speech, a greedy match would find it far faster than a lean one, and the previous solution of /'[^']*'/ is actually far superior.

Additionally, making a match nongreedy does not alter the fact that a regexp will match as soon as possible. This means that a lean match is no more guaranteed to match the shortest possible string than a greedy match is to match the longest possible. For example, take the following, fortunately fictional, company and regexp:

```
$company = "Greely, Greely, and Spatsz";
$partners = $company =~ /Greely.*?Spatsz/;
```

Upon execution, $partners contains the entire string. The reason for this is simple: while it is true that matching from the second Greely would produce a shorter match, the regexp engine doesn't see the second Greely—it sees the first, matches, and then matches the second Greely with .*?. It can only start from the second once it has stepped past the first, to use the stepping-stone analogy. To fix this problem, we need to match repeatedly from each Greely and then take the shortest result. Unfortunately, to do that we need more advanced tools, specifically a custom zero-width assertion. We cover those in the section "Overlapping Matches and Zero-Width Patterns" later in the chapter.

Repetition and Anchors

We have already mentioned anchors, but a few examples of their use in combination with repetition bears discussion. For instance, a common task in Perl scripts is to strip off trailing whitespace from a piece of text. We can do that in a regexp by anchoring a repetition of whitespace (as defined by the \s metacharacter) to the end of the string using the $ anchor:

```
~s/\s+$//;    # replace trailing whitespace with nothing
```

Similarly, if we are parsing some input text and want to skip over any line that is blank or contains only whitespace or whitespace plus a comment (which we will define as starting with a #), we can use a regexp like the one in the following short program:

```
#!/usr/bin/perl
# repanchor1.pl
use warnings;
use strict;

while (<>) {
    chomp;   # strip trailing linefeed from $_
    next if /^(\s*(#.*)?)?$/;   # skip blank lines and comments
    print "Got: $_ \n";
}
```

The regexp here is anchored at both ends. The () and ? state that the entire body of the regexp is optional. A completely blank line will therefore satisfy this pattern and trigger the next iteration of the loop.

If the line is not blank, we have to look inside the body. Here we can match zero or more occurrences of whitespace followed optionally by a # and any text at all, represented by .*. This will match a line containing only spaces, a line starting with zero or more spaces, and then a comment starting with #. But it will not match a line that starts with any other character.

The preceding example is needlessly complex and slow, since a comment line forces the regexp engine to read and match every letter of the comment in order to satisfy the .*. It only needs to do that because the regexp is anchored at the end, and the only reason for that is so we can match the case of an empty line with /^$/. Fortunately, we can make the anchors themselves optional. Since anchors do not match characters, this may not be immediately obvious, but it works nonetheless. Here is a better version of the loop using an improved regexp:

```
#!/usr/bin/perl
# repanchor2.pl
use warnings;
use strict;
while (<>) {
    chomp;   # strip trailing linefeed from $_
    next if /^\s*($|#)/;   # skip blank lines and comments
    print "Got: $_ \n";
}
```

This regexp is only anchored at the beginning. It matches zero or more spaces, followed by either the end of the line or a hash. What comes after the comment marker, if there is one, we neither care about nor check. Note that this syntax works because the end anchor obviously cannot have match text after it. If Perl sees word characters following a dollar sign, it knows that this is a variable to be interpolated; if not, it must be an anchor. The apparent conflict of syntax is therefore not a problem in reality.

This loop behaves no differently from the earlier example, but because the regexp does not have to analyze the whole line to find a match, it completes much faster.

Matching Sequential and Overlapping Terms

One task frequently required of regexps is to check for the presence of several tokens within the match text. This basically comes down to a case of logic: do we want all of the terms or just one of them? If we only want to know if one of them is present, we can use alternatives:

```
$text =~ /proton|neutron/;   # true if either proton or neutron present
```

This regexp is matched if $text contains either sort of particle, a classic or condition. If we want to test that both are present, we have more of a problem; there is no and variant. Instead, we have to divide the problem into two halves:

- Is there a proton, and if so is it followed by a neutron?
- Is there a neutron, and if so is it followed by a proton?

Either of these conditions will satisfy our criteria, so all we need to do is express them as alternatives, as before. The search pattern that implements this logic is therefore

```
$text =~ /(proton.*neutron|neutron.*proton)/;
```

Sometimes a single regexp is not the best solution to a problem like this. Although fine for just two terms, we'd have to extend this expression to six alternatives for three, containing things like proton.*neutron.*electron. Four does not even bear thinking about. The same thing can be achieved more easily with conventional Boolean logic:

```
$text =~ /proton/ && $text =~ /neutron/;
```

This is better, and certainly more scalable, but differs from the first example in that it will match overlapping terms, whereas the previous example does not. This is because the engine starts all over again at the beginning of the search text for the second regular expression. That is, it will match protoneutron.

If we want to allow matches to overlap inside a single regexp, we have to get a little more clever and use zero-width look-ahead assertions as provided by the (?=...) extended pattern. When Perl encounters one of these, it checks the pattern inside the assertion as normal, but it does not absorb any of the character into the match text. This gives us the same "start over" semantics as the Boolean logic but within the same pattern, invoking the regular expression engine only once rather than twice.

Pattern Match Modifiers

Pattern match modifiers modify the operation of the regular expression engine in matches, substitutions, and splits. We have already seen the /i and /g modifiers to match regardless of case and match more than once, respectively. The full set of pattern match modifiers is shown in Table 11-7.

Table 11-7. *Pattern Match Modifiers*

Modifier	Description
/i	Case insensitive: match regardless of case.
/g	Global match: match as many times as possible.
/c	Preserve position of last match on failure (only with /g).
/m	Treat text as multiple lines: allow anchors to match before and after newline.
/o	Compile once: interpolate and compile the search pattern only once.
/s	Treat text as single line: allow newlines to match.
/x	Expanded regular expression: allow documentation within search pattern.

▓**Note** This list does not include /e or /ee—these do not apply to the pattern, but rather control how the replacement text in substitutions is treated by Perl. We will encounter them later, when we cover substitution.

The convention of describing modifiers as /x rather than x is just that, a convention, since the delimiters of the search pattern can easily be changed. In addition, any combination of modifiers can be applied at one time; they do not all need a forward slash (or whatever delimiter we are using):

```
$matched =~ /fullmonty/igmosx;  # the full monty!
```

All of the pattern match modifiers can be placed at the end of the regexp. With the exception of /g, they can also all be placed within the search pattern to enable or disable one or more modifiers partway through the pattern. To switch on modifiers, we use the syntax (?<flags>), and to switch them off, we use (?-<flags>). By default no modifiers are active, and specifying them at the end of the pattern is equivalent to specifying them inline at the start:

```
$matched =~ /pattern/igm;      # with explicit modifiers
$matched =~ /(?igm)pattern/;   # with inlined modifiers
```

Without enclosing parentheses, the effect of the inline modifier controls the entire pattern coming after them. So, if we wanted to restrict case-insensitive matches of the word "pattern" to the letters "tt" only, we can use this:

```
$matched =~ /pa(?i)tt(?-i)ern/; # 'tt' is case insensitive
```

We can also limit the extent of the inlined modifier with parentheses to equal effect:

```
$matched =~ /pa((?i)tt)ern/;    # 'tt' is case insensitive
```

Since using parentheses to limit the effect of an inline modifier generates possibly unwanted extractions to number variables, we can use the (?:...) extended pattern instead of parentheses to suppress them. Better still, we can combine it with the inline modifier into one extended pattern. Since this extended pattern includes the pattern it controls within its parentheses, the syntax looks a little different. Here is a better way of phrasing the last example that avoids creating a number variable:

```
$matched =~ /pa(?i:tt)ern/;
```

A key difference between a trailing modifier and an inlined one is that an inline modifier can be interpolated into the search pattern:

```
# set flags to either 'i' or ''
$flags = ENV{'CASE_SENSITIVE'}?'':'i';
# interpolate into search pattern for match
if ($input =~ /(?$flags:help|start|stop|reload)|EXIT/) { ... }
```

We can of course use both inline and trailing modifiers at the same time, so we could equivalently have put /i on the end and then (?-i:...) within the pattern to disable it again.

If this approach seems particularly useful, consider using the qr quoting operator instead to precompile regexps, especially if the intent is to control the modifiers over the whole of the search pattern. We cover qr in detail later in the chapter.

Regular Expression Metacharacters

In addition to character class, repetition, and grouping, search patterns may also contain metacharacters that have a special meaning within the search pattern. In fact, there are two distinct groups of metacharacters. Some metacharacters, like \s and \b, which we have seen already, have special meaning only in regular expression patterns. The rest have special meaning in interpolated strings, which includes patterns. We have already looked at interpolation, so here we cover regular expression metacharacters.

We can loosely subdivide regexp metacharacters because regexps contain two fundamentally different kinds of subpattern: patterns that have width and absorb characters when they match, and patterns that have no width and must simply be satisfied for the match to succeed. We call the first *character class metacharacters*. These provide shortcuts for character classes (for example, \s). The second category of regexp metacharacters are called *zero-width metacharacters*. These match conditions or transitions within the text (for example, \b).

Character Class Metacharacters

Several metacharacters are shortcuts for common character classes, matching a single character of the relevant class just as if the character class had been written directly. Most of the metacharacters in this category have an inverse metacharacter with the opposing case and meaning, as shown in Table 11-8.

Table 11-8. *Character Class Metacharacters*

Metacharacter	Match Property
\d	Match any digit—usually equivalent to the character class [0..9].
\D	Match any nondigit—usually equivalent to the character class [^0-9].
\s	Match any whitespace character—equivalent to the character class [\t\r\n].

Continued

Table 11-8. *Continued*

Metacharacter	Match Property
\S	Match any nonwhitespace character—equivalent to the character class [^ \t\r\n] or [^\s].
\w	Match any "word" or alphanumeric character, which is the set of all upper- and lowercase letters, the numbers 0..9, and the underscore character, _, usually equivalent to the character class [a-zA-Z0-9_] unless Unicode is in effect (see [:word:] in Table 11-9) or the locale pragma has been used (so an é will also be considered a match for \w if we are working in French, but not if we are working in English).
\W	The inverse of \w, matches any "nonword" character. Usually equivalent to the character class [^a-zA-Z0-9_] or [^\w].
[:class:]	POSIX character class, for example, [:alpha:] for alphanumeric characters.
\p	Match a property, for example, \p{IsAlpha} for alphanumeric characters.
\P	Match a nonproperty, for example, \P{IsUpper} for nonuppercase characters.
\X	Match a multibyte Unicode character ("combining character sequence").
\C	Match a single octet, even if interpretation of multibyte characters is enabled (with use utf8).

Character class metacharacters can be mixed with character classes, but only as long as we do not try to use them as the end of a range, since that doesn't make sense. The following is one way to match a hexadecimal digit:

```
$hexchar = qr/[\da-fA-F]/;  # matches a hexadecimal digit
$hexnum = qr/$hexchar+/;    # matches a hexadecimal number
```

The negated character class metacharacters have the opposite meaning to their positive counterparts:

```
$hasnonwordchar =~ /\W+/;     # match one or more nonword characters
$wordboundary =~ /\w\W/;      # match word followed by nonword characters
$nonwordornums =~ /[\W\d]/;   # match nonword or numeric characters
$letters =~ /[^\W\d_]/;       # match any letter character
```

The last two examples illustrate some interesting possibilities for using negated character class metacharacters inside character classes. We get into trouble, however, if we try to use two negated character class metacharacters in the same character class:

```
$match_any =~ /[\W\S]/;       # ERROR: match punctuation?
```

The intent of this pattern is to match anything that is not a word character or a whitespace character. Unfortunately for us, the regular expression engine takes this literally. A word character is not a whitespace character, so it matches \S. Likewise, a space is not a word character, so it matches \W. Since the character class allows either to satisfy it, this will match any character and is just a bad way of saying "any character at all." What we really need to do to is to invert the class and use the positive versions:

```
$match_punctuation =~ /[^\w\s]/;   # ok now
```

The POSIX character classes (introduced in Perl 5.6) and "property" metacharacters provide an extended set of character classes for us to use. If the utf8 pragma has been used, the property metacharacter \p follows the same definition as the POSIX equivalent. Otherwise, it uses the underlying C library functions isalpha, isgraph, and so on. Table 11-9 lists the classes and metacharacters available.

Table 11-9. *POSIX Character Classes and Properties*

Description	POSIX Character Classes	Property Metacharacter
Alphabetical character	[:alpha:]	\p{IsAlpha}
Alphanumeric character	[:alnum:]	\p{IsAlnum}
ASCII character	[:ascii:]	\p{IsASCII} (equivalent to [\x00-\x7f])
Control character	[:cntrl:]	\p{IsCntrl} (equivalent to [\x00-\x20])
Numeric	[:digit:]	\p{IsDigit} (equivalent to \d)
Graphical character	[:graph:]	\p{IsGraph} (equivalent to [[:alnum:][:punct:]])
Lowercase character	[:lower:]	\p{IsLower}
Printable character	[:print:]	\p{IsPrint} (equivalent to [[:alnum:][:punct:] [:space:]])
Punctuation	[:punct:]	\p{IsPunct}
Whitespace	[:space:]	\p{IsSpace} (equivalent to \s)
Uppercase character	[:upper:]	\p{IsUpper}
Word character	[:word:]	\p{IsWord} (equivalent to \w)
Hexadecimal digit	[:xdigit:]	\p{IsXDigit} (equivalent to [/0-9a-fA-F/])

POSIX character classes may only appear inside a character class, but the properties can be used anywhere, just like any other metacharacter. For example, to check for a digit, we can use any of the following:

```
/\d/
/\p{IsDigit}/
/[[:digit:]]/
```

The brackets of the POSIX class are part of the character class, so to use one we need two sets of brackets, as the last of the preceding examples shows. We can also use properties inside character classes, as these three equivalent matches illustrate:

```
/[01\w\s89]/
/[0[:word:]18[:space:]9]/
/[\p{IsWord}0189\p{IsSpace}]/
```

We can negate both the class and the metacharacter to get the opposite sense. For the metacharacter, we just use \P instead of \p. For example, to match anything but a numeric character:

```
/\P{IsDigit}/
```

For the class, we can add a caret after the first colon, but note this is a Perl extension and not part of the POSIX standard:

```
/[[:^IsDigit:]]/
```

These sequences are useful for two reasons. First, they provide a standard way of referring to character classes beyond the ones defined by Perl's own metacharacters. Second, they allow us to write regular expressions that are portable to other regular expression engines (that also comply with the POSIX specification). However, note that most of these classes are sensitive to the character set in use, and the locale. \p{IsUpper} is not the same as [A-Z], which is only one very narrow definition of "uppercase," for example. See Chapter 23 for more information on properties as well as many more examples.

Zero-Width Metacharacters

Zero-width metacharacters match conditions within the match text, rather than actual characters. They are called zero-width because they do not consume any characters when they match.

The zero-width metacharacters can be subdivided again into those that deal with transitions, which consist of \b and \B, and those that alter the behavior of anchors in the search pattern, which are \G, \A, \z, and \Z.

The metacharacter \b matches on a word boundary. This occurs whenever a word character, as matched by \w, falls adjacent to a nonword character, as matched by \W, in either order. It is equivalent to (\w\W|\W\w) except that unlike this pattern, \b does not consume any characters from the match text.

The metacharacter \B matches on a nonword boundary. This occurs whenever two word characters or two nonword characters fall adjacent to each other. It is equivalent to (\w\w|\W\W) except that \B does not consume any characters from the match text.

U\A, \z, and \Z metacharacters are only significant if the /m pattern match modifier has been used. /m alters the meaning of the caret and dollar anchors so that they will match after and before (respectively) a newline character \n, usually in conjunction with the /g global match modifier. \A and \z retain the original meanings of the anchors and still match the start and end of the match text, regardless of whether /m has been used or not. In other words, if we are not using /m, then \A and ^ are identical, and the same is true of \z and $.

The uppercase \Z is a variation on \z. It matches at the end of the match text, before the newline if any is present. Otherwise, it is the same as \z.

The \G metacharacter applies when we use a regular expression to produce multiple matches using the g pattern modifier. It re-anchors the regular expression at the end of the previous match, so that previously matched text takes no part in further matches. It behaves rather like a forwardly mobile \A.

The \G, \A, \z, and \Z metacharacters are all covered in more detail in the section "Matching More Than Once."

None of the zero-width metacharacters can exist inside a character class, since they do not match a character. The metacharacter \b, however, can exist inside a character class. In this context it takes on its interpolative meaning and is interpreted by Perl as a backspace:

```
$text =~ /\b/;     # search for a word boundary in $text
$text =~ /[\b]/;   # search for a backspace in $text
$text =~ /\x08/;   # search for a backspace, expressed as a character code
```

It follows that if we want a literal backspace in a search pattern (however unlikely that might be), we need to put it in a character class to prevent it from being interpreted as a zero-width word boundary or write it out as a character code.

Extracting Matched Text

Regular expressions become particularly useful when we use them to return the matched text. There are two principal mechanisms for extracting text. The first is through special variables provided by Perl's regular expression engine, and the second by adding parentheses to the search pattern to extract selected areas. The special variables have the advantage of being automatically available, but they are limited to extracting only one value. Using them also incurs a performance cost for all uses of the regular expression engine, even if they are referred to only once. Parentheses, by contrast, allow us to extract multiple values at the same time without the performance cost. The catch is that they are also used to group terms within a pattern, as we have already seen—this can be either a double bonus or an unlooked-for side effect.

Having extracted a value with parentheses, we can reuse it in the search pattern itself. This is called a *backreference*, and it allows us to perform matches on quotes or locate repeating sequences of characters within the match text.

Finally, the range operator, . ., is very effective at extracting text from between two regexps. In Chapter 4 we mentioned that we would revisit the use of the range operator with regular expressions; we do that here. Before we leave the subject of extracting text, we will consider a few examples that show how effective this operator can be in combination with regexps.

Special Variables

Perl defines several special variables that correspond to the final state of a successfully matched regexp. The most significant of these are the variables $&, $`, and $', which hold the matched text, *all* the text immediately before the match, and *all* the text immediately after the match, respectively. These are always defined by default after any successful match, and with the use English pragma, can also be called by the names $MATCH, $PREMATCH, and $POSTMATCH. Let's look at an example:

```perl
#!/usr/bin/perl
# special.pl
use warnings;
use strict;

my $text = "One Two Three 456 Seven Eight 910 Eleven Twelve";
    while ($text =~ /[0-9]+/g) {
    print " \$& = $& \n \$` = $` \n \$' = $' \n";
}
```

Let's execute this code and review the results:

> **perl special.pl**

```
$& = 456
$` = One Two Three
$' =  Seven Eight 910 Eleven Twelve
$& = 910
$` = One Two Three 456 Seven Eight
$' =  Eleven Twelve
```

The simple regular expression in this example searches for matches of any combination of digits. The first match, 456, gets assigned to $&. The value of $` is then all the text before the match, which is One Two Three .. The rest of the string after the match, Seven Eight 910 Eleven Twelve, is assigned to $'. When the second match is found, the values of all three variables change. $& is now 910, $` is One Two Three 456 Seven Eight , and $' is Eleven Twelve.

One problem with these variables is that they are inefficient because the regexp engine has to do extra work in order to keep track of them. When we said these variables are defined by default, it is not entirely true. They are, in fact, not defined until used, after which all of them are calculated for every executed regexp, and not just the ones that we refer to. Indeed, the English module provides a -no_match_vars option to suppress the definition of English names for these variables for precisely this reason. In general, they are fine for short scripts but should be avoided for larger applications. Even in a short script, if we make any extensive use of modules, we should avoid them.

If we really want to use the values of $&, $`, and $' without having Perl track them for every regexp, we can do so with the special array variables @- and @+. The zeroth elements of these arrays are set to the start and end positions of $& whenever a match occurs. While harder to use, they do not incur the performance penalty either. This modified version of our previous example uses substr and the zeroth elements of @- and @+ to extract the values $&, $`, and $' would have:

```perl
#!/usr/bin/perl
# substr.pl
use warnings;
```

```
use strict;

my $text = "One Two Three 456 Seven Eight 910 Eleven Twelve";
$text =~ /[0-9]+/;
while ($text =~ /[0-9]+/g) {
    my $prefix = substr($text,0,$-[0]);    # equals $`
    my $match = substr($text,$-[0],$+[0]-$-[0]);    # equals $&
    my $suffix = substr($text,$+[0]);    # equals $'
    print " \$match = $match \n \$prefix = $prefix \n \$suffix = $suffix \n";
}
```

Let's execute this script and review the results:

> **perl substr.pl**

```
$match = 456
$prefix = One Two Three
$suffix =  Seven Eight
$match = 910
$prefix = One Two Three 456 Seven Eight
$suffix =  Eleven Twelve
```

This is certainly better than having Perl do the extractions for us, since we only extract the values we want when required—although it doesn't do anything for the legibility of our programs. Parentheses generally do the job more simply and as efficiently, but for a few cases this can be a useful trick to know.

Parentheses and Numbered Variables

Sometimes we are not so much interested in what the whole search pattern matches, rather what specific parts of the pattern match. For example, we might look for the general structure of a date or address within the text and want to extract the individual values, like the day and month or street and city when we make a successful match. Rather than extract the whole match with $&, we can extract only the parts of interest by placing parentheses around the parts of the pattern to be extracted. Using parentheses we can access the numbered variables $1, $2, and $3, etc., which are defined on the completion of the match. Numbered variables are both more flexible and faster than using special variables.

Perl places the text that is matched by the regular expression in the first pair of parentheses into the variable $1, and the text matched by the regular expression in the second pair of parentheses into $2, and so on. Number variables are defined in order according to the position of the left-hand parenthesis. Note that these variables start from $1, not $0. The latter is used to hold the name of the program and has nothing to do with regular expressions. Let's consider this example:

```
#!/usr/bin/perl
# parentheses.pl
use warnings;
use strict;

my $text= "Testing";
if ($text =~ /((T|N)est(ing|er))/) {
    print " \$1 = $1 \n \$2 = $2 \n \$3 = $3 \n \$4 = $4 \n";
}
```

Let's execute this script and review the results:

> **perl parentheses.pl**

```
Use of uninitialized value in concatenation (.) at test.pl line 6.
 $1 = Testing
 $2 = T
 $3 = ing
 $4 =
```

There are three pairs of parentheses in this example. The first one is that which surrounds the whole regular expression, hence $1 evaluates to the whole matched text, which is Testing. The match caused by the second pair of parentheses, (T|N), which is T, is assigned to $2. The third pair of parentheses, (ing|er), causes $3 to be assigned the value ing. Since we don't have more parentheses, $4 is undefined, hence the warning.

There is no limit to the number of parenthesized pairs that we can use (each of which will define another numbered variable). As shown in our example, we can even nest parentheses inside each other. The fact that $1 contains all the characters of $2 and $3, and more, does not make any difference; Perl will fill out the variables accordingly.

Even if the pattern within the parentheses is optional (it will successfully match nothing at all), Perl assigns a variable for the parentheses anyway, in order to maintain the positional order:

```
$text =~ /^(non)?(.*)/;
# $1 = 'non' or undefined, $2 = all or rest of text
```

Sometimes we don't want to extract a match variable, we just want to use parentheses to define or group terms together. We can prevent Perl from spitting out a value by using the (?:...) notation. This notation works like regular parentheses for the purposes of defining and grouping terms, but it doesn't give rise to a value:

```
#!/usr/bin/perl
# extended.pl
use warnings;
use strict;

my $text= "Testing";
if ($text =~ /((?:T|N)est(ing|er))/) {
    print " \$1 = $1 \n \$2 = $2 \n \$3 = $3 \n \$4 = $4 \n";
}
```

Let's execute this script and review the results:

> **perl extended.pl**

```
Use of uninitialized value in concatenation (.) at extended.pl line 7.
Use of uninitialized value in concatenation (.) at extended.pl line 7.
 $1 = Testing
 $2 = ing
 $3 =
 $4 =
```

Note how the parentheses containing the T|N are no longer associated with a numbered variable, so $2 is shifted to (ing|er), hence its value is ing. The print statement is now trying to use two undefined variables, $3 and $4, resulting in the two warnings.

We know from earlier examples that if we place a quantifier inside parentheses, then all matches are returned concatenated. We have used this fact plenty of times in expressions like (.*). However, quantifiers cannot multiply parentheses. This means that if we place a quantifier outside rather than inside parentheses, the last match is placed in the corresponding numbered variable.

We do not get extra numbered variables for each repetition. To illustrate this, let's consider this modified version of an example that we used earlier on:

```
#!/usr/bin/perl
# overwrite1.pl
use warnings;
use strict;

my $text = "one:two:three:four:five";
# match noncolon characters optionally followed by a colon, 3 times
if ($text =~ /(([^:]+):?){3}/) {
    print " \$1 = $1 \n \$2 = $2 \n";
}
```

Let's execute this script and review the results:

> **perl overwrite1.pl**

```
$1 = three:
$2 = three
```

In this example, only one pair of $1 and $2 will exist after the regexp finishes. Each repeated match overwrites the values found by the previous match, so once the match is finished, we only have three: and $three (the latter containing the word we want without the preceding colon).

If we actually want to extract all the repetitions rather than the last, we will have to write out each repetition explicitly:

```
#!/usr/bin/perl
# overwrite2.pl
use warnings;
use strict;

my $text = "one:two:three:four:five";
# match noncolon characters optionally followed by a colon, 3 times
if ($text =~ /^(([^:]+):?)(([^:]+):?)(([^:]+):?)/) {
    print " \$2 = $2 \n \$4 = $4 \n \$6 = $6 \n";
}
```

Let's execute this script and review the results:

> **perl overwrite2.pl**

```
$2 = one
$4 = two
$6 = three
```

Although this works, it is neither elegant nor particularly legible. A better alternative is to use the /g global pattern match modifier:

```
#!/usr/bin/perl
# repeat3.pl
use warnings;
use strict;

my $text = "one:two:three:four:five";
while ($text =~ /(([^:]+):?)/g) {
```

```
    print " \$1 = $1 \n \$2 = $2 \n";
}
```

Let's execute this script and review the results:

> **perl overwrite3.pl**

```
$1 = one:
$2 = one
$1 = two:
$2 = two
$1 = three:
$2 = three
$1 = four:
$2 = four
$1 = five
$2 = five
```

An alternative, and sometimes simpler, approach to getting the value we want is to use the special variable $+ or $LAST_PAREN_MATCH. This is defined by the regexp engine as holding the value of whatever the last set of parentheses matched, or to put it another way, the same value as the highest numbered variable. Thus, in the extended.pl example, the value of $+ is ing, which is the value of $2 (the highest numbered variable). If we are only interested in what matched the last set of parentheses, $+ will return it for us, irrespective of how many parentheses might have occurred previously.

As we have already mentioned, whenever we use parentheses to extract values, Perl sets the start and end positions of each successful match in the special array variables @- and @+. Each pair of elements in these arrays corresponds to the start and end position of the corresponding numbered variable. So, $-[1] is the position at which $1 matched inside the text, and $+[1] is the position it finished.

One practical upshot of this is that we can find the number of parentheses that matched by counting the size of either array. We don't count the zeroth element for this since it corresponds to $& (not the parentheses), so the number of matches is equal to the index of the highest element:

```
$no_of_parens = $#-;    # count number of matching parentheses
```

Since parentheses are always extracted if they are present (even if they are conditional), this doesn't make a lot of difference for hard-coded patterns. However, for patterns that may vary and thus may contain differing numbers of parentheses, this is a convenient way of handling an arbitrary number of returned numbered variables, without knowing in advance how many parentheses are present.

Purely for illustrative purposes, we could also extract the value of a numbered variable directly using substr. This is effectively what the regexp does for us when we use parentheses. Similarly, we can find the text that matched between one set of parentheses and the text. Here is how we can find the text between $1 and $2:

```
$between1and2 = substr($1,$-[2]-$+[1]);
```

Backreferences

The numbered variables $1 and onwards are defined after a successful match, but they are not available within the regexp itself. In fact, we can refer to an extracted value within the same regexp using a backreference, written as the number of the extracted parameter preceded by a backslash:

```
$text =~ /('|")(.*?)\1/;    # match single or double quoted strings
```

Backreferences are so called because they refer back to an earlier part of the pattern. They give access to the same values as the numbered variables $1 ... , so for each numbered variable defined there is a corresponding backreference. Since they are prefixed by a backslash, they are left alone by interpolation, which attaches no special significance to escaped numerals (to be specific, single-digit escaped numerals). If we have more than nine backreferences, things can get sticky though, and they are handled by the regexp engine instead.

The point of backreferences is, of course, that they can be used in the pattern. In fact, the values of the backreferences can change several times during the course of an attempted match as the regexp engine searches through different possibilities. Consider the quote-finding regexp we gave a moment ago. It will find one single-quoted string or one double-quoted string. Now assume we feed it the following text:

```
Today's quote is "This is the way to the future".
```

Following the "as soon as possible" rule, the regexp finds the unmatched single quote in Today's and goes looking for a mate. At this point, \1 contains a single quote. Eventually the engine runs out of places to look for another single quote, since there is only one. (Fortunately for us, there is no second apostrophe in the match text.) It backtracks, drops the first single quote, and goes looking for another one. Shortly afterwards it finds the double quote, defining the backreference \1 once again, this time as a double quote. Since there are two double quotes, the match succeeds, and the backreference is assigned to the numbered variable $1.

It follows from this that backreferences are defined as and when the corresponding part of the pattern is matched. This means that we cannot use a backreference earlier than the part of the search pattern that gives it a value—it does not make logical sense:

```
$text =~ /\1(.*?)('|")/;   # ERROR: backreference before definition!
```

Of course, in this particular example the problem is obvious. In more complex regexps, it is easier to make this kind of mistake, especially with a lot of backreferences involved.

Interestingly, a backreference can itself be placed inside parentheses. Perl will happily use the value of an earlier backreference within a pattern that defines a later backreference (and numbered variable, if the match succeeds):

```
$text =~ /('|")([^\1]*)\1/;
print "Found quote:$1$2$1\n";
```

This is an example of quote matching that avoids using the lean .*? pattern and uses a character class to exclude precisely the character we don't want to find, as we covered earlier. In this case, the character is whatever was found by the first part of the pattern and is now held in the backreference \1. As this example shows, there is nothing to stop us using a backreference more than once.

When numbered variables were introduced earlier in the section "Parentheses and Numbered Variables," we mentioned that Perl allows us to extract any number of substrings from the match text, one for each pair of parentheses that we use. This is not a problem for numbered variables, which Perl will happily define up to $100 if necessary. Backreferences do have a problem, however, since the backreference \10 is ambiguous: it also represents a form feed character. Perl resolves this conflict of syntax by using one of its "common sense" rules—for the tenth and higher backreference, if the backreference is defined, then its value is substituted at the position of the backreference in the pattern. If the backreference is not defined, Perl assumes that the backreference is not really a backreference but an ASCII octal character code, and so replaces it with the appropriate character. Since most patterns (at least most sensible ones) do not contain more than nine backreferences, this is fairly safe. To bring the count down, parentheses used for grouping only can be replaced with the (?:...) syntax. Note that if we actually wanted to say "backreference 1 followed by a zero," we could do it by using a character class of one character: \1[0].

Why this confusion in syntax? It comes about because Perl draws upon several sources for its features, and brought much of the syntax with it. The use of the backslash to define and escape metacharacters comes from shell scripting languages like csh, which in turn get it from the C programming language. The use of the backslash to define a backreference comes from the venerable Unix utilities sed and awk, both of which are (loosely speaking) regexp engines with a command line. Perl combines the best features of all these tools, but as a result it occasionally has to deal with the conflict of syntax this sometimes causes. Perl cannot just use $1 either, since that would imply interpolation, which happens prior to the pattern being applied to the regular expression engine.

So what do we do if we have a lot of backreferences, and we actually do want to insert an ASCII code? In fact, this is not a problem as long as we don't mind using something other than octal for the character code. The confusion with backreferences comes because both syntaxes use a backslash followed by digits. If we specify a character code in hexadecimal instead, we can use the \x metacharacter, which since x is not a number, is not mistaken for a backreference:

```
$text =~ /^(.)(.)(.)(.)(.)(.)(.)(.)(.)(.)\x08/;   # match 10 chrs followed
                                                  # by a backspace
```

Extracting Lines with the Range Operator

An interesting alternative to extracting text with a single regexp is to extract it using two simpler regexps and the range operator, ... If the intent of a regexp is to read a potentially large body of text between two markers, using the range operator may provide a faster alternative. The drawback is that the range operator works on lines, not within them, so we might have to do some trimming afterward.

Consider the following single regexp that extracts the text between the two literal markers START and FINISH:

```
$text =~ /^START$(.*?)^FINISH$/msg;
```

The intent of this regexp is to extract the text between each START and FINISH in the body of the match text. We use

- The /g pattern match modifier to extract all the matches
- The /s pattern match modifier to allow newlines to match the dot
- The /m pattern match modifier, so the ^ and $ anchors will match newlines within the text (note that this can be combined with /s) and make the extracted text pattern nongreedy

So, we match between each START and FINISH pair and not between the first START and the last FINISH.

Unfortunately, if the text between the two markers is large, then this regular expression will take a long time to analyze and extract each pair. It would be considerably more convenient to match the very simple text START with one search pattern, FINISH with a second, and then to extract the text between the two matches. This is what the range operator allows us to do.

The following program is an example of the range operator in action. It attempts to retrieve records between START and FINISH markers and store the results into an array of matches. Any line inside a record gets added to the current match in progress. Any line outside gets silently dropped.

```perl
#!/usr/bin/perl
# range.pl
use warnings;
use strict;

my @records;    # list of found records
my $collect = "";   # collection variable for records
my $in = 0;   # flag to check if we've just completed a record
while (<>) {
    print "Considering:$_";
```

```perl
    if (/^START/ ... /^FINISH/) {
        # range is true - we are inside a record
        print "In \n";
        # collect lines for record
        $collect .= $_;
        $in = 1;
    } else {
        # false - we are outside a record
        if (not $in) {
            # we were already outside
            print "Out \n";
        } else {
            # we have just left, found a collect
            print "In -> Out \n";
            # add collected lines to list
            push @records, $collect;
            # clear the collection variable
            $collect = "";
            # set flag to say we are out
            $in = 0;
        }
    }
}

foreach (0..$#records) {
    print "Record $_: \n$records[$_] \n";
}
```

The range operator works on a line-by-line basis. Each side can be either a line number or a regexp that must match the line to satisfy that side of the range. In operation, the range operator "remembers" its current state, which is "off" before the left-hand side becomes true; it then returns false and turns "on" when the left-hand side is satisfied, in this case, when the line contains the text START. When the right-hand side is satisfied, the range operator turns "off" again. It is in effect a Boolean toggle switch that is first triggered on and then triggered off.

This script works by keeping track of its own Boolean toggle $in, so it knows whether the range operator has just finished a record or not. If it has, we store the results in @matches, otherwise we do nothing. Although it works, it does have one flaw: if a START immediately follows a FINISH, then the range operator toggles from "on" to "off," and back to "on," with the result that immediately adjacent records get merged together. We have to ensure there is at least one line between records, though whether the line is empty or not, we do not care.

Although it is a lot more verbose, this code can run a lot faster than the single regexp approach, not only because the regexp engine has a much simpler task, but also because we do not need to read all the text we want to match against before we start.

One common task that web servers and web clients have to perform is separating the header from the body of an e-mail message or an HTTP response. Both these protocols use a completely blank line to indicate the end of the header and the start of the body. Here is a short program that uses the range operator to read the header and body into separate array variables:

```perl
#!/usr/bin/perl
# header.pl
use warnings;
use strict;

my (@head, @body);
```

```
while (<>) {
    if (1 .. /^$/) {
        push @head, $_;
    } else {
        push @body, $_;
        last;    # found start of body, quit loop
    }
}

push @body, <>;
print "Head: \n", join('', @head);
print "Body: \n", join('', @body);
```

Here we have used a while loop to read the header, jumping out of it as soon as the header finishes. The range starts at 1, which the range operator compares to $., the line count. This is true for the first line of the file and therefore true immediately, so we don't need to check whether we are before or after the header. It ends at /^$/, which matches the first completely empty line.

The range operator actually comes in two guises, .. and .... The difference between them is that ... will not complete a range from start to finish on a single line; that is, if the left-hand side has just become true, then the right-hand side is not tested even if it would also be true. In the examples we have used here, there is no difference, since all our regexps have been anchored at the start and so cannot simultaneously match. However, in the event that we wanted to handle an e-mail body that had no head (that is, it starts with an empty line as the first line), we would need to choose between .. and ... depending on whether we wanted to recognize the first line as the end of the header or ignore it and look for a second empty line before ending the header and starting the body.

Matching More Than Once

On many occasions we do not just want to find the first or best match available, but all of them. Unmodified, a regexp will only match the requested text once (if it can, that is). Modified by the global /g pattern match modifier, however, it will match as many times as it can.

The pattern match modifier /g turns a regexp into an iterative rather than one-off function. In much the same way that the each operator, when called in list context, returns the next key and value from a hash, a global regexp will match repeatedly. It will also set the numbered variables, backreferences from parenthesized expressions, and the special variables $&, $`, and $' if we are using them. In the case of regexps, next means the next best match according to the rules of the regexp engine.

Regular Expressions and Loops

When called in a scalar context, a global regexp will return true for each successful match, with the numbered variables and the special variables $&, $`, $', and $+ containing the values for each successful match. Likewise, numbered variables are set per match. When called in a straight scalar context (that is, not a while or until loop), only the first match is made and sets the variables on exit:

```
$text = "one two three";
$matched = $text =~ /\b(\w+)\b/g;    # match once...
print $1;    # print first word found which is 'one'
```

However, when called in a list context, all matches are returned as a list:

```
@matches = $text =~ /\b\w+\b/g;    # collect all words
```

This is a handy way to collect successful matches because it requires neither the use of $& or parentheses plus a numbered variable, but it is only effective when we are only interested in the text the whole pattern matches. More conventionally, a global regexp is often combined with a foreach or while loop.

Both foreach and while loops (and for that matter, map and grep statements) can be used to handle the results of a global regexp. There are, however, important differences between them. The following short program contains one of each, both producing the same result:

```perl
#!/usr/bin/perl
# globalloop.pl
use warnings;
use strict;

my $text = "one, two, three, four";

# iterate over matches with foreach and $_
foreach ($text =~ /\b\w+\b/g) {
    print $_, "\n";
}

# iterate over matches with while and $1
while ($text =~ /\b(\w+)\b/g) {
    print $1, "\n";
}
```

Although identical in result, these two loops are different in the way that they execute. The foreach loop extracts all the matching values from the regexp before the loop starts, so the values of the special variables $& and $1 have the values associated with the last successful match for every iteration of the loop. The preceding foreach loop is, in effect, no different from this more explicit loop:

```perl
@matches = $text =~ /\b\w+\b/g;
foreach (@matches) {
    print $_, "\n";
}
```

If we try to extract subpattern matches with parentheses in a foreach loop, then we will be in for a nasty shock. By contrast, the while loop extracts one match from the regexp each time around the loop. The values of the numbered variables are therefore correct for each match in turn, making it suitable for extracting subpattern matches.

Nested Regular Expression Loops

One pitfall that many programmers have fallen into with the /g flag is that there is only one set of the special and numbered variables $&, $1, and so on. When a second regexp is executed, the results overwrite those of the first, which can have disastrous consequences if we were relying on the initial values of the special variables to remain. The following example program illustrates the perils of trying to use variables like $& and $1 in a pair of nested foreach loops:

```perl
#!/usr/bin/perl
# nest1.pl
use warnings;
use strict;

my $text = "one, two, three, four";
```

```perl
# iterate over matches with foreach and $_
foreach ($text =~ /\b(\w+)\b/g) {
    print "outer: got: $_, matched: $&, extracted: $1 \n";
    foreach (/(\w)/g) {
        print "\tinner: got: $_, matched $&, extracted $1 \n";
    }
}
```

When run, this produces the following output:

> **perl nest1.pl**

```
outer: got: one, matched: four, extracted: four
        inner: got: o, matched e, extracted e
        inner: got: n, matched e, extracted e
        inner: got: e, matched e, extracted e
outer: got: two, matched: e, extracted: e
        inner: got: t, matched o, extracted o
        inner: got: w, matched o, extracted o
        inner: got: o, matched o, extracted o
outer: got: three, matched: o, extracted: o
        inner: got: t, matched e, extracted e
        inner: got: h, matched e, extracted e
        inner: got: r, matched e, extracted e
        inner: got: e, matched e, extracted e
        inner: got: e, matched e, extracted e
outer: got: four, matched: e, extracted: e
        inner: got: f, matched r, extracted r
        inner: got: o, matched r, extracted r
        inner: got: u, matched r, extracted r
        inner: got: r, matched r, extracted r
```

The value of $_ is as expected, because foreach loops localize the value of the loop variable (which in this case is $_) within the scope of the loop. Each time the inner loop is entered, the value of $_ in the outer loop is hidden by a local $_ and pops back into view each time the inner loop exits again. However, the values of $& and $1 slavishly hold the results of the last match (because these are foreach loops, see previously) of whichever regexp executed most recently.

Similar problems occur when we use while loops. This program appears to do much the same as the preceding example, but aborts matching of the individual characters after the first character of each word:

```perl
#!/usr/bin/perl
# nest2.pl
use warnings;
use strict;

my $text = "one, two, three, four";

# iterate over matches with foreach and $_
while ($text =~ /\b(\w+)\b/g) {
    print "outer: matched: $&, extracted: $1 \n";
    while ($1 =~ /(\w)/g) {
        print "\tinner: matched $&, extracted $1 \n";
    }
}
```

When we run this program, we do not get quite what we expected:

```
outer: matched: one, extracted: one
        inner: matched o, extracted o
outer: matched: two, extracted: two
        inner: matched t, extracted t
outer: matched: three, extracted: three
        inner: matched t, extracted t
outer: matched: four, extracted: four
        inner: matched f, extracted f
```

The problem here is that we are matching the inner regexp against $1, though it would not have made any difference if we had used $&. After the first match of the inner loop, $1 contains the character that matched. Unaware that its foundations have been shifted, the regexp advances past the first character, finds there are no more, and promptly finishes. In order to make this program work, we need to make a copy of the matched text and use that for the inner loop:

```perl
#!/usr/bin/perl
# nest3.pl
use warnings;
use strict;

my $text = "one, two, three, four";
# iterate over matches with foreach and $_
while ($text =~ /\b(\w+)\b/g) {
    print "outer: matched: $&, extracted: $1 \n";
    my $inner = $1;
    while ($inner =~ /(\w)/g) {
        print "\tinner: matched $&, extracted $1 \n";
    }
}
```

When we run this modified program, we now get the result we were looking for:

```
outer: matched: one, extracted: one
        inner: matched o, extracted o
        inner: matched n, extracted n
        inner: matched e, extracted e
outer: matched: two, extracted: two
        inner: matched t, extracted t
        inner: matched w, extracted w
        inner: matched o, extracted o
outer: matched: three, extracted: three
        inner: matched t, extracted t
        inner: matched h, extracted h
        inner: matched r, extracted r
        inner: matched e, extracted e
        inner: matched e, extracted e
outer: matched: four, extracted: four
        inner: matched f, extracted f
        inner: matched o, extracted o
        inner: matched u, extracted u
        inner: matched r, extracted r
```

The moral of the story is, think carefully about what kind of loop should be used and make copies of any part of the regexp state that we might want to make use of later. It also pays to test code thoroughly, consider empty strings, and expect failures as well as successful matches. It is important to remember that a library subroutine may contain a regexp we are unaware of, so controlling the use of regexps in our own code is not always adequate protection. In general, it pays to extract values from variables like $1 as soon as possible, to avoid any possibility of the value being changed before we need to use it.

Position

Each time a match is made, the regexp engine updates its position within the match text. This is so that previously matched text is not taken into consideration for the next match; otherwise, the next match would just be the first one again. This position can be extracted and, more dangerously, set with the pos function if the match text is held in a scalar variable:

```perl
#!/usr/bin/perl
# position.pl
use warnings;
use strict;

my $text = "one, two, three, four";

# display matches with their positions
while ($text =~ /\b(\w+)\b/g) {
    print "matched $1 at position ", pos($text), "\n";
    pos($text) = 0 if pos($text) > 15;
}
```

This program uses pos to both display and set back to zero the regexp engine's position. It loops indefinitely, matching each word in turn:

```
> perl position.pl
```

```
matched one at position 3
matched two at position 8
matched three at position 15
matched four at position 21
matched one at position 3
matched two at position 8
...
```

The position returned by pos is the index of the character in the match text immediately beyond the text that matched, that is, the first character of the next match attempt. That is why the position of the first match is 3, not 0. To get the start position, we can subtract the length of $& from the value returned by pos, or $1 if we have extracted the pattern in parentheses, as we have in this case.

Note that pos and not reset is the correct way to reset the position of a multiline match. The reset function on its own with no arguments resets one-shot regular expressions that are defined with ? as the delimiter. Although this does for one-shot regexps what pos($text) = 0 does for global regexps, there is no direct link or correlation between the two.

For the curious, the values returned by pos are the same as the value of the first element of the special array @+, which we covered earlier.

Moving the Start Anchor to the Current Position

We have already mentioned the \A, \z, and \Z metacharacters and explained their significance as anchors in conjunction with the /m modifier. The \G metacharacter is another kind of anchor that moves to the current position at the end of each match in a global regexp. It only has significance in conjunction with /g, since the position is not recorded for regexps that only match once.

At first sight, \G would appear to not be terribly useful. After all, a global regexp already advances through the match text without needing to be re-anchored each time. However, the advantage of the \G anchor is that it allows us to forcibly move the position forward to prevent needless backtracking. In turn, this allows us to force a match to complete before the regular expression engine has finished searching for the greediest match. This allows us to process the match text in much smaller bites than we would otherwise be able to do. As an example, consider the following substitution. It replaces leading spaces with an equivalent number of dashes (minus signs) over one or more lines:

```
$text =~ s/^(\s+)/'-' x length($1)/mge;
```

While perfectly fine, it is not as elegant as it could be. To get the right number of dashes, we have to extract the matched spaces and count them to generate a string of dashes of the same length, which means using the /e modifier to execute the replacement text as code.

With \G, we can rewrite this search pattern to match only one space at a time and re-anchor the search at the start of the remaining text:

```
$text =~ s/\G\s/-/mg;
```

This version causes the pattern to match many more times, but the substitution is both easier to read and much faster for Perl to process.

Retaining Position Between Regular Expressions

When matching text with a global regexp, the regular expression engine automatically keeps track of where it is. However, when the search pattern runs out of valid matches and fails, the position is reset and deleted. Trying to use pos to find the end of the last match afterward will only produce an undefined result.

Sometimes, however, we might want to know where the engine stopped so that we can feed the remaining match text to a different search pattern. Fortunately, by using a variant of the /g modifier, /gc, we can tell the regular expression engine to remember the position of the last match. In combination with \G, this allows us to have one pattern pick up where a previous one left off. To illustrate how this works, consider this sample text, and assume we know only the smallest details about it:

```
$text = "3 2 1 liftoff";
```

All we know is that we have a sequence of numbers followed by a message of some kind. We don't know how many numbers, and we do not want to try and match the whole text at one go because it might be large. So we write one regexp to find the numbers, using /gc to retain the position at the end of the last match, then a second using \G to pick up where we left off. Here is a sample program that does just that:

```
#!/usr/bin/perl
# liftoff.pl
use warnings;
use strict;

my $text = "3 2 1 liftoff";

# use /gc to remember position
while ($text =~ /(\d)/gc) {
    print "$1...\n";
}
```

```
# use \G to match rest of text
if ($text =~ /\G\s*(.+)$/) {
    print ucfirst($1), "!\n";
}
```

Running this program displays

```
3...
2...
1...
Liftoff!
```

As with many solutions in Perl, there are other ways to do this. For instance, we could also have copied the value of $' to $text between the two regexps to produce much the same effect without the use of /gc or the \G anchor. However, as we noted earlier, it is generally a good thing to avoid using variables like $' because of the performance loss this causes in all future pattern matches.

Matching In and Across Multiple Lines

The /s and /m modifiers both alter the way in which the regexp engine handles search patterns. The /s modifier causes the newline character, \n, to match a dot, which it would not do otherwise. The latter modifier, /m, alters the meaning of the ^ and $ anchors so that they match either side of a newline, as well as at the start and end of the text overall.

Although neither modifier is tied to global regexps, they both have a lot of uses in combination with the /g modifier. In particular, the combination of /m and /g makes an effective way to re-anchor a search pattern at the start of each newline. This code snippet extracts configuration values from a string (read from a file) that contains one key-value pair per line:

```
#!/usr/bin/perl
# mflag.pl
use warnings;
use strict;

# put <> into slurp mode
undef $/;
# read configuration file supplied on command line into string
my $configuration = <>;

my %config;
# read all configuration options from config string
while ($configuration =~ /^\s*(\w+)\s* = \s*(.+?)\s*$/mg) {
    $config{$1} = $2;
}

print "Got: $_ => '$config{$_}'\n" foreach (sort keys %config);
```

If we run this program on a file of lines like the following:

```
one = sorrow
two = joy
three = one too many
```

It produces

```
> perl mflag.pl mytextfile
```

```
Got: one => 'sorrow'
Got: three => 'one too many'
Got: two => 'joy'
```

This regular expression says, "start, find me a word (optionally surrounded by whitespace) followed by an equals sign and some more text (also optionally surrounded by whitespace), end."

With the /m modifier present, ^ and $ match at the start and end of each line in the string $configuration, so each line read from the file is checked in turn.

Incidentally, the ^, $, and /m modifiers in this code are redundant, since a newline character cannot match any part of the regexp in this particular example. However, the /m modifier causes the expression to execute a lot faster, since the regexp engine first extracts a line and anchors it at each end before commencing the rest of the search. This means that a small part of the whole string is actually involved in each attempted match.

The /s modifier allows a newline to match a dot. This is mainly useful for matching multiple-line records in a document and extracting them in one go:

```perl
#!/usr/bin/perl
# sflag.pl
use warnings;
use strict;

undef $/;
my $database = <>;
my @records;

while ($database =~ /item:(.*?)(?=item:|$)/sg) {
    my $record = $1;
    $record =~ s/\n/ /g;
    push @records, $record;
}

print "Got: $_\n" foreach @records;
```

If we give this program a file of lines like the following:

```
item: this is item one
item: this is
the second item
item: and
a third item
```

when we run it:

> **perl sflag.pl mytextfile**

it produces the following output:

```
Got: this is item one
Got: this is the second item
Got: and a third item
```

The /s modifier allows the .*? to match multiple lines between each instance of item:. We have also used a zero-width look-ahead extended pattern (the (?=...) syntax) to match the next occurrence of item:, so we can find the full extent of each record, without absorbing it into the match. This is important because we will need to start from it on the next iteration.

The /s and /m modifiers are not mutually exclusive. Although /s allows a newline to match a dot, it does not change the fact that it is a newline. The ^ and $ anchors will still match on either side of it. The database example earlier has a flaw in that it will match item: in the middle of a line, when we probably only wanted item: to be a record separator if it starts a line. We can fix that by using /m, /s, and /g together, as this replacement while loop does:

```
while ($database =~ /^item: (.*?)(?=(^item:|\z))/msg) {
    $record = $1;
    $record =~ s/\n/ /g;
    push @records, $record;
}
```

However, be aware that unlike a ^, a $ cannot be used as an anchor in the middle of a pattern—only at the end. In addition, to handle the last record, we have had to provide \z as an alternative match as well, to match the end of the string. We cannot use $ in this case because /m has altered its meaning.

Counting the Total Number of Matches

Sometimes we do not actually want to return matches from a regexp but just determine how many there are. One obvious way to do this is to count matches using a while loop:

```
$count = 0;
while ($atom =~ /\bproton\b/g) {
    $count++;
}
```

Alternatively, if the cumulative size of all the matched text is not excessively large, we can take the scalar result of the regular expression in list context:

```
$count = scalar($atom =~ /\bproton\b/g);
```

Overlapping Matches and Zero-Width Patterns

The regexp engine ordinarily moves over matched text each time it succeeds, enabling us to find all matches in the match text without matching the same text twice. Unfortunately this makes it extremely difficult to find overlapping matches because as soon as the text has matched once, it will not be considered for any further matches. The following example illustrates an instance of when this can be a problem:

```
#!/usr/bin/perl
# vowels1.pl
use warnings;
use strict;

my $text = "beautiful creature";

# find adjacent vowels
while ($text =~ /([aeiou]{2})/g) {
    print "Found adjacent '$1' at position ", pos($text), "\n";
}
```

When run, this finds the "ea" in "beautiful" and "ea" in "creature", but not the "au" in "beautiful". This is because by the time the regexp engine gets to the "u", the "a" has already been matched and passed over:

```
> perl vowels1.pl
```

```
Found adjacent 'ea' at position 3
Found adjacent 'ea' at position 14
```

Fixing this problem would appear to be nearly impossible, but fortunately Perl allows us to cheat using a zero-width assertion. Zero-width assertions require that the text matches, but do not cause the regexp engine to absorb the match by moving its position beyond them. The text matched by the assertion can be matched again on the next pass. The trick here is to turn the entire pattern into a zero-width assertion using the extended pattern (?=...).

In order to explain why zero-width assertions are useful, it's helpful to look at a simple example. The following program has been deliberately "broken" by placing a zero-width assertion around the entire pattern (.):

```
#!/usr/bin/perl
# zerowidthloop.pl
use warnings;
use strict;
my $text = "proton";
while ($text =~ /(?=(.))/g) {
    print "[$1]";
}
```

We would expect this code to go into an infinite loop. The regexp contains no subpatterns that absorb characters, so the position should never move past the first character. Since the position never moves, each successive match ought to start at the beginning of the string and match the same text again, and so on, indefinitely. So this program ought to produce

> **perl zerowidthloop.pl**

```
[p][p][p][p][p][p][p]...
```

However, Perl has a special optimization that deals with this case. If the whole of a global regexp is zero width, then a successful match will move the position one character forward from the start of the match. As a result, the program actually produces

```
[p][r][o][t][o][n]
```

The optimization is useful for avoiding infinite loops, but it has its own uses too. By rewriting our vowel program to use a zero-width assertion, we can deal with overlapping matches correctly:

```
#!/usr/bin/perl
# vowels2.pl
use warnings;
use strict;

my $text = "beautiful creature";
# find adjacent vowels
while ($text =~ /(?=([aeiou]{2}))/g) {
    print "Found adjacent '$1' at position ", pos($text), "\n";
}
```

Now when we run the program, we get the correct result:

> **perl vowels2.pl**

```
Found adjacent 'ea' at position 1
Found adjacent 'au' at position 2
Found adjacent 'ea' at position 12
```

It takes a little effort to understand this completely, but examining what has happened to the position is illuminating. In the first example, the position after the end of the first match was 3, indicating that the next match would start at the t of beautiful (remembering we are counting from zero). In the second example, the position after the first match is 1, which points to the e of beautiful, because the zero-width assertion has matched but not absorbed the characters ea. This is the same position that Perl found the last match (because the b did not match the pattern at all). Perl notices that it is starting from the same place a second time and automatically moves the position by one.

It is important to realize that this "special case" rule applies only to successful matches. The b of beautiful does not match the pattern at all, so it is moved over by the regexp engine following its "as-soon-as-possible" rule. The zero-width assertion only comes into play when a match succeeds, or in other words, only after the first ea has been matched. This is why we do not get the first ea twice. We can see that the rule comes into effect just before the beginning of each match because the position we get is correct for the start of the match just made. The position is not, as we might possibly expect, "ready" for the next match.

As another example, here is a short program that follows on from our discussion of lean matches, and searches for the shortest match in the string Greely Greely & Spatsz:

```perl
#!/usr/bin/perl
# Greely.pl
use warnings;
use strict;

my $company = 'Greely Greely & Spatz';
my $match = $company;    #set to longest possible match

while ($company =~ /(Greely)(?=(.*?Spatz))/g) {
    my $got = $1.$2;        #assemble match from both parts
    $match = $got if length($got) < length($match);
}

print "Shortest possible match is '$match' \n";.
```

Documenting Regular Expressions

If regular expressions have a down side, other than their tendency to avoid doing what we want given the slightest loophole, it is their syntax. Most patterns of any size tend to be hard to read. Take the following expression as an example, borrowed from earlier in the chapter:

```perl
# read a 'key = value' configuration from a configuration string
while ($configuration =~ /^\s*(\w+)\s*=\s*(.+?)\s*$/mg) {
    %config{$1} = $2;
}
```

Although we can work out what this regexp says, namely, "find me a word, optionally surrounded by whitespace, followed by an equals sign and some more text, also optionally surrounded by whitespace," it takes a certain amount of squinting to do so. Fortunately, we can improve the legibility of this expression by using /x.

The /x pattern match modifier allows us to embellish our regexps with extra whitespace (which, significantly, includes newlines) and comments to improve its legibility and describe what it does. The x stands for *extended*. This term is a little misleading, however, since /x does not add any new features to the engine; it merely extends the syntax for patterns:

```
print "hello" =~ /h e l l o/;      # no '/x', no match
print "hello" =~ /h e l l o/x;     # '/x' ignores spaces, produces '1'
print "h e l l o" =~ /h e l l o/x; # '/x' ignores spaces, no match
```

We can also rewrite groups to place alternatives on different lines, just as we can with if statements:

```
$atom =~ {(
    proton
    | electron
    | neutron
)}x and print "Found a particle";
```

Similarly, a # is assumed to start a comment, unless it forms part of a character class:

```
while ($text =~ {
    (
        [aeiou]    # find a vowel
        {2}        # match it twice
        [#]        # then a hash/pound
    )
}/xg) {
    print "Found adjacent '$1' at position ", pos($text), "\n";
}
```

If we want to use literal whitespace or hashes inside an /x modified pattern, we can either escape them to make them literal, or place them inside a character class as in the preceding example. We can escape spaces to make them literal, and, of course, tabs and newlines already have metacharacter representations:

```
$text =~ /
    (\ |\t)?       # start with optional space or tab
    space          # literal word
    \ +separated   # one or more spaces then a word
    \ +text        # one or more spaces then a word
    \n?            # optionally match newline
/x;
```

Unfortunately, we cannot escape a # directly, so we have to express it in octal (\43) or hexadecimal (\x23), or from Perl 5.6, a named Unicode character (\N{NUMBER SIGN}). A character class, as shown in the previous example, is probably clearer than either approach.

Using both whitespace and comments, we can rewrite our regexps to be much more legible. Admittedly, the following may be overdoing it a little, but it serves to illustrate what /x allows us to do:

```
# read configuration from config string
while ($configuration =~ /

    ^      # anchor at start of line. Note '/m' is in effect

    # match config name
    \s*    # absorb leading whitespace, if any
    (\w+)  # return name, alphanumeric only
    \s*    # absorb any whitespace between name and =
           # must have an equals sign
    =      # match '='
```

```
        # match config value, avoiding surrounding whitespace
        \s*   # absorb any whitespace between = and value
        (.+?) # return value
              # - note, nongreedy, \s* takes precedence
        \s*   # absorb whitespace between value and end of line
        $     # anchor at end of line

    /mg)
{
    %config{$1} = $2;
}
```

Although not directly related to the /x modifier, it is worth noting that if we are using the /e modifier, then we can use whitespace and comments in the replacement part of a substitution. This is because the replacement is then evaluated as code and follows Perl's normal syntax rules.

Substitution

Substitution is performed by the s (also called s///) operator. Its syntax is nearly identical to that of the match operator, as we saw when we briefly introduced it earlier in the chapter and in a few examples since. The key difference is that substitution replaces matched text with a replacement string. For example, to replace all neutrons with protons, we might use

```
$atom =~ s/neutron/proton/g;
```

Substitutions permit all the same pattern match modifiers that matches do—like the /g global modifier in this example. Also, like matches, substitutions return the same values and set the same variables if we use parentheses. All these are aspects of the pattern match rather than the substitution, so they apply to matches, substitutions, and splits alike.

Substituting Matched Text and Interpolation

We are not limited to literal text in the replacement string. For instance, we can substitute the matched text with part of itself. As an example, this (admittedly oversimplistic) regexp attempts to turn Perl-style comments into C-style ones:

```
$program =~ s|#(.*)$|/*$1*/|mg;
```

Notice that characters like * do not need to be escaped on the right-hand side of the substitution—it is not a pattern. Given a line like

```
print "Hello World \n";   #standard greeting
```

it should produce

```
print "Hello World \n";   /*standard greeting*/
```

Of course, this does not take into account that # can occur in Perl programs in other ways (for example, as a character class).

This example also illustrates another important aspect of the replacement string—it is interpolated. This means that all the interpolation metacharacters (but not, of course, the regexp metacharacters) can be used in it, and that variables can be interpolated into it. Interpolation of the replacement text happens each and every time a match occurs. This is fortunate because variables like $1 can change value in each successive match.

The following pattern looks for literal periods that are followed by one or more spaces and replaces them with a full stop plus a linefeed:

```
$text =~ s/\.[ ]+/.\n/;   # put each sentence on a new line
```

As a brief note on this expression, we have looked for spaces rather than whitespace to avoid matching and replacing newlines with themselves, which is unnecessary. We have also used a character class to make the space stand out. While the square brackets are unnecessary, a space on its own in a regexp can be hard to spot.

A little known fact about backreferences is that they also work on the right-hand side of a substitution. That is, instead of using $1 in the replacement string, we can use \1:

```
$program =~ s|#(.*)$|/*\1*/|mg;
```

The reason for this is that it is compatible with sed, one of the Unix tools from which Perl evolved and is present for backward compatibility. However, it is not a good idea because \1 really ought to mean Ctrl-A outside of a pattern, and is not compatible with the /e flag for exactly that reason. In other words, don't use it, but be aware that it might pop up in old Perl scripts.

If we want to replace the matched text with part of itself followed by some numeric digits, then we have a slight problem. How do we distinguish the numbered variable from the following characters? For example, this regexp would like to replace Kilo suffixes with the appropriate number of zeros:

```
/\b(\d+)K\b/$1000/g;    # $1000 does not exist
```

In order to fix this problem, we can make the numbered variable explicit by surrounding the numeral(s) that are part of it with curly braces:

```
/\b(\d+)K\b/${1}000/g;   # correct
```

This is just ordinary delimiting of a variable name for interpolation. It just looks a little different because the variable is a number variable.

Evaluating the Replacement String

In addition to substituting replacement text, interpolated or otherwise, we can actually determine the replacement text by evaluating Perl code at the time of the match. This is enabled through the use of the /e evaluation modifier. Note that we do not say "pattern match modifier" because /e has no bearing on the pattern at all, only the replacement text.

To illustrate how /e works, here is an example of a program that uses a substitution and /e (in combination with /g) to replace numbers with qualitative descriptions:

```
#!/usr/bin/perl
# quality.pl
use warnings;

my $text = "3 Stumps, 2 Bails, and 0 Vogons";

$text =~ s/\b(\d+)\b/$1 > 0?$1 > 1?$1 > 2? "Several":"A pair of":"One":"No"/ge;

print $text, "\n";
```

Executing this code produces the following result:

```
Several Stumps, A pair of Bails, and No Vogons
```

The right-hand side of this substitution contains a perfectly normal (if slightly confusing) Perl expression. Admittedly, this regexp could stand being a little more legible. Since this is executable code, we can format it how we like; we do not need the /x modifier to add whitespace and comments:

```
$text =~ s{\b(\d+)\b}
         {
             $1 > 0?(
             $1 > 1?($1 > 2?"Several":"A pair of"
                ):"One"     # $1 == 1
                ):"No"      # $1 == 0
         }ge;    # global, execute
```

The /e modifier is very similar in operation to the block form of eval, in the sense that Perl performs a compile-time syntax check on the replacement string. Perl can do this because in this case it knows interpolation cannot alter the syntax of the right-hand side—so if it is legal at compile time, it will be legal at run time.

Interpolating and Evaluating the Replacement String

Having just said that /e evaluates but does not interpolate the right-hand side, we can add another e and have Perl interpolate the right-hand side too. The /ee modifier first interpolates the right-hand side, and then evaluates the result of the interpolation, much in the same way as eval deals with a double-quoted string argument.

As an example, the following substitution expands any scalar or array variable in the supplied match text (in the same way that interpolation does on literal text), but without processing any metacharacters that might also be present:

```
$text =~ s/ ([\$\@]\w+) /$1/gee;
```

The search pattern will match any standard Perl variable name like $scalar or @array. For each successful match, $1 is first interpolated and replaced with text containing the name of the variable (say, $scalar). This is then evaluated to get the value of the variable, which is then used as the replacement string.

The drawback of /ee is that it is an expensive, and hence slow, operation involving both an interpolation and an eval each time a match occurs. It also suffers from not being syntax checked at compile time, since Perl does not know what the replacement text is going to be when it executes the substitution. It is therefore not an advisable solution for regexps that match often.

Extended Patterns

Extended patterns are an extension to the syntax of regexps covered so far. They enable us to adjust the operation of the regexp engine within the search pattern. Each extended pattern causes the engine to behave in a different way, but only for the region over which it has control.

All extended patterns have a syntax following the rule (?<character>pattern). The <character> determines the effect that the extended pattern has, and pattern is the pattern affected by it. We have already seen two extended patterns, the backreference suppressing cluster and the zero-width look-ahead:

```
(?:these|terms|do|not|create|a|backreference)     # cluster
(?=zerowidthpattern)                              # zero-width look-ahead
```

Perl defines several extended patterns to perform various tasks, as described in Table 11-10. Some of them are noted as experimental, although in practice they have been available consistently from Perl 5.5 through to Perl 5.8 and seem unlikely to vanish. (The current status of the experimental patterns can be found in the perlre manual page.) As they are by nature trickier to use than most regular expression syntax, all of them should be used with some care.

Table 11-10. *Extended Patterns*

Pattern	Description
(?#comment)	Inline comment. The enclosed text is treated as a comment and ignored for the purposes of compiling the search pattern. Commenting is in general better done with the /x modifier, but this provides a way to temporarily "comment out" parts of a search pattern if necessary.
(?:pattern) (?:imsx-ismx:pattern)	Cluster. Probably the most common of the extended patterns. The enclosed pattern is treated as a group but does not generate backreferences or number variables. For example: (?:this|that|other) In many simple cases, we do not particularly care if a number variable is generated or not and can live with the slight inefficiency. However, in complex patterns that use many parentheses to both group and extract values, this notation can be handy to keep the number of extracted variables under 10, after which complications can arise using backreferences (see earlier). This pattern may be combined with inline modifiers by adding the relevant modifier flags, optionally preceded by a minus to turn them off.
(?=pattern)	Zero-width positive look-ahead assertion. The enclosed pattern must be matched for the assertion to succeed, but does not consume any match text. For example: (?=nextup) As this pattern is zero-width, it does not affect the value of $& or $', and does not contribute to backreferences even if inside parentheses. It is used, for example, to "peek" at the next line in a line-by-line match.
(?!pattern)	Zero-width negative look-ahead assertion. The enclosed pattern must not match for the assertion to succeed. As with the positive variant, match text is not consumed. This pattern can be very tricky indeed to use correctly, and reaching for it often indicates we need to rethink the design of our search pattern. Firstly, because the assertion is zero width, we do not absorb any match text even if it is satisfied, so we must take that into account in the pattern immediately following. For example, this text attempts to make sure the last three characters of a string are not "abc". But it doesn't work: $text=~(?!abc)$/; # ERROR: always succeeds, even if $text ends in 'abc' This assertion will succeed at the very end of the match text, because at the end there are no characters left, and this does satisfy the condition. It will still satisfy the condition even if the last three characters really were "abc". To have this assertion work as intended, we need to provide a positive-width pattern for the text that isn't "abc" to match: $text=~/(?!abc)...$/; # OK - note the '...' The trailing dots change the meaning of this pattern from "check the end is not 'abc'" to "look for three characters at the end which are not 'abc'." While these parse the same to a human, the literal-minded regular expression engine needs the extra clarification. Secondly, alternatives do not work as might be expected inside this assertion. For instance, we cannot say "neither 'a' nor 'b'" with $text=~/^(?!a|b)/; # ERROR: matches any character This actually says "not a" or "not b". Since "a" is not "b", and "b" is not "a", anything at all will satisfy one of these conditions and the assertion will always succeed. Like its positive counterpart, this pattern is zero width, so it does not affect Perl's special regular expression variables, backreferences, or number variables.

Pattern	Description
(?<=pattern)	Zero-width positive look-behind assertion. The enclosed pattern must match the immediately preceding text, which may already have been matched by the regular expression engine. For example, to match a word surrounded by whitespace without matching the whitespace: `while ( $text =~ /(?<=\S)(\w+)(?=\S)/g ) { print "$1 "; }` Note that the regular expression engine requires that this pattern be a fixed width to be legal.
(?<!pattern)	Zero-width negative look-behind assertion. The enclosed pattern must not match the immediately preceding text. For example, to match all interpolatable variables in a string: `while ( $text =~ /(?<!\\)([@$\\]\w+)/g ) { print "$1 "; }` This means "find one of the symbols @, $, or \, *not* preceded by a \, followed by one or more word characters." The backslashes are doubled because the pattern is interpolated, and we want a literal \ in each case. As with its positive counterpart, this pattern can often be avoided. Note that the regular expression engine requires that this pattern be fixed width to be legal.

(?{ code })
(??{ code })
	Experimental: evaluated code. These patterns both allow code to be embedded into the search pattern. The difference between them is that (?{ code }) always succeeds and has no effect on the pattern (zero width), whereas the return value of (??{ code }) is substituted into the search pattern (zero or positive width). Code is executed as it is found. If we group a code pattern with another subpattern (say \w) within a repetition (say +), it will be executed for each match. In the case of a greedy repetition, we can actually see the engine absorbing characters as it progresses through the match text:
	<pre>#!/usr/bin/perl
	# codepattern.pl
	use warnings;
	use strict;
	
	my $text=<>;
	
	while ($text=~/
	    (?{$count=0})
	    ((?:\w
	        (?{print ++$count,"=$& "})
	    )+)
	/xg) {
	    print "\nGot $1\n";
	}</pre>Given match text like "one two", this loop will print out
	<pre>1=o 2=on 3=one
	Got one
	1=t 2=tw 3=two
	Got two</pre>The scope of the code within the expression is recursive—that is, if local is used to localize variables within the code, backtracking will cause those changes to be undone. Here is a backtrack-safe version of the previous example:
	`(?{ local $count=$count+1; print "$count=$&\n" })`
	The return value of the evaluated code is placed into the special variable $^R, unless the extended pattern is being used as a control expression. Both patterns are controlled by the use re 'eval' pragma—see later.

Continued

Table 11-10. *Continued*

Pattern	Description
`(?>pattern)`	Experimental: all or nothing. Backtracking will not be performed on the matched text once this pattern matches. This is a useful efficiency tool when we know that the following pattern cannot match any earlier. For example, to match a word followed by whitespace: `/(?>\w+)\s/` This prevents the regular expression engine from reducing the number of characters that match `\w+`, since we know that anything that matches `\w` cannot possibly match `\s`. Suppressing the backtracking allows the pattern to fail faster. For a good example of why this may improve performance, see the example trace in the debugging section. We can also use this pattern in places where backtracking would successfully provide a match, but one which we do not want to allow. In other words, we can force a failure and avoid an inappropriate success.

`(?(pattern)pattern)`
`(?(pattern)pattern:`
`pattern)`
	Experimental: if-then and if-then-else condition. If the control pattern succeeds, match on the second pattern. If it fails, ignore the second pattern. If a third pattern is present, match that instead. The control pattern can be either an integer that refers to an existing backreference (that is, a previous set of parentheses) or a zero-width assertion of any kind, including look-ahead, look-behind, and code.
	For example, this regular expression looks for an equals sign, optionally within quotes. If a quote is seen, another one must be seen to match it:
	`$text=~/(` `# extract whole match into \1 (=> $1)`
	      `(['"]?)` `# optionally match a quote into \2`
	       `\w+` `# match 'key'`
	        `=` `# match '='` `[\w\s]+`
	`# match 'value'`
	      `(?(2)\2)` `.# match the optional quote in \2 if`
	               `# one was found`
	`)/xg`

Evaluated Code and eval Mode

The extended patterns (`?{ code }`) and (`??{ code }`) are not normally permitted to exist in a search pattern that also contains interpolated variables. In a similar manner to the `strict` module, Perl provides the pragmatic `re` module to control three features of the regular expression engine. Each feature is controlled by a different argument: `taint`, `debug`, and the one we are interested in here, `eval`:

```
use re 'eval';
```

Enabling `eval` mode permits the coexistence of interpolated variables and these extended patterns in the same regular expression. This is otherwise a forbidden combination for security reasons (with or without `taint` mode).

Why is it so dangerous? Because interpolation happens before compilation, and the interpolated variables might therefore contain embedded code that is integrated into the pattern before it is executed. This means that any kind of user input that is used in the regexp could cause our program to execute arbitrary code. This is not a good thing for system security. If we really want to allow user input to regexps, see the `quotemeta` function in "String Interpolation" for ways to protect against problems like this.

Interpolated variables that contain patterns compiled with `qr` are not subject to this prohibition, even if the compiled regexp contains embedded code, so the `eval` mode is often unnecessary and should probably be avoided. If we really want to embed code, this is how we could do it (a little more safely:

```
# allow embedded code patterns
use re 'eval';

# compile a pattern with embedded code
$re1 = qr/a pattern (?{ print "that doesn't contain user input"; })/;

# disable embedded code, enable taint mode
no re 'eval';
use re 'taint';

# allow user to enter regexp! We would probably want much stricter
# limits on what they can enter, in reality.
$re2 = qr/<>/;

# process combination of both regexps.
while ($text =~ /$re1$re2/g) {
    ...
}
```

Note that eval mode is not compatible with taint mode, since taint enforces a stricter level of security.

Controlling Tainted Data and Extended Patterns

Perl supports the concept of tainted data, where information gleaned from an external source is considered insecure. Each time a piece of tainted data is used in an expression, the result of that expression is also marked as tainted. If we try to do something potentially dangerous, like execute an external program, Perl will raise a security error and exit. Taint mode is enabled with the -T command-line option and is automatically enabled if we run a Perl script under a different effective user ID.

We cover taint mode further in Chapter 17, but it is relevant here because regular expressions are the only safe way to explicitly untaint a tainted variable.

Untainting Tainted Variables

We can untaint a tainted variable by extracting a substring from it. Although Perl is aware that the match text is tainted, it assumes that by running a regexp across it, we are taking adequate steps to ensure that any security issues are being dealt with and so does not mark the extract text as tainted.

We can use this fact to untaint variables that we know to be secure. For example, to untaint the DOCUMENT_ROOT environment variable, we could use

```
$ENV{DOCUMENT_ROOT} =~ /^(.*)/ &&
  $ENV{DOCUMENT_ROOT} = $1;
```

We can usually justify doing this, because if DOCUMENT_ROOT has been compromised, then the web server is probably already in more trouble than our CGI script.

Maintaining Taintedness in Regular Expressions

Another mode controlled by the pragmatic re module is taint, which disables the taint-removal properties of regular expressions:

```
use re 'taint';

$ENV{DOCUMENT_ROOT} =~ /^(.*)/ &&
$ENV{DOCUMENT_ROOT} = $1;

# document root is still tainted!
```

Like most pragmatic modules, we can also switch off the "do not untaint" feature with no, which allows us to control which patterns are permitted to untaint data:

```
no re 'taint';
```

Regular Expressions vs. Wildcards

Regular expression patterns bear a passing resemblance to file name *wildcards*, which is often a source of confusion to those new to regexps but familiar with wildcards. Both use special characters like ? and * to represent variable elements of the text, but they do so in different ways. The wildcard *.*, for example, would be written .*\..* when expressed as a regular expression (remember that dots are literal in a wildcard's file name).

Unix shell wildcards (which are more capable than those supported by standard Windows shells) equate to regexps as follows:

- The wildcard ? is equivalent to the regexp ..
- The wildcard * is equivalent to the regexp .*.
- Character classes [...] are identically equivalent but only for literal class contents.

Converting from a regexp to a wildcard is not possible except in the simplest cases. Conversely though, we can convert wildcards to regexps reasonably simply, by handling the four characters ?, *, [, and] as special cases and escaping all other punctuation. The following program does just that in the subroutine wild2re:

```perl
#!/usr/bin/perl
# wildre.pl
use warnings;
use strict;

$| = 1;   # enable autoflush for prompt display of prompt (sic)

while (print "Wildcard: " && <>) {
    chomp;
    print "Regular Expression: ", wild2re($_), "\n";
}

sub wild2re {
    my $re = shift;
    $re =~ s/([^\w\s])/($1 eq '?')?'.'
      :($1 eq '*')?'.*'    :($1 eq '[' || $1 eq ']')?$1
        :"\\$1"/eg;
    return "^$re\$";   #anchor at both ends
}
```

And here's an example of it in use:

```
> perl wildre.pl
```

```
Wildcard: file[0-9]*.*
Regular expression: ^file[0\-9].*\..*$
```

It should come as no surprise that the solution to converting wildcards into regexps involves regexps. In this case, we have checked for any character that is neither a word character nor a whitespace character, handled it specially if it is one of the four that we need to pay particular attention to, and escaped it with a backslash if it isn't. We have used parentheses to extract each matching character into the numbered variable $1, the g pattern match modifier to match every occurrence within the string, and the e flag to evaluate the substitution text as Perl code. The result of the evaluation is used as the replacement text. Here the substitution is a multiple if-then-else statement using the ternary operator that tests $1 against each of the possible cases for treatment and returns the appropriate substitution text.

Before returning the completed pattern, we also add anchors to both ends to prevent it from matching in the middle of a file name, since wildcards do not do that. It is simpler to add them afterwards than have the regular expression add them.

To illustrate that there are many solutions to any given problem in Perl, and regular expressions in particular, here is another version of the previous pattern that also does the job:

```
$re =~ s/(.)/($1 eq '?')?'.'
            :($1 eq '*')?'.*'
             :($1 eq '[' || $1 eq ']')?$1
              :"\Q$1"/eg;
```

This alternative version extracts every character in turn, checks for the four special characters, and then uses \Q to escape the character if it is not alphanumeric. This is not quite as efficient, since it takes a little more effort to work through every character, and it also escapes spaces (though for a file name that would not usually be a problem).

Writing Efficient Regular Expressions

Writing a regular expression that works is one thing. Writing one that works quickly is something else. For every fast regexp, there is another that does the same job but runs like a snail. The regexp engine is already very good at determining the most efficient way to carry out a pattern match, but it can only optimize what we give it.

Writing a regular expression so it can match faster is always a good idea. Writing it so it can fail faster is an even better idea. Many patterns are good at matching quickly, but can take a very long time to run through all the possibilities before they concede defeat. In general, there are three ways we can make our regular expressions more efficient:

- Make the search pattern more specific.
- Avoid recompilation of search patterns.
- Use many simple expressions instead of one complex one.

The last of these is actually one way to achieve the second. Recompilation happens when a reused search pattern contains interpolated variables and can be a major cause of performance loss.

Making Regular Expressions More Specific

The more specific a regular expression is, the fewer possibilities the engine will have to run though to find a match. There are two main ways to make regexps more specific. One is to eliminate subpatterns that are too vague, and the other is to anchor the expression, if possible, to limit the possible start and end points of any prospective match.

Eliminating Vague Subpatterns

Patterns such as .* are very flexible, but terrible in terms of speed, since they can match anything. Many regexp programmers reach for expressions like .* because they are quick and simple to use, and they can be "fixed" by making the rest of the search pattern more specific. Unfortunately, this can cause Perl a lot of extra work. Consider the following two almost-equivalent regexps:

```
$text =~ /('|")(.*)\1/ and print $2;    # extract single or double
                                        # string quoted
$text =~ /('|")([^\1]*?)\1/ and print $2;  # ditto...
```

The second of these examples is superior to the first in several ways, not least because it matches the first pair of quotes, not the first and last quotes in the entire text. Since the text might be long, we make the match nongreedy by adding a ?. Then the engine will look for the second quote forward from the first and not backtrack from the end. The first example, by contrast, will be greedy and match the whole text with .*, then backtrack to try to find a match for the backreference \1. As a result, the second example will usually find a single quoted section within a large body of text much faster than the first. The only time the first will win is if the match text contains a pair of quotes near the beginning and end of the overall text.

If we are only matching word characters, \w* is far better, since it can terminate part of a search earlier than would otherwise be the case. \w+ is even better if we actually require a word, since unlike \w*, it has to match at least one character for the rest of the pattern to be considered at all. The trick is to have a very good understanding of the nature of the text we will be matching; the more information we can give the regexp engine, the better it will perform:

```
$text =~ /(.*) = (.*)/;      # bad
$text =~ /(\w*) = (\S*)/;    # better
$text =~ /^(\w+) = (\S+)/;   # even better
```

It is a common misconception that nongreedy matches are intrinsically more efficient than greedy ones. This may be the case, but only because of the nature of the text we wish to match. Take the following two examples:

```
$text =~ /^(.*)\\?/;     # greedy match
$text =~ /^(.*?)\\?/;    # nongreedy match
```

Both examples look for any text (.*) followed by an optional literal backslash (\\?), but they go about it in different ways. Consider the most likely scenario for this application—a series of lines that are optionally suffixed with a backslash to indicate continuation. The first grabs the whole match text and then looks for an optional backslash, starting from the end. The second grabs one character at a time and then looks to see if the next character is a backslash. If it isn't, the engine backtracks, matches another character to .*?, then checks again, and so on, all the way to the end of the match text. In this case, the first, greedy, match is clearly more efficient. Here, using a $ anchor possibly prefixed by optional whitespace would be even more efficient, though we're trying to keep to examples simple for clarity.

Another reason for using caution with the dot (.) match is that it is not matched by a newline, \n, unless we use the /s modifier. It is easy to forget this when writing regexps, which leads us to get tripped up when the match text unexpectedly contains a newline. Writing a more specific pattern can often force us to consider possibilities like this before they happen.

Anchors

Some patterns can be made faster by relatively simple modifications—adding anchors is one such example. If we want to look for the word omega, and we know that omega is only going to occur at the end of the string, we can anchor it:

```
$text =~ /omega$/;
```

Without the $ to anchor the pattern, the regular expression engine must check for omega anywhere in the string. In the second case, the engine can check that the last letter in the string is an a. If it is not, it can fail immediately.

Anchors are a very effective way of speeding up matches. Even if we cannot anchor a search pattern directly, we can sometimes anchor it to something else with a little more thought. For instance, omega might not occur at the end of the line, but we happen to know that if it does not, it can only be followed by whitespace. This means we can anchor it using

```
$text =~ /omega\s*$/;
```

Similarly, to check for alpha at or near the beginning of the line, we can say

```
$text =~ /^\s*alpha/;
```

The study Function

Perl provides a built-in function called study, which attempts to improve the speed of the regular expression engine by analyzing the match text (note: not the pattern) in advance. For some cases, this can provide a useful speed improvement. For others, it is almost entirely useless.

The function works by examining the text and building lists of positions within the text for each character present (so, for example, the a list contains a list of positions for every a present in the text). When the text is matched, the engine checks for literal characters in the search pattern and scans for them in the match text in order of rarity. If the pattern contains a literal q, and this is the rarest character in the match text that is also present in the pattern, the engine will start by looking for instances of q and then go on from there.

Using study is effective when we expect to make a lot of different matches on the same piece of text, since it will benefit all of them. It is also effective when matching a series of short literal strings in large bodies of text like large documents and whole books. For example:

```
undef $/;       # undefine input record separator
$book = <>;     # slurp in large buckets of text
study $book;    # perform prematch analysis of $book

# search for short literal strings
@matches = $book =~ /\b(sharrow|miz|dloan)\b/sig;
```

In this case, the least common characters are probably w and z, so they would be used as the starting point for determining likely matches by the engine.

In practice, study is hard to use effectively. First, it is severely limited by the fact that only one string can be studied at once—if we study a second string, then the first becomes "unstudied" again. Second, it takes time for study to build its lists, which may take longer than the actual search. Lastly, its benefits in terms of speed are only effective when there are a reasonable number of literal characters in the pattern. The function has no beneficial effect for regexps like

```
$text =~ /^\s*\w+[0-9]*/;   # no literal characters to look for!
```

Remember that when considering whether to use study or not, a good source of literal characters can often be found in interpolated variables, especially if they hold user input. It is the pattern after interpolation that determines whether studying the text is beneficial or not.

Avoiding Recompilation with the Empty Pattern

If an empty pattern is supplied to the regexp engine, the engine will resort to a default of the last successfully matched pattern that was passed to it. This is one way to rematch a regexp without recompiling it:

```
if ($text =~ /$complex\b($interpolated)\b$pattern/) {
    do {
        print "Found '$1';
    } while ($text=~//);   # reuse pattern without recompiling it
}
```

It is important to remember that the reused pattern is the last successful one. If the previous match failed, the empty pattern will cause the engine to reuse the pattern before it instead (presuming that that one was successful). If no successful patterns have been seen, the pattern defaults to being truly empty, which is unlikely to be what we want.

The trick is to guarantee that the previously successful pattern is the one we want to use. The preceding example makes sure of this because the empty pattern is only reached inside the if statement that tests the success of the pattern we want to reuse.

Note that the empty pattern only functions in matches and substitutions—it has no special properties in split. Instead, splitting on an empty pattern falls under the rules of zero-width patterns (see the earlier section "Overlapping Matches and Zero-Width Patterns" for details).

Avoiding Recompilation with the Once-Only Modifier

The /o or "once-only" pattern match modifier is an invaluable tool for speeding up regexps that interpolate variables to create the search pattern. By using this modifier, we can tell the engine that the variables cannot and will not change (or more accurately, that it can ignore them even if they have). If we do not expect the variables to change over the lifetime of the program, /o is an effective way to speed up a match:

```
while (/($search_pattern)/g) { ... }   # reinterpolates each time
while (/($search_pattern)/go) { ... }  # quicker - interpolates once
```

The /o modifier allows the regexp engine to cache the results of compiled regexps for reuse, so it is not just effective for global pattern matches like the preceding. It also has a beneficial effect on nonglobal regexps if they are used repeatedly:

```
# get something to search for
$search_string = shift @ARGV;

# once-only optimized pattern inside body of while loop
while (<>) {
    if (/$search_string/o) {
        print "Found '$1' at line $. \n";
    }
}
```

The problem with /o is that it prevents us changing the pattern of interpolation when we do want to. Another solution to the same problem uses the qr operator, which (in a sense) provides the same functionality as /o, but in a more flexible way. We will discuss it in more detail at the end of this section.

The /o modifier is also particularly effective when combined with eval to generate regexp on the fly, but it is not the only way to avoid recompiling search patterns.

Generating Regular Expressions with eval

The eval function is another excellent way of generating regexps on the fly without having to deal with interpolation. Rather than search for several terms at once, we can generate regexps and then evaluate them.

Here is a simple program that accepts an arbitrary number of search terms (each specified with -t). It then scans whatever files we pass it (anything not prefixed with -t) for each of them:

```
#!/usr/bin/perl
# multisearch.pl
use warnings;
use strict;

use Getopt::Long;

my @terms;
GetOptions('term:s' => \@terms);
```

```
die "Usage $0 [-t term [-t term]] file ...\n" unless @terms;

# build regular expressions
my $regexp = "";
foreach (@terms) {
    $regexp .= 'print("$ARGV:$.('.$_.')$_\n") if /\b'.$_.'\b/o;'. "\n";
}

# dump out the loop body for interest
print "Searching with:\n$regexp";

# build loop
my $loop = 'while (<>) { chomp; '.$regexp.'}';

# evaluate loop
eval $loop;
```

The trick in this program comes in the assembling of the regexps. Each term supplied is built into its own regexp, which is in turn built into the condition of an if statement. Although the terms are elements of the @terms array variable, the code constructed by the foreach loop uses their values as literal search patterns, so we can add the /o modifier to further improve the speed of the program.

Another aspect of this program that displays some cunning is the while loop that retrieves lines from the input. Since eval is an expensive call to make, we avoid calling it repeatedly for each line of the input by placing the while loop inside the eval, rather than the other way around. The <> readline operator does not care either way, and the result is a much faster search.

We can use this program to search for several different terms at the same time:

> **perl multisearch.pl -t one -t two search.txt**

In this case, we are looking for instances of one and two. The code generated by the program and placed in $regexp in response to this command line is (as reported by the program)

```
print("$ARGV:$.(one)$_\n") if /\bone\b/o;
print("$ARGV:$.(two)$_\n") if /\btwo\b/o;
```

Note that the final \n on the end of the $regexp.=... line in the program is purely cosmetic, so the preceding prints out nicely on separate lines. If we removed that code, we could remove the trailing \n as well. Now let us assume that search.txt contains the lines

```
one two three
four
five
six
one seven eight
two nine
four three
six
nine five
zero one one
```

When run, we get the following:

```
search.txt:1(one)one two three
search.txt:1(two)one two three
search.txt:5(one)one seven eight
search.txt:6(two)two nine
search.txt:10(one)zero one one
```

Both one and two were found on the first line, so it appears for both of them. The one also appears on lines five and ten, while two additionally appears on line six. Whatever was on the other lines did not contain either term.

Another approach to assembling a regexp using eval, but avoiding the embedded loop, is to generate an anonymous subroutine instead (see Chapter 7 for more on anonymous subroutines). Here's a variant of the multisearch.pl program that works this way:

```perl
#!/usr/bin/perl
# multifind.pl
use warnings;
use strict;

use Getopt::Long;

my @terms;
my $all = 0;    # find any term by default

GetOptions('term:s' => \@terms, 'all' => \$all);

die "Must specify search term" unless @terms;
# build regular expressions and logic
my @regexps = map { "/\\b$_\\b/o" } @terms;
my $logic = join $all?' && ':' || ',@regexps;

# dump out the logic for interest
print "Searching with: $logic \n";

# interpolate an anonymous sub to test logic
my $match = eval "sub {$logic;}";

# scan input
while (<>) {
    print "$ARGV:$.:$_" if &$match;
}
```

We can use this program to search for several different terms at the same time, printing out the lines if any. Here is an example of an any search:

> **perl multifind.pl -t one -t two search.txt**

In this case, we are looking for instances of one or two, and printing out any lines on which either is present. The anonymous subroutine generated by the program in response to this command line contains this logic (as reported by the program):

```
Searching with: /\bone\b/o || /\btwo\b/o
```

Using the same sample text as before, we get an output of

```
search.txt:1:one two three
search.txt:5:one seven eight
search.txt:6:two nine
search.txt:10:zero one one
```

Alternatively, if we can use the --all option (here abbreviated to -a):

> **perl multifind.pl -t one -t two -a search.txt**

the logic is changed to

```
Searching with: /\bone\b/o && /\btwo\b/o
```

and the resulting output is

```
search.txt:1:one two three
```

This approach is basically similar to the first, but by placing the code we want to match within an anonymous subroutine, then calling eval to create it, we avoid having to call eval repeatedly or embed a while loop inside the eval.

Precompiling Search Patterns with qr

The qr quoting operator allows us to precompile regexps and then use them at a later date. This is handy for verifying the legality of a regexp as we saw earlier in the chapter, and it allows us to be more selective about when we recompile a regexp, as we saw earlier when we tackled the /o modifier.

The real value of qr is that it allows us to remove the uglier aspects of regexp syntax to another place where they don't interfere with the legibility of the program. While the /x modifier can help to make a regexp more comprehensible, it still gets in the way of understanding the surrounding code. With qr we can transplant the regexp entirely. We do not even need to use delimiters, although they are necessary if we want to use a modifier:

```
$re = qr/^a.*?pattern/;    # define a regexp

if ($re)   {   ...   }    # use regexp without delimiters
if (/$re/o) {   ...   }    # use regexp with delimiters and modifier
```

Like the match, substitute, and split functions, qr has the same rules regarding delimiters—anything within reason is allowed, and single quotes prevent the contents being interpolated. See the earlier section "Regular Expression Delimiters" for more information.

Using Pattern Match Modifiers with qr

One of the conveniences of qr is that it allows us to attach pattern match modifiers to a regexp, so we don't need to specify them later. That is, we can specify the modifier to qr and then use the regexp without modifiers:

```
$re = qr/^a.*?pattern/ism;
if ($re) {   ...   }    # use regexp with precompiled modifiers
```

If we print out the regexp, we can see what is actually happening. The pattern is embedded into an inline modifier that surrounds and entirely controls it:

```
print qr/^a.*?pattern/;    # produces '(?-xism:^a.*?pattern)'
print qr/^a.*?pattern/ism;    # produces '(?msi-x:^a.*?pattern)'
```

Notice that the inline modifier is thorough (excluding the /o and /g modifiers)—it switches on everything we ask for and switches off anything we did not. This expression will work as we intended, even when combined with other expressions and additional modifiers:

```
$re1 = /^a.*?pattern/ism;
$re2 = /form \s+ and \s+ void/x;

if (/^$re1$re2$/gm) {   ...   }    # combine two regular expressions
```

The /o modifier is not included in the "thorough" inline modifier for a good reason. While it is legal, it does not do anything in qr. In a sense, qr does the same job as /o, since interpolation of the pattern only happens once—at the time the regexp is defined.

The /g modifier is not legal in a qr pattern at all, since it is not legal as an inline modifier. If we try to use /g with qr, we get a "Bareword found where operator expected" syntax error, which can be a little confusing. If this error ever occurs when trying to use qr, check that the /g modifier is not present.

Using qr As a Replacement for the Once-Only Modifier

As we mentioned earlier when we covered the /o modifier, we can use the qr quoting operator to selectively recompile our regexp when we want to, without losing the benefits of once-only compilation the rest of the time:

```perl
#!/usr/bin/perl
# regb.pl
use strict;

undef $/;
my $text = <>;
my ($this,$that,$other) = ('red','green','blue');

my $pattern = qr/($this|$that)/;
while ($text =~ /$pattern/g) {
    if ($1 eq $this) {
        print "Found '$this' - rotating\n";
        ($this, $that, $other)=($that,$other,$this);
        $pattern = qr/($this|$that)/;
    } else {
        print "Found '$that' - staying put\n";
    }
}
```

This code starts off by looking for red or green. The moment it sees red, it starts looking for green or blue. If it sees green, it starts looking for blue or red, and so on, in a cycle. By using qr to compile and recompile the pattern, we get the benefits of /o without the drawbacks.

Checking the Validity of Regular Expressions

If we are taking input from the user and using it as part or all of a search pattern, it can be very hard to determine if the resulting search pattern is valid or not. The simple way to test the validity of a pattern is to try to compile it and see if we get an error. In order to do that without causing the program to grind to a halt, we use an eval:

```perl
#!/usr/bin/perl
# checkre1.pl
use warnings;
use strict;

while (<>) {
    chomp;
    eval {qr/$_/;};
    print $@?"Error in '$_': $@\n": "'$_' is legal \n";
}
```

We can save the result of successful compilations if we adapt the preceding technique slightly. Here is a short program implementing a subroutine that tries to compile a pattern, returning the pattern for use on success or an undefined value on failure:

```perl
#!/usr/bin/perl
# checkre2.pl
use warnings;
```

```
use strict;
while (<>) {
    chomp;
    if (my $re = compile_re($_)) {
        print "Pattern ok: $re \n";
    } else {
        print "Illegal pattern: $@ \n";
    }
}

sub compile_re {
    my $pattern = shift;

    my $re;    # local package variable
    eval { $re = qr/$pattern/; };

        return $re; #undef on error
}
```

We can run this script and feed it a selection of good and bad patterns as follows:

> **perl checkre2.pl**
^good[pat]e(r|n)

Pattern ok: (?-xism:^good[pat]e(r|n))

---

bad[pattern

Illegal pattern: /bad[pattern/: unmatched [ ] in regexp at ...

If we want to allow user input into regexps without allowing them to enter regexp syntax, then we can use quotemeta to escape any potentially dangerous characters (or place \Q...\E around their input within the regexp):

```
#!/usr/bin/perl
# quote.pl
use warnings;
use strict;

$| = 1;

print "Enter a pattern: ";
my $pattern = <>;
chomp $pattern;

print "Enter some search text: ";
my $input = <>;

if ($input =~ /\Q$pattern\E/) {
    print "'$&' found! \n";
}
```

We can run this program and pass it any kind of pattern to search for, even one with regular expression characters:

> **perl quote.pl**

```
Enter a pattern: *ship
Enter some search text: *ship troopers
'*ship' found!
```

It is important to remember that \Q and \E take effect after variables have been interpolated, so the preceding does actually do what it suggests and doesn't escape the dollar of $input.

Debugging Regular Expressions

The re module also provides a debugging mode. We can enable it with

```
use re 'debug'   # or use re qw(debug taint) etc...
```

When enabled, the regexp engine within Perl will produce a stream of diagnostic information about what it is doing, both at the compilation stage and the matching stage. For instance, here is a short program that uses debug mode to print out the processing of a moderately complex regular expression:

```
#!/usr/bin/perl
# debugre.pl
use warnings;
use strict;

use re 'debug';

my $matchtext = "helium contains two protons, two neutrons and two electrons";

my $re = qr/(\w+\s(?:proton|neutron)s?)/;

while ($matchtext =~ /$re/g) {
    print "Found $1 \n";
}
```

The regexp in this program attempts to find a word (\w+) followed by a space (\s) and either a proton or neutron, optionally followed by an s (s?). The whole thing is extracted into $1 by parentheses. When run, this program outputs first a compilation dialog and then a match dialog. The compilation dialog looks something like this:

```
Compiling REx '(\w+\s+(?:proton|neutron)s?)'
size 22 first at 4
    1: OPEN1(3)
    3:   PLUS(5)
    4:     ALNUM(0)
    5:   PLUS(7)
    6:     SPACE(0)
    7:   BRANCH(11)
    8:     EXACT <proton>(16)
   11:   BRANCH(15)
   12:     EXACT <neutron>(16)
   15:   TAIL(16)
   16:   CURLY {0,1}(20)
   18:     EXACT <s>(0)
   20: CLOSE1(22)
   22: END(0)
stclass `ALNUM' plus minlen 8
```

This is the execution plan of a state machine, which is what the regexp engine creates from the patterns that we supply it. The state numbers, which are also the position of the relevant parts of the pattern in the pattern text, are the columns on the left. The numbers in parentheses on the right are transitions to other states (or jumping points to other parts of the pattern text, which is the same thing) that take place in the right circumstances. For example, state 7 is a BRANCH with two possible successors, 8 and 11. The engine will first move to state 8, and if it succeeds, move on to 16. If state 8 fails, the engine returns to state 7 and takes the other branch to state 11.

Of course, we do not need to understand this state machine in detail, but it can be useful for working out what a regexp actually says, as opposed to what we thought it said. Failing that, we can look at the match dialog to see how the pattern is processed against our match text.

The match dialog is a lot longer, so we won't reproduce it in full. However, from the start of the match text to the first match (two protons) it looks like this, with some additional explanatory comments:

```
Matching REx '(\w+\s+(?:proton|neutron)s?)' against 'helium contains two
protons, two neutrons and
two electrons'
  Setting an EVAL scope, savestack=10
  0 <> <helium conta>      |  1:  OPEN1
  0 <> <helium conta>      |  3:  PLUS
                           ALNUM can match 6 times out of 32767...
```

Aha, the engine has found `helium` at position 0 in the match text, matching the `\w+` that ends at position 3 in the pattern. Note that all of `helium` matches at once because `\w+` is greedy.

```
  Setting an EVAL scope, savestack=10
  6 <elium> < contai>      |  5:  PLUS
                           SPACE can match 1 times out of 32767...
```

It is followed by a space at position 6, so that satisfies the `\s` that ends at position 5. So far, so good ...

```
  Setting an EVAL scope, savestack=10
  7 <lium > <contain>      |  7:      BRANCH
  Setting an EVAL scope, savestack=10
  7 <lium > <contain>      |  8:         EXACT <proton>
                           failed...
```

Oops, the next character does not match the start of proton ...

```
  7 <lium > <contain>      | 12:         EXACT <neutron>
                           failed...
```

and it does not match the start of neutron either ...

```
                           failed...
```

so it does not match proton OR neutron ...

```
                           failed...
```

As there are no other alternatives, the match for \s must be wrong, so backtrack . . .

```
5 <heliu> <m conta>    |  5:    PLUS
                       SPACE can match 0 times out of 32767...
```

Now the greediness of \w+ counts against it. The engine tries to match \w+ against one less character, then sees if that allows \s to match. Of course, it does not.

```
Setting an EVAL scope, savestack=10
                              failed...
  4 <heli> <um conta>   |  5:    PLUS
                       SPACE can match 0 times out of 32767...
Setting an EVAL scope, savestack=10
                              failed...
  3 <hel> <ium conta>   |  5:    PLUS
                       SPACE can match 0 times out of 32767...
Setting an EVAL scope, savestack=10
                              failed...
  2 <he> <lium conta>   |  5:    PLUS
                       SPACE can match 0 times out of 32767...
Setting an EVAL scope, savestack=10
                              failed...
  1 <h> <elium conta>   |  5:    PLUS
                       SPACE can match 0 times out of 32767...
Setting an EVAL scope, savestack=10
                              failed...
```

The engine backtracks all the way back down helium, matching \w+ against one less character each time and trying to match \s with the following character . . .

```
                              failed...
```

Oops, run out of characters to backtrack. So the match to \w+ must also be incorrect. Look for somewhere else to match \w+.

```
Setting an EVAL scope, savestack=10
  7 <lium > <contain>   |  1:    OPEN1
  7 <lium > <contain>   |  3:    PLUS
                       ALNUM can match 8 times out of 32767...
```

The next place that fits \w+ is the word contains. The story for the next few messages is a repeat of the earlier failed match that started with helium, since contains is followed by a space, but the space isn't followed by proton or neutron . . .

```
Setting an EVAL scope, savestack=10
 15 <tains> < two pr>   |  5:    PLUS
                       SPACE can match 1 times out of 32767...
Setting an EVAL scope, savestack=10
 16 <ains > <two pro>   |  7:    BRANCH
Setting an EVAL scope, savestack=10
 16 <ains > <two pro>   |  8:        EXACT <proton>
                              failed...
```

```
16 <ains > <two pro>    | 12:        EXACT <neutron>
                            failed...
                          failed...
                        failed...
```

Again, we find that neutron does not match, so (proton|neutron) does not match, so the \s cannot match. Time to backtrack . . .

```
14 <ntain> <s two p>    |  5:    PLUS
                        SPACE can match 0 times out of 32767...
Setting an EVAL scope, savestack=10
                            failed...
13 <ontai> <ns two >    |  5:    PLUS
                        SPACE can match 0 times out of 32767...
Setting an EVAL scope, savestack=10
                            failed...
12 <conta> <ins two>    |  5:    PLUS
                        SPACE can match 0 times out of 32767...
Setting an EVAL scope, savestack=10
                            failed...
11 < cont> <ains tw>    |  5:    PLUS
                        SPACE can match 0 times out of 32767...
Setting an EVAL scope, savestack=10
                            failed...
10 <m con> <tains t>    |  5:    PLUS
                        SPACE can match 0 times out of 32767...
Setting an EVAL scope, savestack=10
                            failed...
 9 <um co> <ntains >    |  5:    PLUS
                        SPACE can match 0 times out of 32767...
Setting an EVAL scope, savestack=10
                            failed...
 8 <ium c> <ontains>    |  5:    PLUS
                        SPACE can match 0 times out of 32767...  Setting an
EVAL scope,
savestack=10
                            failed...
```

We backtrack all the way to the start of contains trying to match \s and failing, exactly as we did before with helium . . .

```
                        failed...
```

but there is no match. Ergo \w+ cannot match any part of contains either. The engine gives up and moves forward again, looking for the next match for \w+ . . .

```
Setting an EVAL scope, savestack=10
16 <ains > <two pro>    |  1: OPEN1
16 <ains > <two pro>    |  3: PLUS
                        ALNUM can match 3 times out of 32767...
```

The next word is two, matching the \w+ . . .

```
Setting an EVAL scope, savestack=10
19 <s two> < proton>     | 5:     PLUS
                           SPACE can match 1 times out of 32767...
```

which is followed by a space, matching the \s . . .

```
Setting an EVAL scope, savestack=10
20 < two > <protons>     | 7:     BRANCH
Setting an EVAL scope, savestack=10
20 < two > <protons>     | 8:         EXACT <proton>
```

Aha, this time the test for proton succeeds. We never test for neutron because proton is given first in the regexp.

```
26 <roton> <s, two >     | 16:        CURLY {0,1}
                           EXACT <s> can match 1 times out of 1...
```

The optional s also matches, so we grab it too. Note how the ? is internally expanded to {0,1}.

```
Setting an EVAL scope, savestack=10
27 <otons> <, two n>     | 20:        CLOSE1
27 <otons> <, two n>     | 22:        END
Match successful!
```

And now we have reached the end of the regexp (CLOSE1). Since there is no more pattern left, we must have matched. Hurrah! We leave the regexp and execute the body of the while loop:

```
Found two protons
```

Transliteration

Transliteration is the process of replacing one letter with another. The synonymous transliteration operators tr and y, sometimes written tr/// or y///, are usually grouped with the regexp operators because of the similarity of their syntax to the substitution operator. Like the substitution operator, they can be used with any suitable delimiters, are bound to the input text with =~, have search and replace criteria, and even accept modifiers. However, the syntax is really the beginning and the end of their similarity.

The left-hand side of a transliteration is not a pattern but a list of characters to be transformed (that is, transliterated), and the right-hand side is the list of characters that they are transformed into. Each character on the left-hand side is converted into the corresponding character on the right, determined by their respective positions in the left and right lists.

As a simple example, this transliteration converts the letter a into the letter z, the letter b into the letter y, and the letter c into the letter x:

```
$text =~ tr/abc/zyx/;
```

If the replacement list is longer than the search list, then the trailing characters are ignored. If it is shorter, Perl repeats the final character until the replacement list is long enough:

```
$text =~ tr/abcd/zy/;
```

This example replaces a with z and all of b, c, and d with y. The replacement list is internally expanded to zyyy.

The return value from a transliteration is a count of the number of successful translations. Since transliteration is faster than a regular expression for finding single characters, one way we could (for instance) count the number of vowels in a piece of text would be with a transliteration:

```
$vowel_count = $text =~ tr/aeiou/aeiou/;
```

This is a useful enough feature that we can omit the replacement list entirely and produce the same effect:

```
$vowel_count = $text =~ tr/aeiou//; # same as above
```

Although the search list of a transliteration is not a pattern, it does allow some of the syntax defining character classes, and accepts both ranges and interpolation metacharacters (but not, ironically, actual character class metacharacters or interpolated variables). Here is a transliteration that uses ranges to uppercase the letters a to f and z:

```
$text =~ tr/a-fz/A-FZ/;
```

In a similar vein, here is a transliteration that replaces tabs and newlines with spaces:

```
$text =~ tr/\t\n/ /;
```

Here is a transliteration that matches the entire range of characters except ASCII 255 and adds one to the ASCII value of each character:

```
$text = "HAL";
$text =~ tr/\x00-\xfe/\x01-\xff/;
# \x00 is a long way of saying \0 that looks better here
print $text;   # produces 'IBM'
```

Finally, here is an implementation of ROT-13, which swaps the first half of the alphabet with the second:

```
$text =~ tr/a-nA-Nm-zM-Z/m-zM-Za-nA-N/;
```

Note that we cannot use a transliteration to say things like "replace a tab with four spaces"—for that we need a substitution (or the Text::Tabs module). Transliteration can only replace a character with another character, never more, and never less without a modifier.

Transliteration lists are compiled by Perl at compile time, so neither the search nor the replace lists are interpolated. If we want to use lists determined at run time, then we must use an eval:

```
eval "tr/$search/$replace/";
```

As with its regular expression siblings, the transliteration operator will use $_ by default if no explicit match text is supplied:

```
tr/a-z/A-Z/;   # capitalize all lower case characters in $_
```

If the replacement list is empty, characters are transliterated into themselves without change. On its own this is not especially useful, but this behavior is altered by both the /d and /s modifiers.

Transliteration Modifiers

Standard transliterations support three modifiers (c, d, and s) that alter the nature of the transliteration.

The /c or compliment modifier inverts the sense of the search list to include all characters except those listed (somewhat similar to the opening caret of a negated character class). For example, to replace all nonalphabetic characters or whitespace characters with question marks, we could use

```
$text =~ tr/a-zA-Z\t\n/?/c;
```

The /d or delete modifier removes any character in the search list (possibly inverted by /c) that is not transliterated. That is, if the search list is longer than the replacement list, then the replacement list is not extended; the characters on the search list, for which there is no replacement, are then deleted.

```
$text =~ tr/a-zA-Z/A-Z/d;    # uppercase a-z and delete existing A-Z
```

The /s or squash modifier removes duplicate characters in the resulting text if both characters were the product of transliteration. Existing duplicates or duplicates that occur because only one character has been transliterated are left alone. Here is an example that flattens whitespace:

```
$text =~ tr/\t\n/ /s;
# translate any whitespace to literal space and remove resulting duplicates
```

Note that for this example to work, we had to transliterate spaces to themselves in order to be considered for duplicate removal.

To remove existing duplicates, we can transliterate them into themselves by specifying the /s modifier and an empty replacement list. This causes every character to be transliterated into itself, after which duplicates are removed:

```
$text =~ tr/a-zA-Z0-9//s;    # remove duplicate alphanumeric characters
```

All three modifiers may be used in combination with each other. As an example, here is an improved duplicate character eliminator that works for any character at all:

```
$text =~ tr///cs;
```

This works by taking the complement of no characters at all (which is all characters) and translating them into themselves, removing duplicates. Beware, however, of using a complemented nothing as a search list to mean "all characters." Although it does mean this, the width of the search list is still zero, so we only get the expected result if the replacement list is also empty.

Summary

In this chapter, we have explored two of Perl's richest features—interpolation and regular expressions. We first examined the ways in which Perl performs the task of string interpolation, when interpolation occurs, and how to interpolate variables and code.

We then looked at regular expressions, including the match, substitution, and split functions, and basic and advanced definition of search patterns. We saw how to match overlapping terms, compare greedy versus nongreedy matches, convert file wildcards into regular expressions, and match multiple times with the same pattern. We also looked at Perl's advanced special patterns, techniques and strategies for writing efficient regular expressions, and how to debug a regular expression using Perl's built-in regular expression tracer. We also looked at generating regular expressions, precompiling them with the qr operator, and checking their validity before trying to use them.

Finally, we looked briefly at the transliteration function, which shares a great deal in common with the syntax of the match and substitution functions but turns out to have nothing to do with regular expressions.

CHAPTER 12

■ ■ ■

Input and Output with Filehandles

In order to read or write to any kind of data source, we need a way of communicating with it. Filehandles provide that facility, acting as one end of a channel along which data can pass in one or both directions. The other end of the channel is largely abstract, so aside from the details of how we create the filehandle, one filehandle is very much like another. This abstraction allows a lot of different IO programming tasks to be condensed down into one set of concepts. Once we have a filehandle, we can read from it and write to it. If the filehandle points to an actual file or a device that supports the concept of a position, we can also use random access to read or write to different parts of it.

We can do more with filehandles than read or write them, however. One important feature is *file locking*, the process of restricting access to a file by other processes or programs while it is in use. This is often an important issue for CGI scripts, for example. Additionally, we can redirect data streams by replacing filehandles, duplicate filehandles, and even redefine the default filehandle used by functions such as print. All of these issues will be covered in this chapter. In Chapter 13, we look more into manipulating files and directories by name, and also cover directory filehandles, which are superficially similar to but actually quite different from filehandles. Filehandles represent every other kind of input and output we might have to deal with, and they are the primary subject of this chapter.

IO and Filehandles

Filehandles provide a connection between our program and an external data source (or, technically, sink, if we are writing rather than reading). This source may be a file physically present on disk, or it may be something different, such as a serial device, network connection, or the keyboard. Filehandles abstract the details away so all of these wildly different forms of communication can be treated in very similar ways. Although only a small subclass of filehandles actually access a file, the name is used generically, so standard output is a filehandle even though it normally writes to the screen.

At the heart of every filehandle is a *file descriptor*, an integer value that represents the raw data stream and which is used with the operating system. Programmers familiar with C will recognize that Perl's filehandles are very similar to the higher-level buffered input and output provided by streams, which are also based on file descriptors. Indeed, Perl's filehandles wrap file descriptors in much the same way. However, Perl does not make direct use of streams and instead implements much of the same functionality within the interpreter itself. This means that Perl's treatment of filehandles is broadly similar to C, but not identical.

In Perl 5.8, the ground rules for filehandles have changed with the introduction of *PerlIO*, a generic system for managing the properties of filehandles through layers that supply buffering, encoding, and translation. The default configuration in a PerlIO-enabled Perl interpreter is broadly similar to that just described, with the Perl-supplied buffering now provided by the perlio layer. However, we can reconfigure layers to our heart's content, replacing Perl's perlio layer with real Unix stdio buffering if it is available. We can even remove the buffering layer completely and make all our input and output implicitly unbuffered, even for higher-level functions like print. Other layers provide encoding and translation support—the distinction between text and binary files on Windows is handled by the crlf layer, rather than being an embedded feature of the binmode function. Similarly, Unicode is handled by the utf8 layer. We can create our own custom layers and manipulate the layers of a filehandle even while it is still open. Before we get into all the possibilities that this offers, though, it is probably a good idea to get the basics of filehandles down first.

The Filehandle Data Type

Filehandles in Perl are a distinct data type. They are unrelated to scalars and have their own slot in symbol table typeglobs, as we covered in Chapter 5. The reason for this differentiation is that underneath the opaque skin of a filehandle is a structured collection of information that describes the actual connection. By keeping this information private, the filehandle is able to conceal the physical aspects of the device that it is associated with. This allows it to make use of buffering to improve the efficiency of IO operations, storing up writes until there is enough to send and reading larger chunks of data than we asked for. Further attempts to read can then be supplied from memory rather than accessing the data source again. In the case of files, this minimizes the number of disk accesses required, and for other filehandles it minimizes the number of interruptions that the system must undergo.

Filehandles are not scalar values, despite the fact that they represent a single opaque value. As a result, assigning a filehandle to a scalar does not work. By the same token, passing a filehandle into or out of a subroutine also doesn't work. Since there is no special prefix for filehandle variables, only a data type, the only way to pass filehandles around is to refer to them via their typeglob entry. Fortunately, we can create a reference to the typeglob and store it in a scalar variable, then use the reference in place of a regular filehandle.

Standard Filehandles

Perl provides three standard filehandles to all Perl programs automatically, STDIN, STDOUT, and STDERR. All three are automatically open and can be used immediately, without any explicit command to do so.

- Standard input, or STDIN, represents the default input filehandle. In an interactive session, it is usually connected to the keyboard. This is the filehandle that functions like getc (and the readline operator) use by default.

- Standard output, or STDOUT, represents the default output filehandle. In an interactive session, it is usually connected to the screen (also called the *console device*). This is the filehandle that the print and printf functions use by default. Both STDIN and STOUT are "smart" and buffer their connections automatically, buffering whole blocks of data unless they are connected to an interactive device, in which case they only perform line buffering.

- Standard error, or STDERR, is the default error output filehandle. Like STDOUT, it is normally connected to the screen. Unlike STDOUT, it is usually not buffered at all, which ensures that error messages are always written in a timely manner.

For many applications, the standard filehandles are actually all we need, and indeed many of the examples in the book so far make implicit use of them without touching on the subject of IO at all. However, if we want to read or write to anything else, we will need to create a filehandle to access it.

Creating Filehandles

There are two primary ways to create a filehandle in Perl. The most obvious is the open function, which attempts to open a file and create a filehandle to talk to it. The other is to use the IO:: modules, and the IO::File module in particular. The IO:: modules provide an object-oriented interface, which makes them easy to use even if we are not writing object-oriented programs, and for older versions of Perl makes it simpler to create filehandle references.

Creating Filehandles with open

The open function takes a file name and creates a filehandle. Traditionally it takes two arguments, the filehandle to create and the file name, optionally prefixed by an open mode. Without any prefix, files are opened for reading only, as in these two examples:

```
open (MYHANDLE, "myfile"); # explicit file name
open MYHANDLE $filename;    # file name in variable
```

The filehandle MYHANDLE is a package variable that is defined by the call to open. Once open, we can read from the file. For example, reading with the readline operator:

```
while (<MYHANDLE>) {
    print "Received: $_";
}
```

For ordinary files, the return value from open is 1 on success and the undefined value on failure. The filehandle will be created in either case, but if the call to open fails, the filehandle will be unopened and unassigned. In the event that the open fails, the reason is stored in the special variable $! (or $ERRNO if we use English), which produces a message in string context. Since failing to open a file is often a fatal problem for a lot of Perl scripts, open and die are often combined together:

```
open (MYHANDLE, $filename) or die "Can't open $filename: $!\n";
```

Even if we do not want to die, it is a good idea to check the return value of open; failing to check the return value from open can lead to all sorts of problems when we try to use the filehandle.

We can also, from Perl 5.6 onwards, create a filehandle reference and use that in exactly the same way as a regular filehandle. For example:

```
open my $myhandle $filename; # Perl 5.6 or higher only
```

Other than the introduction of the scalar variable, this works exactly the same as the previous example, except that the filehandle will close automatically when the scalar variable $myhandle goes out of scope. This will not work on older versions of Perl, though. When this is a concern, the IO::Handle module, detailed later, provides the same ability to create filehandle references and will also work on older Perl installations. We will come back to the idea of filehandles accessed by reference shortly, in "Referring to Filehandles."

The open function also has a one-argument form. Here, the file name is specified as a package scalar, and open will use the name of the file to create a filehandle of the same name (that is, in the filehandle slot of the typeglob to which the scalar belongs). This does not work for my-declared ones, so its usefulness is somewhat limited:

```
our $FILE = "myfile";
open FILE or die "Failed to open: $! \n";
```

Opening Files for Reading, Writing, and Updating

Without a prefix of any kind, open opens a file for reading only. In order to write to or change the contents of a file, we have to prefix the file name with a file access mode—optionally separated from the file name by spaces. The read mode prefix, <, is usually omitted because it is the default. To write or append to a file, we use the > or >> mode, respectively:

```
open MYHANDLE, ">$file";   # open file for writing
open MYHANDLE, "> $file";  # the same, with optional spacing added
open MYHANDLE, ">>$file";  # open file for appending
```

Both these modes open the file for writing only, but they differ in significant ways. > will create the file if it does not exist, but it destroys any existing content if it does. >> also creates the file if it does not exist, but it will append to the end of the file if it does.

open understands six modes in total: the three standard modes and three "update" variations. The full list with explanations is given in Table 12-1.

Table 12-1. *open File Access Modes*

Mode	Symbol	Description
Read	<	Open the file for read access only, for example: open FH, "<$file"; This is the default mode, and so the < prefix is usually optional. The exception is if the first character of the file name is significant to open; see the upcoming section "Opening Arbitrary File Names." If the file does not exist, then the open fails.
Write	>	Open the file for write access only, for example: open FH, ">$file"; If the file does not exist, then it is created and opened. If the file does exist, then it is truncated and its existing contents are lost. Note that some platforms will not allow the same file to be opened for writing more than once (any Unix-like platform will be fine, however).
Append	>>	Open the file for write access only, for example: open FH, ">>$file"; If the file does not exist, then it is created. If the file does exist, then it is opened and the existing contents are preserved. Any writes to the file will be appended to the end of the existing contents.
Read-Update	+<	Open the file for read and write access, for example: open FH, "+<$file"; This is the standard way to open a file for both read and write access. If the file does not exist, then the open fails. If the file does exist, then its existing contents are preserved, and both read and write will start from the beginning of the file. Note that this is the correct mode to use if we want to open a file and write over the existing contents. The +>> mode appears to do this job, but it will generally append to the end of the file instead, irrespective of the file position.
Write-Update	+>	Open the file for read and write access, for example: open FH, "+>$file"; As with +<, the file is opened for read and write access. If the file does not exist, then it is created. If the file does exist, then it is truncated and its existing contents are lost. Because of this, this mode is usually only used to create new files that will first be written to and later read from.

Mode	Symbol	Description
Append-Update	+>>	Open the file for read and write access, for example: `open FH, "+>>$file";` If the file does not exist, then it is created. If the file does exist, then both read and write commence from the end of the file. On most (but frustratingly not all) platforms, reads may take place from anywhere in the file, presuming the file position is first moved with seek. Writes always append to the end of the file, moving the file position with them. For this reason, this mode is not usually used for read-write access; +< is preferred.

Opening Arbitrary File Names

There are perfectly legal file names that open may have trouble with. For instance, a file could start with a mode sign such as >. This causes problems with the traditional use of open to open a file for reading where the optional < prefix is omitted:

```
$file = ">file";           # tricky file name (starts with a prefix)
open MYHANDLE, $file;      # opens 'file' for writing, prefix in $file is used
open MYHANDLE, "<$file";   # opens '>file' for reading
```

To disambiguate these cases, Perl also provides a three-argument version of open where the mode is supplied separately from the file name. This also allows us to protect leading or trailing spaces, should we be using a file name containing them:

```
$file = " file ";          # leading space
open MYHANDLE, "<$file";   # incorrect, opens 'file'
                           # (leading space stripped after interpolation)
open MYHANDLE, '<', $file; # correct, opens ' file '
                           # (no interpolation, space is preserved)
```

Another way to handle awkwardly named files is to use the system-level open function sysopen instead of open. This will be covered later in the chapter.

Opening Standard Input and Standard Output

The open function treats certain file names as special. For example, if the file name passed to open is a single minus, -, or a minus prefixed with a < symbol, then open will instead open standard input:

```
open MYSTDIN, '-';
```

At first glance, this may not seem particularly useful, but it turns out to be very handy. For a start, we can tell a program to either read from an explicit file name, or from standard input, by selectively passing in either the file name or a minus:

```
$filename = get_filename();        # subroutine, may return undef
open FILE, $filename?$filename:'-'; # open standard input if no file name
```

Perl also makes use of this feature when processing the @ARGV array using the readline operator, <>. See Chapter 14 for more details of using @ARGV in this way.

If the file name passed to open is >-, then standard output is opened instead:

```
open MYSTDOUT, '>-';
```

Again, although not apparently useful, this allows programs to pass in standard output as a file name to functions and subroutines that accept an arbitrary file name.

There is no equivalent way to open standard error in this fashion, at least portably, as it does not have a shorthand file name alias. If we want to explicitly open standard error we can do so, but only by either opening platform-specific files (for example, /dev/stderr on some Unix implementations) or duplicating or aliasing the existing filehandle, which we will cover later in the section "Duplication and Aliasing Filehandles." Note that if we really want to read and write to a file called -, which is rather dubious, we can use the three-argument version of open to do so:

```
open FILE, '+<', '-';   # open a file called '-'.
```

Creating Filehandles with IO::Handle and IO::File

To simplify the creation and use of filehandles, Perl comes with the IO:: family of modules to abstract much of the awkward aspects of filehandles. At the same time, they also provide an object-oriented interface. The IO::Handle module provides basic filehandle support. Support for filehandles representing real files comes from the IO::File module. Directories are handled by IO::Dir, and other special filehandle types are covered by IO::Socket and IO::Pipe.

IO::Handle provides a constructor for creating new anonymous filehandles and a number of methods, such as autoflush, that provide a more convenient interface to variables such as $|. All filehandles are automatically in the IO::Handle namespace, so even "normal" bareword filehandles like STDIN, STDERR, or MYHANDLE can make use of these methods once the IO::Handle module is loaded. Similarly, we can use regular built-in functions like open and print on IO::Handle-derived handles with no change in usage:

```
use IO::Handle;

STDOUT->print("Built-in function"); #does not need IO::Handle
STDOUT->autoflush(1); #added by IO::Handle module

my $fh=new IO::Handle;
open $fh, "myfile.txt" or die "open failed: $!";
```

The last two lines achieve the same end as creating a filehandle by reference (also called an indirect filehandle) as we saw earlier:

```
open my $fh, "myfile.txt" or die "open failed: $!";
```

This syntax is only available from Perl 5.6 onwards, however. By contrast, the IO::Handle version will work on older Perl versions.

A full rundown of IO::Handle is offered later in the chapter. Most of the time, though, we do not use it directly, but one of the several modules built upon it. If we plan to use several of these IO:: modules at once, we can save some typing and use IO instead. This is simply a convenient umbrella module that loads several of the IO:: modules all at once. So, we can say this:

```
use IO::Dir;
use IO::File;
use IO::Handle;
use IO::Pipe;
use IO::Seekable;
use IO::Socket;
```

Or, more tersely:

```
use IO;
```

While convenient, this batch loading is wasteful if we do not actually need all of these modules. In the majority of cases, we should just use the specific IO:: module (or modules) that we need. (An exception to this rule would be persistent environments like Apache's mod_perl, where the same modules can be loaded at startup and used by unlimited Perl handlers.)

Probably the most useful user of IO::Handle is IO::File, which provides generic support for files. Opening a file with IO::File is not dissimilar to opening it with open, but with a much more convenient interface. For example, to open a file in write-only mode, we can supply a single parameter:

```
use IO::File;

$fh = new IO::File;   # create a filehandle object
$fh->open("> myfile") or die "Unable to open: $!";   # open a file
```

We can also create the handle and open the file in a single statement:

```
$fh = new IO::File("> myfile") or die "Unable to open: $!";
```

The filehandle returned from the IO::File new call is a filehandle object that we can use anywhere a regular filehandle goes. In addition, we can manipulate the filehandle with methods from the IO::File, IO::Handle or optional extra IO::Seekable modules:

```
$fh->autoflush(1);                 # IO::Handle
$fh->seek(0, SEEK_END);      # IO::Seekable
$fh->print("Message...\n");    # built-in
$fh->close();                         # IO::File
$fh->open("> $anotherfile");  # IO::File
```

The new method also accepts two arguments, in which case the second argument is the mode to open the file in:

```
$fh->open($anotherfile, ">");
```

The mode may be any of the modes acceptable to open. In addition, it will accept one of the equivalent C-style fopen modes, for which Perl's modes are synonyms. In both cases, IO::File maps the call into an open and returns a filehandle. Finally, the mode may be a combination of numeric flags, which together make up the mode. In this case, IO::File translates the call into a sysopen, and like sysopen we may also supply a permissions mask. The standard open modes are all shorthand codes for their equivalent sysopen mode flags, as Table 12-2 illustrates.

Table 12-2. *open vs. sysopen File Access Modes*

open Mode	fopen Mode	sysopen Flags
<	r	O_RDONLY
>	w	O_WRONLY | O_CREAT | O_TRUNC
>>	a	O_WRONLY | O_APPEND | O_CREAT
+<	r+	O_RDWR
+>	w+	O_RDWR |O_CREAT | O_TRUNC
+>>	a+	O_RDWR |O_APPEND | O_CREAT

Examination of the sysopen flags is revealing. A base mode is always required, and it must be one of O_RDONLY, O_WRONLY, or O_RDWR, which open a file for reading only, writing only (not supported on Windows), or both reading and writing, respectively. To append to a file, we add the O_APPEND flag. Clearly this needs a writable file, so it only combines with O_WRONLY or O_RDWR. Similarly, O_CREAT will create the file if it does not exist, and O_TRUNC will truncate it if it does. By examining this table, we can see why the standard open modes do what they do.

One of the benefits of IO::File is that it allows us to choose whichever method suits us at the time. However, if we want to specify file permissions too, then we must use the sysopen style and supply a numeric mode. We'll cover this and the other flags that can be supplied in a sysopen mode in the section "System-Level IO" later in the chapter.

The DATA Filehandle

Perl defines a special pseudo-filehandle, DATA, that will read input data from within the source file. To create data within a source file, we insert the special token __DATA__ on a line of its own. Everything below this token will not be parsed or compiled by Perl but will instead be made available as input to the DATA pseudo-filehandle, up to the end of the file or an __END__ token, if present.

■Tip We may sometimes see Perl programs use __END__ for this purpose. This may seem confusing since __END__ is supposed to stop Perl parsing, period. The reason for this is for backwards compatibility with the era before Perl 5, where __END__ officially had the role that __DATA__ now does. Consequently __END__ works like __DATA__ in the main source file, but not in other packages or in files included by do or require.

Defining data within a source file can be very convenient. For example, we can define a default configuration file without actually creating or installing a separate file to hold it. It is also convenient for defining large data structures with complex syntax, or where the data is very unlikely to change. Here is an example of a program that stores planetary data in a table and reads it with the DATA filehandle:

```perl
#!/usr/bin/perl
# planets.pl
use warnings;
use strict;

my $columns = <DATA>;
chomp $columns;
my @columns = split /\s*, \s*/, $columns;
shift @columns;   # lose first name

my %table;

while (<DATA>) {
    next if /^#/;   # skip comments
    my @data = split /\s*, \s*/;
    my $name = shift @data;

    foreach (0..$#data) {
        print "$_ : $columns[$_] : $data[$_] \n";
        $table{$name}{$columns[$_]} = $data[$_];
    }
}

foreach (sort keys %table) {
    print "$_\n";
    foreach my $stat (sort keys %{$table{$_}}) {
        print "\t$stat = $table{$_}{$stat}\n";
    }
}
__DATA__
Body    , Radius , Mass    , Distance, Moons, Day        , Year
# The Sun
Sun     , 6.960e8, 1.989e30, 0       , n/a  , 25.36 days , n/a
# The Planets
Mercury , 2.420e6, 3.301e23, 5.791e10, 0    , 58.7 days  , 87.97 days
Venus   , 6.085e6, 4.869e24, 1.082e11, 0    , 243 days   , 224.7 days
```

```
Earth    , 6.378e6, 5.978e24, 1.496e11, 1    , 23.93 hours, 365.3 days
Mars     , 3.375e6, 6.420e23, 2.279e11, 2    , 24.6 hours , 687 days
Jupiter  , 7.140e7, 1.899e27, 7.783e11, 13   , 9.9 hours  , 11.86 years
Saturn   , 6.040e7, 5.685e26, 1.427e12, 10   , 10.2 hours , 28.46 years
Uranus   , 2.360e7, 8.686e25, 2.869e12, 5    , 10.7 hours , 84.02 years
Neptune  , 2.230e7, 1.025e26, 4.498e12, 2    , 15.8 hours , 164.8 years
Pluto    , 3.000e6, 5.000e23, 5.900e12, 1    , 6.3 days   , 248 years
# And the Moon, just for luck
Moon     , 1.738e6, 7.353e22, 1.496e11, n/a  , 27.32 days , 27.32 days


__END__
A comment - this is neither part of the program nor the data (but see below...)
```

If an __END__ token appears after the __DATA__ token, then the data ends as soon as it encounters the __END__, otherwise it finishes at the end of the file. __DATA__ tokens are actually package scoped, so multiple __DATA__ tokens in different files but within the same package concatenate together in the order in which the package files are used or required. To access the data in a different package, we can prefix the filehandle with the package name:

```
# access data in MyPackage
while (<MyPackage::DATA>) {
    ...
}
```

As mentioned earlier, the main source file treats __END__ differently, for compatibility reasons. Consequently, if we use __END__ in the main package, it works like a second __DATA__. If we have already seen a __DATA__ token, however, as is the case in this program, the __END__ is not treated specially and becomes ordinary data. That is, it does *not* signify the end of the data, as it would in any other package. The planets program is actually written to avoid us noticing that it does in fact read both the __END__ and the comment following it as data; the errant lines are eliminated because they do not contain any commas. To prove this, change the hyphen after 'A comment' to a comma and planet 'A comment' will duly appear in the output next time the program is run. If __END__ does not appear to be working correctly, this may be the reason.

Anonymous Temporary Filehandles

We can create a filehandle for a anonymous temporary file using a special variant of the open function (or open method, if we are using IO::File) if we specify undef as the name of the file. The file is anonymous because we do not know its name, nor do we have any way of finding it out. It exists only for so long as the filehandle remains open and is deleted when the filehandle is closed or (in the case of a lexically scoped filehandle reference) falls out of scope.

Clearly it is not useful to create a read-only or write-only filehandle to such a file. Instead, we use the +> or +< mode to create a file that we can both update and read from. (The former makes more sense, as a temporary file that we have only just created is not expected to already have content.) Since the file name is undef, the mode must be specified as a separate argument, making a total of three:

```
open my $tempfh '+>',undef; # open temporary file
print $tempfh "Now you see me";
close $tempfh; # poof!
```

These filehandles can be cloned and duplicated like regular filehandles (we will see how to do this in "Duplicating and Aliasing Filehandles" later) so we can fork a Perl program and have a child process write to the handle, picking up the results later by seeking to the start of the file and reading the contents. Closing the handle destroys the temporary file and the data it contains.

In-Memory Filehandles

From Perl 5.8 onwards, we can take advantage of PerlIO to treat scalar variables like in-memory files. This feature is transparent and occurs automatically if we specify a scalar variable instead of a file name to the open function. In-memory filehandles work just like any other kind of filehandle: we can open them for read, write, or update, seek to different positions in the "file," and so on. At the same time, we can still access or even modify the underlying scalar variable, which has the same effect on the filehandle as changing a file on disk would to a normal filehandle.

Like anonymous temporary files, to use an in-memory filehandle we need to specify the file mode separately. This is true even for read-only filehandles where we must specify a mode of <—it is no longer automatically presumed:

```perl
#!/usr/bin/perl
# inmemoryfiles.pl
use strict;
use warnings;

my $text="The Giant's Game\nThe End Of The World\n";

open MEMFILE, "<", \$text;
print scalar(<MEMFILE>); # produces "The Giant's Game"
close MEMFILE;

my $log="";
open LOGFILE, ">", \$log;
print LOGFILE "The Enemy's Gate";
print LOGFILE " is down\n";
close LOGFILE;
print $log;       # produces "The Enemy's Gate Is Down"
```

This short program exercises two memory filehandles in a read-only and write-only configuration, respectively. If we use a mode like >> or +>>, we can also append to the existing contents of the variable. Note, however, that to reopen a standard filehandle like STDOUT to point to an in-memory file, it must be closed first. This is because the in-memory file is not based upon a file descriptor and thus does not automatically override the one providing the default standard output handle.

Other Filehandles

Before moving on to the details of reading and writing filehandles, it is worth mentioning the other kinds of filehandles supported by Perl. Four other functions in Perl return filehandles: opendir, pipe, socket, and socketpair. In the case of pipe and socketpair, they actually return two filehandles, but these are used in different circumstances.

Directories have their own special filehandle type that recognizes their special nature and allows their contents to be read like files. Directory filehandles can be manipulated much like regular filehandles, with the functions opendir, closedir, seekdir, telldir, rewinddir, and readdir provide the corresponding directory equivalents of their "dir-less" counterparts. IO::Dir wraps these functions in an object-oriented framework much like IO::File, but drops the "dir" suffix so the methods have the same names as their IO::File equivalents. The functions for writing are conspicuously absent because it makes no sense to write to a directory index. We cover directories in detail in the next chapter so that we can keep focused on the broader subject of filehandles here.

Pipes are simply a pair of filehandles wired back to back, one read-only and one write-only. We write into one end and read from the other. Pipes are mainly used for communicating between different processes and external programs, and they are consequently covered in detail in Chapter 21. The open function supports the creation of implicit pipes and the execution of external programs and can also be made to carry out a fork and exec at the same time. These extended uses of the open function are also covered in Chapter 21.

The socket function is the equivalent of open for sockets. Sockets are the backbone of Perl's network programming support and accordingly take up the bulk of Chapter 22. Sockets have more than one mode of operation, but they can operate very much like regular filehandles for the purposes of reading and writing. The socketpair function creates the equivalent of a pipe using sockets, returning two sockets connected back to back. Unlike ordinary pipes, a pair of sockets created this way permits two-way communications.

The term "filehandle" is thus rather more general than it might at first seem, since a handle need not refer to a file or even to a known hardware or network device. The elegance of filehandles is that once created, we can, for most intents and purposes, ignore what they actually represent. This does not mean we do not have to deal with the special circumstances of a filehandle—a network socket has to deal with networking issues that do not apply to a text file. It does mean, however, that for simple reading and writing we can treat all filehandles as basically similar.

Referring to Filehandles

Referring to filehandles correctly has historically been a large source of confusion in Perl. This confusion arises from two sources. First, there is no explicit syntax for the filehandle data type like there is for scalars, arrays, hashes, or typeglobs. Second, what we think of as filehandles in Perl source code are actually symbolic references to typeglobs containing filehandles. Perl's syntax and the use strict module conspire to make this transparent to us, but the conspiracy is not perfect, and so sometimes things do not work as we expect. Once we understand this, a lot of the mystery surrounding Perl's filehandles can be dispelled.

All Perl's built-in functions that take filehandles as arguments allow filehandles to be specified directly or indirectly. Directly just means writing the name of the filehandle, as in

```
print MYHANDLE "Hello Filehandle \n";
```

The print statement knows that MYHANDLE is a filehandle because

- It is the first parameter.
- It is followed by a space.
- It isn't a quoted string.

Unfortunately, if we try to copy this filehandle to a scalar variable, we get an illegal bareword syntax error under use strict:

```
use strict;

$fh = MYHANDLE;    # ERROR: syntax error
```

This is perfectly understandable. Barewords are not allowed in conjunction with use strict, and MYHANDLE is just a string without quotes in this statement. It may also be the name of a filehandle, but that does not mean it looks like a filehandle. Contrary to what the print statement earlier might imply, a bareword is not the syntax for a filehandle. It is actually a special case of a symbolic reference that is permitted by the strict module, precisely for the use of functions that take filehandles.

A filehandle's data type is different from that of a scalar, so we cannot simply store one inside the other, even though a filehandle is intuitively a "single" value. We cannot actually refer to a filehandle at all, only to the typeglob within which it resides. However, since all Perl's file handling functions accept typeglobs and references to typeglobs (both hard and symbolic) as filehandle arguments, we do not notice.

To store and pass filehandles, we need to take a reference to the typeglob of the same name. The reference can be a hard reference or a symbolic reference; either is acceptable to Perl's filehandle functions. Fortunately, treating typeglobs in scalar context generates a symbolic reference for the typeglob, so we can do this:

```
$fh = *MYHANDLE;    # $fh becomes '*main::MYHANDLE'
# symbolic reference OK as filehandle
print $fh "Hello Symbolic Reference to Filehandle \n";
```

Alternatively, we can create a hard reference to the typeglob and use that to indirectly refer to the filehandle:

```
$fh = \*MYHANDLE;    # reference to typeglob
print $fh "Hello Reference to Typeglob \n";
```

The print statement is a little more fastidious than the other filehandle-based functions because its syntax is so flexible in other respects. It will accept a typeglob, filehandle reference, or string stored in a scalar variable. In fact, print is actually an object-oriented method call disguised as a function. Perl blesses all filehandle references (held by the typeglob) into the IO::Handle package and treats print as a method of the class. Actually, loading the IO::Handle module simply augments this built-in behavior with additional features. We can prove this by rewriting the preceding as follows:

```
STDOUT->print("print reveals its true nature");
$fh->print("Hello Reference to Typeglob");
```

When a print statement is compiled, Perl must determine if the first argument could be used to refer to a filehandle or not. If it does, the object-oriented interpretation is used. If not, the currently selected output filehandle is used, and the first argument is reinterpreted as if it were the second.

The print function cannot accept a filehandle name as a literal string since it presumes the name is a value to print out, not a filehandle. This is a rule of convenience because it is the most probable interpretation of the programmer's intent, even if there really is a filehandle of that name. However, an expression inside a block does not trip the convenience rule, and so its value will interpreted as a filehandle:

```
print "STRING";                            # a regular text string
$hno=1; print {'HANDLE'.$hno} "Text...\n"    # print 'Text...' to HANDLE1, etc
print {'STD'.($err?'ERR':'OUT'} "Text...\n"; # STDOUT or STDERR
```

This requirement for a block to differentiate between a filehandle and a string is purely an artifact of this rule of convenience. Other filehandle-based functions do not have to worry about the distinction between first-argument filehandles or text, so they allow the use of strings and string expressions directly. To demonstrate, here are open and the corresponding function close, using a string expression as a filehandle:

```
open 'A'.'B'.'C', '>test.file';
print ABC "Yes, this actually works \n";
close "ABC";    # or even close uc('abc')
```

Since filehandles cannot be stored directly in scalars, typeglobs used to be the only way to pass filehandles into or out of subroutines:

```
# example of passing a filehandle to a subroutine
sub print_to_filehandle {
    $fh = shift;
    print $fh @_;
}

# pass filehandle as typeglob
print_to_filehandle(*STDOUT, "Hello Passed Filehandle \n");
```

```
# pass filehandle as scalar reference to typeglob
$fh = *STDOUT;
print_to_filehandle($fh, "Hello Again");
```

Closer observation of this code reveals that this is just another case of symbolic references. Whether or not we pass a filehandle directly to the subroutine or copy it into a scalar first, it is cast into a scalar by being passed as an argument. This is so that the typeglob is turned into a symbolic reference to itself (*main::STDOUT if we are not in a package), on which print is called as a method. In other words, we are passing a string and not a typeglob.

It is largely on account of this that the IO::Handle and IO::File modules were created, and later the ability to create a filehandle reference directly through open. The drawback with the IO::File and IO::Handle modules is that they add a level of abstraction to file handling, incurring a corresponding performance loss. For most applications, however, the advantages of the IO:: family in simplifying filehandles more than make up for this.

Reading from Filehandles

Once we have a filehandle, we can read from it, presuming that the filehandle is opened for reading and that there is something to read. We can also read a specific numbers of bytes or retrieve them one by one if necessary.

The Readline Operator

The simplest way to read from a filehandle is to use the readline operator, <>:

```
open MYHANDLE, "myfile" or die "Unable to open: $! \n";
$line = <MYHANDLE>;   # read a line
```

In a scalar context, the readline operator reads one line at a time, returning its value. In a list context, however, it reads all the lines at once:

```
@lines = <MYHANDLE>;   # read entire file at one go
```

A line is defined by the input record separator (held in the special variable $/). By default, this is set to the newline character, \n, which takes account of any special translations for the specific platform. This makes it very convenient for reading text files with lines delimited by newlines and is even platform independent. Be aware, however, that this can consume a lot of memory if the file is large.

Redefining the Line Separator

Because of the input record separator, we do not have to read literal lines. By redefining $/ ($INPUT_RECORD_SEPARATOR or $RS with use English), we can read on any delimiter we choose, for example, colons:

```
$/ = ':';
@lines = <MYHANDLE>;   # read file delimited by ':'
```

If we set $/ to an empty string, the readline operator is put into paragraph mode:

```
$/ = "";  # paragraph mode
```

Now the delimiter is matched by one or more completely empty lines in the input, so whole paragraphs will be read each time readline is called. The empty string is almost the same as "\n\n", except that in the latter case, multiple adjacent empty lines are treated as separate delimiters and result in readline returning empty lines itself. The empty string will, by contrast, treat all empty lines between paragraphs as a single delimiter, so long as there are at least two of them.

We can even undefine $/ completely. In this case, the readline operator works in slurp mode and reads an entire file into a single scalar string:

```
undef $/;
$file = <MYHANDLE>;   # read entire file as one scalar
```

This is particularly handy if we want to run a regular expression across the whole file, although it is important to remember that it could cause a severe memory shortage if we use it to read in what turns out to be a very large file.

If we redefine $/, it is a good idea to restore it afterward to avoid unexpected problems else-where. A simple solution is to localize the value of $/ and redefine the local definition—this will automatically restore the old definition at the end of scope, so we do not need to remember to do it explicitly:

```
sub readfile {
    $file = shift;
    if (open FILE, $file) {
        # undefine $/ if called in a scalar context
        local $/ = undef unless wantarray;
        # return file contents as array or single scalar
        return <FILE>;
    }
    return undef;   # failed to open, check $! for the reason
}
```

If the input record separator is defined as a scalar reference to an integer value (which may include a reference to a scalar variable), the readline operator goes into a fixed record mode, reading exactly that many characters each time:

```
$record_size = 32;
$/ = \$record_size;   # or, equivalently, $/ = \32
while (<MYHANDLE>) {
    print "Got $_\n";
    # $_ contains 32 characters unless end of file intervenes
}
```

In this mode, the readline operator is similar in nature to the read function, which we will dis-cuss in a moment.

Aliasing Readline in while Loops

When used in the conditional part of a while loop, the readline operator has the useful property of setting $_. This is a special case for the while loop, which does not ordinarily set $_. We can use this fact to read a file line by line like this:

```
open MYHANDLE, "myfile" or die "Unable to open: $! \n";
while (<MYHANDLE>) {
    print "Read: $_\n";
}
```

Unlike a foreach loop, we cannot provide our own variable after the while keyword to be the loop variable; in this case, it has to be $_. Instead, we can ignore the special case usage and declare and assign to a variable within the parentheses:

```
while (my $line=<MYHANDLE>) { ...
```

See the section "Conditional Loops—while, until, and do" in Chapter 6 for more details.

Counting Line Numbers

The special variable $. contains the number of lines read from the most recently read filehandle. For example, to print out matches in a file in a grep-like manner, we could use $. like this:

```
while (<MYHANDLE>) {
    /$searchpattern/ and print "$.: $_ \n";
}
```

Since $. is a package variable, it persists even after the file has run out of lines, so we can consult it after we have finished reading:

```
@lines = <MYHANDLE>;
print "$. lines read \n";
```

Technically, $. is not the line count but the input record number, as its value is dependent on the input record separator $/, so it does not necessarily reflect the number of lines in the file as we might understand it. So, if $/ is undefined, $. will most likely be 1. The value of $. is reset when the filehandle is closed.

If the range operator, .. or ..., is given a numeric value for either its left or right operand, an implicit comparison to $. is substituted.

Readline and the @ARGV Array

If no filehandle is given to <>, it interprets the elements of the @ARGV array as file names and attempts to open and read from them (as discussed at the start of Chapter 14). In brief, this is how it is done:

```
# read one or more files and print them out, prefixed by file name and line
# number
print "$ARGV:$.:$_" while <>;
```

The name of the file currently being read is held in $ARGV, while the filehandle is stored as ARGV. If @ARGV is empty, <> defaults to standard input by supplying a - behind the scenes, which can also be seen in $ARGV. Conversely, if more than one file is present, each is read in turn, although $. is not reset between files. To fix this, we can use eof and close, resetting $.:

```
while (<>) {
    print "$ARGV: $.: $_";
    close (ARGV) if eof;
}
```

See Chapter 14 for more details and examples of using the readline operator with command-line arguments.

Finer Control over Reading

The readline operator is best suited for reading files with known delimiters or fixed record lengths. For other applications, we may be better off using the read function. This function takes a filehandle, a scalar variable, and a length as arguments, and it attempts to read the number of bytes given by the length into the scalar variable.

```
read MYHANDLE, $text, 60;   # attempt to read 60 bytes into $text
```

The return value of read is either the number of bytes read (which may be less than length if the end of the file was reached), 0 if we are already at the end of the file, and undef if there was an error:

```
$text = <>;
open MYHANDLE, "$text";
$result = read MYHANDLE, $text, 60;   # attempt to read 60 bytes into $text
die "Failed to read: $!" unless defined $result;   # handle an error
print "read $result bytes: $text \n";   # print out the result
```

The current value of $text, if any, is overwritten, and the scalar is shrunk to fit the result. If we want to partially or completely retain the existing contents of $text, we can add an extra offset argument to the read statement. If present, this causes read to write text into the variable from the offset character (offset into the variable, that is, not the file). For example, to concatenate reads without having to use a temporary variable, we can supply the length of the current text as the offset in order to have read place new text at the end of the string:

```
$text = <>;
open MYHANDLE, "$text";
$result;
while ($result = read MYHANDLE, $text, 60, length $text) {
    print "appended $result bytes \n"
}

if (not defined $result) {
    print "Error: $! \n";
} else {
    print "Done \n";
}
```

read and <> both deal with buffered input. The unbuffered system-level equivalent of read is sysread, which behaves in a very similar manner on unbuffered input. It is safe to mix read and <> but not sysread as well. See the section "System-Level IO" for more information.

Detecting the End of File

If we attempt to read beyond the end of a file, an end-of-file condition is encountered. This is a flag set on the filehandle that indicates that no more data is available. Further attempts to read from the file will return with failure.

We can detect the end-of-file condition with the eof function. This takes a filehandle as an argument and returns true or false depending on whether the filehandle has encountered the end-of-file condition or not. For example:

```
$text = <>;
open MYHANDLE, "$text";
if (eof MYHANDLE) {
    print "No more to read \n";
} else {
    ...read some more...
}
```

Operators like the readline operator automatically detect the end-of-file condition and return false when they encounter it. So eof is not necessary for loops like this:

```
while (<>) {
    print "Got: $_ \n";
}
```

The distinction between the end-of-file condition and the actual end of the file is often negligible, but it can be occasionally important. For instance, the file can grow if more data is written into it from another process, but this does not clear the end-of-file condition because our filehandle does not know about it. To clear the condition, we can use seek to move the current position to itself, as documented in the next section:

```
seek MYHANDLE, 0, 1;
```

The end-of-file condition does not just apply to files, but to any filehandle that is open for input. In cases where the filehandle does not refer to an actual file, an end-of-file condition indicates simply that there is no more data to read at the moment. Because this condition may be temporary, the end-of-file condition is transient, and we can only detect it once. If we attempt to read from one of these filehandles after eof has returned true or attempt to use eof twice on the same filehandle, then the end-of-file condition will be cleared and eof will return false. Similarly, an attempt to read will block until more data becomes available.

Reading a Single Character

Single characters can be read with the getc function. Like readline, it takes a filehandle as an argument but returns a single character:

```
$char = getc MYHANDLE;    # get a character from MYHANDLE
$char = getc;             # get a character from STDIN
```

Like print, getc can also be used in the object-oriented style:

```
$fh->getc;
```

IO::Handle and its siblings supply the corresponding ungetc method, though this is only guaranteed to work for one character—do not rely on calling it repeatedly. It takes the ordinal (ASCII code) value of the character as its argument:

```
$fh->ungetc ord($char);   # push $char back onto $fh
```

If getc is not given a filehandle to read from, it defaults to STDIN. However, since terminal buffering means that a typed character will not be sent until the Return key is pressed, this alone is not enough to react to a single key press. In order to do this, we need to control the behavior of the terminal, which we can do in a number of ways, such as using the Term::ReadKey module discussed in detail in Chapter 14.

Writing to Filehandles

The print statement is the primary mechanism for writing to filehandles, although, of course, only to filehandles that are open for output:

```
open OUTPUT, ">output.txt";
print OUTPUT "write to an output filehandle";
```

By default, print writes to standard output. In its simplest usage, we usually call print with one or more things we wish to display. However, this is actually shorthand for printing to standard output:

```
print "Calling Major Tom";         # implicit print to STDOUT
print STDOUT "Calling Major Tom";  # explicit print to STDOUT
```

These statements are not quite identical. In the first, the select function (see "Changing the Default Output Filehandle" later) could be used to change the default filehandle that print uses when no explicit handle is provided. In the second, the STDOUT filehandle is specified directly, so select will not affect it.

We have already looked at the various ways filehandles can be specified to print, so we will not comment further on it here. The print function provides higher-level output, passing through Perl's buffering layer (unless we disable it using PerlIO layers). Lower-level output is handled by syswrite, which is covered in "System-Level IO" later in the chapter.

Buffering and Autoflush Mode

Ordinarily, output to filehandles is buffered, either block buffered if the output is to a noninteractive device like a flat file or line buffered if it is. The distinction between these is that in block buffering, output is saved until a maximum threshold, usually several kilobytes, is reached and then written out all at once. In line buffering, the filehandle buffers output until a newline character is written, at which point the whole line is sent to the output. Interactive devices like screens default to line buffering since that is more logical when communicating with a user.

Block buffering is important for efficiency, but it can be confusing to other programs that are expecting to see the output in a timely manner, such as clients waiting to see the output of a CGI script. Fortunately, the output can be switched from block buffering to line buffering even on filehandles that would normally block-buffer by setting the autoflush flag. For the default output, the special autoflush variable $| ($OUTPUT_AUTOFLUSH with use English) performs this duty:

```
$| = 1;   # set line buffering, 'autoflush' mode
print "Hello World \n";   # write a line
$| = 0;   # restore block buffering
```

Filehandles created with IO::File or IO::Handle can have their autoflush state altered with the autoflush method:

```
$fh->autoflush(1);   # set line buffering. 'autoflush' mode
print $fh "Hello World \n";   # write a line
$fh->autoflush(0);   # restore block buffering
```

If we have used IO::Handle, then we can also use the autoflush method on any filehandle:

```
use IO::File;   # inherits from IO::Handle

# '$$' returns the process ID:
open TMP, "> /tmp/tmp_pid$$" or die "Open failed: $!";
TMP->autoflush(1);
```

It is important to remember that the autoflush flag does not disable buffering. To write to a file or device unbuffered, we can use the system-level IO function syswrite. $| does not disable buffering, it merely allows block-buffered filehandles to be turned into line-buffered ones. For filehandles that are already connected to an interactive device such as a screen, the autoflush flag has no effect. Note also that if the buffering layer has been entirely removed from a filehandle (using PerlIO), then $| cannot affect it as there is no buffer to control—see "Unbuffered Writing" for more information.

Binary and Text Files, Layers, Encodings, and Transforms

Most modern operating systems do not make any distinction between binary and text files. Unfortunately, some operating systems (notably Windows) do. This comes about because of the difference of opinion over the definition of linefeed, as represented by the \n metacharacter. By default, Perl assumes files are textual, so a newline in Perl becomes a single linefeed, a linefeed plus return, or a return plus linefeed, depending on the underlying platform.

Similarly, when a file is read, the appropriate combination of linefeed and return is invisibly converted into a "new line" so that the readline operator will work as expected. If we want to avoid binary data being "reimagined" and have character code 10 (the LF character) actually read or written as a byte of value 10 and not whatever Perl thinks the underlying platform uses, we have to ensure Perl knows what kind of file we are working with—binary or text—before we attempt to read or write it. The same problem also applies to character encodings, in particular Unicode—Perl needs to know whether or not a given string is encoded as one-byte characters or multibyte characters if we expect it to handle the data correctly.

In Perl 5.6 and earlier, the binmode function and the open pragma provide the tools to allow us to handle this problem with the :crlf and :raw line disciplines. From Perl 5.8 onwards, these disciplines have been replaced and augmented by a full-fledged system of customizable layers, incorporating support for UTF-8 encoding, raw unbuffered IO, and custom encoding or translation layers written in either Perl or C. The built-in open function is expanded to allow layers to be specified at the time a handle is first created, while the binmode function and the open pragma extend their reach to allow all of these additional layers to be manipulated. Their syntax is thankfully unchanged, however, so code written for Perl 5.6 and earlier will still work with Perl 5.8 and later.

Default Layers and the PERLIO Environment Variable

The layers that a filehandle is created with by default vary depending on the underlying platform and what optimizations the configuration process determined at the time Perl was built. The bottom-most layer is always unix, however, even on non-Unix platforms. It represents the lowest and rawest access to the file descriptors provided by the operating system. The PerlIO architecture allows for a possible alternative low-level access layer, should one be created.

On top of unix, a Unix Perl will typically instate either perlio or, occasionally, stdio. The latter is essentially the old buffering layer from Perl 5.6 and before, and it is still used in cases where Perl's build configuration tool determines that it might be more efficient than the newer perlio. This is a transient state of affairs, though, and the stdio layer will ultimately be retired completely from Perl 5.10.

A Windows-based Perl will enable the crlf layer, which provides automatic translation to and from DOS-style line endings. We need to switch that off, of course, if we actually want to manage binary data as noted earlier.

On platforms that support it, the mmap layer is also available. This provides access via memory-mapped files, which may be faster in some circumstances at the cost of additional memory. It is not the default ordinarily, but it may be instated at the request of the PERLIO environment variable.

The PERLIO environment variable may be used to control the default layers that Perl uses to create filehandles, in a similar way to the open pragma. It takes one of three values:

- PERLIO=stdio: Request stdio, if available. Fall back to perlio if stdio is not available.

- PERLIO=perlio: Request perlio even if stdio is available.

- PERLIO=mmap: Request memory-mapped files. Fall back to perlio if mmap is not available.

If PERLIO is not set, a Unix-based Perl will default to a setting of stdio (which in turn depends on whether or not stdio is available). A Windows-based Perl will default to the layers unix plus crlf.

Finding the Existing Layers of a Filehandle

The layers present on an existing filehandle may be determined with the get_layers function of the PerlIO package. As this is automatically loaded into Perl (assuming it is modern enough, of course), no special efforts are necessary to load the function. It returns a list of layers as string values for the supplied filehandle. For example:

```
my @stdin_layers = PerlIO::get_layers(STDIN);
```

Layers typically apply to both sides of a filehandle and are maintained as a single list for both input and output by functions like binmode. However, using the open pragma, we may set different layers for input and output. In this case, we might validly want to retrieve the list for input or output independently.

```
my @in_layers = PerlIO::get_layers($fh);
my @out_layers = PerlIO::get_layers($fh, output => 1);
```

Note that there is no equivalent set_layers function. open (the function and the pragma) and binmode are the provided mechanism for layer manipulation.

Establishing Layers at Filehandle Creation

Layers may be set when a filehandle is created by specifying them as part of the second argument to the three-argument version of open. A traditional three-argument open splits the file mode from the file name and looks like this:

```
open FH, "<", "input.txt";
```

To establish layers as well, we simply add them to the file mode, like this:

```
open FH, "<:raw:utf8", "input.txt"
```

This tells Perl that the data read from this filehandle is to be treated without special consideration for treatment of line endings (raw) and contains Unicode text encoded in UTF-8. We can similarly open a filehandle for writing with the same conditions:

```
open FH, ">:raw:utf8", "output.txt"
```

If a fundamental layer such as unix, perlio, or stdio is specified, all existing layers for the filehandle are wiped out, since these layers must appear at the bottom of the stack:

```
open FH, ">:unix:crlf", "output.txt"
```

This means that opening a filehandle with an explicit unix layer creates a raw unbuffered filehandle, for instance. Here we have an unbuffered output filehandle with line-ending processing enabled (which has no effect on Unix but will alter the written data for Windows, for instance). See the section "System-Level IO" found later in the chapter for more details.

The binmode Function

When working with text files, we can let Perl deal with the complications of line endings for us; the default configuration of the filehandle will automatically enable the :crlf layer if the platform requires it. If we are working with a binary file on such a platform, then we need to tell Perl to prevent this automatic translation from taking place. The simplest way to do this is to use the binmode function with a filehandle:

```
binmode HANDLE;   # make HANDLE a binary filehandle
```

This sets the HANDLE filehandle to be binary in both directions (or, technically, sets the :raw layer/discipline). We can also do this explicitly by setting the discipline directly:

```
binmode HANDLE ':raw';   # make HANDLE a binary filehandle
```

Similarly, we can switch on line-ending translation using the :crlf discipline, assuming the underlying platform cares:

```
binmode HANDLE ':crlf';   # make HANDLE a DOS text filehandle
```

This is the limit of what we can do with binmode in older versions of Perl, but from Perl 5.8 onwards PerlIO gives binmode the ability to add and remove layers from an arbitrarily long list.

Setting the unix layer will make the specified handle unbuffered. So this is one way to cause output to go directly to the screen:

```
binmode STDOUT, ':unix'; # make STDOUT unbuffered
```

Note that this is different from setting $|=1. The latter tells the buffering layer to automatically flush the buffer at the conclusion of every print statement in Perl. Here there is no buffering layer for $| to control.

Manipulating Layers with binmode

With PerlIO, we can use `binmode` to specify any layers we want. The specified layers are added to the existing layers defined for the filehandle (both input and output). So, for example, to mark a filehandle as handling UTF-8 encoded data, we could put

```
binmode HANDLE ':utf8';
```

This handle will now handle data as Unicode characters, reading and writing native Unicode data within Perl to and from the handle. The text or binary property of the handle is not affected, so if `:crlf` is already set, then the preceding statement augments it, producing a text-mode Unicode-encoded handle. Of course, this only matters on platforms where `:crlf` actually makes a difference—Unix platforms don't care.

Setting `:raw` on a PerlIO handle will clear all transforming layers—anything that makes the handle "nonbinary." This includes `:crlf` and `:utf8` and any custom transforms or encodings we might have added. To set this handle back to unencoded text mode, we can therefore specify `:raw` (to clear the `:utf8`) and then `:crlf` after it. As this example illustrates, we are also able to specify multiple layers at once, either space-separated or directly concatenated:

```
binmode HANDLE ':raw:crlf'; # clear all nonbinary layers, then add :crlf
```

Both `:utf8` and `:crlf` are actually pseudolayers, meaning that they do not actually add layers to the handle but merely set a flag in whatever the topmost layer actually is to note that the layer should be handled differently. The `:bytes` pseudolayer clears the `:utf8` layer, but it will not remove `:crlf` or other transforming layers as `:raw` does. If `:utf8` is not enabled, `:bytes` has no effect. Given after the initial `:utf8` statement earlier, the following will put the filehandle back in its original state again, but this would have no effect on the handle after the second `:raw:crlf` example:

```
binmode HANDLE ':bytes';
```

Alternatively, we can add the special pseudolayer `:pop`, which, like `:bytes`, does not add a layer. Instead, it removes the topmost layer or pseudolayer (in which case it actually just clears a flag). The rest of the configured layers are left intact. So, given the handle in the state left by our initial `:utf8` statement, to remove it and nothing else we would use

```
binmode HANDLE ':pop'; # cancels previous :utf8 only
```

Using `:pop`, we can remove all layers, even the buffering or raw system layers like `:perlio`, `:stdio`, or `:unix`. This allows us to convert a filehandle from buffered to unbuffered operation and back again if we want to. Removing all the layers from a filehandle is possible, but obviously leaves it in an unusable state.

The open Pragma

Perl supplies a pragmatic module called open.pm, not to be confused with the open function. open performs a similar job to `binmode` but allows the default layers for input and output to be set independently. Any new filehandle inherits the settings laid down by open, using the default input and output layers as appropriate. A handle that is opened for both reading and writing uses both settings, applying them to the corresponding read or write operations.

For example, to set the input discipline to text and the output to binary, we could use

```
use open IN => ':crlf', OUT => ':raw';
```

This sets a default input discipline of `:crlf` and a default output discipline of `:raw` for all filehandles that are opened in the same lexical scope as the declaration.

In Perl 5.6 and earlier, only `:crlf` and `:raw` are defined by the open module. From Perl 5.8 onwards, the full range of layers provided by PerlIO may be set (except `:pop`, because that makes no sense), including our own custom layers if we so desire. The open pragma is not so useful in Perl 5.8, since we can now specify layers at the time we open a filehandle, but it is still handy if we intend to create many filehandles all with the same layers configured. In Perl 5.8, we can also set both input and output using IO, or equivalently just omit it and specify the layers:

```
use open IO => ':utf8'; # specify default UTF8 encoding
use open ':crlf :utf8'; # specify both CRLF and UTF8 encoding
```

Specifying and Creating Custom Layers

Layers are the primary mechanism for setting character encodings. These encodings are managed and defined by the Encode:: family of modules. Existing encodings are described in Encode::Supported, and new encodings may be created by subclassing from Encode::Encoding. To use an encoding as a layer, we use the encoding layer:

```
open INPUT "<:encoding(iso-8859-15)", "its_greek_to_me.txt";
```

While the encode layer is specifically designed to interoperate with character encodings, the general-purpose via layer allows us to insert a transformation layer to carry out any kind of processing that we like. The PerlIO::via::QuotePrint layer is provided as standard with Perl, but many more are available from CPAN. For instance, this is how we can use the PerlIO::via::Base64 module:

```
use PerlIO::via::Base64;
open OUTPUT,'>:via(Base64)','mime_encoded.out' or die "open failed: $!\n";
```

This works because the top-level PerlIO module understands that "via" means that it should look for the package Base64 in the PerlIO::via namespace. So long as the module satisfies the interface requirements for a PerlIO layer, it will now be automatically used to filter and transform all data being written to this filehandle. If we need to customize the behavior of the layer, we can still use it as normal. For example, this is one way to set the line ending for the preceding Base64 layer:

```
use PerlIO::via::Base64 eol => "\n";
```

In fact, the mechanism is a little more generic than this. First, if we create or use a module that resides directly in the PerlIO namespace, such as PerlIO::gzip (also available from CPAN), we can use it without the via qualification and pass arguments to it (which have the same effect as an equivalent import list):

```
use PerlIO::gzip;
open INPUT,'<:gzip','data.gz' or die "open failed: $!\n";
```

If the gzip layer is passed none as an argument, it will handle ZIP-encoded files (that is, without a gzip header):

```
open INPUT,'<:gzip(none)','data.zip' or die "open failed: $!\n";
```

Of course, we can write gzipped data in the same way by attaching the layer to an output filehandle.

Second, if the layer name contains a namespace qualifier (that is, ::), it will be taken as a explicit fully qualified name. That means that our previous Base64 example is really just shorthand for

```
open OUTPUT,'>:via(PerlIO::via::Base64)','mime_encoded.out';
```

With this syntax, there is no longer a need to place our translation layer modules into the PerlIO namespace, and we can simply say

```
use My::Transforming::Layer qw(initialization parameters);
open OUTPUT,'>:via(My::Transforming::Layer)','mime_encoded.out';
```

In order to create a layer, we need to create an object class that adheres to the interface described in the PerlIO::via manual page. There are many optional methods that we can choose to overload or leave unimplemented, and a few mandatory methods: PUSHED, FLUSH, WRITE, and one of READ or FILL.

By way of a simple example, this model implements a shrinkspace layer that removes contiguous whitespace characters. It does this for both input and output, so it is not a reversible transform like QuotedPrint:

```perl
package PerlIO::via::shrinkspace;
use strict;

# layer constructor - return an object of the class
sub PUSHED {
    my ($class,$mode,$fh) = @_;
    my $self = { buffer => '' };
    return bless $self, $class;
}

# input method - read a line from stream and return a processed line
sub FILL {
    my ($self,$fh) = @_;
    my $line = <$fh>;
    # return undef or empty list (depending on context) if at end of file
    return unless defined $line;
    chomp $line;
    $line =~ s/\s+/ /g;
    return $line;
}

# output method - take supplied data and process it outwards
sub WRITE {
    my ($self,$data,$fh) = @_;
    $data =~ s/\s+/ /g;
    $data =~ s/^\s// if $self->{buffer} =~ /\s$/;
    $self->{buffer} .= $data;
    return length($data);
}

# output flush method - actually write data to filehandle
sub FLUSH {
    my ($self,$fh) = @_;
    return -1 unless print $fh $self->{buffer};
    $self->{buffer} = '';
    return 0;
}

1;
```

To instantiate the layer, we implement PUSHED, which is called when the layer is pushed onto the filehandle's layer stack using open or binmode. The key job of PUSHED is to return an appropriate object on which the other methods, FILL, WRITE, and FLUSH, can be called. It is passed the mode of the filehandle in the manner of sysopen (r, w+, and so on) and the filehandle, which here means the top of the immediately preceding PerlIO layer. If we have cleanup work to do, we can also implement POPPED to handle the layer being removed again.

For input, we implement FILL to read a line of data, do something with it, and return it. If we do not want to implement a line-based layer (if, for example, we are not processing textual data), we can instead supply READ, which can be used to provide a sysread-like interface for the layer. Generally speaking, FILL is simpler to use if we are only interested in processing text.

For output, the layer buffers data inside the object within the WRITE method. It remains here until FLUSH is called. It is not necessary to use all the arguments passed to each method; notably we do not need to use the filehandle in WRITE, since we do not intend to write out until FLUSH is called.

To use our filter, we now just say (assuming it is called PerlIO/via/shrinkspace.pm somewhere in the @INC path)

```
use PerlIO::via::shrinkspace;
open INPUT, "<:via(shrinkspace)", "spaced.txt";
```

Similarly, to strip spaces during file output, we add the layer to an output filehandle:

```
#!/usr/bin/perl
# shrinkoutspace.pl
use strict;
use warnings;

use lib '.';
use PerlIO::via::shrinkspace;

my $unspaced="";
open OUTPUT, ">:via(shrinkspace)", \$unspaced;
print OUTPUT "This  text  is  spaced   out";
close OUTPUT;
print $unspaced." no longer\n";
```

which generates

```
This text is spaced out no longer
```

There is much more to the PerlIO layer interface than this simple example. See perldoc PerlIO::via for a detailed rundown of the available methods and some other implementation ideas.

Random Access

If a filehandle refers to an actual file, then we can use random access methods to move about within the file, thereby selectively reading or writing to different parts of it. To achieve this, we make use of the file pointer, which is a position within the file that is associated with the filehandle. Using the built-in functions seek and tell, we can set and retrieve the current position of the file pointer to allow reads or writes to take place at a specific point within the file. If we prefer, we can load the IO::Seekable module to add the same functionality to IO::File-derived filehandles in an object-oriented style. IO::Seekable merely wraps the underlying built-in functions, so the usage is identical. Only the syntax differs.

seek to a Specific Place Within a File

The seek function allows us to change the position of the file pointer associated with our filehandle, so that it points to a different part of the file. It takes three parameters: the filehandle to modify, the new position, and a relationship flag (also known as the whence flag). It will work with either a filehandle or an expression that evaluates to the name of the filehandle as a string.

The actual effect of seek depends on the value of the whence flag, which can be 0, 1, or 2, as shown in Table 12-3.

Table 12-3. *seek Flag Values*

Flag	Effect
seek FH, $pos, 0	Seek to the absolute position given by $pos. For example, seek FH, 0, 0 moves the pointer to the beginning of the file.
seek FH, $pos, 1	Seek forward ($pos > 0) or backward ($pos < 0) by the number of bytes given by $pos from the current position. For example, seek FH, 60, 1 moves the file pointer forward 60 bytes. Note that seeking beyond the end of the file and then writing to the file extends it, but this does not guarantee the new extent is "zeroed" out.
seek FH, $pos, 2	Seek relative to the end of the file. If $pos is negative, seek backwards $pos bytes from the end of the file. If it is zero, seek to the end of the file. If it is positive, attempt to seek forward past the end of the file. For example, seek FH, -60, 2 moves the file pointer to a position 60 characters before the end of the file.

seek returns a true value if it succeeds, and 0 otherwise, for example, if we try to seek to before the beginning of the file. This will cause the file pointer to land at the end of the file, if the file is not open for writing. Alternatively, if it is open for writing, the file will be extended to satisfy the pointer, so an easy way to create a large file is to open it for writing and then move the pointer to a large value:

```
open (BIGFILE, "> bigfile");
seek BIGFILE, 100 * 1024 * 1024, 0;  # move the pointer to the  100MB point

syswrite BIGFILE, 'end';              # write to the file, thereby setting its
                                      # size to 100MB (plus three characters)
close BIGFILE;
```

■**Note** On some filing systems, particularly on Unix platforms, this does not actually assign 100MB of disk space; it actually creates a sparse file that contains only the beginning and the end, a file with a hole in it, so to speak.

Since the meanings of the values 0, 1, and 2 are not particularly memorable, we can use labels for them instead if we use the Fcntl module. This defines three constants, SEEK_SET, SEEK_CUR, and SEEK_END, for 0, 1, and 2, respectively:

```
use Fcntl qw(:seek);   # get SEEK_ constants
seek MYHANDLE, $position, SEEK_SET;
seek MYHANDLE, $moveby, SEEK_CUR;
```

Note that seek is not the same as the sysseek function. The seek function works with buffered filehandles, whereas sysseek works at the system level. Using both interchangeably is not a good idea. For more information on sysseek, see the section "System-Level IO" found later in this chapter.

Clearing the End-of-File Condition with seek

Using seek has the occasionally useful side effect of resetting the end-of-file condition on a filehandle (as read by eof), since by moving the file pointer we are explicitly overriding its position. This can be handy for monitoring the end of growing log files, among other applications. The end-of-file condition on non–position-based filehandles is transient, so this is not an issue here, but for filehandles associated with files, it is permanent since files are assumed not to grow. To clear it, we can use seek.

The simplest way to remove the end-of-file condition without actually moving the file pointer is to seek to the current position:

```
seek MYHANDLE, 0, 1;    # (possibly) reset eof.
```

This works because although we have moved the position to the end of the file, no attempt has been made to read data there. It is the attempt to read rather than the position of the file pointer that causes the end-of-file condition to be raised.

After calling seek, we can attempt to read the file again from the current position and see if any new data has been written. If it has not, we will just raise the end-of-file condition once more. Here is a short program that uses this technique and a sleep to periodically check for output, essentially similar in intent to the Unix command tail -f:

```
#!/usr/bin/perl
# tail.pl
use strict;
use warnings;

die "Give me a file\n" unless @ARGV and -f $ARGV[0];
open LOGFILE, $ARGV[0];

while (1) {
    # read lines while there are lines to read
    print "$.: $_" while <LOGFILE>;

    # got an 'eof' - sleep, reset 'eof', then loop back and try again
    sleep(1);
    seek LOGFILE, 0, 1;
}
```

Writing at the End of File

When multiple programs or processes are all writing to the same file, we cannot always guarantee that our file pointer is actually pointing at the end of the file. In order to make sure that anything we write goes at the end of the file, we can seek to the end explicitly using SEEK_END and a distance of 0:

```
seek MYHANDLE, 0, SEEK_END;
```

If several processes have the same file open in an append mode, lines will not overlap each other, but the order in which they appear cannot be determined. If the file is not open in an append mode, even this cannot be guaranteed. In order to assure that different processes do not overwrite each other, we also need to use some form of file locking, for instance, with flock. Here is a short logging program that uses this technique in combination with file locking to make absolutely sure that it is writing to the current end of the file:

```
#!/usr/bin/perl
#logging.pl
use warnings;
use strict;

use Fcntl qw(:seek :flock);

# open file for update, position is at current end of file
open LOGFILE, ">>", "/tmp/mylog" or die "Unable to open: $! \n";

# lock file for exclusive access
flock LOGFILE, LOCK_EX;
```

```
# now seek to end of file explicitly, in case it changed since the open
seek LOGFILE, 0, SEEK_END;

# write our log message
print LOGFILE "Log message...\n";

# remove lock and close file
flock LOGFILE, LOCK_UN;
close LOGFILE;
```

This program takes advantage of file locking to prevent any other program or process extending the file while it is still busy writing to it. So long as all processes that access the file cooperate with flock, all will be well. It also takes advantage of the fact that flock causes all buffered output on the filehandle to be flushed on both locking and unlocking operations. In this sample program, the close would have done that for us anyway, but the principle still applies.

Finding the Current Position

The tell function is the counterpart to seek. It returns the current value of the file pointer. It takes one parameter (a filehandle) and returns the current position, in bytes, within the file:

```
$position = tell MYHANDLE;
```

Like seek, tell will work on either a filehandle or an expression that evaluates to the name of the filehandle as a string. If no filehandle is given, tell defaults to the last file opened:

```
open (MYHANDLE, "myfile") or die "could not open myfile: $!";
$line = <MYHANDLE>;
print "The first line was ", tell," characters long \n";
```

If the filehandle has no file pointer associated with it, which is the case with serial connections and sockets, the returned pointer value is -1 (rather than undef, which we might have expected):

```
$position = tell MYHANDLE;
print "The file position is", $position >- 1?$position:" not applicable";
```

Object-Oriented Random Access

Programmers who are using filehandles generated by the IO::File module can make use of the object-oriented methods supplied by the IO::Seekable module for filehandles that can have their file positions modified. These methods are direct object-oriented replacements for the standard Perl functions:

```
$fh->seek($position, 0);        # seek to absolute position
$fh->seek($distance, SEEK_CUR); # seek forward 'distance' bytes
$pos = $fh -> tell();           # find current position
```

Truncating and Resizing Files

To make a file longer, we can use the seek function to move beyond the current end of the file or simply append more data to it, so long as we have the file opened in a writable state. However, we cannot make a file shorter this way.

One simple, albeit destructive, way to make a file shorter is to simply write a new file over it, using an open mode that destroys the original contents of the file. If we want to retain part of the original file, we can read it first, then close and reopen the file for writing. For example, this code snippet replaces a file of more than ten lines with the last ten lines in the file:

```perl
#!/usr/bin/perl
# lastten.pl
use warnings;
use strict;

print "Reading...";
open READ, "myfile" or die "Cannot open: $! \n";
my @lines = <READ>;
print "$. lines read \n";
close READ;

exit if $#lines < 9;

print "Writing...";
open WRITE, "> myfile" or die "Cannot write: $! \n";
print WRITE $_ foreach @lines[-10..-1];
print "done \n";
close WRITE;
```

This works fine, and it could well be simpler if we want to modify the contents of the file while at the same time shortening it. However, if we just want to make a file shorter without otherwise altering its contents, we can use the function truncate.

truncate is a very simple function. It takes a filehandle or an expression giving the name or reference of a filehandle, which must be open for writing, and a length:

```perl
truncate FILE, 100;   # truncate file to first 100 bytes
```

Since opening a file for writing truncates it automatically to nothing, use the +< or read-update mode to truncate an existing file:

```perl
open FILE, '+< myfile';
truncate FILE, 100;
close FILE;
```

truncate works on bytes, not lines, so it is good for setting an exact length but useless for truncating to the first n lines of a file. Unfortunately, simply counting the lengths of the lines is not enough, since the newline character in Perl may in reality be one or two characters in the file; as we observed before, both Windows and MacOS use two characters for the line ending. So the only reliable and simple way to truncate the file accurately is to read it up to the desired number of lines and then use seek to find out where the last line ended:

```perl
#!/usr/bin/perl
# truncate.pl
use warnings;
use strict;

die "Specify a file \n" unless @ARGV;
die "Specify a length \n" unless defined($ARGV[1]) and ($ARGV[1] >= 1);
my $file = $ARGV[0];
my $truncate_to = int($ARGV[1]);

print "Reading...";
open READ, "$file" or die "Cannot open: $! \n";
while (<READ>) {
    last if $. == $truncate_to;
}
my $size = tell READ;
print "$. lines read ($size bytes) \n";
exit if $. < $truncate_to;   # already shorter
```

```
close READ;

print "Truncating to $size bytes...";
open WRITE, "+< $file" or die "Cannot write: $! \n";
truncate WRITE, $size;
print "done \n";
close WRITE;
```

This program truncates the given file to the given number of lines. It only reads lines to move the file pointer, so it doesn't do anything with the returned lines. Once it has finished, it checks $. to determine if the file is actually long enough to need truncating. If it is, it finds the current position, which will be the character immediately after the end of the line terminator of the last line, reopens the file for modification, and truncates it.

Interestingly, truncate will extend a file if the new length is longer than the old, so a better name for truncate would have been setlength. The extended bytes, if any, are filled with zeros or null characters, which makes it a better solution to extending a file than seek if a complete and empty file is desirable. Note that truncate can fail with undef if the disk runs out of capacity or we reach a quota limit imposed by the operating system. That is not an issue for the preceding example, since it is making the file shorter, so in that case we did not check (though to be really thorough, we ought to anyway).

File Locking

In situations where more than one program or process may wish to write to the same file at the same time, we need to take care that different processes do not tread on each other's toes. For example, several clients may attempt to execute a script simultaneously. CGI scripts are a common class of Perl program that fall into this category.

As an example of a Perl application that fails as a result of not using file locking, take this hit counter CGI script, designed to be used in a server-side include:

```
#!/usr/bin/perl -T
# badcounter.cgi
use warnings;
use strict;

# script assumes file exists, but may be empty
my $counter = "/home/httpd/data/counter/counter.dat";

open(FILE, "+< $counter") or die "Cannot access counter: $! \n";
my $visitors = <FILE>;
chomp $visitors;
seek FILE, 0, 0;
print FILE $visitors ?++ $visitors:1;
close(FILE);

print "Content-type: text/html\n\n";
print $visitors, "\n";
```

Without protection, the counter will only register one hit if two instances of the script are executed at the same time. Instance 1 adds one to the count, writes, and closes file. However, when instance 2 adds one to the count, it overwrites the value left by instance 1 and closes the file, having updated it once.

To avoid this problem, we need to use *file locks*, so other processes will not attempt to work with a file while we are busy with it. With a lock in place, other processes that attempt to place their own locks on the file must wait (or block) until our process finishes its business and unlocks the file.

By adhering to the file lock mechanism, processes can avoid overwriting each other, preventing the kind of problems inherent in the preceding example.

Establishing File Locks

Perl provides file locking through the `flock` function. `flock` is modeled on but not necessarily implemented by, the C `flock` system call; Perl uses whatever locking facilities are available and presents them to us through its own `flock`. `flock` takes a filehandle and an operation as arguments. The filehandle is the filehandle of the file we want to lock, and the operation is a numerical flag representing the type of lock that we want to establish. There are two basic lock operations, shared and exclusive, plus an `unlock` operation and finally a nonblocking flag. This can be combined with one of the other three to allow a process to continue executing, rather than wait for the lock to become available. Numerically, these are represented by the numbers 1, 2, 8, and 4 respectively, but for convenience's sake we can import descriptive symbols from the `Fcntl` module:

```
use Fcntl ':flock';   # import LOCK_ symbols
```

The four flags are listed in Table 12-4.

Table 12-4. *flock Operations*

Flag	Number	Function

LOCK_SH	1	Establish a shared lock, also known as a read lock:
		`flock FH, 1;`
		`flock FH, LOCK_SH;`
		When LOCK_SH is in effect, other processes may also establish a shared lock but may not establish an exclusive or write lock. This is the lock to use when we want to read a file while ensuring that its contents do not change.

LOCK_EX	2	Establish an exclusive lock, also known as a write lock:
		`flock FH, 2;`
		`flock FH, LOCK_EX;`
		When LOCK_EX is in effect, no other process can establish a lock. This is the lock to use when we want to change the contents of a file and prevent other processes reading it while we do.

LOCK_UN	8	Unlock a previously established lock:
		`flock FH, 8;`
		`flock FH, LOCK_UN;`
		This unlocks a lock that has been previously established. Since the process owns the lock that it is unlocking, this use of `flock` never blocks.

LOCK_NB	4	Do not block when attempting to acquire a lock:
		`flock FH, 5;`
		`flock FH, LOCK_SH|LOCK_NB;`
		`flock FH, 6;`
		`flock FH, LOCK_EX|LOCK_NB;`
		Normally an attempt to establish a shared or exclusive lock will block on the `flock` statement until whichever process currently holding the lock releases it. By combining LOCK_NB with the lock operation, we can have our program do something else while waiting:
		`until (flock FH, LOCK_EX|LOCK_NB) {`
		`    print "Waiting for lock...\n";`
		`    sleep 5;   die "Handle no longer valid" unless defined(fileno *FH);`
		`}`
		Note that to be safe we also check that the filehandle is still valid before trying to lock it again.

Using flock, we can rewrite our counter script so that it functions correctly. All that we need to do is to add an exclusive lock (LOCK_EX) immediately after we open the file and unlock it again (LOCK_UN) immediately before we close it:

```
#!/usr/bin/perl -T
# counter.cgi
use warnings;
use strict;

use Fcntl ':flock';

# script assumes file exists but may be empty
my $counter = "/home/httpd/data/counter/counter.dat";

open(FILE,"+< $counter") or die "Cannot access counter: $!\n";
flock(FILE, LOCK_EX);
my $visitors = <FILE>;
chomp $visitors;
seek FILE, 0, 0;
print FILE $visitors ?++ $visitors:1;
flock(FILE, LOCK_UN);
close(FILE);

print "Content-type: text/html\n\n";
print $visitors, "\n";
```

From Perl 5.004, flock flushes the output of any filehandle that it successfully locks or unlocks to ensure that file writes are properly synchronized. In this case, the close would have flushed remaining output anyway; however, for larger applications this additional feature of flock is extremely convenient.

File Locking Issues and Caveats

It is important to remember that locks established by flock are advisory only. Another program is totally free to ignore the lock if it so chooses (by not checking for it). All participants therefore have to observe locks for them to be effective. Many operating systems also support mandatory locking schemes, but these are largely platform specific.

Another potential problem with flock is that its exact behavior may vary depending on what file locking mechanisms are available on the underlying platform. Most platforms support a flock system call, so Perl's flock can map directly onto it. However, in the event that a true flock is not available, Perl must resort to an emulation based on the less versatile lockf or, if that is not available, basic calls to fcntl. From Perl 5.5, Perl prefers fcntl due to the fact lockf requires files to be writable to lock them. fcntl also has an advantage over the flock system call in that it will work on network-mounted (for example, NFS) file systems, which some implementations of flock do not. We may want to support this, in which case we should use fcntl rather than flock in Perl.

In addition, locks established with a flock emulation will not survive across duplicated filehandles and may not survive a fork. Consult the flock, fcntl, or other file locking documentation of the operating system for details of how the platform supports file locking.

Changing the Default Output Filehandle

The default output filehandle is normally STDOUT, but we can change this by using the select function. This takes a single filehandle (which may not be derived from an expression) as an argument and switches it for the current default:

```
select MYHANDLE;
print "Message to MYHANDLE \n";    # write to MYHANDLE;
```

With no arguments, `select` returns the current default output filehandle, which makes it useful for storing the existing output filehandle should we wish to restore it at a later date:

```
# save existing default output
$original_out = select;

# select a new default output and use it
select NEWOUT;
$| = 1;   # set autoflush on filehandle NEWOUT
print "write data to new default output";

# restore original default output
select $original_out;
```

Or, more tersely:

```
$original_out = select(NEWOUT);
$| = 1;
select $original_out;
```

Or, even more tersely, avoiding a temporary variable but edging into illegibility:

```
select( (select(NEWOUT), $| = 1)[0] );
```

This relies on the fact that the two statements `select(NEWOUT)` and `$|=1` generate a two-element list. The outer `select` uses the first element (the original filehandle) to restore the default filehandle after both statements have executed. The `IO::Handle` module and its descendants package this into an object method, so if we have `IO::Handle` loaded, we can also say

```
NEWOUT->autoflush(1);
```

Note that the `select` function also has an entirely different four-argument form that is used to select between multiple inputs, and which has nothing whatsoever to do with its usage here.

Using Special Variables to Configure Other Filehandles

The special variables that are related to output operate on a per-filehandle basis, each filehandle having its own set of output properties associated with it. The special variables bring out and make available the properties of whatever filehandle is currently selected; changing the value of a special variable affects that filehandle only. For instance, to switch on `autoflush` mode on a filehandle other than `STDOUT`, we can use

```
# enable autoflush on MYHANDLE
select MYHANDLE;
$| = 1;
# STDOUT is not affected
select STDOUT;
```

Similarly, we can set or read the values of the special variables $. (line number), $/ (input record separator), $\ (output record separator), $, (output field separator), and $" (interpolated output field separator) on a per-filehandle basis. The special format variables such as $~ (format name) are also associated with individual file names. See "Reports—The 'R' in Perl" in Chapter 18 for more information on these.

Automatically Restoring the Default Filehandle

As an alternative to using the `select` function directly, we can make use of the `SelectSaver` module. This provides an object-oriented interface to `select` that has the advantage of automatically resetting the default output filehandle to its original state when the `SelectSaver` object is destroyed. In other words, statements like `select STDOUT` become unnecessary after we have finished with another filehandle:

```
use SelectSaver;

...
# scope of SelectSaver defined by 'if' statement
if ($redirect) {
    my $saver = new SelectSaver(NEWOUT);
    $| = 1;
    print "Message to NEWOUT handle"
}
# $saver goes out of scope here, object destroyed
print "Message to original default output handle";
```

`SelectSaver` works by remembering what filehandle was currently selected when the object was created. When the variable `$saver` falls out of scope at the end of the block, the object is destroyed and, as part of its cleanup, restores the filehandle that was originally selected.

Using Default Variables vs. IO::Handle Methods

If the intention is to modify the output properties of a filehandle rather than to make it the default output, a preferred approach is to use the `IO::Handle` methods inherited by filehandles generated by `IO::File`. These also allow the properties of filehandles to be modified, without the need to select them first:

```
# set autoflush on an IO::Handle based filehandle
$fh->autoflush(1);
```

The advantage of this technique is that it is simpler to read—selecting a filehandle just to modify its output properties is not very elegant. All the standard variables that relate to output can be set on a filehandle this way. See the section titled "IO::Handle Methods and Special Variables" for a rundown.

Duplicating and Aliasing Filehandles

If we supply `open` with a mode containing an ampersand, it will duplicate an existing filehandle. For example, to duplicate `STDIN`, we could write

```
open(NEWIN, "&STDIN") or die "Open failed: $! \n";
```

The mode of the new filehandle should be the same as that of the old, in this case read-only. Once duplicated, either handle may be used to read or write to the associated data stream. To duplicate a filehandle that is open in read-update mode, we can use

```
open(DUPLICATE, "+< &ORIGINAL");
```

This actually maps to the `dup` system call (or its nearest equivalent). Both filehandles, `DUPLICATE` and `ORIGINAL`, refer to the same file. However, each is independent of the other, with its own buffering and file position. This allows us to work at two different points within the same file simultaneously. To avoid potential conflicts, we can use file locking via `flock` to prevent the filehandles from treading on each other's toes; as well as preventing overwrite, `flock` also flushes all buffered output whenever a file is locked or unlocked. (See the section "Writing at the End of File" for an example.)

Duplication works on numeric file descriptors as well as filehandles. If we happen to have the file number instead, we can use that in place of the filehandle name. For instance, STDOUT and STDERR initially always have the file numbers 1 and 2 (STDIN is 0). We could save a copy of STDOUT and STDERR before redirecting them with

```
open(OLDOUT, "> &1");   # duplicate fileno 1 (STDOUT)
open(OLDERR, "> &2");   # duplicate fileno 2 (STDERR)
```

While this creates a new filehandle pointing to the same place as the original, the underlying file descriptor is also duplicated (as we can prove by calling fileno on the cloned handle). This means that operations that depend on the file descriptor—such as file locking—will not affect the other filehandle. When this is a concern we can create an alias for a filehandle by using &= in place of & with the file number.

```
open(ALIAS, "> &=MYHANDLE");
```

The ALIAS filehandle in this example uses the same underlying file descriptor as MYHANDLE, so using flock on ALIAS will affect MYHANDLE, and vice versa. Again, we can use a file descriptor in place of the filehandle.

If we happen to only have a file descriptor, and we want to create a filehandle to manage it, we can create one using this technique. Alternatively, if we are using IO::Handle or IO::File, we can use the new_from_fd method of IO::Handle:

```
$fh = IO::Handle->new_from_fd(fileno MYHANDLE);
```

■Note These special modes only work with the two-argument form of open; they do not work with the mode separated from the file name, which is why we concatenated the mode and file number in the open example earlier.

If we happen to have entirely lost the original standard input or standard output that we started out with, we can attempt to reacquire them by opening the special file - (or >- for STDOUT). See the earlier section "Opening Standard Input and Standard Output" for details.

Redirecting Filehandles

To redefine the default output filehandle, we can use select, but this only allows us to change the output filehandle from STDOUT to something else. It does not allow us to change the input filehandle from STDIN or the error filehandle STDERR. Even if we select a different output filehandle, output will still go to the original STDOUT if it is explicitly given:

```
select NEWOUT;
print STDOUT "This still goes to standard output";
```

The solution to these problems is to replace the filehandles themselves. For instance, to temporarily redirect standard output and standard error to a log file, we first need to make copies of the current filehandles, which we can do with the & notation. Since both filehandles are write-only, the correct mode to use is > &:

```
open(OLDOUT, "> &STDOUT");
open(OLDERR, "> &STDERR");
```

Having duplicated the original filehandles, we can now redirect them to the new file:

```perl
open(STDOUT, "> $logfile");
open(STDERR, "> $logfile");
```

Both filehandles will likely be block buffered. At this point we can enable autoflush for both of them, to get line buffering using select:

```perl
select STDOUT;
$| = 1;
select STDERR;
$| = 1;
```

Finally, after we have finished printing to the log file, we can restore the original STDOUT and STDERR by redirecting them back again:

```perl
close(STDOUT); open(STDOUT, "> &OLDOUT");
close(STDERR); open(STDERR, "> &OLDERR");
```

Note that it is important to close the filehandles before we redirect them. If we do not do this, data buffered on those filehandles may not get flushed unless (and until) the program terminates. If we are going to redirect back to the underlying file descriptors of the original STDOUT and STDERR later, we do not need to worry.

In this example, we have redirected the standard output and error filehandles, but any filehandle can be duplicated and/or redirected in this fashion. Here is an example of duplicating a filehandle that is open in read-update mode:

```perl
open(MYDUPLICATE, "+< &MYHANDLE");
```

It is important not to duplicate a filehandle with modes it does not have. Although Perl will let us duplicate a read-only filehandle into a write-only one, the results are unpredictable and unlikely to be what we want; buffering may give the impression that something is working when in fact it is not.

Redirecting the standard filehandles is subtly different, in one way, from redirecting other filehandles. System filehandles are only closed if the open succeeds, so in the event that the open fails, the original filehandle remains open and intact. This threshold that defines system filehandles is governed by the special variable $^F (or $SYSTEM_FD_MAX with use English). It contains the value of the highest system file number, usually 2 corresponding to STDERR. Attempts to open an existing filehandle on a new file whose file number is higher than $^F will cause the file to be closed before the new one is opened. In the event the open fails, the original file remains closed.

Caching Many Filehandles

If we try to open many filehandles all at the same time, we may run into an operating system limit. The FileCache module provides a solution to this problem by allowing filehandles to be cached. If we attempt to access a file for which a filehandle already exists, the cached handle is used. If we attempt to access a file for which no filehandle exists, and we have reached our limit, a filehandle is closed to make room for the new filehandle.

FileCache works by supplying one method, cacheout, which takes the name of a file as a parameter. We never use a filehandle directly, but supply the name of the file instead. This short example illustrates the technique, caching two filehandles:

```perl
#!/usr/bin/perl
# cache.pl
use warnings;
use strict;
no strict 'refs';
```

```
use FileCache;

my $myfile = "/tmp/myfile.txt";
my $anotherfile = "/tmp/anotherfile.txt";

cacheout $myfile;
print $myfile "Message to my file \n";
cacheout $anotherfile;
print $anotherfile "Message to another file \n";
print $myfile "Second message to my file \n";

close $myfile;
close $anotherfile;
```

The module works by creating filehandles with exactly the same name as the path of the file with which it is associated. This allows the scalar holding the file name to be used as a filehandle, and it also allows FileCache to look up the filehandle in an internal hash to see if it exists or not when we request that the file be opened.

Files are opened in write mode (>) if they do not currently exist, or update mode (>>) if they do. Consequently, this module is no use for handling multiple files in a read-write mode. However, it is a short and relatively simple module, so adapting it for caching other kinds of filehandle modes should be a reasonable proposition.

The maximum number of files that can be opened by the FileCache module is determined from the operating system (the /usr/include/sys/param.h header file on Unix systems). In the event that the value in this file is wrong (which does happen) or that this file does not exist (for example, on a Windows- or MacOS-based system), we can override it by setting the value of $FileCache::cacheout_maxopen:

```
if ($FileCache::cacheout_maxopen <= 16) {
    $FileCache::cacheout_maxopen = 64;
}
```

If the FileCache module cannot determine a value for the maximum allowed open files at all, it defaults to 16. So, a value of 16 in $FileCache::cacheout_maxopen is usually a sign that the maximum number of open files needs to be established in some other way and then be supplied to the FileCache module.

Note that just because we can set this value to allow the maximum number of open files possible does not mean that we necessarily ought to, since filehandles consume valuable system resources. If we use this module, we might want to take advantage of the caching mechanism to actually restrict the number of active filehandles:

```
$FileCache::cacheout_maxopen = 32 if $FileCache::cacheout_maxopen > 32;
```

IO::Handle Methods and Special Variables

IO::Handle is a generic filehandle module that provides an easier interface to filehandles than the standard Perl interface. It is the basis of the IO::File module, among others, and provides methods for using and configuring filehandles, which are loosely categorized into creation methods, built-in methods, configuration methods, and utility methods.

The creation methods presented in Table 12-5 create new IO::Handle objects.

Table 12-5. *IO::Handle Constructors*

Method	Action
new	Create a new IO::Handle object, for example: $fh = new IO::Handle; To create a filehandle and associate it with an open file, use IO::File's new instead.
new_from_fd	Create a new IO::Handle object and associate it with the given file descriptor. For example: $fh = IO::Handle->new_from_fd(1); $fh = IO::Handle->new_from_fd(fileno MYHANDLE); The file descriptor is the underlying file number that represents the raw connection to the file or device. It can be specified explicitly, for example, 0, 1, or 2 for STDIN, STDOUT, or STDERR, or derived from an existing filehandle via fileno. Note that this is the underlying functionality behind the open functions &= mode.

Each of these built-in function methods is a wrapper for the equivalent built-in function, as listed in Table 12-6.

Table 12-6. *IO::Handle Wrappers for Built-In Functions*

Method	Action
close	Close the file.
eof	Test for end-of-file condition.
fileno	Return file descriptor (file number) of filehandle.
format_write	Write a format string (equivalent to write).
getc	Get a single character.
read	Read a specific number of bytes.
print	Print to the file.
printf	Format a string and print to the file.
stat	Return information about the file.
sysread	Perform a system-level read.
syswrite	Perform a system-level write.
truncate	Truncate or extend the file.

The configuration methods configure an aspect of the filehandle, and they have a one-to-one correlation to one of Perl's special variables, which performs the equivalent function on the currently selected default output filehandle, as chosen by select. In each case, the original value is returned. The methods and their related special variables fall into two groups: those that work on a per-filehandle basis and those that are global in effect and apply to all filehandles.

The special variables and IO::Handle methods listed in Table 12-7 are specified on a per-filehandle basis.

Table 12-7. *IO::Handle Filehandle Methods*

Method	Variable	Action

autoflush	$|	Set the autoflush flag. Takes a Boolean parameter, for example:
		`$fh->autoflush(1);    # enable autoflush`
		`$fh->autoflush(0);    # disable autoflush`
		Or:
		`select $fh; $| = 1;`

format_page_number	$%	The current page number of the currently selected output channel.
format_lines_per_page	$=	The current page length (printable lines) of the currently selected output channel.
format_lines_left	$-	The number of lines left on the page of the currently selected output channel.
format_name	$~	The name of the current report format for the currently selected output channel.
format_top_name	$^	The name of the current top-of-page format for the currently selected output channel.

input_line_number	$.	The current line number. For example:
		`$lineno = $fh->input_line_number();`
		Or:
		`select $fh; $lineno = $.;`
		Note that although it is possible to set this value, it should usually be treated as read-only.

The special variables and IO::Handle methods listed in Table 12-8 are global but can be set via the appropriate method.

Table 12-8. *IO::Handle Global Methods*

Method	Variable	Action
format_line_break_characters	$:	The current set of characters after which a string may be broken to fill continuation fields (starting with ^) in a format.
format_formfeed	$^L	Which formats output as a form feed.

format_field_separator	$,	The string output between items in a print statement. By default, nothing. To print out comma-separated values, set to ,:
		`$old = $fh->output_field_separator(',');`
		Or:
		`$, = ',';`

output_record_separator	$\	The string output after the end of a print statement. By default, nothing. To print out lines automatically terminated by newlines, set to "\n":
		`$old = $fh->output_record_separator("\n");`
		Or:
		`$\ = "\n";`

Method	Variable	Action
input_record_separator	$/	The string used to separate lines for the readline operator. By default, it is \n. To read in paragraph mode, set to an empty string. To read a whole file at one go (slurp mode), set to undef: $old = $fh->input_record_separator(undef); Or: $/ = ''; # paragraph mode undef $/; # slurp mode

Finally, Table 12-9 lists the utility methods.

Table 12-9. *IO::Handle Utility Methods*

Method	Action
fdopen FILENO	Associate the filehandle with the given filehandle name, IO::Handle object, or file descriptor, for example: $fh->fdopen(1); $fh->fdopen(fileno STDOUT); $fh->fdopen($other_fh); This is the underlying function behind the new_from_fd method.
opened	Return true if the filehandle is currently open, false otherwise. For example: if ($fh->opened) { $line = $fh->getline; } else { # cannot read... }
getline	Return the next line from a file, for example: $line = $fh->getline(); print "$_ \n" while $fh->getline(); This is equivalent to the readline operator when called in a scalar context, even when called in a list context.
getlines	Return all available lines from a file, for example: @lines = $fh->getlines(); This is equivalent to the readline operator when called in a list context. If called in a scalar or void context, this method will croak with an error.
ungetc CHAR	Push a character back into the input buffer, for example: $fh->ungetc(ord $char); The character must be specified as an ASCII code, rather than as a string. Only one character is guaranteed to be pushed back; attempting to push back more than one without an intermediate read may fail.
write BUF, LEN, OFFSET	Equivalent to the syswrite function, this writes a given number of characters to the filehandle, for example: # write all of string to filehandle $fh->write $string; # write first 20 chars of string to filehandle $fh->write $string, 20; # write chars 20 to 40 of string to filehandle $fh->write $string, 20, 20; See syswrite in "System-Level IO" for more information. Note that the built-in Perl write function is mapped to the format_write method, since this makes more logical sense.

Continued

Table 12-9. *Continued*

Method	Action
error	Return true if the filehandle has experienced any errors since it was opened, or the last called to clearerr.
clearerr	Clear the filehandle's error condition (including end of file), for example: $fh->clearerr;
sync	Synchronize in-memory state of all opened files with their states on disc and update all other file system changes. For example: $fh->sync; Note that this is a kernel-level function, which is not supported on all platforms. It does not work on a per-file-system basis and does not flush buffered output at the filehandle level—use flush for that.
flush	Flush buffered output at the application level, for example: $fh->flush; This method will flush any data that has been buffered by either block or line buffering down to the operating system. It does not guarantee that the data is actually written; however, sync does that.
printflush ARGS	Enable autoflush mode, print arguments to filehandle, and then restore the original autoflush state, for example: $fh->printflush("This works", "just", "like print");
blocking 0|1	Set blocking or nonblocking mode on the filehandle, for example: $fh->blocking(0); # enable nonblocking mode $blocking = $fh->blocking(); # retrieve mode This returns the value of the previous setting or the current setting if no flag is specified.
untaint 0|1	Set or unset untainting mode. For example: $fh->untaint(1); # trust data read from $fh This method only has an effect when taint mode has been enabled (-T). Ordinarily, when taint mode is enabled, any data read from a filehandle is considered tainted and a potential security risk. Setting the untaint flag marks the filehandle as being a source of trusted data, so any data read from it is considered untainted. This should not be done lightly—do not use this method just to get a program to work.

System-Level IO

Conventional input and output uses buffered filehandles that optimize file accesses by reducing the number of reads or writes that actually take place. The advantage of this is that file handling is a much more efficient process from the operating system's point of view and for the most part is transparent to us. The disadvantage is that sometimes we want to read and write data with immediate effect, in which case buffering can get in the way.

Buffering is a feature of the standard input/output library, more conventionally known as the stdio library. To avoid buffering, we need a way to bypass the stdio library and access filehandles directly. Fortunately, Perl allows us to do just this with the sys family of built-in functions, sysread, syswrite, and sysseek.

Handling filehandles at the system level also allows us a greater degree of control over them; for instance, we can carry out things like nonblocking IO much more easily. Much of this control comes from the sysopen function.

■**Tip** The standard IO functions use buffered IO, and the system-level functions bypass these buffers. Mixing buffered and nonbuffered functions in the same code is extremely dangerous and highly inadvisable, as inconsistent file positions and corrupted data can very easily be the result. As a general rule, use one set of functions or the other, never both, on the same filehandle.

Opening Filehandles at the System Level

Opening files at the system level is handled by sysopen. Like open, it takes a filehandle name and a file name as an argument. Unlike open, it does not take a mode string like > or +< but a numeric mode made up of several mode flags whose values specify the desired attributes of the filehandle. The Fcntl module defines labels for these numeric flags, such as O_WRONLY for write only access or O_CREAT to create the file if it does not exist. The mode cannot be combined with the file name as it is with open; instead it comes after the file name as an additional third parameter:

```
use Fcntl;   # import standard symbols
sysopen SYSHANDLE, $filename, O_WRONLY | O_CREAT;
```

The standard open modes can all be expressed in terms of a sysopen mode value; < is equivalent to O_RDONLY, and > is equivalent to O_WRONLY| O_CREAT| O_TRUNC. The following two statements are actually identical but phrased differently:

```
# open a file write-only with 'open'
open HANDLE, "> $filename";
# open a file write-only with 'sysopen'
sysopen HANDLE, $filename, O_WRONLY|O_CREAT|O_TRUNC;
```

Note that sysopen does not create a different sort of filehandle to open. In particular, it does not create an unbuffered handle. Whether or not the filehandle is buffered or unbuffered depends on how we read and write it. Functions like read, getc, and the readline operator work via the standard IO buffers, while functions like sysread and syswrite bypass them. sysopen itself has no opinion on the use of buffers or not—it merely provides a lower-level way to create filehandles.

■**Tip** For the curious coming from a C background: while it is true that sysopen uses the open system call to generate an unbuffered file descriptor, it then uses fdopen to create a filehandle from that file descriptor and returns this to Perl. So sysopen does create a filehandle, even though it does not use the fopen system call.

For many applications, we only need to supply three parameters to sysopen. (In fact, in many cases we can get away with two, because an open mode flag of 0 is usually equivalent to O_RDONLY. However, it is dangerous to assume this. Always use the Fcntl symbols.) We can also supply a fourth optional parameter describing the permissions of the file in cases where the file is created. We will come to that in a moment.

Open Mode Flags

sysopen allows us to specify all manner of flags in the open mode, some generically useful, others very specific, and a few more than a little obscure. The main point of using sysopen rather than open is to gain access to these flags directly, allowing us to create open modes other than the six standard combinations supported by open. Some are relevant only to particular kinds of file, such as terminal devices. The following tables show the flags that are combined to make up the various modes used by open.

Always specify one (and only one) of the **primary modes**:

O_RDONLY	Open file for reading only.
O_RDWR	Open file for reading and writing.
O_WRONLY	Open file for writing only (not supported on Windows).

These are **additional modes**:

O_APPEND	Open file for appending.
O_CREAT	Create file if it does not exist.
O_TRUNC	Truncate file on opening it (writing).

See Table 12-2 in the section "Creating Filehandles with IO::Handle and IO::File" earlier in the chapter for a comparison of open and sysopen modes to see how these mode flags are combined to create the six modes of open. Some other useful flags we can *only* access with sysopen include the following:

Text and binary files	O_BINARY O_TEXT	Use binary mode (no newline translation). Use text mode (do newline translation).
Nonblocking IO	O_NONBLOCK O_NDELAY	Enable nonblocking mode. Alias (usually) for O_NONBLOCK. Semantics may vary on platforms for filehandles that are associated with networking.
Additional Modes	O_EXCL	Create file only if it does not already exist (meaningful only with O_CREAT). If it does exist, fail rather than open it.

Nonblocking IO

One of the main reasons for using sysopen over open is for nonblocking IO. Normally when a read or write (including a system read or write performed by sysread or syswrite) is performed, the system will wait for the operation to complete. In the case of reading, Perl will wait for input to arrive and only return control to our application when it has something for us. Frequently, however, we do not want to wait because we want to do other things in the meantime, so we use sysopen and the O_NONBLOCK flag (although it should be noted that the O_NONBLOCK flag is not recognized by Windows at present):

```
use Fcntl;

# open serial port read only, nonblocking
sysopen SERIAL, '/dev/ttyS0', O_RDONLY|O_NONBLOCK;

# attempt to read characters
my $key;
while (sysread SERIAL, $key, 1) {
    if (defined $key) {
        print "Got '$key' \n";
    } else {
        warn "No input available \n";
```

```
        # wait before trying again
        sleep(1);
    }
}

# close the port
close SERIAL;
```

When nonblocking mode is enabled, it attempts to read from a filehandle. When no data is available, it will raise the EAGAIN error in $!. We can get the symbol for EAGAIN from the POSIX module, so a better way to write the preceding example would have been

```
use POSIX qw(EAGAIN);
use Fcntl;

# open serial port read only, nonblocking
sysopen SERIAL, '/dev/ttyS0', O_RDONLY|O_NONBLOCK;

# attempt to read characters
my $key;
    while (sysread SERIAL, $key, 1) {
        if (defined ($key)) {
            print "Got '$key' \n"
        } else {
            if ($!==EAGAIN) {
                warn "No input available \n";

                # wait before trying again
                sleep(1);
            } else {
                warn "Error attempting to read: $! \n";
                last;
            }
        }
    }
}

# close the port
close SERIAL;
```

In this case, we have used sysread to read an individual character directly from the serial port. We could also have used read or even getc to do the same thing via the filehandle's buffers. This probably would have been better, as the filehandle will read in several kilobytes of characters if it can, then return them to us one by one. From our perspective there is no difference, but from the point of view of the serial port it makes a lot of difference.

The Permissions Mask

Since it works at a lower level than open, sysopen also allows us to specify a numeric permissions mask as a fourth argument to sysopen, either in the conventional octal format or as a combination of flags defined by the :mode import label:

```
# permissions mode, as octal integer
open HANDLE, $filename, O_WRONLY|O_CREAT, 0644;
# permissions mode, as set of Fcntl flags:
open HANDLE, $filename, O_WRONLY|O_CREAT,
  S_IRUSR|S_IWUSR|S_IRGRP|S_IROTH;
```

If the open creates the file (generally because O_CREAT is present in the open mode), its permissions are set according to the permissions mask, as modified by the umask value as discussed earlier in the chapter. Otherwise, the permissions mask has no effect.

Using sysopen via IO::File

It is not actually necessary to use sysopen directly to make use of its features. The new method of IO::File automatically uses sysopen if we give it a numeric mode instead of a string:

```
# 'IO::File' open for read/write using 'open'
$fh = new IO::File ($filename, '+<');

# 'IO::File' open for read/write using 'sysopen'
$fh = new IO::File ($filename, O_RDWR);
```

Since new can automatically detect a numeric mode flag and pass it to sysopen instead of open, we can also pass in the permissions mask too:

```
# 'IO::File' open for read/write using 'sysopen' with permissions mask
$fh = new IO::File ($filename, O_RDWR, 0644);
```

The advantage of IO::File is, of course, that it makes filehandles much easier to manipulate and to pass in and out of subroutines. This makes it a good choice for programming regardless of whether we choose to use open or sysopen underneath.

Unbuffered Reading

Reading at the standard IO level is handled by Perl functions such as read and print. The unbuffered system-level equivalents are sysread and syswrite.

sysread looks suspiciously similar to read at first glance. Like read, it takes a filehandle to read from, a scalar variable to store the result in, a length giving the amount of data to read (or attempt to read), and an optional offset. However, sysread bypasses the buffered IO layer that normally underlies read and accesses the file descriptor directly using the operating system's read call:

```perl
#!/usr/bin/perl
# sysread.pl
use warnings;
use strict;

use POSIX;

my $result;

die "Usage: $0 file \n" unless @ARGV;
sysopen HANDLE, $ARGV[0], O_RDONLY|O_NONBLOCK;
# read 20 chrs into $result
my $chrs = sysread HANDLE, $result, 20;
if ($chrs == 20) {
    # got all 20, try to read another 30 chrs into $result after the first 20
    $chrs += sysread HANDLE, $result, 30, 20;
    print "Got '$result' \n";
    if ($chrs < 50) {
        print "Data source exhausted after $chrs characters \n";
    } else {
        print "Read $chrs characters \n";
    }
} elsif ($chrs > 0) {
    print "Got '$result' \n";
```

```
     print "Data source exhausted after $chrs characters \n";
} else {
     print "No data! \n";
}
```

The return value from sysread is the number of characters successfully read. This may be less than the number requested if the data source runs out, and 0 if there is no data to read. However, note that if O_NONBLOCK is not set, then sysread will wait for more data to arrive rather than returning 0. If there is some data but not enough to satisfy the request, then sysread will return when it exhausts the data source. As stated before, Windows does not recognize O_NONBLOCK, so this example will not work properly on that platform.

A moment ago we said that sysread bypasses the buffered IO that *normally* underlies read. The reason for that qualification is that if we have a sufficiently modern Perl, which provides support for PerlIO layers, we have the option to remove the buffering layer, which is either perlio or stdio depending on the way Perl was built, and use a filehandle that maps directly to the raw file descriptor. Here is how we could create an unbuffered handle for reading:

```
open HANDLE, "<:unix", $ARGV[0]; #requires PerlIO
```

Or to modify an existing handle:

```
binmode STDIN, ":unix"; #requires PerlIO
```

This works because the unix layer, being a foundation layer, wipes out all existing layers when we set it on a handle. With the handle unbuffered, read now works almost identically to sysread (with the bonus that we can still use eof to check for end of file). Of course, only sysread will work for both new and older Perl versions.

In fact, the preceding sysread example is more of an example of how to use sysopen (to get a nonblocking filehandle) than it is of how to use sysread, as we could just as easily have used read in this example with the same effect. The key difference between the two is that read would read as much data as possible in the first call, but it would only return to us the requested quantity. Any extra data is stored in the buffer. The second call would simply retrieve data from the buffer and only cause a genuine read of the file if insufficient data is waiting. Of course, we might not want to buffer the data; we may want to share the filehandle between different processes instead. In cases like that, we would use sysread.

There is no system-level definition of the end-of-file condition, but we can do the equivalent for checking for a zero return from sysread instead.

Unbuffered Writing

The counterpart to sysread is syswrite, which writes data directly to the filehandle rather than into the filehandle's buffer using the operating system's write call. This is very useful in all kinds of applications, especially those that involve sending short bursts of information between different processes. If we have PerlIO available, we can use print on an unbuffered filehandle to similar effect (as we will in a moment), but this is only available in recent Perl versions. For backwards compatibility, syswrite is the portable choice.

syswrite takes a filehandle, some data, a length, and an optional offset as parameters. It then writes data from the string to the filehandle up to the end of the text contained in the scalar or the value supplied as the length, whichever is shorter. If an offset is supplied, syswrite starts writing data from that character position. For example, this code snippet writes out the contents of the scalar $data to HANDLE (presumably a serial or network connection) at a rate of 500 characters per second:

```
$pos = 0; $span = 500; $length = length($data);
while ($pos <= $length) {
     syswrite HANDLE, $data, $span, $pos;
```

```
    $pos += $span;
    sleep 1;
}
```

Unlike sysread, the length is also an optional parameter. If omitted, the length of the supplied data is used instead, making syswrite a close analogue for an unbuffered print, only without the ability to accept a list of arguments. We can invent a sysprint that will work like print using syswrite, though:

```
# an unbuffered print-a-like

sub sysprint {
    # check for a leading filehandle and remove it if present
    $fh = (defined fileno($_[0]))?shift:*STDOUT;
    # use $, to join arguments, just like print
    $joiner = $, ?$, :'';
    syswrite $fh, join($joiner, @_);
}

sysprint(*STDOUT, "This ", "works ", "like ", "print ", "(sort of) ", "\n");
```

If we have access to PerlIO, we can simplify much of the preceding by simply removing the buffered layer (stdio or perlio, depending on the circumstances) and creating or modifying the output filehandle to be intrinsically unbuffered. To do this, we set the special unix layer on the filehandle (even on non-Unix platforms). As unix is fundamentally the lowest-level layer possible, this has the effect of wiping out any and all layers we might otherwise have.

For example, this short program prints out ten dots, one a second:

```
#!/usr/bin/perl

binmode(STDOUT,":unix"); #requires PerlIO
for (0..9) {
    print "."; sleep 1;
}
print "\n";
```

Because we set the unix layer on STDOUT, each dot appears when we print it. If we remove or comment out the binmode line, nothing visibly happens for ten seconds, then all ten dots appear at once.

See "Communicating Between Processes" in Chapter 21 for another example where sysread and syswrite are useful for avoiding deadlocks.

System-Level File Positioning

The system-level equivalent of the seek and tell functions is sysseek, which carries out both roles. Like seek, it takes a filehandle, a position, and a whence flag that is set to either 0, 1, or 2, or the Fcntl equivalent symbols SEEK_SET, SEEK_CUR, and SEEK_END:

```
# seek using whence numbers
sysseek HANDLE, 0, 0;   # rewind to start
sysseek HANDLE, 0, 2;   # seek to end of file
sysseek HANDLE, 20, 1;  # seek forward 20 characters

# seek using Fcntl symbols
use Fcntl qw(:seek);

sysseek HANDLE, 0, SEEK_SET;   # rewind to start
sysseek HANDLE, 0, SEEK_END;   # seek to end of file
sysseek HANDLE, 20, SEEK_CUR;  # seek forward 20 characters
```

The old file position is returned by sysseek. To find the current position using sysseek, we can simply seek to it using a whence flag of SEEK_CUR and a position of zero:

```
use Fcntl qw(:seek);
$pos = sysseek HANDLE, 0, SEEK_CUR;
```

Apart from buffering, sysseek is identical in operation to seek. However, tell and sysseek can (and often do) return radically different values for the file position. This is because the position returned by tell is determined by the amount of data read by our application, whereas the position returned by sysseek is determined by the amount of data read by Perl, which includes the data buffered by the filehandle. We can calculate the amount of data currently buffered by taking the difference between the two values:

```
print "There are ", tell(HANDLE) - sysseek(HANDLE, 0, 1), " bytes in the buffer \n";
```

Needless to say, mixing up system-level file positioning with standard IO file positioning is rarely a good idea for precisely this reason.

fcntl and ioctl

No discussion of system-level IO would be entirely complete without a brief look at the fcntl and ioctl functions. These provide very low-level access to filehandles, retrieving and setting parameters that are often otherwise inaccessible to us. fcntl is more generic, and it works across most kinds of filehandle. The ioctl function is targeted at special files, such as character and block devices, and is much more Unix specific.

Returned values, if any, are placed into a passed scalar variable; the return value is used to indicate success or failure only. Both functions return undef on failure and set the error in $!. Otherwise, they either return a positive value (if the underlying system call returns one) or the special return value "0 but true", which returns 0 in a numeric context but tests true otherwise. To get the original underlying return value (which is -1 for failure, 0 or a positive value for success), we can write

```
# calculate original numeric return value from system 'fcntl'
$result = int (fcntl(HANDLE, $action, $value) || -1);
```

Both functions will return a fatal error if used on a platform that does not support the underlying system calls. On Windows, they return 0, but do not actually do anything, although they are not fatal.

Setting Filehandle Attributes with fcntl

The fcntl function (not to be confused with the Fcntl module) performs miscellaneous actions on a filehandle. It takes three parameters: a filehandle, an action to perform, and a value. For actions that retrieve information, this value must be a scalar variable, into which fcntl places the results of the call. The names of the actions are defined, appropriately enough, in the Fcntl module. For example, we can use fcntl to set a filehandle into nonblocking mode after we have opened it:

```
use POSIX;
use Fcntl qw(:mode);

# get the current open mode flags
my $mode;
fcntl HANDLE, F_GETFL, $mode;

# add O_NONBLOCK and set
fcntl HANDLE, F_SETFL, $mode | O_NONBLOCK;
```

Following is a reasonably complete list of actions (some platform specific) supported by fcntl. Because of platform variations, the actual actions available may vary from this list. Consult the system documentation (man fcntl) for details.

F_DUPFD	Duplicate the file descriptor, returning the new descriptor. A low-level version of open's & mode.

The following actions get or set the close-on-exec flag. This flag determines whether the filehandle survives across an exec call. Normally STDIN, STDOUT, and STDERR survive and other filehandles are closed. The threshold for new filehandles can be set with the special variable $^F. The F_SETFD action allows the flag of an individual, already extant filehandle to be modified.

F_GETFD	Read the close-on-exec flag. File descriptors with this flag set are closed across a call to exec.
F_SETFD	Set the close-on-exec flag. For example, to preserve a filehandle across exec we would use fcntl HANDLE, F_SETFD, 0;.

The following actions get and set the mode flags of the filehandle, as specified by open modes like > or sysopen mode flags like O_RDONLY:

F_GETFL	Get the open mode flags, as set by open or sysopen. A combination of flags such as O_RDONLY, O_CREAT, O_APPEND, and so on.
F_SETFL	Set the open mode flags. Usually only the flags O_APPEND, O_ASYNC (Linux/BSD), and O_NONBLOCK can be set, others are unaffected. See earlier for an example.

The following actions, which handle discretionary file locking, are similar to but *not* the same as the flock system call (unless flock is implemented in terms of fcntl, which is sometimes the case). For most purposes, flock is a lot simpler and more portable, but it may not work on network-mounted file systems (for example, via NFS). See the flock discussion earlier in the chapter for a more detailed comparison of the two approaches (and how Perl's own flock relates to them).

F_GETLK	Determine if a file is locked or not. The parameter needs to be a scalar variable, into which details of the lock are written. The l_type field is set to F_UNLCK if no lock is present.
F_SETLK	Set a lock, returning immediately with undef on failure. The parameter needs to be a packed flock structure containing the lock details. $! is set to the reason for the failure if the lock attempt fails.
F_SETLKW	Set a lock, waiting for the file to become available if necessary. Returns undef if interrupted.

The lock type can be one of F_RDLCK, F_WRLCK, or F_UNLCK, which have the obvious meanings. There is no nonblock flag as there is for flock because that function is handled by F_SETLK and F_SETLKW. However, the values passed and returned to these actions are packed lock structures (not simple values), so we need to use pack and unpack to create arguments that are suitable for fcntl when using these actions. Here is a short script that implements a generic locking subroutine, three specific lock subroutines that use it, and a quick demonstration of using them:

```perl
#!/usr/bin/perl
# fcntl.pl
use warnings;
use strict;

use Fcntl;
# generic lock subroutine
sub _do_lock {
    my ($locktype, $fh, $block) = @_;
    $block |= 0;   # don't block unless asked to

    # is this a blocking or nonblocking attempt
    my $op = $block?F_SETLKW:F_SETLK;

    # pack a structure suitable for this operation
    my $lock = pack('s s l l s', $locktype, 0, 0, 0, 0);

    # establish the chosen lock in the chosen way
    my $res = fcntl($fh, $op, $lock);
    seek($fh, 0, 0);
    return $res;
}

# specific lock types
sub read_lock { return _do_lock(F_RDLCK, @_); }
sub write_lock { return _do_lock(F_WRLCK, @_); }
sub undo_lock { return _do_lock(F_UNLCK, @_); }

# called like this:
open MYHANDLE, "+> myfile" or die "Failed to open: $! \n";

# block write lock
write_lock(*MYHANDLE, 1) or die "Failed to lock: $! \n";

print MYHANDLE "Only I can write here \n";
# undo (can''t block anyway)
undo_lock(*MYHANDLE) or die "Failed to unlick: $! \n";
close MYHANDLE;
```

Assuming the platform supports it, the O_ASYNC mode flag can be specified in sysopen (or enabled using fcntl and F_SETLF) to have signals generated by open file descriptors whenever reading or writing becomes possible. This allows us to write synchronous IO routines that can respond to asynchronous events. These actions allow the target and type of signal generated to be configured:

F_GETOWN	Get the process ID (or process group) that is receiving signals (SIGIO or SIGURG) on this file descriptor, if the O_ASYNC mode flag is enabled. By default, the process ID is that of the process that opened the filehandle, that is, us.
F_SETOWN	Set the process ID (or process group) that will receive signals on this file descriptor, if O_ASYNC is enabled.
F_GETSIG	(Linux only) Get the signal type generated by filehandles with O_ASYNC enabled. The default of zero generates a SIGIO signal, as does a setting of SIGIO.
F_SETSIG	(Linux only) Set the signal type generated by filehandles with O_ASYNC enabled.

The POSIX module also defines symbols for the various signal names.

Controlling Devices with ioctl

The ioctl function closely resembles fcntl, both in syntax and in operation. Like fcntl, it takes a filehandle, an action, and a value (which in the case of retrieval actions must be a scalar variable). It also returns "0 but true" on success and undef on failure, setting $! to the reason if so. Also like fcntl, attempting to use ioctl on a platform that does not support it will cause a fatal error.

The ioctl function is an interface for controlling filehandles that are associated with devices, such as serial ports, terminals, CR-ROM drives, and so on. ioctl is a very low-level tool for analyzing and programming the device underlying a filehandle, and it is relatively rare that we need to use it. Most of the useful ioctl actions are already encapsulated into more convenient modules or handled by the POSIX module. However, in a few cases it can be useful, so long as we realize that it is not very portable (many platforms do not support it).

The different actions supported by ioctl can be considerable (as well as highly platform dependent) since different devices categories may support their own particular family of ioctl actions—serial ports have one set, terminals have another, and so on. When Perl is built, it analyzes the underlying system and attempts to compile a list of constant-defining functions, each one corresponding to the equivalent C header file. The most common symbols are placed in sys/ioctl.ph. Other ioctl symbols may be defined in different header files—on a Linux system, CR-ROM ioctls are defined in the header file linux/cdrom.ph. Here's how we can eject a CD on a Linux box:

```
#!/usr/bin/perl
# ioctl.pl
use warnings;
use strict;

# require 'linux/cdrom.ph';

open CDROM, '/dev/cdrom';
ioctl CDROM, 0x5309, 1;   # the ioctl number for CDROMEJECT
# ioctl CDROM, &CDROMEJECT, 1;
close CDROM;
```

For a complete list of ioctl actions, consult the system documentation for the device type in question—Linux defines ioctls in the manual page ioctl_list. Serial port definitions can also be found in the header files compiled by Perl, /usr/lib/perl5/5.6.0/<platform-type>/bits/ioctls.ph for the actions, ioctl_types.ph for flags such as TCIOM_RTS, and TCIOM_CD in a standard Unix Perl 5.6 installation. Terminal definitions are covered by the POSIX routines POSIX::Termios and documented in the POSIX module manual page.

Many of the more common actions performed by ioctl are often better handled elsewhere, for instance, by several of the standard Perl library modules covered in this chapter. In Chapter 15, the POSIX getattr and setattr routines and the POSIX::Termios module are covered.

POSIX IO

The POSIX module provides a direct interface to the standard C library upon which Perl is built, including all of the file handling routines. Most of the time we never need to bother with these, since Perl already supports most of them in its own file functions. However, directly accessing POSIX calls can occasionally come in handy.

The POSIX module provides three main categories of routines that relate to file handling and IO. The first works on filehandles, and the majority of these are identical in every respect to the standard Perl file functions. The second works on file descriptors and is the basis of the system-level IO functions. The third is specifically aimed at talking to terminals and interactive devices, and we discuss it further in Chapter 15.

Intuitively, we might expect Perl's sys file functions to return and operate on file descriptors (not filehandles), since they are after all supposed to be "system" level. In fact they do, by using fileno to determine the underlying file descriptor and then using the appropriate system-level POSIX call. So, even though we have a filehandle complete with buffers, we may never actually use them. The advantage of this approach is that we can use filehandles and still carry out unbuffered IO without ever having to worry about file descriptors unless we really want to.

POSIX Filehandle Routines

The POSIX module provides interfaces to the standard filehandle routines as a convenience to programmers who are migrating from C and are used to routines like fopen, flush, fstat, fgetpos, and so on. In actuality, all of these routines either map directly onto Perl's built-in functions (POSIX::getc simply calls CORE::getc, for example) or methods in the IO::File, IO::Handle or IO::Seekable modules. (For instance, open goes to IO::File, ungetc goes to IO::Handle, and ftell goes to IO::Seekable.)

In short, there is really no reason to use these functions, and we are almost certainly better off using Perl's built-in functions and the IO:: family of modules. However, for those who have a lot of experience with the POSIX library calls and are interested in a quick port with minimal fuss, the POSIX module does provide their equivalents in Perl.

POSIX File Descriptor Routines

The POSIX routines that operate on file descriptors are summarized in Table 12-10. Note that we can use fdopen to create a filehandle from a file descriptor that was created using open or creat. We can use fileno to get a file descriptor from a filehandle for use in these routines.

Table 12-10. *POSIX File Descriptor Routines*

Routine	Purpose
close fd	Close a file descriptor created by open or create.
creat fd, perm	Create a file with an open mode of O_WRONLY|O_CREAT|O_TRUNC. Takes a permissions mask as a second parameter. Shorthand for open.
fdopen fd	Create a filehandle from a file descriptor—equivalent to the open mode &=<fd>.
stat fd	Return "stat" information for the file descriptor. The returned list of values is identical to that returned by Perl's stat.
dup fd	Duplicate an existing file descriptor, returning the number of the new file descriptor. Equivalent to the open mode &<fd>, except it returns a file descriptor.
dup2 oldfd, newfd	Make newfd a duplicate of oldfd, closing newfd first if it is currently open. No direct Perl equivalent.
open file, mode, perm	Open a file descriptor. Identical to sysopen except that it returns a file descriptor, not a filehandle. sysopen can be simulated by following open with fdopen on the generated file descriptor.
Pipe	Create a pair of file descriptors connected to either end of a unidirectional pipe. Returns a list of two descriptors; the first is read-only, the second is write-only. Identical to Perl's pipe except that it returns file descriptors, not filehandles.
read fd, $buf, length	Read from a file descriptor. Identical to Perl's sysread except that it uses a file descriptor and not a filehandle.
write fd, $buf, length	Write to a file descriptor. Identical to Perl's syswrite except that it uses a file descriptor and not a filehandle.

Note that importing these functions into our own applications can cause problems, since many of them have the same name as a Perl counterpart that uses filehandles rather than file descriptors. For that reason, these routines are better called through their namespace prefix:

```
$fd = POSIX::open($path, O_RDWR|O_APPEND|O_EXCL, 0644);
@stat = POSIX::fstat $fd;
$fd2 = POSIX::dup $fd;
POSIX::close $fd;
```

Technically, the directory handling functions such as opendir also deal in file descriptors rather than filehandles, since it makes no sense to buffer the data read from a directory. However, Perl also handles this for us automatically, so we should never have to worry about it.

Moving Between POSIX and Standard IO

Occasionally, we might want to work with both a POSIX file descriptor and a filehandle for the same file. For example, we may want to make use of functions in the POSIX library or third-party C libraries that expect file descriptors as arguments. This takes a lot of care and attention to pull off, because as we remarked when we started, mixing buffered and unbuffered operations can corrupt data and confuse the file position.

Generating a filehandle from a file descriptor involves wrapping it in a stdio file structure containing a pair of buffers. In C, this is done by the fdopen system call. In Perl, we can do the same thing with the special &= open mode, which takes a file descriptor as an argument:

```
# wrap a file descriptor in a new filehandle
open HANDLE, "&= $descriptor";
```

Much the same thing happens implicitly when we duplicate a filehandle with open. The & mode is a shorthand for extracting the file descriptor of a filehandle and then creating a new filehandle structure around it:

```
# duplicate a filehandle the quick way
open NEWOUT, "& STDOUT";

# duplicate a filehandle the explicit way
$stout = fileno STDOUT;
open NEWOUT, "& $stout";
```

Note that there is a difference between & and &=. &= associates a new filehandle with an existing file descriptor. Closing any filehandle associated with that descriptor closes all of them. & creates a new file descriptor that is associated with the same file, but is nonetheless a different descriptor. The file descriptors and their associated filehandles share file positions but they can be closed independently of each other. See "Creating Filehandles with open" at the start of the chapter for more on these special modes.

Extracting the file descriptor from a filehandle is trivial; we just use the fileno function:

```
$descriptor = fileno HANDLE;
```

We can also use fileno to find out if filehandles are duplicated, since they will have the same file descriptor:

```
if (fileno(HANDLE1) == fileno(HANDLE2)) {
    print "Handles are duplicated \n";
}
```

Summary

In this chapter, we looked at using filehandles for input to and output from our Perl programs. We saw that Perl provides us with a rich suite of functions for manipulating filehandles. We examined various ways of creating, referring to, reading, and writing to filehandles. We also discussed Perl's handling of binary and text mode on platforms where the distinction matters and the extended capabilities provided by PerlIO to manipulate filehandle layers. Also covered here were changing the default output filehandle, duplicating and aliasing filehandles, redirecting filehandles, and caching filehandles.

We then looked into the extra possibilities for control that we gain when manipulating filehandles at the system level, including performing unbuffered reading and writing. Finally, we examined the `fcntl` and `ioctl` functions and the `POSIX` module, and we discussed when and why we might need to use them.

This chapter provides the foundations from which we can investigate more specific input and output. The next three chapters cover manipulating files and directories, the command line and interacting with shells, and input and output to terminals. Later on we cover networking, a subject in its own right. It should come as no surprise that these subjects require a lot of coverage—after all, at their most basic, any program that actually does something useful invariably involves getting input from somewhere, doing something with it, and sending the results somewhere else.

## CHAPTER 13

Files and Directories

There are plenty of applications involving files that do not involve opening a filehandle. Examples include copying, moving, or renaming files, and interrogating files for their size, permissions, or ownership. In this chapter, we cover the manipulation of files and directories in ways other than opening filehandles to read or write them using Perl's built-in functions. We also look at the various modules provided as standard with Perl to make file handling both simpler and portable across different platforms, finding files with wildcards through file name globbing, and creating temporary files.

While the bulk of this chapter is concerned with files, we also spend some time looking at directories, which while fundamentally different entities to files, turn out to provide broadly similar techniques to manipulate them.

Querying and Manipulating Files

Files are located in a file system, which stores attributes for every file it references. The most obvious attribute a file has is a file name, but we can also test filing system entries for properties such as their type (file, directory, link) and access permissions with Perl's file test operators. To retrieve detailed information about a file's attributes, we also have the stat and lstat functions at our disposal. Perl also provides built-in functions to manipulate file permissions, ownership, and create or destroy file names within the file system. However, the built-in functions are limited in how versatile they can be on different platforms, because the concepts they embody originate with Unix in mind and are not always portable in themselves.

In addition to the built-in functions, Perl provides a toolkit of modules for handling files portably, regardless of the underlying platform. Some wrap built-in functions, like File::stat, or aggregate many file test operations into a single function call, like File::CheckTree. Others provide useful features such as finding or comparing files, like File::Find and File::Compare. Most of these modules are built on top of File::Spec, which provides basic support for cross-platform file name handling. It is almost always a good idea to use these modules in place of a built-in function whenever portability is a concern.

Beyond basic file handling, Perl also provides the glob function for retrieving file names through wildcard specifications. The built-in glob function is actually implemented in terms of a family of standard modules—each handling a different platform—that we can also use directly for greater control.

A final but important aspect of file handling is the creation and use of temporary files. Apparently simple on the surface, there are several ways to create a temporary file, each with its own advantages, drawbacks, and portability issues.

Getting User and Group Information

Perl provides built-in support for handling user and group information on Unix platforms through the getpwent and getgrent families of functions. This support is principally derived from the underlying C library functions of the same names, which are in turn dependent on the details of the implementation provided by the operating system. All Unix platforms provide broadly the same features for user and group management, but they vary slightly in what additional information they store. While Perl makes a reasonable attempt to unify all the variations, the system documentation is the best source of information on what values these functions return.

Unix platforms define user and group information in the /etc/passwd and /etc/group files, but this oversimplifies the actual process of looking up user and group information for two reasons. First, if a shadow password file is in use, then the user information in /etc/passwd will not contain an encrypted password in the password field. Second, if alternative sources of user and group information are configured (such as NIS or NIS+), then requesting user or group information may initiate a network lookup to retrieve information from a remote server. The order in which local and remote information sources are consulted is typically defined by the file /etc/nsswitch.conf.

Support for other security models and platforms is not provided through built-in functions, but through extension modules. Windows programmers, for example, can make use of the Win32::AdminMisc module to gain access to the Win32 Security API. Windows and other non-Unix platforms do not support getpwent or getgrent, though the Cygwin environment does provide a veneer of Unix security that allows these functions to work on Windows platforms with limited functionality, enough for Perl programs that use them to function. Access Control Lists (ACLs) and other advanced security features are beyond the reach of the built-in functions even on Unix platforms, but they can be handled via various modules available from CPAN.

User Information

Unix platforms store local user information in the /etc/passwd file (though as noted previously they may also retrieve information remotely). The format varies slightly but typically has a structure like this:

```
fred:RGdmsaynFgP56:301:200:Fred A:/home/fred:/bin/bash
jim:Edkl1y7NMtO/M:302:200:Jim B:/home/jim:/bin/ksh
mysql:!!:120:120:MySQL server:/var/lib/mysql:/bin/csh
```

Each line contains the following fields: name, password, user ID, primary group ID, comment/GECOS, home directory, and login shell. In this case, we are not using a shadow password file, so the password field contains an encrypted password. The first two lines are for regular users, while the third defines an identity for a MySQL database server to run as. It does not need a password since it is not intended as a login user, so the password is disabled with !! (* is often also used for this purpose).

The getpwent function (pwent is short for "password entry") retrieves one entry from the user information file at a time, starting from the first. In list context, it returns no less than ten fields:

```
($name, $passwd, $uid, $gid, $quota, $comment, $gcos, $dir, $shell, $expire)
    = getpwent;
```

Since the format and source of user information varies, not all these fields are always defined, and some of them have alternate meanings. A summary of each field and its possible meanings is given in Table 13-1; consult the manual page for the passwd file (typically via man 5 passwd) for exact details of what fields are provided on a given platform.

Table 13-1. *getpwent Fields*

Field		Meaning
Name	**Number**	
name	0	The login name of the user.
passwd	1	The encrypted password. Depending on the platform, the password may be encrypted using the standard Unix crypt function or the more secure MD5 hashing algorithm. If a shadow password file is in use, this field returns an asterisk. Additionally, disabled accounts often prefix passwords with ! to disable them.
uid	2	The user ID of this user.
gid	3	The primary group of this user. Other groups can be found using the group functions detailed later.
quota	4	The disk space quota allotted to this user. Frequently unsupported. On some systems this may be a change or age field instead.
comment	5	A comment, usually the user's full name. On some systems this may be a class field instead. The comment field is often called the gcos field, but this is not technically accurate; this or the next item may therefore actually contain the comment.
gcos	6	Also known as GECOS, originally standing for "General Electric Computer Operating System," although the original meaning is now of historical interest. An extended comment containing a comma-separated series of values—for example, the user's name, location, and work/home phone numbers. Frequently unimplemented, but see note on comment.
dir	7	The home directory of the user, for example, /home/name.
shell	8	The preferred login shell of the user, for example, /usr/bin/bash.
expire	9	The expiry date of the user account. Frequently unsupported, often undefined.

In scalar context, getpwent returns just the name of the user, that is, the first field. To illustrate, we can generate a list of user names with a program like the following:

```perl
#!/usr/bin/perl
# listusers.pl
use warnings;
use strict;

my @users;
while (my $name = getpwent) {
    push @users, $name;
}
print "Users: @users \n";
```

Supporting getpwent are the setpwent and endpwent functions. The setpwent function resets the pointer for the next record returned by getpwent to the start of the password file. It is analogous to the rewinddir function in the same way that getpwent is analogous to both opendir and readdir combined. Since there only is one password file, it takes no arguments:

```perl
setpwent;
```

The endpwent function is analogous to closedir: it closes the internal file pointer created whenever we use getpwent (or getpwnam/getpwuid, detailed in the upcoming text). We cannot get access to this internal filehandle, but it may be freed in order to recapture consumed resources. Additionally, if a network query was made, then this will close the connection:

```
endpwent;
```

The getpwnam and getpwuid functions look up user names and user IDs from each other. getpwnam takes a user name as an argument and returns the user ID in scalar context or the full list of ten in a list context:

```
$uid = getpwnam($username);
@fields = getpwname($username);
```

Similarly, getpwuid takes a numeric user ID and returns either the name or a list of fields, depending on context:

```
$username = getpwuid($uid);
@fields = getpwuid($uid);
```

Both functions also have the same effect as setpwent in that they reset the position of the pointer used by getpwent, so they cannot be combined with it in loops.

Since ten fields is rather a lot to manage, Perl supplies the User::pwent module to provide an object-oriented interface to the pw functions. It is one of several modules that all behave similarly; others are User::grent (for group information), Net::hostent, Net::servent, Net::netent, Net::protoent (for network information), and Stat (for the stat and lstat functions).

User::pwent works by overloading the built-in getpwent, getpwnam, and getpwuid functions with object-oriented methods returning a pw object, complete with methods to extract the relevant fields. It also has the advantage of knowing what methods actually apply, which we can determine using the pw_has class method. Here is an object-oriented user information listing program, which uses getpwent to illustrate how the User::pwent module is used:

```perl
#!/usr/bin/perl
# listobjpw.pl
use warnings;
use strict;

use User::pwent qw(:DEFAULT pw_has);

print "Supported fields: ", scalar(pw_has), "\n";

while (my $user = getpwent) {
    print 'Name     : ', $user->name, "\n";
    print 'Password: ', $user->passwd, "\n";
    print 'User ID : ', $user->uid, "\n";
    print 'Group ID: ', $user->gid, "\n";

    # one of quota, change or age
    print 'Quota    : ', $user->quota, "\n" if pw_has('quota');
    print 'Change   : ', $user->change, "\n" if pw_has('change');
    print 'Age      : ', $user->age, "\n" if pw_has('age');
    # one of comment or class (also possibly gcos is comment)
    print 'Comment : ', $user->comment, "\n" if pw_has('comment');
    print 'Class    : ', $user->class, "\n" if pw_has('class');

    print 'Home Dir: ', $user->dir, "\n";
    print 'Shell    : ', $user->shell, "\n";
```

```perl
    # maybe gecos, maybe not
    print 'GECOS   : ',$user->gecos,"\n" if pw_has('gecos');

    # maybe expires, maybe not
    print 'Expire  : ', $user->expire, "\n" if pw_has('expire');

    # separate records
    print "\n";
}
```

If called with no arguments, the pw_has class method returns a list of supported fields in list context, plus a space-separated string suitable for printing in scalar context. Because we generally want to use it without prefixing User::pwent:: we specify it in the import list. However, to retain the default imports that override getpwent and the like, we also need to specify the special :DEFAULT tag.

We can also import scalar variables for each field and avoid the method calls by adding the :FIELDS tag (which also implies :DEFAULT) to the import list. This generates a set of scalar variables with the same names as their method equivalents but prefixed with pw_. The equivalent of the preceding object-oriented script written using field variables is

```perl
#!/usr/bin/perl
# listfldpw.pl
use warnings;
use strict;

use User::pwent qw(:FIELDS pw_has);

print "Supported fields: ", scalar(pw_has), "\n";

while (my $user = getpwent) {
    print 'Name    : ', $pw_name, "\n";
    print 'Password: ', $pw_passwd, "\n";
    print 'User ID : ', $pw_uid, "\n";
    print 'Group ID: ', $pw_gid, "\n";

    # one of quota, change or age
    print 'Quota   : ', $pw_quota, "\n" if pw_has('quota');
    print 'Change  : ', $pw_change, "\n" if pw_has('change');
    print 'Age     : ', $pw_age, "\n" if pw_has('age');

    # one of comment or class (also possibly gcos is comment)
    print 'Comment : ', $pw_comment, "\n" if pw_has('comment');
    print 'Class   : ', $pw_class, "\n" if pw_has('class');

    print 'Home Dir: ', $pw_dir, "\n";
    print 'Shell   : ', $pw_shell, "\n";

    # maybe gcos, maybe not
    print 'GCOS    : ', $pw_gecos, "\n" if pw_has('gecos');
    # maybe expires, maybe not
    print 'Expire  : ', $pw_expire, "\n" if pw_has('expire');

    # separate records
    print "\n";
}
```

We may selectively import variables if we want to use a subset, but since this overrides the default import, we must also explicitly import the functions we want to override:

```
use User::grent qw($pw_name $pw_uid $pw_gid getpwnam);
```

To call the original getpwent, getpwnam, and getpwuid functions, we can use the CORE:: prefix. Alternatively, we could suppress the overrides by passing an empty import list or a list containing neither :DEFAULT or :FIELDS. As an example, here is another version of the preceding script that invents a new object method, has, for the Net::pwent package, then uses that and class method calls only, avoiding all imports:

```
#!/usr/bin/perl
# listcorpw.pl
use warnings;
use strict;

use User::pwent();

sub User::pwent::has {
    my $self = shift;
    return User::pwent::pw_has(@_);
}

print "Supported fields: ", scalar(User::pwent::has), "\n";

while (my $user = User::pwent::getpwent) {
    print 'Name     : ', $user->name, "\n";
    print 'Password: ', $user->passwd, "\n";
    print 'User ID : ', $user->uid, "\n";
    print 'Group ID: ', $user->gid, "\n";

    # one of quota, change or age
    print 'Quota    : ', $user->quota, "\n" if $user->has('quota');
    print 'Change   : ', $user->change, "\n" if $user->has('change');
    print 'Age      : ', $user->age, "\n" if $user->has('age');

    # one of comment or class (also possibly gcos is comment)
    print 'Comment : ', $user->comment, "\n" if $user->has('comment');
    print 'Class    : ', $user->class, "\n" if $user->has('class');

    print 'Home Dir: ', $user->dir, "\n";
    print 'Shell    : ', $user->shell, "\n";

    # maybe gcos, maybe not
    print 'GECOS    : ', $user->gecos, "\n" if $user->has('gecos');

    # maybe expires, maybe not
    print 'Expire  : ', $user->expire, "\n" if $user->has('expire');
    # separate records
    print "\n";
}
```

As a convenience, the Net::pwent module also provides the getpw subroutine, which takes either a user name or a user ID, returning a user object either way:

```
$user = getpw($user_name_or_id);
```

If the passed argument looks numeric, then getpwuid is called underneath to do the work; otherwise, getpwnam is called.

Group Information

Unix groups are a second tier of privileges between the user's own privileges and that of all users on the system. All users belong to one primary group, and files they create are assigned to this group. This information is locally recorded in the /etc/passwd file and can be found locally or remotely with the getpwent, getpwnam, and getpwuid functions as described previously. In addition, users may belong to any number of secondary groups. This information, along with the group IDs (or gids) and group names, is locally stored in the /etc/group file and can be extracted locally or remotely with the getgrent, getgrnam, and getgrgid functions.

The getgrent function reads one entry from the group's file each time it is called, starting with the first and returning the next entry in turn on each subsequent call. It returns four fields, the group name, a password (which is usually not defined), the group ID, and the users who belong to that group:

```perl
#!/usr/bin/perl
# listgr.pl
use warnings;
use strict;

while (my ($name, $passwd, $gid, $members) = getgrent) {
    print "$gid: $name [$passwd] $members \n";
}
```

Alternatively, calling getgrent in a scalar context returns just the group name:

```perl
#!/usr/bin/perl
# listgroups.pl
use warnings;
use strict;

my @groups;
while (my $name = getgrent) {
    push @groups, $name;
}
print "Groups: @groups \n";
```

As with getpwent, using getgrent causes Perl (or more accurately, the underlying C library) to open a filehandle (or open a connection to an NIS or NIS+ server) internally. Mirroring the supporting functions of getpwent, setgrent resets the pointer of the group filehandle to the start, and endgrent closes the file (and/or network connection) and frees the associated resources.

Perl provides the User::grent module as an object-oriented interface to the getgrent, getgrnam, and getgrid functions. It works very similarly to User::pwent, but it provides fewer methods as it has fewer fields to manage. It also does not have to contend with the variations of field meanings that User::pwent does, and it is consequently simpler to use. Here is an object-oriented group lister using User::getgrent:

```perl
#!/usr/bin/perl
# listbigr
use warnings;
use strict;

use User::grent;

while (my $group = getgrent) {
    print 'Name    : ', $group->name, "\n";
    print 'Password: ', $group->passwd, "\n";
    print 'Group ID: ', $group->gid, "\n";
    print 'Members : ', join(', ', @{$group->members}), "\n\n";
}
```

Like User::pwent (and indeed all similar modules like Net::hostent, etc.), we can import the
:FIELDS tag to variables that automatically update whenever any of getgrent, getgrnam, or getgrgid
are called. Here is the previous example reworked to use variables:

```perl
#!/usr/bin/perl
# listfldgr.pl
use warnings;
use strict;

use User::grent qw(:FIELDS);

while (my $group = getgrent) {
    print 'Name    : ', $gr_name, "\n";
    print 'Password: ', $gr_passwd, "\n";
    print 'Group ID: ', $gr_gid, "\n";
    print 'Members : ', join(', ', @{$group->members}), "\n\n";
}
```

We can also selectively import variables if we only want to use some of them:

```perl
use User::grent qw($gr_name $gr_gid);
```

In this case, the overriding of getgrent and the like will not take place, so we would need to
call User::grent::getgrent rather than just getgrent, or pass getgrent as a term in the import list.
To avoid importing anything at all, just pass an empty import list.

The Unary File Test Operators

Perl provides a full complement of file test operators. They test file names for various properties,
for example, determining whether they are a file, directory, link, or other kind of file, determining
who owns them and what their access privileges are. All of these file tests consist of a single minus
followed by a letter, which determines the nature of the test and either a filehandle or a string containing the file name. Here are a few examples:

```perl
-r $filename    # return true if file is readable by us
-w $filename    # return true if file is writable by us
-d DIRECTORY    # return true if DIRECTORY is opened to a directory
-t STDIN        # return true if STDIN is interactive
```

Collectively these functions are known as the -X or file test operators.

The slightly odd-looking syntax comes from the Unix file test utility test and the built-in
equivalents in most Unix shells. Despite their strange appearance, the file test operators are really
functions that behave just like any other built-in unary (single argument) Perl operator, including
support for parentheses:

```perl
print "It's a file!" if -f($filename);
```

If no file name or handle is supplied, then the value of $_ is used as a default, which makes for
some very terse if somewhat algebraic expressions:

```perl
foreach (@files) {
    print "$_ is readable textfile\n" if -r && -T;   # -T for 'text' file
}
```

Only single letters following a minus sign are interpreted as file tests, so there is never any confusion between file test operators and negated expressions:

```perl
-o($name)    # test if $name is owned by us
-oct($name)  # return negated value of $name interpreted as octal
```

The full list of file tests follows, loosely categorized into functional groups. Note that not all of these tests may work, depending on the underlying platform. For instance, operating systems that do not understand ownership in the Unix model will not make a distinction between -r and -R, since this requires the concept of real and effective user IDs. (The Win32 API does support "impersonation," but this is not the same thing and is supported by Windows-specific modules instead.) They will also not return anything useful for -o. Similarly, the -b and -c tests are specific to Unix device files and have no relevance on other platforms.

This tests for the existence of a file:

-e	Return true if file exists. Equivalent to the return value of the stat function.

These test for read, write, and execute for effective and real users. On non-Unix platforms, which don't have the concepts of real and effective users, the uppercase and lowercase versions are equivalent:

-r	Return true if file is readable by effective user ID.
-R	Return true if file is readable by real user ID.
-w	Return true if file is writable by effective user ID.
-W	Return true if file is writable by real user ID.
-x	Return true if file is executable by effective user ID.
-X	Return true if file is executable by real user ID.

The following test for ownership and permissions (-o returns 1, others ' ' on non-Unix platforms). Note that these are Unix-based commands. On Windows, files are owned by "groups" as opposed to "users":

-o	Return true if file is owned by our real user ID.
-u	Return true if file is setuid (chmod u+S, executables only).
-g	Return true if file is setgid (chmod g+S. executables only). This does not exist on Windows.
-k	Return true if file is sticky (chmod +T, executables only). This does not exist on Windows.

These tests for size work on Windows as on Unix:

-z	Return true if file has zero length (that is, it is empty).
-s	Return true if file has non-zero length (opposite of -z).

The following are file type tests. While -f, -d, and -t are generic, the others are platform dependent:

-f	Return true if file is a plain file (that is, not a directory, link, pipe, etc.).
-d	Return true if file is a directory.
-l	Return true if file is a symbolic link.
-p	Return true if file is a named pipe or filehandle is a pipe filehandle.

Continued

-S	Return true if file is a Unix domain socket or filehandle is a socket filehandle.
-b	Return true if file is a block device.
-c	Return true if file is a character device.
-t	Return true if file is interactive (opened to a terminal).

The -T and -B tests determine whether a file is text or binary (for details see "Testing Binary and Text Files" coming up shortly):

-T	Return true if file is a text file.
-B	Return true if file is not a text file.

The following tests return timestamps, and also work on Windows:

-M	Return the age of the file as a fractional number of days, counting from the time at which the application started (which avoids a system call to find the current time). To test which of two files is more recent, we can write `$file = (-M $file1 > -M $file2)? $file1: $file2;`
-A	Return last access time.
-C	On Unix, return last inode change time. (Not creation time, as is commonly misconceived. This does return the creation time, but only so long as the inode has not changed since the file was created.) On other platforms, it returns the creation time.

Link Transparency and Testing for Links

This section is only relevant if our chosen platform supports the concept of symbolic links, which is to say all Unix variants but not most other platforms. In particular, Windows "shortcuts" are an artifact of the desktop and unfortunately have nothing to do with the actual filing system.

The stat function, which is the basis of all the file test operators (except -l) automatically follows symbolic links and returns information based on the real file, directory, pipe, etc., that it finds at the end of the link. Consequently, file tests like -f and -d return true if the file at the end of the link is a plain file or directory. Therefore we do not have to worry about links when we just want to know if a file is readable:

```
my @lines;
if (-e $filename) {
    if (-r $filename) {
        open FILE, $filename;   # open file for reading
        @lines = <FILE>;
    } else {
        die "Cannot open $filename for reading \n";
    }
} else {
    die "Cannot open $filename - file does not exist \n";
}
```

If we want to find out if a file is actually a link, we have to use the -l test. This gathers information about the link itself and not the file it points to, returning true if the file is in fact a link. A practical upshot of this is that we can test for broken links by testing -l and -e:

```
if (-l $file and !-e $file) {
    print "'$file' is a broken link! \n";
}
```

This is also useful for testing that a file is not a link when we do not expect it to be. A utility designed to be run under "root" should check that files it writes to have not been replaced with links to /etc/passwd, for example.

Testing Binary and Text Files

The -T and -B operators test files to see if they are text or binary. They do this by examining the start of the file and counting the number of nontext characters present. If this number exceeds one third, the file is determined to be binary; otherwise, it is determined to be text. If a null (ASCII 0) character is seen anywhere in the examined data, then the file is assumed to be binary.

Since -T and -B only make sense in the context of a plain file, they are commonly combined with -f:

```
if (-f $file && -T $file) {
    ...
}
```

-T and -B differ from the other file test operators in that they perform a read of the file in question. When used on a filehandle, both tests read from the current position of the file pointer. An empty file or a filehandle positioned at the end of the file will return true for both -T and -B, since in these cases there is no data to determine which is the correct interpretation.

Reusing the Results of a Prior Test

The underlying mechanism behind the file test operators is a call to either stat or, in the case of -l, lstat. In order to test the file, each operator will make a call to stat to interrogate the file for information. If we want to make several tests, this is inefficient, because a disc access needs to be made in each case.

However, if we have already called stat or lstat for the file we want to test, then we can avoid these extra calls by using the special filehandle _, which will substitute the results of the last call to stat (or lstat) in place of accessing the file. Here is a short example that tests a file name in six different ways based on one call to lstat:

```
#!/usr/bin/perl
# statonce.pl
use warnings;
use strict;

print "Enter filename to test: ";
my $filename = <>;
chomp $filename;

if (lstat $filename) {
    print "$filename is a file \n" if -f _;
    print "$filename is a directory \n" if -d _;
    print "$filename is a link \n" if -l _;

    print "$filename is readable \n" if -r _;
    print "$filename is writable \n" if -w _;
    print "$filename is executable \n" if -x _;
} else {
    print "$filename does not exist \n";
}
```

Note that in this example we have used lstat, so the link test -l _ will work correctly. -l requires an lstat and not a stat, and it will generate an error if we try to use it with the results of a previous stat:

```
The stat preceding -l _ wasn't an lstat...
```

Caching of the results of stat and lstat works for prior file tests too, so we could also write something like this:

```
if (-e $filename) {
    print "$filename exists \n";
    print "$filename is a file \n" if -f _;
}
```

Or:

```
if (-f $filename && -T _) {
    print "$filename exists and is a text file \n";
}
```

The only drawback to this is that only -l calls lstat, so we cannot test for a link this way unless the first test is -l.

Access Control Lists, the Superuser, and the filestat Pragma

The file tests -r, -w, and -x and their uppercase counterparts determine their return value from the results of the stat function. Unfortunately, this does not always produce an accurate result. Some of the reasons that these file tests may produce incorrect or misleading results include

- An ACL is in operation.
- The file system is read-only.
- We have superuser privileges.

All these cases tend to produce "false positive" results, implying that the file is accessible when in fact it is not. For example, the file may be writable, but the file system is not.

In the case of the superuser, -r, -R, -w, and -W will always return true, even if the file is set as unreadable and unwritable, because the superuser can just disregard the actual file permissions. Similarly, -x and -X will return true if any of the execute permissions (user, group, other) are set. To check if the file is really writable, we must use stat and check the file permissions directly:

```
$mode = ((stat $filename)[2]);
$writable = $mode & 0200;   # test for owner write permission
```

▓Tip Again, this is a Unix-specific example. Other platforms do not support permissions or support them in a different way.

For the other cases, we can try to use the filetest pragma, which alters the operation of the file tests for access by overriding them with more rigorous tests that interrogate the operating system instead. Currently there is only one mode of operation, access, which causes the file test operators to use the underlying access system call, if available:

```
use filetest 'access';
```

This modifies the behavior of the file test operators to use the operating system's access call to check the true permission of a file, as modified by access control lists, or file systems that are mounted read-only. It also provides an access subroutine, which allows us to make our own direct tests of file names (note that it does not work on filehandles). It takes a file name and a numeric flag containing the permissions we want to check for. These are defined as constants in the POSIX module and are listed in Table 13-2.

Table 13-2. *POSIX File Permission Constants*

Constant	Description
R_OK	Test file has read permission.
W_OK	Test file has write permission.
X_OK	Test file has execute permission.
F_OK	Test that file exists. Implied by R_OK, W_OK, or X_OK.

Note that F_OK is implied by the other three, so it need never be specified directly (to test for existence, we can as easily use the -e test, or -f if we require a plain file).

While access provides no extra functionality over the standard file tests, it does allow us to make more than one test simultaneously. As an example, to test that a file is both readable and writable, we would use

```
use filetest 'access';use POSIX;
...
$can_readwrite = access($filename, R_OK|W_OK);
```

The return value from access is undef on failure and "0 but true" (a string that evaluates to zero in a numeric context and true in any other) on success, for instance, an if or while condition. On failure, $! is set to indicate the reason.

Automating Multiple File Tests

We often want to perform a series of different file tests across a range of different files. Installation scripts, for example, often do this to verify that all the installed files are in the correct place and with the correct permissions.

While it is possible to manually work through a list of files, we can make life a little simpler by using the File::CheckTree module instead. This module provides a single subroutine, validate, that takes a series of file names and -X style file tests and applies each of them in turn, generating warnings as it does so.

Unusually for a library subroutine, validate accepts its input in lines, in order to allow the list of files and tests to be written in the style of a manifest list. In the following example, validate is being used to check for the existence of three directories and an executable file installed by a fictional application:

```
$warnings = validate(q{
    /home/install/myapp/scripts -d
    /home/install/myapp/docs -d
    /home/install/myapp/bin -d
    /home/install/myapp/bin/myapp -fx
});
```

validate returns the number of warnings generated during the test, so we can use it as part of a larger installation script. If we want to disable or redirect the warnings, we can do so by defining a signal handler:

```
$SIG{__WARN__} = { };   # do nothing
$SIG{__WARN__} = {print LOGFILE @_};   # redirect to install log
```

The same file may be listed any number of times, with different tests applied each time. Alternatively, multiple tests may be bunched together into one file test, so that instead of specifying two tests one after the other, they can be done together. Hence, instead of writing two lines:

```
/home/install/myapp/bin/myapp -f
/home/install/myapp/bin/myapp -x
```

we can write both tests as one line:

```
/home/install/myapp/bin/myapp -fx
```

The second test is dependent on the first, so only one warning can be generated from a bunched test. If we want to test for both conditions independently (we want to know if it is not a plain file, and we also want to know if it is not executable), we need to put the tests on separate lines.

Tests may also be negated by prefixing them with a !, in which case all the individual tests must fail for the line to succeed. For example, to test whether a file is neither setuid or setgid:

```
validate(q{
    /home/install/myapp/scripts/myscript.pl    !-ug
})
```

Normal and negated tests cannot be bunched, so if we want to test that a file name corresponds to a plain file that is not executable, we must use separate tests:

```
validate(q{
    /home/install/myapp/scripts/myscript.pl    -f
    /home/install/myapp/scripts/myscript.pl    !-xug
})
```

Rather than a file test operator, we can also supply the command cd. This causes the directory named at the start of the line to be made the current working directory. Any relative paths given after this are taken relative to that directory until the next cd, which may also be relative:

```
validate(q{
    /home/install/myapp      cd || die
        scripts         -rd
        cgi             cd
        guestbook.cgi   -xg
        guestbook.cgi   !-u
        ..              cd
        about_us.html   -rf
        text.bin        -f || warn "Not a plain file"
});
```

■Tip validate is insensitive to extra whitespace, so we can use additional spacing to clarify what file is being tested where. In the preceding example, we have indented the files to make it clear which directory they are being tested in.

We can supply our own warnings and make tests fatal by suffixing the file test with || and either warn or die. These work in exactly the same way as their Perl function counterparts. If our own error messages are specified, we can use the variable $file, supplied by the module, to insert the name of the file whose test failed:

```
validate(q{
    /etc         -d  || warn "What, no $file directory? \n"
    /var/spool   -d  || die
})
```

This trick relies on the error messages being interpolated at run time, so using single quotes or the q quoting operator is essential in this case.

One of the advantages of File::CheckTree is that the file list can be built dynamically, possibly generated from an existing file tree created by File::Find (detailed in "Finding Files" later in this chapter). For example, using File::Find, we can determine the type and permissions of each file and directory in a tree, then generate a test list suitable for File::CheckTree to validate new installations of that tree. See the section "Finding Files" and the other modules in this section for pointers.

Interrogating Files with stat and lstat

If we want to know more than one attribute of a file, we can skip multiple file test operators and instead make use of the stat or lstat functions directly. Both functions return details of the file name or filehandle supplied as their argument. lstat is identical to stat except in the case of a symbolic link, where stat will return details of the file pointed to by the link and lstat will return details of the link itself. In either case, a 13-element list is returned:

```
# stat filehandle into a list
@stat_info = stat FILEHANDLE;

# lstat file name into separate scalars
($dev, $ino, $mode, $nlink, $uid, $gid, $rdev, $size,
    $time, $mtime, $ctime, $blksize, $blocks) = lstat $filename;
```

The stat function will also work on a filehandle, though the information returned is greatly influenced by the type of filehandle under interrogation:

```
my @stdin_info=stat STDIN; # stat standard input
opendir CWD, ".";
my @cwd_info=stat CWD;      # stat a dir handle
```

Note The lstat function will not work on a filehandle and will generate a warning if we try. lstat only makes sense for actual files since it is concerned with symbolic links, a filing system concept that does not translate to filehandles.

The thirteen values are always returned, but they may not be defined or have meaning in every case, either because they do not apply to the file or filehandle being tested or because they have no meaning on the underlying platform. Thirteen values is a lot, so the File::stat module provides an object-oriented interface that lets us refer to these values by name instead. The full list of values, including the meanings and index number, is provided in Table 13-3. The name in the first column is the conventional variable name used previously and also the name of the method provided by the File::stat module.

Table 13-3. *stat Fields*

Method	Number	Description
dev	0	The device number of the file system on which the file resides.
ino	1	The inode of the file.
mode	2	The file mode, combining the file type and the file permissions.
nlink	3	The number of hard (not symbolic) references to the inode underneath the file name.
uid	4	The user ID of user that owns the file.
gid	5	The group ID of group that owns the file.

Continued

Table 13-3. *Continued*

Method	Number	Description
rdev	6	The device identifier (block and character special files only).
size	7	The size of the file, in bytes.
atime	8	The last access time, in seconds.
mtime	9	The last modification time, in seconds.
ctime	10	The last inode change time, in seconds.
blksize	11	The preferred block size of the file system.
blocks	12	The number of blocks allocated to the file. The product of $stat_info[11]*$stat_info[12] is the size of the file as allocated in the file system. However, the actual size of the file in terms of its contents will most likely be less than this as it will only partially fill the last block—use $stat_info[7] (size) to find that.

Several of the values returned by stat relate to the "inode" of the file. Under Unix, the inode of a file is a numeric ID, which it is allocated by the file system, and which is its "true" identity, with the file name being just an alias. On platforms that support it, more than one file name may point to the same file, and the number of hard links is returned in the nlink value and may be greater than one, but not less (since that would mean the inode had no file names). The ctime value indicates the last time the node of the file changed. It may often mean the creation time. Conversely, the access and modification times refer to actual file access.

On other platforms, some of these values are either undefined or meaningless. Under Windows, the device number is related to the drive letter, there is no inode, and the value of nlink is always 1. The uid and gid values are always zero, and no value is returned for either blocksize or blocks, either. There is a mode, though only the file type is useful; the permissions are always 777. While Windows NT/2000/XP supports a fairly complex permissions system, it is not accessible this way; the Win32::FileSecurity and Win32::FilePermissions modules must be used instead. Accessing the values returned by stat can be a little inconvenient, not to mention inelegant. For example, this is how we find the size of a file:

```perl
$size = (stat $filename)[7];
```

Or, printing it out:

```perl
print ((stat $filename)[7]);   # need to use extra parentheses with print
```

Unless we happen to know that the eighth element is the size or we are taking care to write particularly legible code, this leads to unfriendly code. Fortunately, we can use the File::stat module instead.

Using stat Objects

The File::stat module simplifies the use of stat and lstat by overriding them with subroutines that return stat objects instead of a list. These objects can then be queried using one of File::stat's methods, which have the same names as the values that they return.

As an example, this short program uses the size, blksize, and blocks methods to return the size of the file supplied on the command line:

```perl
#!/usr/bin/perl
# filesize.pl
use warnings;
use strict;

use File::stat;
```

```
print "Enter filename: ";
my $filename = <>;
chomp $filename;
if (my $stat = stat $filename) {
    print "'$filename' is ", $stat->size,
          " bytes and occupies ", $stat->blksize * $stat->blocks,
          " bytes of disc space \n";
} else {
    print "Cannot stat $filename: $| \n";
}
```

As an alternative to using object methods, we can import 13 scalar variables containing the results of the last stat or lstat into our program by adding an import list of :FIELDS. Each variable takes the same name as the corresponding method prefixed with the string st_. For example:

```
#!/usr/bin/perl
# filesizefld.pl
use warnings;
use strict;

use File::stat qw(:FIELDS);

print "Enter filename: ";
my $filename = <>;
chomp($filename);
if (stat $filename) {
    print "'$filename' is ", $st_size,
          " bytes and occupies ", $st_blksize * $st_blocks,
          " bytes of disc space \n";
} else {
    print "Cannot stat $filename: $| \n";
}
```

The original versions of stat and lstat can be used by prefixing them with the CORE:: package name:

```
use File::stat;

...

my @new_stat = stat $filename;    # use new 'stat'
my @old_stat = CORE::stat $filename;    # use original 'stat'
```

Alternatively, we can prevent the override from happening by supplying an empty import list:

```
use File::stat qw();    # or '', etc.
```

We can now use the File::stat stat and lstat methods by qualifying them with the full package name:

```
my $stat = File::stat::stat $filename;
print "File is ", $stat->size(), " bytes \n";
```

Changing File Attributes

There are three basic kinds of file attribute that we can read and attempt to modify: ownership, access permissions, and the access and modification timestamps. Unix and other platforms that support the concept of file permissions and ownership can make use of the chmod and chgrp functions to modify the permissions of a file from Perl. chmod modifies the file permissions of a file for the three categories: user, group, and other. The chown function modifies which user corresponds to the user permissions and which group corresponds to the group permissions. Every other user and group falls under the other category. Ownership and permissions are therefore inextricably linked and are combined into the mode value returned by stat.

File Ownership

File ownership is a highly platform-dependent concept. Perl grew up on Unix systems, and so it attempts to handle ownership in a Unix-like way. Under Unix and other platforms that borrowed their semantics from Unix, files have an owner, represented by the file's user ID, and a group owner, represented by the file's group ID. Each relates to a different set of file permissions, so the user may have the ability to read and write a file, whereas other users in the same group may only get to read it. Others may not have even that, depending on the setting of the file permissions.

File ownership is handled by the chown function, which maps to both the chown and chgrp system calls. It takes at least three parameters, a user ID, a group ID, and one or more files to change:

```perl
my @successes = chown $uid, $gid, @files;
```

The number of files successfully changed is returned. If only one file is given to chown, this allows a simple Boolean test to be used to determine success:

```perl
unless (chown $uid, $gid, $filename) {
    die "chown failed: $! \n";
}
```

To change only the user or group, supply -1 as the value for the other parameter. For instance, a chgrp function can be simulated with

```perl
sub chgrp {
    return chown(shift, -1, @_);
}
```

Note that on most systems (that is, most systems that comprehend file ownership in the first place), usually only the superuser can change the user who owns the file, though the group can be changed to another group that the same user belongs to. It is possible to determine if a change of ownership is permitted by calling the sysconf function:

```perl
my $chown_restricted = sysconf(_PC_CHOWN_RESTRICTED);
```

If this returns a true value, then a chown will not be permitted.

chown needs a user or group ID to function; it will not accept a user or group name. To deduce a user ID from the name, at least on a Unix-like system, we can use the getpwnam function. Likewise, to deduce a group ID from the name, we can use the getgrnam function. We can use getpwent and getgrent instead to retrieve one user or group respectively, as we saw in the section "Getting User and Group Information" earlier in the chapter. As a quick example, the following script builds tables of user and group IDs, which can be subsequently used in chown:

```perl
#!/usr/bin/perl
use warnings;
use strict;

# get user names and primary groups
my (%users, %usergroup);
while (my ($name, $passwd, $uid, $gid) = getpwent) {
    $users{$name} = $uid;
    $usergroup{$name} = $gid;
}
```

```
# get group names and gids
my (%groups, @groups);
while (my ($name, $passwd, $gid) = getgrent) {
    $groups{$name} = $gid;
    $groups[$gid] = $name;
}

# print out basic user and group information
foreach my $user (sort {$users{$a} <=> $users{$b}} keys %users) {
    print "$users{$user}: $user, group ", $usergroup{$user},
        " (", $groups[$usergroup{$user}], ")\n";
}
```

File Permissions

Perl provides two functions that are specifically related to file permissions, chmod and umask. As noted earlier, these will work for any Unix-like platform, including MacOS X, but not Windows, where the Win32::FileSecurity and Win32::FilePermissions modules must be used. The chmod function allows us to set the permissions of a file. Permissions are grouped into three categories: user, which applies to the file's owner, group, which applies to the file's group owner, and other, which applies to anyone who is not the file's owner or a member of the file's group owner. Within each category each file may be given read, write, and execute permission.

chmod represents each of the nine values (3 categories × 3 permissions) by a different numeric flag, which are traditionally put together to form a three-digit octal number, each digit corresponding to the respective category. The flag values within each digit are 4 for read permission, 2 for write permission, and 1 for execute permission, as demonstrated by the following examples (prefixed by a leading 0 to remind us that these are octal values):

0200	Owner write permission
0040	Group read permission
0001	Other execute permission

The total of the read, write, and execute permissions for a category is 7, which is why octal is so convenient to represent the combined permissions flag. Read, write, and execute permission for the owner only would be represented as 0700. Similarly, read, write, and execute permission for the owner, read and execute permission for the group, and execute-only permission for everyone else would be 0751, which is 0400 + 0200 + 0100 + 0040 + 0010 + 0001.

Having explained the permissions flag, the chmod function itself is comparatively simple, taking a permissions flag, as calculated previously, as its first argument and applying it to one or more files given as the second and subsequent arguments. For example:

```
chmod 0751, @files;
```

As with chown, the number of successfully chmodded files is returned, or zero if no files were changed successfully. If only one file is supplied, the return value of chmod can be tested as a Boolean result in an if or unless statement:

```
unless (chmod 0751, $file) {
    die "Unable to chmod: $! \n";
}
```

The umask function allows us to change the default permissions mask used whenever Perl creates a new file. The bits in the umask have the opposite meaning to the permissions passed to chmod. They unset the corresponding bits in the permissions from the permissions used by open or sysopen when the file is created and the resulting permissions set. Thus the permission bits of the umask mask the permissions that open and sysopen try to set. Table 13-4 shows the permission bits that can be used with umask and their meanings.

Table 13-4. *umask File Permissions*

umask Number	File Permission
0	Read and write
1	Read and write
2	Read only
3	Read only
4	Write only
5	Write only
6	No read and no write
7	No read and no write

umask only defines the access permissions. Called without an argument, it returns the current value of the umask, which is inherited from the shell and is typically set to a value of 002 (mask other write permission) or 022 (mask group and other write permissions):

```
$umask = umask;
```

Alternatively, umask may be called with a single numeric parameter, traditionally expressed in octal or alternatively as a combination of mode flags as described previously. For example:

```
umask 022;
```

Overriding the umask explicitly is not usually a good idea, since the user might have it set to a more restrictive value. A better idea is to combine the permissions we want to restrict with the existing umask, using a bitwise OR. For example:

```
umask (022 | umask);
```

The open function always uses permissions of 0666 (read and write for all categories), whereas sysopen allows the permissions to be specified in the call. Since umask controls the permissions of new files by removing unwanted permissions, we do not need to (and generally should not) specify more restrictive permissions to sysopen.

File Access Times

The built-in utime function provides the ability to change the last access and last modification time of one or more files. It takes at least three arguments: the new access time, in seconds since 1970/1/1 00:00:00, the new modification time, also in seconds, and then the file or files whose times are to be changed. For example:

```
my $onedayago=time - 24*60*60;
utime $onedayago, time(), "myfile.txt", "my2ndfile.txt";
```

This will set the specified files to have a last access time of exactly a day ago and a last modification time of right now. From Perl 5.8, we can also specify undef to mean "right now," so to emulate the Unix touch command on all C or C++ files in the current directory, we could use

```
utime undef, undef, <*.c>, <*.cpp>
```

The Fcntl Module

The Fcntl module provides symbolic constants for all of the flags contained in both the permissions and the file type parts of the mode value. It also provides two functions for extracting each part, as an alternative to computing the values by hand:

```
use Fcntl qw(:mode);        # import file mode constants

my $type = IFMT($mode);     # extract file type
my $perm = IFMODE($mode);   # extract file permissions

printf "File permissions are: %o \n", $perm;
```

The file type part of the mode defines the type of the file and is the basis of the file test operators like -d, -f, and -l that test for the type of a file. The Fcntl module defines symbolic constants for these, and they are summarized in Table 13-5.

Table 13-5. *Fcntl Module File Test Symbols*

Name	Description	Operator
S_IFREG	Regular file	-f
S_IFDIR	Directory	-d
S_IFLNK	Link	-l
S_IFBLK	Block special file	-b
S_IFCHR	Character special file	-c
S_IFIFO	Pipe or named fifo	-p
S_IFSOCK	Socket	-S
S_IFWHT	Interactive terminal	-t

Note that Fcntl also defines a number of subroutines that test the mode for the desired property. These have very similar names, for example, S_IFDIR and S_ISFIFO, and it is easy to get the subroutines and flags confused. Since we have the file test operators, we do not usually need to use these subroutines, so we mention them only to eliminate possible confusion.

These flags can also be used with sysopen, IO::File's new method, and the stat function described previously, where they can be compared against the mode value. As an example of how these flags can be used, here is the equivalent of the -d file test operator written using stat and the Fcntl module:

```
my $mode = ((stat $filename)[2]);
my $is_directory = $mode & S_IFDIR;
```

Or, to test that a file is neither a socket or a pipe:

```
my $is_not_special = $mode & ^(S_IFBLK | S_IF_CHR);
```

The Fcntl module also defines functions that do this for us. Each function takes the same name as the flag but with S_IF replaced with S_IS. For instance, to test for a directory, we can instead use

```
my $is_directory = S_ISDIR($mode);
```

Of course, the -d file test operator is somewhat simpler in this case.

The permissions part of the mode defines the read, write, and execute privileges that the file grants to the file's owner, the file's group, and others. It is the basis of the file test operators like -r, -w, -u, and -g that test for the accessibility of a file. The Fcntl module also defines symbolic constants for these, summarized in Table 13-6.

Table 13-6. *Fcntl Module File Permission Symbols*

Name	Description	Number
S_IRUSR	User can read.	00400
S_IWUSR	User can write.	00200
S_IXUSR	User can execute.	00100
S_IRGRP	Group can read.	00040
S_IWGRP	Group can write.	00020
S_IXGRP	Group can execute.	00010
S_IROTH	Others can read.	00004
S_IWOTH	Others can write.	00002
S_IXOTH	Others can execute.	00001
S_IRWXU	User can read, write, execute.	00700
S_IRWXG	Group can read, write, execute.	00070
S_IRWXO	Others can read, write, execute.	00007
S_ISUID	Setuid.	04000
S_ISGID	Setgid.	02000
S_ISVTX	Sticky (S) bit.	01000
S_ISTXT	Swap (t) bit.	10000

For example, to test a file for user read and write permission, plus execute permission, we could use

```
$perms_ok = $mode & S_IRUSR | S_IWUSR | S_IRGRP;
```

To test that a file has exactly these permissions and no others, we would instead write

```
$exact_perms = $mode == S_IRUSR | S_IWUSR | S_IRGRP;
```

The file permission flags are useful not only for making sense of the mode value returned by stat, but also as inputs for the chmod function. Consult the manual page for the chmod system call (on Unix platforms) for details of the more esoteric bits such as sticky and swap.

Linking, Unlinking, Deleting, and Renaming Files

The presence of file names can be manipulated directly with the link and unlink built-in functions. These provide the ability to edit the entries for files in the file system, creating new ones or removing existing ones. They are not the same as creating and deleting files, however. On platforms that support the concept, link creates a new link (entry in the filing system) to an existing file, it does not create a copy (except on Windows, where it does exactly this). Likewise, unlink removes a file name from the filing system, but if the file has more than one link, and therefore more than one file name, the file will persist. This is an important point to grasp, because it often leads to confusion.

Linking Files

The link function creates a new link (sometimes called a *hard* link, to differentiate it from a *soft* or *symbolic* link) for the named file. It only works on platforms that support multiple hard links for the same file:

```
if (link $currentname, $newname) {
    print "Linked $currentname to $newname ok \n";
} else {
    warn "Failed to link: $! \n";
}
```

link will not create links for directories, though it will create links for all other types of files. For directories, we can create symbolic links only. Additionally, we cannot create hard links between different file systems and not between directories on some file systems (for example, AFS). On Unix, link works by giving two names in the file system the same underlying inode. On Windows and other file systems that do not support this concept, an attempt to link will create a copy of the original file.

On success, link returns true, and a new file name will exist for the file. The old one continues to exist and can either be used to read or alter the contents of the file. Both links are therefore exactly equivalent. Immediately after creation, the new link will carry the same permissions and ownership as the original, but this can subsequently be changed with the chmod and chown built-in functions to, for example, create a read-only and a read-write entry point to the same data.

Deleting and Unlinking Files

The opposite of linking is unlinking. Files can be unlinked with the built-in unlink function, which takes one or more file names as a parameter. If no file name is supplied, unlink uses $_:

```
unlink $currentname;   # single file

foreach (<*.*>) {
    unlink if /\.bak$/;   # unlink $_ if it ends '.bak'
}

unlink <*.bak>;   # the same, via a file glob
```

On platforms where unlinking does not apply (because multiple hard links are not permissible), unlink simply deletes the file. Otherwise, unlink is not necessarily the same as deleting a file, for two reasons. First, if the file has more than one link, then it will still be available by other names in the file system. Although we cannot (easily) find out the names of the other links, we can find out how many links a file has through stat. We can establish in advance if unlink will really delete the file or just remove one of its links by calling stat:

```
my $links = (stat $filename)[3];
```

Or more legibly with the File::stat module:

```
my $stat = new File::stat($filename);
my $links = $stat->nlink;
```

Second, on platforms that support it (generally Unix-like ones), if any process has an open filehandle for the file, then it will persist for as long as the filehandle persists. This means that even after an unlink has completely removed all links to a file, it will still exist and can be read, written, and have its contents copied to a new file. Indeed, the new_tmpfile method of IO::File does exactly this if it is possible and true anonymous temporary files are not available—"Temporary Files" covers this in detail later in this chapter. On other platforms (for example, Windows), Perl will generally reject the attempt to unlink the file so long as a process holds an open filehandle on it. Do not rely on the underlying platform allowing a file to be deleted while it is still open; close it first to be sure.

The unlink function will not unlink directories unless three criteria are met: we are on Unix, Perl was given the -U flag, and we have superuser privilege. Even so, it is an inadvisable thing to do, since it will also remove the directory contents, including any subdirectories and their contents from the filing system hierarchy, but it will not recycle the same space that they occupy on the disc. Instead they will appear in the lost+found directory the next time an fsck filing system check is performed, which is unlikely to be what we intended. The rmdir built-in command covered later in the chapter is the preferred approach, or see the rmtree function from File::Path for more advanced applications involving multiple directories.

Renaming Files

Given the preceding, renaming a file is just a case of linking it to a new name, then unlinking it from the old, at least under Unix. The following subroutine demonstrates a generic way of doing this:

```
sub rename {
    my ($current, $new) = @_;
    unlink $current if link($current, $new);
}
```

The built-in rename function is essentially equivalent to the preceding subroutine:

```
# using the built-in function:
rename($current, $new);
```

This is effective for simple cases, but it will fail in a number of situations, most notably if the new file name is on a different file system from the old (a floppy disk to a hard drive, for instance). rename uses the rename system call, if available. It may also fail on (non-Unix) platforms that do not allow an open file to be renamed.

For a properly portable solution that works across all platforms, consider using the move routine from the File::Copy module. For the simpler cases it will just use rename, but it will also handle special cases and platform limitations.

Symbolic Links

On platforms that support it, we can also create a soft or symbolic link with the built-in symlink function. This is syntactically identical to link but creates a pointer to the file rather than a direct hard link:

```
if (symlink $currentname, $newname) {
    die "Failed to link: $! \n";
}
```

The return value from symlink is 1 on success or 0 on failure. On platforms that do not support symbolic links (a shortcut is an invention of the Windows desktop, not the file system), symlink produces a fatal error. If we are writing code to be portable, then we can protect against this by using eval:

```
$linked = eval {symlink($currentname, $newname);};
if (not defined $linked) {
    warn "Symlink not supported \n";
} else {
    warn "Link failed: $! \n";
}
```

To test whether symlink is available without actually creating a symbolic link, supply an empty file name for both arguments:

```
my $symlinking = eval {symlink('',''); 1};
```

If the symlink fails, eval will return undef when it tries to execute the symlink. If it succeeds, the 1 will be returned. This is a generically useful trick for all kinds of situations, of course.

Symbolic links are the links that the -l and lstat functions check for; hard links are indistinguishable from ordinary file names because they *are* ordinary file names. Most operations performed on symbolic links (with the notable exceptions of -l and lstat of course) are transferred to the linked file, if it exists. In particular, symbolic links have the generic file permissions 777, meaning everyone is permitted to do everything. However, this only means that the permissions of the file that the link points towards take priority. An attempt to open the link for writing will be translated into an attempt to open the linked file and check its permissions rather than those of the symbolic link. Even chmod will affect the permissions of the real file, not the link.

Symbolic links may legally point to other symbolic links, in which case the end of the link is the file that the last symbolic link points to. If the file has subsequently been moved or deleted, the symbolic link is said to be "broken." We can check for broken links with

```
if (-l $linkname and !-e $linkname) {
    print "$linkname is a broken link! \n";
}
```

See "Interrogating Files with stat and lstat" earlier in the chapter for more on this (and in particular why the special file name _ cannot be used after -e in this particular case) and some variations on the same theme.

Copying and Moving Files

One way to copy a file to a new name is to open a filehandle for both the old and the new names and copy data between them, as this rather simplistic utility attempts to do:

```
#!/usr/bin/perl
# dumbcopy
use warnings;
use strict;

print "Filename: ";
my $infile = <>;
chomp $infile;
print "New name: ";
my $outfile = <>;
chomp $outfile;
open IN, $infile;
open OUT, "> $outfile";
print OUT <IN>;
close IN;
close OUT;
```

The problem with this approach is that it does not take into account the existing file permissions and ownerships. If we run this on a Unix platform and the file we are copying happens to be executable, the copy will lose the executable permissions. If we run this on a system that cares about the difference between binary and text files, the file can become corrupted unless we also add a call to binmode. Fortunately, the File::Copy module handles these issues for us.

The File::Copy module provides subroutines for moving and copying files without having to directly manipulate them via filehandles. It also correctly preserves the file permissions. To make use of it, we just need to use it:

```
use File::Copy;
```

File::Copy contains two primary subroutines, copy and move. copy takes the names of two files or filehandles as its arguments and copies the contents of the first to the second, creating it if necessary. If the first argument is a filehandle, it is read from; if the second is a filehandle, it is written to. For example:

```
copy "myfile", "myfile2";   # copy one file to another
copy "myfile", \*STDOUT;     # copy file to standard output
copy LOG, "logfile";         # copy input to filehandle
```

If neither argument is a filehandle, copy does a system copy in order to preserve file attributes and permissions. This copy is directly available as the syscopy subroutine and is portable across platforms, as we will see in a moment.

copy also takes a third, optional argument, which if specified determines the buffer size to use. For instance, to copy the file in chunks of 16K, we might use

```
copy "myfile", "myfile2", 16 * 1024;
```

Without a buffer size, copy will default to the size of the file, or 2MB, whichever is smaller. Setting a smaller buffer will cause the copy to take longer, but it will use less memory while doing it.

move takes the names of two files (not filehandles) as its arguments and attempts to move the file named by the first argument to have the name given as the second. For example:

```
move "myfile", "myfile2";   # move file to another name
```

If possible, move will rename the file using the link and unlink functions. If not, it will copy the file using copy and then delete the original. Note, however, that in this case we cannot set a buffer size as an optional third parameter.

If an error occurs with either copy or move, the file system may run out of space. Then the destination file may be incomplete. In the case of a move that tried to copy the file, this will lose information. In this case, attempting to copy the file and then unlinking the original is safer.

On platforms that care about binary and text files (for example, Windows), to make a copy explicitly binary, use binmode or make use of the open pragmatic module described earlier in the chapter.

Here is a rewritten version of the file copy utility we started with. Note that it is not only better, but also it is considerably smaller:

```perl
#!/usr/bin/perl
# smartcopy.pl
use warnings;
use strict;

use File::Copy;

print "Filename: ";
my $infile = <>;
chomp $infile;
print "New name: ";
my $outfile = <>;
chomp $outfile;

unless (copy $infile, $outfile) {
    print "Failed to copy '$infile' to '$outfile': $! \n";
}
```

As a special case, if the first argument to copy or move is a file name and the second is a directory, then the destination file is placed inside the directory with the same name as the source file.

Unix aficionados will be happy to know that the aliases cp and mv are available for copy and move and can be imported by specifying one or both of them in the import list:

```perl
use File::Copy qw(cp mv);
```

System Level Copies and Platform Portability

As well as the standard copy, which works with either file names or filehandles, File::Copy defines the syscopy subroutine, which provides direct access to the copy function of the underlying operating system. The copy subroutine calls syscopy if both arguments are file names and the second is not a directory (as seen in the previous section); otherwise, it opens whichever argument is not a filehandle and performs a read-write copy through the filehandles.

The syscopy calls the underlying copy system call supplied by the operating system and is thus portable across different platforms. Under Unix, it calls the copy subroutine, as there is no system copy call. Under Windows, it calls the Win32::CopyFile module. Under OS/2 and VMS, it calls syscopy and rmscopy, respectively. This makes the File::Copy module an effective way to copy files without worrying about platform dependencies.

Comparing Files

The File::Compare module is a standard member of the Perl standard library that provides portable file comparison features for our applications. It provides two main subroutines, compare and compare_text, both of which are available when using the module:

```
use File::Compare;
```

The compare subroutine simply compares two files or filehandles byte for byte, returning 0 if they are equal, 1 if they are not, and -1 if an error was encountered:

```
SWITCH: foreach (compare $file1, $file2) {
    /^0/ and print("Files are equal"), last;
    /^1/ and print("Files are not equal"), last;
    print "Error comparing files: $! \n";
}
```

compare also accepts a third optional argument, which if specified defines the size of the buffer used to read from the two files or filehandles. This works in an identical manner to the buffer size of File::Copy's copy subroutine, defaulting to the size of the file or 2MB, whichever is smaller, if no buffer size is specified. Note that compare automatically puts both files into a binary mode for comparison.

The compare_text function operates identically to compare but takes as its third argument an optional code reference to an anonymous comparison subroutine. Unlike compare, compare_text compares files in text mode (assuming that the operating system draws a distinction), so without the third parameter, compare_text simply compares the two files in text mode.

The comparison subroutine, if supplied, should return a Boolean result that returns 0 if the lines should be considered equal and 1 otherwise. The default that operates when no explicit comparison is provided is equivalent to

```
sub {$_[0] ne $_[1]}
```

We can supply our own comparison subroutines to produce different results. For example, this comparison checks files for case-insensitive equivalence:

```
my $result = compare_text ($file1, $file2, sub {lc($_[0]) ne lc($_[1])});
```

Similarly, this comparison uses a named subroutine that strips extra whitespace from the start and end of lines before comparing them:

```
sub stripcmp {
    ($a, $b) = @_;
    $a =~s/^\s*(.*?)\s*$/$1/;
    $b =~s/^\s*(.*?)\s*$/$1/;
    return $a ne $b;
}
my $result = compare_text ($file1, $file2, \&stripcmp);
```

For those who prefer more Unix-like nomenclature, cmp may be used as an alias for compare by importing it specifically:

```
use File::Compare qw(cmp);
```

Finding Files

The File::Find module provides a multipurpose file-finding subroutine that we can configure to operate in a number of different ways. It supplies one subroutine, find, which takes a first parameter of either a code or hash reference that configures the details of the search and one or more subsequent parameters defining the starting directory or directories to begin from. A second, finddepth, finds the same files as find but traverses them in order of depth. This can be handy in cases when we want to modify the file system as we go, as we will see later.

If the first parameter to either find or finddepth is a code reference, then it is treated as a wanted subroutine that tests for particular properties in the files found. Otherwise, it is a reference to a hash containing at least a wanted key and code reference value and optionally more of the key-value pairs displayed in Table 13-7.

Table 13-7. *File::Find Configuration Fields*

Key	Value	Description
wanted	<code ref>	A reference to a callback subroutine that returns true or false depending on the characteristics of the file. Note that passing in a code reference as the first parameter is equivalent to passing {wanted => $coderef} Since find does not return any result, a wanted subroutine is required for find to do anything useful. The name is something of a misnomer, as the subroutine does not return a value to indicate whether a given file is wanted.
bydepth	0|1	A Boolean flag that when set causes files to be returned in order of depth. The convenience subroutine finddepth is a shorthand for this flag.
follow	0|1	A Boolean flag that when set causes find to follow symbolic links. When in effect, find records all files scanned in order to prevent files being found more than once (directly and via a link, for example) and to prevent loops (a link linking to its parent directory). For large directory trees, this can be very time consuming. For a faster but less rigorous alternative, use follow_fast. This option is disabled by default.
follow_fast	0|1	A Boolean flag that when set causes find to follow symbolic links. Like follow, follow_fast causes find to follow symbolic links. Unlike follow, it does not check for duplicate files, and so is faster. It still checks for loops, however, by tracking all symbolic links. This option is disabled by default.
follow_skip	0|1|2	A three-state flag that determines how find treats symbolic links if either follow or follow_fast is enabled: A setting of 0 causes find to die if it encounters a duplicate file, link, or directory. The default of 1 causes any file that is not a directory or symbolic link to be ignored if it is encountered again. A directory encountered a second time causes find to die. A setting of 2 causes find to ignore both duplicate files or directories. This flag has no effect if neither follow nor follow_fast is enabled.
no_chdir	0|1	A Boolean flag that when set causes find not to change down into each directory as it scans it. This primarily makes a difference to the wanted subroutine, if any is defined.

Key	Value	Description
untaint	0|1	A Boolean flag that when set causes find to untaint directory names when running in taint (-T) mode. This uses a regular expression to untaint the directory names, which can be overridden with untaint_pattern.
untaint_pattern	\<pattern\>	The pattern used to untaint directory names if untaint is enabled. The default pattern, which attempts to define all standard legal file name characters, is qr/^([-+@\w.\/]+)$/ If overridden, the replacement regular expression search pattern compiled with qr. In addition, it must contain one set of parentheses to return the untainted name and should probably be anchored at both ends. Files with spaces inside the file name will fail unless this pattern is overridden. If multiple parentheses are used, then only the text matched by the first is used as the untainted name.
untaint_skip	0|1	A Boolean flag that when set causes find to skip over directories that fail the test against untaint_pattern. The default is unset, which causes find to die if it encounters an invalid directory name.

The following call to find searches for and prints out all files under /home, following symbolic links, untainting as it goes, and skipping over any directory that fails the taint check. At the same time, it pushes the files it finds onto an array to store the results of the search:

```perl
my @files;
find({
    wanted => sub {
        print $File::Find::fullname;
        push @files, $File::Find::fullname;
    },
    follow => 1, untaint => 1, untaint_skip => 1
}, '/home');
```

The power of find lies in the wanted subroutine. find does not actually return any value, so without this subroutine the search will be performed but will not actually produce any useful result. In particular, no list of files is built automatically. We must take steps to store the names of files we wish to record within the subroutine if we want to be able to refer to them afterwards. While this is simple enough to do, the File::Find::Wanted module from CPAN augments File::Find and fixes this detail by providing a find_wanted subroutine. Used in place of find, it modifies the interface behavior of the wanted subroutine to return a Boolean value, which it uses to build a list of values when the return value is true. The list is then returned from find_wanted. To specify a wanted subroutine, we can specify a code reference to an anonymous subroutine (possibly derived from a named subroutine) either directly or as the value of the wanted key in the configuration hash. Each file that is located is passed to this subroutine, which may perform any actions it likes, including removing or renaming the file. For example, here is a simple utility script that renames all files in the target directory or directories using lowercase format:

```perl
#!/usr/bin/perl
# lcall.pl
use warnings;
use strict;

use File::Find;
use File::Copy;
```

```
die "Usage: $0 <dir> [<dir>...] \n" unless @ARGV;
foreach (@ARGV) {
    die "'$_' does not exist \n" unless -e $_;
}

sub lcfile {
    print "$File::Find::dir - $_ \n";
    move ($_, lc $_);
}

finddepth (\&lcfile, @ARGV);
```

In order to handle subdirectories correctly, we use finddepth so files are renamed first and the directories that contain them second. We also use the move subroutine from File::Copy, since this deals with both files and directories without any special effort on our part.

Within the subroutine, the variable $_ contains the current file name, and the variable $File::Find::dir contains the directory in which the file was found. If follow or follow_fast is in effect, then $File::Find::fullname contains the complete absolute path to the file with all symbolic links resolved to their true paths. If no_chdir has been specified, then $_ is the absolute pathname of the file, same as $File::Find::fullname; otherwise, it is just the leafname of the file.

If follow or follow_fast is set, then the wanted subroutine can make use of the results of the lstat that both these modes use. File tests can then use the special file name _ without any initial file test or explicit lstat. Otherwise, no stat or lstat has been done, and we need to use an explicit file test on $_. As a final example, here is a utility script that searches for broken links:

```
#!/usr/bin/perl
# checklink.pl
use warnings;
use strict;

use File::Find;

my $count = 0;

sub check_link {
    if (-l && !-e) {
        $count++;
        print "\t$File::Find::name is broken \n";
    }
}

print "Scanning for broken links in ", join(', ', @ARGV), ":\n";
find(\&check_link, @ARGV);
print "$count broken links found \n";
```

Note that it has to do both an explicit -l and -e to work, since one requires an lstat and the other a stat, and we do not get a free lstat because in this case as we do not want to follow symbolic links. (In follow mode, broken links are discarded before the wanted subroutine is called, which would rather defeat the point.)

Another way to create utilities like this is through the find2perl script, which comes as standard with Perl. This emulates the syntax of the traditional Unix find command, but instead of performing a search, it generates a Perl script using File::Find that emulates the action of the original command in Perl. Typically, the script is faster than find, and it is also an excellent way to create the starting point for utilities like the examples in this section. For example, here is find2perl being used to generate a script, called myfind.pl, that searches for and prints all files ending in .bak that are a week or more old, starting from the current directory:

```
> find2perl . -name '*.bak' -type f  -mtime +7 -print > myfind.pl
```

We don't need to specify the -print option in Perl 5.8 since it is now on by default, but it doesn't do any harm either. find2perl takes a lot of different options and arguments, including ones not understood by find, to generate scripts that have different outcomes and purposes such as archiving. This command is, however, a fairly typical example of its use. This is the myfind.pl script that it produces:

```
#! /usr/bin/perl -w
    eval 'exec /usr/bin/perl -S $0 ${1+"$@"}'
        if 0; #$running_under_some_shell

use strict;
use File::Find ();

# Set the variable $File::Find::dont_use_nlink if you're using AFS,
# since AFS cheats.

# for the convenience of &wanted calls, including -eval statements:
use vars qw/*name *dir *prune/;
*name   = *File::Find::name;
*dir    = *File::Find::dir;
*prune  = *File::Find::prune;

# Traverse desired file systems
File::Find::find({wanted => \&wanted}, '.');
exit;

sub wanted {
    my ($dev, $ino, $mode, $nlink, $uid, $gid);

    /^.*\.bak\z/s
    && (($dev, $ino, $mode, $nlink, $uid, $gid) = lstat($_))
    && -f _
    && (int(-M _) > 7)
    && print("$name\n");
}
```

Often we want to make a record of the files that are of interest. Since the wanted subroutine has no way to pass back values to us, the caller, this means adding files to a global array or hash of some kind. Since globals are undesirable, this is an excellent opportunity to make use of a closure: a subroutine and a my-declared variable nested within a bare block. Here is an example:

```
#!/usr/bin/perl
# filefindclosure.pl
use strict;
use warnings;
use File::Find;

die "Give me a directory\n" unless @ARGV;

{ # closure for processing File::Find results
    my @results;

    sub wanted { push @results, $File::Find::name }
    sub findfiles {
        @results=();
```

```
        find \&wanted, $_[0];
        return @results;
    }
}

foreach my $dir (@ARGV) {
    print("Error: $dir is not a directory\n"), next unless -d;
    my @files=findfiles($dir);
    print "$_ contains @files\n";
}
```

For more recent versions of Perl, File::Find implements its own warnings category to issue diagnostics about any problems it encounters traversing the filing system, such as broken symbolic links or a failure to change to or open a directory. We might not find these warnings that helpful, so we can disable them (but leave all other warnings enabled) with

```
use warnings;
no warnings 'File::Find';
```

Deciphering File Paths

The File::Basename module provides subroutines to portably dissect file names. It contains one principal subroutine, fileparse, which attempts to divide a file name into a leading directory path, a basename, and a suffix:

```
use File::Basename;

# 'glob' all files with a three character suffix and parse pathname
foreach (</home/*/*.???>) {
    my ($path, $leaf, $suffix) = fileparse($_, '\.\w{3}');
    ...
}
```

The path and basename are determined according to the file naming conventions of the underlying file system, as determined by the operating system or configured with fileparse_set_fstype. The suffix list, if supplied, provides one or more regular expressions, which are anchored at the end of the file name and tested. The first one that matches is used to separate the suffix from the basename. For example, to find any dot + three letter suffix, we can use \.\w\w\w, or as in the preceding example, \.\w{3}.

To search for a selection of specific suffixes, we can either supply a list or combine all combinations into a single expression. Which we choose depends only on which is more likely to execute faster:

```
fileparse ($filename, '\.txt', '\.doc');   # list of suffixes
fileparse ($filename, '\.(txt|doc));       # combined regular expression

fileparse ($filename, '\.htm', '\.html', \.shtml);   # list of suffixes
fileparse ($filename, '\.s?html?));        # combined regular expression
```

Remember when supplying suffixes that they are regular expressions. Dots in particular must be escaped if they are intended to mean a real dot (however, see the basename subroutine detailed next for an alternative approach).

In addition to fileparse, File::Basename supplies two specialized subroutines, basename and dirname, which return the leading path and the basename only:

```
my $path = dirname($filename);
my $leaf = basename($filename, @suffixes);
```

basename returns the same result as the first item returned by fileparse except that metacharacters in the supplied suffixes (if any) are escaped with \Q...\E before being passed to fileparse. As a result, suffixes are detected and removed from the basename only if they literally match:

```
# scan for .txt and .doc with 'fileparse'
my ($path, $leaf, $suffix) = fileparse($filename, '\.(txt|doc)');
```

Or:

```
# scan for .txt and .doc with 'basename'
my $leaf = basename($filename, '.txt', '.doc');
```

dirname returns the same result as the second item returned by fileparse (the leading directory) on most platforms. For Unix and MSDOS, however, it will return . if there is no leading directory or a directory is supplied as the argument. This differs from the behavior produced by fileparse:

```
# scan for leading directory with 'fileparse'
print (fileparse('directory/file'));      # produce 'file'
print (fileparse('file')[1]);             # produce 'file'
print (fileparse('directory/')[1];        # produce 'directory/'
```

Or:

```
# scan for leading directory with 'dirname'
print dirname('directory/file');      # produce 'file'
print dirname('file');                # produce '.'
print dirname('directory/');          # produce '.'
```

The file system convention for the pathname can be set to one of several different operating systems with the fileparse_set_fstype configuration subroutine. This can take one of the following case-insensitive values shown in Table 13-8, each corresponding to the appropriate platform.

Table 13-8. *File::Basename File System Conventions*

Value	Platform
AmigaOS	Amiga syntax
MacOS	Macintosh (OS9 and earlier) syntax
MSWin32	Microsoft Windows long file names syntax
MSDOS	Microsoft DOS short file names (8.3) syntax
OS2	OS/2 syntax
RISCOS	Acorn RiscOS syntax
VMS	VMS syntax

If the syntax is not explicitly set with fileparse_set_fstype, then a default value is deduced from the special variable $^O (or $OSNAME with use English). If $^O is none of the preceding file system types, Unix-style syntax is assumed. Note that if the pathname contains / characters, then the format is presumed to be Unix style whatever the file system type specified.

For a more comprehensive approach to portable file name handling, the low-level File::Spec module provides an interface to several different filing system and platform types. It is extensively used by other modules, including File::Basename and the File::Glob modules (and in fact most of the File:: family of modules). We do not usually need to use it directly because these other modules wrap its functionality in more purposeful and friendly ways, but it is useful to know it is there nonetheless. Specific filing system support is provided by submodules like File::Spec::Unix, File::Spec::Win32, and File::Spec::Mac. The correct module is used automatically to suit the platform of execution, but if we want to manage Macintosh file names on a Windows system, accessing the platform-specific module will give us the ability to do so.

Several functions of `File::Spec` are worth mentioning here, because they relate to the handling of pathnames. The module is an object-oriented one to allow it to be easily used in other file system modules, and so the functions are actually provided as methods, not subroutines—a functional but otherwise identical interface to the available subroutines is offered by the `File::Spec::Functions` module. None of the methods shown in Table 13-9 actually touch the filing system directly. Instead, they provide answers to questions like "Is this filing system case insensitive?" and "Is this an absolute or relative file name?"

Table 13-9. *File::Spec Methods*

Method	Description
`File::Spec->curdir()`	Return the native name for the current working directory—that is, . on most platforms. For the actual path, we need Cwd.
`File::Spec->rootdir()`	Return the native name for the root directory. On Unix, that's /. On Windows and Mac, it depends on the currently active volume.
`File::Spec->devnull()`	The name of the null device, for reading nothing or dumping output to nowhere. /dev/null on Unix, nul on Windows.
`File::Spec->canonpath($path)`	Clean up the passed path into a canonical form, removing cruft like redundant . or trailing / elements appropriately. It does not remove .. elements—see `File::Spec->no_upwards(@files)`.
`File::Spec->updir()`	Return the native name for the parent directory—that is, .. on most platforms. For the actual path, Cwd and File::Basename are needed.
`File::Spec->no_upwards(@files)`	Examine the list of files and remove upwards directory elements (typically ..—see `File::Spec->updir()`) along with the preceding directory element.
`File::Spec->case_tolerant()`	Return true if the platform differentiates upper- and lowercase, false otherwise.
`File::Spec->file_name_is_absolute()`	Return true if the file name is absolute on the current platform.
`File::Spec->path()`	Return the current path, as understood by the underlying shell. This is the PATH environment variable for Unix and Windows, but it varies for other platforms.
`File::Spec->rel2abs($path,$to)`	Return the absolute path given a relative path and, optionally, a base path to attach the relative path to. If not specified, the current working directory is used.
`File::Spec->abs2rel($path,$from)`	The inverse of rel2abs, this takes an absolute path and derives the relative path from the optional base path supplied as the second argument. Again, the current working directory is used if only one argument is supplied.

In addition to these routines, we also have access to `catfile`, `catdir`, `catpath`, `join`, `splitdir`, `splitpath`, and `tmpdir`. With the exception of `tmpdir`, these are all involved in the construction or deconstruction of pathnames to and from their constituent parts. The `File::Basename` and `File::Path` modules provide a more convenient interface to most of this functionality, so we generally would not need to access the File::Spec methods directly. The tmpdir method returns the location of the system-supplied temporary directory, /tmp on most Unix platforms. It is used by modules that create temporary files, and we discuss it in more detail later on.

To call any of these methods, for example path, we can use either the object-oriented approach:

```
use File::Spec; # object-oriented
print File::Spec->path();
```

or use the equivalent functional interface:

```
use File::Spec::Functions; # functional
print path();
```

By default, File::Spec::Functions automatically exports canonpath, catdir, catfile, curdir, rootdir, updir, no_upwards, file_name_is_absolute, and path. We can choose to import all functions with :ALL or select individual functions in the usual way.

File Name Globbing

The majority of operating system shells support a wildcard syntax for specifying multiple files. For instance, *.doc means all files ending with .doc. Perl provides this same functionality through the file glob operator glob, which returns a list of all files that match the specified wildcard glob pattern:

```
my @files = glob '*.pod';   # return all POD documents in current directory
```

The glob pattern, not to be confused with a regular expression search pattern, accepts any pattern that would normally be accepted by a shell, including directories, wildcard metacharacters such as asterisks (zero-or-more), question marks (zero-or-one), and character classes. The following examples demonstrate the different kinds of glob operation that we can perform:

```
# match html files in document roots of all virtual hosts
my @html_files = glob '/home/sites/site*/web/*.html';
# match all files in current directory with a three-letter extension
my @three_letter_extensions = '*.???';
# match all files beginning with a to z
my @lcfirst = '[a-z]*';
# match 'file00 to file 49'
my @numbered_files = glob 'file[0-4][0-9]';
# match any file with a name of three or more characters
my @three_or_more_letter_files = glob '???*';
```

The order in which files are returned is by default sorted alphabetically and case sensitively (so uppercase trumps lowercase). We can alter this behavior by passing flags to the File::Glob module, which underlies glob, as well as allow more extended syntaxes than those in the preceding examples.

Before embarking on a closer examination of the glob function, keep in mind that while the underlying platform-specific glob modules do a good job of presenting the same interface and features, the opendir, readdir, and closedir functions are more reliable in cross-platform use, if more painstaking to use. This is particularly important with older versions of Perl (especially prior to version 5.6) where glob is less portable.

glob Syntax

The glob operator can be used with two different syntaxes. One, the glob built-in function, we have already seen:

```
my @files = glob '*.pl'  # explicit glob
```
The other is to use angle brackets in the style of the readline operator:
```
my @files = <*.pl>       # angle-bracket glob
```

How does Perl tell whether this is a readline or a glob? When Perl encounters an angle bracket construction, it examines the contents to determine whether it is a syntactically valid filehandle name or not. If it is, the operator is interpreted as a readline. Otherwise, it is handled as a file glob. Which syntax we use is entirely arbitrary. The angle bracket version looks better in loops, but it resembles the readline <> operator, which can create ambiguity for readers of the code:

```
foreach (<*.txt>) {
    print "$_ is not a textfile!" if !-T;
}
```

One instance we might want to use glob is when we want to perform a file glob on a pattern contained in a variable. A variable between angle brackets is ambiguous, so at compile time Perl guesses it is a readline operation. We can insert braces to force Perl to interpret the expression as a file glob, but in these cases it is often simpler to use glob instead:

```
@files = <$filespec>;      # ERROR: attempts to read lines
@files = <${filespec}>;    # ok, but algebraic
@files = glob $filespec;   # better
```

The return value from the globbing operation is a list containing the names of the files that matched. Files are matched according to the current working directory if a relative pattern is supplied; otherwise, they are matched relative to the root of the file system. The returned file names reflect this too, incorporating the leading directory path if one was supplied:

```
@files = glob '*.html';   # relative path
@files = glob '/home/httpd/web/*.html';   # absolute path
```

glob combines well with file test operators and array processing functions like map and grep. For example, to locate all text files in the current directory, we can write

```
my @textfiles = grep {-f && -T _} glob('*');
```

The glob function does not recurse, however. To do the same thing over a directory hierarchy, we can use the File::Find module with a wanted subroutine containing something similar:

```
sub wanted {
    push @textfiles, $File::Find::name if -f && -T _;
}
```

The glob operator was originally a built-in Perl function, but since version 5.6 it is implemented in terms of the File::Glob module, which implements Unix-style file globbing and overrides the built-in core glob. An alternative module, File::DosGlob, implements Windows/DOS-style globbing, with some extensions.

Unix-Style File Globbing

The standard glob does file globbing in the style of Unix, but it will still work on other platforms. The forward slash is used as a universal directory separator in patterns and will match matching files on the file system irrespective of the native directory separator. On Windows/DOS systems, the backslash is also accepted as a directory separator.

We automatically trigger use of the File::Glob module whenever we make use of the glob operator in either of its guises, but we can modify and configure the operator more finely by using the module directly. File::Glob defines four import tags that can be imported to provide different features, listed in Table 13-10.

Table 13-10. *File::Glob Import Tags*

Label	Function
:glob	Import symbols for the flags of glob's optional flag argument. See Table 13-11 for a list and description of each flag.
:case	Treat the file glob pattern as case sensitive. For example, *.doc will match file.doc but not file.DOC.
:nocase	Treat the file glob pattern as case insensitive. For example, *.doc will match both file.doc and file.DOC.
:globally	Override the core glob function. From Perl 5.6 this happens automatically. This will also override a previous override, for example, by File::DosGlob. For example, to import the optional flag symbols and switch the file globbing operator to a case-insensitive mode, we would write `use File::Glob qw(:glob :nocase);`

If not explicitly defined, the case sensitivity of glob is determined by the underlying platform (as expressed by the special variable $^O). The :case and :nocase labels allow us to override this default. For individual uses, temporary case sensitivity can be controlled by passing a flag to the glob operator instead, as we will see next.

Extended File Globbing

The glob operator accepts a number of optional flags that modify its behavior. These flags are given as a second parameter to glob and may be bitwise ORed together to produce multiple effects. To import a set of constants to name the flags, use File::Glob, explicitly specifying the :glob label:

```
use File::Glob qw(:glob);
```

The core glob function takes only one argument, a prototype, which is still enforced even though it is now based on a two-argument subroutine. To supply flags, we call the glob subroutine in the File::Glob package, where the prototype does not apply. For example, to enable brace expansions and match case insensitively, we would use

```
my @files = File::Glob::glob $filespec, GLOB_BRACE|GLOB_NOCASE;
```

The full list of flags is displayed in Table 13-11.

Table 13-11. *File::Glob Operator Flags*

Flag	Function
GLOB_ALPHASORT	Along with GLOB_NOSORT, this flag alters the order in which files are returned. By default, files are returned in case-sensitive alphabetical order. GLOB_ALPHASORT causes an alphabetical sort, but case-insensitively, so upper- and lowercase file names are adjacent to each other. See also GLOB_NOSORT.
GLOB_BRACE	Expand curly braces. A list of alternatives separated by commas is placed between curly braces. Each alternative is then expanded and combined with the rest of the pattern. For example, to match any file with an extension of .exe, .bat, or .dll, we could use `my @files = *.{exe, bat, dll}` Likewise, to match Perl-like files: `my @perl_files = *.{pm, pl, ph, pod}` See also "DOS-Style File Globbing" later for an alternative approach.
GLOB_CSH	File globbing in the style of the Unix C Shell csh. This is a combination of all four of the FreeBSD glob extensions for convenience: `GLOB_BRACE|GLOB_NOMAGIC|GLOB_QUOTE|GLOB_TILDE`

Continued

Table 13-11. *Continued*

Flag	Function
GLOB_ERR	Cause glob to return an error if it encounters an error such as a directory that it cannot open. Ordinarily glob will pass over errors. See "Handling Globbing Errors" for details.
GLOB_LIMIT	Cause glob to return a GLOB_NOSPACE error if the size of the expanded glob exceeds a predefined system limit, typically defined as the maximum possible command-line argument size.
GLOB_MARK	Return matching directories with a trailing directory separator /.
GLOB_NOCASE	Perform case-insensitive matching. The default is to assume matches are case sensitive, unless glob detects that the underlying platform does not handle case-sensitive file names, as discussed earlier. Note that the :case and :nocase import labels override the platform-specific default, and GLOB_NOCASE then applies on a per-glob basis.
GLOB_NOCHECK	Return the glob pattern if no file matches it. If GLOB_QUOTE is also set, the returned pattern is processed according to the rules of that flag. See also GLOB_NOMAGIC.
GLOB_NOMAGIC	As GLOB_NOCHECK, but the pattern is returned only if it does not contain any of the wildcard characters *, ?, or [.
GLOB_NOSORT	Disable sorting altogether and return files in the order in which they were found for speed. It overrides GLOB_ALPHASORT if both are specified. See also GLOB_ALPHASORT.
GLOB_QUOTE	Treat backslashes, \, as escape characters and interpret the following character literally, ignoring any special meaning it might normally have. On DOS/Windows systems, backslash only escapes metacharacters and is treated as a directory separator otherwise. See also "DOS-Style File Globbing" later for an alternative approach.
GLOB_TILDE	Expand the leading tilde, ~, of a pattern to the user home directory. For example, ~/.myapp/config might be expanded to /home/gurgeh/.myapp/config.

Handling Globbing Errors

If glob encounters an error, it puts an error message in $! and sets the package variable File::Glob::GLOB_ERROR to a non-zero value with a symbolic name defined by the module:

GLOB_NOSPACE	Perl ran out of memory.
GLOB_ABEND	Perl aborted due to an error.

If the error occurs midway through the scan, and some files have already been found, then the incomplete glob is returned as the result. This means that getting a result from glob does not necessarily mean that the file glob completed successfully. In cases where this matters, check $File::Glob::GLOB_ERROR:

```
@files = glob $filespec;
if ($File::Glob::GLOB_ERROR) {
    die "Error globbing '$filespec': $! \n";
}
```

DOS-Style File Globbing

DOS-style file globbing is provided by the File::DosGlob module, an alternative to File::Glob that implements file globs in the style of Windows/DOS, with extensions. In order to get DOS-style globbing, we must use this module explicitly, to override the Unix-style globbing that Perl performs automatically (for instance, if we are running on a Windows system, we may receive wildcard input from the user that conforms to DOS rather than Unix style):

```
use File::DosGlob;          # provide File::DosGlob::glob
use File::DosGlob qw(glob);  # override core/File::Glob's 'glob'
```

Unlike File::Glob, File::DosGlob does not allow us to configure aspects of its operation by specifying labels to the import list, and it does not even override the core glob unless explicitly asked, as shown in the second example earlier. Even if we do not override glob, we can call the File::DosGlob version by naming it in full:

```
@dosfiles = File::DosGlob::glob ($dosfilespec);
```

Even with glob specified in the import list, File::DosGlob will only override glob in the current package. To override it everywhere, we can use GLOBAL_glob:

```
use File::DosGlob qw(GLOBAL_glob);
```

This should be used with extreme caution, however, since it might upset code in other modules that expects glob to work in the Unix style.

Unlike the DOS shell, File::DosGlob works with wildcarded directory names, so a file spec of C:/*/dir*/file* will work correctly (although it might take some time to complete).

```
my @dosfiles = glob ('my\dos\filepath\*.txt');  # single quoted
```

The module also understands DOS-style backslashes as directory separators, although these may need to be protected:

```
my @dosfiles = <my\\dos\\filepath\\*.txt>;      # escaped
```

Any mixture of forward and backslashes is acceptable to File::DosGlob's glob (and indeed Perl's built-in one, on Windows); translation into the correct pattern is done transparently and automatically:

```
my @dosfiles = <my/dos/filepath\\*.txt>;        # a mixture
```

To search in file names or directories that include spaces, we can escape them using a backslash (which means that we must interpolate the string and therefore protect literal backslashes):

```
my @programfiles = <C:\\Program\ Files\\*.*>;
```

If we use the glob literally, we can also use double quotes if the string is enclosed in single quotes (or the q quoting operator):

```
my @programfiles = glob 'C:/"Program Files"/*.*';
```

This functionality is actually implemented via the Text::ParseWords module, covered in Chapter 19.

Finally, multiple glob patterns may be specified in the same pattern if they are separated by spaces. For example, to search for all .exe and .bat files, we could use

```
my @executables = glob('*.exe *.bat');
```

Temporary Files

There have always been two basic approaches for creating temporary files in Perl, depending on whether we just want a scratchpad that we can read and write or want to create a temporary file with a file name that we can pass around. To do the first, we can create a filehandle with IO::File that points to a temporary file that exists only so long as the filehandle is open. To do the second, we can deduce the name of a unique temporary file and then open and close it like an ordinary file, using the POSIX tmpnam function.

From Perl 5.6.1, we have a third approach that involves using File::Temp, which returns both a file name and a filehandle. From Perl 5.8, we have a fourth, an anonymous temporary file that we can create by passing a file name of undef to the built-in open function. This is essentially the same as the first approach, but using a new native syntax. We covered anonymous temporary files in the last chapter, so here we will examine the other three approaches.

Creating a Temporary Filehandle

Temporary filehandles can be created with the new_tmpfile method of the IO::File module. new_tmpfile takes no arguments and opens a new temporary file in read-update (and binary, for systems that care) mode, returning the generated filehandle. In the event of an error, undef is returned and $! is set to indicate the reason. For example:

```
my $tmphandle = IO::File->new_tmpfile();
unless ($tmphandle) {
    print "Could not create temporary filehandle: $! \n";
}
```

Wherever possible, the new_tmpfile method accesses the operating system tmpfile library call (on systems that provide it). This makes the file truly anonymous and is the same interface provided by open in sufficiently modern versions of Perl. On these generally Unix-like systems, a file exists as long as something is using it, even if it no longer has a file name entered in the file system. new_tmpfile makes use of this fact to remove the file system entry for the file as soon as the file-handle is created, making the temporary file truly anonymous. When the filehandle is closed, the file ceases to exist, since there will no longer be any references to it. This behavior is not supported on platforms that do not support anonymous temporary files, but IO::File will still create a temporary file for us. See Chapter 12 for more information on filehandles and temporary anonymous files.

Temporary File Names via the POSIX Module

While IO::File's new_tmpfile is very convenient for a wide range of temporary file applications, it does not return us a file name that we can use or pass to other programs. To do that, we need to use the POSIX module and the tmpnam routine. Since POSIX is a large module, we can import just tmpnam with

```
use POSIX qw(tmpnam);
```

The tmpnam routine takes no arguments and returns a temporary file name guaranteed to be unique at the moment of inquiry. For example:

```
my $tmpname = tmpnam();
print $tmpname;    # produces something like '/tmp/fileV9vJXperl'
```

File names are created with a fixed and unchangeable default path, defined by the P_tmpdir value given in the C standard library's studio.h header file. This path can be changed subsequently, but this does not guarantee that the file does not exist in the new directory. To do that, we might resort to a loop like this:

```
do {
    my $tmpname = tmpnam();
    $tmpname =~ m|/ ([^/]+) $| && $tmpname = $1;    # strip '/tmp'
    $tmpname = $newpath.$tmpname;    # add new path
} while (-e $tmpname);
```

This rather defeats the point of tmpnam, however, which is to create a temporary file name quickly and easily in a place that is suitable for temporary files (/tmp on any vaguely Unix-like system). It also does not handle the possibility that other processes might be trying to create temporary files in the same place. This is a significant possibility and a potential source of race conditions. Two processes may call tmpnam at the same time, get the same file name in return, then both open it. To avoid this, we open the temporary file using sysopen and specify the O_EXCL flag, which requires that the file does not yet exist. Here is a short loop that demonstrates a safe way to open the file:

```
# get an open (and unique) temporary file
do {
    my $tmpname = tmpnam();
    sysopen TMPFILE, $tmpname, O_RDWR|O_CREAT|O_EXCL;
} until (defined fileno(TMPFILE));
```

If another process creates the same file in between our call to tmpnam and the sysopen, the O_EXCL will cause it to fail; TMPFILE will not be open, and so the loop repeats (see the next section for a better approach). Note that if we only intend to write to the file, O_WRONLY would do just as well, but remember to import the symbols from the POSIX or Fcntl modules. Once we have the file open, we can use it:

```
# place data into the file
print TMPFILE "This is only temporary \n";
close TMPFILE;

# use the file - read it, write it some more, pass the file name to another
# process, etc.

# remember to tidy up afterwards!
unlink $tmpname;
```

Since we have an actual tangible file name, we can pass it to other processes. This is a common approach when reading the output of another command created with a piped open. For example, here is an anonymous FTP command-line client, which we can use to execute commands on a remote FTP server:

```
#!/usr/bin/perl -w
# ftpclient.pl
use warnings;
use strict;
use POSIX qw(O_RDWR O_CREAT O_EXCL tmpnam);
use Sys::Hostname; # for 'hostname'

die "Simple anonymous FTP command line client\n".
    "Usage: $0 <server> <command>\n" unless scalar(@ARGV)>=2;

my ($ftp_server,@ftp_command)=@ARGV;

# get an open and unique temporary file
my $ftp_resultfile;
do {
    # generate a new temporary file name
    $ftp_resultfile = tmpnam();
```

```
    # O_EXCL ensures no other process successfully opens the same file
    sysopen FTP_RESULT, $ftp_resultfile, O_RDWR|O_CREAT|O_EXCL;
    # failure means something else opened this file name first, try again
} until (defined fileno(FTP_RESULT));

# run ftp client with autologin disabled (using -n)
if (open (FTP, "|ftp -n > $ftp_resultfile 2>&1")) {
    print "Client running, sending command\n";

    # command: open connection to server
    print FTP "open $ftp_server\n";
    # command: specify anonymous user and email as password
    my $email=getlogin.'@'.hostname;
    print FTP "user anonymous $email\n";
    # command: send command (interpolate list to space arguments)
    print FTP "@ftp_command\n";

    close FTP;
} else {
    die "Failed to run client: $!\n";
}

print "Command sent, waiting for response\n";
my @ftp_results = <FTP_RESULT>;
check_result(@ftp_results);
close FTP_RESULT;
unlink $ftp_resultfile;
print "Done\n";

sub check_result {
    return unless @_;

    print "Response:\n";
    # just print out the response for this example
    print "\t$_" foreach @_;
}
```

We can use this (admittedly simplistic) client like this:

```
$ ftpclient.pl ftp.alphacomplex.com get briefing.doc
```

Using File::Temp

As of Perl 5.6.1, we have a better approach to creating temporary files, using the File::Temp module. This module returns the name and filehandle of a temporary file together. This eliminates the possibility of a race condition. Instead of using sysopen with the O_EXCL flag, as we showed in the previous section, File::Temp provides us with the following much simpler syntax using its tempfile function:

```
my ($FILEHANDLE, $filename) = tempfile();
```

However, tempfile can take arguments that we can use to gain more control over the created temporary file, as shown in the following:

```
my ($FILEHANDLE, $filename) = tempfile($template, DIR => $dir, SUFFIX = $suffix);
```

The template should contain at least four trailing Xs, which would then be replaced with random letters, so $template could be something like filenameXXXXX. By specifying an explicit directory with DIR, we can specify the directory where we want the temporary file to be created. Otherwise, the file will be created in the directory specified for temporary files by the function tmpdir in File::Spec.

Finally, at times we might need our temporary file to have a particular suffix, possibly for subsequent processing by other applications. The following will create a temporary file called fileXXXX.tmp (where the four Xs are replaced with four random letters) in the directory /test/files:

```
my ($FILEHANDLE, $filename) = tempfile("fileXXXX", DIR => "/test/files",
                                        SUFFIX => ".tmp");
```

However, the recommended interface is to call tempfile in scalar instead of list context, returning only the filehandle:

```
my $FILEHANDLE = tempfile("fileXXXX", DIR => "/test/files", SUFFIX => ".tmp");
```

The file itself will be automatically deleted when closed. No way to tamper with the file name means no possibility of creating a race condition.

To create temporary directories, File::Temp provides us with the tempdir function. Using the function without argument creates a temporary directory in the directory set by tmpdir in File::Spec:

```
my $tempdir = tempdir();
```

As with tempfile, we can specify a template and explicit directory as arguments to tempdir. Here also the template should have at least four trailing Xs that will be translated into four random letters. The DIR option overrides the value of File::Spec's tmpdir:

```
my $tempdir = tempdir("dirXXXX", DIR => "/test/directory");
```

This will create a temporary directory called something like /test/directory/dirdnar, where dnar are four random letters that replaced the four Xs. If the template included parent directory specifications, then they are removed before the directory is prepended to the template. In the absence of a template, the directory name is generated from an internal template.

Removing the temporary directory and all its files, whether created by File::Temp or not, can be achieved using the option CLEANUP => 1.

In addition to the functions tempfile and tempdir, File::Temp provides Perl implementations of the mktemp family of temp file generation system calls. These are shown in Table 13-12.

Table 13-12. *File::Temp Functions*

Funtion	Description
mkstemp	Using the provided template, this function returns the name of the temporary file and a filehandle to it: `my ($HANDLE, $name) = mkstemp($template);` If we are interested only in the filehandle, then we can use mkstemp in scalar context.
mkstemps	This is similar to mkstemp but accepts the additional option of a suffix that is appended to the template: `my ($HANDLE, $name) = mkstemps($template, $suffix);`
mktemp	This function returns a temporary file name but does not ensure that the file will not be opened by a different process: `my $unopened = mktemp($template);`
Mkdtemp	This function uses the given template to create a temporary directory. The name of the directory is returned upon success and undefined otherwise: `my $dir = mktemp($template);`

Finally, the `File::Temp` module provides implementations of the POSIX's `tmpname` and `tmpfile` functions. As mentioned earlier, POSIX uses the value of `P_tmpdir` in the C standard library's `studio.h` header file as the directory for the temporary file. `File::Temp`, on the other hand, uses the setting of `tmpdir`. With a call to `mkstemp` using an appropriate template, `tmpname` returns a filehandle to the open file and a file name:

```
my ($HANDLE, $name) = tmpname();
```

In scalar context, `tmpname` uses `mktemp` and returns the full name of the temporary file:

```
my $name = tmpname();
```

While this ensures that the file does not already exist, it does not guarantee that this will remain the case. In order to avoid a possible race condition, we should use `tmpname` in list context.

The `File::Temp` implementation of the POSIX's `tmpfile` returns the filehandle of a temporary file. There is no access to the file name, and the file is removed when the filehandle is closed or when the program exits:

```
my $HANDLE = tmpfile();
```

For further information on `File::Temp`, consult the documentation.

Querying and Manipulating Directories

Directories are similar to files in many ways; they have names, permissions, and (on platforms that support it) owners. They are significantly different in others ways, however. At their most basic, files can generally be considered to be content, that is, data. Directories, on the other hand, are indices of metadata. Record based, each entry in a directory describes a file, directory, link, or special file that the directory contains. It only makes sense to read a directory in terms of records and no sense at all to write to the directory index directly—the operating system handles that when we manipulate the contents.

Accordingly, operating systems support a selection of functions specifically oriented to handling directories in a record-oriented context, which Perl wraps and makes available to us as a collection of built-in functions with (reasonably) platform-independent semantics. They provide a more portable but lower-level alternative to the `glob` function discussed earlier in the chapter.

Directories can also be created and destroyed. Perl supports these operations through the functions `mkdir` and `rmdir`, which should be synonymously familiar to those with either a Windows or a Unix background. For more advanced applications, the `File::Path` module provides enhanced directory-spanning analogues for these functions.

A discussion of directories is not complete without the concept of the current working directory. All of Perl's built-in functions that take a file name as an argument, from `open` to the unary file test operators, base their arguments relative to the current working directory whenever the given file name is not absolute. We can both detect and change the current working directory either using Perl's built-in functions or with the more flexible `Cwd` module.

Reading Directories

Although directories cannot be opened and read like ordinary files, the equivalent is possible using directory handles. For each of the file-based functions `open`, `close`, `read`, `seek`, `tell`, and `rewind`, there is an equivalent that performs the same function for directories. For example, `opendir` opens a directory and returns a directory handle:

```
opendir DIRHANDLE, $dirname;
```

Although similar to filehandles in many respects, directory handles are an entirely separate subspecies; they only work with their own set of built-in functions and even occupy their own internal namespace within a typeglob, so we can quite legally have a filehandle and a directory handle with the same name. Having said that, creating a filehandle and a directory handle with the same name is more than a little confusing.

If opendir fails for any reason (the obvious ones being that the directory does not exist or is in fact a file), it returns undef and sets $! to indicate the reason. Otherwise, we can read the items in the directory using readdir:

```
if (opendir DIRHANDLE, $dirname) {
    print "$dirname contains: $_ \n" foreach readdir DIRHANDLE;
}
```

readdir is similar in spirit to the readline operator, although we cannot use an equivalent of the <> syntax to read from a directory filehandle. If we do, Perl thinks we are trying to read from a filehandle with the same name. However, like the readline operator, readdir can be called in either a scalar context, where it returns the next item in the directory, or in a list context, where it returns all remaining entries:

```
my $diritem = readdir DIRHANDLE;  # read next item
my @diritems = readdir DIRHANDLE;  # read all (remaining) items
```

(Another example of list context is the foreach in the previous example.)

Rather than return a line from a file, readdir returns a file name from the directory. We can then go on to test the file name with file test operators or stat/lstat to find out more about them. However, if we do this, we should take care to append the directory name first or use chdir; otherwise, the file test will not take place where we found the file but in the current working directory:

```
opendir DIRHANDLE, '..';  # open parent directory
foreach (readdir DIRHANDLE) {
    print "$_ is a directory  \n" if -d "../$_";
}
closedir DIRHANDLE;
```

Or, using chdir:

```
opendir DIRHANDLE, '..';  # open parent directory
chdir '..';  # change to parent directory
foreach (readdir DIRHANDLE) {
    print "$_ is a directory \n" if -d;  # use $_
}
closedir DIRHANDLE;
```

Note that when finished with a directory handle, it should be closed, again using a specialized version of close, closedir. In the event closedir fails, it also returns undef and sets $! to indicate the error. Otherwise, it returns true.

Directory Positions

Directory filehandles also have positions, which can be manipulated with the functions seekdir, telldir, and rewinddir, direct directory analogues for the file position functions seek, tell, and rewind. Keep in mind that the former set of functions only work on directories (the plain file counterparts also work on directories, but not very usefully), and a directory position set with seekdir must be deduced from telldir, in order to know what positions correspond to the start of directory entries:

```
# find current position of directory handle
my $dpos = telldir DIRHANDLE;
# read an item, moving the position forward
my $item = readdir DIRHANDLE;
# reset position back to position read earlier
```

```
seekdir DIRHANDLE, $dpos;
# reset position back to start of directory
 rewinddir DIRHANDLE;
```

Although they are analogous, these functions are not as similar to their file-based counterparts as their names might imply. In particular, seekdir is not nearly as smart as seek, because it does not accept an arbitrary position. Instead, seekdir is only good for setting the position to 0, or a position previously found with telldir.

Directory Handle Objects

As an alternative to the standard directory handling functions, we can instead use the IO::Dir module. IO::Dir inherits basic functionality from IO::File, then overloads and replaces the file-specific features with equivalent methods for directories.

```
my $dirh = new IO::Dir($directory);
```

Each of the standard directory handling functions is supported by a similarly named method in IO::Dir, minus the trailing dir. Instead of using opendir, we can create a new, unassociated IO::Dir object and then use open:

```
my $dirh = new IO::Dir;
my $dirh->open ($directory);
```

Likewise, we can use read to read from a directory filehandle, seek, tell, and rewind to move around inside the directory, and close to close it again:

```
my $entry = $dirh->read;    # read an entry
my $dpos = $dirh->tell;     # find current position
$dirh->seek($dpos);         # set position
$dirh->rewind;              # rewind to start
my @entries = $dirh->read;  # read all entries
```

Directories As Tied Hashes

As an alternative to the object-oriented interface, IO::Dir also supports a tied hash interface, where the directory is represented by a hash and the items in it as the keys of the hash. The values of the hash are lstat objects created via the File::stat package, called on the key in question. These are created at the moment that we ask for it so as not to burden the system with unnecessary lstat calls. If the main purpose of interrogating the directory is to perform stat-type operations (including file tests), we can save time by using this interface:

```
# list permissions of all files in current directory
my %directory;
tie %directory, IO::Dir, '.';

foreach (sort keys %directory) {
    printf ("$_ has permissions %o \n", $directory{$_}->mode & 0777);
}
untie %directory;
```

IO::Dir makes use of the tied hash interface to extend its functionality in other ways too. Assigning an integer as the value of an existing key in the hash will cause the access and modification time to be changed to that value. Assigning a reference to an array of two integers will cause the access and modification times to be altered to the first and second, respectively. If, on the other hand, the entry does not exist, then an empty file of the same name is created in the directory, again with the appropriate timestamps:

```
# set all timestamps to the current time:
my $now = time;

foreach (keys %directory) {
    $directory{$_} = $now;
}

# create a new file, modified one day ago, accessed now:
$directory{'newfile'} = [$now, $now-24 * 60 * 60];
```

Deleting a key-value pair will also delete a file, but only if the option DIR_UNLINK is passed to the tie as a fourth parameter:

```
# delete backup files ending in .bak or ~
tie %directory, IO::Dir, $dirname, DIR_UNLINK;

foreach (keys %directory) {
    delete $directory{$_} if /(\.bak|~)$/;
}
untie %directory;
```

With DIR_UNLINK specified, deleting an entry from the hash will either call unlink or rmdir on the items in question, depending on whether it is a file or a directory. In the event of failure, the return value is undef and $! is set to indicate the error, as usual.

Finding the Name of a Directory or File from Its Handle

As a practical example of using the directory functions, the following example is a solution to the problem of finding out the name of a directory or file starting from a handle, assuming we know the name of the parent directory:

```
sub find_name {
    my ($handle, $parentdir) = @_;

    # find device and inode of directory
    my ($dev, $ino) = lstat $handle;
    open PARENT, $parentdir or return;
    foreach (readline PARENT) {
        # find device and node of parent directory entry
        my ($pdev, $pino) = lstat '../$_';
        # if it is a match, we have our man
        close PARENT, return $_ if ($pdev == $dev && $pino == $ino);
    }
    close PARENT;
    return;   # didn't find it...strange!
}

my $name = find_name (*HANDLE, "/parent/directory");
close HANDLE;
```

First, we use lstat to determine the device and inode of the parent directory—or possibly the symbolic link that points to the directory, which is why we use lstat and not stat. We then open the parent and scan each entry in turn using lstat to retrieve its device and inode. If we find a match, we must be talking about the same entry, so the name of this entry must be the name of the file or directory (or a name, on Unix-like platforms where multiple names can exist for the same file).

We can adapt this general technique to cover whole file systems using the File::Find module, though if we plan to do this a lot, caching the results of previous lstat commands will greatly improve the run time of subsequent searches.

Creating and Destroying Directories

The simplest way to create and destroy directories is to use the mkdir and rmdir functions. These both create or destroy a single directory, starting at the current working directory if the supplied name is relative. For more advanced applications, we can use the File::Path module, which allows us to create and destroy multiple nested directories.

Creating Single Directories

To create a new directory, we use the built-in mkdir function. This takes a directory name as an argument and attempts to create a directory with that name. The pathname given to mkdir may contain parent directories, in which case they must exist for the directory named as the last part of the pathname to be created. If the name is absolute, it is created relative to the root of the filing system. If it is relative, it is created relative to the current working directory:

```
# relative - create directory 'scripts' in current working directory
mkdir 'scripts';
# absolute - create 'web' in /home/httpd/sites/$site, which must already exist
mkdir "/home/httpd/sites/$site/web";
# relative - create directory 'scripts' in subdirectory 'lib' in current
# working directory. POSSIBLE ERROR: 'lib' must already exist to succeed.
mkdir 'lib/scripts';
```

mkdir may be given an optional second parameter consisting of a numeric permissions mask, as described earlier in the chapter. This is generally given as an octal number specifying the read, write, and execute permissions for each of the user, group, and other categories. For example, to create a directory with 755 permissions, we would use

```
mkdir $dirname, 0755;
```

We can also use the mode symbols from the Fcntl module if we import them first. Here is an example of creating a directory with 0775 permissions, using the appropriate Fcntl symbols:

```
use Fcntl qw(:mode);
# $dirname with 0775 permissions
mkdir $dirname, S_RWXU | S_RWXG | S_ROTH | S_XOTH;
```

The second parameter to mkdir is a permissions mask, also known as umask, not a generic file mode. It applies to permissions only, not the other specialized mode bits such as the sticky, setuid, or setgid bits. To set these (on platforms that support them), we must use chmod after creating the directory.

The setting of umask may also remove bits; it is merged with the permissions mask parameter to define the value supplied to mkdir. The default permissions mask is 0777 modified by the umask setting. (A umask setting of octal 022 would modify the stated permissions of a created directory from 0777 to 0755, for example.) This is generally better than specifying a more restricted permissions mask in the program as it allows permissions policy to be controlled by the user.

Creating Multiple Directories

The mkdir function will only create one directory at a time. To create multiple nested directories, we can use the File::Path module instead.

File::Path provides two routines, mkpath and rmtree. mkpath takes a path specification containing one or more directory names separated by a forward slash, a Boolean flag to enable or disable a report of created directories, and a permissions mask in the style of mkdir. It is essentially an improved mkdir, with none of the drawbacks of the simpler function. For example, to create a given directory path:

```
use File::Path;

# create path, reporting all created directories
my $verbose = 1;
my $mask = 0755;
mkpath ('/home/httpd/sites/mysite/web/data/', $verbose, $mask);
```

One major advantage mkpath has over mkdir is that it handles preexisting directories in stride, using them if present and creating new directories otherwise. It also handles directory naming conventions of VMS and OS/2 automatically. In other respects, it is like mkdir, using the same permission mask and creating directories from the current working directory if given a relative pathname:

```
# silently create scripts in lib, creating lib first if it does not exist.
mkpath "lib/scripts";
```

If mkpath is only given one parameter, as in the preceding example, the verbose flag defaults to 0, resulting in a silent mkpath. And like mkdir, the permissions mask defaults to 0777.

mkpath can also create multiple chains of directories if its first argument is a list reference rather than a simple scalar. For instance, to create a whole installation tree for a fictional application, we could use something like this:

```
mkpath ([
    '/usr/local/apps/myapp/bin',
    '/usr/local/apps/myapp/doc',
    '/usr/local/apps/myapp/lib',
], 1, 0755);
```

In the event of an error, mkpath will croak and return with $! set to the reason of the failed mkdir. To trap a possible croak, put the mkpath into an eval:

```
unless (defined eval {mkpath(@paths, 0, 0755)}) {
    print "Error from mkpath: $@ ($!) \n";
}
```

Otherwise, mkpath returns the list of all directories created. If a directory already exists, then it is not added to this list. As any return from mkpath indicates that the call was successful overall, an empty list means simply that all the directories requested already exist. Since we often do not care if directories were created or not, just so long as they exist, we usually do not actually check the return value, only trap the error as in the preceding example.

Destroying Single Directories

To delete a directory, we use the rmdir function, which returns 1 on success and 0 otherwise, setting $! to indicate the reason for the error. rmdir takes a single directory name as an argument or uses the value of $_ if no file name is given:

```
rmdir $dirname;    # remove dirname

rmdir;    # delete directory named by $_
```

rmdir typically fails if the given name is not a valid pathname or does not point to a directory (it might be a file or a symbolic link to a directory). It will also fail if the directory is not empty.

Deleting nested directories and directories with contents is more problematic. If we happen to be on a Unix system, logged in as superuser, and if we specified the -U option to Perl when we started our application, then we can use unlink to remove the directory regardless of its contents.

In general, however, the only recourse we have is to traverse the directory using opendir, removing files and traversing into subdirectories as we go. Fortunately, we do not have to code this ourselves, as there are a couple of modules that will greatly simplify the process.

Destroying Multiple or Nonempty Directories

As well as mkpath, the File::Path module provides a second routine, rmtree, that performs (loosely speaking) the opposite function.

rmtree takes three parameters: the first, like mkpath, is a single scalar directory path. It comprises one or more directories separated by forward slashes, or alternatively a reference to an anonymous array of scalar directory paths. Paths may be either absolute or relative to the current working directory.

The second is, just like mkpath, a Boolean verbosity flag, set to false by default. If enabled, rmtree reports on each file or directory it encounters, indicating whether it used unlink or rmdir to remove it, or whether it skipped over it. Symbolic links are deleted but not followed.

The third parameter is a safety flag, also Boolean and false by default. If true, rmtree will skip over any file for which the program does not have write permission (or more technically, the program's effective user ID does not have write permission), except for VMS, which has the concept of "delete permission." Otherwise, it will attempt to delete it anyway, which depends not on the file's permissions or owner but on the permissions of the parent directory, like rmdir.

Consider the following simple script, which simply wraps rmtree:

```
#!/usr/bin/perl
# rmtree.pl
use strict;
use warnings;
use File::Path;

my $path=$ARGV[0];

my $verbose = 0;
my $safe = 1;
rmtree $path, $verbose, $safe;
```

With an array reference instead of a scalar pathname, all the paths in the array are deleted. We can remove $path from the preceding script and replace all of the script below it with

```
# remove all paths supplied, silently and safely.
rmtree(\@ARGV, 0, 1);
```

On success, rmtree returns the number of files deleted. On a fatal error, it will croak like mkpath and can be trapped in the same way. Other, nonfatal, errors are carped (via the Carp module) and must be trapped by a warning signal handler:

```
$SIG{__WARN__} = handle_warnings();
```

If the safety flag is not set, rmtree attempts to force the permissions of file directories to make them deletable. In the event of it failing to delete them afterwards, it may also be unable to restore the original permissions, leading to potentially insecure permissions. In all such cases, the problem will be reported via carp and trapped by the warning signal handler if present.

Finding and Changing the Current Directory

All of Perl's directory handling functions from opendir to rmdir understand both absolute and relative pathnames. Relative is in relation to the current working directory, which initially is the directory that the shell was in when it started our application. Desktop icons, for example, provided by Windows shortcuts, supply the ability to specify the working directory before running the program the shortcut points to. Perl programs started from other processes inherit the current working directory, or CWD for short, of the parent. In a command shell, we commonly find the `cd` command changes the current working directory.

We can change the current working directory in Perl with the `chdir` function. `chdir` takes a directory path as its argument and attempts to change the current working directory accordingly. If the path is absolute, it is taken relative to the root directory; otherwise, it is taken relative to the current working directory. It returns true on success and false on failure. For example:

```
unless (chdir $newdir) {
    "Failed to change to $newdir: $! \n";
}
```

Without an argument, `chdir` changes to the home directory, equivalent to entering "cd" on its own on the command line. An argument of `undef` also behaves this way, but this is now deprecated behavior since it is too easy to accidentally feed `chdir` an undefined value through an unset variable that was meant to hold a file name.

On Windows things are a bit more complicated, since Windows preserves a current directory for each drive available to the system. The current directory as understood by Perl is therefore a combination of the currently selected drive and the current working directory on that drive. If we pass a directory to `chdir` without a drive letter, we remain on the current drive.

There is no direct way in Perl to determine what the current working directory is, since the concept means different things to different platforms. Shells often maintain the current working directory in an environment variable that we can simply check, such as `$ENV{PWD}` (the name is derived from the Unix `pwd` command, which stands for "print working directory"). More formally, we can use either the `POSIX` module or the more specialized `Cwd` module to find out.

Using the `POSIX` module, we can find the current working directory by calling the `getcwd` routine, which maps onto the underlying `getcwd` or `getwd` (regional variations may apply) routine provided by the standard C library. It takes no parameters and returns the current working directory as a string:

```
use POSIX qw(getcwd);
my $cwd = getcwd;
```

This will work for most, but not all, platforms—a credible `getcwd` or `getwd`-like function must be available for the `POSIX` module to use it. Alternatively, we can use the `Cwd` module. This is a specialized module dedicated to all issues surrounding the current working directory in as portable a way as possible. It supplies three different ways to determine the current directory:

`getcwd` and `fastcwd` are pure Perl implementations that are therefore maximally portable. `cwd` attempts to use the most natural and safe method to retrieve the current working directory supported by the underlying platform, which might be `getcwd` or some other operating system interface, depending on whether it be Unix, Windows, VMS, OS/2, and so on.

`getcwd` is an implementation of the real `getcwd` as provided by POSIX written purely in Perl. It works by opening the parent directory with `opendir`, then scanning each file in turn through `readdir` and `lstat`, looking for a match with the current directory using the first two values returned (the `dev` and `lno` fields). From this it deduces the name of the current directory, and so on all the way to the top of the filing system. This makes `getcwd` slow, but it will work in the absence of additional cooperation from the operating system. `getcwd` avoids using `chdir`, because having `chdir`ed out of the current directory, permissions may not allow it to `chdir` back in again. Instead it assembles an increasingly long string of `/../../../` to access each directory in turn. This makes it safe but slow.

`fastgetcwd` is also a pure Perl implementation. It works just like `getcwd` but assumes `chdir` is always safe. Instead of accessing each parent directory through an extending string of `/..`, it uses `chdir` to jump up to the parent directory and analyze it directly. This makes it a lot faster than `getcwd`, but it may mean that the current working directory changes if `fastgetcwd` fails to restore the current working directory due to its permissions.

cwd attempts to use the best safe and "natural" underlying mechanism available for determining the current working directory, essentially executing the native command to return the current working directory—on a Unix platform this is the pwd command, on Windows it is command /c cd, and so on. It does not use the POSIX module. If all else fails, the Perl-only getcwd covered previously is used. This makes it the best solution for most applications, since it takes advantage of OS support if any is available, but it can survive happily (albeit slowly) without. However, it is slower than the POSIX module because it usually executes an external program.

All three methods will return the true path to the file, resolving and removing any symbolic links (should we be on a platform that supports them) in the pathname. All four functions (including the alias getfastcwd) are automatically imported when we use the module and are called in the same way, taking no parameters and returning the current working directory:

```
use Cwd;            # import 'getcwd', 'fastcwd', 'fastgetcwd', and 'cwd'

$cwd = getcwd;      # slow, safe Perl
$cwd = fastcwd;     # faster but potentially unsafe Perl
$cwd = getfastcwd;  # alias for 'fastcwd'
$cwd = cwd;         # use native platform support
```

If we only want to use one of these functions, say cwd, we can tell the module to export just that one function with

```
use Cwd qw(cwd);
```

Sometimes we want to find the path to a directory other than the one we are currently in. One way to do that is to chdir to the directory in question, determine the current working directory, and then chdir back. Since this is a chore, the Cwd module encapsulates the process in abs_path (alias realpath) and fast_abs_path functions, each of which can be imported into our application by explicitly naming them. Both take a path to a file or directory and return the true absolute path to it, resolving any symbolic links and instances of . or .. as they go:

```
use Cwd qw(abs_path realpath fast_abs_path);

# find the real path of 'filename'
$absdir = abs_path('symboliclink/filename');

# 'realpath' is an alias for 'abs_path'
$absdir = realpath('symboliclink/filename');

# find the real path of our great grand parent directory
$absdir = fast_abs_path('../../..');
```

The cwd function is actually just a wrapper to abs_path with an argument of .. By contrast, fast_abs_path is a wrapper for getcwd that uses chdir to change to the requested directory beforehand and chdir again to restore the current working directory afterward.

In addition to the various cwd functions and the abs_path routines, Cwd supplies one more routine, chdir, that improves the standard built-in chdir by automatically tracking changes in the environment variable $ENV{PWD} in the same manner as some shells do. We can have this chdir override the standard chdir by importing it specifically:

```
# override system 'chdir'
use Cwd qw(chdir);
```

After this, chdir will automatically update $ENV{PWD} each time we use it. The original chdir is still available as CORE::chdir, of course.

Summary

In this chapter, we covered Perl's interaction with the filing system, including the naming of files and directories, testing for the existence of files, using the built-in `stat` and `lstat` functions, and deleting, renaming, copying, moving, comparing, and finding files.

Doing all of this portably can be a challenge, but fortunately Perl helps us out, first by natively understanding Unix-style filenaming conventions on almost any platform, and second by providing the `File::` family of modules for portable file system operations. `File::Spec` and `File::Spec::Functions` are the underlying foundation for these modules, while modules like `File::Basename` and `File::Copy` provide higher-level functionality we can use for portable file system manipulation.

We also looked at Perl's `glob` operator and the underlying `File::Glob::` modules that modern Perls invoke when we use it. We went on to look at the creating and use of temporary files, a special case of filing system interaction that can be very important to get right. Finally, we took a special look at the particular properties and problems of managing directories, which are like files in some ways but quite unlike them in many others.

## CHAPTER 14

Command Line and Shell Interaction

This chapter and the next explore interacting with Perl through the command line. This is a broader subject than it might at first appear, since it covers everything from command-line processing to properties of shells and terminal programming. A desktop icon can be configured to trigger a command too, so even in a graphical world command-line processing can still be relevant. Perl was partly inspired by Unix commands like sed and awk and so inherits a lot of shell-like sensibilities and syntax. Not surprisingly, therefore, Perl turns out to be quite good at command-line processing.

We begin by looking at how we read command-line options into our Perl programs, starting with the special array @ARGV and then the Getopt::Std and Getopt::Long modules. Following that we see how to find and possibly set the invoked program name and look at examining and affecting the environment with the special hash %ENV. Finally, we look at various ways that we can create command shells written in Perl itself, as well as blending features of the underlying shell into Perl.

Parsing Command-Line Arguments

When any Perl program is started, Perl passes any *command-line arguments* specified to the program in the special array @ARGV, which is automatically predefined by Perl to contain the list of arguments before execution starts. Perl does not perform any special processing on passed arguments, nor does it look for special arguments—how we deal with passed arguments is entirely up to us. Of course, Perl scripts can still be started with arguments even when they are being run from other programs, so all this still applies even if our script is not being started interactively.

Command-Line Conventions

There is, of course, more than one syntax for command-line options, depending on the shell and platform in use. Although there are several different conventions, they all work on the idea of *options* (sometimes called *switches*) and values. In the Unix world, an option is an argument that is, traditionally, one character long, prefixed with a minus, potentially accompanied by a following value:

```
> program -a 1 -b -2 -c -d
```

Options and values are distinct because options have a minus prefix, whereas values do not. If an option is followed by another option, it doesn't have a value. We can also have trailing arguments, values that do not belong to an option and have meanings in their own right.

```
> program -a 1 -b -2 -c -d file.txt file2.txt
```

How do we know if file.txt is a value belonging to the -d option or a stand-alone argument? We don't, just by inspection. The documentation and usage information for this program will have to tell us.

In general, the fewer characters we have to type to execute a command, the better. As it happens, the POSIX standard defines a fairly flexible convention for single-letter, single-minus options that allows bundling of valueless options and also permits values to follow options directly (with no space) or after an equals sign:

```
> program -a1 -b=-2 -cd
```

The advantage of eliminating a space as the option/value separator is that we can specify otherwise tricky values like negative numbers without ambiguity. The option `-cd` is a bundle of the options `-c` and `-d`. Because options are always single letters, and neither of these example options takes a value, the application can determine that the option is really a bundle of two.

A more recent convention for processing command-line arguments is provided by so-called GNU long options. In the following example, a double minus is used as the prefix for long option names that may be descriptive words rather than just single letters:

```
> program --option1=1 --option2=-2 --option3 --option4
```

Long names break the single-letter rule for option names and so prevent both bundling and appending a value directly to an option. The advantage is that they are easier to remember and considerably easier to understand. For instance, a long option like `--verbose` is much more comprehensible than `-v`. If we do have so many options that we are running out of letters, a friendly program will provide both, one for clarity and one for speed of typing once the user has learned how to use the command.

In these examples, we used `-` and `--`, but strictly speaking these are a Unix convention. In the Windows world, the original prefix was the forward slash, so we would be typing commands like this:

```
> program /a1 /b=-2 /c /d
```

More modern Windows command-line applications, particularly those inspired by or ported from Unix, understand both `-` and `/`. However, prefixes aside, the principle is just the same. It is important to realize that, unlike wildcards, `-` and `/` are not characters interpreted by the shell (be it a DOS or Unix shell). They are just a convention for the application itself to take note of and handle itself, and as such we are free to handle any kind of prefix or prefixes we like. Adhering to a consistent and recognizable convention is just friendlier for anyone else who wants to use our programs.

Another aspect of Windows shells that can cause problems is that, in general, they do not understand single quotes as a Unix shell would. First this means that whenever we need to include quoted text inside a value, we must use double quotes for both the value and the internal text and make sure to escape internal quotes with backslash characters. Second, characters with meaning to the shell also have to be escaped; we can't rely on single quotes to prevent the shell from expanding values via interpolation as we can in Unix. Perl's own `-e` option, which takes arbitrary Perl code as its value, is particularly vulnerable to issues like this.

Simple option processing is easy to arrange in Perl without additional support just by inspecting the contents of the `@ARGV` array. However, once we start adding concepts like options that may take optional values, options that may be defined many times, or options that only accept numeric values, things become more complex. Fortunately, a lot of the hard work in defining consistent command lines can be done for us by the `Getopt::Std` and `Getopt::Long` modules. Both these modules provide extensive support for command-line argument processing, as well as syntax checking.

The @ARGV Array

The `@ARGV` array contains all the arguments that were passed to our program when it was started. The definition of what defines an "argument" depends not on Perl, but on the shell that was used to start our program. However, in most cases spaces separate arguments from one another (Unix shell programmers may care to look up the `IFS` environment variable in the shell documentation). For example, if we were to run a Perl program called `myscript` like this:

```
> perl myscript -u sventek -p cuckoo
```

this results in an @ARGV array containing the four values -u, sventek, -p, and cuckoo. Unlike the C language, the first argument is not the program name. Instead, Perl places that information in the special variable $0 (or $PROGRAM_NAME with the English module), which is the convention used by Unix shells. Unlike shells, Perl does not put the next argument in $1, and it actually uses $1 and onward for quite a different purpose, as we saw in Chapter 11.

Perl's reason for assigning the program name to $0 and removing it from the argument list is twofold. In part, it is in deference to shell programming, but more significantly it allows us to do clever things with @ARGV that the presence of the program name would make inconvenient. Most notable among these is reading input from files passed in @ARGV automatically using the readline operator. From the shell programmer's perspective, @ARGV is similar to the shell variable $* with the program name removed. To C or C++ programmers, @ARGV is a smarter version of char *argv[ ], where we no longer need a separate int argc to tell us how many arguments the array contains.

To check the number of arguments, we can either use scalar or find the highest element in the array (remember that Perl indexes from zero):

```
scalar(@ARGV);  # number of arguments passed
$#ARGV;         # highest element = no. of arguments -1
```

In the preceding example, we are obviously passing arguments that are key-value pairs, so we would probably want to turn them into a hash. This won't work if an odd number of elements were passed, so we need to check for that before blindly turning @ARGV into a hash. We probably ought to also check that all the keys start with a minus, since that is the convention we are following. The following code handles all these issues:

```perl
#!/usr/bin/perl
# turntohash.pl
use warnings;
use strict;

my %args;

if (scalar(@ARGV)%2) {
    die "Odd number of arguments passed to $0";
} else {
    %args = @ARGV;   # convert to hash
    foreach (keys %args) {
        # check each of the keys
        die "Bad argument '$_' does not start with -" unless /^-/;
    }
}
```

This example has its limitations, however. It doesn't handle multiple instances of the same argument. For example, it overrides earlier definitions with later ones. Additionally, we don't make any attempt to check that the arguments have valid names, though we could easily do that within the loop. However, for simple argument parsing, it does the job without requiring the help of an external module like Getopt::Std.

Passing Arguments to Perl Itself

Since Perl passes everything supplied on the command line to our own programs, we cannot pass arguments to Perl itself when we run a script directly, although the *shebang* line (typically #!/usr/bin/perl) handles this problem for us elegantly, if we are able to use it. Otherwise, there are two possible solutions to this problem. One is to simply start our script via Perl while supplying any arguments we like to Perl:

```
> perl -w -Mstrict -MMyModule myperlscript -u sventek -p cuckoo
```

Note that Perl determines the name of the program to run, `myperlscript`, because it is the first bare argument (that is, first value that does not belong to a preceding option) to appear on the command line. All arguments that appear after it are deemed arguments to the program, not to Perl, and so this command does not do what we want:

```
> perl -w myperlscript -Mstrict -MmyModule # ERROR: -M passed to script, not Perl
```

The only rule here is to ensure that options meant for Perl are specified early enough on the command line.

If the name of the program (in this case, `myperlscript`) happens to resemble a command-line option or an optional value for the preceding option, we can make it explicit by using the special `--` argument:

```
> perl -Mstrict -MMyModule -w -- myperlscript -name sventek -pass cuckoo
```

The `--` argument is a convention, at least in the Unix world, which means that nothing should be processed beyond this point. Perl uses `--` to separate its own arguments from the script name and the script's own arguments. When using the `-s` option (see the next section) to set variables from the command line, `--` should also be used to stop feeding arguments to `-s` and to leave them in `@ARGV`. The program itself is placed after, not before, the `--`.

We can also specify arguments to pass to Perl by setting the environment variable `PERL5OPT`:

```
setenv PERL5OPT "-Mstrict -MPOSIX -w"    # Unix (csh)
export PERL5OPT="-Mstrict -MPOSIX -w"    # Unix (ksh/bash)
PERL5OPT="-Mstrict -MPOSIX -w"; export PERL5OPT   # Unix (older ksh)
set PERL5OPT = -Mstrict -MPOSIX -w   # DOS/Windows
```

Perl sees the value of `PERL5OPT` when it starts, and this is used with every Perl script, removing the need to type it in on a program-by-program basis. See Chapter 1 for more on Perl's environment variables.

Setting Variables from @ARGV

The `-s` option causes Perl to cease scanning the command line for options and to treat all options after it as variables set to the value following the option, or 1 if there is no following value. For example:

```
> perl -s -debug -- myscript.pl
```

This sets the variable `$debug` inside the script `myscript.pl` to the value 1. Alternatively, to set a different debug level, we could use

```
> perl -s -debug = 2 -- myscript.pl
```

The `$debug` variable in this example is a global package variable; we can access it from within the script as `$main::debug`, or declare it with `use vars` or `our` (the preferred way from Perl 5.6 onward). There is no limit to how many variables we may specify in this way.

An interesting, if slightly odd, use of `-s` is in the shebang line of a script:

```
#!/usr/bin/perl -s
...
```

This causes Perl to interpret any command line passed to the script as a series of variables to define, and is potentially useful for debugging applications that otherwise do not take arguments.

Reading Files from @ARGV

One of the most common classes of command-line utilities consists of scripts that process one or more files given as arguments. The Unix commands `cat`, `more`, and `strings` all fall under this banner, as do the DOS utilities `type`, `dir`, and `del`.

Since this is such a common use of command-line arguments, Perl caters for it with a special shortcut when we use the <> operator to read from standard input. Specifically, if we use <>, Perl tries to open each element in @ARGV as a file in turn and returns the lines read. If @ARGV is empty, <> reads from standard input. This allows us to write incredibly terse and concise scripts because we can eliminate the need to open filehandles or check that the arguments are really files; Perl will handle it for us. For example, here is a simple version of the Unix cat or DOS type command implemented in Perl:

```
print while <>;
```

Short, isn't it? We can try out this one-line program on any text file, and it will dutifully print out its contents. It works because <> attempts to read input from the contents of the @ARGV array, taking each entry to be a file name. Before we continue, it is worth comparing the preceding code with this very similar-looking example:

```
print <>;
```

While this produces the same result, it does so by evaluating <> in list context, which has the effect of reading all the lines in all the files into memory first, and then supplying that list of lines to print. As a result, it could consume enormous quantities of memory, depending on the files involved. The first example reads one line at a time only, so it does not have this problem. Returning to the first example, if nothing is contained in @ARGV, then standard input is used instead. Either way, the while loop aliases each line read to $_, which the print prints out:

```
> perl -e "print while <>" file1.txt file2.txt
```

Indeed, this is such a common task that Perl lets us place an implicit while (<>) {...} loop around code with the -n or -p options (other options that work in conjunction with -n and -p are -a, -l, and -o). So we could just have said

```
> perl -ne "print" file1.txt file2.txt
```

Just as with normal file reads, the line count variable, $., also works here, so we can print out a file with line numbers by modifying our program to read

```
#!/usr/bin/perl
# cat.pl
use warnings;
use strict;

print "$. : $_" while <>;
```

Or, as a command-line script:

```
> perl -ne 'print "$.:$_"' file1.txt file2.txt
```

Note the single quotes, which allow us to use double quotes for the interpolated string. In Windows shells, single quotes do not work this way, and so we must use double quotes and escape the inner double quotes:

```
> perl -ne "print \"$.:$_\"" file1.txt file2.txt
```

This version will also work fine in Unix, but involves more punctuation than is really necessary. Another option would be to use the qq quoting operator, of course:

```
> perl -ne "print qq[$.:$_]" file1.txt file2.txt
```

This all very well, but we can't tell where the first file ends and the second begins. The current file being processed is stored in the scalar variable $ARGV, so we can improve our one-line program still further by including the file name too:

```
print "$ARGV:$.:$_" while <>;
```

Note that if we pass more than one file, the script will happily read each of them in turn under the same filehandle. We do not see it directly in the preceding examples, but it is defined automatically by Perl and made available to us, if we need to refer to it, as ARGV. Perl does all the opening and closing of files read in this way behind the scenes, so all the files are treated as being part of the same file access from our point of view. This is why variables like $. do not reset from one file to the next. Depending on what we want to do, this can be an advantage or a problem, but if we want to fix this issue we can do so with the eof function:

```perl
#!/usr/bin/perl
# bettercat.pl
use warnings;
use strict;

while (<>) {
    print "$ARGV:$.:$_";
    close (ARGV) if eof;
}
```

This works by closing the current file (via the automatically defined ARGV) if there is no more data to read in it. Calling eof without a parameter or parentheses applies it to the file last read, which here happens to be the same file pointed to by ARGV. We could also have said eof(ARGV) to produce the same effect, but note that eof() with empty parentheses is quite different from eof with no parentheses—it will only detect the end of all input, or in other words, the end of the last file.

We can manipulate the @ARGV array before using <> to read the file names in it any way we like, for example, to remove non–file-name parameters. Here is a simple string-matching program in the style of the Unix grep command that does just that. The first argument is the pattern to search for. Anything after that is a file to search in, so we just remove the first argument with shift and let <> see the rest:

```perl
#!/usr/bin/perl
# simplegrep1.pl
use warnings;
use strict;

die "Usage: $0 <pattern> <file> [<file> ...]\n" unless scalar(@ARGV)>1;
my $pattern = shift @ARGV;    # get pattern from first argument
while (<>) {
    print "$ARGV:$. $_" if /$pattern/o; #o - compile pattern once only
    close (ARGV) if eof;
}
```

Note that when we come to use this program, * will work fine for Unix shells, since they automatically expand the wildcard and pass an actual list of files to our program. On Windows systems, the standard shell is not so smart and just passes the * as is. If we want to trap these instances, we can check for occurrences of *, ?, and so on and use the glob function (covered last chapter) in conjunction with the File::DosGlob module to make up for the shell's shortcomings.

@ARGV and Standard Input

In the previous example, the script needs two arguments to perform its function, so die is executed if fewer are received. This ensures the user has entered both a pattern and a file name before the program attempts to carry out its job. But what if we want to have the program read from standard input and not a file?

Handily, Perl can be made to open standard input in place of a file with the special file name -. We can insert this into @ARGV before we use <> in the event that only one argument is passed. The result is that the <> operator always gets a file name to read from, but the file name in this case is really the standard input to the program. Here's a modification to the preceding script that handles this possibility:

```
$pattern = shift @ARGV;
die "Usage: $0 <pattern> [<file> ...]\n" unless @ARGV>1;
@ARGV=('-') unless @ARGV;   # not actually necessary - see below
```

When Perl sees the file name - in @ARGV, it interprets it as a request to read from standard input. We can even supply it in the command line, which allows us to use the script in these (admittedly Unix-like) ways:

> **cat filename | simplegrep pattern -**
> **simplegrep pattern - < filename**

In fact, the explicit line to add - to @ARGV in the preceding example is not needed because Perl will do it for us automatically if nothing is present in @ARGV at all. If we print $ARGV, we can see that this is the case. This happens when <> is first used, so as long as @ARGV is empty before we use the readline operator, standard input is taken care of for us, and all we have to do is change the usage line to allow only one argument:

```
#!/usr/bin/perl
# simplegrep2.pl
use warnings;
use strict;

die "Usage: $0 <pattern> [<file> ...]\n" unless scalar(@ARGV);
my $pattern = shift @ARGV;    #get pattern from first argument
while (<>) {
    print "$ARGV:$.$_" if /$pattern/;
    close (ARGV) if eof;
}
```

We do not get this automatic use of - if @ARGV has any values in it. In these cases, we could push - onto the end of the array to have a script automatically switch to reading standard input once it has exhausted the contents of the files named explicitly beforehand.

Simple Command-Line Processing with Getopt::Std

Hand-coded command-line processing is fine when only a few relatively simple command-line arguments are required, but it becomes tricky to handle a larger number of arguments or a more complex syntax. In these cases, it is a far better idea to make use of one of the Getopt modules to simplify the task. Fortunately, the standard Perl library comes with two modules specifically designed to simplify the task of reading and parsing command-line arguments: Getopt::Std and Getopt::Long. While both modules modify @ARGV in the process of extracting options from it, neither module precludes reading files through <> as described earlier. After the command-line options are processed, anything left in (or inserted into) @ARGV can then be used with <> as before.

The Getopt::Std module is a simpler and lighter-weight module that provides support for single-character arguments, with or without values, in compliance with the POSIX standard. It is also in the style of the getopt feature of Unix shells from which it and its larger sibling derive their names. Parsed arguments are defined as global scalar variables based on the argument name or, if supplied, stored in a hash as key-value pairs.

The Getopt::Long module is a much more comprehensive and larger module that provides support for long argument names, stricter argument value checking, abbreviations, aliases, and other various features. It supports both POSIX-style arguments and (as its name suggests) GNU long arguments, but is possibly overkill for simple scripts. Since it provides a superset of the features of Getopt::Std, we will cover the simpler module first.

Getopt::Std provides two functions to define the list of expected arguments. The first is getopt, which allows us to specify a set of options that take parameters. Any other options (as defined by the fact that they start with -) are considered to be Boolean options that enable something and take no argument. The second is the more versatile getopts, which allows us to explicitly define both Boolean and value options and so can emit a warning about anything that does not appear to be either.

Basic Processing with getopt

The function getopt lets us define a set of arguments that all take an optional value. It is somewhat simplistic in its operation and exists as a compatible Perl equivalent of the getopt command implemented by all Unix shells. To use getopt, we supply it with a list of letters that correspond to the options that we wish to process. Any option that is not in the list is assumed to be a Boolean flag. For example:

```
use Getopt::Std;
getopt("atef");
```

This defines the options -a, -t, -e, and -f as arguments that take parameters. Then getopt will accept a value immediately after the argument, or separated by either a space or an equals sign. That is, all of the following are acceptable:

```
-abc
-a = bc
-a bc
```

When a program containing this code is called, the command line is parsed and a global scalar variable of the form $opt_X is set, where X is the name of the argument. If we create a script containing the preceding code and feed it some arguments, we can see this in action:

> **perl myscript -a bc -e fg -k 99**

This creates three global scalar variables, assuming that Perl will allow it. If we have use strict or use strict vars in effect, then we need to predeclare these variables with our (or use vars, prior to Perl 5.6) in order to avoid a run-time error. The equivalent direct assignments would have been

```
$opt_a = "bc";  # option a given value bc
$opt_e = "fg";  # option e given value fg
$opt_k = 1;     # 'k' not in list of arguments, therefore Boolean
```

The moment getopt sees something that is not an option or an option value, it terminates and leaves the remainder of @ARGV untouched. In this example, @ARGV is left holding the trailing argument 99, because it is neither an option nor a value belonging to the preceding valueless -k option.

Creating global scalar variables is inelegant. As an alternative, we can supply getopt with a reference to a hash as its second argument, say %opt. This causes getopt to populate the hash with the parsed values instead. The processed arguments appear as keys and values in %opts. Again, given the same example arguments as before, $opts{'k'} is defined to be 1 and @ARGV ends up containing 99 as the only unprocessed argument. The following script shows this in action and also prints out the parsed arguments and whatever is left in @ARGV afterwards, if anything:

```
#!/usr/bin/perl
# getopt.pl
use strict;
use warnings;

use Getopt::Std;

my %opts;
```

```
getopt("atef",\%opts);

print "Arguments:\n";
foreach (keys %opts) {
    print "\t$_ => $opts{$_}\n";
}

print "ARGV:\n";
foreach (@ARGV) {
    print "\t$_\n";
}
```

Let's execute this script and review the results:

> **perl getopt.pl -a bc -e fg -k 99**

```
Arguments:
    e => fg
    a => bc
    k => 1
ARGV:
    99
```

It is worth noting that if we had put -k 99 as the first argument in the list, the 99 and everything following it, including the -a and -e options and their arguments, would have remained unprocessed in @ARGV.

If we don't specify a value for an argument that takes one, it defaults to 1, so -a and -a1 are effectively equivalent.

Smarter Processing with getopts

The more advanced getopts allows us to define both Boolean and value options. It can also check for invalid options, which immediately makes it more useful than getopt, and permits us to bundle options together. This provides POSIX-compliant command-line processing. It is inspired by and similar to the getopts built-in command of more modern Unix shells like bash.

Like getopt, options are defined by a string containing a list of characters. This time, however, value options are suffixed with a colon, with any letter not so suffixed taken to be Boolean. To define three Boolean flags, a, e, and t, and a value option f, we would use

```
getopts ("aetf:");    # 'aet' Boolean, 'f' value, defines $opt_X scalars

if ($opt_a) {
    ...
}
```

Like getopt, getopts takes an optional second parameter of a hash to hold the parsed values; otherwise, it defines global scalar variables of the form $opt_X.

```
getopts("aetf:",\%opts);    # ditto, puts values in %opts
```

The order of letters is not important, so the following are all equivalent:

```
getopts("f:ate");
getopts("af:et");
getopts("taf:e");
```

Any option that is not specified in the list will cause getopts to emit the warning Unknown option :X, where X is the option in question. Since this is a warning, we can trap it using one of the techniques discussed in Chapter 16, for example, by defining and assigning a subroutine to $SIG{__WARN__} if we want to process the unrecognized option ourselves or make the warning fatal by turning it into a die.

We mentioned bundles a moment ago. *Bundling* is the term used to describe several single-letter arguments combined into a contiguous string, and it is applicable only if all but the last of the concatenated arguments do not take a value. Unlike getopt, getopts permits bundling (but at the cost of not permitting the value to follow immediately after the option). That is, instead of entering

```
> perl myscript -a -t -e
```

we can enter

```
> perl myscript -ate
```

A value option can be bundled, but only if it is the last option in the bundle. It follows from this that we can only permit one value option in any given bundle. With the specification f:ate, we can legally enter

```
> perl myscript -aetf value    # ok
> perl myscript -taef value    # also ok, different order
```

but not

```
> perl myscript -fate value    # value does not follow f argument
```

The -- argument is recognized and processed by Getopt::Std, causing it to cease processing and to leave all remaining arguments in @ARGV. The -- itself is removed. We can pass on the remaining arguments to another program using system, exec, or open, or read them as files using <> if we wish:

```
> perl myscript -aetf value -- these arguments are not processed
```

This leaves @ARGV containing these, arguments, are, not, and processed.

Advanced Command-Line Processing with Getopt::Long

The Getopt::Long module performs the same role as Getopt::Std but with better parsing, error checking, and richer functionality. It handles single-letter options—including bundling—and in addition supports GNU long options.

The key distinguishing feature between the two modules is that Getopt::Long accepts the double-minus–prefixed long-option naming style. To illustrate what we mean, here are two versions of a putative length argument. Only the first can be handled by Getopt::Std, but both can be parsed by Getopt::Long:

```
-l    # traditional short option
--length = value    # more descriptive long option
```

The Getopt::Long module is very flexible and implements a number of optional features such as abbreviation, case sensitivity, and strict- or loose-option matching. In order to control the behavior of the module, we can make use of the Getopt::Long::Configure subroutine.

Basic Processing with GetOptions

The module Getopt::Long defines one function, GetOptions, to parse the contents of @ARGV. In its simplest form, it takes a list of options and scalar references, placing the value of each option into the corresponding reference. Without additional qualification, each option is handled as a Boolean flag and the associated scalar is set to 1 if seen. The following code snippet defines two Boolean options, verbose and background:

```perl
#!/usr/bin/perl
# definebool.pl
use warnings;
use strict;

use Getopt::Long;

my ($verbose, $background);   # parse 'verbose' and 'background' flags
GetOptions (verbose => \$verbose, background => \$background);

print "Verbose messages on \n" if $verbose;
```

After this code is executed, the variables $verbose and $background are either undefined or set to the value 1. We can easily use them in conditions, as illustrated previously.

If the command line was processed successfully, GetOptions returns with a true value; otherwise, it returns undef. We can therefore use it in conditions and terminate the program if all is not well. For example:

```perl
# print some help and exit if options are not valid
usage(), exit unless GetOptions (verbose => \$verbose, background => \$bg);
```

A warning will be raised by GetOptions for anything that it does not understand, so we are saved from the task of having to describe the problem ourselves (although we still have to provide the usage subroutine, presumably to list the valid options and command-line syntax to help the user).

If we do not supply a reference, GetOptions will define a global scalar with the name $opt_<option name> instead, in the same manner to Getopt::Std. This mode of use is generally deprecated on the basis that defining global variables is not good programming practice. GetOptions also accepts a hash reference as its first parameter and will store parsed arguments in it, if present. This is similar to Getopt::Std, but the arguments are inverted compared to getopt or getopts:

```perl
#!/usr/bin/perl
# hashref.pl
use warnings;
use strict;

use Getopt::Long;

my %opts;
GetOptions(\%opts, 'verbose', 'background');
```

One special case bears mentioning here. We might want to handle the case of a single minus (conventionally used to mean "take input from standard input, not a file"), as used by several Unix commands and demonstrated earlier with Getopt::Std. We can do that using an option name of an empty string:

```perl
GetOptions('' => \$read_from_stdio);
```

For the time being we have limited our discussion to scalars, but GetOptions is also capable of handling multiple values in both list and hash forms. We'll see how to do that a little later, after we have dealt with option prefixes and defining option values.

Option Prefixes

With the exception of the single bare minus option, options can be specified with either a single or a double minus, or if we define it first, any prefix we like. The double-minus prefix is treated as a special case compared to all other prefixes, however. Options that have been prefixed with a double minus are treated as case insensitive by default, whereas all other prefixes are case sensitive, though we can alter case sensitivity using Getopts::Long::Config. This means that --o and --O both define the option o, whereas -o and -0 define the options o and 0. The double-minus prefix is also treated differently in option bundling.

The archaic prefix + is also accepted by default but is now deprecated. We can explicitly disallow it, as well as redefining the prefixes we do allow (for instance the backslash), by specifying our own prefix. There are two ways to do this, the first of which is to specify the new prefix as the first argument to GetOptions. However, this is deprecated in modern usage. A better way is to use the Getopt::Long::Configure subroutine. To redefine the prefix this way, we put something like

```
# configure a prefix of '/'
Getopt::Long::Configure ("prefix=/");
```

The second way to specify a prefix is to configure the prefix_pattern option of Getopt::Long, which allows us to specify a range of prefixes. It takes a regular expression as an argument, so we need to express the options we want to allow in terms of a regular expression. To allow single, double, and backslash prefixes, we can use (-|--|\/), as in this example:

```
# configure prefixes of --, - or / (but not +
Getopt::Long::Configure ("prefix_pattern=(--|-|\/)");
```

Note that because prefix_pattern is used in a regular expression, we must use parentheses to encapsulate the options and escape any characters that have special significance for regular expressions.

An alternative to simply disabling a prefix is to handle it ourselves before calling GetOptions. For example, a few utilities use + to explicitly negate an option. We can handle that by replacing + with --no and defining the option to be Boolean:

```
#!/usr/bin/perl
# negate.pl
use warnings;
use strict;

use Getopt::Long;
# translate + negation to Getopt::Long compatible --no negation
foreach (@ARGV) {
    s/^\+/--no/;    # substitute elements of @ARGV directly
}

my %opts;
GetOptions (\%opts, 'verbose', 'background');
```

This requires defining the options we want to be able to negate as negatable Boolean values. We see how to do that, as well as handle other types of option, next.

Defining Option Values

All the options we have seen so far have been Boolean options. By adding extra information to the option name in the form of attributes, we can define (and enforce) different kinds of options, including negatable options, incremental options, and integer value options.

Negatable Boolean Options

A *negatable Boolean option* is one that can be switched off as well as switched on. The Boolean options we have seen so far are one-way—once we have specified what they are, they cannot be undone. That might seem like a strange thing to want to do, but if we are editing a previous command line or calling an external program from within another, it is often more convenient to disable an option explicitly than check through the arguments to see if it has been set to start with. Some features just make more sense enabled by default too, so we might want to define options simply to turn them off.

Negatable Boolean options are defined by suffixing the option name with an exclamation mark. We can use this to create an option that is normally on, but which we can turn off by prefixing the option name with no:

```
$quiet = 1;
GetOptions ("quiet!" => \$quiet);
```

This now allows us to specify -noquiet to switch off quiet mode:

> **perl myscript -noquiet**

And -quiet to turn it on again:

> **perl myscript -noquiet -otheroption -quiet**

Sometimes it is useful to know whether an option variable is not set because that is its default value or because it was explicitly cleared by the option. Since disabling a negatable option sets the corresponding value to zero, setting the original value to the undefined value allows us to check whether the option was specified on the command line or not:

```
#!/usr/bin/perl
# check.pl
use warnings;
use strict;
use Getopt::Long;

my $option = undef;   # make it undef explicitly, just to make it clear
GetOptions ("option!" => \$option);

if (defined $option) {
    # the option was seen on the command line
} else {
    # the option was not specified
}
```

Since undef evaluates as false in a conditional context, we can still determine whether an option has been set in places where we don't care whether the option was specified or not, and still retain that information for use in places where we do. If we are using a hash to define all our options, then there is no need to go this far; we can just test the option name with exists to see if it has been set:

```
#!/usr/bin/perl
# exists.pl
use warnings;
use strict;

use Getopt::Long;
my %opts;
GetOptions (\%opts, 'option!');
if (exists $opts{'option'}) {   # the option was seen on the command line
}
```

Incremental Options

Incremental options increase by one each time they are seen on the command line, starting from the original value. A classic case of such an option is a *verbose* flag, where the level of information a program returns increases according to the level of verbosity set, which is equal to the number of verbose options we use.

In order to prevent Perl returning an undefined value error, the starting value of an incremental option variable should be initialized to a defined value, most probably zero. Here is an example of implementing a verbose option as an incremental option:

```
#!/usr/bin/perl
# increment.pl
use warnings;
use strict;

use Getopt::Long;

my $verbose = 0;   # default verbosity = off
GetOptions ("verbose+" => \$verbose);
```

Now, to set different levels of verbosity, we just specify the option the required number of times:

```
> perl increment.pl -verbose                    # $verbose == 1
> perl increment.pl -verbose -verbose           # $verbose == 2
> perl increment.pl -verbose -verbose -verbose  # $verbose == 3
```

In fact, we can save a lot of typing and just specify -v several times, or even just -vvv, because GetOptions can also handle abbreviations for us, as we will see.

Integer, Floating-Point, and String Options

To define an option that takes a value, we modify the option name by suffixing it either with an equals sign for a mandatory value or with a colon if the value is optional. Following the equals sign or colon we then specify s, i, or f to acquire a string (that is, anything other than a space), an integer, or a floating-point value:

```
GetOptions("mandatorystring=s"  => \$option1);
GetOptions("optionalstring:s"   => \$option2);
GetOptions("mandatoryinteger=i" => \$option3);
GetOptions("optionalfloat:f"    => \$option4);
```

The Getopt::Long module allows options and values to be separated by either a space or an equals sign. In most cases, it does not matter which we use, with the single exception of negative numbers (more about these in a moment):

```
--mandatorystring = text -nextoption ...
--mandatorystring text -nextoption ...
```

The distinction between a mandatory and optional value is, of course, that we can omit the value if it is optional. If we specify an option (say, -mandatorystring) but leave out a mandatory value, GetOptions emits a warning:

```
Option option requires an argument
```

The integer and floating-point variations are similar, but check that the supplied value is an integer or floating-point value. Note that we cannot supply a hexadecimal (or octal or binary) integer. This will cause GetOptions to emit a warning, for example:

```
Value "0xff" invalid for option integer (number expected)
```

Options with optional values will parse the following argument only if it does not look like an option itself. This can be important if we want to accept a negative integer as a value. For example, consider the following option and value, as typed on a command line:

```
> perl myscript -absolutezero -273
```

If we define absolutezero as a mandatory value (say, an integer) with a name of absolutezero=i, then -273 is interpreted as the value of absolutezero by GetOptions. However, if we make the value optional with absolutezero:i, then GetOptions will interpret the - of -273 as an option prefix and assume that absolutezero has no value.

We can solve this problem in three ways. The first, as we have just seen, is to make the value mandatory by specifying the name with an equals sign. The second is to use = as a separator between the option name and the value. For example:

```
> perl myscript -absolutezero=-273
```

The last is simply to disallow the - character as an option prefix by redefining the prefix (or prefixes) that GetOptions will recognize, as we discussed earlier.

Abbreviations

GetOptions automatically performs abbreviation matching on its options. That is, if an option can be abbreviated and still be uniquely identified, we can abbreviate it all the way down to a single character, so long as it is still unique. For example, the option verbose, if defined on its own, can be specified as -verbose, -verbos, -verbo, -verb, -ver, -ve, or -v. If we want to prevent this behavior, we use the Configure subroutine to disable it:

```
Getopt::Long::Configure("no_auto_abbrev");
```

Abbreviation down to single characters is great, but this doesn't work if we have two options that start with the same letter such as

```
GetOptions(verbose => \$verbose, visible => \$visible);
```

To specify either option, we now have to specify at least -ve or -vi respectively. The best way to avoid this problem is simply to give our options more distinct names, but if we can't avoid it, we can optionally define an alias.

Aliases

Aliases take the form of a pipe-separated list of names (|). For example, to provide an internationally friendly color option, we could use

```
GetOptions("color|colour" => \$color);
```

The first name in the list is the *true* name, in the sense that this is the name used to define the $opt_N variable or the key of the options hash (if specified) supplied as the first argument. Any of the names in the list will now set this option.

Similarly, we can use an alias to allow one of two options to be recognized by a single letter if neither can be abbreviated:

```
GetOptions("verbose|v" => \$verbose, "visible" => \$visible);
```

Now we can say -v for verbose and -vi for visible. Note that if we want to combine an alias list with an option value specifier, we just put the specifier on the end of the list—we don't need to apply it to every alias. The following short program implements an incrementable verbose option and a negatable visible option:

```
#!/usr/bin/perl
# visible.pl
use warnings;
use strict;

use Getopt::Long;

my ($verbose, $visible) = (0, -1);
```

```
GetOptions(
    "verbose|v+" => \$verbose,
    "visible!" => \$visible,
);

print "Verbose is $verbose\n";
print "Visible is $visible\n";
```

Interestingly, since visible is negatable as novisible, and it is the only such option, we can abbreviate it to just -nov. Even just -n will work in this case, as there are no other options that begin with n.

Handling Option Values

We have already seen how to read option values into scalar variables, and we mentioned at the time that GetOptions can also handle multiple values as lists and hashes. It does this in a rather cunning way by checking the type of reference that we supply for each option and handling it as appropriate. Take the following short program:

```
#!/usr/bin/perl
# filenames.pl
use strict;
use warnings;

use Getopt::Long;

my @filenames;

GetOptions("file=s" => \@filenames);

print scalar(@filenames)," files entered\n";

foreach (@filenames) {
    print "\t$_\n";
}
```

We can specify the file option as many times as we like, the result of which is a list of file names held in the array @filenames. We don't even have to be consistent about the prefix:

> **perl filename.pl -f foo.txt --f bar.doc -file baz.pl --file clunk.txt**

This doesn't allow us to pass several values to a single option, however. If we wanted to do that, we could use a comma as a separator and then use split ourselves after GetOptions has done its work. If that seems inconvenient, wait until we come to handling values via code references . . .

In a similar manner to handling a list of values by supplying an array reference, we can also handle a list of key-value pairs by supplying a hash reference. When GetOptions sees a hash reference, it automatically looks for an equals sign in the value and tries to split it into a key and value:

```
#!/usr/bin/perl
# config.pl
use warnings;
use strict;

use Getopt::Long;

my %config;

GetOptions("config=s" => \%config);
```

```
print scalar(keys %config)," definitions\n";
foreach (sort keys %config) {
    print "\t$_ => $config{$_}\n";
}
```

Now we can use the `config` option several times to build a hash of configuration variables:

> `perl config.pl --config verbose = 3 --config visible = on`

`GetOptions` also allows a code reference in place of a reference to a scalar, array, or hash. This lets us do in-line processing of values as `GetOptions` processes them. For example, to allow comma-separated values to define a list, we can define a subroutine to split the supplied value and plug it into the target array:

```
#!/usr/bin/perl
# splitval1.pl
use warnings;
use strict;

use Getopt::Long;

our @file;   # same name as option, 'use vars @file' if Perl < 5.6

sub parsevalue {
    # allow symbolic references within this sub only
    no strict 'refs';

    my ($option, $value) = @_;
    push @$option, split(',', $value);
}

GetOptions("file=s" => \&parsevalue);

print scalar(@file)," files entered\n";
foreach (@file) {
    print "\t$_\n";
}
```

In this example, we have defined a subroutine `parsevalue` and given its reference to `GetOptions`. When it encounters a `file` option, it passes the name of the option (`file`) and the value to `parsevalue` as parameters. In turn, `parsevalue` splits the value using a comma as the separator and pushes the result onto a variable with the same name as the option. To achieve that, we have used a symbolic reference for which we have to (within the subroutine only) disable `strict` references. We can now enter file names either one by one with separate `file` options or in one big comma-separated list:

> `perl splitval2.pl --file first --file second,third -f fourth,fifth`

The `parsevalue` subroutine is an example of a generic argument processor. It will work with any option because it uses the name of the option to deduce the array to update. The only catch to this is that we have to define the options as global variables using `our` rather than `my`, since symbolic references do not resolve to lexically scoped variables. To avoid symbolic references entirely, we can put most of the processing work in `parsevalue` but use a temporary anonymous subroutine to assign the result to our variable of choice:

```
#!/usr/bin/perl
# splitval2.pl
use warnings;
use strict;
```

```
use Getopt::Long;

my @file;    # lexical, no longer needs to be the same name

sub parsevalue {
   my ($option, $value) = @_;
   return split(',', $value);
}

GetOptions("file=s" => sub {push @file, parsevalue(@_)});
```

We can invoke this version of the program in exactly the same way as the first one, as shown previously.

Documenting Options

In the event of an error occurring when parsing the command line, neither Getopt::Std nor Getopt::Long support displaying usage information beyond warning of specific problems. It is traditional (and polite) to supply the user with some help about what the problem is, and at the very least a brief description of the command-line syntax—the "usage." For example, for a script that takes two optional flags and a list of file names, we might write

```
unless (GetOptions(\%opts, 'verbose', 'visible')) {
   print "Usage: $0 [-v|-verbose] [-vi|-visible] <filename>\n";
}
```

We can create a short HERE document to describe each option with brief information on its meaning and use, and for a command-line tool of any seriousness maintaining this document is an essential part of its creation. Here is a subroutine that displays a friendlier usage message:

```
use File::Basename qw(basename);

sub usage {
   my $tool=basename($0);

   print STDERR "@_\n" if @_;
   print STDERR <<_USAGE_END;
Usage: $tool -h[elp] | [-v[erbose]] [-vi[sible]] <filename>
   -h  | --help       this text
   -v  | --verbose    enable verbose diagnostics
   -vi | --visible    make actions visible

Type 'perldoc $tool' for more information
_USAGE_END
}
```

This usage subroutine uses File::Basename to print out just the name of our command and not the whole path to it. It also allows us to pass in an additional message, which is printed out first, so we can generate our own usage errors too:

```
usage("You must specify a filename") unless @ARGV;
```

Finally, it reminds the user that more documentation is available in the source that can be read with perldoc (this assumes we have any, of course).

We can also use the Pod::Usage module to place the usage information into the source file itself as POD (literally, "Plain Old Documentation"). This can be effective in some situations, although it is also fairly limited in what it allows us to do. See Chapter 18 for more information on POD and the various Pod modules, including Pod::Usage.

Bundling Options

Bundling, as explained earlier, is the combination of several options into one, a part of the POSIX standard that both Getopt::Std and Getopt::Long support. For example, we can specify -a, -b, -c, and -f options with

> **`perl myscript -abcf filename`**

The module Getopt::Long supports two kinds of bundling, neither of which is enabled by default. To enable the simplest, we call the Configure subroutine:

```perl
#!/usr/bin/perl
# bundle1.pl
use warnings;
use strict;

use Getopt::Long;

Getopt::Long::Configure("bundling");

my ($a, $b, $c, $file);
GetOptions(a => \$a, b => \$b, c => \$c, "file=s" => \$file);
```

This enables traditional single-letter bundling with the single-minus prefix (in fact, any prefix except the double minus). Any sequence of letters prefixed with a single minus is treated as a collection of single-letter options, not a complete option name or abbreviation:

```perl
-abc    # equivalent to -a -b -c, not -abc
```

We can even combine values into the bundle as long as they look like values and not options (this presumes that we defined a, b, and c as value parameters):

```perl
-a1b32c80    # equivalent to -a 1 -b 32 -c 80
```

However, a double minus will never be treated as a bundle, so --abc will always set the option abc.

The second kind of bundling causes GetOptions to try to match single-minus prefixed options to long names first, and only treat them as a bundle if no long option name matches. In this case, -abc would match the abc option just as --abc does. Here is a short example program that uses this form of bundling:

```perl
#!/usr/bin/perl
# bundle2.pl
use warnings;
use strict;

use Getopt::Long;

Getopt::Long::Configure("bundling_override");

my ($a, $b, $c, $abc) = (0,0,0,0); # initialize with zero

GetOptions(a => \$a, b => \$b, c => \$c, "abc:s" => \$abc);

print "a: $a\n";
print "b: $b\n";
print "c: $c\n";
print "abc: $abc\n";
```

Executing this program with various different arguments demonstrates how and when the override takes effect:

```
-a -b -c    # sets 'a', 'b', and 'c'
-ab -c      # sets 'a', 'b', and 'c'
-abc        # matches 'abc', sets 'abc'
-acb        # doesn't match 'abc' - sets 'a' 'b' and 'c'
--a         # matches 'a' - sets 'a'
--ab        # abbreviation - sets 'abc'
-A          # doesn't match anything, warns of unknown 'A'
--A         # case insensitive - sets 'a'
--abcd      # doesn't match anything, warns of unknown 'abcd'
-abcd       # sets 'a', 'b', and 'c', warns of unknown option 'd'
```

As the last example illustrates, the long name abc is only matched with a single-minus prefix if we specify it completely and exactly, so the letters a to d are interpreted as bundled options instead. Bundles also disable abbreviations, as in effect abbreviations are no longer uniquely identifiable. For example, -ab sets a and b rather than being interpreted as an abbreviation for -abc. However, we can still abbreviate --abc as --ab if we use a double-minus prefix, since this disables any attempt at bundling.

An upshot of bundling is that we can no longer derive single-letter abbreviations for long options automatically, so if we want to support both a -v and a --verbose option with the same meaning, we now have to spell them out as alternatives. For legibility within our program, it makes sense to put the long name first, so it will control the name of the variable or hash key generated as a result. For example:

```
Getopt::Long::Configure("bundling");
GetOptions(qw[
    help|h
    debug|d+
    verbose|v+
    visible|vi!
    message|msg|m=s
]);
```

Case Sensitivity

By default, Getopt::Long automatically treats double-minus–prefixed options as case insensitive. This is not the case for any other prefix, most notably the single-minus prefix, which is considered case sensitive. However, we can set the sensitivity of double-minus–prefixed options by configuring ignore_case in our program before we call GetOptions. For example:

```
Getopt::Long::Configure("ignore_case");       # default behavior
Getopt::Long::Configure("no_ignore_case");    # '--Option' case sensitive
```

We can set the sensitivity of all options, including double-minus–prefixed ones, with ignore_case_always:

```
Getopt::Long::Configure("ignore_case_always");
Getopt::Long::Configure("no_ignore_case_always");
```

Clearing either configuration value with no_ also clears the other, so no_ignore_case and no_ignore_case_always are actually the same. However, no_ignore_case_always sounds better if we then specify ignore_case too. For instance, the default configuration is equivalent to

```
Getopt::Long::Configure("no_ignore_case_always", "ignore_case");
```

If we want to reverse the normal state of affairs and make long options case sensitive and short options case insensitive, we could do that with the following two configuration changes:

```
#!/usr/bin/perl
# casesens.pl
use warnings;
use strict;

use Getopt::Long;

my %opts;

Getopt::Long::Configure("ignore_case_always", "no_ignore_case");
GetOptions(\%opts, 'verbose', 'visible', 'background');
```

Of course, the point of long options is that their name is descriptive and unique, so the case should not matter. Therefore, it is doubtful that this configuration is actually all that desirable, even if it is possible.

Handling Unrecognized Option and Value Arguments

When GetOptions encounters an option that it does not recognize, it (usually) issues a warning. However, how it reacts to a value that it does not recognize is another matter. If a value is expected as an optional or mandatory suffix to an option, it is easy to verify that it follows whatever format the option was defined with. But a value that is encountered when no value was expected does not fall under these rules.

In fact, GetOptions has three modes of operation for dealing with unexpected situations such as these.

permute Mode

In permute mode (the default unless POSIXLY_CORRECT has been defined in the environment), unexpected value arguments are simply ignored and left in the @ARGV array. Processing continues past the unknown argument, while further options and values are parsed as normal. At the exit of the subroutine, @ARGV contains all the arguments that were not used as either options or values. permute mode is set explicitly by calling

```
Getopt::Long::Configure('permute');
```

The permute mode gets its name because its effect is equivalent to permuting the command line by moving all the unrecognized value arguments to the end. That is, the following two command lines are equivalent, assuming that none of the options take a value:

```
> perl myscript -a one -b two -c three
> perl myscript -a -b -c one two three
```

Having GetOptions return unrecognized values (if not options) in @ARGV can be useful, for example, in combination with the <> operator, as we discussed earlier in the chapter.

However, in permute mode we can handle these unrecognized arguments ourselves by defining a special subroutine and passing a reference to it to GetOptions. This works in a very similar way to the handling of normal options with code references that we looked at earlier. In deference to the fact that this is in the spirit of the <> operator, the name for the option used to trigger this subroutine is <>. The following script simply builds an array called @oob_values containing the unrecognized values; without the subroutine, the @ARGV array would contain these values instead:

```
#!/usr/bin/perl
# unrecog.pl
use warnings;
use strict;

use Getopt::Long;
```

```
my ($verbose, $size, @oob_values);

sub handle_unknown {
    # push extra values onto out-of-band value list
    push @oob_values, @_;
}

GetOptions(
    "verbose+" => \$verbose,        # verbose option
    "size=i"   => \$size,           # size option
    "<>"       => \&handle_unknown, # unknown values
);

print "Verbose ", $verbose?'on':'off',"\n";
print "Size is ", (defined $size)?$size:'undefined',"\n";
print "Extras: ", join(',', @oob_values),"\n" if @oob_values;
```

Interestingly, handle_unknown is called as each unknown value is encountered, which means that the values of the other option variables may change from one call to the next. It is the current value of these options that we make use of in the processing. For example, the value of $verbose is 0, 1, and then 2 each time handle_unknown is called in the following command line:

> **perl unrecog.pl this -v that -v other**

Setting permute mode automatically disables require_order mode. Setting the environment variable POSIXLY_CORRECT to a true value disables permute and enables require_order (see the upcoming section "POSIX mode").

require_order Mode

In require_order mode, the first encounter with an unknown value argument causes GetOptions to cease processing the rest of @ARGV and return immediately—as if a naked double minus, --, had been encountered. This mode is set explicitly by calling

Getopt::Long::Configure("require_order");

Unlike permute mode, it is not possible to define an unknown argument handler in this mode. Setting require_order mode automatically disables permute mode and is the default if the environment variable POSIXLY_CORRECT is defined.

pass_through Mode

In pass_through mode, unrecognized option arguments are passed through untouched in the same way that unrecognized value arguments are passed. This allows unrecognized options and their values to be passed on as arguments to other programs executed from inside Perl. The pass_through mode is not enabled by default but can be set explicitly by calling

Getopt::Long::Configure("pass_through");

The pass_through mode can be combined with either of the require_order or permute modes. In the case of require_order mode, enabling pass_through mode will cause GetOptions to stop processing immediately, but it will not cause GetOptions to emit a warning and will leave the unrecognized option in @ARGV. In the case of permute mode, all unrecognized options and values are collected and left at the end of @ARGV after GetOptions returns. If a <> subroutine has been defined, both unrecognized option and value arguments are passed to it.

Irrespective of which mode is in use, the bare double minus -- always terminates the processing of @ARGV immediately. The -- itself is removed from @ARGV, but the following arguments are left as is. This applies even if we are using permute mode and have defined a <> subroutine to handle unknown value arguments.

POSIX Mode

The Getopt::Long module was written with the POSIX standard for command-line arguments in mind, which is the origin of the double-minus prefix for long option names, among other things. This module is more flexible than the POSIX standard strictly allows, however, which can be very convenient or a nuisance, depending on our aims. In order to satisfy both camps, the module can be put into a POSIX-compliant mode, which disables all the nonstandard features by defining the environment variable POSIXLY_CORRECT:

```
setenv POSIXLY_CORRECT 1    # Unix (csh)
export POSIXLY_CORRECT=1    # Unix (newer ksh/bash)
POSIXLY_CORRECT=1; export POSIXLY_CORRECT   # Unix (older ksh)
set POSIXLY_CORRECT = 1   # Windows
```

We can also set POSIX mode from within Perl by adding POSIXLY_CORRECT to the %ENV hash. In order for this to work properly, we have to define the variable in a BEGIN block before the use statement, so that the variable is defined before the module is used:

```
BEGIN {
    $ENV{'POSIXLY_CORRECT'} = 1;
}

use Getopt::Long;
```

Enabling POSIX mode has the following effects:

- The archaic + prefix is suppressed. Only - and -- are recognized by default. (The configuration option prefix_pattern is set to (--|-).)

- Abbreviation matching is disabled. (The configuration option auto_abbrev is unset.)

- Non-option arguments, that is, arguments that do not start with an option prefix and are not values of a preceding option, may not be freely mixed with options and their values. Processing terminates on encountering the first non-option argument. (The configuration option require_order is set.)

As the preceding shows, the primary effect of POSIXLY_CORRECT is to alter the default values of several of the module's configuration options. We could, of course, configure them ourselves directly, but defining the environment variable is more convenient and will also keep up to date should the module change in the future. We can always alter the configuration afterwards, say to reenable abbreviations, if we choose.

Generating Help and Version Messages

As a convenience, Getopt::Long also provides two additional subroutines, VersionMessage and HelpMessage. The first generates a simple version message by extracting the script or module version from $VERSION. The second generates basic usage information by extracting and printing the SYNOPSIS section of the embedded POD documentation, if present. For example:

```
use Getopt::Long qw(GetOptions HelpMessage VersionMessage);

my %opts
GetOptions(\%opts,
    help    => sub { HelpMessage() },
    version => sub { VersionMessage(
                        -message => "You are using:",
                        -exitval => 'NOEXIT'
                    ) },
    flag    => \$opts{flag}
);
```

The HelpMessage subroutine uses the pod2usage subroutine from Pod::Usage to do the actual work and will accept a numeric exit status, string message, or a list of named options as arguments that are passed down to that function. Specifically, it understands -output to send output to a given file name or filehandle, -message to define an additional prefixed message, and -exitval to define the exit status. If the exit status is NOEXIT, control is returned to the program.

VersionMessage emulates Pod::Usage in that it will accept a string message, numeric exit status, or a list of key-value pairs, but it does not actually make use of the module to carry out its job. Only the options previously noted are handled. See Chapter 18 for more information on Pod::Usage.

Summary of Configuration Options

We have already mentioned the Configure subroutine in Getopt::Long and described most of its options. Most options are Boolean and can be set by specifying their name to Getopt::Long::Configure, or cleared by prefixing their name with no_. The prefix and prefix_pattern options both take values that are specified with an equals sign. The Configure subroutine will accept any number of options at one time. For example, to enable bundling and to change the allowed prefixes to a single minus or a forward slash, we can use

```
Getopt::Long::Configure("bundling", "prefix_pattern = (-|\/)");
```

In more recent versions of Getopt::Long, since version 2.24, we can also configure Getopt::Long at the time we first use it. The special token :config is used to mark genuine imports from configuration options:

```
use Getopt::Long qw[HelpMessage :config bundling prefix_pattern=(-|\/)];
```

Note that it is also perfectly acceptable to call Configure more than once if need be.

Table 14-1 shows a short summary of each option. Options that have a default value and a POSIX default value alter their default behavior if the environment variable POSIXLY_CORRECT is set.

Table 14-1. *Getopt::Long::Configure Options*

Option Name	Default Values	Action
auto_abbrev	set POSIX: unset	Allow long option names to be abbreviated so long as the abbreviation is unique. Not compatible with single-minus options when bundling is in effect.
bundling	unset	Interpret single-minus option names as bundles of single-character options. Clearing bundling also clears bundling_override.
bundling_override	unset	Interpret single-minus options as long names if possible, or bundles otherwise. Setting or clearing this option also sets or clears bundling.
default	n/a	Reset all options to their default value, as modified by POSIXLY_CORRECT.
getopt_compat	set POSIX: unset	Allow the archaic + as well as - and -- to start options. A shortcut for prefix_pattern.
ignore_case	set	Ignore case of long (double-minus–prefixed) options. Clearing this also clears ignore_case_always.
ignore_case_always	unset	Ignore case of all options, however prefixed. Clearing this also clears ignore_case; however, ignore_case may subsequently be set.
pass_through	unset	Allow unknown options to pass through as well as values, rather than raise a warning. Used with permute or require_order.

Option Name	Default Values	Action
permute	set POSIX: unset	Allow unknown values to pass through. Exclusive with require_order.
prefix	n/a	Set the prefix string for options, for example, - or /. Only one prefix can be specified. To set alternative prefixes, use prefix_pattern.
prefix_pattern	(-|--|\+) POSIX: (-|--)	Set the list of prefix strings for options. This is a regular expression pattern, therefore special characters like + must be escaped and the whole list enclosed in parentheses.
require_order	unset POSIX: set	Terminate processing on first unrecognized value (or option if pass_through set). Exclusive with permute.

Getting and Setting the Program Name

The name of the script for which Perl was invoked is given by the special variable $0, or $PROGRAM_NAME with the English module loaded. This is the full pathname to the script, so it is frequently shortened to just the basename (sometimes called leafname) with File::Basename:

```
use File::Basename qw(basename);
my $program_name=basename $0;
```

We can assign to $0 to change the name of the program within Perl. On some, but not all, platforms, this will also change the external name of the program, for example, as listed by the ps command on Unix:

```
$0="aliasedname.pl"; #(try to) change our name
```

Perl knows some tricks for several platforms to enable the external visibility of assignment to $0 to work, even in circumstances where it would not normally work. However, as this varies from one platform to another, the only way to know for certain if a given platform will support it is to try it.

In practice, it is usually possible to find the original name from the operating system, so this is a poor technique for disguising the origins of a program. It is more suitable for providing status information after the program name.

Reading from the Environment

Command-line arguments are maybe the most obvious means of passing information into a command-line Perl program, but the environment is equally important.

The special variable %ENV is one of the main sources of information available to a Perl program when it starts. This hash, defined by Perl automatically, contains key-value pairs of the script's environment. This is, for example, the primary mechanism for transmitting details of a client request from a web server to a CGI script run by that server.

Even in programs designed to be executed from a shell, the environment is an excellent way to configure less commonly used features to avoid creating excessive numbers of options and values. For instance, rather than creating a --debug option, we could instead look for an environment variable ENABLE_DEBUG to enable the same feature. Care should be taken over choosing the names of these variables, to minimize the possibility of conflicts with other programs.

We can dump out the contents of Perl's environment with a short script or directly on the command line:

```
> perl -we 'foreach (sort keys %ENV) { print "$_ => $ENV{$_}\n"}'
```

In an xterm window running on a Linux X Window System desktop, this produces something like

```
DISPLAY => :0.0
ENV => /home/gurgeh/.bashrc
HISTFILESIZE => 1000
HOME => /home/gurgeh
HOSTDISPLAY => localhost.localdomain:0.0
HOSTNAME => localhost.localdomain
HOSTTYPE => i386
LOGNAME => gurgeh
MAIL => /var/spool/mail/gurgeh
OSTYPE => Linux
PATH => /usr/local/bin:/bin:/usr/bin:/usr/X11R6/bin:.
SHELL => /bin/bash
SHLVL => 6
TERM => xterm
TZ => Ikroh/Chiark_Orbital
USER => gurgeh
WINDOWID => 62914563
```

In a Windows DOS or NT shell, we would instead type (because Windows does not understand single quotes)

```
> perl -e "foreach (sort keys %ENV) { print qq($_ => $ENV{$_}\n); }"
```

This would produce something like the following:

```
ALLUSERSPROFILE => C:\Documents and Settings\All Users
APPDATA => C:\Documents and Settings\Ken Wronkiewicz\Application Data
CLASSPATH => C:\WINNT\System32\QTJava.zip
COMMONPROGRAMFILES => C:\Program Files\Common Files
COMPUTERNAME => WIREMONSTER2
COMSPEC => C:\WINNT\system32\cmd.exe
DIRCMD => /a
HOMEDRIVE => C:
HOMEPATH => \
INCLUDE => C:\Program Files\Microsoft Visual Studio\VC98\atl\include;C:\Program
Files\Microsoft Visual Studio\VC98\mfc\include;C:\Program Files\
Microsoft Visual Studio\VC98\include
LIB => C:\Program Files\Microsoft Visual Studio\VC98\mfc\lib;C:\Program Files\
Microsoft Visual Studio\VC98\lib
LOGONSERVER => \\WIREMONSTER2
MSDEVDIR => C:\Program Files\Microsoft Visual Studio\Common\MSDev98
NUMBER_OF_PROCESSORS => 1
OS => Windows_NT
OS2LIBPATH => C:\WINNT\system32\os2\dll;
...
```

The exact contents of %ENV can vary wildly depending on the underlying platform, the operating system, and the chosen shell and user preferences. However, we can usually expect $ENV{PATH} to be defined, as well as (on a Unix system at least) HOME, USER, TERM, SHELL, and OSTYPE (though the latter is often better deduced by looking at the special variable $^O or $OSNAME with use English). Keep in mind when using environment variables that no environment variable is guaranteed to exist in every platform, and that the same concept is often embodied in different variables from one platform to another.

Configuring Programs via %ENV

One major reason for examining %ENV is to allow users to create local definitions for our own environment variables. This provides a simple and easy way to configure a script without having to go to the trouble of looking for and reading a configuration file. This sort of configuration is common on Unix systems. For example, to provide a program with a default location for locating scripts but allow that default to be overridden if the environment variable MY_SCRIPTDIR is set, we might write

```
$default_scriptdir = "/usr/local/myapp/scripts";
$scriptdir = $ENV{MY_SCRIPTDIR}?$ENV{MY_SCRIPTDIR}:$default_scriptdir;
```

More creatively, we can scan for any environment variable with a specific prefix, say MY_, and create a configuration hash based on it:

```
foreach (keys %ENV) {
    # regular expressions are covered in Chapter 11
    /^MY_(.*)/ and $conf{$1} = $ENV{$_};
}
```

This is an ideal mechanism for establishing defaults, too, if we iterate over a list of keys in a default hash:

```
%defaults = {
    SCRIPTDIR => '/usr/local/myapp/scripts',
    # other defaults...
}

foreach (keys %defaults) {
    $conf{$1} = (defined $ENV{"MY_$1"})?$ENV{"MY_$1"}:$defaults{$1};
}
```

We can modify, add, or delete entries in %ENV just as we can with any other hash. %ENV is not a copy of the script's environment; it actually is the script's environment. This means that any changes we make to %ENV change the environment for any child processes that are started after the change, for example, with fork. It is not possible to change the environment of the parent, and therefore Perl scripts cannot return information back to the parent via the environment. (Even though Windows platforms emulate fork through threads, this behavior is maintained for consistency.)

Handling Tainted Input from %ENV

Taint mode is a security feature that marks data retrieved from an external source as potentially dangerous. If tainted data is passed in an unsafe operation, which primarily means any attempt to run or communicate with an external process or file, Perl will raise a fatal security error. The main use of tainting is in CGI and other server-side applications that may be executed by unknown and unauthenticated third parties. We cover it here because one of the primary sources of input for CGI scripts is the environment, as we noted earlier.

Taint mode is enabled with the -T option, and is automatically switched on if the real and effective user IDs are different, which is typical on Unix-based web servers. The concept of real and effective user IDs doesn't apply to non-Unix platforms, so there the -T option needs to be supplied or specified in Perl's startup configuration (via PERL5OPT, for example).

All the values in the %ENV hash fall into the category of insecure input, so attempting to use them in a potentially insecure operation will cause a fatal error. To prevent this, we must either avoid using %ENV, place operations into the safe block, or untaint the values explicitly. Regular expressions can be used to untaint data, though this should be used with extreme caution. To untaint DOCUMENT_ROOT, for instance, a variable we might expect to trust since it is set by the web server and should not change, we could use

```
$ENV{DOCUMENT_ROOT} =~ /(.*)/ and $docroot = $1;
```

Of course, sometimes we might want to avoid untainting data simply because we used a regular expression on it. To avoid this, we can use the re pragmatic module described in the discussion on regular expressions in Chapter 11. More on taint mode and CGI programming can be found in Chapters 15 and 23.

The Env.pm Module

Perl provides a module, Env.pm, that simplifies the handling of the %ENV hash by allowing us to import environment variables into our program as scalar or array variables. In its simplest form of usage, we can use it to pull in several environment variables as scalars:

```
# import environment variables via Env.pm
use Env qw(PATH HOME TERM);

# environment variables now available as scalars:
print $PATH, $HOME, $TERM;
```

Note that it does not matter if the environment variable exists yet. As soon as it is defined, either by the imported name or the %ENV hash, the new value will be reflected in both places.

We can also read and write environment variables in arrays if we prefix the variable name with @:

```
use Env qw(@PATH);          # access path via array
$first_dir = $PATH[0];      # find name of first directory in path
unshift @PATH, $scriptdir;  # add a new directory to start of path
```

The separator used by the Env module for splitting environment variables is the value of $Config::Config{path_sep}, which by default is set to a colon. This is the standard separator for most multiple-value environment variables (and path information variables in particular) on Unix. We can change it to handle other kinds of variables, for example, comma-separated values:

```
use Env qw(@PATH);
$Config::Config {'path_sep'} = ',';
use Env qw(@MY_CSV_VAR);
```

Note, however, that all variables are stored as scalar strings in the %ENV hash underneath whatever labels we give them. This means that any alteration to an array variable causes the module to rebuild and then resplit the variable to regenerate the array. That will cause problems if we changed the separator in the meantime.

Interestingly, we can access the same variable in both scalar and array form by importing both names:

```
#!/usr/bin/perl
# config.pl
use warnings;
use strict;

use Env qw($PATH @PATH);
```

```
$sep = $Config::Config{'path_sep'};
# add current directory if not already present
unless ($PATH =~ /(^|$sep)\.($sep|$)/) {
    push @PATH, '.';
}
```

Since both variables access the same underlying environment variable, a change to either (or the underlying $ENV{PATH}) will change the other too.

■**Tip** For the curious, the Env module is a good example of a simple tied object class. Each imported variable is actually an object in disguise that simply accesses the environment variable of the same name. Ties and tied objects are covered in more detail in Chapter 19.

Writing Shells in Perl

Shells are a particular subclass of interactive program that are worth a little special attention. To most people, a shell is what they type commands into. More accurately, a shell is a command interpreter that provides an interface between the user, the operating system, and its services. On a Unix machine, there are many shells to choose from, including the Bourne shell, sh; C shell, csh; Korn shell, ksh; and the Bourne Again shell, bash. Windows has several shells available, the standard one being COMMAND.COM. Windows NT/2000/XP has a (slightly, some would say) improved shell, cmd.exe.

Perl was partly created as a better solution to the various different shells and scripts that existed on Unix systems beforehand. Its major advantage is that, unlike all the shells mentioned previously, scripts written in Perl do not depend on any given Unix or Windows shell being available (though, of course, Perl itself needs to be available).

Perl does not have a shell mode as such, but it is very easy to create one by running Perl with suitable arguments. Perl also comes with a couple of modules that close the gap between Perl and the shell it is running in. The module Shell.pm allows unrecognized functions in Perl code to be evaluated by the underlying shell, effectively integrating the shell's own abilities into Perl. This is interesting, although potentially dangerous too, and manifestly not portable. Conversely, ExtUtils::Command goes the other way, providing emulations of several important Unix commands that will function on Windows platforms, allowing us to use commands like rm, mv, cp, and chmod on non-Unix platforms.

If we simply want a shell to try out Perl commands, then we can use the Perl debugger as a passable shell by typing

> `perl -dwe 1`

This debugs the program 1, with warnings enabled. In the process, it provides a prompt at which we can define subroutines and evaluate expressions. For more advanced uses, there are several shell programs and modules available from CPAN and elsewhere, two of the most popular being perlsh, available from http://www.bgw.org/projects/perlsh/, and psh, available from http://www.focusresearch.com/gregor/psh/ and also from CPAN in the Psh package.

Simple Perl Shells

Creating a Perl shell is actually remarkably easy, and this shell can be a useful tool to wrap modules of our own devising to provide a flexible interface to their API. If we don't require any particular degree of sophistication, we can generally create a shell script that runs Perl as a shell in a single line. Here is an example that will work on Unix or Windows, and which uses the -n switch to put an implicit while (<>) {...} around the code we specify with -e:

> `perl -nwe "eval $_; print q|perl> |"`

To explain this in more detail, the e switch specifies a line of code for Perl to execute, in this case an eval followed by a prompt. The w enables warnings, which is always a good idea, and the n puts the code specified by e into a permanent loop. When run, this takes Perl code typed in by the user and evaluates it—a very simple shell. The only catch to this is that it doesn't display the prompt the first time around. Here's a slightly improved shell that fixes that problem and also adds strict syntax checking for good measure:

```
> perl -Mstrict -we "while(1) { print q|perl> |; eval <> }"
```

This is very similar to the previous example, except that we have used an explicit loop, moving the implicit <> inside the loop as an explicit eval after the prompt. Alternatively, we can use a BEGIN block, as this example shows:

```
> perl -nwe 'BEGIN { print "perl> " } eval $_; print "perl> "';
```

On Windows, we must escape the dollar sign:

```
> perl -nwe "BEGIN { print q|perl> | } eval \$_; print q|perl> |";
```

The implementations for Unix and Windows are slightly different as Unix systems exchange the single and double quotes and remove the backslash from $_, which is protected only because the outer quotes are doubled. While this shell is not very capable or useful, it can provide the foundation for many more focused shell applications. To get a usable generic shell, though, we need to do some more coding.

Writing a More Useful Shell

Here is a simple Perl script that implements a shell using the ReadLine module (for more on this module see the next chapter). This enables us to take advantage of the readline library on our system to provide features such as a history list or in-line editing to make the user's life easier. If the library isn't present, the script will still work, it just won't be as powerful.

```perl
#!/usr/bin/perl
# shell1.pl
use warnings;
use strict;

# create readline object
use Term::ReadLine;
my $term = new Term::ReadLine "Perl Shell";

# switch off any highlighting
$term->ornaments(0);

# enable autoflush (output appears instantly)
$|=1;

# evaluate entered expressions until 'quit'
do {
    my $input = $term->readline("perl> ");
    print("\n"),last if $input eq "quit";
    eval $input;
} while (1);
```

As this script shows, it is possible to create a reasonably capable Perl shell with only a few lines of Perl code. The biggest drawback with this shell application is that it evaluates each line as we enter it, so it's no good for multiline statements like foreach loops (or indeed the preceding do...while loop) unless we concatenate the statement onto one line.

We can fix this in two ways. First, we can teach the shell to understand the backslash character, \,
for line continuation, so it is possible for us to type something like this and get the expected output:

> **perl shell1.pl**

```
perl> print "Hello\
perl> World\n"
```

Second, we can look for curly braces on the start and end of lines and keep a count of the
number of open braces that haven't been close yet, so we can legitimately type the following:

> **perl shell1.pl**

and get this output:

```
perl> for (1..10) {
perl> print "$_";
perl> }
```

Here is an improved version of our first shell that handles both these cases and makes a few
other improvements on the way:

```perl
#!/usr/bin/perl
# shell2.pl
use warnings;
use strict;

# create readline object
use Term::ReadLine;

my $term = new Term::ReadLine "Perl Shell";

# switch off any highlighting
$term->ornaments(0);

# Enable autoflush (output appears instantly)
$|=1;

# Declare some variables
my $this;    # current line
my $input;   # accumulated input
my $bracing = 0;    # number of unclosed open braces

# Evaluate entered expressions until 'quit'
while (($this = $term->readline("perl> ")) ne "quit") {
    if ($this =~ s/\\$//) {
        # if the line ends with '\', collect more lines
        $input = $this;
        # keep track of the braces even so
        $bracing += ($this =~ /{\s*$/);
        $bracing -= ($this =~ /^\s*}/);
        # get the next line and redo
        $this = $term->readline(" > ");
        redo;
    } else {
```

```
            # doesn't end with '\'
            $input.= $this;
            # keep track of the braces
            $bracing += ($this =~ /{\s*$/);
            $bracing -= ($this =~ /^\s*}/);
            # if braces outstanding, collect more lines
            if ($bracing) {
                $this = $term->readline("{$bracing} > ");
                redo;
            }
    }

    if ($input =~ s/^!\s*//) {
        # input beginning with '!' is a system command
        system $input;
    } elsif ($input =~ s/^\?\s*//) {
        # input beginning with `?` is a 'perldoc' query
        if ($input =~ /^([A-Z]|perl)/) {
            # straight perldoc if it's capitalized or starts 'perl'
            system "perldoc",$input;
        } else {
            # otherwise assume it's a function
            system "perldoc","-f",$input;
        }
    } else {
        # Evaluate it as Perl code
        eval $input;
        warn($@),undef $@ if $@;
    }

    $input="";
}
```

This script contains a few points of interest. First, it uses the redo command to restart the loop without executing the condition in the while loop. This is how the input line is grown without being overridden at the start of the loop. The backslash continuation (the first clause in the upper if statement) is basically similar to the example we saw back when we discussed loops in Chapter 6. The other clause handles lines that don't end with a backslash and gets another line if there are still braces outstanding. For the sake of simplicity, we don't check for multiple opening or closing braces on the same line, since it is actually quite tricky to handle all possible cases.

Whenever the code cannot immediately be executed, be it because a backslash was used or braces are still outstanding, the shell needs to read another line. It does this by calling readline again, this time with a modified prompt to indicate that the next line is extending previously entered input. In the case of a backslash, we change the prompt from perl> to just > so the user is clued in to the change in behavior. In the case of braces, we indicate the level of nesting by putting the value of $bracing into the prompt. In both cases, we read another line and concatenate it to the input previously read. We then restart the loop with redo, skipping the readline in the while condition.

If there are no outstanding braces or backlashes, we go to the evaluation part of the loop. Here we have embellished things slightly, just to illustrate how features can be added. The second if statement checks the input for a leading ! or ?. Since the conditions are substitution statements that substitute the ! or ? for nothing, they are stripped in the process of matching. In the case of !, the shell passes the rest of the input to the real shell to execute—this allows us to "break out" of our Perl shell if we want to execute a shell command. In the case of ?, the shell passes the rest of the input to perldoc and provides us with a basic help system. To keep the command flexible but simple, we check the start of the input following the ? and make a guess as to whether it is a manual page (beginning with perl), a module (which almost always begin with a capital letter, with the exception of pragmatic modules like strict and vars), or a function name (none of the above). This isn't perfect, partly for the reasons just given, but it's not bad for a start.

With this shell, we can enter loops and if statements, and even define subroutines line by line and still have the shell understand them:

```
perl> sub hello {
{1} > print "Hello World\n"
{1} > }
perl>
perl> hello()
```

Hello World

```
perl>
```

We can also read in modules with use and then make use of them, for example:

```
perl> use Term::ReadKey
perl> ReadMode 4
perl> use CGI qw(:standard)
perl> use vars '$cgi';
perl> $cgi = new CGI
perl> ...
```

The one thing we have to watch out for is that my and our declarations will not last past the current statement, because they are lexically scoped and exist only inside the scope of the eval. To create variables that last from one command to the next, we need to declare them with use vars. This is probably a candidate for a special command if we decided to extend the shell.

Integrating the Shell into Perl

The standard Perl library comes with a module called Shell.pm, which provides the ability for unrecognized function names to be passed to the underlying shell for execution rather than simply raising an error. (Whether or not this is a good idea is highly debatable.)

Here is an example script for a shell that integrates the Unix ls, mv, and rm commands into Perl. It scans the directory supplied as its argument (or the current directory otherwise) and lowercases the file names of all files and directories it finds, deleting any files that end with a tilde. To find the files, it uses ls (the argument -1 makes sure that ls returns a simple list of files, one per line—usually it will do this anyway when talking to a program but it never hurts to be explicit); to rename them it uses mv, and to delete them it uses rm:

```
#!/usr/bin/perl
# xshell1.pl
use warnings;
use strict;

use Shell;

my $dir = (@ARGV)?$ARGV[0]:".";
my @files = split "\n",ls(-1);

foreach (@files) {
    print "File $_ ";
```

```
    if (/~$/) {
        # delete files ending in ~
        rm($_);
        print "deleted";
    } else {
        # rename to lowercase
        my $newname = lc $_;
        if ($newname ne $_) {
            mv($_,lc $_);
            print "renamed $newname";
        } else {
            print "ok";
        }
    }
    print "\n";
}
```

When pointed at a directory containing the files File1, FILE2, File3~, fIlE4, and FIle5~, this script, when run, looks like this:

> **perl xshell1.pl**

```
File FIle5~ deleted
File File1 mv: 'File1' and 'file1' are the same file
renamed file1
File File3~ deleted
File fIlE4 mv: 'fIlE4' and 'file4' are the same file
renamed file4
File file2 ok
File test.pl ok
```

The Shell module works regardless of what the underlying shell actually is, though, of course, the underlying shell may support entirely different commands. Consequently, this is not a very portable solution.

Unrestrained access to the underlying shell is also potentially dangerous—we could end up executing all kinds of dangerous commands without meaning to as a result of even a minor bug in our code. A better solution is to restrict the shell commands to those we actually want to allow. We can do that by passing the Shell module a list of the commands we want to access:

```
use Shell qw(ls mv rm);
```

Now we can make use of the ls, mv, and rm commands, but nothing else will be interpreted as a shell command. As a bonus, we can omit the parentheses and use the commands as functions rather than subroutines, because importing their names predeclares them:

```
#!/usr/bin/perl
# xshell2.pl
use warnings;
use strict;

use Shell qw(ls mv rm);

my $dir = (@ARGV)?$ARGV[0]:".";
my @files = split "\n",ls -1;
```

```
foreach (@files) {
    print "File $_ ";
    if (/~$/) {
        # delete files ending in ~
        rm $_;
        print "deleted";
    } else {
        # rename to lowercase
        my $newname = lc $_;
        if ($newname ne $_) {
            mv $_,lc($_);
            print "renamed $newname";
        } else {
            print "ok";
        }
    }
    print "\n";
}
```

If we set the variable $Shell::capture_stderr, we can also capture the standard error of the shell command and retrieve it along with the normal output of the command (if any). This isn't entirely portable, however, though it should work in most shells. For example, to list a directory that may not exist:

```
use Shell qw(ls);
$Shell::capture_stderr = 1;
ls $ARGV[0];
```

The catch with this is that should the command generate error output as well as normal output, both will be mixed together. Consequently, this approach is better left to situations where the command either generates normal output or an error message, where the two can be easily distinguished.

Emulating Unix Commands on Windows

Another module related to shell commands that comes as standard with Perl is the ExtUtils::Command module. This provides something of the opposite role to Shell, implementing Unix commands in Perl such that they can be executed on Windows systems. Table 14-2 presents a list of the implemented commands; the ellipsis (...) indicates that more than one parameter can be passed.

Table 14-2. *ExtUtils::Command Commands*

Name	Parameters	Action
cat	file...	Type out the contents of the file(s).
mv	file... newfile|directory	Rename file(s) to newfile or directory.
cp	file... newfile|directory	Copy file(s) to newfile or directory.
touch	file...	Update modification time of the file(s).
rm_f	file...	Delete the file(s).
rm_rf	(file|directory)...	Recursively delete files/directories.
mkpath	directorypath...	Create each chain of directories passed.
eqtime	srcfile dstfile	Give dstfile the same times as srcfile.
chmod	mode file...	Change the permissions on the file(s).
test_f	file	Test that file is a file (not a link/directory).

Here's one example of how these commands can be used:

```
> perl -MExtUtils::Command -e mv filename newfilename
```

Just because the commands implemented by ExtUtils::Command are designed to work directly from the command line does not mean that we cannot use them as portable file manipulation tools within our own programs too. However, ExtUtils::Command was not written with programmatic use in mind, so all the subroutines in it use @ARGV as the source for their arguments, requiring us to wrap them with local subroutines that convert arguments passed in @_ to a local copy of the @ARGV array.

As an example, here is the script we introduced earlier using the Shell module, rewritten to be portable by using ExtUtils::Command instead:

```perl
#!/usr/bin/perl
# xshell3.pl
use warnings;
use strict;

use ExtUtils::Command ();   # empty list - no import

# programmatic wrappers for ExtUtils::Command subroutines
sub mv   { local @ARGV = @_;ExtUtils::Command::mv();   }
sub cp   { local @ARGV = @_;ExtUtils::Command::cp();   }
sub rm_f { local @ARGV = @_;ExtUtils::Command::rm_f(); }

my $dir = (@ARGV)?$ARGV[0]:".";
my @files = <$dir/*>;

foreach (@files) {
    print "File $_ ";
    if (/~$/) {
        # delete files ending in ~
        rm_f $_;
        print "deleted";
    } else {
        # rename to lowercase
        my $newname = lc $_;
        if ($newname ne $_) {
            mv $_,lc($_);
            print "renamed $newname";
        } else {
            print "ok";
        }
    }
    print "\n";
}
```

A key reason for the existence of this module is to allow Perl modules to compile and build themselves without having to cater for different platforms in their Makefiles. The ExtUtils::Command module makes heavy use of modules in the File:: hierarchy to attempt cross-platform portability.

Summary

In this chapter, we looked at getting information into programs through the command line and the environment. We first looked at the special array @ARGV: how to use it to pass arguments to Perl, how to set variables from it, and how it handles files. We then examined two modules that we can use for processing command-line options. We looked first at the simpler Getopt::Std and its two functions getopt and getopts, before examining in more detail the Getopt::Long module. We saw, among other things, how to define option values, use abbreviations and aliases, document and bundle options, and handle unrecognized options and values.

We followed this up with a look at the special array %ENV and examined how to use it to read values from the environment. We can also change the contents of %ENV to alter the environment seen by any external programs that we invoke from within our Perl code. We can also use the Env module to wrap %ENV in a more convenient interface.

In the last part of the chapter, we examined many aspects of using shells with Perl. We saw how to write our own simple Perl shells, how to invoke the Perl debugger as a quick-and-dirty shell with no additional programming effort, and how to integrate shell commands directly into Perl using the Shell module. Finally, we covered the ExtUtils::Command module, which allows us to implement Unix commands such that they can be executed on Windows.

## CHAPTER 15

Terminal Input and Output

Once upon a time, a *terminal* was a beige-colored box with a monochrome screen and a keyboard. In those days, computer rooms were populated with mainframes capable of supporting many simultaneous user sessions, and so, in order to allow simultaneous users, many terminals could be wired up to the computer, each with its own screen and keyboard. In order to save the computer from having to worry about every little detail of user input, such as scrolling the screen or dealing with the effect of a delete, terminals became progressively smarter, handling most of the minutiae of user input themselves and only sending the user's input to the computer when they hit the Return key. This meant the mainframe itself only had to take note of a user when they actually finished typing a command, rather than for each and every key press.

Terminals quickly became smarter, gaining abilities like being able to reposition the cursor, clear selected parts of the screen, scroll both down and up, and support colors. The object of all this was to relieve the computer of the work of dealing with the screen—instead of moving lines on the display, the computer could just tell the terminal to "insert a line here." Terminal commands took the form of *escape sequences*, terse sequences of characters precede by an escape.

In the era of the graphical user interface this might all seem entirely historical, but not so. Terminals are inherently bound up with the concept of interactive character input and output. Anywhere that we use a character-based interface, from a Unix xterm to a DOS shell, to the initial dialog on a serial connection to establish a PPP network connection, we are actually working through a virtual terminal that emulates the features of a real hardware terminal. This is why we can enter text and delete it at a command-line prompt without having to actually program code to handle the Delete key—the terminal emulation underlying our shell or application deals with it automatically. Terminal IO programming is a particular subset of general IO programming that is specifically directed towards the needs and issues of communicating through a terminal—that is, reading input from a keyboard and writing output to a screen, whatever that keyboard and screen actually turn out to be.

Determining Whether a Script Is Interactive

Programs fall into two broad categories—those that interact with an actual user, possibly through a terminal, and those that merely carry on relations with other programs and don't require a terminal. Since we often use the same program in both capacities, it is useful to be able to tell, from within the program, how it is being used.

Fortunately, Perl has a function designed precisely for this purpose, -t. This is one of the -X unary operators that variously test file names and filehandles for properties such as being a directory, executable, or writable by us, and so on. -t tests filehandles to see if they are connected to a terminal or not. So by testing STDIN with -t, we can check whether we are getting input from a terminal, and therefore (presumably) a user, or whether our input is coming from a nonterminal device, which most likely means from another program:

```
$interactive = -t STDIN;
```

Of course, just because standard input is coming from a terminal does not necessarily mean that standard output is going to one. So, if we want to prompt the user when our program is being used interactively, both STDIN and STDOUT should be checked:

```
#!/usr/bin/perl
use strict;
use warnings;

my $is_interactive=-t STDIN && -t STDOUT;

print "We are ",($is_interactive?"interactive"
                 :"not interactive"),"\n";
```

This short program sets a global variable, $is_interactive, to record whether the input and output of the program is attached to an interactive session. If it is, it will print "We are interactive", or "We are not interactive" otherwise. We can test it in this latter mode by running it through this short test script:

```
#!/usr/bin/perl
# testinteractive.pl
use strict;
use warnings;

# interactive - passes STDOUT
system "./checkinteractive.pl";

# not interactve -passes end of pipe
open PIPE,"./checkinteractive.pl |";
print <PIPE>;
close PIPE;
```

As this example illustrates, invoking a program with system does not put it into a noninteractive state because the invoked program is passed the current input and output (and error) filehandles that are active in the invoking program itself—in the first case the output handle seen by checkinteractive.pl is the STDOUT of testinteractive.pl. Opening a program through a piped open is a different matter altogether. The PIPE filehandle is not associated with a terminal, so when we run this script, we see "We are interactive" followed by "We are not interactive."

Reading from the Keyboard

Simple line-based input can be achieved with the <> or readline operator. The standard Perl library also provides enhanced support for reading complete lines with Term::ReadLine, which attempts to use a built-in readline library if one is present, and which supports the idea of command history. However, this limits us to complete lines and requires waiting for the user to type something, since the default behavior of terminals is to wait until Return has been pressed before bothering us with whatever was typed.

If we want to be more responsive, we use the extension module Term::ReadKey. This module handles nonblocking reads, timeouts, allows character to be typed without echoing them back to the screen, and several other useful features besides. Term::Complete is also at our disposal, a module that implements word completion. We'll be taking a look at both of these in due course.

Before embarking on a discussion of Term::ReadKey, it is worth mentioning some of the alternatives. On a Unix system, the ever-versatile stty command provides another way to access and program terminals, and if we only wish to deal with Unix platforms, often simply calling stty is suffice. For example, to disable echoing, we can use

```
system "stty -echo";
```

and to reenable it:

```
system "stty echo";
```

The advantage of stty is that as a tool provided by the operating system it can reliably deal with local platform issues for us, but it doesn't stand a chance of working on a non-Unix platform. Another utility that is potentially useful if we happen to know we are running inside an X terminal is xwininfo.

For portable applications, an all-Perl solution is a good idea, if only as a backup plan. Since Term::ReadKey works with most, but not all, platforms, we can compromise and use stty where available and Term::ReadKey as a fallback.

Simple Input

The simplest way to read input from the keyboard is the <> readline operator, which reads a single line of text from the current input filehandle. This is usually STDIN, so the following—assuming there is nothing in @ARGV, as discussed last chapter—are equivalent:

```
print <>;
print <STDIN>;
```

Note that if we do have something in @ARGV, the first attempts to open the elements of @ARGV as files, whereas the second reads from standard input, so the distinction can be important. Also note that if STDIN isn't a terminal, then either version may block waiting for input if insufficient input has arrived yet. We cover this in more detail shortly.

Controlling Terminal Input with Term::ReadKey

For situations where simple input techniques like <> will not do on their own, we can use the Term::ReadKey module, available from CPAN. This provides a much greater degree of control over the characteristics of the terminal and attempts to provide a degree of cross-platform support, so a script written under Unix still has a good chance of working on Windows or other platforms. As well as providing functionality to read terminal input into our programs, it also provides limited control over the properties of the terminal itself, such as whether or not it should echo typed characters to the screen and determining the key to perform a delete operation.

The Term::ReadKey module tries to implement as many of its features as possible for the platform it finds itself running on. However, not all terminals are created equal, so a DOS shell may not support the same features as a Unix shell. Since Unix has always had a fairly detailed idea of what a terminal ought to be, on account of growing up with them (so to speak), most of these features tend to work on Unix-like systems and, to a lesser degree, on other platforms.

Two particular subroutines in the Term::ReadKey package are available for reading input into our program. The ReadKey subroutine reads and returns a single character from the input available, waiting if necessary for it to be typed. In contrast, ReadLine reads entire lines and returns the input as a string. However, the biggest determinant of the behavior of both subroutines is the *read mode* of the terminal, which Term::ReadKey also allows us to control. Before discussing actual input, therefore, we need to look at read modes and find out what they do.

Read Modes

Central to the operation of Term::ReadKey is the concept of *read mode*. The read mode is an aspect of the terminal itself as opposed to the way it is used, and it controls how the terminal receives and processes input characters. There are six modes in total, numbered 0 to 5, with the meanings given in Table 15-1.

Table 15-1. *Term::ReadKey Read Modes*

Mode	Name	Meaning
0	restore	Restore the original read mode setting.
1	normal	Set normal cooked mode. Typed characters are echoed to the screen, and control characters are interpreted.
2	noecho	Set no-echo cooked mode. Typed characters are not echoed to the screen. Control characters are interpreted.
3	cbreak	Character-break mode. Typed characters are returned immediately to the program and are not echoed to the screen.
4	raw	Set raw mode. Control characters are read like normal characters, not interpreted.
5	ultra-raw	As with raw, but LF to CR/LF translation is disabled.

Some of these modes are more obvious than others. The normal mode is just what we expect from a normal command line—characters are echoed as we type them and an action is initiated only when we press Return. In addition, control characters are intercepted and handled by the terminal, rather than simply added to the input.

The noecho mode is the same as normal mode, with the exception that characters are not echoed. This makes it suitable for things like password input. By contrast, cbreak mode causes the terminal to immediately return characters as they are entered, without echoing them to the screen. This makes it suitable for single key-press applications like menu selections.

Both the raw and ultra-raw modes disable the handling of control characters by the terminal. Instead, they are sent back like any other typed character for our program to handle. The ultra-raw mode is identical to raw except that it disables the automatic translation of linefeeds into carriage-return/linefeed pairs on Unix systems. Note that this is quite different from the :crlf discipline/layer discussed in the last chapter—here we are concerned with whether or not the cursor actually moves down one line and moves to the start of the next line, a more specific issue than whether or not we have reached the end of a line in a file. If the filehandle supplied to ReadKey or ReadLine happens to be a serial connection, parity is also disabled.

The default setting is 0, which is to say, whatever mode the terminal was in when the program was started. To change the read mode, we use the ReadMode function from Term::ReadKey. This is automatically imported when the module is used and takes a single parameter of either a number or the corresponding named synonyms:

```
use Term::ReadKey;
```

```
ReadMode 1;            # set normal cooked mode
ReadMode 2;            # set no-echo mode
ReadMode 'noecho';     # same as above, but more legible
ReadMode 'restore';    # restore the mode to whatever it started as
```

The read mode when we start can be any of these values, though it is most likely to be 1. However, if we have been called from another program, then that program may have changed the read mode before calling us. For example, we might be the program another_program being called from this Perl script:

```
use Term::ReadKey;
```

```
ReadMode 'noecho';     # suppress output
system("another_program");
ReadMode 'restore';    # restore terminal to original settings
```

If we do change the terminal read mode, then it is a good idea to restore it again before we finish, since it is not restored automatically just because we exit. Recall that it is a property of the terminal, not our program or the Term::ReadKey module. If we do not restore the mode, we can cause problems for the program that called our code, or even the user if we run it directly. For example, if we were to run the preceding script from a shell and omit the ReadMode 'restore';, then it would return to the user with echoing disabled, so that any further commands typed would be invisible to them. Obviously this is not a good thing, so to be sure that no unexpected incidents occur, we should restore the read mode as a matter of course.

Restoring settings is one good use for an END block. With the following additional definition, we can ensure that our program will restore the terminal before it exits wherever in the program it does so, so long as it exits normally:

```
END {
    ReadMode 'restore';
}
```

To handle abnormal exits, we can do the same thing in __DIE__ and signal handlers.

The restore mode has one additional property; when used, it causes the next mode to be set to become the default. In the preceding case, our program exits before this can become relevant, but the following sequence of calls shows it in action:

```
ReadMode 0;    # 'restore' - restores to the default mode
ReadMode 1;    # sets mode 1, changes default mode to 1
ReadMode 4;    # sets mode 4 ('raw' mode)
ReadMode 0;    # restores the mode to mode 1
```

It is important to realize that since the read mode is a property of the terminal, it affects all kinds of input, including the <> readline operator, not just the ReadKey and ReadLine subroutines covered next.

Reading a Single Character

Frequently we want to read not a line, but a single character from the keyboard, to make a menu selection, for example. We might think to use the built-in function getc, but while this only reads one character, it still requires a return for the terminal emulation to process it and feed it to our program. A more flexible solution is the ReadKey subroutine from Term::ReadKey:

```
$character = ReadKey 0;
```

The subroutine ReadKey takes two parameters: a mode and an optional filehandle. If no file-handle is specified, ReadKey defaults to standard input—the preceding is equivalent to

```
$character = ReadKey 0, STDIN;
```

The mode of ReadKey, which is not related to the terminal read mode, can be one of 0, as shown here, -1, or a positive value:

- Mode 0 is the blocking mode—ReadKey will wait indefinitely until we enter at least a return or interrupt the program. Any platform that Perl can run on supports this mode. This is equivalent to Perl's built-in getc.

- A mode of -1 causes ReadKey to enter nonblocking mode. In this case, ReadKey does not wait for input but grabs whatever is in the input buffer and returns the first character immediately. If nothing is available, presumably because we have not typed anything, ReadKey returns undef.

- A mode with a positive value represents a wait of the given number of seconds, which can be fractional. For example, to wait for half a second (but return sooner if a key is pressed in the time limit), we could use

```
$character = Readkey 0.5;
```

■**Note** Using very small delay values in a loop is generally a bad idea unless essential, since it forces the operating system to do extra work polling for input.

On exit, $character will contain the first character that we typed, or more correctly, the first character that was available in the keyboard buffer, which may already have characters waiting (and which can be filled by things other than the keyboard, to boot).

Contrary to what we might expect, ReadKey does not necessarily return immediately after a character is typed. In fact, it may appear to wait until we enter return. This is not due to an error in our program but to a property of the terminal itself. In order to persuade the terminal to react instantly, we also need to use another read mode, cbreak. The following short script demonstrates how cbreak mode can be combined with ReadKey to react instantly to a typed character:

```perl
#!/usr/bin/perl
# hitakey.pl
use warnings;
use strict;

use Term::ReadKey;

ReadMode 'cbreak';

print "Hit a key: ";
my $selection = ReadKey 0;

print "You typed $selection\n";
ReadMode 'restore';
```

With cbreak mode, the familiar effect of seeing typed characters immediately echoed to the screen does not occur. We can use this fact to create a prompt that checks the entered value before we echo it (or choose not to). For example, we could implement a screen-based menu system with selections from 1 to 9 and check the user's input with a script like this (we have omitted the actual menu options for brevity, since they're not the point here):

```perl
#!/usr/bin/perl
# menu.pl
use warnings;
use strict;

use Term::ReadKey;

ReadMode 'cbreak';

print "Enter an option 1 to 9: ";
my $selection = 0;
do {
    $selection = int (ReadKey 0);
} until ($selection >= 1 and $selection <= 9);

print "You typed $selection\n";
ReadMode 'restore';
```

The cbreak mode can be used with any of the modes of ReadKey to produce interesting effects. For example, this script echoes each character as we type it, but it also prints a dot for every half second that nothing is typed:

```perl
#!/usr/bin/perl
# dot.pl
use warnings;
use strict;

use Term::ReadKey;
ReadMode 'cbreak';

# enable autoflush
$| = 1;

my $char;
do {
    $char = ReadKey 0.5;
    print defined($char) ? $char : '.';
} until (lc($char) eq 'q');

ReadMode 'restore';
```

To actually get our characters to appear on the screen when we print them, we also have to put Perl into autoflush mode by setting the autoflush variable $| to 1. Without this, we would see nothing until we entered either a return (which incidentally does not quit the program) or a lower or uppercase q to stop the program. Eventually the amount of output would become large enough to trigger an automatic write, but this is hardly the effect we are looking for. We enable autoflush to achieve immediate output.

It so happens that the raw and ultra-raw modes will also work with instant effect when used with ReadKey, but this is not their intended purpose, and in fact they may cause unexpected side effects when used in this way. The real point of the raw and ultra-raw modes is to disable the processing of control characters by the terminal, which will be covered in the forthcoming section "Getting and Setting Control Characters."

Single characters can also be retrieved using the getch method from the Term::Screen module. This is a third-party module that provides a lot of terminal screen handling features that are otherwise inconvenient to write. We cover this topic in the forthcoming section "Writing to the Screen."

Reading Complete Lines

Whereas ReadKey returns single characters to us, complete lines are read by ReadLine. However, this subroutine only works completely on Unix platforms (on others it works in blocking mode but not with nonblocking, instead returning an error warning that nonblocking mode is not supported). For other platforms, we can use the Term::ReadLine module instead, which is discussed later. Not to be confused with Term::ReadLine, Term::ReadKey's ReadLine subroutine is very similar to using the <> operator, but with the additional flexibility of being able to avoid waiting for input.

Like ReadKey, ReadLine takes a reading mode as an argument, followed by an optional filehandle. To use it in its simplest guise, to read from standard input, we just write

```perl
$input=ReadLine 0;   # implicitly read from STDIN
$input=ReadLine 0, *STDIN; # with an explicit filehandle
```

This is (more or less) identical to writing

```perl
$input = <STDIN>;
```

However, like ReadKey, ReadLine also accepts a mode of -1 for nonblocking input and a positive value for a timeout in seconds. Using nonblocking causes ReadLine to read whatever is in the input buffer, up to the first return, and to return that. If nothing is in the input buffer or there is an input but not a complete line, then ReadLine will return the undefined value. Note that this is still true even if we have cbreak set as the terminal read mode, since that only causes the terminal to return characters to ReadLine immediately—ReadLine still wants to see an end-of-line character before it returns anything to us.

A positive value causes ReadLine to wait for a set length of time for input and return undef if nothing was entered in the prescribed time limit. For example:

```
print "Give your name - you have 10 seconds to comply: ";
$name = ReadLine 10;
die "Too Slow! Access Denied" unless defined $name;
```

If a nonblocking mode is used, it applies to the first character only—once a character is typed, the call will block until a return is entered. This applies even if we hit Delete.

Note For more advanced ways to read lines of input from the user, including history lists and editable command lines, skip ahead to the section "Advanced Line Input with Term::ReadLine."

Passwords and Invisible Input

If we set the read mode to either cbreak or noecho, we can write a script that accepts input from the user but does not echo the characters typed back to the terminal. The cbreak mode is more suitable for single character input like the hitakey.pl example offered earlier. The mode noecho is more suitable for entering complete lines, where we do not want to know what the user is typing until they press Return. A good example of this kind of application is a password entry prompt:

```
#!/usr/bin/perl
# password.pl
use warnings;
use strict;

use Term::ReadKey;

ReadMode 'noecho';
print "Enter your password: ";
my $password = ReadLine 0;
print "Thanks!\n";
ReadMode 'restore';
```

This makes use of the ReadLine subroutine that comes with Term::ReadKey to read a complete line from the user. Note that we could equally have used cbreak mode here, the only difference being that with cbreak, characters would have been sent back to our program as soon as they were typed. We can't use the password until we have all of it, so in this case cbreak gains us nothing and just causes extra work for the computer.

Finding and Setting the Screen Size

Sometimes it is useful to know how big the terminal screen actually is, for example, when paging output. This might actually be a screen size, or it might correspond to the effective screen size of a terminal window on a graphical desktop. Whatever the screen actually is, we can determine its size with GetTerminalSize, which takes a filehandle and returns four values describing the size. Standard output is used if no handle is passed, except for Windows, where the handle is obligatory:

```
($cwidth, $cheight, $pwidth, $pheight) = GetTerminalSize STDOUT;
```

Astute readers will have noticed this doesn't have much to do with reading key presses or any kind of input. Rather, it is supported by Term::ReadKey since it is a useful thing to be able to find out.

Since it is an output issue rather than an input one (screens are not generally much use for input), the supplied filehandle ought to be open for output and should correspond to some kind of terminal; serial ports don't have display dimensions.

The width and height of the screen in characters is returned in the first two values, with the width and height of the screen in pixels returned in the second two (though this will be zero in cases where the screen doesn't support pixels). Since we are primarily concerned with character IO here, we can discard the second two values and just write

```
($width, $height) = GetTerminalSize;
```

We can use our knowledge of the screen height to page through output, writing exactly a screenful of output before pausing. The following script does exactly this and uses ReadKey in cbreak mode to allow the user to scroll another screenful by pressing any key. As a small improvement on this basic design, we have prefixed each output line with its line number and have also checked the pressed key and exited immediately if it is either q or Q:

```perl
#!/usr/bin/perl
# page.pl
use warnings;
use strict;

use Term::ReadKey;

my ($width, $height) = GetTerminalSize;

my $count = 0;

ReadMode 'cbreak';

while (<>) {
    print "$.: $_";   # $. added to make example more interesting
    if (++$count == $height) {
        last if lc(ReadKey 0) eq 'q';
        $count = 0;
    }
}

ReadMode 'restore';
```

Having demonstrated how to page text in Perl, it is worth pointing out that all operating systems offer a pager program (more or less on Unix, for instance), so if all we want to do is page output, we can call that program and feed it the output we want to page using a piped open.

On Unix systems, we can also set the screen size using SetTerminalSize, supplying the same four arguments. We may not care about the pixel size (and attempting to set it frequently doesn't really do anything), but SetTerminalSize requires we set it anyway, so it is a good idea to preserve the old values and reuse them just in case:

```perl
# get screen size
($x, $y, $w, $h) = GetTerminalSize;

# set screen size to 80x24
SetTerminalSize (80, 24, $w, $h);
```

This does not, fairly obviously, actually change the size of the screen, but indicates to the terminal what size we would prefer it to be. In some cases, like a Unix shell window running under the X Window system, this might cause the shell window to actually resize itself, but we cannot depend on that behavior. Otherwise, the only effect of SetTerminalSize is to cause the operating system to notify any other programs that it is reading that terminal through a SIGWINCH (window change) signal.

It may happen that another application will try to change the terminal size in a similar manner to the way that SetTerminalSize does. This might happen, for example, if the user resizes a terminal window on the desktop. In this case, we may receive a SIGWINCH signal ourselves (assuming that our platform supports it—Windows does not). Ordinarily, this would be ignored, but we can respond to it and handle the new screen size with a signal handler:

```
# establish global width/height
($width, $height) = GetTerminalSize;

# set up a signal handler to catch screen size changes
$oldwinch = $SIG{WINCH};

sub window_changed {
    ($width, $height) = GetTerminalSize;

    # handle the new size - Text::Wrap might be useful here...
    redraw($width, $height);

    # call the old handler by its code reference, if there was one
    &$oldwinch if $oldwinch;

    # in case the OS clears the handler
    $SIG{WINCH} = \&window_changed;
}

$SIG{WINCH} = \&window_changed;
```

As an alternative to Term::ReadKey, the Term::Size and Term::Screen packages available from CPAN also provide functionality for getting or setting the terminal size—see later.

Serial Connections and Terminal Speed

It might happen to be that the terminal we are talking to is actually a serial connection connected to a program or user elsewhere. If we expect to be handling potentially slow connections, we could then modify the amount of data we actually send, giving slow connections more condensed information. In these cases, we can find out the speed of the terminal with GetSpeeds, which takes a filehandle as an argument (or defaults standard input otherwise) and returns two values, namely the input speed and the output speed:

```
($baud_in, $baud_out) = GetSpeeds SERIAL_CONNECTION;
```

If the filehandle is not a serial connection, then this call returns an empty list, which in the preceding case results in two undefined scalars.

Serial connections are also affected by the raw and ultra-raw read modes. Specifically, the terminal will attempt to override any parity settings, if any are in effect. This can be slightly surprising if we are reading a serial connection in raw mode, but since setting parity is now something of a rarity, it is unlikely to be that much of a problem in practice.

Line Ending Translation

As we are now well aware, different operating systems do not use the same line terminator. Under Unix, it is simply a linefeed, or LF for short. Under Windows, it is a return (to be technically accurate carriage return) and linefeed, or CR LF for short. The Macintosh and VMS are different again, using LF CR. Needless to say, this can be confusing.

In order to deal with the possibility of seeing CR LF (or LF CR) rather than LF on the end of lines, terminals usually convert CR LF into LF when they see it, returning only the LF to the application (on some systems this is done in cooperation with the underlying C library too).

Most of the time this is just what we need, because it eliminates another source of compatibility issues for us without us having to worry about it. However, if we actually want to turn this feature off, we can do so by putting the terminal into ultra-raw mode:

```
ReadMode 'raw';      # regular 'raw' mode
ReadMode 'ultra-raw'; # disables CR/LF->LF translation
```

The catch is that ultra-raw mode is in all other respects like raw mode, which is not necessarily what we wanted to use. On a Windows system, this is exactly the same as the regular raw mode, since Windows applications expect to see CR LF and so do not remove the CRs. On a Unix system, this disables the translation so that a CR LF sent to the terminal is passed unchecked as CR LF to the application.

Getting and Setting Control Characters

One of the principal differences between a terminal (whether it be a real screen-and-keyboard terminal or a window on a desktop) and regular IO devices is that terminals can handle a lot of things by themselves without needing the program connected to them to tell them how to do so. An obvious example of this is echoing typed characters to the screen; the terminal deals with that automatically without our involvement.

Less obvious but more interesting are terminal operations like pausing and resuming scrolling, and interrupting the running application. Each terminal operation may be associated with a control character, such as Ctrl-C to interrupt a program or Ctrl-S to pause scrolling. When a terminal is in a cooked mode, which is to say any read mode other than raw or ultra-raw, each time a character is typed the terminal looks it up in the list of operations to see if it triggers a particular event. (On Unix, these definitions are kept in the /etc/termcap, /etc/terminfo, and etc/gettydefs files.)

Using the Term::ReadKey subroutine GetControlChars we can, on platforms that support it, access the list of terminal operations and which keys are associated with which functions. Like most of the subroutines in Term::ReadKey, an optional filehandle can be supplied; otherwise, standard input is used. A list of key-value pairs is returned by GetControlChars, with the key name being the hash key and the key code associated with it being the value. For example, to find out which key code generates an interrupt, we can use

```
%controlchars = GetControlChars;
print "INTERRUPT is ", ord($controlchars{INTERRUPT});
```

Similarly, we can dump out the entire list to the screen with a small program, though since not all platforms support this function, we might not actually get any output:

```perl
#!/usr/bin/perl
# getcontrolchars.pl
use strict;
use warnings;

use Term::ReadKey;

my %controlchars = GetControlChars;
foreach (sort keys %controlchars) {
    print "$_\t=>" , ord ($controlchars{$_}), "\n";
}
```

Executing this script produces a list resembling (but possibly not exactly the same, depending on where and on what we run the program) the following:

```
DISCARD => 15
EOF => 4
EOL => 0
```

```
EOL2 => 0
ERASE => 127
ERASEWORD => 23
INTERRUPT => 3
KILL => 21
MIN => 1
QUIT => 28
QUOTENEXT => 22
REPRINT => 18
START => 17
STOP => 19
SUSPEND => 26
SWITCH => 0
TIME => 0
```

This list of operations and characters comes from the terminal and represents the internal mapping that it is using to process control characters. Many of the operations returned in the list may not be assigned and so have a character value of zero (or 255, depending on the platform) in the returned array—these characters are discarded by the terminal.

■Tip If the terminal is not a real terminal, which is usually the case, what it receives may already have been processed by something else first. For instance, the X Window system defines its own character mapping (the xrdb utility can do this), which takes effect before our terminal emulation even sees the character. Likewise, PC keyboards actually generate 16-bit values, which are translated by the operating system into characters before we get to see them.

On Unix platforms only, we can also alter which control characters trigger which operations, using SetControlChars. This takes a list of key-value pairs as arguments and applies them to the terminal's built-in list. Each pair consists of a name, as returned by GetControlChars, followed by the character or character value. A value of zero disables the operation. For example, we can redefine or disable the Delete key by setting the ERASE operation:

```
SetControlChars ERASE => 0;    # disables delete
SetControlChars ERASE => 2;    # sets delete to Control-B
```

In the following program, we extract and print the list of control characters, alter some of them, and then print it out again. Note that the attempted alterations will not produce any effect on Windows systems (and will, in fact, generate an error):

```perl
#!/usr/bin/perl
# setcontrolchars.pl
use warnings;
use strict;

use Term::ReadKey;
my %oldcontrolchars = GetControlChars;

sub dump_list {
    my %controlchars = GetControlChars;
    foreach my $key (sort keys %controlchars) {
        print "$key\t => ",ord($controlchars{$key}),"\n";
    }
    print "\n";
}
```

```
dump_list;

# disable interrupt, suspend and erase (delete)
# change eof to whatever suspend is (i.e., Ctrl-D to Ctrl-Z)
SetControlChars INTERRUPT => 0,
                EOF => $oldcontrolchars{SUSPEND},
                SUSPEND => 0,
                ERASE => 0;

dump_list;

# reset control characters to their old values
SetControlChars %oldcontrolchars;

dump_list;
```

This program disables the interrupt operation, which is normally bound to Ctrl-C, and changes the end-of-file (or more accurately end-of-transmission, EOT) character, by default Ctrl-D under Unix, to Ctrl-Z, which is more like Windows.

Advanced Line Input with Term::ReadLine

Perl provides a module called Term::ReadLine as part of the standard library. Although it does little by itself, it provides an interface to a system readline library, if one is installed. Two libraries are currently available (at least on Unix systems), the standard Perl readline library and the much more capable third-party GNU Readline library. GNU Readline is also available under Windows as a Cygwin package.

Whichever library is installed, we can use Term::ReadLine to access it—if the GNU library is installed, Term::ReadLine will automatically use it, so we do not have to cater for different libraries in our own code. The module Term::ReadLine will work with no underlying readline library, but few of the advanced features supported by a real readline library, like editable command lines or command-line history traversal, will be available. By writing our programs to use Term::ReadLine, however, we can transparently and automatically make use of these features if our program is run on a system where they are installed.

Also supported by Term::ReadLine are several standard methods, listed in Table 15-2, which we can call on terminal objects created with the module.

Table 15-2. *Term::ReadLine Methods*

Name	Function
ReadLine	Return the name of the underlying library module.
new	Create a new terminal object.
readline	Read a line. This is the central method of the module.
addhistory	Add a new line to the input line history.
IN/OUT	Return the input and output filehandles of the terminal, respectively. See also findConsole.
MinLine	Set a limit on the shortest length of an input line before it is allowed in the input line history.
findConsole	Return an array of two strings containing the appropriate file name strings for opening the input and output, respectively. See also IN/OUT.
Attribs	Return a reference to a hash of internal configuration details.
Features	Return a reference to a hash of supported features.

In addition, Term::ReadLine supplies some *stub methods*. Without an underlying library, these have no useful effect, but if one is present, they will become active and perform the relevant function. The stubs ensure that we can call these methods even if the library we are using doesn't support one or more of them. If we want to check if a given method is supported (as we probably should), we can use the Features method to find out (see Table 15-3).

Table 15-3. *Term::Readline Feature Methods*

Name	Function
tkRunning	Enable or disable the tk event loop while waiting for input. Perl-Tk only.
ornaments	Enable, disable, or change the decoration of the prompt and input text when using readline.
NewTTY	Switch the terminal to a new pair of input and output filehandles.

In addition to the standard methods, the underlying library may define other methods that are unique to it. The GNU library in particular defines a very extensive set of calls, in fact more than we have time to touch on here. For full details, see perldoc Term::ReadLine::Gnu.

Each library adds its own set of features to the list returned by Features, so we can also test for them before trying to use the corresponding methods. Before calling any methods, however, we first have to create a terminal object.

Creating a Terminal Object

The Term::ReadLine module is object oriented, so to use it we first instantiate a terminal object. We give this object a name, presumably a descriptive name for the program, and then optionally typeglobs for the filehandles that we wish to use for input and output:

```
use Term::ReadLine;

# use STDIN and STDOUT by default
$term = new Term::ReadLine "Demo";
# use filehandles IN and OUT explicitly
$term = new Term::ReadLine "Demo", *IN, *OUT;

# use a serial connection (same filehandle for both input and output)
$serialterm = new Term::ReadLine "Remote", *SERIAL, *SERIAL;
```

Once we have created a terminal object, we can use it to both read and write to the terminal. The following script shows the general idea:

```
#!/usr/bin/perl
# termobject.pl
use warnings;
use strict;

use Term::ReadLine;

my $term = new Term::ReadLine "My Demo Application";
print "This program uses ", $term->ReadLine,"\n";

my $input=$term->readline("Enter some text: ");
print "You entered: $input\n";
```

First we load in the Term::ReadLine module. Then, just for curiosity's sake, we use the ReadLine method to determine the name of the underlying package, if any. Then we use the readline method (note the difference in case) to read a line from the terminal, optionally supplying a prompt.

When this program is run, it causes Term::ReadLine to look for and load an underlying readline library if it can find one. If it can, it passes control to it for all other functions. The library in turn provides editing functionality for the actual input of text. If we are using the GNU library, we can take advantage of its more advanced features like editable command lines automatically, since they are provided for us by the library. In our own code, we don't have to raise a finger, which is the point, of course.

If we happen to be using a terminal that isn't connected to standard input and standard output, we need to direct output to the right filehandle, which means passing print the right filehandle. The preceding happens to work because the terminal is connected to standard out, so a simple print works. We really ought to direct output to the terminal's output, irrespective of whether it is standard out not. Fortunately, we can find both the input and output filehandles from the terminal object using the IN and OUT methods:

```
$input_fh = $term->IN;
$output_fh = $term->OUT;

print $term->OUT "This writes to the terminal";
```

Once created, the filehandles used by the terminal can (usually) be changed with the newTTY method. This takes two typeglobs as arguments and redirects the terminal to them:

```
$term->newTTY *NEWIN *NEWOUT;
```

It is possible, though unlikely, that this will not work if the library does not support the switch. To be sure of success, we can interrogate Term::ReadLine to find out whether the newTTY feature (or indeed any feature) is actually supported.

Supported Features

Due to the fact that different readline implementations support different features of Term::ReadLine, we can interrogate the module to find out what features are actually supported. The Features method provides us with this information, as we briefly mentioned earlier. It returns a reference to a hash with the keys being the features supported:

```
#!/usr/bin/perl
# readlinefeatures.pl
use warnings;
use strict;

use Term::ReadLine;

my $term = new Term::ReadLine "Find Features";
my %features = %{$term->Features};

print "Features supported by ",$term->ReadLine,"\n";
foreach (sort keys %features) {
    print "\t$_ => \t$features{$_}\n";
}
```

Let's execute this script with Term::ReadLine::Gnu (available from CPAN) installed and review its output:

```
> perl readlinefeatures.pl
```

```
Features supported by Term::ReadLine::Gnu
    addHistory =>    1
    appname =>    1
```

```
attribs =>     1
autohistory =>     1
getHistory =>    1
minline =>   1
newTTY =>    1
ornaments =>    1
preput =>    1
readHistory =>     1
setHistory =>    1
stiflehistory =>     1
tkRunning =>    1
writeHistory =>     1
```

We should not confuse these features with callable methods. Some, though not all, of these features correspond to methods supported by the underlying library. Unfortunately, the feature names do not always match the names of the methods that implement them. For example, the method to add a line of history is addhistory, not addHistory.

We can use the feature list to check that a feature exists before trying to use it. For example, to change a terminal to use new filehandles, we could check for the newTTY feature, using it if present, and resort to creating a new object otherwise:

```perl
sub switch_tty {
    my ($term,*IN,*OUT) = @_;
    $features = $term->Features;
    if ($features->{newTTY}) {
        $term->newTTY(*IN,*OUT);
    } else {
        $name = $term->appname;
        $term = new Term::ReadLine $name,*IN,*OUT;
    }
    return $term;
}
```

Regardless of which features are actually supported, Term::ReadLine defines stub methods for a selected subset so that calling them will not cause an error in our program, even if they don't have any useful effect.

Setting the Prompt Style and Supplying Default Input

The readline method takes a prompt string as its argument. This string is printed to the screen using ornaments (if any have been defined) that alter the look of the prompt and the entered text. For example, GNU Readline underlines the prompt text by default.

Ornamentation can be enabled, disabled, or redefined with the ornaments method. Enabling and disabling the currently defined ornaments is achieved by passing 1 or 0 (a true or false value) to ornaments:

```perl
#!/usr/bin/perl
# ornament.pl
use warnings;
use strict;

use Term::ReadLine;

my $term = new Term::ReadLine "Ornamentation";

# disable ornaments
```

```perl
$term->ornaments(0);
my $plain = $term->readline("A plain prompt: ");
print "You entered: $plain\n";

# enable default ornaments
$term->ornaments(1);
my $fancy = $term->readline("A fancy prompt: ");
print "You entered: $fancy\n";
```

Alternatively, the current ornamentation can be redefined by passing four parameters containing terminal capabilities (as deduced by the `Term::Cap` module—see later) as a string. The first two are applied before and after the prompt, and the second two before and after the input text. For example:

```perl
# define ornaments (md = bold, me = normal)
$term->ornaments('md, me, ,');
$userd = $term->readline("A user-defined prompt: ");
print "You entered: $userd\n";
```

In this example, we have used `md`, which is the terminal capability code for bold, and `me`, which is the terminal capability code to return to `normal`. We don't want to change the input line, so we have left those two entries blank. If we have no termcap library, this will fail, since `Term::Cap` is used to determine how to handle ornaments. To enable the `ornaments` subroutine to work without generating a warning, add the following:

```perl
# disable warnings for platforms with no 'termcap' database
$Term::ReadLine::termcap_nowarn = 1;
```

The GNU version of `readline` supports a second optional parameter that contains the default input text. This is known as the *preput* text, and we can test to see if it is supported by checking for the `preput` feature. Since passing extra parameters is not an error, not checking is fine—we simply won't see the default text. Here is a short example of supplying some default text to the `readline` method:

```perl
#!/usr/bin/perl
# defaulttext.pl
use warnings;
use strict;

use Term::ReadLine;

my $term = new Term::ReadLine "Default Input";

my $input = $term->readline("Enter some text: ", "Default Text");
print "You entered: $input\n";
```

If the preput text is supplied and the library supports it, the input line is automatically filled with the default text. The user can then either delete and replace or edit (because GNU readline supports in-line editing) the default text or just press Return to accept it.

Command-Line History

The `Term::ReadLine` module provides support for command-line history—that is, a record of what has been typed beforehand. This can be used to allow the user to step backward or forward through previous commands, typically using the up and down cursor keys. This functionality is provided automatically (assuming a library is present which supports it), so again we do not have to do anything special to provide it.

We can control the history several ways, however. First, we can lie about previously entered commands by using the addhistory method:

```
$term->addhistory("pretend this was previously entered text");
```

If we have the GNU readline library, we can also remove a line from the history by giving its line number to remove_history:

```
$term->remove_history(1);   # remove line 1 from history, GNU only
```

We can also, using the GNU library, retrieve the whole history as an array with GetHistory:

```
@history = $term->GetHistory;
```

We can then step through this array and pass the index numbers to remove_history if desired. Of course, to prevent the line numbers changing as we proceed, traversing the array in reverse order is recommended. For example, this loop traverses the history array, removing all lines that have less than three characters:

```
@history = $term->GetHistory;
# traverse in reverse order, to preserve indices in loop
foreach my $item (reverse 0..$#history) {
    $term->remove_history($item) if length($history[$item])<3);
}
```

We can actually do this automatically with the standard MinLine method, which should work regardless of the underlying library. Additionally, we can disable the history entirely by passing an undefined value to it:

```
$term->MinLine(3);     # only record lines of three plus characters
$term->MinLine(undef);   # disable history
```

The GNU readline library goes far beyond these features, however. It also provides support for editing, moving around, saving, loading, and searching the history. For a complete, if terse, list of available features, see the Term::ReadLine::Gnu documentation.

Word Completion

Some shell programs support the concept of *completion*, where the shell attempts to deduce the rest of a partially entered word from the first few letters. We can provide the same feature within our own Perl programs with either the GNU Readline library or the somewhat simpler (but less able) Term::Complete module.

This module supplies the Complete function, which takes a prompt and a list of words for matching against. This is an example of how we might use it:

```
#!/usr/bin/perl
# complete.pl
use warnings;
use strict;

use Term::Complete;

my @terms = qw(one two three four five six seven eight nine ten);
my $input = Complete("Enter some number words: ",@terms);

print "You entered: $input\n";
```

Completion is triggered by pressing the Tab key. When this occurs, Term::Complete attempts to match the text entered so far against one of the words in the completion list. If there is a unique match, it fills in the rest of the word. For example, if we were to enter e and then press Tab,

Term::Complete would automatically fill in ight for eight, since that is the only word that begins with e.

If there is not a unique match, then Tab will produce no useful effect. Instead, we can enter Ctrl-D to have Term::Complete return a list of valid matches. If we were to enter t then Ctrl-D, then the available completions two, three, and ten would be displayed, one per line:

```
Enter some number words: t^D
ten
three
two
Enter some number words: t
```

The Term::Complete module supplies several functions that allow various keys to be redefined, with the curious exception of Tab for completion. None of these functions are exported by the module, so we must access them via their full names. They are as listed in Table 15-4.

Table 15-4. *Term::Complete Functions*

Function	Keystroke	Action
Term::Complete::complete	Ctrl-D	List matching completions, if any.
Term::Complete::kill	Ctrl-U	Erase whole line.
Term::Complete::erase1	Delete	Delete last character.
Term::Complete::erase2	Backspace	Delete last character.

The Term::ReadLine::Gnu package provides a more comprehensive completion mechanism but depends on the GNU Readline library being installed on the system. This may be more trouble than we want to go to, especially on a non-Unix or non-Windows system. It is also a much more involved library to program and is beyond the scope of this book—consult the documentation and the manual page for the bash shell (which makes extensive use of GNU Readline) if available.

Writing to the Screen

Perl provides a lot of different approaches to writing to a terminal screen, from simply printing to standard output, through low-level terminal control modules like Term::Cap and the POSIX::Termios interface, to very high-level modules like the third-party Curses module. Somewhere in the middle we can find modules like Term::ANSIColor and the third-party Term::Screen, which provide a slightly simpler interface to the features of the low-level modules.

The Term::ANSIColor module handles the specific problem of using colors and other text attributes like blinking, bold, or underline. Other commands can be sent to the screen by interrogating the terminal capabilities with Term::Cap. However, since Term::Cap is a rather low-level module, the third-party Term::Screen module provides a few of these facilities in a more convenient form. If we plan to do a lot of screen output, however, such as writing a complete text-based GUI application, then we might want to look at the Curses module.

Terminal Capabilities

Terminal capabilities ultimately determine the number of ways we can talk to it. There are many different kinds of terminals, both real and simulated, each with its own particular range of features. Even if a terminal supports all the usual features, it may not do it in the same way as another. In order to make sense of the huge range of possible terminals and different terminal features and options, Unix machines make use of a terminal capability or *termcap* database. A given terminal has a terminal type associated with it. Interested applications can look up items in the database to find out how to tell the terminal to do things like move the cursor or change the color of text.

We send commands to terminals in the form of ANSI escape sequences, a series of characters starting with an escape (character 27, or \e). To switch on blue text, for example, we could use

```
print "\e[34m--this is blue text--\e[0m\n";
```

Of course, this relies on the terminal supporting ANSI escape sequences, which is likely on a Unix system but is not the case for a DOS shell—if characters like e[32m appear on the screen, it's a safe bet that ANSI isn't supported, so the rest of this discussion is likely to be academic.

Remembering that \e[...m is the sequence for changing screen colors and that 34 is the number for blue is hardly convenient, however. Worse, while things like the color blue are standard across all terminals (all color terminals, that is), many other terminal capabilities vary widely in the precise escape sequences that control them. For that reason, rather than write escape sequences explicitly, we use Term::Cap to find them out for us.

Using Term::Cap

The Term::Cap module is an interface to the terminal capability or *termcap* database commonly found on Unix systems that allows us to issue commands to terminals based on what kind of terminal we are using. To use it, we create a terminal capability object using Term::Cap, then pass that object information about what we want to do, along with the filehandle of the terminal we want to do it on. In order to use the module, therefore, we first have to create a terminal capability object (or *termcap object* for short) that points to the entry in the termcap database that we want to use. We also need a termcap database for Term::Cap to work with, so again, this is academic for platforms that do not possess one.

Creating a Termcap Object

Using the Tgetent method, Term::Cap creates terminal capability objects. In order to use it, we must pass it a hash reference, which it blesses, populates with capability strings, and returns to us. In order to work out which entry to look up, Tgetent needs to know the terminal name, for example, ansi for a standard ANSI terminal, vt100 for a terminal that adheres to the VT100 standard, and so on. Unix shell tools like xterm use their own terminal mode, for example, xterm, which is a superset of the ANSI terminal that also knows a few things particular to living inside a window, such as resizing the screen.

In general, we want Term::Cap to look up the entry for whatever terminal it is our program happens to be running in, which it can normally deduce from the environment. To tell Tgetent to look at the environment, we pass it an anonymous hash containing a key-value pair of TERM and undef:

```
#!/usr/bin/perl
# anonhash.pl
use warnings;
use strict;

use Term::Cap;

# create a terminal capability object - warns of unknown output speed
my $termcap = Term::Cap->Tgetent({ TERM => undef });

print "Capabilities found: ",join(',',sort(keys %{$termcap})),"\n";
```

Just to demonstrate what this actually does, we have looked at the hash that the termcap object actually is and printed out its keys. That's usually a rather rude way to treat an object, but it serves to illustrate our point. Run from a Unix xterm window, this program produces the following output:

```
OSPEED was not set, defaulting to 9600 at ./termcap1.pl line 7
Capabilities found:
OSPEED,PADDING,TERM,TERMCAP,_AL,_DC,_DL,_DO,_IC,_LE,_RI,_UP,_ae,_al,_am,_as,_bc,
_bl,_cd,_ce,_cl,_cm,_co,_cr,_cs,_ct,_dc,_dl,_do,_ei,_ho,_ic,_im,_is,_it,_k1,_k2,
_k3,_k4,_k5,_k6,_k7,_k8,_k9,_kI,_kN,_kP,_kb,_kd,_ke,_kh,_kl,_km,_kr,_ks,_ku,_le,
_li,_md,_me,_mi,_mr,_ms,_nd,_pc,_rc,_sc,_se,_sf,_so,_sr,_ta,_te,_ti,_ue,_up,_us,
_xn,_xo
```

Note Note that we avoided actually printing out the values of the hash, which contain the ANSI escape sequences themselves, because printing them would cause the terminal to react to them. This would likely confuse it and probably leave it in an unusable state. Escape sequences are not interesting to look at in any case; the whole point of the termcap database is that we don't need to look at them directly.

To safely dump out the values of the capabilities, we can substitute the escape characters with a plain text equivalent like <ESC> that will not be interpreted by the terminal. For the terminally curious (so to speak), this loop will achieve that:

```
foreach my $cap (sort keys %$termcap) {
    my $value=$termcap->{$_};
    $value =~ s/\e/<ESC>/g;
    print "$cap => $value\n";
}
```

Disregarding the warning (which we'll come to in a moment) and the uppercased entries, each of the underscore prefixed entries is a capability of this terminal, and the value of that entry in the hash is the ANSI escape sequence that creates that effect. By using this object, we can generate valid escape sequences to do the things we want without worrying about what the correct sequence is for any given terminal. In fact, we can disregard the terminal type altogether most of the time, which is the idea, of course.

If we want to pretend we're an ANSI terminal rather than anything else, or we just happen to know that the terminal we're using (remembering that we could be in some sort of shell window that doesn't correspond to any specific terminal) happens to be ANSI compatible, we could write

```
$termcap = Term::Cap->Tgetent({TERM =>'ansi'});
```

Tgetent also seeks the output speed of the terminal because terminal capabilities may be defined to be dependent on the speed of the connection. If it isn't told, it will complain with a warning but retrieve the terminal capability information anyway based on an assumed speed of 9600 bps. In order to silence this, we can feed it a speed from the POSIX module:

```
#!/usr/bin/perl
# speed.pl
use warnings;
use strict;

use POSIX;
use Term::Cap;

# set the line speed explicitly - but 'POSIX::B9600' may not be defined
my $termcap1 = Term::Cap->Tgetent({
    TERM => undef,
    OSPEED => POSIX::B9600
});
```

Better, we can use the POSIX::Termios package to ask the terminal directly, then feed that value to Term::Cap:

```
# interrogate the terminal for the line speed, no need for a constant
my $termios = new POSIX::Termios;
$termios->getattr(fileno(STDOUT));
my $termcap2 = Term::Cap->Tgetent({
    TERM => undef,
    OSPEED => $termios->getospeed
});
```

The POSIX::Termios is a very low-level way to control a terminal directly. Modules like Term::ReadKey use it, along with Term::Cap, behind the scenes to perform many of their functions. We can also use it directly, and we will cover it in more detail later. Of course, this might seem a pointless exercise if we know we will be talking to a screen or a shell window that doesn't have a line speed, but Term::Cap is not able to assume that, and it can't determine this from the terminal type, since that's just an emulation. Additionally, we should not assume that our application won't one day run on a real terminal on the end of a real serial connection.

Clearing the Screen, Moving the Cursor, and Other Tricks

Given an object representing the terminal's capabilities, we can use it to make the terminal do things. One of the first obvious things to do is clear the screen. The terminal capability code for that is cl, so we feed that to the Tputs method of Term::Cap along with the number 1 to tell Tputs to generate a code that does clear the screen (rather than doesn't, strangely—the command needs a parameter), and the filehandle of the terminal:

```
$termcap->Tputs('cl', 1, *STDOUT);
```

Similarly, to move the cursor about, we use the cm (cursor move) capability with the Tgoto method. For instance, to move the cursor to position x = 3 and y = 5, we would use

```
$termcap->Tgoto('cm', 3, 5, *STDOUT);
```

Then, to write some text in bold, we could use

```
$termcap->Tputs('md', 1, *STDOUT);
print "Bold Text";
```

We can use any capability of the terminal in this way, so long as we have a thorough knowledge of terminal capability codes. Since that is rather a lot of work to go to, we might be given to wonder if someone has already done all this work and parceled up the most common features for us. Fortunately, someone has—see Term::Screen and the Curses module later in the chapter.

Writing in Colors

Most terminal emulations support the ANSI standard for escape sequences that control aspects of the terminal such as cursor position or the appearance of text. Unlike a lot of other escape sequences, the color and text attribute sequences are fairly standard across all terminals. Instead of writing ANSI sequences by hand or resorting to Term::Cap, we can make use of the Term::ANSIColor module from CPAN instead.

This module works by defining an attribute name for each of the escape sequences related to text representation, such as bold for bold text and on_red for a red background. We can use these attributes to create text in any style we like, with the twin advantages of simplicity and legibility.

There are two basic modes of operation. The first is a functional one, using the subroutines color and colored to generate strings containing ANSI escape sequences, passing the names of the attributes we want to create as the first argument. The second uses constants to define each code separately, and we will see how to use it shortly. Before we look at a short example of using the

`Term::ANSIColor` module, a short word of warning. The effects of using the module will be dependent on the settings of your terminal. For example, if your terminal is set to print red on white, the following example will exhibit no noticeable difference. In the meantime, here is a short example of how `color` can be used to generate red text on a white background:

```
#!/usr/bin/perl
# text.pl
use warnings;
use strict;

use Term::ANSIColor;

print color('red on_white'),'This is Red on White';
```

The argument to `color` is a list of attribute names, in this case the attributes red and on_white to produce red-on-white text. Here we have passed them as space-separated terms in a string, but we can also supply the attributes as a list:

```
@attributes = 'red';
push @attributes, 'on_white';
print color(@attributes), 'Or supply attributes as a list...';
```

Note that `color` does not print anything by itself. It returns a string to us and leaves it to us to print it or otherwise use it. Similarly, here is how we can produce bold underlined text:

```
print color('bold underline'),'This is bold underlined';
```

We can generate any of the color sequences supported by the ANSI standard using `Term::ANSIColor`, all of which have been given convenient textual names for easy access. Table 15-5 lists all the names defined by `Term::ANSIColor`. Note that several attributes have synonyms, and that case is irrelevant—RED works as well as red.

Table 15-5. *Term::ANSIColor Attributes*

Name	Action
clear, reset	Reset and clear all active attributes.
bold	Start bolding.
underline, underscore	Start underlining.
blink	Start blinking.
reverse	Reverse both foreground and background colors logically. If no colors are set, invert white on black to black on white.
concealed	Conceal text.
black, red, green, yellow, blue, magenta	Put text into given color. May be combined with a background color.
on_black, on_red, on_green, on_yellow, on_blue, on_magenta	Put text background into given color. May be combined with a foreground color.

The problem with `color` is that it does not switch off what it switches on. If we run the preceding programs, then whatever escape sequences were in effect at termination continue on after the end of the program. This means that without special care and attention, we can end up typing bold underlined green on cyan text at our shell prompt, or even worse. In order to prevent this, we need to remember to clear the active attributes before we finish:

```
print color('red on_white'),'This is Red on White', color('reset');
```

This is another case where an END block is potentially useful, of course:

```
# make sure color is switched off before program exits
END { print color('reset') }
```

However, passing reset to the end of all our print statements is clumsy. The colored function solves this problem by automatically adding escape codes to clear the active attributes to the end of the returned string, at a slightly higher cost in terms of characters output. With colored, we don't need to reset the screen ourselves, so the following is visually equivalent but simpler to write than the previous example:

```
print colored('This is Red on White', 'red on_white');
```

The text to be encapsulated comes first, so we can still pass attributes as a list if we like:

```
my @attributes = ('red', 'on_white');
print colored('Or as a list of attributes...', @attributes);
```

It is important to realize, however, that reset (or the synonymous clear) resets all active ANSI sequences, not just the ones we issued last. This is more obvious with color than colored, which might give the impression that we can switch from green-on-black to red-on-white and back to green-on-black using a reset, which is not the case:

```
print colored('green on black, colored('red on white'), 'and back', 'green');
```

In this example, the and back will be white on black, not green, because the reset generated by the internal call to colored overrides the original color setting and then resets it. The reset added by the outer call to colored is therefore redundant.

The function colored has been written with multiline text in mind. Ordinarily, it places codes at the beginning and end of the string passed as its first argument. If, however, the package variable $Term::ANSIColor::EACHLINE is set to a string of one or more characters, then colored splits the line on each occurrence of this separator and inserts codes to clear and then reestablish the passed attributes on either side of it. The most obvious use of this feature is, of course, to set the separator to \n, as in

```
#!/usr/bin/perl
# multicolor.pl
use warnings;
use strict;

use Term::ANSIColor;

$Term::ANSIColor::EACHLINE = "\n";

my $text = "This is\nan example\nof multiline\ntext coloring\n";

print colored($text, 'bold yellow');
```

There is no reason why we should just apply this to lines. As a slightly different example of what we can do, here is a way to display binary numbers with the 1s emphasized in bold. It works by making the separator 0 and using bold cyan as the attribute:

```
#!/usr/bin/perl
# boldbin.pl
use warnings;
use strict;

use Term::ANSIColor;

my $number = rand 10_000_000;
```

```
# my $bintext = sprintf '%b', $number;   # if Perl >=5.6
my $bintext = unpack 'B32', pack('d', $number);

$Term::ANSIColor::EACHLINE ='0';

print colored($bintext, 'bold cyan');
```

The second mode of operation bypasses color and colored entirely by importing symbols for each attribute directly into our own namespace with the :constants label. To use this mode, we need to import the constants from the module by using the :constants tag:

```
use Term::ANSIColor qw(:constants);
```

By doing this, we create a host of constant subroutines, one for each attribute. The constants are all uppercase, so instead of calling color or colored, we can now print out attributes directly. Here is red-on-white text, generated using constants:

```
#!/usr/bin/perl
# constants.pl
use warnings;
use strict;

use Term::ANSIColor qw(:constants);

print RED, ON_WHITE, "This is Red on White", RESET;
```

The values of these constants are strings, so we can also concatenate them with the . operator:

```
$banner = BLUE.ON_RED.UNDERSCORE."Hello World".RESET;
print $banner,"\n";
```

As these examples show, constants suffer from the same problem as color, in that we have to explicitly switch off whatever attributes we switch on. However, if we leave out the commas and set the variable $Term::ANSIColor::AUTORESET, then the module will automatically figure things out and add the reset for us:

```
# automatically append reset code
$Term::ANSIColor::AUTORESET = 1;

# look, no commas!
print RED ON_WHITE "This is Red on White";
```

This is clever, but mysterious. We might be given to wonder how this works, since this doesn't look like a legal print statement. The answer is that the "constants" are not strings but subroutines. Unlike constants declared with the use constant pragma, these subroutines take arguments, and without parentheses they behave like list operators, absorbing whatever is to their right. With the commas in place, each subroutine is called without arguments. Without the commas removed, each is called with the rest of the statement as its argument and returns a string based on its own name prefixed to whatever the rest of the line returned. By working out if they were called with or without arguments, each subroutine can work out whether it needs to append a reset or not. Perl evaluates this statement right to left, so the argument to RED is the return value from ON_WHITE.

Having explained the way this works, we might choose to avoid this syntax, since RED in this example looks exactly like a filehandle to the reader (Perl knows it is a subroutine, of course). As an alternative, we can define the output record separator to produce a similar effect and retain the commas:

```
local $/ = RESET;   # automatically suffix all 'print' statements with a reset
print RED, ON_WHITE, "This is Red on White";
```

The advantage of the "constants" approach is that Perl can check our code at compile time, rather than at run time, since a misspelled constant will cause a syntax error unlike an attribute string passed to color or colored. The disadvantage is that we end up with a lot of attribute constants in the namespace of our code, which isn't always desirable.

Higher-Level Terminal Modules

The Term::Cap module gives us the ability to send a range of commands to terminals without having to worry about what kind of terminal we are actually talking to, although it is a little too low level for convenient use. Fortunately, there are several third-party solutions that build on basic terminal capabilities to make our job easier. Just two are mentioned here—Term::Screen, which is a friendly wrapper around Term::Cap that implements many of the most common functions in an easy-to-use form, and Curses, a terminal programming library vast enough that it has entire books dedicated to it.

Term::Screen

The third-party Term::Screen module (available at the nearest CPAN mirror) encapsulates a lot of the most common terminal functionality into a simpler and easy-to-use form, if we want to spend significant time exerting control over the terminal screen and want to avoid writing all our own Term::Cap subroutines. Although it is not a standard module, it does use Term::Cap to do all the actual work, so wherever Term::Cap works, Term::Screen ought to. It actually uses the Unix stty command to do the dirty work, so it won't work for other platforms. However, it is designed to be subclassed, so an MS-DOS module is a distinct possibility, if not supplied (at least, not yet).

As an example, here is how we can clear the screen and move the cursor with Term::Screen. Notice that it is a lot simpler and more legible than the Term::Cap version we saw earlier:

```perl
#!/usr/bin/perl
# movecurs.pl
use warnings;
use strict;

use Term::Screen;

my $terminal = new Term::Screen;
$terminal->clrscr();
$terminal->at(3,4);
$terminal->puts("Here!");
$terminal->at(10,0);
$terminal->puts("Hit a key...");
my $key = $terminal->getch();
$terminal->at(10,0);
$terminal->puts("You pressed '$key'");
$terminal->at(11,0);
```

This example also demonstrates the getch method, an alternative to using ReadKey from the Term::ReadKey module that we covered earlier. getch is more convenient, since it doesn't involve messing about with the terminal read mode, but of course it requires having Term::Screen installed. Of course, Term::ReadKey is not a standard module either.

As an added convenience, Term::Screen's output methods are written so that they return the terminal object created by new Term::Screen. This means they can be used to call other methods, allowing us to chain methods together. For example, we could have concatenated much of the preceding example script into

```perl
$terminal->clrscr->at(3,4)->puts("Here!")->at(10,0)->puts("Hit a key...");
```

The Term::Screen module provides a toolkit of methods for working with terminals. Table 15-6 summarizes these, along with the arguments they take.

Table 15-6. *Term::Screen Methods*

Name	Action
resize (rows, cols)	Resize the screen, in the same way that Term::ReadKey's SetTerminalSize does.
at (row, col)	Move the cursor to the given row and column of the screen.
normal	Set the text style to normal. For example, $terminal->normal() puts the terminal into normal.
bold	Set the text style to bold.
reverse	Set the text style to reverse.
clrscr	Clear the screen and move the cursor to 0,0.
clreol	Clear from the cursor position to the end of the line.
clreos	Clear from the cursor position to the end of the screen.
il	Insert a blank line before the line the cursor is on.
dl	Delete the line the cursor is on. Lower lines move up.
ic (char) exists_ic	Insert a character at the cursor position. Remainder of line moves right. The method exists_ic returns true if this actually exists as a termcap capability, false otherwise.
dc exists_dc	Delete the character at the cursor position. Remainder of line moves left. The method exists_dc returns true of this actually exists as a termcap capability, false otherwise.
echo noecho	Enable or disable echoing of typed characters to the screen, in the same way that Term::ReadKey's ReadMode does.
puts (text)	Print text to the screen. Identical to print except that it can be chained with at as illustrated previously.
getch	Return a single character in raw mode.
key_pressed	See if a key has been pressed without actually reading it.
flush_input	Clear any current data in the input buffer.
stuff_input	Insert characters into the input of getch for reading. Note that this only works for getch—it does not put characters into the real input buffer.
def_key (cap, keycode)	Define a function key sequence. char is the character generated by the definition (and read by getch). keycode is what the function key actually generates. The definition causes keycode to be translated into char by the terminal.
get_fn_keys	Define a default set of function key definitions.

All of these methods are fairly self-explanatory, with the exception of def_key. This programs the function keys (which includes the cursor keys and keys like Insert and Home) of a keyboard to return a given character, if the terminal is programmable. The *keycode* is a particular escape sequence such as \e[11~ for function key one or \e[A for the up cursor key, and the cap is a terminal capability such as ku for cursor up. That is, to swap the up and down cursor keys, we could write

```
$terminal->def_key('ku', "\e[B~");
$terminal->def_key('kd', "\e[A~");
```

A list of common escape sequences generated by function keys can be found in the Term::Screen module itself, inside the get_fn_keys method. As well as being informative, when called this also resets the definitions to their defaults, handy if we just swapped our cursor keys around:

```
$terminal->get_fn_keys();
```

This is certainly useful, but it does have one liability—with the exception of the ic and dc methods, it assumes that the given capability exists, and does not check for it. However, since all the capabilities it supports are fairly standard, it is likely that they will work as advertised.

If even Term::Screen is not up to the task, we might consider turning to the very capable and feature-rich Curses module. However, Curses depends on an implementation of the curses library on our platform—Term::Screen only needs Term::Cap, which is a standard Perl library module.

The Curses Library

The *Curses* library is the granddaddy of all screen manipulation libraries. It supports everything we have discussed so far, including all the tricky details of terminal capabilities, mouse input, and text-based windows as well as many other features. Most Unix platforms have a Curses library installed, and several ports exist to other platforms such as Windows, including the free *GNU ncurses* implementation.

Perl supports Curses libraries through the Curses module, available as usual from any CPAN mirror. As well as the Curses library, the module also supports the extension Panel library, which adds overlapping window support to Curses. Assuming that we have these libraries and the Curses module installed, we can write windowed terminal applications using Curses. The actual features of a given Curses library depend on the implementation (early implementations do not support Windows, for example), but all libraries support the same general set of operations.

The C interface to Curses tends to support four different subroutines for each function: the basic feature, the basic feature within a window, the basic feature combined with a cursor movement, and the basic feature combined with a cursor movement within a window. For example, the addstr subroutine, which writes text to the screen, comes in four different flavors, each with a different set of arguments, as these four different C statements demonstrate:

```
addstr("Text..."); /* write text at cursor */
mvaddstr(3, 5 ,"Text"); /* move cursor, write text */
waddstr(window, "Text..."); /* in window write text at cursor */
mvwaddstr(window, 3, 5, "Text"); /* in window move cursor, write text */
```

The Curses module simplifies this by providing an object-oriented interface for programming windows and by wrapping all of the variants into one Perl subroutine. In order to work out which one we actually want, the Curses module merely inspects the number of arguments and their type.

Since Curses is a huge library, we cannot hope to document it all here. Instead, we will look at a few simple examples that demonstrate the basics of writing Curses applications in Perl.

A Simple Curses Application

A simple Curses program starts with initscr, which initializes the screen for use by Curses. After this, we can configure the terminal in any way we like, for example, to switch echoing off. We can send output to the screen with addstr, followed by refresh to tell Curses to actually draw it. Finally, when we are finished, we call endwin to reset the terminal for normal use again. Here is a short example program that lists environment variables one by one and shows the basic structure of a Curses program:

```perl
#!/usr/bin/perl
# curses1.pl
use warnings;
use strict;

use Curses;

initscr();   # initialize the screen to use curses
cbreak();    # go into 'cbreak' mode
noecho();    # prevent key presses echoing
# move and addstr as separate actions
attron(A_BOLD|A_UNDERLINE);
move(2,5);
addstr("Environment Variable Definitions:");
attroff(A_BOLD|A_UNDERLINE);
move(15,5);
addstr("Hit a key to continue, 'Q' to finish...");

# enable color
start_color();

# define some color pairs
init_pair(1, COLOR_WHITE,COLOR_BLACK);
init_pair(2, COLOR_YELLOW,COLOR_BLACK);
init_pair(3, COLOR_BLACK,COLOR_CYAN);

OUTER: while (1) {
    foreach (sort keys %ENV) {
        attron(COLOR_PAIR(3));   # set black-on-cyan
        addstr(5,8," $_ ");      # move and write variable name
        clrtoeol();              # delete anything beyond it
        attron(COLOR_PAIR(2));   # set yellow-on-black
        addstr(6,8,$ENV{$_});    # move and write variable value
        clrtoeol();              # delete anything beyond it
        move(9,79);              # move the cursor out of the way
        refresh();               # send output to the screen
        last OUTER if (lc(getch) eq 'q');
    }
}

attron(COLOR_PAIR(1)); # set white-on-black
move(9,5);
addstr("All Done");
refresh();                  # send output to the screen

END { endwin; }        # end Curses properly even on abnormal termination
```

This is what this application looks like:

There are a few points to note about this application:

- First, every Curses program that does not create windows (see later) must start with `initstr`. Similarly, all Curses programs must end with `endwin` to reset the terminal into a usable state afterwards.

- Second, nothing appears on the screen until we call `refresh`. Up until this point, Curses carries out all the changes in an internal buffer, recording what parts of the screen have been changed. When we call `refresh`, all the changes—and only the changes—made since the last `refresh` (or `initscr`) are sent to the terminal in one go. This allows Curses to make efficient use of bandwidth in situations that involve a slow serial or network connection.

- Third, if no coordinates are specified to subroutines that output to the screen, then the current cursor position is used instead. This can be seen earlier, for example, in the `move` and `addstr` pairs.

- Fourth, we can enable and disable text attributes like bold or underline by using `attron` and `attroff`. The different attributes can be numerically `or`ed together to switch several attributes on or off together.

- Fifth, to use colors in Curses, we need to first call `start_color`. Curses handles colors in pairs, setting both foreground and background at once. We define color pairs using `init_pair`, which takes an arbitrary pair number and a foreground and background color. These pairs can be used with `attorn` (and `attroff`) using the `COLOR_PAIR` macro. The whole interface is more sophisticated than this quick example, of course.

- Last, as we discussed earlier, most Curses features take variable numbers of arguments and determine what to do based on how many there are. To write at a given position of the screen, we can therefore use `move` and then `addstr` with one argument or supply the coordinates and the string as three arguments to `addstr`. The `clrtoeol` subroutine also accepts coordinates, though we haven't used them here.

Now that we have seen how to create a Curses application that manages the whole screen, we can look at creating and managing windows in Curses.

Curses Windows

The Curses module has two modes of operation. The simple mode, which we have just seen, is suitable for full-screen programs where the entire screen is used as a single window. The object-oriented version is useful if we are programming Curses windows, where each window is effectively a small screen in its own right. In this case, we do not use initscr but create and call methods on window objects. The homogenization of the Curses module interface means that we still use the same names for the methods as we did for the functions. Here is how we create a window in Curses:

```
# create a new 20x10 window, top left corner at coordinates 5,5
my $window = new Curses (10, 20, 5, 5);
```

Once we have created a window, we can move the cursor around in it, write to it, refresh it, and set attributes on it, just as we can with the whole screen. Here is a short program that creates a window, writes to it, and then moves it across the screen each time we press a key:

```perl
#!/usr/bin/perl
# curses2.pl
use warnings;
use strict;

use Curses;

# create a 3x20 window with top corner at 0,0
my $window = new Curses(3, 20, 0, 0);

cbreak();   # go into 'cbreak' mode
noecho();   # prevent key presses echoing
curs_set(0) # hide the cursor

# define some colors
start_color();
init_pair(1,COLOR_YELLOW,COLOR_BLUE);
init_pair(2,COLOR_GREEN,COLOR_BLUE);
# put something in the window
$window->attron(COLOR_PAIR(1));
$window->clear();
$window->box(0,0);
$window->attron(COLOR_PAIR(2));
$window->addstr(1, 1, " This is a Window ");
$window->attroff(COLOR_PAIR(2));

$window->refresh();
getch;

foreach (5..25) {
    $window->mvwin($_, $_);
    $window->refresh();
    last if (lc(getch) eq 'q');
}

END { endwin; }   # end Curses properly even on abnormal termination
```

Another Curses feature used for the first time in this program is the curs_set function, which controls the visibility of the cursor. As this is a windowed application, we pass it a value of zero to render the cursor invisible. This is what the application looks like after we have entered a few key presses:

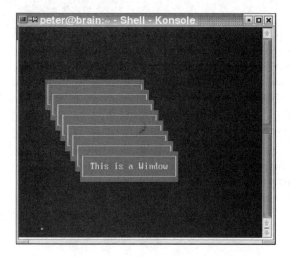

One irritating aspect of this application is that it leaves a trail of old window borders across the screen as the window moves. To avoid this trailing effect, we would need to delete the old window first—fortunately Curses's refresh mechanism means that blanking the whole block and then replacing the window in its new position is as efficient as trying to work out the parts that have changed. However, this doesn't take account of the possibility that something else might be underneath the window. To solve that problem, we can make use of Panels, an extension to Curses frequently supplied as a secondary library that provides intelligent windows that can stack and overlap.

Third-Party Extensions to Curses

Curses is a popular library and has been around for some time now. Consequently, a lot of other libraries and Perl modules have been written that build on Curses to provide everything from simple menus to complete GUI toolkits. Checking CPAN for modules providing more advanced Curses-based features is well worth the time before embarking on a Curses-based project—the Curses::Forms module (for data entry) and Curses::Widgets module (for button bars, dialog boxes, and other "GUI" components) in particular. Other Curses modules include Cdk, which uses a third-party C library built on Curses, and PV.

Programming the Terminal Directly with POSIX

For occasions when modules like Term::ReadKey won't do, and we have to program the terminal directly, we can use the POSIX module. However, while many platforms support some POSIX compliance, they may not be able to handle programming the terminal directly. On Unix, these techniques will usually work; other platforms may not be so fortunate.

Whereas Term::Cap interrogates the termcap database, POSIX::Termios is concerned with the terminal itself. That is, Term::Cap can tell us what the Delete key ought to be; POSIX::Termios can tell us what it actually is right now. To use it, we first need to create a termios object, then associate that object with the filehandle of the terminal we want to manipulate:

```
use POSIX;
my $termios = new POSIX::Termios;
```

We then tell the object to read the attributes of a terminal by passing a filehandle number to getattr. This can be either a simple integer such as 0 for STDIN, 1 for STDOUT, or 2 for STDERR, or a file number extracted from a filehandle with fileno:

```perl
# three different ways to get the attributes of STDIN
$termios->getattr;
$termios->getattr(0);
$termios->getattr(fileno(STDIN));
```

Once we have the attributes in our termios object, we can retrieve them with functions like getospeed (for the terminal output speed) and getcc (for the control characters) and set them with functions like setospeed and setcc. All this just changes values in a hash, however. Once we have finished modifying the attributes, we set them on a filehandle by using setattr. Here is a short program that redefines a few properties of STDIN and STDOUT by way of an example:

```perl
#!/usr/bin/perl
# termios.pl
use warnings;
use strict;

use POSIX qw(:termios_h);

my $stdin = fileno(STDIN);
my $stdout = fileno(STDOUT);

print "\nInterrogating STDIN:\n";
my $termios_stdin = new POSIX::Termios;
$termios_stdin->getattr($stdin);

# redefine the erase (delete) key
print "\tErase key is ", $termios_stdin->getcc(VERASE), "\n";
print "Set Erase to Control-D:\n";
$termios_stdin->setcc(VERASE,4);
print "\tErase key is ", $termios_stdin->getcc(VERASE), "\n";

# set the terminal to no-echo
my $lflag = $termios_stdin->getlflag;
printf "\tLocal flag is %b\n", $lflag;
# Perl<5.6: print "\tLocal flag is ",unpack("B16",pack('n',$lflag)),"\n";
# print "Set Terminal Mode to Noecho\n";
$termios_stdin->setlflag($lflag & ~(ECHO | ECHOK));
printf "\tLocal flag is %b\n",$termios_stdin->getlflag;

# Perl<5.6: print "\tLocal flag is ",
# unpack("B16",pack('n', $termios_stdin->getlflag)),"\n";
# set changes on STDIN
print "Setting STDIN from termios object\n";
$termios_stdin->setattr($stdin,POSIX::TCSANOW);

# restore original local flag (enable echo)
$termios_stdin->setlflag($lflag | ECHO | ECHOK);
printf "\tLocal flag is %b\n",$termios_stdin->getlflag;
# Perl<5.6: print "\tLocal flag is
# ",unpack("B16",pack('n', $termios_stdin->getlflag)),"\n";
print "Setting STDIN from termios object\n";
$termios_stdin->setattr($stdin, POSIX::TCSANOW);

print "\nInterrogating STDOUT:\n";
my $termios_stdout = new POSIX::Termios;
$termios_stdout->getattr($stdout);
my $old_stdout=new POSIX::Termios;
$old_stdout->getattr($stdout);
```

```
# set the output speed
print "\tOutput speed is ",$termios_stdout->getospeed,"\n";
print "Set speed to 9600 bps:\n";
$termios_stdout->setospeed(POSIX::B9600);
print "\tOutput speed is ", $termios_stdout->getospeed,"\n";

# set changes on STDOUT
print "Setting STDOUT from termios object\n";
$termios_stdout->setattr($stdout, POSIX::TCSANOW);
```

When run, this script should produce output similar to the following:

```
Interrogating STDIN:
        Erase key is 127
Set Erase to Control-D:
        Erase key is 4
        Local flag is 1000101000111011
Set Terminal Mode to Noecho
        Local flag is 1000101000010011
Setting STDIN from termios object
        Local flag is 1000101000111011
Setting STDIN from termios object

Interrogating STDOUT:
        Output speed is 15
Set speed to 9600 bps:
        Output speed is 13
Setting STDOUT from termios object
```

For more information on the POSIX module and in particular the subroutines and arguments of the POSIX::Termios module, consult the system POSIX manual page and the Perl documentation under perldoc POSIX.

Summary

In this chapter, we saw how to communicate with a terminal, real or virtual, and learned how to determine whether a script is interactive. Controlling terminal input using the Term::ReadKey module was covered, as well as how to read individual characters from the keyboard (or any input device) interactively, without waiting for the Return key to be pressed. After this, we moved on to reading complete lines and looked at the various ways the Term::ReadLine module expands the capabilities of Perl's built-in readline operator to handle passwords and invisible input, serial connections, line ending translation, and control characters. We also looked at interrogating the terminal to discover its size.

The latter part of the chapter discussed terminal capabilities and the creation of terminal objects, their supported features, and maintaining a history of command lines. We also looked at the Term::Screen module, saw how to write in colors and use ornaments, and then looked at the Curses library, the basis for many terminal-oriented applications. Finally, we explored ways to program a terminal directly via POSIX, when no higher-level interface can do the job.

## CHAPTER 16

Warnings and Errors

Wish as we might, warnings and errors are an inevitable part of the software development life cycle. Like any programming language, Perl generates warnings and errors and provides tools and mechanisms to help us identify problems and control what happens in the event that a warning or error is generated. Some warnings and errors can be issued at compile time—a common example is a syntax error. Others only occur during run time. Some may occur at either phase, depending on what Perl can figure out during compilation.

Errors are always fatal and always issued whenever they occur. We can carry out cleanup tasks if we supply an END block, but we cannot stop the error from terminating the program unless we place the code in which it occurs inside an eval. In this case, the return value of the eval will be false and the special variable $@ set to the error message that Perl raised within the eval.

Warnings are a different matter. They are never fatal, unless we choose to make them so, and in Perl 5.5 and earlier, they were divided into two broad categories, optional and mandatory. Mandatory warnings, as their name suggests, are always issued whether or not we asked for them. Optional warnings are issued only if we enabled them with the -w option or the equivalent special variable $^W. From Perl 5.6 onwards, the warnings pragma allows much greater flexibility in how warnings are handled, including the ability to disable even mandatory warnings—now called default warnings—and enable or disable warnings by category. We can even devise our own warnings categories if we so wish.

As well as Perl's own errors, we often need to deal with system errors, numeric Errno values returned to us through the special variables $! or $?. These errors are neither fatal nor issue any warning, so we need to make sure we deal with them. If we have a lot of checking to do, the Fatal module can help to automate some of the task for us.

Enabling Warnings

Global warnings are traditionally enabled from the command line. We can use the -w switch:

```
> perl -w myscript.pl
```

This enables warnings in the script and any modules that it loads. We can, of course, also use PERL5OPT for this purpose, first introduced back in Chapter 1. On any Unix platform, and in fact most others too, we can specify the -w option on the first line too, if it starts with the special #! notation:

```
#!/usr/bin/perl -w
```

We can achieve a similar effect within the application by setting the variable $^W (although since Perl 5.6 this is superseded by and inferior to the warnings pragma):

```
#!/usr/bin/perl
$^W=1;
...
```

Even though $^W sets the same underlying control variable as -w, as a variable assignment, it only takes effect at run time. It therefore cannot affect warnings during compile time. We could place the assignment inside a BEGIN block, but this lacks elegance:

```
BEGIN { $^W=1; }
```

From Perl 5.6 onwards, the warnings pragma is an altogether better way to enable warnings, and it takes over from $^W as the preferred mechanism for enabling or disabling warnings within code:

```
#!/usr/bin/perl
use warnings;
...
```

The difference between this example and the previous one is that warnings are not enabled in modules that this script happens to use. While it is perfectly valid for the invoker of our program to tell Perl to enable warnings globally with -w, it is considered bad form for the code itself to make that decision on behalf of modules that it is only the user of. $^W still works and is equivalent to -w; it is simply the usage model that is discouraged.

The application can switch global warnings off again by unsetting $^W. As $^W is a global special variable, we would typically do this within a block (for example, a subroutine) using the local keyword. In fact, this is one of the relatively few places where local is exactly the right tool for the job:

```
sub mywarningpronesub {
    local $^W = 0;
    ...
}
```

The more modern way to achieve the same end is

```
sub mywarningpronesub {
    no warnings;
    ...
}
```

The preceding two examples seem exactly the same, but they differ in the same way that local differs from my—the effect of creating a locally altered $^W propagates into any subroutines called from within the block, even if they are in other packages. By contrast, no warnings affects only the code in the block and does not affect code in called subroutines. This means we won't inadvertently disable a warning from a subroutine we call that we would rather have seen just because we wanted to suppress a warning in our own code. In addition, no warnings will disable all warnings, even mandatory/default ones that $^W and -w cannot influence.

Note that where both -w and $^W and the warnings pragma are attempting to control warnings, the warnings pragma always wins.

The warnings pragma is actually a lot more versatile than this, and it has the potential to allow us to enable or disable warnings selectively. It also works at compile time, unlike $^W. We will cover it in more detail at the end of the chapter.

Forcing Warnings On or Off

If we want to prevent warnings from being disabled by the application, we can replace the -w option with -W, which has exactly the same effect but ignores any attempts by the program or a loaded module to disable them again, even temporarily:

```
> perl -W myscript.pl
```

The exact reverse is also possible, disabling warnings completely and preventing code from enabling them again with -X. This is not an option to make frequent use of (fixing the warnings is a much better idea) but can sometimes help in otherwise verbose output or in well-understood production environments. For example:

```
> perl -X myscript.pl
```

The -W and -X options completely override all instances of -w, the use warnings pragma, and the special variable.

Enabling Better Diagnostics

Occasionally, the errors and warnings emitted by Perl are less than completely transparent. We can't get Perl to fix a problem for us, but we can ask it for a more detailed description of the error or warning with the diagnostics pragma. When enabled, Perl will provide a complete (and frequently very long) description of any warning or error rather than the normal terse message. To enable it, we just write

```
use diagnostics;
```

As an example, the following program generates a void context warning, because the statement return value is not used, and it performs no other task:

```
#!/usr/bin/perl
use diagnostics;

2**2;
```

Since generating diagnostic warnings implies generating warnings in the first place, use diagnostics automatically enables global (not lexically scoped) warnings. That said, we can still disable them with no warnings or $^W=0 later on. As a result, we do not need to enable warnings in this program explicitly—we get them automatically. This is the warning that Perl produces from the preceding program when the warnings pragma is enabled:

```
Useless use of a constant in void context at ./diagnostics.pl line 4 (#1)
```

And here is what the diagnostics pragma has to say about it:

```
(W void) You did something without a side effect in a context
that does nothing with the return value, such as a statement that
doesn't return a value from a block, or the left side of a scalar
comma operator. Very often this points not to stupidity on your
part, but a failure of Perl to parse your program the way you
thought it would. For example ....

(...and so on)
```

As this truncated output shows, the diagnostic output is frequently quite detailed.

We can learn more about a warning without generating such verbose output by looking it up with perldoc perldiag. This references the perldiag.pod manual page, which contains the text of all the diagnostics displayed by the diagnostics pragma.

The (W void) prefix at the start of the message indicates that this is a warning (as opposed to a fatal error) in the void category. We can use this information with the warnings pragma to selectively enable or disable this warning, as we will see later.

By default, use diagnostics will generate diagnostics for warnings at both the compile and run-time stage. It is not possible to disable diagnostics during the compile stage (no diagnostics does not work), but they can be enabled and disabled at run time with enable diagnostics and disable diagnostics:

```
use diagnostics;
disable diagnostics;

sub diagnose_patient {
    enable diagnostics;
    my $undefined_filehandle;
    print $undefined_filehandle "It's worse than that, he's dead Jim";
    disable diagnostics;
}
```

Optionally, -verbose may be specified to have the diagnostics pragma output an introduction explaining the classification of warnings, errors, and other salient information:

```
use diagnostics qw(-verbose);
```

Two variables may also be set to control the output of the diagnostics module prior to using use on it. $diagnostics::PRETTY enhances the text a little for browsing. $diagnostics::DEBUG is for the overly curious. Both are unset by default but can be enabled with

```
BEGIN {
    $diagnostics::PRETTY=1;
    $diagnostics::DEBUG=1;
}
```

Getting Warning Diagnostics After the Fact

It is not a terribly good idea to enable use diagnostics in programs that generate a lot of warnings. Fortunately, we can collect the terse warning messages generated during execution of our program and expand them later, at our leisure. The command-line tool splain (as in "explain," but punchier) will generate diagnostic messages from warnings if they have been stored in a file:

```
> perl myscript.pl 2>warnings.log
> splain -v -p < warnings.log
```

The -v (verbose) and -p (pretty) options are optional; they have the same meanings as they do for the diagnostics pragma if specified.

Generating Warnings and Errors

We can generate our own (nonfatal) warnings and (fatal) errors using the warn and die functions. Both functions take a list of arguments, which are passed to print and sent to standard error.

The key distinction between them is, of course, that die causes the application to exit, whereas warn merely emits a message and allows the application to continue running. The die function returns the value of $! to the caller, which can be retrieved through $? if the caller is also a Perl script. If $! is not set but $? is, then die shifts it right eight places ($? >> 8) and returns that as the exit code, to propagate the exit code from a child process to the parent. The value returned by die (or exit) can also be modified through $? (we will come to this a little later).

If the message passed to either warn or die ends with a newline, then it is printed verbatim, without embellishment. If, however, no trailing newline is present, then Perl will add details of the file and line number to the end of the message (plus a newline). Consider the following examples:

```
> perl -e "warn \"Eek! A Mouse\n\""
```

```
Eek! A Mouse!
```

```
> perl -e "warn \"Eek A Mouse\""
```

```
Eek! A Mouse! at -e line 1.
```

If no message at all is passed to warn or die, then they consult the value of $@ to see if an error has been trapped by an eval statement (see later). In this case, they use the message contained in $@ and append \t...caught or \t...propagated to it, respectively. If even $@ is not defined, then they get creative; die simply produces

```
Died at <file> line <line>.
warn produces the paranoid:
Warning: something's wrong at <file> line <line>.
```

Of course, giving either function no arguments is questionable at best, unless we are checking explicitly the result of an eval:

```
die if !eval($evalstr) and $@;
```

As a special case for evaluated code, if the die function is passed a reference (not a message), then this reference is set into the variable $@ outside the eval. The main point of this is to allow object-oriented programs to raise exceptions as objects rather than messages:

```
eval {
    ...
    die new MyModule::PermissionsException;
}

if ($@) {
    if ($@ == MyModule::PermissionsException) {
        ...
    } else {
        ...
    }
}
```

If die is given a reference as an argument and it is not in an eval, then it simply prints the reference by converting it into a string, as usual.

Intercepting Warnings and Errors

An error is always fatal, so the only way to intercept it nonfatally is by enclosing the code that raises it within an eval statement. For example, this is how we could deal with a fatal error by converting it into a warning instead:

```
my $result=eval $code_in_a_string;
if ($@) {
    warn "Fatal error in evaluated code: $@\n";
}
```

The special variable $@ is given the text of the error message that Perl would ordinarily have issued. Warnings are not recovered by this variable, but we can trap them with a warnings pseudo-handler.

Warnings and errors, whether issued by Perl directly or generated by applications through the warn or die functions, can also be trapped within program code using the __WARN__ and pseudo-signal handlers, by defining values for them in the %SIG signal handler hash. For example, we could suppress warnings completely, even under -W, by creating a warnings handler that does nothing:

```
BEGIN {
    $SIG{__WARN__} = sub{};
}

2*2; # does not produce void context warning even under -W
```

To ensure the handler is used even at compile time, we enclose it in a BEGIN block. This is a deliberately simplistic example, however. Actually, disabling warnings even under -W should not be done lightly, if at all.

A more useful warnings handler might embellish the warning before printing it or redirect it to a file:

```
$SIG{__WARN__} = sub{ print WARNLOG, "$0 warning: ", @_, "\n" };
```

We can even call warn from inside the handler, since the handler itself is disabled while it is executing:

```
$SIG{__WARN__} = sub { warn "$0 warning: ", @_; };
```

The die handler is defined in much the same way, but unlike a warn handler, we cannot suppress it completely—to do that we need an eval as illustrated previously—only change the message by calling die a second time. Any other action will cause Perl to carry on and continue dying with the original arguments. This means that we can use a die handler to perform cleanup actions, but we cannot use it to avoid death.

```
$SIG{__DIE__} = sub {
    # send real message to log file
    print LOGFILE "Died: @_";
    # Give the user something flowery
    die "Oh no, not again";
}
```

This approach is useful in things like CGI programs, where we want the user to know something is wrong but do not want to actually give away potentially embarrassing details. (In fact, the CGI::Carp module is an extension of the Carp module covered later in this chapter that exists precisely for this purpose and implements a smart __DIE__ handler that is worth a look to prevent exactly this kind of eventuality.)

Warnings and Errors with Calling Context

The Carp module is one of Perl's most enduringly useful modules. It's primary subroutines carp and croak work exactly like warn and die but return details of the calling context rather than the one in which they occurred. They are therefore ideal for library code and module subroutines, since the warning or error will report the line in the code that called them rather than a warning or error in the module source itself.

Both routines track back up the stack of subroutine calls looking for a call from a suspect package, which by default means the first call not in the package itself or its ancestry (as determined by @ISA). They then use and return the details of that call. The upshot of this is that irrespective of how many subroutine or method calls might have occurred within the package, it is the calling package that resulted in the carp or croak that is reported:

```perl
package My::Module;

sub mymodulesub {
    carp "You called me from your own code";
}
```

When called, say from a script named `owncode.pl`, the `mymodulesub` subroutine in this module will generate a message like

```
You called me from your own code at ./owncode.pl line N.
```

From the point of view of an application developer, this gives them a message that originates in their own code, and not in a library module from which they have no immediate means to trace the error or warning back to the call that caused it.

The `cluck` and `confess` subroutines are more verbose versions of `carp` and `croak`. They generate messages for the file and line number they were actually called at (unlike `carp` and `croak`, but like `warn` and `die`) and generate a full stack trace of subroutine calls in reverse order, from the subroutine they were called from back up to the top of the program.

Here is a short program that demonstrates `carp`, `cluck`, and `confess`. To make things interesting, we have used three subroutines, each in their own package, to illustrate the effect of calling these subroutines at different points:

```perl
#!/usr/bin/perl
# carpdemo.pl
use warnings;

{
    package Top;
    use Carp qw(cluck);
    sub top {
        cluck "Called 'top'";
        Middle->middle();
    }

    package Middle;
    use Carp;
    sub middle {
        carp "Are we there yet? Called 'middle'";
        Bottom->bottom();
    }

    package Bottom;
    use Carp qw(carp confess shortmess);
    #our @CARP_NOT=qw(Middle); #see @CARP_NOT later

    sub bottom {
        shortmess("Here we are");
        carp "Called 'bottom'";
        confess "I did it!";
    }
}

Top->top();
```

This is the output generated from this program:

```
Called 'top' at ./carpdemo.pl line 9
        Top::top('Top') called at ./carpdemo.pl line 30
Are we there yet? Called 'middle' at ./carpdemo.pl line 10
Here we are at ./carpdemo.pl line 17
Called 'bottom' at ./carpdemo.pl line 17
I did it! at ./carpdemo.pl line 26
        Bottom::bottom('Bottom') called at ./carpdemo.pl line 17
        Middle::middle('Middle') called at ./carpdemo.pl line 10
        Top::top('Top') called at ./carpdemo.pl line 30
```

We can see in this example that each call to carp or shortmess reports itself in the context of the caller rather than the subroutine being called. So we see Called 'bottom' at line 17, rather than at line 25 where the call to carp actually resides. None of these packages inherit from each other, so carp only has to step back one level in the subroutine stack to find the context to report. If these packages did inherit from each other, all the carp calls would report themselves at the last line of the program, where the outermost call originated.

Redefining the Calling Context

Since packages in the inheritance hierarchy of the package that invokes carp, cluck, croak, or confess are considered to be within the context of the package (that is, trusted), Carp will search up the calling stack until it finds a subroutine in a package that is not a relation.

We can override this behavior and define our own trust relationships by defining a package variable called @CARP_NOT. This takes the place of @ISA for determining context in any package in which it is placed. Changing the trust relationship is useful, for example, to augment is-a relationships with has-a relationships. In the previous example, we had a commented-out assignment to @CARP_NOT in the Bottom package. If we enable it and run the program again, the output changes in the fourth and fifth lines to

```
Here we are at ./carpdemo.pl line 10
Called 'bottom' at ./carpdemo.pl line 10
```

This is because the Middle package is now trusted by the Bottom package, so the calling context now steps up one more level in the calling stack and finds the call from top in package Top at line 10 instead. Only these two lines change, because the trust relationship only affects carp and shortmess for calls between Middle and Bottom.

Trust works both ways, so we can equally define Bottom as a trusted package of Middle and see exactly the same results:

```
...package Middle;
use Carp;
our @CARP_NOT=qw(Bottom); #same effect
...
```

If we were to similarly tell Middle it could trust Top, the initial call to Top->top would be reported as the context instead. This is because trust is transitive; if Bottom trusts Middle, it trusts what Middle trusts too. Without any @CARP_NOT arrays defined, @ISA is used, so this simply becomes a case of trusting the family—if two packages have a common ancestor, they trust each other.

However, adding Top to the @CARP_NOT array in Bottom would not have the same effect, since Middle still does not trust Top or vice versa. A direct call from Top to Bottom, on the other hand, would be treated as trusted.

Forcing a Full Stack Trace

If the symbol verbose is imported into the application, then carp and croak are automatically upgraded into cluck and confess, that is, a stack trace is generated by all four subroutines. We do not typically want to do this within applications, but it is very handy on the command line if we want to get extra detail on a problem:

```
> perl -MCarp=verbose myscript.pl
```

Since carp and cluck are essentially improved versions of warn, they can, like warn, be trapped by assigning a handler to $SIG{__WARN__}. Similarly, croak and confess can be caught with $SIG{__DIE__}.

Developers who are engaged in writing server-side applications like CGI scripts should instead make use of the CGI::Carp module. This overrides the default subroutines provided by Carp with versions that are formatted to be compatible with the format of a web server's error log.

Warnings Categories

The warnings pragma is more than just a lexically scoped alternative to the -w option and special variable $^W, even though this is a good reason by itself for us to use it. By default, with no argument list, all warnings are enabled. This is actually equivalent to

```
use warnings qw(all);
```

By supplying alternative and more specific category names to the warnings pragma, and especially using no, we can enable or disable warnings selectively. For example, the following disables all warnings related to void context, including the Useless use of .... in void context message we saw earlier:

```
no warnings qw(void);
```

Since this is a lexically scoped declaration, we can use it inside a subroutine in the same way we can selectively enable symbolic references with no strict 'refs'. The effect of the pragma extends only within the body of the subroutine or block in which it is declared.

Enabling and Disabling Warnings by Category

We can enable or disable warnings as often as necessary, with only the warning categories cited being affected. The effects of multiple warning pragmas stack up cumulatively (with each one removing its effects again when its scope ends), and several categories may also be given at once. For example:

```
no warnings 'void';
no warnings 'untie';
no warnings 'uninitialized';
use warnings 'untie';
```

This has the same cumulative effect as the following single declaration:

```
no warnings qw(void uninitialized);
```

We can also programmatically check whether a given category of warnings is enabled or not, with warnings::enabled:

```
my $we_are_checking_for_void = warnings::enabled('void');
```

Defining and Using Custom Warnings Categories

We can also manage our own category, if we are programming modules. A new warnings category can be dynamically added, with a category name equal to the module's package (or to be more precise, the package currently in effect). For example, this creates a new warnings category called My::Module:

```
package My::Module;
use warnings::register;
...
```

To issue warnings in our new module category, call warnings::warn rather than the core warn to have the warning emitted under the custom category rather than as a regular uncategorized warning:

```
...
warnings::warn("This warning is in the 'My::Module' category");
```

With one argument, warnings::warn will use the current package as the category, assuming that we registered it beforehand. To issue a warning outside the package, or to issue a warning in one of Perl's predefined warnings categories, we insert the category name in front of the warning message. Here is a short example of registering a new category, Ship::Announcement, and then issuing a warning using it:

```
#!/usr/bin/perl
use strict;
use warnings;

{
    package Ship::Announcement;
    use warnings::register;
}

warnings::warn("Ship::Announcement" =>
    "Pinback, it's your turn to feed the alien");
```

Interestingly, we can also use a blessed object reference as a category. Perl will simply extract the object's class using ref and use that as the category name. This means we can write code like this:

```
#!/usr/bin/perl
# objectwarn.pl
use strict;
use warnings;

{
    package Ship::Announcement;
    use warnings::register;

    sub new {
        my ($class,$msg)=@_;
        $msg ||= "No message";
        return bless \$msg, (ref($class) or $class);
    }
}
my $msg = new Ship::Announcement("Please return to the Bomb Bay immediately");

warnings::warn($msg => $$msg);
```

We can also issue a warning in one of Perl's predefined warnings categories:

```
warnings::warn(void => "This warning is in the 'void' category");
```

The real point of defining our own warnings category in a module is, of course, that we can now selectively control warnings from the module independently. Code that uses our module would now ideally be able to switch warnings from our module on and off by issuing appropriate pragmas:

```
use warnings qw(Ship::Announcement);
no warnings qw(Ship::Announcement);
```

However, the warn subroutine does not honor these pragmas and will always issue a warning, so long as the warning category actually exists. To control whether or not a warning is issued based on whether or not the category is enabled, we need to use the enabled or warnif subroutines instead.

Conditional Warnings

We can check whether or not a given warnings category is enabled with the warnings::enabled function. This returns a true value if the warning is currently active, or a false value otherwise. We can use this to issue a warning only if the category is enabled—it is important to remember that warnings::warn on its own does not take heed of whether or not a category is enabled or disabled. If we do not pass an argument to warnings::enabled, then it will use the current package name as the category, just as warnings::warn does:

```
package Ship::Malfunction;
...

if (warnings::enabled()) {
    warnings::warn("Abandon Ship!");
}
```

We can also use it to issue a warning in a different category to the one being checked, as this snippet of code illustrates:

```
use warnings "Ship::Announcement", "Ship::Malfunction";

if (warnings::enabled("Ship::Malfunction")) {
    warnings::warn("Ship::Announcement" => "Abandon Ship!");
} else {
    warnings::warn("Ship::Ignored" =>
        "We'll find out what it is when it goes bad");
}
```

If we do not need to issue warnings in a different category, then we can use warnings::warnif as a shorter way to express the same concept:

```
warnings::warnif("Ship::Malfunction" => "Abandon Ship!"); # explicit category

warnings::warnif("Abandon Ship!"); # implicit category = current package
```

If we want to issue warnings conditionally, we should always use warnif in preference to warn. If we want to make a warning mandatory and impossible to disable even with a bare no warnings pragma (-X will still work), we use warn instead of warnif.

The warnif and enabled subroutines also work on object references, just as warnings::warn does. This has interesting possibilities for subclassed object classes, since we can enable warnings for each subclass individually even though the actual warning is issued in the parent class. This is because the warnings category is derived from the package an object is blessed into, which is what-ever subclass the object belongs to. Imagine adding this method to the Ship::Announcement package in the previous object example:

```
sub announce {
    my $self=shift;
    warnings::warnif($self => $$self);
}
```

If called with a `Ship::Announcement` object, the `warnif` subroutine will check that the `Ship::Announcement` category is enabled. If we created a subclass called `Ship::Announcement::Important`, then `warnif` would instead check for that warnings class—even though the same subroutine is called in both cases.

Making Warnings Fatal

The `warnings` pragma also allows us to change the severity level of a warnings category to convert all warnings in that category into fatal errors. To do this, we prefix any warning or list of warnings we want to be made fatal with the special `FATAL` keyword. For example:

```
use warnings FATAL => "Ship::Malfunction", "Ship::Status";
```

The fatality is established at the place the category is used, not by the category itself, so a given category can be fatal in one place and nonfatal in another (and, of course, not enabled at all in a third):

```
use warnings qw(Ship::Announcement Ship::Malfunction);
...
{
    use warnings "Ship::Status", FATAL => "Ship::Malfunction";
    ...
}
...
no warnings Ship::Malfunction;
```

Once a warning is marked fatal in a given scope, it stays fatal within that scope. So if we were to disable the `Ship::Malfunction` category within the block and then reenable it, it would return as a fatal warning. To downgrade a fatal error back to a nonfatal one, we use the corresponding `NONFATAL` keyword:

```
use warnings FATAL => "Ship::Malfunction";      # mark fatal
no warnings "Ship::Malfunction";                # disabled
use warnings "Ship::Malfunction";               # still fatal
use warnings NONFATAL => "Ship::Malfunction";   # now nonfatal
```

We can make Perl's own warnings fatal and then nonfatal again in the same way:

```
use warnings FATAL => qw[deprecated severe redefine];
```

```
use warnings FATAL => 'all', NONFATAL => 'io', FATAL => 'exec','unopened';
```

The second example makes all warnings fatal, then makes the `io` category nonfatal, then within the `io` category the `exec` and `unopened` categories are made fatal again. To see how these categories are related to each other, let's take a look at Perl's complete list of predefined warning categories.

Predefined Warning Categories

All of Perl's internal warnings are assigned to a category. By enabling or disabling these categories, we can control what warnings the interpreter will issue. Here is a list of all the currently defined categories:

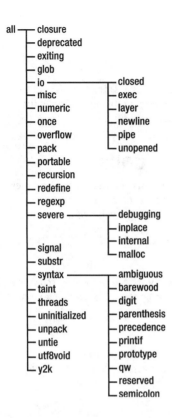

As this is a hierarchical list, we can disable all types of input/output warnings through the io master category, or just except unopened filehandle warnings with the unopened category. So to enable all warnings, then disable all input/output warnings but keep warnings concerning unopened filehandles, we can write

```
use warnings;
no warnings qw(io);
use warnings qw(unopened):
```

The all category is at the top of the tree and contains, appropriately enough, all categories. Since it is implied if the warnings pragma is used without an argument, we do not usually have a reason to specify it explicitly. It is chiefly useful for making all warnings fatal, as noted earlier.

More commonly, we might want to disable a specific category temporarily because we know the warning is incorrect in a specific case. For instance, if we want to use qw to define a list of words that validly include commas, we can tell Perl to not complain about this possible mistake but keep all other warnings enabled. The example that follows disables qw warnings only within the subroutine block where the use of qw would otherwise trip the error:

```
#!/usr/bin/perl
# noqwcommawarn.pl
use strict;
use warnings;

sub first3list {
    no warnings 'qw';
```

```
        return qw[one,two,three a,b,c first,second,third]
};

print join(" ", first3list()),"\n";
```

To find out what category a given warning belongs to, we can use `diagnostics` to print out the description of the warning, which includes the warning type and category at the beginning of the first line. We can also and equivalently look up the warning in `perldoc perldiag`.

Handling Error Results from System Calls

Many of Perl's functions make calls to the operating system in order to carry out their task. Examples of such functions include `open` and `close`. None of these functions cause fatal errors or even produce warnings if they fail. Instead, they return an undefined value and set the value of the special variable `$!`.

System Error Numbers and Names

`$!`, also known as `$ERRNO` if we have used the `English` module, is directly related to the C `errno` value and holds the error status of the last system function called. In a string context, it returns a textual description, which we can use in our own messages:

```
warn "Warning - failed: $! \n";
```

In a numeric context, it returns the actual value of `errno`, which we can use programmatically. In order to use symbolic names rather than numbers for errors, it is convenient to use the `Errno` module:

```
use Errno qw(EAGAIN);

if ($!) {
    # check for EAGAIN in numeric comparison
    sleep(1), redo if $! == EAGAIN;
    # die, using $! in string context
    die "Fatal error: $!\n";
}
```

We can avoid importing error symbols and just write them explicitly:

```
sleep(1), redo if $! == Errno::EAGAIN;
```

`Errno` also defines the hash variable `%!`, which looks like a Perl special variable but actually is not. It allows us to check for errors by looking them up as keys in the hash and determining if they are set to a true value. Because `$!` can only hold one error at a time, there can only be one key with a true value, so this is really just an alternative syntax to using `==`:

```
sleep(1), redo if $!{EAGAIN};
```

The `Errno` module is smart in that it understands which errors are actually available on the platform that Perl is running on, so we can check for the existence of a particular symbol with `exists`:

```
#!/usr/bin/perl
# errno.pl
use warnings;
use strict;

use Errno;
```

```
print "EAGAIN = ", Errno::EAGAIN, "\n" if exists &Errno::EAGAIN;
print "EIO = ", Errno::EIO, "\n" if exists &Errno::EIO;
```

The symbols defined by Errno are subroutines, in the style of use constant, not scalars. Alternatively, we can use %!:

```
# continuation of errno.pl
foreach (qw[EAGAIN EIO EVMSERR EKETHUMP]) {
    warn "$_ not supported\n" unless exists $!{$_};
}
```

This will generate the warning EKETHUMP not supported on all platforms except those with excessive black pudding combat training. EVMSERR should only be defined on a VMS system.

Before making too much use of $!, be aware that the error number and name for a particular system error condition may not be consistent on all platforms. Most Unix implementations define the same numbers for the more common error types, but the more esoteric the error, the higher the likelihood of the number being inconsistent. For other platforms, the probability is higher still, so writing code that relies on specific values for the error number is likely to be nonportable unless a lot of care is taken. Consult the platform's errno.h for specific details of a particular operating system's definitions.

Setting the System Error Number

In a few cases, it can be advantageous to actually set the value of $!. Although it can be treated either numerically or as a string, $! can only be assigned a numeric value. Despite this, we can still produce a textual message from it:

```
$! = 1;
print "$!";   # display 'Operation not permitted'.
```

Setting $! should not be done lightly, since we can obscure a previous error that we ought to be handling. It sometimes happens that a system error is serious enough that we cannot proceed beyond it, and the correct course of action is to exit ourselves. This is one common reason to assign to $!:

```
if ($?) {
    $! = $? >> 8;
    die "Child exited abnormally: $!";
}
```

Or more briefly using exit:

```
exit ($?>>8) if $?;
```

Overriding $! is often done in an END block, in order to intercept a fatal error and adjust the exit status seen by the outside world before the program terminates.

It is important to remember to shift down the value of $? before assigning it to $!; otherwise, the return value will not be what we expect. In fact, the bottom 8 bits will get used as the exit status, and these are usually all blank, unless a signal occurred. This can be demonstrated by executing a command like

```
$ perl -e 'exit 1025'
$ echo $?
```

The shell will most likely return 1 from the echo command, illustrating that the top 8 bits are simply ignored.

While manipulating $! can be very useful, the die function automatically derives it from the value of $? if it is not currently set and $? is, so we do not have to worry in these cases—Perl will do the right thing automatically.

Handling Errors in Evaluated Code

Code evaluated inside an eval statement, which includes code evaluated indirectly via do, require, or even use (if the module contains a BEGIN block), may also set the variable $!. However, if the code fails to compile at all (in the event of a syntax error), then the special variable $@ is set to a textual description of the syntax error, as we saw earlier. The return value from eval is undef in this case, but it may also be undef in many cases that set $!, if the return value is determined by a function like open that returns undef itself. In order to properly handle an eval, therefore, we need to check both variables.

```
eval $evalstr;
if ($@) {
    die "Eval error: $@\n";
} elsif ($!) {
    die "Error: $!\n";
}
```

In the event of success, eval returns the value of the last expression that it evaluated, not a Boolean-oriented success or failure as we might like. Since this can frequently be 0 or undef, a common trick for checking eval for errors is to explicitly add a final statement of 1 to guarantee that the eval will always return true on success. A syntax error of any kind, on the other hand, will cause eval to return undef, since it never gets to the 1.

For instance, the following example will determine if the symlink function is supported on our platform:

```
$symlink_ok = eval {symlink("", ""); 1}
```

This works because in the event of the success or failure of the symlink, the eval will always return 1. It will return undef due to a fatal error raised by Perl in the event that the platform does not support symlink. In this case, symlink will return 0 but not raise a fatal error if it is supported, since we cannot link an empty file name to itself. The added 1 allows us to ignore the issue of a successful compile but a failed call. Of course, if we actually want to return a meaningful value from the eval, this is not going to work, but for many cases it's a useful trick.

Extended System Error Messages

Some platforms set the variable $!. However, also supply additional error information in the special variable $^E, also called $EXTENDED_OS_ERROR with the English module loaded. Currently only OS/2, Windows, and VMS support this feature (see Table 16-1).

Table 16-1. *Platforms Supporting $^E*

Platform	Description
OS/2	$^E is set to the last call to the OS/2 API either via the underlying C run-time libraries or directly from Perl. Incidental causes of $! being set are not carried over to $^E.
VMS	$^E may provide more specific information about errors than $!. This is particularly true for the VMS-specific EVMSERR, which we mentioned briefly in the example earlier.
Windows	$^E contains the last error returned by the Win32 API, as opposed to $!, which is more generic. It may contain additional information or a better description of the error, but it may also be empty even after an error due to the nonunified nature of the Win32 error reporting system.

For all other platforms, $^E is identical to $!. The best approach for handling $^E therefore is to add it to an error message if it is set and is not equal to the message returned from $!:

```
$message = $!;
$message.= "\n $^E" if $^E ne $!;
warn $message;
```

Finer-grained control may be possible by checking $^O ($OSNAME with use English) and dealing with errors in a platform-specific way, but this is overkill for most applications.

Errno and the POSIX Module

The POSIX module provides a direct interface from Perl to the underlying C standard library. Many of the functions in this library set errno and therefore the value of $! in Perl, and they can be handled in the same way as standard Perl functions like open and close. The POSIX module supplies its own errno function, which is just an explicit numeric evaluation of $! (literally expressed as $!+0), which serves to illustrate how closely $! is linked to the errno value.

The POSIX module also defines constants for the standard system errors like EAGAIN, EINVAL, EPERM, and so on, which we can import with the errno_h tag, along with the errno subroutine:

```
use POSIX qw(:errno_h);
```

In general, the Errno module is preferred over this approach, since it has better portability across different platforms (it allows us to check for the availability of a given error, for instance). However, for programs that make extensive use of the POSIX module, this may be an acceptable alternative.

All (modern) Unix systems conform closely to the POSIX standard, so the POSIX module works well on these platforms. Windows and other platforms can make some use of the module, but many aspects of it (in particular the API) will not be available. In particular, this module has no direct correspondence to the somewhat approximate POSIX compatibility layer in Windows NT.

Checking the Exit Status of Subprocesses and External Commands

Child processes run by Perl (for example, external commands run via system, backticks, and forked processes) return their status in the special variable $? when they exit. This is traditionally a 16-bit value (though it's 32 bit on Windows), containing two 8-bit values:

```
my $exitcode = $? >> 8;     # exit code
my $exitsignal = $? & 127;  # signal that caused exit
```

The *exit code* is the exit value returned by the subprocess. It should be zero for success, and a number corresponding to an error code on failure. The signal is often 0, but if set indicates that the child died because of a signal that it could neither trap nor ignore; for example, 2 would correspond to a SIGINT, and 9 would be a SIGKILL. Here is one way we could check for and handle a process that was either terminated by a signal or returned with an exit code (the command is in @args):

```
my $result = system(@args);
if (my $signal = $? & 127) {
    warn "External command exited on signal $signal\n";
} elsif (our $! = $? >> 8) {
    # assign $! numerically
    $! = $exitcode;

    # display it textually
    warn "External command existed with error: $!\n";
}
```

We take advantage of the special properties of $! to generate a textual message from the returned exit code, but note that this is only appropriate if the exit code corresponds to an errno value.

$? also controls the exit status from our own applications, although it is only set as the program exits. We can intercept and change the exit status of an application by redefining it in an END block. For example, to pretend that all is well (even if it technically isn't):

```
END {
    $? = 0 if $? and $ENV{'ALLS_WELL_THAT_ENDS_BADLY'};
}
```

Making Nonfatal System Errors Fatal

The Fatal module provides a simple and effective way to promote system-level errors to fatal errors in Perl. It can become inconvenient to provide error handling logic for every instance, so the Fatal module provides a convenient way to handle error conditions for many operations without coding. To use it, we simply pass an import list of the functions we want it to handle for us. For example, to trap errors from open and close:

```
use Fatal qw(open close);
```

Fatal works on the assumption that an undefined or empty value return is a sign of failure, so it will only trap functions like open and close that adhere to this rule. However, most of Perl's functions that make calls to the operating system, and therefore set $! on failure, do exactly this. We can even trap a failed print this way, something that we rarely do because of the loss in clarity this would otherwise cause:

```
use Fatal qw(print open close sysopen);
```

The Fatal module simply wraps the functions named in its import list with versions that emit errors. As such, it also works on our own subroutines, so long as they have been previously declared or defined and adhere to the same return value convention:

```
use Fatal qw(mysubroutine);
```

This works well if we never want to check for failures ourselves, but otherwise it can be overly limiting since it prevents us from making any more considered choices about how to handle a given error situation.

Rather than simply making all failures into fatal errors—which we must catch with a signal handler to prevent our application exiting—we can use Fatal to supplement our own error checking. In this mode, a fatal error is generated only if the return value of a wrapped subroutine or system operation is not checked explicitly. The mechanism, again simple, makes use of Perl's understanding of void context, which is reflected within subroutines as an undefined value from the wantarray function.

The wrappers generated by Fatal will check for and react to the context if we add the special label :void (for void context) to the import list. Any subroutines or functions listed before this label are treated as before and always issue an error on failure. Any subroutines or functions listed afterward issue an error only if their return value is ignored:

```
use Fatal qw(sysopen :void open close);

# OK - error handled by wrapper
open FILE, "> /readonly/area/myfile";

# OK - error handled in our code
unless (open FILE, "> /readonly/area/myfile") {
    ... handle error explicitly
}
```

```
# ERROR: block is never executed - Fatal wrapper intercepts
unless (sysopen FILE, "/readonly/area/myfile", O_RDWR|O_CREAT) {
    ...
}
```

Note that the last example will not generate an error at either compile time or run time—the Fatal wrapper will simply always intercept a failed sysopen, and our unless clause will never be called.

Error Logs and System Logs

We frequently want to arrange for errors and logging messages to go to a file rather than directly to the screen. This is simple enough to arrange both within and outside Perl. Outside, we can usually make use of output redirection in the shell to create a log file. Most modern shells (including NT's cmd.exe) allow standard error (filehandle number 2) to be directed with

> **perl myscript.pl 2>error.log**

From inside Perl, we can redirect the STDERR filehandle in a number of ways, which we cover in more detail in Chapter 5. Here is one simple way of doing it, by simply reopening STDERR to a new location:

```
open STDERR, "> /tmp/error.log" or print STDERR "Failed to open error log: $!";
```

▓**Tip** Note that if this open fails, the original STDERR filehandle remains intact. Since this is likely to be our fall-back option, we allow the open to fail but issue a warning about it on the original STDERR.

On Unix and Unix-like platforms, we may also make use of the system log, run by the system log daemon syslogd and generally configured by a file called /etc/syslog.conf or similar. Perl provides a standard interface to the Unix system log through the Sys::Syslog module:

```
use Sys::Syslog;
```

To open a connection to the system log daemon, use openlog. This takes three arguments: a program identifier, so we can be uniquely identified, a string containing optional options, and a syslog service, for example, user:

```
openlog 'myapp', 0, 'user';
```

Instead of 0 or '', the options can also be a comma-separated combination of cons, pid, nowait, and ndelay, which are passed to the underlying socket, for example, cons,pid,nowait. Once a connection is established, we can log messages with syslog, which takes a priority as its first argument and a printf-style format and values as the second and further arguments. The syslog daemon itself takes the priority, for example, error, and uses it to determine where the message is sent to, as determined by its own configuration (the file /etc/syslog.conf on most Unix systems).

```
syslog('debug', 'This is a debug message');
syslog('info', 'Testing, Testing, %d %d %d', 1, 2, 3);
syslog('news|warning', 'News unavailable at %s', scalar(localtime));
syslog('error', "Error! $!");
```

The value of $! is also automatically substituted for the %m format, in syslog only, so the last example can also be written as

```
syslog('error', 'Error! %m');
```

The socket type used to the connection may also be set (for openlog) or changed (even in between calls to syslog) with setlogsock, which we could use to switch between local and remote logging services. The default is to use an Internet domain socket (but note that a Unix domain socket is often better both from a security and a performance point of view. It is potentially possible to overrun syslog on an Internet domain socket, resulting in lost messages):

```
setlogsock ('unix');   # use a Unix domain socket
setlogsock ('inet');   # use an Internet domain socket
```

The return value from setlogsock is true if it succeeds or 0 if it fails. Consult the system documentation for more information on the system log and how to use and configure it.

On Windows NT/2000/XP, we can make use of the Win32::Eventlog module, available from CPAN, which provides an interface to the NT system log. For some reason known only to the developers of Windows, this log is a binary file and cannot be easily read except with the eventvwr utility. Be that as it may, here is a short example of using the Win32::EventLog module:

```
#!/perl/bin/perl
# win32.pl
use Win32::EventLog;
use strict;

my $e = new Win32::EventLog($0);
my %hash = (
    Computer  => $ENV{COMPUTERNAME},
    EventType => EVENTLOG_ERROR_TYPE,
    Category  => 42,
    Data      => "Data about this error",
    Strings   => "this is a test error"
);
$e->Report(\%hash);
```

For more information about programming the Windows event log, see perldoc Win32::Eventlog.

Summary

In this chapter, we examined Perl's errors and warnings, how and when Perl generates them, and how we can control them. Warnings can be enabled either globally or selectively, forced on or off from outside the program, and with the new lexical warnings pragma, limited in scope to just the source file and enclosing block where they are declared.

Errors cannot be simply switched off, but we can manage them to some extent with END blocks and the __DIE__ signal pseudo-handler. We can also trap warnings with the __WARN__ signal pseudo-handler. Neither mechanism is a true signal, but the semantics are implemented the same way.

We looked at the Carp module, which generates more useful information than the core die and warn functions, and the Fatal module, to conveniently wrap functions and subroutines in wrapper routines without needing to go to the trouble of implementing our own error handling code, unless we choose to. We also looked at system errors, the special variables $! and $?, the Errno module, intercepting the exit status before an application exits, and working with the system log on both Unix and Windows platforms.

Finally, we looked at handling warnings categories with the warnings pragma and saw how to define our own warnings categories so that we can provide tighter control over when and where warnings are generated from our own code.

CHAPTER 17

■■■

Debugging, Testing, and Profiling

Perl comes with a comprehensive and fully featured debugger. Unlike other languages, however, the debugger is not a separate tool but simply a special mode of the Perl interpreter, which makes use of an external library called perl5db.pl. To enable it, we use the -d option, after which we may step through code, set breakpoints, examine, and execute code selectively from inside the debugger.

In addition to the debugger, Perl supplies a number of modules designed for debugging support or that are simply useful for debugging. In particular, the Safe module allows us to create a restricted environment for Perl scripts to run in, and the Test::Harness module in conjunction with Test, Test::Simple, or Test::More allows us to create automated testing scripts, among other things.

It isn't always necessary to reach for the debugger at the first sign of trouble. With a little thought, it is relatively simple to build debugging support into the application itself which, if done correctly, can greatly help in tracking down problems. It also makes us think about what could go wrong, which itself helps to prevent bugs.

Regardless of whether we implement our own debugging framework, it is always a good idea to minimize the amount of trouble we can get into by using the pragmatic modules Perl supplies to aid in developing our code in the first place.

Debugging Without the Debugger

Before reaching for the debugger, it is worth taking some basic precautions that will prevent many problems from occurring in the first place: increasing the interpreter's sensitivity to code, checking for taintedness, or using the regular expression debugger when the trouble resides within a regular expression.

We can also build debug support into an application directly. While this will not have the generic flexibility of Perl's debugger, generating contextually aware debug messages is a good way to keep code well maintained and track the issues that we really care about. After all, we are in the best position to know how our own code is supposed to behave.

Pragmatic Debugging Modules

The strict and warnings pragmatic modules are the two most important for debugging. We looked at warnings in the last chapter, so they won't be covered again here. We looked at strictness earlier on, so here is a quick recap of what it does:

- use strict vars: Variables must be declared with my or our or written explicitly as package variables.
- use strict subs: Bareword strings are not allowed because of their possible conflict with subroutine names.
- use strict refs: Symbolic references are prohibited.

To enable all three of these syntax checks at once, simply use

```
use strict;
```

To enable only some of them or disable one temporarily, qualify the pragma:

```
use strict 'vars';  # enable strict variables
no strict 'refs';   # allow symbolic references
```

Frequently, the use statement is seen without quotes around the trailing mode arguments. This is only legal before strict subs are enabled, though, and becomes an illegal use of barewords immediately afterwards.

Taint Checks

Taint checks are the other main line of defense for any Perl application that is designed to run on a public server or can be accessed by an unprivileged user. With taint checks enabled, Perl monitors all data input from a source outside the program and considers it untrusted. Taint checks are turned on with the -T command-line switch, which is commonly combined with -w:

```
> perl -Tw mytaintcheckedapp.pl
```

In Perl 5.6 and earlier, there is no way to make taint violations nonfatal, on the grounds that it was far better to force the programmer to clean up the code than merely warn of a potential security problem. From Perl 5.8 onwards, this rule has been relaxed with the introduction of the -t option, which operates just like -T but issues its diagnostics as warnings rather than errors:

```
> perl -tw mytaintcheckedapp.pl
```

The taintedness propagates to the results of any expressions involving tainted data. If we then try to have Perl send output outside the program, the tainted data will cause a fatal error rather than permit the operation to succeed. One of the most common kinds of taint violation is relying on the value of the PATH environment variable to find an external program. Even though our code may not directly refer to it, Perl considers all values in %ENV to be untrustworthy. To solve the problem, we must either use an explicit path for the external program or set PATH inside our application to a value that is not derived from an external source.

On Unix, taint mode is enabled automatically if Perl detects that a process is being run under an effective user ID that is different from the real user ID. The effective user ID can differ from the real one for one of two reasons: the application has been given a different effective user ID by having its setuid bit set, or the application—having started with superuser privileges—voluntarily chooses to drop its privileges once it has carried out essential startup tasks and changes its own user ID to a less privileged one. In both cases, the user ID under which the application runs is not the same as the one that was used to start it. See the chmod Unix manual page for more on the setuid bit, and the POSIX module and special variables $< and $> in perldoc perlvar for more on handling real and effective user IDs.

There is no way to disable taint mode from within the program once it has been enabled. Instead, to untaint data—including any values supplied by the environment to variables like %ENV or @INC—it must be passed through a regular expression and extracted as match text. See Chapter 11 for the details on how to do this.

The Regular Expression Debugger

Perl's regular expression engine also comes with its own debugging support, which is entirely independent of the Perl debugger. To enable it, we add the following to any Perl script or application:

```
use re qw(debug);
```

See Chapter 11 for more information on this and other aspects of debugging regular expressions.

Applications That Debug Themselves

It makes a lot of sense to build an application with debugging in mind, since debug support that is tailored to the design of an application is frequently more effective than a generic debugging tool, however powerful it is. The amount of debug support we want to provide depends on the size of the code and the complexity of the task that it is attempting to solve. For a simple script, a single subroutine will probably do, but for something larger, a more designed solution may be necessary.

A Simple Debugging System

It pays to add debug support early on when writing code. One typical approach is to write a debug subroutine and then call it at appropriate moments:

```
# simple debug
sub debug {
    print STDERR @_,"\n";
}
...
debug "The value of 'scalar' is $scalar";
```

This simple debug routine mimics print but sends its output to standard error. But it also cannot be switched off. If we are happy to edit the code to enable or disable debugging, we can define two subroutines and keep one of them commented:

```
sub debug {}
# sub debug { print STDERR @_, "\n"; }
```

This will not suffice if we want to be able to enable debugging from outside the program. A better debugging subroutine might use the environment to enable or disable debug messages, as this one does:

```
# a better debug
sub debug {
    print STDERR @_, "\n" if $ENV{DEBUG};
}
```

This debug routine only prints out messages if the DEBUG environment variable is set. Alternatively, we can create two debug subroutines as before and selectively enable one or the other depending on the value of the environment variable:

```
#!/usr/bin/perl
# aliasdebug.pl
use strict;
use warnings;
use subs 'debug';

sub debug_off {}
sub debug_on { print STDERR @_,"\n"; }
*debug = $ENV{DEBUG}? \&debug_on : \&debug_off;

debug "Debugging is enabled";
```

This technique makes use of typeglob aliasing to invent a debug subroutine that refers either to the empty definition or the debugging version. Since the subroutine is not declared by its definition (since the aliasing happens at run time), we also need a use subs declaration so Perl does not complain about the last line not using parentheses. We could have put the typeglob alias inside a BEGIN block to achieve the same result.

A Better Debugging System

This section offers a simple script that implements a multilevel debugging scheme, so we can assign different levels of debug to different messages. Thus, level 2 messages only appear with level 2 debug or higher, but level 1 messages appear for any debug level. We have also implemented it as a closure, so that the debug level can only be changed through the debug subroutine itself or the more specific debug_level, which also returns the debug level if we wish to know it programmatically:

```perl
#!/usr/bin/perl
# debug.pl
use warnings;
use strict;

# define a debugging infrastructure
{ my $debug_level = $ENV{DEBUG};
  $debug_level |= 0;   # set to 0 if undefined

  # return, and optionally set, debug level
  sub debug_level (;$) {
      $debug_level = $_[0] if @_;
      return $debug_level;
  }
  # print debug message or set debug level
  sub debug (;$@) {
      # remove first argument (if present)
      my $level = shift;

      # @_ will contain more elements if 2+ arguments were passed
      if (@_) {
          # 2+ argument calls print debug message if permitted
          print STDERR @_, "\n" if $level <= debug_level();
      } else {
          # one and no-argument calls set level
          debug_level($level?$level:1);
      }
  }
}
```

Having created these debug subroutines and their hidden debug-level variable, we can now use it like this:

```perl
# continuation of debug.pl
# set debugging level explicitly
debug_level(1);
# send some debug messages
debug 1, "This is a level 1 debug message";
debug 2, "This is a level 2 debug message (unseen)";
# change debug level with single argument 'debug'
debug 2;
debug 2, "This is a level 2 debug message (seen)";
# return debugging level programmatically
debug 0, "Debug level is: ", debug_level;
# set debug level to 1 with no argument 'debug'
debug;
debug 0, "Debug level now: ", debug_level;
```

We have the choice of letting the environment determine the debugging level or overriding it with our own value inside the program. This is clearly a lot better than the first attempt, but it is also a lot bigger, which is a waste if we are not actually going to use the debugger. If we want to have the debug support enabled only if we actually intend to use it, we can selectively define the debug routine with an alias as we did earlier.

We will be using this debug.pl script as sample code for some other debugging tools Perl makes available to us—notably compiler backend modules—later on in the chapter.

Creating Debug Logs

We might also want to create a *debug log* rather than have debugging messages go to standard error. This is not a problem, as we can just redirect standard error in the shell. On Unix we can use

```
> DEBUG=1 perl myscript.pl 2> error.log
```

And on Windows:

```
> set DEBUG=1
> perl myscript.pl 2> error.log
```

We could also write the application to use another environment variable for a log name:

```
> DEBUG=1 DEBUG_LOG="error.log" perl myscript.pl
```

Again, on Windows this needs to be changed to

```
> set DEBUG=1
> set DEBUG_LOG="error.log"
> perl myscript.pl
```

All the application needs to do is check for the DEBUG_LOG environment variable and send a logging message to it:

```
*DEBUG = *STDERR unless defined($ENV{'DEBUG_LOG'})
    and open DEBUG "> $ENV{DEBUG_LOG}";
```

We guarantee the existence of the DEBUG filehandle by aliasing it to STDERR in the event that the log could not be opened.

Adding Calling Context to Debug Messages

A final useful feature that we can add to debugging messages is to include the location that they were issued from. This is invaluable for finding precisely where a debugging message is coming from, and it is particularly useful when locating debugging messages in a large application of many modules and files. We can find this information easily through the caller function, covered in some detail back in Chapter 7. With no arguments, it returns the details of the current caller, which in the preceding examples would be the debug subroutine itself. To return the details of the subroutine containing the debug message, we need to go back up the calling stack one frame by passing 1 to caller. The caller function returns a list of ten values, of which the first four are the most useful:

```
($pkg, $file, $line, $sub) = caller(1);
```

Armed with these values, we can create a debug message that reports the file name line number or possibly the subroutine name, as in this case:

```
sub debug {
    my $sub=(caller 1)[3];
    print STDERR "** $sub | ", @_, "\n";
}
```

The subroutine name is fully qualified and includes the package, so $pkg is not required. We make several assumptions, however. First, since only the subroutine name is reported, we assume here that the subroutine in question is small enough so that we do not need to spend much time searching it to locate the debug call. Second, we also assume that the package corresponds to a known file name and is not spread across several files—usually true, but not always. Finally, we assume that only subroutines will be calling it; there will be no useful context if this debug is called outside a subroutine.

A more general debug message might use the file and line numbers as well:

```
sub debug {
    ($pkg, $file, $line, $sub) = caller(1);
    print STDERR "** $sub ($file:$line) | ", @_, "\n";
}
```

We can, of course, construct a more complex conditional message if we like. In any event, we can substitute this code for the print statement in any of the previous debug examples to give us context-specific debug messages with relative ease.

Before moving on, it is worth mentioning the Carp module, covered in the previous chapter, which contains several routines designed to return context-sensitive messages that can serve for debug routines like the preceding ones.

The Perl Debugger

The Perl debugger is a tool for analyzing Perl programs during the course of their execution. It allows us to step line by line through a Perl program, examining the state of variables and calling subroutines interactively. We can set breakpoints in the code and let the program run until it encounters one, passing control back to us in the debugger. We can also execute arbitrary code, define new subroutines, and even use the debugger as a basic Perl shell if we want to.

The main functionality of the debugger is actually implemented in an external source file called perl5db.pl. This file provides routines that plug into the "debugging" hooks in the Perl interpreter to provide debugging services. When debugging is enabled, the Perl interpreter makes use of these generic hooks to provide information to whatever external debugging support has been provided. As a result, we can customize the debugger by modifying the external source file or replace the debugger with an entirely different support library altogether. One such replacement is the Perl profiler, which we also cover in this chapter.

Starting the Debugger

To start the Perl debugger, we use the -d option. For example, to debug a program called mybuggyscript.pl, we would use

> `perl -d mybuggyscript.pl`

We can combine -d with other flags, for example, the taint and warnings flags, for really conscientious debugging:

> `perl -Twd mybuggyscript.pl`

By combining -d and -e, we can debug code supplied directly on the command line. Since the debugger allows us to type in and execute arbitrary code, this makes for a simple but effective Perl shell, as we saw back in Chapter 14. Although we have to supply some valid Perl code, it does not have to do anything useful. The value 1 is therefore a legal Perl program, which we pass in with -e:

> `perl -dwe 1;`

Alternative debug support libraries are accessed by giving the -d flag an argument. One possible use for this is as a customized replacement debugger created by modifying the perl5db.pl script that provides the standard debugger. Another is to use an existing alternative like the Perl profiler, called DProf, which we can do with

> `perl -d:DProf rapidoffensiveunit.pl`

Assuming we start the standard debugger, it will load in the Perl script (or code, in the case of -e), execute any `BEGIN` blocks it finds and provide us with a prompt, ready to execute the first line of code in the program proper. For example:

> `perl -d config.pl`

This is using the `config.pl` script example from Chapter 6. It produces a standard startup message, the first line of the script (in this case a hash variable declaration), and a prompt:

```
Default die handler restored.
Loading DB routines from perl5db.pl version 1.22
Editor support available.
Enter h or 'h h' for help, or 'man perldebug' for more help.
main::(config.pl:3):    my %config=();
  DB<1>
```

The line `my %config=()` is the line that is about to be executed. The 3 is the line number in the file at which this statement was found. The `DB<1>` tells us that the command we are about to execute is the first command; we can go back and reexecute commands later with `!<command no>`.

▮**Tip** The debugger will only start up if the program compiles successfully. If it has errors that prevent this, we will have to fix them before we can use the debugger. Assuming that the program is at least good enough to compile, we can execute debugging commands.

Entering Commands

The debugger provides commands to do everything from pulling Perl data apart and scrutinizing it to rewriting the program interactively. Debugger commands are single letters followed in some cases by space-separated arguments. One particularly useful command is `h`, which displays a summary of the currently supported debugger commands (like many things in Perl, the debugger evolves from release to release):

    DB<1> **h**

In more recent versions of the debugger, this produces a one-page summary of all commands available:

```
List/search source lines:           Control script execution:
  l [ln|sub]  List source code         T           Stack trace
  - or .      List previous/current line  s [expr]    Single step [in expr]
  v [line]    View around line         n [expr]     Next, steps over subs
  f filename  View source in file      <CR/Enter>   Repeat last n or s
  /pattern/ ?patt?   Search forw/backw  r            Return from subroutine
  M           Show module versions     c [ln|sub]   Continue until position
Debugger controls:                     L            List break/watch/actions
  o [...]      Set debugger options    t [expr]     Toggle trace [trace expr]
  <[<]|{[{]|>[>] [cmd] Do pre/post-prompt  b [ln|event|sub] [cnd] Set breakpoint
  ! [N|pat]    Redo a previous command  B ln|*      Delete a/all breakpoints
  H [-num]     Display last num commands  a [ln] cmd  Do cmd before line
  = [a val]    Define/list an alias    A ln|*       Delete a/all actions
  h [db_cmd]   Get help on command     w expr       Add a watch expression
```

```
 h h            Complete help page          W expr|*    Delete a/all watch exprs
 |[|]db_cmd  Send output to pager           ![!] syscmd Run cmd in a subprocess
 q or ^D        Quit                        R           Attempt a restart
Data Examination:      expr     Execute perl code, also see: s,n,t expr
  x|m expr        Evals expr in list context, dumps the result or lists methods.
  p expr          Print expression (uses script's current package).
  S [[!]pat]      List subroutine names [not] matching pattern
  V [Pk [Vars]]   List Variables in Package.  Vars can be ~pattern or !pattern.
  X [Vars]        Same as "V current_package [Vars]".
  y [n [Vars]]    List lexicals in higher scope <n>.  Vars same as V.
For more help, type h cmd_letter, or run man perldebug for all docs.
```

Extended information is generated by h h, which is the output generated by older editions. Since the output of h h is quite long, we might want to page it by prefixing it with |, so the full command is |h h. For this to work, the platform needs to have a valid pager program configured. Unix users will be fine, but those on other platforms may need to configure the pager (consult the upcoming section "Configuring the Debugger" to see how to configure a pager program).

Simple Debugging Commands: Single Stepping

Possibly the two most useful debugger commands are s, which single-steps through a program one line at a time, and n, which executes the next line. The distinction between these two is that s will step into subroutines and offer them to us to execute line by line, whereas n will call the subroutine and offer the next line in the current context. Here is an example of how we can use s to step through a Perl script, in this case the config.pl script from Chapter 6. Note that the bold lines are entered in response to the <> being executed:

```
    DB<1> s
```

```
    main::(config.pl:4):    while (<>) {
```

```
    DB<1> s
```

```
Dante=Too Cool To Kill
main::(config.pl:5):           chomp; #strip linefeed
```

```
    DB<1>
```

```
main::(config.pl:7):        next if /^\s*$/;
# skip to the next iteration on empty lines
```

```
    DB<1> p $_
```

```
Dante=Too Cool To Kill
```

```
    DB<2> s
```

```
main::(config.pl:8):          next if /^\s*#/;
# skip to the next iteration on comments
```

```
  DB<2> s
```

```
main::(config.pl:9):          my ($param, $value) = split("=", $_,2);
# split on first '='
```

```
  DB<2> s
```

```
main::(config.pl:10):          print("No value for parameter '$_'\n"),
next unless $value;
```

```
  DB<2> x $param
```

```
0   'Dante'
```

```
  DB<3> x $value
```

```
0   'Too Cool To Kill'
```

```
  DB<3> s
```

```
main::(config.pl:12):          $config{$param} = $value;
```

```
  DB<3> s
```

```
main::(config.pl:4):    while (<>) {
```

```
  DB<3> s
```

```
Joe=I am the Law
main::(config.pl:5):          chomp;   # strip linefeed
```

```
  DB<3> s
```

```
main::(config.pl:7):          next if /^\s*$/;   # skip to the next iteration on empty lines
```

```
    DB<3> s
```

```
    main::(config.pl:8):        next if /^\s*#/;
# skip to the next iteration on comments
```

```
    DB<3> s
```

```
    main::(config.pl:9):        my ($param, $value)=split("=",$_,2);
# split on first '='
```

```
    DB<3> s
```

```
main::(config.pl:10):        print("No value for parameter '$_'\n"),
next unless $value;
```

```
    DB<3> s
```

```
    main::(config.pl:12):        $config{$param} = $value;
```

```
    DB<3> s
```

```
    main::(config.pl:4):    while (<>) {
```

```
    DB<3> x %config
```

```
0  'Joe'
1  'I am the Law'
2  'Dante'
3  'Too Cool To Kill'
```

```
    DB<4>
```

As it happens, just entering return reexecutes the last s or n we used, so we did not need to type s after the first time.

This example output also shows the p command, which prints out values in exactly the same way that Perl's print statement does; and the x command, which examines the contents of values, expanding and printing their contents prefixed with an index number if they are arrays or hashes. The x command will descend any number of levels in order to fully display the contents of an array or hash, which makes it very useful.

Running Arbitrary Code

Any line that is not recognized as a debugger command is executed as Perl code:

```
DB<1> print "Hello Debugger World\n", 2+2, " is 4\n";
```

```
Hello Debugger World
4 is 4
```

In the rare cases where we want to execute code that looks like a debugger command, we can disambiguate it by prefixing the line with anything that is not a valid debugger command, such as ;. For example, the debugger command x examines (dumps out) the contents of variables, so if we want to execute a subroutine called x, we can use

```
DB<2> ;x 1,2,3
```

This calls x with arguments 1,2,3, rather than the debugger's examine command. Note that having subroutines with single-letter names is not terribly sensible in the first place.

Multiline Commands

We can come up with very long debugging commands if we need to specify a lot of arguments or execute code within the debugger, for example, to define a subroutine. If we want to be able to do this without entering the entire command on a single line, we can use a backslash at the end of the line to continue the command on the next line. For example, to define a handy environment dumping command, we can define a subroutine:

```
DB<7> sub dumpenv { \
  cont:     foreach (sort keys %ENV) { \
  cont:        print "$_ => $ENV{$_}\n"; \
  cont:     } \
  cont:  }

DB<8> dumpenv
DISPLAY => :0.0

ENV => /home/gurgeh/.bashrc
HOME => /home/gurgeh
...
```

If we make a mistake and forget a trailing slash at any point, the debugger will complain, and we'll have to start again. If we have ReadLine support enabled (automatically provided by the Term::ReadLine module if we have it installed, see Chapter 15), then we can use the up cursor key to reenter each line again, which is quicker than typing it. If we want to use this subroutine a lot, we can also define it in an external configuration file so it is automatically available whenever we start the debugger.

Debugging Commands

Having seen how to make use of simple debugging commands like the s, p, and x commands, we can now take a more detailed look at all the commands that are executable from the Perl debugger prompt. In order to make them a little more digestible, we have loosely and informally organized them into the functional groups presented in Tables 17-1 through 17-11.

Table 17-1. *Debugger Help Commands*

Command	Action
h	Display a summary of all debugger commands. To display information on a single option, for example, the x command, type h followed by the command letter: h x Rather intelligently, the h command correctly substitutes the current values of recallCommand and shellBang for the commands whose letters are determined by these configuration options.
man [page]	Call the system manual page viewer for the given page or perldoc if no such viewer is available. The actual viewer can be configured by setting $DB::doccmd to the viewer command. If no page is supplied, it calls the viewer on itself (for help on using the viewer, for example, man man or perldoc perldoc). Non-Unix platforms may experience problems such as leaving the screen in a strange state if they don't support any sensible definition of manual pages. Using a separate window for documentation is a better idea in this case.

Table 17-2. *Debugger Variable Display Commands*

Command	Action
p [expr]	Print the expression expr to the debugger's output terminal, defined by $DB::OUT, which is independent of STDOUT (see the later section "Tracing and Terminals"). For example: p $param,'=', $value p works exactly like the print statement (though it only adheres to the values of $/ and $, if they are set in the same command). References and complex data structures are printed out as-is, in the style of print. For a more useful display of complex data, use x.

x [expr]	Evaluate and print out expr as a list, formatting the output prettily. Nested array and hash references are listed recursively. For example:
	DB<1> **$href={ 'top'=>{ middle=>['left','right', { bottom => 1 }]}}**
	DB<2> **x $href**
	    0 HASH(0x8223380)
	       'top' => HASH(0x822335c)
	       'middle' => ARRAY(0x82232cc)
	          0 'left'
	          1 'right'
	          2 HASH(0x825276c)
	       'bottom' => 1

V [pkg [vars]], X [vars]	These commands list the contents of the named variables from the named package. If vars is omitted, list all variables from the named package. If pkg is also omitted, it lists variables in the current package. For example, to display the current value of $DB::doccmd: DB<1> **V DB doccmd** $doccmd = 'man' To list all variables in DB, the debugger's own package: DB<1> **V DB** To list all variables in the current package: DB<1> **V** To list variables selectively in the current package, use the X command instead, which omits the pkg argument: DB<1> **X param value config**

Command	Action
V [pkg [vars]], X [vars]	Note that the prefix $, @, %, etc., should not be supplied to either of X or V, and that all variables with a corresponding name will be displayed, for example, $config, @config, and %config, if they exist. If the variable name starts with ~ or !, the name is used as a regular expression and is matched against the names of the variables in the package. Matching (or in the case of !, nonmatching) variables are dumped. Remember to use anchors (^ or $) to match variables with prefixes or suffixes.
T	Display the calling stack, listing the callers of the current subroutine in the spirit of the caller function. If there is no stack to display, it produces nothing. (Although the debugger itself is at the top of the stack, it removes itself from this output.)

Table 17-3. *Debugger Source Code Display Commands*

Command	Action
w	List a "window" of lines around the current line. The window is chosen to be a sensible range of lines determined by the context around the current line. When debugging a loop or subroutine, w returns the code of the loop or subroutine if it is of a reasonable size.

l	List the next window of lines in the current source file. Again, this is determined by context and will usually follow the window given by w. If there is no next window, l will return lines roughly similar to those returned by w.
	 If a number is specified, list that line number. For example, to list line 7:
	     DB<1> **l 7**
	 If a start and increment are specified with a +, lines are listed starting from line number start and listing lines lines in total. For example, to list lines 3 to 7:
	     DB<1> l 3+4
	 Alternatively, if a start and end range are specified with -, list lines starting from line number start and ending at line number end. For example, to list lines 3 to 7:
	     DB<1> **l 3-7**
	 Finally, if a subroutine name is specified, list the first window of lines of the named subroutine. For example:
	     DB<1> **l mysubroutine**

-	List the previous window of lines in the current source file. This is the reverse of l and will usually list the previous window before that given by w. If there is no previous window -, like l, it will return lines roughly similar to w.
.	List the last line to be executed by the debugger.
f filename	Switch to viewing the named file (or eval expression), which must be loaded (or to be more precise, present as a key in the %INC hash). If the file name does not precisely match an entry in %INC, it is used as an unanchored regular expression. For example, to find and view CGI.pm, we need only put DB<1> **f CGI** Normally the debugger will show the appropriate file for the current execution context of the application being debugged. This command is helpful for setting breakpoints in other files. The keys of %INC hold file names, not package names with colons, so f Term::ReadKey will not work, but f Term/ReadKey will. eval statements are remembered and numbered in the order that they are defined and can be accessed by number, for example f 3 for the third eval statement.

Continued

Table 17-3. *Continued*

Command	Action
/pattern	Search forward for the regular expression pattern in the source file. Searches are case insensitive and return the next match forward from the position where the last match was found. For example: DB<1> /$param A match may be repeated by entering a single / or ?. A second optional / may also be specified, which has no effect (and notably regular expression flags may not be put after it). Without metacharacters or regular expression terms, this is equivalent to a case-insensitive text match.
?pattern	Search backward for the regular expression pattern in the source file. As with /pattern, further matches are carried out from the position of the last successful match, and a single ? or / will rematch with the same pattern.
m expr	Display the list of methods that may be called on the object (blessed reference) or package name that is the result of expr. Inherited methods are marked with the module from which they are inherited. For example, m CGI displays all the methods defined for the CGI module, assuming it is loaded; typing use CGI at the debugger prompt will do that if it isn't.

Table 17-4. *Debugger Command History Commands*

Command	Action

! [[-]number]	Repeat or recall a previous command. Without arguments, repeat the last command:
	   DB<1> !
	With a numeric argument, repeat the command with that number. To repeat the third command:
	   DB<1> !3
	With a negative numeric argument, repeat the (n+1)th previous command. To repeat the command before last:
	   DB<1> !-1
	The character used for this command is the same as that used for executing temporary shells from within the debugger, but it can be reconfigured with the recallCommand option.

H [-number]	List previous commands. Without arguments, list all previous commands:
	   DB<1> H
	An argument of zero or any positive number also lists all previous commands. A negative number lists that many previous commands, including the H command itself. To list the previous command, therefore, use
	   DB<1> H -2
	To list the six previous commands, excluding the H, use
	   DB<1> H -7

= [alias cmd]	Define command alias. Without arguments, list currently defined aliases:
	   DB<1> =
	With one argument, give the command that the alias is an alias to:
	   DB<1> = next
	With arguments, define a command alias. For example, to define aliases for the next, step, and alias commands:
	   DB<10> = next n
	   next = n
	   DB<11> = alias =
	   alias = =
	   DB<12> alias step s
	   step = s
	Aliases can be made to other aliases. Redefining an alias will then alter the effect of all secondary aliases.

Table 17-5. *Debugger Code Execution Commands*

Command	Action
s	Single-step execute the next line, stepping into subroutines if present. Subroutine calls in expressions will also be single-stepped into.
n	Single-step execute the next line, executing and stepping over subroutine calls. If a subroutine call forms part of a larger expression, it will still be stopped after, so breaks in mid-expression are possible.
<return>	Repeat the last s or n command, whichever was more recently issued. This allows us to effectively use s and n to set a "stepping mode" and then use return to execute lines in that mode.

c [line|sub]	Continue executing lines in nonstop mode, optionally setting a once-only breakpoint at the specified line number or subroutine. Without an argument, it executes the program continuously until it exits or a previously set breakpoint or watchpoint is encountered:
	    DB<1> **c**
	With a line number, enter continuous execution until the given line number is reached:
	    DB<1> **c 12**
	On return (which will only happen if one of the preceding criteria is met), c displays a list of the lines that were executed. The subroutine name variant is similar but stops inside the next call to the named subroutine.

r	Continue executing lines in nonstop mode until the return from the current subroutine. This implicitly sets a once-only breakpoint on the next line after the statement that led to the subroutine.
q (^D/^C)	Quit the debugger. Ctrl-D (or Ctrl-C on Windows) is an alias for q.
R	Restart the debugger by causing it to "exec" itself (this may not work well on some platforms, for example, Windows). The command history, breakpoints, actions, and debugger options are preserved; other states may be lost.
|	Page output of debugger command or arbitrary code by piping the output DB::OUT to the currently defined pager program, as given by $DB::pager (|more on most Unix platforms). For example: DB<1> **|V DB** This dumps out all variables in the debugger's own DB package, leading to potentially large output that is paged for easier reading.
||	The same as |, except that the debugger also uses select to make DB::OUT the currently selected output filehandle for the duration of the command. This is mostly relevant to executing arbitrary code: DB<1> **|| print "This goes to DB::OUT, not STDOUT";**
! [shell cmd]	Run a shell command using the shell defined by $ENV{SHELL}, with a command equivalent to $ENV{SHELL} -c 'shell cmd'. Non-Unix systems may need to reconfigure the shell used first before this will work. Note that this is the same character as the repeat command, but it can be redefined with shellBang.
!! [shell cmd]	Run a shell command in a subprocess, using the shell defined by $ENV{SHELL} and using DB::IN and DB::OUT as standard input and output; this is useful if standard input and output have been redirected. See also the shellBang configuration option, which sets the character used for this command and the preceding one.

Table 17-6. *Debugger Trace Mode Command*

Control	Action
t [expr]	Without arguments, this toggles tracing mode from on to off, and vice versa: DB<1> **t** With tracing mode enabled, the lines that were executed by the last c or n are listed out when the debugger next returns, giving a complete trace of all code executed. Without this, only the line due to be executed next is listed. If an expression is supplied, trace through that expression. See "Tracing and Terminals" for more information.

Table 17-7. *Debugger Breakpoint Commands*

Command	Action
b [line] [condition] b sub [condition] b postpone sub b compile sub b load file	Set a breakpoint to cause the debugger to return to the user from continuous execution, as entered by the c command. The most common form of breakpoints are those set on line numbers. For example, to set a breakpoint at line 10: DB<1> **b 10** Line number breakpoints may optionally be followed by a condition, which will cause the breakpoint to be triggered only if the condition also holds. The condition is an arbitrary Perl expression of the kind that is used in if or while statements. For example, to break only when the %config hash has at least three key-value pairs defined: DB<1> **b 10 keys(%config)>2** The line number may also be omitted, in which case the breakpoint is set on the next line to be executed. An optional condition may still be set in this case: DB<1> **b keys(%config)>2**
b [line] [condition] b sub [condition] b postpone sub b compile sub b load file	A subroutine breakpoint is set by using b with the name of the subroutine to break in. Execution is halted by the debugger on entry to the subroutine but before the first statement in the subroutine is executed: DB<1> **b mysubroutine** As with line breakpoints, a condition may be specified: DB<1> **b mysubroutine keys(%config)>2** A subroutine reference (supplied in a variable) may also be supplied; however, conditions are not supported in this case: DB<1> **b $mysubref** Lesser variants of the b command are b postpone sub, which sets the breakpoint only after the subroutine has been compiled. b compile sub also waits for the subroutine to compile, but then it sets a breakpoint at the first line of execution. b load file breaks when the named file is loaded by use, require, or do. Note that this effective way of breaking inside a BEGIN block is specified prior to starting the debugger in a configuration file or PERL5DB.
L	List all breakpoints and actions currently defined.
S	List all subroutines currently defined, including those defined interactively in the debugger. This is obviously handy for setting breakpoints.
d [line]	Delete the breakpoint at the specified line number, as returned by the L command. If no line number is specified, delete the breakpoint on the next line to be executed, if any is present.
D	Delete all existing breakpoints.

Table 17-8. *Debugger Action Command*

Command	Action
a [[line] action]	With two arguments, set an action to be done before the line given by line is executed. The action is any arbitrary Perl code (not, however a debugger command), for example: DB<1> **a 10 print "Got to line 10!\n";** With one or no arguments, delete the action from the specified line number or the next line to be executed if the line number is omitted. For example: DB<1> **a 10** Actions are a very effective way of adding temporary code to an application without actually editing it. With actions, we can add additional debug messages and set variables to experimental values, without disturbing the source code.
A	Delete all existing actions.

Table 17-9. *Debugger Watchpoint Commands*

Watchpoint	Action
| W [expr] | Without arguments, delete all existing watch expressions (watchpoints). With an argument, sets a watch expression or watchpoint for the debugger to study during execution. If the value of the expression changes, the debugger breaks program execution and returns control to the user. Typically, c is used to continue execution until a breakpoint or watchpoint is encountered. If a watchpoint is encountered, the debugger will display the old and new values of the expression that triggered the break:<br>```
DB<1> W $value
main::(config.pl:5):            chomp;   # strip linefeed
DB<2> c
nokeyvaluepairhere
No value for parameter 'nokeyvaluepairhere'
key=value
Watchpoint 0:   $value changed:
old value:  undef
new value:  'value'
main::(config.pl:10): print("No value for parameter '$_'\n"),next
unless $value;
DB<2> c
Watchpoint 0:   $value changed:
old value:  'e'
new value:  undef
main::(config.pl:4):    while (<>) {
```<br>Each watchpoint set incurs a performance penalty, since the Perl interpreter must track each value watched. Though there is no limit, it makes sense to only watch one or two values at a time. |
```

Table 17-10. *Debugger Advanced Action Commands*

Prompt	Action
< [action]	Set an action, which can be any arbitrary Perl code, to execute immediately before the debugger prompt is displayed. (We cannot specify debugger commands, however; the { command does that.) For example, to display the current time and date: DB<1> **< print scalar(localtime)** < clears any existing actions set to execute before the prompt. However, see <<. If no action is specified, existing actions are cleared.

<<	Append an action to execute immediately before the debugger prompt is displayed and after any existing actions. For example, to add the current working directory:
	
	   DB<1> **use POSIX qw(getcwd);**
	   DB<2> **<< print ' ',getcwd**

< ?	List the actions currently set to execute before the prompt. For example: Tue Dec 26 15:06:35 2000 /home/gurgeh DB<74> < ? pre-perl commands: < -- print scalar(localtime) < -- print ' ',getcwd
> [action]	Set an action to execute immediately after a debugger command to execute program code (that is, s, n, c, r, etc.) has been entered but before any results are displayed. For example: DB<30> **> print "Here we go! \n"** As with >, this command clears any and all actions already set to be executed after the prompt. To add to an existing action, use <<. If no action is specified, existing actions are cleared but no new one is set.
>>	Append an action to execute immediately after a debugger command to execute program code has been given and after any already set actions.

>?	List the actions currently set to execute after the prompt. For example:
	
	   DB<1> **>?**
	post-perl commands:
	       > -- print "Here we go!\n"

{ [cmd]	Set a debugger command to be executed before each debugger prompt. This works identically to the < command except that it takes a debugger command as an argument instead of arbitrary Perl code. For example, to examine the contents of a variable step-by-step: DB<1> **{ x %config** If no command is specified, all existing commands are removed, the same as < and >. Note that setting commands like s, n, c, and r is perfectly possible but can potentially have interesting, if not entirely helpful, effects.
{{ cmd	Append a new debugger command to be executed before each debugger prompt and after any already set commands.

{ ?	List debugger commands set to execute before the prompt. For example:
	
	   DB<1> **{ ?pre-debugger commands:**
	       { -- x %config

Table 17-11. *Debugger Configuration Commands*

Command	Action

O	Any number of options may be set with one O command, each option separated from the last by a space. Boolean options may be set on simply by giving their name:
	`DB<1> O inhibit_exit`
	`        inhibit_exit = '1'`
	To clear a Boolean option or set a non-Boolean option, use an equals sign followed by the new value:
	`DB<1> O pager=|less inhibit_exit=0`
	`        pager = '|less'`
	`        inhibit_exit = '0'`
	Options may be queried by suffixing them with ?:
	`DB<1> O pager?`
	For more information on configuration options, read on.

Configuring the Debugger

The Perl debugger supports a collection of configuration options that control how it presents output and deals with situations during the course of debugging. These options may be set in a variety of different ways, interactively with the O command, through the environment via the `PERLDB_OPTS` environment variable, or in a `.perldb` configuration script.

Interactively

First and most obviously, the O command detailed earlier can be used to set one or more configuration options interactively from inside the debugger, for example:

`DB<101> O pager=\|less recallCommand=[ warnlevel=2 dielevel=1 NonStop ]`

Through the Environment

Second, options may be specified in the environment variable `PERLDB_OPTS`, which takes the form of a string with the options to be set in the same format as the O command; for example, on a Unix shell:

`> PERLDB_OPTS="NonStop warnlevel=2 dielevel=1" perl -d...`

The Windows equivalent is somewhat less terse:

`> set PERLDB_OPTS=NonStop warnlevel=2 dielevel=1`
`> echo %PERLDB_OPTS%`

`NonStop warnlevel=2 dielevel=1`

The .perldb Script

Finally, we can create a configuration file containing arbitrary code, including subroutine definitions useful for debugging and use statements to pull in modules that supply useful debugging features.

This file is called `.perldb` on Unix systems, or `perldb.ini` on Windows, and must be placed in either the current directory or our home directory (as defined by the `HOME` or `LOGDIR` environment variables). On `Unix` systems, it must also be executable and owned by either the superuser or the user running the debugger. Last, it must not give write permission to "others." To arrange that under Unix, we can use

```
> chmod go-w .perldb
```

On Windows NT, use

```
> attrib +r perldb.ini
```

This makes the file read-only for everyone. Alternatively, we can edit perl5db.pl to remove the check in the subroutine is_safe_file (this is potentially a reason for creating a custom debugger). Doing so obviously entails some risk, which is why the check is.

The reason for these security precautions is that an insecure database configuration file is a security hazard, since the code in it is added to any application if the -d option can be triggered. If Perl detects that our configuration file is insecure on a Unix platform, it refuses to run it and returns the message

```
perldb: Must not source insecure rcfile ./.perldb.
        You or the superuser must be the owner, and it must not
        be writable by anyone but its owner.
```

The content of the file is actually Perl code run within the DB package, not a configuration file in the traditional sense. To set up aliases, we plug in new entries to the %DB::alias hash, and to set options, we call the subroutine parse_options (which is supplied by DB).

Aliases take the form of regular expression substitutions, substituting the replacement text for the matching part of the command given in the debugger. We can define more powerful aliases than the = command allows. For example, many debuggers support the stop at and stop in commands to set breakpoints on lines and in subroutines, respectively. Since these are two-word commands, the = command has trouble defining them, but we can define both in a single alias in a .perldb file:

```
# This is a .perldb configuration file
$DB::alias{'stop'} = 's/stop (at|in)/b/';
```

To set options, use the parse_options subroutine:

```
# set some options
parse_options("pager =|less NonStop AutoTrace");
```

The .perldb file is processed before the contents of PERL_DBOPTS are considered, so PERL_DBOPTS will override options specified in the .perldb file. However, if we define a subroutine called afterinit within the file, it will be called after the PERLDBOPTS options have been processed:

```
# these options will override PERL_DBOPTS
sub afterinit {
    parse_options("AutoTrace");
}
```

Since this is a conventional Perl script (if used in an unconventional setting), we can place anything in here:

```
# generally useful stuff

use re 'debug';    # enable regular expression traces

sub dumpenv {
    foreach (sort keys %ENV) {
        print "$_ => $ENV \n";
    }
}
```

Debugger Configuration Options

Configuration options fall into four loose categories: *Debugger, Readline, Output,* and *Terminal*, listed in Tables 17-12 through 17-15. Debugger options are related to the operation of the debugger itself. ReadLine Library options control the interface between the debugger and the Term::ReadLine module. Output options are related to the Dumpvalue module, which implements the output display of the x, X, and V commands. Finally, Terminal options control how the debugger connects to terminals for debugging output; this is where the DB::OUT filehandle connects to for debugging output.

■**Tip** The default value returned by O for a number of these values is N/A. This reflects the fact that no explicit value has been set, and that the default is being used, rather than that the value of these options is the string N/A.

Table 17-12. *Debugger Options*

Option	Meaning
recallCommand	Set the character used for the recall/repeat command (by default !). For example: DB<1> **O recallCommand=P**
shellBang	Set the character used for the shell and subprocess commands (by default ! and !!). For example: DB<1> **O shellBang=Z** Note that this is case sensitive; Z is not the same as z.
pager	Set the command used to run external pagers by the | command (by default |more on Unix). It should start with a | to pipe output. For example: DB<1> **O pager=|less**
dieLevel warnLevel signalLevel	These three options control how the debugger deals with signals. The dieLevel and warnLevel options deal with the die and warn pseudohandlers. The signalLevel deals with real signals: DB<1> **O dieLevel=1 warnLevel=1** The default of 0 has the debugger leave most signals alone, since many programs install their own handlers to deal with these conditions. Setting 1 will generate a backtrace for dies, warnings, and other signals, respectively and embellish warnings originating from evaled code. Setting 2 will cause the debugger to intercept and rephrase all warnings and errors, irrespective of their origin. In general, don't change these values unless the situation merits it.
inhibit_exit	If true (default), this prevents stepping from passing over the end of the script (be it the actual end or an exit). If false, the debugger will leave the script and lose context information like global variables.
PrintRet	If true (default), this prints out the return value from subroutines that have just been terminated via the r command. If false, nothing is printed.
frame	Control the printing of messages on entry and exit from subroutines, in addition to the normal trace messages for line numbers. The default is 0, which does nothing. Other values are made up of different bits, which set different display options: bit 1 (1): Not used. bit 2 (2): Print messages on entry. bit 3 (4): Print function arguments. bit 4 (8): Execute tied and overloaded arguments to get their string representations. bit 5 (16): Print return value. (This affects subroutines returning as a result of any debugger command. The PrintRet configuration option applies only to returning explicitly from a subroutine with r.)

Continued

Table 17-12. *Continued*

Option	Meaning
frame	A frame of 2 (bit 2) or 6 (bits 2 and 3) is the most common. When combined with NonStop, it allows us to generate an execution trace of subroutine and function calls within a program: 　DB<1> O NonStop frame=6
maxTraceLen	This is the maximum length by which to truncate the argument list to, when bit 3 of the frame option is set. The default is 400, which is likely to be long enough for most simple arguments. Set to something shorter to be briefer: 　DB<1> O frame=6 maxTraceLen=60
NonStop	If true, the debugger executes programs continuously (as if c were typed automatically) until interrupted by a breakpoint or watchpoint, or programmatically by $DB::signal or $DB::single. Note that watchpoints and breakpoints can be set prior to entering the debugger via the .perldb script.

Table 17-13. *Debugger Readline Options*

Option	Action
tkRunning	If the debugger is running within a tk environment, setting this value to 1 will enable tk events to be processed while the debugger is waiting for input. See the Term::ReadLine section in Chapter 15 for more information.
ornaments	The ANSI escape sequences used to highlight the prompt. See Chapter 6 for details on how to disable or configure these. Note that this can only be done from inside a .perldb script, and it may cause strange effects in a non-ANSI shell.
ReadLine	Set to 0 to disable use of the ReadLine library. This is primarily useful for debugging applications, which use ReadLine themselves. Default is 1.

Table 17-14. *Debugger Output Options*

Option	Action
arrayDepth	Print only the number of elements specified. If undefined (the default), print all elements.
hashDepth	Print only the number of key-value pairs specified. If undefined (the default), print all pairs.
compactDump	If set to a positive value, and if the length of the line is less than the value, this causes arrays and hashes to be displayed on one line. If set to 1, a suitably large value (400+) is used. Only arrays and hashes that do not contain references will be compacted. The default is off.
veryCompact	If true, this prints arrays and hashes that do not contain references on one line irrespective of how long the resulting line is. The default is off. Setting veryCompact effectively overrides compactDump.
globPrint	If true, print out the contents of globs (treat them as specialized references). Otherwise, do not. The default is off.
DumpDBFiles	If true, print out the arrays holding debugged files. The default is off.
DumpPackages	If true, print out package symbol tables. The default is off.
DumpReused	If true, print out values multiple times if multiple references to them are encountered. Otherwise, REUSED_ADDRESS is inserted instead of repeating the dump. The default is off.

Option	Action
quote	Print out strings in the configured style. The default is auto, which uses double- or single-quoted strings, whichever is more appropriate for the string (that is, if it contains a double quote, single quotes are used). It can also be set to single or double quotes with quote=" or quote='.
HighBit	If true (default), this prints out characters with their high bit (bit 8) set as-is. Otherwise, it masks out the high bit and prints the result.
undefPrint	If true (default), this represents undefined values with the string undef; otherwise, it represents them as empty strings.
UsageOnly	If true, this generates a simple per-package memory usage report. The default is off.

Table 17-15. *Debugger Terminal/Tracing Options*

Option	Action
AutoTrace	If true, this enables tracing by default, in the same way that the t command toggles tracing on. The default is 0, off.
LineInfo	A file or pipe to send line number information to (that is, the debugger output of actual source code lines). To create a trace file, set to LineInfo=trace.log. To send to an external program (which uses a shorter message), prefix the program name with a pipe. This is how external editors that support Perl debugging interface to the debugger: LineInfo=|debugger.
TTY	This is the name of the terminal to use for debugging output (for example, con on Windows). By default, the output is sent to the current terminal. Note that commands like p and x send their output to this device and not to standard output. So if that is redirected, debugging output still goes to the debugging terminal.
noTTY	If set to a true value, the debugger automatically starts up in NonStop mode. It then connects to the terminal specified by TTY when execution is broken by a break-point, watchpoint, or programmatic return like $DB::single. The third-party module Term::Rendezvous may also be used to search for a suitable terminal at the point of interrupt.

Tracing and Terminals

The debugger supports two different kinds of tracing. *Line tracing* consists of numbered lines of source code and is controlled by the AutoTrace option. *Frame tracing* reports the entry and exit details from subroutines and is controlled by the frame configuration option. By default, both go to the same destination, the terminal attached to the DB::OUT filehandle. This is usually the same terminal that the program itself is attached to, but importantly, it is not affected by redirecting standard output or standard error within the program or from the command line. (For those confused as to what terminals have to do with anything, please refer to Chapter 15, where all will become clear.)

Tracing can be used interactively, but it is most useful for generating noninteractive traces from running programs. We can stop the debugger from entering an interactive section with the NonStop option; in combination with AutoTrace, we can produce a line trace to the screen with

```
> PERLDB_OPTS='NonStop AutoTrace' perl -d myscript.pl
```

The frame option is a combined flag that contributes additional information to the trace, depending on which bits are set. If frame is set to 2, the debugger will log all subroutines entered during the course of the program's execution. With NonStop or noTTY also set, this allows us to generate an execution trace of subroutine calls:

```
> PERLDB_OPTS='NonStop frame=2' perl -d myscript.pl
```

In this example, there is no line tracing, so the output we see will contain only subroutine call trace messages. If we wanted line tracing too, we would enable it by adding the AutoTrace option as well. Setting other bits in the frame value produces other values. 22 prints subroutine arguments (4) and return values (16). Here is an example with both AutoTrace and a frame of 22:

```
> PERLDB_OPTS='NonStop frame=22 AutoTrace' perl -d myscript.pl
```

All of these examples output tracing information to the screen, mixed in with the normal standard output and standard error of the program. Since the debugger uses its own filehandle for output, redirecting standard output and standard error will not redirect the tracing output. To get a trace log, we instead use the LineInfo option. This controls where tracing output is sent (both line and frame, despite the name). For example, to redirect tracing to a trace log and debug messages (printed out by the program itself) to a debug log, we could use

```
> PERLDB_OPTS='NonStop frame=2 AutoTrace LineInfo=trace.log' \
perl -d myscript.pl 2> debug.log
```

The normal standard output of the program will appear on the screen, while tracing information will go to trace.log and error output from the program itself will end up in debug.log. If we wanted to capture standard output too, we would do this:

```
> PERLDB_OPTS='NonStop frame=2 AutoTrace LineInfo=trace.log' \
perl -d myscript.pl > output.log 2> debug.log
```

In this instance, we have also redirected standard output from the program to a file called output.log.

Two other configuration options control how the debugger interacts with terminals: TTY and noTTY. The TTY option determines where nontrace debugger output goes (for example, output from the p and x commands, which could be triggered as actions). The value of the TTY option is expected to be interactive, for example, another terminal window or a serial port; both DB::IN and DB::OUT are attached to it. The related noTTY option prevents the debugger from attaching to the device named by TTY unless and until the debugger is entered interactively—it takes no argument.

Entering the Debugger Programmatically

Just as setting breakpoints and watchpoints from the debugger is useful for breaking the flow of execution, we can also have the program trigger a break itself. This is especially useful for compile-time statements executed in BEGIN blocks, since the debugger will not ordinarily break in these. Instead it executes them and halts on the first line of normal execution. This is also useful if we have specified the NonStop or noTTY configuration options.

To have a program pass control back to the debugger, set the variable $DB::single. This puts the debugger (if running) into single-step mode and therefore out of continuous execution mode. For example:

```perl
#!/usr/bin/perl -T
# an example start to an about-to-be debugged application
# allow debugger to break during compile phase
use warnings;

BEGIN { $DB::single = 1; }

# now load modules with complex 'BEGIN' blocks so we can debug them
use CGI;
```

```
use DBI;
use SomeOtherModule;
...
```

If the debugger is not present, setting this variable has no other effect than to create it when the application is not being debugged.

The debugger enters interactive mode in one of two slightly different ways, depending on the value that is given to $DB::single. Setting $DB::single=1 gives rise to a debugging prompt as if an s had just been typed. Pressing Return will cause further s commands to be executed. Alternatively, setting $DB::single=2 enters the debugger's interactive mode as if an n has just been typed. Further returns will therefore produce n commands.

As an alternative to setting $DB::single to break within a BEGIN block, we can also set one of two more specialized breakpoints. First, the load breakpoint can be used to break in a use statement at the point the file is loaded. For example:

```
DB<1> b load CGI.pm
```

We can also use the compile breakpoint to break on the compilation of a subroutine:

```
DB<1> b compile mysubroutine
```

Another way to trigger a return to the debugger's prompt is to set the value of the variable $DB::signal (note, not single) to a suitable signal number. Both the program and debugger will behave as if the given signal had just been raised, with the debugger's behavior taking precedence (determined by the value of the signalLevel configuration option). For example:

```
# define a signal handler
$SIG{10} = sub { print "Hello Debugger \n"; }

# simulate a USR1 signal when debugging
$DB::signal = 10;
```

Both the subroutine and the setting of $DB::signal can be defined in the debugger itself. In particular, we could set a debugger action to define $DB::signal at a given line.

Independently of $DB::single, the t command can be simulated by setting the value of $DB::trace to either 0 or 1, enabling or disabling tracing. This allows us to toggle tracing within a program without setting breakpoints. For example, we can define our own tracing environment variable so we can generate trace output selectively in NonStop mode without further debugger configuration:

```
...
# trace the next bit
$DB::trace = 1 if $ENV{DO_TRACING};
...
# finished tracing the bit of interest
$DB::trace = 0 if $ENV{DO_TRACING};
...
```

Using Debugger Hooks

Perl grants extra access to the internals of the interpreter to code in the DB package. By placing our own code into this package, we can create our own debugger alternatives. We can also extend the capabilities of our own debugging modules.

As a practical example, we can access the list of arguments passed to a subroutine from the DB package, which allows us to determine not only where a subroutine was called, but also how. This information is not normally reported by a die or warn, but by placing code into the DB package we can create our own stack trace that reports the subroutine stack, as well as the arguments that were passed at each stage.

Here is a module that does just this by registering a handler for the __DIE__ hook. The subroutine is in the package My::StackTrace, but its body is placed into the special DB package in order to gain access to the subroutine arguments in the @DB::args array, an array Perl does not otherwise make available to us:

```perl
# StackTrace.pm
package My::StackTrace;
use strict;
use FileHandle;
require 5.000;

# register the subroutine below as a die handler
$SIG{__DIE__} = 'My::StackTrace::DumpStack';

sub DumpStack {
    my $msg = shift;

    # enable extended argument processing via the debugger hooks
    # built into Perl by accessing DB::args from witin the DB package
    package DB;

    # for inclusion in HTML error documents
    print "<PRE><HR />\n" if $ENV{REMOTE_HOST};
    print "\n$msg\n";

    my $i = 1;
    while (my ($pack,$file,$line,$subname,$hasargs,$wantarray) = caller($i++)) {
        my @args = @DB::args;
        my @tmp = caller($i);

        print "$file:$line ";
        print "(in $tmp[3])" if $tmp[3];

        my $routine = $pack.'::'. $subname;
        print "\n\t&$routine (";

        # for subroutines that convey password data, hide the arguments
        # when dumping the trace, for security.        if ($hasargs) {
            if ($routine =~/SQL_OpenDatabase/ ||
                $routine =~/RPC::PlClient::new/ ||
                $routine =~/DBD::Proxy::dr::connect/ ||
                $routine =~/DBI::connect/
            ) {
                print scalar(@args)," arguments hidden for security";
            } else {
                print join(", ", @args);
            }

        print ")\n";
    }
    print "\n\n";
    print "<HR /></PRE>\n" if $ENV{"REMOTE_HOST"};

    exit;   # transmute death into a graceful exit
}

1;
```

This module provides an improved stack trace. Here is a short example program that makes use of it and puts it through its paces:

```perl
#!/usr/bin/perl
# StackTrace.pl
use warnings;
use strict;

use StackTrace;

sub a {push @_, shift @_; b(@_);}
sub b {push @_, shift @_; c(@_);}
sub c {push @_, shift @_; d(@_);}
sub d {push @_, shift @_; e(@_);}
sub e {
    push @_, shift @_;
    print "@_";
    die "Sudden death";
}

a('Testing', 1, 2, 3);
```

The output from this program is

```
1 2 3 Testing
Sudden death at ./stacktrace.pl line 12.

./stacktrace.pl:8 (in main::d)
        &main::main::e(1, 2, 3, Testing)
./stacktrace.pl:7 (in main::c)
        &main::main::d(Testing, 1, 2, 3)
./stacktrace.pl:6 (in main::b)
        &main::main::c(3, Testing, 1, 2)
./stacktrace.pl:5 (in main::a)
        &main::main::b(2, 3, Testing, 1)
./stacktrace.pl:15
        &main::main::a(1, 2, 3, Testing)
```

Debugging and Informational Modules

In addition to the Perl debugger, the Perl standard library supplies a number of different modules that are handy for debugging and developing programs in various controlled ways. Here we will examine two of them, Dumpvalue and Safe.

The Dumpvalue Module

The Dumpvalue module provides the basis for the Perl debugger's configurable output in the x, X, and V commands and is the source of the "Output" configuration options such as arrayDepth, compactDump, and globPrint. Since the Dumpvalue module is an independent part of the Perl library, we can also make use of it outside the debugger.

Dumpvalue works through an object-oriented interface, with a dumper object that has configuration options identical to those detailed in Table 17-14 in the "Debugger Configuration Options" section. Basic value output is supported by the dumpValue and dumpValues methods, which dump out one value and a list of values, respectively. For both methods, the value or values must be scalars. For example:

```perl
#!/usr/bin/perl
# dumpval.pl
use warnings;
use strict;

use Dumpvalue;

my $dumper = new Dumpvalue(compactDump => 1, globPrint => 1);

my %myhashvariable = (
    'top' => {
        middle => [
            'left', 'right', {
                'bottom' => 1
            }
        ]
    }
);

# dump one variable
$dumper->dumpValue(\%myhashvariable)
```

This produces

```
0  HASH(0x8223380)
   'top' => HASH(0x822335c)
      'middle' => ARRAY(0x82232cc)
         0  'left'
         1  'right'
         2  HASH(0x825276c)
             'bottom' => 1
```

The dumpValues method works similarly but treats its list of arguments as a top-level array:

```perl
# dump several variables
$dumper->dumpValues ($var1, $var2, \@anarray, \%anotherhash);

# dump each element of an array:
$dumper->dumpValues (@myarrayvariable);
```

The Dumpvalue module works well with modified tracing arrangements, especially if it is encapsulated in tracing subroutines. For example, the following script illustrates a simple trace subroutine that implements level-based tracing based on the value of the putative environment variable TRACE_ON:

```perl
#!/usr/bin/perl
# trace.pl
use warnings;
use strict;

{
    use Dumpvalue;

    # private dumper object for 'trace' subroutine
    my $dumper = new Dumpvalue (compactDump => 1);
```

```
        my $level = $ENV{TRACE_ON};
        $level |= 0;    # default to no tracing

        sub trace {
            $dumper->dumpValues(@_) if $_[0] <= $level;
        }
    }

my %hash = (one => 1, two => 2);
my @array = (1..10);

# a level 2 trace statement
trace 2, \%hash, \@array;
```

We can run this program, setting the value of TRACE_ON to 2 in the environment, with a command like this:

> **TRACE_ON=2 perl trace.pl**

generating the following output:

```
0  2
1  HASH(0x81269c0)
   'one' => 1
   'two' => 2
2  ARRAY(0x8126ac8)
   0  1
   1  2
   2  3
   3  4
   4  5
   5  6
   6  7
   7  8
   8  9
   9  10
```

The other output method supported by Dumpvalue is dumpvars, which prints out details of package variables. This method is the basis of the X and V debugger commands and takes this form:

dumpvars(pkg, var, var...);

As with the X command, we can give just a package name to dump all variables or specify a list of variables (minus data type prefixes) to dump. If the variable name starts with ~ or !, the name is applied as a regular expression and all matching (or in the case of !, nonmatching) names are dumped. For example:

```
#!/usr/bin/perl
# dumpvars.pl
use strict;
use warnings;

use Dumpvalue;

my $dumper = new Dumpvalue(compactDump => 1, globPrint => 1);

# dump out '@INC', '%INC', and '%ENV':
$dumper->dumpvars('main', 'INC', 'ENV');
```

```
# dump out everything else
$dumper->dumpvars('main', '!(INC|ENV)');
# dump out anything that ends in a digit: handy after a regexp!
$dumper->dumpvars('main', '~\d$');
```

The other methods supported by dumper objects all relate to configuration options, as listed in Table 17-16.

Table 17-16. *Dumpvalue Methods*

Method	Action
set_quote('"'|"'"|, 'auto')	Set options to handle printout with the given quote type. Strings are rendered to use either single quotes, double quotes, or (with auto) whichever is most logical. The content of the string is adjusted to fit the quote type.
set_unctrl('quote'|'unctrl')	Set the unctrl option to vary how nonalphanumeric characters are represented, quote when the quote type is a double quote. The quote option attempts to escape all characters in a way that allows them to be interpolated back again. The unctrl option represents them in a more human readable form, for example, ^D is equivalent to Ctrl-D.
compactDump(0|1|number)	Set or clear the compactDump option.
veryCompact(0|1)	Set or clear the veryCompact option. This also sets the compactDump option.
set (option => value, ...)	Set or clear general options, for example: $dumper->set(tick => 'auto');
get (option, option, ...)	Get general options, for example: @opts = $dumper->get('tick', 'HighBit', 'printUndef');

Similar functionality is provided by the Data::Dumper module, which is also handy for serialization. They both produce legible output for values, so we can use either for this purpose. Data::Dumper is covered in Chapter 5.

The Safe Module

The Safe module creates a protective *compartment* for the execution of Perl code. Within the compartment, a different namespace prevails, and code within the compartment is not allowed to access variables in other namespaces, even the main namespace. This is a similar idea to the Java "sandbox" concept: code outside the compartment may place variables into it, but access to anything outside the compartment from within is strictly forbidden.

Additionally, an *operator mask* is applied to the compartment, which enables us to disable the operators available inside. The default mask is the :default mask. We first covered it back in Chapter 4 when we covered the OpCode module, and we provide some more details on operator masks here.

Creating Compartments

The new method is used to create a compartment. Once created, we then invoke either the reval (meaning *restricted* eval) method to execute code within the compartment, or alternatively, the rdo (meaning *restricted* do) method to execute an external file from within the compartment. Both methods are identical in operation to their functional counterparts eval and do. For instance, reval returns the value of the last expression evaluated on success and sets $@ on an error.

Here is an example of creating a simple unmodified compartment and executing a script from within it:

```
use Safe;

my $compartment = new Safe;
$compartment->reval($string_to_eval);
$compartment->rdo('myscript.pl');
```

If the code executed in the compartment attempts to reach outside its bounds or use an operator forbidden by the compartment, it fails with an error. This happens at the compile stage in the case of operators and potentially at either compile or run time in the case of variable access. Since we have not altered the operator mask assigned to the compartment, it has the default mask set.

Sharing Variables and Subroutines

Variables may be shared between the outside world and the compartment using the share and share_from methods. The share method accepts a list of package variables defined in the current package (that is, global variables) and imports them into the compartment's namespace:

```
# note, variables cannot be lexical - declare with 'our', not 'my'
our $scalar = "This is a scalar";
our (@array, %hash);
sub external {
    # external subroutine...
};
$compartment->share('$scalar', '@array', '%hash', '&external');
```

Alternatively, variables can be imported into the compartment namespace from another named package with share_from. This takes a package name as its first argument and an array reference to a list of variable names similar to that accepted by share:

```
$compartment->share_from(
    My::Package => ['$scalar', '@array', '%hash', '&external']
);
```

The variables (for example, $My::Package::scalar) must already exist in the named package to be imported into the compartment successfully.

Variables may be retrieved from the compartment in the reverse direction using the varglob method. This returns a typeglob of a symbol inside the compartment. For example, to alias a compartment typeglob to an external typeglob:

```
*compartmentvar = $compartment->varglob('varname');
```

Variables with the name varname (for example, $varname, @varname, the subroutine varname, etc.) may now be accessed by the equivalent names $compartmentvar and so on. Alternatively, to set the variable $scalar inside the compartment without aliasing:

```
${$compartment->varglob('scalar')} = "This is a scalar";
```

This allows external code to access variables inside the compartment without needing to know the root namespace of the compartment. If we really want to know the root namespace, the root method can be used like so:

```
$cmp_ns = $compartment->root();
```

Using this with symbolic references would allow us to set variables inside the compartment. However, this is not encouraged, as the point of the compartment is to keep the namespace anonymous to prevent accidental cross-talk.

Operator Masks

Other methods of the compartment object relate to the control of the operator mask and are direct interfaces to the functions of the Opcode module covered in Chapter 4. In brief, they are as described here:

Method	Purpose
$c->permit(OP, ...)	Add the listed operators to those allowed in the compartment.
$c->permit_only(OP, ...)	Allow only the listed operators to be executed within the compartment—all others are denied.
$c->deny(OP, ...)	Remove the listed operators from those allowed in the compartment.
$c->deny_only(OP, ...)	Deny only the listed operators in the compartment; all others are allowed.

As an example, the following method call removes the system and backtick opcodes from the permitted list:

```
$c->deny('system', 'backtick');
```

Similarly, to explicitly enable a more relaxed set of operators, including open, close, and stat:

```
# :browse is a superset of :default plus some others
$c->allow_only(':browse', ':filesys_open');
```

Note that opcodes are not operators: they are the foundations upon which operators are implemented and may not have the same names; backtick is the opcode for the backtick operator, which is either literal backquotes or the qx operator. See also the use ops pragma in Chapter 4.

The Safe Module in Use

As an example of how we can use the Safe module, here is a short utility that creates and uses a compartment to deny the use of backtick quotes (which includes the qx operator) and to log all uses of system:

```
#!/usr/bin/perl
# loggedsystem.pl
use warnings;
use strict;

use Safe;
my $compartment = new Safe;

$compartment->deny('system', 'backtick');

use subs qw(system);

sub system {
    warn "About to execute: @_ \n";
    CORE::system @_;
}

# offer our 'system' to the compartment
$compartment->share('&system');

# test line to prove compartment is working
```

```
$compartment->reval('system("ls")');
$compartment->reval('CORE::system("ls")');
warn $@ if $@;

# process command line
foreach (@ARGV) {
    die "'$_' not found or not executable \n" unless -x;
    $compartment->rdo($_);
    warn $@ if $@;
}
```

Windows users should exchange the Unix command ls in this example with the DOS command dir if they want to see output from this example.

Note that both rdo and reval use eval internally, so to check for errors we need to inspect the value of $@, rather than $!. In both cases the code may not even compile (because it uses a forbidden operator), so checking $@ is vital for using compartments successfully.

If we give this program a name like logsystem, we could use it like this:

```
> logsystem perl myscript.pl
```

The point of this is that not only have we replaced the original system with our own logging version, but we have also prevented the script we execute from bypassing us by disabling the core system function inside the compartment. If the script tries to use CORE::system to get around our logger, it will be denied access by the compartment.

Debugging Perl Itself

Perl comes with a built-in debug mode to debug the interpreter that is distinct from the Perl debugger we have already seen, but this mode is only available if it was enabled when Perl was built. Alternatively, we can use one of the compiler backend modules in the standard library or on CPAN to extract, analyze, and manipulate the opcode tree that our code is compiled into internally, instead of executing it.

Debugging the Perl Interpreter

Although not generally available in prebuilt Perl distributions, it is possible to create a Perl interpreter that includes internal debugging support. This has nothing to do with debugging using the -d option, but rather allows us to debug the interpreter itself as it executes code. We can use this to generate various kinds of information with the -D option. If internal debug support is not available, then the -D option will also not be available.

The -D option takes a collection of single-letter identifiers as parameters. Each parameter enables a different debugging feature, and we may enable as many as we see fit. Table 17-17 summarizes the perlrun manual page.

Table 17-17. *-D Option Arguments*

1	p	Tokenizing and parsing
2	s	Stack snapshots
4	l	Context (loop) stack processing
8	t	Trace execution
16	o	Method and overloading resolution
32	c	String/numeric conversions

Continued

Table 17-17. *Continued*

64	P	Print preprocessor command for -P
128	m	Memory allocation
256	f	Format processing
512	r	Regular expression parsing and execution
1024	x	Syntax tree dump
2048	u	Tainting checks
4096	L	Memory leaks (only if Perl was compiled with -DLEAKTEST)
8192	H	Hash dump—usurps values()
16384	X	Scratchpad allocation
32768	D	Cleaning up
65536	S	Thread synchronization

Options have both a numeric and symbolic value, and we may combine either as a value to the -D option. For example, to enable trace execution and stack snapshots, we can use any of the following:

```
> perl -Dst ...
> perl -Dts ...
> perl -D10 ...
```

If Perl has not been built with internal debugging support, this will not work. However, we can generate much of the same information, albeit not always in an identical manner, with some of the compiler backend modules in the B:: family.

The Compiler Backend

Perl provides a collection of compiler backend modules. All of these modules, which reside in the B:: namespace, operate at the boundary between compilation and execution. Essentially, they wait until Perl has finished compiling our code and then interrupt the normal progression to the execution phase to do something else with the compiled program. At this point, the program exists in memory as a tree of opcodes and operands in the symbol table, and so a sufficiently savvy module can step in and analyze the compiled code. This is what a compiler backend does.

Loosely speaking, there are two kinds of compiler backend: those that analyze the opcode tree and report on it, and those that turn the compiled program into some other executable form. This second group is made up of essentially Perl-to-something-else compilers and currently consist of B::C and B::CC, which convert Perl into C, and B::Bytecode, which converts Perl into executable Perl bytecode. They are covered in Chapter 20. Here we are interested in the backends that analyze our compiled code.

Invoking a Compiler Backend Module

To invoke any backend module, we use the compiler frontend module, O. Grandiose though it sounds, all the O module does is define a CHECK block that invokes the backend module we pass to it and flip on the "compile check" flag so that the interpreter does not go on to execute the program once the backend module is finished. Typically, it used from the command line. For example, here is how we can use it to invoke B::Terse to generate a terse dump of the compiled opcode tree for a simple statement print 6*9:

```
> perl -MO=Terse -e "print 6*9"
```

This is what it prints out:

```
LISTOP (0x816e0a0) leave [1]
    OP (0x816def8) enter
    COP (0x816df38) nextstate
    LISTOP (0x816e218) print
        OP (0x816e0d8) pushmark
        SVOP (0x816e1c0) const [2] IV (0x81523bc) 54
```

Notice that Perl has optimized the expression at compile time because it has detected that the multiplication consists of two constants and compressed it to a constant 54. The first three lines are part of the interpreter's startup and shutdown process, so we are just left with a `print` statement. Let's try two variables instead:

> **perl -MO=Terse -e "print $$ * $<"**

This gives us

```
LISTOP (0x816df98) leave [1]
    OP (0x816df18) enter
    COP (0x816df38) nextstate
    LISTOP (0x816e0a0) print
        OP (0x816dec8) pushmark
        BINOP (0x816e218) multiply [3]
            UNOP (0x816e1c0) null [15]
                PADOP (0x816e0d8) gvsv  GV (0x816ad6c) *$
            UNOP (0x8155fc0) null [15]
                PADOP (0x816def8) gvsv  GV (0x815238c) *<
```

The two variables we picked were $$, the process ID, and $<, the user ID. Both of these are numeric, and while multiplying them is not likely to provide particularly useful information, they both happen to be predefined by Perl and not optimizable at compile time. We can see that in each case the scalar SV value is extracted from the GV typeglob in the symbol table before been fed to the binary multiply operation.

Of the backends that are not concerned with compiling Perl into something else, roughly half are concerned with deconstructing the compiled code and rendering it in various forms and levels of information, and the other half analyze the code for various statistical or quality-based metrics.

Rendering Compiled Code

The B::Terse module seen earlier is one of several modules that dumps out the compiled code of a program. It is handy to see how Perl actually creates the opcode tree, and it is not so long as to be impossible to comprehend. However, it is also light on details. In fact, while B::Terse was historically a stand-alone module, it is now a wrapper for the more flexible B::Concise module. This is what B::Concise does by default with our example expression:

```
8   <@> leave[1 ref] vKP/REFC ->(end)
1      <0> enter ->2
2      <;> nextstate(main 1 -e:1) v ->3
7      <@> print vK ->8
3         <0> pushmark s ->4
6         <2> multiply[t3] sK/2 ->7
-            <1> ex-rv2sv sK/1 ->5
4               <#> gvsv[*$] s ->5
```

```
-              <1> ex-rv2sv sK/1 ->6
5                  <#> gvsv[*<] s ->6
```

Here we can see much the same information as before, but now we can see the opcode flags, the running order, and the progression of states. If we feed the -exec option to B::Concise:

> **perl -MO=Concise,-exec -e'print $$ * $<'**

we can see the running order instead:

```
1  <0> enter
2  <;> nextstate(main 1 -e:1) v
3  <0> pushmark s
4  <#> gvsv[*$] s
5  <#> gvsv[*<] s
6  <2> multiply[t3] sK/2
7  <@> print vK
8  <@> leave[1 ref] vKP/REFC
-e syntax OK
```

We can also supply -basic, which is the same as B::Terse, and -tree, which creates a tree diagram:

```
<8>leave[1 ref]-+-<1>enter
                |-<2>nextstate(main 1 -e:1)
                `-<7>print-+-<3>pushmark
                          `-<6>multiply[t3]-+-ex-rv2sv---<4>gvsv[*$]
                                            `-ex-rv2sv---<5>gvsv[*<]
-e syntax OK
```

As their names suggest, both modules abbreviate the details of the opcodes they display for the sake of brevity. The B::Debug module, on the other hand, goes into gory but unstructured detail. Here is what it has to say about the multiplication opcode in the preceding examples:

```
BINOP (0x816e220)
        op_next      0x816e0a8
        op_sibling     0x0
        op_ppaddr     PL_ppaddr[OP_MULTIPLY]
        op_targ      3
        op_type      55
        op_seq     7086
        op_flags     6
        op_private     2
        op_first     0x816e1c8
        op_last     0x8155fc0
```

There is a great deal of information here, much of which is only likely to be of interest to programmers engaged in debugging Perl itself. But we can see that this is a binary operation, that it has a first and last operand, what kind of operation it is, what comes next, what the type is, and what its flags value is. This value corresponds to the G_ flags described in perlapi.

In the opposite direction, we have the B::Showlex backend. This simply extracts and lists out the lexical variables referenced in the code:

> **perl -MO=Showlex -e'print $$ * $<'**

This generates output including

```
0: SPECIAL #1 &PL_sv_undef
1: GV (0x816aeec) *$
2: GV (0x815238c) *>
3: NULL (0x81523bc)
-e syntax OK
```

Without qualification, the file-scope lexical variables are listed. We can also print out lexical variable data for a specific subroutine, for example, the debug subroutine from the debug.pl script we looked at earlier:

> `perl -MO=Showlex,debug debug.pl`

The B::Graph module available from CPAN is one of many modules that attempts to make more, or at least prettier, sense of Perl's opcode tree. This particular module generates graph definitions that can be read and rendered by the GraphViz module.

Analyzing Compiled Code

Rather than render or dump out the details of our compiled programs, we can use other compiler backends to analyze and compile statistical data from it. The B::Lint and B::Xref modules that come with the standard Perl library are both useful tools in this respect.

Linting with B::Lint

The B::Lint module generates extra warnings for code details that are not considered serious enough to warn about by Perl itself; the name is derived from the lint tool that performs a similar task for C. Many of these are actually perfectly legal and even common idioms, but they may also happen to be mistakes. Eight different style checks are available that we can enable all together:

> `perl -MO=Lint app.pl`

Or selectively:

> `perl -MO=Lint,context,undefined-subs app.pl`

The full list of checks is listed in Table 17-18.

Table 17-18. *B::Lint Style Checks*

Name	Check
bare-subs	Use of a subroutine without parentheses in a bareword context allowed by use strict subs. Hash keys and the left side of => are the common culprits.
context	Use of an array in an implicitly scalar context, such as comparing @ARGV to 1.
dollar-underscore	Explicit use of $_ or implicit use of $_ with print.
implicit-read	Implicit read of a special variable, typically $_, as in an unbound regular expression match.
implicit-write	Implicit write to a special variable, typically $_, as in an unbound regular expression substitution or split.
private-names	Use of underscore-prefixed nonlocal subroutines or variables, as _subname() implies a private subroutine.
regexp-variables	Use of the resource-hungry regular expression variables $`, $&, or $'.

Continued

Table 17-18. *Continued*

Name	Check
undefined-subs	Use of an as-yet undefined subroutine. Does not play well with code that uses an AUTOLOAD subroutine.
all	All of the preceding.
none	None of the preceding.

By default, only code in the supplied program and the main package is checked. Use the -u option to add a list of additional modules to check:

```
> perl -MO=Lint,context,undefined-subs,-u,My::Module app.pl
```

Cross-Referencing with B::Xref

The B::Xref module allows us to generate a cross-reference report listing every variable and subroutine in a Perl program. Such reports can be very illuminating in understanding the construction of large applications. By way of example, here is how we can generate a cross-reference report for the debug debug.pl we presented earlier in the chapter:

```
> perl -MO=Xref debug.pl
```

And following is the output that this command produces. For each file of interest, the report lists the subroutines found and within them each lexical and package variable:

```
File debug.pl
  Subroutine (definitions)
    Package Internals
      &SvREADONLY            s0
      &SvREFCNT               s0
      &hash_seed              s0
      &hv_clear_placeholders s0
    Package PerlIO
      &get_layers             s0
    Package Regexp
      &DESTROY               s0
    Package UNIVERSAL
      &VERSION                s0
      &can                    s0
      &isa                    s0
    Package main
      &debug                  s29
      &debug_level            s14
  Subroutine (main)
    Package (lexical)
      $debug_level            i7, 8
    Package main
      %ENV                    7
  Subroutine debug
    Package (lexical)
      $level                  i19, 22, 27, 27
    Package main
      &debug_level            &22, &27
      *STDERR                 22
      @_                      19, 22, 22
  Subroutine debug_level
```

```
        Package (lexical)
           $debug_level              12, 13
        Package main
           @_                        12
debug.pl syntax OK
```

The comma-separated number sequences look cryptic but turn out to be very simple. The numbers themselves are line numbers, with 0 indicating a definition outside the scope of the file. s means a subroutine definition, i means the introduction of a variable, and & means the call of a subroutine (or method).

We can see here that debug_level, which exists in package main, is called from subroutine debug at lines 20 and 25 of the script. The lexical variable $level is introduced at line 17 and used on lines 20 and 25 (twice). Since we are usually interested primarily in where definitions are used, we can get a shorter report with

> **perl -MO=Xref,-d debug.pl**

This switches off the initial Subroutine (definitions) section and leaves us with the usage information within each subroutine body. We can also use -d to generate raw machine-parsable output and -oFILE to write to the named file.

As a tool for analyzing the sense of compiled code, the B::Fathom module available from CPAN is also worthy of consideration. It makes an impressive, although not infallible, attempt to determine how legible our Perl code is:

> **perl -MO=Fathom debug.pl**

Here is what it had to say about debug.pl:

```
 74 tokens
 26 expressions
 10 statements
  3 subroutines
readability is 2.56 (very readable)
debug.pl syntax OK
```

The readability metric is calculated from a number of factors, but whitespace is not one of them. A good score is desirable, but it is not in itself a guarantee of legible code.

Regenerating Perl from Compiled Code

One last compiler backend module worth mentioning is B::Deparse. This takes Perl as input, compiles it, and turns it back into Perl again. For example, this is what the debug.pl script presented earlier in the chapter looks like after it has been put through the compile-deparse cycle:

```perl
use warnings;
use strict 'refs';
{
    my $debug_level = $ENV{'DEBUG'};
    $debug_level |= 0;
    sub debug_level (;$) {
        $debug_level = $_[0] if @_;
        return $debug_level;
    }

    sub debug (;$@) {
        my $level = shift @_;
```

```
        if (@_) {
            print STDERR @_, "\n" if $level <= debug_level();
        }
        else {
            debug_level $level ? $level : 1;
        }
    }
    ;
}
```

This is recognizable as the same program, down to the variable names and the subroutine prototypes. Not all Perl code is so easily reconstructed, but B::Deparse can handle a great deal already and is steadily improving.

This is more useful than it might sound. For a start, it has definite debugging applications when code does not seem to behave the way we want it to. Compiling and regenerating the code might reveal the difference between reality and our expectations. The Data::Dumper module is now also a client of B::Deparse and can use it to serialize Perl data structures incorporating code references.

Automated Testing

Perl provides several modules as part of its standard library that allow us to easily implement and carry out automated tests. The Test::Harness module provides a mechanism to perform tests mechanically, running through a series of specified tests and checking the results for a satisfactory outcome. The complementary Test module provides a simple toolkit of features to enable us to write scripts that produce output compatible with what the Test::Harness module expects. Competing for our affections are the Test::Simple and Test::More modules, modern alternatives to the Test module that seek to replace it with simplified usage and more extensible features. The advantage of Test is that it has been available since Perl version 5.0 and so is guaranteed to be present in all except the most archaic installations. Conversely, when developing a module that is in any event only compatible with Perl 5.8 or higher, Test::Simple is a better choice. Beyond these, CPAN offers more advanced testing modules for unit testing, and Test::Inline, which allows test code to be embedded within the module it is testing.

The main application of many of these modules is in creating installable module packages. When we use the h2xs utility to set up a basic module infrastructure for development and distribution, it automatically puts together a framework, including a makefile that makes use of Test::Harness. However, the module can be used independently too. How we implement tests to be compatible with the expectations of Test::Harness is up to us. We will first look at writing tests using the older Test module before moving on to its replacements Test::Simple and Test::More. Then we will see how Test::Harness can be used to invoke them to test our module.

Writing a Test Script

It is not actually necessary to use a test module to create tests compatible with Test::Harness, but since the manual approach is hard work, it makes sense to use Test or one if its alternatives.

The Test Module

To use the Test module, we first need to pass a list of key-value pairs to the plan subroutine. The only required pair key is tests, which defines the number of test results that the test script returns. Typically, this is placed in a BEGIN block to make sure it initializes before any program code is evaluated:

```
#!/usr/bin/perl
# mytest.pl
use strict;
```

```
use warnings;

use Test;
BEGIN {plan tests => 8}
```

(Here plan is a subroutine, with arguments of tests and 8. The list operator-style syntax is just an affectation to allow us to write plan tests as an English expression.)

This specifies that this test script will return eight results, and we will have to ensure that we do indeed return eight results during the course of the script. Normally, tests are fatal to Test::Harness if they fail, but we can make tests we expect to fail nonfatal by marking them as todo tests. To do this, we add a todo key to the list passed to plan, followed by a reference to an array of test numbers:

```
BEGIN {plan tests => 8, todo => [7, 8]}
```

This marks tests 7 and 8 as nonfatal. The implication is that these tests apply to features that do not yet work; we can write the test for them anyway, and update the code later. If a test starts to work, it should be taken off the todo list so that a future failure causes Test::Harness to register a fatal problem.

Finally, we can pass a subroutine to be called on failed tests with the onfail key:

```
BEGIN {plan tests => 8, todo => [7, 8], onfail =>
    sub {warn 'Oh no, not again'}
}
```

Test passes a hash containing the keys package, repetition, and result to the subroutine specified by onfail, so we have the option of recording more sophisticated diagnostics if we so choose. Regardless of whether todo or onfail is specified, having given plan a number of tests to expect, we now need to perform them. Test provides two subroutines to return test results compatible with Test::Harness, namely ok and skip.

The ok subroutine performs tests and takes between one and two arguments. The one argument form simply returns its value and produces an ok result if that result is true:

```
ok (0);   # an automatic failure
ok (1);   # an automatic success
ok (mysubtotest($testarg1, $testarg2));   # test for true result
```

This is suitable for tests that can be deemed to have succeeded if they return any true result. For other tests, we supply a two-argument form. The first argument is the test to perform and the second is the expected result. Both arguments can be expressions, and the expected result can validly be 0 or even undef. For example:

```
# test subroutine call against expected value
use My::Rhyme;
$farming_wife = new My::Rhyme('reason');
ok($farming_wife->count('blind mice'), 3);

# test the results of two calls for equality
ok(search_here('needle', 'haystack'), search_there('needle', 'haystack'));

# test against undef - a function with arguments expected to fail
ok(reassemble_humpty(king => ['horses', 'men']), undef);
```

The second argument may also be a regular expression, in which case the test result is matched against it:

```
$re_pattern = compile_pattern('test');
$match_text = match_on('default_text');
ok($match_text, qr/$re_pattern/);
```

Other than the regular expression case, the two arguments to ok are equivalent; the ok subroutine simply tests them for equality, so it does not matter which way around we put them. However, the convention is to put the test first and the expected result second.

The skip subroutine works exactly like ok, but takes a single initial argument that determines whether or not the test should be considered. If it evaluates to a false value, the test result is used as normal. If it evaluates to a string value, it is used to describe the reason for the test; otherwise, skip is automatically used. Either way, the reason is placed after the ok message, prefixed by a #. For example:

```
use Platform::Specific::Package qw(incompatible wise_men);
$message = incompatible($^O);
skip($message, 3, wise_men);
```

In this case, the subroutine incompatible should return 0 or undef if the platform is supported; it should return a message like Sorry, not supported on this platform if it isn't. Of course, the test script itself can define this subroutine if the package does not.

Test scripts that wish to check if they are being run through Test::Harness can check for the environment variable HARNESS_ACTIVE, which the Test::Harness module sets when it calls test scripts. If it isn't running, then scripts can alter their output or simply refuse to run:

```
die "Not being run by Test::Harness" unless defined $ENV{HARNESS_ACTIVE};
```

A test script can execute any code it likes and define any subroutine it needs to perform the necessary tests. After all, it is an ordinary Perl script, just one that generates a specific output. It should avoid printing output to STDOUT explicitly, relying on the ok or skip subroutines instead, but may print its own messages to STDERR. Doing this selectively is a good use for the HARNESS_ACTIVE environment variable.

It is possible to issue diagnostic messages—additional text for human consumption—so long as we make sure to prefix our additional messages with a #. This will cause Test::Harness to ignore the output rather than attempting to interpret it as a test result.

Simple Tests with Test::Simple

Test::Simple and Test::More are alternatives to the Test module. They are compatible with each other in that Test::More will do everything the simpler module does, with the same defined interface. Test::Simple is intended to be a gentle introduction to testing for those daunted by extensive manual pages, while Test::More provides the more advanced features a veteran tester requires.

Whichever module we choose, we first need to tell how many tests we will be running, which we can do by passing the word "tests" and the desired number in the import list. A typical test script might start like this:

```
#!/usr/bin/perl
# mysimpletest.pl
use strict;
use warnings;

use Test::Simple tests => 8;
```

Test::Simple provides exactly one subroutine, ok, which takes one or two parameters. The first is the test, and the second is simply a name for the test. The output of ok is "ok" or "not ok", followed by the test name if we supplied one:

```
ok write_file($file);        # test subroutine, no test name
ok (-f $file,"file created"); # test file exists, test named
```

The first argument, the test, is always evaluated in scalar context (as ok has a prototype of $$) and so will count lists or hashes, with empty ones evaluating to false and therefore a failed test. The following are thus equivalent:

```
ok (@array,"not empty");
ok (scalar(@array),"not empty");
```

When run, our test program will print out the correct 1..8 preamble (for 8 tests) and then print out "ok" or "not ok" with optional trailing test name for each test we have supplied. Test::Simple also causes an END block to be registered that exits with an appropriate exit status when our test program ends: 0 for success, 255 for a fatal error such as a die, and a positive number indicating the number of failed tests otherwise. This makes it convenient to call even from outside Test::Harness.

This is actually the limit of what Test::Simple does—it is deliberately simple so as to make writing tests trivial, and thus encourages more module writers to write them. For more useful testing functionality, we replace Test::Simple with Test::More and carry on programming—all existing tests will work as before.

Better Tests with Test::More

Anywhere we write Test::Simple we can exchange it for Test::More. By doing this, we can gain access to more useful test subroutines. These loosely divide into wrappers for Perl keywords that turn them into tests, and ways to express tests more conveniently in general.

The Plan

Just like Test and Test::Simple, the first order of business is usually to define the number of tests we will be performing. However, during development of the test driver, we may not know exactly how many test cases we require. In order to prevent this being a failure, for development only, we pass no_plan on the import list:

```
use Test::More 'no_plan'; # number of tests not yet finalized
```

If none of the tests in a test script are applicable, and we can determine this in the compile phase prior to loading the module, we can just have Test::More abort the test instead. The if pragma is one way to establish this condition:

```
use if  $ENV{NO_FOO_TESTS}, Test::More => qw(skip_all);
use if !$ENV{NO_FOO_TESTS}, Test::More'=> tests, 8;
```

Tests for Module Initialization

Since most test scripts test a module, the first thing they need to do is test that the module loads correctly. Rather than make us wrap the usual functions use, require, can, or isa with test logic, we can use testing versions of the same features provided to us by Test::More:

Normal Function	As a Test
use My::Module qw(import list);	BEGIN { use_ok My::Module => qw(import list) }
require "My/Module.pm";	require_ok "My/Module.pm";
My::Module->can("method1");	can_ok My::Module => "method1", "method2";
My::Module->isa("Alleged::Parent");	isa_ok My::Module => "Alleged::Parent";

use_ok is a special case since only the real use has the property of being in an implicit BEGIN block. We therefore need to wrap our test version with an explicit block. Semantically the end result is the same. can_ok and isa_ok are handy for testing modules that dynamically adjust their inheritance or autoload methods on demand.

Tests for Basic Scalars

The is and isnt subroutines improve on ok for direct comparisons by allowing Test::More to know what the compared value is. These two tests are equivalent, but the second one allows Test::More to print out the generated and expected values on a failure:

```
ok ($value eq '42', "the answer"); # this is fine
is ($value, 42, "the answer");     # but this is better
```

Since this is always a positive comparison, we can invert the sense with isnt:

```
isnt ($value, 54, "blindfold scrabble");
```

As the first example suggests, the comparison is a string comparison even if the test operands are numeric. If we know we want to carry out a numeric comparison or want to use a different comparison operator, we can use the generic cmp_ok routine. This takes an additional parameter, which is a string containing the desired operation. To carry out the preceding test with a numeric operator, we would use

```
cmp_ok ($value, "==", 42, "the answer"); # better still for numeric
```

The regular expression comparison offered by the Test module's version of ok is here implemented as like and unlike:

```
like ($six_small_black_ships, qr/one_big_white_ship/);
unlike ($sweet_smelling_liquid, qr/tea/);
```

Of course, like is and isnt, these are really just specializations of cmp_ok, this time with the =~ and !~ operators.

Tests for Arrays, Hashes, and Complex Data Structures

These test routines work fine for scalar comparisons but are not useful for arrays, hashes, or complex data structures. But we are also provided for here, as demonstrated in Table 17-19.

Table 17-19. *Array, Hash, and Complex Tests*

Test	Meaning
eq_array	Compare the elements of two arrays, in order.
eq_set	Compare the elements of two arrays, out of order. Unlike eq_array, so long as the two arrays contain the same values, the order does not matter. Duplicate values are considered distinct, however, and each one must have a corresponding value in the other array.
eq_hash	Compare the keys and values of two hashes.
is_deeply	Compare the structures pointed to by two references.

These routines are all recursive, following references and comparing the data structures they point to with the appropriate eq_array or eq_hash criteria. This applies also to eq_set—only the top-level arrays may have their elements out of order with respect to each other.

Explicit Pass and Fail

If we have written tests with our own logic and simply want to say whether or not the test succeeded for failed, we can do so with the pass and fail subroutines. These are more elegant than simply printing out the "ok" or "not ok" text explicitly. It can also read better than ok for some kinds of test. For example:

```
if ($error_text=my_complex_test()) {
    fail "Test failed - $error_text";
```

```
} else {
    pass "Test succeeded";
}
```

The single argument is the test name, with the same meaning as the second argument to ok. We could achieve the same effect by passing 1 or 0 as the first argument to ok, but pass and fail are more elegant.

Diagnostic Output

We can generate diagnostic output that won't upset Test::Harness with the diag routine. This takes a multiline string as an argument and prefixes each line with a # before outputting it:

```
if ($error_text=my_complex_test()) {
    fail "Test failed";
    diag "The reason was '$error_text'";
}
```

Skipping Tests

We can tell Test::More to skip tests with the skip routine. This is radically different from the Test module's approach, however. Rather than simply calling skip in place of ok, we use the routine to tell the module how many of the tests immediately following should be skipped, and wrap both the condition and the tests it affects with a block that is given the special label SKIP. The actual tests themselves are not touched, which makes it easy for us to enable or disable a test with a precondition such as in this example:

```
SKIP: {
    if ($^O eq 'MSWin32') {
        skip "test not supported on Windows", 2;
    }

    ok not_on_windows_test_1();
    ok not_on_windows_test_2();
}
```

This approach makes it easy to "comment out" tests without actually completely removing them—the test output will remind us that tests are being skipped, so we will be reminded to reenable them later. More usually, this allows tests to be skipped for platforms on which they are not applicable or when the feature under test requires the presence of an optional module that is not installed. Note that it is fine to nest such blocks—the label is not used literally by Perl but has meaning to the module instead.

Tests to Do

We can also mark tests as "to do" tests, meaning that they are tests for features that are yet to be implemented. Like skipped tests, a special block is used, this time labeled TODO. Also like skipped tests, we can use this block to predefine a set of tests as "to do" tests without rewriting them in any way. Unlike skipped tests, the mechanism we use to do this is to set a package variable $TODO, which is automatically exported into our test script. Since we want to constrain the effect of this variable, the best approach is usually to use local to create a scoped temporary value:

```
TODO: {
    local $TODO="not yet implemented";

    is(get_a_string(), "expected result");
    ok(return_a_true_value,"test of truth");
}
```

The value of $TODO should be set to a string describing why the tests it affects are "to do" tests. This is reflected in the output generated by the tests when they are invoked. Note that a "to do" test that actually succeeds is considered an error by Test::Harness, since it should not be possible for a test to succeed if the feature it is testing has not been implemented.

Customs Tests with Test::Builder

The engine that powers both Test::More and Test::Simple is the Test::Builder module. This provides a wide range of capabilities of which those we have just seen are just convenient wrappers and extrapolations. If we want to create our own test modules or manipulate the underlying test object, we can. The module creates a singleton object that is automatically instantiated when the module is used and is invoked by the subroutines we have just covered. We can retrieve it with

```
my $builder=Test::More->builder(); # or the same for Test::Simple
```

Having the underlying object allows us to call methods that are not directly accessible through the subroutines provided by its clients. For instance, Test::More's isnt subroutine is implemented using Test::More's isnt_eq method, which compares using string comparisons. The isnt_num method, which is not available as a Test::More routine, carries out a numeric comparison instead, which is useful when a value needs to evaluated in numeric context, like this check on the special variable $!:

```
use POSIX qw(:errno_h);
do_a_filesystem_test(); #
$builder->isnt_num($! => ENOENT);
```

We can also use Test::Builder directly to create My::Custom::Test::Module with an array of convenience tests to suit our own particular purposes. Capabilities of Test::Builder not available through Test::More can be made accessible this way. We can also add our own new test routines for scripts to use. Since Test::Builder is designed to be a singleton, we don't inherit from it but create a local internal builder object. We supply an import method so that our new tests are exported to the test script and use it to name each new test we are providing:

```
package My::Custom::Test::Module;
use strict;
use warnings;
use Test::Builder;

my $builder = Test::Builder->new;

sub import {
    my $self = shift;
    my $package = caller;

    #tell builder where to export to
    $builder->exported_to($package);
    #pass on import arguments to 'plan'
    $builder->plan(@_);
    #pass our own routines up for export
    $self->export_to_level(1, $self, qw[is_eq is_numeq]);
}

### our extended test routines ###

sub is_eq ($$;$) {
    return $builder->is_eq(@_);
}
```

```perl
sub is_numeq ($$;$) {
    return $builder->is_num(@_);
}

1;
```

This `import` routine is interesting in that while `Test::Builder` uses the `Exporter` module, the arguments passed to the module when we load it are instead passed on to the `plan` method, which is why we can state the number of tests as part of the import list. The actual exports are stated explicitly as arguments to the `export_to_level` method and have nothing to do with the arguments actually passed to the `import` method. A smarter `import` method could take a list of subroutines to export and discriminate them from plan instructions, but test scripts don't usually require this level of sophistication.

The builder object provides many methods that we can use to adjust the test before or as it is running. For instance, we can direct the test output to a specific file or filehandle with the `output` method. `Test::More` does not provide this, but we can make it available with our own test module:

```perl
sub setlog ($) {
    $builder->output($file_or_$filehandle);
}
```

Tests may use as many test modules as they like. As long as we follow the preceding template, it is fine for a test script to use our own test module and `Test::More` together:

```perl
#!/usr/bin/perl
use Test::More;
use My::Custom::Test::Module;
...
```

Writing Tests Inline

The `Test::Inline` module, available from CPAN, provides us with the appealing ability to write test code embedded within the POD documentation (see Chapter 18) of the module that it is testing. We can also test code examples to ensure that our documentation is current with the implementation.

A specialized POD translator then extracts the test code and generates test scripts from it. `Test::More` is used to drive the generated scripts, so any feature provided by `Test::More` can be used in embedded tests. The module distribution comes with pod2test, which does the work of extraction, so there is no need to actually use `Test::Inline` within our own code.

Tests are marked using the special POD formats `testing` and `example`. For an embedded test, we can use a POD =for paragraph:

```
=for testing
is(my_function(1,2,3),'expected result');
is(my_function(4,5,6),'other expected result');
```

Or we can use a =begin...=end documentation block:

```
=begin testing

is(my_function(1,2,3),'expected result');
is(my_function(4,5,6),'other expected result');

=end testing
```

In either case, a POD reader will not display the tests because the output format is not "testing." Only pod2test looks for the "testing" format, so only it will pay attention to these sections. Be sure not to include any empty lines between the =for and any tests that belong to it, however, or they will appear in the documentation. To space things out, use the =begin...=end block instead.

Writing Testable Code Examples

An embedded code example is different in that we actually do want it to appear in the documentation. It would be nice to be able to test these code examples, though, if only to ensure that they are keeping in step with the module if it changes its interface in any way.

We often want to provide a sample code section but not a complete working example, since the latter is excessive and unnecessary in documentation with many examples. Fortunately, we are catered for. Initialization code we do not want to display (if any) is placed in an optional initial =for example paragraph. The code we actually want to be seen in documentation is placed between =for example begin and =for example end paragraphs, with a leading blank line to ensure it is displayed rather than absorbed into the preceding =for example begin paragraph.

As an example, take this embedded test, to which we have also added a title:

```
=head2 Example of method_example

=for example
my $object=new Object::For::Example();

=for example begin

my $result=$object->method_example(1,2,3);

=for example end

=cut
```

If we do not need any initialization, we can omit the initial =for example paragraph. It is critical to use =for and not =begin...=end for the actual example code, however, since the latter will swallow all the paragraphs contained within and cause them to not be displayed except by the nonexistent "example" POD formatter. This is not the result we are looking for.

When turned into a test, the preceding code will simply be compiled, but not run. We can turn it into a full-fledged test by adding a =for example_testing paragraph as well:

```
=head2 Tested example of method_example

=for example
my $object=new Object::For::Example();

=for example begin

my $result=$object->method_example(1,2,3);

=for example end

=for example_testing
is($result,'expected result');

=cut
```

Now this example will be correctly initialized, executed, and the return result checked. The heading and the actual example are displayed by POD readers, but the initialization code and the tests are only seen by pod2test when it converts them into test scripts.

The distinction between testing and example_testing is that example_testing will only be able to use code contained in the example itself, whereas testing can see only "real" Perl code. We can also use example_testing in a =begin...=end block if we have a lot of testing to do and want to use some blank lines to break it up.

Once we have written our embedded tests, we can create the test script with a command like

>**pod2test Object/For/Example.pm > object_for_example_embeddedtests.t**

We can now run the generated test script either directly or via Test::Harness to invoke the inlined tests and code examples. The test script does not reference the original inlined code, however, so we need to rerun pod2test every time we change it.

Harnessing Tests

Once we have one or more test scripts, however we chose to implement them, we can process them through the Test::Harness module. The module supplies one single subroutine, runtests, which takes one or more script names as arguments. For cross-platform compatibility, it is a good idea if the script paths are absolute, but it is not a hard and fast requirement.

Using this module, we can create a master test script whose job it is to run all our other test scripts and collate and analyze their results for us. For example, here is a script that uses Test::Harness to run through a series of test scripts supplied on the command line:

```
#!/usr/bin/perl
use warnings;
use Test::Harness;
runtests(@ARGV);
```

As this Unix-specific example shows, Test::Harness is not a hard module to use. A slightly more complex example might keep all its scripts in a particular subdirectory relative to the location of the master script:

```
#!/usr/bin/perl
use warnings;
use Find::Bin qw($Bin);
use Test::Harness;

runtests glob "$Bin/t/*.pl";
```

The runtests routine expects to get output for each test run consisting of a series of lines. The first line should be a test range of the form 1..N. It should then be followed by a series of ok or not ok lines, with # Skip... plus a reason optionally appearing after ok lines, and continue in this manner for as many tests as the range specified. For example:

```
1..8
ok 1
not ok 2 my second test
ok 3  # 'Skip': not implemented on this platform
ok
ok
ok
not ok 7 my tricky test
# a comment on this test...
ok 8 the end #this is the last test
```

Test results should be followed by a test number, although it is permissible to omit them. If a number is present, a test name is also permissible, as in "my second test" previously. A comment may also be provided after a # after the test number and optional name. Comments may also appear on their own and are typically used for diagnostic output that is to be displayed when the test harness is run in verbose mode.

Note that the Test module generates numbered tests, with the number coming after the "ok" (or "not ok") and before the skip comment. This is optional, and we do not need to supply it, but if we do it ought to start at 1 and increment monotonically.

If an entire test script wishes to have itself skipped, it can return a range 1..0, optionally by a reason:

```
1..0    # Skipped: bottled out at the last moment
```

runtests will then analyze and produce a statistical analysis of the test results. If all tests were successful, it prints some timing information supplied by the Benchmark module. If any tests failed, it dies with output similar to the following:

```
FAILED tests 2, 7
Failed 2/8 tests, 75.00% okay
```

If a test does not return a zero exit code, runtests will also report this. It does not die as a result. The HARNESS_IGNORE_EXITCODE environment variable, if set, suppresses this message.

Two package variables may be set in test scripts to control the operation of the harness:

$Test::Harness::verbose	This turns verbose mode on or off, depending on whether it is assigned a true or false value.
$Test::Harness::switches	This holds a string of extra command-like options to pass to each test script when it is invoked; it has the same effect on invoked test scripts as PERL5OPT but without affecting the script running the harness.

Test::Harness also makes use of several environment variables, if defined, as listed in Table 17-20.

Table 17-20. *Test::Harness Environment Variables*

Environment Variable	Effect
HARNESS_VERBOSE	Display the complete standard output of tests rather than just those parts that have significance to Test::Harness. The environment variable is overridden by explicitly setting $Test::Harness::verbose.
HARNESS_PERL_SWITCHES	Can be used to specify extra options to pass Perl when executing each test. One obvious definition for this variable is -w, to force warnings to be enabled. The environment variable is overridden by explicitly setting $Test::Harness::switches.
HARNESS_IGNORE_EXITCODE	If true, instructs runtests not to check or report on tests that return non-zero exit codes.
HARNESS_COLUMNS	Set the width for output. Defaults to 80 or the value of $ENV{COLUMNS}, if set by the shell.
HARNESS_OK_SLOW	Output a test result once a second. Useful for slow connections or for visually checking output.
HARNESS_COMPILE_TEST	If true, will cause runtests to use the perlcc utility to attempt to compile the test as a stand-alone executable before running it. The object of this is to see whether it works as a stand-alone application, but as perlcc is still relatively new, it might not.
HARNESS_FILELEAK_IN_DIR	Specify the name of a directory in which runtests will check for new files. If a test generates files but does not clean them up afterward, runtests will report them. For example: LEAKED FILES: temp.file
HARNESS_NOTTY	If true, this environment variable tells runtests to treat its output as a nonterminal device, even if it is a terminal.

As previously mentioned, Test::Harness also sets the environment variable HARNESS_ACTIVE. Tests and applications can check for this variable if need be to determine if they are being tested or being run outside of Test::Harness.

Harnessing Tests from the Command Line

Perl from version 5.8.3 onward comes with the command-line program prove to provide a simple way to invoke tests via Test::Harness without needing a module distribution makefile (or indeed, a module). It takes a list of scripts or directories containing scripts as arguments, and runs every script it finds. With no arguments at all, it looks in the current working directory for any files ending in a .t extension. For example, to run a single test script:

> **prove mytestscript.pl**

Or to run all scripts ending in .t in a "t" subdirectory:

> **prove t**

We can also supply the options shown in Table 17-21 to prove.

Table 17-21. *prove Options*

Option	Effect
-b, --blib	Same effect as use blib, add the blib and lib subdirectories of the current location to @INC. Useful for testing unpacked module distributions (only). See also -l.
-d, --debug	Display debug information about the tests as prove runs them.
-D, --dry	Perform a dry run and output the file names of the test scripts that would be run, without actually running them. Useful to check the effects of -r.
--ext=<ext>	Add more extensions to the default list that prove searches for when given a directory argument. For example, --ext=.pl will also find Perl scripts like mytestscript.pl. No effect on explicitly named files.
-h, --help	Display brief usage information for prove.
-H, --man	Display extended manual page for prove.
-I	Same effect as perl -I, add a path to @INC.
-l, --lib	Add lib to @INC. See also -b.
-r, --recurse	Recurse into subdirectories when scanning directories for tests. Only applicable if a directory was supplied in the command line. Any files matching the extensions specified by --ext are added to the list of tests to run.
-s, --shuffle	Run tests in a random order to prevent inadvertent intertest dependencies from generating false positive results.
-T	Same effect as perl -T, enable taint errors.
-t	Same effect as perl -t, enable (nonfatal) taint warnings.
-v, --verbose	Display diagnostic output from test scripts, not just output significant to Test::Harness. See HARNESS_VERBOSE.
-V, --version	Display the version of prove.

Any or all of these options may also be set as defaults by citing them within the PROVE_SWITCHES environment variable. This has the same connotations and format as PERL5OPT and is simply the options and values as they would be written on the command line.

Testing Coverage

Writing tests is all very well, but without a clear idea of what needs to be tested, we may omit important functions. Worse still, it is hard to write tests that ensure that every clause of every conditional
statement is actually followed and produces the right results. Writing tests is actually very hard work,
not because the tests are hard, but because achieving full testing of a whole module is much harder
than it looks, even for the author of the module. At the top end of the scale, do not be surprised to
spend 70% of all development time writing tests, and only 30% writing the actual module or script.

The degree to which a test suite tests its module is called its *coverage*. The Devel::Cover module from CPAN attempts to calculate the coverage of a test suite by analyzing what operations are
called in the compiled code tree generated by the Perl interpreter before it executes it. It will also
test the completeness of POD documentation via the Pod::Coverage module, if it is also installed.

While still in alpha, Devel::Cover is already very useful and is well worth a look for developers
who want to get their test suites right. Here are some ways we can use it:

```
> perl -MDevel::Cover myscript.pl -option=value ...
> PERL5OPT="-MDevel::Cover" myscript.pl -option=value ...
```

Or, we can analyze an unpacked module distribution through its makefile. By setting PERL5OPT,
we can have any Perl program we invoke automatically generate coverage data:

```
> PERL5OPT="-MDevel::Cover" make test
```

If we only care about generating coverage for Test::Harness scripts, we can instead say something like

```
> HARNESS_PERL_SWITCHES = "-MDevel::Cover" make test
```

As these examples show, we do not generally use Devel::Cover within a script, but load it into
memory directly on the command line. Of course, myperlscript.pl could be a test script or even a
test harness script that runs a complete test suite. The effect of this command is to generate a database file, called cover_db by default, that contains the results of the coverage analysis. By default,
modules on Perl's @INC path are not analyzed by anything else. We can control this and other features by passing options:

```
> perl -MDevel::Cover=-ignore,Namespace::Regex,-db,myscript_db myscript.pl
> perl -MDevel::Cover=-coverage,statement,branch,subroutine,pod myscript.pl
```

Unless the -silent option is specified, Test::Harness is in use, or the module is loaded from
PERL5OPT, a report will also automatically be generated. We can also generate the report independently
with the cover script, which post-processes the coverage database and generates human-readable
reports that we can look at to see how well our testing is doing. We can pass most of the same options
here too:

```
> cover -coverage statement,branch,subroutine,pod myscript_db
```

As an example, consider this simple Perl script:

```perl
#!/usr/bin/perl
# testcoverage.pl
use strict;
use warnings;

sub heads () {
    my $head="Head";
    $head.="s";
    return $head;
}
```

```
sub tails () {
    return ucfirst lc "TAILS";
}

if (rand > 0.5) {
    print heads();
} else {
    print tails();
}

print "\n";
```

The report generated by this program for the "heads" branch is

```
--------------------------- ------ ------ ------ ------ ------ ------ ------
File                        stmt branch  cond    sub   pod   time  total
--------------------------- ------ ------ ------ ------ ------ ------ ------
myscript.pl                 85.7   50.0   n/a   75.0   n/a  100.0   80.0
Total                       85.7   50.0   n/a   75.0   n/a  100.0   80.0
--------------------------- ------ ------ ------ ------ ------ ------ ------
```

Since there is only one source file involved, there is only one entry, and the total is simply the
same results repeated. For more complex programs with multiple modules, we would get a line for
each module involved. 85.7% of the statements in the program and 50% of the branches were executed—there is only one condition, and we followed only one branch of it. If we had taken the tails
branch, only 71% of the statements would have been executed (as we can prove if we reanalyze the
script until a Tails result comes up).

This script has no POD, so there are no results from it. The key figure is the total coverage,
80%—ideally we want 100%, although this is not always possible for reasons covered in the
Devel::Cover documentation. For the full list of options supported by the Devel::Cover and the
cover script, see their respective manual pages.

Profiling

Profiling is the process of collecting timing statistics for an application. In general this occurs in two
steps. First, a raw data file of timing information is generated by running the application in a profiling mode. Second, an analysis tool is then used to read the raw statistics and generate a report.

Perl does not provide a separate profiling tool. Instead, the Devel::DProf module is provided to
alter the behavior of the Perl interpreter itself to generate the raw statistics. Once the file has been
generated, the dprofpp tool can be used to analyze the results.

We do not necessarily have to use the profiler to generate timing information, however. First, for
very simple cases, we can get away with using the times function, which is the basis of the profiler's
statistics as well as other timing modules. Second, we can use the Benchmark module to generate timing statistics for repeated execution. As its name suggests, the Benchmark module is not so much
aimed at providing detailed timing information as performance statistics; it is handy for testing the
speed of a Perl script or application on different platforms.

Profiling Perl Applications

To profile an application, we use the Devel::DProf module. This is implemented as an alternative
debugger module, which hooks into Perl's debugging interface via the -d option. To specify the

profiler rather than the normal debugger, we suffix the -d option with :DProf to specify the profiler module:

```
> perl -d:DProf myscript.pl
```

This will generate a file of raw profile statistics called tmon.out in the current directory. There are no options that can be supplied to the profiler, not even one to change the name of the output file.

The profiler is essentially a statistics collection package built around the times function, generating a file of raw data as its output. In order to make sense of this file, we need to use a profile analyzer such as dprofpp, which is supplied as standard with Perl.

Note that not all modules in the Devel family can be used in this way. Only modules that define a DB subroutine are actually designed to work with Perl's debugging interface. The Devel::DProf module is the only such alternative supplied with Perl as standard, though other third-party modules exist on CPAN.

Generating Profile Reports

On its own, the profile information produced by the Devel::DProf module is not of much use to us. Fortunately, Perl provides a profile analysis tool called dprofpp that can interpret profile files and generate various kinds of report from them. This tool is written in Perl, so it will work anywhere that Perl does.

By default, dprofpp looks for a file called tmon.out, the name of the profile file generated by Devel::DProf. It then prints out the details of the 15 most time-consuming subroutines. This is a common enough occurrence that we can frequently just type

```
> perl -d:DProf myscript.pl
> dprofpp
```

We can even have dprofpp run the profiling stage for us, generating and analyzing the tmon.out file in one easy step. The following command is equivalent to the preceding two:

```
> dprofpp -p myscript.pl
```

The usual output of dprofpp is a table of subroutines and associated timing statistics (we say usual because the -S, -T, and -t options cause dprofpp to generate an execution tree instead). For example, here is a short script that lists installed files using the ExtUtils::Installed module. We use it an example because it is both short and takes a little time to run, and so it generates some meaningful statistics (on a Unix platform):

```
#!/usr/bin/perl
# installed.pl
use warnings;
use strict;

use ExtUtils::Installed;

my $inst = ExtUtils::Installed->new();
print join "\n", $inst->modules();
```

drofpp is then executed like so:

```
> dprofpp -p installed.pl
```

The output reports something similar to the following (the times are of course entirely dependent on the hardware we run the script on):

```
Total Elapsed Time = 3.638225 Seconds
User+System Time = 1.178225 Seconds

Exclusive Times
%Time    ExclSec    CumulS    #Calls    sec/call    Csec/c    Name
19.5     0.230      0.239     76        0.0030      0.0031    ExtUtils::Packlist::read
12.7     0.150      0.149     1         0.1496      0.1493    SelfLoader::_load_stubs
11.0     0.130      0.269     9         0.0144      0.0299    ExtUtils::Installed::BEGIN
10.3     0.122      0.755     2         0.0608      0.3776    File::Find::_find_dir
9.34     0.110      0.138     68        0.0016      0.0020    ExtUtils::MM_Unix::parse_version
8.49     0.100      0.634     1864      0.0001      0.0003     ExtUtils::Installed::_ANON_
5.94     0.070      0.067     566       0.0001      0.0001    ExtUtils::MM_Unix::canonpath
5.09     0.060      0.080     4         0.0150      0.0200    ExtUtils::MakeMaker::BEGIN
4.24     0.050      0.076     283       0.0002      0.0003     ExtUtils::MM_Unix::catdir
3.39     0.040      0.151     283       0.0001      0.0005     ExtUtils::MM_Unix::catfile
1.70     0.020      0.020     2         0.0100      0.0100    Exporter::export
1.70     0.020      0.020     1         0.0200      0.0200    vars::BEGIN
1.70     0.020      0.030     8         0.0025      0.0037    ExtUtils::MM_Unix::BEGIN
1.70     0.020      0.289     2         0.0100      0.1445    main::BEGIN
0.85     0.010      0.010     71        0.0001      0.0001    strict::bits
```

The columns in this report have the meanings listed in Table 17-22.

Table 17-22. *Profile Report Columns*

Column	Action
%Time	The percentage of time spent in this subroutine as a fraction of the total run time, not including time spent in subroutines called from this one. The -I option alters this column to include time spent.
ExclSec	The amount of time spent in this subroutine, not including time spent in subroutines called from this one.
CumulS	The amount of time spent in this subroutine, including time spent in subroutines called from this one. This contrasts with ExclSec.
#Calls	The total number of calls made to this subroutine during the course of execution. The sec/call and Csec/c values are computed from this plus ExclSec and CumulS, respectively.
sec/call	Time spent on average per call to this subroutine, not including time spent in subroutines called from this one, that is, sec/cal=ExclSec/#Calls. This is in contrast with Csec/c.
Csec/c	Time spent on average per call to this subroutine, including time spent in subroutines called from this one, that is, Csec/c=CumulS/#Calls. Contrast with sec/call.
Name	The name of the subroutine, if available. Anonymous subroutines are still listed under _ANON_ in the package in which they are created. However, see the -A and -R command-line options in Table 17-25.

The dprofpp utility understands a number of command-line options that alter the way that it computes statistics and the way in which it displays them. These can be loosely categorized into five groups: sorting, display, subroutines, timing, and interpretation options. The options belonging to these groups are defined in Tables 17-23 through 17-27, respectively.

Table 17-23. *dprofpp Sorting Options*

Option	Action
-a	Sort subroutines alphabetically (sort on Name column).
-l	Sort by number of subroutine calls (sort on #Calls column).
-U	Do not sort. Subroutines are listed in the order they are found in the profile file. This is more efficient if we want to do our own sorting later, in which case we probably also want to use -q.
-v	Sort by average call time (sort on sec/call column).
-z	The default sort order. Sort by percentage of time used (sort on %Time column).

Table 17-24. *dprofpp Display Options*

Option	Action
-O number	Limit the number of subroutines displayed to number. The number may be optionally separated from the option by a space. The default is 15, equivalent to -O 15. Setting this value to a negative number will display all subroutines: > **dprofpp -O-1**
-q	Suppress column headings. This stops dprofpp from generating the column headings line and also the Total and User+System elapsed time lines, making the output easier for machine parsing.
-S	Generate an execution tree showing all subroutine calls instead of a normal profile report, including timing statistics. Multiple calls, even if not consecutive, are listed only once, with a repeat count. This differs from -t, and it means that the execution tree is not a literal description of the chain of subroutine calls but a hierarchical form of the standard profile report. Contrast with -T and -t.
-T	Generate an execution tree showing all subroutine calls instead of a normal profile report, without statistics. Multiple consecutive calls are listed separately. Contrast with -S and -t.
-t	Generate an execution tree showing all subroutine calls instead of a normal profile report, without statistics. Multiple consecutive calls are listed only once with a repeat count. This generates a shorter and generally more readable report than -T. Contrast with -S and -T.

Table 17-25. *dprofpp Subroutine Options*

Option	Action
-A	In older releases of Perl, this causes dprofpp to assign the time spent autoloading a subroutine definition to the subroutine entry *::AUTOLOAD. The default is to include the autoload time in the first call to the subroutine. Newer releases of Perl automatically assign time to AUTOLOAD separately, so this option is redundant.
-g subname	Profile only the named subroutine and the subroutines that it calls. This is handy for profiling a specific part of the application. This isolates calls to subroutines from the named subroutine from calls to them from elsewhere. For example: > **dprofpp -p myscript.pl -g mysubname**
-R	Count calls to anonymous subroutines in the same package separately. The default is to accumulate all anonymous subroutine calls together into an __ANON__ entry. Note that for obvious reasons, dprofpp is not able to give a name for an anonymous subroutine.

Option	Action

-R	At the time of writing there is a bug in the dprofpp, but the original line 556 in the file, shown here:
	
	`if ($opt_R and ($name =~/::(__ANON__|END)$/)) {`
	
	can be changed to
	
	`if ($opt_R and ($name =~/(__ANON__|END)$/)) {`
	
	This will allow it to work. In future versions of dprofpp, this bug may well be fixed.

Table 17-26. *Benchmark Module Timing Options*

Option	Action
-E	Display the percentage of time not including time spent in subroutines called from them. This affects only the %Time column and therefore the sort order if sorting by percentage time (-z, the default). This is the default.
-I	Display the percentage of time including time spent in subroutines called from them. This affects only the %Time column and therefore the sort order if sorting by percentage time (-z, the default).
-s	Display system time only, rather than User+System time, in contrast with -u and -r. See "Collecting Timing Information Directly" later for an explanation of the distinction between user and system time.
-r	Display elapsed real time, rather than User+System time, in contrast with -s and -u. Note that this value is likely to be fairly meaningless for profiling.
-u	Display user time only, rather than User+System time. Contrast with -s and -r.

Table 17-27. *Benchmark Module Interpretation Options*

Option	Action
-F	Generate fake exit timestamps for profiles that are missing them, possibly due to the influence of goto (dprofpp reports that the profile is "garbled"). Note that the results of using this option are indeterminate.
-p scriptname	Run the profiler on the script to generate a tmon.out file and then generate a report from it. The tmon.out file is left after the command has completed generating a report from it.
-Q	In combination with the -p option, run the profiler to create a tmon.out file, but do not generate a report from the results. For example: `> dprofpp -p myscript.pl -Q`
-V	Print the version number of dprofpp and exit. If a tmon.out file is present, then the version number found in the XS_VERSION field inside the file is also reported.

Collecting Timing Information Directly

Perl provides two functions that return information to us about the current time. The time function returns the number of seconds since midnight, January 1, 1970, GMT (the notional moment that Unix was born). Unfortunately, while this is useful for computing real times, it is no use for computing execution times because it does not take into account the fact that system time is split between many processes (including operating system calls) and only measures to the nearest second.

> **Tip** Before leaving the subject of time, it is worth mentioning the Time::HiRes module, available from CPAN, which replaces both the time and sleep functions with versions that work down to the microsecond. If we want to work with real time at a higher resolution, this is a very useful module to install.

To examine time from the point of view of the application, we use the times function. This function returns not one but four values to us:

```
($user, $system, $cuser, $csystem) = times;
```

The $user and $system values refer to the user and system time of the current process. The $cuser and $csystem values refer to the user and system time used by child processes (see Chapter 22). These will have values if we have used system, fork, the forking version of open, and so on; otherwise, the value will be zero. In and of itself this is not useful, but if we call times twice and take the difference between the returned values, then we can compute the user and system time taken between the two calls.

The distinction between user and system time is actually that user time is time spent running the application itself, the time is spent in user space. system time is time spent by the operating system dealing with requests from our application. For example, calls to the time function cause the operating system to retrieve the current time, so the time spent doing this is system time. By contrast, adding and subtracting numbers does not require operating system services, and so this is user time. The total of user and system time equals to the total time spent.

As an example of the use of both user and system time, consider the following program, which computes the time taken for a loop by calling times before and after it:

```perl
#!/usr/bin/perl
# gettime.pl
use warnings;
use strict;

my ($user1, $system1) = times;
my ($a, $t);

# repeat a loop one million times
foreach (1..1_000_000) {
    # incur some user time
    $a += 2**2000;
    # incur some system time
    $t = time;
}
my ($user2, $system2) = times;

# compute times
my $user = $user2 - $user1;
my $system = $system2 - $system1;
my $total = $user + $system;

print "Time taken: user = $user system = $system total = $total \n";
```

The body of the loop contains two lines. The first line computes 2 to a high power and consumes a little user time. There are no calls to the operating system involved here, and therefore no system time is taken to do this. The second line uses the Perl time function, which makes a call to the operating system and so does consume system time. The assignment also consumes a little user time, but not much compared to computing 2 to the power of 2000. If we run this program, we get a result similar to the following:

```
Time taken: user=3.05 system=0.52 total=3.57
```

If we run this repeatedly, we get a slightly different result, simply depending on what else the processor and operating system are involved with at that particular point in time and how accessible the system clock was. The total tends to be almost exactly the same because we are only counting time spent actually running this program, not other processes that may also be running elsewhere. The wall clock time taken may be quite different from the total, but it is not relevant for calculating timing information:

```
Time taken: user=3.01 system=0.57 total=3.58
Time taken: user=2.79 system=0.78 total=3.57
Time taken: user=3.06 system=0.52 total=3.58
Time taken: user=3.03 system=0.54 total=3.57
Time taken: user=3.08 system=0.49 total=3.57
```

It is because of these variations that serious testing of application performance is better performed by the Benchmark module.

Performance Testing with Benchmark

The Benchmark module is a standard part of the Perl library that allows us to write performance tests for our code. It operates on the same basic principles as the profiler and uses the times function detailed previously as the basis for its results. However, it is not aimed at highlighting underperforming code, but generating accurate and consistent performance statistics, which it does by repeatedly running code to generate a more representative average time.

Benchmark can be used to run simple time comparisons, showed earlier using times. We do this by creating new raw Benchmark objects with new, which contain absolute times. Then we compare them with timediff to generate a relative Benchmark we can actually use:

```
$start = new Benchmark;
...do time consuming things...
$finish = new Benchmark;

$difference = timediff($start, $finish);

print "Time taken: ", timestr($difference);
```

The real meat of the module is in the timeit, timethis, timethese, and countit subroutines, however.

Benchmark works by generating Benchmark objects that encapsulate times internally. We can generate these objects with subroutines like timethis and timethese, and then print them out in a friendly format using the timestr subroutine. A summary of the methods and subroutines available follows; subroutines prefixed with * are not imported by default and must be given explicitly along with any other subroutines if not qualified by package. For example:

```
# need to import 'timesum' and therefore also 'timediff' and 'timestr'
use Benchmark qw(timesum timediff timestr);
```

Or:

```
# use 'timesum' via package, no need to import 'timediff' or 'timestr'
use Benchmark;
...
print timestr Benchmark::timesum ($difference1, $difference2);
```

The Benchmark module provides the three methods listed in Table 17-28.

Table 17-28. *Benchmark Module Methods*

Method	Action
new	Class method. Create a new raw Benchmark object containing absolute times. timediff is needed to convert two of these into a useful result Benchmark object. For example: `$start = new Benchmark;`

debug	Object or class method. Set debugging either globally or per object:
	`# enable debugging on this Benchmark object`
	`$start -> debug(1);`
	
	`# switch off debugging globally`
	`debug Benchmark 0;`

iters	Object method. Return the number of iterations used to generate this benchmark (for Benchmark objects generated by the timeit, timethis, timethese, and countit subroutines). For example:
	`$result = timeit(1000, 'mysubroutine');`
	`$count = $result->iters;`

Basic benchmarking can be done just using the new and timediff functions, as noted previously. We can also compute sums of differences with timesum, as detailed in Table 17-29.

Table 17-29. *Benchmark Module Time Functions*

Function	Action

timediff	Compute the difference in times between two raw Benchmark objects (as created by new) and return a new Benchmark object containing the difference. For example:
	`$difference = timediff($start, $end);`
	`print timestr $difference;`

timesum	Compute the sum of times of two relative Benchmark objects (computed themselves with timediff), returning a new Benchmark object. For example:
	`$diff1 = timediff ($start1, $end1);`
	`$diff2 = timediff ($start2, $end2);`
	`$total = Benchmark::timesum ($diff1, $diff2);`
	Note that this subroutine is not imported by default.

timestr	Generate a friendly string representation of a Benchmark object calculated from timediff (or potentially timesum) earlier. This is the easy way of turning a Benchmark object into something we can review. For example:
	`print  timestr $difference;`
	A second optional style argument determines the contents of the returned string; the default is auto:
	all: Produce all times.
	none: Produce no times.
	noc: Produce parent process times only.
	nop: Produce child process times only.
	auto: Produce child process times only if they are non-zero (that is, all or noc).
	A third parameter may be used to define the format of the output times; it takes the form of a sprintf style format, only without a leading %. The default is 5.2f. For example:
	`print timestr ($difference, 'noc', '10.5f');`
	See the sections "timeit" and "countit" for some examples of the strings produced by timestr.

Benchmark calculations are performed by the timeit, timethis, timethese, and countit subroutines. Additionally, the cmpthese subroutine generates a table of results from the output of timethese.

timeit

Given a number of iterations and some code to test, timeit runs the code for that number of iterations and returns a Benchmark object containing the result. For example:

```
# time one thousand iterations of '2**rand'
$result = timeit(1000, "2**rand");
```

The code may be either given as a string, in which case it is evaled to produce the code to test, or it may be a referenced to a subroutine:

```
# time an anonymous subroutine
$result = timeit(1000, sub {2**rand});

# time a named subroutine
$result = timeit(1000, \&mysubroutine);
```

Note that either of these approaches allows compile-time checking of the code, unlike the eval version, but passing arguments is not possible this way. To achieve that, we need to define a new subroutine to pass test arguments for the benchmark:

```
sub testmysubroutine {
    mysubroutine('testing', 1, 2, 3);
}
$result = timeit(1000, \&testmysubroutine);
```

Or use an eval string:

```
$result = timeit(1000, "mysubroutine 'test', 1, 2, 3");
```

A test subroutine will incur a slight additional cost, but it should be negligible compared to the actual subroutine unless it is very fast and we are testing it a large number of times.

As a concrete example, this program benchmarks a simple expression by executing it one million times:

```
#!/usr/bin/perl
# timeit.pl
use Benchmark;

sub mysubroutine { my $timewaster = time**rand; }

my $result = timeit(1000000, 'mysubroutine');

print "Executed ", $result->iters, " iterations in ", timestr($result),"\n";
```

The output of this program is (but times may vary) something like

```
Executed 1000000 iterations in  8 wallclock secs ( 7.54 usr +  0.46 sys = 8.00 CPU)
@ 125000.00/s (n=1000000)
```

timethis

This subroutine combines timeit with timestr and prints the results to standard output. timethis takes four arguments; a count and code string, just as timeit does, followed by an optional title and optional style, which has the same meaning and values as the style argument of timestr earlier. For example:

```
# default output
timethis(1000, \&mysub);

# customized output
timethis(1000, \&mysub, "Testing!", 'toc');
```

If the count is negative or zero, then timethis uses countit (discussed later) instead of timeit, with the count interpreted as a minimum number of seconds to run for. Note that time is taken as User+System time, not real ("wallclock") time, so the actual time taken may be longer. In addition, the last iteration will likely carry the actual time incurred over the limit since the limit will expire while it is in progress.

The return value of timethis is a Benchmark object, with the same meaning as the result returned from timeit. If no title is specified, it defaults to timethis COUNT, where COUNT is the value of the first argument. The real point of the title is for use by the timethese subroutine, discussed next.

timethese

This subroutine carries out bulk benchmark calculations by calling timethis multiple times. The arguments of timethese are counts. This is applied to every individual benchmark and may be negative to define a minimum time. As with timethis, a hash reference with a list of tests to perform is passed to timestr. It has the same meaning and values as timestr's style argument.

The hash of tests consists of key-value pairs, the keys of which are names for the tests and which are used as the titles in timethis, and values which are the actual tests, evaluable strings, or code references. For example:

```
$resulthashref = timethese (1000, {
    'Test 1' => sub {time()**rand()**rand()},
    'Test 2' => "2 + 2 + 2 + 2 + 2 + 2 + 2 + 2",
    'Test 3' => \&mysub,
}, 'all');
```

The return value from timethese is a hash reference containing the same keys as the test hash and with the Benchmark result objects as the values. This hash can be passed to cmpthese to generate a comparative report.

See the example output of cmpthese for an example of the output produced by timethese (which is called by cmpthese).

cmpthese

cmpthese carries out bulk benchmark calculations and then generates a comparative report of percentage differences between each pair of tests. This subroutine can be passed either arguments identical to those accepted by timethese, in which case it simply calls timethese to get either a hash of results or the hash reference containing the results from a previous timethese:

```
cmpthese(1000, {
    'Test 1' => sub { time()**rand()**rand() },
    'Test 2' => "2 + 2 + 2 + 2 + 2 + 2 + 2 + 2",
    'Test 3' => \&mysub,
}, 'all');
```

Or:

```
cmpthese($resulthashref);
```

The return result of cmpthese is a hash reference of results, the same as that returned by timethese, potentially useful if we passed in explicit arguments rather than a result hash reference.

As a practical example, the following benchmark program determines whether there is any noticeable difference between a named subroutine, an anonymous subroutine, and an evaluated code fragment. An arbitrary calculation that Perl cannot optimize away, the current time to the power of a random number, serves our purposes for this example:

```
#!/usr/bin/perl
# cmpthese.pl
use warnings;
use strict;

use Benchmark qw(cmpthese);
sub mysubroutine {
    my $timewaster = time**rand;
}

cmpthese(1000000, {
    'Anon Test' => sub {my $timewaster = time**rand},
    'Eval Test' => 'my $timewaster = time**rand',
    'Ref Test'  => \&mysubroutine,
}, 'all');
```

In order to get accurate results, we have to push up the number of iterations so that a significant number of seconds elapse, so we give the test one million iterations (a slower computer may want to tone this number down a little). The output of this program consists of the output from timethese, followed by a comparative table:

```
Benchmark: timing 1000000 iterations of Anon Test, Eval Test, Ref Test...
 Anon Test:  6 wallclock secs ( 5.22 usr  0.74 sys +  0.00 cusr
  0.00 csys = 5.96 CPU)
@ 167785.23/s (n=1000000)
 Eval Test:  6 wallclock secs ( 5.27 usr  0.49 sys +  0.00 cusr
  0.00 csys = 5.76 CPU)
@ 173611.11/s (n=1000000)
  Ref Test:  7 wallclock secs ( 5.09 usr  0.62 sys +  0.00 cusr
  0.00 csys = 5.71 CPU)
@ 175131.35/s (n=1000000)

Rate        Anon    Test      Eval    Test    Ref Test
Anon   Test   167785/s      --      -3%     -4%
Eval      Test    173611/s    3%      --      -1%
Ref       Test    175131/s    4%      1%      --
```

Apparently an anonymous subroutine is fractionally faster that a named one, with eval bringing up the rear, though there's not much in it.

Conceivably, cmpthese can be used with a self-assembled hash of keys and values. This will work so long as the keys are descriptive labels and the values are Benchmark result objects computed by timethis, timethese, countit or timediff, and timesum. However, the result is unlikely to be useful unless the same count value is used for each benchmark result in the hash.

Note that there is no way to silence the output of timethese and just display the comparative table.

countit

This subroutine computes the number of iterations possible in the given time. It takes two arguments, a time to compute against and the code to compute. It returns the number of iterations that fit into the given time, including the iteration in process when the time expired. For example:

```perl
#!/usr/bin/perl
# countit.pl
use warnings;
use strict;

use Benchmark qw(countit timestr);
sub mysubroutine {
    my $timewaster = time**rand;
}

my $result = countit(10, 'mysubroutine');

print "Executed ", $result->iters, " iterations in ",
  timestr($result, 'noc'), "\n";
```

The Benchmark module also contains a caching mechanism for storing the results of null loops, that is, loops containing no body (or at least no body that performs useful work, as determined by Perl's optimization algorithms). This allows the module to subtract its own overheads from the benchmarks it computes. The cache is controlled by the functions listed in Table 17-30.

Table 17-30. *Benchmark Module Cache Functions*

Function	Action
enablecache	Enable caching of times. for null loops. Each iteration count used for a null loop is cached and reused if requested a second time: Benchmark::enablecache;
disablecache	Do not cache null loop times. Benchmark::disablecache;
clearcache	Clear the cached time for the null loop for the given number of iterations. For example: Benchmark::clearcache(1000);
clearallcache	Clear all cached times for the null loop: Benchmark::clearallcache;

In general, we can ignore this caching; it happens automatically and without our intervention. If we want to disable it for any reason, we can do so with Benchmark::disablecache.

Summary

In this chapter, we covered debugging and optimizing our Perl applications. We first looked at ways to avoid debugging programs by using the features Perl provides us to minimize the probability of creating bugs in the first place and examined ways to build debug support directly into a program to enable the generation of more context-sensitive and meaningful debug information. We then went on to look at Perl's debugger, including how to start it, how to use it once it is started, how to configure debug options, and how to programmatically switch between running and single-step modes from within the program being debugged. We also looked at generating program traces using the debugger, without entering the debugger's interactive mode.

Perl provides many modules that have application to debugging, including some that are used internally by the debugger itself. We examined two: the Dumpvalue module for dumping out the contents of complex data structures, and the Safe module for creating isolated compartments in which we can run Perl code with restricted access to data as well as built-in operators and functions. We then looked at debugging the Perl interpreter itself using compiler backends like B::Terse and B::Xref to analyze the opcode tree that results from the compilation of our Perl code.

We then looked at writing and automating tests with the Test::Harness module and either Test, Test::Simple, Test::More, or possibly one of several other modules in the Test:: namespace that are available from CPAN. Testing is an important part of development that is all too easy to skip over. With these modules, developers now have both reason and opportunity to test their code easily and conveniently.

Finally, we covered various aspects of profiling and timing, including Perl's own profiler, an alternative debugging backend that takes the place of Perl's debugger to generate timing information instead of providing debug support. For gathering general timing information, we can also gather timing information directly using the times function or using the suite of convenience timing routines provided by the Benchmark module.

CHAPTER 18

■ ■ ■

Text Processing, Documentation, and Reports

We have seen a lot of Perl's native capabilities in terms of interpolation and regular expressions. However, these are just the start of Perl's text processing capabilities.

Perl comes with a standard library of text processing modules that solve many common problems associated with manipulating text. These include such tasks as tab expansion, determining abbreviations, and paragraph formatting. While not necessarily advanced, they provide a simple way of performing useful functions without reinventing the wheel.

Another class of text processing modules is dedicated to understanding Perl's documentation syntax known as POD, or *Plain Old Documentation*. The Pod:: family of Perl modules enable us to perform various functions such as create, transform, and generally manipulate POD documentation in many different ways. We also look at processing a very special subclass of documents, source files, using Perl source filters.

The final part of this chapter deals with Perl's support for reports. These allow us to format text using special layout definitions. Formats are a built-in feature of the Perl interpreter that enable us to do many handy things with text, and we will explore, among other things, format structure, page control, and the format data type.

Text Processing

Perl's standard library contains several handy text processing modules that solve many common problems and can save a lot of time. These modules are often overlooked when considering Perl's text processing capabilities simply because the core language already provides such a rich set of functionality.

The main text processing modules are all members of the Text:: family of which those listed in Table 18-1 are the most common.

Table 18-1. *Standard Text Processing Modules*

Module	Function
Text::Tabs	Convert tabs to and from spaces.
Text::Abbrev	Calculate unique abbreviations from a list of words.
Text::Balanced	Match nested delimiters.
Text::ParseWords	Parse text into words and phrases.
Text::Wrap	Convert unformatted text into paragraphs.
Text::Soundex	Convert similar sounding text into condensed codes.

Many of Perl's other standard modules have more than a little to do with text processing of one kind or another. We make a brief note of them and where they are covered at the end of this section. In addition, CPAN offers many more modules for handling text. Searching in the Text:: namespace will uncover many modules designed for basic processing requirements, while namespaces like XML:: or Parser:: offer more advanced task-specific modules.

Expanding and Contracting Tabs with Text::Tabs

The Text::Tabs module is the simplest of the text processing modules. It provides two subroutines, unexpand for converting sequences of spaces into tab characters and expand for converting tab characters into spaces. Here is how they work:

```
# convert spaces into tabs
$tabbed_text = unexpand($spaced_text);

# convert tabs into spaces
$spaced_text = expand($tabbed_text);
```

Both of these subroutines work on either single strings, as just shown, or lists of strings, as in

```
@tabbed_lines = unexpand(@spaced_lines);
```

Any tabs that already exist in the text are not affected by unexpand, and similarly existing spaces are not touched by expand. The gap between stops (the stop gap, so to speak) is determined by the variable $tabstop, which is set to the desired tab width, 4 by default. This is actually imported into our own package by default so we can set it with

```
$tabstop = 8;   # set a tab width of eight characters
```

That said, it is better from a namespace pollution point of view to import only the subroutines and set $tabstop as a package variable:

```
use Text::Tabs qw(expand unexpand);
$Text::Tabs::tabstop = 8;
```

Calculating Abbreviations with Text::Abbrev

It is occasionally useful to be able to quickly determine the unique abbreviations for a set of words, for instance, when implementing a command-line interface. Assuming we wish to create our own, rather than use an existing solution like Term::Complete or (sometimes) Term::Readline, we can make use of the Text::Abbrev module to precompute a table of abbreviations and their full-name equivalents.

The Text::Abbrev module supplies one function, abbrev, which works by taking a list of words and computing abbreviations for each of them in turn by removing one character at a time from each word and recording the resultant word stalk in a hash table. If the abbreviation has already been seen, it must be because two words share that abbreviation, and it is removed from the table. If a supplied word is an abbreviation of another, it is recorded and the longer abbreviations remain, pointing to the longer word. This short script shows the module in action:

```
#!/usr/bin/perl
# abbrev.pl
use warnings;
use strict;
use Text::Abbrev;

my $abbreviations = abbrev(@ARGV);
```

```
foreach (sort keys %{$abbreviations}) {
    print "$_ => $abbreviations->{$_} \n";
}
```

When run, this script produces a hash of unique abbreviations. In the output that follows, the abbreviations for gin, gang, and goolie are calculated. The single letter g is not present because it does not uniquely identify a word, but ga, gi, and go are:

> **abbrev.pl gin gan goolie**

```
        ga => gang
        gan => gang
        gang => gang
        gi => gin
        gin => gin
        go => goolie
        goo => goolie
        gool => goolie
        gooli => goolie
        goolie => goolie
```

The abbrev function returns either a list suitable for creating a hash or a hash reference, depending on whether it was called in list or scalar context:

```
%abbreviations = abbrev('gin', 'gang', 'goolie');
$abbreviations = abbrev('gin', 'gang', 'goolie');
```

We can also pass in a reference to a hash or a typeglob (deprecated) as the first argument. However, the original contents, if any, are not maintained:

```
# overwrite previous contents of $abbreviations
abbrev($abbreviations, 'ghost', 'ghast', 'ghoul');
```

Note that the Term::Complete module combines abbreviations with a command-line entry mechanism (although it does not use Text::Abbrev to determine abbreviations). If we don't need anything more complex, this is a simpler solution than rolling our own with Text::Abbrev. See Chapter 15 for more details.

Parsing Words and Phrases with Text::ParseWords

Many applications that accept textual input need to be able to parse the text into distinct words for processing. In most simple cases, we can get away with using split. Since this is such a common requirement, split even splits using whitespace as a default. For instance, this rather terse program carves up its input text into a list of words, separated by whitespace and split using split with no arguments:

```
#!/usr/bin/perl
# splitwords.pl
use warnings;
use strict;

my @words;
push @words, split foreach(<>);
print scalar(@words), "words: @words \n";
```

This approach falls short if we want to handle more advanced constructs like quotes. If two or more words are surrounded by quotes, we often want to treat them as a single word or phrase, in which case we can't easily use split. Instead we can use the Text::ParseWords module, which handles quotes and produces a list of words and phrases using them.

Parsing Space-Separated Text

The Text::ParseWords module supports the parsing of text into words and phrases, based on the presence of quotes in the input text. It provides four subroutines:

shellwords	Process strings using whitespace as a delimiter, in the same manner as shells.
quotewords	Handle more general cases where the word separator can be any arbitrary text.
nested_quotewords	Similar to quotewords, word separator can be any arbitrary text.
parse_line	A simpler version of quotewords, which handles a single line of text and which is actually the basis of the other three.

The first, shellwords, takes one or more lines of text and returns a list of words and phrases found within them. Since it is set to consider whitespace as the separator between words, it takes no other parameters:

```
@words = shellwords(@input);
```

Here is a short program that shows shellwords in action:

```perl
#!/usr/bin/perl
# shell.pl
use warnings;
use strict;

use Text::ParseWords qw(shellwords);

my @input = (
    'This is "a phrase"',
    'So is\ this',
    q('and this'),
    "But this isn\\'t",
    'And neither \"is this\"',
);

print "Input: ", join('',@input),"\n";

my @words = shellwords(@input); print scalar(@words), " words:\n";
print "\t$_\n" foreach @words;
```

When run, this program should produce the following output:

```
> shell.pl
```

```
Input: This is "a phrase" So is\ this 'and this' This isn\'t Neither \"is this\"
11 words:
        This
        is
        a phrase
```

```
So
is this
and this

This
isn't

Neither
"is
this"
```

This program demonstrates several points. First, we can define phrases with double quotes, or single quotes if we use the q function. Second, we can also define phrases by escaping spaces that we want shellwords to overlook. In order to have shellwords process these backslashes, we have to use single quotes (or q) around the string as a whole to avoid interpolation from evaluating them first. Finally, to have shellwords ignore a quote, we can escape it, but to escape a single quote, we have to use double quotes around the string and escape it twice (once for interpolation, once for shellwords). Of course, a lot of this is simpler if the text is coming from a variable rather than a literal string.

Parsing Arbitrarily Delimited Text

The quotewords subroutine is a more flexible version of shellwords that allows the word separator to be defined. It takes two additional parameters, a regular expression pattern describing the word separator itself and a keep flag that determines how quotes are handled. This is how we might use it to emulate and modify the result of shellwords. Note the value of the keep flag in each case:

```perl
# emulate 'shellwords' with 'quotewords'
@words = quotewords('\s+', 0, @lines);

# emulate 'shellwords' but keep quotes and backslashes
@words = quotewords('\s+', 1, @lines);
```

As a more complete example, here is a short program that parses a file of colon-delimited lines (like those found in /etc/passwd) into a long list of fields:

```perl
#!/usr/bin/perl
# readpw.pl
use warnings;
use strict;

use Text::ParseWords;

my (@users, @fields);
if (open PASSWD,"/etc/passwd") {
    @users = <PASSWD>;
    chomp @users;   # remove linefeeds
    @fields = quotewords(':', 0, @users);
    close PASSWD;
}
print "@fields";
```

The keep parameter determines whether quotes and backslashes are removed once their work is done, as real shells do, or whether they should be retained in the resulting list of words. If false, quotes are removed as they are parsed. If true, they are retained. The keep flag is almost but not quite Boolean. If set to the special case of `delimiters`, both quotes and characters that matched the word separator are kept:

```
# emulate 'shellwords' but keep quotes and backlashes and also store the
# matched whitespace as tokens too
@words = quotewords('\s+', 'delimiters', @lines);
```

Batch-Parsing Multiple Lines

The preceding `/etc/passwd` example works, but it assembles all the resultant fields of each user into one huge list of words. Far better would be to keep each set of words found on each individual line in separate lists. We can do that with the `nested_quotewords` subroutine, which returns a list of lists, one list for each line passed in. Here is a short program that uses `nested_quotewords` to do just that:

```
#!/usr/bin/perl
# password.pl
use Text::ParseWords;

my @ARGV = ('/etc/passwd');
my @users = nested_quotewords(':', 0, <>);

print scalar(@users)," users: \n";
print "\t${$_}[0] => ${$_}[2] \n" foreach @users;
```

This program prints out a list of all users found in `/etc/passwd` and their user ID. When run it should produce output that starts something like the following:

> **perl password.pl**

```
16 users:
        root => 0
        bin => 1
        daemon => 2
        adm => 3
        ...
```

In this case, we could equally well have used `split` with a split pattern of a colon since quotes do not usually appear in a password file. However, the principle still applies.

Parsing a Single Line Only

The fourth function provided by `Text::ParseWords` is `parse_line`. It parses a single line only but is otherwise identical in operation to `quotewords`, and it takes the same parameters with the exception that the last can only be a scalar string value:

```
@words = parse_line('\s+', 0, $line);
```

The `parse_line` subroutine provides no functional benefit over `quotewords`, but if we only have one line to parse, for example, a command-line input, then we can save a subroutine call by calling it directly rather than via `quotewords` or `shellwords`.

Parsing Brackets and Delimiters with Text::Balanced

Added to the Perl standard library for Perl 5.6, `Text::Balanced` is also available for older Perls from CPAN. It provides comprehensive abilities to match delimiters and brackets with arbitrary levels of nesting. Matching nested delimiters is traditionally a hard problem to solve, so having a ready-made solution is very welcome.

Extracting an Initial Match

All of the routines provided by Text::Balanced work in essentially the same way, taking some input text and applying one or more delimiters, brackets, or tags to it in order to extract a match. We can also supply an initial prefix for the routine to skip before commencing. This prefix, by default set to skip whitespace, is a regular expression, so we can create quite powerful match criteria.

Quotes and Single-Character Delimiters

To match delimiters and brackets, we have the extract_delimited and extract_bracketed routines. These operate in substantially similar ways, the only difference being that the latter understands the concept of paired characters, where the opening and closing delimiters are different. Here is a simple example of extracting the first double-quoted expression from some input text:

```
#!/usr/bin/perl
# quotebalanced1.pl
use strict;
use warnings;
use Text::Balanced qw(extract_delimited);

my $input=qq[The "quick" brown fox "jumped over" the lazy "dog"];

my ($extracted,$remainder)=extract_delimited($input,'"','The ');
print qq[Got $extracted, remainder <$remainder>\n];
```

The first argument to extract_delimited is the text to be matched. The second is the delimiter; only the first character is used if more than one is supplied. The third (optional) parameter is the prefix to skip before starting the extraction. Without it, only whitespace is skipped over. This program will generate the following output:

```
Got "quick", remainder < brown fox "jumped over" the lazy "dog">
```

The remainder starts with the space immediately following the second quote, and the extracted text includes the delimiters. If we don't care about the remainder, we do not have to ask for it. All the extract_ functions will notice when they are called in a scalar context and will return just the extracted text, so we can write

```
my $extracted=extract_delimited($input,'"','The ');
```

If we want to match on more than one kind of delimiter, for example, single and double quotes, we replace the delimiter with a character class, like this:

```
my $extracted=extract_delimited($input,q/["']/,'The ');
```

This reveals that the delimiter is actually a regular expression, and indeed we could also write qr/["']/ here, or use even more advanced patterns. Whichever quote character is found is looked for again to complete the match, so any number of intervening single quotes may occur between an initial double quote and its terminating twin.

We are not just limited to quotes as delimiters—any character can be used. We can also pass undef as a delimiter, in which case the standard Perl quotes are used. The following statements are equivalent:

```
my $extracted=extract_delimited($input,q/["'`]/,'The '); #explicit

my $extracted=extract_delimited($input,undef,'The '); #implict ',"  and `
```

In order to match the first set of quotes, we supplied the prefix 'The ' to extract_delimited. Given the position of the first quote, the routine then finds the second. This is not very flexible, however. What we would really like to do is specify a prefix that says "skip everything up to the first double quote." Luckily, this turns out to be very easy because the prefix is a regular expression, and this is simply expressed as [^"]+, or "anything but a double quote":

```
my ($extracted,$remainder)=extract_delimited($input,'"','[^"]+');
```

Substituting this line for the original will generate exactly the same output, but now it is no longer bound to the specific prefix of the input text. If we are curious to know what the prefix actually matched, we can get it from the third value returned:

```
my ($extracted,$remainder,$prefix)=extract_delimited($input,'"','[^"]+');
```

We can supply a precompiled regular expression for the third parameter as well:

```
my ($extracted,$remainder)=extract_delimited($input,'"',qr/[^"]+/);
```

This emphasizes the regular expression, which improves legibility. It also allows us to specify trailing pattern match modifiers, which allows us to specify this alternate regular expression, which is closer to the literal meaning of "skip everything up to the first quote":

```
my ($extracted,$remainder)=extract_delimited($input,'"',qr/.*?(?=")/s);
```

This pattern starts with a nongreedy match for anything. Since a dot does not ordinarily match a newline, the /s modifier is required to permit the prefix to match an arbitrary number of initial lines without double quotes in them. This pattern also makes use of a positive look-ahead assertion (?=") to spot a quote without absorbing it. Combined with the nongreedy pattern, this will match all text up to the first quote.

By default, the backslash character, \, escapes delimiters so that they will not be considered as delimiters in the input text. A fourth parameter to extract_delimited allows us to change the escape character or individually nominate a different escape character for each delimiter. For example:

```
extract_delimited($input,q/['"`]/,undef,'');      # no escape character
extract_delimited($input,q/['"`]/,undef,q/\033/); # ASCII 27 (ESC)
extract_delimited($input,q/['"`]/,undef,q/'"`/);  # escape is delimiter
```

The last example defines a list of quote characters that is identical to (that is, in the same order as) the delimiters specified in the character class of the second parameter. If more than one escape character is specified, then each delimiter is escaped with the corresponding escape character. If not enough escape characters are supplied, then the last one is used for all remaining delimiters. In this example, the escape character for each delimiter is the same as the delimiter, so now we double up a character to escape it.

We can generate a customized regular expression that can take the place of extract_delimited for preset criteria. To do this, we make use of gen_delimited_pat, which takes delimiter and optional escape character arguments:

```
my $delimiter_re=gen_delimited_pat(q/['"`]/,q/'"'/);
```

The regular expression generated by this statement will match quote strings using any of the quote characters specified, each one of which is escapable by doubling it up. This is a convenient way to pregenerate regular expressions and does not even require that Text::Balanced is available in the final application:

```
$input =~ /($delimiter_re)/ and print "Found $1\n";
```

Or, to emulate extract_delimited more closely:

```
$input =~/^($prefix)($delimiter_re)(.*)$/ and
  ($prefix,$extracted,$remainder)=($1,$2,$3);
```

The regular expression is in an optimized form that is much longer than one we might otherwise write but which is the most efficient at finding a match. It does not extract text though, so we need to add our own parentheses to get the matched text back.

Brackets and Braces

The extract_bracketed function is identical in use and return values, except that the delimiters are one or more of the matched brace characters (), [], {}, or <>. Here is an adapted version of the previous example that extracts bracketed text:

```
#!/usr/bin/perl
# bracebalanced.pl
use strict;
use warnings;
use Text::Balanced qw(extract_bracketed);

my $input=qq[The (<quick brown> fox) {jumped} over the (<lazy> dog)];

my ($extracted,$remainder)=extract_bracketed($input,'()<>{}',qr/[^()<>{}]+/);
print qq[Got "$extracted", remainder "$remainder"\n];
```

When run, this program will produce the following output:

```
Got "(<quick brown> fox)", remainder " {jumped} over the (<lazy> dog)"
```

As before, the prefix is simply defined as text not containing any of the delimiters. If we changed the delimiter to not detect (, the text extracted would instead be <quick brown>. Interestingly, since Perl already knows about matched delimiter characters for quoting operators, we only need to specify the opening characters:

```
my ($extracted,$remainder)=extract_bracketed($input,'(<{',qr/[^()<>{}]+/);
```

It would be a mistake to think that extract_bracketed just looks for a closing delimiter character, though. One of its major benefits is that it understands nested braces and will only match on the corresponding closing brace. Take this adjusted example, where all the braces are round:

```
#!/usr/bin/perl
# nestedbracebalanced.pl
use strict;
use warnings;
use Text::Balanced qw(extract_bracketed);

my $input=qq[The ((quick brown) fox) (jumped) over the ((lazy) dog)];

my ($extracted,$remainder)=extract_bracketed($input,'(',qr/[^()]+/);
print qq[Got "$extracted", remainder "$remainder"\n];
```

When run, this matches the correct closing brace, after fox, not the first one after brown:

```
Got "((quick brown) fox)", remainder " (jumped) over the ((lazy) dog)"
```

In situations where more than one brace type is significant, all brackets must nest correctly for the text to be successfully extracted. For example, if ( ) and <> are both considered delimiters, then this text will not match because there is no matching >:

```
my $input=''(supply < demand)';
```

Only those characters listed as delimiters (and their corresponding closing characters) are managed this way, so if we do not consider < and > to be delimiters, then they are not considered and this text would match.

We can even handle quoted delimiters and ignore them rather than treating them as delimiters if we include a quote character in the list of delimiters. For example:

```
my ($extracted,$remainder)=extract_bracketed($input,q[("')],qr/[^()]+/);
```

This will match on round brackets only but disregard any round brackets found within single- or double-quoted strings. Interestingly, if the letter q is included, any character acceptable as a Perl quoting delimiter for quotelike operators such as // or {} is also recognized. If not specified as an acceptable brace delimiter, characters like { and } will instead operate like quotes, causing their contents to be skipped rather than processed for valid delimiters.

XML and Other Tagged Delimiters

The extract_tagged function does for tags what extract_bracketed does for brace characters. It is broadly similar in use: it returns the same values of ($extracted,$remainder,$prefix), but it has a slightly expanded list of up to five parameters. Here are some examples of it:

```
extract_tagged($text);                          # match any XML tag.
extract_tagged($text,"<FOO>")                   # match <FOO>...</FOO>
extract_tagged($text,"<[a-z]+>")                # match any lowercase XML tag
extract_tagged($text,"/start","/end")           # match /start.../end
extract_tagged($text,"[FOO]","[/FOO]",$prefix)  # skip prefix then match
                                                # [FOO]...[/FOO]
```

As these examples show, while XML tags are the default target, any kind of delimiter tags can be fined, including regular expressions matches. We can also pass in undef for any parameters for which we just want to accept the defaults. For example:

```
extract_tagged($text,"{FOO}",undef,$prefix)     # skip prefix then match
                                                # {FOO}...{/FOO}
extract_tagged($text,undef,undef,$prefix)       # skip prefix then match
                                                # any XML tag.
```

Tags must balance, just as braces must balance for extract_bracketed. The composition of the start tag and the end tag is specified and analyzed for punctuation versus alphanumeric characters, and the general rule for tags is inferred from it. The end tag, if not specified, is autogenerated by inserting a / before the alphanumeric part, so (abc) is automatically paired with (/abc) and sets (...) and (/...) as the general rule. Remarkably, this will even work for tags like <[a-z]+> as in the preceding example.

For example, the following program looks for and extracts the first lowercased XML tag:

```
#!/usr/bin/perl
# extractlctagged.pl
use strict;
use warnings;
use Text::Balanced qw(extract_tagged);

my $input=qq[<TEXT>The quick brown <subject>fox</subject> jumped
over the lazy <object>dog<?object></TEXT>];
```

```
my ($extracted,$remainder)=
  extract_tagged($input,"<[a-z]+>",undef,".*?(?=<[a-z]+>)");
print qq[Got "$extracted"\nRemainder "$remainder"\n];
```

Running this program will produce

```
Got "<subject>fox</subject>"
Remainder " jumped over the lazy <object>dog</object></TEXT>"
```

To match any XML-compliant tags, we would replace the extract_tagged call in this example with

```
my ($extracted,$remainder)=extract_tagged($input,undef,undef,".*?<[^<>]+>");
```

This would try to match the entire input text because of the initial <TEXT>, but the <subject> and <object> tags both match the general rule for tags, and so this match would fail, because the closing tag for <object> was <?object>, and not the expected </object>. (We can see the reason for the failure by printing out $@, as we will see later. $@ is set by Text::Balanced whenever a match cannot be made.)

The fifth parameter to extract_tagged is a hash of configuration options that allow us to alter the match behavior to handle common alternate inputs. For instance, HTML (as opposed to XHTML) allows some tags to be left unclosed. If we want to be able to handle these, we can tell extract_tagged not to require the closing tag. For example, this will not only match paragraph tags <p>...</p>, but also end the paragraph if a second <p> is seen:

```
my $paragraph=extract_tagged($text,"<p>","</p>",".*?(?=<p>)", {
    reject => ["<p>"],
    fail   => MAX
});
```

Here the reject option instructs the routine to fail if a second <p> is seen. The criteria are specified within a list reference so that we can specify multiple reject criteria at the same time if we wish. The fail option MAX instructs it to succeed and return all the characters matched up until that point rather than fail. This caters for both a closing tag and a new opening one. Alternatively, we can say fail => PARA to cut off the returned characters at the next blank line.

We can also use the ignore option to have extract_tagged disregard character sequences that would otherwise match the start tag specification. This is generally useful when the start tag is a regular expression or the "match any XML tag" default. For example, to handle the <object> tag by simply ignoring it, we could put

```
my $paragraph=extract_tagged($text,undef,undef,".*?(?=<[^<>]+>)",{
    ignore => ["<object>"],
});
```

If we expect to use the same parameters to extract_tagged frequently, we can generate a custom match that is routine-specific to the match we want to make with gen_extract_tagged. This takes the exact same arguments, minus the first input text argument, and allows us to rewrite this:

```
my ($extracted,$remainder)=
  extract_tagged($text,"<TOP>","<BOTTOM>",qr/.*?(?=<TOP>)/);
```

as this:

```
my $topbottom_match=
  gen_extract_tagged("<TOP>","<BOTTOM>",qr/.*?(?=<TOP>)/);
my ($extracted,$remainder)=$topbottom_match->($input);
```

The returned value is actually a closure (that is, a code reference) blessed into the `Text::Balanced::Extractor` class, and hence is invoked as a method call and not a subroutine. These routines become very useful in multiple match scenarios using `extract_multiple`. We can also create a special tag matcher for the `<object>...=<?object>` example and process it along with XML tags instead of ignoring it.

Perl-Style Quoted Text

The `extract_quotelike` function extracts Perl-style quoted strings from the input text. It is essentially a smarter version of `extract_delimited` that understands not just the standard quote characters, but also Perl's quotelike operators q, qq, and qr, hence its name. It will also parse any quotelike operator such as `m//`, `s///`, `tr///`, or any of their alternate quote syntaxes like `s{}{}`.

Since it is a specialized function, we cannot specify delimiters, and in fact we can only specify the text to be matched and the initial prefix. Perhaps to make up for this, this function returns up to ten values in list context, although not all of them will contain meaningful values depending on what kind of quoted text was found.

```
my ($extracted,$remainder,$matchedprefix,
    $typeofquote,
    $startdelim1,$text1,$enddelim1,
    $startdelim2,$text2,$enddelim2,
    $endflags) = extract_quotelike($input,$prefix);
```

The first three values here are the familiar extracted text, remainder, and matched prefix that we have already seen. The fourth value holds the operator, if any, that was found. For a regular quoted string it is undefined, but it will hold the appropriate value for a q, qq, qr, s, m, y, or tr operator. The next three values describe the delimiters and the text of the first found string. For a regular quoted string, this is the string and its delimiters. For a match or substitution, it is the delimiters and pattern of the match. The three values following this have the same meaning except for the second found string; this only has meaning for substitutions and transliterations, the only two operators to have the concept of a "second" string. Finally, any pattern match modifiers found are returned. This only has meaning for matches, substitution, or transliteration, of course.

Clever though it is, `extract_quotelike` is only really useful for parsing text containing Perl code. To handle ordinary quoted text, we actually want `extract_delimited` instead.

Variables and Code

The final two extraction routines are `extract_variable` and `extract_codeblock`. The first of these simply matches any kind of Perl variable, including method calls and subroutine calls, via a code reference. It has the usual semantics:

```
my (extracted,$remainder,$matchedprefix)=extract_variable($input,$prefix);
```

Like `extract_quotelike`, this is only useful if we are parsing Perl code. Of course, in these cases it is very useful indeed.

The `extract_codeblock` function is essentially a combination of `extract_quotelike` and `extract_bracketed` that will correctly parse strings containing nested braces and quoted strings that may contain braces that should not be considered significant for the purposes of matching. Its usage is identical to `extract_bracketed` except that a fourth argument may be specified to describe an outer delimiter that is not included in the delimiter set passed as the second argument. This allows code to be "marked up" in enclosing text using a special delimiter that is not considered special within the code block itself. Only after the code block matches its initial delimiter again is the closing outer delimiter looked for once more.

For example, this statement matches on (), {}, or [] braces, but looks for an outer set of <> braces to mark the beginning and end of the code:

```
my ($extracted,$remainder,$matchedprefix)=
   extract_codeblock($input, q/{}()[]/ , qr/.*?(?=<)/, "<>");
```

Even though the code block might actually contain < and > characters, they are not recognized as delimiters. Whatever the first brace inside the outer <....> turns out to be, the closing > is only matched when that brace is matched again, taking into account any nesting of delimiters that takes place within the block.

The default bracket delimiter for extract_codeblock is just {}, so with only the input text as an argument, or with a second argument of undef, other kinds of brace are not recognized. This is different from the default {}()[] of extract_bracketed.

Both extract_codeblock and extract_quotelike may be more feature-full than we actually require. If we only need to deal with real quote characters and do not need the outer delimiter feature, we can achieve a similar effect more simply and with greater flexibility using extract_bracketed with a delimiter string containing the quote and brace characters we want to handle.

Extracting Multiple Matches

All of the extractor functions we have looked at so far take note of and maintain the match position of input text that is stored in a variable. This is the same position that the pos function and the \G regular expression metacharacter reference and that the /g modifier sets. As a result, all of the extract_ functions can be used in loops to extract multiple values. Here is a modified version of one of our earlier examples, now rewritten into a do...while loop:

```perl
#!/usr/bin/perl
# whilequotebalanced.pl
use strict;
use warnings;
use Text::Balanced qw(extract_delimited);

my $input=qq[The "quick" brown fox "jumped over" the lazy "dog"];
my ($extracted,$remainder);

do {
    ($extracted,$remainder)=extract_delimited($input,'"',qr/[^"]+/);
    print qq[Got $extracted, remainder <$remainder>\n];
} while ($extracted and $remainder);
```

When run, this version of the program will print out

```
Got "quick", remainder < brown fox "jumped over" the lazy "dog">
Got "jumped over", remainder < the lazy "dog">
Got "dog", remainder <>
```

Note the criteria of the while condition. We terminate the loop if we run out of input text, indicated by an empty remainder, or we get an undef returned for the extracted text, indicating an error. In the latter case, we can look at $@ to see what the problem was.

For more advanced requirements, we can use the extract_multiple function. This wraps one or more extraction functions and applies the input text to each of them in turn. For example, this program applies extract_bracketed repeatedly to the input text we used earlier:

```perl
#!/usr/bin/perl
# bracebalanced1.pl
use strict;
use warnings;
use Text::Balanced qw(extract_multiple extract_bracketed);

my $input=qq[The (<quick brown> fox) {jumped} over the (<lazy> dog)];
```

```
my @matches=extract_multiple(
    $input,
    [ \&extract_bracketed ],
    undef, 1
);
print "Got ",scalar(@matches)," matches\n";
print $_+1,"='",$matches[$_],"'\n" foreach (0..$#matches);
```

When run, this program will output the following:

```
Got 3 matches
1='(<quick brown> fox)'
2='{jumped}'
3='(<lazy> dog)'
```

Of the four arguments supplied to extract_multiple, the first is the input text as usual. If it is undefined, $_ is used. The second we will pass over for a moment. The third parameter defines how many matches to make; it has the same meaning as the third argument of split. A positive number will cause only that many matches to take place (in scalar context, the number of matches is forced to 1, and a warning is issued if more are requested).

The fourth determines if unmatched text is discarded or returned. If true, it is discarded. If unspecified or false, it is returned. The unmatched text is able to take the place of prefix text in many cases; the unmatched text is assembled character by character each time extract_multiple is unable to advance through the input text using any of the supplied extractors. If we modified the last argument to 0, for example, the first string returned would be "The ".

Note If we don't need to specify the fourth argument and don't want to limit matches, then we can omit both the third and fourth arguments and just specify the input text.

The second argument is the most complex. It is a reference to an array of extraction functions. Here we have only one. Only the input text is passed, but if we are happy to use an extraction function with its settings, we can just specify it as a code reference. An extraction function can also be a closure generated by gen_extract_tagged, a regular expression, or a literal text string. Each is automatically detected and handled correctly, as demonstrated in this modified call:

```
my @matches=extract_multiple(
    $input,
    [ \&extract_bracketed,
      qr/THE/i,
      'over'
    ],
    undef, 1
);
```

This will display the following:

```
Got 6 matches
1='The'
2='(<quick brown> fox)'
3='{jumped}'
4='over'
5='the'
6='(<lazy> dog)'
```

Note that there are no spaces before or after the extracted text. That is because the default prefix matched by extract_bracketed is whitespace. It is matched inside the extractor but not returned as matched text.

What if we want to use different parameters to the defaults? This is not a problem, but we need to use an anonymous subroutine to wrap our extractor subroutines with the arguments we want. The first argument should be $_[0], to get the input text passed in by extract_multiple. For example:

```
my @matches=extract_multiple(
    $input,
    [ sub { extract_bracketed($_[0],'()<>{}',qr/[^()<>{}]+/) } ],
    undef, 1
);
```

As a final nicety, if an extractor is specified as a hash reference to a hash of one key-value pair, the value is used as the extractor, and on a successful match the extracted text is returned in a reference blessed into the class named by the key:

```
my @matches=extract_multiple(
    $input, [
        { Parsed::String::QUOTED    => \&extract_delimited }
        { Parsed::String::BRACKETED => \&extract_bracketed },
    ]
);
```

This allows smart extraction algorithms to tokenize extracted text conveniently and is very useful for implementing parsers.

Handling Failed Matches

If any of Text::Balanced's functions fail, an undef is returned to the caller. In a list context, the undef is followed by the original input text, so the usual semantics of ($extracted,$remainder) remain consistent even in a failed match. To find out the actual reason for the failure, we look at the special variable $@, which is assigned an object of class Text::Balanced::ErrorMsg with two attributes:

$@->{error}	A diagnostic error message indicating the reason for failure
$@->{pos}	The position in the input text where the error occurred

In a string context, both values are combined into a single diagnostic error message. For example, in our earlier mismatched XML tag example where we wrote <object>dog<?object>, $@ would be set to

```
Found unbalanced nested tag: <object>, detected at offset 66
```

There are over 20 possible reasons for Text::Balanced to fail and set $@. On a successful match, $@ will always be undef, so any other value is an indication of failure.

Formatting Paragraphs with Text::Wrap

The Text::Wrap module provides text-formatting facilities to automate the task of turning irregular blocks of text into neatly formatted paragraphs, organized so that their lines fit within a specified width. Although not particularly powerful, it provides a simple and quick solution.

It provides two subroutines: wrap handles individual paragraphs and is ideally suited for formatting single lines into a more presentable form, and fill handles multiple paragraphs and will work on entire documents.

Formatting Single Paragraphs

The wrap subroutine formats single paragraphs, transforming one or more lines of text of indeterminate length and converting them into a single paragraph. It takes three parameters: an initial indent string, which is applied to the first line of the resulting paragraph; a following indent string, applied to the second and all subsequent lines; and finally a string or list of strings.

Here is how we could use wrap to generate a paragraph with an indent of five spaces on the first line and an indent of two spaces on all subsequent lines:

```
$para = wrap('     ', '  ', @lines);
```

Any indentation is permissible. Here is a paragraph formatted (crudely) with HTML tags to force the lines to conform to a given line length instead of following the browser's screen width:

```
$html = wrap("<p>  ", "<br>", $text);
```

If a list is supplied, wrap concatenates all the strings into one before proceeding—there is no essential difference between supplying a single string over a list. However, existing indentation, if there is any, is not eliminated, so we must take care to deal with this first if we are handling text that has already been formatted to a different set of criteria. For example:

```
s/^\s+// foreach @lines;   # strip leading whitespace from all lines
```

The list can be of any origin, not just an array variable. For example, take this one-line reformatting application:

```
print wrap("\t", "", <>);   # reformat standard input/ARGV
```

Tabs are handled by Text::Wrap to expand them into spaces, a function handled by Text::Tabs, previously documented. When formatting is complete, spaces are converted back into tabs, if possible and appropriate. See the section "Expanding and Contracting Tabs with Text::Tabs" for more information.

Customized Wrapping

The Text::Wrap module defines several package variables to control its behavior, including the formatting width, the handling of long words, and the break text.

The number of columns to format is held in the package variable Text::Wrap::columns and has a default value of 76, which is the polite width for things like e-mail messages (to allow a couple of > quoting prefixes to be added in replies before 80 columns is reached). We can change the column width to 39 with

```
$Text::Wrap::columns = 39;
```

Words that are too long to fit the line are broken up (URLs in text documents are a common culprit). This behavior can be altered to a fatal error by setting the variable with the following line:

```
$Text::Wrap::huge = 'die';
```

Alternatively, long words can be left as-is, causing them to overflow the width, with

```
$Text::Wrap::huge = 'overflow';
```

We can also configure the *break text*, that is, the character or characters that separate words. The break text is a regular expression, defined in the package variable $Text::Wrap::break, and is by default \s, to match any whitespace character. To allow a comma or a colon, but not a space to break text, we could redefine this to $Text::Wrap::break = '[:,]';.

A limited debugging mode can also be enabled by setting the variable $Text::Wrap::debug:

```
$Text::Wrap::debug = 1;
```

The `columns`, `break`, and `huge` variables can all be exported from the `Text::Wrap` package, if desired:

```
use Text::Wrap qw($columns $huge);$columns = 39;
$huge = 'overflow';
```

As with any module symbols we import, this is fine for simple scripts but is probably unwarranted for larger applications—use the fully qualified package variables instead.

Formatting Whole Documents

Whole documents can be formatted with the `fill` subroutine. This will chop the supplied text into paragraphs first by looking for lines that are indented, indicating the start of a new paragraph, and blank lines, indicating the end of one paragraph and the start of another. Having determined where each paragraph starts and ends, it then feeds the resulting lines to `wrap`, before merging the resulting wrapped paragraphs back together.

The arguments passed to `fill` are the same as those for `wrap`. Here is how we would use it to reformat paragraphs into unindented and spaced paragraphs:

```
$formatted_document = fill("\n", "", @lines);
```

If the two indents are identical, `fill` automatically adds a blank line to separate each paragraph from the previous one. Therefore, the preceding could also be achieved with

```
$formatted_document = fill("", "", @lines);
```

If the indents are not identical, then we need to add the blank line ourselves:

```
$formatted_document = fill("\t", "", @lines);
# indent each new paragraph with a tab, paragraphs are continuous

$formatted_document = fill("\n\t", "", @lines);
# indent each new paragraph with a tag, paragraphs are separated
```

All the configurable variables that affect the operation of `wrap` also apply to `fill`, of course, since `fill` uses `wrap` to do most of the actual work. It is not possible to configure how `fill` splits text into paragraphs.

Note that if `fill` is passed lines already indented by a previous `wrap` operation, then it will incorrectly detect each new line as a new paragraph (because it is indented). Consequently, we must remove misleading indentation from the lines we want to reformat before we pass them to `fill`.

Formatting on the Command Line

`Text::Wrap`'s usage is simple enough for it to be used on the command line:

```
> perl -MText::Wrap -e "fill('','',<>)" -- textfile ...
```

Here we have used the special argument `--` to separate Perl's arguments from the file names to be fed to the formatter. We can supply any number of files at once and redirect the output to a file if we wish. A related module that may be worth investigating is `Text::Autoformat`, which is specifically tailored for command-line uses like this.

Matching Similar Sounding Words with Text::Soundex

The `Text::Soundex` module is different in nature from the other modules in the `Text::` family. While modules such as `Text::Abbrev` and `Text::ParseWords` are simple solutions to common problems, `Text::Soundex` tackles a different area entirely. It implements a version of the *Soundex* algorithm developed for the U.S. Census in the latter part of the 19th century as an aid for phonetically indexing surnames and popularized by Donald Knuth of TeX fame.

The Soundex algorithm takes words and converts them into tokens that approximate the sound of the word. Similar-sounding words produce tokens that are either the same or close together. Using this, we can generate Soundex tokens for a predetermined list of words, say a dictionary or a list of surnames, and match queries against it. If the query is close to a word in the list, we can return the match even if the query is not exactly right, misspelled, for example.

Tokenizing Single Words

The Text::Soundex module provides exactly one subroutine, soundex, that transforms one word into its Soundex token. It can also accept a list of words and will return a list of the tokens, but it will not deal with multiple words in one string:

```
print soundex "hello";          # produces 'H400'
print soundex "goodbye";        # produces 'G310'
print soundex "hilo";           # produces 'H400' - same as 'Hello'
print join ',', soundex qw(Hello World);
                                # produces 'H400,W643'
print soundex "Hello World"     # produces 'H464'
```

The following short program shows the Soundex algorithm being used to look up a name from a list given an input from the user. Since we are using Soundex, the input doesn't have to be exact, just similar:

```
#!/usr/bin/perl
# surname.pl
use warnings;
use strict;

use Text::Soundex;

# define an ABC of names (as a hash for 'exists')
my %abc = (
    "Hammerstein" => 1,
    "Pineapples" => 1,
    "Blackblood" => 1,
    "Deadlock" => 1,
    "Mekquake" => 1,
    "Rojaws" => 1,
);

# create a token-to-name table
my %tokens;
foreach (keys %abc) {
    $tokens{soundex $_} = $_;
}
# test input against known names
print "Name? ";
while (<>) {
    chomp;
    if (exists $abc{$_}) {
        print "Yes, we have a '$_' here. Another? ";
    } else {
        my $token = soundex $_;
        if (exists $tokens{$token}) {
            print "Did you mean $tokens{$token}? ";
        } else {
            print "Sorry, who again? ";
```

```
        }
    }
}
```

We can try out this program with various different names, real and imaginary, and produce different answers. The input can be quite different from the name if it sounds approximately right:

> **perl surname.pl**

```
Name? Hammerstone
Did you mean Hammerstein? Hammerstein
Yes, we have a 'Hammerstein' here. Another? Blockbleed
Did you mean Blackblood? Mechwake
Did you mean Mekquake? Nemesis
Sorry, who again?
```

Tokenizing Lists of Words and E-Mail Addresses

We can produce a string of tokens from a string of words by splitting up the string before feeding it to soundex. Here is a simple query program that takes input from the user and returns a list of tokens:

```
#!/usr/bin/perl
# soundex.pl
use warnings;
use strict;

use Text::Soundex;

while (<>) {
    chomp;   #remove trailing linefeed
    s/\W/ /g;   #zap punctuation, e.g. '.', '@'
    print "'$_' => '@{[soundex(split)]}'\n";
}
```

We can try this program out with phrases to illustrate that accuracy does not have to be all that great, as a guide:

> **perl soundex.pl**

```
definitively inaccurate
'definitively inaccurate' => 'D153 I526'
devinatovli inekurat
'devinatovli inekurat' => 'D153 I526'
```

As well as handling spaces, we have also added a substitution that converts punctuation into spaces first. This allows us to generate a list of tokens for an e-mail address, for example.

The Soundex Algorithm

As the previous examples illustrate, Soundex tokens consist of an initial letter, which is the same as that of the original word, followed by three digits that represent the sound of the first, second, and third syllable, respectively. Since one has one syllable, only the first digit is non-zero. On the other hand, seven has two syllables, so it gets two non-zero digits. Comparing the two results, we can notice that both one and seven contain a 5, which corresponds to the syllable containing "n" in each word.

The Soundex algorithm has some obvious limitations though. In particular, it only resolves words up to the first three syllables. However, this is generally more than enough for simple "similar sounding" type matches, such as surname matching, for which it was designed.

Handling Untokenizable Words

In some rare cases, the Soundex algorithm cannot find any suitable token for the supplied word. In these cases, it usually returns nothing (or to be more accurate, undef). We can change this behavior by setting the variable:

```
$Text::Soundex::soundex_nocode:
```

```
$Text::Soundex::soundex_nocode = 'Z000';   # a common 'failed' token
print soundex "=>";   # produces 'Z000'
```

If we change the value of this variable, we must be sure to set it to something that is not likely to genuinely occur. The value of Z000 is a common choice, but it matches many words including Zoo. A better choice in this case might be Q999, but there is no code that is absolutely guaranteed not to occur. If we do not need to conform to the Soundex code system (we might want to pass the results to something else that expects valid Soundex tokens as input), then we can simply define an impossible value like _NOCODE_ or ?000, which soundex cannot generate.

Other Text Processing Modules

As well as the modules in the Text:: family, several other Perl modules outside the Text:: hierarchy involve text processing or combine text processing with other functions.

Several of the Term:: modules all involve text processing in relation to terminals. For instance, Term::Cap involves generating ANSI escape sequences from capability codes, while Term::ReadLine provides input line text processing support. These modules are all covered in Chapter 15.

Writing sed Scripts with Perl

Many Unix shell scripts make use of the sed command to carry out text processing. The name is short for *stream editor*, and a typical sed command might look like this:

```
sed 5q file.txt
```

This prints out the first five lines of a file, rather like the head command.

Perl comes with a script called psed that provides a complete implementation of sed written in Perl. As it has no dependency on the real sed, it will work on platforms like Windows for which sed is not available (short of installing a Unix shell environment like Cygwin):

```
psed 5q file.txt
```

When invoked under the alternate name s2p, this script instead takes the supplied sed arguments and generates a stand-alone Perl script that performs the same operation:

```
s2p 5q file.txt > printtop5.pl
```

Of course, the script generated is not terribly efficient compared to simply reimplementing the script in Perl to start with. Under either name, the script can also be given the option -f to parse and process a sed script in a file rather than a directly typed command and -e to specify additional commands (with or without -f).

Documenting Perl

Documentation is a good idea in any programming language. Like most programming languages, Perl supports simple comments. However, it also attempts to combine the onerous duties of commenting code and documenting software into one slightly less arduous task through the prosaically named *POD* or *Plain Old Documentation* syntax.

Comments

Anything after a # is a comment and ignored by the Perl interpreter. Comments may be placed on a line of their own or after existing Perl code. They can even be placed in the middle of multiline statements:

```
print 1 *   # depth
4*   # width
9;   # height
```

Perl will not interpret a # inside a string as the start of a comment, but because of this we cannot place comments inside HERE documents. While we cannot comment multiple lines at once, like C-style /*...*/ comments, POD offers this ability indirectly.

POD: Plain Old Documentation

POD is a very simple markup syntax for integrating documentation with source code. It consists of a series of special one-line tokens that distinguish POD from source code and also allows us to define simple structures like headings and lists.

In and of itself, POD does nothing more than give us the ability to write multiline comments. However, its simple but flexible syntax also makes it very simple to convert into user-friendly document formats. Perl comes with the following POD translator tools as standard:

pod2text	Render POD in plain text format.
pod2html	Render POD into HTML.
pod2man	Render POD into Unix manual page (nroff) format.
pod2latex	Render POD into Latex format.

Many more translators are available from CPAN, of course, including translators for RTF, XML, PostScript, PDF, DocBook, OpenOffice, as wells as alternate translators for HTML, text, and so on. The perldoc utility is just a friendlier and more specialized interface to the same translation process, as are pod2usage and podselect, all of which are covered in this section.

POD Paragraphs

POD allows us to define documentation paragraphs, which we can insert into other documents—most usually, but by no means exclusively, Perl code. The simplest sequence is =pod ... =cut. The =pod token states that all of the following text is to be taken as POD paragraphs, until the next =cut or the end of the file:

```
...
$scalar = "value";
=pod

This is a paragraph of POD text embedded into some Perl code. It is not indented,
so it will be treated as normal text and word wrapped by POD translators.
```

```
=cut

print do_something($scalar);
...
```

Within the delimited section, text is divided into paragraphs, which are simply blocks of continuous text (potentially including linefeeds). A paragraph ends and a new one begins only when a completely empty line is encountered. All POD tokens will absorb a paragraph that immediately follows them, which is why there is a blank line after the =cut in the preceding example. While the blank line preceding the =cut is not necessary, maintaining blank lines on both sides helps to visually discriminate the POD directive.

Some tokens such as =item and =head1, covered shortly, use the attached paragraph for display purposes. Others, like =pod and =cut, ignore it. This lets us document the POD itself, as the text immediately following =pod or =cut is not rendered by POD processors.

```
=pod this is just a draft document

mysubname - this subroutine doesn't do much of anything
at all and is just serving as an example of how to document it with
a POD paragraph or two

=cut end of draft bit
```

Since nonblank following lines are included in the text attached to the token, the preceding =pod token could also be written, with identically equivalent meaning, as follows:

```
=pod this is
just a draft
document
```

The same rule applies to all POD tokens except =cut. While POD translators will absorb text on the line or lines immediately following a =cut, the Perl interpreter itself will only ignore text following a =cut on the same line. As a consequence, we cannot spread a "cut comment" across more than one line and expect code to compile.

Paragraphs and Paragraph Types

If a paragraph is indented, then we consider it to be preformatted, much in the same way that the HTML <pre> tag works. The following example shows three paragraphs, two of which are indented:

```
=pod

        This paragraph is indented, so it is taken as
        is and not reformatted by translators like:

pod2text - the text translator
pod2html - the HTML translator
pod2man - the Unix manual page translator

        Note that 'as is' also means that escaping does not work, and that
        interpolation doesn't happen. What we see is what we get.

This is a second paragraph in the same =pod...=cut section. Since it is
not indented it will be reformatted by translators.

=cut
```

Headings

Section headings can be added with the =head1 and =head2 tokens, plus =head3 and =head4 in more recent releases of the POD translators. The heading text is the paragraph immediately following the token and may start (and end) on the same line:

```
=head1 This is a level one heading
```

  Or:

```
=head2 This is
 a level
two heading
```

  Or:

```
=head2
As is this
```

Heading tokens start a POD section in the same way that =pod does if one is not already active. POD sections do not nest, so we only need one =cut to get back to Perl code. In general the first form is used, but it's important to leave an empty line if we do not want the heading to absorb the following paragraph:

```
=head1 ERROR: This heading has accidentally swallowed up
       this paragraph, because there is no separating line.
=head2 ERROR: Worse than that, it will absorb this second level heading too
       so this becomes one long level one heading.
=cut
```

This is how we should really do it:

```
=head1 This is a level one heading

This is a paragraph following the level one heading.

=head2 This is a level two heading

    This a preformatted paragraph following the level two heading.

=cut
```

How the headings are actually rendered is entirely up to the translator. By default the text translator pod2text indents paragraphs by four spaces, level two headings by two, and level one headings by none—crude, but effective. The HTML translator pod2html uses tags like <h1> and <h2> as we might expect.

Lists

Lists can be defined with the =over ... =back and =item tokens. The =over token starts a list and can be given a value such as 4, which many formatters use to determine how much indentation to use. The list is ended by =back and is optional if the POD paragraph is at the end of the document. =item defines the actual list items of which there should be at least one, and we should not use this token outside of an =over ... =back section. Here is an example three-item list:

```
=over 4

=item 1

This is item number one on the list
```

```
=item 2

This is item number two on the list

=item 3

This is the third item

=back
```

Like =pod and =head*n*, =over will start a POD section if one is not active.

The numbers after the =item tokens are purely arbitrary; we can use anything we like for them, including meaningful text. However, to make the job of POD translators easier, we should stick to a consistent scheme. For example, if we number them, we should do it consistently, and if we want to use bullet points, then we should use something like an asterisk. If we want named items, we can do that too. For example, a bullet-pointed list with paragraphs:

```
=over 4

=item *
This is a bullet pointed list

=item *
With two items

=back
```

A named items list:

```
=over 4

=item The First Item

This is the description of the first item

=item The Second Item

This is the description of the second item

=back
```

A named items list without paragraphs:

```
=over 4

=item Stay Alert

=item Trust No one

=item Keep Your Laser Handy

=back
```

POD translators will attempt to do the best they can with lists, depending on what they think we are trying to do and the constraints of the document format into which they are converting. The pod2text tool will just use the text after the item name. The pod2html tool is subject to the rules of HTML, which has different tags for ordered, unordered, and descriptive lists (<ol>, <ul>, and <dl>) so it makes a guess based on what the items look like. A consistent item naming style will help it make a correct guess.

Although =over will start a new POD section, =back will end the list but not the POD section. We therefore also need a =cut to return to Perl code:

```
=over 4

=item * Back to the source
=back

=cut
```

Character Encodings

If documentation is written in a different character set than the default Latin-1, POD translators can be told to render it using an alternate character encoding with the =encoding token. For example:

```
=encoding utf8
```

Typically, this is used to state the encoding of a whole document and should be placed near the top, before any renderable text.

Translator-Specific Paragraphs

The final kinds of POD token are the =for and =begin ... =end tokens. The =for token takes the name of a specific translator and an immediately following paragraph (that is, not with an intervening blank line), which is rendered only if that translator is being used. The paragraph should be in the output format of the translator, that is, already formatted for output. Other translators will entirely ignore the paragraph:

```
=for text
This is a paragraph that will appear in documents produced by the pod2text format.

=for html <font color = red>
<p>But this paragraph will appear in <b>HTML</b> documents
</font>
```

Again, like the headings and item tokens, the paragraph can start on the next line, as in the first example, or immediately following the format name, as in the second.

Since it is annoying to have to type =for format for every paragraph in a collection of paragraphs, we can also use the pair of =begin..=end markers. These operate much like =pod...=cut but mark the enclosed paragraphs as being specific to a particular format:

```
=begin html

<p>Paragraph1

<p><table>......
......</table>

<p>Paragraph2

=end
```

If =begin is used outside an existing POD section, then it starts one. The =end ends the format-specific section but not the POD, so we also need to add a =cut to return to Perl code, just as for lists.

```
=begin html

<p>A bit of <b>HTML</b> document
```

```
=end

=cut
```

The =begin and =end tokens can also be used to create multiline comments, simply by providing =begin with a name that does not correspond to any translator. We can even comment out blocks of code this way:

```
=begin disabled_dump_env

foreach (sort keys %ENV) {
    print STDERR, "$_ => $ENV{$_}\n";
}

=end

=begin comment

This is an example of how we can use POD tokens to create comments.
Since 'comment' is not a POD translator type, this section is never
used in documents created by 'pod2text', 'pod2html', etc.

=end
```

Some extension modules also understand specific format names. For example, the Test::Inline module looks for the special name test to mark the location of in-line tests.

Using POD with __DATA__ and __END__

If we are using either a __DATA__ or a __END__ token in a Perl script, then we need to take special care with POD paragraphs that lie adjacent to them. POD translators require that there must be at least one empty line between the end of the data and a POD directive for the directive to be seen (rather like POD directives themselves, in fact); otherwise, it is missed by the translation tools. In other words, write this:

```
...
__END__

=head1

...
```

and not this:

```
...
__END__
=head1

...
```

Interior Sequences

We mentioned earlier that POD paragraphs could either be preformatted (indicated by indenting) or normal. Normal paragraphs are reformatted by translators to remove extraneous spaces, newlines, and tabs. Then the resulting paragraph is rendered to the desired width if necessary.

In addition to basic reformatting, normal paragraphs may also contain *interior sequences*. Each sequence consists of a single capital letter, followed by the text to treat specially within angle brackets. For example:

```
=pod
```

This is a B<paragraph> that uses I<italic> and B<bold> markup using the
BE<lt>textE<gt> and IE<lt>text<gt> interior sequences. Here is an example
code fragment: C<substr $text,0,1> and here is a filename: F</usr/bin/perl>.
All these things are of course represented in a style entirely up to the
translator. See L<perlpod> for more information.

```
=cut
```

To specify a real < and >, we have to use the E<lt> and E<gt> sequences, reminiscent of the <
and > HTML entities. The full, loosely categorized list of interior sequences supported by POD
follows:

Style:

Sequence	Formatting
B<text>	Bold/Strong text (options, switches, program names).
I<text>	Italic/Emphasized text (variables, emphasis).
S<text>	Text contains nonbreaking spaces and cannot be word-wrapped.
C<code>	Code/Example text (listings, command examples).
F<file>	File names.

Cross-references and hyperlinks:

Sequence	Formatting
L<name>	A cross-reference link to a named manual page and/or section
L<page>	Other manual page
L<page/name>	Section or list item in other manual page
L<page/"name">	The same as preceding entry
L</name>	Section or list item in current manual page
L<"name">	The same as preceding entry

A section title is the text after a =head POD directive, with any spaces replaced with underscores. A list item title is the text after an =item POD directive. In case of conflicts, the first match
will usually be linked to. Markup (if the title contains any) may be omitted in the link name.

Either a leading / or quotes are necessary to distinguish a section or list item name from manual page names.

L<text|name>	Equivalent to the L<name> sequence, but with an alternative text description for the link

The descriptive text is given first. The original link name is given second, after a pipe symbol,
and describes the nature of the link. For example:

```
L<text|name>
L<text|name/item>
L<text|name/"section">
L<text|"section">
L<text|/"section">
```

Under this syntax we cannot use explicit / or | characters, but see E<escape> later.

Miscellaneous:

X<index>	An index entry. Ignored by most formatters, it may be used by indexing programs.
Z<>	A zero-width character. Useful for breaking up sequences that would otherwise be recognized as POD directives.

Special characters and escape sequences:

E<escape>	A named or numbered entity, styled on the &entity; syntax of HTML.

These escapes are usually only necessary inside another sequence or immediately after a capital letter representing an escape sequence; for instance, B<text> is written literally as BE<lt>textE<gt>. In particular, the following special names are supported:

E<lt>	<
E<gt>	>
E<sol>	/
E<verbar>	|

Otherwise, a generic number or name can be specified:

E<number>	ASCII character code
E<html>	HTML entity (for example, "copy")

Most translators will handle the preceding four named entities but are not necessarily going to support generic entities. The obvious exception to this is, of course, the HTML translator, which doesn't have to do any work other than add a & and ; to the name.

POD Tools and Utilities

Perl provides a collection of modules in the Pod:: family that perform translations from POD into other formats and also provides utility modules for checking syntax. Most of these modules are wrapped by utility scripts that Perl provides as standard. The pod2html tool, for example, is merely a wrapper for the Pod::Html module.

Translator Tools

We have already mentioned pod2text and pod2html. Perl also comes with other translators and some POD utilities too. All the translators take an input and optional output file as arguments, plus additional options to control their output format. Without either, they take input from standard input and write it to standard output.

The list of POD translators supplied with Perl is as follows:

pod2text	Translates POD into plain text. If the -c option is used and Term::ANSIColor is installed (see Chapter 15), colors will also be used.
pod2html	Translates POD into HTML, optionally recursing and processing directories and integrating cross-links between pages.

| pod2latex | Translates POD into Latex, either a single document or a collection of related documents. |
| pod2man | Translates POD into Unix manual pages (compatible with nroff/troff). |

For more details on these translators, we can consult the relevant perldoc page using the now familiar command line:

> **perldoc <translatorname>**

In addition to the standard translators, there are many POD translation tools available from CPAN; including translators for RTF/Word, LaTex, PostScript, and plenty of other formats. Even a mildly popular format will likely have a POD translator.

Retrieval Tools

In addition to the translators, Perl provides three tools for extracting information from PODs selectively. Of these, perldoc is by far the most accomplished. Although not strictly a translator, perldoc is a utility that makes use of translators to provide a convenient Perl documentation lookup tool.

To attempt to retrieve usage information about the given Perl script, we can use the pod2usage tool. For example:

> **pod2usage myscript.pl**

The tool searches for a SYNOPSIS heading within the file and prints it out using pod2text. A verbosity flag may be specified to increase the returned information:

-v 1	(default) SYNOPSIS only
-v 2	SYNOPSIS plus OPTIONS and ARGUMENTS (if present)
-v 3	All POD documentation

A verbosity of 3 is equivalent to using pod2text directly. If the file is not given with an absolute pathname, then -pathlist can be used to provide a list of directory paths to search for the file in.

A simpler and more generic version of pod2usage is podselect. This tool attempts to locate a level 1 heading with the specified section title and extracts the subdocument from under that title in each file it is passed:

> **podselect -s='How to boil an egg' *.pod**

Note that podselect does not do any translation, so it needs to be directed to a translator for rendering into reasonable documentation.

POD Verification

It is easy to make simple mistakes with POD, omitting empty lines or forgetting =cut, for example. Fortunately, POD is simple enough to be easy to verify as well. The podchecker utility scans a file looking for problems:

> **podchecker poddyscript.pl**

If all is well, then it will return the following:

poddyscript.pl pod syntax OK.

Otherwise, it will produce a list of problems, which we can then go and fix, for example:

```
*** WARNING: file does not start with =head at line N in file poddyscript.pl
```

This warning indicates that we have started POD documentation with something other than a =head1 or =head2, which the checker considers to be suspect. Likewise:

```
*** WARNING: No numeric argument for =over at line N in file poddyscript.pl
*** WARNING: No items in =over (at line 17) / =back list at line N in file
poddyscript.pl
```

This indicates that we have an =over ... =back pair, which not only does not have a number after the over, but also does not even contain any items. The first is probably an omission. The second indicates that we might have bunched up our items so they all run into the =over token. If we had left out the space before =back, we would instead have got this error:

```
*** ERROR: =over on line N without closing =back at line EOF in file poddyscript.pl
```

The module underlying podchecker is Pod::Checker, and we can also use it in code:

```
# function syntax
$ok = podchecker($podfile, $checklog, %options);

# object syntax
$checker = new Pod::Checker %options;
$checker->parse_from_file($podpath, $checklog);
```

Both file arguments can be either file names or filehandles. By default, the POD file defaults to STDIN and the check log to STDERR, so a very simple checker script could be

```
use Pod::Checker;
print podchecker?"OK":"Fail";
```

The options hash, if supplied, allows one option to be defined: enable or disable the printing of warnings. The default is on, so we can get a verification check without a report using STDIN and STDERR:

```
$ok = podchecker(\*STDIN, \*STDERR,'warnings' => 0);
```

The actual podchecker script is more advanced than this, but not by all that much.

Creating Usage Info and Manual Pages from POD

The pod2usage tool allows us to dump out just the SYNOPSIS section from a POD document, the SYNOPSIS plus OPTIONS and ARGUMENTS (if either are present), or the whole manual page. We can make use of the Pod::Usage module to provide the same capabilities within our own scripts.

The pod2usage subroutine is automatically exported when using Pod::Usage and is the single interface to its features. While it has a number of different calling conventions, it is typically used with Getopt::Std or Getopt::Long, as in this example:

```
#!/usr/bin/perl
# podusagedemo.pl
use strict;
use warnings;
use Pod::Usage;
use Getopt::Long qw(:config bundling no_ignore_case);
```

```
=head1 NAME

A demonstration of Pod::Usage

=head1 SYNOPSIS

  podusagedemo.pl -h | -H | -l | -r [<files>]

=head1 OPTIONS

  -h|--help      this help
  -H|--morehelp  extended help
  -l|--left      go left
  -r|--right     go right

=head1 ARGUMENTS

One or more files may be specified as arguments, otherwise
standard input is used. (Both this section and OPTIONS are
are displayed by the -h option)

=head1 DESCRIPTION

This is the extended help displayed by the -H option

=cut

my %opts;

pod2usage(-verbose=>0) unless GetOptions(\%opts,qw[
    h|help H|m|morehelp l|left r|right
]);
pod2usage(-verbose=>1)  if  $opts{h};
pod2usage(-verbose=>2)  if  $opts{H} or $opts{m};
pod2usage(-verbose=>2, "Cannot go both left and right")
  if $opts{l} and $opts{r};

# ...
```

A verbose level of 0 corresponds to the SYNOPSIS only, which just displays the command line preceded by Usage:. A verbose level of 1 prints out the OPTIONS and ARGUMENTS sections as well, similarly preceded by Options: and Arguments: respectively. This happens when the -h option is used. An -H or a -m will generate the whole documentation, using highlighting and a pager in the manner of perldoc or the pod2usage tool. The help output, verbose level 1, looks like this:

> **./podusagedemo.pl -h**

```
Usage:
      podusagedemo.pl -h | -H | -l | -r [<files>]

Options:
      -h|--help      this help
      -H|--morehelp  extended help
      -l|--left      go left
      -r|--right     go right
```

Arguments:
    One or more files may be specified as arguments, otherwise standard
    input is used. (Both this section and OPTIONS are displayed by -h)

We can also build the calls to pod2usage directly into the call to GetOptions:

```
my %opts;
GetOptions(
    'h|help'        => sub { pod2usage(-verbose=>1) },
    'H|m|morehelp'  => sub { pod2usage(-verbose=>2) },
    'l|left'        => \$opts{l},
    'r|right'       => \$opts{r},
);
```

Although it is usually clearer to call pod2usage with named arguments like -verbose and -message, we can also call it with a single numeric or string argument. A numeric argument will be treated as an exit status and will cause the program to exit displaying the synopsis (that is, verbose level 0). A string argument will be used as the message, as if -message had been specified, again with a verbose level of 0.

The pod2usage subroutine also understands the options and defaults shown in Table 18-2.

Table 18-2. *pod2usage Options*

Option	Purpose
-msg	Alias for -message.
-exitval	Set an explicit exit status for pod2usage. Otherwise, 2 if verbose level is 1, or 1 if verbose level is 2 or 3. The special value NOEXIT causes pod2usage to return control to the program rather than exiting.
-input	File name or filehandle to get POD documentation from. For example, *DATA. Otherwise, the source file is used.
-output	File name or filehandle to write generated documentation to. Otherwise, standard output is used if the exit status is 0 or 1, and standard error if the exit status is 2 or higher. Note the default exit status is 2.
-pathlist	Search path to locate the file name specified to -input if it is not locally present. May be specified as a reference to an array or a colon-delimited path. Defaults to $ENV{PATH}. This option allows programs to self-document themselves even when the documentation is located in an external POD file.

There is no requirement to specify separate OPTIONS or ARGUMENTS sections. If desired, either section can be bundled into the SYNOPSIS to have them appear even for verbose level 0. In this case, level 1 simply becomes identical to level 0.

Recent versions of Getopt::Long provide the HelpMessage and VersionMessage subroutines. HelpMessage is essentially a wrapper around pod2usage, while VersionMessage emulates pod2usage syntax and options, but it is fully contained within Getopt::Long. See Chapter 14 for more information.

Programming POD

Perl provides a number of modules for processing POD documentation. These modules form the basis for all the POD utilities, and they are described briefly in Table 18-3.

Table 18-3. *POD Modules*

Module	Action
Pod::Checker	The basis of the podchecker utility. See earlier.
Pod::Find	Search for and return a hash of POD documents. See the section "Locating Pods."
Pod::Functions	A categorized summary of Perl's functions, exported as a hash.
Pod::Html	The basis for the pod2html utility.
Pod::Latex	The basis for the pod2latex utility.
Pod::Man	The basis for both the pod2man and the functionally identical pod2roff utilities.
Pod::Parser	The POD parser. This is the basis for all the translation modules and most of the others too. New parsers can be implemented by inheriting from this module.
Pod::ParseLink	A module containing the logic for converting L<...> POD links into URLs.
Pod::ParseUtils	A module containing utility subroutines for retrieving information about and organizing the structure of a parsed POD document, as created by Pod::InputObjects.
Pod::InputObjects	The implementation of the POD syntax, describing the nature of paragraphs and so on. In-memory POD documents can be created on the fly using the methods in this module.
Pod::Perldoc	The basis for the perldoc utility. Also incorporates a family of plug-in submodules handling format conversions, some of which require Pod::Simple (available from CPAN).
Pod::PlainText	The basis for the pod2text utility.
Pod::Plainer	A compatibility module for converting new-style POD into old-style POD.
Pod::Select	A subclass of Pod::Parser and the basis of the podselect utility, Pod::Select extracts selected parts of POD documents by searching for their heading titles. Any translator that inherits from Pod::Select rather than Pod::Parser will be able to support the Pod::Usage module automatically.
Pod::Text	The basis of the pod2text utility.
Pod::Text::Color	Convert POD to text using ANSI color sequences. The basis of the -color option to pod2text. Subclassed from Pod::Text. This uses Term::ANSIColor, which must be installed (see Chapter 15).
Pod::Text::Overstrike	Convert POD to text using overstrike escape sequences, where different effects are created by printing a character, issuing a backspace, and then printing another.
Pod::Text::Termcap	Convert POD to text using escape sequences suitable for the current terminal. Subclassed from Pod::Text. Requires termcap support (see Chapter 15).
Pod::Usage	The basis of the pod2usage utility; this uses Pod::Select to extract usage-specific information from POD documentation by searching for specific sections, for example, NAME, SYNOPSIS.

In addition to the modules listed here, the Pod::Simple family of modules on CPAN is also worthy of attention. Pod::Simple provides a revised and refactored toolkit for writing and using POD translators with a flexible and extensible interface.

Another module of interest to developers working on ensuring that documentation for a module is complete is Pod::Coverage. This module can be used to test whether or not POD documentation fully covers all the subroutines defined within it. The Devel::Cover module, covered in Chapter 17, will automatically invoke Pod::Coverage if available. This is generally a more convenient interface, and it analyzes the coverage of our tests at the same time.

Using POD Parsers

Translator modules, which is to say any module based directly or indirectly on Pod::Parser, may be used programmatically by creating a parser object and then calling one of the parsing methods:

```
parse_from_filehandle($fh, %options);
```

Or:

```
parse_from_file($infile, $outfile, %options);
```

For example, assuming we have Term::ANSIColor installed, we can create ANSIColor text documents using this short script:

```perl
#!/usr/bin/perl
# parseansi.pl
use Pod::Text::Color;

my $parser = new Pod::Text::Color(
    width => 56,
    loose => 1,
    sentence => 1,
);

if (@ARGV) {
    $parser->parse_from_file($_, '-') foreach @ARGV;
} else {
    $parser->parse_from_filehandle(\*STDIN);
}
```

We can generate HTML pages, plain text documents, and manual pages using exactly the same process from their respective modules.

Writing a POD Parser

Writing a POD parser is surprisingly simple. Most of the hard work is already done by Pod::Parser, so all that's left is to override the methods we need to replace in order to generate the kind of document we are interested in. Particularly, there are four methods we may want to override:

command	Render and output POD commands.
verbatim	Render and output verbatim paragraphs.
textblock	Render and output regular (nonverbatim) paragraphs.
interior_sequence	Return rendered interior sequence.

By overriding these and other methods, we can customize the document that the parser produces. Note that the first three methods display their result, whereas interior_sequence returns it. Here is a short example of a POD parser that turns POD documentation into an XML document (albeit without a DTD):

```perl
#!/usr/bin/perl
# parser.pl
use warnings;
use strict;

{
    package My::Pod::Parser;

    use Pod::Parser;
    our @ISA = qw(Pod::Parser);

    sub command {
        my ($parser, $cmd, $para, $line) = @_;
        my $fh = $parser->output_handle;

        $para =~s/[\n]+$//;
        my $output = $parser->interpolate($para, $line);
        print $fh "<pod:$cmd> $output </pod:$cmd> \n";
    }

    sub verbatim {
        my ($parser, $para, $line) = @_;
        my $fh = $parser->output_handle;

        $para =~s/[\n]+$//;
        print $fh "<pod:verbatim> \n $para \n </pod:verbatim> \n";
    }

    sub textblock {
        my ($parser, $para, $line) = @_;
        my $fh = $parser->output_handle;

        print $fh $parser->interpolate($para, $line);
    }

    sub interior_sequence {
        my ($parser, $cmd, $arg) = @_;
        my $fh = $parser->output_handle;

        return "<pod:int cmd=\"$cmd\"> $arg </pod:int>";
    }
}

my $parser = new My::Pod::Parser();

if (@ARGV) {
    $parser->parse_from_file($_) foreach @ARGV;
} else {
    $parser->parse_from_filehandle(\*STDIN);
}
```

To implement this script, we need the output filehandle, which we can get from the output_handle method. We also take advantage of Pod::Parser to do the actual rendering work by using the interpolate method, which in turn calls our interior_sequence method. Pod::Parser provides plenty of other methods too, some of which we can override as well as or instead of the ones we used in this parser; see the following for a complete list:

> **perldoc Pod::Parser**

The Pod::Parser documentation also covers more methods that we might want to override, such as begin_input, end_input, preprocess_paragraph, and so on. Each of these gives us the ability to customize the parser in increasingly detailed ways.

We have placed the Parser package inside the script in this instance, though we could equally have had it in a separate module file. To see the script in action, we can feed it with any piece of Perl documentation—the POD documentation itself, for example. On a typical Unix installation of Perl version 5.6 or higher, we can do that with

```
> perl mypodparser /usr/lib/perl5/5.8.6/pod/perlpod.pod
```

This generates an XML version of perlpod that starts like this:

```
<pod:head1>NAME</pod:head1>
perlpod - plain old documentation

<pod:head1>DESCRIPTION</pod:head1>
A pod-to-whatever translator reads a pod file paragraph by paragraph,
and translates it to the appropriate output format. There are
three kinds of paragraphs:
<pod:int cmd="L">verbatim|/"Verbatim Paragraph"</pod:int>,
<pod:int cmd="L">command|/"Command Paragraph"</pod:int>, and
<pod:int cmd="L">ordinary text|/"Ordinary Block of Text"</pod:int>.

...
```

By comparing this with the original document, we can see how the parser is converting POD tokens into XML tags.

Locating PODs

The Unix-specific Pod::Find module searches for POD documents within a list of supplied files and directories. It provides one subroutine of importance, pod_find, which is not imported by default. This subroutine takes one main argument—a reference to a hash of options including default search locations. Subsequent arguments are additional files and directories to look in. The following script implements a more or less fully featured POD search based around Pod::Find and Getopt::Long, which we cover in detail in Chapter 14.

```
#!/usr/bin/perl
# findpod.pl
use warnings;
use strict;

use Pod::Find qw(pod_find);
use Getopt::Long;

# default options
my ($verbose,$include,$scripts);
my $display = 1;

# allow files/directories and options to mix
Getopt::Long::Configure('permute');

# get options
GetOptions('verbose!' => \$verbose,
    'include!' => \$include,
    'scripts!' => \$scripts,
```

```
    'display!' => \$display,
);

# if no directories specified, default to @INC
$include = 1 if !defined($include) and (@ARGV or $scripts);

# perform scan
my %pods = pod_find({
    -verbose => $verbose,
    -inc => $include,
    -script => $scripts,
    -perl => 1
}, @ARGV);

# display results if required
if ($display) {
    if (%pods) {

        print "Found '$pods{$_}' in $_\n foreach sort keys %pods;
    } else {
        print "No pods found\n";
    }
}
```

We can invoke this script with no arguments to search @INC or pass it a list of directories and files to search. It also supports four arguments to enable verbose messages, disable the final report, and enable Pod::Find's two default search locations. Here is one way we can use it, assuming we call the script findpod:

> **perl findpod.pl -iv /my/perl/lib 2> dup.log**

This command tells the script to search @INC in addition to /my/perl/lib (-i), produce extra messages during the scan (-v), and redirect error output to dup.log. This will capture details of any duplicate modules that the module finds during its scan. If we only want to see duplicate modules, we can disable the output and view the error output on screen with this command:

> **perl findpod.pl -i --nodisplay /my/perl/lib**

The options passed in the hash reference to pod_find are all Boolean and all default to 0 (off). They have the meanings listed in Table 18-4.

Table 18-4. *pod_find Options*

Option	Action
-verbose	Print out progress during scan, reporting all files scanned that did not contain POD information.
-inc	Scan all the paths contained in @INC. Implies -perl.
-script	Search the installation directory and subdirectories for POD files. If Perl was installed as /usr/bin/perl, then this will be /usr/bin for example. This implies -perl.
-perl	Apply Perl naming conventions for finding POD files. This strips Perl file extensions (.pod, .pm, etc.), skips over numeric directory names that are not the current Perl release, and so on.

The hash generated by findpod.pl contains the file in which each POD document was found as the key and the document title (usually the module package name) as the value.

Source Filters

An intriguing feature of Perl is the ability to preprocess source code before it is even compiled. This capability is provided by the `Filter::Util::Call` module, which uses an underlying C-based interface to the Perl interpreter itself to intercept source code after it is read in but before it is compiled.

Here is an example of it in use to implement a filter that carries out a simple substitution. The filter itself is implemented by the `filter` method, while the `import` method performs the task of installing the filter with a specified pair of match and replacement strings:

```
package Class::Filter::Replace;
use strict;
use Carp qw(croak);
use Filter::Util::Call;

sub import {
    my ($self,$replace,$with)=@_;
    unless ($replace) {
        croak("use ".__PACKAGE__." 'original' [, 'replacement'];");
    }
    $with ||= ""; #replace with nothing

    my $filter={
        replace => $replace,
        with    => $with,
    };

    filter_add($filter);
}

sub filter {
    my $status=filter_read(); # set $_ from input
    s/$_[0]->{replace}/$_[0]->{with}/go if $status > 0;
    return $status; # 0 = end of file, <0 = error
}

1;
```

We can now use this filter to preprocess source code. Here, we set the filter to replace all instances of the word Goodbye with Hello. Since the filter is installed at compile time by virtue of `use`, it affects the code immediately following it:

```
#!/usr/bin/perl
use strict;
use warnings;

use Class::Filter::Replace Goodbye => 'Hello';

my $Goodbye="so long";
print "Goodbye, I must be going, $Hello\n";
```

Running this program prints out the following:

```
Hello, I must be going, so long
```

We can also use a filter directly on any source code from the command line:

```
> perl -MClass::Filter::Replace=Goodbye,Hello unfiltered.pl
```

While this filter might look like we could easily register multiple objects in the same class, this is not so. In fact, the class is a singleton, because Filter::Util::Call will permit only one filter per class. What actually happens here is that the class is extracted from the context of filter_add, and the hash reference is passed as a hash reference to the filter method, which is called as a class method, not as an object instance method. This is why we did not bother to bless the hash reference $filter into the class before passing it on.

A filter consists of either an object class that inserts itself by name into the filter interface with filter_add and provides a filter method for Filter::Util::Call to call back, as earlier, or a simple subroutine that carries out the same task as the filter method and is inserted by code reference. Here is the code reference version of the preceding filter:

```
package Closure::Filter::Replace;
use strict;
use Carp qw(croak);
use Filter::Util::Call;

sub import {
    my ($self,$replace,$with)=@_;
    croak("use ".__PACKAGE__." 'original' [, 'replacement'];")
      unless $replace;
    $with ="" unless $with;

    my $filter=sub {
        my $status=filter_read(); #populates $_
        s/$replace/$with/g if $status > 0;
        return $status;
    }

    filter_add($filter);
}

1;
```

To read source in other than a line-by-line basis, we can either supply a size argument to filter_read or make use of filter_read_exact. Both uses cause the filter to try to read a block of the requested number of bytes; filter_read may come back with less if it cannot initially read enough, while filter_read_exact will block and not stop trying until the end of file or an error is encountered:

```
my $status=filter_read($size); #block mode, nonblocking

my $status=filter_read_exact($size); #block mode, blocking
```

Note that both filter_read and filter_read_exact append to the current value of $_, so multiple calls to filter_read within the filter subroutine will not reset it to an entirely new value each time. The status is always returned with a value of 0 for end of file, greater than 0 for a successful read, and less than 0 for an error. Hence in this example we perform the substitution only if $status > 0.

If a filter wishes to disable itself, perhaps because it should only apply to a certain part of the source, it can do so by calling filter_del. For example:

```
if (/__(DATA|END)__/) {
    filter_del();
}
```

The Filter::Simple module provides a third way to define a filter. While not as flexible, it is a lot simpler to use and will suit many applications. For instance, we can rewrite the preceding examples as follows:

```perl
package Simple::Filter::Replace;
use strict;
use Carp qw(croak);
use Filter::Simple;

my ($replace,$with);

sub import {
    $replace = $_[1];
    unless ($replace) {
        croak("use ".__PACKAGE__." 'original' [, 'replacement'];");
    }
    $with = $_[2] || "";
}

FILTER { s/$replace/$with/g };

1;
```

The key to this module is the special FILTER block. This is processed by Filter::Simple using its own internal filter to generate a filter out of our code. We can get a lot smarter too, because the module colludes with Text::Balanced to give us the ability to register filters to process only code, only quoted strings, or a number of other selections with a FILTER_ONLY specification:

```perl
use Filter::Simple;

FILTER_ONLY
    code   => sub { s/ucfirst/lcfirst/g },
    string => sub { s/Goodbye/Hello/g };
```

The full list of filter types is offered in Table 18-5.

Table 18-5. *Filter::Simple Filter Types*

Filter Type	Effect
all	Everything, same as FILTER.
code	Filter code, excluding quotelike operators.
executable	code plus quotelike.
quotelike	Filter quotelike operators q, qq, qr.
regex	Filter regular expression patterns.
string	Filter literal strings in quotes or quotelike text.

The all filter is identical to FILTER, so we could previously have written

```perl
FILTER all => sub { s/$replace/$with/g };
```

We can specify all of these filters except code more than once, with cumulative effect:

```perl
use Filter::Simple;

FILTER_ONLY
    code   => sub { s/ucfirst/lcfirst/g },
```

```
string => sub { s/Goodbye/Ciao/g }
string => sub { s/Ciao/Au Revoir/g },
string => sub { s/Au Revoir/Hello/g };
```

While Perl modules are the primary type of source filter, we can also use external commands. The `Filter::exec` module (which is available in the `Filter` distribution on CPAN, but not as standard) is one way we can invoke an external program to filter our code. For instance, if we happened to have a gzipped Perl script, we could run it on a Unix platform with this command:

```
> perl -MFilter::exec=gunzip,-c myscript.pl.gz
```

The `Filter::sh` module is similar, but it takes a single string as the command, invoking an intermediate shell to execute it:

```
> perl -MFilter::sh='gunzip -c' myscript.pl.gz
```

Although functional, these modules mostly serve as examples of how to implement filters. As further demonstration, the `Filter::cpp` module provides support for C-style preprocessor macros, `Filter::tee` outputs the post-processed source code for inspection, and `Filter::decrypt` provides support for running encrypted source files. Each of these modules uses an underlying factory module that subclasses `Filter::Util::Call` to register the filter, for instance, `Filter::exec` invokes `Filter::Util::Exec`.

The `Filter::Util::Call` interface is used by several modules in the standard distribution. The `Switch` module uses it to implement new semantics and keywords in Perl, by translating them into real Perl keywords before the interpreter gets to look at them. The `B::Byteloader` module uses a filter to convert compiled code saved in binary form back into a parsed opcode tree.

Reports: The "R" in Perl

Reports are a useful but often overlooked feature of Perl. They provide a way to generate structured text such as tables or forms using a special layout description called a *format*. Superficially similar in intent to the `print` and `sprintf` functions, the strength of formats comes from their ability to describe layouts in physical terms, making it much easier to see how the resulting text will look and making it possible to design page layouts visually rather than resorting to character counting with `printf`.

Formats and the Format Data Type

Intriguingly, formats are an entirely separate data type with their own typeglob slot, separate from scalars, arrays, hashes, and filehandles. Like filehandles, they have no prefix or other syntax to express themselves and as a consequence often look like bareword filehandles, which can occasionally be confusing.

A format is compiled from a format definition, a series of formatting or picture lines containing literal text and placeholders, interspersed with data lines that describe the information used to fill placeholder and comment lines. As a simple example, here is a format definition that defines a single pattern line consisting mainly of literal text and a single placeholder, followed by a data line that fills that placeholder with some more literal text:

```
This is a @<<<<< justified field

"left"
```

To turn a format definition into a format, we need to use the `format` function, which takes a format name and a multiline format definition, strongly reminiscent of a here document, and turns it into a compiled format. A single full stop on its own defines the end of the format. To define the very simple format example earlier, we would write something like this:

```
format MYFORMAT =
This is a @<<<<< justified field
"left"
.
```

The trailing period is very important. It is the end token that defines the end of the implicit HERE document. A format definition will happily consume the entire contents of a source file if left unchecked.

To use a format, we use the write function on the filehandle with the same name as the format. For the MYFORMAT example earlier, we would write the following:

```
# print format definition to filehandle 'MYFORMAT'
write MYFORMAT;
```

This requires that we actually have an open filehandle called MYFORMAT and want to use the format to print to it. More commonly we want to print to standard output, which we can do by either defining a format called STDOUT or assigning a format name to the special variable $~ ($FORMAT_NAME with the English module). In this case, we can omit the filehandle, and write will use the currently selected output filehandle, just like print:

```
$~ = 'MYFORMAT';
write;
```

We can also use methods from the IO:: family of modules, if we are using them. Given an IO::Handle-derived filehandle called $fh, we can assign and use a format on it like this:

```
$fh->format(MYFORMAT);
$fh->format_write();
```

The write function (or its IO::Handle counterpart format_write) generates filled-out formats by combining the picture lines with the current values of the items in the data lines to fill in any placeholder present.

Format SyntaxFormats consist of a collection of picture and data lines, interspersed with optional comments, combined into a HERE-style document that is ended with a single full stop.

Of the three, comments are by far the simplest to explain. They resemble conventional Perl comments and simply start with a # symbol, as this example demonstrates:

```
format FORMNAME =
# this is a comment. The next line is a picture line
This is a pattern line with one @<<<<<<<<<<.
# this is another comment.
# the next line is a data line
"placeholder"
# and don't forget to end the format with a '.':
.
```

Picture and data lines take a little more explaining. Since they are the main point of using formats at all, we will start with picture lines.

Picture Lines and Placeholders

Picture lines consist of literal text intermingled with placeholders, which the write function fills in with data at the point of output. If a picture line does not contain any placeholders at all, it is treated as literal text and can be printed out. Since it does not require any data to fill it out, it is not followed by a data line. This means that several picture lines can appear one after the other, as this static top-of-page format illustrates:

```
STATIC_TOP =
This header was generated courtesy of Perl formatting
See Chapter 18 of Pro Perl for details
-------------------------------------------
.
```

Placeholders are defined by either an @ or a ^, followed by a number of <, |, >, or # characters that define the width of the placeholder. Picture lines that contain placeholders must be followed by a data line (possibly with comments in between) that defines the data to be placed into the placeholder when the format is written.

Formats do not support the concept of a variable-width placeholder. The resulting text will always reserve the defined number of characters for the substituted value irrespective of the actual length of the value, even if it is undefined. It is this feature that makes formats so useful for defining structured text output—we can rely on the resulting text exactly conforming to the layout defined by the picture lines. For example, to define a ten-character field that is left justified, we would use

```
This is a ten character placeholder: @<<<<<<<<<
$value_of_placeholder
```

Note that the @ itself counts as one of the characters, so there are nine < characters in the example, not ten. To specify multiple placeholders, we just use multiple instances of @ and supply enough values in the data line to fill them. This example has a left-, center-, and right-justified placeholder:

```
This picture line has three placeholders: @<<<@|||@>>>
$first, $second, $third
```

The second example defines three four-character-wide placeholders. The <, |, and > characters define the justification for fields more than one character wide; we can define different justifications using different characters, as we will see in a moment.

Programmers new to formats are sometimes confused by the presence of @ symbols. In this case, @ has nothing to do with interpolation; it indicates a placeholder. Because of this, we also cannot define a literal @ symbol by escaping it with a backslash, that is, an interpolation feature. In fact, the only way to get an actual @ (or indeed ^) into the resulting string is to substitute it from the data line:

```
# the '@' below is actually a placeholder:
This is a literal '@'
# but we can make it a literal '@' by substituting one in on the data line:
'@'
```

Simple placeholders are defined with the @ symbol. The caret ^ or "continuation" placeholder, however, has special properties that allow it to be used to spread values across multiple output lines. When Perl sees a ^ placeholder, it fills out the placeholder with as much text as it reasonably can and then truncates the text it used from the start of the string. It follows from this that the original variable is altered and that to use a caret placeholder we cannot supply literal text. Further uses of the same variable can then fill in further caret placeholders. For example, this format reformats text into 38 columns with a > prefix on each line:

```
format QUOTE_MESSAGE =
> ^<<<<<<<<<<<<<<<<<<<<<<<<<<<<<<<<<<<
$message
^<<<<<<<<<<<<<<<<<<<<<<<<<<<<<<<<<<<<
$message
^<<<<<<<<<<<<<<<<<<<<<<<<<<<<<<<<<<<<
$message
^<<<<<<<<<<<<<<<<<<<<<<<<<<<<<<<<<<<<
$message
.
```

This creates a format that processes the text in the variable $message into four lines of 40 characters, fitting as many words as possible into each line. When write comes to process this format, it uses the special variable $: to determine how and where to truncate the line. By default it is set to \n- to break on spaces, newlines, or hyphens, which works fine for most plain text.

There are a number of problems with this format—it only handles four lines, and it always fills them out even if the message is shorter than four lines after reformatting. We will see how to suppress redundant lines and automatically repeat picture lines to generate extra ones with the special ~ and ~~ strings shortly.

Justification

It frequently occurs that the width of a field exceeds that of the data to be placed in it. In these cases, we need to decide how the format will deal with the excess, since a fixed-width field cannot shrink (or grow) to fit the size of the data. A structured layout is the entire point of formats. If the data we want to fill the placeholder is only one-character wide, we need no other syntax. As an extreme case, to insert six single-character items into a format, we can use

```
The code is '@@@@@@'
# use first six elements of digits, assumed to be from 0 to 9.
@digits
```

For longer fields, we need to choose how text will be aligned in the field through one of four justification methods, listed in Table 18-6, depending on which character we use to define the width of the placeholder.

Table 18-6. *Placeholder Justification Styles*

Placeholder	Alignment	Example
<	Left justified	@<<<<
>	Right justified	@>>>>
|	Center justified	@||||
#	Right-justified numeric	@####

The <, |, and > justification styles are mostly self-explanatory; they align values shorter than the placeholder width to the left, center, or right of the placeholder. They pad the rest of the field with spaces. (Note that padding with other characters is not supported. If we want to do that, we will have to generate the relevant value by hand before it is substituted.) If the value is the right length in any case, then no justification occurs. If it is longer, then it is truncated on the right irrespective of the justification direction.

The numeric # justification style is more interesting. With only # characters present, it will insert an integer based on the supplied value—for an integer number it substitutes in its actual value, but for a string or the undefined value it substitutes in 0, and for a floating-point number it substitutes in the integer part. To produce a percentage placeholder, for example, we can use the following:

```
Percentage: @##%
$value * 100
```

If, however, we use a decimal point character within the placeholder, then the placeholder becomes a decimal placeholder, with floating-point values point-justified to align themselves around the position of the decimal point:

```
Result (2 significant places): @####.##
$result
```

This provides a very simple and powerful way to align columns of figures, automatically truncating them to the desired level of accuracy at the same time.

If the supplied result is not a floating-point number, then the fractional places are filled in with 0, and for strings and undefined values the ones column is also filled in with 0.

The actual character used by the decimal placeholder to represent the decimal point is defined by the locale, specifically the LC_NUMERIC value of the locale. In Germany, for instance, the conventional symbol to separate the integer and fractional parts is a comma, not a full stop. Formats are in fact the only part of Perl that directly accesses the locale in this way, possibly because of their long history; all other parts of the language adhere to the use locale directive. Although deprecated in modern Perl, we can also use the special variable $# to set the point character.

The final placeholder format is the * placeholder. This creates a raw output placeholder, producing a complete multiple-line value in one go and consequently can only be placed after an @ symbol; it makes no sense in the context of a continuation placeholder since there will never be a remainder for a continuation to make use of. For example:

```
> @* <
$multiline_message
```

In this format definition, the value of $multiline_message is output in its entirety when the format is written. The first line is prefixed with a >, and the last is suffixed with <. No other formatting of any kind is done. Since this placeholder has variable width (and indeed, variable height), it is not often used, since it is effectively just a poor version of print that happens to handle line and page numbering correctly.

Data Lines

Whenever a picture line contains one or more placeholders it must be immediately followed by a data line consisting of one or more expressions that supply the information to fill them. Expressions can be numbers, string values, variables, or compound expressions:

```
format NUMBER =
Question: What do you get if you multiply @ by @?

6, 9
Answer: @#
6*9
.
```

Multiple values can be given either as an array or a comma-separated list:

```
The date is: @###/@#/@#
$year, $month, $day
```

If insufficient values are given to fill all the placeholders in the picture line, then the remaining placeholders are undefined and padded out with spaces. Conversely, if too many values are supplied, then the excess ones are discarded. This behavior changes if the picture line contains ~~ however, as shown later.

If we generate a format using conventional quoted strings rather than the HERE document syntax, we must take special care not to interpolate the data lines. This is made more awkward because in order for the format to compile, we need to use \n to create newlines at the end of each line of the format, including the data lines, and these do need to be interpolated. Separating the format out onto separate lines is probably the best approach, though as this example shows, even then it can be a little hard to follow:

```
# define page width and output filehandle
$page_width = 80;
$output = "STDOUT_TOP";
```

```
# construct a format statement from concatenated strings
$format_st = "format $output = \n".
'Page @<<<'. "\n".
'$='. "\n".
('-'x$page_width). "\n".
".\n";   # don't forget the trailing '.'

# define the format - note we do not interpolate, to preserve '$='
eval $format_st;
```

Note that continuation placeholders (defined by a leading caret) need to be able to modify the original string in order to truncate the start. For this reason, an assignable value such as a scalar variable, array element, or hash value must be used with these fields.

Suppressing Redundant Lines

The format and write functions support two special picture strings that alter the behavior of the placeholders in the same picture line, both of which are applied if the placeholders are all continuation (caret) placeholders.

The first is a single tilde, or ~ character. When this occurs anywhere in a picture line containing caret placeholders, the line is suppressed if there is no value to plug into the placeholder. For example, we can modify the quoting format we gave earlier to suppress the extra lines if the message is too short to fill them:

```
format QUOTE_MESSAGE =
> ^<<<<<<<<<<<<<<<<<<<<<<<<<<<<<<<<<<<
$message
^<<<<<<<<<<<<<<<<<<<<<<<<<<<<<<<<<<<<~
$message
^<<<<<<<<<<<<<<<<<<<<<<<<<<<<<<<<<<<<~
$message
^<<<<<<<<<<<<<<<<<<<<<<<<<<<<<<<<<...~
$message
.
```

In this example, the bottom three picture lines have a ~ suffix, so they will only be used if $message contains sufficient text to fill them after it has been broken up according to the break characters in $:. When the format is written, the tildes are replaced with spaces. Since they are at the end of the line in this case, we will not see them, which is why conventionally they are placed here. If we have spaces elsewhere in the picture line, we can replace one of them with the tilde and avoid the trailing space.

We modify the last picture line to indicate that the message may have been truncated because we know that it will only be used if the message fills out all the subsequent lines. In this case, we have replaced the last three < characters with dots.

The ~ character can be thought of as a zero-or-one modifier for the picture line, in much the same way that ? works in regular expressions. The line will be used if Perl needs it, but it can also be ignored if necessary.

Autorepeating Pattern Lines

If two adjacent tildes appear in a pattern line, then write will automatically repeat the line while there is still input. If ~ can be likened to the ? zero-or-one metacharacter of regular expressions, ~~ can be likened to *, zero-or-more. For instance, to format text into a paragraph of a set width but an unknown number of lines, we can use a format like this:

```
format STDOUT =
^<<<<<<<<<<<<<<<<<<<<<<<<<<<<~~
```

```
$text
.
```

Calling write with this format will take the contents of $text and reformat it into a column 30 characters wide, repeating the pattern line as many times as necessary until the contents of $text are exhausted. Anything else in the pattern line is also repeated, so we can create a more flexible version of the quoting pattern we gave earlier that handles a message of any size:

```
format QUOTE =
>~~^<<<<<<<<<<<<<<<<<<<<<<<<<<<<<<<
$message
.
```

Like ~, the ~~ itself is converted into a space when it is output. It also does not matter where it appears, so in this case we have put it between the > quote mark and the text, to suppress the extra space on the end of the line it would otherwise create.

Note that ~~ only makes sense when used with a continuation placeholder, since it relies on the continuation to truncate the text. Indeed, if we try to use it with a normal @ placeholder, Perl will return a syntax error, since this would effectively be an infinite loop that repeats the first line. Since write cannot generate infinite quantities of text, Perl prevents us from trying.

Formats and Filehandles

Formats are directly associated with filehandles. All we have to do is write to the filehandle, and the associated format is invoked. It might seem strange that we associate a format with a filehandle and then write to the filehandle, rather than specifying which format we want to use when we do the writing, but there is a certain logic behind this mechanism. There are in fact two formats that may be associated with a filehandle. The main one is used by write, but we can also install a top-of-page format that is used whenever Perl runs out of room on the current page and is forced to start a new one. Since this is associated with the filehandle, Perl can use it automatically when we use write rather than needing to be told.

Defining the Top-of-Page Format

Perl allows two formats to be associated with a filehandle. The main format is used whenever we issue a write statement. The top-of-page format, if defined, is issued at the start of the first page and at the top of each new page. This is determined by the special variable $= (length of page) and $- (the number of lines left). Each time we use write, the value of $- increases. When there is no longer sufficient room to fit the results of the next write, a new page is started, a new top-of-page format is written, and only then is the result of the last write issued.

The main format is automatically associated with the filehandle of the same name so that the format MYFORMAT is automatically used when we use write on the filehandle MYFORMAT. Giving it the name of the filehandle with the text _TOP appended to it can similarly associate the top-of-page format. For instance, to assign a main and top-of-page format to the filehandle MYFORMAT, we would use something like this:

```
format MYFORMAT =
...main format definition...
.

# define a format that gives the current page number
format MYFORMAT_TOP =
This is page @<<<
$=
-----------------------
.
```

Assigning Formats to Standard Output

Since standard output is the filehandle most usually associated with formats, we can omit the format name when defining formats.

```
format STDOUT=
The magic word is "@<<<<<<<<<";
$word
.

format STDOUT_TOP=
Page @>
$#
-----------
.
```

We can also omit STDOUT for the main format and simply write

```
format =
The magic word is "@<<<<<<<<<";
$word
.
```

This works because standard output is the default output filehandle. If we change the filehandle with select, format creates a format with the same name as that filehandle instead. The write function also allows us to omit the filehandle; to write out the formats assigned to whatever filehandle is currently selected, we can simply put

```
write;
```

Determining and Assigning Formats to Other Filehandles

We are not constrained to defining formats with the same name as a filehandle in order to associate them. We can also find their names and assign new ones using the special variables $~ and $^.

The special variable $~ ($FORMAT_NAME with use English) defines the name of the main format associated with the currently selected filehandle. For example:

```
$format = $~;
```

Likewise, to set the current format we can assign to $~:

```
# set standard output format to 'MYFORMAT';
$~ = 'MYFORMAT';

use English;
$FORMAT_NAME = 'MYFORMAT';    # more legibly
```

The variable is set to the name of the format, not to the format itself, hence the quotes.

The special variable $^ ($FORMAT_TOP_NAME with use English) performs the identical role for the top-of-page format:

```
# save name of current top-of-page format
$topform = $^;
# assign new top-of-page format
$^ = 'MYFORMAT_TOP';
# write out main format associated with standard out,
# (using top-of-page format if necessary)
write;
# restore original top-of-page format
$^ = $topform;
```

Setting formats on other filehandles using the variables $~ and $^ requires special maneuvering with select to temporarily make the target filehandle the current filehandle:

```
# set formats on a different filehandle
$oldfh = select MYHANDLE;
$~ = 'MYFORMAT';
$^ = 'MYFORMAT_TOP';
select $oldfh;
```

The IO::Handle module (and subclasses like IO::File) provide a simpler object-oriented way of setting reports on filehandles:

```
$fh = new IO::File ("> $outputfile");
...
$fh->format_name ('MYFORMAT');
$fh->format_top_name ('MYFORMAT_TOP');
...
write $fh;   # or $fh->format_write ();
```

Page Control

Perl's reporting system uses several special variables to keep track of line and page numbering. We can use these variables to produce line and page numbers and set them to control how pages are generated. There are four variables of particular interest, and these are listed in Table 18-7.

Table 18-7. *Format Page Control Variables*

Variable	Corresponds To
$=	The page length
$%	The page number
$-	The number of lines remaining
$^L	The formfeed string

$= (or $FORMAT_LINES_PER_PAGE with use English) holds the page length and by default is set to 60 lines. To change the page length, we can assign a new value:

```
$= = 80;   # set page length to 80 lines
```

Or more legibly:

```
use English;
$FORMAT_LINES_PER_PAGE = 80;
```

If we want to generate reports without pages, we can set $= to a very large number. Alternatively, we can redefine $^L to an empty string and avoid (or subsequently redefine to nothing) the "top-of-page" format.

$% (or $FORMAT_PAGE_NUMBER with use English) holds the number of the current page. It starts at 1 and is incremented by one every time a new page is started, which in turn happens whenever write runs out of room on the current page. We can change the page number explicitly by modifying $%, for example:

```
$% = 1;   # reset page count to 1
```

$- (or $FORMAT_LINES_LEFT with use English) holds the number of lines remaining on the current page. Whenever write generates output, it decrements this value by the number of lines in the format. If there are insufficient lines left (the size of the output is greater than the number of lines

left), then $- is set to 0, the value of $% is incremented by one, and a new page is started, starting
with the value of $^L and followed immediately by the top-of-page format, if one is defined. We can
force a page break on the next write by setting $- to 0:

```
$- = 0;    # force a new page on the next 'write'
```

Finally, $^L (or $FORMAT_FORMFEED with use English) is output before the top-of-page format by
write when a new page is started. By default it is set to a formfeed character, \f. See the section
"Creating Footers" for a creative use of $^L.

As an example of using the page control variables, here is a short program that paginates its
input file, adding the name of the file and a page number to the top of each page. It also illustrates
creating a format dynamically with eval so we can define not only the height of the resulting pages,
but also their width.

```perl
#!/usr/bin/perl
# paginate.pl
use warnings;
use strict;
no strict 'refs';
use Getopt::Long;

# get parameters from the user
my $height = 60;  # length of page
my $width = 80;   # width of page
my $quote = "";   # optional quote prefix
GetOptions ('height|size|length:i', \$height,
    'width:i', \$width, 'quote:s', \$quote);
die "Must specify input file" unless @ARGV;

# get the input text into one line, for continuation
undef $/;
my $text = <>;

# set the page length
$= = $height;

# if we're quoting, take that into account
$width -= length($quote);

# define the main page format - a single autorepeating continuation field
my $main_format = "format STDOUT = \n".
                  '^'.$quote.('<' x ($width-1))."~~\n".
                  '$text'. "\n".
                  ".\n";
eval $main_format;

# define the top of page format
my $page_format = "format STDOUT_TOP = \n".
                  '@'.('<' x ($width/2-6)). ' page @<<<'. "\n".
                  '$ARGV,$%'. "\n".
                  '-'.'x$width. "\n".
                  ".\n";
eval $page_format;

# write out the result
write;
```

To use this program, we can feed it an input file and one or more options to control the output, courtesy of the Getopt::Long module, for example:

```
> perl paginate.pl input.pl -w 50 -h 80
```

Creating Footers

Footers are not supported as a concept by the formatting system; there is no "bottom-of-page" format. However, with a little effort we can improvise our own footers. The direct and obvious way is to keep an eye on $- and issue the footer when we get close to the bottom of the page. If the footer is smaller in lines than the output of the main format, we can use something like the following, assuming that we know what the size of output is:

```
print "\nPage $%\n" if $- < $size_of_format;
```

This is all we need to do, since the next attempt to write will not have sufficient space to fit and will automatically trigger a new page. If we want to make sure that we start a new page on the next write, we can set $- to 0 to force it:

```
print ("\nPage $% \n"), $- = 0 if $- < $size_of_format;
```

A more elegant and subtle way of creating a footer is to redefine $^L. This is a lot simpler to arrange but suffers in terms of flexibility since the footer is fixed once it is defined, so page numbering is not possible unless we redefine the footer on each new page.

For example, if we want to put a two-line footer on the bottom of 60-line pages, we can do so by putting the footer into $^L (suffixed with the original formfeed) and then reducing the page length by the size of the footer, in this case to 58 lines:

```
# define a footer.
$footer = ('-'x80). "\nEnd of Page\n";
# redefine the format formfeed to be the footer plus a formfeed
$^L = $footer. "\f";

# reduce page length from default 60 to 58 lines
# if we wanted to be creative we could count the instances of '\n' instead.
$= -= 2;
```

Now every page will automatically get a footer without any tracking or examination of the line count. We still have to add a footer to the last page manually. The number of lines remaining to fill on the last page is held by $-, so this turns out to be trivial:

```
print ("\n" * $-);  # fill out the rest of the page (to 58 lines)
print $footer;      # print the final footer
```

As mentioned earlier, arranging for a changing footer such as a page number is slightly trickier, but it can be done by remembering and checking the value of $- after each write:

```
$lines = $-;
write;
redefine_footer() if $- > $lines;
```

This will work for many cases but will not always work when using ~~, since it may cause write to generate more lines than the page has left before we get a chance to check it.

Combining Reports and Regular Output

It is possible to print both unformatted and formatted output on the same filehandle.

However, while write and print can be freely mixed together, print knows nothing about the special formatting variables such as $=, $-, and $% that track pagination and trigger the top-of-page format. Consequently, we must take care to track line counts ourselves if we want pages to be of even length, by adjusting $- ourselves.

For instance:

```
write;
foreach (@extra_lines) {
    print $_, "\n";
    --$-;    # decrement $-.
}
```

Unfortunately, this solution does not take into account that $- might become negative if there is not enough room left on the current page. Due to the complexities of managing mixtures of write and print, it is often simpler to either use formline or create a special format that is simply designed to print out the information we were using print for.

Generating Report Text with formline

The formline function is a lower-level interface to the same formatting system used by write. formline generates text from a single picture line and a list of values, the result of which is placed into the special variable $^A. For example, this is how we could create a formatted string containing the current time using formline:

```
($sec, $min, $hour) = localtime;
formline '@#/@#/@#', $hour, $min, $sec;
$time = $^A;
print "The time is: $hour:$min.$sec \n";
```

In this case, it would probably be easier to use sprintf, but we can also use formline to create text from more complex patterns. For instance, to format a line of text into an array of text lines wrapped at 20 characters, we could use formline like this:

```
$text = get_text();    # get a chunk of text from somewhere

@lines;
while ($text) {
    formline '^<<<<<<<<<<<<<<<<<<<<', $text;
    push @lines, $^A;
}
```

The formline function is only designed to handle single lines, so it ignores newlines and treats the picture text as a single line. This means that we cannot feed formline a complete format definition and expect it to produce the correct result in $^A.

Strangely, there is no simple way to generate text from write, other than by redirecting filehandles, since write sends its results to a filehandle. However, we can produce a version of write that returns its result instead.

```
sub swrite ($@) {
    my $picture = shift;
    formline ($picture, @_);
    return $^A;
}
```

This function is a friendly version of formline, but it is not a direct replacement for write, since it only operates on a single picture line and expects a conventional list of values as an argument. However, it is convenient and simple to use.

Summary

This chapter dealt with text processing in depth, building on the concepts of regular expressions and interpolation to carry out advanced text manipulation. To begin with, we looked at text processing modules, including Text::Tab, Text::Abbrev, Text::ParseWords, and the versatile Text::Balanced. We also looked at rewrapping text with Text::Wrap and tokenizing it with Text::Soundex.

Source code is an important subclass of text document. We covered Perl's Plain Old Documentation (POD) syntax, and saw how to construct it, format it, render it, and write our own tools to parse it. From here we went on to look at preprocessing source files using a source filter. We covered the Filter::Util::Call module and also saw how to simplify some aspects of filter development with the Filter::Simple module.

Finally, we looked at reports, the "R" in Perl, which provide us with a way to create simple templates to format the way output is rendered. We looked at the format data type, formats and filehandles, format structure (including justification), and page control.

CHAPTER 19

■■■

Object-Oriented Perl

Objects are a way to hide complexity behind an opaque value. Concealed behind the interface it presents to us, the value holds not only data, but also all the code necessary to access, manipulate, and store it. All objects belong to an object *class*, and the class defines what kind of object they are. The code that implements an object's features also belongs to the class, and the objects—sometimes called *object instances*—are simply values that belong to a given class. They "know" what kind of object they are, and therefore which class the subroutines that can be used through them come from. In Perl, an object class is just a package, and an object instance is just a reference that knows its class and references the data that defines the state of that particular instance.

Perl was not originally an object-oriented language; only from version 5 did it acquire the necessary features (symbolic references and packages) to implement them. As a result, Perl's object-oriented features are relatively basic and not compulsory. Perl takes a belt-and-braces approach to object-oriented programming, espousing no particular object-oriented doctrine (of which there are many), but permitting a broad range of different object-oriented styles. Despite this, and arguably because of it, Perl is more powerful as an object-oriented language than it is often given credit for.

Many object-oriented languages take a much stricter line. Being strict is the entire point for some languages. Java, for instance, requires that everything be an object, even the main application. Other languages have very precise views about what kind of object model they support, how multiple inheritance works, how public and private variables and methods are defined, how objects are created, initialized, and destroyed, and so on. Perl's disposition inherits much from languages like Lisp, which combine a deliberately very simple syntax with the ability to extend it in almost any direction. As such, Perl does not endorse any particular model of object-oriented programming, which makes it both extremely flexible and highly disconcerting to programmers used to a different object-oriented style.

Because Perl does not dictate how object-oriented programming should be done, it can leave programmers who expect a more rigorous framework confused, because what they previously considered to be fundamentals of an object-oriented language are now given to them to express and implement as they see fit. However, during the course of this chapter, we hope to show that by learning the basics of how Perl implements objects, a programmer can wield Perl in a highly effective way to implement object-oriented programs.

In this chapter, we introduce object-oriented programming from the Perl perspective. We then go on to using objects (which need not imply an object-oriented program), and then tackle the meat of the chapter—writing object classes, including constructors and destructors, properties and attributes, and single and multiple inheritance. We also take a look at a uniquely Perlish use of objects—mimicking a standard data type by `tieing` it to an object-oriented class. The DBM:: modules are a well-known example, but there are many other interesting uses for tied objects too.

Introducing Objects

Object-oriented programming is an entirely different method of implementing libraries and applications from the traditional or functional approach. Object orientation allows us to cleanly abstract the actual implementation of a library so that it can be easily reused and adapted through inheritance. Although we can achieve the same ends in functional implementations, it is typically a lot harder to maintain. In order to appreciate how Perl implements and provides for object-oriented programming, therefore, a basic grasp of object-oriented concepts is necessary.

Object Concepts

Perl's hands-on approach means that we can strip away a lot of the jargon that tends to accrete around the implementation of object orientation; the lack of any dogmatic adherence to a particular style or mechanism actually reduces the amount of learning a programmer needs to write object-oriented Perl. However, some concepts are fundamental to all object-oriented programming. The following sections are a short discussion of the most important ones in general terms, accompanied by Perl's perspective on them.

Classes

An *object class* provides the implementation of an object. It consists of *class methods*, routines that perform functions for the class as a whole, and *object methods*, routines that perform functions for individual objects (also called *object instances*). It may also contain package variables, or in object-oriented terminology, *class attributes*. The details of the class are hidden behind the interface provided by these methods, in the same way that a functional module hides its implementation from us.

All object classes contain at least one important class method: a constructor that generates new object instances. In addition, it may have a destructor, for tidying up associated resources when an object instance is destroyed.

Perl implements object classes with packages. In fact, a package is just an object class by another name. This basic equivalence is the basis for much of Perl's simple and obvious approach to objects in general. A class method is just a subroutine that takes a package name as its first argument, and an object method is a subroutine that takes an object name as its first argument. Perl automatically handles the passing of this first argument when we use the arrow (->) operator.

Objects

Objects are individual instances of an object class, consisting of an opaque value representing the state of the object but abstracting the details. Because the object implicitly knows what class it belongs to, we can call methods defined in the object class through the object itself, in order to affect the object's state. Objects may contain, within themselves, different individual values called *object attributes* (or sometimes instance attributes).

Perl implements objects through references; the object's state is held by whatever it is that the reference points to, which is up to the object's class. The reference is told what class it belongs to with the bless function, which marks the references as belonging to a particular class. Since a class is a package, method calls on the object (using ->) are translated by Perl into subroutine calls in the package. Perl passes the object as the first argument so the subroutine knows which object to operate on.

The storage of object attributes is up to the actual data type used to store them; typically the data type is a hash variable, and the attributes are simply keys of the hash. Of course, the point of object orientation is that the user of an object does not need to know anything about this.

Inheritance, Multiple Inheritance, and Abstraction

One important concept of object-oriented programming, and the place where objects score significant gains over functional programming, is *inheritance*. An object's classes may inherit methods and class attributes from parent classes, in order to provide some or all of their functionality, a technique also known as *subclassing*. This allows an object class to implement only those features that differentiate it from a more general parent without having to worry about implementing the classes contained in its parent. Inheritance encourages code reuse, allowing us to use tried and tested objects to implement our core features rather than reinventing the wheel for each new task. This is an important goal of any programming environment, and one of the principal motivations behind using object-oriented programming.

Multiple inheritance occurs when a subclass inherits from more than one parent class. This is a contentious issue, since it can lead to different results depending on how parent classes are handled when two classes both support a method that a subclass needs. Accordingly, not all object-oriented languages allow or support it. Some, like Java, permit a class to inherit from two parents, but only in constrained circumstances: one direct parent, one interface implementation. Dynamic inheritance occurs when an object class is able to change programmatically the parent or parents from which it inherits. It also occurs when a new subclass is created on the fly during the course of execution. Again, not all languages allow or support this.

An important element of inheritance is that the subclass does not need to know the details of how the parent class implements its features, only how to use them to implement its own variation—the interface. This gives us *abstraction*, an important aspect of object-oriented programming that allows for easy reuse of code; the parent class should be able to change its implementation without subclasses noticing. Note that this does not mean that the *programmer* of the subclass need know nothing of the parent—any design assumptions made (and hopefully documented) in the parent had better be reflected in the subclass if we expect the outward behavior to remain consistent.

Inheritance in most object-oriented languages happens through some sort of declaration in the class. In Perl, inheritance is supported through a special array that defines "is a" relationships between object classes. Logically enough, it is called @ISA, and it defines what kind of parent class a given subclass is. If anything is in the @ISA array of a package, then the object class defined by that package "is a" derived class of it.

Perl allows for multiple inheritance by allowing an object class to include more than one parent class name in its @ISA array. When a method is not found in the package of an object, its parents are scanned in order of their place in the array until the method is located. If a parent also has an @ISA array, it is searched too. Multiple inheritance is not always a good thing, and Perl's approach to it has problems, but it makes up for it by being blindingly simple to understand.

Inheritance in Perl can also be dynamic, since @ISA has all the properties of a regular Perl array variable, so it can be modified during the course of a program's execution to add new parent classes, remove existing ones, entirely replace the parent class(es), or reorder them.

Public and Private Methods and Data

Both object classes and object instances may have *public* and *private* data and methods. Public data and methods make up the defined interface for the object class and the objects it implements that external code may use. Private data and methods are intended for use only by the object class and its objects themselves (such as supporting methods and private state information). Making parts of an object class private is also known as *encapsulation*, though that is not an exclusively object-oriented concept. Good object-oriented design suggests that all data should be encapsulated (accessed by methods, as opposed to being accessed directly). In other words, there should generally be no need for directly accessible—that is, public—data in a class or object.

Perl does not have any formal definition of public and private data; it operates an open policy whereby all data and methods are visible to the using package. There is no "private" declaration, though my can by used to declare file-scoped variables, which are effectively private. Instead, the using package is expected to abide by the intended and documented interface and not abuse the fact that it can circumvent it if it chooses.

If we really want to, we can enforce various types of privacy (for example, with a closure), but only by implementing it by hand in the object class. Strangely, by not having an explicit policy on privacy, Perl is a lot simpler than many object-oriented languages that do, because dubious concepts like `friend` classes and selective privacy simply do not exist.

Polymorphism

Another concept that is often associated with objects is *polymorphism*. This is the ability of many different object classes to respond to the same request but in different ways. In essence, this means that we can call an object method on an object whose class we do not know precisely and get some form of valid response. The class determines the actual response of the object, but we do not need to know which class the object is contained in, in order to call the method. Inheritance provides a very easy way to create polymorphic classes. By inheriting and overriding methods from a single parent class, many subclasses can behave the same way to the user. Because they inherit a common set of methods, we can know with surety that the parent interface will work for all its subclasses.

In Perl, polymorphism is simply a case of defining two or more methods (subroutines), in different classes (packages) with the same name, and handling the same arguments. A method may then be called on an object instance of any of the classes without needing to know which class the object actually belongs to. So long as each class honors the contract, the calling code does not need to differentiate.

In some cases, we might want to use a method that may or may not exist; either we can attempt the call with -> inside an `eval` or use the special `isa` and `can` methods supported by all objects in order to determine what an object is and isn't capable of. These methods are provided for by the `UNIVERSAL` object, from which all objects (and indeed all Perl code) implicitly inherit.

Overloading

Overloading is the ability of an object class to substitute for existing functionality supplied by a parent class or the language itself. There are two types of overloading, *method overloading* and *operator overloading*.

Method overloading is simple in concept. It occurs whenever a subclass implements a method with the same name as a parent's method. An attempt to call that method on the subclass will be satisfied by the subclass, and the parent class will never see it. Its method is said to have been overloaded. In the context of multiple inheritance, some languages also support parameter overloading, where the correct method can be selected by examining the arguments passed to the method call and comparing it to the arguments accepted by the corresponding method in each parent class.

Operator overloading occurs when an object class implements special methods for the handling of operators defined in the core language. When the language sees that an object is used as an operand of an operator, it replaces the regular use of the operator with the version supplied by the class. For instance, this allows us to "add" objects together using +, even though objects, being opaque values, cannot be added. The object class supplies a meaning for the operator and returns a new object reflecting the result operation.

Perl supports both kinds of overloading. Method overloading is simply a case of defining a subroutine with the same name as the subroutine to be overloaded in the parent. The subclass can still access the parent's method if it wishes, by prefixing the method name with the special `SUPER::` prefix. There is no such thing as parameter overloading in Perl, since its parameter passing mechanism (the @_ array) does not lend itself to that kind of examination. However, a method can select a parent class at run time by analyzing the arguments passed to it. (For those who cannot do without, there are modules on CPAN that provide parameter overloading in Perl. Why build it into the language when it can be added on demand?)

Operator overloading is also supported through the overload pragmatic module. With this module, we can implement an object replacement for any of Perl's built-in operators, including all the arithmetic, logical, assignment, and dereferencing operators.

Adaptability (Also Called Casting or Conversion)

Objects may sometimes be reclassified and assigned to a different class. For instance, a subclass will often use a parent class to create an object, then adjust its properties for its own needs before reclassifying the object as an instance of itself rather than its parent. Objects can also be reclassified en route through a section of code; for example, an object representing an error may be reclassified into a particular kind of error or reclassified into a new class representing an error that has already been handled. All of these operations are instances of dynamic inheritance.

In Perl, objects can be switched into a new class at any time, even into a class that does not exist. We can bless a reference into any class simply by naming the class. If we also create and fill an @ISA array inside this class, then it can inherit from a parent class too, enabling us to create a functional subclass on the fly.

Programming with Objects

Although Perl supports objects, it does not require that we use them exclusively; it is possible and feasible to use objects from otherwise entirely functional applications. Using objects is therefore not inextricably bound up with writing them. So, before delving into implementation, we will take a brief look at using objects from the outsider's perspective, with a few observations on what Perl does behind the scenes.

Creating Objects

All object classes contain at least one method known as a *constructor*—a class method that creates new object instances based on the arguments passed to it. In many object-oriented languages (C++ and Java being prime examples), object creation is performed by a keyword called new. For C++, new has specific meaning in relation to memory allocation, but since Perl already handles this transparently, there is no need to implement a special keyword for constructing objects. Perl allows us to give a constructor any name, since it is just a subroutine. Of course, new is a perfectly valid subroutine name, and so we can use

```
$object = My::Object::Class->new(@args);
```

In deference to other languages that provide a new keyword, Perl also allows us to invert this call and place the new before the package name separated by a space:

```
$object = new My::Object::Class(@args);
```

This statement is functionally identical to the preceding one but bears a stronger resemblance to traditional constructors in other languages. However, since Perl does not give new any special meaning, a constructor method may have any name and take any arguments to initialize itself. We can therefore give our constructor a more meaningful name. We can have multiple constructors too if we like; it is all the same to Perl:

```
$object = old My::Object::Class(@args);
$object = create_from_file My::Object::Class($filename);
$object = empty My::Object::Class ();
```

This alternate syntax is also used by the print statement, which, as we observed back in Chapter 3, is really an object-oriented method of the IO::Handle class that is built into the core language.

Using Objects

The principal mechanism for accessing and manipulating objects is the -> operator. In a non–object-oriented context, this is the dereferencing operator, and we use it on an unblessed reference to access the data it points to. For example, to access a hash by reference:

```
$value = $hashref->{key};
```

However, in object-oriented use, -> becomes a class access operator, providing the means to call class and object methods (depending on whether the left-hand side is a class name or an object) and access properties on those objects. The only distinction is that the right-hand side is now a subroutine name instead of a hash key:

```
$object_result = $object->method(@args);

$class_result = Class::Name->classmethod(@args);
```

The returned results of these calls may be objects (in which case they might be either constructors or simply methods that return the object passed to them) or just regular Perl data types.

Since an object is at heart a reference, the two uses of -> are not as far apart as they might at first seem. If an object is implemented as a hash reference, for example, we can still write

```
$value = $object->{hash_key};
```

The difference is that a blessed reference allows us to call methods because the reference is associated with a package. A regular reference is not associated with anything, and so cannot have anything called through it.

Accessing Properties

Since an object is just a blessed reference, we can access the underlying properties of the object by dereferencing it just like any other reference, as we just saw. In object-oriented terms, this is called accessing the object's attributes (also called properties) directly. If the object is implemented in terms of a hash, the hash key is the name of the property:

```
$value = $object->{property_name};
```

Similarly, we can set a property or add a new one with

```
$object->{property_name} = $value;
```

We can also undef, delete, push, pop, shift, unshift, and generally manipulate the object's properties using conventional list and hash functions. If the underlying data type is different, say an array or even a scalar, we can still manipulate it, using whatever processes are legal for that kind of value.

However, this is really nothing to do with object orientation at all, but rather the normal non–object-oriented dereferencing operator. Perl uses it for object orientation so that we can think of dereferencing an object in terms of accessing an object's public data. In other words, it is a syntactic trick to help keep us thinking in object-oriented terms, even though we are not actually performing an object-oriented operation at heart.

One major disadvantage of accessing an object's data directly is that we break the interface defined by the object class. The class has no ability to control how we access the object's data; neither can it spot attempts to access invalid properties or set invalid values. Worse, it breaks the rules of good object-oriented programming, because our code is now dependent on this implementation detail. If the object implementation changes to use an array instead of a hash, or simply renames the keys it uses, our code will break. It is better to use methods defined by the class to access and store properties on its objects whenever possible. (These methods are called *accessors* and *mutators* in object-oriented parlance.) The object should be an abstract opaque data type.

> ■**Note** One exception to this rule is for performance reasons, when object methods that do no more than return a property value are called very frequently—consider an object class that manages sets of other objects numbering in the thousands. In this case, accessing the property through the hash key saves much time by avoiding thousands of method calls to an accessor method. However, such use of a class should be documented by the programmer to indicate that direct access is valid for the nominated key, and that the name of the property will not change—that is, the name of the hash key is part of the documented interface of the class. This guarantee does not have to extend to all properties of the class, just those for which direct access is desirable.

Calling Class Methods

A class method is a subroutine defined in the class, which operates on a class as a whole, rather than a specific object of that class. The most common type of class method is a constructor, which asks the class to create a new instance of an object, but any method that performs a function on behalf of the class, such as setting a piece of global information (that is, class data) used by all instances of the class, is a class method too.

To call a class method, we use the -> operator on the package name of the class, which we give as a bare, unquoted string, just as we do with use:

```
$result = My::Object::Class->classmethod(@args);
```

The inverted syntax we used before will also work with any other class method. The preceding statement can again be rewritten to the equivalent:

```
$result = classmethod My::Object::Class(@args);
```

Although universally applicable, this syntax should only be used for constructors, where its ordering makes logical sense. (Think of constructors with names like cloned, cached, or encoded for an idea of how classes with multiple constructors can take advantage of this syntax.)

The subroutine that implements the class method is called with the arguments supplied by us, plus the package name, which is passed first. In other words, this class method call and the following subroutine call are handled similarly for classes that do not inherit:

```
# method call - correct object-oriented syntax
My::Class->method(@args);

# subroutine call - does not handle inheritance
My::Class::method('My::Class', @args);
```

> ■**Note** Many object-oriented languages implement method calls with the same underlying mechanic but conceal the passing of the object into the method, instead representing it with a keyword such as this. Perl dispenses with this special keyword on the grounds that it would redundantly increase the complexity of the language.

For classes that do not inherit, Perl uses the @ISA array to search for a matching method if the class in which the method is looked for does not implement it. This is because the -> operator has an additional important property that differentiates a method call from a subroutine call. A subroutine call has no such magic associated with it.

It might seem redundant that we pass the package name to a class method—after all, it has no instance data to make it special—since the method surely already knows what package it is in and could refer to it with __PACKAGE__ even without knowing. Again, however, this is only true for classes that do not inherit. If a parent method is called because a subclass did not implement a class method (a result of using the -> operator), then the package name passed will be that of the subclass, not that of the parent. This is crucial, because it means that the parent method can call another method defined in the parent but overloaded by the subclass, in which case it is the version in the subclass that gets called.

Calling Object Methods

An object method is a subroutine defined in the class that operates on a particular object instance. To call an object method, we use the -> operator on an object of a class that supports that method:

```
$result = $object->method(@args);
```

The subroutine that implements the object method is called with the argument we supply, preceded by the object itself (a blessed reference, and therefore a scalar). The following calls are nearly, but not quite, the same:

```
# method call - correct object-oriented syntax
$object->method(@args);

# subroutine call - does not handle inheritance
My::Object::Class::method($object, @args);
```

Just as with class methods, if the package into which the object is blessed does not provide the named method, the -> operator causes Perl to search for it in any and all parent classes, as defined by the @ISA array.

Nesting Method Calls

If the return value from a method (class or object) is another object, we can call a second method on it directly. This allows us to chain method calls together:

```
print "The top card is ", $deck->card(0)->fullname;
```

This particular chain of method calls is from the Game::Deck example, which we provide later in the chapter. It prints out the name of the playing card on the top of the deck of playing cards represented by the $deck object. Game::Deck supplies the card method, which returns a playing card object. In turn, the playing card object (Game::Card, not that we need to know the class) provides the fullname method. We will return to this subject again when we cover "has-a" versus "is-a" relationships.

Determining the Class of an Object

An object is a blessed reference. Calling the ref function on an object returns not the actual data type of the object, but the class into which it was blessed:

```
$class = ref $object;
```

If we really need to know the actual underlying data type—which in a well-designed object-oriented application should usually be never, but it can be handy for debugging—we can use the reftype subroutine supplied by the attributes or Attribute::Handlers modules. See the section "References" in Chapter 5 for details.

However, knowing what class an object belongs to does not always tell us what we want to know; for instance, we cannot easily use it to determine if an object belongs to a subclass of a given parent class, or even find out if it supports a particular method or not. Fortunately, Perl provides a way to determine these inherited characteristics.

Determining Inherited Characteristics

Determining the nature and abilities of an object is a common requirement, so Perl provides the UNIVERSAL object class, which all objects automatically inherit from (and, in fact, all modules, object-oriented or not). UNIVERSAL is a small class that contains only three methods for identifying the class, capabilities, and version of an object or object class. Because Perl likes to keep things simple, this class is actually implemented in Perl code as a module in the standard library.

Determining an Object's Ancestry

The isa method, provided by UNIVERSAL to all objects, allows us to determine whether an object belongs to a class or a subclass of that class, either directly or through a long chain of inheritance. Consider this example:

```
if ($object->isa("My::Class")) {
    $class = ref $object;
    if ($class eq "My::Class") {
        print "Object is of class My::Class \n";
    } else {
        print "Object is a subclass of My::Class \n";
    }
}
```

We can also use isa on a class name or string variable containing a class name:

```
$is_child = My::Object::Subclass->isa("MyObjectClass");
$is_child = $packagename->isa($otherpackagename);
```

These statements return true if the object or class on which the isa method is called is either in the same class or a subclass of that class (as determined by the contents of @ISA for the class and the @ISA of each successive parent in the ancestry of the class).

Before writing class names into our code, however, we should consider the issue of code maintenance. Explicitly hard-coding class names is an obstacle to portability and can trip up otherwise functional code if used in an unexpected context. If the class name is derived programmatically, it is more acceptable. For example:

```
$is_child = $luke->isa(ref $vader); # object in class or subclass
```

Since isa searches the @ISA, it needs to do some work to return an answer to us. For a single call, this time is probably insignificant, but if we want to repeatedly analyze the ancestry of an object class, we might be better off extracting the complete ancestry to start with and recording it for later use. Fortunately, we don't need to do this ourselves, as this is what the Class::ISA module does. This is how we can retrieve the complete ancestry of an object class as a list of packages:

```
my @ancestry = Class::ISA::super_path(__PACKAGE__);
```

Or:

```
my @ancestry=__PACKAGE__->Class::ISA::super_path();
```

The list returned will contain all the ancestors of the requested package—in this case the current package, as determined by __PACKAGE__. It does not contain the UNIVERSAL package from which all objects implicitly inherit, neither does it contain the package for which the request was issued. To add the latter, we simply replace super_path with self_and_super_path, or even more simply just prefix the array with the package name. For instance, to find the full ancestry of an object:

```
my @full_ancestry=(Class::ISA::self_and_super_path(ref $object), 'UNIVERSAL');
```

Alternatively, we can extract a hash of class names and versions; the value of each hash element is derived by calling the VERSION method on each class (which in turn inherits from UNIVERSAL::VERSION and looks for $VERSION if not defined otherwise). The value is undefined if the package does not provide a version:

```
my %versions=Class::ISA::self_and_super_versions(__PACKAGE__);
foreach (sort keys %versioned) {
    print "$_ version ",
          (defined($versions{$_}) ? $versions{$_} : "undefined"),
          "\n";
}
```

Determining an Object's Capabilities

Knowing an object's class and being able to identify its parents does not tell us whether or not it supports a particular method. For polymorphic object classes, where multiple classes provide versions of the same method, it is often more useful to know what an object can do rather than what its ancestry is. The UNIVERSAL class supplies the can method to find out:

```
if ($object->can('method')) {
    return $object->method(@args);
}
```

If the method is not found in either the object's class or any of its parents, can will return undef. Otherwise, it returns a code reference to the method that was found:

```
if ($methodref = $object->can('method')) {
    $object->$methodref(@args);
}
```

We can also use can on an object class to determine whether it or any of its ancestors provides a specified method:

```
foreach (@methods) {
    $can{$_} = My::Object::Class->can('method');
}
```

Again, the package name may also be given in a string variable. This is permitted even under strict references, though we will need to relax this restriction if we want to actually call the method named in the variable:

```
$result = $package->$methodname(@args)
  if $package->can($methodname);
```

Alternatively, we can simply try to call the method and see if it works or not, wrapping the call in an eval to prevent it from generating a fatal error:

```
$result = eval {$object->method(@args)};
if ($@) {
    # error - method did not exist
}
```

It is worth noting that this will have quite a different effect if an AUTOLOAD subroutine is present in the class or any parent class. We cover autoloading in object classes later in the chapter.

Determining an Object's Version

The final method provided by the UNIVERSAL object is VERSION, which looks for a package variable called $VERSION in the class on which it is called:

```perl
# version of a class
my $package_version = $packagename->VERSION;

# version of an object's class
my $object_version = $object->VERSION;

# test version
if ($packagename->VERSION < $required_version) {
    die "$packagename version less than $required_version";
}
```

In practice, we usually don't need to call VERSION directly, because the use and require statements do it for us, providing we supply a numeric value rather than an import list after a package name:

```perl
# use class only if it is at least version 1
require My::Object::Class 1.00;
```

Note that use differs from require in that, apart from using an implicit BEGIN block, it imports from the package as well, if an import method is available. However, since an object-oriented class should rarely define anything for export—it breaks the interface and causes problems for inheritance—the import mechanism is usually used to configure the class at load time instead, if it is used at all.

However, in some cases we can use VERSION to alter behavior depending on the version of another module. For instance, we can use a new and improved implementation of a method with more recent versions of the other module and resort to a previous one for older versions. For example, here is a hypothetical object having a value assigned to one of its attributes. The old class did not provide an accessor method for this attribute, so we are forced to access the attribute directly from the underlying hash. From version 1 onward all attributes are accessed by method:

```perl
if ($object->VERSION < 1.00) {
    # old version - set attribute directly
    $object->{'attribute'} = $value;
} else {
    # new version - use the provided method instead
    $object->attribute($value);
}
```

Note that we could have done the same thing with can, but this is slower since it tests the entire object hierarchy of parents looking for a method. It is also less clear, since without additional comments it is not obvious why we would be checking for the availability of the method in the first place. In these cases, checking the version is the better approach.

Writing Object Classes

Writing an object class is no more difficult than writing a package, just with slightly different rules. Indeed, an object class is just a package by a different name. Like packages, object classes can spread across more than one file, but more often than not an object class is implemented in a single module with the same name (after translation into a pathname) as the package that implements it.

The first and most obvious difference between a package and an object class is that the latter usually has at least one constructor method. In addition, all the subroutines take an object or a class name as a first parameter. The package may also optionally define a DESTROY block for destroying objects, analogous to the END block in ordinary packages.

A final difference, and arguably one of the most crucial, is that object classes can inherit methods from one or more parent classes, as we will see.

Constructors

The most important part of any object class is its constructor: a class method whose job it is to generate new instances of objects. Typically the main (or only) constructor of an object class is called new, so we can create new objects with any of the following statements:

Using traditional object-oriented syntax:

```
$object = new My::Object::Class;
$object = new My::Object::Class('initial', 'data', 'for', 'object');
```

Or, using class method call syntax:

```
$object = My::Object::Class->new();
$object = My::Object::Class->new('initial', 'data', 'for', 'object');
```

This new method is just a subroutine that accepts a class name as its first parameter (supplied by the -> operator) and returns an object. At the heart of any constructor is the bless function. When given a single argument of a reference, bless marks it as belonging to the current package. Here is a fully functional (but limited, as we will see in a moment) constructor that illustrates it in action:

```
#Class.pm
package My::Object::Class;
use strict;

sub new {
    my $self = {};  # create a reference to a hash
    bless $self;    # mark reference as object of this class
    return $self;   # return it.
}
```

The problem with this simple constructor is that it does not handle inheritance. With a single argument, bless puts the reference passed to it into the current package. However, the constructor may have been called by a subclass, in which case the class to be blessed into is the subclass, not the class that the constructor is defined in. Consequently, the single argument form of bless is rarely, if ever, used. Instead, correctly written object classes use the two-argument version of bless to bless the new object into the class passed as the first argument. This enables inheritance to work correctly:

```
sub new {
    my $class = shift;
    my $self = {};
    bless $self, $class;
    return $self;
}
```

Or, equivalently but much more tersely:

```
sub new {
    return bless {}, shift;
}
```

We can initialize an object when we create it by passing arguments to the constructor. Here is a package that implements the bare essentials of a playing card class. It takes two additional parameters—a name and a suit:

```
# card1.pm
package Game::Card;
use strict;
```

```perl
sub new {
    my ($class, $name, $suit) = @_;
    my $self = bless {}, $class;

    $self->{name} = $name;
    $self->{suit} = $suit;
    return $self;
}

1;
```

The underlying representation of the object is a hash, so we store attributes as hash keys. We could also check that we actually get passed a name and suit, but in this case we are going to handle the possibility that a card has no suit (a joker, for example) or even no name (in which case it is, logically, a blank card). A user of this object could now access the object's properties (in a non–object-oriented way) through the hash reference:

```perl
#!/usr/bin/perl
# ace.pl
use warnings;
use strict;

use Game::Card;

my $card = new Game::Card1('Ace', 'Spades');
print $card->{name};   # produces 'Ace';
$card->{suit} = 'Hearts';   # change card to the Ace of Hearts
```

Just because we can access an object's properties like this does not mean we should. If we changed the underlying data type of the object (as we are about to do), this code will break. A better way is to use *accessor* and *mutator* methods, which we cover in the appropriately titled section "Accessors and Mutators" shortly.

Choosing a Different Underlying Data Type

Objects are opaque values implemented in terms of references, so we are free to choose any type of reference as the basis for an object class. The usual choice is a hash, since this provides a simple way to store arbitrary data by key; it also fits well with the "properties" or "attributes" of objects, the named values that can be set and retrieved on objects. But other types of reference are possible too.

Using an Array

The class that follows uses an array as its underlying implementation, with a constructor that returns a blessed array reference:

```perl
# Card.pm
package Game::Card;
use strict;

use Exporter;

our @ISA = qw(Exporter);
our @EXPORT = qw(NAME SUIT);

use constant NAME => 0;
use constant SUIT => 1;
```

```perl
sub new {
    my ($class, $name, $suit) = @_;
    my $self = bless [], $class;

    $self->[NAME] = $name;
    $self->[SUIT] = $suit;
    return $self;
}

1;
```

This object is functionally identical to the hash-based one (although, since at this point it belongs to a class that only implements a constructor, not a terribly useful one), but it has a different internal representation. In this simple example, we want to allow users to access properties directly but not with an explicit numeric index, so we export constants to represent the attributes. Now the code to use the class looks like this. (Note that by accessing the object properties directly we are forced to change the code that uses the object. This is why methods are better, as we mentioned earlier.)

```perl
#!/usr/bin/perl
# arrayuse.pl
use warnings;
use strict;

use Game::Card;    # imports 'NAME' and 'SUIT'

my $card = new Game::Card('Ace', 'Spades');
print $card->[NAME];    # produces 'Ace'
$card->[SUIT] = 'Hearts';    # change card to the Ace of Hearts
print " of ", $card->[SUIT];    # produces ' of Hearts'
```

The advantage of the array-based object is that arrays are a lot faster to access than hashes are, so performance is improved. The disadvantage is that it is very hard to reliably derive a subclass from an array-based object class because we need to know what indices are taken and which are safe to use. Though this is possible, it requires extra effort and outweighs the benefits of avoiding a hash. It also makes the implementation uglier, which is usually a sign that we are on the wrong track. For objects that we do not intend to use as parent classes, however, arrays can be an effective choice.

Using a Typeglob

We can also create an object based on a typeglob and use it to provide object-oriented methods for a filehandle. Indeed, this is exactly the approach taken by the IO::Handle class, which is the basis of object-oriented filehandle classes such as IO::File, IO::Dir, and IO::Socket.

Here is the actual constructor used by the IO::Handle module, with additional comments:

```perl
sub new {
    # determine the passed class, by class method, object method,
    # or preset it to 'IO::Handle'.
    my $class = ref($_[0]) || $_[0] || "IO::Handle";
    # complain if no or more than one argument was passed
    @_ == 1 or croak "usage: new $class";
    # create an anonymous typeglob (using gensym from the Symbol module)
    my $io = gensym;
    # bless it into the appropriate subclass of 'IO::Handle'
    bless $io, $class;
}
```

Perl automatically dereferences the reference to a filehandle contained in a typeglob when it is passed to a file handling function, so we can pass the objects returned from this handle to Perl's IO functions, and they will use them just as if they were regular filehandles.

Using a Scalar

Limited though it might seem, we can also use a scalar to implement an object. For instance, here is a short but functional "document" object constructor, which takes a filehandle as an optional argument:

```
# Document.pm
package Document;
use strict;

# scalar constructor
sub new {
    my $class = shift;

    my $self;
    if (my $fh = shift) {
        local $/ = undef;
        $$self = <$fh>;
    }

    return bless $self, $class;
}
```

We can extend this class to implement methods that operate on text, but we hide the details behind the object. As an added benefit, we can pass the object reference instead of the text data, which can be significantly more efficient if there is a lot of data. As we will see later, we can implement a method to overload Perl's string context evaluation for the class so that when printed (for example), the object reference behaves exactly like a regular scalar variable containing the same text.

Using a Subroutine

Finally, we can also use a subroutine as our object implementation, blessing a reference to the subroutine to create an object. In order to do this, we have to generate and return an anonymous subroutine on the fly in our constructor. This might seem like a lot of work, but it provides us with a way to completely hide the internal details of an object from prying eyes. We will see an example of this kind of object later in the chapter under the section "Keeping Data Private."

Methods

As we have already observed, methods are just subroutines that are designed to be called with the -> operator. There are two broad types:

- Class methods perform tasks related to the class as a whole and are not tied to any specific object instance.
- Object methods perform a task for a particular object instance.

Although in concept these are fundamentally different ideas, Perl treats both types of method as just slightly different subroutines, which differ only in the way that they are called and in the way they process their arguments. With only minor adjustments to our code, we can also create methods that will operate in either capacity and even as a subroutine too, if the design supports it.

Class Methods

A *class method* is a method that performs a function for the class as a whole. Constructors, which we have already seen examples of, are a common example, and frequently they are the only class methods an object class provides. Here is another, which sets a pair of global resources that apply to all objects of the class:

```perl
$MAX_INSTANCES = 100;

sub set_max {
    my ($class, $max) = @_;
    $MAX_INSTANCES = $max;
}

sub get_max {
    return $MAX_INSTANCES;
}
```

We would call these class methods from our own code with

```perl
My::Object::Class->set_max(1000);
print "Maximum instances: ", My::Object::Class->get_max();
```

Setting and returning class data like this is probably the second most common use for a class method after constructors. Only class-level operations can be performed by a class method, therefore all other functions will be performed by object methods.

A special case of a class method that can set class data is the import method, which we dwelt on in the previous chapter. We will take another look at import methods when we come to discuss class data in more detail later on in the chapter.

Object Methods

An object method does work for a particular object, and receives an object as its first argument. Traditionally we give this object a name like $self or $this within the method, to indicate that this is the object for which the method was called. Like many aspects of object-oriented programming in Perl (and Perl programming in general), it is just a convention, but a good one to follow. Other languages are stricter; a variable called self or sometimes this is automatically provided and so we don't have a choice about the name.

Here is a pair of object methods that provide a simple object-oriented way to get and set properties (also known as attributes, but either way they are values) on an object. In this case the object is implemented as a hash, so within the class this translates into setting and getting values from the hash:

```perl
# get a property - read only
sub get {
    my ($self, $property) = @_;

    return $self->{$property}; # undef if no such property!
}

# set a property - return the old value
sub set {
    my ($self, $property, $value) = @_;
    $oldvalue = $self->property if exists $self->{$property};
    $self->{$property} = $value;
    return $oldvalue; # may be undef;
}
```

In practice, the users of our objects could simply dereference them and get to the hash values directly. However, we do not want to encourage this since it bypasses our interface. So instead we provide some methods to do it for them. These methods are still very crude though, since they do not check whether a property is actually valid or not. We will look at some better ways of handling properties later.

As a more practical example, here is a pair of search methods that belong to the Document object class we created a constructor for earlier, along with the constructor and the rest of the package, to make it a complete example. Note that the wordsearch method itself makes an object-oriented call to the search method to carry out the actual work:

```perl
# Document.pm
package Document;
use strict;

# scalar constructor
sub new {
    my $class = shift;

    my $self;
    if (my $fh = shift) {
        local $/ = undef;
        $$self = <$fh>;
    }

    return bless $self, $class;
}

# search a document object
sub search {
    my ($self, $pattern) = @_;

    my @matches = $$self =~ /$pattern/sg;
    return @matches;
}
# search and return words
sub wordsearch {
    my ($self, $wordbit) = @_;

    my $pattern = '\b\w*'.$wordbit.'\w*\b';
    return $self->search($pattern);
}

1;
```

We can use this object class to perform simple searches on documents read in by the constructor, in an object-oriented style:

```perl
#!/usr/bin/perl
# search.pl
use warnings;
use strict;

use IO::File;
use Document;

my $fh = new IO::File('file.txt');
my $document = new Document($fh);
```

```
# find words containing e or t
print join(' ', $document->wordsearch('[et]'));
```

If the file file.txt contains this text:

```
This is a file of text to
test the Document object
on.
```

The program produces

```
file text to test the Document object
```

This is not a very well-developed object class; it does not allow us to create an object from anything other than a filehandle, and it needs more methods to make it truly useful. However, it is the beginning of a class we could use to abstract simple text operations on documents. Already it has removed a lot of the ugliness of regular expression code and abstracted it behind the class implementation, with relatively little effort.

Multiple-Context Methods

Class methods expect a package name as their first argument, whereas object methods expect an object. Other than this, however, they are identical. Since we can determine an object's class by using ref, it's easy to write a method that works as both a class and an object method.

The most common kind of method we can develop with this approach is a class method that is adapted to work from objects as well, by extracting the class of the object from it using ref and using that instead. For example:

```
sub classmethod {
    my $self = shift;
    my $class = (ref $self)?(ref $self):$self;
    ...
}
```

Or, more tersely, using a logical ||:

```
sub classmethod {
    my $self = shift;
    my $class = ref $self || $self;
    ...
}
```

Or, even more tersely:

```
sub classmethod {
    my $class = (ref $_[0]) || $_[0];
    ...
}
```

The methods that use this trick the most are constructors that allow us to create a new object from an old one. This allows users to create new objects without even knowing exactly what they are—abstraction taken to the extreme. Here is a version of the Game::Card constructor that does this:

```
sub new {
    my ($class, $name, $suit) = @_;
    $class = (ref $class) || $class;

    $self = bless {}, $class;
```

```
    $self->{name}= $name;
    $self->{suit} = $suit;

    return $self;
}
```

We can also create a subroutine that can be called as a subroutine, in addition to being called as a method. This takes a little more thought, since the first argument is whatever we pass to the subroutine when we use it as such. If the subroutine gets no arguments at all, it knows it must have been called as a subroutine and not a method. For example, if a constructor takes no initialization data, we can do this:

```
# a constructor that may be called as a subroutine
sub new {
    my $class = (ref $_[0]) || $_[0] || __PACKAGE__;
    return bless {}, $class;
}
```

The first line of this subroutine translates as "if we were passed an object, use the class returned as its reference; otherwise, if we were passed anything at all use that as the class, we must have been called as a subroutine, so use the name of the package we are in." We can construct an object from this subroutine using any of the following means:

```
# as class method:
$object = My::Flexible::Constructor::Class->new;
$object = new My::Flexible::Constructor::Class;

# as object method:
$object = $existing_flexible_object->new;

# as subroutine:
$object = My::Flexible::Constructor::Class::new;
```

Here is another version of the Game::Card constructor that also handles being called as a subroutine. Because it takes additional arguments, we have to make some assumptions in order to work out what the first argument is. In this case we will assume that the class name, if supplied, will start with Game::. This is a limitation, but one we are willing to accept in this design:

```
sub new {
    my ($class, $name, $suit) = @_;
    $class = (ref $class) || $class;

    # check for the first argument and adjust for subroutine call
    unless ($class =~ /^Game::/) {
        ($class, $name, $suit) = (__PACKAGE__, $class, $name);
    }

    $self = bless {}, $class;
    $self->{name} = $name;
    $self->{suit} = $suit;
    return $self;
}
```

Of course, whether or not this is actually worth doing depends on whether we actually expect a method to be called as a subroutine. If this is not part of the design of our object class, we should probably avoid implementing it, just to discourage non–object-oriented usage.

Object Data

Object properties, also called object attributes, are values that are stored within the object. We do not necessarily know how they are stored, but we know what they are because the object class documentation will (or at least, should) tell us.

If we know the object's underlying implementation, we can access and set these values directly. The attribute becomes just an array element or hash value:

```
print $card->{suit};
$card->{name} = 'Queen';
```

This is very bad, however, for several reasons. First, since we are bypassing the object class by not calling a method to do this, the object will have no knowledge of what we are doing. Hence it cannot react or correct us if we do something unexpected, like add a season attribute. The design of this class is not supposed to include an attribute for season, but it has no way of knowing what we are doing. Second, if the names of the attributes change, or the implementation alters in any way, we may find that our code breaks. For instance, if we alter the class to use an array rather than a hash as its underlying data type, all our code will instantly break.

Both problems are symptomatic of violating the principle of *encapsulation*, which dictates that the implementation of the object should be hidden behind the interface. They derive from the fact that we, as users of the class, are determining how the object is accessed, when we should really be using an interface provided for us by the class. In other words, we should be using object methods to both get and set the values of the object's attributes.

Tip A related concept to both class and object data is the idea of private class and object data. Perl does not provide a strict mechanism for enforcing privacy, preferring that we respect the design of the object class and don't attempt to work around the provided interface. For cases where we do want to keep data private, we can resort to several options, which we will cover a little later in the chapter.

Accessors and Mutators

The methods that are provided to get and set object attributes are known in object-oriented circles as *accessors* and *mutators*. Despite this jargon, they are really just subroutines that set values in a hash, array, or whatever data type we used to implement the object.

Here is an example of accessor and mutator methods for the suit attribute of the Game::Card class (we can just duplicate them for the name attribute):

```
# get passed card object and return suit attribute
sub get_suit ($) {
    return shift->{suit};
}

# set suit attribute on passed card object
sub set_suit ($$) {
    $_[0]->{suit} = $_[1];
}
```

Note that the prototypes here are purely for our reading benefit. While Perl accepts them, the interpreter does not know, at the time it compiles the call, which object class will actually be called as a result. Consequently, Perl cannot verify that the prototype is correct. If we were to call the method as a subroutine without using ->, the prototype would be honored, but, of course, we would lose the ability to inherit. (This limitation of prototypes will be lifted in Perl 6.)

Having separate accessor and mutator methods can be a little awkward, however, especially if we have a lot of attributes to deal with. An object with 20 possible attributes needs 40 subroutine definitions to handle them. A popular alternative is to combine accessors and mutators into one method, using the number of arguments passed to determine what to do. For example:

```perl
sub suit ($;$) {
    my ($self, $suit) = @_;

    if ($suit) {
        my $oldsuit = $self->{suit};
        $self->{suit} = $suit;
        return $oldsuit;
    }

    return $self->{suit};
}
```

This accessor/mutator method gets the current value of the suit attribute if no value is passed or sets it if one is. As a bonus, it also makes a note of and returns the old value of the attribute. We do not need to check whether the attribute exists because we know (because we wrote the class and defined the behavior of its interface) that the constructor always sets the hash keys up, even if they have undefined values.

This method does not allow us to unset the suit either, in this case intentionally. If we want to permit the suit to be unset, we will have to check to see if we were passed a second argument of undef as opposed to no second argument at all. We can do that by replacing the line

```perl
if ($suit) {
```

with

```perl
if (scalar(@_)>1) {
```

Or, more tersely:

```perl
if ($#_) {
```

Either replacement checks that at least two arguments were passed to the method, without checking what the second argument is, so undef can be passed as the new attribute value, as can an empty string. However, since the fullname method concatenates this attribute into a string, we probably do not want to allow undef, so this is probably the best variation to use:

```perl
sub suit ($;$) {
    my ($self, $suit) = @_;

    if (defined $suit) {
        my $oldsuit = $self->{suit};
        $self->{suit} = $suit;
        return $oldsuit;
    }

    return $self->{suit};
}
```

This will allow an empty string to set the attribute, but not undef.

Generic Accessors/Mutators

Combining accessors and mutators into one method is an improvement over the case of separate accessors and mutators methods, at least in terms of the number of subroutines we define, but it comes at the cost of increased code complexity.

We do not really want to have to repeat the same subroutine 20 times for each attribute we might want to set or get. However, since all the attributes are essentially just different cases of key-value pairs, we can write one generic accessor/mutator and make all the actual attribute methods wrappers for it, as this example demonstrates (again the prototype is purely for show):

```perl
sub _property ($$;$) {
    my ($self, $attr, $value) = @_;

    if (defined $value) {
        my $oldv = $self->{$attr};
        $self->{$attr} = $value;
        return $oldv;
    }

    return $self->{$attr};
}

sub suit ($;$) { return shift->_property('suit', @_); }
sub name ($;$) { return shift->_property('name', @_); }
```

Now each new method we want to add requires just one line of code. Better still, the relationship between the name of the method and the name of the hash key has been reduced to one single instance. The setting and getting of attributes is also fully abstracted now. Subclasses that make use of a parent class containing this method can set and get their own properties without needing to know how or where they are stored. This is a very attractive benefit for a properly written object class.

The underscore at the start of _property is meant to imply that this subroutine is not meant for public consumption: it is a private method for the use of the class only. Perl does not enforce this, but by naming it this way (and not including it in the user documentation), we make our intention clear. If a user of the class chooses to ignore the design and use it anyway, they cannot say they have not been warned.

Having a generic accessor/mutator method gives us great power to develop our object class. Anything we implement in this method will apply to all attributes supported by the object. As an example, here is another version that allows new attributes to be created, but only if another force flag is added. We also add a nonfatal flag to determine whether or not an attempt to set a nonexistent attribute is fatal:

```perl
sub _property ($$;$$$) {
    my ($self, $attr, $value, $force, $nonfatal) = @_;

    if (defined $value) {
        if ($force || exists $self->{$attr}) {
            my $oldv = $self->{$attr};
            $self->{$attr} = $value;
            return $oldv;
        } else {
            croak "Attempt to set non-existent attribute '$attr'"
                unless $nonfatal;
            return undef;
        }
    }

    return (exits $self->{$attr})?$self->{$attr}:undef;
}
```

To handle fatal errors, we have made use of croak, from the Carp module; we will need to add a use Carp; line to our object class for it to work. As we covered in Chapter 16, croak reports errors in the context of the caller rather than the place at which the error occurs. This is very useful in packages, and object classes are no exception.

If we are using accessors and mutators for attribute access, we should use them everywhere, including inside the object itself. Here is another version of the constructor for the Game::Card class, written to use the methods of the class rather than initializing them directly. We have also added a prototype (purely for documentation) at the same time:

```perl
sub new ($;$$) {
    my ($class, $name, $suit) = @_;
    $class = (ref $class) || $class;

    my $self = bless {}, $class;
    $self->name($name);
    $self->suit($suit);
    return $self;
}
```

This further protects the object class against alterations, this time of itself. However, it does come at a performance penalty of an additional subroutine call. For the preceding constructor, this is minor and acceptable, but if we are writing a method that uses a loop to access or modify attributes, we may want to compromise and access the attributes directly (only because we're inside the object class) for speed.

Class Data

Class data is associated with a class as a whole, rather than with an individual object, and is used to define properties that affect the class as a whole. This can include things like global constants that never change or changing values like serial numbers or a maximum limit on the number of permitted objects.

As an example, here is an object class that generates serial numbers for objects. It keeps a record of the next serial number in the start key of the global variable %conf and increments it each time a new object is created:

```perl
# extract from Serial.pm
package Serial;
use strict;

use Carp;

our %conf = (
    'start'     => 1,
    'increment' => 1,
);

sub new {
    my $class = (ref $_[0]) || $_[0];
    $conf{start} = $_[1] if defined $_[1];

    my $self=bless {}, $class;
    $self->{serial} = $conf{start};
    $conf{start} += $conf{increment};
    return $self;
}

sub serial {
    return shift->{serial};
}

1;
```

Having built this class, we can use it to create new Serial objects, as this short script does. If we pass in a serial number, the count is reset to that point:

```
#!/usr/bin/perl
# serial1.pl
use warnings;
use strict;

use Serial;

my @serials;
foreach (1..10) {
    push @serials, new Serial;
}

print $serials[4]->serial, "\n";
my $serial = new Serial(2001);
print $serial->serial, "\n";
```

The value of the two serial numbers displayed by this program, produces the following output:

```
5
2001
```

This shows us that the fifth serial number (index 4, counting from zero) is 5, as we would expect if the loop generated successive serial numbers starting from 1, with an increment of 1. The second serial number has the value 2001 as we specifically requested. If we generated another serial number object, it would have a serial number of 2002.

Although it might not seem terribly useful, this is actually a perfectly functional and usable object class because we can inherit from it. Any object can add serial number functionality to itself by inheriting from this object and making sure to call the new method of Serial from its own new method. We will see more about this later.

The class data of the Serial object class is declared with our, which means that it is package data and therefore accessible outside of the class. We can configure the object class itself by altering these values. For example, to reset the serial number to 42 and the increment to 7:

```
$Serial::conf{start} = 42;
$Serial::conf{increment} = 7;
```

Now when we call new we will get serial numbers 42, 49, 56, and so on. However, just as we do not really want to allow users to control object data directly, neither do we want to allow users to set class data without supervision. The better approach is to implement a class method to set, and check, new values for class data. Here is a configure method that we can add to the Serial object class to handle this for us:

```
# extract from Serial.pm
sub configure {
    my $class = shift;

    while (my ($key, $value) = (shift, shift)) {
        $key eq 'start' and $conf{start} = int($value), last;
        $key eq 'increment' and do {
            $value = int($value);
            croak "Invalid value '$_'" unless $value;
            $conf{increment} = $value;
            last;
```

```
        };
        croak "Invalid name '$key' in import list";
    }
}
```

Better still, we can now change the definition of %conf to make it inaccessible from outside the class with my:

```
my %conf = (
    start     => 1,
    increment => 1,
);
```

Defined this way, the configuration hash is inaccessible to external users, and has become private class data—only the configure method can alter it, because only it is in the same lexical scope. We can now call this method to configure the class, as shown by this modified version of our script:

```
#!/usr/bin/perl
# serial_a.pl
use warnings;
use strict;

use Serial;

Serial->configure(start => 42, increment => 7);

my @serials;
foreach (1..10) {
    push @serials, new Serial;
}

print $serials[4]->serial, "\n";
my $serial = new Serial(2001);
print $serial->serial, "\n";
```

The output from this version of the script is (as a little arithmetic would lead us to expect)

```
70
2001
```

This class method ensures that we only try to set the two configuration values the class actually supports, and also it checks that we do not try to set an increment of zero (which would cause all objects to have the same serial number, of course); neither check would be possible if we simply reached in and changed the hash values directly.

Inheriting Class Data

In the class method shown previously, we ignored the class passed in because we want to set the class data of this particular class, even if the method was called through a subclass. This means that different objects from different classes, all inheriting from Serial, will all have different and distinct serial numbers. However, if we wanted to set class data on a per-class basis, the assignments in this method would be altered to something like

```
${"${class}::conf"}{start} = int($value);   # or ${$class.'::conf'}...,
                                             # or ${"${class}::conf"}
```

This sets the value of $conf{start} as a package variable in whichever package the call to the configure method actually originated; in this version of the class, each class that inherits from Serial would have its own configuration and its own sequence of serial numbers.

If we have classes inheriting from each other, each with the same class data values, we need to pay attention to this kind of detail, or we can easily end up setting class data in the wrong class. See the section "Nonobject Classes" for an example of a class that works this way. An alternative approach that gets around these difficulties is to set class data via objects; we will also look at that in a moment.

Setting Class Data Through Import Methods

We briefly mentioned the import method earlier in the chapter and discussed it at some length in Chapter 10. From the point of view of object-oriented programming, the import method is just another class method, with the unusual property that the use statement calls it, if present. We can easily adapt our earlier example of the configure method to work as an import method too, simply by renaming it import. However, calling Serial->import to configure a variable is confusing, so instead we can just create an import method that calls the configure method, leaving it available under the old name:

```
sub import {
    shift->configure(@_);
}
```

We could also just alias it, if we like typeglobs:

```
*import = \&configure;
```

Either way, we can now configure the Serial class with

```
use Serial qw(start => 42, increment => 7);
```

Everything that applies to the import method also applies to the unimport method, of course, for when we use no rather than use. This is a lot less common, but it is ideal for controlling Boolean flags, as the next example illustrates.

Nonobject Classes

All the classes we have looked at so far have been object classes, containing at least one constructor. However, we can create classes that work entirely on class data. This might seem like a strange idea, but it makes sense when we also include the possibility of inheritance. Just as inheriting object methods from a parent class allows us to abstract details of an object's workings, we can inherit class methods to abstract class data manipulations.

The following class continues the theme of the previous section by implementing both import and unimport methods to create a set of Boolean flags stored as class data. It provides methods to get, set, delete, and create new variables, as well as a list method to determine which variables exist, or are set or unset. It is also an example of a package containing only class data, with no constructor at all. Rather than being an object class in its own right, it is designed to be inherited by other object classes to provide them with class data manipulating methods.

```
# Booleans.pm
package Booleans;
use strict;
no strict 'refs';

use Carp;

# establish set boolean vars
sub import {
```

```perl
    my $class = shift;
    ${"${class}::conf"}{$_} = 1 foreach @_;
}

# establish unset boolean vars
sub unimport {
    my $class = shift;
    ${"${class}::conf"}{$_} = 0 foreach @_;
}

# private method -- does all the actual work for set, unset, and delete
# only variables already established may be altered here.
sub _set ($$$) {
    my $class = (ref $_[0]) || $_[0];
    unless (exists ${"${class}::conf"}{$_[1]}) {
        croak "Boolean $_[1] not imported";
    }

    if (defined $_[2]) {
        ${"${class}::conf"}{$_[1]} = $_[2]?1:0;
    } else {
        delete ${"${class}::conf"}{$_[1]};
    }
}

# return variable value
sub get ($$) {
    my $class = (ref $_[0]) || $_[0];
    return ${"${class}::conf"}{$_[1]};
}

# set a variable
sub set ($$) {
    shift->_set(@_, 1);
}

# clear a variable
sub unset ($$) {
    shift->_set(@_, 0);
}

# delete an existing variable
sub delete ($$) {
    shift->_set(@_, undef);
}

# invent a new variable -- _set doesn't allow this
sub create ($$$) {
    ${"$_[0]\:\:conf"}{$_[1]} = $_[2] ? 1 : 0;
}

# return a list of all set, all unset or all variables
sub list ($;$) {
    my ($class,$set)=@_;

    if (defined $set) {
        # return list of set or unset vars
```

```perl
        my @vars;
        foreach (keys %{"${class}::conf"}) {
            push @vars,$_ unless ${"${class}::conf"}{$_} ^ $set;
        }
        return @vars;
    } else {
        # return list of all vars in set
        return keys %{"$_[0]\:\:conf"};
    }
}

1;
```

Having no constructor, this class cannot be instantiated directly. It is designed to be inherited by other classes, which can use the methods it supplies to set their own Boolean flags. This accounts for all the occurrences of

```perl
%{"${class}::conf"}
```

This is a symbolic reference that resolves to the %conf hash in the package that was first accessed through the method call, so every class that makes use of this class gets its own %conf hash, rather than sharing one in Booleans.

Indeed, we do not even declare a %conf hash here since it is not necessary, both because we do not expect to use the module directly and because we always refer to the hash by its full package-qualified name, so no our or use vars declaration is necessary. This is an important point, because it means that a subclass can have a conf array just by subclassing from Booleans. It need not declare the hash itself. It is still free to do so, but the point of this class is that all Boolean variable access should be via the methods of this class, so it should never be necessary.

We can test out this class with a short script that does use the module directly, just to prove that it works:

```perl
#!/usr/bin/perl
# booleans.pl
use warnings;
use strict;

use Booleans qw(first second third);
no Booleans qw(fourth fifth);

print "At Start: \n";
foreach (Booleans->list) {
    print "\t$_ is\t:", Booleans->get($_), "\n";
}

Booleans->set('fifth');
Booleans->unset('first');
Booleans->create('ninth', 1);
Booleans->delete('fourth');

print "Now: \n";
foreach (Booleans->list) {
    print "\t$_ is\t:", Booleans->get($_), "\n";
}

print "By state: \n";
print "\tSet variables are: ", join(', ', Booleans->list(1)), "\n";
print "\tUnset variables are: ", join(', ', Booleans->list(0)), "\n";
```

The output of this program is

```
At Start:
        first is      :1
        fifth is      :0
        fourth is     :0
        third is      :1
        second is     :1
Now:
        first is      :0
        fifth is      :1
        ninth is      :1
        third is      :1
        second is     :1
By state:
        Set variables are: fifth, ninth, third, second
        Unset variables are: first
```

Clearly the most immediately useful improvement we could make to this class is to have list return the flags in the order of creation (if only for cosmetic purposes), but it serves to prove that the class, such as it is, performs as designed.

Accessing Class Data via Objects

We sometimes want to allow users of our object class to find out the contents of our class data, and even in some cases set it. The lazy way to do this is simply to access the data directly, but as we have already noted, this is not object oriented and therefore bad practice. Better is to use a class method, as we did earlier. Both approaches suffer from the fact that we need to use the class name to access either the data or the method to manipulate it, which varies between a class and its subclasses.

An alternative approach that avoids all this complexity, as well as avoids instances of constructing package variable names on the fly with expressions like ${class}::variable, is to store references to the class data in the objects. We can then access and set the class data through the object using an accessor/mutator-style method.

In order to use this approach, we need to add some private attributes to the object instance that contains references to the class data. The key point of this technique is that we establish a relationship between the object and its class data in the constructor at the moment the object is created. From this point on, so long as we use the object to access the class data, there is no ambiguity as to which class we are referring to, and we do not need to figure out package prefixes or object class names. The object "knows" which class data applies to it.

Here is a modified version of the constructor for the Serial class that provides references for the class data of the class. The key lines are those containing the definitions for the _next and _incr attributes:

```
# part of xxx_serial2/Serial.pm
sub new {
    my $class = (ref $_[0]) || $_[0];
    $conf{start} = $_[1] if defined $_[1];

    my $self = bless {}, $class;
    $self->{serial} = $conf{start};
    $self->{'_next'} = \$conf{start};
    $self->{'_incr'} = \$conf{increment};
    $conf{start} += $conf{increment};
    return $self;
}
```

We create the two new attributes by assigning references to the hash values we want to provide access for. We give them underscored names, to indicate that these are intended for private use, not for public access. Finally, we provide object methods that use these new attributes. Here is an accessor/ mutator object method that we can append to our Serial class that performs this duty for us:

```
sub next ($;$) {
    my ($self, $new) = @_;
    ${$self->{'_next'}} = $new if $new;
    return ${$self->{'_next'}};
}
```

Now, if we want to change the serial number for the next object created, we can find any existing Serial object (or subclass thereof) and use the next method, as this short script illustrates:

```
#!/usr/bin/perl
# serial2.pl
use warnings;
use strict;

use Serial;

my $serial = new Serial;
print "First serial number is ", $serial->serial, "\n";
$serial->next(10000);
my $serial2 = new Serial;
print "Second serial number is ", $serial2->serial, "\n";
```

When we run this script, we get the expected output:

```
First serial number is 1
Second serial number is 10000
```

When we use the Serial class directly, the next method has exactly the same effect as configuring the increment through the configure class method. However, if we create a subclass for this class, we can now choose whether to keep the references to Serial's class data or replace them with references to class data for the subclass. If we change the references to point to class data for the new class, the next method will adapt automatically because it works through the reference. When we cover inheritance more fully, we'll develop a subclass of Serial that makes use of this.

Inheritance and Subclassing

Inheritance is the cornerstone of code reuse in object-oriented programming. By inheriting the properties and methods of one class into another, we can avoid having to reimplement code a second time, while at the same time retaining abstraction in the existing implementation. A well-designed object class can allow classes that inherit from it, also known as subclasses, to carry out their own tasks using the parent class as a foundation without knowing more than the bare minimum of how the parent is actually implemented. If a subclass can perform a task purely in terms of methods supplied by the parent, it need know nothing at all. Inheritance is thus a powerful tool for abstraction, which in turn allows us to write more robust and more reusable object classes. There is no need to reinvent the wheel, particularly if the wheel is already working and is well tested.

Perl's inheritance mechanism is, yet again, both matter-of-fact and extremely powerful. It consists of two parts: the special package variable @ISA, that defines inheritance simply by naming the class or classes from which an object class inherits methods and/or class data, and the -> operator, which searches the packages named by @ISA whenever the immediate class does not provide a method.

There are many different forms of inheritance in the object-oriented world, but all of them revolve around the basic principles of abstraction and propagation of method calls from subclasses to their parents. Some, but not all, languages permit *multiple inheritance*, where a subclass can inherit from more than one parent. Similarly, some but not all languages permit *dynamic inheritance* (a class's parents can be changed by the class at will). Perl permits both of these mechanisms in the @ISA array. Adding more than one package to @ISA is multiple inheritance; modifying the contents of @ISA programmatically is dynamic inheritance. It is this kind of simple implementation of complex concepts that makes Perl such an endearing language.

One limitation (or strength, depending on how we look at it) of Perl's approach is that subclasses always know who their parents are, but parents have no idea who their children are. There is no way for a parent class to determine what classes may be using it, nor any mechanism, short of returning undef from a constructor, to bar inheritance. Perl's attitude is that classes ought to be inheritable and that knowledge of subclasses is neither necessary nor desirable for good object-oriented programming.

In addition to whatever classes they may explicitly inherit from, all classes inherit automatically from the UNIVERSAL object, which as we mentioned nearer the start of the chapter, provides the can, isa, and version methods for all objects. We can place our own methods in this special package if we wish, to give all objects new capabilities.

Inheriting from a Parent Class

The basis of all inheritance is the @ISA array, a special package variable, which if defined, describes the package or packages from which an object class will inherit methods. To inherit from a parent class, we need only specify its package name in the @ISA array. For example:

```
package Sub::Class;
use Parent::Class;
our @ISA = qw(Parent::Class);
```

@ISA works hand in glove with the -> operator, which actually enacts the process of searching for inherited methods. Any method call for a method that is not implemented by this class will automatically be forwarded up to the parent class. If it also does not implement the method, then its parent class(es) are searched until Perl runs out of ancestors or a matching method is found.

As an alternative to referencing the @ISA array directly, we can use the base pragma. The following has the same effect as the previous example, but it is one line shorter. It also refers to the parent class in exactly one place only, which is intuitively more elegant:

```
package Sub::Class;
use base Parent::Class;
```

The base pragma is important in two other ways. First, in combination with the fields pragma, it allows us to create objects using pseudohashes or restricted hashes (see Chapter 5). This is a generic mechanism used to quickly and conveniently implement simple object-oriented classes. Many of the object-oriented classes provided by the Perl standard library are implemented this way, and we will come back to touch on it again later.

Secondly, while the base pragma modifies @ISA just as the explicit assignment does, it does so during the compilation phase, because use is implicitly in a BEGIN block. Unlike the explicit assignment, any existing contents of the @ISA array are also retained intact. This means we can use it multiple times and that all parent classes will be present in the @ISA array at the end of the compilation phase, so CHECK and INIT blocks will be able to make use of parent classes. By contrast, the explicit assignment to @ISA only occurs at run time. We could, of course, put it in a BEGIN block, but the base pragma is simply more elegant.

Overloading and Calling Overloaded Methods

We frequently want to implement our own version of a method supplied by a parent, but in doing so, we also often want to take advantage of the parent's method, to carry out tasks related to the parent's implementation of our object. We do not necessarily need to know what these are (that is the point of abstraction), but we would still like to have them done for us.

By overriding (or in object-oriented terms, *overloading*) a method in a parent class, we suppress the call to the parent method. If we still need to make use of the parent method we now need to call it explicitly from the replacement method. For instance, if we are in a package that is a subclass of Parent::Class, we might write

```
sub a_method {
    my $self = shift;
    $self->Parent::Class::a_method(@_);
    ... do our own thing ...
}
```

The effect of the method call here is to call a_method in the parent class, but with the package or object specified by $self. Unless this class itself has subclasses this will be the package name or an object instance of the class, not that of the parent's. From the parent's perspective, there is not (or should not) be any difference. Our class is a subclass of it and therefore has all the same properties except that which it overrides.

Many objects only have one parent class but still name the parent class explicitly, as in the preceding example. This is an irritation—there is only one parent, and so we should not have to mention it. Furthermore, it binds the subclass explicitly to the parent class. Only the @ISA array should need to know this information. Fortunately, we can make use of the special package prefix SUPER::, which allows us to refer to the parent class without explicitly naming it:

```
sub a_method {
    my $self = shift;

    $self->SUPER::a_method(@_);
    ... do our own thing ...
}
```

Note that this is subtly but significantly different from writing the incorrect

```
SUPER->a_method(@_); # ERROR, parent package name passed
```

In this case, the call to a_method gets the package that SUPER resolved to as its first argument—this is not the object making the call, not even the package that the call is being made from.

The SUPER:: package does not actually exist, but it evaluates at run time to all of the packages (since we may have more than one) from which this package inherits. Perl carries out another search for the method, starting from each of the packages in @ISA in turn, until it either finds the method or runs out of object classes to search. If we only inherit from one parent class, then SUPER:: is almost (but not quite) the same as $ISA[0]:::

```
$self->$ISA[0]::a_method(@_);
```

The difference is subtle, but important. All objects implicitly inherit from the UNIVERSAL object, but only SUPER:: takes this into account when searching for methods. $ISA[0]:: does not.

Overloading and Calling Overloaded Constructors

Constructors are an important special case of overriding and inheriting from a parent class. Because Perl does not offer a special naming convention for constructors, and in particular does not insist that a constructor have the name of the class, it does not suffer from the requirement to spell out constructors for every subclass. If we call new on a subclass and it does not provide a new, the parent class new is called. Inheritance of constructors works just like an ordinary method, because in Perl constructors *are* ordinary methods, just ones that happen to return a new object of the class.

Because a parent constructor method gets the class name of the subclass as its first argument, it can create objects in the subclass without knowing what the subclass is. The fact that it is a subclass is sufficient in itself. A subclass frequently needs to do its own initialization beyond that which the parent's constructor carries out though, so in this case we want to write a constructor in the subclass and have it call the parent constructor to actually create the object. The subclass never uses bless itself, it just augments the object returned by the parent constructor (which is already blessed into the subclass).

To achieve this, we must call the constructor in the parent class with our own class name as the first argument:

```
sub new {
    my $self = shift;
    my $class = (ref $self) || $self;

    $self = $class->SUPER::new(@_);
    ... do our own thing ...

    return $self;
}
```

If the parent class is well behaved and allows inheritance to take place properly, it should return an object blessed into whatever package asked for it. We do not even need to know what the package is, because it was passed in. It might be our own class, but it might equally be a subclass. By avoiding naming a package explicitly, we handle all these possibilities without having to overtly worry about any of them.

Writing Inheritable Classes

In order for an object class to be inheritable, we need to implement it so that it does not contain or refer to any noninheritable elements. Although this takes a little extra work, it pays dividends because we create object classes that can be reused and customized by implementing subclasses that add to and override the methods of the original.

In addition, the very act of writing an object class with inheritance in mind helps us develop it more robustly and exposes weaknesses in the design that might otherwise pass unnoticed until much later. The three golden rules for writing inheritable objects are

- Do not refer directly to class data.
- Always write constructors to use the passed class name.
- Never, ever, export anything.

A fourth less formal but handy rule of thumb is

- Work through the passed object.

This is a more general form of rule 2, but directed towards object methods rather than constructors. Class methods are off the hook a little here, Since we do not usually expect a class method to be inherited (they work on a class-wide basis), they tend to be more class specific. Having said that, it is better if we can write our class methods to be inheritable too.

Finally, a fifth rule of thumb is

- Call parent constructors as the first substantive act of a constructor.

Following this rule ensures that resources are properly allocated by the parent class (or classes) before we do our own initialization. It also ensures that the parent class will not overwrite an attribute after we set it in the inherited class. Of course, we might need to do some initialization to call a parent constructor, but as a general rule of thumb it is a good one to stick to.

More on Class Data Through Objects

As we saw earlier, if we do not want to refer to the same class data in every subclass, we need to take special steps involving symbolic references (though we could also use the qualify_to_ref subroutine provided by the Symbol module). The problem with either approach is that we are committed to that model. We cannot choose whether we want to access the original parent's class data or our own version in further subclasses. Grandchildren get the grandparent's data or their own, depending on how the parent decides to implement its class data accessors and mutators.

The solution is to allow the class to be accessed indirectly, through the objects that we build, which we do by building references to the class data as properties of the objects of the class. We have already seen this in action earlier in the chapter when we altered the constructor and accessor/mutator methods of the Serial module to work with class data through object properties. Here is the constructor of the last version of the Serial class again as a reminder:

```perl
sub new {
    my $class = (ref $_[0]) || $_[0];
    $conf{start} = $_[1] if defined $_[1];

    my $self = bless {}, $class;
    $self->{serial} = $conf{start};
    $self->{'_next'} = \$conf{start};
    $self->{'_incr'} = \$conf{increment};
    $conf{start} += $conf{increment};
    return $self;
}
```

The essential point of this design, from an inheritance point of view, is that any object classes that inherit this constructor may override it with their own constructor. This can choose to either leave the references defined in the object alone or replace them with new references. Here is a complete subclass that does just this, as well as adding a new read-only attribute, at the time of creation:

```perl
# MySerial.pm
package MySerial;
use strict;

use Serial;

our @ISA = qw(Serial);

my $next = 1;
my $plus = 1;

sub new {
    my $class = shift;

    # call Serial::new
    my $self = $class->SUPER::new(@_);

    # override parent serial with our own
    $self->{serial} = $next;
```

```perl
    # replace class data references
    $self->{'_next'} = \$next;
    $self->{'_incr'} = \$plus;

    # add a creation time
    $self->{time} = time;

    return $self;
}

sub time {
    return shift->{time};
}

1;
```

To test out this new subclass, we can use a modified version of our last test script:

```perl
#!/usr/bin/perl
# myserial.pl
use warnings;
use strict;

use MySerial;

my $serial = new MySerial;
print "Serial number ", $serial->serial, " created at ",
scalar(localtime $serial->time), "\n";
$serial->next(10000);
sleep(1);
my $serial2 = new MySerial;
print "Serial number ", $serial2->serial," created at ",
scalar(localtime $serial2->time), "\n";
```

The output of this script should look like (depending on the time the script is executed) the following:

```
Serial number 1 created at Mon Jan  1 12:11:17 2001
Serial number 10000 created at Mon Jan  1 12:11:18 2001
```

What makes this subclass interesting is that it can continue to use the methods provided by the parent class, which use the object properties to access the class data. We do not even need to replace the class data with the same kinds of variables—in the original it was a hash of two key-value pairs. In the subclass it is two discrete scalar variables. By altering these properties, the subclass effectively reprograms the parent's methods to work with the class data that the subclass wants to use. We have moved the choice of which class data is accessed from the parent to the subclass.

There is one remaining flaw in the subclass constructor—it sets the attributes of the parent object class directly. In order to enable the subclass to set its class data without referring directly to the hash, we should provide a method to set the class data and a method to set the serial number. Here are two methods that, when appended to the Serial class, will do the job for us:

```perl
# private method to set location class data
sub _set_config {
    my ($self, $nextref, $incrref) = @_;
```

```
    $self->{'_next'} = $nextref;
    $self->{'_incr'} = $incrref;
}

# private method to set serial number
sub _set _serial {
    $self->{serial} = shift;
}
```

We have avoided implementing a method to set the serial number up to now because it is not a feature we want to allow publicly. Therefore, we have given it a leading underscore and called it _set_serial to emphasize that it is for the use of subclasses only. The underscore prefix is only a convention, not a requirement, but it is a commonly used one. The method to set the class data is similarly only for the use of subclasses, so we have called it _set_config. The subclass constructor can now be modified to use these methods, resulting in this new, correctly object-oriented, constructor:

```
# part of MySerial.pm
sub new {
    my $class = shift;

    # call Serial::new
    my $self = $class->SUPER::new(@_);

    # override parent serial with our own
    $self->_set_serial($next);

    # replace class data references
    $self->_set_config(\$next, \$plus);

    # add a creation time
    $self->{time} = time;

    return $self;
}
```

Not only is this more correct, it is simpler to understand too. It is not quite perfect though—the time attribute assumes that the Serial class uses a hash as its underlying representation. We may be happy to live with that, but if we wanted to fix that too, we could make use of the private _property method we created earlier in the section "Generic Accessors/Mutators" for the easy creation of, and access to, attributes. By adding this method to the Serial class, we could then replace the line setting the time attribute:

```
$self->{time} = time;
```

to

```
$self->_property(time => time);
```

Exports

Avoiding exports from object classes almost goes without saying. If we export any variable or subroutine from an object class, it is accessible from outside the method calling scheme, breaking the design. Avoiding exports is, of course, very easy; we just don't do it. In particular, the Exporter should not be used.

There is one exception to this rule, however, which comes about when we design an object class to be used both with objects, and with a functional interface, as the CGI module does. Here we generally use a default object created inside the package as global data (that is, a singleton), and use it whenever an explicit object is not passed to us. To do that requires writing the required methods so they can also be called as functions. For example:

```perl
package My::FunctionalObject;
use strict;
use Exporter;

our @ISA = qw(Exporter);
our @EXPORT_OK = qw(method_or_function);

my $default_object = new My::FunctionalObject;

sub new {
    ...
}
sub method_or_function {
    my $self = (ref $_[0])?shift:$default_object;

    return $self->do_something_else (@_);
}
```

This hypothetical method relies on the fact that, if called as a function, its first argument will not be a reference. It uses this fact to test whether it had been called as a function or method, and it sets $self to be either the passed object or the default object accordingly. So long as we design all our methods/subroutines so that the first argument passed in the argument list can never be a reference, this technique will work very well.

Writing an Inheritable Debug Class

As an extended practical example of an inheritable object class, this section presents an object class for implementing a generic debugging mechanism for objects. It also exercises most of the concepts we have introduced so far in the chapter.

We frequently want to include debugging support in our code, where messages are conditionally logged depending on the value of a debugging flag. In the case of object classes, we have two different places to put such a flag, as class data in the class itself for overall debugging of all objects in that class, or at a per-object level, using object properties. In the case of class-level debugging, we also have the choice of handling all classes with a single debugging flag or giving each class its own debugging flag.

This is more than just a debugging design issue; all data must fall into one of these three categories. Debugging support is thus a good general example of how to handle data in an object-oriented context. It pays to consider inheritance here, because it is better to create a generic debugging module and use it in many places rather than repeat it for each object class we create.

Class-Level Debugging

Class-level debugging revolves around a class data variable, which controls whether debug messages will be printed on a class-wide basis. The debug method itself, which prints out the messages, can work as either a class or object method.

Here is a simple example that provides two new methods for multilevel debugging support. Any method within the class can use them, and any inheritors of the class can also use them to enable debugging for the class:

```
package My::Debuggable::Class;
use switch;

my $debug_level = 0;

# accessor/mutator
sub debug_level {
    my ($self, $level) = @_;
    $debug_level = $level;
}

# debug method
sub debug {
    my ($self, $level) = (shift, shift);
    print STDERR @_, "\n" if $level <= $debug_level;
}
```

We can now write methods that use these debugging methods like so:

```
sub a_method {
    my $self = shift;

    $self->debug(1, "This is a level one debug message");
    ...
}
```

Or, from elsewhere:

```
My::Debuggable::Class->debug_level(2);
My::Debuggable::Class->debug(1, "A debug message");
$my_debuggable_class_object->debug(2, "Another debug message");
```

We can also inherit the debug methods into a subclass:

```
package Other::Class;

use Debuggable;
our @ISA = qw(Debuggable);

__PACKAGE__->debug_level(1);
```

Or, from elsewhere:

```
Other::Class->debug_level(1);
$other_class_object->debug(1, "Debug message");
```

This class provides a global debugging switch. Since all objects are controlled by the same debug flag, they are all controlled together, irrespective of which subclass they are in. If we want to enable debugging on a per-class basis, we can do by replacing the private $debug_level with a constructed package variable name, as this adjusted debugging class does:

```
# Debugpack.pm
package Class::Debuggable;
use strict;
no strict 'refs';

# accessor/mutator
sub debug_level {
    my ($self, $level) = @_;
    my $class = (ref $self) || $self;
```

```perl
        ${"${class}::debug_level"} = $level;
}

# debug method
sub debug {
    my ($self, $level) = (shift, shift);
    print STDERR @_, "\n" if $level <= ${"${class}::debug_level"};
}

1;
```

Since we use symbolic references to compute the name of the class-specific debugging flag, we disable strict references for this class only. Now when we enable or disable the debug level for a particular object class, only the objects of that class will notice:

```perl
# set different debug levels for different classes
Class::One->debug_level(2);
Class::Two->debug_level(1);
Class::Three->debug_level(0);
```

Object-Level Debugging

To debug at the object level, we need to create a debug attribute associated with the object, which we can do in the constructor. The following debugging class implements an object-level debugging scheme and uses an object attribute instead of class data. The object attribute is stored as a hash key, so any object class that inherits from it must use a hash as its underlying representation, which is an important limitation we need to be aware of when using it. (If a generic accessor/mutator mechanism is available to us, we could use that to overcome this limitation, but if we plan to stick to hashes for our objects, then we may consider this simpler implementation acceptable.)

The class also provides a constructor, for classes that want to inherit from it and do not need to inherit from any other parent class, and a separate initializer to create the debugging flag attribute independently for objects that already exist. This gives us maximum flexibility when using the class in combination with others.

```perl
# Object/Debuggable.pm
package Object::Debuggable;
use strict;
no strict 'refs';

# constructor - for new objects
sub new {
    my ($self, $level) = @_;
    my $class = (ref $self) || $self;

    $self = bless {}, $class;
    $self->initialize($level);

    return $self;
}

# initializer - for existing objects
sub initialize {
    my ($self, $level) = @_;
    $self->{debug_level} = $level;
}
```

```perl
# accessor/mutator
sub debug_level {
    my ($self, $level) = @_;

    if (defined $level) {
        $self->{debug_level} = $level;
    }

    return $self->{debug_level};
}

# debug method
sub debug {
    my ($self, $level) = (shift, shift);
    print STDERR @_, "\n" if $level <= $self->{debug_level};
}

1;
```

Implementing a Multiplex Debug Strategy

With a little thought, we can create a debugging class that supports all three of the debugging modes we have seen so far. This class implements a single global debugging flag that affects all classes and objects that inherit from it, a per-class debugging flag, and individual debugging flags for each object:

```perl
# Debuggable.pm
package Debuggable;
use strict;
no strict 'refs';
# global debugging flag -- all classes
my $global_level = 0;

# object constructor
sub new {
    my ($self, $level) = @_;
    my $class = (ref $self) || $self;

    $self = bless {}, $class;
    $self->initialize($level);
    return $self;
}

# initializer for existing objects
# (actually just a wrapper for debug_level)
sub initialize {
    my ($self, $level) = @_;
    $self->debug_level($level);
}

# get/set global debug level
sub global_debug_level {
    my ($self, $level) = @_;

    if (defined $level) {
        # set new level, return old one
```

```perl
        my $old = $global_level;
        $global_level = $level;
        return $old;
    }

    # return current global debug level
    return $global_level;
}

# get/set class debug level
sub class_debug_level {
    my ($self, $level) = @_;
    my $class = (ref $self) || $self;

    if (defined $level) {
        # set new level, return old one
        my $old = ${"${class}::class_debug"};
        ${"${class}::class_debug"} = $level;
        return $old;
    }

    # return current class debug level
    return ${"${class}::class_debug"};
}

# get/set object debug level
sub debug_level {
    my ($self, $level) = @_;
    my $class = ref $self;

    # check to see if we were called as class method
    unless (my $class = ref $self) {
        # '$self' is a class name
        return $self->class_debug_level($level);
    }

    if (defined $level) {
        # set new level, return old one
        my $old = $self->{'debug_level'};
        $self->{'debug_level'} = $level;
        return $old;
    }

    # return current object debug level
    return $self->{'debug_level'};
}

sub debug {
    my ($self, $level) = (shift, shift);

    # if no message, set the (class or object) debug level itself
    return $self->debug_level($level) unless @_;

    # write out debug message if criteria allow
    # object debug is allowed if object, class, or global flag allows
    # class debug is allowed if class or global flag allows
    my $class = (ref $self) || $self;
```

```perl
    print STDERR @_, "\n" if
    $level <= $global_level || (
        defined ${"${class}::class_debug"} and
            $level <= ${"${class}::class_debug"}
    ) || (
        ref($self) and $level <= $self->{'debug_level'}
    );
}

1;
```

This class attempts to handle almost any kind of debugging we might want to perform. We can set debugging globally, at the class level, or on individual objects. If we do not have an object already, we can use the constructor; otherwise, we can just initialize debugging support with `initialize`, which operates as either a class or object method and sets the class-wide or object-specific flag appropriately. In fact, it just calls `debug_level`, which does exactly the same thing, but `initialize` sounds better in a constructor.

The three accessor/mutator methods all work the same way and perform the same logic, applied to their particular debugging flag—global, class, or object—with the exception of the object-level accessor/mutator, which passes class-level requests to the class method if it is called with a package name rather than an object.

The `debug` routine itself now checks all three flags to see if it should print a debug message. If any one of the three is higher than the level of the message, it is printed; otherwise, it is ignored. Class-level debugging messages ignore the object-level debug flag, since in their case there is no object to consult. As a convenience, if we supply no message at all, we can set and get the debug level instead. Since we simply pass the request to `debug_level`, and `debug_level` in turn passes class method calls to `class_debug_level`, we can in fact handle all of the module's functionality except the global flag through `debug`.

To demonstrate all this in action, here is a short script, complete with its own embedded test object class (which does nothing but inherit from `Debuggable`) that tests out the features of the module:

```perl
#!/usr/bin/perl
# debugged.pl
use warnings;
use strict;
# a test object class
{
    package Debugged;
    use Debuggable;
    our @ISA = qw(Debuggable);
    sub new {return bless {}, shift;}
}

# create a test object from the test class
my $object = new Debugged;   # defined below so no 'use'

# set debug levels globally, at class level, and on the object
Debugged->global_debug_level(0);
Debugged->class_debug_level(2);
$object->debug_level(1);

# print class and object-level debug messages
Debugged->debug(1, "A class debug message");
$object->debug(1, "A debug message");
```

```
# find current debug levels with _level methods
print "Class debug level: ", Debugged->class_debug_level, "\n";
print "Object debug level: ", $object->debug_level, "\n";

# find current debug levels with no-argument 'debug'
print "Class debug level: ", Debugged->debug, "\n";
print "Object debug level: ", $object->debug, "\n";

# switch off class and object debug with 1-argument 'debug'
Debugged->debug(0);
$object->debug (0);
```

The output from this program is

```
A class debug message
A debug message
Class debug level: 2
Object debug level: 1
Class debug level: 2
Object debug level: 1
```

Inheriting from an object class and then using the subclass as a substitute for the parent class is a good test of inheritance. If the module is written correctly, everything the parent class does should work identically for the subclass. However, to really appreciate this, we really need to discuss inheritance properly.

Private Methods

A *private* method is one that can only be called from the class in which it is defined, or alternatively, a method that can only be called from a subclass. Both concepts are implemented as specific features in many object-oriented languages. Typically, Perl does not provide any formal mechanism for defining either type of method. However, its pragmatic approach makes both easy to implement, simply by checking the class name within the method. The catch is that although easy to do, this kind of privacy is enforced at run time, rather than at compile time. Pragmatism is good, but it has its drawbacks too.

To make a method private to its own class, we can check the package name of the caller and refuse to execute unless it's our own, as returned by the __PACKAGE__ token. Here is the _property method we developed for the Game::Card class from earlier in the chapter, adapted to enforce privacy rather than just implying it with a leading underscore:

```
# _property method private to methods of this class
sub _property ($$;$) {
    my ($self, $attr, $value) = @_;
    my $class = ref $self;
    croak "Attempt to call private method if $class ne __PACKAGE__";

    if ($value) {
        my $oldv = $self->{$attr};
        $self->{$attr} = $value;
        return $oldv;
    }

    return $self->{$attr};
}
```

To restrict access to subclasses and ourselves only, we can make use of the isa method. This returns true if a class is a subclass of the named class, so we can use it to create a subclass-private method like this. This version of _property takes this approach, which makes it much more suitable in an inheritable parent class.

```
# _property method private to methods of this class
sub _property ($$;$) {
    my ($self, $attr, $value) = @_;
    my $class = ref $self;
    croak "Attempt to call private method unless $class->isa(__PACKAGE__)";
    if ($value) {
        my $oldv = $self->{$attr};
        $self->{$attr} = $value;
        return $oldv;
    }

    return $self->{$attr};
}
```

Extending and Redefining Objects

Perl's objects are dynamic in more than one way. First, we can change their ancestry by manipulating the @ISA array. Second, and more interestingly, we can call bless on an object a second time to alter the package to which it belongs. While we should never need to do this for subclassing an object class, we can use bless to create specialized subclasses, to indicate particular situations.

Extending a Parent Class

Properly designed parent classes should be able to create objects in any requested subclass on demand, by virtue of the two-argument form of bless. For example, say we want to extend the DBI module to batch up do requests and then execute them all at once. We could just place our methods directly into the DBI class to ensure that a database handle object (of class DBI) can use them. This is a bad idea, however, because we might break the implementation of the parent class if it happens to define a method with the same name. This is, again, a case of defining the class interface from outside the class, which is an object-oriented no-no. Instead, the DBI module can bless a returned handle into our own class rather than the DBI class:

```
# Extended/DBI.pm
package Extended::DBI;
use strict;

use DBI;
our @ISA = qw(DBI);

my @cache;

sub do_later {
    my ($dbh, $statement) = @_;

    push @cache, $statement;
    if (@cache == 4) {
        $dbh->do($_) foreach @cache;
        @cache = ();
    }
}
```

```perl
sub do_now {
    return map {$dbh->do($_)} @cache;
}
```

```perl
1;
```

We can now write code to use the `Extended::DBI` class in place of `DBI`:

```perl
use Extended::DBI;
```

```perl
my $dbh = Extended::DBI->connect($dsn, $user, $password);
$dbh->do_later($statement);
$dbh->do_later($another_statement);
...
$dbh->do_now();
```

This works because while we call the `DBI` class method `connect` to create the database handle, we pass the name of the class into which we want the returned handle blessed. Inside `connect`, the new database handle is blessed into the class we asked for, `Extended::DBI`. The new handle works just like a regular `DBI` handle, but we can now cache and execute `do` statements with it too.

Constructing Subclasses on the Fly

Another interesting case of extending a parent object is writing the parent object such that it extends itself in order to reflect the circumstances under which it was created. There is no particular reason why a constructor cannot create an object of a different class from the one it is in or the one passed to it. If we define an `@ISA` array for a newly invented class (which we can do simply by assigning it with a fully qualified package name), we can also have this new class inherit its methods from another class. This gives us the possibility of creating different versions of a parent class for different occasions.

For example, a common approach taken by other object-oriented languages is to represent errors as objects (generically known as *exception* objects) rather than as raw numbers or some other basic data type, so errors can be handled in a more object-oriented style without relying on an arbitrary `system` error value. While Perl does not support such a concept natively, we can create an error object class that supports various different methods for handling errors. We can then subclass this class on the fly when a new type of error occurs. By choosing this approach, we need not create subclasses for every error type, and we automatically support any new errors that may arise without needing to change our code.

The following example demonstrates an object class that translates system errors, as communicated by the special variable `$!` (or `$ERRNO`, if using the `English` module), into objects whose class is based on the common name for the error, `ENOENT` for error number 2, for example. Each object class is created on the fly if it does not exist, and an `@ISA` array is placed into it to subclass it from the class name passed to the constructor (which is either the parent class itself or something that inherits from it, either way, the methods of our class can be called from the new subclass). The key parts of the module are the `new` constructor and the `_error_from_errno` subroutine:

```perl
# ErrorClass.pm
package ErrorClass;
use strict;

use Errno;
no strict 'refs';

my %errcache;
```

```perl
sub new {
    my ($class, $error) = @_;
    $class = (ref $class) || $class;
    $error = $error || $!;
    # construct the subclass name
    my $subclass = $class. '::'. _error_from_errno($error);

    # cause subclass to inherit from us
    unless (@{$subclass. '::ISA'}) {
        @{$subclass. '::ISA'} = qw(ErrorClass);
    }

    # return reference to error, blessed into subclass
    return bless \$error, $subclass;
}

# return the integer value of the error
sub number {
    my $self = shift;
    return int($$self);
}

# return the message of the error
sub message {
    my $self = shift;
    return ''.$$self;
}

# accessor/mutator
sub error {
    my ($self, $error) = @_;
    if (defined $error) {
        my $old = $$self;
        $$self = $error;
        return $old;
    }
    return $$self;
}

# subroutine to find the name of an error number
sub _error_from_errno {
    my $errno = int(shift);

    # do we already know this one by name?
    if (defined $errcache{$errno}) {
        return $errcache{$errno};
    }

    # otherwise, search for it in the export list
    my ($name, $number);
    foreach $name (@Errno::EXPORT_OK) {
        $number = Errno->$name;
        $errcache{$number} = $name;
        return $name if $errno == $number;
    }
```

```
    # unlikely, but just in case...
    return 'UNKNOWN';
}

1;
```

The class works by using the `Errno` package to find names for errors, and then scanning each in turn by calling the constant subroutine defined by `Errno`. When it finds a match, it creates a new subclass comprising the passed class name and the error name, and then it blesses the error into that class before returning it. It also caches the error numbers and error names as it searches so it can avoid calling too many subroutines in future.

It is interesting to see just how easily a class can be created in code. The only thing that exists in the subclasses we create is a definition for the `@ISA` array—everything else is inherited. Despite this, they are still fully functional object classes, with methods that can be called, and if we wish, they can even be subclassed.

The `ErrorClass` object class is also an example of an object based on a scalar value, in this case, the value of `$!`. If no initial value is given, the constructor defaults to using the current value of `$!` as the basis for the object it is about to return. `$!` is an interesting value because it has divergent integer and string definitions. This object simply blesses that value, which retains its dual nature even when copied to a new variable and allows the integer and string aspects of it to be retrieved by different accessors. Here is a short script that demonstrates how this class can be used:

```
#!/usr/bin/perl
# error.pl
use warnings;
use strict;

use ErrorClass;

# generate an error
unless (open IN, "no.such.file") {
    my $error = new ErrorClass;

    print "Error object ", ref $error, "\n";
    print "\thas number ", $error->number, "\n";
    print "\thas message '", $error->message, "'\n";

    print "It's not there! \n" if $error->isa("ErrorClass::ENOENT");
}
```

Running this script produces this output:

```
Error object ErrorClass::ENOENT
        has number 2
        has message 'No such file or directory'
It's not there!
```

The last line of this script demonstrates the real point of the class. Rather than checking numbers or using the `Errno` module to call a constant subroutine to determine the numeric value of the error, we convert the error into an object. We can now, in a properly object-oriented way, check the type of an error by looking to see what kind of error object it is.

Multiple Inheritance

In object-oriented circles, the whole idea of multiple inheritance is fiercely debated, with many languages banning it outright. The idea of multiple inheritance (inheriting from several parent classes at once) seems simple enough, but while multiple inheritance is very powerful, it is also a very quick route to object-oriented chaos. It becomes less clear where an inherited method is inherited from, it becomes more complicated to ensure that objects destruct their resources in the right order, and it becomes possible to have complicated inheritance trees where two parents can inherit from the same grandparent (also called diamond inheritance). All of these issues make designing object classes for multiple inheritance much more difficult and more prone to error. Perl abstains from this debate—although it does allow it, it doesn't take great pains to support it either.

To inherit from more than one class is very simple indeed; we just place more than one class into the @ISA array:

```
package My::Subclass;

use Parent::Class::One;
use Parent::Class::Two;

our @ISA = qw(Parent::Class::One Parent::Class::Two);
```

The base pragma allows us to instead write

```
use base Parent::Class::One;
use base Parent::Class::Two;
```

When we come to call a method on My::Subclass, Perl will first check that the package actually implements it. If it does, there is no problem; the method is called and its value returned. If it does not, Perl checks for the method in the parent classes in @ISA, in the order in which they are defined. This means that Parent::Class::One is searched first, including all the classes that it in turn inherits from. If none of them satisfy the method call, Parent::Class::Two is searched. If both packages (or an ancestor thereof) define the method, then only the one found in Parent::Class::One is called, and the version in Parent::Class::Two is never seen.

The manner of searching is therefore crucially affected by the order in which packages are named in @ISA. The following statement is at first sight the same as the preceding one, but in actuality it differs in the order in which packages are searched, leading to potentially different results:

```
our @ISA = qw(Parent::Class::Two Parent::Class::One);
```

Writing Classes for Multiple Inheritance

Inheriting more than one class into our own is easy; we just add the relevant package names to our @ISA array. Writing a class so that it is suitable for multiple inheritance takes a little more thought. By definition, we can only return one object from a constructor, so having multiple constructors in different parent classes gives the subclass a dilemma; it cannot call a constructor in each parent class, since that will yield it several objects of which it can only return one. It also cannot just call one parent constructor, since that will prevent the other parent classes from doing their part in the construction of the inherited object. The same problem, but to a lesser degree, also affects other methods: do we call all the parent methods that apply or just one? And in that case, how do we choose which one?

In the case of constructors, the best way to implement the class so that it can easily be a co-parent with other classes is to separate the construction of the object from its initialization. We can then provide a separate method to initialize the object if another constructor has already created it. For example, here is the constructor for the Game::Card class we displayed at the start of the chapter:

```perl
sub new {
    my ($class, $name, $suit) = @_;
    $class = (ref $class) || $class;

    my $self = bless {}, $class;

    $self->{name} = $name;
    $self->{suit} = $suit;

    return $self;
}
```

This constructor is fine for single inheritance, but it's no good for multiple inheritance, since the only way a subclass constructor can initialize the name and suit properties is to create an object containing them through this method in the parent class, which returns an object. If the subclass constructor has already created an object through another parent's constructor, say via the Serial module, it ends up with two objects, one create by each parent, and no way to combine them. (In fact it can, because both modules happen to use hash-based objects and the key names do not conflict. But this requires the subclass to rely on fundamental assumptions about the underlying data of the object, which is bad for abstraction.)

Instead, we split the constructor in two, like this:

```perl
sub new {
    my $class = shift;
    $class = (ref $class) || $class;

    my $self = bless {}, $class;
    $self->initialize(@_);
    return $self;
}

sub initialize {
    my ($self, $name, $suit) = @_;

    $self->{name} = $name;
    $self->{suit} = $suit;
}
```

With this done, we can now create a subclass that inherits from the Serial, Game::Card, and Debuggable object classes all at the same time, in order to create a serialized debuggable game card class:

```perl
# Debuggable.pm
package Game::Card::Serial::Debuggable;
use strict;

use Game::Card;
use Serial;
use Debuggable;

our @ISA = qw(Serial Debuggable Game::Card);

sub new {
    my $class = shift;
    $class = (ref $class) || $class;
```

```
    my $self = $class->Serial::new;
    $self->Debuggable::initialize();
    $self->Game::Card::initialize(@_);
    return $self;
}
```

We can test that this combined subclass works using the following script:

```
#!/usr/bin/perl
# dsgamecard.pl
use warnings;
use strict;

use Game::Card::Serial::Debuggable;

my $card = new Game::Card::Serial::Debuggable('Ace', 'Spades');

print $card->fullname, " (", $card->serial, ") \n";
$card->debug(1);
$card->debug(1, "A debug message on object #", $card->serial, "\n");
```

The output from this script should be

```
Ace of Spades (1)
A debug message on object #1
```

Although a simplistic example, classes like this are actually genuinely useful, just for the fact that they combine the features of multiple parent classes. Both the Serial and Debuggable object classes can be added to any other object to add serial numbers and debugging support. This is one of the more common uses of multiple inheritance and a great example of how object-oriented programming helps encourage code reuse.

In this example, we used the Serial module to create the object. In practice, it does not matter which of the three parents actually creates our object (unless, of course, one of them does not have a separate initializer method). Analyzing the pattern here, we can see that in fact we could call initializer methods on all three parent objects, Serial::initialize, Debuggable::initialize, and Game::Card::Initialize, and create the object ourselves:

```
sub new {
    my $class = shift;
    $class = (ref $class) || $class;

    my $self = bless {}, $class;
    $self->Serial::initialize();
    $self->Debuggable::initialize();
    $self->Game::Card::initialize(@_);
    return $self;
}
```

Better still, we can split this constructor into two as well, so we use its initializer method in further multiply inheriting subclasses. Since we already have a new constructor (in fact, several identical ones) that calls the initializer automatically, we actually only need

```
sub initialize {
    my $self = shift;

    $self->Serial::initialize();
    $self->Debuggable::initialize();
```

```
    $self->Game::Card::initialize(@_);
    return $self;
}
```

One problem with this scenario is how to deal with arguments if more than one parent `initialize` method needs arguments. In this case, we did not need to worry about that because only the `Game::Card` class needs arguments to initialize it. Since the resulting hash has unique keys, we can't have more than one initializer try to create the same key. Given this, though, we could pass in key-value pairs and have each initializer subroutine (which doesn't have to be called `initialize`) remove the keys that applied to its own initialization, returning those that do not apply to it. If all the classes involved have well-defined behaviors, this can work very well.

All the object classes involved here have to use a hash as their underlying data representation, since they all presume a hash. However, this is a problem for regular inheritance too, rather than being a specific issue for multiple inheritance. As a rule, alternative object implementations can be good for isolated classes, but they do not work well when inheritance enters the picture. It is possible, with some more effort, to have all of these classes get and set their values not by directly accessing the hash but through a generic accessor and mutator mechanism provided by a grandparent class. The access to the underlying data is itself abstracted from the parent classes, so now we can have any kind of underlying data type we like again. See the section "Generic Accessors/Mutators" earlier in the chapter for more on this.

Calling Multiply Inherited Methods

The normal algorithm Perl follows to resolve a call to a method not present in the immediate class (that is, a subroutine not in the immediate package) is to search the `@ISA` array from first element to last. For each parent class, if it does not provide the method, its own `@ISA` is searched, and so on recursively. Perl will there completely explore all ancestors of each parent class in `@ISA` before moving on to the next.

If more than one parent class provides a method, the order of the parent classes in `@ISA` determines which one is found first. As soon as the search finds a match, it is terminated. and Perl calls the located method. Since we ideally only want to implement a given method in one place, this is usually the desired effect—even the possibility of having a method resolved by a different class is a risky proposition, more so because simply reordering `@ISA` is enough to cause it to happen. Since we do not always have control over the naming of parent class methods, we need to be aware of this possibility.

Automating Multiple Initialization with EVERY

It is not always true that we want to resolve a method call to the first successful match, however. In fact, we might want to call not one but all of the matching methods in each parent class that supports it. A very good example of this is the `Game::Card::Serial::Debuggable` constructor we just looked at. Here, an `initialize` method calls the `initialize` method on all of its parent classes in order to completely initialize the object.

While this works, it is not very scalable. It would be convenient if our object class could just know to call parent initializers automatically. Luckily, the `NEXT` module provides just this functionality with the pseudoclass `EVERY`. Typically of Perl, this useful piece of object-oriented semantics is implemented simply as an `AUTOLOAD` routine. When we call a method with any of the special names it recognizes, it dynamically searches the packages defined by `@ISA` looking for a suitable match.

In the case of `EVERY`, the search is made in each directly or indirectly inherited class. Two different search algorithms are available: `EVERY` calls methods first-to-last in the `@ISA` array, and youngest-to-oldest in the ancestry, so all methods in immediate parent classes are called before any method in a grandparent class. `EVERY::LAST` changes this to a first-to-last, oldest-to-youngest algorithm, identical to the normal `@ISA` method search except that, of course, it does not terminate on the first match. As such it is more appropriate to constructor and initialization methods, while `EVERY` is more appropriate to destructors and other end-of-life methods.

Since we want to call every initializer rather than simply the first one Perl finds, we want to replace the call to initialize in our original Game::Card constructor with a derived one computed by the NEXT module. In our particular examples so far, it makes no difference which search algorithm is used, as our ancestry is only one level deep. Since we want to deal with distant descendant subclasses that might need initialize called on their parent before it gets called on them, we should use EVERY::LAST:

```
package Game::Card;
use NEXT;

sub new {
    my $class = shift;
    $class = (ref $class) || $class;

    my $self = bless {}, $class;
    $self->EVERY::LAST::initialize(@_);
    return $self;
}
```

...

This version of the constructor will seek out and call every initialize method defined in the calling class or any and every ancestor of it. So now we do not need to write any initialization code in our Game::Card::Serial::Debuggable class *at all*. We merely need to inherit from the three classes we want to use, Game::Card, Serial, and Debuggable. The new constructor in Game::Card will now cause the initialize method in itself and the ones in Serial and Debuggable to be called automatically when we create a new card object.

Since this behavior is essential for all three classes to initialize correctly, and we don't want to require the use of Game::Card just to ensure that Serial initializes automatically, this is a good time to consider moving the constructor to a grandparent class with a name like Multiply::Inheriting. The only job of this class is to provide a constructor for initializing objects in classes that use this style of multiple inheritance:

```
package Multiply::Inheriting;
use NEXT;

sub new {
    my $class = shift;
    $class = (ref $class) || $class;

    my $self = bless {}, $class;
    $self->EVERY::LAST::initialize(@_);
    return $self;
}

1;
```

Now all classes that want to make use of this style of multiple inheritance can simply use it and not define a constructor themselves.

```
package Game::Card;
use Multiply::Inheriting;
our @ISA=qw(Multiply::Inheriting); #inherit 'new'

sub initialize {
    my ($self, $name, $suit) = @_;
```

```
    $self->{name} = $name;
    $self->{suit} = $suit;
}
```

...

For an example of where we would use EVERY instead of EVERY::LAST, see the section "Destroying Objects" later in the chapter.

Passing on a Method Call with NEXT

We can also use the NEXT pseudoclass, also provided by the NEXT module, to write methods that will restart the method search as if they had not been found in the first place. This allows a parent class to "decline" a method if it determines that it cannot satisfy it. Done correctly, this can get classes in the same inheritance tree to cooperate in cases where a method call handled by the first class found would be more appropriately handled by the second. Clearly getting this right can be very tricky, which is why multiple inheritance is often considered a bad idea in many circles. The following short example illustrates the general idea:

```
#!/usr/bin/perl
use strict;
use warnings;
use NEXT;

{
    package First::Parent;
    sub new { print __PACKAGE__,"\n"; shift->NEXT::new(@_); };

    package Second::Parent;
    sub new { print __PACKAGE__,"\n"; return bless {},__PACKAGE__ };
}

package Child;
our @ISA=qw(First::Parent Second::Parent);

my $obj=new Child;
```

When run, this program will print out

```
First::Parent
Second::Parent
```

The new constructor in the second parent actually constructs the object, but it is not called directly. Instead, the constructor in the first parent is found by the method call, but it is then redispatched, locating the second. As with EVERY, this is actually the work of a very clever AUTOLOAD routine rather than any native intelligence of the interpreter itself.

NEXT operates very much like SUPER does, except that it uses the context of the original class called to search adjacent sibling classes rather than only parent classes of the class in which it is invoked. Unlike SUPER, however, NEXT does not consider a failure to find a next class a fatal error. This allows several classes to dispatch onwards without worrying about whether there is a next method or not. If we want NEXT to behave like SUPER, we can instead use NEXT::ACTUAL, which will, like SUPER, generate a fatal error if there is no next method to dispatch to. A good example of where this is useful is in AUTOLOAD methods, as we will see shortly.

Note that if a grandparent class is inherited twice via different parent classes into the same subclass, NEXT can cause it to be called twice, once for each chain of ancestry between it and the child. This is called *diamond inheritance* and is almost always a very bad idea, indicating structural issues with the factoring of the object classes. However, if we find that we have no choice and want to avoid the duplicate call, then we can replace NEXT with NEXT::DISTINCT. This works exactly the same as NEXT but will only call a given method once in each class. We can as before make failure to find any method fatal with NEXT::DISTINCT::ACTUAL or NEXT::ACTUAL::DISTINCT.

Drawbacks with Multiple Inheritance

Multiple inheritance can get messy very quickly, which is one of the reasons why many languages disapprove of it. The normal inheritance hierarchy is rooted at the top and spreads out and down, with each subclass adding and overriding the methods of its parent. Multiple inheritance stands this arrangement on its head, with each subclass inheriting methods from more than one parent, which in turn may inherit methods from more than one grandparent.

This is problematic for two reasons. The first, and nastiest, is that we can end up with a cyclic dependency, where an ancestor inherits from one of its descendants. This is possible to do in single inheritance too, but it is easier to do it accidentally with multiple inheritance. Fortunately, Perl can detect this and aborts if we try to create a cyclic dependency.

The second is simply that an object with multiple inheritance can quickly become hard to understand and even harder to debug; because their behavior is no longer predictable, we do not know in advance which parent object will satisfy a given method call without studying all the parent methods and their grandparents and the contents of the @ISA arrays of all the objects concerned.

A particularly nasty but all too common example of object inheritance that is hard to predict is where two parent classes inherit from the same grandparent, or in more general cases, where two ancestors inherit from the same common ancestor. We now end up with recombinant branches where a method in the common ancestor can potentially be called by either of two different routes from the original subclass, entirely dependent on the order of parent classes in the @ISA array. There are arguments for designing applications that use object hierarchies like this, but in general recombinant inheritance is a sign that the design of our classes is overcomplex and that there is probably a different organization of classes that would better suit our purposes.

In many languages, methods can be selected not just by their name, but also by the type and number of arguments that they accept. Perl does not support this model natively, so prototypes of inherited classes are ignored. Having said this, the Class::Multimethods module on CPAN does provide an argument-list based mechanism for searching for methods in parent classes, if we have a compelling need for it.

The bottom line for designing classes with multiple inheritance is therefore to keep them as simple as possible and to avoid complex inverted trees of parent classes if at all possible.

A UNIVERSAL Constructor

As we have already seen, all object classes implicitly inherit from the UNIVERSAL class and therefore can always make use of the can, isa, and VERSION methods that it provides.

With a little thought, we can also add our own methods to UNIVERSAL to make them generic across all the methods in our application. This is not something to be done without considering the possible consequences, because it can cause unexpected problems by inadvertently satisfying a method call that was intended for a different parent class.

Having said this, there are some methods that we can place into UNIVERSAL that are so common among objects that it is worth creating a generic method for them. The methods will be stored in a particular module, and the documentation of that module should make clear that methods are added to UNIVERSAL when it is used. For instance, we introduced the concept of initializer methods when we talked about multiclassing. The constructor we created as a result of this was totally generic; so we could place it in UNIVERSAL to give all our object classes a new constructor that calls an initializer, then just define an initializer rather than a constructor. The advantage is that we don't need to manipulate @ISA to get the desired behavior.

To place anything into UNIVERSAL, we only have to specify it as the package name. Here is an example object class that adds a generic new constructor to all objects:

```
# Universal/Constructor.pm
package UNIVERSAL;
use strict;
sub new {
    my $class = shift;
    $class = (ref $class) || $class;

    my $self = bless {}, $class;
    $self->initialize(@_);
    return $self;
}

sub initialize { }

1;
```

To use this constructor, we now only have to use the module and provide an initializer method if we want to actually perform some initialization:

```
package My::Class;
use strict;
use Universal::Constructor;

sub initialize {
    my ($self, $value1, $value2) = @_;

    $self->{attr1} = $value1;
    $self->{attr2} = $value2;

    return $self;
}

1;
```

Note that we don't need an @ISA definition for this class because it implicitly inherits from UNIVERSAL already. We could similarly, assuming we based all our objects on a hash, create universal accessors, universal mutators, or a universal accessor/mutator of the types we created before. If any object wants to have its own constructor, it only has to override the new provided by our universal class, or just not use it at all.

Whether or not putting methods into UNIVERSAL is a good idea is debatable. Certainly, over-complex or task-specific methods are a bad idea, as is any kind of class data. If most of our object classes all use the same methods, then it can be a workable approach, but in the end it is only one line less than using a different package name and placing it in an @ISA definition.

It is also possible that we want to avoid having another class satisfy a method provided by the UNIVERSAL package. It would be strange, but not impossible, for a parent class to provide a can method (an object that defines an AUTOLOAD method might want to do this to return a true result for methods that it supports but has not yet defined). If we need to avoid calling it, we can explicitly add UNIVERSAL to the start of the @ISA array for our object class (or at the least in front of the class with the troublesome can method). For example:

```
our @ISA = qw(UNIVERSAL Problem::Parent Other::Class);
```

Alternatively, we can fully qualify a method to ensure it comes from the correct class:

```
my $has_method = $object->UNIVERSAL::can('method');
```

Container Classes: Has-A vs. Is-A

So far we have only talked about one kind of relationship between objects, the is-a relationship. However, not all object relationships can be expressed in terms of is-a. It may be true that a tire is-a wheel, but it does not make sense to say that a deck of playing cards is-a playing card, or vice versa. The other form of relationship is has-a; a deck of cards has-a collection of cards in it.

Since an object is just a scalar value, one object has another just by storing it as an attribute. Objects that store and manage many other objects this way are sometimes called *containers* or *container objects*.

Extending the Game::Card example, let's consider a new class, Game::Deck, that manages a list of Game::Card objects. This new class allows us to create a new deck of cards of our chosen suits and names and then deal cards from it. We can also replace them on the top or bottom, peek at any card in the deck, and print out the whole deck:

```perl
# Game/Deck.pm
package Game::Deck;
use strict;

use Game::Card;

### Constructor

sub new {
    my ($class, $suits, $names, $cardclass) = @_;
    my $self = bless {}, $class;

    if ($suits) {
        # create cards according to specified arguments

        # these allow us to specify a single suit or name
        $suits = \$suits unless ref $suits;
        $names = \$names unless ref $names;

        # record the names and suits for later
        $self->{suits} = $suits;
        $self->{names} = $names;

        # generate a new set cards
        my @cards;
        foreach my $suit (@$suits) {
            foreach my $name (@$names) {
                my $card = new Game::Card($name, $suit);
                bless $card, $cardclass if defined $cardclass;
                push @cards, $card;
            }
        }

        # add generated cards to deck
        $self->{cards} = \@cards;
    } else {
        # initialize an empty deck
        $self->{cards} = [];
    }

    return $self;
}
### Cards, Suits and Names
```

```perl
# return one or more cards from deck by position
sub card {
    my ($self, @range) = @_;

    return @{$self->{'cards'}} [@range];
}

sub suits {
    return @{shift->{'suits'}};
}

sub names {
    return @{shift->{'names'}};
}

### Deal and Replace

# shuffle cards randomly
sub shuffle {
    my $self = shift;

    # create a hash of card indices and random numbers
    my %order = map {$_ => rand()} (0..$#{$self->{'cards'}});

    # rebuild the deck using indices sorted by random number
    my @newdeck;
    foreach (sort {$order{$a} <=> $order{$b}} keys %order) {
        push @newdeck, $self->{'cards'}[$_];
    }

    # replace the old order with the new one
    $self->{'cards'} = \@newdeck;
}

# deal cards from the top of the deck
sub deal_from_top {
    my ($self, $qty) = @_;
    return splice @{$self->{'cards'}}, 0, $qty;
}

# deal cards from the bottom of the deck
sub deal_from_bottom {
    my ($self, $qty) = @_;
    return reverse splice @{$self->{'cards'}}, -$qty;
}

# replace cards on the top of the deck
sub replace_on_top {
    my ($self, @cards) = @_;
    unshift @{$self->{'cards'}}, @cards;
}

# replace cards on the bottom of the deck
sub replace_on_bottom {
    my ($self, @cards) = @_;
    push @{$self->{'cards'}}, reverse @cards;
}
```

```
### Nomenclature

# return string for specified cards
sub fullnames {
    my ($self, @cards) = @_;

    my $text;
    foreach my $card (@cards) {
        $text .= $card->fullname. "\n";
    }
    return $text;
}

# return string of whole deck ('fullname' for Deck class)
sub fulldeck {
    my $self = shift;
    return $self->fullnames (@{$self->{'cards'}});
}

# print out the whole deck
sub print {
    my ($self, @range) = @_;

    if (@range) {
        print $self->fullnames (@{$self->{'cards'}}[@range]);
    } else {
        print $self->fulldeck;
    }
}

1;
```

To use this class, we first call the constructor with a list of suits and card names. We can then manipulate the deck according to our whims. Here is a short script that puts the class through its paces. Note how simple the construction of a standard 52-card deck is:

```
#!/usr/bin/perl
# gamedeck.pl
use warnings;
use strict;

use Game::Deck;

# create a standard deck of playing cards
my $deck = new Game::Deck(
    ['Spades', 'Hearts', 'Diamonds', 'Clubs'],
    ['Ace', 2..10, 'Jack', 'Queen', 'King'],
);

# spread it out, shuffle it, and spread it out again
print "The unshuffled deck looks like this: \n";
$deck->print;
$deck->shuffle;
print "After shuffling it looks like this: \n";
$deck->print;

# peek at, deal, and replace a card
print "Now for some card cutting... \n";
```

```
print "\tTop card is ", $deck->card(0)->fullname, "\n";
my $card = $deck->deal_from_top(1);
print "\tDealt ", $card->fullname, "\n";
print "\tTop card is now ", $deck->card(0)->fullname, "\n";
$deck->replace_on_bottom($card);
print "\tReplaced ", $card->fullname, " on bottom \n";
print "The deck now looks like this: \n";
$deck->print;
```

As we briefly mentioned earlier in the chapter, if the result of calling an object method is another object, then we can chain method calls together and avoid storing the intermediate objects in temporary variables. We can see this happening in the preceding script in this expression:

```
$deck->card(0)->fullname
```

Because the has-a relationship fits this model very well, the meaning of this expression is obvious just by inspection, "give me the full name of the first card in the deck."

The concept of the deck implemented by this object class extends readily to other kinds of deck, for example, a hand of cards is really just a small deck; it has an order with a top and bottom card, we can deal from it, and so on. So, to deal a hand of cards, we just create a hand deck and then deal cards from the main deck, adding them to the hand. This extension to the test script shows this in action (we have dealt from the bottom just for variety):

```
# gamedeck.pl (continued)
# deal a hand of cards - a hand is just a small deck
my $hand = new Game::Deck;
my @cards = $deck->deal_from_bottom(7);
$hand->replace_on_top(@cards);
print "Dealt seven cards from bottom and added to hand: \n";
$hand->print;
```

This example demonstrates how effective a has-a relationship can be when it fits the requirement for the design of a class.

Autoloading Methods

There is no intrinsic reason why we cannot use the autoloader to load methods on their first use, just as we can load subroutines on their first use in ordinary non–object-oriented packages; both the SelfLoader and AutoLoader modules, covered in Chapter 10, will work just as well with methods as they do with subroutines. Before choosing this route, however, be aware that the autoloading routine should manage its return value carefully to allow an object class to cooperate in multiple inheritance scenarios (that is, in situations where we actually want to decline a method call and allow another class to handle it).

Typically, a method autoloader is useful for accessor or mutator methods when we do not want to define them all at once (or indeed at all, unless we have to). Fortunately, Perl searches for methods in parent classes before it resorts to the autoloader; otherwise, this technique would be impractical.

As an example of how we can adapt a class to use autoloading, here is a generic accessor/mutator method and the first two of a long line of specific methods that use it, borrowed from an edition of the Game::Card object class.

```
sub _property {
    my ($self, $attr, $value) = @_;

    if (defined $value) {
        my $oldv = $self->{$attr};
        $self->{$attr} = $value;
```

```
        return $oldv;
    }

    return $self->{$attr};
}

sub propone { return shift->_property(propone => @_); }
sub proptwo { return shift->_property(proptwo => @_); }
...
```

Even though this is an efficient implementation, it becomes less than appealing if we have potentially very many attributes to store. Instead, we can define an AUTOLOAD method to do it for us. Here is a complete and inheritable object class that takes this approach, allowing us to set and get any attribute we please by calling an appropriately named method:

```
# Autoloading.pm
package Autoloading;
use strict;

sub new {return bless {}, shift}

sub _property {
    my ($self, $attr, $value) = @_;

    if ($value) {
        my $oldv = $self->{$attr}{$value};
        $self->{$attr} = $value;
        return $oldv;
    }

    return $self->{$attr};
}

sub AUTOLOAD {
    our $AUTOLOAD;

    my $attr;
    $AUTOLOAD =~ /([^:]+)$/ and $attr = $1;

    # abort if this was a destructor call
    return if $attr eq 'DESTROY';

    # otherwise, invent a method and call it
    eval "sub $attr {return shift->_property('$attr', \@_);}";
    shift->$attr(@_);
}

1;
```

To test out this class, we can use the following script:

```
#!/usr/bin/perl
# autol.pl
use warnings;
use strict;

use Autoloading;
```

```
my $object = new Autoloading;

$object->name('Styglian Enumerator');
$object->number('say 6');

print $object->name, " counts ", $object->number, "\n";
```

The output should be

```
Styglian Enumerator counts say 6
```

This class is, in essence, very similar to examples we covered using the discussion on autoloading in Chapter 10, only now we are in an object-oriented context. Because of that, we have to take an additional step and suppress the call to DESTROY that Perl will make when an object falls out of scope. Otherwise, if this class is inherited by a subclass that defines no DESTROY method of its own, we end up creating an attribute called DESTROY on the object (shortly before it becomes recycled). In this case, it would not have done any harm, but it is wasteful.

Another problem with this class is that it is not very selective; it allows any method to be defined, irrespective of whether the class or any subclass actually requires or intends to provide that method. To fix this, we need to add a list of allowed fields to the class and then check them in the autoloader. The following modified example does this and also creates an object reference to the list of allowed fields (which is created as a hash for easy lookup) to allow the method to be properly inherited:

```
package Autoloading;
use strict;
use Carp;

# 'standard' list of attributes -- expanded later
my %attrs=map {$_ => 1} qw(name number rank);

sub new {
    my $class=shift;

    my $self=bless {}, $class;
    $self->{'_attrs'}=\%attrs;

    return $self;
}

# this generic accessor/mutator is called by the subroutines that
# are created by the AUTOLOAD subroutine, below. It is not intended
# to be called directly, as hinted by the leading underscore.
sub _property ($$;$) {
    my ($self,$attr,$value)=@_;

    $self->{$attr}=$value if defined $value;

    return $self->{$attr};
}

sub AUTOLOAD {
    our $AUTOLOAD;

    my $attr;
    $AUTOLOAD=~/([^:]+)$/ and $attr=$1;
```

```
        # abort if this was a destructor call
        return if $attr eq 'DESTROY';

        # otherwise, invent a method and call it
        my $self=shift;
        if ($self->{'_attrs'}{$attr}) {
            eval "sub $attr {return shift->_property('$attr',\@_);}";
            $self->$attr(@_);
        } else {
            my $class=(ref $self) || $self;
            croak "Undefined method ${class}::$attr called";
        }
}

sub add_attrs {
    my $self=shift;

    map { $self->{'_attrs'}{$_}=1 } @_;
}

1;
```

This module presets the attributes name, number, and rank as allowed. So any attempt to set a different attribute, for example size, on this class (or a subclass) will be met with an appropriate error, directed to the line and file of the offending method call by the Carp module. (For Perl 5.8 onwards, we could use a restricted hash to enforce this too—see Chapter 5.) Here is a script that tests it out:

```
#!/usr/bin/perl
# auto2.pl
use warnings;
use strict;

use Autoloading;

my $object = new Autoloading;

$object->name('Styglian Enumerator');
$object->number('say 6');
$object->size('little');    #ERROR
print $object->name, " counts ", $object->number, "\n";
print "It's a ", $object->size, " one.\n";
```

When we run this program we get:

```
Undefined method Autoloading::size called at auto2.pl line 12
```

This works fine for most cases, but how about multiple inheritance? The catch with an AUTOLOAD routine is that, even if it declines to handle the missing method, the interpreter will not resume searching for it. Even if the method really does exist in another parent class, the AUTOLOAD subroutine terminates the search if it is encountered first. To solve this problem, we can use the NEXT module, covered earlier, and specifically the NEXT::ACTUAL pseudoclass. This allows us to pass on the method call we wish the autoloader to decline to handle as if it had never been called in the first place. We simply use NEXT and replace the previous croak statement with

```
$self->NEXT::ACTUAL();
```

(We use NEXT::ACTUAL rather than NEXT so that a fatal error will result if no other class can provide the method either. Note that with this mechanism in place we can have AUTOLOAD subroutines in multiple parent classes and still have the right one pick satisfy our call for us.)

Subclasses of the Autoloading class can create their own set of attributes simply by defining a new hash and assigning a reference to it to the special _attrs key. However, any subclass that wishes to also allow methods permitted by the parent needs to combine its own attribute list with that defined by the parent. This is done most easily by calling the constructor in the parent and then appending new fields to the hash attached to the _attrs hash key.

Since this is a generic requirement for all subclasses, the first thing we should do is add a method to the Autoloading class that performs this function for subclasses. Here is a method that does what we want, taking a list of attributes and adding them to the hash. Again, we have it working through the object attribute to preserve inheritance:

```perl
# added to 'Autoloading' class
sub add_attrs {
    my $self = shift;

    $self->{'_attrs'}{$_}=1 foreach @_;
}
```

Having added this method to the parent Autoloading class, we can now have subclasses use it to add their own attributes. Here is a subclass that uses it to add two additional attributes to those defined by the parent class:

```perl
#!/usr/bin/perl
# Autoloading::Subclass
package Autoloading::Subclass;
use warnings;
use strict;

use Autoloading;
our @ISA = qw(Autoloading);

my @attrs = qw(size location);

sub new {
    my $class = shift;

    my $self = $class->SUPER::new();
    $self->add_attrs(@attrs);
    return $self;
}

1;
```

If we adjust our test script to use and create an object of this new class, it now works as we intended:

```
Styglian Enumerator counts say 6
It's a little one.
```

Although in this example our main autoloading class defines its own attributes, by removing the hard-coded attributes defined in the Autoloading module, we could create a generic autoloading module suitable for adding to the @ISA array of any object wishing to make use of it.

Keeping Data Private

In other (some might say *proper*) object-oriented languages, methods, class data, and object data may be declared private or public, in some cases with varying degrees of privacy (somewhere between absolute privacy and complete public access). Perl does not support any of these concepts directly, but we can provide for all of them with a little thought. We have already seen and covered private methods in the discussion on inheritance. Private class and object data are, however, another matter.

Private Class Data

Keeping class data private is very simple indeed, we just declare our global variables with my to give them a lexical scope of the file that contains them and prevent them having entries in the symbol table. Since code in the same file can access them, no other object class can touch class data declared this way (not even by declaring the same package name in a different file).

If we want to keep class data private to only a few methods within a file, we can do that too by adding some braces to define a new lexical scope, then defining a lexically scoped variable and methods to use it within them. To emphasize the fact that it is private to the class, we use underscores for the variable name. As with method names, this not enforced but merely a common convention used to indicate the intention of privacy to readers of the code. Here is a simple example:

```perl
package My::Class;
use strict;

# create private data and methods to handle it

{
    my $_class_private_data;
    sub _set_data {shift; $_class_private_data = shift;}
    sub _get_data {return $_class_private_data;}
}

# methods outside the scope of the private data must use the methods
# provided to access it

sub store_value {
    my ($self, $value) = @_;
    $self->_set_data($value);
}

sub retrieve_value {
    my $self = shift;
    return $self->_get_data();
}

1;
```

Strictly speaking, this is not object-oriented programming at all, but a restriction of scope within a file using a block, a technique we have seen before. However, "private class data" does not immediately translate into "lexical variables and block scope" without a little thought.

Private Object Data

Perl's general approach to privacy is that it should be respected, rather than enforced. While it is true that we can access the data underlying any blessed reference, the principles of object-oriented programming request that we do not, and if we do so, it is on our own head if things break later.

However, if we really want to enforce the privacy of object data, there are a few ways that it can be accomplished. One popular way is to implement the object not in terms of a reference to a basic data type like a hash or array, but as a reference to a subroutine, which alone has the ability to see the object's internal data.

This technique is known as a closure, and it was introduced in Chapter 7. Closures in object-oriented programming are no different except that each reference to a newly created closure is turned into an object. The following example demonstrates one way of implementing an object as a closure:

```perl
# Closure.pm
package Closure;
use strict;

use Carp;

my @attrs = qw(size weight shape);

sub new {
    my $class = shift;
    $class = (ref $class) || $class;

    my %attrs = map {$_ => 1} @attrs;

    my $object = sub {
        my ($attr, $value) = @_;

        unless (exists $attrs{$attr}) {
            croak "Attempt to ", (defined $value)?"set":"get",
            " invalid attribute '$attr'";
        }

        if (defined $value) {
            my $oldv = $attrs{$attr};
            $attrs{$attr} = $value;
            return $oldv;
        }

        return $attrs{$attr};
    };
    return bless $object, $class;
}

# generate attribute methods for each valid attribute
foreach my $attr (@attrs) {
    eval "sub $attr {\$_[0]('$attr', \$_[1]);}";
}

1;
```

The class starts by defining an array of three attributes. The new constructor maps these to a my-declared hash and then creates an anonymous generic accessor/mutator subroutine to serve as the object that checks the passed attribute is valid. As this subroutine is defined in the same scope as the hash, it is the only way to access that hash once the constructor has returned. Finally, for convenience, three attribute-specific accessor/mutators are defined with eval that simply call the generic accessor/mutator as a subroutine (since it is a code reference, after all).

Here is a short script to show it in action:

```
#!/usr/bin/perl
# closure.pl
use warnings;
use strict;

use Closure;

my $object = new Closure;

$object->size(10);
$object->weight(1.4);
$object->shape('pear');
print "Size:", $object->size,
      " Weight:", $object->weight,
      " Shape:", $object->shape, "\n";

print "Also size:", &$object('size'), "\n";
```

When run, the output of this script should be

```
Size:10 Weight:1.4 Shape:pear
Also size:10
```

This object class uses a constructor to create and return a blessed code reference to a closure. The closure subroutine itself is just what it seems to be: a subroutine, not a method. However, it is defined inside the scope of the new method, so the lexical variables $class and %attrs created at the start of new are visible to it. At the end of new, both lexical variables fall out of scope, but %attrs is used inside the anonymous subroutine whose reference is held by $object, so it is not recycled by the garbage collector. Instead, the variable becomes persistent, surviving as long as the object created from the closure reference does, and becomes the internal storage for the object's attributes. Each time new is called, a fresh %attrs is created and used by a new closure subroutine, so each object is distinct and independent.

We generate the accessor/mutator methods using an eval and also demonstrate that, with a little ingenuity, we can avoid naming the attributes in more than one place. This code is evaluated when the module is compiled, so we do not lose any performance as a result of doing it this way.

Another efficiency measure we could use, in order to improve the preceding example, is to reduce the size of the closure subroutine, since Perl holds a compiled copy of this code for every object we create. With a little inspection, we can see that by passing a reference to the %attrs hash to an external subroutine we can reduce the size of the closure and still retain its persistent data. In fact, we can reduce it to a single line:

```
package Closure;
use strict;
use Carp;

sub new {
    # get the name of the implementing subclass
    my $class=shift;
    $class=(ref $class) || $class;

    unless ($class->can('attributes')) {
        # if we don't have an attributes method, import() was not called with
        # a list of attributes on this class (or any superclass).
        croak "No attributes defined or inherited by this object class";
```

```
    }

    # get the hard-wired attributes from the subclass
    my @attrs=$class->attributes();

    # prep the private attribute hash
    my %attrs=map {$_ => undef} @attrs;

    # create the closure
    my $object=sub {
        return _property_sub(\%attrs,@_);
    };

    # return a blessed code reference object
    return bless $object,$class;
}

sub _property_sub {
    my ($href,$attr,$value)=@_;

    # is this a valid attribute?
    unless (exists $href->{$attr}) {
        croak "Attempt to ",(defined $value)?"set":"get",
            " invalid attribute '$attr'";
    }

    # actually set or get the attribute
    if (defined $value) {
        my $oldv=$href->{$attr};
        $href->{$attr}=$value;
        return $oldv;
    }

    return $href->{$attr};
}
```

The _property_sub subroutine in this example bears more than a little resemblance to the _property method we used in earlier examples. Here though, the first argument is an ordinary hash reference, and not the blessed hash reference of an object. Observant readers may notice that the list of predefined attributes and the foreach loop that defines the attribute-specific attributes is missing this time around. We are going to do something better in a moment, but if we just add them back we can test this version of the Closure class with the same script as before, and with the same results. However, note the last line of that test script:

```
print "Also size:", &$object('size'), "\n";
```

As this shows, we can call the closure directly rather than via one of its officially defined accessor methods. This does no harm, but if we wanted to put a stop to it, we could do so by checking the identity of the caller. There are several ways we can do this, of which the fastest is probably to use the caller function to determine the package of the calling subroutine. If it is the same package as the closure's, then it must be an accessor; otherwise, it is an illegal external access. Here is a modified version of the anonymous subroutine from the new constructor that performs this check:

```
    # create the closure
    my $object=sub {
        croak "Attempt to bypass accessor '$_[0]'" if caller ne __PACKAGE__;
        return _property_sub(\%attrs,@_);
    };
```

Now if we try to access the size attribute directly, we get

```
Attempt to bypass accessor 'size' ...
```

Now we have an object class that cannot be used in any way other than the way we intended. However, it still has an explicit list of attributes. We should be able to do better than that, and we can. We mentioned earlier in the chapter that the import mechanism is perfectly positioned to feed information like desired attributes to a module when it is first used. By defining an import subroutine, we can turn this closure class into a generic reusable mechanism for creating closure subclasses:

```perl
# continuation of package Closure
sub import {
    my ($package,@attrs)=@_;

    return unless @attrs;

    # we allow only the direct subclass to define attributes.
    return unless $package eq __PACKAGE__;
    $package=caller;

    foreach my $attr (@attrs) {
        # the method name is the attribute name prefixed by the package
        my $method=$package.'::'.$attr;
        unless (defined &$method) {
            eval "sub $method { \$_[0]->('$attr', \$_[1]); };";
        }
    }

    # create a class method that returns the attribute names for this class.
    # unlike a package variable, the method is read-only.
    my $attributes_method=$package.'::attributes';
    eval "sub $attributes_method { return qw(@attrs) };";
    # we check for this method in 'new' to see if attributes were defined here.
}
```

This import subroutine carries out the same task as our original list of attributes and the eval loop, creating the corresponding accessor/mutator methods for each attribute passed to the import subroutine. This now allows us to write subclasses like this:

```perl
package Volume;
use base Closure qw(height width depth);
1;
```

We can test this subclass with

```perl
#!/usr/bin/perl -w
# closuresubclasstest.pl
use strict;
use Volume;

my $volume=new Volume();
$volume->height('quite big really');
print $volume->height(),"\n";
```

Destroying Objects

When all references to an object are eliminated, Perl will perform garbage collection and reclaim the memory it is using. This is also known more generally as *resource deallocation*.

However, for some objects this is not enough; if they make use of shared memory segments, filehandles, wrap C code via XSUBS, or are responsible for resources that are not directly held within the object itself, then we need to free them explicitly.

Whenever Perl garbage-collects a blessed reference, it checks for a destructor method in the object's class. If one is defined, it is called before garbage collection takes place. Objects are destroyed before unblessed references and other data types, so destructors can run safe in the knowledge that Perl has yet to clean up any nonobject data they might reference. As an example, here is a destructor for a putative object that contains a local filehandle and a network socket:

```perl
sub DESTROY {
    $self = shift;

    # close a filehandle...
    close $self->{filehandle};
    # shut down a network socket
    shutdown $self->{socket};
}
```

Any system resource held by an object instance should be destroyed, freed up, deallocated, or otherwise returned in the class destructor.

We can also use destructors for purely informational purposes. Here is a destructor for the Serial object class, which takes advantage of the fact that each object has a unique serial number to log a message to the effect that it is being destroyed:

```perl
# destructor for 'Serial' class ...
sub DESTROY {
    my $self = shift;
    print STDERR ref($self), " serial no ", $self->serial, " destroyed\n";
}
```

With this destructor added to the object class, we can now run a program like this to create a collection of serial objects:

```perl
#!/usr/bin/perl
# serialdestroy.pl
use warnings;
use strict;

use Serial;

my @serials;
foreach (1..5) {
    push @serials, new Serial;
}

my $serial = new Serial(2001);
```

When the program ends, Perl calls the destructor for each object before discarding the reference, resulting in the following output:

```
Serial serial no 5 destroyed
Serial serial no 4 destroyed
Serial serial no 3 destroyed
Serial serial no 2 destroyed
Serial serial no 1 destroyed
Serial serial no 2001 destroyed
```

Other than the fact that it is called automatically, a DESTROY method is no different from any other object method. It can also, from a functional programming point of view, be considered the object-oriented equivalent of an END block. Note that like END, these objects were destroyed in inverse order to their initial creation.

Destructors and Inheritance

We never normally need to call a destructor directly, since it is called automatically whenever the object passes out of scope and is garbage collected. However, in the case of inherited classes, we have a problem, since destructors are called the same way any other method is called (Perl searches for it and calls the first one it finds in the hierarchy of objects from child to parent). If a subclass does not define a destructor, then the destructor in the parent class will be called, and all is well. However, if the subclass does, it overrides the parent's destructor.

In order to make sure that all aspects of an object are properly destroyed, we need to take steps to call parent destructors if we don't define a destructor for ourselves. For objects that inherit from only one parent, we can do that calling the method SUPER::DESTROY:

```
sub DESTROY {
    $self = shift;

    # destroy our own resources (for example, a subhash of values for this class):
    delete $self->{'our_own_hash_of_data'};

    # call parent's destructor
    $self->SUPER::DESTROY;
}
```

We should take care to destroy our own resources first. When writing constructors, it is good practice to call the parent constructor before doing our own initialization. Similarly, when we destroy an object, we should destroy our own resources first and then call the parent destructor (reverse order). The logic behind this is simple; we may need to use the parent class to destroy our resources, and destroying the parts of the object it relies on may prevent us from doing that.

Alternatively, and more interestingly, we can rebless the object into the class of its parent. This is analogous to peeling an onion where each subclass is a layer. Once the subclass has destroyed the object's resources that pertain to it, what is left is, at least for the purposes of destruction, an object of the parent class:

```
sub DESTROY {
    my $self = shift;

    # destroy our own resources
    undef $self->{our_own_hash_of_data};

    bless $self, $ISA[0];
}
```

The parent object's class name is defined by the element in the @ISA array—we require that we have only one, so it must be element index zero. What actually happens here is that we catch Perl's garbage collection mechanism with our DESTROY method, remove the resources we are interested in, and then toss the object back to the garbage collector by allowing the reference to go out of scope a second time. But as we reblessed the object, Perl will now look for the DESTROY method starting at the parent class instead.

Although elegant, this scheme does have one major flaw: it fails if any subclass uses multiple inheritance. In this case, reblessing the object can cause considerable confusion when the object fails to be passed on to sibling subclass destructors. Both the examples in the following section would potentially fail if the first parent destructor reblessed the object before the second sees it.

Destructors and Multiple Inheritance

In objects classes that use multiple inheritance, we have to get more involved, since SUPER:: will only call one parent destructor:

```
sub DESTROY {
    $self = shift;

    ...destroy our own resources...

    $self->First::Parent::Object::DESTROY;
    $self->Second::Parent::Object::DESTROY;
}
```

This is a little ugly, however, since it involves writing the names of the parent packages explicitly. If we change the contents of the @ISA array, then this code will break. It also depends on us knowing that the parent object or objects actually have a DESTROY method. A better way to do it is to iterate through the @ISA array and test for parent DESTROY methods:

```
sub DESTROY {
    $self = shift;

    ...destroy our own resources...

    foreach (@ISA) {
        if ($destructor = $_->can('DESTROY')) {
            $self->$destructor;
        }
    }
}
```

We typically want to destroy our own resources before calling parent destructors. This is the inverse order to initialization, where we generally want to call the parents' initializers on an object instance before augmenting it with our own initialization logic.

Handling Multiply Inherited Destructors with NEXT and EVERY

Since writing destructors for object classes in multiple-inheritance scenarios can be more than a little tricky, the NEXT module again comes to our rescue with simplified semantics to make the job a little easier. Essentially we have two strategies: use NEXT in each DESTROY block to redispatch the method search to the next block in line, or rename all DESTROY blocks into ordinary methods and use EVERY in the top-level superclass to call them all. In both cases, the destructors will be called in the correct order, first-to-last and youngest-to-oldest. Here is how we would rewrite the previous example with NEXT:

```
sub DESTROY {
    $self = shift;
```

```
    ...destroy our own resources...

    $self->NEXT::DESTROY();
}
```

Of course, for this to work, all the inherited classes involved must each invoke NEXT::DESTROY or the chain will be broken. The alternative is to create a superclass with a universal destructor in it and have it call all destructor subroutines, now renamed to something else such as destroy:

```perl
#!/usr/bin/perl
# everydestructor.pl
use strict;
use warnings;

{
    package Ancestor;
    use NEXT;
    sub new     { return bless {}, ref($_[0]) || $_[0]; }
    sub DESTROY { print "We'll all"; shift->EVERY::destroy(); }
    sub destroy { print " we go\n"; }

    package Parent;
    our @ISA=qw(Ancestor);
    sub destroy { print " when"; }

    package Child;
    our @ISA=qw(Parent);
    sub destroy { print " go together"; }
}

my $object=new Child;
```

When the program terminates, it will print (as its dying action) "We'll all go together when we go." This shows that the DESTROY method of Ancestor is called first, then the destroy methods in the correct youngest-to-oldest order, finishing with the Ancestor's own destroy method. Notice that unlike the NEXT-based approach, only the Ancestor package needs access to the functionality of the NEXT module here.

Overloading Operators

So far we have looked at objects from the point of view of methods. We can get quite a long way like this, but sometimes it becomes desirable to be able to treat objects as if they were conventional data types. For instance, if we have an object class, which can in some sense be added or concatenated with another object of the same type, we would like to be able to say

```perl
$object1 += $object2;
```

Or, rather than presuming we have an add method for the purpose:

```perl
$object1->add($object2);
```

Unfortunately, we cannot add objects or easily apply any other operator to them, because they are at heart just references, and they obey the same rules that normal references do. Furthermore, objects represent opaque values, so we should not even be able to express the idea of adding them—it is nonsensical. Instead, we need to redefine the + operator (and by inference, the += operator) in such a way that the object's class can provide the implementation for us.

Basic Overloading

This redefinition of standard operators for objects is known as operator overloading, and Perl supports it through the overload module. Presuming that we have an add method for a given object class, we can assign it to the + operator so that when an object of our class is added to anything, it is called to perform the actual "addition" instead of the default + operator supplied by Perl. Here is an example of an object class that handles addition and addition assignment operations:

```perl
# addition.pm
package My::Value::Class;
use strict;

use overload '+'  => \&add,
             '+=' => \&addassign;

sub new {
    my ($class, $value) = @_;
    my $self = bless {}, $class;

    return $self;
}

sub value {
    my ($self, $value) = @_;
    $self->{value} = $value if defined $value;
    return $value;
}

sub add {
    my ($operand1, $operand2) = @_;
    my $result=$operand1->new;
    $result->value($operand1->value + $operand2->value);
    return $result;
}

sub addassign {
    my ($operand1, $operand2) = @_;

    $operand1->value($operand1->value + $operand2 - value);
}

1;
```

The add and addassign methods handle the + and += operators, respectively. Unfortunately they only work when both operands are objects of type My::Value::Class. If one operand is not of the right type, then we have to be more cautious. Perl automatically flips the operands around so that the first one passed is always of the object type for which the method has been called. Since binary operations take two operands, we have broken our usual habit of calling the object $self; $operand1 makes more sense in this case.

Consequently, we only have to worry about the type of the second operand. In this case, we can simply treat it as a numeric value and combine it with the value attribute of our object. To test the operand to see if it is of a type we can add as an object, we use ref and isa:

```perl
sub add {
    my ($operand1, $operand2) = @_;

    my $result = $operand1->new;
```

```
        if (ref $operand2 and $operand2->isa(ref $operand1)) {
            $result->value($operand1->value + $operand2->value);
        } else {
            $result->value($operand1->value + $operand2);
        }
        return $result;
}
```

Determining the Operand Order and Operator Name

For some operations, the order of the operands can be important, a good example being subtraction and another being concatenation. In order to deal with this, operator methods are called with a third Boolean flag that indicates whether the operands are given in reverse order, or to put it another way, if the object for which this method is implemented came second rather than first. If set, this flag also tells us by implication that the first operand was not of the correct object class (and possibly not even an object).

As an example, here is a concatenation method that uses this flag. It also checks the type of the other operand passed and returns a different type of result depending on the order. If a plain string was passed as the first argument, a plain string is returned; otherwise, a new object is returned. To keep the example simple, we have presumed an object whose textual representation is in the attribute name:

```
sub concatenate {
    my ($operand1, $operand2, $reversed) = @_;

    if ($reversed) {
        # if string came first, return a string
        return $operand2.$operand1->{name};
    } else {
        # if object came first, return an object
        my $result = $operand1->new();
        $result->{name} = $operand1->{name}.$operand2;
        return $result;
    }
}
```

Now all we have to do is overload the concatenation operator with this method:

```
use overload '.' => \&concatenate;
```

Occasionally, we might also want to know the operator name that triggered the method. This is actually passed in a fourth argument to all operator methods, though it is not usually required. The obvious and probably most common application is for errors (another is for the nomethod operator method discussed later). For example, to reject operands unless they both belong to the right class (or subclass), we do this:

```
sub an_operator {
    my ($op1, $op2, $rev, $name)=@_;

    unless (ref $op2 and $op2->isa(__PACKAGE__)) {
        croak "Cannot use '$name' on non-",
        __PACKAGE__, " operands";
    }
}
```

Overloading Comparisons

An interesting operator to overload is the `<=>` operator, for comparison. By providing a method for this operator, we can allow sort to work with our objects. For example, dealing only with an object-to-object comparison:

```
use overload '<=>' => \&compare;

sub compare {
    my ($operand1, $operand2) = @_;
    return $operand1->{'value'} <=> $operand2->{'value'};
}
```

With this method in place, we can now say (at least for objects of this class)

```
@result = sort @objects;
```

and get a meaningful result.

This is a more useful operator to overload than it might seem even from the preceding, because the overload module can deduce the correct results for all the other numeric comparison operations based on it. Likewise, if we define an operator method for cmp, all the string comparison operations can be deduced for it. This deduction is called *autogeneration* by the overload module, and we cover it in more detail in a moment.

Overloading Conversion Operations

The numeric and string conversion of objects are two operators, which we may overload, even though we do not normally think of them as operators. However, objects, being references at heart, do not have useful numeric or string values by default; by overloading these operations, we can create objects that can take part in numeric calculations or be printed out.

Overloading String Conversion

String conversion happens whenever a Perl value is used in a string context, such as concatenation or as an argument to a print statement. Since objects ordinarily render themselves as a class name plus a memory address, which is generally less than meaningful, providing a string representation for them can be an extremely useful thing to do.

String conversion is not an operator in the normal sense, so the string conversion operator is represented as a pair of double quotes. Here is how we can assign an operator method for string conversion:

```
use overload '""' => \&render_to_string;
```

We now only have to create an operator method that produces a more sensible representation of the object. For example, this method returns the object name, as defined by a name attribute, enclosed within double quotes:

```
sub render_to_string {
    my $self = shift;
    return '"'.$self->{name}.'"';
}
```

Alternatively, this more debugging-oriented renderer dumps out the contents of the hash being used to implement the object (in the case of other representations we would need to use different methods, of course):

```
sub render_to_string {
    my $self = shift;
    $out = "$self:\n";
```

```
    map {
        $out .= "\t$_ => $self->{$_} \n"
    } keys %{$self};

    return $out;
}
```

Finally, here is an object class that uses a converter to translate date values into different formats, depending on what format we require:

```perl
# DateString.pm
package DateString;
use strict;

# construct date object and values
sub new {
    my ($class, $time, $format) = @_;
    $class = ref $class || $class;

    $time = time() unless $time;
    my ($d, $m, $y) = (localtime($time))[3, 4, 5];
    my $self = bless {
        day    => $d,
        month  => $m+1,      # months 0-11 to 1-12
        year   => $y+1900,   # years since 1900 to year
        format => $format || 'Universal'
    }, $class;

    return $self;
}

# only the format can be changed
sub format {
    my ($self, $format) = @_;

    if ($format) {
        $self->{format} = $format;
    }

    return $self->{format};
}

# the string conversion for this class
sub date_to_string {
    my $self = shift;
    my $format = shift || $self->{format};

    my $string;
    SWITCH: foreach ($self->{format}) {
        /^US/ and do {
            $string = sprintf "%02d/%02d/%4d", $self->{month}, $self->{day},
                        $self->{year};
            last;
        };

        /^GB/ and do {
            $string = sprintf "%02d/%02d/%4d", $self->{day}, $self->{month},
                        $self->{year};
```

```
            last;
        };

        # universal format
        $string = sprintf "%4d/%02d/%02d",
        $self->{year}, $self->{month}, $self->{day};
    }
    $string .= " ($self->{format})";
}

# overload the operator to use convertor
use overload '""' => \&date_to_string;

1;
```

To show how this class operates, here is a short program that prints out the current date in Universal, English, and US format:

```
#!/usr/bin/perl
# datestring.pl
use warnings;
use strict;

use DateString;

my $date = new DateString(time);
print "$date \n";
$date->format('GB');
print "$date \n";
$date->format('US');
print "$date \n";
```

Here is what the script produces, assuming we run it on February 14, 2005:

```
2005/02/14 (Universal)
14/02/2005 (GB)
02/14/2005 (US)
```

We wrote these conversion methods in the style of conventional object methods, using shift and $self. This does not mean they do not receive four arguments like other overloaded operator methods, simply that we do not need or care about them. There is only one operand.

Overloading Numeric Conversion

Just as we can overload string conversion, we can overload numeric conversion. Numeric conversion takes place whenever a data value is used in a numeric context (such as addition or multiplication) or as an argument to a function that takes a numeric argument.

There are two numeric conversion operators, both of which are specially named since, like string conversion, they do not correspond to any actual operator. The standard numeric conversion is called 0+, since adding anything to zero is a common trick for forcing a value into a numeric context. Here's how we can assign an operator method for numeric conversions:

```
"0+" => \&render_to_number;

sub render_to_number {
    my $self = shift;
    return 0+ $self->{'value'}};
}
```

Similarly, here is a numeric converter for the date class we converted into a string earlier. The numeric value of a date is not obvious, so we will implement it in terms of a 32-bit integer with two bytes for the year and one byte each for the month and day:

```perl
sub date_as_version {
    $self = shift;
    $year_h = $self->year / 256;
    $year_l = $self->year % 256;
    return pack('C4', $year_h, $year_l, $self->month, $self->day);
}
```

This conversion is not useful for display, but it will work just fine for numeric comparisons, so we can compare date objects using traditional operators like < and == rather than by overloading these operators to have a special meaning for dates:

```perl
die "Date is in the future" if $day > $today;    # date objects
```

The second numeric conversion handles translation into a Boolean value, which takes place inside the conditions of while and until loops and also in the ?: operator, unless we overloaded that too. References are always true, since they always have values, so to test objects meaningfully, we need to provide a Boolean conversion. The operator is called bool and is used like this:

```perl
"bool" => \&true_or_false;
```

The meaning of truth or falsehood in an object is, of course, very much up to the object. The return value should map to either true or false in Perl, for example, 1 for true and the empty string for false:

```perl
sub true_or_false {
    my $self = shift;
    return $self->{'value'}?1:'';
}
```

Note that if we do not provide an overload method for Boolean conversion, the overload module will attempt to infer it from string conversion instead.

Falling Back to Nonoverloaded Operators

Earlier in the chapter, we introduced the ErrorClass object class, which encapsulated errno values inside an object. While we could compare the object class as a string or convert it into a number, we had to call methods in the object class to do so. It would be much nicer if this could be handled for us.

Here is an extension to the ErrorClass object that does just that. For the sake of this example, we will give it the file name ErrorClass/Overload.pm, though it actually adds overloaded methods to the base ErrorClass object class:

```perl
# ErrorClass/Overload.pm
package ErrorClass;
use strict;

use ErrorClass;

use overload (
    '""'     => \&error_to_string,
    '0+'     => \&error_to_number,
    fallback => 1,
);

sub error_to_string {
    my $class = (ref $_[0]) || $_[0];
```

```perl
    my $package = __PACKAGE__;
    $class =~ /$package\:\:(\w+)/ and return $1;
}

sub error_to_number {
    return shift->number;
}

1;
```

This extension package provides two new methods in the ErrorClass class, error_to_string and error_to_number, which overload the string and numeric conversion operators. We have also set the fallback flag to permit conversion methods to be called when no overloaded object method is available. Instead of complaining that there is no eq string comparison operation for ErrorClass objects, for example, Perl will "fall back" to the ordinary string comparison, converting ErrorClass objects into strings in order to carry it out. Without this, we would be able to print out ErrorClass objects and convert them into integers with int, because these are direct uses of the conversion operators, but we would not be able to write a line like this:

```perl
print "It's not there! \n" if $error eq 'ENOENT';
```

Without fallback, this operation will fail because the eq operator is not overloaded for ErrorClass objects. With fallback, the error will be converted into a string, and then eq will compare it to the string ENOENT. In fact, this handles all the string comparison operators, including cmp. Similarly, the numeric conversion operation allows Perl to fall back to all the normal numeric comparison operators.

Here is a modified version of the test script for the ErrorClass module that shows how we can use these new overloaded conversions to simplify our programming with ErrorClass objects:

```perl
#!/usr/bin/perl
# overload.pl
use warnings;
use strict;

use ErrorClass::Overload;

# generate an error
unless (open STDIN, "no.such.file") {
    my $error = new ErrorClass;

    print "Error object ", ref $error, "\n";
    print "\thas number ", $error->number, "\n";
    print "\thas message '", $error->message, "'\n";
    print "Text represetation '", $error, "'\n";
    print "Numeric representation = ", int($error), "\n";
    print "It's not there! \n" if $error eq 'ENOENT';
}
```

Running this script should produce this output:

```
Error object ErrorClass::ENOENT
        has number 2
        has message 'No such file or directory'
Text representation 'ENOENT'
Numeric representation = 2
It's not there!
```

Operator Overloading and Inheritance

Operator methods are automatically inherited by child classes, just like other methods, but the hard reference syntax we have used so far does not allow us to specify that an inherited method should be used; it requires us to specify a reference to a specific method subroutine. We can have Perl search parent classes for the implementation of an overloaded operator by supplying the name of the method rather than a reference to it. Here is how we would overload the <=> operator with an inherited method:

```
use overload '<=>' => "compare";
```

The method name is essentially a symbolic reference, which is looked up using the -> operator internally. This may or may not be a good thing; it allows inheritance, but a hard reference has the advantage of producing a compile-time error if the method does not exist.

Inheriting methods for operators rather than inheriting the overloaded operator assignments can have a serious affect on performance. If autogeneration (discussed next) is enabled, inheritance can cause Perl a lot of needless extra work as it tries to construct new methods from existing ones. Ordinarily, the search for methods is quick since we only need to see what references exist in the list of overloaded operators. But with inheritance, a search through the hierarchy for each method not implemented in the class is performed—for large inheritance trees that can cause a lot of work.

Autogenerated Operations

When we started out with the overload module, we provided methods to handle both the + and += operators. However, we actually only needed the + operation overloaded, because the overload module is smart enough that it can infer operations that have not been overloaded from those that have been.

For instance, the current behavior for the operation += can be inferred from the + operator, since $a += $b is just shorthand for $a = $a + $b, and Perl knows how to do that for our object class. Similarly, if Perl knows how to do subtraction, it also knows how to do a unary minus (since that is just 0-$a) and -=. The ++ and -- operators can likewise be inferred from + and -; they are just $a = $a + 1 and $a = $a - 1. The overload module can even infer abs from -. That said, we could often supply more efficient versions of these operators, but autogeneration means that we do not have to.

Unfortunately, just because an operator can be deduced does not mean that it should be. For instance, we may have a date class that allows us to compute differences between dates expressed as strings, as in

```
'1 Jan 2006' - '30 Dec 2005' = '2 days'
```

A binary subtraction makes sense in this context, but a unary minus does not. There is no such thing as a negative date. In order to distinguish it from the binary subtraction operator, the unary minus is called neg when used in the list supplied to the overload module. So, one way we can implement subtraction but forbid negation is

```
use overload '-' => \&subtract,
neg => sub {croak "Can't negate that!"};
```

This is awkward if we need to prevent several autogenerated operators, not least because we have to work out what they are to disable them. Instead, to prevent the overload module autogenerating operator methods, we can specify the fallback flag. The default value is undefined, which allows autogeneration to take place, but it dies if no matching operator method could be found or autogenerated.

The fallback flag is intimately connected to autogeneration. If set to 1, Perl reverts to the standard operation rather than fail with an error, which is very useful for object classes that define only conversion operations like the ErrorClass::Overload extension we showed earlier.

If fallback is set to 0, however, autogeneration is disabled completely, but errors are still enabled. (Unfortunately, there is no way to disable both errors and autogeneration at the same time.) A better way to disable negation is like this:

```
use overload '-' => \&subtract,
fallback => 0;
```

We also have the option to supply a default method (for when no other method will suit) by specifying an operator method for the special nomethod keyword. This operates a little like an AUTOLOAD method does for regular methods and is always called if a method can neither be called nor autogenerated. The fourth argument comes in very handy here, as this nomethod operation method illustrates:

```
sub no_operator_found {
    my $result;

    # deal with some operators here
    SWITCH: foreach ($_[3]) {
        /^ <=> / and do {$result = 0,  last};   # always lexically equal
        /^cmp/ and do {$result = 0, last};    # always numerically equal
        # insert additional operations here

        # croak if the operator is not one we handle
        croak "Cannot $_[3] this";
    }
    return $result;
}

use overload '-' => \&subtract,
            '+' => \&add,
            nomethod => \&no_operator_found;
```

We can also use this with the fallback flag, in which case autogeneration is disabled. Only explicit addition and subtraction (plus numeric and string comparisons through the nomethod operation) are enabled:

```
use overload '-' => \&subtract,
            '+' => \&add,
            fallback => 0,
            nomethod => \&no_operator_found;
```

Overloadable Operators

Not every operator provided by Perl can be overloaded. Conversely, some of the things that we might normally consider functions actually can be overloaded. Table 19-1 summarizes the different categories of operators understood by the overload module and the operators within each category that it handles.

Table 19-1. *Overloadable Operators*

Operator Category	Operators
with_assign	+ - * / % ** << >> x .
assign	+= -= *= /= %= **= <<= >>= x= .=
str_comparison	< <= > >= == !=
3way_comparison	<=> cmp

Continued

Table 19-1. *Continued*

Operator Category	Operators
num_comparison	lt le gt ge eq ne
binary	& | ^
unary	neg ! ~
mutators	++ --
func	atan2 cos sin exp abs log sqrt
conversion	bool "" 0+

For more details on these categories and the overload pragma, see perldoc overload.

Automating Object Class Development

There is a veritable cornucopia of object-oriented development modules available for Perl, all of which aim to automate much of the process of creating new object classes. Most of them are in the Class:: namespace, and many of them are dedicated to implementing different kinds of object semantics.

Two useful third-party modules available from CPAN are Class::MethodMaker, which can automatically generate object properties and methods, and Class::Multimethods, which gives Perl the ability to select methods from multiple parent classes based on the type and number of arguments passed (a feature present in several other object-oriented languages but absent from Perl). Class::Contract allows for object classes to be designed and implemented according to the contract of their defined interface. If none of these suffice, there are nearly 200 others of varying ability and maturity available for consideration.

Aside from CPAN, Perl comes with two basic object class construction mechanisms that can simplify the development of object classes. First, there are the base and fields pragmatic modules, which allow us to create objects based on pseudohashes or restricted hashes (depending on how new our Perl is). Various extension modules are available on CPAN that build on these two modules to provide more advanced object semantics. Second, the Class::Struct module provides a simple way to create objects with attributes of predeclared data types—scalar, array, hash, etc.—and auto-generates appropriate accessors and mutators for them.

Building Object Classes with fields and base

The fields pragma allows us to declare hash-based objects with a restricted list of attributes. The returned object reference behaves like a hash, but any attempt to get or set an invalid hash key will provoke a fatal error. If possible, invalid accesses are checked at compile time and produce syntax errors; otherwise, they are detected at run time. Here is another version of the Game::Card class created using the fields pragma:

```
package Game::Card;
use strict;
use fields qw(name suit _up_sleeve);

sub new {
    my $proto=shift;
    my $class=ref($proto) || $proto;

    my Game::Card $self=fields::new($class);
    $self->initialize(@_);
```

```
    return $self;
}

sub initialize {
    my Game::Card $self=shift;
    my ($name,$suit)=@_;
    $self->{name} = $name;
    $self->{suit} = $suit;
}
```

We can use this object class in code like this:

```
#!/usr/bin/perl
# fieldsgamecard.pl
use strict;
use warnings;
use Game::Card;

my Game::Card $card=new Game::Card(Ace => 'Spades');
print $self->{name};
print $self->{number}; # ERROR: nonexistent attribute;
```

Notice the typed declaration in this example. This is a hint to the Perl interpreter to tell it that this variable will be holding an object reference of the specified class. Using this information, Perl can detect hash key accesses through the reference and flag invalid keys as compile-type syntax errors. If we leave out the type, the code will still work, but the error will be detected only at run time. The typed declaration in the new and initialize methods has the same effect—if we try to assign a hash key that wasn't declared in the list of fields, Perl will reject it.

We have already used the base pragma to define class inheritance, but its true purpose comes to light when it is used in conjunction with fields. Using it, we can add additional attributes to sub-classes of fields-based classes like this:

```
package Amber::Trump;
use strict;
use base Game::Card qw(location alive);
```

And:

```
#!/usr/bin/perl
# fieldssubclass.pl
use strict;
use warnings;
use Amber::Trump;

my Amber::Trump $prince=new Amber::Trump('Corwin');
$prince->{suit}='black and silver';
$prince->{location}='Earth';
$prince->{alive}='yes';
```

We added a special attribute _up_ sleeve to our fields-based Game::Card class. As the leading underscore implies, this is meant to be a private attribute of the class and not visible outside it, even to subclasses. The fields and base pragmas enforce this implication, so an attempt to access this private information from the subclass will cause an error. If the object is declared as a typed scalar, this will even be a compile-time syntax error. If we want to provide extra logic in the constructor to handle the new attributes, we can define it in the subclass as usual. We can also add an initialize method as we designed one into this class:

```
sub initialize {
    my Amber::Trump $self=shift;
    my ($name,$suit,$location,$alive)=@_;

    $self->SUPER::initialize($name,$suit);
    $self->{location} = $name;
    $self->{alive} = $suit;
}
```

The underlying data type of a `fields`-based class is either the older pseudohash mechanism or the new restricted hash, depending on whether we are using Perl prior to version 5.10 (technically, 5.9) or not. The `base` pragma ensures that whatever mechanism is actually used to create the object, inheritance is handled correctly. This means that we cannot define an attribute that collides with an attribute already in place in a parent class, for example, and it also means that the mapping of hash keys to index values is correctly extended when pseudohashes are in use.

The `Class::Fields` module, available from CPAN, provides expanded semantics to the `fields` and `base` modules. These include the ability to programmatically extract the available attributes of a class and analyze their derivation (are they inherited, and if so from which parent class) and their visibility (public, private, or protected). In addition, we can declare attributes as public, private, and protected rather than supply them as a list to the `fields` pragma, and we can perform a number of other high-level object manipulations that will be more familiar to programmers of other object-oriented languages. An alternative is `Class::Struct::FIELDS`, which combines the capabilities of fields-based objects with the convenience of the `Class::Struct` module, which we tackle next.

Building Object Classes with Class::Struct

The `Class::Struct` provides much more limited but considerably simpler object class generation features than modules like `Class::MethodMaker`. Several object classes provided by Perl are based on it, including all the `hostent`, `netent`, `protoent`, and `servent` modules, as well as `stat` and several others. All of these modules make good working examples of how `Class::Struct` is used.

The module provides one subroutine, `struct`. The name is taken from C's `struct` declaration, after which the module is patterned. To use it, we supply a list of attributes and their data types, indicated by the appropriate Perl prefix, $ for scalars, @ for arrays, and % for hashes. In return, it defines a constructor (`new`) and a complete set of accessor/mutator methods for each attribute we request. For example, this is how we can create a constructor and six accessor/mutator methods for an address class in one statement:

```
# Address.pm
package Address;
use strict;

use Class::Struct;
struct (
    name => '$',
    address => '@',
    postcode => '$',
    city => '$',
    state => '$',
    country => '$',
);

1;
```

This object class creates objects with five scalar attributes and one array attribute whose value is stored as an array reference. When we use this module, `struct` is called and the class is fully defined. The constructor new, generated on the fly by struct, accepts initialization of the object with named arguments, so we can create and then print out the fields of an object created by this class using a script like the following:

```perl
#!/usr/bin/perl
# address.pl
use warnings;
use strict;

use Address;

my $address = new Address(
    name => 'Me Myself',
    address => ['My House', '123 My Street'],
    city => 'My Town',
);

print $address->name," lives at: \n",
    "\t", join("\n\t", @{$address->address}), "\n",
    "in the city of ", $address->city, "\n";
```

This produces the following output:

```
Me Myself lives at:
        My House
        123 My Street
in the city of My Town
```

Getting and setting attributes on these automatically generated objects is fairly self-evident. Each accessor/mutator follows the pattern of accessor/mutator methods we have seen before. Scalars are retrieved by passing no arguments and set by passing one:

```perl
$name = $address->name;   # get an attribute
$address->name($name);    # set an attribute
```

Array and hash attributes return a reference to the whole array or hash if no arguments are passed; otherwise, they return the value specified by the passed index or hash key if one argument is passed and set the value specified if two:

```perl
$arrayref = $address->address;
$first_line = $address->address(0);
$address->address(0, $firstline);
$hashref = $address->hashattr;
$value = $address->hashattr('key');
$address->hashattr('key', $value);
```

The underlying object representation of this class is an array. If we want to be able to inherit the class reliably, we are better off using a hash, which we can do by passing struct (the name of the class we want to create methods for), followed by the attributes we want to handle in a hash or array reference. If we pass an array reference, the class is based on an array. If we pass a hash reference, it is based on a hash like so:

```perl
# AddressHash.pm
package Address;
use strict;

use Class::Struct;
```

```
struct Address => {
    name => '$',
    address => '@',
    postcode => '$',
    city => '$',
    state => '$',
    country => '$',
};
```

```
1;
```

We can create and then print out the fields of the object created by this version of the class using the same script, producing the same output as before.

In fact, we do not even need the package Address at the top of this module, since struct creates subroutines in the package passed to it as the first argument anyway.

We can also use objects as attributes by the simple expedient of naming an object class instead of a Perl data type prefix. Here's a modified Address class that replaces the address array attribute with a subclass called Address::Lines with an explicit house and street attribute:

```
# AddressNest.pm
package Address;
use strict;

use Class::Struct;

struct 'Address::Lines' => [
    house => '$',
    street => '$',
];

struct (
    name => '$',
    address => 'Address::Lines',
    postcode => '$',
    city => '$',
    state => '$',
    country => '$',
);
```

```
1;
```

Since we can chain together object calls if the result of one method is another object, we can modify the test script to be

```
#!/usr/bin/perl
# addressnest.pl
use warnings;
use strict;

use AddressNest;

my $address = new Address(
    name => 'Me Myself',
    city => 'My Town',
);

$address->address->house('My House');
$address->address->street('123 My Street');
```

```
print $address->name, " lives at: \n",
    "\t", $address->address->house, "\n",
    "\t", $address->address->street, "\n",
    "in the city of ", $address->city, "\n";
```

We can, if we choose, optionally prefix the attribute type with an asterisk, to make *$, *@, *%, or *Object::Class. When present, this causes the accessor for the attribute to return references rather than values. For example, if we used name => '*$' in the arguments to struct, we could do this:

```
$scalar_ref = $address->name;
$$scalar_ref = "My New Name";
$new_scalar = "A Different Name Again";
$address->name(\$newscalar);
```

The same referential treatment is given to array, hash, and object attributes, for example, with address => '*@':

```
$first_element = $address->address(0);
$$first_element = "My New House";
```

If we want to provide more precise control over attributes, we can do so by redefining the accessor/mutator methods with explicit subroutines. Be aware, however, that Perl will warn about redefined subroutines if warnings are enabled. If we need to override a lot of methods, however, the benefits of using Class::Struct begin to weaken, and we are probably better off implementing the object class from scratch.

As a final example, if we want to create a class that contains attributes of one type only (most probably scalars), we can create very short class modules, as this rather terse but still fully functional example illustrates:

```
# AddressMap.pm
use strict;

use Class::Struct;
struct Address => { map {$_ => '$'}
    qw (name house street city state country postcode)
};

1;
```

For completeness, here is the test script for this last class; note that it is very similar to our first example, which was mostly made up of scalars. Again, it produces the same output as all the others:

```
#!/usr/bin/perl
# addressmap.pl
use warnings;
use strict;

use AddressMap;

my $address = new Address(
    name => 'Me Myself',
    house => 'My House',
    street => '123 My Street',
    city => 'My Town',
);

print $address->name," lives at:\n",
    "\t", $address->house, "\n",
    "\t", $address->street, "\n",
    "in the city of ", $address->city, "\n";
```

To combine the capabilities of `Class::Struct` with the inheritance and restricted access abilities of the `fields` and `base` pragmas, we can make use of the `Class::Struct::FIELDS` module, available from CPAN. This module integrates the features of both approaches, with some necessary restrictions on use to allow them to interoperate correctly. The resultant objects generated by this module behave just like regular `Class::Struct` objects, but they are based on pseudohashes or restricted hashes generated by the `fields` pragma.

Ties and Tied Objects

One of the more intriguing parts of Perl's support for object-oriented programming is the tied object. Tied objects are somewhat at odds with the normal applications of object orientation. In most object-oriented tasks, we take a functional, non–object-oriented problem and rephrase it in object-oriented terms. Ties go the other way, taking an object class and hiding it behind a simple non–object-oriented variable.

Tied objects allow us to replace the functionality of a standard data type with an object class that secretly handles the actual manipulations, so that access to the variables are automatically and transparently converted into method calls on the underlying object. The object can then deal with the operation as it sees fit. Perl allows us to tie any standard data type, including scalars, arrays, hashes, and filehandles. In each case, the operations that the underlying object needs to support vary.

There are many possible uses for `tie`, from hashes that only allow certain keys to be stored (as used by the `fields` module), to the DBM family of modules, which use tied hash variables to represent DBM databases. The Perl standard library provides several tied classes, including the `fields` module and the DBM family of modules, and there are many, many tied class implementations available from CPAN. Before implementing a tied class, it is worth checking to see if it has already been done.

Tied object classes are a powerful way to use objects to provide enhanced features in places that are otherwise hard to reach or difficult to implement. The `tie` makes the object appear as a conventional variable. This allows us to replace ordinary variables with "smart" ones, so any Perl code that works with the original data type will also work with the tied object, oblivious to the fact that we have replaced it with something else of our own design.

Using Tied Objects

Variables are bound to an underlying object with the `tie` function. The first argument to `tie` is the variable to be bound, and the second is the name of the object class, which will provide the functionality of the tied variable. Further arguments are passed to the constructor that is, in turn, used to create the object used to implement this particular variable, which is, of course, determined by the type of variable being tied. For example, to tie a scalar variable to a package called `My::Scalar::Tie`, we could put

```
my $scalar;
tie $scalar, 'My::Scalar::Tie', 'initial value';
```

The `initial value` argument is passed to the constructor; in this case, it is expected to be used to set up the scalar in some way, but that is up to the constructor. Similarly, to tie a hash variable, this time to a DBM module, we use the following:

```
tie %dbm, 'GDBM_File', $filename, $flags, $perm;
```

The `GDBM_File` module implements access to DBM files created with the gdbm libraries. It needs to know the name of the file to open, plus, optionally, open flags and permissions (in exactly the same way that the sysopen function does). Given this, the module creates a new database object that contains an open filehandle for the actual database handle as class data. If we tie a second DBM database to a second variable, a second object instance is created, containing a filehandle for the second database. Of course, we only see the hash variable, all the work of reading and writing the database is handled for us by the DBM module (in this case GDBM_File).

The return value from tie is an object on success, or undef on failure:

```
$object = tie $scalar, 'My::Scalar::Tie', 'initial value';
```

We can store this object for later use, or alternatively (and more conveniently) we can get it from the tied variable using tied:

```
$object = tied $scalar;
```

Handling Errors from tie

Many, though not all, tied object modules produce a fatal error if they cannot successfully carry out the tie (the database file does not exist, or we did not have permission to open it, for example). To catch this, we therefore need to use eval. For example, this subroutine returns a reference to a tied hash on success or undef on failure:

```
sub open_dbm {
    my $filename = shift;
    my %dbm;

    eval {tie %dbm, 'GDBM_File', $filename};
    if ($@) {
        print STDERR "Dang! Couldn't open $filename: $@";
        return undef;
    }

    return \%dbm;
}
```

This is not a property of tie, but rather a general programming point for handling any object constructor that can emit a fatal error, but it's worth mentioning here because it is easy to overlook.

Accessing Nested References

The special properties of a tied variable apply only to that variable; access to the internal values of a tied hash or array is triggered by our use of the tied variable itself. If we extract a reference from a tied hash or array, the returned value is likely to be a simple untied reference, and although attempts to manipulate it will work, we will really be handling a local copy of the data that the tied hash represents and not the data itself.

The upshot of this is that we must always access elements through the tied variable, and not via a reference. In other words, the following is fine:

```
$tied{key}{subkey}{subsubkey1} = "value1";
$tied{key}{subkey}{subsubkey2} = "value2";
$tied{key}{subkey}{subsubkey3} = "value3";
```

But this is probably not:

```
$subhash = $tied{key}{subkey};
$subhash->{subsubkey1} = "value1";
$subhash->{subsubkey2} = "value2";
$subhash->{subsubkey3} = "value3";
```

Although this appears to work, the extraction of the hash reference $subhash actually causes the tied variable to generate a local copy of the data that the hash represents. Our assignments to it therefore update the local copy but have no effect whatsoever on the actual data that the tied hash controls access to.

Having said that we cannot use internal references, this is not absolutely the case. It is perfectly possible for the tied object class to return a newly tied hash that accesses the nested data we requested, in which case we can use the subreference with impunity, just like the main tied variable. However, this is a lot of effort to go to, and most tied object classes do not go to the lengths necessary to implement it.

Testing If a Variable Is Tied

The tied function returns the underlying object used to implement the features of the tied variable, or it returns undef otherwise. The most frequent use for this is to test whether a tie succeeded. For example, here is another way to trap and test for a failed tie:

```
eval {tie %hash, My::Tied::Hash}
handle_error($@) unless tied %hash;
```

We can also call methods on the underlying object class through tied. For example, wrapping tied and an object method call into one statement:

```
(tied %hash)->object_method(@args);
```

Just because we can call an underlying method does not mean we should, though. If the tied object class documentation provides additional support methods (and most tied classes of any complexity do), calling these is fine. But calling the methods that implement the tie functionality itself is a bad idea. The whole point of the tie is to abstract these methods behind ordinary accesses to the variable; sidestepping this is therefore breaking the interface design.

Untying Objects

Tied objects consume system resources just like any other object, or indeed variable. When we are finished with a tied object, we should dispose of it so that the object's destructor method, if any, can be called. In the case of the DBM:: modules, this flushes any remaining output and closes the database filehandle.

In many instances, the only reference to the underlying object is the tie to the variable, so by undoing the tie between the variable and the object, we cause Perl to invoke the garbage collector on the now unreferenced object. Appropriately enough, the function to do this is untie:

```
untie %hash;
```

untie always succeeds, unless the destructor emits a fatal error, in which case we need to trap it with eval. The fact it never returns a failed result makes writing a test very easy:

```
handle_error($@) unless eval {untie %hash};
```

If we pass untie on a variable that is not tied, nothing happens, but untie still succeeds. However, if we want to check explicitly, we can do so, for example:

```
untie %hash if tied %hash;
```

Writing Tied Objects

Tied object classes work by providing methods with predefined names for each operation that Perl requires for the data type of the variable being tied. For instance, for tied scalars, an object class needs to define a constructor method called TIESCALAR, plus the additional methods listed in Table 19-2.

Table 19-2. *Required Tied Scalar Methods*

Method	Description
FETCH	An accessor method that returns a scalar value
STORE	A mutator method that stores a passed scalar value
DESTROY	Optionally, a destructor for the object

Scalars are the simplest class to tie because we can essentially only do two things to it—read it, which is handled by the FETCH method, and write it, which is handled by the STORE method. We can also tie arrays, hashes, and filehandles if we define the appropriate methods.

Some methods are always mandatory; we always need a constructor for the class, with the correct name for the data type being tied. We also always need a FETCH method, to read from the object. Others are required only in certain circumstances. For instance, we do not need a STORE method if we want to create a read-only variable, but it is better to define one and place a croak in it, rather than have Perl stumble and emit a less helpful warning when an attempt to write to the object is made.

Standard Tied Object Classes

Creating the supporting methods for every required operation can be tedious, particularly for arrays, which require 13 methods in a fully implemented object class.

Fortunately, Perl removes a lot of the grunt work of creating tied object classes by providing template object classes, listed in Table 19-3, in the standard library that contain default methods we can inherit from, or override, with our own implementations. The default methods mostly just croak when they are not implemented, but each module also provides a minimal, but functional, Std object class (see Table 19-4) that implements each data type as an object of the same type blessed and returned as a reference.

Table 19-3. *Base Tie Classes*

Module	Data Type
Tie::Scalar	Tied scalars
Tie::Array	Tied arrays
Tie::Hash	Tied hashes
Tie::Handle	Tied handles (file, directory, socket, and so on)

Table 19-4. *"Standard" Tie Classes*

Module	Data Type
Tie::StdScalar	Minimal tied scalar class
Tie::StdArray	Minimal tied array class
Tie::StdHash	Minimal tied hash class
Tie::StdHandle	Minimal tied handle class

In addition, we can make use of three enhanced tied hash classes, shown in Table 19-5.

Table 19-5. *Extended Tie Classes*

Module	Description
`Tie::RefHash`	Tied hashes that allow references to be used as the hash keys, overcoming the usual restriction of hash keys to static string values.
`Tie::SubstrHash`	Tied hashes that permit only a fixed maximum length for both keys and values, and in addition to this, limit the total number of entries allowed in the hash.
`Tie::Memoize`	Tied hashes that cache previously requested values for faster subsequent accesses. Useful for wrapping computationally expensive but invariant calculations.

Tied Object Methods

The methods we need to define for each data type vary, but loosely fall into the categories of constructor/destructor, accessor/mutator, function implementations, and specialized operations that apply to specific data types. All tied object classes need a constructor, and they may implement a destructor. All types except filehandles may also (and usually should) define an accessor and mutator. Arrays, hashes, and filehandles also need to define methods for Perl's built-in functions that operate on those data types, for instance, pop, shift, and splice for arrays; delete and exists for hashes; and print, readline, and close for filehandles.

We are free to define our own methods in addition to the ones required by the tie and can call them via the underlying object, if we desire. We can also create additional class methods; the only one required (for all classes) is the constructor. Note that the UNTIE method was added to the standard set in Perl 5.6.1; if used by a Perl older than this, it will not be called automatically, so tied object classes that need to work on a wider range of Perl versions should not rely on it. (Since it is an ordinary subroutine, an older Perl will not warn us that it is not implemented.)

The standard library modules define default versions of all these methods, but we may choose to implement a tied object class without them, or even want to override them with our own methods. The following summaries list the methods required by each data type, along with a typical use of the tied variable that will trigger the method, with some brief explanations:

Methods and Uses for Scalars

Here are the creator/destructor methods for scalars:

Method	Use
`TIESCALAR class, list`	`tie $scalar, Class::Name, @args;`
`DESTROY self`	`undef $scalar;`
`UNTIE self`	`untie $scalar;`

The accessor/mutator methods for scalars are as follows:

Method	Use
`FETCH self`	`$value = $scalar;`
`STORE self, value`	`$scalar = $value;`

Scalars are the simplest tied object class to implement. The constructor may take any arguments it likes, and the only other method that needs to handle an argument is STORE. Note that the constructor is the only method we call directly, so we cannot pass extra arguments to the other methods even if we wanted to; all information required must be conveyed by the object.

Methods and Uses for Arrays

Arrays require the same methods as scalars, but they take an additional index argument for both FETCH and STORE. These are the constructor/destructor methods for arrays:

Method	Use
TIEARRAY class, list	tie @array, Class::Name, @list;
DESTROY self	undef @array;
UNTIE self	untie @array;

The accessor/mutator methods for arrays are as follows:

Method	Use
FETCH self, index	$value = $array[$index];
STORE self, index, value	$array[$index] = $value;
DELETE self, index	delete $array[$index];
EXISTS self, index	exists $arrat[$index];

Interestingly, tied arrays may implement semantics for delete and exists. Even though these make no sense for real arrays, it is possible they might mean something to a tied array class. It would be possible to implement delete in terms of splice, for instance.

Prior to Perl 5.8.1, negative index values are automatically converted into appropriate positive values by calling FETCHSIZE (covered in a moment) to determine the actual size of the array and then subtracting the index from it, as happens for built-in arrays. From 5.8.1 onwards this behavior can be disabled by setting a package variable in the tied class $NEGATIVE_INDICES to a true value, for example:

```
package My::Tied::Class
use base Tied::Array;
our $NEGATIVE_INDICES=1;
```

This change permits classes that want to treat negative indices as special cases the ability to do so. For older Perls, this variable, of course, has no effect, and the index seen by FETCH, STORE, DELETE, and EXISTS is always positive.

We also need implementations for the push, pop, shift, unshift, and splice functions if we want to be able to use these functions on our tied arrays:

Method	Use
PUSH self, list	push @array, @list;
POP self	$value = pop @array;
SHIFT self	$value = shift @array;
UNSHIFT self, list	unshift @array, @list;
SPLICE self, offset, length, list	splice @array, $offset, $length, @list;

Finally, we need methods to handle the extension or truncation of the array. Unique to arrays are the EXTEND, FETCHSIZE, and STORESIZE methods, which implement implicit and explicit alterations the extent of the array; real arrays do this through $#array, as covered in Chapter 5. The extension/truncation methods for arrays are as follows:

Method	Use
CLEAR self	@array = ();
EXTEND self, size	$array[$size] = $value;
FETCHSIZE self	$size = $#array;
STORESIZE self, size	$#array = $size;

Methods and Uses for Hashes

Hashes are more complex than arrays, but ironically are easier to implement. Here are the constructor/destructor methods for hashes:

Method	Use
TIEHASH class, list	tie %hash, Class::Name, @list;
DESTROY self	undef %hash;
UNTIE self	untie %hash;

Like arrays, the FETCH and STORE methods take an additional argument, this time of a key name. The accessor/mutator methods for hashes are as follows:

Method	Use
FETCH self, key	$value = $hash{$key};
STORE self, key, value	$hash{$key} = $value;
SCALAR self	$hasvalues = %hash;

The SCALAR method was added in Perl 5.8.3. Prior to this, tied hashes were always false in scalar context. From 5.8.3 onwards, if a SCALAR method is not defined and an iterator has been not defined by each, FIRSTKEY is called to determine if the hash has any values. If each has an active iterator, FIRSTKEY is not called, and the hash is automatically true in scalar context. (It is not possible for each to have an iterator if there are no values, ergo the hash cannot be empty.)

The delete and exists functions are implemented through the DELETE and EXISTS methods. In addition, CLEAR is used for deleting all the elements from a hash. The defined function is implemented in terms of FETCH, so there is no DEFINED method. This is also why there is no EXISTS or DEFINED method for arrays or scalars, since both operations are equivalent to defined for anything except hashes. The following lists the function implementation methods for hashes:

Method	Use
CLEAR self	%hash = ();
DELETE self, key	$done = delete $hash{$key};
EXISTS self, key	$exists = exists $hash{$key};

The FIRSTKEY and NEXTKEY methods need a little more explanation. Both methods are needed for the each keyword, which retrieves each key-value pair from a hash in turn. To do this, the class must define some form of iterator that stores the current position, so that the next key produces a meaningful result. This iterator should be reset when FIRSTKEY is called and incremented when NEXTKEY is called. Both methods should return the appropriate key and value as a list. Finally, when there are no more key-value pairs to return, NEXTKEY should return undef. The each iteration methods are as follows:

Method	Use
FIRSTKEY self	($key, $value) = each %hash; # first time
NEXTKEY self, lastkey	($key, $value) = each %hash; # second and subsequent times

Methods and Uses for Filehandles

Filehandles are unique amongst tied variables because they define neither an accessor or mutator method. Instead, the constructor makes available some kind of resource, typically with open, pipe, socket, or some other method that generates a real filehandle. The constructor/destructor methods for filehandles are listed here:

Method	Use
TIEHANDLE class, list	tie $fh, Class::Name, @args;
DESTROY self	undef $fh;
UNTIE self	untie $fh;

Whatever the creator method does, the CLOSE method needs to be defined to undo whatever it creates.

The only other methods required are for the standard filehandle functions: print, printf, and write for output and read, readline, and getc for input, as appears in the following list. If we are implementing a read-only or write-only filehandle, we need only define the appropriate methods, of course.

Function Implementation Method	Use
READ self, scalar, length, offset	read $fh, $in, $size, $from
READLINE self	$line = <$fh>
GETC self	$char = getc $fh
WRITE self, scalar, length, offset	write $fh, $out, $size, $from
PRINT self, list	print $fh @args
PRINTF self, format, list	printf $fh $format @values
CLOSE self	close $fh

An Example Tied Hash Class

The tied hash class that follows demonstrates a basic use of the tied functionality provided by Perl by creating hashes that can have read, write, or delete access enabled or disabled. In order to demonstrate the fundamentals of tied object classes, it explicitly defines methods for all the possible access types for a hash, and does not use Tie::Hash. Despite this, it is still very simple to understand.

The design follows a common theme for a lot of tied classes, where the actual data is stored as an element of a hash that represents the object, with other elements holding flags or values that configure how the real data is handled. This is a general template that works well for all manner of "smart" scalars, arrays, hashes, and filehandles.

```perl
# Permission/Hash.pm
package Permission::Hash;
use strict;

use Carp;

sub TIEHASH {
    my ($class, %cfg) = @_;

    my $self = bless {}, shift;

    $self->{value} = ();
    foreach ('read', 'write', 'delete') {
        $self->{$_} = (defined $cfg{$_})?$cfg{$_}:1;
    }

    return $self;
}

sub FETCH {
    my ($self, $key) = @_;
    croak "Cannot read key '$key'" unless $self->{read};
    return $self->{value}{$key};
}

sub STORE {
    my ($self, $key, $value) = @_;
    croak "Cannot write key '$key'" unless $self->{write};
    $self->{value}{$key} = $value;
}

sub EXISTS {
    my ($self, $key) = @_;
    croak "Cannot read key '$key'" unless $self->{read};
    return exists $self->{value}{$key};
}

sub CLEAR {
    my $self = shift;
    croak "Cannot delete hash" unless $self->{delete};
    $self->{value} = ();
}

sub DELETE {
    my ($self, $key) = @_;
    croak "Cannot delete key '$key'" unless $self->{delete};
    return delete $self->{value}{$key};
}
```

```perl
sub FIRSTKEY {
    my $self = shift;
    my $dummy = keys %{$self->{value}};    #reset iterator
    return $self->NEXTKEY;
}

sub NEXTKEY {
    return each %{shift->{value}};
}

1;
```

Because we are creating a tied hash that controls access to a real hash, most of the methods are very simple. We are relaying the operation requested on the tied variable to the real variable inside. This class could be improved a lot, notably by adding proper accessor/mutator methods for the three flags. We could also add other permission types. A more interesting and complex example would be to set the flags on each key, rather than for the hash as a whole. Here is a short script that puts the Permission::Hash class through its paces:

```perl
#!/usr/bin/perl
# permhash.pl
use warnings;
use strict;

use Permission::Hash;

my %hash;
tie %hash, 'Permission::Hash', read => 1, write => 1, delete => 0;

$hash{one}   = 1;
$hash{two}   = 2;
$hash{three} = 3;

print "Try to delete a key... \n";
unless (eval {delete $hash{three}; 1} ) {
    print $@;
    print "Let's try again... \n";
    (tied %hash)->{delete} = 1;
    delete $hash {three};
    print "It worked! \n";
    (tied %hash)->{delete} = 0;
}

print "Disable writing... \n";
(tied %hash)->{write} = 0;
unless (eval {$hash{four} = 4; 1} ) {
    print $@;
}
(tied %hash)->{write} = 1;

print "Disable reading... \n";
(tied %hash)->{read} = 0;
unless (defined $hash{one}) {
    print $@;
}
(tied %hash)->{read} = 1;
```

When run, this script should produce output resembling the following:

```
Try to delete a key...
Cannot delete key 'three' at permhash.pl line 12
Let's try again...
It worked!
Disable writing...
Cannot write key 'four' at permhash.pl line 23
Disable reading...
Cannot read key 'one' at permhash.pl line 30
```

Many more practical variants on this design can easily be implemented. In the case of hashes alone, we can easily create case-insensitive hashes (apply lc to all passed keys) or accumulative hashes (make each value an array and append new values to the end in STORE), or restrict the number of keys (count the keys and check whether the key already exists in STORE, before creating a new one) or the names of the keys (pass a list of acceptable keys to the constructor, then check that any key passed to STORE is in that list) that can be assigned. Restricted hashes provide much of the capabilities cited in this last example, but with our own tied object class we can customize the behavior of the hash in any way we like.

An Example Class Using Tie::StdHash

The standard Tie modules provide inheritable methods for all the required actions needed by each type of tied variable, but for the most part, these simply produce more informative error messages for methods we do not implement ourselves. They are a useful safety net for developing tied classes, but not much more.

However, each of these packages comes with internal Std and Extra subclasses that implement minimal but functional tied objects of the same class. For example, Tie::Scalar contains Tie::StdScalar and Tie::ExtraScalar. With these classes we need only overload the methods that we need to augment the behavior of—everything else is already taken care of. As a very practical example, here is the actual implementation of Tie::StdHash, as defined inside the Tie::Hash module:

```perl
package Tie::StdHash;
@ISA = qw(Tie::Hash);

sub TIEHASH  { bless {}, $_[0] }
sub STORE    { $_[0]->{$_[1]} = $_[2] }
sub FETCH    { $_[0]->{$_[1]} }
sub FIRSTKEY { my $a = scalar keys %{$_[0]}; each %{$_[0]} }
sub NEXTKEY  { each %{$_[0]} }
sub EXISTS   { exists $_[0]->{$_[1]} }
sub DELETE   { delete $_[0]->{$_[1]} }
sub CLEAR    { %{$_[0]} = () }

1;
```

In this class, each method is simply given a primitive implementation that implements the semantics of the data type it is standing in for. By itself, therefore, this class takes a hash and replaces it with an object that implements a hash—in other words, no change in behavior. The point, of course, is to overload some of these methods. Note that the DESTROY and UNTIE methods are not provided with a default implementation, as there is no basic equivalent functionality for them to simulate.

We can use this object class to implement our own tied hash classes, as long as we are willing to accept the implementation of the object as a directly tied hash. If we want to store additional information "to the side" of the hash, for example to store flags or metadata that we do not want to store in the hash directly, we can make use of Tie::ExtraHash instead. This operates identically to Tie::StdHash, except that the internal storage is changed to an array and a reference to the hash is stored in the first element. The default methods simply reference the hash in element 0 rather than directly, so STORE and FETCH become

```perl
sub STORE    { $_[0][0]{$_[1]} = $_[2] }
sub FETCH    { $_[0][0]{$_[1]} }
```

The first argument, $_[0], is a reference to the array. The second, [0], accesses the hash, and {$_[1]} the requested key in the hash. Tie::ExtraHash and its equivalents for scalars, arrays, and filehandles does not in any way make use of the array except as a means to reach the hash. We are therefore free to use any other elements to store metadata as we see fit. We just need to remember to convert access to the hash.

As a practical example, here is a hash class based on Tie::StdHash that will limit either the total number of hash keys allowed or restrict keys to one of a specific list provided when the object is initialized (in a similar manner to pseudohashes or restricted hashes, but now fully within our control). It overloads just three of the possible methods:

```perl
# Limit/Hash.pm
package Limit::Hash;
use strict;

use Carp;
use Tie::Hash;
our @ISA = qw(Tie::StdHash);

sub TIEHASH {
    my ($class, @keys) = @_;

    my $self = $class->SUPER::TIEHASH;
    croak "Must pass either limit or key list" if $#keys == -1;
    if ($#keys) {
        $self->{'_keys'} = {map {$_ => 1} @keys};
    } else {
        croak ",", $keys[0], "' is not a limit" unless int($keys[0]);
        $self->{'_limit'} = $keys[0]+1;   #add one for _limit
    }

    return $self;
}

sub FETCH {
    my ($self, $key) = @_;
    croak "Invalid key '$key'"
        if defined($self->{'_keys'}) and
            (!$self->{'_keys'}{$key} or $key =~ /^_/);
    return $self->SUPER::FETCH($key);
}

sub STORE {
    my ($self, $key, $value) = @_;
    croak "Invalid key '$key'"
        if defined($self->{'_keys'}) and
            (!$self->{'_keys'}{$key} or $key =~ /^_/);
    croak "Limit reached"
        if defined($self->{'_limit'}) and
            (!$self->{'_limit'} or
```

```
            $self->{'_limit'} <= scalar(%{$self}));
    $self->SUPER::STORE($key, $value);
}

1;
```

The constructor examines the arguments passed to it and either establishes a limit or a list of valid keys. If a limit was passed, we add one to it to allow for the _limit key itself, which also resides in the hash. If no arguments are passed at all, the constructor complains. Otherwise, two special keys are created in the hash to hold the configuration.

The only other methods we override are FETCH and STORE. Each method checks that the key is valid, and prevents "private" underscore prefixed keys from being set. If the key passes the check, we pass the request to the FETCH and STORE methods of Tie::StdHash, our parent.

Technically, we do not need to pass the method request up to the parent object from our versions of TIEHASH, FETCH, and STORE since they are obvious implementations. However, it is good practice to use parent methods where possible, so we do it anyway.

```
# limithash.pl
#!/usr/bin/perl
use warnings;
use strict;

use Limit::Hash;

tie my %hash, 'Limit::Hash', 'this', 'that', 'other';

$hash{this} = 'this is ok';
$hash{that} = 'as is this';
print $hash{this}, "\n";
$hash{'invalid-key'} = 'but this croaks';
```

When run, this script should produce the following:

```
this is ok
Invalid key 'invalid-key' at limithash.pl line 13
```

A Tied Constant Scalar Class

There are many ways to create constant scalars in Perl, for instance, typeglob-aliasing a reference to a constant string. A constant scalar tied class is another solution to this problem. As the example that follows illustrates, the implementation is trivial if we use Tie::StdScalar—we just overload STORE:

```
package Constant::Scalar;
use base Tie::StdScalar;

sub STORE { die "Attempt to modify constant"; }

1;
```

We could go on to extend this class to "lock" or "unlock" the value much as we did with the Permissions::Hash example earlier. Although it is slower than the typeglob approach, the tied constant scalar permits us to add additional functionality like this in an elegant and intuitive way.

Caveats of Tied Objects

Useful though tied objects are, they do not come without caveats. One drawback of a tied object class is that it is slower than the equivalent native data type. A real hash is very fast in Perl, and a restricted hash is not much slower. But a tied hash, array, scalar, or filehandle requires a method call for every kind of manipulation, and this will always be less efficient than the native equivalent.

Tied objects strive to implement the semantics of ordinary data types, but with additional intelligence. However, there are a few cases where a tied object will not behave like a fundamental data type that we may need to be aware of. One of the more subtle ones is that autovivification of arrays and hashes no longer works when the array or hash is actually a tied object. With a real array or hash, we can say

```
$array[0][1][2][3]='deep down array value';
$hash{key}{deep}{deeper}{waydown}='deep down hash value';
```

This will not work with a tied hash or array unless all the intermediate data structures already exist, at least currently. (It may be supported beyond Perl 5.10.)

Prior to Perl 5.8.3, hashes always evaluated to a false value in scalar context, so we cannot test whether or not a tied hash has any keys with a construct like this one:

```
if (%tied_hash) { ... # possible ERROR: always always false prior to 5.8.3
```

In a sufficiently modern Perl, the SCALAR method is implemented so tied hashes can provide an answer to this question. Failing this, Perl checks to see if each built-in function has been called for the underlying data and has an active iterator, in which case the hash evaluates to a true value. If each does not have an active iterator, FIRSTKEY is called and the hash evaluates to true if FIRSTKEY returns a value. Since FIRSTKEY may trigger initialization code for empty tied hashes in our tied object implementation, this behavior is worth keeping in mind.

Summary

Object-oriented development is an important subject in any language, and no less so in Perl. Despite its roots as a hybrid of shell programming and C, Perl turns out to be surprisingly capable as an object-oriented language, thanks in part to also having concepts originated by Lisp in its ancestry. Perl implements almost all of its object semantics in terms of the method call operator -> and the @ISA array, on top of which everything else can be built. Because of this, it is able to jettison large parts of object mechanics and terminology that are seen as fundamental in other languages. The result is a language that provides only basic object support, yet permits almost any kind of object-oriented philosophy to be used.

After introducing the basic ideas behind object-oriented programming, we looked at creating objects with constructors and using objects by calling class and object methods. We then learned how to determine what inherited characteristics an object possesses, for example, its ancestry, capabilities, and version. After this, we saw how to write object classes; specifically we looked at constructors and choosing an underlying data type. As well as this, we looked at class, object, and multiple-context methods.

From here, we discussed object and class data, which involved learning about accessors and mutators, along with inheriting and setting class data. Then we learned about class and object-level debugging, and implemented a multiplex debug strategy.

Subclassing and inheriting from object classes is one of the main reasons to write them, and accordingly we spent some time looking at inheritance and strategies for extending and redefining the behavior of objects. We also looked at the potential and pitfalls of multiple inheritance, defining methods in the UNIVERSAL package, autoloading methods on demand, passing method calls on to sibling classes, and writing destructors to intelligently clean up object resources when the object is no longer in use.

Many languages provide the ability to overload operators to give objects the same semantics as fundamental data types in numerical or string operations such as addition or concatenation. Perl is no exception and provides this feature through the overload pragma. We saw how to use overload to add objects together and control the results of numerical and string conversions (also called "stringification").

While Perl makes it easy for us to create our own kind of objects, we can usually use an existing module to supply most of the desired functionality. The standard Perl library provides two means to this end with the fields pragma and the Class::Struct module; CPAN provides a host of more advanced solutions if these are not adequate to our needs. If all else fails, we can always design our own strategy for object development.

In the last part of the chapter, we looked at tied object classes, which allow us to disguise object classes behind apparently normal fundamental built-in data types. Tied objects allow us to implement sophisticated behaviors behind the familiar semantics of scalar, array, hash, or filehandle operations. We looked at some example tied object implementations, including a lockable hash and a constant scalar and summarized the capabilities available to us for different kinds of tied data.

CHAPTER 20

■ ■ ■

Extending and Embedding Perl

Sometimes it is more convenient to reach outside Perl for a feature than implement it as Perl code. A classical example is system libraries that we want to make use of from within Perl. As these libraries are not Perl themselves, we need a way to interact with them. Another common case is algorithms that are faster when implemented as pure C than we can manage within Perl. Modules that make use of external code this way are known as *extensions*. Whatever the reason for using C, C++, or another language, we need some glue to bind the compiled code into our Perl. The glue is called XSUBs, or XS for short, and Perl provides plenty of support to help us write extensions using it.

In this chapter, we will see how to integrate a Perl interpreter into a C or C++ program and how to use C or C++ code from within Perl. Both subjects spend a lot of their conceptual time at the border between Perl and C, and so readers interested in either subject will find value in both sections. In particular, Perl provides an extensive library of C macros and routines for reading, writing, creating, and manipulating Perl data structures in C, as well as manipulating the stack of the Perl interpreter. Whichever direction we are interested in proceeding, managing Perl data from C is more than likely to become important.

While binding C into Perl using XS is relatively easy, it is easier still with the Inline module. Not only can this versatile module automate most of the work necessary to glue Perl and C together, but also it can manage C++, Java, Python, and a number of other languages with equal aplomb with the appropriate supporting module from CPAN. Even with the help of Inline, some knowledge of XS concepts and Perl's C interface will undoubtedly prove useful, however.

We will also spend some time in this chapter looking at various ways in which we can compile Perl programs into C executables and Perl bytecode, along with some of the drawbacks and caveats inherent to the process.

Using Perl from C or C++

To embed Perl into a C or C++ program involves linking the program code against the library that implements the Perl interpreter (for which the perl executable is merely a frontend). However, the interpreter library was built a certain way, depending on our build-time choices, and will not necessarily work correctly if linked against with code compiled a different way.

Therefore, the first thing we need to do is make sure we are building Perl the way we want it to be used as an embedded interpreter. This means that we don't build a threaded interpreter if we want to use it within a program that must run on a nonthreaded platform, for example. Assuming we have a satisfactory interpreter library ready to go, we can now set up our source code to build in a way that is compatible with it.

Setting Up to Build Against Perl

In order to make use of our interpreter, we must make sure to compile source code that uses it with the same definitions and compiler flags that Perl was built with. So when we include header files from the Perl distribution, they provide the same definitions to us as they did when we built the interpeter library.

Luckily, Perl is fully aware of how it was built and can answer any question about it through the -V option or the Config.pm module. For example, to find out what external libraries Perl was linked with, we can execute the following:

> **perl -V:lib**

This will generate something like

```
libs='-lnsl -lgdbm -ldb -ldl -lm -lcrypt -lutil -lpthread -lc';
```

This indicates that this is a threaded Perl interpreter, among other things. We can similarly extract values for the compiler flags with -V:ccflags, the linker flags with -V:ldflags, the actual name of the interpreter library with -V:libperl, and so on. Using the -V option without a qualifying name will dump out all of the compiler and linker flags, so we can see what is available. As presented, these values work as makefile macros, but we can extract just the value and lose the name=...; by adding colons, -V::libs:, for example.

While we could go about generating build commands with these, there is a better way. Since embedding a Perl interpreter is a common task and always requires these flags, the Extutils::Embed module is available to do all the hard work for us. Here is how we get the compiler options:

> **perl -MExtUtils::Embed -e ccopts**

The ccopts subroutine extracts all of the values related to compiler options and returns something like (depending on the platform and where we installed Perl) this:

```
-D_REENTRANT -D_GNU_SOURCE -DTHREADS_HAVE_PIDS -fno-strict-aliasing -pipe
-I/usr/local/include -D_LARGEFILE_SOURCE -D_FILE_OFFSET_BITS=64
-I/installed/perl/lib/5.8.5/i686-linux-thread-multi/CORE
```

To get the linker flags, we substitute ccopts with ldopts:

> **perl -MExtUtils::Embed -e ldopts**

which returns a result along the lines of

```
-Wl,-E  -L/usr/local/lib
/installed/perl/lib/5.8.5/i686-linux-thread-multi/auto/DynaLoader/DynaLoader.a
-L/installed/perl/lib/5.8.5/i686-linux-thread-multi/CORE -lperl -lnsl -ldl
-lm -lcrypt -lutil -lpthread -lc
```

We can also extract the compiler name with

$ perl -V::cc:

The extra colons suppress the leading and trailing characters and leave us with just the value in quotes. We can use this directly or in a makefile. In fact, generating makefile macros automatically is a common requirement, and we can generally do something like the following to achieve it (this particular example is specific to gmake, but most make tools provide a similar feature):

```
# gmake makefile for embed.c

CC=$(shell perl -V::cc:)
CCFLAGS=$(shell perl -MExtUtils::Embed -e ccopts)
LD=$(shell perl -V::ld:)
LDFLAGS=$(shell perl -MExtUtils::Embed -e ldopts)

all: embed

embed.o: embed.c
        $(CC) $(CCFLAGS) -o $@ -c $?

embed: embed.o
        $(LD) -o $@ $? $(LDFLAGS)
```

For Windows, Perl ships with a utility called genmake, which generates an nmake-compatible makefile. To use it, we just pass it the names of the source file or files that comprise our program:

> **perl genmake embed.c**

Either way, we now have a makefile that will build a C program with an embedded Perl interpreter for us. Now we just need to write one.

Creating and Invoking a Perl Interpeter

To create a Perl interpreter, we need to create a Perl interpreter instance, then invoke it to execute the code we want it to run. We need to perform some steps first to ensure that the interpreter is initialized correctly, and once we are done with the interpreter, we need to cleanly dispose of it. Fortunately, this can all be done with a few lines of code, as all the hard work has already been done for us by the EXTERN.h and perl.h header files that come in every Perl installation.

To demonstrate, the following short C program creates and invokes a Perl interpreter to evaluate and print out the current time using the Perl built-in function localtime:

```
/* embed.c */
#include <EXTERN.h>
#include <perl.h>

PerlInterpreter *my_perl;

int main(int argc, char **argv, char **env)
{
    /* initialize */
    PERL_SYS_INIT3(&argc,&argv,&env);

    /* create the interpreter */
    my_perl = perl_alloc();
    perl_construct(my_perl);
    PL_exit_flags |= PERL_EXIT_DESTRUCT_END;

    /* invoke perl with arguments */
    int perl_argc = 3;
    char *code="print scalar(localtime).\"\\n\"";
    char *perl_argv[] = {argv[0], "-e",code};
    perl_parse(my_perl, NULL, perl_argc, perl_argv, env);
    perl_run(my_perl);
```

```
        /* clean up */
        perl_destruct(my_perl);
        perl_free(my_perl);

        /* finish */
        PERL_SYS_TERM();
}
```

The PERL_SYS_INIT3 and PERL_SYS_TERM macros perform some essential startup and shutdown tasks that are necessary to create and dispose of a Perl interpreter cleanly. We should always use them at the start and end of our program.

We create and destroy an individual interpreter with perl_alloc, perl_construct, perl_destruct, and perl_free. In order to have Perl execute END blocks when the interpreter is destroyed, we bitwise-OR include PL_EXIT_DESTRUCT_END in PL_exit_flags (a special macro defined in the Perl headers). This is important because in a normal Perl interpreter this step is taken care of when the program terminates, a safe assumption for the Perl executable, but almost certainly not true for our embedded interpreter. Note that the use of my_perl as the pointer variable is not arbitrary; unless we redefine it, this is the name that macros like PL_exit_flags expect to work with.

In the middle of the program, we actually invoke the interpreter using perl_parse and perl_run. The perl_parse function carries out the task of setting up the interpreter using command-line options. This makes a very simple and convenient interface to set the interpreter up because it is identical to invoking Perl in normal use. Here we initialize a completely new list of arguments using -e to pass in some arbitrary code for the interpreter to execute for us. We can just as easily use -M to load in (pure Perl) modules or any other options that we desire. The second argument to perl_parse, currently NULL, is used to pass in a function pointer for managing modules that are not pure Perl—we will come back to it later.

Before going further, it is worth taking a quick look at the perlclib manual page. This describes many Perl-supplied C functions that should be used in place of the standard C library equivalents that we may be more familiar with. The reason for using these functions is that they are guaranteed to work consistently across all platforms, and so minimize portability problems that may arise from using native functions. For example, do not use malloc and free, but safemalloc and safefree, when talking to the interpreter. Instead of strcmp, use savepv. And so forth—see perldoc perlclib for details.

Evaluating Expressions

We typically want to extract values from the interpreter after having it evaluate code rather than have Perl print them out. We can achieve this with a collection of other macros that are described at length in the perlguts and perlapi manual pages. There are very many of these macros, but perhaps the most useful are eval_pv, which evaluates a string expression, and get_sv, which retrieves a scalar variable.

Here is an expanded example that shows eval_pv and get_sv in action. To keep our manipulations separate from the interpreter startup and shutdown code, it's been split off into the separate subroutine do_stuff:

```
/* embedeval.c */
#include <EXTERN.h>
#include <perl.h>

PerlInterpreter *my_perl;

void do_stuff(void);

int main(int argc, char *argv[], char *env[])
{
```

```
    char *perl_argv[] = {argv[0], "-e","0"};

    /* initialize */
    PERL_SYS_INIT3(&argc,&argv,&env);

    /* create the interpreter */
    my_perl = perl_alloc();
    perl_construct(my_perl);
    PL_exit_flags |= PERL_EXIT_DESTRUCT_END;

    /* invoke perl with arguments */
    perl_parse(my_perl, NULL, 3, perl_argv, env);
    perl_run(my_perl);

    do_stuff();

    /* clean up */
    perl_destruct(my_perl);
    perl_free(my_perl);

    /* finish */
    PERL_SYS_TERM();
}

void do_stuff(void)
{
    SV *intscalar, *strscalar;
    int intval;
    char *strval;
    AV *thetime,*anotherarray;
    SV *isdst_sv,*hour_sv;
    I32 thehour,theminute;

    /* evaluate an expression */
    eval_pv("($int,$str)=(6,'Number 6')",TRUE);

    /* get the result */
    intscalar=get_sv("int",FALSE); /*get $int*/
    intval=SvIV(intscalar);        /*extract integer slot*/
    strscalar=get_sv("str",FALSE); /*get $str*/
    strval=SvPV(strscalar,PL_na);  /*allocate and extract string slot*/
    printf("The answer is %d (%s)\n",intval,strval);
}
```

In this example, we initialize the Perl interpreter with the arguments -e and 0. This simply makes the interpreter ready to evaluate arbitrary expressions, since without it the interpreter will attempt to read code from standard input—just as typing perl on the command line with no arguments does.

The eval_pv function evaluates arbitrary Perl code for us, and it is the equivalent of Perl's eval function. We can use it as many times as we like, with cumulative effect, so we could also have written the following:

```
eval_pv("$int=5",TRUE);
eval_pv("$int++",TRUE);
eval_pv("$str='Number '.int)",TRUE);
```

If the second argument is given as the macro TRUE, the interpreter will die if it encounters a fatal error, just as Perl would in normal (that is, non-evaled) code. Rather than letting the interpreter abort, we can choose to handle the error ourselves in C if the second argument of eval_pv is changed to FALSE. This makes eval_pv behave exactly like Perl's eval, and we can check the value of the special variable $@ via the macro ERRSV:

```
eval_pv("This is not Perl!",FALSE);
if (SvTRUE(ERRSV)) {
    printf ("Error from eval: %s\n", SvPV(ERRSV, PL_na)) ;
}
```

The Perl eval function returns a value, although we are not obliged to use it. Since eval_pv is eval in C, it also returns a value, which allows us to write

```
strscalar=eval_pv("'Number' '.int), FALSE);
if (! SvTRUE(ERRSV)) {
    strval = SvPV(strscalar,PL_na);
}
```

eval_pv is really a wrapper for the more generic eval_sv, which evaluates the string part of a scalar value. In other words, it is equivalent to

```
eval_sv(newSVpv("$int=5",0), FALSE);
```

The means by which we get values back from the interpreter varies depending on what kind of data type we are looking for. Here we are dealing with scalars and used the SvIV and SvPV macros to extract C data types from the Perl scalar. We will take a closer look at working with scalars next and then go on to consider arrays, hashes, and complex data structures.

Working with Scalars

The get_sv function extracts a scalar variable from the symbol table of the interpreter. As scalars are composite values, the return type is a pointer to an SV—short for *scalar value*—the C data type of a Perl scalar. We can only extract package variables this way, so if we had declared $int and $str with my, we would not be able to extract them.

get_sv returns a pointer to an SV, which is the Perl data type for a scalar. From this we can extract any of the value slots such as integer, floating-point number, or string using an appropriate macro. SvIV extracts the integer value as we have already seen, while SvNV extracts the floating-point value. SvPV is a little different, since it returns a pointer to a string. We pass the special value PL_na to tell Perl we don't care how long the string is. We could also use SvPV_nolen instead of SvPV to similar effect:

```
strval = SvPV(strscalar, PL_na);
strval = SvPV_nolen(strscalar);
```

The second FALSE argument to get_sv indicates that no space should be allocated for this variable. If we used TRUE, we could create the scalar in the symbol table at the same time. Specifically, it will create a scalar if not already present and return a pointer to it:

```
newscalar = get_sv("doesnotexistyet", TRUE);
```

We would more likely want to use newSVpv, newSViv or one of their many variants to give the new variable a value at the same time. Note that unlike the preceding, the following statements create the data structure but do not add it to the symbol table, so the interpreter will not be able to see them yet:

```
intscalar = newSViv(6);              /* integer */
fltscalar = newSVnv(3.14159);        /* floating point */
strscalar = newSVpv("Number 6", 0);  /* 0=calculate length */
strscalar = newSVpvf("Number %d", 6); /* printf-style */
```

There are many more variants on these available in the Perl API. The newSVpvf macro is particularly handy to know about, however, because it makes constructing strings easy using C's sprintf function. The regular newSVpv requires a length argument, but the macro will automatically calculate the string length if we supply a zero as we did here. As we saw earlier, we can use SvTRUE to test a scalar for "truth" in the Perl sense of that word. We can also call macros like SvCUR to retrieve the length of the string.

What about references? From the perspective of C, a reference is simply a scalar value whose value is another SV. The "outer" SV is a wrapper for the SV inside. We can dereference it to get the "inner" scalar with SvRV (which returns NULL if the scalar isn't a reference) and create a reference to a scalar with newSVrv or newRV_inc. The abbreviation for references is therefore RV, but there is no RV data type in C. Instead, references are SVs, just like regular scalars, and test an SV to see if it is an RV or not with macros like SvROK. We will return to them later in this chapter.

Working with Arrays

Handling Perl arrays is done with get_av and a range of functions like av_fetch, av_pop, av_push, av_unshift, and av_delete, among others. We can also create arrays in C using newAV and populate it with av_store or av_make.

Following is an example of how we can use some of these functions. Since the interpreter startup and shutdown code remains the same, we will just swap out the do_stuff subroutine with a new one:

```
void do_stuff (void) {
    AV *thetime,*anotherary; /*AV is C type for arrays*/
    SV *isdst_sv;            /*array elements are SVs*/
    I32 thehour,theminute;   /*explicitly 32-bit int'*/

    /* create an array */
    eval_pv("@time=localtime",TRUE);
    thetime = get_av("time",FALSE); /* the array */
    theminute = SvIV(* av_fetch(thetime, 1, FALSE));
    thehour = SvIV(* av_fetch(thetime, 2, FALSE));
    printf("It is %d:%d \n",thehour,theminute);
    printf("@time has %d elements\n",av_len(thetime)+1);
    isdst_sv=av_pop(thetime); /* pop a value */
    printf("@time has %d elements\n",av_len(thetime)+1);
}
```

Notice that most of the code in this subroutine works with arrays directly from C—only the first statement actually runs any Perl code. It also does not mention the interpreter instance by name, because the macros reference my_perl implicitly—this is why we created it as a global variable in the first place.

The av_fetch function does the job of accessing array elements by index. We can also pop and unshift them and, of course, push and shift new SV* values too. If the last argument to av_fetch is a TRUE rather than FALSE as here, then it also serves to create the array element if the array does not yet hold it (just as it would in Perl).

We can also use av_store to set an SV* into the array. The return value is of type SV**, a pointer to the SV pointer passed as the last argument, or NULL if the store failed for any reason. For example, to replace the SV at index 2 of the array, we would write

```
if (av_store(thetime,2,new_hour_sv)==NULL) {
    /* failed! */
}
```

The av_fetch function also returns NULL if the array element does not exist. We took a shortcut here, since we passed TRUE as the last argument to eval_pv so we know the evaluation must have succeeded and @time must exist. In more complex code, we would be better advised to check the return value rather than dereference the return value directly as was done here.

We can also loop through an array, which turns out to be nothing more complicated than finding the array length and then iterating through it with a normal C for loop. The next iteration of do_stuff that follows works with @INC. First we add and remove a new element at a high index, then we loop through the array and print out the paths from it:

```
void do_stuff(void) {
    AV *inc = get_av("INC",TRUE); /* get @INC array */
    SV **valuep;

    /* store value at index 1000 */
    if (av_store(inc, 1000, newSVpv("newvalue",8))==NULL) {
        exit(99); /* NULL=failed store */
    }

    /* test for and retrieve value at index 1000 */
    if (av_exists(inc, 1000)) {
        valuep = av_fetch(inc, 1000, FALSE);
        printf("1000: %s\n", SvPV(*valuep, PL_na));
        printf("length of @INC is %d\n---\n", av_len(inc));
        av_delete(inc, 1000, FALSE); #flag arg needed but ignored
    }

    /* loop over array values and print them out */
    printf("length of @INC is now %d\n---\n", av_len(inc));
    for (int index=0; index<=av_len(inc); index++) {
        valuep = av_fetch(inc, index, FALSE);
        if (value != NULL) {
            printf("%d: %s\n", index, SvPV(*valuep, PL_na));
        }
    }
}
```

In this code, we test for a failed store or fetch by testing for a return value of NULL. The return value is of type SV**, so assuming it is not NULL we must dereference the pointer to get a value that we can pass to macros like SvPV. Interestingly, the first printout of the array length will report 1000, but the second, after we delete our added element, is something like 5 (depending on how many paths @INC normally has).

Working with Hashes

Working with hashes and references is very similar to arrays and scalars, so now that we know the basics of handling scalar and array values, we can easily extend them to these data types too.

We can store and fetch hash keys with hv_get and hv_store, test them with hv_exists, delete them with hv_delete, and create a new hash in C with newHV. We also have a collection of hv_iter* routines to manage the iterator with. The following subroutine manipulates the %ENV hash, first by adding and then removing a new key, then by printing out the contents using the iterator:

```
void do_stuff(void) {
    HV *env = get_hv("ENV",TRUE); /* get %ENV hash */
    SV value, *valuep;  /* key value */
    I32 length;         /* key length */
    char *key;          /* key name */
```

```
    /* store, retrieve, and delete  a new key*/
    hv_store(env, "newkey", 6, newSVpv("newvalue",8), TRUE);
    if (hv_exists(env, "newkey", 6)) {
        valuep = hv_fetch(env, "newkey", 6, TRUE);
        printf("newkey => %s\n---\n", SvPV(*valuep, PL_na));
        hv_delete(env, "newkey", 6, G_DISCARD);
    }

    /* iterate over keys and print them out*/
    hv_iterinit(env);
    while ((value = hv_iternextsv(env, &key, &length))) {
        printf("%-20s => %s\n", key, SvPV(value, PL_na));
    }
}
```

The hv_iternextsv function is actually a convenient combination of several other steps, hv_iternext, hv_iterkey, and hv_iterval. There are many, many other functions and macros that we can use to manipulate and test Perl data from C, but this provides a taste of what is possible. The G_DISCARD flag tells Perl to throw away the value and return NULL; otherwise, we get a pointer to the SV value of the key we deleted (if it was present in the hash).

Working with Complex Data Structures

It is relatively simple to create complex data structures, though we may have to keep an eye on our reference counts as we mentioned when we talked about arrays.

Since an array or hash held as a value of another array or hash is really stored through a reference, nesting arrays and hashes is simply a case of wrapping an AV* or HV* value with a scalar RV. To do that, we use newRV_inc or newRV_noinc and recast the pointer to an SV*, as illustrated in this version of do_stuff, which stores an array in an element of a second array and in the value of a hash key:

```
void do_stuff(void)
{
    SV *scalar,*reference;
    AV *array,*array2;
    HV *hash;
    SV **valuep;

    /* create an array of 10 elements */
    array = newAV();
    for (int i=0; i<10; i++) {
        scalar = newSVpvf("value %d",i+1);
        av_push(array, scalar);
    }

    /* create reference for array ref count is already
       1 from creation so we do not increment it again */
    reference = newRV_noinc((SV *)array);

    /* add reference to a new array */
    if (array2 = newAV()) {
        av_push(array2, reference);
    }

    /* add reference to hash. As the array also holds the
       reference we increment the ref count if successful */
    if (hash = newHV()) {
```

```
                SvREFCNT_inc(reference);
                if (hv_store(hash, "array", 6, reference, 0)==NULL) {
                    SvREFCNT_dec(reference);
                }
            }
        }

        /* extract array from hash */
        if (valuep = hv_fetch(hash, "array", 6, FALSE)) {
            SV *svref = *valuep;
            if (SvOK(svref) && SvROK(svref)) {
                SV *sv = SvRV(svref);
                if (SvTYPE(sv) == SVt_PVAV) {
                    AV *av = (AV *) sv; /*recast*/
                    SV **svp;
                    if (svp = av_fetch(av, 2, FALSE)) {
                        printf("Got '%s' from index 2 of
                            array\n",SvPV(*svp,PL_na));
                    }
                }
            }
        }
    }
}
```

This example manages the reference counts, allowing for the fact that newly constructed data types have a default reference count of 1 to start with, and takes care not to increment them unnecessarily. When we add the array reference to the hash as well as the second array, we do need to increment the count, however.

It also extracts the array reference from the hash, dereferences it, and prints out the string value of one of the scalars stored in it. We happen to know how we created the data structure, but since we should usually check what we are doing we use SvOK and SvROK to verify that the scalar is valid and is indeed a reference. The SvTYPE macro tells us what kind of thing the reference was pointing to. We compare it to SVt_PVAV to check for an array—to check for a hash we would instead use SVt_PVHV. Once we know we have an array, we can recast back to an AV* and access it as normal.

Using C Using Perl Using C

If we want to use Perl modules that themselves make use of underlying C code (also called *extensions*), we have to go back and adjust the workings of our interpreter a little. In order to know how to load in the C library part of a Perl extension, the interpreter needs some additional help, which we provide by supplying a function pointer as the second argument to perl_parse. The function performs the job of bootstrapping the external C part of any extensions we want to use. Typically, we use the Dynaloader to dynamically load any modules on demand, so this is the only module we need to handle for most cases.

Following is a new version of the embedded interpreter, incorporating code using the Scalar::Util and Socket modules. We use the dualvar function to create a scalar variable with divergent integer and string values within Perl and getservbyname to look up a service. Of course, both of these tasks could be done from C directly, and in the second case without involving Perl at all—but they serve our purposes for this simple example.

Note the EXTERN_C declarations—these are the new code we added—the macro is present so it can be defined to nothing for C and extern C for C++. The xs_init function defined here is passed to perl_parse to carry out the required initialization. The main routine is unchanged apart from the addition of xs_init as the second argument:

```
/* embedeval.c */
#include <EXTERN.h>
#include <perl.h>

PerlInterpreter *my_perl;

void do_stuff(void);

EXTERN_C void boot_DynaLoader (pTHX_ CV* cv);
EXTERN_C void xs_init(pTHX)
{
    char *file = __FILE__;
    dXSUB_SYS;

    /* DynaLoader is a special case */
    newXS("DynaLoader::boot_DynaLoader", boot_DynaLoader, file);
}

int main(int argc, char **argv, char **env)
{
    /* initialize */
    PERL_SYS_INIT3(&argc,&argv,&env);

    /* create the interpreter */
    my_perl = perl_alloc();
    perl_construct(my_perl);
    PL_exit_flags |= PERL_EXIT_DESTRUCT_END;

    /* invoke perl with arguments */
    char *perl_argv[] = {argv[0], "-e","0"};
    perl_parse(my_perl, xs_init, 3, perl_argv, env);
    perl_run(my_perl);

    do_stuff();

    /* clean up */
    perl_destruct(my_perl);
    perl_free(my_perl);

    /* finish */
    PERL_SYS_TERM();
}

void do_stuff(void)
{
    SV *scalar;
    int intval;
    char *strval;

    /* load a module with eval_pv */
    eval_pv("use Scalar::Util 'dualvar'",TRUE);
    eval_pv("use Socket",TRUE);
    /* evaluate an expression */
    eval_pv("$value=dualvar(6,'Number 6')",TRUE);
    eval_pv("$ssh_service=getservbyname('ssh','tcp')",TRUE);
    /* get the result */
    scalar=get_sv("value",FALSE); /*get $value*/
```

```
        intval=SvIV(scalar);            /*extract integer slot*/
        strval=SvPV(scalar,PL_na);      /*allocate and extract string slot*/
        printf("The answer is %d (%s)\n",intval,strval);
        printf("SSH port is %d\n",SvIV(get_sv("ssh_service",FALSE)));
}
```

The ExtUtils::Embed module allows us to generate the necessary extra glue for extensions using the -e xsinit option. By default it writes the glue code to a file called perlxsi.c, which we can choose to maintain separately from our other source if we wish or to embed it into the interpreter code as we did previously. This is the simplest way we can use it:

> **perl -MExtUtils::Embed -e xsinit**

Without a specific list of modules, this just generates code to initialize Dynaloader plus any statically linked extensions (which can be none at all, as in the preceding example). If we have specific dynamically loaded modules in mind, we can instead generate code to handle them directly and skip Dynaloader. For example, to bind the Socket module and an extension of our own called My::Extension, we could use this:

> **perl -MExtUtils::Embed -e xsinit -o init_xs.c Socket My::Extension**

Here we also used the -o option to change the output file name. This command generates a file called init_xs.c containing

```
#include <EXTERN.h>
#include <perl.h>

EXTERN_C void xs_init (pTHX);

EXTERN_C void boot_Socket (pTHX_ CV* cv);
EXTERN_C void boot_My__Extension (pTHX_ CV* cv);

EXTERN_C void
xs_init(pTHX)
{
        char *file = __FILE__;
        dXSUB_SYS;

        newXS("Socket::bootstrap", boot_Socket, file);
        newXS("My::Extension::bootstrap", boot_My__Extension, file);
}
```

While this is convenient, bear in mind that the code is generated without regard to whether the named modules have a dynamic library component to them or indeed actually exist.

Calling Subroutines

We can call Perl subroutines from C too. To do so, we need to manage the interpreter's stack, since C does not understand Perl's calling conventions or concepts like void, scalar, or list context. As usual, macros are available to help:

```
void do_stuff(void)
{
    dSP;                          /* declare local stack pointer (SP) */
    int count;                    /* number of return arguments */

    /* Perl sub to split a string and return first N parts, reversed */
    eval_pv("sub rsplit ($$;$) { return reverse split $_[0],$_[1],$_[2] }",TRUE);
```

```
        ENTER;                          /* prepare to call sub */
        SAVETMPS;                       /* note existing temporaries */

        PUSHMARK(SP);                   /* note where stack pointer started */
        XPUSHs(sv_2mortal(newSVpv(",",1)));
        XPUSHs(sv_2mortal(newSVpv("one,two,three",13)));
        XPUSHs(sv_2mortal(newSViv(2)));
        PUTBACK;                        /* update global stack pointer */

        count = call_pv("rsplit", G_ARRAY); /* call, get number return values */
        printf("Got %d results\n",count);

        SPAGAIN;                        /* query the stack */
        for (int i=0; i<count; i++) {
            char *part = POPp;
            printf("result %d is '%s'\n",i,part); /* pop (string) results */
            safefree(part);             /* free allocated memory */
        }
        PUTBACK;                        /* clean up global stack */

        FREETMPS;                       /* free any temporaries created by us */
        LEAVE;                          /* finish up */
}
```

Quite a lot is going on here, but a lot of it is boilerplate code—we write it and forget it. The dSP, ENTER, and SAVETMPS macros carry out essential setup work, creating a local stack pointer and noting existing temporary (that is, mortal) values. The PUSHMARK(SP) macro starts a counter to keep track of how many arguments we push onto the stack. The PUTBACK macro uses that count to update the real stack pointer from our locally modified copy.

Between PUSHMARK(SP) and the first PUTBACK we supply our arguments. There are many macros available to do this, depending on what we are trying to do. XPUSHs simply puts a scalar value onto the stack. The X means "extend the stack" and differentiates this macro from PUSHs, which assumes the stack has already been extended (we could alternatively choose to extend the stack several places then fill in the blanks, so to speak). We push three mortal SVs using the newSVpv and newSViv macros to generate them from C data types.

That takes care of the buildup—now we need to look at the call to the subroutine and the handling of the return values. Calling a named subroutine is done with call_pv. It takes the subroutine name as its first argument and a set of flags as its second. In this case, we need to tell the interpreter that we want to call the subroutine in array context, so we set G_ARRAY. We can also use G_SCALAR or G_VOID—the last of which is important to stop Perl generating values we don't need, which wastes time. The return value from this call is the number of return values waiting for us on the stack.

There are many ways to read values back too. Here we use one of the simpler techniques. First we use SPAGAIN to move the stack pointer to the right place to get to the return values. POPp is one of several macros that extracts a scalar and converts it to a C data type, in this case a pointer value (that is, a string). We could also use POPi for an integer, POPn for a floating-point number, POPs to get the SV itself, or POPl for a long integer. Notice the use of safefree here: if we return new string values, we should also free the memory the interpreter used to create them. The safefree function is Perl's version of free, which we should always use in preference to the native function—see perldoc perlclib for more on this and other preferred Perl versions of standard functions.

We now need to clean up. First we use PUTBACK a second time to reset the global stack pointer from our local copy. FREETMPS cleans up the temporary values that we created and marked as mortal (and which we can tell from others that may exist because we used SAVETMPS to note where ours started). Finally, we use LEAVE to restore the stack pointer to its original condition—the idea being that our call should leave the stack in the same state it was in beforehand.

There are many permutations on this basic theme, far too many to elaborate on in detail. One useful alternative is call_sv, which allows us to call a scalar containing a code reference rather than a named subroutine. We only need to change two lines of code to do this. First:

```
eval_pv("sub rsplit ($$;$) { return reverse split $_[0],$_[1],$_[2] }",TRUE);
```

becomes this:

```
SV *cref=eval_pv("sub ($$;$) { return reverse split $_[0],$_[1],$_[2] }",TRUE);
```

And secondly:

```
count = call_pv("rsplit", G_ARRAY);
```

becomes this:

```
count = call_sv(cref, G_ARRAY);
```

This allows us to call anonymous subroutines, which if we create them from C do not even get entered into the interpreter's symbol table. For more advanced examples, see the perlcall manual page and perlapi for the complete list of available macros.

Using C or C++ from Perl

Perl provides extensive support for building modules to interface to an underlying C or C++ library. Such modules are known as *extensions*, and while this term can also apply to pure Perl modules, in practice it is used almost exclusively to describe a Perl module that depends on an underlying library.

The glue that binds Perl to C or C++ is the XSUB, which stands for *extension subroutine*. XSUBs are written in a special language called XS, in files with (usually) an .xs extension, and are compiled into C code with the XSUB preprocessor xsubpp that comes standard with Perl. XS is made up of a few declarative section headers and a lot of macros that are actually defined by Perl's header files. XSUBs can be simple declarations that map to an existing C or C++ subroutine or contain compiled code that implements functionality directly. This C or C++ code has access to the Perl interpreter's data, so we can use all the techniques we saw in the previous section to extract Perl data or write it back from C within the XSUB code, including the macros listed in perlapi and the Perl equivalents of C library functions detailed in perlclib.

While XSUBs are the fundamental link between Perl and C, we do not always need to write them ourselves. The h2xs utility, in collaboration with xsubpp and the C::Scan module, can often extract function signatures from C headers and generate XSUB definitions to map them into Perl without us needing to write a line of code ourselves. More interestingly, the Inline module provides an interface to inline foreign language code directly into Perl source files. It natively supports C and is essentially a wrapper for the XSUB autogeneration approach just mentioned, but it also has supporting modules for Java, Tcl, Python, and a host of other languages available from CPAN. We will return to Inline in "Inlining C and Other Languages into Perl" at the end of this section.

Creating Extensions with h2xs

The primary tool for setting up to build Perl extensions is h2xs. This script, which we first saw in Chapter 10, is designed to automatically create the correct directory structure and supporting files to create a Perl module. Previously we used the -X option to suppress the XS support that is the primary function of h2xs and used it to create the basic directory structure for a distributable module:

```
> h2xs -X -n My::PurePerl::Module
```

To make h2xs generate the additional support for XSUBs, we drop the -X. If we give the tool some actual C headers and source files to work with, it will automatically generate files based on what it finds. But we can also build our own XSUBs from scratch, which is often required in any case since what h2xs deduces from C source is not always all that close to what we actually require.

For example, say we want to create an extension called Heavy::Fraction, which does not bind against any existing C code. We can set up the module structure with

> **h2xs -b 5.6.0 -n Heavy::Fraction**

The -n option provides the module name, which is necessary if we are not converting an existing header from which a name can be derived. The -b option tells h2xs what the earliest version of Perl we will be supporting is. Here we chose 5.6.0. This should create all the appropriate files and generate the following output:

```
Writing Heavy-Fraction/ppport.h
Writing Heavy-Fraction/lib/Heavy/Fraction.pm
Writing Heavy-Fraction/Fraction.xs
Writing Heavy-Fraction/fallback/const-c.inc
Writing Heavy-Fraction/fallback/const-xs.inc
Writing Heavy-Fraction/Makefile.PL
Writing Heavy-Fraction/README
Writing Heavy-Fraction/t/Heavy-Fraction.t
Writing Heavy-Fraction/Changes
Writing Heavy-Fraction/MANIFEST
```

The only files we need to immediately concern ourselves with here are Fraction.pm, where we can place any additional Perl code our module will be providing, Fraction.xs, the XS file where our C code and XSUB definitions and declarations will go, and Makefile.PL. This is the file from which we generate our makefile:

> **perl Makefile.PL**

The makefile generated by this command contains targets for the generated C code that use xsubpp to regenerate them from the XS file. We can then build the extension with

> **make**
> **make test**

If we have sufficient privileges or are installing to a location under our control (as described in Chapter 10), we can also use

> **make install**

The contents of Makefile.PL look like this:

```
use 5.006;
use ExtUtils::MakeMaker;
# See lib/ExtUtils/MakeMaker.pm for details of how to influence
# the contents of the Makefile that is written.
WriteMakefile(
    NAME            => 'Heavy::Fraction',
    VERSION_FROM    => 'lib/Heavy/Fraction.pm', # finds $VERSION
    PREREQ_PM       => {}, # e.g., Module::Name => 1.1
    ($] >= 5.005 ?     ## Add these new keywords supported since 5.005
      (ABSTRACT_FROM => 'lib/Heavy/Fraction.pm', # retrieve abstract from module
       AUTHOR        => 'Peter Wainwright <peter@cybrid.net>') : ()),
    LIBS            => [''], # e.g., '-lm'
    DEFINE          => '', # e.g., '-DHAVE_SOMETHING'
    INC             => '-I.', # e.g., '-I. -I/usr/include/other'
    # Un-comment this if you add C files to link with later:
```

```
    # OBJECT              => '$(O_FILES)', # link all the C files too
);
if (eval {require ExtUtils::Constant; 1}) {
    # If you edit these definitions to change the constants used by this module,
    # you will need to use the generated const-c.inc and const-xs.inc
    # files to replace their "fallback" counterparts before distributing your
    # changes.
    my @names = (qw());
    ExtUtils::Constant::WriteConstants(
        NAME            => 'Heavy::Fraction',
        NAMES           => \@names,
        DEFAULT_TYPE    => 'IV',
        C_FILE          => 'const-c.inc',
        XS_FILE         => 'const-xs.inc',
    );
} else {
    use File::Copy;
    use File::Spec;
    foreach my $file ('const-c.inc', 'const-xs.inc') {
        my $fallback = File::Spec->catfile('fallback', $file);
        copy ($fallback, $file) or die "Can't copy $fallback to $file: $!";
    }
}
```

We can enable or disable the generation of various parts of this file and the accompanying files in the module distribution with flags like -A (disable autoloader), -C (disable Changes file), and --skip-ppport (do not generate ppport.h or use Devel::PPPort).

For C++, we need to override the default compiler and linker with the C++ compiler and tell xsubpp to generate C++-compliant code. This is easy enough—the following additions to the argument list of WriteMakefile will do the trick (assuming our compiler is g++, of course):

```
WriteMakefile(
    ...
    'CC'        => "g++",       # define 'CC' macro
    'LD'        => "\$(CC)",    # derive 'LD' from 'CC'
    'XSOPT'     => "-C++",      # define 'XSOPT' macro
);
```

■**Note** Other xsubpp options that may prove useful for C++ are -heirtype, which recognizes and translates nested C++ namespaces (that is, types with :: in their name), and -except, which adds exception handling stubs to the generated code.

It is valid to insert makefile macros into these definitions, for example, we base LD on CC so if we change CC we also change LD. If our make tool defines a standard macro for the C++ compiler like CPP, we would also write

```
    'CC'        => "\$(CPP)", # derive 'CC' from 'CPP'
```

Additional typemap files (should we have any) can be specified with a TYPEMAPS argument and an associated array reference of typemap file names. We will come back to these later.

If we have extra C sources we want built along with the code generated from the XS file, we can add them by uncommenting and editing the OBJECT line to contain the object file to which the source file is compiled. The default make rules will do the rest for us.

Converting C Constants to Perl Constants

The h2xs script is capable of parsing #define directives into Perl constants, but without help, not much more. If we take a header file defines.h with lines like these:

```
#define ONE 1
#define TWO 2
#define THREE 3
```

and run a command like this:

> **h2xs -n My::Defines defines.h otherheader.h**

we will get a simple module that, once compiled, defines three Perl constants, ONE, TWO, and THREE. The defines.xs file inside the directory My-Defines contains the directive

```
#include <defines>
```

Obviously, this header is required for the generated C code to compile, so we copy it into the My-Defines directory. Glancing at Makefile.PL, we see that the @names array under the ExtUtils::Constant section now reads

```
my @names = (qw(ONE THREE TWO));
```

This tells the extension which #define constants we want to map into Perl constants. We can now use these constants in our code:

```
use My::Defines;
print "2 = ",TWO,"\n";
```

In fact, if we look in the test script My-Defines/t/My-Defines.t, we will find that a test case has already been set up to test the constants are defined correctly.

Converting Function Prototypes to XSUBs

If we install the C::Scan module and the Data::Flow module on which it depends, we can upgrade h2xs into a tool that can not only convert #define directives, but also scan the source for enums and function prototypes too. To enable this functionality once the extra modules are installed, we just need to add the -x argument:

> **h2xs -n My::Functions functions.h**

Given a functions.h with these contents:

```
void subone(int, int);int subtwo(char *input);
```

we end up with a file My-Functions/Functions.xs containing XSUB declarations suitable for mapping onto the implementations of subone and subtwo, presumably in functions.c or another implementation file:

```
void
subone(arg0, arg1)
        int     arg0
        int     arg1

int
subtwo(input)
        char *  input
```

Depending on how complete the function prototype is, the more information the XSUB will contain. So while a function prototype does not need to name its arguments, the XSUB will use the names if it finds them. Otherwise, it will use arg0, arg1, and so on.

In order to use these functions, we can just compile the module. We need to add the separate implementation file to `Makefile.PL`, by uncommenting and completing the `OBJECTS` argument:

```
OBJECT          => 'functions.o', # link all the C files too
```

A default rule will be used to build this object file from `functions.c`. If we need to customize the build options, we can do so either by adding the appropriate definitions to `Makefile.PL` or supplying them in arguments to `hx2s`. We can add any compiler and linker options, include paths, libraries, and library search paths, we need this way. To add extra compiler flags, use `-F` or `--cpp-flags`. To add extra libraries, use `-l`. For example:

```
> h2xs -n My::Functions -F "-I/other/include -std=c99" \
-L/other/lib -lm -lnsl -lsocket source/*.h
```

We can now compile the module and use the C functions from our Perl code like normal Perl subroutines, for example:

```
use My::Functions;
my $my_number = subtwo("my_string");
```

To find out what these definitions mean, we need to learn about how to define an XSUB.

Defining XSUBs

Rather than pregenerating an XS file, we can create our own XSUB definition file by following a few simple rules. An XS file contains four main sections:

- Mandatory include directives for Perl headers
- Optional C or C++ code, including more include directives if required
- An XS `MODULE` and `PACKAGE` declaration to mark the start of XS code
- XSUB declarations

Let's examine each of these in turn.

Mandatory Headers

The mandatory headers should look familiar if we have already looked at calling Perl from C. They are the same two headers we have seen before, accompanied by a third header, `XSUB.h`, that is required when writing extensions:

```
#include <EXTERN.h>
#include <perl.h>
#include <XSUB.h>
```

These three lines should be at the start of every XS file. For C++, since Perl's headers are C and not C++, we modify this slightly to

```
#ifdef __cplusplus
extern "C" {
#endif
#include "EXTERN.h"
#include "perl.h"
#include "XSUB.h"
#ifdef __cplusplus
}
#endif
```

If we added a definition for `XSOPT` of `-C++` in our `Makefile.PL`, this will be generated for us automatically.

Optional C or C++ Code

Following this we can add any conventional C (or C++, if applicable) code that we like. For binding to a precompiled library, we would include appropriate headers to import the function prototypes so that we can check our XSUB declarations against them. For a simple example, it is simplest to embed the code, so here is a subroutine to calculate the highest number of times one number will fit into another:

```
int heavyfraction (int num1, int num2) {
    int result;

    if (num1 > num2) {
        result = num1 / num2;
    } else {
        result = num2 / num1;
    }

    return result;
}
```

Start of XS Code

The end of the C section and the start of the XSUB section is marked by a MODULE and PACKAGE declaration. This tells xsubpp in what module distribution the resulting extension is packaged, and in what Perl namespace it belongs in, as determined by a Perl package declaration. Typically, the module corresponds to the root namespace of the packages defined, and in many cases where there is only one package they are simply the same. For example:

```
MODULE = Heavy::Fraction    PACKAGE = Heavy::Fraction
```

We can create multiple .pm files each with its own package declaration by redeclaring the package name with different values, but each time we must include the module first. Since this usually never changes, we often see things like this:

```
MODULE = Heavy::Fraction  PACKAGE = Heavy::Fraction

... XSUBs ...

MODULE = Heavy::Fraction  PACKAGE = Heavy::Fraction::Heavy

... XSUBS ...

MODULE = Heavy::Fraction  PACKAGE = Heavy::Fraction::Utility

... XSUBS ...
```

XSUB Definitions

Once we have at least one MODULE and PACKAGE declaration, we can actually write an XSUB. The simplest XSUB declarations simply provide the definitions to bind the C function to a Perl subroutine. To bind heavyfraction, we would write

```
int
heavyfraction(num1, num2)
    int num1
    int num2
```

The XS file format is quite precise about this layout—we must put the return type on a separate line and specify the argument list without types, which instead appear indented after it. Other than that, there are no semicolon terminators; this is essentially a K&R-style C function prototype. We can put all of the preceding together and build the Heavy::Fraction module. As a finishing touch, we can add these lines to the test script t/Heavy-Fraction.t and upgrade the plan to two tests:

```
my $result=Heavy::Fraction::heavyfraction(10,2);
ok($result==5);
```

If all goes well, we should be able to build the extension and run the test driver successfully. The curious might like to look at the generated Fraction.c file to see what xsubpp actually did with the Fraction.xs file.

Although int is a C data type and not a Perl integer, xsubpp automatically knows how to convert all the basic C data types to and from Perl scalars, so we do not need to add any logic to do it ourselves. Any standard C data type will work here—double, float, short, long, char *, and so on are all mapped transparently. We can also write C functions that take and return Perl types like SV *.

For more complex types, we need to add some extra glue in a typemap file, which we cover in "Mapping Basic C Types into Perl" later in the chapter. For now, we can rely on xsubpp to know how to handle our C types for us.

Ignoring the C Function Return Value

Since XSUBs map to a C function prototype, the return type is automatically mapped and converted to a Perl scalar in the generated code. Although it is relatively rare, we might occasionally want to disregard the return value of a C function that we are binding to (presumably not under our control or we could just rewrite it) on the grounds that it serves no useful purpose and therefore wastes Perl's time reading it back.

Since we cannot simply declare the subroutine void, we instead use NO_OUTPUT to tell xsubpp not to build the code to manage the return value:

```
NO_OUTPUT int
returns_a_useless_value()
```

This example XSUB also takes no arguments, so it has no list of argument declarations either. At a bare minimum, therefore, a C subroutine that takes no arguments and returns no values can be bound to in just two lines of XS code. Of course, most useful subroutines will both take arguments and return values. We can manage fixed and variable numbers of both input arguments and output values, but we can only do so much with a simple XSUB declaration—for more advanced uses we will need to add some code.

Adding Code to XSUBs

An XSUB declaration allows us to map a Perl subroutine call onto a preexisting C subroutine of the same name. However, sometimes we do not want to make a direct mapping, either because we need to wrap the C routine in some additional logic before providing it to Perl or because we want to improve on C's calling semantics. C, after all, can only return a single value, while Perl is happy to handle a list.

We can also forego the C subroutine altogether and embed the C code directly into the XSUB definition. The following example embeds some simple C code that returns the number of times the lower of the two numbers passed will fit into the larger:

```
int
heavyfraction(num1, num2)
    int num1
    int num2
CODE:
    if (num1 > num2) {
```

```
        RETVAL = num1 / num2;
    } else {
        RETVAL = num2 / num1;
    }
OUTPUT:
    RETVAL
```

The code in the CODE section is all standard C, apart from the special variable RETVAL. This macro is automatically defined to be a variable of the same type as the functions return type—in this case, int—and it is automatically placed into a scalar and pushed onto Perl's stack after our code completes so that Perl can receive the computed value when no CODE or PPCODE is present. The OUTPUT block here declares what the XSUB returns to Perl. Here it is technically not needed, since RETVAL is automatically returned for any XSUB with a nonvoid return type. It is good form to include it though, because it helps to underline that our subroutine is returning a value.

In this example, we can make use of just the argument variables and RETVAL to perform the calculation. If we need to create any intermediate values, which is highly likely, we will need to declare them. We can simply declare a local variable at the top of the CODE block, but we are better advised to use PREINIT, so that the generated code places them at the start of the generated function correctly. The next example replaces RETVAL with an explicit and more meaningfully named variable, to illustrate both use of PREINIT and returning something other than RETVAL:

```
int
difference(num1, num2)
    int num1
    int num2
PREINIT:
    int delta;
CODE:
    delta = abs(num1 - num2);
OUTPUT:
    delta
```

We can place simple expressions into the OUTPUT section too, which allows us to create this alternative implementation with no CODE section at all:

```
int
difference(num1, num2)
    int num1
    int num2
OUTPUT:
    abs(num1-num2);
```

Returning Multiple Values

CODE and OUTPUT work well when we only have one return value to pass back. The generated C code will manage the job of postprocessing the return value into a suitable form to be placed on the Perl interpreter stack, based on the declared return value of the XSUB. If we have more than one value to pass back though, we cannot use the C function prototype. Instead, we replace CODE with PPCODE, delete the OUTPUT section, and manage the stack ourselves:

```
int
countdown_list(message, from=10, to=0)
    int from
    int to
PREINIT:
    int delta, i;
PPCODE:
```

```
    if (to < from) {
        delta = from - to + 1;
        EXTEND(SP, delta);
        for (i=to; i>=from; i--) {
            XST_mIV(i, 0);
        }
        XSRETURN(delta);
    } else {
        XSRETURN_UNDEF;
    }
```

Since we want to return several values to the Perl stack, we need to make room for them, which the EXTEND macro does for us. To actually place the return values on the stack, we use XST_mIV, which wraps up an integer value in a scalar SV, marks it as mortal, puts it on the stack, and increments the stack pointer all in one operation. Finally, we use XSRETURN to tell Perl how many values are coming back to it.

In this example, we also use XSRETURN_UNDEF to return undef if the input parameters are not to our liking. We can return any single value this way from either a PPCODE or CODE section. It has the effect of immediately returning just like an explicit return keyword. We could modify the preceding example to handle the from and to values being equal this way:

```
PPCODE:
    if (to == from) XSRETURN_IV(to);
    if (to < from) {
        ...
```

Handling Output Arguments

Sometimes a function argument is used for output rather than input. For example, an int * is passed to provide an integer in which the length of a buffer is returned. There is no need for Perl to follow this idiom and pass a variable to be written to since we can return values as SVs or return multiple arguments instead.

We can change the default mapping to tell xsubpp not to treat such arguments as input arguments with the NO_INIT keyword.

For example, take a C function with a void return type and two arguments: an integer for input and a pointer to an integer for output:

```
void convert_int(int input, int *output);
```

We can turn this into a conventional subroutine that returns the integer rather than requiring Perl to pass in a second scalar variable parameter with

```
void
convert_int(input, output)
    int input
    int &output = NO_INIT
OUTPUT
    output
```

Now we can call the function in Perl with

```
my $output=convert_int($input);
```

Detecting Calling Context

In a Perl subroutine, we can use wantarray to detect the calling context. When we call Perl from C, we can communicate this context through call_pv or call_sv by setting one of the G_SCALAR, G_ARRAY, or G_VOID flags. To detect the calling context in a call from C to Perl, we use the GIMME_V macro, which returns the appropriate G_ flag.

In Perl, we frequently use wantarray to return an array reference instead of a list in scalar context rather than have the list counted, as would otherwise be the case:

```
return wantarray? @result : \@result;
```

We can adapt our countdown_list XSUB to make the same determination like this:

```
int
countdown_list(message, from=10, to=0)
    int from
    int to
PREINIT:
    int delta, i;
PPCODE:
    if (GIMME_V == G_VOID) XSRETURN_UNDEF;

    if (to < from) {
        delta = from - to + 1;
        if (GIMME_V == G_ARRAY) {
            EXTEND(SP, delta);
            for (i=to; i>=from; i--) {
                XST_mIV(i, 0);
            }
            XSRETURN(delta);
        } else { /* G_SCALAR */
            AV* array=newAV();
            for (i=to; i>=from; i--) {
                av_push(array, newSViv(i));
            }
            XPUSHs(sv_2mortal(newRV_noinc((SV*)array)));
            XSRETURN(1);
        }
    } else {
        XSRETURN_UNDEF;
    }
```

In void context, we simply return undef without bothering to carry out any computation at all. In array context, we build up the stack as before. In scalar context, we create a Perl array in C, then add scalar values to it. Once we have finished constructing the array, we create a reference to it and push the reference onto the stack. As we only have one value, we use XPUSHs to do the job, but we could also have used EXTEND(1) followed by PUSHs. There are a bewildering number of macros available to manipulate the stack, so these are only some of the ways we can achieve our ends.

Correctly counting references is important when returning Perl data types back to the interpreter. A new data type like the array created in this example automatically has a reference count of 1, even though it is not (yet) referred to by anything the interpreter knows about. When we create the reference for it, we have the choice of incrementing the array's reference count by one with newRV_inc, or leaving it alone with newRV_noinc. It would be incorrect to increment the count to 2, since only the reference knows about the array, so we use newRV_noinc in this case. As a technical note, the scalar reference also has a reference count of 1 on creation, so we do not need to increment its count either.

Assigning Default Input Values

We can define default values for some of the input arguments so that they do not have to be supplied in Perl. This turns out to be very simple. For example:

```
int
count_down(message, from=10, to=0)
    int from
    int to
PREINIT:
    int i;
CODE:
    if (to < from) {
        for (i=to; i>=from; i--) {
            printf("%d...\n",i);
        }
        printf("Liftoff!\n");
        RETVAL = 0; /*launched ok*/
    } else {
        RETVAL = 1; /*abort can't count*/
    }
OUTPUT:
    RETVAL
```

This gives us the ability to call an XSUB with a variable number of arguments, so long as we supply at least the minimum and no more than the maximum. The only proviso with default input values is that we must place the defaulted arguments after any mandatory ones.

Defining Variable Arguments and Prototypes

Perl subroutines support accepting unlimited numbers of arguments. C is normally quite a different story, but fortunately we can make use of the *varargs* feature of C to create an XSUB that takes variables arguments just like Perl. In C, we declare a subroutine to use variable arguments with an ellipsis (...), and the same convention is understood by XS too. Here is a simple example that calculates the average value of an arbitrary list of supplied integers:

```
int
average(...)
PREINIT:
    int argno;
CODE:
    RETVAL = 0;
    for (argno=0; argno<items; argno++) {
        RETVAL += SvIV(ST(argno));
    }
    RETVAL = RETVAL / items;
}
OUTPUT:
    RETVAL
```

The trick to this code is the items variable. When xsubpp sees the ellipsis in the declaration, it automatically sets up items with the number of arguments that we passed from Perl. These arguments are on the Perl stack as we enter the function, so we use the ST macro to retrieve them, passing it the position of the argument we are interested in. Here we simply loop through them.

Because the types of the arguments are not known in advance, the generated C code cannot automatically map Perl types to C ones as it can for fixed arguments. The arguments on the stack are therefore scalar values of type SV* (even a list is passed as scalars, and an array reference is a scalar anyway). To perform a numeric calculation we are interested in, we need to extract the integer value with SvIV.

If we want to require some fixed arguments as well as a variable list, we can do so by putting them first on the line, just like a C varargs declaration:

```
int
fixed_and_varargs(nargs, returnval, ...)
    int nargs
    char &returnval = NO_INIT
...
```

The fixed arguments are handled separately, so we can continue to use items and ST to access the variable arguments as before. Alternatively, if we just have a fixed number of optional parameters, we can use a default value of NO_INIT for the optional parameters:

```
int
fixed_and_fixedoptionalargs(mandatory, optional = NO_INIT)
    int mandatory
    int optional
```

The value of items will be 1 if only the mandatory argument was passed and 2 if the optional one was passed too.

Regular Perl subroutines can have optional prototypes, and so can XSUBs. In fact, prototypes are automatically provided for XSUBs unless we choose to disable them with

```
PROTOTYPES: DISABLED
```

Any XSUB below this line will not get a prototype. We can use ENABLED to reenable prototypes later on in the same XS file. We can also give a specific prototype to a particular XSUB with a one-line PROTOTYPE: section, with the prototype immediately following. For example:

```
PROTOTYPE: $;$$$
```

This says pass one scalar, then one to three optional scalar arguments. This is different from the default prototype for an ellipsis, which does not place a limit on the number of passed arguments. Within the XSUB, we can find out how many arguments we actually got with items, as before. We could also generate the same prototype by declaring three trailing arguments with default values.

If we really want to map a return value through supplied arguments (rather than via RETVAL or through stack manipulation), we can do that too. Since we have to have a variable passed in to be able to assign to it, we can define the prototype appropriately, for example:

```
PROTOTYPE: $\$;$$$
```

We can require that a passed argument be an array or hash reference, just as with a regular prototype. In this case, we need to either define the XSUB with a corresponding argument of type SV * and dereference it in C or provide a typemap to convert from the array reference to something else. We give an example of that later on in the chapter. Intriguingly, we can even pass callbacks this way by prototyping a code reference and then having the XSUB call it with eval_sv.

Using Perl Types as Arguments and Return Values

While xsubpp understands a wide range of C types automatically, it's also possible to use Perl's own C data types. For instance, we can define an XSUB that takes and returns an SV *. The advantage of defining an XSUB that uses Perl types is that we can take advantage of Perl concepts such as undef that do not translate well into C.

For instance, we can create a routine that normally returns an integer, but in the case of an error returns undef. Returning an SV * rather than an int makes this easy. For completeness, this very simple example also takes an SV * as input, though an int would have been equally convenient:

```
SV *
positive_or_undef(in)
    SV *in
CODE:
    if (SvIV(in) < 0) {
        RETVAL = &PL_sv_undef;
    } else {
        RETVAL = in;
    }
OUTPUT:
    RETVAL
```

Here PL_sv_undef is a predefined SV that contains an undef value, as seen from Perl. We assign its address to RETVAL, an SV * to return undef to Perl.

There is nothing to stop us receiving or returning array, hash, or code references, so long as we write the XSUB to handle the Perl data structures from C. But if we want to do many conversions of the same types, then we might be better off implementing a typemap to handle the conversion. To see how to do that, it is useful to first look at how xsubpp handles the simpler C types we have been using so far.

Mapping Basic C Types into Perl

The xsubpp script is able to convert between C data types such as int, double, or char * and Perl scalars not through some innate magical knowledge, but because it makes use of a list of standard conversions held in a file called typemap in the ExtUtils directory under the standard library. This file contains all the definitions necessary to convert C types to and from Perl.

We can add our own supplementary typemap file by adding a TYPEMAP argument to the WriteMakefile call in our Makefile.PL:

```
WriteMakefile(
    NAME             => 'Heavy::Fraction',
    ...
    TYPEMAP          => ['heavytypemap','lighttypemap']
);
```

The value of the TYPEMAP argument is an array reference of typemap files. Without path information, these files are looked for in the root directory of the distribution, that is, in the top Heavy-Fraction directory we created with h2xs for our example module earlier in the chapter. Note that it is perfectly acceptable to create a new typemap file for each type we want to handle, containing just the definitions to handle that one type.

Each typemapping consists of an equivalency statement, with the C type on the left and the Perl type on the right, an INPUT definition to convert the Perl type to the C type, and an OUTPUT definition to go in the other direction. These three sections are traditionally gathered together into separate parts of the typemap file, with the equivalencies at the top, the input conversions in the middle, and the output conversions at the bottom.

In order to see how types are mapped, we will take a look at some examples from the default typemap file.

Stating Type Equivalency

The statements of equivalency are all grouped together at the top, and if we look here we see, among other things, the following:

```
int                    T_IV
char *                 T_PV
```

This says that a C int is converted to and from a T_IV. A short and a long are also converted to this type. A char * is converted to a T_PV. Each of these Perl types is a conversion target whose meaning is defined by the input and output conversions that come afterward. Perl defines several types that we can use for the right-hand side of these statements, so if we have a C type we can convert to an already defined Perl type, we can just add an equivalency line. For example, a percentage type might allow an integer from 0 to 100, so we convert it to an unsigned integer with

```
percentage              T_UV
```

With this line added to an included typemap, we can use percentage as an input parameter or a return type and xsubpp will be able to handle it transparently, just as it already does for integers. We do not need to add anything else, as the default typemap already provides input and output conversions for T_UV.

If none of the standard definitions will do, we will have to provide our own conversion logic. All we have to do is provide the means to get the C types we want to handle into a C type defined by Perl, and vice versa, and the xsubpp tool will be able to do the rest.

Input Conversion

The input section of the typemap file is marked by the keyword INPUT. After this, we find a definition for each of the Perl types on the right-hand side of the equivalency statements in the first section. Each conversion maps the Perl type to all possible C types that it can be related to. Here is where we find the conversions to turn a Perl scalar into an integer:

```
T_IV
        $var = ($type)SvIV($arg)
```

And a Perl scalar into a pointer value:

```
T_PV
        $var = ($type)SvPV_nolen($arg)
```

The Perl type appears at the start of a line, on its own. This defines the start of the conversion definition. What follows is perfectly ordinary C code (it can even include if statements and for loops) and is defined using normal C syntax except for the "scalar variables." These are not, in fact, scalar variables at all, but macros that are expanded into suitable forms by xsubpp. They are given this look to give them familiarity:

- $var is replaced with the C-typed output variable. We need to assign a properly typed expression to it for the conversion to succeed.

- $arg is the Perl input variable. Notice that it is *always* an SV*, though it might turn out to be a reference SV that is pointing to something more complex like an AV*, an HV*, or something more esoteric.

- $type is the C type defined on the left-hand side of the equivalency statement. This is how a single INPUT definition can handle more than one conversion. For these conversions, it is simply used to perform an explicit recast.

Since SvPV_nolen is used to extract the string from the SV for the conversion from T_PV, it is implicit that any C type that is defined as equivalent to it understands a null-terminated string. If it doesn't, we need to create our own mapping. Similarly, anything that is associated with T_IV is by implication handled by simply recasting an integer value into that type. If this is not the case, we need a different mapping.

Armed with this information, we can create our own input conversion. As a simple example, we can take our percentage type and convert it into an integer with our own Perl type, using the exact same conversion but with our own mapping. First, we change the Perl type to one of our own devising. (Recall that the ones already in the default typemap have meaning only because they have INPUT and OUTPUT definitions.) For example, we can put this in our local typemap file:

```
percent    T_PERCENT
```

Now we just add

```
T_PERCENT
        $var = ($type)SvUV($arg);
```

This converts a Perl SV into a C variable of type percent. We can do a little better than this, though. A percentage can only legally be a value between 0 and 100, so we can add C code to check for this:

```
T_PERCENT
        {
            IV tmp_$var = SvUV($arg);
            if (tmp$var >=0 && tmp$var <=100) {
                $var = ($type)SvUV($arg);
            } else {
                Perl_croak(aTHX_ \"$var is not in range 0..100\");
            }
        }
```

This conversion demonstrates several tricks that we can employ. First, we can declare local variables if we use an outer { ... } block. (We do not need to use this block, however, if we do not have any need to declare a variable. The if...else statement can exist just fine without it.) Second, we can base the name of a temporary variable on the name of the real variable $var—the substitution is made by xsubpp before the C compiler sees it. Third, we can throw an error with Perl_croak.

Output Conversion

The output section of the typemap file is marked by the keyword OUTPUT. After this, we again find a definition for each of the Perl types on the right-hand side of the equivalency statements in the first section. Each conversion maps all possible C types to the Perl type. Here is where we find the conversions to turn an integer into a Perl scalar:

```
T_IV
        sv_setiv($arg, (IV)$var);
```

And a pointer value into a Perl scalar:

```
T_PV
        sv_setpv((SV*)$arg, $var);
```

We find $var and $arg here too, but now we are converting the value in $var, the C type, to $arg, which is an SV*. Again, notice that the destination variable must always be a Perl scalar of type SV*, though it might be generated as a reference to an AV* and so on. We might do this, for example, to convert a char** into an array reference. The SV* variable that gets substituted for $arg is predefined and preallocated by the time our conversion code is seen, so we use sv_setiv and sv_setpv to simply set the appropriate slot of the scalar from our C data.

For our percent type, the conversion is identical to the normal unsigned integer conversion:

```
T_PERCENT
        sv_setuv($arg, (UV)$var);
```

Mapping C Structs into Perl

Now that we understand the basics of typemaps, we can look at taking more complex data types like structs and converting them to and from Perl. There are several modules on CPAN that will attempt to handle this transparently for us, notably Inline::Struct, but if we can't use a prepackaged solution, there are two basic approaches that we can take:

- Create a custom Perl type and define INPUT and OUTPUT conversions for it.

- Map the C type to T_PTROBJ, which stores a passed pointer as a void *, and manage all the conversion logic from within the CODE sections of XSUBs (which being C, can access the native C type directly).

The first approach assumes conversion to and from a Perl scalar, since that is how typemaps operate. The second approach allows us to be more flexible about how and what we convert, but we don't get transparent conversion just by naming the types in an XSUB.

Let's look at the first approach. Assume we have a C data type declared as follows:

```
typedef struct {
    int number;
    char *name;
} serial_t;
```

First, we add the equivalency statement to the first section of our local typemap file:

```
serial_t  T_SERIAL
```

Then we add an input conversion somewhere within the INPUT section. We have free choice of what the Perl equivalent of this structure is—it could be an array reference of two elements, a string of the form "name: number", or any other representation. We will choose a hash reference with keys of "name" and "number", and at the same time see how to handle a blessed hash reference too.

For this implementation, if either key is not present, we will convert to 0 and an empty string, respectively. We know that $arg should contain the reference to a hash and that $var is a variable of type serial_t:

```
T_SERIAL
        if (SvROK($arg) && SvTYPE(SvRV($arg)) == Svt_PVHV) {
            SV** tmpsvp;
            tmpsvp = hv_fetch((HV*)SvRV($arg),"name",4,FALSE);
            $var.name = (tmpsvp==NULL)
                ? "" : SvPV_nolen(*tmpsvp);
            tmpsvp = hv_fetch((HV*)SvRV($arg),"number",6,FALSE);
            $var.number = (tmpsvp==NULL)
                ? 0  : SvIV(*tmpsvp);
        } else {
            Perl_croak(aTHX_ \"$var is not a hash reference\");
        }
```

If we wanted to additionally ensure that the passed hash reference was blessed into a particular Perl class, or a subclass, we could replace the first line with

```
if (SvROK($arg) && sv_derived_from($arg, "Serial")) {
```

Similarly, the OUTPUT section should contain code to create a hash reference containing the appropriate keys:

```
T_SERIAL
        {
            HV *serial = newHV();
            hv_store(serial,"name", 4, newSVpv($var.name, 0), 0);
```

```
        hv_store(serial,"number",6,newSViv($var.number), 0);
        $var = newSVrv((SV*)serial, "Serial");
    }
```

The second argument to newSVrv is passed to bless, so this blesses the hash reference into the package Serial. If we leave it as NULL, then we just get a regular unblessed hash reference.

So, how about the second approach? The standard typemap defines a Perl type T_PTROBJ, which simply assigns a pointer to any kind of structure to an SV using sv_setref_pv. The result of this mapping is that an XSUB gets to manipulate the native data type directly. For example, to create a new serial_t structure, we could write this into an XS file:

```
serial_t *
newserial(name, nummber)
    char *name;
    int number;
CODE:
    RETVAL = (serial_t *)Safemalloc(sizeof(serial_t));
    RETVAL->name = savepv(name);
    RETVAL->number = number;
OUTPUT:
    RETVAL;
```

And to access the number member:

```
int
number(serial)
    serial_t *serial;
CODE:
    RETVAL = serial->number;
OUTPUT:
    RETVAL
```

In Perl, we can now write code like this:

```
use Serial;
my $serial=newserial("Number 6" => 6);
my $number=$serial->number();
```

Converting this into a Serial object in Perl is simply a matter of writing a new subroutine that wraps newserial and blesses a reference to the returned scalar, to pick one of several possible approaches.

We are creating new C variables dynamically here, so we need to allocate memory. safemalloc and savepv are supplied by Perl's API to provide equivalents of C memory allocation functions that will always play nicely with the Perl interpreter. The savepv function is the Perl supplied version of strdup, for example. We should generally always use the functions provided by Perl for this purpose.

Mapping C++ Object Classes

Dealing with C++ objects is not so different from C objects. Since C++ classes are by definition opaque values, we cannot reasonably make use of a typemap to do all the work for us, so we are left with the T_PTROBJ approach.

Since handling objects is a common requirement, we can make use of the perlobject.map file by Dean Roehrich. This is a useful aid to creating a Perl/C++ class extension that includes a O_OBJECT type, among other types, which automatically takes care of converting between a blessed Perl object of the Perl class and a pointer to a C++ object instance. It is nearly identical to this example typemapping adapted from the perlxs manual page (most of which should now be understandable to us):

```
INPUT
O_OBJECT
if (sv_isobject($arg) && (SvTYPE(SvRV($arg)) == SVt_PVMG)) {
    $var = ($type)SvIV((SV*)SvRV($arg));
} else {
    Perl_warn(aTHX_
        \"${Package}::$func_name() -- $var is not a blessed SV reference\" );
    XSRETURN_UNDEF;
}

OUTPUT
O_OBJECT
sv_setref_pv($arg, CLASS, (void*)$var);
```

The only mysterious entity here is Svt_PVMG, which is simply the return value of SvTYPE for a blessed Perl reference, though it is interesting to note the use of Perl_warn with an apparently interpolated string (it isn't, of course, but the text is expanded by xsubpp). This typemap will handle the casting of the blessed scalar to and from an object of the correct C++ type. We still have to supply the logic to manage the transformation from the opaque C++ reference to Perl object, though.

The equivalency statement for a C++ class MyClass would look like this:

```
MyClass *     O_OBJECT
```

Let's assume we also call the Perl extension MyClass.pm and create an example constructor, object method, and destructor to map to this C++ class. The key detail to add is to prefix the XSUB subroutine name with a class name and ::. This tells xsubpp that we are mapping onto a C++ class and causes two new macros to be defined:

- THIS: The C++ object instance
- CLASS: The C++ class type

Constructors

We can set up a constructor to be called by Perl with an XSUB called new, which tells xsubpp that this XSUB is a constructor. A typical constructor might be as follows:

```
MyClass *
MyClass::new(from = NO_INIT)
    MyClass *from
PROTOTYPE: $;$
CODE:
    if (items > 1) {
        RETVAL = new MyClass(from);
    } else {
        RETVAL = new MyClass();
    }
OUTPUT:
    RETVAL
```

This constructor takes an optional argument, which is of the same C++ class (that is, an object to clone) and calls the appropriate version of the C++ constructor accordingly. Note the default argument value of NO_INIT—this tells xsubpp to construct code to allocate memory for a MyClass object if we pass in the corresponding Perl object, but to not bother if no Perl object was passed. The typemap takes care of converting the returned pointer into a blessed SV *.

Why do we test items against 1 rather than 0? This is one way to define an optional argument, as we saw earlier. However, because this is a C++ XSUB, there is an implicit first argument. For object methods, it defines an object pointer in THIS. For a constructor, it defines CLASS. However, we already took care of the class in the typemap, so we don't need to refer to it here.

Methods

A method to call the C++ object from the blessed Perl reference that encapsulates it is simple now that we can create the object. Here is an example method that passes an integer and expects another integer back:

```
int
MyClass::convertint(in)
    int in
CODE:
    RETVAL = (int)(THIS->convert_an_int(in));
OUTPUT:
    RETVAL
```

The C++ object is accessed through THIS, which is the implicit first argument, and we call the object method as normal. If the method happens to return a long or similar integer-like type, we can always cast it, as we have in this example. It is worth noting that the Perl method, here convertint, does not have to line up with the C++ method, here convert_an_int.

How about C++ operator methods? These might seem to be a different problem altogether, but in fact we just wrap them like ordinary methods and then use Perl's overload module to map the Perl name for the operator to Perl's equivalent operator type, which we can do in the h2xs-generated Perl module that accompanies the XS file (MyClass.pm in this example).

We can have xsubpp do this job for us by adding an OVERLOAD: line and adjusting the XSUB slightly, in particular adding a third argument to denote which side of the Perl expression we are on (should we care). For example:

```
bool_t
operator_isequal(lhs,rhs,onright)
    MyClass *lhs    MyClass *rhs
    IV onright
OVERLOAD: == eq
CODE:
    RETVAL operator==(*lhs,*rhs);
OUTPUT:
    RETVAL
```

This handles both the numeric and string equality operators in Perl. The return type here is bool_t, which we are assuming is the return type of the operator== method in the C++ class and which happens to be predefined in the default typemap. We should adjust this accordingly if the return type is different (for example, int).

To handle the stringify operator (""), specify \"\"., To enable automatic fallback operator generation, specify FALLBACK: TRUE just after the MODULE and PACKAGE declaration in the XS file.

Destructors

To map a Perl DESTROY block to the destructor of a C++ class is possibly the simplest XSUB of all. We just write

```
void
MyClass::DESTROY()
```

The xsubpp script will handle the rest.

Inlining C and Other Languages into Perl

The Inline module, which we mentioned briefly at the start of this chapter, is a convenient wrapper around the functionality of xsubpp and the C::Scan module that encapsulates the process of generating the XS file for us. Better still, it allows us to place the C code bodily within a Perl source file rather than in a separate file. Furthermore, we can embed almost any language if we install the appropriate support module. By default, Inline automatically provides Inline::C, but we can add Inline::CPP to inline C++, Inline::Java to inline Java, Inline::Python to inline Python, and so on. Each of these support modules implements the interface defined by the Inline module and provides support for a specific language.

The embedded code is compiled the first time the program is run, so we do not even need to have a "make" step to use it. Here is a simple script that demonstrates one way we can inline C code:

```perl
#!/usr/bin/perl
# inlinefraction.pl
use strict;
use warnings;

use Inline C => qq[
int heavyfraction (int num1, int num2) {
    int result;

    if (num1 > num2) {
        result = num1 / num2;
    } else {
        result = num2 / num1;
    }

    return result;
}
];

print heavyfraction(10,3);
```

The first time we run this script, there will be a pause as Inline extracts the embedded code, determines the XSUB mappings to be generated for it, and passes the resulting sources to the underlying C compiler. On subsequent invocations, the program will run at full speed, as the C has already been compiled.

Depending on how we want to organize the code, we can inline the C code in a variety of ways. First, there are HERE documents, essentially a syntactic variant on the previous example:

```perl
use Inline C => <<_END_OF_C;
int heavyfraction (int num1, int num2) {
    ...
}
_END_OF_C
```

Or, we can use an intermediate string variable, so long as we make sure it is defined at compile time, for example, by importing it from our own module designed for the purpose:

```perl
use My::C::Repository qw($codestring);
use Inline 'C' => $codestring;
```

Equivalently, but at run time instead of compile time, we can use the language-neutral bind method of the Inline module to the same effect. This approach is useful if we don't want to compile the code unless we intend to use it. Of course, this also means that there will be a delay the first time the use of this code is triggered.

```
my $codestring='int heavyfraction ...';
Inline->bind(C => $codestring);
```

Without any qualifying argument, Inline will look for code beneath a special marker named for the language being inlined, after the __END__ marker:

```
use Inline 'C';

print heavyfraction(10,3);

__END__
__C__
int heavyfraction (int num1, int num2) {
...
```

With the special keyword DATA, we can place code into a __DATA__ section before the __END__ marker, if it is present:

```
use Inline C => 'DATA';

print heavyfraction(10,3);

__DATA__
__C__
int heavyfraction (int num1, int num2) {
...

__END__
```

Finally, we can use the Inline::Files module to remove the need for the special tokens entirely. Implemented as a Perl source filter, it removes the inlined code from the Perl source before the interpreter gets to compile it, leaving Perl's __DATA__ and __END__ free for other uses:

```
use Inline::Files;
use Inline C;

__C__
int heavyfraction (int num1, int num2) {
...

__DATA__
Now we can put real data here again

__END__
Now we can put real end notes here again
```

The special token FILE or BELOW can also be used to explicitly request this augmented style of inlined section; we can also still use the DATA section or HERE documents as before.

Just to prove the versatility of Inline, here is a reimplementation of heavyfraction as embedded Python. For this to work, we need to install Inline::Python and, of course, Python itself, if it is not already available:

```
#!/usr/bin/perl
# inlinepython.pl
use strict;
use warnings;

use Inline Python => <<_END_OF_PYTHON;
def heavyfraction(x,y):
```

```
    if x > y:
        return x / y
    else:
        return y / x
_END_OF_PYTHON

print heavyfraction(10,3);
```

Configuring the Inline Module

The `Inline` module has several configuration options that we can specify for either all languages or an individual language. Here is how we can have `Inline` always rebuild C, while at the same time telling it to look in the `__DATA__` section for the source:

```
use Inline C => 'DATA', FORCE_BUILD => 1;
```

We can configure `Inline` without invoking its compilation features using the `Config` keyword. The following is identical in operation to the previous example, but it splits the configuration and invocation into two separate statements:

```
use Inline C => 'Config', FORCE_BUILD => 1;
use Inline C => 'DATA';
```

To configure all languages at once, we just omit the language:

```
use Inline Config => FORCE_BUILD => 1;
```

The available configuration options are listed in Table 20-1.

Table 20-1. *Inline Module Configuration Options*

Option	Description
DIRECTORY	Location of temporary build directory for derived files. Defaults to _Inline.
FORCE_BUILD	Force Inline to reextract and rebuild inlined sources. Defaults to 0.
INC	Additional include paths, for example, -I/usr/include/extradir.
LIBS	Additional libraries, for example, -llight -lheavy.
WARNINGS	Enable warnings. Defaults to 1.

While we would not typically want to configure `FORCE_BUILD` within our code, we can preload and configure the module on the command line. For example:

```
> perl -MInline=Config,FORCE_BUILD,1 inlinefraction.pl
```

This will force a rebuild for all inlined language types. We can specify a specific language (should we have inlined several into the same application) as before and configure several at once by specifying `-MInline=lang,...` for each language in turn.

Collaborating with XSUBs

To configure `Inline` to collaborate with another module containing C or C++ extensions, we can use the special `with` token. This causes `Inline` to import the function signatures from the other module and make the underlying library routines available to the inlined code as well. For instance, we could write this into a Perl source file:

```
use Inline with => Heavy::Fraction;
```

This would import our example XS extension from earlier in the chapter and make the `heavyfraction` routine directly callable from within C (or C++) code inlined into this source file.

Creating Distributable Inlined Modules

To create a distributable module that uses inlined code, we need to set up Makefile.PL to compile the foreign language section up front. This is because normally the inlined code is only handled when an application is run. This clearly won't do for a module.

Fortunately, the solution is simple. We just replace ExtUtils::MakeMaker with Inline::MakeMaker, a subclass of the original module that integrates support for inlined code. Once this is done, we can use make and make dist as usual to create a distributable module archive.

See perldoc Inline-FAQ and Inline::C-Cookbook for more information and examples.

Compiling Perl

One of the most often-requested Perl tools is a Perl-to-C compiler, or at least a Perl-to-something-more-compact compiler. In fact, Perl comes with three, in the form of compiler backends in the B:: family of modules.

- The B::C module performs a straight translation of a compiled tree of Perl opcodes and operands into C statements to construct the same tree from scratch. It then invokes an embedded Perl interpreter allocated and constructed in C to process the reconstructed tree.

  The advantage of this approach is that the resulting C program will do exactly what the original Perl program did and can run without Perl present. The drawback is that it will be much bigger than the Perl interpreter (a copy of which is linked in to the program) and might not even be any faster. B::C is not guaranteed to generate viable C code in every case, but it is successful most of the time.

- The B::CC module performs starts the same way, from the compiled Perl code, but it generates low-level C code that mimics the operation of the interpreter directly.

  Like the B::C module, the resulting program should run without needing Perl, and because it does not need to link in the interpreter, it should be both smaller and faster. The drawback is that the module is still experimental and is quite likely to not generate code that functions entirely correctly.

- The B::Bytecode module converts a compiled tree of opcodes and operands into bytecode; the opcode tree converted into a compact binary form. This compact form can be regenerated back into the compiled tree with the Byteloader module. This module is a translator (implemented using Filter::Util::Call) that simply converts from a compressed representation of Perl rather than the usual human-readable form.

We can invoke any of the backends through the O module, just as we did for the other B:: modules back in Chapter 17. For instance, this compiles the Perl script app.pl into an executable called app.exe:

```
> perl -MO=C,-oapp.exe app.pl
```

And this converts the script into bytecode, along with a two-line prefix to load the Byteloader to have the bytecode executed:

```
> perl -MO=Bytecode,-oapp.plc app.pl
```

The .plc extension means "compiled Perl" and is traditional for a bytecode-encoded Perl program. To execute this compiled code, we can invoke the Byteloader module like this:

```
> perl -MByteLoader app.plc
```

Alternatively, we can add a short snippet of Perl to the top of the file to do the job for us:

```
#!/usr/bin/perl
use ByteLoader 0.05;
```

All the backends are set up to understand an import list that consists of options and arguments like a command line. Here, -o determines the output file name (otherwise, we get the traditional a.out). However, it is more convenient to use the perlcc script, which conveniently encapsulates the process of generating the C code, compiling it, and even running it if we so desire. Here are the same compilations done via perlcc:

```
> perlcc -o app.exe app.pl
> perlcc -B -o app.plc app.pl
```

The perlcc script automatically adds the two-line prefix for the bytecode version, so we do not need to add it ourselves.

To use B::CC instead of B::C, we specify the -O option:

```
> perlcc -O -o app.exe app.pl
```

For the Perl-to-C compilers only, the intermediate C code can be preserved for the overly curious with the -S option:

```
> perlcc -o app.exe -S app.pl
```

Likewise, we can specify additional libraries to link against with the -L and -l options, which have the same meanings as they do to a regular linker. The -c option can be used to generate the intermediate C code without going on to compile it to an executable.

For all three backends, -e can be used to compile a one-liner, -v can be used to increase the output of the tool, and -log can be used to send that output to a log file. Adding -r causes the resulting program to be executed immediately after the compiler has finished its work (not, obviously, in conjunction with -c).

There is no intermediate code for the bytecode compiler—the byte code essentially is the intermediate code—but we can convert it into a (slightly) more readable form with the B::Disassembler module or the disassemble front-end script (found in the B directory in the standard library alongside the compiler backend modules) that invokes it for us. The assemble script carries out the opposite conversion for those who feel compelled to tinker with Perl "assembly language" instead of just writing Perl like normal people. It also has the more practical application of allowing us to update bytecode generated by an older version of the B::Bytecode backend to work with a more modern Perl installation, without needing to go back to the original sources.

We can also, technically, compile Perl into Perl with the B::Deparse module. Although this might not sound interesting, it does have some useful applications. First, the Data::Dumper module can use it to encode code references in serialized data. Second, it can be a useful tool in debugging some uncooperative code, by transforming it into the code it really is, rather than what it looks like. See Chapter 17 for more details.

Naturally, several more sophisticated means of compiling Perl into C are available from CPAN. One in particular that may be worth investigating is PAR, a toolkit for archiving Perl code loosely inspired by Java's *jar* files. PAR also comes with a utility called pp that will create a self-contained executable in the manner of perlcc, but with superior results. PAR has many other useful tricks too, especially for creating module distributions.

Summary

In this chapter, we looked at how to integrate a Perl interpreter into C or C++ code and use it to evaluate Perl code, call Perl subroutines, and manipulate Perl data structures. We also looked at integrating C code into Perl by writing an extension module in XS, the language of extension subroutines, or XSUBs. In both cases, a good basic understanding of the macros and functions that Perl provides through its C header files is essential. While there are very many of these functions, in this chapter we have covered a good selection of the most common of them along with a range of their possible uses. We looked in particular at the h2xs program and the xsubpp XSUB compiler and how we can use these Perl-provided tools to automate some or all of the process of binding C and Perl together.

The Inline module is a very convenient wrapper for much of the preceding and understands how to drive xsubpp from within an ordinary Perl script. Using it, we can have our code automatically invoke a compiler to generate the bindings to external C libraries and compile embedded C code at the point of execution, notably without a makefile involved. Inline can also provide integration to many other languages including Java, Basic, PHP, and Python. We looked at a simple implementation of a Python-based extension by way of example.

Finally, we saw how to compile Perl programs into C executables or alternatively into Perl bytecode. Either approach makes use of a compiler backend module, either B::C or B::CC for C code, or B::Bytecode for binary bytecode that can be regenerated into a compiled Perl opcode tree with the Byteloader module.

CHAPTER 21

■ ■ ■

Processes, Signals, and Threads

In this chapter, we look at managing multiple strands of execution within a single application, both with multiple separate processes and with lighter-weight threads. We also cover the related subject of communicating between processes, both within the same application and between applications. In particular, we examine signals and interprocess communication, also known as IPC.

Signals are the operating system's basic mechanism for indicating error conditions and other events asynchronously. We can receive them, for example, as a result of errors in low-level system calls or abnormal termination of socket filehandles. Unless we handle it or state that we wish to ignore it, such a signal will terminate the running application. Ignoring a signal is easy but not always wise, so in this chapter we will see how to write special subroutines called *signal handlers* to manage signals sensibly. We can also raise signals against other processes, either once in the same application or elsewhere. Not all signals are errors. On Unix platforms, for example, we can use an alarm signal to trigger an event over a period of our choosing.

In the main part of the chapter, we look at writing Perl applications that manage multiple concurrent strands of execution. First we examine creating and handling multiple separate processes. While this is chiefly of interest to Unix programmers, Perl now has quite credible emulation for multiprocessing applications under Windows too. One of the major problems with multiple processes is getting information between them, so we also look at message queues, semaphores, and shared memory, three different solutions to the problem of interprocess communication.

After processes we look at threads, specifically the new *interpreter threads* introduced with Perl 5.8. While processes exist in relative isolation, with completely separated data and execution environments, threads share everything within the same process. This makes them very lightweight by comparison and easy to share data between. In most languages, it also makes them much trickier to program since it is easy for threads to overwrite the same data. However, interpreter threads enable Perl to keep data used by different threads partitioned away from each other unless we specify that data is to be shared. This greatly simplifies the task of programming threads and making most Perl modules thread-compatible even if they have no special knowledge or understanding of them.

Signals

Much like hardware interrupts, signals are exceptional events that happen independently of whatever code a program happens to be executing at the time. They are said to be "out of band," since they also cannot be deferred for handling at a later point in time. Either the program recipient of a thread handles it, or the operating system will handle it by terminating the program.

Typically, the operating environment defines default triggers and behaviors for most signals. A Unix shell, for instance, maps some signals to key sequences, such as KILL to Ctrl-C, and STOP to Ctrl-Z. Other processes, as well as the kernel, have the ability to send signals to any designated process.

Every process keeps an index table of each possible signal and its response to each. Whenever a process receives a signal, it stops normal execution and executes the behavior defined for that signal. Depending on the signal, that behavior may be to take some action and then return control back to the interrupted routine. Alternatively, the response might be to do some cleaning up and exit the program or to explicitly ignore the signal.

Perl allows the programmer to redefine the behaviors of most signals in any of these ways as necessary. The signal index is stored in Perl as the hash variable %SIG, with the key value being the signal name and the value being either

- A code reference to a subroutine to execute

- A scalar return value

By assigning various values to signals in the hash, we can control how an application responds to different signals. To elaborate a little on what kind of signals we have available, we can dump out a list of them by printing out the keys of the %SIG hash:

```
> perl -e "print join q/ /,sort keys %SIG"
```

At the system level, each signal is denoted as an integer, rather than the name we see here. If we need to cross-reference the numeric and names, we can discover them via kill -l (provided we're on a Unix platform, of course) or through the position of the name in Perl's Config variable sig_name, which is a space-delimited string:

```
#!/usr/bin/perl
# siglist.pl
use warnings;
use strict;

use Config;

my @signals = split ' ', $Config{sig_name};
for (0..$#signals) {
    print "$_ $signals[$_] \n" unless $signals[$_] =~ /^NUM/;
}
```

This generates a list of all signals and their associated number, skipping over real-time signal numbers beginning NUM (in the range between RTMIN and RTMAX):

```
0 ZERO
1 HUP
2 INT
3 QUIT
4 ILL
5 TRAP
6 ABRT
7 BUS
8 FPE
9 KILL
10 USR1
...
```

Many of these signals are obscure, unlikely, or only occur if we have certain features enabled. The signal SIGPWR, for example, applies to power failure situations and SIGIO occurs only with file-handles set to asynchronous mode using O_ASYNC. The most commonly used signals are as listed in Table 21-1 (but note that not all of these signals work on non-Unix platforms).

Table 21-1. *Standard Signals and Their Meanings*

Name	Key	Meaning
SIGHUP	HUP	**Hangup** Controlling terminal or process has terminated (for example, a modem, hence "hang up"). Often redefined in daemons to tell them to reread their configuration files and restart operations.
SIGINT	INT	**Interrupt** Instruct the process to interrupt what it is doing and exit. This signal is trappable (which means we can redefine its handler) so that a process can perform any necessary clean-up before doing so. Pressing Ctrl-C on the keyboard is often the manual way to send this signal.
SIGQUIT	QUIT	**Quit** A higher priority signal to shut down and, depending on the system's configuration, may produce a core dump. This signal, too, is trappable.
SIGKILL	KILL	**Kill** An explicit command to tell the process to immediately exit. This signal is not trappable. (Would we really want to take away the kernel's ability to terminate runaway processes?)
SIGUSR1	USR1	**User-defined signal** While this signal is never used by the kernel, the default behavior for any process receiving the signal is to exit.
SIGUSR2	USR2	**User-defined signal** A second signal for process definition. Like USR1, the default behavior is to exit.
SIGPIPE	PIPE	**Broken pipe** A pipe that a process was either reading from or writing to has been closed by the other end.
SIGALRM	ALRM	**Alarm** An alarm timer for this process has expired. Not supported on Microsoft platforms.
SIGTERM	TERM	**Terminate** Like INT, this instructs the process to exit and is trappable. This signal has a higher priority than INT, but lower than QUIT and KILL.
SIGCHLD	CHLD	**Child exit** A child process has exited.
SIGFPE	FPE	**Floating-point exception** The floating-point processor was asked to perform an illegal operation.
SIGSEGV	SEGV	**Invalid memory reference** An attempt was made to read or write an invalid address in memory.
SIGCONT	CONT	**Continue** Resume execution if stopped by a STOP signal.
SIGSTOP	STOP	**Stop** The process is halted until it receives a CONT, at which point it resumes operational. This signal is not trappable.
SIGIO	IO	**Asynchronous IO event** If a filehandle is set for asynchronous operation (O_ASYNC), this signal is raised whenever an event (for example, more input) occurs on it.
SIGWINCH	WINCH	**Window changed** The window or terminal in which the console of a process is running has changed size (the user resizing a window can do this). Chapter 15 discusses this in more detail.

For a complete list of signals, there is no substitute for the system documentation (usually `man 7 signal` on Unix). Even on Unix, some signals are platform dependent. The same documentation should inform us of the default behavior of each signal. Regardless, by manipulating the contents of the %SIG hash, we can override these defaults for most signal types and install our own mechanisms for handling signals.

Safe vs. Unsafe Signals

Between Perl 5.6 and 5.8, the way Perl handled signals was overhauled significantly. In the old implementation, a signal could interrupt Perl in the middle of executing an opcode. This made it very tricky to handle signals safely, especially if any significant manipulation of Perl's state happened as a result of the signal. In such cases, the interpreter could find itself in an inconsistent state, with unpredictable consequences.

Perl 5.8 introduces so-called safe signals, which guarantee that signals will only be delivered to the running application in between opcodes. This means that if Perl is busy reading or writing to a filehandle, it will finish the current IO operation before handling the signal. Similarly, if the program is in the middle of a sort operation, the operation will complete first.

The advantage of safe signals is that signal handling is much more robust. The disadvantage is that since some operations can take a long time, receipt of a signal may not occur quickly. For the most part, this is not an issue, but in a few applications, it might be more important to handle a signal quickly than try to keep Perl happy (typically this would be situations where the program is always going to terminate as a result of the signal and never attempt to resume). For these applications, we can set the environment variable PERL_SIGNALS to unsafe:

```
> PERL_SIGNALS=unsafe immediatesignalapp.pl
```

To explicitly request safe signals, we can set the variable to safe instead. Prior to Perl 5.8, this variable has no effect (and signals are always "unsafe").

Signal Handling

A string or subroutine reference may be set as values of the %SIG hash to control what happens when a given signal is received:

Value	Action
DEFAULT or undef	Perform the default behavior as determined by the system.
IGNORE	Instruct the process to take no action in response to the signal. Untrappable signals are unaffected by this setting (such as KILL).
\&subreference sub { codeblock }	If a subroutine reference or an anonymous subroutine is set as the value of a signal, then it is called whenever that signal is received. We can then decide how to handle it ourselves, including ignoring it, raising a different signal, dying, and so on.
subroutine	If the name of the subroutine is set as a string, this will be evaluated as &main::subroutine when the signal is received.

For example, to ignore SIGPIPE signals, we would put the following:

```
$SIG{PIPE} = 'IGNORE';
```

To restore the default handling for SIGINT signals:

```
$SIG{INT} = 'DEFAULT';
```

To find out the current setting of SIGALRM (remembering that undef is equal to DEFAULT):

```
$alarming = $SIG{ALRM};
```

To set a subroutine as a signal handler:

```
$SIG{USR1} = \&usr1handler;
```

The last of these is, of course, the most interesting. Signal handlers, when called, receive the name of the signal that called them as an argument, so we can assign multiple signals to the same handler or handle each signal individually.

```
$SIG{HUP}  = \&handler;
$SIG{STOP} = \&handler;
$SIG{USR1} = \&handler;
```

If we set a text string that is not DEFAULT or IGNORE, then it is taken as a symbolic reference to a subroutine in the main (not the current) package. So be careful about spelling. Thus

```
$SIG{INT} = 'DEFLAT';
```

actually means

```
$SIG{INT} = \&main::DEFLAT;
```

This will silently fail unless we are using the -w flag with Perl, in which case it will merely complain on STDERR that the handler DEFLAT is undefined. Although this is a perfectly legal way to set a signal handler, the fact that it defaults to the main package can cause confusion when handling signals inside packages—even if the package defines a subroutine with the same name, it won't get called. Note also that though this is a form of symbolic reference, it is not trapped by the use strict refs pragma. Conversely, if we try to set a signal that does not exist, Perl will complain with an error, for example:

```
No such signal SIGFLARE at...
```

A practical example for redefining trappable signals would be when our program creates temporary files. A well-behaved program should clean up after itself before exiting, even when unexpectedly interrupted. In the following example, we will redefine the INT handler to remove a temporary PID file before exiting. This will keep the program from leaving PID files around when the user interrupts the program with a Ctrl-C:

```
$SIG{INT} = sub {
    warn "received SIGINT, removing PID file and exiting.\n";
    unlink "$ENV{HOME}/.program.pid";
    exit 0;
};
```

The die and warn Pseudo-Handlers

In addition to the standard signals, the %SIG hash also allows us to set handlers for Perl's error reporting system, specifically the warn and die functions together with derivatives of them like carp and croak (supplied by the Carp module). These are not true signal handlers but hooks into Perl's internals, which allow us to react to events occurring within Perl. The %SIG hash makes a convenient interface because, aside from some minor differences in behavior, they operate very similarly to signals.

Neither the warn or die hooks are present as keys in the %SIG hash by default—we have to add them:

```
$SIG{__WARN__} = \&watchout;
$SIG{__DIE__}  = \&lastwillandtestament;
```

Both handlers may customize the error or warning before passing it on to a real warn or die (the action of the handler is suppressed within the handler itself, so calling warn or die a second time will do the real thing). A warning handler may choose to suppress the warning entirely; die handlers, however, cannot avert death, but only do a few things on its deathbed, so to speak. See Chapter 16 for more on die and warn, and registering handlers for them.

The hook mechanism is not extensible; the __ prefix and suffix merely distinguish these special handlers from true signal handlers. They do not, however, allow us to create arbitrary signals and handlers.

Writing Signal Handlers

Signal handlers are just subroutines. When they are called, Perl passes them a single parameter: the name of the signal. For example, here is a program containing a very simple signal handler that raises a warning whenever it receives an INT signal, but otherwise does nothing with it:

```perl
#!/usr/bin/perl
# inthandler1.pl
use warnings;
use strict;

sub handler {
    my $sig = shift;
    print "Caught SIG$sig! \n";
}

# register handler for SIGINT
$SIG{INT} = \&handler;

# kill time
while (1) { sleep 1; }
```

Note that since the handler handled the exception, the program does not exit. If we still want the handler to exit after performing whatever other actions we need done, we must add the exit command to the end of our handler. Here is another handler that implements this scheme, using a private counter. It will catch the first two signals but defer to the normal behavior on the third reception:

```perl
#!/usr/bin/perl
# inthandler2.pl
use warnings;
use strict;

{
    # define counter as closure variable
    my $interrupted = 0;

    sub handler {
        foreach ($interrupted) {
            $_ == 0 and warn("Once..."), $interrupted++, last;
            $_ == 1 and warn("Twice..."), $interrupted++, last;
            $_ == 2 and die ("Thrice!");
        }
    }
}

# register handler for SIGINT
$SIG{INT} = \&handler;
```

```
# kill time
while (1) { sleep 1; }
```

A few platforms (BSD systems, typically) cancel signal handlers once they have been called. If we want these systems to be maximally portable, we have to reinstall the handler before we exit it, if we wish it to be called again:

```
handler {
    $sig = shift;

    # reinstate handler
    $SIG{$sig} = \&handler;

    ... do stuff ...
}
```

To prevent another signal from coming in before we have redefined it, we will do that first in every handler. Since this does no harm even on platforms that do not need it, it is a good piece of defensive programming if we are worried about portability.

Avoiding Overcomplex Handlers

The preceding handlers are good examples of signal handlers in the sense that they do very little. Signals implicitly herald a critical event, so executing complex code, and especially anything that causes Perl to allocate more memory to store a value, is a bad idea.

Avoiding Memory Allocation

For example, the following signal counting handler is not a good idea; it allocates a new key and value for the hash each time a signal it has not seen previously arrives.

```
%sigcount;

sub allocatinghandler {
    $sigcount {$_[0]}++;
}
```

This modified version is fine though, as we have guaranteed that all the keys and all the values of the hash already exist, so no new memory needs to be allocated within the handler:

```
%sigcount = map { $_ => 0 } keys %SIG;

sub nonallocatinghandler {
    $sigcount{$_[0]}++;
}
```

The rule of thumb for any signal handler is to do the absolute minimum necessary.

Uninterruptible Signal Handlers

Unlike the warn and die hooks, real signal handlers do not suppress signals while they are running, so if we want to avoid being interrupted a second time while we are still handling a signal, we have to find a way to avoid further signals. One way to do this is simply disable the handler for the duration of the handler:

```
sub handler {
    $SIG{$_[0]} = 'IGNORE';
    ... do something ...
    $SIG{$_[0]} = \&handler;
}
```

A better way is to localize a fresh value for the signal value in $SIG using local. This has the same effect as reassigning it explicitly, but with the advantage that the old value is restored immediately on exiting the handler without our intervention:

```
sub handler {
    local $SIG{$_[0]} = 'IGNORE';

    ... do something...
}
```

We can suppress signals in normal code using the same principles, for instance, by temporarily reassigning a signal to a new handler or value. We can do that by either making a record of the old one or using local to suppress it if we happen to be in a section of code that is scoped appropriately:

```
$oldsig   = $SIG{INT};
$SIG{INT} = 'IGNORE';

... code we do not want interrupted ...

$SIG{INT} = $oldsig;
```

As always, these techniques only work on trappable signals.

Aborting System-Level Operations

On many versions of Unix, as well as a few other platforms, signals that occur during some system calls, and in particular during input and output operations, may cause the operation to restart on the return from the signal handler. Frequently, we would rather abort the whole operation at this point, since resuming is likely to be either pointless or plain wrong. Unfortunately, the only way to abort the interrupted code from inside a signal handler is to use die or CORE::exit. Moreover, to be able to resume normal execution at a point of our choice rather than jump into a die handler or exit the program, we have to put the die (or rather, the context of the die) inside an eval, since that will exit the eval and resume execution beyond it. So the code we want to abort must all be inside an eval:

```
sub handler {
    $SIG{$_[0]} = 'DEFAULT';
    die;
}

$result = eval {
    $SIG{INT} = \&handler;
    ...read from a network connection...
    $SIG{INT} = 'DEFAULT';
    1;   # return true on completion
}

warn "Operation interrupted! \n" unless $result;
```

If the code in the eval completes successfully, it returns 1 (because that is the last expression in the eval). If the handler is called, the die causes the eval to return undef. So we can tell if the handler was called or not by the return value from eval, and therefore we can tell if the code was interrupted. We can vary this theme a little if we want to return an actual result from the eval; so long as we do not need to validly return a false value, we can always use this technique. Note that even though the die itself is not in the eval, the context in which it is called is the eval's context, so it exits the eval, not the program as a whole.

This approach also works for setting and canceling alarms to catch system calls that time out; see the later section "Alarms" for more information.

Flexibly Installing Signal Handlers

We have already seen how to install a signal handler by hand; simply set the value of the relevant signal in the signal hash:

```
$SIG{INT} = \&handler;
```

While fine for a single signal, this is cumbersome for handling many of them. One way to set up multiple signals is to assign a new hash to %SIG, for example:

```
%SIG = (%SIG, INT => IGNORE, PIPE => \&handler, HUP => \&handler);
```

There is, however, a better way, with the sigtrap pragmatic module. This takes a list of signal actions and signals, and assigns each signal the action that immediately preceded it. sigtrap provides two handlers of its own: a stack-trace handler, the default action, and die, which does what it implies. It also provides several keywords for common groups of signals, as well as a keyword for currently unassigned signals.

The default action is stack-trace, so the following three pragmas all have the same effect; normal-signals is the group comprising the SIGINT, SIGHUP, SIGPIPE, and SIGTERM signals:

```
use sigtrap qw(INT HUP PIPE TERM);
use sigtrap qw(stack-trace INT HUP PIPE TERM);
use sigtrap qw(stack-trace normal-signals);
```

Alternatively, we can choose to set a die handler. Here are two examples of using die with the signals that sigtrap categorizes under error-signals:

```
use sigtrap qw(die ABRT BUS EMT FPE ILL QUIT SEGV SYS TRAP);
use sigtrap qw(die error-signals);
```

We can also supply our own handler, by prefixing it with the keyword handler:

```
use sigtrap qw(handler myhandler ALRM HUP INT);
```

If we want to be sure the handler exists before installing it, we can drop the qw and use a subroutine reference in a regular list:

```
use sigtrap handler => \&myhandler, qw(ALRM HUP INT);
```

We may assign different handlers to different signals all at the same time; each signal is assigned the handler before it in the list. The signals at the front are assigned stack-trace if the first item in the list is not die or a handler of our own devising:

```
use sigtrap qw(
    stack-trace normal-signals ALRM USR2
    die error-signals
    handler usrhandler USR1 USR2
    die PWR
    handler inthandler INT HUP
);
```

We can specify as many handlers and signals as we like. In addition, later assignments supplant earlier ones, so handler inthandler INT HUP replaces the assignment to stack-trace of these signals in the first line (in the guise of normal-signals). If we want to assign a handler to all signals only if they have not already been assigned or ignored, we can precede the signals we want to trap conditionally with the untrapped keyword. For example, to call the stack-trace handler for normal signals not already trapped:

```
use sigtrap qw(stack-trace untrapped normal-signals);
```

The opposite of untrapped is any; this cancels the conditional assignment of untrapped:

```
use sigtrap qw(stack-trace untrapped normal-signals any ALRM USR1 USR2);
```

If sigtrap is not passed any signal names at all, it defaults to a standard set that was trapped in previous incarnations of the module. This list is also defined as old-interface-signals. The following are therefore equivalent:

```
use sigtrap qw(stack-trace old-interface-signals);
use sigtrap;
```

Sending Signals

The traditional Unix command (and C system call) for sending signals is kill, a curious piece of nomenclature that comes about from the fact that the default signal sent by the kill command was 15--SIGTERM, which caused the program to exit. Despite this, we can send any signal using Perl's kill function.

The kill command takes at least two arguments. The first is a signal number or a signal name given as a string. The second and following arguments are the IDs of processes to kill. The return value from kill is the number of processes to which a signal was delivered (which, since they may ignore the signal, is not necessarily the number of processes that acted on it):

```
# tell kids to stop hogging the line
kill 'INT', @mychildren;

# a more pointed syntax
kill INT => @mychildren, $grandpatoo;

# commit suicide (die would be simpler)
kill KILL => $$;    # $$ is our own process ID
kill (9, $$);       # put numerically

# send our parent process a signal
kill USR1 => getppid
```

Sending a signal to a negative process ID will send it to the process group of that process (including any child processes the process may have, and possibly the parent process that spawned it too, unless the process used setpgrp). For example, this instruction will send an HUP signal to every other process in the same process group:

```
kill HUP => -$$;
```

The HUP signal in particular is useful for a parent process to tell all its children to stop what they are doing and reinitialize themselves. The Apache web server does exactly this in forked mode (which is to say, on Unix but not Windows) if we send the main process a HUP. Of course, the main process does not want to receive its own signal, so we would temporarily disable it:

```
sub huphandler {
    local $SIG{HUP} = 'IGNORE';
    kill HUP => -$$;
}
```

The signal 0 (or ZERO) is special. It does not actually send a signal to the target process or processes at all but simply checks that those process IDs exist. Since kill returns the number of processes to which a signal was successfully sent, for signal 0 it reports the number of processes that exist, which makes it a simple way to test if a process is running:

```
kill(0 => $child) or warn "Child $child is dead!";
```

Alarms

Alarms are a particularly useful kind of signal that is issued whenever an internal timer counts down to zero. We can set an alarm with the `alarm` function, which takes an integer number of seconds as an argument:

```perl
# set an alarm for sixty seconds from now
alarm 60;
```

If the supplied number is zero, the previous alarm, if any, is canceled:

```perl
# cancel alarm
alarm 0;
```

Setting the alarm will cause the process to exit (as per the default behavior of the signal), unless we also set a new handler for the signal:

```perl
alarmhandler {
    print "Alarm at ", scalar(localtime), "\n";
}

$SIG{ALRM} = \&alarmhandler;
```

Please note that specifying a time interval does not mean that the timer will raise a SIGALRM in exactly that interval. What it says is that sometime after that interval, depending on the resolution of the system clock and whether our process is in the current context, a signal will be sent.

A Simple Use of Alarms

We can only ever have one `alarm` active at a time, per process, so setting a new alarm value resets the timer on the existing alarm, with zero canceling it as noted previously. Here is a program that demonstrates a simple use of alarms, to keep reprompting the user to input a key:

```perl
#!/usr/bin/perl
# alarmkey.pl
use strict;
use warnings;

use Term::ReadKey;

# Make read blocking until a key is pressed, and turn on autoflushing (no
# buffered IO)
ReadMode 'cbreak';
$| = 1;

sub alarmhandler {
    print "\nHurry up!: ";
    alarm 5;
}
$SIG{ALRM} = \&alarmhandler;
alarm 5;

print "Hit a key: ";
my $key = ReadKey 0;
print "\n You typed '$key' \n";

# cancel alarm
alarm 0;

# reset readmode
ReadMode 'restore';
```

We use the Term::ReadKey module to give us instant key presses without returns and set $| = 1 to make sure the Hurry up! prompt appears in a timely manner. In this example, the alarm 0 is redundant because we are about to exit the program anyway, but in a larger application this would be necessary to stop the rest of the program being interrupted by Hurry up! prompts every five seconds.

Using Alarms to Abort Hung Operations

We can also use alarms to abort an operation that has hung or is taking too long to complete. This works very similarly to the eval-and-die example we gave earlier for aborting from a section of code rather than continuing it—this time we use alarms instead to catch an interrupt. Here is a code snippet that aborts from an attempt to gain an exclusive lock over the file associated with the file-handle HANDLE if the lock is not achieved within one minute:

```
sub alarmhandler {
    die "Operation timed out!";
}

sub interrupthandler {
    die "Interrupted!";
}

$SIG{ALRM} = \&alarmhandler;
$SIG{INT} = \&interrupthandler;

$result = eval {
    # set a timer for aborting the lock
    alarm 60;

    # block waiting for lock
    flock HANDLE, LOCK_EX;

    # lock achieved! cancel the alarm
    alarm 0;

    ... read/write to HANDLE ...

    flock HANDLE, LOCK_UN;
    1;   # return true on completion
}

warn @_ unless $result;
```

The alternative approach to this is to turn the lock into a nonblocking lock, then check the return value, sleep for a short while, and then try again. The signal approach is more attractive than this solution in some ways, since it spends less time looping. It is, though, limited by the fact that we can no longer use an alarm for any other reason until we have stopped using the alarm here for this purpose.

POSIX Signal Functions

Before leaving the subject of signals, some programmers may find it useful to examine the sigaction, sigprocmask, sigpending, and sigsuspend functions provided by the POSIX module. These provide a Perl interface to the standard C library functions of the same name, but with the addition of the POSIX::SigAction and POSIX::SigSet object classes to simplify the creation and manipulation of the underlying C language structures. As of Perl 5.8, sigaction is an atomic operation and can also take an argument of a code reference, DEFAULT or IGNORE, just like the %SIG hash.

In general, there should be no need to use these functions over Perl's built-in signal support (which in any case maps down to them on platforms where they are supported). But for certain cases, such as XSUB programming, the subject of Chapter 20, they might come in useful. See the POSIX manual page for details (the object classes are documented near the end) and the sigaction manual page on supporting platforms.

Starting New Processes

Perl supports the creation of new processes through the fork function, which is an interface to the operating system's underlying fork function. Forking, a pre-Unix concept, is universal on all Unix-like operating systems. Other platforms like Windows (and pre-OS X Macintosh) use a thread-based model and have no native equivalent of fork. Instead, Perl provides an emulation of fork that allows us to "fork" a new process even though the operating system does not understand the concept in those terms. (From Perl 5.8, interpreter threads are used to implement fork. Since interpreter threads do not automatically share data, they are very good at pretending to be forked processes. That said, if we can guarantee Perl 5.8 or better, we should be able to use threads instead on both platforms anyway.)

The fork function spawns a clone of itself, creating a *child* process (the original process is called the main or *parent* process). The cloning is total, as the child shares the same application code and has its own copies of every variable and filehandle. After the fork, there are two near-identical copies of the original process running, the only immediate difference being the return value from fork. For the child, it is zero. For the parent, it is the process ID of the child if the fork was successful, or undef if not. As a result, fork is always found in close proximity to an if statement, for example:

```perl
if ($pid = fork) {
    print "Still in the parent process - we started a child with ",
        "process ID $pid\n";
} else {
    print "This is the child process\n";
    # terminate child and return success (zero) to the parent
    exit 0;
}
```

What the preceding example does not do, though, is check the return value for a failure of the fork operation. If the fork failed entirely, it will return undef, and we should always check for this possibility (which might occur if the system has reached a limit on processes or does not have enough memory to create the new process). So, we can check it using defined:

```perl
$pid = fork;
die "Failed to fork: $! \n" unless defined $pid;
if ($pid) {
    # parent
    ...
} else {
    # child
    ...
}
```

Replacing the Current Process

We can replace the current process with a completely different one by using the exec function. This replaces the current process in its entirety with the external command supplied as the argument. Even the original process ID is taken over by the new process:

```perl
exec 'command', @arguments;
```

While exec does have uses in a single-processing application, it is more often used with fork to run an external command as a subprocess of the original application. We will show some examples of this in action a little later in the chapter.

Code never needs to check the return value from exec, since if it succeeds the original process will not be there to return a status to in any case. The only time that a program will continue past an exec is if the exec fails:

```
exec @command;          # hand over to the next act
die "Exec failed: $!\n"; # exec must have failed
```

Several of Perl's built-in functions perform automatic fork+execs. These include the system and backtick functions and certain variants of open. We cover all of these later on in the chapter.

Process IDs

The process ID of the current process can always be found from the special variable $$ (also called $PID or $PROCESS_ID with the English module loaded):

```
print "We are process $$\n";
```

For Unix, a child process can find the process ID of the parent process that created it with the getppid function (this is not implemented on Windows as it is not meaningful):

```
$parent = getppid;
print "Our parent is $parent \n";
```

This allows us to use kill to send a signal to the parent process:

```
kill "HUP", $parent;
```

On Windows, there is one caveat to be aware of: handles (the Windows equivalents of Unix PIDs) are unsigned 32-bit integers, while Perl's 32-bit integers are signed. Due to this, handles are occasionally interpreted as a negative integer. This interferes with the semantics of signals, where any signal sent to a negative integer goes to the entire process group, not just a specific process, with rather different results than those desired. Process groups are explained in more detail in the next section.

Process, Groups, and Daemons

Whenever a parent process uses fork (either directly or implicitly) to create a child, the child inherits the process group of the parent. The significance of process groups comes in when signals are sent to a group rather than a single process. If it is intended to be an independent process, then the parent may have its own group ID (which is generally the same as its process ID); otherwise, it will have inherited the process group from its own parent.

We can find the process group of a process by using the getpgrp function (like getppid, this is not implemented on Windows or some other non-Unix platforms), which takes a process ID as an argument. To find our own process group, we could write

```
$pgid = getpgrp $$; #but...
```

We can also supply any false value, including undef, to get the process group for the current process. This is generally a better idea because not all versions of the underlying getpgrp function are the same, and the only value they have in common is 0. Since Perl maps directly to the underlying function, only 0 is truly portable:

```
$pgid = getpgrp 0; #...these are better
$pgid = getpgrp;
```

We usually do not need to find out the process group, since we already know the child will be in the same group as the parent. What we often want to do, however, is change the group to isolate a child from the parent. We can do this with setprgrp, which takes a process ID and a process group ID as arguments:

```
setpgrp $pid, $pgid;
```

In practice, the only process we ever want to change the group for is our own, when we want to divorce a child process from the fate of its parent. Specifically, this insulates the former child from any signals sent to the process group of the parent, so the child will live on even if the parent terminates (and signals its children to do so also). Such child processes are said to be *daemons*, running independently of the original process that created them.

While in theory we can join any existing group, we generally want to create our own group. Process group IDs are just numbers, and they usually have the same value as the process ID that owns that group. To put ourselves in our own group, therefore, we simply need to give ourselves a process group ID that is equal to our process ID:

```
setpgrp $$, $$;
```

Just as before, we can use a false value for both IDs to default to the current process ID, so we can also say

```
setpgrp 0, 0;
```

Or even just the following (though not quite as portable):

```
setpgrp;
```

Both calls will put the child process into its own group. By doing this, we isolate the child from the process group that the parent originally belonged to. Here is a quick example of a daemon that performs the role of a backseat driver (that is, it keeps shouting out directions when we're trying to concentrate):

```perl
#!/usr/bin/perl
# backseat.pl;
use warnings;
use strict;

if (my $pid = fork) {
    print "Backseat daemon started with ID $pid \n";
    sleep 1;    # give child time to leave group
    kill 9,-$$; # parent suicides gratuitously
}

setpgrp 0, 0;

# child loops in background
while (1) {
    alarm 60;
    foreach (int rand(3)) {
        $_ == 0 and do { print("Go Left! \n");       last };
        $_ == 1 and do { print("Go Right! \n");      last };
        $_ == 2 and do { print("Wait, go back! \n"); last };
    }
    sleep rand(3)+1;
}
```

This is a simplistic example, so there is only one child process. If the parent just exited grace-fully, then the child would simply transfer its affections to the init process (PID 1 on most Unix platforms). However, this parent is badly behaved and kills itself and all its children by sending sig-nal 9 (SIGKILL) to its process group. The child survives, however, because by the time the parent does this, it has dissociated itself from the group and does not receive the signal. If we comment out the setpgrp line, the child dies when the parent does and the daemon is not created.

If we do not want to print a friendly message, we can also simplify the fork statement to just

```
fork and exit;   # isn't self-documenting code great?
```

Handling Children and Reaping Exit Codes

When a child exits, the operating system keeps a record of its exit status and retains the child process in the process table. The exit status remains until the parent recovers, or reaps it. If we fail to do this, the dead children turn into zombies when the parent exits (no, really—this is all serious Unix terminology, honest) and hang around the process table, dead but not buried. Using the ps command on a system where this is happening reveals entries marked zombie or defunct.

Perl's built-in functions (other than fork) automatically deal with this issue for us, so if we cre-ate extra processes with open, we do not have to clean up afterwards. For fork and the IPC::Open2 and IPC::Open3 modules (both of which we cover later), we have to do our own housekeeping.

Waiting for an Only Child

To reap an exit status, we use either the basic wait or more complex waitpid functions. If we, as the parent process, want to wait for a child to finish before continuing, then there is no problem, we simply use the wait function to cease execution until the child exits:

```
# fork a child and execute an external command in it
exec @command unless fork;

# wait for the child to exit
$child_pid = wait;
```

The process ID of the child is returned by wait, if we need it, not the exit status. Instead, we find it in $?.

Getting the Exit Status

When wait returns, it sets the exit code of the child in the special variable $?. As we covered back in Chapter 16, this is a 16-bit value comprised of two 8-bit values, the exit status in the top half and the signal that caused the child to exit (if any) plus the coredump flag in the bottom half. (This is inci-dentally identical to the value returned by the Unix wait system call.) To get the actual exit code and signal number, we therefore need to use

```
my $exitsig = $? & 127;    # signal is lower 7 bits
my $cored   = $? & 128;    # coredump flag
my $exitcode = $? >> 8;    # exit code is upper 8 bits
```

If we import the appropriate symbols from the POSIX module, we can also use some conven-ience functions (with the same names as the macros familiar to C programmers) to extract these values:

```
use POSIX qw(:sys_wait_h);

$exitsig = WSTOPSIG($?);
$exitcode = WEXITSTATUS($?);
```

Only one of the exit codes and the signals will be set, so for a successful exit (that is, an exit code of zero), $? will be zero too. This is a convenient Boolean value, of course, so we can test $? for truth to detect a failed process, whether it exited with a non-zero status or aborted by a signal. Of course, since such codes are often left to the discretion of the developer to respect, we cannot always rely on that.

In some cases, particularly if we wrote the external command, the returned code may be an errno value, which we can assign to $! for a textual description of the error. In the parent process:

```
wait;
$exitcode = $? >> 8;
if ($exitcode) {
    $! = $exitcode; #assign to $! to 'recreate' error
    die "Child aborted with error: $! \n";
}
```

If there are no child processes, then wait returns immediately with a return value of -1. However, this is not generally useful since we should not be in the position of calling wait if we did not fork first, and if we did attempt to fork, we should be testing the return value of that operation. If we are handling more than one process, we should use waitpid instead.

Handling Multiple Child Processes

If we have more than one child process, then wait is not always enough, because it will return when any child process exits. If we want to wait for a particular child, then we need to use waitpid:

```
$pid = fork;
if ($pid) {
    waitpid $pid, 0;
} else {
    ...child...
}
```

Two arguments are taken by waitpid. The first is the process ID of the child to wait for. The second argument is a flag that effects the operation of waitpid. The most common flag to place here is WNOHANG, which tells waitpid not to wait if the child is still running but return immediately with -1. This argument is one of several constants defined by the POSIX module, and we can import it either from the :sys_wait_h group or directly:

```
use POSIX qw(:sys_wait_h);
```

Or:

```
use POSIX qw(WNOHANG);
```

We can use this to periodically check for a child's exit without being forced to wait for it:

```
$pid = fork;
if ($pid) {
    while (waitpid $pid, WNOHANG) == -1) {
        print "Waiting for $pid...\n";
        sleep 5;
    }
} else {
    ...child...
}
```

This works for a single child process, but if we have several children to tidy up after, we have to collect all their process IDs into a list and check all of them. This is not convenient. Fortunately, we can pass -1 to `waitpid` to make it behave like `wait` and return with the value of the first available dead child:

```
# wait until any child exits
waitpid -1, 0;

# this is the nonblocking version
waitpid -1, WNOHANG;
```

We do not necessarily want to keep checking for our children exiting, particularly if their exit status is irrelevant and we only want to remove them from the process table. What we need is a way to call `waitpid` when the child exits without having to check periodically in a loop. Fortunately, we can install a signal handler for the `SIGCHLD` signal that allows us to do exactly this. However, since more than one child could exit at once, calling `waitpid` only once may not be enough. An efficient signal handler thus needs to keep calling `waitpid` until there are no exit codes left to collect, yielding a design like this:

```
sub waitforchildren {
    my $pid;
    do {
        $pid = waitpid -1, WNOHANG;
    } until ($pid! == -1);
}

$SIG{CHLD} = \&waitforchildren;
```

This is tedious, but necessary if we are to manage child processes responsibly and portably. On some systems we can get away with simply ignoring `SIGCHLD` and have the operating system remove dead children for us:

```
$SIG{CHLD} = 'IGNORE';
```

Or, if we can let the child change its process group, we can let `init` reap children instead. This is not portable across all systems, though, so in general the preceding solutions are preferred.

▓Note For the technically curious, Perl maps the built-in `waitpid` to an appropriate native function, `waitpid` or possibly `wait4`. Which is chosen depends on the platform.

POSIX Flags and Functions

The `POSIX` module defines several symbols and functions other than `WNOHANG` for use with the `wait` and `waitpid` system calls. We import all of them when we import with the `:sys_wait_h` tag:

```
use POSIX qw(:sys_wait_h);
```

There are actually two flags. One is `WNOHANG`, which we have already seen. The other, `WUNTRACED`, also returns process IDs for children that are currently stopped (that is, have been sent a `SIGSTOP`) and have not yet been resumed. For example:

```
$possibly_stopped_pid = waitpid -1, WNOHANG | WUNTRACED;
```

In addition, the convenience functions listed in Table 21-2 are defined.

Table 21-2. *Convenience Functions*

Function	Action
WEXITSTATUS	Extract the exit status if the processed has exited. Equivalent to $? >> 8. For example: `$exitcode = WEXITSTATUS($?);` The exit code is zero if the process was terminated by a signal.
WTERMSIG	Extract the number of the signal that terminated the process if the process aborted on a signal. For example: `$exitsignal = WTERMSIG($?);` The signal number is zero if the process exited normally (even if with an error).

WIFEXITED	Check that the process exited, as opposed to being aborted by a signal. The opposite of WIFSIGNALED. For example:
	`if (WIFEXITED $?) {`
	`    return WEXITSTATUS($?)`
	`} else {return -1};`

WIFSIGNALED	Check that the process terminated on a signal, as opposed to exited. The opposite of WIFEXITED. For example:
	`if (WIFSIGNALED $?) {`
	`    print "Aborted on signal ",`
	`    WTERMSIG($?), "\n";`
	`} elsif (WEXITSTATUS $?) {`
	`    print "Exited with error ",`
	`    WEXITSTATUS($?), "\n";`
	`} else {`
	`    # exit code was 0`
	`    print "Success! \n";`
	`}`

WSTOPSIG	Extract the number of the signal that stopped the process if we specified WUNTRACED and the process returned is stopped as opposed to terminated. For example: `$stopsig = WSTOPSIG($?)` This is usually SIGSTOP, but not necessarily.

WIFSTOPPED	If we specified WUNTRACED as a flag, this returns true if the returned process ID was for a stopped process:
	`if (WIFSTOPPED $?) {`
	`    print "Process stopped by signal ",`
	`    WSTOPSIG($?),"\n";`
	`} elsif (...){`
	`    ...`
	`}`

Communicating Between Processes

Communicating between different processes, or interprocess communication (IPC), is a subject with many facets. Perl provides many possible ways to establish communications between processes, from simple unidirectional pipes, through bidirectional socket pairs, to fully fledged control over an externally executed command.

In this section, we are going to discuss the various ways in which different processes can communicate with one another and the drawbacks of each approach while paying particular attention to communications with an externally run command. The open function provides a simple and easy way to do this, but it can also be a dangerous one if we do not do some thorough screening. Instead we can turn to the forking version of open or use the IPC::Open2 or IPC::Open3 library modules for a safer approach.

Before covering the more advanced ways to establish communications between processes and external programs, we will cover the obvious and simple methods like system and do. They may not be sophisticated, but sometimes they are all we need to get the job done.

Very Simple Solutions

If we simply want to run an external program, we do not necessarily have to adopt measures like pipes (covered in the next section) or child processes; we can just use the system function:

```
system "command plus @arguments";
```

However, if system is passed a single argument, it checks it to see if it contains shell-special characters (like spaces, or quotes), and if present, starts a shell as a subprocess to run the command. This can be dangerous if the details of the command are supplied by the user; we can end up executing arbitrary commands like rmdir. A better approach is to pass the arguments individually, and this causes Perl to execute the command directly, bypassing the shell:

```
system 'command', 'plus', @arguments;
```

However, system only returns the exit code of the command, which is great if we want to know if it succeeded or not but useless for retrieving its output. For that, we can use the backtick operator qx or the equivalent backtick quotes:

```
# these two statements are identical. Note both interpolate too.
$output = `command plus @arguments`;
$output = qx/command plus @arguments/;
```

Unfortunately, both variants of the backtick operator create a shell, and this time there is no way to avoid it, since there is no way to pass a list of arguments. If we really want to avoid the shell, we have to start getting creative using a combination of open, pipe, and fork. Fortunately, Perl makes this a little simpler for us, as we will see shortly.

Not to be overlooked, we can also execute external programs with do if they are written in Perl. This function is essentially an enhanced version of eval that reads its input from an external file rather than having it written directly into the code. Its intended purpose is for loading in library files (other than modules, for which use or require are preferred), which do not generate output. If the script happens to print things to standard output, that will work too, so long as we don't want to control the output.

```
$return_value = do './local_script.pl';
```

The do command has a lot of disadvantages, however. Unlike eval, it does not cache the code executed for later use, and it is strictly limited in what it can do. For more useful and constructive forms of interprocess communication, we need to involve pipes.

Pipes

A pipe is, simply put, a pair of file handles joined together. In Perl, we can create pipes with the pipe function, which takes two filehandle names as arguments. One filehandle is read-only, and the other is write-only. By default, Perl attempts to buffer IO. This is also the case when we want a command to respond to each line without waiting for a series of lines to come through to flush the buffer. So we would write

```
pipe (READ, WRITE);
select WRITE;
$| = 1;
```

Or, using IO::Handle:

```
use IO::Handle;
pipe (READ, WRITE);
WRITE->autoflush(1);
```

We can also create pipes with the IO::Pipe module. This creates a "raw" IO::Pipe object that we convert into a read-only or write-only IO::Handle by calling either the reader or writer method:

```
use IO::Pipe;

my $pipe = new IO::Pipe;
if (fork) {
    $pipe->reader;
    # $pipe is now a read-only IO::Handle
} else {
    $pipe->writer;
    # $pipe is now a write-only IO::Handle
}
```

The most common use for pipes is for IPC (interprocess communication, mentioned earlier), which is why we bring them up here rather than in Chapter 12. As a quick example and also as an illustration of pipes from the filehandle perspective, here is a program that passes a message back and forth between a parent and child process using two pipes and a call to fork:

```
#!/usr/bin/perl
# message.pl
use warnings;
use strict;

pipe CREAD, PWRITE;    # parent->child
pipe PREAD, CWRITE;    # child->parent

my $message = "S";

if (fork) {
    # parent--close child end of pipes
    close CREAD;
    close CWRITE;

    syswrite PWRITE, "$message \n";
    while (<PREAD>) {
        chomp;
        print "Parent got $_ \n";
        syswrite PWRITE, "P$_ \n";
        sleep 1;
    }
} else {
    # child--close parent end of pipes
    close PREAD;
    close PWRITE;

    while (<CREAD>) {
        chomp;
        print "Child got $_ \n";
        syswrite CWRITE, "C$_ \n";
    }
}
```

As this example shows, both processes have access to the filehandles of the pipes after the fork. Each process closes the two filehandles that it does not need and reads and writes from the other two. In order to ensure that buffering does not deadlock the processes waiting for each other's message, we use the system-level `syswrite` function to do the actual writing, which also absolves us of the need to set the `autoflush` flag. When run, the output of this program looks like this:

```
Child got : S
Parent got: CS
Child got : PCS
Parent got: CPCS
Child got : PCPCS
Parent got: CPCPCS
```

...

Note that this program works because each process reads exactly one line of input and produces exactly one line of output, so they balance each other. A real application where one side or the other needs to read arbitrary quantities of data will have to spend more time worrying about deadlocks; it is all too easy to have both processes waiting for input from the other.

Opening and Running External Processes

If the first or last character of a file name passed to open is a pipe (|) symbol, the remainder of the file name is taken to be an external command. A unidirectional pipe connects the external process to our program. Input to or output from the external process is connected to our process based on the position of the pipe symbol. If the symbol precedes the command, the program's input (STDIN) is connected to an output statement in our process. If the symbol appends the command, the program's output (STDOUT) is accessed with an input type statement from our process.

If the pipe character occurs at the start of the file name, then the input to the external command is connected to the output of the filehandle, so printing to the filehandle will send data to the input of the command. For example, here is a standard way of sending an e-mail on a Unix system by running the `sendmail` program and writing the content of the e-mail to it through the pipe:

```
# get e-mail details from somewhere, e.g., HTML form via CGI.pm
my ($from_addr, $to_addr, $subject, $mail_body, $from_sig) = get_email();

# open connection to 'sendmail' and print e-mail to it
open (MAIL, '|/usr/bin/sendmail -oi -t') || die "Eep! $! \n";
print MAIL <<END_OF_MAIL;
From: $from_addr;
To: $to_addr
Subject: $subject

$mail_body
$from_sig
END_OF_MAIL

# close connection to sendmail
close MAIL;
```

If, on the other hand, the pipe character occurs at the end, then the output of the external command is connected to the input of the filehandle. Reading from the filehandle will receive anything that the external command prints. For example, here is another Unix-based example of using an open to receive the results of a `ps` (list processes) command:

```
#!/usr/bin/perl
# pid1.pl
use warnings;
use strict;

my $pid = open (PS,"ps aux|") || die "Couldn't execute 'ps': $! \n";
print "Subprocess ID is: $pid \n";
while (<PS>) {
    chomp;
    print "PS: $_ \n";
}
close PS;
```

The return value of open when it is used to start an external process this way is the process ID of the executed command. We can use this value with functions such as waitpid, which we covered earlier in the chapter.

Note that it is not possible to open an external program for both reading and writing this way, since the pipe is unidirectional. Attempting to pass a pipe in at both ends will only result in the external command's output being chained to nothing, which is unlikely to be what we want. One solution to this is to have the external command write to a temporary file and then read the temporary file to see what happened:

```
if (open SORT, "|sort > /tmp/output$$") {
    ... print results line by line to SORT ...
    close SORT;

    open(RESULT, '/tmp/output$$')
    ... read sorted results ...
    close RESULT;

    unlink '/tmp/output$$';
}
```

Another, better, solution is to use the IPC::Open2 or IPC::Open3 module, which allows both read and write access to an external program. The IPC:: modules are also covered in this chapter, under the section "Bidirectional Pipes to External Processes."

Bidirectional Pipes

Standard pipes on Unix are only one-way, but we can create a pair of filehandles that look like just a pipe, but one that can flow in both directions. Perl provides a number of functions to create and manage sockets, which are bidirectional networking endpoints represented in our applications as filehandles. They can be used to communicate between different processes and different systems across a network, and a large part of Chapter 22 is concerned with them. Here, however, we are interested in their use for local interprocess communications.

The socketpair function stands apart from the other socket functions because it does not have any application in networking applications. Instead, it creates two sockets connected back to back, with the output of each connected to the input of the other. The result is what looks and feels like a bidirectional pipe. (Unfortunately, Windows programmers are out of luck here—the concept is not valid on these platforms.)

Sockets have domains, types, and protocols associated with them. The domain in Perl can be either the Internet or Unix, the type a streaming socket, datagram socket, or raw socket, and the protocol can be something like PF_INET or PF_UNIX (these constants actually stand for **P**rotocol **F**amilies). This is the general form of socketpair being used to create a parent and child filehandle:

```
socketpair PARENT, CHILD, $domain, $type, $protocol;
```

However, most of this is fairly irrelevant to `socketpair`; its sockets do not talk to network interfaces or the file system, they do not need to listen for connections, they cannot be bound to addresses, and finally they are not bothered about protocols, since they have no lower-level protocol API to satisfy. Consequently, we generally use a Unix domain socket, since they are more lightweight than an Internet domain socket. We make it streaming so we can use it like an ordinary filehandle, and not bother with the protocol at all. The actual use of `socketpair` is thus almost always

```
use Socket;

socketpair PARENT, CHILD, AF_UNIX, SOCK_STREAM, PF_UNSPEC;
```

Here is a version of the message passing program we showed earlier using a pair of sockets rather than two pairs of pipe handles:

```perl
#!/usr/bin/perl
# socketpair.pl
use warnings;
use strict;

use Socket;

socketpair PARENT, CHILD, AF_Unix, SOCK_STREAM, PF_UNSPEC;

my $message = "S";

if (fork) {
    syswrite PARENT, "$message \n";
    while (<PARENT>) {
        chomp;
        print "Parent got: $_ \n";
        syswrite PARENT, "P$_ \n";
        sleep 1;
    }
} else {
    while (<CHILD>) {
        chomp;
        print "Child got : $_ \n";
        syswrite CHILD, "C$_ \n";
    }
}
```

In fact, we could also close the parent and child socket handles in the child and parent processes respectively, since we do not need them—we only needed one end of each pipe. We can also use the socket in only one direction by using the `shutdown` function to close either the input or the output:

```
shutdown CHILD, 1;    # make child read-only
shutdown PARENT, 0;   # make parent write-only
```

The difference between `close` and `shutdown` is that `close` only affects the filehandle itself; the underlying socket is not affected unless the filehandle just closed was the only one pointing to it. In other words, `shutdown` includes the socket itself, and hence all filehandles associated with it are affected.

This program is a lot more advanced in the way that it manufactures the conduit between the two processes, because it uses Perl's socket support to create the filehandles, but the benefit is that it makes the application simpler to write and generates fewer redundant filehandles.

Avoiding Shells with the Forked Open

One problem with using open to start an external process is that if the external command contains spaces or other such characters that are significant to a shell, open will run a shell as a subprocess and pass on the command for it to interpret, so that any special characters can be correctly parsed. The problem with this is that it is potentially insecure if the program is to be run by untrusted users, and it will fail if taint mode is enabled through the -T option, as, for example, is the case with a CGI script. Functions such as exec and system allow us to separate the parameters of a command into separate scalar values and supply them as a list, avoiding the shell.

Unfortunately, open does not directly allow us to pass in a command as a list. Instead it allows us to use exec to actually run the command by supplying it with the magic file names |- or -|. This causes open to create a pipe and then fork to create a child process. The child's standard input or standard output (depending on whether |- or -| was used) is connected to the filehandle opened in the parent. If we then use exec to replace the child process with the external command, the standard input or output is inherited, connecting the external process directly to the filehandle created by open in the parent.

The return value from open in these cases is the process ID of the child process (in the parent) and zero (in the child), the same as the return value from fork, enabling us to tell which process we are now running as.

Of course, it is not obligatory to run an external command at this point, but this is by far the most common reason for using a forked open. It is also by far the most common reason for using exec, which replaces the current process by the supplied command. Since exec allows the command to be split up into a list (that is, a list containing the command and arguments as separate elements), we can avoid the shell that open would create if we used it directly (or handed it a scalar string with the complete command and arguments in it). Here's an example of running the Unix ps command via a forked open:

```perl
#!/usr/bin/perl
# pid2.pl
use warnings;
use strict;

my $pid = open (PS, "-|");
die "Couldn't fork: $! \n" unless defined $pid;
if ($pid) {
    print "Subprocess ID is: $pid \n";
    while (<PS>) {
        chomp;
        print "PS: $_\n";
    }
    close PS;
} else {
    exec qw[ps -ef];    # no shells here
}
```

Or, more tersely and without recording the process ID:

```perl
#!/usr/bin/perl
# pid3.pl
use warnings;
use strict;

open (PS, "-|") || exec 'ps', '-ef';
while (<PS>) {
```

```
    chomp;
    print "PS: $_ \n";
}
close PS;
```

Bidirectional Pipes to External Processes

Perl provides a pair of modules, IPC::Open2 and IPC::Open3, that provide access to bidirectional pipes. These modules have the added advantage that the subroutines they supply, open2 and open3, permit the external commands to be given as a list, again avoiding an external shell.

As we know from Chapter 12, all applications get three filehandles for free when they start and are represented by STDIN, STDOUT, and STDERR. These are the three filehandles all applications use, and they are also the three filehandles with which we can talk and listen to any external process. This is what the piped open does, but only for one of the filehandles. However, due to the facts that STDIN is read-only and STDOUT and STDERR are write-only, we can in theory create pipes for each of them, since we only need a unidirectional conduit for each handle. This is what the open2 and open3 subroutines provided by IPC::Open2 and IPC::Open3 do. The difference between them is that open2 creates pipes for standard input and output, whereas open3 deals with standard error too.

Using either module is very simple. In the old style of Perl IO programming, we supply typeglobs (or typeglob references) for the filehandles to associate with the external command, followed by the command itself:

```
use IPC::Open2;

my $pid = open2(*RD, *WR, @command_and_arguments);
```

Or:

```
use IPC::Open3;

my $pid = open3(*WR, *RD, *ERR, @command_and_arguments);
```

Confusingly, the input and output filehandles of open2 are in a different order in open3. This is a great source for errors, so check carefully, or only use open3 to avoid getting them the wrong way around.

Since typeglobs are considered somewhat quaint these days, we can also pass in IO::Handle objects for much the same effect:

```
use IPC::Open2;
use IO::Handle;

my $in = new IO::Handle;
my $out = new IO::Handle;
my $pid = open2($in, $out, 'command', 'arg1', 'arg2');
print $out "Hello there \n";
my $reply = n;
```

In a similar vein but without the explicit calls to IO::Handle's new method, we can have open2 or open3 create and return the filehandles for us if we pass in a scalar variable with an undefined value:

```
use IPC::Open3;

my ($in,$out,$error);
my $pid = open3($out, $in, $error, 'command', 'arg1', 'arg2');
print $out "Hello there \n";
my $reply = n;
```

Both open2 and open3 perform a fork-and-exec behind the scenes, in the same way that a forked open does. The return value is the process ID of the child that actually executed (with exec) the external command. In the event that establishing the pipes to the external command fails, both subroutines raise a SIGPIPE signal, which we must catch or ignore (this we have covered earlier on in the chapter). Neither subroutine is concerned with the well being of the actual external command, however, so if the child aborts or exits normally, we need to check for ourselves and clean up with waitpid:

```
use POSIX qw(WNOHANG);

my $pid = open2($in, $out, 'command', @arguments);
until (waitpid $pid, WNOHANG) {
    # do other stuff, and/or read/writes to $in & $out
}
```

Note that this particular scheme assumes we are using nonblocking reads and writes; otherwise, the waitpid may not get called. We can also check for a deceased external process by detecting the EOF condition on the input or error filehandles (or by returning nothing from a sysread), but we still need to use waitpid to clean up the child process.

If we do not want to do anything else in the meantime, perhaps because we have another child process busy doing things elsewhere, we can simply say

```
# wait for child process to finish
waitpid $pid, 0;
```

If the write filehandle is prefixed with >&, then the external command is connected directly to the supplied filehandle, so input that arrives on it is sent directly to the external command. The filehandle is also closed in our own process. Similarly, if <& is given to the read or error filehandles, they are connected directly to the application. Here's a script that illustrates this in action:

```
# Usage: myscript.pl 'somecommand @args'

use IPC::Open3;

print "Now entering $ARGV[0] \n";
my $pid = open3('>&STDIN', '<&STDOUT', '<&STDERR', @ARGV);
waitpid $pid, 0;
print "$ARGV[0] finished. \n";
```

Note that we use standard input for the writing handle and standard output for the reading handle. That's because this script is a middleman in the transaction; input comes in from standard input but then goes out to the external command, and vice versa for standard output.

With a little embellishment, this script could be made useful, for example, logging uses of various commands, checking arguments, or processing tainted data.

We do not have to redirect all three filehandles, only the ones we don't want to deal with:

```
sub open2likeopen3 {
    return open3(shift, shift, '>&STDERR', @_);
}
```

This implements a subroutine functionally identical to open2 (unless we already have redirected standard error, that is) but with the arguments in the same order as open3.

Handling Bidirectional Communications

Some external commands will communicate with us on a line-by-line basis. That is, whenever we send them something, we can expect at least one line in response. In these cases, we can alternate between writing and reading as we did with our pipe and socketpair examples earlier. Commands like ftp are a good example of this kind of application.

However, many commands can accept arbitrary input and will not send any output until they have received all of the input. The only way to tell such a command that it has all the input it needs is to close the filehandle, so we often need to do something like this:

```
@instructions = <ARGV>;
($in, $out);

# send input and close filehandle
$pid = open2($in, $out, 'command', @arguments);
print $out @instructions;
close $out;
# receive result
@result = n;
close $in;

# clean up and use the result
waitpid $pid, 0;
print "Got: \n @result";
```

If we want to carry out an ongoing dialog with an external process, then an alternating write-read-write process is not always the best way to approach the problem. In order to avoid deadlocks, we have to continually divert attention from one filehandle to the other. Adding standard error just makes things worse.

Fortunately, there are two simple solutions, depending on whether we can (or want to) fork or not. First, we can use the select function or the vastly more convenient IO::Select module to poll multiple input filehandles, including both the normal and error output of the external command plus our own standard input. Alternatively, we can fork child processes to handle each filehandle individually. We can even use threads, if we have a version of Perl that is built to use them. We go into more detail on threads later on.

Sharing Data Between Processes

The problem with forked processes, as we have observed before and will observe again when we get to threads, is that they do not share data easily. Consequently, to communicate with each other or share resources, processes need to either establish a channel for communication or find some common point of reference that can be seen by all the processes concerned.

In this section, we are going to discuss the IPC facilities provided by Unix systems and their near cousins, generically known as *System V IPC*, after the variant of Unix in which it first appeared. There are three components to System V IPC: *message queues*, *semaphores*, and *shared memory segments*. System V IPC is now a fairly venerable part of Unix and is not generally portable to non-Unix platforms that do not comply with POSIX. Some parts of it are also implemented through pipes and socket pairs for ease of implementation. It still has its uses, though, in particular because the objects that we can create and access with it are persistent in memory and can survive the death of the applications that use them. This allows an application to store all its mission-critical data in shared memory and to pick up exactly where it left off if it is terminated and restarted.

Like most parts of Perl that interface to a lower-level library, IPC requires a number of constants that define the various parameters required by its functions. For IPC, these constants are defined by the IPC::SysV module, so almost any application using IPC includes the statement

```
use IPC::SysV;
```

Note that we do not actually have to be on a System V Unix platform to use IPC, but we do have to be on a platform that has the required IPC support. In general, Perl will not even have the modules installed if IPC is not available, and we will have to find alternative means to our goal, some of which are illustrated during the course of the other sections in this chapter. Even on Unix systems IPC is not always present. If it is, we can usually find out by executing this command:

```
> ipcs
```

If IPC is available, this will produce a report of all currently existing shared memory segments, semaphores, and message queues, usually in that order.

The common theme between IPC message queues, semaphores, and shared memory segments is that they all reside persistently in memory and can be accessed by any process that knows the resource ID and has access privileges. This differentiates them from most other IPC strategies, which establish private lines of communication between processes that are not so easily accessed by other unrelated processes.

Strictly speaking, Perl's support for IPC is available in the language as the function calls msgctl, msgget, msgrcv, msgsnd, semctl, semget, semop, shmctl, shmget, shmread, and shmwrite. These are merely wrappers for the equivalent C calls, and hence are pretty low level, though very well documented. However, since these functions are not very easy to use, the IPC:: family of modules includes support for object-oriented IPC access. In the interests of brevity, we will concentrate on these modules only in the following sections.

IPC::SysV

The IPC::SysV module imports all of the specified SysV constants for use in our programs in conjunction with the other IPC modules. Table 21-3 presents a summary of the most widely used constants. To see the full set of what IPC::SysV can export, we can do a perldoc -m on the module and consult development man pages for further information. Error constants are imported with the core module Errno.

Table 21-3. *Widely Used SysV Constants*

Constant	Purpose
GETALL	Return an array of all the values in the semaphore set.
GETNCNT	Return the number of processes waiting for an increase in value of the specified semaphore in the set.
GETPID	Return the PID of the last process that performed an operation on the specified semaphore in the set.
GETVAL	Return the value of the specified semaphore in the set.
GETZCNT	Return the number of processes waiting for the specified semaphore in the set to become zero.
IPC_ALLOC	Currently allocated.
IPC_CREAT	Create entry if key doesn't exist.
IPC_EXCL	Fail if key exists.
IPC_NOERROR	Truncate the message and remove it from the queue if it is longer than the read buffer size (normally keeps the message, and returns an error) when applied to message queues.
IPC_NOWAIT	Error if request must wait.
IPC_PRIVATE	Private key.
IPC_RMID	Remove resource.

Continued

Table 21-3. *Continued*

Constant	Purpose
IPC_SET	Set resource options.
IPC_STAT	Get resource options.
IPC_W	Write or send permission.
MSG_NOERROR	The same as IPC_NOERROR.
SEM_UNDO	Specify the operation be rolled when the calling process exits.
SETALL	Set the value of all the semaphores in the set to the specified value.
SETVAL	Set the value of the semaphore in the set to the specified value.
S_IRUSR	00400: Owner read permission.
S_IWUSR	00200: Owner write permission.
S_IRWXU	00700: Owner read/write/execute permission.
S_IRGRP	00040: Group read permission.
S_IWGRP	00020: Group write permission.
S_IRWXG	00070: Group read/write/execute permission.
S_IROTH	00004: Other read permission.
S_IWOTH	00002: Other write permission.
S_IRWXO	00007: Other read/write/execute permission.
ftok	Convert a pathname and a process ID into a key_t-type SysV IPC identifier.

Messages Queues

At one time, message queues were the only effective way to communicate between processes. They provide a simple queue that processes may write messages into at one end and read out at the other. We can create two kinds of queues, private and public. Here is an example of creating a private queue:

```
use IPC::SysV qw(IPC_PRIVATE IPC_CREAT S_IRWXU);
use IPC::Msg;

my $queue = new IPC::Msg IPC_PRIVATE, S_IRWXU | IPC_CREAT;
```

The new constructor takes two arguments. The first is the queue's identifier, which for a private queue is IPC_PRIVATE. The second is the permissions of the queue, combined with IPC_CREAT if we wish to actually create the queue. Like files, queues have a mask for user, group, and other permissions. This allows us to create a queue that we can write to, but applications running under other user IDs can only read from.

For a private queue, full user permissions are the most obvious, and we specify these with S_IRWXU. This is defined by the Fcntl module, but IPC::SysV imports the symbols for us, so we don't have to use Fcntl ourselves. We could also have said 0700 using octal notation. (Permissions are discussed in detail in Chapter 13.)

If the queue is private, only the process that created the queue and any forked children can access it. Alternatively, if it is public, any process that knows the queue's identifier can access it. For a queue to be useful, therefore, it needs to have a known identifier, or key, by which it can be found. The key is simply an integer, so we can create a public queue, which can be written to by processes running under our user ID (that is, this application) and only read by others with something like the following:

```
# create a queue for writing
my $queue = new IPC::Msg 10023, 0722 | IPC_CREAT;
```

Another process can now access this message queue with

```
my $queue = new IPC::Msg 10023, 0200;
```

On return, $queue will be a valid message object for the queue, or undef if it did not exist. Assuming success, we can now read and write the queue to establish communications between the processes. If we had created a private queue (not specifying the SysV ID key) and we want to send the message queue's key to another process so we can establish communications, we can extract it with id:

```
my $queue = new IPC::Msg IPC_PRIVATE, 0722 | IPC_CREAT;
my $id = $queue->id;
```

To send a message, we use the snd method:

```
$queue->snd($type, $message, $flags);
```

The message is simply the data we want to send. The type is a positive integer, which can be used by the rcv method to select different messages based on their type. The flags argument is optional, but it can be set to IPC_NOWAIT to have the method return if the message could not be sent immediately (in this case, $! will be set to EAGAIN). It is possible for error code constants to be imported by the module.

To receive a message, we use the rcv method:

```
my $message;
$queue->rcv(\$message, $length, $type, $flags);
```

The first argument must be a scalar variable into which the message is read. The second defines the maximum length of the message to be received. If the message is larger than this length, then rcv returns undef and sets $! to E2BIG. The type allows us to control which message we receive and is an integer with the following possible meanings:

Integer Value	Meaning
0	Read the first message on the queue, regardless of type.
> 0	Read the first message on the queue of the specified type. For example, if the type is 2, then only messages of type 2 will be read. If none are available, this will cause the process to block until one is. However, see IPC_NOWAIT and MSG_EXCEPT later.
< 0	Read the lowest and furthest forward message on the queue with a type equal to or less than the absolute value of the specified type. For example, if the type is -2, then the first message with type 0 will be returned; if no messages of type 0 are present, the first message of type 1, or if no messages of type 1 are present, the first message of type 2 is returned.

The flags may be one or more of the following:

Flag	Action
MSG_EXCEPT	Invert the sense of the type so that for zero or positive values it retrieves the first message not of the specified type. For instance, a type of 1 causes rcv to return the first message not of type 1.
MSG_NOERROR	Allow outsize messages to be received by truncating them to the specified length, rather than returning E2BIG as an error.
IPC_NOWAIT	Do not wait for a message of the requested type if none are available but return with $! set to EAGAIN.

Put together, these two functions allow us to set up a multilevel communications queue with differently typed messages for different purposes. The meaning of the type is entirely up to us; we can use it to send different messages to different child processes or threads within our application. Also it can be used as a priority or *out-of-band* channel marker, to name a few some examples.

The permissions of a queue can be changed with the set method, which takes a list of key-value pairs as parameters:

```
$queue->set (
    uid => $user_id,        # i.e., like 'chmod' for files
    gid => $group_id,       # i.e., like 'chgrp' for files
    mode => $permissions,   # an octal value or S_ flags
    qbytes => $queue_size   # the queue's capacity
)
```

We can also retrieve an IPC::Msg::stat object, which we can in turn create, modify, and then update the queue properties via the stat method:

```
my $stat = $queue->stat;
$stat->mode(0722);
$queue->set($stat);
```

The object that the stat method returns is actually an object based on the Class::Struct class. It provides the following get/set methods (the * designates portions of the stat structure that cannot be directly manipulated):

Method	Purpose
uid	The effective UID queue is running with
gid	The effective GID queue is running with
cuid*	The UID queue was started with
cgid*	The GID queue was started with
mode	Permissions set on the queue
qnum*	Number of messages currently in the queue
qbytes	Size of the message queue
lspid*	PID of the last process that performed a send on the queue
lrpid*	PID of the last process that performed a receive on the queue
stime*	Time of the last send call performed on the queue
rtime*	Time of the last receive call performed on the queue
ctime*	Time of the last change performed on the stat data structure

Note that changes made to the object returned by the stat method do not directly update the queue's attributes. For that to happen, we need to either pass the updated stat object or individual key-value pairs (using the keys listed previously as stat methods) to the set method.

Finally, we can destroy a queue, assuming we have execute permission for it, by calling remove:

```
$queue->remove;
```

If we cannot remove the queue, the method returns undef, with $! set to indicate the reason, most likely EPERM. In keeping with good programming practices, it is important that the queue be removed, especially since it persists even after the application exits. However, it is equally important that the correct process do so, and no other process pulls the rug out from under the others.

Semaphores

IPC semaphores are an in-memory set of numeric flags (also known as semaphore sets) that can be read and written by different processes to indicate different states. Like message queues, they can be private or public, having an identifier by which they can be accessed with a permissions mask controlling who can access them.

Semaphores have two uses: first, as a set of shared values, which can be read and written by different processes; and second, to allow processes to block and wait for semaphores to change value, so that the execution of different processes can be stopped and started according to the value of a semaphore controlled by a different process.

The module that implements access to semaphores is IPC::Semaphore, and we can use it like this:

```
use IPC::SysV qw(IPC_CREAT IPC_PRIVATE S_IRWXU);
use IPC::Semaphore;

my $size = 4;
my $sem = new IPC::Semaphore(IPC_PRIVATE, $size, IPC_CREAT | S_IRWXU);
```

This creates a private semaphore set with four semaphores and owner read, write, and execute permissions. To create a public semaphore set, we provide a literal key value instead:

```
my $sem = new IPC::Semaphore(10023, 4, 0722 | IPC_CREAT);
```

Other processes can now access the semaphore with

```
my $sem = new IPC::Semaphore(10023, 4, 0200);   # or S_IRDONLY
```

As with message queues, we can also retrieve the key of the semaphore set with the id method:

```
$id = $sem->id;
```

Once we have access to the semaphore, we can use and manipulate it in various ways, assuming we have permission to do so. A number of methods exist to help us do this, and these are listed here:

Name	Action
getall	Return all values as a list. For example: `my @semvals = $sem->getall;`

getval	Return the value of the specified semaphore. For example:
	`# first semaphore is 0, so 4th is 3`
	`my $sem4 = $sem->getval(3);`

setall	Set all semaphore values. For example, to clear all semaphores: `$sem->setall( (0) x 4 );`

setval	Set the value of the specified semaphore. For example:
	`# set value of 4th semaphore to 1`
	`$sem->setval(3, 1);`

set	Set the user ID, group ID or permissions of the semaphore, for example:
	`$sem->set(`
	`    uid => $user_id,`
	`        gid => $group_id,`
	`    mode => $permissions,`
	`);`

Alternatively we can get, manipulate, and set a stat object as returned by the stat method in the same manner as IPC::Msg objects.

Name	Action

stat	Generate a IPC::Semaphore::stat object we can manipulate and then use with set. For example:
	`$semstat = $sem->stat;`
	`$semstat->mode(0722);`
	`$sem->set($semstat);`

getpid	Return the process ID of the last process to perform a semop operation on the semaphore set.
getncnt	Return the number of processes that have executed a semop and are blocked waiting for the value of the specified semaphore to increase in value. `$ncnt = $sem->getncnt;`
getzcnt	Return the number of processes that have executed a semop and are blocked waiting for the value of the specified semaphore to become zero.

The real power of semaphores is bound up in the op method, which performs one or more semaphore operations on a semaphore set. This is the mechanism by which processes can block and be unblocked by other processes.

Each operation consists of three values: the semaphore number to operate on, an operation to perform, and a flag value. The operation is actually a value to increment or decrement by, and it follows these rules:

- If the value is positive, the semaphore value is incremented by the supplied value. This always succeeds, and never blocks.

- If the supplied value is zero, and the semaphore value is zero, the operation succeeds. If the semaphore value is not zero, then the operation blocks until the semaphore value becomes zero. This increases the value returned by getzcnt.

- If the value is negative, then the semaphore value is decremented by this value, unless this would take the value of the semaphore negative. In this case, the operation blocks until the semaphore becomes sufficiently positive enough to allow the decrement to happen. This increases the value returned by getncnt.

We can choose to operate as many semaphores as we like. All operations must be able to complete before the operation as a whole can succeed. For example:

```
$sem->op(
    0, -1, 0,   # decrement semaphore 1
    1, -1, 0,   # decrement semaphore 2
    3,  0, 0,   # semaphore 3 must be zero
);
```

The rules for blocking on semaphores allow us to create applications that can cooperate with each other; one application can control the execution of another by setting semaphore values. Applications can also coordinate over access to shared resources. This a potentially large subject, so we will just give an simple illustrative example of how a semaphore can coordinate access to a common shared resource:

1. Application 1 creates a semaphore set with one semaphore, value 1, and creates a shared resource, for example, a file or an IPC shared memory segment. However, it decides to do a lot of initialization, and so it doesn't access the resource immediately.

2. Application 2 starts up, decrements the semaphore to 0, and accesses the shared resource.

3. Application 1 now tries to decrement the semaphore and access the resource. The semaphore is 0, so it cannot access it and therefore blocks.

4. Application 2 finishes with the shared resource and increments the semaphore, an operation that always succeeds.

5. Application 1 can now decrement the semaphore since it is now 1, and so the operation succeeds and no longer blocks.

6. Application 2 tries to access the resource a second time. First it tries to decrement the semaphore, but is unable to, and blocks.

7. Application 1 finishes and increments the semaphore.

8. Application 2 decrements the semaphore and accesses the resource.

And so on . . .

Although this sounds complex, in reality it is very simple. In code, each application simply accesses the semaphore, creating it if not present, then adds two lines around all accesses to the resource to be protected:

```
sub access_resource {
    # decrement semaphore, blocking if it is already zero
    $sem->op(0, -1, 0);
    ... access resource ...
    # increment semaphore, allowing access by other processes
    $sem->op(0, 1, 0);
}
```

If we have more than one resource to control, we just create a semaphore set with more semaphores.

The basis of this approach is that the applications agree to cooperate through the semaphore. Each one has the key for the semaphore (because it is given in a configuration file, for instance), and it becomes the sole basis for contact between them. Even though the resource being controlled has no direct connection to the semaphore, each application always honors it before accessing it. The semaphore becomes a gatekeeper, allowing only one application access at a time.

If we do not want to block while waiting for a semaphore, we can specify IPC_NOWAIT for the flag value. We can do this on a "per semaphore basis" too, if we want, though this could be confusing. For example:

```
sub access_resource {
    return undef unless $sem->op(0, -1, IPC_NOWAIT);
    ... access resource ...
    $sem->op(0, 1, 0);
}
```

We can also set the flag SEM_UNDO (if we import it from IPC::SysV first). This causes a semaphore operation to be automatically undone if the process exits, either deliberately or due to an error. This is helpful in preventing applications that abort while locking a resource and then never releasing it again. For example:

```
$sem->op(0, -1, IPC_NOWAIT | SEM_UNDO);
die unless critical_subroutine();
```

As with message queues, care must be given to not leave unused segments around after the last process exits.

We will return to the subject of semaphores when we come to talk about threads, which have their own semaphore mechanism, inspired greatly by the original IPC implementation described previously.

Shared Memory Segments

While message queues and semaphores are relatively low-level constructs made a little more accessible by the IPC::Msg and IPC::Semaphore modules, shared memory has altogether more powerful support module in the form of IPC::Shareable. The key reason for this is that IPC::Shareable implements shared memory through a tie mechanism, so rather than reading and writing from a memory block, we can simply attach a variable to it and use that.

The tie takes four arguments, a variable (which may be a scalar, an array, or a hash), IPC::Shareable for the binding, and then an access key, followed optionally by a hash reference containing one or more key-value pairs. For example, the following code creates and ties a hash variable to a shared memory segment:

```
use IPC::Shareable;

our %local_hash;
tie %local_hash, 'IPC::Shareable', 'key', {create => 1}

$local_hash{hashkey} = 'value';
```

This creates a persistent shared memory object containing a hash variable that can be accessed by any application or process by tie-ing a hash variable to the access key for the shared memory segment (in this case key):

```
# in a process in an application far, far away...
%other_hash;
tie %other_hash, IPC::Shareable => 'key';

$value = $other_hash{hashkey};
```

A key feature of shared memory is that, like memory queues and semaphores, the shared memory segment exists independently of the application that created it. Even if all the users of the shared memory exit, it will continue to exist so long as it is not explicitly deleted (we can alter this behavior, though, as we will see in a moment).

Note that the key value is actually implemented as an integer, the same as semaphores and message queues, so the string we pass is converted into an integer value by packing the first four characters into a 32-bit integer value. This means that only the first four characters of the key are used. As a simple example, baby and babyface are the same key to IPC::Shareable.

The tied variable can be of any type, including a scalar containing a reference, in which case whatever the reference points to gets converted into a shared form. This includes nested data structures and objects, making shared memory ties potentially very powerful. However, each reference becomes a new shared memory object, so a complex structure can quickly exceed the system limit on shared memory segments. In practice, we should only try to tie relatively small nested structures to avoid trouble.

The fourth argument can contain a number of different configuration options that determine how the shared memory segment is accessed, as listed in Table 21-4.

Table 21-4. *IPC::Shareable Configuration Options*

Option	Function
create	If true, create the key if it does not already exist. If the key does exist, then the tie succeeds and binds to the existing data, unless exclusive is also true. If create is false or not given, then the tie will fail if the key is not present.
exclusive	Used in conjunction with create. If true, allow a new key to be created but do not allow an existing key to be tied to successfully.

Option	Function
mode	Determine the access permissions of the shared memory segment. The value is an integer, traditionally an octal number or a combination of flags like S_IRWXU | S_IRGRP.
destroy	If true, cause the shared memory segment to be destroyed automatically when this process exits (but not if it aborts on a signal). In general, only the creating application should do this or be able to do this (by setting the permissions appropriately on creation).
size	Define the size of the shared memory segment, in bytes. In general, this defaults to an internally set maximum value, so we rarely need to use it.
key	If the tie is given three arguments, with the reference to the configuration options being the third, this value specifies the name of the share memory segment: `tie %hash, 'IPC::Shareable' {key => 'key', ...};` For example: ```tie @array, 'IPC::Shareable', 'mysharedmem', {
create => 1,
exclusive => 0,
mode => 722,
destroy => 1,
}```

Other than the destroy option, we can remove a shared memory segment by calling one of three methods implemented for the IPC::Shareable object that implements the tie (which may be returned by the tied function), as shown in Table 21-5.

Table 21-5. *IPC::Shareable Methods*

Method	Purpose
remove	Remove the shared memory segment, if we have permission to do so.
clean_up	Remove all shared memory segments created by this process.
clean_up_all	Remove all shared memory segments in existence for which this process has permissions to do so. For example: ```# grab a handle to the tied object via the 'tied'
command
$shmem = tied $shared_scalar;
use the object handle to call the 'remove' method on
it
print "Removed shared scalar" if $shmem->remove;```

We can also lock variables using the IPC::Shareable object's shlock and shunlock methods. If the variable is already locked, the process attempting the lock will block until it becomes free. For example:

```
$shmem->lock;
$shared_scalar = "new value";
$shmem->unlock;
```

Behind the scenes this lock is implemented with IPC::Semaphore, so for a more flexible mechanism, use IPC::Semaphore objects directly.

As a lightweight alternative to IPC::Shareable, we can make use of the IPC::ShareLite module, naturally available from CPAN. This provides a simple store-fetch mechanism using object methods and does not provide a tied interface. However, it is faster than IPC::Shareable.

Threads

Threads are, very loosely speaking, the low fat and lean version of forked processes. Like processes, each thread is a separate strand of execution. Also like processes, newly created threads are owned by the parent thread that created them. They also have unique identifiers, though these are thread IDs rather than process IDs. We can even wait for a thread to finish and collect its exit result, just like `waitpid` does for child processes.

However, threads run within the same process and share the same interpreter, code, and data. Nothing is duplicated except the thread of execution. This makes them much more lightweight, so we can have very many of them, and we don't need to use any of the workarounds that forked processes need.

Thread support for Unix platforms is still considered experimental, but as of Perl 5.8 it is increasingly robust. Windows versions of Perl are implicitly capable of threads, and in fact `fork` is implemented with threads on that platform—the process ID returned by `fork` is actually a thread ID. With a few caveats, there is no reason we cannot now write threaded Perl applications, so long as we built Perl with thread support initially, of course.

Checking for Thread Support

To find out if threads are available programmatically, we can check for the `usethreads` key in the `%Config` hash:

```
BEGIN {
    use Config;
    die "Threadbare!\n" unless $Config{usethreads};
}
```

This tells us threads are supported, but not which kind. If we need to check that we have interpreter threads rather than the older 5.005 threads, we can also (or instead) check for `useithreads`:

```
BEGIN {
    use Config;
    die "No interpreter threads!\n" unless $Config{useithreads};
}
```

From the command line, we can check if threads are present by trying to read the documentation. The `Thread` module is present for both types of thread. The `threads` module will only be present if interpreter thread support is enabled:

```
> perldoc threads
```

The `threads` module is the basis of handling threads in Perl. It is an object-oriented module that represents threads as objects, which we can create using `new` and manipulate with methods. In addition, it provides a number of functions that operate on a per-thread basis. The older `Thread` module exists even with interpreter threads as a portability aid for programs written to the old interface. However, since data is automatically shared in the older implementation and automatically kept private with interpreter threads, this gesture is unlikely to work for threaded programs of any complexity.

Thread modules come in two flavors, pragmatic and application oriented. Basic support for threads is supplied by the pragmatic `threads` and `threads::shared` modules, the latter of which provides the ability to share data between threads. These two modules interface directly into the interpreter's thread mechanics and are necessary to enable threads and shared data in our application. Although they are pragmatic, both modules also provide methods and subroutines for stating, stopping, querying, and manipulating threads.

Application-oriented thread modules live in the `Thread::` namespace. The `Thread::Semaphore` and `Thread::Queue` modules, which both come standard with Perl (and which are covered later in the chapter) are two good examples, but there are plenty more interesting examples on CPAN for the curious.

Creating Threads

Threads resemble forked processes in many ways, but in terms of creation they resemble, and indeed are, subroutines. The standard way of creating a thread, the `create` method, takes a subroutine reference and a list of arguments to pass to it. The subroutine is then executed by a new thread of execution, while the parent thread receives a thread object as the return value. The following code snippet illustrates how it works:

```
use threads;

sub threadsub {
    my $self = threads->self;
    ...
}

my $thread = threads->create(\&threadsub, @args);
```

The `new` method is an alias, so we can also say

```
my $thread = new threads(\&threadsub, @args);
```

This creates a new thread, with `threadsub` as its entry point, while the main thread continues on. The alternative way to create a thread is with the `async` function, whose syntax is analogous to an anonymous subroutine. This function is not imported by default, so we must name it in the import list to the `Thread` module:

```
my $thread = async {
    my $self = threads->self;
    ...
};
```

Just like an anonymous subroutine, we end the `async` statement with a semicolon. The block may not need it, but the statement does.

The choice of `create`/`new` or `async` depends on the nature of the thread we want to start; the two approaches are identical in all respects apart from their syntax. If we only want to start one instance of a thread, then `async` should be used. Otherwise, `create` or `new` is better if we want to use the same subroutine for many different threads:

```
my $thread1 = new threads \&threadsub, $arg1;
my $thread2 = new threads \&threadsub, $arg2;
my $thread3 = new threads \&threadsub, $arg3;
```

or, with a loop:

```
# start a new thread for each argument passed in @ARGV:
@threads;
foreach (@ARGV) {
    push @threads, threads->create(\&threadsub, $_);
}
```

Because interpreter threads make a copy of the data in the original thread to create the new thread, we do not normally need to take any special action to create new threads, and code that is not thread-aware is automatically thread-safe. However, if we have any non-Perl data in a thread, Perl cannot deal with it directly—this particularly affects extension modules with XSUBs—and we may have a problem. To solve it, we can make use of the special `CLONE` method in any package that needs to deal with special cases:

```
package Special::Thread::Module;

sub CLONE {
    # handle any special thread cloning needs for this package
}
```

If present, this method is called—in every loaded package that defines or inherits it—just after the thread is created and just before its entry point is called. We can also use this method to adjust or "thin down" data that we do not need to have cloned to conserve memory.

Identifying Threads

Since we can start up many different threads all with the same subroutine as their entry point, it might seem tricky to tell them apart. However, this is not so.

First, we can pass in different arguments when we start each thread to set them on different tasks. An example of this would be a filehandle, newly created by a server application, and this is exactly what the example of a threaded server in Chapter 22 does. Second, a thread can create a thread object to represent itself using the self class method:

```
my $self = threads->self;
```

With this thread object, the thread can now call methods on itself, for example tid, which returns the underlying thread number:

```
my $self_id = $self->tid;
```

or all in one statement:

```
my $self_id = threads->self->tid;
```

It is possible to have more than one thread object containing the same thread ID, and this is actually common in some circumstances. We can check for equivalence by comparing the IDs, but we can do better by using the equals method:

```
print "Equal!\n" if $self->equal($thread);
```

or, equivalently:

```
print "Equal!\n" if $thread->equal($self);
```

Thread identities are useful for many purposes, one of the most useful being thread-specific data.

Sharing Data Between Threads

There is one major difference between the older implementation of threads provided in Perl 5.6 and earlier and the interpreter threads available in Perl 5.8 onward: data is automatically shared in the older model, and never shared, unless we ask for it, in the newer one. The older model mirrors the behavior of the underlying thread support provided by the operating system, but there is no reason for Perl to mimic this behavior in its own threads, so instead the interpreter tracks the use of data by threads and duplicates unshared data as needed. This is actually more convenient, at least for code that was not written with threads in mind, since it means that by default threads can never inadvertently interfere with each other by overwriting each other's data.

To actually share data, we make use of the threads::shared module, which provides the share function to mark a variable as shared across all threads. In actuality, this simply switches off the smart duplication of data that the interpreter would ordinarily carry out, for indicated variables only. If the threads module has *not* been loaded previously, share and other functions like lock and cond_wait that are also provided by this module are exported as nonfunctional stubs. This means our code will still run in a nonthreaded context, but it also means we must make sure to load threads first:

```
use threads;
use threads::shared;
```

Once a variable is shared, each thread will see the same underlying storage when the variable is accessed, rather than getting its own copy:

```
my $answer = 42;
share($answer);
my @array = (1,2,3);
share(@array);
```

If we know in advance which variables we want to share, which is generally the case, we can use the shared attribute instead:

```
my $answer : shared = 42;
my @array : shared = qw(1 2 3);
my %hash : shared = (one => 1, two => 2, three => 3);
```

We are not limited to sharing declared variables. We can also create a new anonymous reference and share it all in one go. However, since the subroutine normally expects a variable argument, we must call it with & to suppress the prototype:

```
my $aref = &share([1 2 3]);
```

Either way, once a variable is shared, all threads have access to the same data. In order to prevent them from overwriting each other and coordinate access to the shared data, we now need to apply a lock so that only one thread can access it at any given moment.

Variable Locks

When multiple threads share data, we sometimes have problems stopping them from treading on each other's toes. Since data is not shared between threads by default, we can largely ignore this problem for code that does not choose to share data, but the problem still exists when sharing common resources among a pool of threads.

The lock subroutine does handle this, however. It takes any variable as an argument and places a lock on it so that no other thread may lock it for as long as the lock persists, which is defined by its lexical scope. The distinction between *lock* and *access* is important; any thread can simply access the variable by not bothering to acquire the lock, so the lock is only good if all threads abide by it. Just like flock for filehandles, a thread variable lock is advisory, not compelled.

It is not necessarily given that because data is shared it needs to be locked. Any number of threads can read the same data without risk of conflict, after all. It is important to place a lock on the data for code that writes or modifies it, but it is not always necessary to place a lock for code that only reads it. If we write our code so that only one thread can ever update the shared data, we may not need a lock at all.

If we have three shared variables, all of which are involved in any transaction, we can lock just one of them to control access to all three or invent a new lock variable solely for the purpose—it does not matter what approach we use, so long as we do it consistently.

As a short and incomplete example, this subroutine locks a filehandle used for output, so that only one thread can write to the filehandle at a time:

```
my $sharedfh : shared = IO::File->open("> app.log");

sub writelog {
    lock $sharedfh;
    print $sharedfh, @_;
}
```

The shared and locked properties of a variable are distinct from its value, so it does not matter what (or when) we assign to the variable, or even whether we assign to it at all.

It is not necessary to explicitly unlock the variable, and in fact not possible either. The lock is released as soon as it goes out of scope, which in this case is at the end of the subroutine. Any lexical scope is acceptable, however, so we can also place locks inside the clauses of if statements, loops, map and grep blocks, and eval statements. We can also choose to lock arrays, hashes, or globs:

```perl
lock @array;
lock %hash;
lock *glob;
```

Alternatively, we can lock just an element, which gives us a form of record-based locking, if we define a record as an array element or hash value:

```perl
my %ghash : shared;

sub varlocksub {
    my $key = shift;
    lock $ghash{$key};
    ...
}
```

In this version, only one element of the hash is locked, so any other thread can enter the subroutine with a different key and the corresponding value at the same time. If a thread comes in with the same key, however, it will find the value under lock and key (so to speak) and will have to wait.

While it is possible and perfectly legal to place a lock on a hash or array, locking a hash does not imply a lock on any of its keys, and locking an array does not imply locking any of its elements. Similarly, locking a key or element does not imply a lock on the hash or array to which it belongs.

Subroutine Locks

In Perl 5.6, the locked and method attributes provided serialized access to a subroutine. Neither of these attributes exist for interpreter threads, and we can no longer lock a subroutine by reference, either. But we can lock a variable associated with the subroutine, for example, the code reference of an anonymous subroutine:

```perl
my $subref : shared = sub {
    lock $subref;
    print "This is thread ",threads->self->tid,"\n";
}
```

This is just syntactic sugar: it doesn't really matter what the variable is, so long as we relate it somehow to the subroutine to lock. We can equally use a closure, like in this example:

```perl
#!/usr/bin/perl -w
# locksub.pl
use strict;
use warnings;
use threads;
use threads::shared;

{ my $lock : shared;
  sub mysub {
      print "Thread ",threads->self->tid()," waiting for access\n";
      lock $lock;
      print "I am thread ",threads->self->tid(),"\n";
      sleep 1;
      threads->detach();
```

```
    }
}

foreach (1..5) {
    threads->create(\&mysub);
}

do {
    sleep 1;
    print "Waiting for threads:",(map { " ".$_->tid } threads->list),"\n";
} while (threads->list);
```

The closure hides the lock variable where external code cannot get to it. Here each thread tries to execute the mysub subroutine, but only one thread can hold the lock on the closure variable $lock at any given time, and so access to the subroutine is serialized. Each thread sleeps for a second and then detaches itself to let the main thread know it is done. Meanwhile, the main thread waits for all the child threads to detach before exiting. This is a simplistic thread management scenario, of course—semaphores and queues are more sophisticated techniques we will look at in a moment.

It is not usually necessary to lock object methods this way because object instances are generally created on a per-thread basis and are not shared between threads—if we need to coordinate method access to other shared variables, then we would lock on those variables in any case. There are currently limitations on the sharing of blessed object references, so it is often inadvisable to share them in any case—see the threads::shared manual page for details. (In our IO::File example earlier, we were safe because the lock works even if the blessed nature of the glob reference is lost between threads—no IO::File methods got called.)

Thread Management

Perl keeps a list of every thread that has been created. We can get a copy of this list, as thread objects, with the threads->list class method:

```
@threads = threads->list;
```

One of these threads is our own thread. We can find out which by using the equal method:

```
$self = threads->self;
foreach (@threads) {
    next if $self->equal($_);
    ...
}
```

Just because a thread is present does not mean that it is running, however. Perl keeps a record of the return value of every thread when it exits and a record of the thread for as long as that value remains unclaimed. This is similar to child processes that have not had waitpid called for them. The threaded equivalent of waitpid is the join method, which we call on the thread we want to retrieve the exit value for:

```
my $return_result = $thread->join;
```

The join method will block until the thread on which join was called exits. If the thread aborted (for example by calling die), then the error will be propagated to the thread that called join. This means that it will itself die unless the join is protected by an eval:

```
my $return_result = eval { $thread->join; }
if ($@) {
    warn "Thread unraveled before completion\n";
}
```

As a convenience for this common construct, the Thread module also provides an eval method, which wraps join inside an eval for us:

```
my $return_result = $thread->eval;
if ($@) {
    warn "Thread unraveled before completion\n";
}
```

It is bad form to ignore the return value of a thread, since it clutters up the thread list with dead threads. If we do not care about the return value, then we can tell the thread that we do not want it to linger and preserve its return value by telling it to detach:

```
$thread->detach;
```

This is the thread equivalent of putting a child process in its own process group—the parent no longer gets the exit status when the child exits. The catch is that if the thread dies, nobody will notice, unless a signal handler for the __DIE__ hook has been registered and it checks threads->self for the dying thread. If we join a moribund thread from the main thread without precautions, we do have to worry about the application dying as a whole.

As a slightly fuller and more complete (although admittedly not particularly useful) example, this short program starts up five threads, then joins each of them in turn before exiting:

```
#!/usr/bin/perl
# join.pl
use warnings;
use strict;
# check we have threads
BEGIN {
    use Config;
    die "No interpreter threads!\n" unless $Config{useithreads};
}
use threads;

# define a subroutine for threads to execute
sub threadsub {
    my $self = threads->self;
    print "Thread ", $self->tid, " started \n";
    sleep 10;
    print "Thread ", $self->tid, " ending \n";
}

# start up five threads, one second intervals
my @threads;
foreach (1..5) {
    push @threads, new threads \&threadsub;
    sleep 1;
}

# wait for the last thread started to end
while (my $thread = shift @threads) {
    print "Waiting for thread ", $thread -> tid, " to end... \n";
    $thread->join;
    print "Ended \n";
}

# exit
print "All threads done \n";
```

Typically, we care about the return value, and hence would always check them. However, in this case we are simply using join to avoid terminating the main thread prematurely.

Condition Variables, Semaphores, and Queues

Locked variables have more applications than simply controlling access. We can also use them as conditional blocks by having threads wait on a variable until it is signaled to proceed. In this mode the variable, termed a condition variable, takes on the role of a starting line; each thread lines up on the block (so to speak) until the starting pistol is fired by another thread. Depending on the type of signal we send, either a single thread is given the go-ahead to continue, or all threads are signaled.

Condition variables are a powerful tool for organizing threads, allowing us to control the flow of data through a threaded application and preventing threads from accessing shared data in an unsynchronized manner. They are also the basis for other kinds of thread interaction. We can use *thread semaphores*, provided by the Thread::Semaphore module, to signal between threads. We can also implement a *queue* of tasks between threads using the Thread::Queue module. Both these modules build upon the basic features of condition variables to provide their functionality but wrap them in a more convenient form.

To get a feel for how each of these work, we will implement a basic but functional threaded application, first using condition variables directly, then using semaphores, and finally using a queue.

Condition Variables

Continuing the analogy of the starting line, to "line up" threads on a locked variable we use the cond_wait subroutine. This takes a locked variable as an argument, unlocks it, and then waits until it receives a signal from another thread. When it receives a signal, the thread resumes execution and relocks the variable.

To have several threads all waiting on the same variable, we need only have each thread lock and then cond_wait the variable in turn. Since the lock prevents more than one thread executing cond_wait at the same time, the process is automatically handled for us. The following code extract shows the basic technique applied to a pool of threads:

```
my $lockvar;   # lock variable - note it is not locked at this point

sub my_waiting_thread {
    # wait for signal
    {
        lock $lockvar;
        cond_wait $lockvar;
    }

    # ...the rest of the thread, where the work is done
}

for (1..10) {
    threads->create(\&my_waiting_thread);
}
```

This code snippet shows ten threads, all of which use the same subroutine as their entry point. Each one locks and then waits on the variable $lockvar until it receives a signal. Since we don't want to retain the lock on the variable after we leave cond_wait, we place both lock and cond_wait inside their own block to limit the scope of the lock. This is important since other threads cannot enter the waiting state while we have a lock on the variable; sometimes that is what we want, but more often it isn't.

Having established a pool of waiting threads, we need to send a signal to wake one of them up, which we do with cond_signal:

```
# wake up one thread
cond_signal $lockvar;
```

This will unlock one thread waiting on the condition variable. The thread that is restarted is essentially random; we cannot assume that the first thread to block will be the first to be unlocked again. This is appropriate when we have a pool of threads at our disposal, all of which perform the same basic function. Alternatively, we can unlock all threads at once by calling cond_broadcast thusly:

```
# everybody up!
cond_broadcast $lockvar;
```

This sends a message to each thread waiting on that variable, which is appropriate for circumstances where a common resource is conditionally available and we want to stop or start all threads, depending on whether they are available or not. It is important to realize, however, that if no threads are waiting on the variable, the signal is discarded; it is not kept until a thread is ready to respond to it. It is also important to realize that this has nothing (directly) to do with process signals, as handled by the %SIG array; writing a threaded application to handle process signals is a more complex task (see the Thread::Signal module for details).

Note that the actual value of the lock variable is entirely irrelevant to this process, so we can use it for other things. For instance, we can use it to pass a value to the thread at the moment that we signal it. The following short threaded application does just this, using a pool of service threads to handle lines of input passed to them by the main thread. While examining it, pay close attention to the two condition variables that lay at the heart of the application:

- $pool: Used by the main thread to signal that a new line is ready. It is waited on by all the service threads. Its value is programmed to hold the number of threads currently waiting, so the main thread knows whether or not it can send a signal or if it must wait for a service thread to become ready.

- $line: Used by whichever thread is woken by the signal to $pool. Lets the main thread know that the line of input read by the main thread has been copied to the service thread and that a new line may now be read. The value is the text of the line that was read.

The two condition variables allow the main thread and the pool of service threads to cooperate with each other. This ensures that each line read by the main thread is passed to one service thread both quickly and safely:

```
#!/usr/bin/perl
# threadpool.pl
use warnings;
use strict;

use threads;
use threads::shared;

my $threads = 3; # number of service threads to create
my $line : shared= "";
                # parent lock variable and input line set to "" here, we
                # assign each new line of input to it, and set it to 'undef'
                # when we are finished to tell service threads to quit
my $pool : shared = 0;
                # child lock variable and pool counter set to 0 here,
                # service threads increment it when they are ready for input
```

```perl
# a locked print subroutine--stops thread output mingling
{
  my $lock : shared;
  sub thr_print {
      lock $lock;
      print @_;
  }
}

# create a pool of three service threads
foreach (1..$threads) {
    threads->create(\&process_thing);
}

# main loop: Read a line, wait for a service thread to become available,
# signal that a new line is ready, then wait for whichever thread picked
# up the line to signal to continue
while ($line = <>) {
    chomp $line;
    thr_print "Main thread got '$line'\n";

    # do not signal until at least one thread is ready
    if ($pool==0) {
        thr_print "Main thread has no service threads available, yielding\n";
        threads->yield until $pool>0;
    }
    thr_print "Main thread has $pool service threads available\n";

    # signal that a new line is ready
    {
        lock $pool;
        cond_signal $pool;
    }
    thr_print "Main thread sent signal, waiting to be signaled\n";
    # wait for whichever thread wakes up to signal us
    {
        lock $line;
        cond_wait $line;
    }
    thr_print "Main thread received signal, reading next line\n";
}

thr_print "All lines processed, sending end signal\n";
# set the line to special value 'undef' to indicate end of input
$line = undef;
{
    lock $pool;
    # tell all threads to pick up this 'line' so they all quit
    cond_broadcast $pool;
}
thr_print "Main thread ended\n";
exit 0;

# the thread subroutine--block on lock variable until work arrives
sub process_thing {
    my $self=threads->self;
    my $thread_line;
```

```perl
    thr_print "Thread ",$self->tid," started\n";
    while (1) {
        # has the 'quit' signal been sent while we were busy?
        last unless (defined $line);

        # wait to be woken up
        thr_print "Thread ",$self->tid," waiting\n";
        {
            lock $pool;
            $pool++;
            cond_wait $pool; #all threads wait here for signal
            $pool--;
        }

        # retrieve value to process
        thr_print "Thread ",$self->tid," signaled\n";
        $thread_line = $line;

        # was this the 'quit' signal? Check the value sent
        last unless (defined $thread_line);

        # let main thread know we have got the value
        thr_print "Thread ",$self->tid," retrieved data, signaling main\n";
        {
            lock $line;
            cond_signal $line;
        }

        # do private spurious things to it
        chomp ($thread_line=uc($thread_line));
        thr_print "Thread ",$self->tid," got '$thread_line'\n";
    }
    thr_print "Thread ",$self->tid," ended\n";
}
```

Once the basic idea of a condition variable is understood, the way in which this application works becomes clearer. However, there are a few aspects still worth pointing out. In particular, the $pool variable is used by the main thread to ensure that it only sends a signal when there is a service thread waiting to receive it. To achieve this, we increment $pool immediately before cond_wait and decrement it immediately afterwards. By doing this, we ensure that $pool accurately reflects the number of waiting service threads; if it is zero, the main thread uses yield to pass on execution until a service thread becomes available again.

The means by which the application terminates is also worth noting. Threads do not necessarily terminate just because the main thread does, so in order to exit a threaded application cleanly, we need to make sure all the service threads terminate, too. This is especially important if resources needed by some threads are being used by others. In this application, the main thread uses cond_signal to signal the $pool variable and wake up one service thread when a new line is available. Once all input has been read, we need to shut down all the service threads, which means getting their entire attention. To do that, we give $line the special value undef and then use cond_broadcast to signal all threads to pick up the new "line" and exit when they see that it is undef. However, this alone is not enough because a thread might be busy and not waiting. To deal with that possibility, the service thread subroutine also checks the value of $line at the top of the loop, just in case the thread missed the signal.

Finally, this application also illustrates the use of the locked subroutine attribute. The thr_print subroutine is a wrapper for the regular print function that only allows one thread to print at a time.

This prevents the output of different threads from getting intermingled. For simple tasks like this one, locked subroutines are an acceptable solution to an otherwise tricky problem that would require at least a lock variable. For longer tasks, locked subroutines can be a serious bottleneck, affecting the performance of a threaded application, so we should use them with care and never for anything likely to take appreciable time.

As of Perl 5.8.3, cond_wait can take two shared variable arguments; the first is the signal variable, the second the lock variable:

```
cond_wait $sigvar,$lockvar;
```

It works identically to the one-argument form, except for the division of responsibility. The objective is to allow us to signal the same variable several times and unlock more than one thread concurrently, by having different threads use different lock variables for the same signal variable. The number of different lock variables in play is equal to the total number of concurrent threads the signal variable can trigger.

Also from Perl 5.8.3 onwards, the threads module also provides the cond_timedwait function. It works identically to its untimed counterpart earlier, but it takes an additional timeout value in seconds. The return value of cond_timedwait is true if a signal was received and false if the timeout was reached first. This lets us write code that can periodically stop waiting to do other tasks:

```
{
    lock $line;
    while (! cond_timedwait($line,10)) {
        thr_print "Yawn...\n";
    }
}
```

As with cond_wait, we can split the signal and lock variables if we wish:

```
cond_timedwait $sigvar,$lockvar,$timeout;
```

This works identically to the two-argument form, except for the division of responsibility. As with cond_wait, this form of the function allows us to signal the same variable several times and unlock more than one thread concurrently.

Semaphores

Although it works perfectly well, the preceding application is a little more complex than it needs to be. Most forms of threads whatever language or platform they reside on support the concept of semaphores, and Perl is no different. We covered IPC semaphores earlier, and thread semaphores are very similar. They are essentially numeric flags that take a value of zero or any positive number and obey the following simple rules:

- Only one thread may manipulate the value of a semaphore in either direction at a time.

- Any thread may increment a semaphore immediately.

- Any thread may decrement a semaphore immediately if the decrement will not take it below zero.

- If a thread attempts to decrement a semaphore below zero, it will block until another thread raises the semaphore high enough.

Perl provides thread semaphores through the Thread::Semaphore module, which implements semaphores in terms of condition variables—the code of Thread::Semaphore is actually quite short as well as instructive. It provides one class method, new, and two object methods, up and down. new creates a new semaphore:

```
$semaphore = new Thread::Semaphore;    # create semaphore, initial value 1
$semaphore2 = new Thread::Semaphore(0) # create semaphore, initial value 0
```

up increments a semaphore:

```
$semaphore->up;        # increment semaphore by 1
$semaphore->up(5);     # increment semaphore by 5
```

Finally, down decrements a semaphore, blocking if necessary:

```
$semaphore->down;      # decrement semaphore by 1
$semaphore->down(5);   # decrement semaphore by 5
```

Depending on our requirements, we can use semaphores as binary stop/go toggles or allow them to range to larger values to indicate the availability of a resource. Here is an adapted form of our earlier threaded application, rewritten to replace the condition variables with semaphores:

```perl
#!/usr/bin/perl
# semaphore.pl
use warnings;
use strict;

use threads;
use Thread::Semaphore;

my $threads = 3;         # number of service threads to create
my $line : shared = "";  # input line

my $main = new Thread::Semaphore;     # proceed semaphore, initial value 1
my $next = new Thread::Semaphore(0);  # new line semaphore, initial value 0

# a locked print subroutine--stops thread output mingling
{ my $lock : shared;
  sub thr_print {
      lock $lock;
      print @_;
  }
}

# create a pool of three service threads
foreach (1..$threads) {
    threads->create(\&process_thing);
}

# main loop: read a line, raise 'next' semaphore to indicate a line is
# available, then wait for whichever thread lowered the 'next' semaphore
# to raise the 'main' semaphore, indicating we can continue.
while ($line = <>) {
    chomp $line;
    thr_print "Main thread got '$line'\n";

    # notify service threads that a new line is ready
    $next->up;
    thr_print "Main thread set new line semaphore, waiting to proceed\n";

    # do not proceed until value has been retrieved by responding thread
    $main->down;
    thr_print "Main thread received instruction to proceed\n";
}

thr_print "All lines processed, sending end signal\n";
```

```perl
# set the line to special value 'undef' to indicate end of input
$line = undef;
# to terminate all threads, raise 'new line' semaphore to >= number of
# service threads: all service threads will decrement it and read the
# 'undef'
$next->up($threads);
thr_print "Main thread ended\n";
exit 0;

# the thread subroutine--block on lock variable until work arrives
sub process_thing {
    my $self = threads->self;
    my $thread_line;

    thr_print "Thread ", $self->tid, " started\n";
    while (1) {
        # try to decrement 'next' semaphore--winning thread gets line
        thr_print "Thread ", $self->tid, " waiting\n";
        $next->down;

        # retrieve value to process
        thr_print "Thread ", $self->tid, " signalled\n";
        $thread_line = $line;

        # was this the 'quit' signal? Check the value sent
        last unless (defined $thread_line);

        # let main thread know we have got the value
        thr_print "Thread ", $self->tid, " retrieved data, signaling main\n";
        $main->up;

        # do private spurious things to it
        chomp ($thread_line=uc($thread_line));
        thr_print "Thread ", $self->tid, " got '$thread_line'\n";
    }
    thr_print "Thread ", $self->tid, " ended\n";
}
```

The semaphore version of the application is simpler than the condition variable implementation, if only because we have hidden the details of all the cond_wait and cond_signal functions inside calls to up and down. Instead of signaling the pool of service threads via a condition variable, the main thread simply raises the next semaphore by one, giving it the value 1. Meanwhile, all the service threads are attempting to decrement this semaphore. One will succeed and receive the new line of input, and the others will fail, continuing to block until the semaphore is raised again. When it has copied the line to its own local variable, the thread raises the main semaphore to tell the main thread that it can proceed to read another line. The concept is recognizably the same as the previous example but is easier to follow.

We have also taken advantage of the fact that semaphores can hold any positive value to terminate the application. When the main thread runs out of input, it simply raises the "next" semaphore to be equal to the number of service threads. At this point, all the threads can decrement the semaphore, read the value of $line that we again set to undef, and quit. If a thread is still busy, the semaphore will remain positive until it finishes and comes back to decrement it—we have no need to put in an extra check in case we missed a signal.

Queues

Many threaded applications, our example a case in point, involve the transport of data between several different threads. In a complex application, incoming data might travel through multiple threads, passed from one to the next before being passed out again: a bucket-chain model. We can create pools of threads at each stage along the chain in a similar way to the preceding example application, but this does not improve upon the mechanism that allows each thread to pass data to the next in line.

The two versions of the application that we have produced so far are limited by the fact that they only handle a single value at a time. Before the main thread can read another line, it has to dispose of the previous one. Even though we can process multiple lines with multiple service threads, the communication between the main thread and the service threads is not very efficient. If we were communicating between different processes, we might use a pipe, which buffers output from one process until the other can read it; the same idea works for threads, too, and takes the form of a *queue*.

Perl provides support for queues through the Thread::Queue module, which implements simple thread queues in a similar way to the semaphores created by Thread::Semaphore. Rather than a single numeric flag, however, the queue consists of a list to which values may be added at one and removed from the other. At heart this is essentially no more than a shift and pop operation. Using conditional variables and locking the module, however, creates a queue that values may be added to and removed from safely in a threaded environment, following rules similar to those for semaphores:

- Only one thread may add or remove values in the queue at a time.

- Any thread may add values to a queue immediately.

- Any thread may remove values from a queue immediately if there are enough values available in the queue.

- If a thread attempts to remove more values than are available, it will block until another thread adds sufficient values to the queue.

The Thread::Queue module provides a constructor and four object methods to create and manage queues. The new constructor creates a new queue:

```
$queue = new Thread::Queue;
```

Values can be added to the queue, singly or in bulk, with the enqueue method:

```
$queue->enqueue($value);    # add a single value
$queue->enqueue(@values);   # add several values
```

A single value can be removed with dequeue. If no value is available, the method will block until one is available:

```
$value = $queue->dequeue;   # remove a single value, block
```

If we don't want to risk getting blocked, dequeue_nb removes a single value from a queue, if available, but returns undef immediately, without blocking, if nothing is available:

```
$value = $queue->dequeue_nb;   # remove a single value, don't block
if (defined $value) {
    ...
}
```

Finally, to check the number of values in the queue without actually removing one, we have the following pending:

```
print "There are ",$queue->pending," items in the queue\n";
```

Using a queue, we can rewrite our threaded application again to separate the main thread from the pool of service threads. Since the queue can take multiple values, the main thread no longer has to wait for each value it passes on to be picked up before it can continue. This simplifies both the code and the execution of the program. The queue has no limit, however, so we make sure not to read too much by checking the size of the queue and yielding if it reaches a limit we choose. Here is a revised version of the same application using a queue:

```perl
#!/usr/bin/perl
# queue.pl
use warnings;
use strict;

use threads;
use Thread::Queue;
use Thread::Semaphore;

my $threads = 3;         # number of service threads to create
my $maxqueuesize = 5;    # maximum size of queue allowed

my $queue = new Thread::Queue;    # the queue
my $ready = new Thread::Semaphore(0);   # a 'start-gun' semaphore
                                        # initialized to 0 each service
                                        # thread raises it by 1

# a locked print subroutine - stops thread output mingling
sub thr_print : locked {
    print @_;
}

# create a pool of service threads
foreach (1..$threads) {
    threads->create(\&process_thing, $ready, $queue);
}

# wait for all service threads to increment semaphore
$ready->down($threads);
# main loop: Read a line, queue it, read another, repeat until done
# yield and wait if the queue gets too large.
while (<>) {
    chomp;
    thr_print "Main thread got '$_'\n";

    # stall if we're getting too far ahead of the service threads
    threads->yield while $queue->pending >= $maxqueuesize;

    # queue the new line
    $queue->enqueue($_);
}

thr_print "All lines processed, queuing end signals\n";

# to terminate all threads, send as many 'undef's as there are service
# threads
$queue->enqueue( (undef)x$threads );
thr_print "Main thread ended\n";
exit 0;
```

```perl
# the thread subroutine--block on lock variable until work arrives
sub process_thing {
    my ($ready,$queue)=@_;

    my $self=threads->self;
    my $thread_line;

    thr_print "Thread ",$self->tid," started\n";
    $ready->up; #indicate that we're ready to go

    while (1) {
        # wait for queue to deliver an item
        thr_print "Thread ",$self->tid," waiting\n";
        my $thread_line=$queue->dequeue();

        # was this the 'quit' signal? Check the value sent
        last unless (defined $thread_line);

        # do private spurious things to it
        chomp ($thread_line=uc($thread_line));
        thr_print "Thread ",$self->tid," got '$thread_line'\n";
    }
    thr_print "Thread ", $self->tid, " ended\n";
}
```

Since the service threads block if no values are waiting in the queue, the problem of having service threads wait is solved for us—we previously dealt with this using condition variables and semaphores. However, we don't need a return semaphore anymore because there is no longer any need for a service thread to signal the main thread that it can continue; the main thread is free to continue as soon as it has copied the new line into the queue.

The means by which we terminate the program has also changed. Originally, we set the line variable to undef and broadcast to all the waiting threads. We replaced that with a semaphore, which we raised high enough so that all service threads could decrement it. With a queue, we use a variation on the semaphore approach, adding sufficient undef values to the queue so that all service threads can remove one and exit.

We have added one further refinement to this version of the application—a "start-gun" semaphore. Simply put, this is a special semaphore that is created with a value of zero and is incremented by one by each service thread as it starts. The main thread attempts to decrement the semaphore by a number equal to the number of service threads, so it will only start to read lines once all service threads are running. Why is this useful? Because threads have no priority of execution. In the previous examples, the first service threads will start receiving and processing lines before later threads have even initialized. In a busy threaded application, the activity of these threads may mean that the service threads may never get the time to initialize themselves properly. In order to make sure we have a full pool of threads at our disposal, we use this semaphore to hold the main thread back until the entire pool is assembled.

Monitoring Thread Status

The Thread::Status module is a handy way to get debugging information from a threaded application. While it can be loaded directly into an application, it is more usual to load it from the command line:

```
> perl -MThread::Status mythrapp.pl
```

This will print to standard error, every five seconds, a report of all running threads. We can also control the output destination, output format, and number of stack frames (callers):

```
> perl -Mthread::Status=output,status.log,format=xml,callers=3 mythrapp.pl
```

Thread::Status does have one drawback, however: it currently requires Thread::Signal. This was a standard module prior to Perl 5.8 that is now mostly deprecated as a result of the introduction of "safe" signals.

In the older implementation of threads, applications that needed to handle process signals need to use the Thread::Signal module in order to have signals delivered to threads reliably. The newer implementation does not quite replace it, however, so the older version is available from CPAN if needed (for example, for Thread::Status).

Summary

In this chapter, we first looked at sending and receiving signals from Perl processes and writing signal handlers to deal with signals intelligently. We saw how the die and warn functions can be trapped with pseudo-signal handlers and investigated strategies and caveats in the implementation of signal-handling subroutines. We also examined the alarm signal and used it to trigger timed events to abort hung processes.

We went on to example multiprocessing applications and the use of fork, both explicitly and implicitly via open, to start up child processes. When creating child processes, it is very important to manage them properly and in particular collect or *reap* their exit status when they terminate. Alternatively, a child process can be made independent of its parent by changing its process group, also called *daemonizing* it. We also looked at communicating between processes using pipes, paired sockets, and Unix System V IPC: message queues, semaphores, and shared memory segments.

While fork is a standard Unix system call, Windows has no equivalent concept, and so Perl instead emulates fork using interpreter threads. This turns out to be a fairly impressive emulation that allows many multiprocessing Perl applications to run on Windows and Unix almost identically.

Finally, we looked at Perl's implementation of threads, newly overhauled in Perl 5.8. The new implementation of threads is called interpreter threads, and it differs from the older version in Perl 5.6 and earlier, in that data is not automatically shared between threads unless and until we ask for it. This is very different to most languages, notably C and C++, and means that the majority of Perl code will run in a threaded environment unaltered without needing to be aware of threads. Windows Perl is automatically threaded because it needs threads to emulate the fork system call. For Unix, we may need to rebuild Perl with thread support enabled in order to use it, as we covered back in Chapter 1.

■ ■ ■

Networking

The basics of networking are not greatly different from input and output to any other kind of device or file. A filehandle that provides abstract access to a network socket shares many of the properties of a filehandle that provides access to a file or a serial port—not least that they can all be represented as filehandles. However, programs designed to work across a network have a new range of problems and challenges to solve beyond those encountered by local file system and device access.

In this chapter, we look at the basics of establishing network connections with sockets and how to create them using Perl's built-in networking functions. While we do not always need to go to the lowest level of network programming and manipulate sockets directly, we often need to configure them to operate in a particular way, so we also look at socket options and why we might need to use them.

We look at both the TCP/IP and UDP protocols, and we create simple clients and servers for each with Internet domain sockets, with Perl's built-in functions, and also with the IO::Socket module. We also look at Unix domain sockets, which, while not directly related to networking between computers, share a great deal in common with their Internet domain relatives. A real server application typically handles multiple requests from clients simultaneously, so we also explore creating a multiplexing server capable of handling more than one connection at a time.

In the final part of the chapter, we discuss retrieving information about the networking environment, including host names, network services, and protocols, and take a special look at determining the local hostname, a more complex problem than it might at first seem.

We will not spend significant time elaborating on the nature and properties of networking protocols here, but if necessary a short rundown of networking concepts can be found in Chapter 1 of *Pro Apache*, Third Edition (Wainwright, Peter; Apress, 2004). Chapter 12 of that book also covers embedding Perl code into an Apache server (versions 1.3 and 2.0) using mod_perl, another way to write Perl applications that communicate over a network.

Beyond the basics covered here, CPAN provides a vast array of modules to simplify different kinds of network programming, from protocol-specific modules like LWP, Net::FTP, and HTTP::Daemon (to name but three) to general-purpose modules like IO::All, which provides a single interface to manage all kinds of IO tasks, including network connections. It is well worth checking out CPAN before reinventing the wheel, but even when using these higher-level modules, a basic understanding of the underlying technology and concepts is invaluable.

Sockets

Sockets are the operating system's abstract interface to the networking layer, mapping the details of a network connection into something that looks and feels exactly like a filehandle. Within Perl we can manipulate sockets at a very low level using Perl's built-in functions and the Socket module, which provides the glue between Perl and the operating system's native socket support libraries; or we can take advantage of higher-level modules like IO::Socket to manage some of the work for us.

Socket Types and Protocols

There are two basic kinds of sockets: *Internet domain* or INET sockets, and *Unix domain* sockets (the latter of which we saw in some nonnetwork applications using `socketpair` in Chapter 21). Internet domain sockets are associated with an address, port number, and protocol, allowing us to establish connections across the network. Unix domain sockets, by contrast, appear as files in the local filing system and are used to communicate between processes running on the same machine.

Sockets have a type associated with them that determines the nature of the data that they can handle—streaming data or discrete datagrams, for example. The type of data a socket will handle in turn usually determines the possible protocols that can be used. For instance, streaming sockets use the connection-oriented TCP/IP protocol, since TCP provides the flow control, state, and session management necessary to stream data reliably and in a reproducible order.

Most operating systems now provide support for the IPv6 protocol and reflect this support in their implementation of sockets. Some handle other protocols such as IPX, X25, or AppleTalk, all of which we can use through an appropriately configured socket. The nature of the protocol tends to dictate the kinds of data we can transmit and receive, and so the type of socket we create. Here we are chiefly interested in streaming sockets used with the TCP/IP protocol and datagram sockets used with the UDP protocol. We can also create a very low-level "raw" socket that works directly with the IP protocol. Other socket types will be available, but which ones depend on the underlying operating system.

The Socket Module

Since Perl's socket support is an interface to the native C libraries, it can support any type of socket the system can. Non-Unix platforms may have varying support for sockets, so it can be important to check the actual features available. At the very least, standard Internet domain sockets should be supported.

The built-in socket functions are a very direct interface, essentially just the veneer over the underlying C-based functions. One consequence of this is that the idiosyncrasies of the platform's implementation may poke through, in particular the large number of numeric values for the various arguments of the socket functions. In addition, the address information arguments required by functions like `bind`, `connect`, and `send` need to be in a packed `sockaddr` format that is acceptable to the underlying C library functions. Fortunately, the `Socket` module provides constants for all of these socket arguments (extracted from the system header files when the extension was compiled), so we do not need to memorize those numeric values. It also provides conversion utilities like `inet_aton` and `inet_ntoa` that convert string addresses into the packed form required and returned by the C functions.

A summary of Perl's socket functions is given in the next sections, some directly supported by Perl, the rest provided by `Socket.pm`. Each of them is explained in more detail during the course of the chapter.

General Socket Functions

These functions apply to both servers and clients:

Function	Description
socket	Create a new socket filehandle in the specified domain (Internet or Unix) of the specified type (streaming, datagram, raw, etc.) and protocol (TCP, UDP, etc.). For example: `socket(ISOCK, PF_INET, SOCK_STREAM, $proto);`

Function	Description
shutdown	Close a socket and all filehandles that are associated with it. This differs from a simple close, which only closes the current process's given filehandle, not any copies held by child processes. In addition, a socket may be closed completely or converted to a read-only or write-only socket by shutting down one half of the connection. For example: `shutdown(ISOCK, SOCK_RDWR);`
socketpair	Generate a pair of Unix domain sockets linked back to back. This is a quick and easy way to create a full-duplex pipe (unlike the pipe function) and is covered in more detail in Chapter 21. For example: `socketpair(RSOCK, WSOCK, SOCK_STREAM, PF_UNSPEC);`

Server Functions

These functions create and manage server sockets:

Function	Description
bind	Bind a newly created socket to a specified port and address. For example: `bind ISOCK, $packed_addr;`
listen	(*Stream sockets only.*) Set up a queue for receiving incoming network connection requests on a bound socket. For example: `listen ISOCK, $qsize;`
accept	(*Stream sockets only.*) Accept and create a new communications socket on a bound and listened-to server socket. For example: `accept CNNCT, ISOCK;`

Client Functions

These functions create and manage client sockets:

Function	Description
connect	Connect a socket to a remote server at a given port and IP address, which must be bound and listening to a specified port and address. While datagram sockets can't really connect, this sets the default destination. For example: `connect ISOCK, $packed_addr;`

Socket Options

These functions get and set options on sockets:

Function	Description
getsockopt	Retrieve a configuration option from a socket. For example: `$opt = getsockopt ISOCK, SOL_SOCKET, SO_DONTROUTE;`
setsockopt	Set a configuration option on a socket. For example: `setsockopt ISOCK, SOL_SOCKET, SO_REUSEADDR, 1;`

Input and Output

These functions provide socket-specific input and output:

Function	Description
send	Send a message. For UDP sockets, this is the only way to send data, and an addressee must be supplied, unless a default destination has already been set by using the connect function. For TCP sockets, no addressee is needed. For example: `send ISOCK, $message, 0;`
recv	Receive a message. For a UDP socket, this is the only way to receive data, and it returns the addressee (as a sockaddr structure) on success. TCP sockets may also use recv. For example: `$message = recv ISOCK, $message, 1024, 0;`

Conversion Functions

These functions convert socket configuration data to and from the format understood by the underlying socket functions provided by the operating system:

Function	Description
inet_aton	Convert a hostname (for example, www.myserver.com) or textual representation of an IP address (for example, 209.165.161.91) and turn it into a 4-byte packed value for use with INET sockets. If a host name is supplied, a name lookup, possibly involving a network request, is performed to find its IP address (this is a Perl extra and not part of the C call). Used in conjunction with pack_sockaddr_in. For example: `my $ip = inet_aton($hostname);`
inet_ntoa	Convert a 4-byte packed value into a textual representation of an IP address, for example, 209.165.161.91. Used in conjunction with unpack_sockaddr_in.
pack_sockaddr_in	Generate a sockaddr_in structure suitable for use with the bind, connect, and send functions from a port number and a packed 4-byte IP address. For example: `my $addr = pack_sockaddr_in($port, $ip);` The IP address can be generated with inet_aton.
unpack_sockaddr_in	Extract the port number and packed 4-byte IP address from the supplied sockaddr_in structure: `my ($port, $ip) = unpack_sockaddr_in($addr);`

sockaddr_in	Call either unpack_sockaddr_in or pack_sockaddr_in depending on whether it is called in a list (unpack) or scalar (pack) context:
	`my $addr = sockaddr_in($port, $ip);`
	`my ($port, $ip) = sockaddr_in($addr);`
	The dual nature of this function can lead to confusion, so using it in only one direction or using the pack and unpack versions explicitly is recommended.

pack_sockaddr_un	Convert a pathname into a sockaddr_un structure for use with Unix domain sockets: `my $addr = pack_sockaddr_un($path);`
unpack_sockaddr_un	Convert a sockaddr_un structure into a pathname: `my $path = unpack_sockaddr_un($addr);`

Function	Description

sockaddr_un	Call either unpack_sockaddr_un or pack_sockaddr_un depending on whether it is called in a list (unpack) or scalar (pack) context:
	my $addr = sockaddr_un($path);
	my ($path) = sockaddr_un($addr);
	This function is even more confusing than sockaddr_in, since it only returns one value in either case—the context (scalar or list) tells the function which direction it is working in. Using it for packing only or using the pack and unpack versions explicitly is definitely recommended.

Special IP Addresses

In addition to the utility functions, Socket supplies four symbols for special IP addresses in a prepacked format suitable for passing to pack_sockaddr_in:

Symbol	Description
INADDR_ANY	Tell the socket that no specific address is requested for use, we just want to be able to talk directly to all local networks.
INADDR_BROADCAST	Use the generic broadcast address of 255.255.255.255, which transmits a broadcast on all local networks.
INADDR_LOOPBACK	The loopback address for the local host, 127.0.0.1.
INADDR_NONE	An address meaning "invalid IP address" in certain operations. Usually 255.255.255.255. This is invalid for TCP, for example, since TCP does not permit broadcasts.

Creating Sockets

The procedure for creating sockets is the same for both Unix and INET sockets; it only differs depending on whether we are opening a client or server connection.

Server sockets typically follow three steps: creating the socket, initializing a socket data structure, and binding the socket and the structure together:

```
socket(UNIXSOCK, PF_UNIX, SOCK_STREAM, 0)
    or die "socket error: $!\n";
my $sock_struct = sockaddr_un('/tmp/server.sock');
bind(UNIXSOCK, $sock_struct)
    or die "bind error: $!\n";
```

We may or may not also need to insert a setsockopt call to fully configure the socket appropriately, but these three steps are always required as a minimum. This socket is not used for communication, however. Instead, we use listen to receive incoming connection requests from clients and accept to acknowledge them.

Opening client connections is similar: create the socket, create the packed remote address, and connect to the server:

```
socket(INETSOCK, PF_INET, SOCK_STREAM, getprotobyname('tcp'))
    or die "socket error: $!\n";
my $paddr = sockaddr_in($port, inet_aton($ip));
connect(INETSOCK, $paddr)
    or die "connect error: $!\n";
```

Socket Options

The socket specification defines a number of options that may be set for sockets to alter their behavior. For direct manipulation of socket options, we can make use of Perl's built-in getsockopt and setsockopt functions, which provide low-level socket option handling capabilities.

The getsockopt function takes three arguments: a socket filehandle, a protocol level, and the option to set. Protocol level refers to the level of the desired protocol layer in the network stack. TCP, for instance, is a higher-level protocol than IP, and so has a higher value. We needn't bother with the particular values, though, since constants are available. setsockopt takes the same three arguments, but it can also include a value to set the option to. Leaving that argument out effectively unsets that option.

Options can be one of a number of values, including those listed in Table 22-1.

Table 22-1. *Socket Options*

Option	Description
SO_ACCEPTCONN	The socket is listening for connections.
SO_BROADCAST	The socket is enabled for broadcasts (used with UDP).
SO_DEBUG	Debugging mode enabled.
SO_LINGER	Sockets with data remaining to send continue to exist after the process that created them exits, until all data has been sent.
SO_DONTROUTE	The socket will not route. See also MSG_DONTROUTE in the upcoming section "Reading from and Writing to Sockets."
SO_ERROR	(*Read only.*) The socket is in an error condition.
SO_KEEPALIVE	Prevent TCP/IP closing the connection due to inactivity by maintaining a periodic exchange of low-level messages between the local and remote sockets.
SO_DONTLINGER	Sockets disappear immediately, instead of continuing to exist until all data has been sent.
SO_OOBINLINE	Allow "out-of-band" data to be read with a regular recv—see the upcoming section "Reading from and Writing to Sockets."
SO_RCVBUF	The size of the receive buffer.
SO_RCVTIMEO	The timeout value for receive operations.
SO_REUSEADDR	Allow bound addresses to be reused immediately.
SO_SNDBUF	The size of the send buffer.
SO_SNDTIMEO	The timeout period for send operations.
SO_TYPE	The socket type (stream, datagram, etc.).

Of these, the most useful is SO_REUSEADDR, which allows a given port to be reused, even if another socket exists that's in a TIME_WAIT status. The common use for this is to allow an immediate server restart, even if the kernel hasn't finished its garbage collection and removed the last socket:

```
setsockopt SERVER => SOL_SOCKET, SO_REUSEADDR => 1;
```

The SO_LINGER option is also useful, as is its opposite, SO_DONTLINGER. Usually the default, SO_DONTLINGER causes sockets to close immediately when a process exits, even if data remains in the buffer to be sent. Alternatively, we can specify SO_LINGER, which causes sockets to remain open as long as they have data still to send to a remote client.

```
setsockopt SERVER => SOL_SOCKET, SO_DONTLINGER => 1;
```

SO_KEEPALIVE informs the kernel that TCP messages should be periodically sent to verify that a connection still exists on both ends. This feature can be handy for connections going through a NAT firewall, since that firewall has to maintain a table of connection translations, which are expired automatically after an interval with no activity. It also provides a periodic link test for those applications that keep predominantly idle connections but need to be assured that a valid connection is maintained.

```
setsockopt SERVER => SOL_SOCKET, SO_KEEPALIVE => 1;
```

SO_BROADCAST sets or tests a socket for the ability to broadcast, an option that is only applicable to UDP sockets. SO_TYPE is a read-only option that returns the socket type. SO_ERROR indicates that the socket is in an error condition, though $! is an alternative.

The getsockopt function simply retrieves the current value of a socket option:

```
my $reusable = getsockopt SERVER => SOL_SOCKET, SO_REUSEADDR;
```

The expert network programmer can use getsockopt and setsockopt at lower levels in the protocol stack by supplying a different level as the protocol-level argument. The Socket module does not define symbols for these levels since they have nothing directly to do with sockets. So to get useful names, we must include the sys/socket.ph definition file:

```
require 'sys/socket.ph'.
```

This file defines symbols for all the system constants related to networking on the platform in question, including SOL_ symbols for lower-level protocols. The most interesting for us are the following:

Symbol	Description
SOL_IP	IP version 4 protocol
SOL_TCP	TCP protocol
SOL_UDP	UDP protocol
SOL_IPV6	IP version 6 protocol
SOL_RAW	"Raw" protocol (SOCK_RAW)
SOL_IPX	IPX protocol
SOL_ATALK	Appletalk protocol
SOL_PACKET	"Packet" protocol (SOCK_SEQPACKET)

Each protocol defines its own set of options. The only one of immediate interest to us here is TCP_NODELAY, which disables buffering at the TCP protocol level, essential for sending things like typed characters in real time across network connections:

```
setsockopt CONNECTION, SOL_TCP, TCP_NODELAY, 1;
```

Reading from and Writing to Sockets

Reading from and writing to sockets is handled by the recv and send functions, respectively. This is used with datagram sockets more often than with other types. As Perl merely wraps the C function, the syntax and behaviors are the same, so detailed information can be found in the C manual pages (for Unix, see recv(2) and send(2)).

The send function takes four arguments: a socket filehandle, a message, a numeric flag (which in most cases can be 0), and an addressee, in the form of a sockaddr_in or sockaddr_un structure:

```
send SOCKET, $message, $flags, $addressee;
```

Since stream sockets are connected, we can omit the last argument for that type. For other types, the addressee is a `sockaddr` structure built from either a host and port number or a local pathname, depending on the socket domain:

```
my $inetaddr = sockaddr_in($port, inet_aton($hostorip));
my $unixaddr = sockaddr_un($pathname);
```

The `flags` argument is a little more interesting; it is combined from a number of flags with symbols (defined by the `Socket` module) that alters the form or way in which the message is sent:

Send Flag	Description
MSG_OOB	Send an out-of-band (that is, high-priority) message.
MSG_DONTROUTE	Ignore the local network gateway configuration and attempt to send the message directly to the destination.
MSG_DONTWAIT	Do not wait for the message to be sent before returning. If the message would have blocked, the error `EAGAIN` (see the `Errno` module in Chapter 16) is returned, indicating we must try again later.
MSG_NOSIGNAL	TCP sockets only. Do not raise a `SIGPIPE` signal when the other end breaks the connection. The error `EPIPE` is still returned.

For example:

```
use Errno qw(EAGAIN EPIPE);

$result = send SOCKET, $message, MSG_DONTWAIT|MSG_NOSIGNAL, $addressee;
if ($result == EAGAIN) {
    ...
}
```

The `recv` function also takes four arguments, but instead of an addressee, it specifies a length for the data to be received. It resembles the `read` function in several ways; the arguments are a socket filehandle, as before, then a scalar variable into which the message is placed, followed by an expected length, followed up by a `flags` argument as before. The return value on success is the `sockaddr` structure for the client:

```
my $message;        # scalar to store message in
my $length = 1024;  # expected maximum length
my $sender = recv SOCKET, $message, $length, $flags;
```

The `length` argument is in fact somewhat arbitrary, since the size of the message is determined when it is read and adjusted accordingly. However, the supplied length is used to preallocate storage for the received message, so a size that is equal to or larger than the expected message size will allow Perl to operate slightly more efficiently. However, configuring for too large a message is also wasteful, so choose a reasonable value.

The `flags` argument allows us to modify the way in which we receive messages:

Receive Flag	Description
MSG_OOB	Receive an out-of-band message rather than a message from the normal message queue, unless OOB messages are being put at the head of the queue of normal messages by setting the `SO_OOBINLINE` socket option (see "Configuring Socket Options").
MSG_PEEK	Examine and return the data of the next message on the socket without removing it.

Receive Flag	Description
MSG_WAITALL	Wait until a message has been completely received before attempting to retrieve it.
MSG_ERRQUEUE	Retrieve a message from the error queue rather than the normal message queue.
MSG_NOSIGNAL	TCP sockets only. Do not raise a SIGPIPE signal when the other end breaks the connection. The error 'EPIPE' is still returned.

For example:

```
my $message;
my $sender = recv SOCKET, $message, 1024, MSG_PEEK|MSG_WAITALL;
```

Note that depending on the socket implementation, the send and recv methods may accept more or different flags from those listed previously. However, these are reasonably typical for most platforms, and certainly most Unix platforms.

Closing Sockets

Like all other in-memory variables, Perl performs reference counting on sockets and will close them automatically should all the existing references go out of scope. However, in keeping with good programming practice, we should explicitly release unneeded resources. Since sockets are filehandles, we can close them like any other filehandle:

```
close INETSOCK;
```

There is a caveat to this rule, however: close only affects the filehandle for the process that called it. Any other children with a handle to the socket, which can easily happen if the socket was opened by a parent process that then forked, will still have access to it. As a result, the socket remains open. This allows us to close a socket without worrying whether sibling processes are still using it, but if we need to really close the socket, a workaround exists in the shutdown function:

```
shutdown(INETSOCK, 2);
```

This call closes the named socket completely for all processes with handles to it. Sockets can provide bidirectional communication, however, and shutdown also allows us to shut down one channel independently of the other. To make the socket read-only, we call shutdown with a second argument of 1. To make it write-only, we call it with a second argument of 0. The Socket module also defines constants for these values, which make them slightly friendlier:

```
shutdown SOCKET, SHUT_RD;     # shutdown read
shutdown SOCKET, SHUT_WR;     # shutdown write
shutdown SOCKET, SHUT_RDWR;   # shutdown completely
```

The IO::Socket Module

Although the Socket module makes using the socket functions possible, it is a deliberately low-level module. To make common tasks simpler to program, the IO::Socket module and its children, IO::Socket::INET and IO::Socket::Unix, provide a friendlier and simpler interface that automatically handles the intricacies of translating host names into IP addresses and thence into the sockaddr structure, as well as translating protocol names into numbers and even services into ports.

All the socket functions are represented as methods; new sockets are created, bound, listened to, or connected with the new method, and all other functions become methods of the resulting filehandle object:

```
my $socket = new IO::Socket::INET($server_address_and_port);
```

Or:

```
my $socket = new IO::Socket::UNIX($path_to_peer);
```

Followed by (depending on the type and domain of the socket created):

```
$socket->accept;
$udpsocket->send("Message in a Datagram", 0, $addressee);
$tcpsocket->print("Hello Network World!\n");
$socket->close;
```

We are leaving the exact details of the socket creation parameters vague here since there are a lot of permutations depending on the type of socket and the domain in which it operates. We will see examples of all the various kinds of sockets during the course of this chapter. The main distinction between these socket objects and the native Perl functions is in the way they are created and configured.

Configuring Socket Options

Options can be set on sockets at creation time using the new method, but the IO::Socket modules also support getsockopt and setsockopt methods. These are direct interfaces to the functions of the same name and behave identically to them, though the syntax differs slightly. For example:

```
$connection->setsockopt(SOL_SOCKET, SO_KEEPALIVE => 1);
```

The IO::Socket modules also allow us to configure aspects of the socket when we create it, though not with the same flexibility as getsockopt and setsockopt. The arguments differ for Internet and Unix domain sockets, in accordance with their different behaviors.

The full range of options accepted by the new method of IO::Socket::INET is given in Table 22-2.

Table 22-2. *IO::Socket::INET Constructor Options*

INET Options	Description
LocalAddr LocalHost	(*Server only.*) The local address or hostname to serve, optionally followed by the port number or service name (which may additionally be followed by a default in parentheses) prefixed by a colon. For example: `127.0.0.1` `127.0.0.1:4444` `127.0.0.1:myservice(4444)` `www.myserver.com` `www.myserver.com:80` `www.myserver.com:http`
LocalPort	(*Server only.*) The local port number or service name, if not given in LocalAddr/ LocalHost format. For example: `80` `http`
Listen	(*Server only.*) The size of the queue to establish on the bound server socket. The maximum possible size is defined on a platform basis by the constant SOMAXCONN. Default: 5
Multihomed	(*Server only.*) Boolean value. Listen for connections on all locally available network interfaces. Default: false
ReuseAddr Reuse	(*Server only.*) Boolean value. Set the SO_REUSEADDR option to free up the address to which the socket is bound for immediate reuse. Reuse is the older name, deprecated in favor of ReuseAddr. Default: false

INET Options	Description
ReusePort	(*Server only.*) Boolean value. Where supported, set the `SO_REUSEPORT` option to free up the port to which the socket is bound for immediate reuse. Default: false
PeerHost	(*Client only.*) The remote address or hostname to connect to, optionally followed by a port number or service name (which may additionally be followed by a default in parentheses) prefixed by a colon. For example: `127.0.0.1` `127.0.0.1:4444` `127.0.0.1:myservice(4444)` `www.myserver.com` `www.myserver.com:80` `www.myserver.com:http`
PeerPort	(*Client only.*) The remote port number or service name, if not given in `PeerAddr`/`PeerHost`. For example: `80http`
Proto	The protocol number or, more sensibly, name. For example: `tcp` `udp` `icmp` The type is set implicitly from the socket type if it is `SOCK_STREAM`, `SOCK_DGRAM`, or `SOCK_RAW`. Default: `tcp`
Timeout	Timeout value for socket operations, in seconds. Default: 0 (no timeout).
Type	The socket type. For example: `SOCK_STREAM` (for TCP) `SOCK_DGRAM` (for UDP) `SOCK_RAW` (for ICMP) `SOCK_SEQPACKET` The socket type is set implicitly from the protocol if it is `tcp`, `udp`, or `icmp`. Default: `SOCK_STREAM`

If only one argument is passed to the `new` method of `IO::Socket::INET`, it is assumed to be a client's peer address, including the port number or service name.

```
my $server = new IO::Socket::INET($server_address_and_port);
```

The `new` method of `IO::Socket` does not have this shorthand; defining the socket domain is mandatory.

The `new` method of the `IO::Socket::Unix` module is considerably simpler. It takes only four arguments, as listed in Table 22-3, three of which we have already seen.

Table 22-3. *IO::Socket::Unix Constructor Options*

Unix Option	Description
Local	(*Server only.*) The pathname of the socket connection in the file system, for example: `/tmp/myapp_socket` The pathname should be somewhere that the server has the ability to create a file. A previous file should be checked for and removed first if present.

Continued

Table 22-3. *Continued*

Unix Option	Description
Listen	(*Server only.*) Specify that this is a server socket, and set the size of the queue to establish on the bound server socket. The maximum possible size is defined on a platform basis by the constant SOMAXCONN. Note that unlike INET sockets, it is the setting of this parameter, not Local or Peer, that causes the module to bind and listen to the socket. It is not implied by Local. Default: 5
Peer	(*Client only.*) The pathname of the socket connection in the file system, for example: /tmp/myapp_socket
Type	The socket type, for example: SOCK_STREAM SOCK_DGRAM SOCK_RAW SOCK_SEQPACKET Default: SOCK_STREAM

If using new via the parent IO::Socket module, we must also supply a domain for the socket:

```
my $socket = new IO::Socket(Domain => PF_INET, ...);
```

This may be from the PF_ family of constants, for example, PF_INET or PF_UNIX (or indeed PF_APPLETALK, etc.). These are not to be confused with the AF_ constants (as supplied to gethostbyaddr or getnetbyaddr, which are of the address family of symbols).

Implementing Servers and Clients

Now that we have looked at of the basics of sockets and covered their creation and configuration with both the Socket and IO::Socket approaches, we can use them to create both servers and clients. We will first look at streaming connections using TCP/IP, then move on to connectionless UDP sockets, and also look at UDP broadcasting. For good measure, we will also cover Unix domain sockets.

TCP/IP Clients and Servers

The TCP protocol is a connection-oriented protocol that guarantees reliable and consistently ordered communications between a server and a client. A server is simply an application that listens for and accepts incoming connections from client applications. Once the connection is established, the two ends may then carry out whatever service the server is there to perform— receive a file, send a web page, relay mail, and so on.

To establish a TCP/IP connection, the server first creates a TCP socket to listen for incoming connections by first creating the socket with socket, and then assigning it to server duty with the bind function. The resulting socket is not connected, nor can it be used for communications, but it will receive notification of clients that connect to the address and port number to which it is bound. To receive connections, we use the listen function, which creates an internal queue for incoming connections to collect. Finally, we use the accept function to pull a connection request from the queue and create a socket filehandle for it. With it, we can communicate with the remote system. Behind the scenes, TCP sends an acknowledgment to the client, which creates a similar socket to communicate with our application.

A Simple TCP/IP Server

The following simple application demonstrates one way to create a very simple TCP server operating over an INET socket, using Perl's built-in socket functions:

```perl
#!/usr/bin/perl
# tcpinetserv.pl
use strict;
use warnings
use Socket;

my $proto = getprotobyname('tcp');
my $port = 4444;

# Create 'sockaddr_in' structure to listen to the given port
# on any locally available IP address
my $servaddr = sockaddr_in($port, INADDR_ANY);

# Create a socket for listening on
socket SERVER, PF_INET, SOCK_STREAM, $proto
    or die "Unable to create socket: $!";

# bind the socket to the local port and address
bind SERVER, $servaddr or die "Unable to bind: $!";

# listen to the socket to allow it to receive connection requests
# allow up to 10 requests to queue up at once.
listen SERVER, 10;

# now accept connections
print "Server running on port $port...\n";
while (accept CONNECTION, SERVER) {
    select CONNECTION; $| = 1; select STDOUT;
    print "Client connected at ", scalar(localtime), "\n";
    print CONNECTION "You're connected to the server!\n";
    while (<CONNECTION>) {
        print "Client says: $_\n";
    }
    close CONNECTION;
    print "Client disconnected\n";
}
```

We use the Socket module to define the constants for the various socket functions—PF_INET means create an INET socket (we could also have said PF_UNIX for a Unix domain socket or even PF_APPLTALK for a Macintosh Appletalk socket). SOCK_STREAM means create a streaming socket, as opposed to SOCK_DGRAM, which would create a datagram socket. We also need to specify a protocol. In this case we want TCP, so we use the getprotobyname function to return the appropriate protocol number—we explore this and similar functions at the end of the chapter.

Once the constants imported from Socket are understood, the socket function becomes more understandable; it essentially creates a filehandle that is associated with a raw, unassigned socket. To actually use it for something, we need to program it. First, we bind it to listen to port 4444 on any locally available IP address using the bind function. The bind function is one of the esoteric socket functions that requires a packet C-style data structure, so we use the sockaddr_in function to create something that is acceptable to bind from ordinary Perl values. The special INADDR_ANY symbol tells bind to listen to all local network interfaces; we could also specify an explicit IP address with inet_aton:

```
# bind to the loopback address
# (will only respond to local clients, not remote)
bind SERVER, inet_aton('127.0.0.1');
```

The listen function enables the socket's queue to receive incoming network connections and sets the queue size. It takes the socket as a first argument and a queue size as the second. In this case, we said 10 to allow up to ten connections to queue; after that, the socket will start rejecting connections. We could also use the special symbol (again defined by Socket) of SOMAXCONN to create a queue of the maximum size supported by the operating system:

```
# create a queue of the maximum size allowed
listen SERVER, SOMAXCONN;
```

Having gone through all this setup work, the actual server is almost prosaic—we simply use "accept" to generate sockets from the server socket. Each new socket represents an active connection to a client. In this simple example, we simply print a hello message and then print out whatever the client sends until it disconnects. In order to make sure that anything we send to the client is written out in a timely manner, we set autoflush on the socket filehandle. This is an important step, since our response to the client may never reach them because our socket is waiting for enough data to fill the buffer before flushing it to the client. IO buffering is enabled in Perl by default. Alternatively, we could have used the syswrite function, which explicitly bypasses any buffering.

A TCP/IP Server Using IO::Socket

The IO::Socket module simplifies much of the basic work of socket manipulation by relieving us from having to do all of the low-level sockaddr_in manipulation socket function calls. Returning to the server example we just saw, let's rewrite it using IO::Socket:

```
#!/usr/bin/perl
# tcpioinetserv.pl
use warnings;
use strict;

use IO::Socket;

my $port = 4444;

my $server = IO::Socket->new(
    Domain    => AF_INET,
    Proto     => 'tcp',
    LocalPort => $port,
    Listen    => SOMAXCONN,
);

print "Server running on port $port...\n";
while (my $connection = $server->accept) {
    print "Client connected at ", scalar(localtime), "\n";
    print $connection "You're connected to the server!\n";
    while (<$connection>) {
        print "Client says: $_";
    }
    close $connection;
    print "Client disconnected\n";
}
```

This is both simpler and easier to read. Note that we didn't need to specify a socket type, since the IO::Socket module can work it out from the protocol—TCP means it must be a SOCK_STREAM.

It also has the advantage that autoflushing is enabled by default on the newly created sockets, so we don't have to do it ourselves.

As a slightly simplified case for when we know we want an INET socket, we can use the IO::Socket::INET module directly, obviating the need for the Domain argument:

```
my $server = new IO::Socket::INET(
    Proto     => 'tcp',
    LocalPort => $port,
    Listen    => SOMAXCONN,
);
```

The filehandles returned by either approach work almost identically to "ordinary" filehandles for files and pipes, but we can distinguish them from other filehandles with the -S file test:

```
print "It's a socket!" if -S CONNECTION;
```

Filehandles returned by the IO::Socket modules also support all the methods supported by the IO::Handle class, from which they inherit, so we can, for example, say

```
$socket->autoflush(0);
$socket->printf("%04d %04f", $int1, $int2);
$socket->close;
```

See Chapter 12 for more on the IO::Handle module and the other modules in the "IO" family.

Our preceding example lacks one primary attribute necessary for a true multiuser server—it can only handle one connection at a time. A true server would either fork or use threads to handle each connection, freeing up the main process to continue to accept new connections. We will come back to this later on in the chapter.

A Simple TCP/IP Client

Implementing a client is simpler than creating a server. We start out by creating an unconnected stream socket of the correct domain and protocol with socket. We then connect the socket to the remote server with the connect function. If the result of the connect is not a failure, then this is all we have to do, apart from use the socket. Once we're done, we need to close the socket, in order to maintain our status as good denizens on the host.

The following application demonstrates a very simple INET TCP client, using Perl's built-in socket functions:

```
#!/usr/bin/perl
# tcpinetclient.pl
use warnings;
use strict;

use Socket;

my $proto = getprotobyname('tcp');
my $host = inet_aton('localhost');
my $port = 4444;
# Create 'sockaddr_in' structure to connect to the given
# port on the IP address for the remote host
my $servaddr = sockaddr_in($port, $host);

# Create a socket for connecting on
socket SERVER, PF_INET, SOCK_STREAM, $proto
    or die "Unable to create socket: $!";

# bind the socket to the local port and address
connect SERVER, $servaddr or die "Unable to connect: $!";
```

```
# enable autoflush
select SERVER; $| = 1; select STDOUT;

# communicate with the server
print "Client connected.\n";
print "Server says: ", scalar(<SERVER>);
print SERVER "Hello from the client!\n";
print "Server says: ", scalar(<SERVER>);
print SERVER "And goodbye!\n";
print "Server says: ", scalar(<SERVER>);
close SERVER;
```

The initial steps for creating the client are identical to the server. First, we create a socket of the right type and protocol. We then connect it to the server by feeding connect the socket filehandle and a sockaddr_in structure. However, in this case the address and port are those of the server, not the client (which doesn't have a port until the connection succeeds). The result of the connect is either an error, which returns undef and we catch with a die, or a connected socket. If the latter, we enable autoflush on the server connection to ensure data is written out in a timely manner, read a message from the server, send it a couple of messages, and close the connection.

Clients may bind to a specific port and address if they wish to, just like servers, but may not listen on them. It is not common that we would want to create a bound client, since one possible use is to prevent two clients on the same machine from talking to the server at the same time. This implies that SO_REUSEADDR is not set for the socket.

A TCP/IP Client Using IO::Socket

Again, we can use the IO::Socket module to create the same client in a simpler fashion, avoiding the need to convert the hostname to a packed Internet address with inet_aton and setting autoflush:

```
#!/usr/bin/perl
# tcpioinetclient.pl
use warnings;
use strict;

use IO::Socket;

my $host = 'localhost';
my $port = 4444;

my $server = IO::Socket->new(
    Domain   => PF_INET,
    Proto    => 'tcp',
    PeerAddr => $host,
    PeerPort => $port,
);
die "Connect failed: $!\n" unless $server;

# communicate with the server
print "Client connected.\n";
print "Server says: ", scalar(<$server>);
print $server "Hello from the client!\n";
print "Server says: ", scalar(<SERVER>);
print $server "And goodbye!\n";
print "Server says: ", scalar(<SERVER>);
close $server;
```

As with the server, we can also eliminate the `Domain` argument by using the `IO::Socket::INET` module directly:

```
my $server = new IO::Socket::INET(
    Proto     => 'tcp',
    PeerAddr => $host,
    PeerPort => $port,
);
```

In fact, if we use `IO::Socket::INET`, we can omit the protocol too and combine the address and port together. This gives us a single argument, which we can pass without a leading name:

```
my $server = new IO::Socket::INET("$host:$port");
```

This one-argument version only works for creating INET TCP clients, since all other uses of the `IO::Socket` modules require at least one other argument. Fortunately, creating an INET TCP client is a common enough requirement that it's still a useful shortcut.

Reading and Writing TCP/IP Sockets

Socket filehandles that represent the ends of a TCP connection are trivial to use for input and output. Since TCP streams data, we can read and write it in bytes and characters, just as we do with any normal filehandle:

```
# send something to the remote socket
print SOCKET "Send something to the other end\n";

# get something back
my $message = <SOCKET>;
```

As we mentioned in the previous examples, Perl buffers IO by default, since the message will only reach the client as we fill the buffer and force a flush. For that reason, we need to either use the `syswrite` function or set `autoflush`ing to 1 after selecting our handle:

```
select SOCKET; $| = 1; select STDOUT;
```

Or:

```
SOCKET->autoflush(1);
```

The `IO::Socket` module automatically sets `autoflush` on socket filehandles that it creates, so we don't have to worry about this when we use it. However, autoflushing is not the same as unbuffered, so if we wanted to send individual key presses in real time, we might also want to set the `TCP_NODELAY` option as an additional measure. (From Perl 5.8 onwards, we could also remove the buffering layer.)

We can use `send` and `recv` to send messages on TCP connections, but we don't usually want to—the whole point of a streaming socket is that it is not tied to discrete messages. These functions are more useful (indeed, necessary) on UDP sockets. On a TCP connection, their use is identical—except that we do not need to specify a destination or source address since TCP connections, being connection oriented, supply this information implicitly.

Determining Local and Remote Addresses

We occasionally might care about the details of either the local or the remote addresses of a connection. To find our own address, we can use the `Sys::Hostname` module, which we cover at the end of the chapter. To find the remote address, we can use the `getpeername` function. This function returns a packed address `sockaddr` structure, which we will need to unpack with `unpack_sockaddr_in`:

```
my ($port, $ip) = unpack_sockaddr_in(getpeername CONNECTION);
print "Connected to: ", inet_ntoa($ip), ", port $port\n";
```

We can use this information for a number of purposes, for example, keeping a connection log or rejecting network connections based on their IP address:

```
# reject connections outside the local network
inet_ntoa($ip) !~ /^192\.168\.1\./ and close CONNECTION;
```

A quirk of the socket API is that there is no actual "reject" capability—the only way to reject a connection is to accept it and then close it, which is not elegant but gets the job done. This does open the possibilities of Denial of Service (DoS) attacks though, and care needs to be taken to protect against this, for example, by limiting the number of new connections accepted over a period of time.

The IO::Socket::INET module also provides methods to return the local and remote address of the socket:

```
# find local connection details
my $localaddr = $connection->sockaddr;
my $localhost = $connection->sockhost;
my $localport = $connection->sockport;

# find remote connection details
my $remoteaddr = $connection->peeraddr;
my $remotehost = $connection->peerhost;
my $remoteport = $connection->peerport;
```

As with other methods of the IO::Socket::INET module, unpacking the port number and IP address is done for us, as is automatic translation back into an IP address, so we can do IP-based connection management without the use of unpack_sockaddr_in or inet_ntoa:

```
# reject connections outside the local network
$remoteaddr =~ /^192.168.1/ and close CONNECTION
```

We can also reject by host name, which can be more convenient, but which can also be unreliable because it may require DNS lookups on which we cannot necessarily rely. The only way to verify that a host name is valid is to use gethostbyname on the value returned by peerhost and then check the returned IP address (or possibly addresses) to see if one matches the IP address returned by peeraddr. Comparing both forward and reverse name resolutions is a good security practice to employ. See the end of the chapter and the discussion on the host functions for more details.

UDP Clients and Servers

Unigram Data Protocol, or UDP, provides a nonguaranteed transmission protocol for use in applications where data integrity is not required (or can be handled by the application). This makes UDP a much lighter protocol than TCP, which must maintain state in order to handle retransmissions. UDP servers frequently make use of broadcasts to provide the same information to many clients at once without needing to maintain details of each client receiving the information. As its name suggests, UDP is not suitable for streaming information (which implies a consistent and ordered transfer of information) and instead communicates discrete packets called datagrams.

UDP may not seem terribly useful, but there are applications where it has clear advantages over the more complex TCP protocol. The Network Time Protocol, or NTP, is a typical example of the use of UDP. Each time update can be transferred as an individual packet of information, so packet ordering is not important, and it is not critical if a client misses a packet—it can run on its own clock until the next time it receives a packet.

A Simple UDP Server

Here is an example of a simple INET UDP server, written using Perl's built-in socket functions.
It is similar to the TCP server, creating a server socket and binding it, but it differs in that we don't
listen to it (that call is restricted to stream and sequential packet sockets):

```perl
#!/usr/bin/perl
# udpinetserv.pl
use warnings;
use strict;

use Socket;

my $proto = getprotobyname('udp');
my $port = 4444;

# Create 'sockaddr_in' structure to listen to the given port
# on any locally available IP address
my $servaddr = sockaddr_in($port, INADDR_ANY);

# Create a socket for listening on
socket SERVER, PF_INET, SOCK_DGRAM, $proto
    or die "Unable to create socket: $!";

# bind the socket to the local port and address
bind SERVER, $servaddr or die "Unable to bind: $!";

# now receive and answer messages
print "Server running on port $port...\n";
my $message;
while (my $client = recv SERVER, $message, 1024, 0) {
    my ($port, $ip) = unpack_sockaddr_in($client);
    my $host = gethostbyaddr($ip, AF_INET);
    print "Client $host:$port sent '$message' at ", scalar(localtime), "\n";
    send SERVER, "Message '$message' received", 0, $client;
}
```

The key difference with this server is that because UDP is connectionless, we do not generate
new filehandles with accept and then communicate over them. Instead, we read and write messages directly using the send and recv functions. Each of those functions takes optional flags (which
we did not use, hence the argument of 0 on both calls), and they are documented in the operating
system manual pages:

```
> man 2 recv
> man 2 send
```

Every message we receive comes with the sender's address attached. When we retrieve a message with recv, we get the remote address of the client (as a sockaddr_in structure for INET servers
or a sockaddr_un structure for Unix domain ones), which we can feed directly to the send function to
return a response.

A UDP Server Using IO::Socket

Again, we can use the IO::Socket module to do the same thing in a clearer way:

```perl
#!/usr/bin/perl
# udpioinetserv.pl
use warnings;
use strict;
```

```perl
use IO::Socket;

my $port = 4444;

my $server = new IO::Socket(
    Domain    => PF_INET,
    LocalPort => $port,
    Proto     => 'udp',
);

die "Bind failed: $!\n" unless $server;

print "Server running on port $port...\n";
my $message;
while (my $client = $server->recv($message, 1024, 0)) {
    my ($port, $ip) = unpack_sockaddr_in($client);
    my $host = gethostbyaddr($ip, AF_INET);
    print "Client $host:$port sent '$message' at ", scalar(localtime), "\n";
    $server->send("Message '$message' received", 0, $client);
}
```

The send and recv methods of IO::Socket are simply direct interfaces to the functions of the same name, so the client address passed to the send method is a sockaddr_in (or sockaddr_un, in the Unix domain) structure. We'll cover both send and recv in more depth shortly.

A Simple UDP Client

Whereas TCP clients create a dedicated connection to a single host with each socket, a UDP client can broadcast packets to any host it wishes with the same socket. Consequently, we do not use connect but use send and recv immediately on the created socket:

```perl
#!/usr/bin/perl
#udpinetclient.pl
use warnings;
use strict;

use Socket;

my $proto = getprotobyname('udp');
my $host  = inet_aton('localhost');
my $port  = 4444;

# Create a socket for sending & receiving on
socket CLIENT, PF_INET, SOCK_DGRAM, $proto
    or die "Unable to create socket: $!";

# Create 'sockaddr_in' structure to connect to the given
# port on the IP address for the remote host
my $servaddr = sockaddr_in($port, $host);

# communicate with the server
send CLIENT, "Hello from client", 0, $servaddr or die "Send: $!\n";
my $message;
recv CLIENT, $message, 1024, 0;
print "Response was: $message\n";
```

The UDP socket is free to communicate with any other UDP client or server on the same network. In fact, we can bind and listen to a UDP socket and use it as a client to send a message to another server as well.

A UDP Client Using IO::Socket

The IO::Socket version of this client is as follows:

```perl
#!/usr/bin/perl
# udpioinetclient.pl
use warnings;
use strict;

use IO::Socket;

my $host = 'localhost';
my $port = 4444;

my $client = new IO::Socket(
    Domain   => PF_INET,
    Proto    => 'udp',
);

die "Unable to create socket: $!\n" unless $client;

my $servaddr = sockaddr_in($port, inet_aton($host));
$client->send("Hello from client", 0, $servaddr)
    or die "Send: $!\n";
my $message;
$client->recv($message, 1024, 0);
print "Response was: $message\n";
```

We can also use IO::Socket::INET directly and omit the Domain argument:

```perl
my $client = new IO::Socket::INET(Proto => 'udp');
```

Unfortunately, because the send and recv methods are direct interfaces to the send and recv functions, the recipient address is still a sockaddr_in structure, and we have to do the same contortions to provide send with a suitable addressee that we do for the built-in function version. This aside, IO::Socket still makes writing UDP clients simpler, if not quite as simple as writing TCP clients.

UDP Broadcasts

One of the key benefits of UDP is that we can broadcast with it. In fact, broadcasting is trivially easy to do, as it simply involves sending messages to the broadcast address of the network we want to communicate with. For the 192.168 network, the broadcast address is 192.168.255.255:

```perl
my $port = 444;
my $broadcast = '192.168.255.255';
my $broadcastaddr = ($port, inet_aton($broadcast));
```

The special address 255.255.255.255 may therefore be used to broadcast to any local network. The prepacked version of this address is given the symbolic name INADDR_BROADCAST by the Socket and IO::Socket modules:

```perl
$udpsocket->send("Hello Everybody", 0, INADDR_BROADCAST);
```

Standard UDP makes no provision for narrowing the hosts to which a broadcast is sent—everything covered by the broadcast address will get the message. An enhancement to UDP, called Multicast UDP, provides for selected broadcasting, subscribers, and other enhancements to the standard UDP protocol. However, it is more complex to configure and requires multicast-aware routers and gateways if broadcasts are to travel beyond hosts on the immediate local network. The `IO::Socket::Multicast` module found on CPAN provides a programming interface to this protocol.

Unix Domain Clients and Servers

Unix domain sockets are the other type of socket that we can create. Whereas Internet domain sockets allow remote communications via networking, Unix domain sockets work through the local filing system. This restricts communications to local processes, but they otherwise behave in a similar manner to Internet domain sockets. When we only want to communicate locally, the absence of network support makes this a lighter-weight implementation, with correspondingly higher performance, than making a network connection to `localhost`. The advantage is that we can write substantially the same application code to use a socket and largely ignore the underlying type except when we need to make a distinction.

Of course, as their name implies, a potential drawback of Unix domain sockets is that they may not be supported on non-Unix operating systems.

A Simple Unix Domain Server

Writing an application to use a Unix domain socket is almost identical to writing it to use an INET socket:

```perl
#!/usr/bin/perl
# unixserv.pl
use warnings;
use strict;

use Socket;

my $file = '/tmp/unixserv_socket';

# Create 'sockaddr_un' structure to listen the local socket
my $servaddr = sockaddr_un($file);

# remove an existing socket file (if present)
unlink $file;
# Create a socket for listening on
socket SERVER, PF_UNIX, SOCK_STREAM, 0
    or die "Unable to create socket: $!";
# bind the socket to the local socket
bind SERVER, $servaddr or die "Unable to bind: $!";

# listen to the socket to allow it to receive connection requests
# allow up to 10 requests to queue up at once.
listen SERVER, 10;

# now accept connections
print "Server running on file $file...\n";
while (accept CONNECTION, SERVER) {
    select CONNECTION; $| = 1; select STDOUT;
    print "Client connected at", scalar(localtime), "\n";
```

```
    print CONNECTION "You're connected to the server!\n";
    while (<CONNECTION>) {
        print "Client says: $_";
    }
    close CONNECTION;
    print "Client disconnected\n";
}
```

First, we create a socket, but now we make it a Unix domain socket by specifying PF_UNIX for the socket domain. We also do not specify a protocol—unlike INET sockets, Unix domain sockets do not care about the protocol ahead of time—so instead we give it a value of 0.

Before we create the socket, we clear away the file name created, if any, by the previous incarnation of the server; otherwise, we may not be able to create the new socket. The address for bind still needs to be converted into a form it will accept, but since we are converting a Unix domain address (a file name), we use sockaddr_un rather than sockaddr_in. Other than these changes, the server is identical.

A Unix Domain Server Using IO::Socket

The IO::Socket implementation of this server is similarly changed in only the barest details from the INET version. One important, but perhaps not obvious, difference is that an explicit Listen argument must be given to the new method for the socket to be bound and listened to. Without this, the server will generate an "invalid argument" error from accept. This is not the case with INET sockets, though we can specify a Listen argument if we want.

```perl
#!/usr/bin/perl
# iounixserv.pl
use warnings;
use strict;

use IO::Socket;

my $file = '/tmp/unixserv_socket';

# remove previous socket file, if present
unlink $file;
my $server = IO::Socket->new(
    Domain    => PF_UNIX,
    Type      => SOCK_STREAM,
    Local     => $file,
    Listen    => 5,
);

die "Could not bind: $!\n" unless $server;

print "Server running on file $file...\n";
while (my $connection = $server->accept) {
    print $connection "You're connected to the server!\n";
    while (<$connection>) {
        print "Client says: $_\n";
    }
    close $connection;
}
```

A Simple Unix Domain Client

The Unix domain version of the client is also almost identical to its INET counterpart:

```perl
#!/usr/bin/perl
# unixclient.pl
use warnings;
use strict;

use Socket;

my $file = '/tmp/unixserv_socket';

# Create 'sockaddr_un' structure to connect to the given
# port on the IP address for the remote host
my $servaddr = sockaddr_un($file);

# Create a socket for connecting on
socket SERVER, PF_UNIX, SOCK_STREAM, 0
    or die "Unable to create socket: $!";

# bind the socket to the local socket
connect SERVER, $servaddr or die "Unable to connect: $!";

# enable autoflush
select SERVER; $| = 1; select STDOUT;

# communicate with the server
print "Client connected.\n";
print "Server says: ", scalar(<SERVER>);
print SERVER "Hello from the client!\n";
print SERVER "And goodbye!\n";
close SERVER;
```

Again, we create a socket in the Unix domain and specify a protocol of 0. We provide connect with a Unix domain address compiled by sockaddr_un and connect as before. Together, this server and client operate identically to their INET counterparts—only they do it without consuming network resources. The only drawback is that a remote client cannot connect to our Unix domain–based server. Of course, in some cases, we might actually want that, for security purposes, for example.

A Unix Domain Client Using IO::Socket

The IO::Socket version of this client is

```perl
#!/usr/bin/perl
# iounixclnt.pl
use warnings;
use strict;

use IO::Socket;

my $file = '/tmp/unixserv_socket';

my $server = IO::Socket->new(
    Domain   => PF_UNIX,
    Type     => SOCK_STREAM,
    Peer     => $file,
);
```

```
die "Connect failed: $!\n" unless $server;

# communicate with the server
print "Client connected.\n";
print "Server says: ", scalar(<$server>);
print $server "Hello from the client!\n";
print $server "And goodbye!\n";
close $server;
```

Determining Local and Remote Pathnames

When called on a Unix domain socket, getpeername should return the name of the file being accessed by the other end of the connection. This would normally be the same as the file used for this end, but the presence of symbolic or hard links might give the client a different pathname for its connection than that being used by the server.

```
# get remote path
my $remotepath = unpack_socket_un(getpeername);
```

The IO::Socket::Unix module provides the peerpath and hostpath to return the name of the file used by the local and remote sockets, respectively:

```
my $localpath = $server->hostpath;
my $remotepath = $server->peerpath;
```

Writing Multiplexed Servers

So far in this chapter, we have covered networking fundamentals implementing simple single-client TCP/IP servers that are capable of handling only one connection at a time.

For UDP this isn't too much of a limitation, since UDP works on a message-by-message basis. For TCP it is severely limiting, however, because while one client has the server's attention, connection requests from other clients must wait in the queue until the current client disconnects. If the number of requests exceeds the size of the queue specified by listen, connection requests will begin to bounce.

In order to solve this problem, we need to find a way to multiplex the server's attention, so that it can handle multiple clients at once. Depending on our requirements, we have three options:

- Give the server the ability to monitor all client connections at once. This involves using the select function to provide one loop with the ability to respond to any one of several connections whenever any one of them becomes active. This kind of server is called a nonforking or polling server. Although it is not as elegant or efficient as a forking or threading server, a polling server does have the advantage that it will work on any platform.

- Dedicate a separate process to each connection. This involves the fork function, and it consists of forking a new child process to manage each connection. This kind of server is called a forking server. However, fork may not be available on all platforms. (In particular, use at least Perl 5.8 if planning to use a forking server on a Windows platform.)

- Spawn a new thread to handle each connection. This is a similar idea to the forking server, but is much more resource-efficient, since threads are much more lightweight than separate processes. This kind of server is called a threaded server. However, like the fork function, threads are not always available to us (depending on how Perl was built).

We will consider and give an example of each kind of server in the following section, illustrating the basic similarities and differences between them.

Polling Servers

If we want to write a single process server that can handle multiple connections, we need to use the select function, or more conveniently, the IO::Select module. Both the function and the module allow us to monitor, or poll, a collection of filehandles for events, in particular readiness to be read. Using this information, we can build a list of filehandles and watch for activity on all of them. One of the filehandles is the server socket, and if input arrives on it, we accept the new connection. Otherwise, we read from an existing client's filehandle and do whatever processing we need to, based on what it sends. Developing a selecting server is actually simple, once the basics of the select function are understood.

Neither select nor IO::Select is restricted to network applications, of course. As they use filehandles, they will work on any kind of input or output. While we are primarily interested in networking here, it is worth remembering that we can apply the function and module to local file-handles too, should the need arise.

The select Function

The select function has two completely different uses in Perl. The standard use takes one argument that changes the default output filehandle. The select function we are interested in here has a four-argument version, which takes three bitmasks (read, write, and exceptions) and an optional timeout value. We can use this version of select to continuously scan multiple filehandles simulta-neously for a change in their condition and react whenever one of them becomes available for reading or writing or else enters an error condition. Be aware, however, that at least Perl 5.8 is nec-essary to use select reliably on a Windows platform; while select is a standard operating-system call on Unix, Perl needs to emulate it for Windows, and the emulation provided by older Perls is unfortunately not very useful.

The bitmasks represent the file numbers (also called file descriptors) of the filehandles that we are interested in; the first bit refers to file descriptor 0 (usually STDIN), the second to 1 (STDOUT), and the third to 2 (STDERR). Every new filehandle that we create contains inside it a low-level file descrip-tor, which we can extract with fileno.

Using select effectively first requires extracting the file numbers from the filehandles we want to monitor, which we can do with fileno, then building bitmasks from them, which we can do with vec. The following code snippet creates a mask with bits set for standard input and a handle created with one of the IO:: modules, for example, IO::Socket:

```
my @handles;
$mask = 0;

push @handles, \*STDIN;
vec($mask, fileno(STDIN), 1);
push @handles, $handle;
vec($mask, fileno($handle), 1);
```

We can now feed this mask to select. The @handles array is going to be useful later, but we will disregard it for now.

The select function works by writing into the passed arguments new bitmasks indicating the filehandles that are actually in the requested state; for each bit set to 1, it will be turned off if the handle is not readable or writable, or does not have an exception (meaning an unusual condition, such as out-of-band data for a network socket or data on an error stream such as STDERR), and left at 1 otherwise. To preserve our mask for a later date, we have to assign it to new scalars that select will assign its result to. If we don't want to know about writable file descriptors, which is likely, we can pass undef for that bitmask:

```perl
my ($read, $except) = ($mask, $mask);
while (my $got = select $read, undef, $except) {
    $except?handle_exception:handle_read;
    my ($read, $except) = ($mask, $mask);
}
```

Here handle_read and handle_exception are subroutines, which we have yet to write. We can also write, more efficiently but marginally less legibly, the following:

```perl
while (my $got = select $read = $mask, undef, $except = $mask) {
    $except?handle_exception:handle_read;
}
```

If select is not given a fourth argument for a timeout, it will wait forever for something to happen, at which point the number of interesting file descriptors is returned. If a fourth parameter of a timeout in seconds is specified, $got may contain 0 if the timeout occurred before any input did:

```perl
my ($read, $except);
while ('forever') {
    while (my $got = select $read = $mask, undef, $except = $mask, 60) {
        $except?handle_exception:handle_read;
    }
    print "Nothing happened for an entire minute!\n";
}
```

The only remaining aspect to deal with is how to handle the result returned by select. We can again use vec for this, as well as the @handles array we created earlier but have not until now used. In essence, we scan through the array of filehandles, checking for the bit that represents its file descriptor in the mask. If it is set, that file descriptor is up to something and we react to it:

```perl
handle_read {
    foreach (@handles) {
        vec($read, fileno $_) and read_from_client($_);
    }
}
```

Both select and the IO::Select module are unbuffered operations. That is, they operate directly on file descriptors. This means that buffers are ignored, and buffered IO functions such as print and read may produce inconsistent results; for example, there may be input in the filehandle buffer but not at the system level, so the file descriptor shows no activity when there is in fact data to be read.

Therefore, rather than using print, read, and other buffered IO functions, we must typically use system-level IO functions like sysread and syswrite, which write directly to the file descriptor and avoid the buffers. Simply setting $| = 1 is not adequate, although if we have a PerlIO-enabled Perl, we may be able to remove the buffering layer as noted in Chapter 12. This is not portable to older Perl versions, of course.

An advantage of forked and threaded servers is that they do not need to use system IO, since each process or thread is dedicated to a single filehandle and can choose to wait on it indefinitely.

The IO::Select Module

The IO::Select module provides a friendlier interface to the select function. Instead of building bitmasks, we just create an object and add filehandles to it. The module does the work of constructing the bitmasks for us internally. For example:

```perl
use IO::Select;

my $selector = new IO::Select(\*STDIN, $handle);
```

To scan for active filehandles, we then use the can_read method. The return value is an array of the filehandles (not file descriptors as with select) that are currently in the requested state:

```
my @handles = $selector->can_read;
```

We can now iterate commands for each handle:

```
foreach (@handles) {
    read_from_client $_;
}
```

The counterpart to can_read, can_write, scans for writable filehandles. It is less frequent that we might want to use this, but it can be useful when writing a lot of data over a slow connection. The has_exception method checks for filehandles that are in an exception state (for example, pending out-of-band data for a network socket, or waiting data on an error stream such as STDERR).

To add a new handle, for example, from an accept, we use add:

```
$selector->add($server->accept);
```

Similarly, to remove a handle, we use remove:

```
$selector->remove($handle);
```

These are the primary methods provided by IO::Select. The remaining methods, listed in Table 22-4, are less commonly used but still useful to know about.

Table 22-4. *IO::Select Methods*

Method	Description
exists	Called with a filehandle, this method returns the filehandle if it is present in the select object, and undef if not. For example: `$selector->add($fh) unless $selector->exists($fh);`
handles	Return an array of all the filehandles present in the select object: `my @handles = $selector->handles;`
count	Return the number of filehandles present in the select object: `my $handles = $selector->count;`
bits	Return a bitmask representing the file numbers of the registered filehandles, suitable for passing to the select function: `my $bitmask = $selector->bits;`

select	A class method. Perform a select in the style of the select function but using IO::Select objects rather than bitmasks. Three array references are returned, each holding the handles that were readable, writable, and exceptional (so to speak), respectively. An optional fourth argument containing a timeout in seconds may also be supplied. For example:
	`my ($readers, $writers, $excepts) = select IO::Select(`
	`    $read_selector, $write_selector,`
	`    $except_selector, 60    # timeout`
	`);`
	
	`foreach (@{$readers}) {`
	`    ...`
	`}`
	This function is essentially similar to calling can_read, can_write, and has_exception on three different select objects simultaneously. It mimics the simultaneous polling of these three conditions with three different bitmasks that the select function performs. Note that the same select object can be passed for all three select object arguments.

Armed with this interface, we can now build a simple multiplexing server based on the select function.

A Simple Polling Server

Here is an example of a simple INET polling TCP server. It uses IO::Select to monitor a collection of filehandles and reacts whenever one of them becomes active. The first handle to be monitored is the server socket, and we check for it especially when an input event occurs. If the server socket is active, it means a new connection request has arrived, so we accept it. Otherwise, it means a client has sent us something, so we respond:

```perl
#!/usr/bin/perl
# ioselectserv.pl
use warnings;
use strict;

use IO::Socket;
use IO::Select;

my $serverport = 4444;

# create a socket to listen on
my $server = new IO::Socket(
    Domain    => PF_INET,
    Proto     => 'tcp',
    LocalPort => $serverport,
    Listen    => SOMAXCONN,
);

die "Cannot bind: $!\n" unless $server;

# create a 'select' object and add server fh to it
my $selector = new IO::Select($server);

# stop closing connections from aborting the server
$SIG{PIPE} = 'IGNORE';

# loop and handle connections
print "Multiplex server started on port $serverport...\n";
while (my @clients = $selector->can_read) {
    # input has arrived, find out which handles(s)
    foreach my $client (@clients) {
        if ($client == $server) {
            # it's a new connection, accept it
            my $newclient = $server->accept;
            syswrite $newclient, "You've reached the server\n";

            my $port = $newclient->peerport;
            my $name = $newclient->peerhost;
            print "New client $port:$name\n";
            $selector->add($newclient);
        } else {
            # it's a message from an existing client
            my $port = $client->peerport;
            my $name = $client->peerhost;
            my $message;
            if (sysread $client, $message, 1024) {
                print "Client $name:$port sent: $message";
                syswrite $client, "Message received OK\n";
            } else {
```

```
            $selector->remove($client);
            $client->shutdown(SHUT_RDWR);
            print "Client disconnected\n";    # port, name not defined
        }
      }
    }
}
```

This passable server handles new connections, carries out a simple exchange of messages with a client, and drops them when they disconnect. The select call causes Perl to raise SIGPIPE signals that will cause our application to abort if not trapped. In this case, we choose to ignore them and detect the closing of the connection by getting a read event on a filehandle with no data—sysread returns 0 bytes read. As discussed in Chapter 12, this is the only reliable way to check for closed connections at the system level, as eof does not work on unbuffered connections.

A Simple Forking Server

The alternative to using a single process to read from multiple connections is to use multiple processes to read from a single connection. The following server uses fork to generate an individual child process for each child connection:

```perl
#!/usr/bin/perl
# ioforkserv.pl
use warnings;
use strict;

use IO::Socket;

$| = 1;              # autoflush on
$SIG{CHLD}='IGNORE'; # tell OS to clean up dead children

my $port = 4444;

my $server = IO::Socket->new(
    Domain    => PF_INET,
    Proto     => 'tcp',
    LocalPort => $port,
    Listen    => SOMAXCONN,
    Reuse     => 1,
);

die "Bind failed: $!\n" unless $server;

print "Multiplex server running on port $port...\n";
while (my $connection = $server->accept) {
    my $name = $connection->peerhost;
    my $port = $connection->peerport;
    if (my $pid = fork) {
        close $connection;
        print "Forked child $pid for new client $name:$port\n";
        next;   # on to the next connection
    } else {
        # child process - handle connection
        print $connection "You're connected to the server!\n";
        while (<$connection>) {
            print "Client $name:$port says: $_";
            print $connection "Message received OK\n";
```

```
    }
    print "Client $name:$port disconnected\n";
    $connection->shutdown(SHUT_RDWR);
  }
}
```

When the server receives a connection, it accepts it and then forks a child process. It then closes its copy of the connection since it has no further use for it—the child contains its own copy and can use that. Having no further interest in the connection, the main process returns to the accept call and waits for another connection.

Meanwhile, the child communicates with the remote system over the newly connected socket. When the readline operator returns a false value, an indication of the end-of-file condition, the child determines that the remote end has been closed and shuts down the socket.

If the remote end shuts down without cleanly closing the connection, a SIGPIPE signal is received by the client, which will die because of it, raising a SIGCHLD to the main process in turn. This simple server ignores SIGCHLD so that the whole server does not die as a result—a more sophisticated server would likely handle the signal more elegantly than this, or better, install a handler into $SIG{PIPE} to allow the child process to handle the error condition instead. We could also choose to ignore SIGPIPE signals in the child; the abnormal termination would cause the child process to end anyway. (A more sophisticated server would also reap the exit statuses of finished children with wait or waitpid, as covered in the previous chapter.)

Because each connection communicates with a separate child process, each connection can coexist with all the others. The main process, freed from the responsibility of handling all the communication duty, is free to accept more connections, allowing multiple clients to communicate with the server simultaneously.

A Simple Threaded Server

The alternative to forking processes is to use threads. Like forking, threads may or may not be available on our platform, so which we use may be as much a matter of circumstance as choice. (Instructions on how to build a thread-capable Perl are included in Chapter 1.)

Assuming we do have threads, we can write a multiplexed server along very similar lines to the forking server. The threaded version is, however, simpler, as well as considerably less resource-hungry. Following is a threaded version of the preceding forking server:

```
#!/usr/bin/perl
# iothreadserv.pl
use warnings;
use strict;

BEGIN {
    use Config;
    die "No thread support!\n" unless $Config{usethreads};
}
use threads;
use IO::Socket;

$| = 1;                # autoflush on
$SIG{PIPE}='IGNORE';   # Ignore clients that do not cleanly drop connection

my $port = 4444;

my $server = IO::Socket->new(
    Domain      => PF_INET,
    Proto       => 'tcp',
```

```
        LocalPort => $port,
        Listen    => SOMAXCONN,
        Reuse     => 1,
);

die "Bind failed: $!\n" unless $server;

print "Multiplex server running on port $port...\n";
while (my $connection = $server->accept) {
    my $name = $connection->peerhost;
    my $port = $connection->peerport;

    my $thread = threads->create(\&connection, $connection, $name, $port);
    print "Created thread ",$thread->tid," for new client $name:$port\n";
    $thread->detach;
}

# child thread - handle connection
sub connection {
    my ($connection, $name, $port) = @_;
    $connection->autoflush(1);
    print $connection "You're connected to the server!\n";
    while (<$connection>) {
        print "Client $name:$port says: $_";
        print $connection "Message received OK\n";
    }
    $connection->shutdown(SHUT_RDWR);
}
```

> ■**Note** This implementation is designed for Perl's newer threaded model (from Perl 5.8 onwards). For the older "5.005" threads, we would replace use threads with use Thread and threads->create with new Thread. Otherwise, the code is identical.

When the server receives a connection, it accepts it and spawns a new thread to handle it. We pass the connection filehandle to the new thread on startup. We don't need to lock access to any variables, since each thread cares only about its own connection. We also pass in the name of the host and the port number, though we could have easily passed these inside the thread as well.

The main thread is only concerned with accepting new connections and spawning child threads to deal with them. It doesn't care about what happens to them after that (though again a more complex server probably would), so it uses the detach method to renounce all further interest in the child. Since all the threads run in the same process, we tell the server to ignore SIGPIPE signals; otherwise, an abnormally terminated connection would bring down the whole server. Contrast this to the forked server where SIGPIPE is received by the child process and a SIGCHLD received (and ignored) by the master process.

Threads all run in the same process, so there are no process IDs to manage, no child processes to ignore, and no duplicate filehandles to close. In fact, all the threads have access to all the same filehandles, but since each thread only cares about its own particular filehandle, none of them treads on the others' toes. It's a very simple design and it works remarkably well.

Getting Network Information

All systems have network information configured locally (unless, of course, they are diskless workstations, in which case their configuration was loaded from the network and stored in memory). This information includes things like host names, IP addresses, and network services.

General information about addresses (both hostnames and resolved IPs), networks, services, and protocols can usually be accessed through a standard suite of operating system functions to which Perl provides a direct mapping. For finding the name of our own system (which is more complex than it might at first appear), we can use the Sys::Hostname module.

Hostname queries may also make use of name resolution services like DNS and NIS/NIS+, as well as local configuration files. This is because they use the underlying operating system calls to do the actual work rather than attempting to parse local configuration files. Not only does this make them more portable, but also it allows them to work with both local and remote hostnames.

A lot of the functions detailed here, particularly for hosts and networks, are wrapped and made easier to use by the utility functions inet_aton and inet_ntoa, covered in the section "Sockets" earlier in the chapter. The IO::Socket module further abstracts the details of service, protocol, and network configuration from the user; in these cases, we may be able to avoid actually calling any of these functions directly.

System Network Configuration

All networked systems hold information about hosts, services, networks, and protocols. Unix systems keep this information in a set of specially formatted files in the /etc directory, while Windows NT/2000/XP stores them under a directory similar to \WinNT\system32\drivers\etc:

Hosts	/etc/hosts
Networks	/etc/networks
Services	/etc/services
Protocols	/etc/protocols

To extract information from these files, Unix defines a standard set of C library functions, analogues of which are available within Perl as built-in functions. Because Perl tries to be a platform-independent language, many of these functions also work on other systems such as Windows or VMS, though they don't always read the same files or formats as the Unix equivalents.

Perl provides no fewer than 20 built-in functions for making inquiries of the system network configuration. They are divided into four groups of five, for hosts, networks, services, and protocols, respectively. Each group contains three functions for getting, resetting, and closing the related network information file, plus two functions for translating to and from the name of the host, network, service, or protocol from its native value. The following table summarizes all 20 functions (those marked with * are not supported on Windows platforms, and many applications will not run because of their use):

	Read	Reset	Close	From Name	To Name
Hosts	gethostent	sethostent	endhostent*	gethostbyname	gethostaddr
Networks	getnetent	setnetent	endnetent*	getnetbyname	getnetbyaddr
Services	getservent	setservent	endservent*	getservbyname	getservbyport
Protocols	getprotoent	setprotoent	endprotoent*	getprotobyname	getprotobynumber*

Perl's versions of these functions are smart and pay attention to the contexts in which they are called. If called in a scalar context, they return the name of the host, network, service, or protocol. For example:

```
# find the service assigned to port 80 (it should be 'http')
my $protocol = getprotobyname('tcp');
my $servicename = getservbyport(80, $protocol);
```

The only exception to this is the -name functions, which return the other logical value for the network information being queried—the IP address for hosts and networks, the port number for services, and the protocol number for protocols:

```
# find out what port this system has 'http' assigned to
my $httpd_port = getservbyname('http', $protocol);
```

Called in a list context, each function returns a list of values that varies according to the type of information requested. We can process this list directly, for example:

```
#!/usr/bin/perl
# listserv.pl
use warnings;
use strict;

while (my ($name, $aliases, $port, $proto) = getservent) {
    print "$name\t$port/$proto\t$aliases\n";
}
```

Alternatively, we can use one of the four Net:: family modules written for the purpose of making these values easier to handle. Each module overrides the original Perl built-in function with a new object-oriented version that returns an object, with methods for each value:

```
#!/usr/bin/perl
# listobjserv.pl
use warnings;
use strict;

use Net::servent;

while (my $service = getservent) {
    print 'Name    : ', $service->name, "\n";
    print 'Port No: ', $service->port, "\n";
    print 'Protocol: ', $service->proto, "\n";
    print 'Aliases: ', join(', ', @{$service->aliases}), "\n\n";
}
```

These four modules all accept an optional fields argument that imports a variable for each part of the returned list. For the Net::servent module, the variables are the subroutines prefixed with s_, so the alternative way of writing the preceding is this:

```
#!/usr/bin/perl
# listfldserv.pl
use warnings;
use strict;

use Net::servent qw(:FIELDS);

while (my $service = getservent) {
    print 'Name    : ', $s_name, "\n";
    print 'Port No: ', $s_port, "\n";
```

```
    print 'Protocol: ', $s_proto, "\n";
    print 'Aliases: ', join(', ', @s_aliases), "\n\n";
}
```

Importing the variables still overrides the core functions, however. We can get them back by prefixing them with CORE::, as in the following:

```
($name, $aliases, $proto) = CORE::getprotobyname($name_in);
```

Alternatively, we can gain access to the object methods without the overrides by passing an empty import list:

```perl
#!/usr/bin/perl
# listcorserv.pl
use warnings;
use strict;

use Net::servent ();

while (my $service = Net::servent::getservent) {
    print 'Name    : ', $service->name, "\n";
    print 'Port No: ', $service->port, "\n";
    print 'Protocol: ', $service->proto, "\n";
    print 'Aliases: ', join(', ', @{$service->aliases}), "\n\n";
}
```

We will cover each of the four kinds of network information in a little more detail in the following sections.

Hosts

Host information consists of an IP address followed by a primary name and possibly one or more aliases. On a Unix server, this is defined in the /etc/hosts file, of which a semitypical example might be the following:

```
127.0.0.1       localhost   localhost.localdomain   myself
192.168.1.10    borahorzagobachul.culture.gal       horza
192.168.1.102   sleepersevice.culture.gal           sleeper
192.168.1.103   littlerascal.culture.gal            rascal
192.168.1.1     hub.chiark.culture.gal      hub     chiark
```

Host information is also available via DNS, NIS, NIS+, files, and a number of other name resolution protocols; the gethostent, gethostbyname, and gethostbyaddr functions will all use these automatically if they are configured on the system.

gethostent

Whatever the eventual origin of the information, each definition (or "entry," hence gethostent) comprises an IP address, a primary name, and a list of aliases. The gethostent function retrieves one of these in turn from the local host configuration, starting from the first:

```perl
#!/usr/bin/perl
# listhost.pl
use warnings;
use strict;

while (my ($name, $aliases, $type, $length, @addrs) = gethostent) {
    print "$name\t[$type]\t$length\t$aliases\n";
}
```

The output of this program consists of lines resembling the following, one for each host found:

```
www.alpha-complex.com   [2]     4         computer.alpha-complex.com alpha-complex.com
```

Here the name and aliases are as listed previously in the example hosts file. The type and length are the address type (2, or AF_INET, for Internet addresses, which is in fact the only supported type) and length (4 for IPv4 and 16 for IPv6). The format of the address or addresses is a packed string of 4 bytes (or octets) describing the IP address. To get a string representation, we need to process it with unpack or use the Socket module's inet_ntoa subroutine, which we'll come back to in a moment or two.

If gethostent is called in a scalar context, it instead just returns the name:

```perl
#!/usr/bin/perl
# listhostnames.pl
use warnings;
use strict;

my @hosts;
while (my $name = gethostent) {
    push @hosts, $name;
}
print "Hosts: @hosts\n";
```

endhostent

gethostent resembles the opendir and readdir directory functions, except that the open happens automatically and there is no filehandle that we get to see. However, Perl does keeps a filehandle open internally, so if we only want to pass partway through the defined hosts, we should close that filehandle with

```
endhostent;
```

If the resolution of the request involves a network lookup to a remote DNS or NIS server, endhostent will also close down the resulting network connection.

sethostent

We can also carry out the equivalent of rewinddir with the sethostent function:

```
sethostent 1;
```

When querying the local host file, this rewinds to the start of the file again. If we are making network queries, this tells the operating system to reuse an existing connection if one is already established. More specifically, it tells the operating system to open and maintain a TCP connection for queries rather than use a one-off UDP datagram for the query. In this case, we can shut down the TCP connection with

```
sethostent 0;
```

Rather than scanning host names one by one, we can do direct translations between name and IP address with the gethostbyname and gethostbyaddr functions. Both these functions will cause the operating system to make queries of any local and remote name resolution services configured.

gethostbyaddr, gethostbyname

In list context, both functions return a list of values like gethostent. In scalar context, they return the name (for gethostbyaddr) or address (for gethostbyname) :

```
($name, $aliases, $type, $length, @addrs) = gethostbyname($name);
$name = gethostbyaddr($addr, $addrtype);
$addr = gethostbyname($name);
```

In the event that the host could not be found, both functions return undef (or an empty list, in list context) and set $? (not, incidentally, $!) to indicate the reason. We can use $? >> 8 to get a real exit code that we can assign to $!, however (see Chapter 16 for more on this and the Errno module).

The addrtype parameter of gethostbyaddr specifies the address format for the address supplied. There are two formats we are likely to meet, both of which are defined as symbolic constants by the Socket module:

AF_INET	Internet (IPv4) address
AF_INET6	IPv6 Internet address

In all cases, the addresses returned (and in the case of gethostbyaddr, the address we supply) are in packed form. This isn't (except by sheer chance) printable, and it isn't very convenient to pass as a parameter either. We can use pack and unpack to convert between "proper" integers and addresses (the following example is for IPv4 or AF_INET addresses, on a little-endian machine):

```
$addr = pack('C4', @octets);
@octets = unpack('C4', $addr);
```

More conveniently, we can make use of the inet_aton and inet_ntoa functions from the Socket module to convert between both addresses and hostnames and IP strings of the form n1.n2.n3.n4. For example, this short script looks up and prints out the IP addresses for the hostnames given on the command line:

```perl
#!/usr/bin/perl
# hostlookup.pl
use warnings;
use strict;

use Socket qw(/inet/);

die "Give me a hostname!\n" unless @ARGV;

while (my $lookup = shift @ARGV) {
    my ($name, $aliases, $type, $length, @addrs) = gethostbyname($lookup);
    if ($name) {
        foreach (@addrs) {
            $_ = inet_ntoa($_);
        }
        if ($name eq $lookup) {
            print "$lookup has IP address: @addrs\n";
        } else {
            print "$lookup (real name $name) has IP address: @addrs\n";
        }
    } else {
        print "$lookup not found\n";
    }
}
```

We could use this script like this:

```
> perl hostlookup.pl localhost rascal hub chiark
```

And we would get (assuming the preceding host file example and no network lookups) this output:

```
localhost has IP address: 127.0.0.1
rascal (real name rascal.culture.gal) has IP address: 192.168.1.103
hub (real name hub.chiark.culture.gal) has IP address: 192.168.1.1
chiark (real name hub.chiark.culture.gal) has IP address: 192.168.1.1
```

Likewise, to look up a host by address:

```
$localhostname = gethostbyaddr(inet_aton('127.0.0.1'));
```

Or to find the true name, using a hostname lookup:

```
$localhostname = gethostbyaddr(inet_aton('localhost'));
```

While we're examining this particular example, it is worth noting that for finding the hostname of our own system we are better off using the Sys::Hostname module, described later in the chapter.

One word of warning—be aware that both gethostbyname and gethostbyaddr reset the pointer used by gethostent in the same way that sethostent does, so they cannot be used in a loop of gethostent calls.

The Net::hostent Module

The object-oriented override module for the host query functions is Net::hostent. It provides both an object-oriented alternative and, on request, a collection of imported scalar variables that are set by each request. Strangely, however, it only provides an object-oriented interface for gethostbyname and gethostbyaddr, not gethostent, so to avoid resetting the pointer of gethostent we have to take a two-stage approach. Here is a short program to list all hosts in the object-oriented style:

```perl
#!/usr/bin/perl
# listobjhost.pl
use warnings;
use strict;

use Net::hostent;
use Socket qw(inet_ntoa);

my @hosts;
while (my $host = gethostent) {
    push @hosts, $host;
}

while (my $host = shift @hosts) {
    $host = gethostbyname($host);
    print 'Name      : ', $host->name, "\n";
    print 'Type      : ', $host->addrtype, "\n";
    print 'Length    : ', $host->length, " bytes\n";
    print 'Aliases   : ', join(', ', @{$host->aliases}), "\n";
    print 'Addresses: ', join(', ', map {inet_ntoa($_)}
        @{$host->addr_list}), "\n\n";
}
```

And again, using variables:

```perl
#!/usr/bin/perl
# listfldhost.pl
use warnings;
use strict;
```

```perl
use Net::hostent qw(:FIELDS);
use Socket qw(inet_ntoa);

my @hosts;
while (my $host = CORE::gethostent) {
    push @hosts, $host;
}

while (my $host = shift @hosts) {
    $host = gethostbyname($host);
    print 'Name      : ', $h_name, "\n";
    print 'Type      : ', $h_addrtype, "\n";
    print 'Length    : ', $h_length, " bytes\n";
    print 'Aliases   : ', join(', ', @h_aliases), "\n";
    print 'Addresses: ', join(', ', map{inet_ntoa($_)} @h_addr_list), "\n\n";
}
```

If we only want to import some variables, we can pass them directly in the import list, but we must also import the overrides we want to use if so:

```perl
use Net::hostent qw($h_name @h_aliases @h_addr_list gethostent);
```

We use the CORE:: prefix here partly to remind ourselves that gethostent is not being overridden and partly to protect ourselves in case a future version of the Net::hostent module extends to cover it.

gethostbyname and gethostbyaddr also return objects. gethostbyaddr automatically makes use of the Socket module to handle conversions, so we can supply an IP address like 127.0.0.1 without needing to worry about whether it will be understood. In addition, the Net::hostent module supplies a shorthand subroutine, gethost, which calls either gethostbyname or gethostbyaddress, depending on whether its argument looks like an IP address or a hostname.

Networks

Networks are simply groups of IP addresses that have been assigned a network name. For example, for the host file example given earlier, 127 and 192.168.1 are potential groupings that may be given a network:

```
loopback    127.0.0.0
localnet    192.168.1.0
```

getnetent

Networks are therefore essentially very much like hosts, with getnetent the equivalent of gethostent:

```perl
($name, $aliases, $type, $netaddr) = getnetent;
```

Or, in scalar context:

```perl
$netname = getnetent;
```

All these values have the same meanings as the same values returned by gethostent et al., but only for networks, of course. The $netaddr is now an IP address for the network, and unlike hosts, where there is only one, this refers to many.

```perl
use Socket qw(/inet/);

$netip = inet_ntoa($netaddr);
$netaddr = inet_aton('192.168');
```

endnetent, setnetent

The setnetent function resets the pointer in the network information file to the start or (in the case of NIS+ lookups) preserves an existing network connection if one happens to be active. Like sethostent, it takes a Boolean flag as a parameter and switches between TCP and UDP connections for network requests. For file-based access, using getnetbyname or getnetbyaddr also resets the pointer of getnetent in the local network file. The endnetent function closes the network information file or network connection.

getnetbyaddr, getnetbyname

getnetbyname and getnetbyaddr work similarly to their host counterparts, except for network addresses. Like gethostbyname, getnetbyname will do a remote lookup if the host network configuration is set to do that, although this is considerably rarer.

```
$netaddr = getnetbyname('mynetwork');
$netname = getnetbyaddr('192.168.1', AF_INET);   # from 'Socket'
```

The Net::netent Module

The object-oriented override module for the network query functions is Net::netent. Like Net::hostent, it does not override getnetent, only getnetbyaddr and getnetbyname. Since both these functions reset the pointer of getnetent, we have to collect names (or addresses) first, then run through each one with getnetbyname or getnetbyaddr. Here's a script that dumps out network information in the same vein as the object-oriented host script earlier:

```perl
#!/usr/bin/perl
# getobjnet.pl
use warnings;
use strict;

use Net::netent;
use Socket qw(inet_ntoa);

my @nets;
while (my $net = CORE::getnetent) {
    push @nets, $net;
}
while (my $net = shift @nets) {
    $net = getnetbyname($net);
    print 'Name     : ', $net->name, "\n";
    print 'Type     : ', $net->addrtype, "\n";
    print 'Aliases  : ', join(', ', @{$net->aliases}), "\n";
    print 'Addresses: ', $net->addr_list, "\n\n";
}
```

Note that this script will happily return nothing at all if we don't have any configured networks, which is quite possible. The field-based version of this script is as follows:

```perl
#!/usr/bin/perl
# getfldnet.pl
use warnings;
use strict;

use Net::netent qw(:FIELDS);
use Socket qw(inet_ntoa);

my @nets;
while (my $net = CORE::getnetent) {
```

```
    push @nets, $net;
}

while (my $net = shift @nets) {
    $net = getnetbyname($net);
    print 'Name     : ', $n_name, "\n";
    print 'Type     : ', $n_addrtype, "\n";
    print 'Aliases  : ', join(', ', @n_aliases), "\n";
    print 'Addresses: ', $n_net, "\n\n";
}
```

In addition, Net::netent defines the getnet subroutine. This attempts to produce the correct response from whatever is passed to it by calling either getnetbyname or getnetbyaddr depending on the argument. Like gethost, it automatically handles strings that look like IP addresses, so we can say

```
$net = gethost('192.168.1');
print $net->name;   # or $n_name;
```

Network Services

All networked hosts have the ability to service network connections from other hosts in order to satisfy various kinds of requests: anything from a web page to an e-mail transfer. These services are distinguished by the port number that they respond to; web service (HTTP) is on port 80, FTP is on port 21, SMTP (for e-mail) is on port 25, and so on.

Rather than hard-code a port number into applications that listen for network connections, we can instead configure a service, assign it to a port number, and then have the application listen for connections on the service port number. On Unix systems, this association of service to port number is done in the /etc/services file, a typical sampling of which looks like this:

```
tcpmux      1/tcp   # TCP port service multiplexer
ftp-data   20/tcp
ftp        21/tcp
telnet     23/tcp
smtp       25/tcp   mail
time       37/tcp   timserver
time       37/udp   timserver
nameserver 42/tcp   name    # IEN 116
whois      43/tcp   nicname
domain     53/tcp   nameserver    # name-domain server
domain     53/udp   nameserver
finger     79/tcp
www        80/tcp   http    # World Wide Web HTTP
www        80/udp   # Hypertext Transfer Protocol
```

A real services file contains a lot more than this, but this is an indicative sample. We can also define our own services, though on a Unix system they should be at least port 1024 or higher, since many ports lower than this are allocated as standard ports for standard services. Furthermore, only the administrator has the privileges to bind to ports under 1024. For example:

```
myapp    4444/tcp  myserver   # My server's service port
```

getservent

Each entry consists of a primary service name, a port number, and a network protocol, and an optional list of aliases. The getservent function retrieves one of these in turn from the local host configuration, starting from the first. For example, as we showed earlier in the general discussion:

```
#!/usr/bin/perl
# listserv.pl
use warnings;
use strict;

while (my ($name, $aliases, $port, $proto) = getservent) {
    print "$name\t$port/$proto\t$aliases\n";
}
```

Here name, aliases, and port are reasonably self-evident. The protocol is a numeric value describing the protocol number—6 for TCP, 7 for UDP, for example. We can handle this number and convert it to and from a name with the protocol functions such as getprotoent and getprotobynumber, which we will come to in a moment.

endservent, setservent

setservent resets the pointer for the next getservent to the start of the services file, if given a true value. endservent closes the internal filehandle. These are similar to their network and host counterparts, but they are far less likely to open network connections for queries (DNS and NIS do not do this, but NIS+ conceivably might).

getservbyport

Services are related to ports, not addresses, so the function getservbyport returns a list of parameters for the service defined for the named port, or an empty list otherwise. Since ports may be assigned to different services using different network protocols, we also need to supply the protocol we are interested in:

```
my $protocol = getprotobyname('tcp');
my ($name, $aliases, $port, $proto) = getservbyport(80, $protocol);
# or ($name, $aliases, $port, $proto) = getservbyname('http', $protocol);
```

Or, in scalar context, for our user-defined service:

```
my $name = getservbyport(4444, $protocol);
my $port = getservbyname('myserver', $protocol);
```

The Net::servent Module

The object-oriented override module for service queries is Net::servent, and we saw examples of using it in both the object-oriented style and with imported variables earlier. Unlike the host and network modules, Net::servent does override getservent, so we can iterate through services without having to collect names or port numbers into a list first and then run through the result with getservbyname or getservbyport.

In addition, Net::servent defines getserv as a convenience subroutine that maps a passed argument onto either getservbyproto or getservbyname depending on whether the passed argument looks numeric or not.

Network Protocols

Protocols are defined in terms of numbers at the network level—0 for IP, 6 for TCP, 17 for UDP, and so on. These are designated standards defined in RFCs. Locally, these numbers are associated with a user-friendly name, so instead of referring to "protocol number 6," we can say "tcp" instead. For example, here are a few entries from a typical /etc/protocols file on a Unix server:

```
ip        0    IP       # Internet pseudo protocol number
icmp      1    ICMP     # Internet control message protocol
igmp      2    IGMP     # Internet Group Management
ipencap   4    IP-ENCAP # IP encapsulated in IP (officially 'IP')
```

```
tcp       6     TCP     # transmission control protocol
udp      17     UDP     # user datagram protocol
```

This file is not one we are expected to ever add to, although we can create a protocol if we want. We can, however, interrogate it.

getprotoent

We can list the protocol definitions defined for the local system with getprotoent, which works in the familiar way, reading the first entry in the list and then each subsequent entry every time it is called. In scalar context, it returns the protocol name:

```
my $firstprotoname = getprotoent;
```

In list context, it returns a list of values consisting of the primary name for the protocol, the port number, and any aliases defined for it. This short script illustrates how we can use it to dump out all the protocol details defined on the system:

```
#!/usr/bin/perl
# listprot.pl
use warnings;
use strict;

while (my ($name, $aliases, $proto) = getprotoent) {
    print "$proto $name ($aliases)\n";
}
```

endprotent, setprotoent, getprotobyaddr, getprotobyname

endprotoent closes the internal filehandle, and setprotoent resets the pointer for the next entry to be returned by getprotoent to the start of the file if given a true value, as usual. Also as usual, calling getprotobyname and getprotobynumber also resets the pointer. As with their similarly named brethren, getprotobyname and getprotobynumber return the port number and port name, respectively, in a scalar context. For example:

```
my $proto_name = getprotobynumber($proto_number);
```

Or in the reverse direction:

```
my $proto_number = getprotobyname($proto_name);
```

In list context, they return the same values as getprotoent.

The Net::protoent Module

The object-oriented override module for protocols is Net::protoent, which overrides the getprotoent, getprotobyname, and getprotobynumber functions with equivalents that return objects. Here is the object-oriented way of listing protocol information using Net::protoent:

```
#!/usr/bin/perl
# listobjproto.pl
use warnings;
use strict;

use Net::protoent;

while (my $protocol = getprotoent) {
    print "Protocol: ", $protocol->proto, "\n";
    print "Name     : ", $protocol->name, "\n";
    print "Aliases : ", join(', ', @{$protocol->aliases}), "\n\n";
}
```

As with the other Net:: modules that provide object-oriented wrappers for Perl's network information functions, we can also import variables that automatically take on the values of the last call. The equivalent field-based script is

```perl
#!/usr/bin/perl
# listfldproto.pl
use warnings;
use strict;

use Net::protoent qw(:FIELDS);

while (my $protocol = getprotoent) {
    print "Protocol: ", $p_proto, "\n";
    print "Name    : ", $p_name, "\n";
    print "Aliases : ", join(', ', @p_aliases), "\n\n";
}
```

In addition, Net::protoent defines the getproto subroutine as a convenient way to produce a valid response from almost any passed value. Numeric values are passed to getprotobynumber; anything else is presumed to be a name and passed to getprotobyname.

Determining the Local Hostname

Determining the local hostname for a system can sometimes be a tricky problem. First, a system can happily have more than one network interface and therefore more than one name. Second, the means by which the hostname is defined varies wildly from one operating system to another.

If we just want to open a network connection to a service or application (such as a web server) running on the local machine, we can often get away with simply connecting to the local loopback IP address. However, this is not enough if we need to identify ourselves to the application at the other end.

On most Unix platforms, we can execute the hostname command to find the name of the host, or, failing that, use uname -n. Alternatively, we can use the gethostbyname function to try to identify the true name of the local host from one of its aliases. The standard localhost alias should work on any system that has it defined as the hostname for the loopback address in either DNS or the hosts file. Be aware, though, that it may not always return a fully qualified name.

Because of this complex melange of alternative and interlocking approaches, Perl comes with the Sys::Hostname module. This attempts all of the preceding methods and more in turn, with different tests depending on the underlying platform. It provides a single subroutine, hostname, which hides all of these mechanics from us and allows us simply to say the following:

```perl
#!/usr/bin/perl
# hostname.pl
use warnings;
use strict;

use Sys::Hostname;

print "We are: ", hostname, "\n";
```

This will try to produce the correct result on almost any platform (even, interestingly, Symbian's EPOC) and is probably the best solution for both simplicity and portability.

Summary

In this chapter, we covered networking with Perl. We started by explaining how to use the Socket and IO::Socket modules to create network clients and servers. Specifically, we covered

- Using Socket.pm. We covered how to create simple servers and clients that connect and listen to specified sockets. We showed how to do this using TCP, UDP, and Unix domain sockets.
- Using IO::Socket. We repeated every example used previously in the simpler format used with the IO::Socket module.
- Broadcasting with UDP and how to send packets to multiple destinations simultaneously.

Later, we covered how to use forking, threading, and polling to create network servers that can deal with multiple requests from clients. We had examples of each type of server included in the text, which can be adapted to any other projects.

In the last section of this chapter, we looked at retrieving different kinds of network information. We also discussed the following topics:

- Getting host information, including a portable way to discover the local hostname, and how to discover the IP address of a specified hostname and to acquire any aliases it might have
- Getting network information and discovering what host or IP address is part of what network, and whether network names have been defined
- How to discover what network services are available on our system
- How to examine the network protocols available to our system, even though it is very rare to ever update this information

The examples throughout this chapter performed similar tasks in different ways (including how to write the applications in an object-oriented style), and we will now move on to discuss web server programming and various other network services in the following chapter.

CHAPTER 23

■ ■ ■

Unicode, Locale, and Internationalization

There are many different languages in the world, each with its own unique set of characters; grammatical sentence structure; local conventions for the representation of dates, times, and decimal points; and myriad other details. In this chapter, we cover two of the major tools at our disposal for handling different languages and country-specific formats, Unicode and locale.

The Unicode Standard is the result of an attempt to encode all the known symbols in the world, ancient and modern, into a single unified database. Perl provides excellent support for handling Unicode, including an implicit understanding of multibyte characters, commonly known as *wide characters*. Wide characters are necessary because traditional encodings, including Latin 1, the default encoding for the Web as well as Perl source, are designed to fit each character they handle into a single byte, giving only 256 possible characters. Clearly the entire world's symbology is going to need something a little larger. As we discuss Unicode, we will also revisit Perl's support for character encodings and see how to translate Unicode strings to and from other character sets. We will even see how to encode Perl source code.

Localization, abbreviated L10N (because there are ten letters between the "l" and "n"), is concerned with not just the native language of the user of an application, but also where they are in the world—a French speaker can be in France, Belgium, Switzerland, or Canada, to name just a few of the countries where French is spoken. The combination of language and country is called a *locale*, and each locale has different conventions and standard formats for representing quantities like time and currency. By making use of the locale support provided by the operating system, we can write Perl programs that are locale-aware. Perl can automatically make use of some details of a locale to reconfigure the behavior of built-in functions, but we can also query additional details of a locale to discover the words for "yes" and "no" or the name of the local currency. Locale is primarily supported by Unix platforms, but while Windows handles locale differently, it can still be taught to support locale-oriented programs.

We also take a look at internationalization, abbreviated I18N, which takes the concept of locales and adds to it the ability to generate messages for the correct language and, if necessary, country. This is a lot more complex than it might at first seem, since different languages have different ideas about sentence structure, what is single and what is plural, and how the number zero is handled, to name some of the simpler problems that arise. To internationalize an application, we need to create lexicons of messages and message construction routines that are capable of handling all the various different ways even the simplest message needs to be rendered under different languages.

We start off with an examination of character sets. In order to develop software that is aware of alternative character sets, character encodings, or Unicode, it is helpful to know a little about the background of how character sets came to be. From there we can look at the Unicode standard, what it provides, and the problems that it was designed to solve.

A Brief History of Symbols

A collection of distinct characters or symbols is a character repertoire. It is defined by giving a name to each character and associating that name with a visible representation. For many characters, for instance alphanumeric letters, their name when written down is their visible representation, which makes it tricky to draw a distinction. Punctuation is a better example: "~" is "a tilde" and "!" is "an exclamation mark."

On its own, a character repertoire is not something a computer can understand. A *character code* is a numeric value, specifically an integer, associated with a character. Since computers fundamentally only understand numbers, this provides the means to translate each member of a character repertoire into a form that a computer is able to process.

Finally, a *character set* is the combination of these two concepts, a table that maps every character in a character repertoire to a numeric value. Implicitly, it also provides the inverse mapping of every numeric value (in a given range) to a character. It follows from this that every integer counting from zero is a code for a character and so the numeric value associated with a character is also known as its *code position* or *code point*, since it serves as an index for the character set table. For instance, in standard ASCII a capital A has a character code 65, so it is the 66th entry in the character set, counting from zero.

Building Character: ASCII and ISO 8859

Historically, the most established character set was the ASCII standard, a character set represented by numeric codes in the range 0 to 127 and storable in a single byte. This was important, as a byte was the optimum size for 8-bit computers to handle. ISO 8859 later built on ASCII to provide a family of related character sets with codes 0–127 defined identically, and 128–159 explicitly undefined (they do not map to printable characters and are typically used as control characters). Codes 160–255 provided different characters for different language groups, but still in a single byte.

ISO 8859-1, also known as Latin 1, is the default encoding for many applications, including the Web, and is also called Western European. It defines characters suitable for a large number of European countries and has room for a couple of African ones too, but it has no Euro symbol. Other members of the family—there are 16 siblings in all—replace various subsets of Latin 1 with different characters to provide support for other language groups. Some languages, like German, appear more than once (and English is effectively supported in all 16), but different members of the family make different trade-offs between characters and symbols. ISO-8859-15 and ISO 8859-16, the newest members, throw out symbols to make room for more language support.

The ISO 8859 is sufficiently pervasive that it is worth reviewing what it actually contains. Table 23-1 offers the full list of defined character sets.

Table 23-1. *The ISO 8859 Family*

Encoding	Alphabet	Languages
ISO 8859-1	Latin 1	West European: Albanian, Basque, Catalan, Danish, Dutch (partial), English, Faeroese, Finnish (partial), French (partial), German, Icelandic, Irish, Italian, Norwegian, Portuguese, Rhaeto-Romanic, Scottish, Spanish, Kurdish, Swedish African: Afrikaans, Swahili No Euro symbol
ISO 8859-2	Latin 2	Central and Eastern European: Czech, German, Hungarian, Polish, Slovak, Slovenian
ISO 8859-3	Latin 3	South European: Turkish, Maltese, and Esperanto Superceded by Latin 5 for Turkish
ISO 8859-4	Latin 4	North European (Baltic): Estonian, Latvian, Lithuanian, Greenlandic, Sámi

Encoding	Alphabet	Languages
ISO 8859-5	Cyrillic	Russian, Ukranian, Belarusian
ISO 8859-6	Arabic	Arabic (partial)
ISO 8859-7	Greek	Greek (ancient and modern)
ISO 8859-8	Hebrew	Hebrew
ISO 8859-9	Latin 5	Modified Latin 1: added Turkish, no Icelandic
ISO 8859-10	Latin 6	Modified Latin 4 (Nordic): Sámi, Inuit, Icelandic
ISO 8859-11	Thai	Thai
ISO 8859-12	Undefined	Not defined
ISO 8859-13	Latin 7	Baltic Rim: Modified Latin 4/6, more glyphs
ISO 8859-14	Latin 8	Celtic: Gaelic, Breton
ISO 8859-15	Latin 9	Modified Latin 1, includes Euro and all French/Finish letters, but fewer glyphs
ISO 8859-16	Latin 10	South-East European: Albanian, Croatian, Finnish, French, German, Hungarian, Irish Gaelic, Italian, Polish, Romanian, Slovenian

Naturally, this is not the whole story. Windows uses its own standard, for instance, where character sets are known as *code pages*. Of the many available, code page 1252 loosely corresponds to ISO 8859-1, but uses character codes 128–159 to represent special characters (ISO 8859 states that these codes should not represent printable characters).

Meanwhile, elsewhere in the world, languages with character sets totally unrelated to ASCII cannot be represented with any member of the ISO 8859 family. Japanese has several character sets, including ISO 2202, Shift-JIS, and others. Taiwanese uses Big5, Hindi uses ISCII, and so on. All of these character sets have many more than 256 characters, so the character codes must necessarily be bigger than a single byte can encode.

To deal with all these different character sets, the concept of character encodings was invented. Since character codes alone do not tell us what character set they require, the generator of a piece of textual data must include with the data the details of the character set in which it is encoded. For example, a web server does this by including a `Charset:` header with every document it sends to a client, and a client can tell a server what character sets it will accept with an `Accept-Charset:` header. In some cases, character set information can be embedded into text so that the rendering application knows to render one piece of text as Latin 1, another as Greek (ISO 8859-7), and a third as Hirigana, all in the same document. But this is really a makeshift solution, and so a better one was designed—*Unicode*.

Unicode and the Universal Character Set

The modern Unicode Standard is the culmination of two separate efforts to create a true universal character set. The ISO 10646 project defined one single Universal Character Set or UCS. In this scheme, character codes are 32-bit values, subdivided into 65,536 planes of 65,536 characters (16 bits) each. Plane 0, where the top 16 bits are all zero, is known as the Basic Multilingual Plane. It defines the character codes for practically all modern languages, as well as a selection of special characters, sigils, and miscellaneous symbols.

Meanwhile, the first Unicode Standard was published by the Unicode Consortium, an alliance of software developers. It defined not just character codes, but also metadata like the direction of text (left-to-right or right-to-left). Seeing the benefit of synergy, the two standards merged and the Unicode Standard became the definition for all character codes—called *code points* in Unicode terminology—of the Basic Multilingual Plane, Plane 0 of the UCS. For this reason, Unicode is sometimes thought of as a standard for 16-bit character codes, but as we will see, this is not exactly true, because the standard itself only defines an abstract character code and says nothing directly about how that character code should be stored or transmitted.

Blocks and Scripts

Plane 0 is where all the character sets defined by previous standards like the ISO 8859 family end up, and it is itself subdivided into blocks of contiguous characters. Many blocks are 128 or 256 characters in size, but by no means all. For the curious, the complete list is defined in the file `Blocks.txt`, which is located in the `unicode` or `unicore` (from Perl 5.8 onwards) subdirectory within Perl's standard library.

Within a block, Unicode character codes, also sometimes called code points, are defined with the notation U+code where `code` is the character code in hexadecimal. The first block, U+0000 to U+007F, is called *Basic Latin* and corresponds to ASCII. The second, U+0080 to U+00FF, is called *Latin 1 Supplement*, and together with Basic Latin it corresponds to Latin 1. The fact that the numeric value of these codes exactly aligns with ISO 8859-1 is not an accident, as we will see when we come to discuss encoding Unicode.

Unicode and the UCS break the assumption that every code has a character and every character a single code. While blocks are simple contiguous sequences of characters, scripts are an abstract association of related characters that may span more than one block, while only using selected characters from each. To pick a simple example, Unicode defines two blocks as Cyrillic:

```
0400..04FF; Cyrillic
0500..052F; Cyrillic Supplement
```

The first of these blocks corresponds to ISO 8859-5. The second, as its name suggests, provides characters for which there was insufficient room in that standard. While this is convenient for backwards compatibility with 8-bit encodings, it does not allow us to refer to a single collection of character codes as *Cyrillic*.

This problem is solved by *scripts*. A script (here in the sense of a character font, rather than a program) may include characters from several blocks, but it may only include some characters from each. Where two blocks contain encodings for the same character, a script will select a code from just one of them to represent the character.

The Cyrillic script includes most but not all of the codes from the preceding two blocks, plus U+1D2B. The Latin script is a good deal more complex, including characters from many different blocks. By doing this, it provides a consistent and complete definition for Latin alphabets that is not limited by the constraints of the ISO 8859 standard. But the script defines only letters—notably, it does not include numbers or punctuation.

Other scripts include Common, where common symbols reside. Every language represented by ISO 8859 (and others) has a script, and even Braille and Linear B are supported. The file `Scripts.txt` in the `unicode/unicore` directory contains the complete list, as understood by Perl.

While Plane 0 is filling up, vast stretches of empty space in the UCS do not as yet have any kind of character associated with them. They may be assigned in the future, and indeed the work of codifying the world's symbology is not yet complete. This means that character codes we specify may not actually be legal according to the ISO 10646 and Unicode Standards.

The Encoding of Unicode

Since Unicode character codes are 4-digit hexadecimal numbers, we can see that they can be represented by 16-bit values, which is correct assuming that we are currently in Plane 0 of the UCS, where Unicode reigns. But this code is an abstract one, and it does not necessarily mean that all Unicode characters are encoded, recorded, or transmitted as 16-bit values. That's determined by the character encoding. Previously, encodings switched between different character sets. For Unicode, encodings may apply to the same Unicode character codes, but they now determine how those codes are stored and transmitted, and in particular how many bytes for each character are needed to do it.

For many languages, we only need 8 bits to encode each character, as provided by ISO 8859. For others, notably Asian languages, at least 16-bit values are necessary. As a result, there are several encoding schemes available, some fixed length, with all characters taking up the same number of bytes, and some variable length. For instance, the UCS-2 and UCS-4 fixed-length encodings defined by ISO 10646 allow 2-byte and 4-byte character codes, respectively. In UCS-2, a mechanism is defined to switch the current plane to provide access to characters in other planes. UCS-4 provides access to all planes simultaneously, but it is twice as big.

Both UCS-2 and UCS-4 also have the major disadvantage that programs not expecting Unicode character input will completely fail to comprehend text encoded in either standard, since traditionally characters only took up one byte. UTF-8 addresses this issue by defining a variable length encoding where the most common characters are encoded using 1 byte, while less common characters require more. UTF-8 allows for up to six characters for an encoding, although only codes up to 4 bytes long are currently defined.

UTF-8 solves the backwards-compatibility problem by defining character codes for all the characters defined by ISO 8859-1 in the very same positions as the earlier standard. As a result, if a UTF-8-encoded character stream does not include any characters that require an encoding of greater than one byte, it is 100% compatible with Latin 1, and it will be understood by programs expecting single-byte character input. Only if a multibyte character occurs does special action need to be taken.

It is important to remember that UTF-8 is not Unicode, just a particular encoding that is currently the most popular and practical for compatibility reasons. We have already mentioned UCS-2 and UCS-4. Other encodings include the following:

- UTF-16: A variable-length encoding that encodes characters using either 16-bit or 32-bit values. Unlike UTF-8, byte order is significant, and UTF-16LE and UTF-16BE define the big-endian and little-endian versions of this encoding. Alternatively, the Byte-Order-Mark (BOM) value 0xFFFE may be prefixed to define the byte order (since bytes will arrive as 0xFE 0xFF for big-endian UTF-16 and 0xFF 0xFE for little-endian UTF-16).

- UTF-32: A 32-bit encoding that is identical in effect to UCS-4. UTF-32LE and UTF-32BE determine the byte order, or alternatively the BOM, which is FFFE0000 (little endian) or 0000FEFF (big endian).

- UTF-7: A 7-bit encoding for use where the transmission or storage medium is not 8-bit safe. This typically means legacy ASCII-aware infrastructure that predates ISO 8859.

More information on Unicode can be found at http://www.unicode.org. The UTF-8 encoding is described in http://www.ietf.org/rfc/rfc2279.txt.

Unicode in Perl

Having examined Unicode's background, it is time to look at how Perl manages Unicode. The good news is that, as least as of Perl 5.8, Perl intuitively understands Unicode and can transparently handle much of the hard work.

Perl has comprehensive support for Unicode built into the interpreter and is capable of storing wide characters, requiring more than one byte to store their character code, in an internal variable-width format that corresponds to UTF-8. String data is stored as single-byte character codes using the native character encoding when possible, but if Perl encounters a character that cannot be stored in that encoding, the string in which it occurs is transparently and automatically upgraded to a UTF-8 encoded format.

For the most part, we can leave it to Perl to figure out when support for wide characters is necessary, and so we do not need to worry about what form Perl is storing string data internally. However, for the curious, the Unicode data files that Perl uses as the basis of all Unicode knowledge can be found either in a directory under the standard library called unicore in Perl 5.8 onwards or unicode prior to Perl 5.8—on a Unix platform a typical location is /usr/lib/perl5/5.6.1/unicode or /usr/lib/perl5/5.8.5/unicore, while on Windows look for a directory like C:/Perl/lib/unicore. We will return to these files later in the chapter.

Unicode support in Perl 5.6 was a code-oriented feature, and the use utf8 pragma was used to switch Perl code into and out of Unicode-aware operation. This proved to be inelegant, so Perl 5.8 instead makes the data itself Unicode-aware and sets a UTF-8 flag on each string or filehandle that contains or needs to be aware of wide characters. Perl's string-based functions and operators now transparently adapt to manage wide characters whenever they encounter a string or filehandle that demands it. As a result, we rarely need to query the UTF-8 flag or explicitly convert strings between byte-oriented and wide-character interpretations.

Writing in Unicode

Perl supports the generation of Unicode symbols through interpolation. To support Unicode, two new interpolation sequences are provided: \x{code}, which interpolates a hexadecimal Unicode character code, and \N{name}, which interpolates from a name defined by the Unicode Standard. With either notation, we can create strings with Unicode characters.

As a practical example, take the following example, which prints a string containing a Psi character in the Cyrillic alphabet using the \x{code} notation:

```
#!/usr/bin/perl
# unicodex.pl
binmode STDOUT,":utf8";
print "\x{470} is a Cyrillic capital Psi\n";
```

To print this string out, we have to tell Perl that standard output is capable of handling Unicode characters; otherwise, Perl will conclude that the string cannot be printed, and we will get a "Wide character" warning instead of output. We enable this feature by setting the UTF-8 layer on the STDOUT filehandle with binmode, as we saw back in Chapter 12.

We can also create Unicode characters with the built-in chr function. Given a character code greater than 255, chr will automatically deduce we want a wide character and generate a wide-character string:

```
my $Psi=chr(0x470);
```

When \x is used with braces, it defines a Unicode character, so the string must by necessity be promoted to a UTF-8 string, even if the encodings in question are only single byte. \x{40} is not the same as \x40—the former represents a Unicode character that will promote the string that contains it to a wide-character internal format, whereas the latter represents a character code in the currently active native 8-bit format. The fact that both encodings may happen to represent the same character (@) is immaterial to whether Perl subsequently treats the string as 8-bit or variable-width encoded.

The Unicode Standard defines a character repertoire, which as we discussed at the start of the chapter means that every character has a name. We can use these names in place of the character codes with the charnames pragma, which gives the ability to specify characters using full names, short names, or within individual scripts. To use the full official names defined by the standard, we specify a :full argument, like so:

```
#!/usr/bin/perl
# unicodefull.pl
use charnames qw(:full);    # use Unicode with full names
```

```
print "\N{CYRILLIC CAPITAL LETTER PSI} is a Cyrillic capital Psi\n";
print "\N{GREEK CAPITAL LETTER PSI} is a Greek capital Psi\n";
print "\N{CYRILLIC SMALL LETTER PSI} is a Cyrillic small psi\n";
```

As the term suggests, full names are always verbose and in uppercase (or more correctly are case insensitive), and so we must spell out exactly what character we mean with keywords like SMALL and CAPITAL for case. Alternatively, we can import short names, which provide shortcuts to the official names and which use case in the name to determine the case of the resulting character:

```
#!/usr/bin/perl
# unicodeshort.pl
use charnames qw(:short);   # use Unicode with short names
print "\N{Cyrillic:Psi} is a capital Psi in Cyrillic\n";
print "\N{Greek:Psi} is a capital Psi in Greek\n";
print "\N{Cyrillic:psi} is a lowercase psi in Cyrillic\n";
```

Finally, we can import character names from specified scripts, in which case we can use an even shorter name. The scripts we specify help Perl to disambiguate which script we mean, so we can omit it unless we happen to import two scripts and use a character with the same name in each. The following program allows us to just say Psi because we exclusively select Cyrillic character names:

```
#!/usr/bin/perl
# unicodescript.pl
use charnames qw(cyrillic); # use explicit Unicode script
print "\N{Psi} is a capital Psi in Cyrillic\n";
print "\N{psi} is a lowercase psi in Cyrillic\n";
```

If we do not fully specify a letter character, then Unicode defines a resolution order that determines which of several possible characters is selected. For instance, if we ask for a letter with both upper- and lowercase forms but do not specify which we want, the uppercase variant will be selected. In terms of the full character name, the search order is

```
SCRIPT CAPITAL LETTER NAME
SCRIPT SMALL LETTER NAME
SCRIPT LETTER NAME
```

With short names in effect, this search order determines which letter is found within a given script, with the qualification that a NAME that is all lowercase ignores a CAPITAL variant, and any other name ignores the SMALL variant. The case used for a short name is disregarded for case-invariant characters, such as numerals.

These names, and their numeric equivalents, will also work in Perl's regular expression engine, which understands wide-character search patterns just as functions like length do. For example:

```
#!/usr/bin/perl
# whiteknight.pl
use charnames ":full";

# interpolate Unicode character into string
my $chess_move = "White moves \N{WHITE CHESS KNIGHT}";

# match UTF-8 string against UTF-8 pattern
print "Check!\n" if $chess_move =~ /\N{WHITE CHESS KNIGHT}/;
```

This short program generates a string containing a white knight chess piece symbol, then matches it with a regular expression containing the same symbol.

Converting Between Names and Codes

The charnames pragma also supplies a pair of useful functions that allow us to retrieve the full Unicode name for a given character code or the character code for a supplied Unicode name. The viacode function takes an integer code value and returns the name for it or undef if the code is invalid. We can use it to create a simple name listing utility like this:

```perl
#!/usr/bin/perl
# uninames.pl
use strict;
use warnings;
use charnames ':full';

die "Usage: $0 <start> <end>\n" unless @ARGV>=1;
my ($start,$end)=@ARGV;
$end=$start unless $end;

die "Bad range $start..$end\n"
    if ($start.$end)=~/\D/ or $end<$start;

for (my $code=$start; $code<=$end; $code++) {
    printf "%6d = U+%04X : %s\n", $code, $code,
        charnames::viacode($code) || '*Invalid*';
}
```

We can use this tool to produce either a single name or a list of sequential names like this:

```
> uninames.pl 1005 1010
```

```
 1005 = U+03ED : COPTIC SMALL LETTER SHIMA
 1006 = U+03EE : COPTIC CAPITAL LETTER DEI
 1007 = U+03EF : COPTIC SMALL LETTER DEI
 1008 = U+03F0 : GREEK KAPPA SYMBOL
 1009 = U+03F1 : GREEK RHO SYMBOL
 1010 = U+03F2 : GREEK LUNATE SIGMA SYMBOL
```

If we try an invalid code, we instead get the following:

```
> uninames.pl 567
```

```
  567 = U+0237 : *Invalid*
```

Here is a script that goes the other way, displaying the character code for the specified name:

```perl
#!/usr/bin/perl
# getcode.pl
use strict;
use warnings;
use charnames ':full';

die "Usage: $0 <name>\n" unless @ARGV;
my $name=uc(join ' ',@ARGV);

my $code=charnames::vianame($name);
if ($code) {
    printf "%6d = %04X : %s\n", $code, $code, $name;
```

```
} else {
    print "   $name is *Invalid*\n";
}
```

This translator is unforgiving, though—it will not return a result unless we give it a complete full name:

```
> ./getcode.pl A
```

```
A is *Invalid*
```

```
> ./getcode.pl LATIN CAPITAL A
```

```
LATIN CAPITAL A is *Invalid*
```

```
> ./getcode.pl LATIN CAPITAL LETTER A
```

```
65 = 0041 : LATIN CAPITAL LETTER A
```

Accessing the Unicode Database

Perl keeps all the data files and scripts that provide support for Unicode in a subdirectory called unicore in the Perl standard library directory. (In Perl 5.6, the subdirectory was called unicode, but it has since been renamed to avoid conflicting with the Unicode:: module family on case-insensitive file systems.)

Many of the files in this directory are text files that together comprise the Unicode Standard specification in machine-parsable format, taken from the Unicode Standard repository at http://www.unicode.org. Script names can be found in Scripts.txt, blocks are defined in Blocks.txt, and so on. Other files here, notably the Perl scripts and the contents of the To and lib subdirectories, are created as part of the Perl installation by the mktables script also located in this directory. If we ever had a reason to modify one of the text files, this script can regenerate all the secondary files for us. Taken together, they comprise the Unicode database.

Modules like the charnames pragma allow us to use the database without worrying about its low-level details. If we need more direct access, we use the Unicode::UCD module, which provides a low-level programmatic view of the Unicode data files. Of most immediate interest are the charblocks, charscripts, charblock, and charscript routines, which as their names suggest access block and script information.

Block and Script Information

The charblocks function returns details of all defined blocks, organized into a hash of arrays, with the name of each block being the block name and the arrays being one or more ranges, themselves arrays with the start and end character codes as the first and second elements. The block name is the third element, but we already have it from the key. The following program dumps this structure out in legible form:

```
#!/usr/bin/perl
# charblocks.pl
use strict;
use warnings;
use Unicode::UCD qw(charblocks);
```

```
my $blkref=charblocks();

foreach my $block (sort keys %$blkref) {
    printf "%40s :", $block;
    my @ranges=@{$blkref->{$block}};
    foreach my $range (@ranges) {
        printf " U+%04X..U+%04X", @$range;
    }
    print "\n";
}
```

Running this program generates a long list of blocks with entries like these:

```
 Cypriot Syllabary : U+10800..U+1083F
             Cyrillic : U+0400..U+04FF
Cyrillic Supplementary : U+0500..U+052F
             Deseret : U+10400..U+1044F
          Devanagari : U+0900..U+097F
            Dingbats : U+2700..U+27BF
```

Each block name can only ever have one range associated with it. However, we can use the charscripts function to generate a similar data structure, and a script can contain many ranges (with a single character being a range from itself to itself). If we replace the call to charblocks in the last script with this line:

```
my $blkref=charscripts();
```

we now get a list of scripts with associated ranges, similar to this:

```
 Cherokee : U+13A0..U+13F4
  Cypriot : U+10800..U+10805 U+10808..U+10808 U+1080A..U+10835
            U+10837..U+10838 U+1083C..U+1083C U+1083F..U+1083F
 Cyrillic : U+0400..U+0481 U+0483..U+0486 U+048A..U+04CE U+04D0..U+04F5
            U+04F8..U+04F9 U+0500..U+050F U+1D2B..U+1D2B
  Deseret : U+10400..U+1044F
```

To retrieve information for a specific block or script, we can use the singular versions of these functions. Both take an argument of either a block or script, respectively, or a character code. With a name, the corresponding range (or ranges in the case of scripts) are looked up and returned as an array of range arrays, just like the values of the hashes generated by the charblocks and charscripts routines. With a value, the corresponding block or script name is returned. The value may be specified either as an integer or in the U+NNNN format, in which case the NNNN is interpreted as a hexadecimal code. Here is a program that looks up block names and code ranges using charblock:

```
#!/usr/bin/perl
# charblock.pl
use strict;
use warnings;
use Unicode::UCD qw(charblock);

die "Usage: $0 <block name|code value|U+NNNN> ... \n"
    unless @ARGV;

foreach my $block (@ARGV) {
    # get the block for a code or the code ranges for a block
    my $ranges=charblock($block);

    if ($ranges) {
        if (ref $ranges) {
```

```perl
            print "Block $block:";
            # mapped name to array of ranges
            foreach my $range (@$ranges) {
                printf " U+%04X..U+%04X", @$range;
            }
        } else {
            # mapped a code to a block name
            print "Code $block is in the block '$ranges'";
        }
    } else {
        print "$block : *Invalid code value or block name*";
    }
    print "\n";
}
```

Using this script, we can generate output like this:

```
> charblock.pl Cyrillic 1234 U+1234 Latin "Basic Latin"
```

```
Block Cyrillic: U+0400..U+04FF
Code 1234 is in the block 'Cyrillic'
Code U+1234 is in the block 'Ethiopic'
Latin : *Invalid code value or block name*
Block Basic Latin: U+0000..U+007F
```

The charscript version of this program is identical in all respects other than replacing the call to charblocks with a call to charscripts. If we do this (and rename block to script throughout), we produce output like this:

```
> charscript.pl Cyrillic 1234 U+1234 Latin "Basic Latin"
```

```
Script Cyrillic: U+0400..U+0481 U+0483..U+0486 U+048A..U+04CE U+04D0..U+04F5
 U+04F8..U+04F9 U+0500..U+050F U+1D2B..U+1D2B
Code 1234 is in the script 'Cyrillic'
Code U+1234 is in the script 'Ethiopic'
Script Latin: U+0041..U+005A U+0061..U+007A U+00AA..U+00AA U+00BA..U+00BA
U+00C0..U+00D6 U+00D8..U+00F6 U+00F8..U+01BA U+01BB..U+01BB
U+01BC..U+01BF U+01C0..U+01C3 U+01C4..U+0236 U+0250..U+02AF U+02B0..U+02B8
U+02E0..U+02E4 U+1D00..U+1D25 U+1D2C..U+1D5C U+1D62..U+1D65 U+1D6B..U+1D6B
U+1E00..U+1E9B U+1EA0..U+1EF9 U+2071..U+2071 U+207F..U+207F U+212A..U+212B
U+FB00..U+FB06 U+FF21..U+FF3A U+FF41..U+FF5A
Basic Latin : *Invalid code value or script name*
```

The charinrange routine combines the features of the preceding functions to provide the ability to test whether a given character is a member of a given script or block. It has the same effect as the \p{...} notation in regular expressions, when the property is a script or block, but it operates on the character code rather than the character(or a string containing the character). For example:

```perl
#!/usr/bin/perl
use strict;
use warnings;
use charnames ':short';
use Unicode::UCD qw(charinrange charblock);

my $char="\N{Cyrillic:Psi}";
```

```
print "In block Cyrillic!\n" # string via interpolation
    if $char =~ /\p{InCyrillic}/;

print "In block Cyrillic!\n" # character code via charinrange
    if charinrange(charblock("Cyrillic"), ord($char));
```

The two tests in this short script are effectively equivalent, but the charinrange version is more efficient if we are interested in testing individual characters. Conversely, the property is easier for testing strings.

Detailed Character Information

The charinfo routine of Unicode::UCD extracts every piece of information the Unicode specification has to say about a given character code, including its block and script, its full name, its general category (which is also a property that it can be matched to), and the upper- or lowercase equivalent, if any exists. This short script uses charinfo to print out all defined values for the supplied character code or codes:

```
#!/usr/bin/perl
# charinfo.pl
use strict;
use warnings;
use Unicode::UCD qw(charinfo);

die "Usage: $0 <code value|U+NNNN> ... \n"
    unless @ARGV;

foreach my $char (@ARGV) {
    my $info=eval { charinfo($char) };

    if ($info) {
        print "Character code U+",(delete $info->{code}),":\n";
        print map {
            $info->{$_} ? sprintf "%13s = %s\n", $_, $info->{$_} : ()
        } sort keys %$info;
    } else {
        print "$char : *Invalid code*\n";
    }
}
```

We can use this script like this:

```
> charinfo.pl 1234
```

```
Character code U+04D2:
          bidi = L
         block = Cyrillic
      category = Lu
 decomposition = 0410 0308
         lower = 04D3
      mirrored = N
          name = CYRILLIC CAPITAL LETTER A WITH DIAERESIS
        script = Cyrillic
```

From this we can see that this is an uppercase letter (both from the name and the category) and that it has a lowercase variant. We can also see from its decomposition that it can be made up from two other unicode characters, which if we look them up turn out to be CYRILLIC CAPITAL LETTER A and COMBINING DIAERESIS.

Its default rendering order is left to right, and it is not mirrored (reflected) if forced into a right-to-left order. By contrast, this is what the Basic Latin numeral 6 returns:

```
./charinfo.pl 54
Character code U+0036:
        bidi = EN
       block = Basic Latin
    category = Nd
     decimal = 6
       digit = 6
    mirrored = N
        name = DIGIT SIX
     numeric = 6
```

As 6 is a digit and not a letter, it is in the Nd category and does not belong to a script. Its default rendering order is neutral, so it can be controlled by the prevailing direction. Being a number, it also has a numeric value but no uppercase or lowercase variant.

Case Mapping, Folding, and Composition Exclusion

The Unicode::UCD module provides three more routines for export, all of which are concerned with case manipulation and conversion, that we will only mention briefly here:

- compexcl returns true if the specified character has a composition exclusion—that is, it should not be combined with a modifier to create a composite character. For example, we can add an accent to a u, for example, but we can't necessarily add one to an ü. Accents are usually available both bundled with characters and as combining characters that modify the appearance of the preceding character, but only if the Unicode database says that such a modification is acceptable.

  This is more complex than it might seem: depending on what script they come from, characters with the same visual representation may have different restrictions. See also the Unicode::Normalize module for routines to decompose characters into their constituents, recompose constituents back into composite characters, and more information on character composition in general.

- casefold returns a structure containing information on how the character's case may be folded, in a locale-independent way.

- casespec returns the valid case mappings of the specified character, possibly modified by the locale currently in effect.

In the rare cases that we might need to check which version of the Unicode Standard Perl is using, we can also extract it with the nonexportable function Unicode::UCD::UnicodeVersion. For example:

```
> perl -MUnicode::UCD -e 'print Unicode::UCD::UnicodeVersion()'
```

Implications of Wide Characters in Perl

Before using Unicode in a Perl application or module, it is important to keep in mind that while Perl will for the most part transparently handle wide-character strings just as easily as traditional 8-bit ones, some features of Perl will not behave in quite the same way once wide-character support is enabled. In particular:

- The chr and ord functions no longer necessarily map between single characters and single bytes, and the return value of ord may exceed 256.

- When an 8-bit encoded string is used in an operation with a UTF-8 encoded string, a copy of the 8-bit encoding is automatically made and upgraded to UTF-8. This is rather like tainting in strings, and it works the same way: a wide-character string "widens" any string that is generated from an operation in which it takes part, even if the resulting string does not contain any wide characters.

- The length of a string is no longer necessarily equal to the number of bytes in the string.

- The . any-character pattern in regular expressions now potentially matches more than one byte. To explicitly match a byte, we must instead use the \C pattern metacharacter.

- Functions like length, index, and substr take longer to execute on UTF-8 strings because they must scan through the string and look for multibyte characters in order to count characters to find the desired position in the string. This is true even if the string only contains single-byte characters and so is compatible with Latin 1, since Perl still has to check.

- Not all Perl features recognize wide-character text. The major exceptions are filing system operations, since the file system is most likely not using Unicode for file names, even their contents are encoded in UTF-8. The %ENV and @ARGV arrays are also not marked as wide-character, even if Unicode is enabled everywhere else. The -C command-line option can be used to tell Perl that @ARGV is encoded in UTF-8, but %ENV is always interpreted as 8-bit Latin 1. The pack and unpack functions also remain byte-oriented but provide the U placeholder to pack and unpack UTF-8 encoded strings.

Reading and Writing Unicode

The PerlIO system provided by Perl 5.8 onwards allows any filehandle to be marked as accepting or not accepting wide characters by setting the :utf8 layer for it. As was discussed back in Chapter 12, layers can be added and removed in a number of different ways. Encoding layers, including the :utf8 layer, are no different.

If we are opening a filehandle for the first time, we can set the layer at the same time, with open:

```
open INUTF8, "<:utf8", "unicode.txt";
```

If we already have a filehandle, like STDOUT, we can use binmode to set the layer on it, as we saw in our first Unicode example:

```
binmode STDOUT,":utf8";
```

Alternatively, we can set the default filehandle layers for all new filehandles with the open pragma. Both of these statements tell Perl to set the :utf8 layer on all new filehandles for both input and output:

```
use open ":utf8"; # mark all new filehandles as UTF8
use open IO => ":utf8"; # likewise
```

If we add an argument of :std to this statement, Perl also marks the STDIN, STDOUT, and STDERR filehandles with whatever the default encoding is for new filehandles.

```
use open ":utf8", ":std"; # also mark STDIN/OUT/ERR
```

The open pragma also has the useful property that if we specify :locale, which implies :std, Perl will enable whatever encoding is set for the locale (as determined from the LC_ALL, LC_CTYPE, or LANG environment variables) as the default for input and output on all filehandles:

```
use open ':locale';
```

We can also use the encoding pragma to automatically mark standard input, standard output, and literal string text (including any text in the __DATA__ section of the source file) as UTF-8. However, while the leading colon is optional for binmode, it is not permitted in the argument to the pragma:

```
#!/usr/bin/perl
# unicodex2.pl

use encoding "utf8";

print "\x{470} is a Cyrillic capital Psi\n";
```

Of course, unless we happen to be using a Unicode-aware shell, the actual output from running any of these scripts is quite likely to be a pair of strange characters corresponding to the 2 bytes that make up the wide character (0x04 and 0x71 in this case) and not an actual Psi character.

The encoding pragma provides an interface between PerlIO and the Encode module, which contains definitions for all character encodings known to Perl. Any encoding can be applied, so we can use the pragma to convert UTF-8 to and from other character encodings. By mentioning a filehandle and a secondary encoding—in the same way as the open pragma—we can produce the same effects as a binmode statement to have different encodings for input, output, and in-code text:

```
use encoding 'iso-8859-5', STDOUT => 'utf8';
```

This statement tells Perl that string literals are encoded in ISO 8859-5 (8-bit Cyrillic), but any data sent to standard output should be encoded as Unicode characters using the UTF-8 encoding.

We can also use the pragma from the command line. Changing the internal encoding of the script is not very practical, but we can make the input and output UTF-8 encoded with

```
> perl -Mencoding=STDIN,utf8,STDOUT,utf8 myscript.pl
```

From Perl 5.8, we also have the -C option to switch on UTF-8 encodings for filehandles and command-line arguments, but not literal text. It takes either a collection of letters or a numeric value as its argument. These arguments are listed in Table 23-2.

Table 23-2. *Arguments to Perl's -C Option*

Letter	Numeric Value	Description
I	1	STDIN marked as :utf8.
O	2	STDOUT marked as :utf8.
E	4	STDERR marked as :utf8.
i	8	All new filehandles marked as :utf8 for input.
o	16	All new filehandles marked as :utf8 for output.
A	32	The contents of the @ARGV array are marked as UTF-8 (that is, wide-character) strings.
L	64	Enable the preceding only if the locale indicates UTF-8 is acceptable (determined, in order, from the environment variables LC_ALL, LC_TYPE, and LANG).
S	7	Shorthand for IOE.
D	24	Shorthand for io.

The previous example can be rewritten using the -C option:

```
> perl -CIO myscript.pl
```

Or, adding the numeric values for input (1) and out (2) together, we can equivalently use

```
> perl -C3 myscript.pl
```

A -C option with no argument or an argument of zero switches on all features, except for A - @ARGV processing, and is equivalent to -CIOEioL or -CLSD. The S and D options are just shorthand for combinations of other letters.

The environment variable PERL_UNICODE also controls this setting. If -C is not specified, PERL_UNICODE is examined for a series of option letters or a numeric value. For example, in most Unix shells, we can type the following:

```
> PERL_UNICODE=3 perl myscript.pl
```

Of course, the real point of this variable is to set the desired behavior as part of the default environment.

Within Perl, the setting of the -C flag can be read as a numeric value with the special variable ${^UNICODE}. This reflects the settings that were in effect when Perl started, and it never changes. In particular, it is not affected by any use of open (pragma or function) or binmode to set the default layers or the layers on the standard filehandles.

If we print a wide-character string to a filehandle that is not so marked, Perl will generate a wide-character warning unless there is a valid mapping for the character into the selected output encoding. Since not every character in a Unicode script can be represented by a more restricted encoding like the ISO 8859 family, this may not always work, even if the output encoding is for the same language.

Unicode and Other Character Sets

Since we can set different encodings for internal text and for filehandles, we can transparently map from one encoding to another in Perl, just by setting the encodings appropriately. For example, this Perl one-line command converts text files written in ISO 8859-5 into Unicode:

```
> perl -C0 -Mencoding=STDIN,iso-8859-5 -ne "print" < cyrillic.txt > utf8.txt
```

The piconv utility that comes with Perl is a version of the standard iconv tool on many Unix platforms that makes use of Perl's Encode module to do the work instead of the operating system's native libraries. We can achieve the same effect as the preceding command with

```
> piconv --from iso-8859-5 --to utf8 < cyrillic.txt > utf8.txt
```

The script is not complex, as it simply wraps Perl's standard encoding functionality with a few command-line options, and the main part of it amounts to less than a hundred lines. Programmers interested in making more direct use of Perl's Encode module may find it worth examining.

It is also interesting to examine what Perl is actually doing with strings encoded in non-Latin 1 character sets. The built-in ord function comes in useful here as it can tell us what character code Perl has chosen to use internally. The short program that follows is written in Cyrillic, as defined by ISO 8859-5. The only practical effect of this is that the character with code 0xD0 assigned to $char is evaluated as a member of ISO 8859-5:

```perl
#!/usr/bin/perl
# map88595touni.pl
use encoding 'cyrillic';

my $char="\xD0"; # no {} braces = 8-bit encoding
printf "U+%04X\n", ord($char);
```

Internally, Perl maps the character to a 16-bit Unicode character when it compiles the string. We can see when we run the program and get this output:

```
U+0430
```

For 8-bit encodings, it is relatively simple to write a script that shows the mapping for each of the 256 possible values to its Unicode equivalent. Since the bottom half always maps directly for ISO 8859 character sets, we can reduce this to the top 128 codes:

```
#!/usr/bin/perl
# mapall88595uni.pl
use encoding 'cyrillic';

foreach my $code (128..255) {
    my $char=chr($code);
    printf "%02X => U+%04X\n", $code, ord($char);
}
```

This generates 128 lines of output of the following form:

```
...
EE => U+044E
EF => U+044F
F0 => U+2116
F1 => U+0451
F2 => U+0452
...
```

Notice that the mapping is not linear and that some characters in this character set are not in the Cyrillic block or the Cyrillic script in the Unicode Standard. U+2116 is, as it turns out, a NUMERO SIGN.

It is always possible (other than in exceptional circumstances) to map a character in any other character encoding into Unicode. However, the reverse transform is not always possible, even for characters that are clearly members of the language for which the encoding is designed. This is because encodings like the ISO 8859 cannot always provide an encoding for every known character of a script. The Unicode character U+0470, which we have been using as an example in this chapter, is a member of both the Cyrillic script and of the Cyrillic block. Even so, it does not have a direct mapping to the 8-bit ISO 8859-5 encoding for Cyrillic:

```
> perl -Mencoding=utf8,STDOUT,iso-8859-5 -e 'print "\x{470}"'
```

```
"\x{0470}" does not map to iso-8859-5.
```

Character code U+0430 (which charinfo tells us is a CYRILLIC SMALL LETTER A), on the other hand, does map:

```
> perl -Mencoding=utf8,STDOUT,iso-8859-5 -e 'print "\x{430}"'
```

a

Of course, unless the shell is currently using ISO 8859-5, we won't actually see the character in the encoding. If we were to now use `ord` to find the character code of this character, we would find that it was 223, or `D0` in hexadecimal, which is the value we began with at the start of this section.

Encoding Perl Source

So far we have looked at strings and filehandles and how they deal with wide-character data. But we can also encode Perl source itself in Unicode or any other native character set that the underlying platform supports. This allows us to use variable and subroutine names—but not the names of packages—using characters outside the usual Latin 1 range, even using wide characters if we want to.

To encode Perl source itself, we again use the `encoding` pragma, but now we make use of the `Filter` option. This assigns the specified encoding to a source filter (provided through the `Filter::Util::Call` interface described in Chapter 18) so Perl code is passed through the `Encode` module before it even gets compiled.

For example, to use Unicode characters in our variable and subroutines, we can use

```
use encoding 'utf8', Filter => 1;
```

Although the `Filter` option fundamentally changes the way the pragma works, it maintains compatibility with the nonfiltered uses too, so we can still set different encodings for `STDIN` and `STDOUT` as before. So, we can write our code—including string literals—in ISO 8859-5 (the 8-bit encoding for Cyrillic), but have Perl print out in UTF-8 with either of the following:

```
use encoding 'iso8859-5', Filter => 1, STDOUT => 'utf8';
use encoding 'cyrillic', Filter => 1, STDOUT => 'utf8';
```

Perl compiles variable and subroutine names into either a Latin 1 or a UTF-8 names, depending on whether the characters that make each name up can be represented in Latin 1 or not, just as it does for string literals. This detail is however mostly moot—the result is that we can write source in any encoding we choose.

■Note If all we want to do is write literal strings in a native 8-bit encoding, we do not need to use the `Filter` option—the `encoding` pragma with a single encoding as its argument does that. We only need to use the `Filter` option if we want to create variables and subroutines using characters outside the Latin 1 encoding.

Sorting in Unicode

While Perl's `sort` function can sort wide-character strings just as it can traditional 8-bit ones, it only provides one possible interpretation of an appropriate sort order, based purely on comparison of character codes via the `cmp` operator, which it uses by default when no explicit sort subroutine is supplied.

Unicode is of course more complex than this, and there is no official relationship between the character code of a character and its "order" in relation to other characters. The `Unicode::Collate` module provides a complete implementation of the Unicode sorting algorithm and can be used to sort UTF-8 encoded strings under a variety of different criteria, such as the following:

- Whether uppercase ranks higher or lower than lowercase
- Which characters should be ignored entirely for the purpose of sorting
- Whether composite characters should be compared according to their composite forms or decomposed into multiple constituent characters first

A simple use of the module is to create a collation object that can be used to sort characters using the default behavior defined by the Unicode Standard. For example:

```
my $sorter=new Unicode::Collate;
my @sorted = $sorter->sort(@unsorted);
```

We can also make use of the `cmp` method inside Perl's built-in `sort` function:

```
my @sorted=sort { $sorter->cmp($a,$b) } @unsorted;
```

The collation object can be customized in many ways when it is created by passing in one or more key-value pairs to adjust its behavior. For example, this collator object ignores whitespace, strips a leading "the " if present, and ranks uppercase letters after lowercase ones:

```
my @sorter=new Unicode::Collate(
    ignoreChar => qr/\s/,
    upper_before_lower => 0,
    preprocess => { $_[0]=~/^the\s+/i },
);
```

This is just a simple example of what we can do with the collator object. For more advanced configuration options, see the `Unicode::Collate` manual page.

Detecting and Converting Wide-Character Strings

Perl's implementation of wide-character support is designed so that, for the most part, we can ignore the way that it works and just use wide characters without any extra effort. However, if we really need to find out whether a given string is marked as UTF-8 or byte-encoded, we can use the `is_utf8` function:

```
#!/usr/bin/perl
# is_utf8.pl

my $tee=chr(0x74);
print "is t wide? ",utf8::is_utf8($tee)?"yes":"no","\n";
my $Psi=chr(0x470);
print "is Psi wide? ",utf8::is_utf8($Psi)?"yes":"no","\n";
```

This script will let us know that, as suspected, the letter "t" is not a wide character, but a Cyrillic Psi is. Of course, it is really the string that is being checked, but these strings only contain one character.

The `is_utf8` function and the other functions mentioned in this section are provided by Perl in the `utf8` package. They are *not* provided by the `utf8` pragma, and as the preceding example shows, we do not invoke use `utf8` to make use of them.

One problem with wide-character support is that it forces Perl to scan through strings that are marked as potentially containing wide characters in order to determine positions. However, we might happen to know that there are no wide characters in a string, and so there is no need for Perl to carry out this extra work. Alternatively, we might want to treat the string as a byte sequence even if it does have wide characters. Either way, we can convert a string to its byte-oriented form with the `encode` function. To go the other way and turn a byte-sequence into a wide character string, we use `decode`. Both functions carry out an in-place conversion of the original string.

```
#!/usr/bin/perl
# utf8encode.pl

my $Psi=chr(0x470); # a one character wide-character string
print "Wide-character length: ",length($Psi),"\n";
print "First character code : ",ord(substr $Psi,0,1),"\n";
```

```
utf8::encode $Psi; # convert to byte-oriented form
print "Byte length: ",length($Psi),"\n";
print "First character code : ",ord(substr $Psi,0,1),"\n";

my $decoded_ok=utf8::decode $Psi; # convert back
print "Wide-character again: ",length($Psi),"\n";
print "First character code : ",ord(substr $Psi,0,1),"\n";
```

When run, the output from this script is

```
Wide-character length: 1
First character code : 1137
Byte length: 2
First character code : 209
Wide-character again: 1
First character code : 1137
```

As expected, when we encode the string, the length changes to 2 and ord on the start of the string returns a number less than 256. Clearly, although the string has not actually changed contents, it will now behave very differently with Perl's string functions, including regular expressions like \w.

The encode function always succeeds, since any wide-character string must obviously have an equivalent byte-oriented form, and it clears the UTF-8 flag to mark the string as a byte-encoded one.

The decode function can fail, however, if the sequence of bytes in the string corresponds to invalid wide-character codes. We should therefore check the return value, which is true on success and false on failure. If the decoding succeeds, the resulting string still may not be marked with the UTF-8 flag, though. This will only happen if a wide character was found in the string, since there is no point slowing down string functions without reason.

There are three other functions in the utf8:: namespace, but we are less likely to find a use for them. upgrade is like the encode function, but does not manage the UTF-8 flag. The corresponding downgrade function performs the opposite operation. Like decode, it can fail. It takes an additional argument, which if *not* true will cause Perl to die on error. Finally, valid checks whether a string can be successfully converted by decode or downgrade.

Unicode in Regular Expressions

The integration of Unicode into the regular expression engine allows us to match text according to Unicode properties, shortcuts for various character classes defined by the Unicode Standard. Properties come in several flavors depending on what part of the standard they implement, for example General, BiDi, or Script. A complete list of available properties can be found in the perlunicode manual page. This occasionally updates, as new properties and scripts are added to the Unicode specification.

To match properties in regular expressions, we use either the \p{PROPERTY} notation for a positive match or \P{PROPERTY} for a negative match, where PROPERTY is the Unicode property we want to match. For example, this matches a control character:

```
print "text contains a control character"
    if $string =~ /\p{Control}/;
```

General properties have short and long names, so Control can also be specified as Cc. Perl 5.6 also prefixed general property names with Is, and so for backwards compatibility, Perl 5.8 onwards allows either form to also be optionally prefixed with Is, so IsControl or IsCc are also valid ways to specify this property.

Many properties come in general and more specific variants, so for example, we can ask for a letter or specify an uppercase letter. Here are a few examples of standard Unicode properties, with a few general categories and some of their more specific variants:

- Letter, L: Letter (equivalent to \w)
  - UppercaseLetter, Lu: Uppercase letter
  - LowercaseLetter, Ll: Lowercase letter
- Mark, M: Marked character (for example, accented)
- Number, N: Number
  - DecimalNumber, Nd: Decimal number (equivalent to \d)
- Punctuation, P: Punctuation
  - DashPunctuation, Pd: Dash character
- Symbol, S: Symbol character
- MathSymbol, Sm: Mathematical symbol
- Separator, Z: Separator
  - LineSeparator, Zl: Line separator
  - ParagraphSeparator, Zp: Paragraph separator
  - SpaceSeparator, Zs: Space separator
- Other, C: Other character (none of L, M, N, P, or Z)
  - Cntrl, Cc: Control character

Single-letter properties like M can be specified without braces, so we can say equally \p{M} or \pM.

Extended properties implement combinations or aliases for standard Unicode properties and basic pattern elements. A few examples are

- ASCII: Equivalent to the character class [\x00-\x7f]
- Math: A mathematical symbol in any script
- WhiteSpace: A whitespace character in any script

Script properties can be used to determine if a character belongs to a particular script:

```
# match on Cyrillic Script
if ($text =~ /\p{Cyrillic}/) { ... }
```

As with general properties, we can use an Is prefix, so IsCyrillic is also valid.

Block properties by contrast can be used to determine if a character belongs to a particular block. Since some blocks have the same names as scripts, block properties are prefixed with In. To test that a character is in the Cyrillic block, as opposed to the Cyrillic script, we use the following:

```
# match on Cyrillic block
if ($text =~ /\p{InCyrillic}/) { ... }
```

Finally, characters with different directional representations (Hebrew and Arabic are written right to left, for instance) can be matched on their bidirectional or Bidi properties, all of which start with Bidi. For example, the BidiL property matches characters normally written in a left-to-right order, while BidiR matches characters normally written in right-to-left order.

Custom Character Properties

New character properties can be implemented simply by defining a subroutine with an Is or In prefix in the main package. A property subroutine should return a text string defining the Unicode characters it matches, using either code ranges or other named properties, blocks, or scripts. For example:

```
#!/usr/bin/perl
use strict;
use warnings;
use charnames qw(:short);

sub IsCyrillicBlock {
return <<_END_;
0400 04FF
0500 0520
1D2B
_END_
}

my $string="\N{Cyrillic:Psi}";

print "IsCyrillicBlock\n" if $string=~/\p{IsCyrillicBlock}/;
```

The number ranges correspond to the Cyrillic or Cyrillic Supplement blocks, plus the one lone character that happens to fall outside either block, so this property will match a character in either block plus the extra character. It is more extensive than the CyrillicScript property, because that only matches some of the characters in each block. In this case it happens that the blocks are contiguous, so we could also just have written

```
sub IsCyrillicBlock {
return <<_END_;
0400 0520
1D2B
_END_
}
```

Unlike built-in properties, however, the Is is not optional for these custom-made properties, and we must specify it in the property name for Perl to find our custom property.

We can also use named properties to describe what character codes we want to use. Any general, extended, script, or block property can be used. Additionally, we may negate a property to subtract one from another. This example uses named properties and subtraction to match the Cyrillic Script, but not any of the characters in the Cyrillic Supplement block:

```
sub IsScriptNotSupplement {
return <<_END_;
+utf8::IsCyrillic
-utf8::InCyrillicSupplement
_END_
}
```

To negate the overall sense of a property, we can of course use the \P{...} notation, but we can also negate the property itself by adding an exclamation mark to the front of the first specification:

```
sub IsNotCyrillicBlock {
return <<_END_;
!0400 0520
-1D2B
_END_
}
```

The first range defines all possible characters except those in the range U+0400 to U+0520. Following it, we can add or subtract further ranges, character codes, or properties as usual using a plus or minus prefix. Here, we subtract U+1D2B to complete the negated version of the property definition.

We can refer to our own property subroutines by prefixing them with main:: rather than utf8::, so we can reuse them in other custom properties, such as this example, which matches any character in the blocks that is not included in the script:

```
sub IsBlockNotScript {
return <<_END_;
+main::IsCyrillicBlock
-utf8::IsCyrillic
_END_
}
```

We can also define custom transformations for the lc, lcfirst, uc, and ucfirst functions by creating subroutines with the names ToUpper, ToLower, and ToTitle. For the default mappings, see the definitions in the To subdirectory in the unicode/unicore directory.

Locale

A locale is a collection of contextual data that describes the preferred language, character set, and formatting styles for decimal numbers, dates, monetary values, and other quantities for a given location. By querying, the applications can transparently customize their output to conform to local conventions, whatever they might be. This process is called localization, abbreviated to L10N, because there are 10 letters between the "l" and "n." Locales are an important part of internationalization, similarly abbreviated to I18N, the process of making applications generate grammatically and contextually correct messages for different languages and countries.

Locale is supported by most Unix-like platforms, and it consists of a number of operating system libraries and a collection of data files that provides locale information for the locales supported on the platform. Any operating system that provides locale functionality also provides a default locale called the *C locale*, or sometimes the equivalent *POSIX locale* (these are essentially the same, but they are defined by different standards). Other locales may or may not be available, depending on whether the data files have been installed or not. On Windows, locales are handled differently, but fortunately modules available from CPAN enable some locale information to be handled the same way irrespective of how the platform manages it.

The locale system is divided into categories, each of which can be configured through a different environment variable. In addition, some variables are used as defaults for others if they happen not to be defined, and there are one or two additional variables supported by particular platforms. There are six primary categories, and the variables that control them are listed in Table 23-3.

Table 23-3. *Locale System Categories*

Category	Variable	Description
Collation	LC_COLLATE	Sorting (collation) order.
Character type	LC_CTYPE	Character set and encoding.
Messages	LC_MESSAGE	Language for OS and external library messages.
Currency	LC_MONETARY	Symbols and formatting for currency values.
Number formats	LC_NUMERIC	Formatting of numeric values (decimal point, thousands separator).
Dates and times	LC_TIME	Local format of time and date strings.

Continued

Table 23-3. *Continued*

Category	Variable	Description
Global override	LC_ALL	Set all the preceding categories, overriding any more specific variable.
Global default	LANG	Set all the preceding categories, unless a more specific category variable is defined.
Messages override	LANGUAGE	Override LC_ALL for category LC_MESSAGE (for the GNU C library only).

In addition to these, we may also set the category variables LC_PAPER, LC_NAME, LC_ADDRESS, LC_TELEPHONE, LC_MEASUREMENT, and LC_IDENTIFICATION. These provide specialized information about preferred paper sizes, and the formatting of names, addresses, and telephone numbers.

In each case, the value of the variable is a locale specification indicating a language, a country, an optional character encoding, and an optional dialect. The language and country are taken from ISO 639, which defines the standard list of short codes for countries. In order to make it easy to discriminate them, the language is always lowercased, and the country is always uppercased. Here are some examples:

- en: English
- en_GB: British English
- fr_BE: Belgian French
- fr_CH: Swiss French
- en_GB.iso885915: British English, ISO 8859-15 encoding
- ru_RU.iso88595: Russian, ISO 8859-5 encoding
- fr_BE@euro: Belgian French (Euro dialect)

These specifications are increasingly specific, with looser locales applying defaults where needed. For instance, while Russian has more than one character set encoding, ISO 8859-5 is the default. To override this and ask for the KO18R encoding instead, we would use ru_RU.ko18r. All of these locale settings are dependent on the operating system's understanding of locale and the locales it has installed.

Possibly the most important aspect of locale is the preferred language and (8-bit) character encoding. In these modern times, these aspects can now be more easily handled by Unicode, but it is still useful for a Unicode application to be aware of the locale's preferred encoding. Perl provides two ways to do this: first, the open pragma allows the locale to be used to determine the default encoding for filehandles with the :locale argument, as covered earlier in the chapter; second, the -C option (introduced in Perl 5.8) can be given an L argument to have the other arguments (O, E, and so on) enabled only if the locale supports UTF-8.

If all we are interested in doing is importing details of the locale's language and character set, then this is all the interaction we need with the locale system. If we want to make use of other aspects of the locale, such as the formatting of floating-point numbers, then we need to enable additional locale support.

Enabling Locales in Perl

To enable locale support in Perl, we merely need to invoke the locale pragma:

```
use locale;
```

This will tell Perl to use locale information, where possible and appropriate, in its built-in functions and modules. For this to work, however, the platform must not only support locales, but also Perl must believe that it does too. This is a build-time configuration issue, and we can check for locale support by looking for d_setlocale, either through the Config module or via the command line:

```
> perl -V:d_setlocale
d_setlocale='define';
```

The value of this parameter will be UNKNOWN if locales are not supported and define if they are.

Perl will read the currently configured locale, as described by the environment variables that control locale settings, use it to read in the data files for that locale, and configure the interpreter accordingly. It will also make the locale details available within the program, so we can query the locale for information beyond that which Perl can apply automatically.

If no appropriate locale is configured, the default locale, C, or POSIX, is used.

Availability of Locales

To find out which locales the operating system supports, we can use the locale utility (available on most Unix platforms) to list them with locale -a. We can similarly extract a list of available character encodings with locale -m. (The exact arguments may vary from one OS to another.) By way of example, here are a few lines of output from running locale with the -a option, with all the different locales of the French language:

```
fr_BE
fr_BE@euro
fr_BE.utf8
fr_CA
fr_CA.utf8
fr_CH
fr_CH.utf8
fr_FR
fr_FR@euro
fr_FR.utf8
fr_LU
fr_LU@euro
fr_LU.utf8
```

Notice here that each locale has an 8-bit and a UTF-8 variant, and for countries that have joined the Euro, there is a euro dialect available too, which affects the currency symbol selected by the LC_MONETARY category. It is easy to differentiate these from their lowercased country code of fr. Similarly, here are all the official languages spoken in Switzerland, distinguished by the uppercased country code of CH:

```
de_CH
de_CH.utf8
fr_CH
fr_CH.utf8
it_CH
it_CH.utf8
```

We can also use the I18N::LangTags module to determine the legality of language tags (which are the language and country portion of the locale, but with a hyphen in place of an underscore). It can also derive alternate and fallback languages and convert locales to language tags:

```perl
#!/usr/bin/perl
# langtags.pl
use strict;
use warnings;

use I18N::LangTags qw(
    implicate_supers
    locale2language_tag
    is_language_tag
);

# check for valid syntax (does not look up)
print "Tag ok\n" if is_language_tag("fr-CH");

# extract the language tag from a locale - returns 'ru-RU'
print "Tag is ",locale2language_tag("ru_RU.ko18r"), "\n";

# expand a list of tags to include generic supersets
my @expanded=implicate_supers('fr-CH','de-CH');
print "Expanded tags: @expanded\n";
```

This last example would print the following:

```
fr-CH fr de-CH de
```

Windows does not support Unix-style locale, but information can be derived from other sources to generate some of the same data. In particular, the Win32::Locale module available from CPAN provides various functions to extract locale information from the operating system, even though Windows handles many aspects of locale very differently from Unix and other platforms:

```perl
print "Windows 'locale' is equivalent to ",
    Win32::Locale::get_locale(),"\n";
```

While it is directly usable, Win32::Locale is more useful to have installed so that other locale-oriented modules may make use of it if they detect it is present.

Another useful module is I18N::LangTags::Detect, which attempts to infer the user's preferred language from not just locale variables, but also other possible sources such as CGI environment variables like HTTP_ACCEPT_LANGUAGE. It will also use Win32::Locale on Windows systems (if it is installed). Here is one way to use it to derive a list of acceptable languages:

```perl
my @ok_langs = I18N::LangTags::implicate_supers(
    I18N::LangTags::Detect::detect()
);
```

Also provided in the I18::LangTags:: family is I18N::LangTags::List. This provides a mapping for each language tag to an English name, which can then be further used with modules like Locale::Language, described later in the chapter.

How Locales Affect Perl

Assuming that Perl is able to parse the configured locale and load the locale data, programs that invoke the locale pragma become transparently aware of the locale.

- LC_COLLATE controls the behavior of the sort function without a sort subroutine and the le, lt, ge, gt and cmp operators.
- LC_CTYPE controls the characters that are considered letters and therefore the characters matched by the regular expression metacharacter \w. It may also affect the operation of lc, lcfirst, uc, and ucfirst.
- LC_TIME has no effect in Perl, but it does affect the POSIX strftime function.
- LC_MESSAGE and LANGUAGE have no effect in Perl, but they may affect the text of error messages returned into $! by C libraries called via extension modules.
- LC_NUMERIC controls the decimal point character used by print, printf, sprintf, and write.

Additionally, and irrespective of whether the locale pragma has been used or not:

- Report formats, as invoked through the write function, always use the current locale (see LC_NUMERIC earlier).

If Perl sees locale variables in the environment but cannot deduce a correct locale from them, it will generate a warning message and fall back to the default locale, C or POSIX. To disable this warning, we can set the PERL_BADLANG environment variable to a false value (an empty string or zero):

```
> PERL_BADLANG=0 perl mylocaleapp.pl
```

However, a bad locale setting may indicate a more serious problem that should really be fixed rather than worked around. In particular, working around a bad locale in Perl will not help C library functions that access locale information.

Locale and Tainting

When locale support is enabled in Perl through the locale pragma, all functions and operators that are influenced by locale, and which return strings as their result, mark those strings as tainted. This is because a badly (or maliciously) configured locale can cause bizarre behavior, for example, by modifying the date and time formats used by the POSIX strftime function to use literal numbers where the values should be.

The tainting effects of locale include interpolated strings that use the case-mapping metacharacters \l, \L, \u, and \U, and their functional equivalents lc, lcfirst, uc, and ucfirst. It also taints extracted text from matches on patterns using the \w regular expression metacharacter—including special variables like $& as well as parentheses—and the original string after modification by a substitution using \w. This can be important, since extracting text from a regular expression is the primary means for untainting tainted data. To successfully untaint (assuming of course that this is safe to do), use a pattern that does not involve \w.

Getting and Setting the Locale

Rather than have Perl read locale configuration information from the environment, we can request a specific locale with the setlocale function. This is a standard library function provided by the operating system and accessed from Perl through the POSIX module. Here is how we can use it to switch four locale categories to different locales:

```
#!/usr/bin/perl
use strict;
use warnings;
use locale;
use POSIX 'locale_h';
```

```
setlocale(LC_COLLATE, 'fr_CH');
setlocale(LC_NUMERIC, 'en_US');
setlocale(LC_MONETARY, 'fr_CH');
setlocale(LC_TIME, 'fr_FR');
```

Slightly counterintuitively, the setlocale function is also used to find out what the locale is currently set to for a given category. To do this, we provide it with only one argument. For example, to find out the current LC_MONETARY locale:

```
print "The monetary locale is ",setlocale(LC_MONETARY), "\n";
```

Although it looks similar, this is not the same as looking up the corresponding environment variable. First, this returns the derived value after all of the locale environment variables have been taken into account. Second, if we feed LC_ALL to this function, we get back a long semicolon-delimited list of all locale settings:

```
LC_CTYPE=en_GB;LC_NUMERIC=C;LC_TIME=en_GB;LC_COLLATE=C;
LC_MONETARY=en_GB;LC_MESSAGES=en_GB;LC_PAPER=en_GB;LC_NAME=en_GB;
LC_ADDRESS=en_GB;LC_TELEPHONE=en_GB;LC_MEASUREMENT=en_GB;
LC_IDENTIFICATION=en_GB
```

Since this is a report of the actual locale settings, it does not reflect how they were set, so we do not see LC_ALL here, nor LANG or LANGUAGE, even if they were used to establish the locale.

Querying the Current Locale

Perl can only deduce appropriate behavior for a small subset of locale-dependent situations, and so there are many more locale settings than Perl is able to make use of automatically. For instance, Perl cannot know when we ask to print a dollar sign whether we are referring to currency or some other use of the symbol.

To find the correct currency symbol for the current locale, we need to query the locale ourselves with the localeconv function provided by the operating system, by way of the POSIX module. The localeconv function returns a reference to a hash of key-value pairs, of which currency_symbol is the one of interest to us. Here is a command that sets the locale in the environment and then asks localeconv for the currency symbol, via Perl:

```
> LC_ALL=fr_FR perl -MPOSIX=localeconv -e "print localeconv()->{currency_symbol}"
```

The symbol may not actually turn out to be a symbol, of course. For example, the preceding command will print EUR since the fr_FR locale does not know about the Euro symbol. If we use fr_FR@euro instead, the locale switches to a character encoding that includes the Euro symbol and will duly print the character corresponding to the Euro character code instead (whether we actually get a Euro or not depends on the encoding supported by the terminal, of course).

localeconv, as its name suggests, returns conversion information defined by the LC_MONETARY and LC_NUMERIC categories. Since it queries the locale directly, it does not rely on Perl understanding the locale implicitly, and so it does not need the locale pragma to be invoked in order to work. This short program prints out all the settings that localeconv can access:

```
#!/usr/bin/perl
# localeconv.pl
use strict;
use warnings;
use POSIX qw(localeconv);

my $conv = localeconv();
```

```perl
for my $var (sort keys %$conv) {
    printf "%17s => %s\n", $var, $conv->{$var};
}
```

This is what this program prints out under the Swiss French locale:

```
> LC_ALL=fr_CH localeconv.pl
```

```
      currency_symbol => Fr.
        decimal_point => .
          frac_digits => 2
      int_curr_symbol => CHF
      int_frac_digits => 2
  mon_decimal_point => .
        mon_grouping =>
  mon_thousands_sep =>
        n_cs_precedes => 1
       n_sep_by_space => 1
          n_sign_posn => 4
        negative_sign => -
        p_cs_precedes => 1
       p_sep_by_space => 1
          p_sign_posn => 4
```

We can also use the I18N::LangInfo module to query the locale for day and month names, the local words for "yes" and "no," and the preferred format for date and time strings. I18N::LangInfo accesses the parts of the locale controlled by LC_TIME and LC_MESSAGE and provides one function, langinfo, plus a collection of symbol names for values that we can query. The available values are system dependent, but they usually include DAY1 to DAY7, MON1 to MON12 for day and month names and their AB-prefixed abbreviations. The full list can usually be found in the /usr/include/localinfo.h header.

By way of an example, this short program prints out all the day and month names, plus the local words for, and the regular expression to match valid input for, "Yes" and "No":

```perl
#!/usr/bin/perl
# langinfo.pl
use strict;
use warnings;
use I18N::Langinfo qw(
    /DAY/ /MON/
    YESSTR NOSTR YESEXPR NOEXPR CODESET
    langinfo
);

print "Code set = ",langinfo(CODESET),"\n";
print "Yes='",langinfo(YESSTR),"' regex='",langinfo(YESEXPR),"'\n";
print " No='",langinfo(NOSTR) ,"' regex='",langinfo(NOEXPR),"'\n";

no strict 'refs';
foreach my $day (1..7) {
    print "Day $day is ", langinfo(&{'DAY_'.$day}),
        " (",langinfo(&{'ABDAY_'.$day}),")\n";
}
foreach my $month (1..12) {
    print "Month $month is ", langinfo(&{'MON_'.$month}),
        " (",langinfo(&{'ABMON_'.$month}),")\n";
}
```

Given a locale like `fr_FR@euro`, this program will print out the following:

```
> LC_ALL=fr_FR@euro ./langinfo.pl
```

```
Code set = ISO-8859-15
Yes='Oui' regex='^[oOyY].*'
 No='Non' regex='^[nN].*'
Day 1 is dimanche (dim)
Day 2 is lundi (lun)
Day 3 is mardi (mar)
Day 4 is mercredi (mer)
Day 5 is jeudi (jeu)
Day 6 is vendredi (ven)
Day 7 is samedi (sam)
Month 1 is janvier (jan)
Month 2 is février (fév)
Month 3 is mars (mar)
Month 4 is avril (avr)
Month 5 is mai (mai)
Month 6 is juin (jun)
Month 7 is juillet (jui)
Month 8 is août (aoû)
Month 9 is septembre (sep)
Month 10 is octobre (oct)
Month 11 is novembre (nov)
Month 12 is décembre (déc)
```

Notice that because we asked for the euro dialect of `fr_FR`, the character set switched to ISO 8859-15, which includes this symbol. Without the dialect, we would have gotten ISO 8859-1. Like `localeconv`, `I18N::LangInfo` is independent of Perl's built-in locale support, and we do not need to use the `locale` pragma in order to make use of it.

Perl's standard library also supplies a number of modules in the `Locale::` family. The most important of these, `Locale::MakeText`, is covered later in the section "Internationalization." The others all provide a map of English names to standard abbreviations for country, language, currency, and character scripts, each defined by a different ISO standard, along with importable subroutines to access the data in each table. Here is a summary of the available modules:

`Locale::Country`	ISO 3166-1	`code2country country2code country_code2code` `all_country_codes all_country_names`
`Locale::Currency`	ISO 4217	`code2currency currency2code` `all_currency_codes all_currency_names`
`Locale::Language`	ISO 632	`code2language language2code` `all_language_codes all_language_names`
`Locale::Script`	ISO 15924	`code2script script2code script_code2code` `all_script_codes all_script_names`
`I18N::LangTags::List`	RFC 3066	`name`

For example, we can list out all the currency codes and their (English) names, as defined by ISO 4217, with this short script:

```perl
#!/usr/bin/perl
# currencies.pl
use strict;
```

```perl
use warnings;
use Locale::Currency qw(all_currency_codes code2currency);

my @codes=all_currency_codes();
print map {
    "'$_' is the ".code2currency($_)."\n"
} @codes;
```

This produces output starting with

```
'adp' is the Andorran Peseta
'aed' is the UAE Dirham
'afa' is the Afghani
'all' is the Lek
'amd' is the Armenian Dram
```

Additionally, `Locale::Constants` provides constants for use in the `Locate::Country` and `Locale::Script` modules, which know how to convert between the 2-letter, 3-letter, and numeric conventions for country and script codes:

```perl
#!/usr/bin/perl
# scripts.pl
use strict;
use warnings;
use Locale::Script qw(
    all_script_names script2code
    LOCALE_CODE_ALPHA_2 LOCALE_CODE_ALPHA_3 LOCALE_CODE_NUMERIC
);

my @scripts = all_script_names();
foreach my $script (sort @scripts) {
    printf "%-37s: 2-ltr='%s' 3-ltr='%s' numeric='%d'\n", $script,
        script2code($script => LOCALE_CODE_ALPHA_2),
        script2code($script => LOCALE_CODE_ALPHA_3),
        script2code($script => LOCALE_CODE_NUMERIC);
};
```

This program generates a listing with lines like these:

```
Cypro-Minoan            : 2-ltr='cm' 3-ltr='cmn' numeric='402'
Cyrillic                : 2-ltr='cy' 3-ltr='cyr' numeric='220'
Deserel (Mormon)        : 2-ltr='ds' 3-ltr='dsr' numeric='250'
Devanagari (Nagari)     : 2-ltr='dv' 3-ltr='dvn' numeric='315'
Egyptian demotic        : 2-ltr='ed' 3-ltr='egd' numeric='70'
```

Also in the preceding table is `I18N::LangTags::List`, which provides a single routine, `name`, that provides the English language name for a language tag. It provides very similar results to `Locale::Language` and also draws on definitions originating outside the ISO 639 standard. The full list of language codes it recognizes is defined in the manual page, along with the standard from which they originate. The returned language names can in general then be converted to a different form using the `language2code` subroutine of `Locale::Language`.

Internationalization

Locales, with or without the help of Unicode, are an essential first step towards making an application or module aware of the language and country of its user, but they cannot provide more than basic help with the problem of communicating with a user in their native language. Issues of grammar, sentence structure, and basic divergences of language use mean that it is rarely possible to simply translate a message into the desired target languages and then print it out according to the locale. The process of fully educating an application to provide grammatically correct and context-sensitive messages is known as internationalization, or I18N for short, because there are 18 letters between the first "i" and the last "n."

The Locale::Maketext module provides a better solution to the problem of internationalization. It gives us the ability to create catalogs of messages, also called *lexicons*, one for each language that we intend to support. A message can be a literal text string, a text string with substitutions, or a subroutine that can implement more advanced behavior in those situations that really demand it. It is aware of locales and can recognize and configure itself from environment variables like HTTP_ACCEPT_LANGUAGE and will make use of the Win32::Locale module to derive locale information on Windows platforms.

Configuring for Internationalization

The first step to setting up a language lexicon is to define a subclass of Locale::Maketext. This should generally be within the namespace of the module or module family to be internationalized, so if the core module of an application is called My::Application, we would choose a name like My::Application::Lexicon or My::Application::I18N. The basic contents of this module are minimal:

```
package My::Application::I18N;
use base qw(Locale::Maketext);

1;
```

The real work is in the lexicon modules. We create one for each locale, inheriting from the preceding module, and named for the lowercased locale. Within each lexicon, message keys and values are provided in a hash variable called %Lexicon. For example, the US English lexicon might look like this:

```
package My::Application::I18N::en_us;
use base qw(My::Application::I18N);

%Lexicon=(
    Welcome => "Welcome!";
    ...
);

1;
```

If we don't want to define lexicons for multiple English locales, we can use just the language rather than the language plus country, in this case en rather than en_us. If Locale::Maketext cannot find a module for the precise locale, it will look for generic language lexicons as a substitute. This means we can define a general-purpose English lexicon and then define specific lexicons for particular dialects as needed.

Lexicon modules can also inherit from other lexicons through the usual @ISA mechanism. If Locale::Maketext sees that a lexicon has parent classes, they are also searched for %Lexicon hash variables if the child class does not supply a requested message. The parents' ancestors are searched in turn, until a message is found or all possible locations for the message turn up empty. So we can, for example, define an en_gb lexicon with British customizations of a general-purpose English lexicon written in en_us. This also makes it very simple to create catalogs of shared messages for use in many different applications.

If the default fallback behavior is not enough, we can define our own list of fallback languages by passing a list of language tags and/or languages to the `fallback_languages` class method, which we can invoke from our master lexicon class. For example, to fall back to English from any locale, including non-English ones:

```
My::Application::I18N->fallback_languages("en-US","en");
```

Notice that the arguments are language tags, identical to the short form of a locale except that a hyphen (minus sign) is used rather than an underscore. (As the use of language tags implies, the fallback functionality is courtesy of the `I18N::LangTags` module, covered earlier in the chapter.)

We can also, if we prefer, instantiate a lexicon object and pass it to `fallback_language_classes`:

```
my $fallback_en=new My::Application::I18N::en->new();
My::Application::I18N->fallback_language_classes($fallback_en);
```

This has the advantage over `fallback_languages` in that once the lexicon object is instantiated it cannot fail to be used in the event that no other lexicon can be found, since we have already created it.

Using Internationalization

To use the newly defined lexicons in a module or application, we create a lexicon object with the `get_handle` method. With an argument like `en` or `fr`, this will generate a lexicon for the requested language. But it is more interesting when no argument is supplied—in this case, the locale is inspected and variables like `HTTP_ACCEPT_LANGUAGE` are consulted to infer the correct language from context. For example:

```
use My::Application::I18N;
my $lexicon=My::Application::I18N->get_handle();
die "No language support available!\n"
  unless $lexicon;
```

Once a lexicon object has been found and instantiated, we can extract messages from it through their key with the `maketext` method. This is the core method of `Locale::Maketext`, because it is the mechanism by which the lexicons we define are invoked to return locale-dependent messages. For example, to extract the simple welcome message earlier, we could use

```
print $lexicon->maketext("Welcome"),"\n";
```

As the language lexicon represented by $lang is determined by the locale, this will print `Welcome` in any English locale, assuming we defined a lexicon for `en` rather than `en_us`; otherwise, the lookup will work for US English but fail for other variants like British or Canadian English. Similarly, we can define a `de` lexicon to return `Wilkommen` in German locales. Any languages not directly supported are handled through the fallback mechanism described previously.

Writing Messages

The L10N's work of internationalization is, of course, writing the actual messages. For simple messages with no variable components, a simple string will do. But more often, we need to generate a message that varies according to context, with placeholders taking the place of values to be substituted in context. For example, take this message returned by a theoretical search engine:

```
Found 16 results for 'Perl'
```

There are two places in this message where a value needs to be filled in. To mark up places in a message that need to be expanded when the message is generated, `Locale::Maketext` offers bracket notation, where variable text is marked by square brackets. The simplest use of bracket notation is to provide numbered placeholders for arguments passed to the maketext method. When the message is retrieved from the lexicon, the values are placed into the message string before it is returned. For example, this would be the English language value for the preceding message:

```
Found [_1] results for '[_2]'
```

The key that triggers this message can be anything we like, as it serves only to retrieve the message value. For example, if the key we used was found_results, the en lexicon would have a key-value pair like this:

```
%Lexicon = (
    found_results => "Found [_1] results for '[_2]'",
    ...
);
```

And it would be retrieved in the program with the following:

```
print $lexicon->maketext(found_results => 16, 'Perl');
```

We would then complete the job by adding all the appropriate translations to the other language lexicons we intend to support. An alternative choice of key is to use the message value for the "primary" language (most likely the language of the developer writing the program):

```
print $lexicon->maketext("Found [_1] results for '[_2]' => 16, 'Perl');
```

This makes the code more legible, since we can see the bracket notation in the key and see, at least for one language, what the result will look like without having to run the program to find out. It also comes in handy if we set up a lexicon to autogenerate missing message values from the key, as described later.

Parameter placeholders work like array indices, with negative numbers counting from the end, so '[_-1]' would expand into the last argument passed. '[_*]' is a special case—it expands into the whole list. If we actually want to use a literal left square bracket, we can escape it with a tilde (not a backslash): ~[. To get a literal tilde, double it up: ~~.

The more interesting use of bracket notation is to invoke a method, which we can do by simply naming it after the opening bracket. Any parameters we want to pass to it come after it, separated with commas, before the closing bracket. The method can be defined anywhere in the lexicon class or a superclass, depending on whether we need it in only one lexicon or in several. In our example, My::Application::I18N::en and My::Application::I18N are both valid places for a method to be defined.

A common requirement for special handling is correctly pluralizing a noun, and the Locale::Maketext module (which lexicons all inherit from) provides a general-purpose method quant to handle this problem, at least for most Western languages. Here is how we can use it in bracket notation:

```
Found [quant,_1,result] results for '[_2]'

Found [quant,_1,result,results] results for '[_2]'
```

The first version selects between the singular and plural of result based on the value of the first argument passed (16 in our earlier example). The second version simply appends an "s" if the quantity is plural, which happens to be correct for "result" but, of course, would not work for "sheep" or "bunny." In all cases, whitespace is significant, so do not be tempted to use spaces around the commas.

We might also want to handle the special case of zero matches, which we can do with a fourth argument:

```
Found [quant,_1,result,results,no results] results for '[_2]'
```

The quant method is used sufficiently frequently that it can also be abbreviated to an asterisk in bracket notation:

```
Found [*,_1,result,results,no results] results for '[_2]'
```

Locale::Maketext supplies a small handful of other useful methods too:

encoding	The character encoding of the current locale, for example: $lexicon->encoding().
language_tag	The language tag of the current locale, for example: $lexicon->language_tag().
numf	Format the supplied number according to the local conventions for the decimal points and thousands separator, for example: [numf,12345.678].
sprintf	A direct interface to Perl's sprintf function, to make use of sprintf-style format strings, for example: [sprintf,"%20s : %-20s",_1,_2].

All of these methods can be called in code or via bracket notation, but as the example suggests, numf and sprintf are more likely candidates for the latter. Like quant, numf also has a shorthand name, #, so the example in the table could also be written as

```
[#,12345.678]
```

If all else fails, we can assign a code reference to a method to be called directly by the maketext method. For example, for a lexicon entry that returns a correctly constructed "results" phrase, we could use this:

```
"[_1] results" => \&count_results
```

This is just a more direct (and more efficient) way of saying

```
"[_1] results" => "[count_results,_*]"
```

Here is one way this method might be implemented. It just calls quant to return the correct phrase for a number of results, and illustrates that quant and other methods like it can be just as easily called in code as through bracket notation:

```
sub count_results {
    my ($lexicon,$count)=@_;
    return $lexicon->quant($count,"result","results","no results");
}
```

Intriguingly, there is nothing to stop us calling maketext itself from one of these subroutines, so we can devise very intricate mechanisms for handling even the trickiest scenarios.

Handling Failed Lookups

In the event that a message is missing in the lexicon of a particular language, Locale::Maketext will ordinarily die with a fatal error. However, if a lexicon contains the special key fail, which can be set explicitly or via the fail_with method, the named method is invoked as an error handler. Depending on our needs, we can define this method in the language lexicon module itself or place it in the master module to be invoked from all lexicons. For example, to install the handler at runtime, we can use

```
$lexicon->fail_with("lexicon_failure");
```

Or in the master module:

```
sub lexicon_failure {
    my ($lexicon, $key, @params)=@_;
    return $fallback_en->maketext($key => @params);
}
```

This particular error handler calls the English fallback lexicon we created earlier, and provides an alternative way to manage fallback situations to the `fallback_languages` and `fallback_language_classes` methods. In a real error handler, we would also likely log the failed lookup so we can take preventative action in a future release.

A convenient error handler called `failure_handler_auto` is actually provided by `Locale::Maketext` itself:

```
$lexicon->fail_with("failure_handler_auto");
```

This handler will try to make sense of the requested key, compile it into a value to evaluate any bracket notation if possible, or just return the key as a last resort. Every failed lookup is recorded in a hash reference assigned to the key `failure_lex` in the lexicon in which the lookup failed. This can be dumped out or otherwise recorded, for example, in an `END` block, to get a log of all failed lookups during the lifetime of the application.

We can also have `Locale::Maketext` automatically handle missing messages by defining them with an *automatic* lexicon.

Automatic Lexicons

If the `%Lexicon` hash contains the special hash-key pair `_AUTO => 1`, then missing messages in the lexicon are invented by creating a new entry with the lookup key as the value:

```
%Lexicon = (
    _AUTO => 1,
    ...
);
```

While this is no substitute for actually defining the message in each supported language, it does allow for a fallback message rather than generating an error. However, it bypasses the regular fallback mechanism, and it does not even consult lexicons in superclasses. It is most useful for application development, as it frees us from the need to define the lexicon as we develop the application—we only need to make calls to the `maketext` method as usual, and the application will use the keys we supply as the message values for all languages, until such time as we pass the lexicon to translators to fill in the values for the other languages we intend to support.

Summary

In this chapter, we looked at Perl's support for character encodings and Unicode in particular. We saw how Perl implements wide characters, how to handle strings and filehandles that are wide-character enabled, and how to convert between Unicode and other native character encodings. We also looked at Unicode character names and querying the Unicode database for details of blocks, scripts, and character properties.

We then turned to the subject of localization, or L10N, and locales, collections of related contextual information that describe the preferred character set of different languages and locations; the preferred local format of dates, times, and numbers; the name of the local currency; names of days and months; and even the local words for "yes" and "no." Locales are well supported in Perl on Unix systems. For Windows, the `Win32::Locale` module can be installed to provide much of the same information.

Finally, we took a brief look at internationalization, or I18N, the process of writing applications so that they are fully aware of their locale and can communicate with the user in their native language. This is trickier than it might at first seem, since different languages have very different ideas about sentence structure, whether zero is singular or plural (or neither), and a myriad of other concerns. In Perl, we can use `Locale::Maketext`, a flexible module that enables us to define catalogs or *lexicons* of messages and, where necessary, message-returning subroutines to generate context-sensitive responses in multiple languages.

Index

forums.apress.com
FOR PROFESSIONALS BY PROFESSIONALS™

JOIN THE APRESS FORUMS AND BE PART OF OUR COMMUNITY. You'll find discussions that cover topics of interest to IT professionals, programmers, and enthusiasts just like you. If you post a query to one of our forums, you can expect that some of the best minds in the business—especially Apress authors, who all write with *The Expert's Voice*™—will chime in to help you. Why not aim to become one of our most valuable participants (MVPs) and win cool stuff? Here's a sampling of what you'll find:

DATABASES
Data drives everything.

Share information, exchange ideas, and discuss any database programming or administration issues.

INTERNET TECHNOLOGIES AND NETWORKING
Try living without plumbing (and eventually IPv6).

Talk about networking topics including protocols, design, administration, wireless, wired, storage, backup, certifications, trends, and new technologies.

JAVA
We've come a long way from the old Oak tree.

Hang out and discuss Java in whatever flavor you choose: J2SE, J2EE, J2ME, Jakarta, and so on.

MAC OS X
All about the Zen of OS X.

OS X is both the present and the future for Mac apps. Make suggestions, offer up ideas, or boast about your new hardware.

OPEN SOURCE
Source code is good; understanding (open) source is better.

Discuss open source technologies and related topics such as PHP, MySQL, Linux, Perl, Apache, Python, and more.

PROGRAMMING/BUSINESS
Unfortunately, it is.

Talk about the Apress line of books that cover software methodology, best practices, and how programmers interact with the "suits."

WEB DEVELOPMENT/DESIGN
Ugly doesn't cut it anymore, and CGI is absurd.

Help is in sight for your site. Find design solutions for your projects and get ideas for building an interactive Web site.

SECURITY
Lots of bad guys out there—the good guys need help.

Discuss computer and network security issues here. Just don't let anyone else know the answers!

TECHNOLOGY IN ACTION
Cool things. Fun things.

It's after hours. It's time to play. Whether you're into LEGO® MINDSTORMS™ or turning an old PC into a DVR, this is where technology turns into fun.

WINDOWS
No defenestration here.

Ask questions about all aspects of Windows programming, get help on Microsoft technologies covered in Apress books, or provide feedback on any Apress Windows book.

HOW TO PARTICIPATE:
Go to the Apress Forums site at **http://forums.apress.com/**.
Click the New User link.